the complete guide to drawing & painting

the complete guide to drawing & painting

Oceana

AN OCEANA BOOK

This book is produced by
Quantum Publishing Ltd
6 Blundell Street
London N7 9BH

This edition printed 2006

ISBN 1-84573-159-X

QUMCGTD

Manufactured in Singapore by
Pica Digital Pte. Ltd

Printed in Singapore by
Star Standard Industries Pte. Ltd

CONTENTS

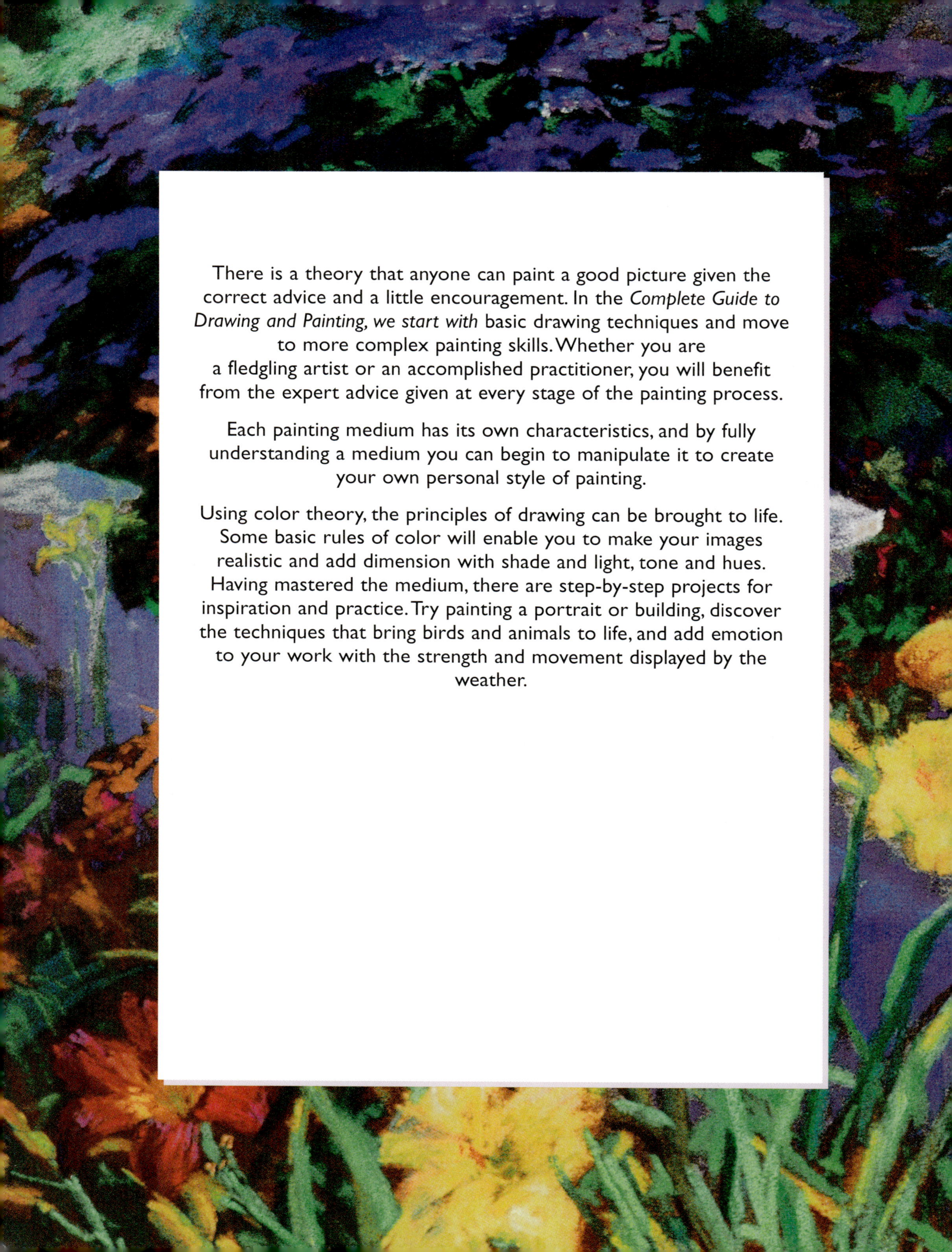

There is a theory that anyone can paint a good picture given the correct advice and a little encouragement. In the *Complete Guide to Drawing and Painting, we start with* basic drawing techniques and move to more complex painting skills. Whether you are a fledgling artist or an accomplished practitioner, you will benefit from the expert advice given at every stage of the painting process.

Each painting medium has its own characteristics, and by fully understanding a medium you can begin to manipulate it to create your own personal style of painting.

Using color theory, the principles of drawing can be brought to life. Some basic rules of color will enable you to make your images realistic and add dimension with shade and light, tone and hues. Having mastered the medium, there are step-by-step projects for inspiration and practice. Try painting a portrait or building, discover the techniques that bring birds and animals to life, and add emotion to your work with the strength and movement displayed by the weather.

INTRODUCTION

Throughout the world, more and more people have taken up painting and drawing, and this book is a complete practical guide whether you are a student of art, or simply interested in learning and improving your technique and approach. As well as dealing with all the traditional areas of art, such as oil and watercolor painting, the book's comprehensive coverage includes some less well-known fields, such as airbrushing, spattering, and scumbling.

The book also aims to help the artist answer questions like—what do I need to know, how do I go about it, and what materials and equipment do I need? The book has a clear introduction to each medium, showing the range of available equipment and a comprehensive range of techniques in a clear step-by-step format with numerous photographs and interesting, informative captions.

Every technique is broken down into a number of steps that are photographed. Each individual step is numbered and given an extensive explanatory caption. By following the numbers through, a complete technique can be built up.

The eventual rewards of making telling, well-drawn, and constructed drawings and paintings are great. Much pleasure and endless joy to others can ensue; the greater your experience and the wider the range of projects undertaken, the better the results. Another great benefit that springs from picture making is that you soon learn to see the world in ways different from others. The dull, olive green tone of a tree in the foreground, alongside the acid yellow greens of fresh spring foliage, will be seen to contrast well with the sun-bathed sea, shimmering turquoise blue in the middle distance. So much more can be gleaned from seeing in this way than by a casual observer.

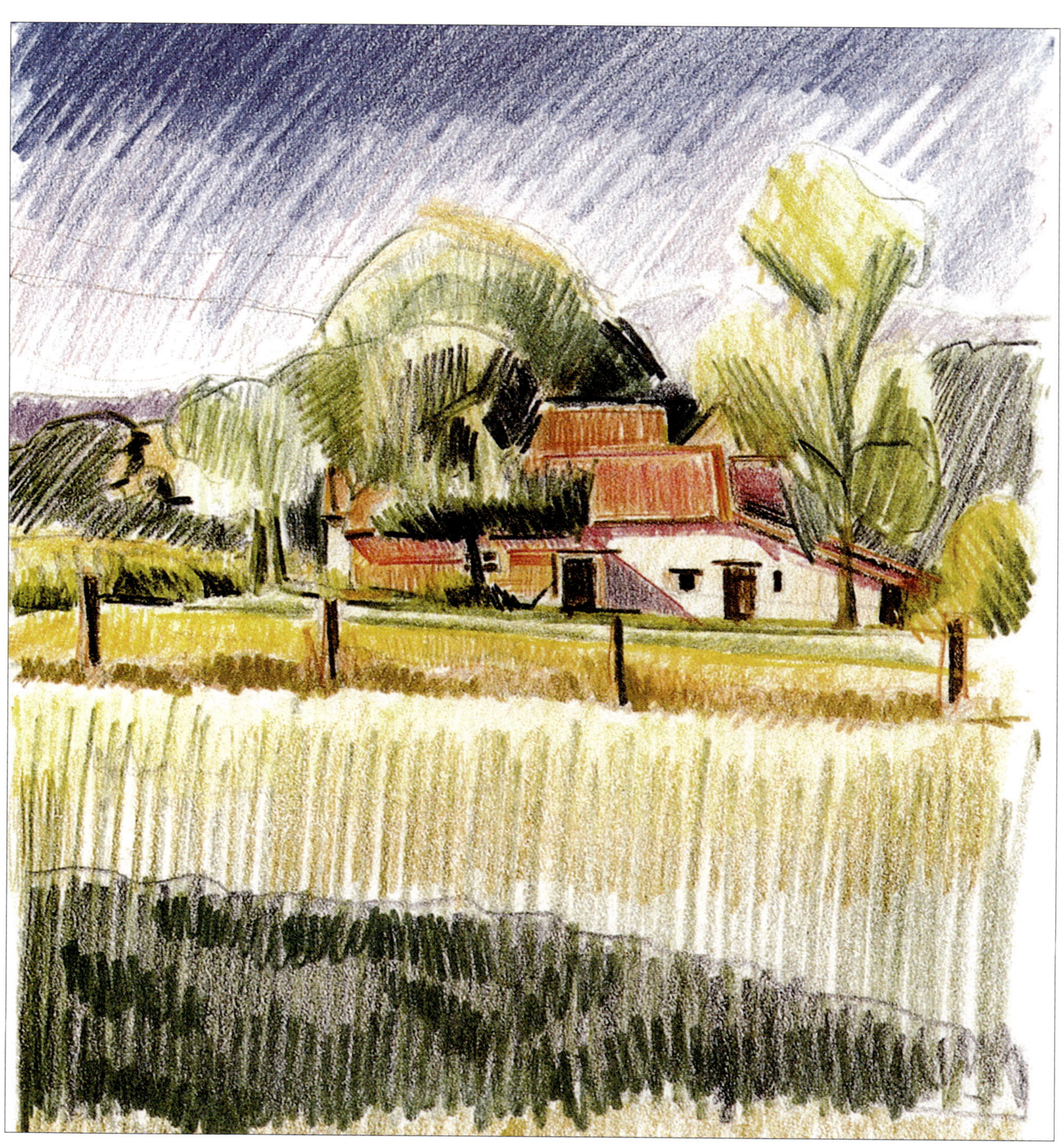

DRAWING

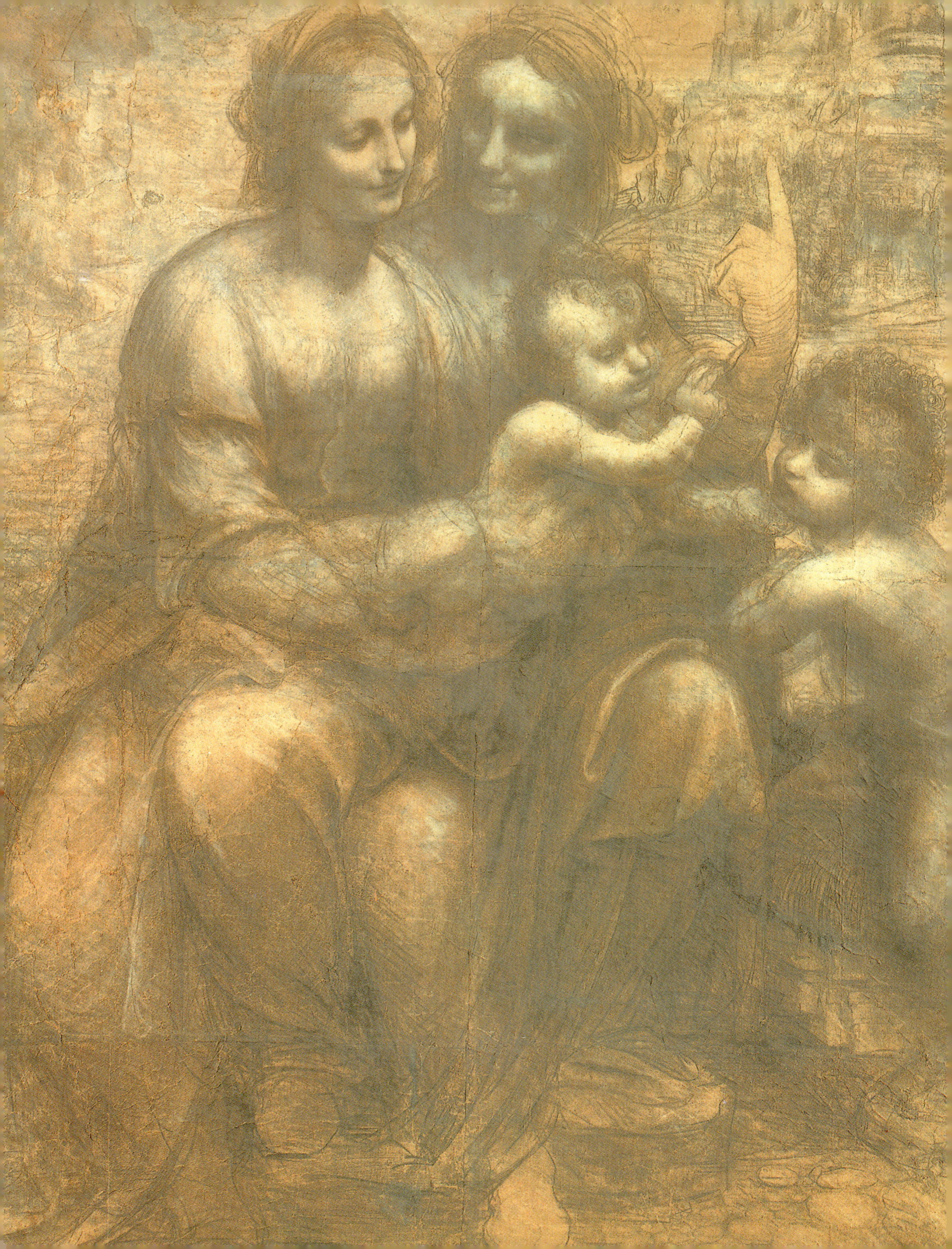

1 INTRODUCTION

It is often a great surprise the first time to discover the range of images and techniques to be found in the art of drawing. The dictionary definition is far too narrow to be of any real value in understanding the breadth of work that an art historian would include in the category of drawn images. However, many people still think that drawing is carried out only with a pencil and that it consists mainly of outlines.

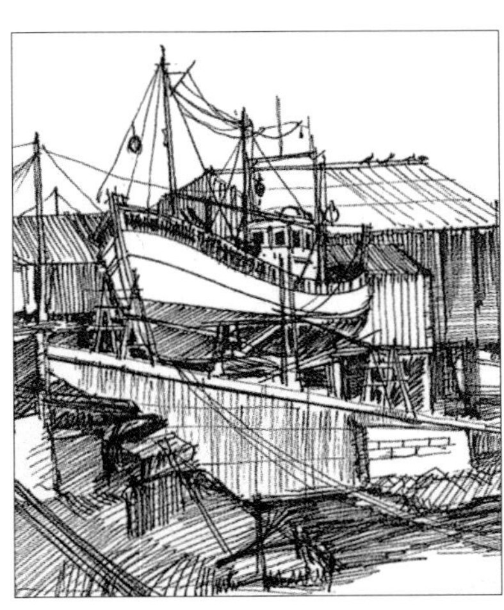

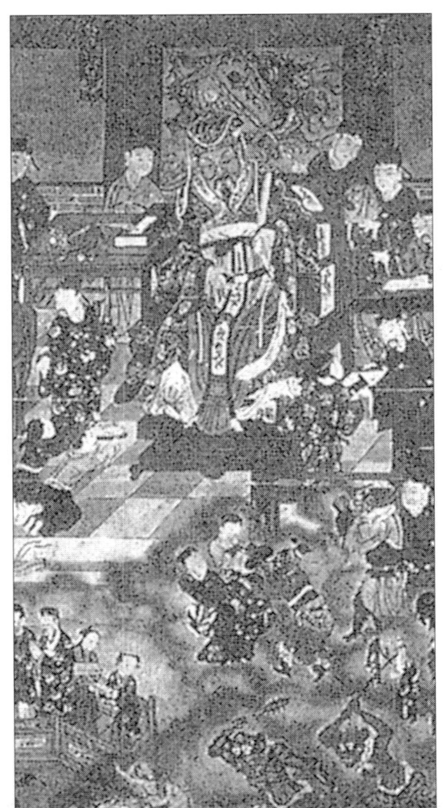

Presented with the image of Ruskin's drawing, *The Market Place, Abbeville*, everyone would agree that this is a drawing. However, Degas' pastel drawing of a woman at her toilet *Apres le bain, femme sèssuyant* might cause some confusion, particularly as this work in pastel is in full color. Close study of the Degas reveals that it is made up of small lines of color, which are quite separate on the surface.

Above *In this drawing of a shipyard, a felt tip pen has been used on a smooth cartridge paper.*

Left *An oriental drawing of* Yama, King of the Seventh Hell. *Yama, being the main subject matter of the painting, is depicted much larger than the other figures.*

Far Left *This drawing by Leonardo da Vinci is one of a series of drawings subject culminating in a painting now in The Louvre in Paris.*

The common link between the Degas and the Ruskin is that both utilize a line. Even though the Degas is in full color the technique that has been employed in the execution of the piece makes it very clearly a drawing, not a pastel painting.

These two examples have been executed with a dry medium. Again, it can be something of a surprise to discover for the first time that a number of wet media are also included in the art of drawing, such as ink used with pen and brush. In the drawing of his wife having her hair combed, Rembrandt applied the large dark areas with a brush, and it is only in those parts of the drawing that are well lit that we find lines drawn with a pen denoting in detail the hands and the heads. The drawing covers a broad spectrum of approaches and is an excellent pointer to the difficulty of making up any hard-and-fast rules about what a drawing is. It would prove just as difficult to try to define drawing in terms of subject matter.

This section of the book deals with representational drawing. Representational drawing is not about techniques or media, as many books seem to suggest. Drawing is about seeing in a particular way which allows for the translation of the three-dimensional world being observed into a two-dimensional form on a plane surface. In explaining this process of translation, this section on drawing deals mainly with the picture-plane representational European system, which has been the predominant pictorial form since the late 15th century. And because the emphasis is on how to see in a particular way and how to translate what you see onto paper on canvas, the principles can be applied to painting, which we will come to later in the book.

Right *Pencil and wash study in the tradition of typographical art. It accurately records an aspect of Trafalgar Square, London, without really making any comment about the life of the city. The same style of drawing could be used to depict any city.*

Most of the visual images we see in our everyday lives—such as on television, in magazine pictures, on the cinema screen, etc.—we see through the picture-plane system, and it is often forgotten that this approach to representing the world has not always dominated our perception, nor was it invented and developed by one single person, but by artists during the Renaissance over a period of approximately 100 years. It is now so universally accepted that it is difficult for many people to imagine any other system of creating images.

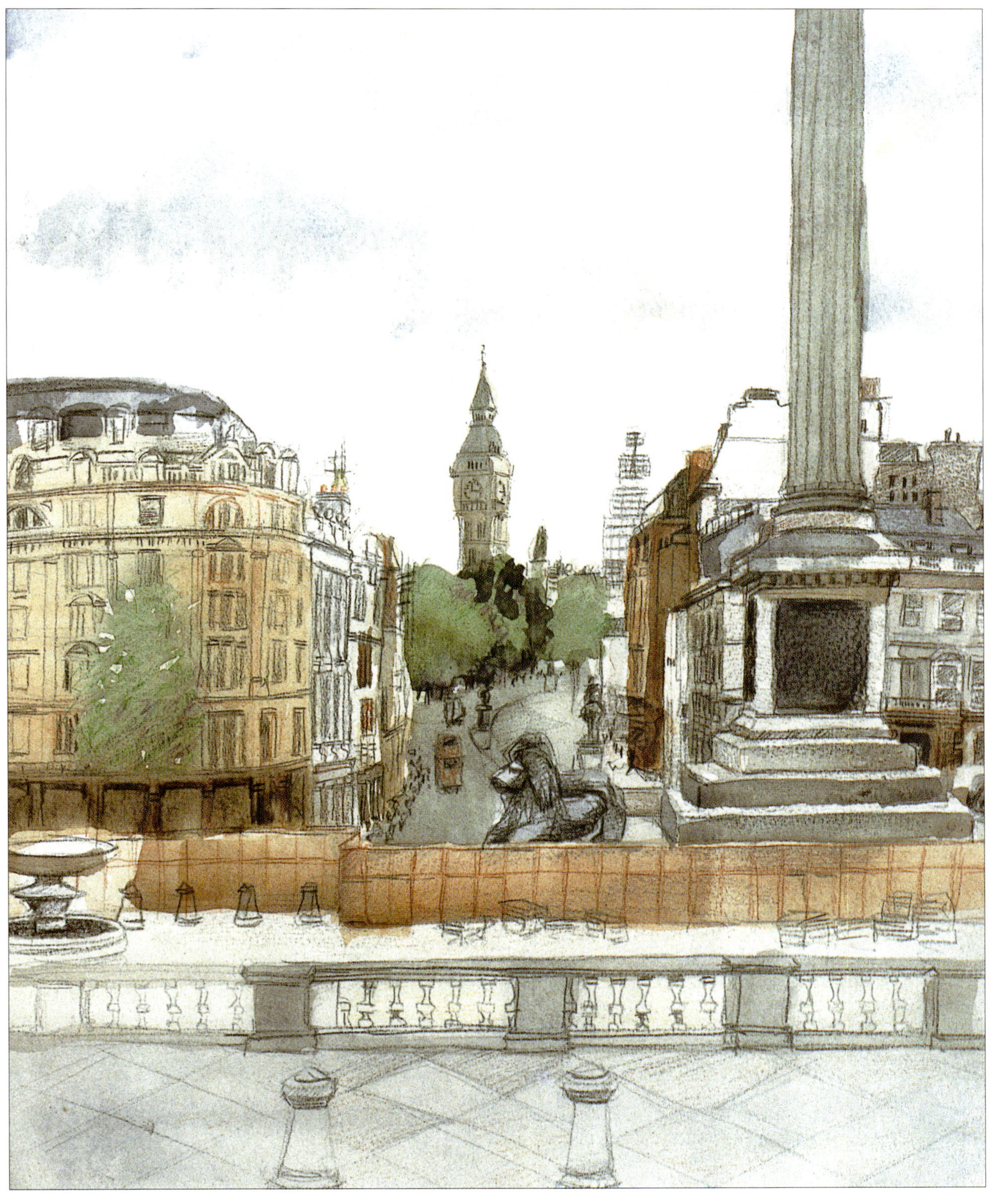

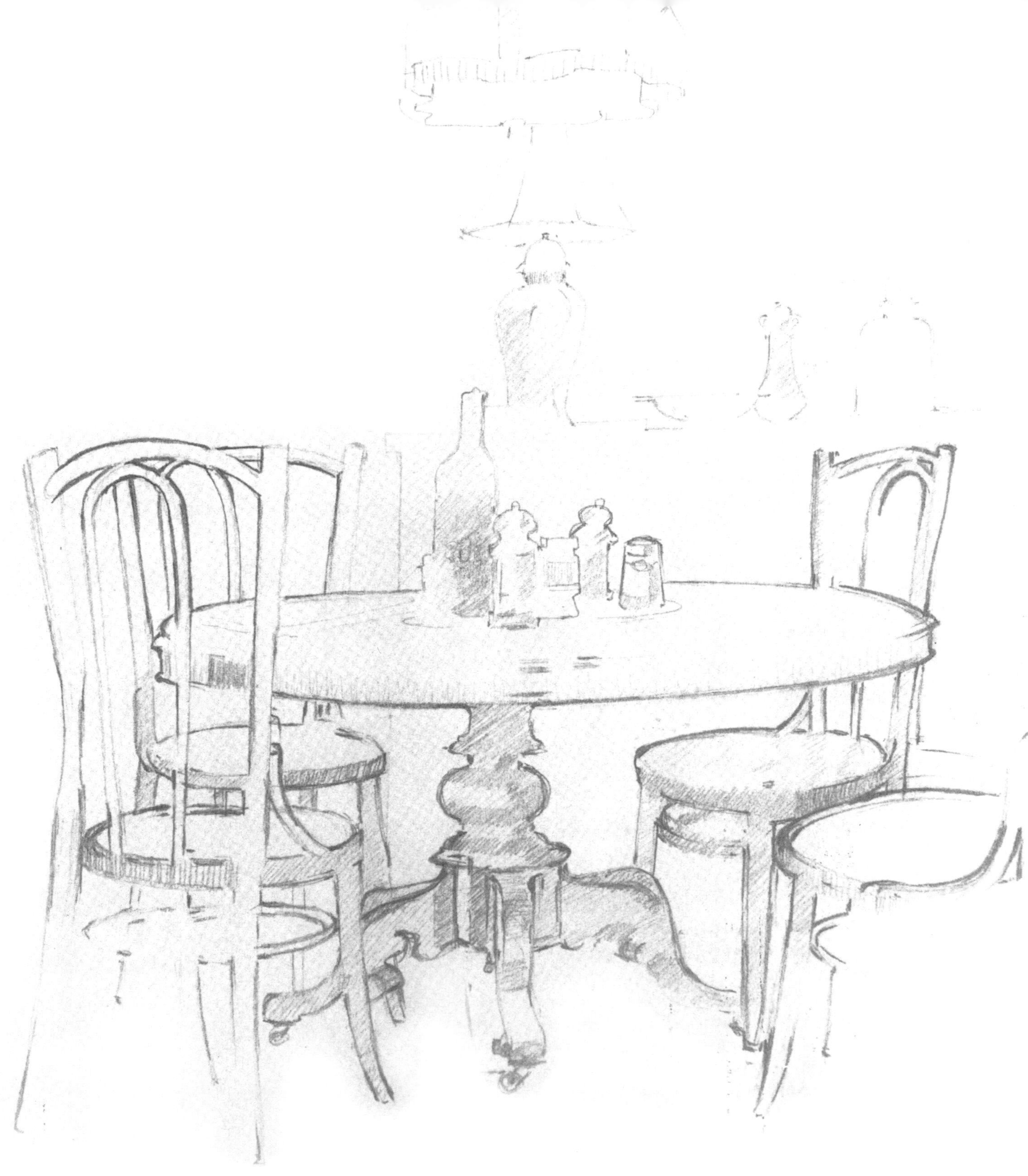

Above: *Pencil representational drawing of a dining room table and chairs.*

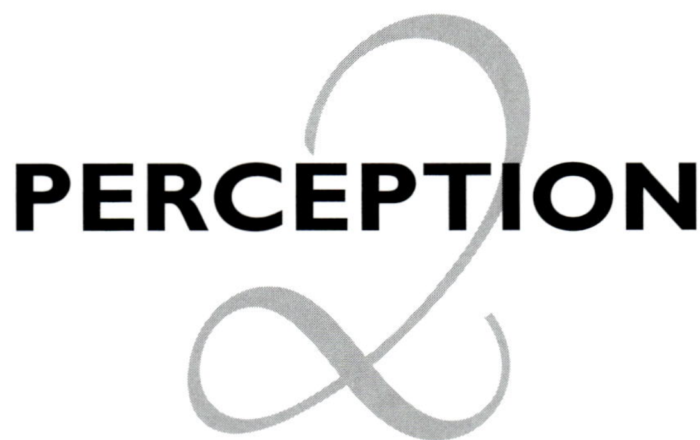

PERCEPTION

It might appear odd that the first exercise in a book about drawing is to write something, but it is essential to be aware of how we use our eyes in our daily lives, and also to discover what adjustments we can make to our perceptual processes to make effective representational drawings.

As an exercise, perhaps at the end of an evening meal, leave the dining table and walk into the adjoining room. Write a full description of the table in the room you have just left. The description will probably be a list of the items you can remember.

Now return to the room. Sit looking at the table in front, and write another description. This will likely be more elaborate and individually detailed.

The reason for writing out the descriptions is simply to make you use your eyes. In the second attempt, you consciously used your eyes to gather more information than your memory could hold. You should by now realize that you are quite observant, capable of assimilating in considerable detail what is visually presented to you, but that you find it much harder to reproduce it all from memory.

A problem arises, however, when you try to translate this method of observation into a drawing. Leaving the objects exactly where they

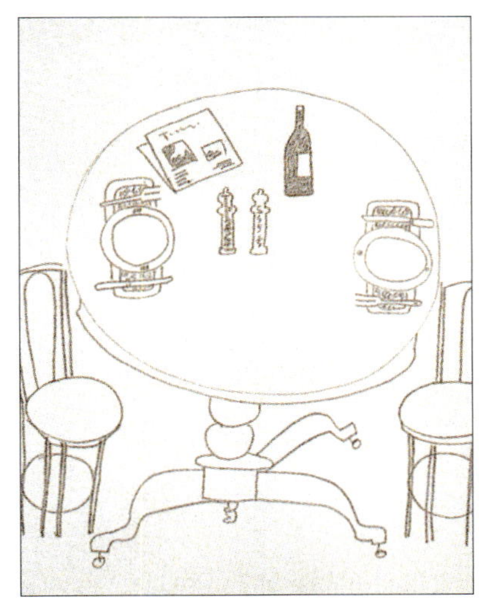

Above: *This pencil drawing was obviously done from memory by an untutored eye. Without the table in front of you, it is very difficult to remember the relationships between objects. Many things are left out, and things have been added that were not actually there.*

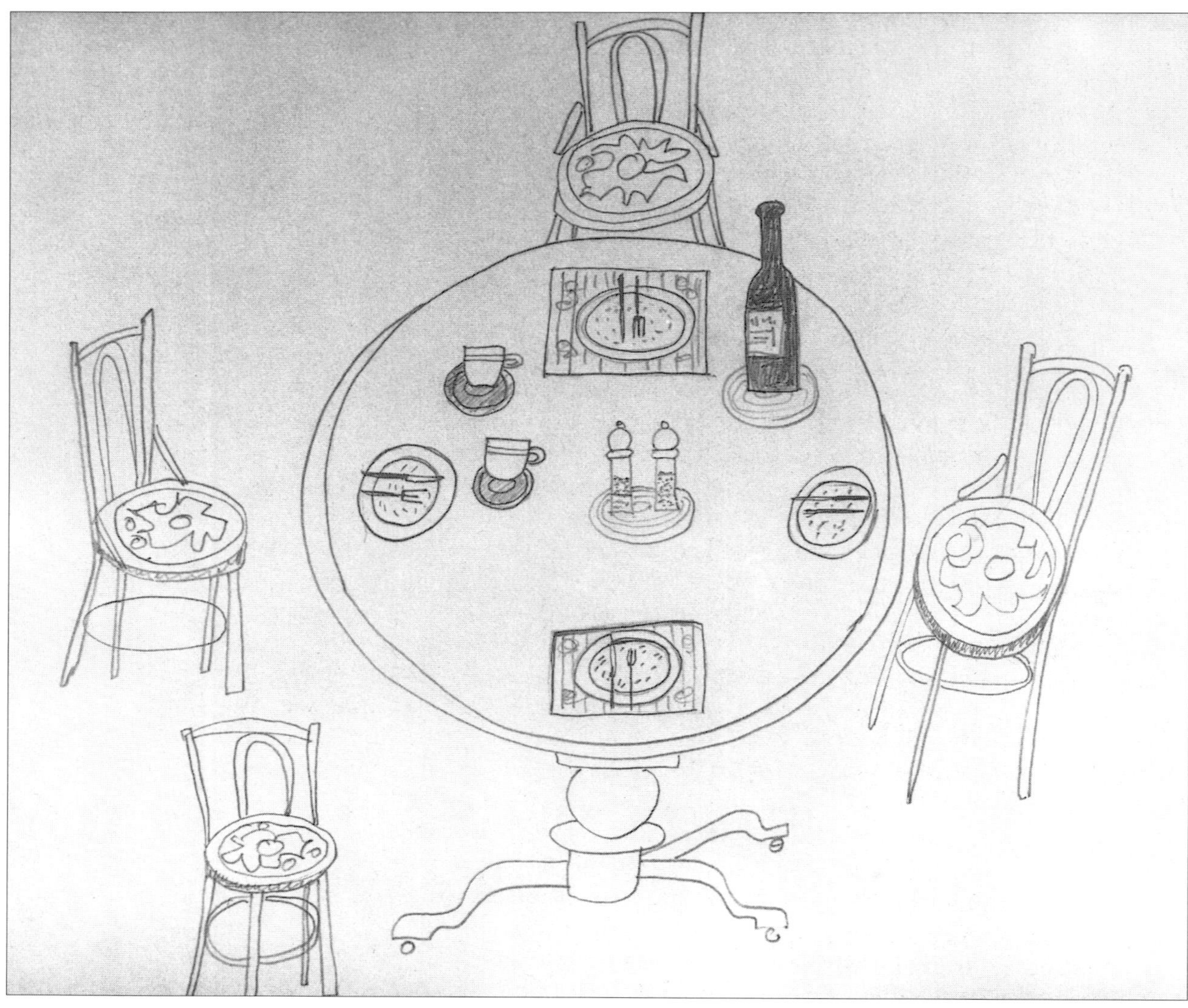

Above: *Here, the drawing was made with the table and chairs in full view. Again, the drawing has not been rendered with any perspective, although all the objects are recorded more tellingly, with the patterns on the plates, the chair seats, and indication that the bottle and saucers are of a darker color. There is clearly far more information in this drawing.*

are on the table, make a drawing of the room in front of you. You will probably end up with a drawing not dissimilar to the one illustrated. Most beginners find it difficult to draw a table from wherever they are viewing it. It is impossible to see it as a complete circle, and there is a strong compulsion to visually tilt the surface so that all the objects you wish to draw can be clearly seen. This is due not to any lack of ability to see, but to using the information seen in a way that is not compatible with the act of drawing, but that corresponds completely with the act of verbal description. For example, to verbally describe all the objects on the table, it is necessary to visually isolate them one by one, find an appropriate word or sentence, and move on to the next object. In your first drawing, most beginners still want to use the visual information in a verbal way.

Now try again to draw the table. Place a chair about eight or ten feet away, sit down, and draw the objects on the table from this one fixed viewpoint. It soon becomes apparent that not all the objects on the table can be fully seen. One object may partly obscure another, and a portion of the table may be partly obscured by a chair that is in your line of vision. You will probably still find an urge to visually tilt the table at a far greater angle than it actually is. You will also probably find that you tend to draw one object first in its entirety, then move on to the next, and that you try to fit the table and chairs around the objects.

This exercise will have been much more difficult than you imagined at first it would be.

The main problem most beginners have in perceiving the interrelationship of all the objects is thus due, in some degree, to the fact that they tend to perceive the world in a solely three-dimensional way. To fully appraise most objects, it is normal to pick them up or walk around them, using your eyes all the time to take in details of color, form, weight, and texture. It is not until beginners actually start to make a representational drawing of what he or she sees from a fixed viewpoint

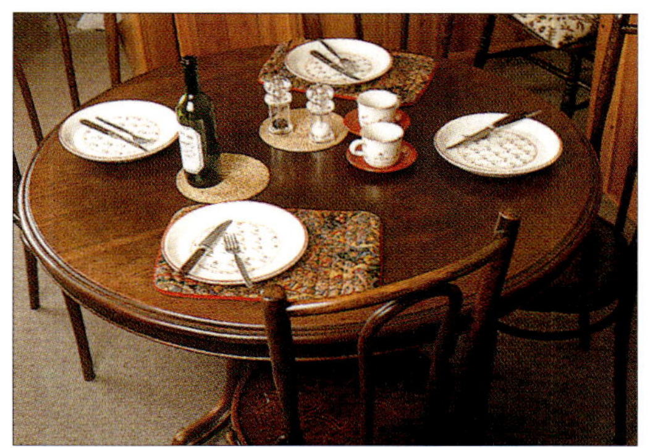

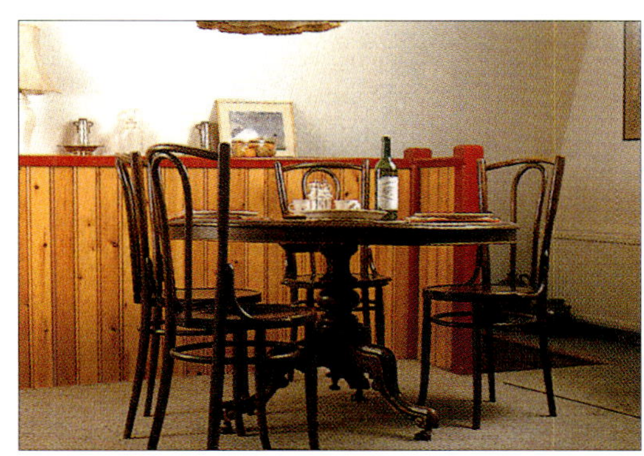

Top Right: *You can see from these two photographs that they have been taken from different angles. In the untutored drawing, the student has attempted to incorporate in one drawing the information gathered from viewpoints that are unrelated. It is obvious that the photographs are of the same table, but the visual information they contain is very different. This is even more apparent when the two photographs are transformed into two line drawings (below).*

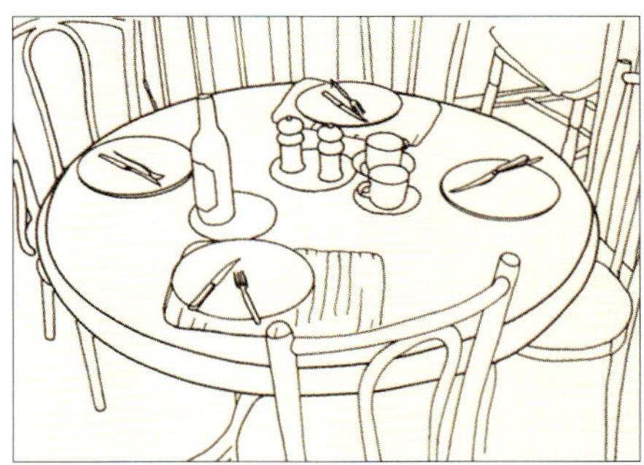

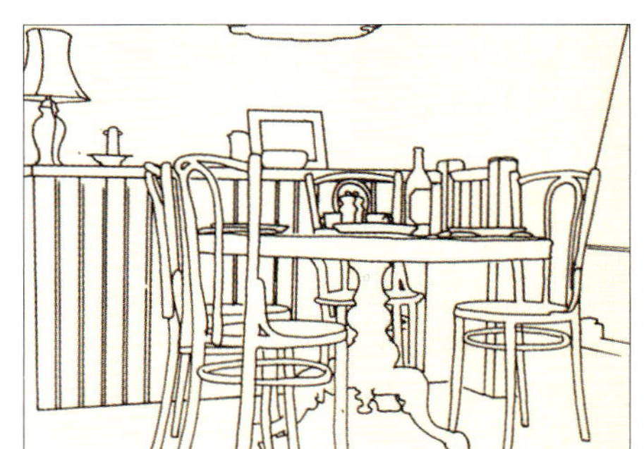

that the full realization occurs that it is impossible to see an object in its entirety. For example, if you were to move the chair on which you sat to do your first drawing, just one foot to the right or to the left, all the visual relationships of the objects on the table—such as the shapes of the objects and the spaces between them—change. From your first position you might, for instance, have been able to see a cup; you knew the handle was there, but you could not see it. From your second position, the cup has not moved, but you can now see the handle. Pictorially, the object has changed. What beginners are always struggling about is their perceived experience of an object as distinct from their actual view of it.

We all receive through our eyes more information than can possibly be shown in a single drawing. We, therefore, have to be selective, using only the visual information that can be recorded from a fixed viewpoint.

Always remember, the art of drawing is to see from one fixed viewpoint and to select from the visual information what is most useful to create a pictorial representation. Drawing is not about seeing better, but about being more selective.

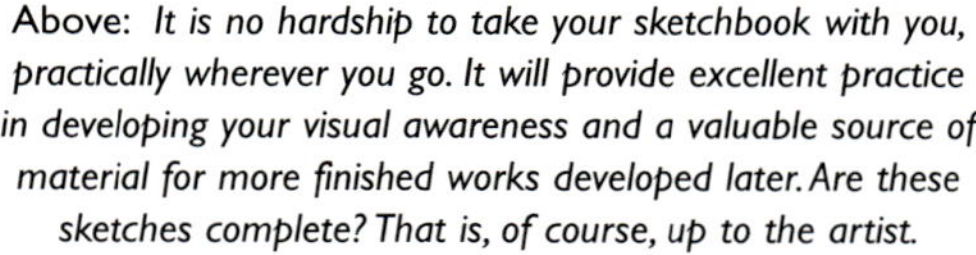

Above: *It is no hardship to take your sketchbook with you, practically wherever you go. It will provide excellent practice in developing your visual awareness and a valuable source of material for more finished works developed later. Are these sketches complete? That is, of course, up to the artist.*

The exercises in this book are designed to help you to start asking yourself the right questions, through your eyes. Each exercise on its own is comparatively simple and should not cause any great difficulty. The art of representational drawing is to utilize the whole or part of these individual exercises at the same time, because a drawing is a combination of all the elements described. Learn by the experience of drawing from life. Do not expect to comprehend every aspect of drawing all at once.

In this book there are outlines of several theories associated with representational drawing—such as perspective, light and shade, tone, etc.—but try to avoid learning these theories in isolation. For example, familiarize yourself with perspective by working on a subject matter that requires some basic knowledge of the subject, such as drawing buildings. When you begin, try to avoid working from photographs or other drawings because in these the threedimensional world has already been translated into two-dimensional—i.e., flat-form. The main purpose of this section of the book is to help you to translate the three-dimensional world you see, by using your eyes, into a two-dimensional or flat (plane) form. Although drawing from

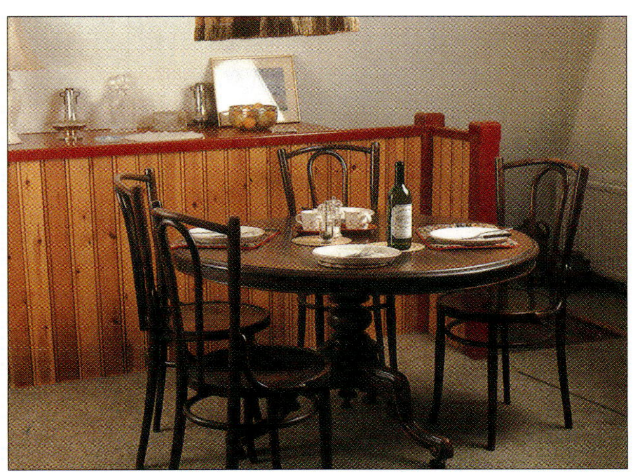

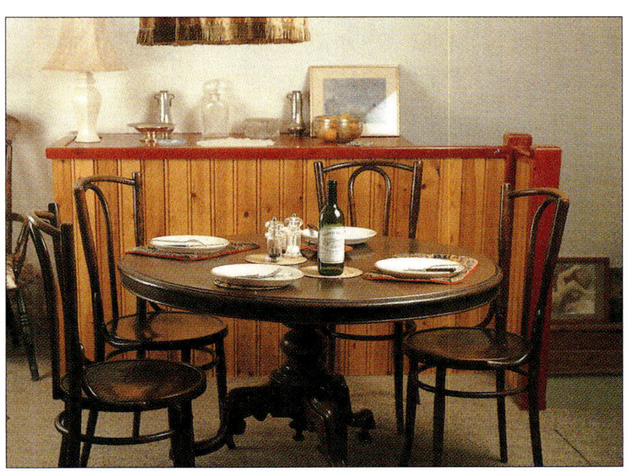

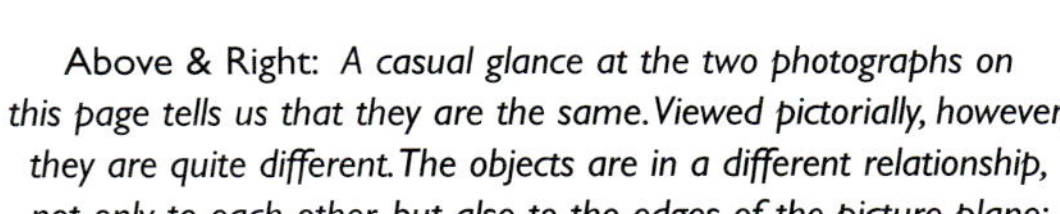

Above & Right: *A casual glance at the two photographs on this page tells us that they are the same. Viewed pictorially, however, they are quite different. The objects are in a different relationship, not only to each other, but also to the edges of the picture plane: consider, for example, the changed relative positions of the bottle and the middle chair. Produce your own line drawings of both these photographs, together with detail drawings of the central section.*

photographs might give you a satisfying result, it cannot help you in the true quest of learning how to see in a pictorial way. Photography can be useful—but can come in later. Practice and first-hand experience are the finest teachers.

This book focuses on the form of representational drawing principally associated with Western culture, although that is not the only method of representing the three-dimensional world in a flat two-dimensional way. The visual conventions of pre-Renaissance culture and of Eastern cultures are markedly different. Even in our own culture, conventions are different in certain aspects of design. Engineers and architects, for example, make very accurate and easily understood drawings—which do not obey any of the conventions of representational drawing—of three-dimensional objects. This book deals primarily with the post-Renaissance conventions, however, and makes no attempt to investigate other methods in any depth.

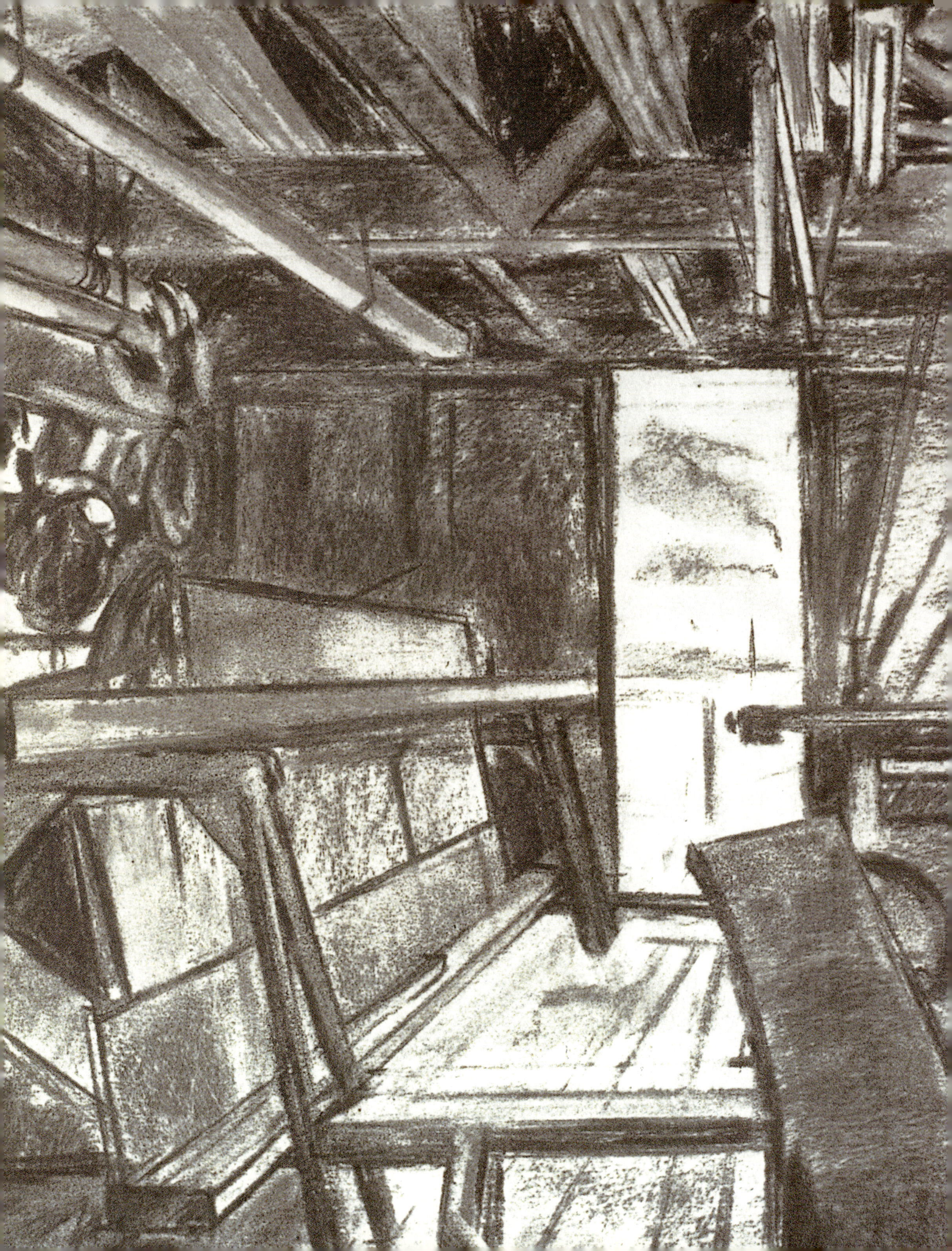

3 BASIC PRACTICE

One great advantage of drawing is that there is no need for a lavish studio or even a room set aside for it, and the equipment used can be of the most simple type. Some of the most beautiful drawings have been done with a piece of burnt stick and colored earths on cave walls. The right pencils, the right ink, and a perfect easel cannot in themselves make anyone draw any better. There is only one requirement: to see.

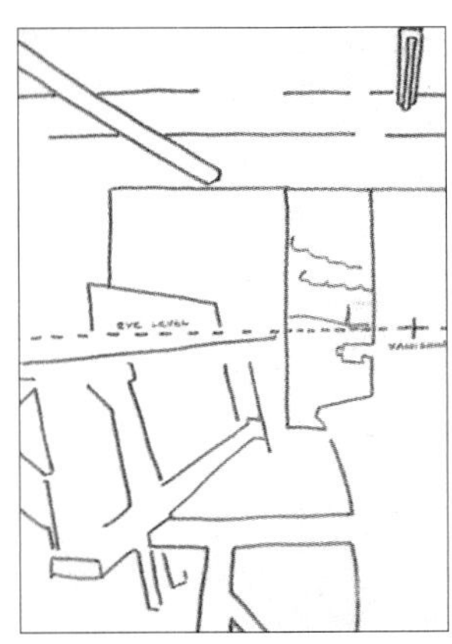

Above *Even this apparently loosely-rendered drawing, on closer inspection, reveals its perspective understructure.*

Collect together four or five cardboard cartons of various sizes, and a couple of bottles, and place them in a natural way on a table that itself should preferably be rectangular. Put your paper on a piece of board and sit on a chair with another chair facing you, propping the board up on that chair, so that it becomes an easel. There is a good reason in this exercise for this odd way of sitting. Look carefully at what is in front of you and try to draw the cartons on the table as accurately as possible from the fixed viewpoint you have chosen.

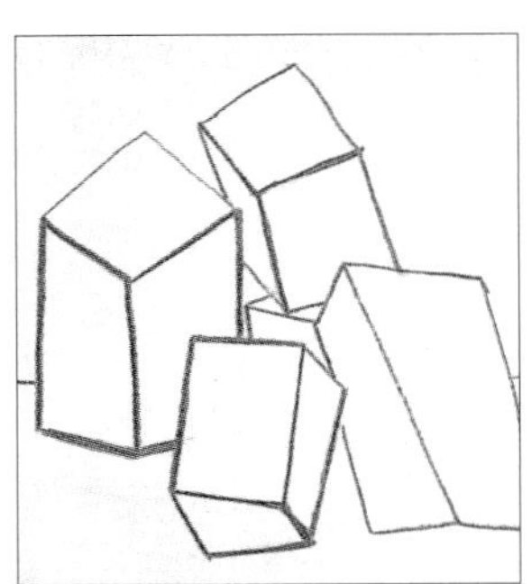

Left *In this drawing, the student has drawn the boxes as five individual objects and their relationship to one another.*

Far Left *In this drawing of a shipwright's shed, the enclosed space of the walls and ceiling creates a box; the end wall with a door is parallel to the picture plane.*

At your first attempt you will almost certainly come up against the problem mentioned in the previous chapter. Your mind, through your previous experience of cartons, knows that they have got sides, tops,

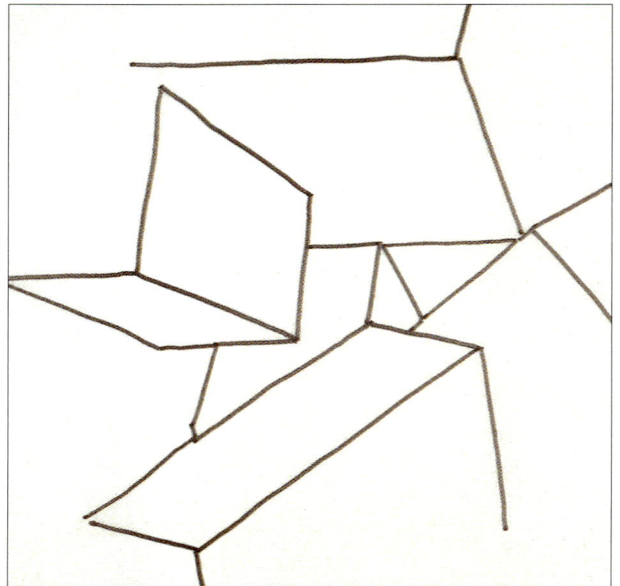

***Above** The second stage in the drawing, after the simple silhouette (as seen in the picture to the Right). It is a careful observation of the center, where all the boxes make a negative shape relative to one another. This is drawn in the correct proportion and relationship to the outer line drawing.*

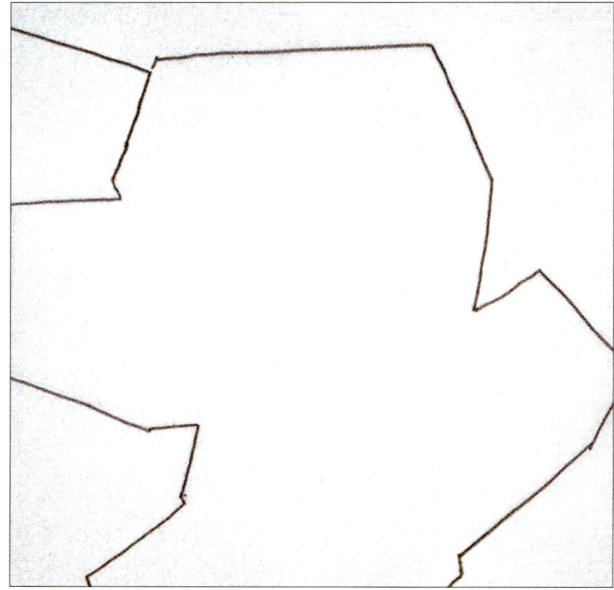

***Above** In this simple line drawing, the five cartons have not been seen as individual shapes but have been approached—along with the table—as a flat silhouette. It is impossible to make a drawing like this without conceiving of the cartons as one total shape.*

and bottoms and will not believe what your eyes are now telling you—that the tops of the cartons do not appear as perfect rectangles. Even though you are looking across the top of the cartons and your eye is giving you that information, in your mind you will try to tilt them up so that their squareness or rectangularity can be fully seen. This is an important insight into how the mind interprets objects.

Try a second drawing. This time, do not look at the cartons individually as boxes but run a line with your pencil from where you have drawn the edge of the table around the shape of all the boxes, making a single outline shape. This time, you are attempting to see them as a whole shape. You have now taken the first step to translating what is three-dimensional form into two-dimensional form.

Now move the boxes around into a different pattern, making sure that there is a gap between one or two of the boxes. Again draw purely linearly, starting from where you draw the edge of the table. When you come to the gap between two boxes, try to become aware not of the next box but of the negative space between the boxes. In your two-dimensional translation, the negative space is just as important a shape on the paper as the positive shape of the box itself.

It can be a helpful exercise to think of your sheet of paper as a flat sheet of glass through which you are viewing the boxes. This can be extremely useful in helping to understand the two-dimensional nature of drawing. If you can obtain a piece of glass or a sheet of clear, stiff plastic, mask off an area as illustrated, the same size as the piece of paper on which you are going to draw. Prop up the piece of glass in front of you so that the boxes are viewed through this glass screen. With a felt-tip pen start marking out the form of the boxes on the glass screen. You will also realize how important a fixed viewpoint is in representational drawing. The slightest movement of the head alters all the relationships between the boxes that you have already drawn on the glass, which is why it is important to maintain a fixed position while you are sketching out the structure of the drawing.

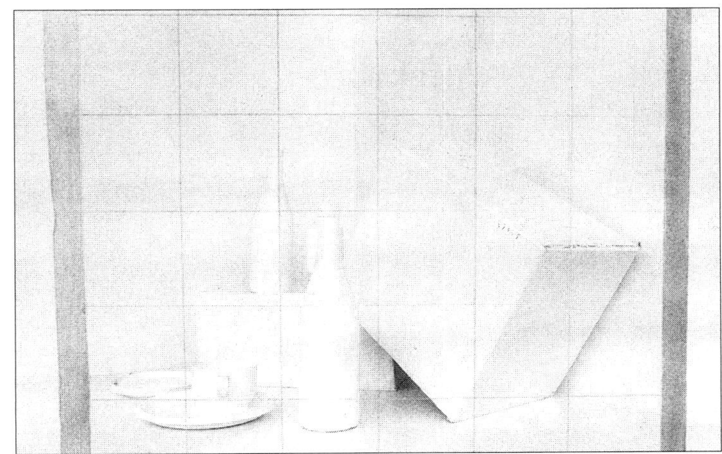

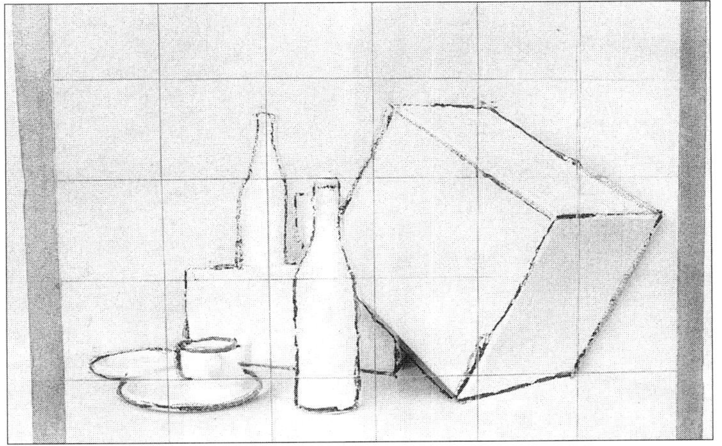

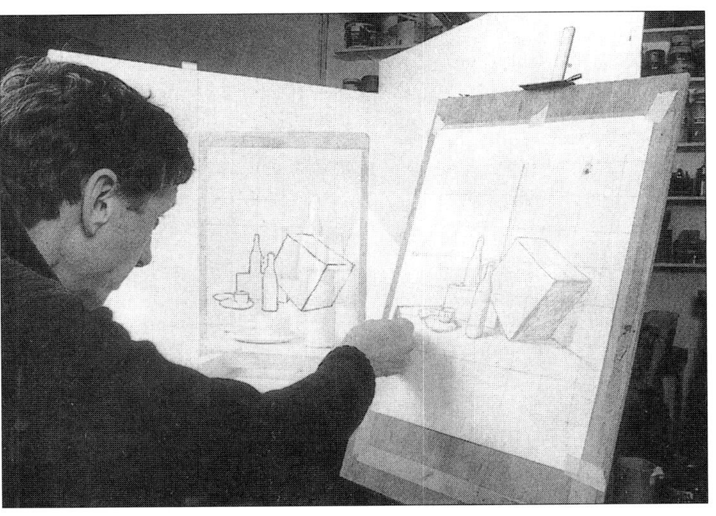

Top *Use a piece of normal window glass or a piece of rigid PVC plastic, approximately 14 x 20 in. (35 x 50 cm). Tape off an area 12 x 16 in. (30 x 40 cm). Cut two slits of equal depth with a saw in two short lengths of 1 x 2 in. (2.5 x 5 cm) timber.*

Middle *Draw the objects onto the glass screen using a felt tip pen or fine brush with a little gouache, making sure that your corners used as a reference are correctly in line.*

Right *Square up your glass screen and paper into 2 in. (5 cm) grids. Your paper and your grid are now exactly the same size and identically squared up.*

Sit so that you can see through the screen and look at your paper without having to move. Note where the objects in your still life are positioned on the grid and draw accordingly.

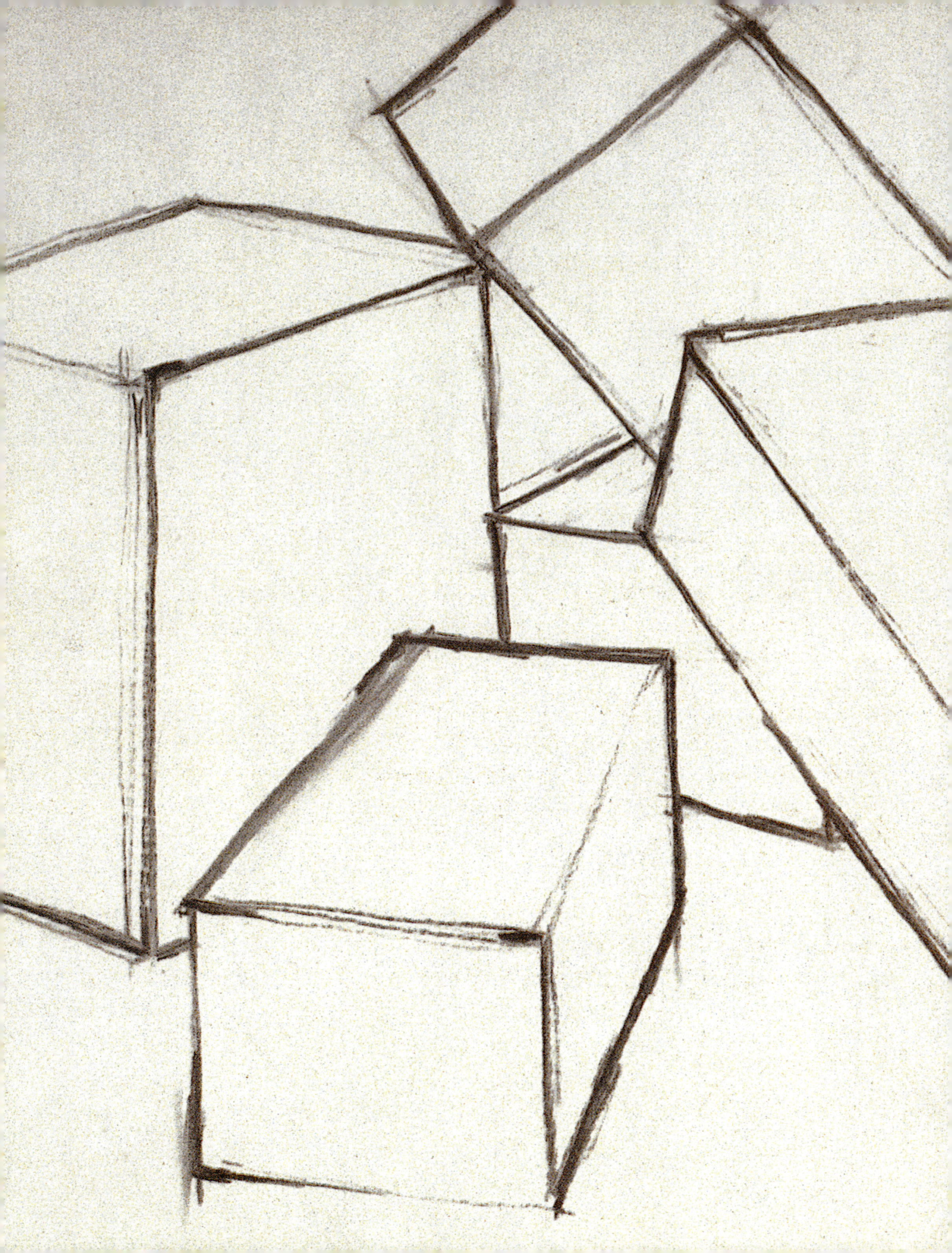

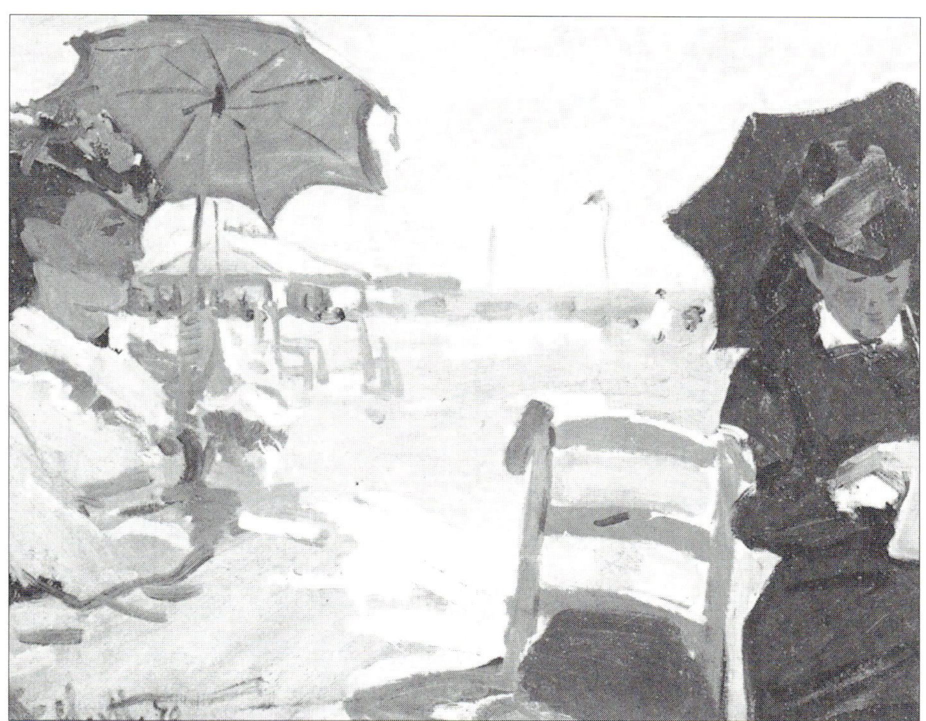

You may well be wondering why you were asked to prop a board up on a chair and draw in that particular manner. The sheet of glass or plastic is acting as a transparent picture-plane. A picture can be thought of as a rectangular surface through which we see the world. This window we call the "picture-plane" and it is the most important concept to understand in representational drawing. How does this glass picture-plane through which we are viewing the boxes relate to our drawing paper?

Left: *This is undoubtedly a drawing of five cartons, but the visual approach to this drawing, and the way in which the cartons are seen, are very different to the first attempt on page 21. Here, the boxes appear to be in the correct size and relationship to one another, as you would expect in a representational drawing. The boxes were seen clearly in the first drawing, but the information was used in a haphazard way. In this image, the observation has been ordered in a way which makes representational drawing possible.*

Above: Beach at Trouville *by Claude Monet (1840–1926) possesses a well-constructed design (as per the Golden Section formulation). But, from what we know of Monet's methods, it is unlikely that he used mathematical devices to locate the proportional divisions.*

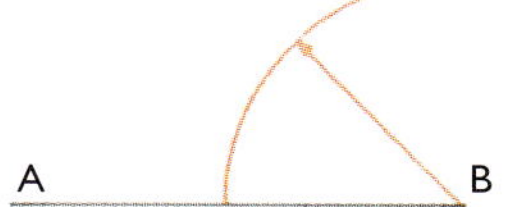

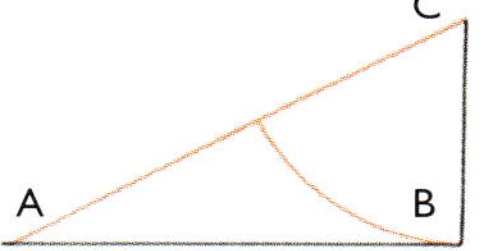

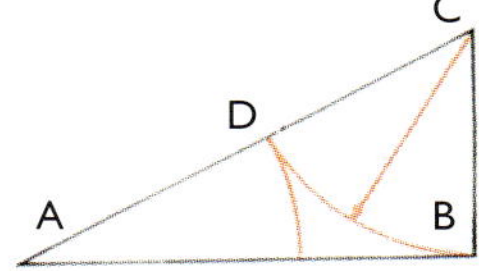

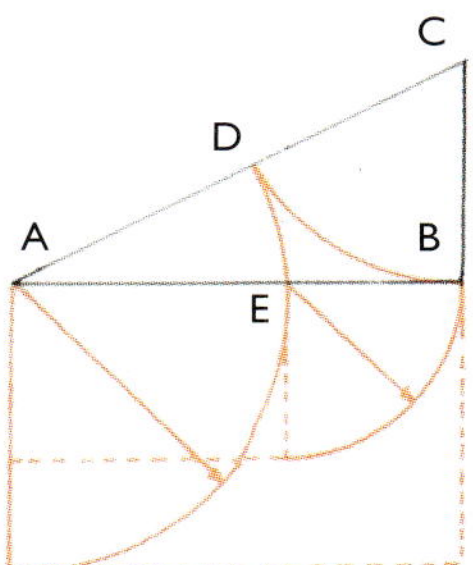

Right: *The Golden Section formulated in Vitruvius'* De Architectura *in the first century* BC *was the basis of the Greek definition of perfect proportion. Vitruvius stated that a harmonious relationship was achieved between unequal parts of a whole, if the smaller was in the same proportion to the larger as the larger was to the whole.*

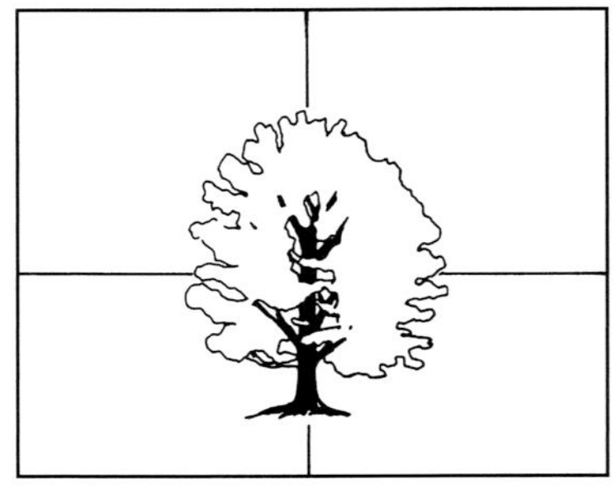
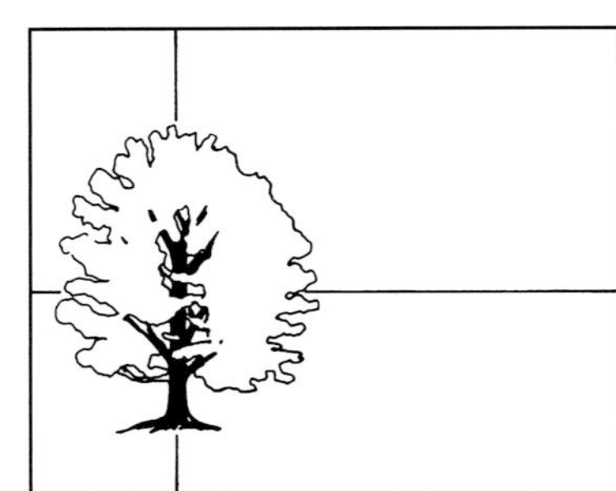
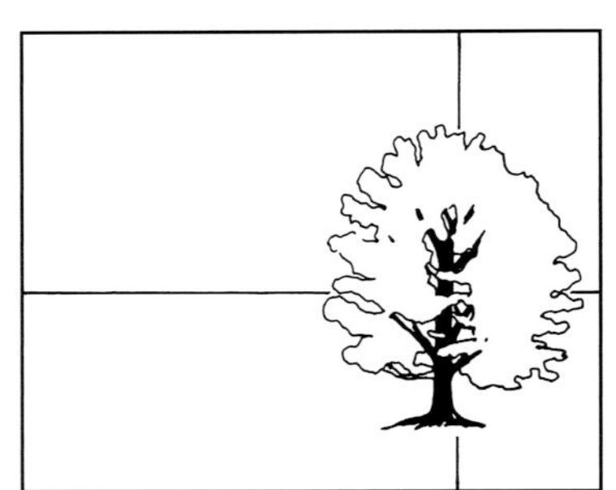
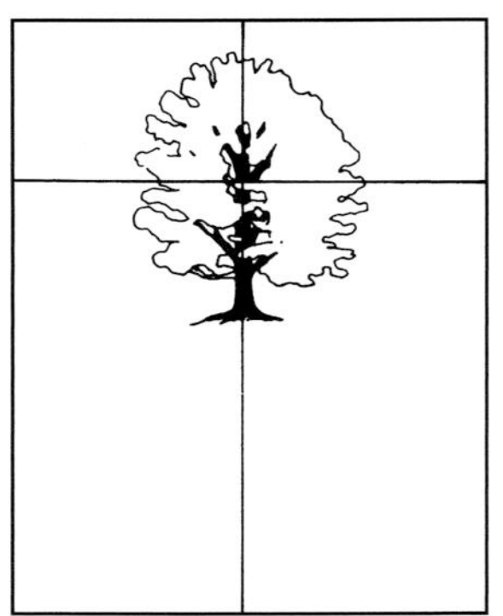
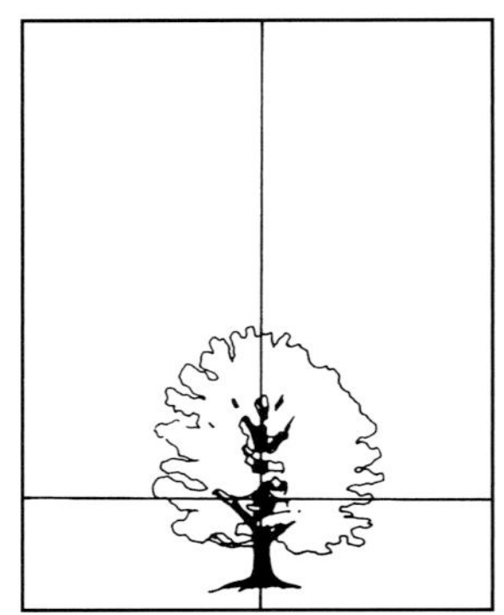
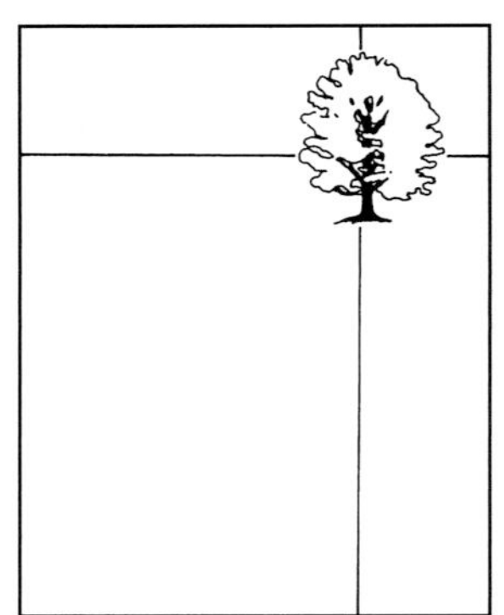
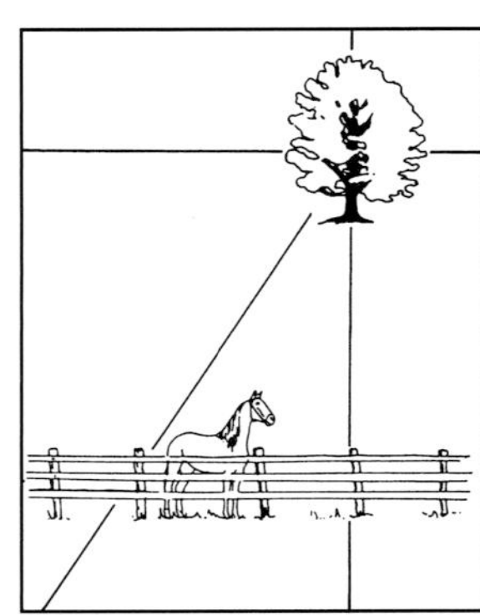

***Above** As the tree is moved to different positions on the picture plane, the composition of the picture is radically changed. Although it is an identical drawing, the composition of each example is quite different, thus illustrating the fact that although the subject matter can be important in making an interesting drawing, it is not necessarily the most important. It is more important that the position of the subject matter on the picture plane will make an interesting composition.*

Rearrange the boxes again and prop up the sheet of glass or plastic as shown. This time, however, notice that on the glass there has been ruled a square grid producing 2 in. (5 cm) squares right across the whole viewing area. Rule up a piece of paper in the same 2 in. (5 cm) squares. Repeat the procedure of looking through the glass screen and note where the significant lines of the boxes—the corners, etc.—are in relation to the grid on the glass screen. Find the corresponding position on your squared-up paper and mark it accordingly. When you have positioned all the most important marks remove the glass screen and continue to finish the drawing from the established marks.

Whenever you make a representational drawing, whether you are attempting a landscape, a figure, or any other subject, your mental and visual processes should correspond to thinking of it as drawing through an imaginary picture-plane, or as through a real picture-plane which you have just physically removed by taking away the glass sheet. The nearer you can get your piece of paper and board to a vertical position, the easier it is to relate this imaginary glass picture-plane to your paper, so it is worth your while spending some time to achieve this.

The fundamental difference between representational drawing and all the other forms of drawing is that the subject matter to be drawn is viewed as through a vertical window on the world. An analytical investigation of this particular approach to drawing was undertaken in the Renaissance by such great masters as Paolo Uccello, Leonardo da Vinci, and many others, and it represented a fundamental change in the way in which painting and drawing was practiced from then on. So much so that pre-Renaissance works look strange to us, as we are so used to looking at drawings and paintings that constitute realistic and convincing representations of the subject matter.

In the Western world, the picture-plane—i.e., representational drawing—was not seriously challenged as a concept from the 15th to the 20th century. Inseparably linked with the concept of the picture-plane, and subservient to it, are the theoretical concepts of composition and linear perspective. These concepts are often incorrectly studied as separate subjects, when in fact they are utterly bound up with each other.

Composition is the overall relation of the objects being drawn to the edges of the picture-plane. In the several illustrations of the same tree given as examples (on page 26), it can be seen that the positive and negative shapes—i.e., pattern—that make up the composition are radically altered by the position of the tree relative to the edges that make up the picture-plane. If the tree is placed centrally and the picture-plane has horizontal format, there are three equal distributions of pattern: from left to right, negative space, approximately equal positive space, approximately equal negative space. By moving the tree to the left or right this relationship in the proportions of the pattern is altered, thereby giving an entirely different "feel" to the drawing. In addition to a relationship between the positive and negative spaces on a horizontal plane (from left to right), there is also a relationship from top to bottom. Take the same tree and place it on a picture-plane that is now vertical in format: the balance of the positive and negative spaces from left to right and from top to bottom again are radically different. Yet each composition contains an identical drawing of the identical tree.

In general, it does not matter how well you draw a tree if the composition of which it

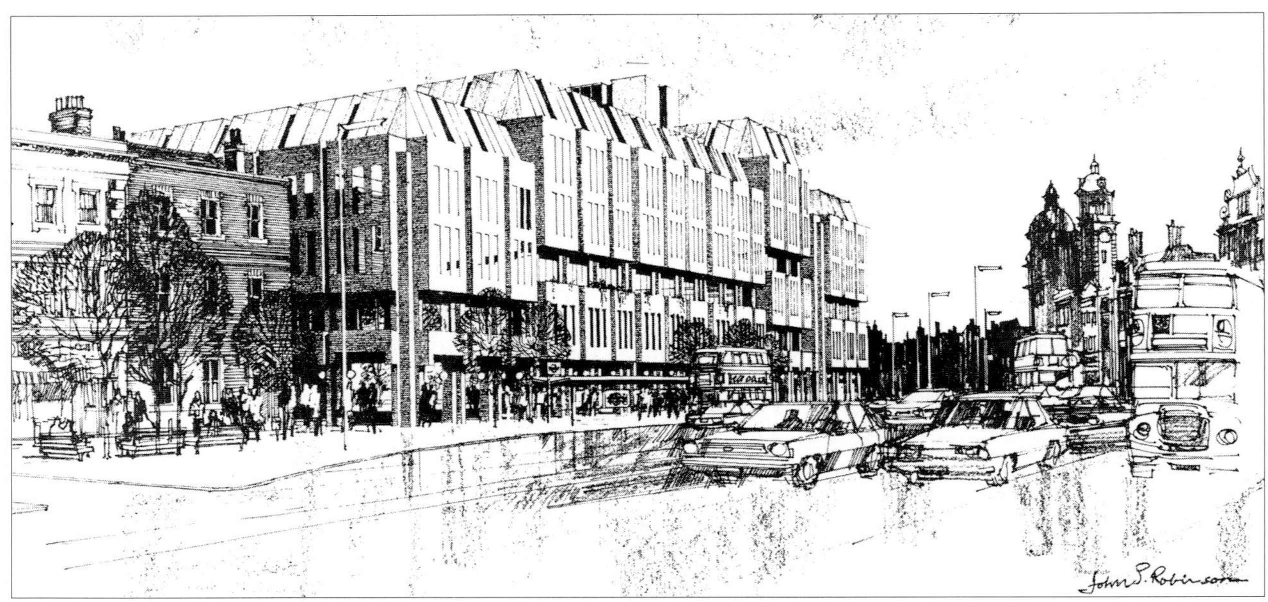

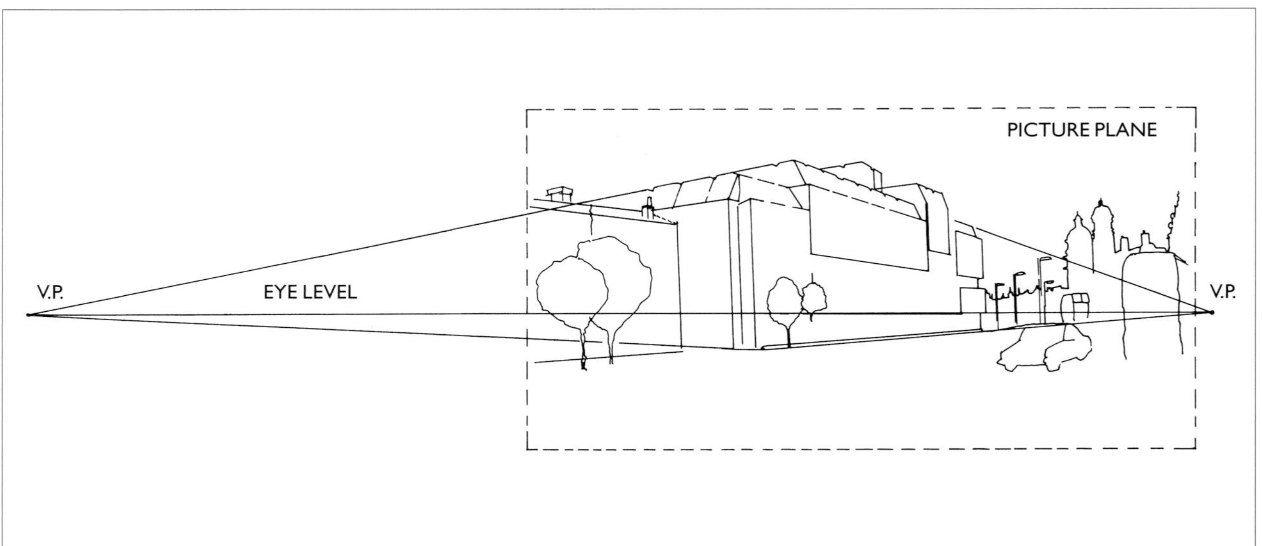

Above *This perspective rendering of an urban development is a fine example of the architect's use of two-point perspective for visualising a proposed development in an existing urban street. The pedestrians and motor vehicles are used in this case to give the drawing a sense of relative scale. A visual device is used to make the pedestrians and motor vehicles slightly smaller than they would actually be to give the proposed building a grander sense of scale. If the opposite effect is required, the pedestrians and vehicles would be drawn larger, therefore reducing the apparent size of the building.*

is a major part is boring and very equally balanced. A less well drawn tree that divides the picture plane into a greater variety of more interesting shapes may be a much more exciting piece of work.

Scale and perspective are really the same thing. Perspective is often thought of, incorrectly, as the mathematical theory much used by architects to render a three-dimensional visualization of a proposed building project. This mathematical theory is indeed one form of perspective which is dealt with more thoroughly at a later stage in this book, but linear perspective is only a mathematical device to be able to work out in a logical manner the relative size of objects as they recede into the distance. For the artist, accurate observation of the relative sizes of objects already deals with most of the problems of perspective and scale.

Perspective is a sense of scale, or the size of an object relative to other objects on the picture-plane, and their size relative to the size of the picture-plane.

To return to the drawing of the tree in our example, the tree is always the same size, what has altered, however, is the size of the picture-plane (piece of paper) on which it is drawn. In the first example the size of the picture-plane has been reduced, and the tree looks exceedingly large. In the next example the size of the picture-plane has been increased, and the tree looks as though it is in the middle distance. In the third example the drawing is on an altogether much larger piece of paper, and our initial perception is that the tree is in the distance. So, to summarize this, scale is not about actual size; it is about relative size.

Both perspective and composition, in conjunction with the picture-plane, are constantly referred to throughout this book, each time relating these very fundamental aspects to the particular subject matter. The way in which perspective, for example, is used in drawing the figure in landscape and still life is fundamentally the same, but has a particular application relative to each of those subjects. This applies equally to the theory of composition. The concept of the picture-plane in representational drawing stays constant whatever the subject matter.

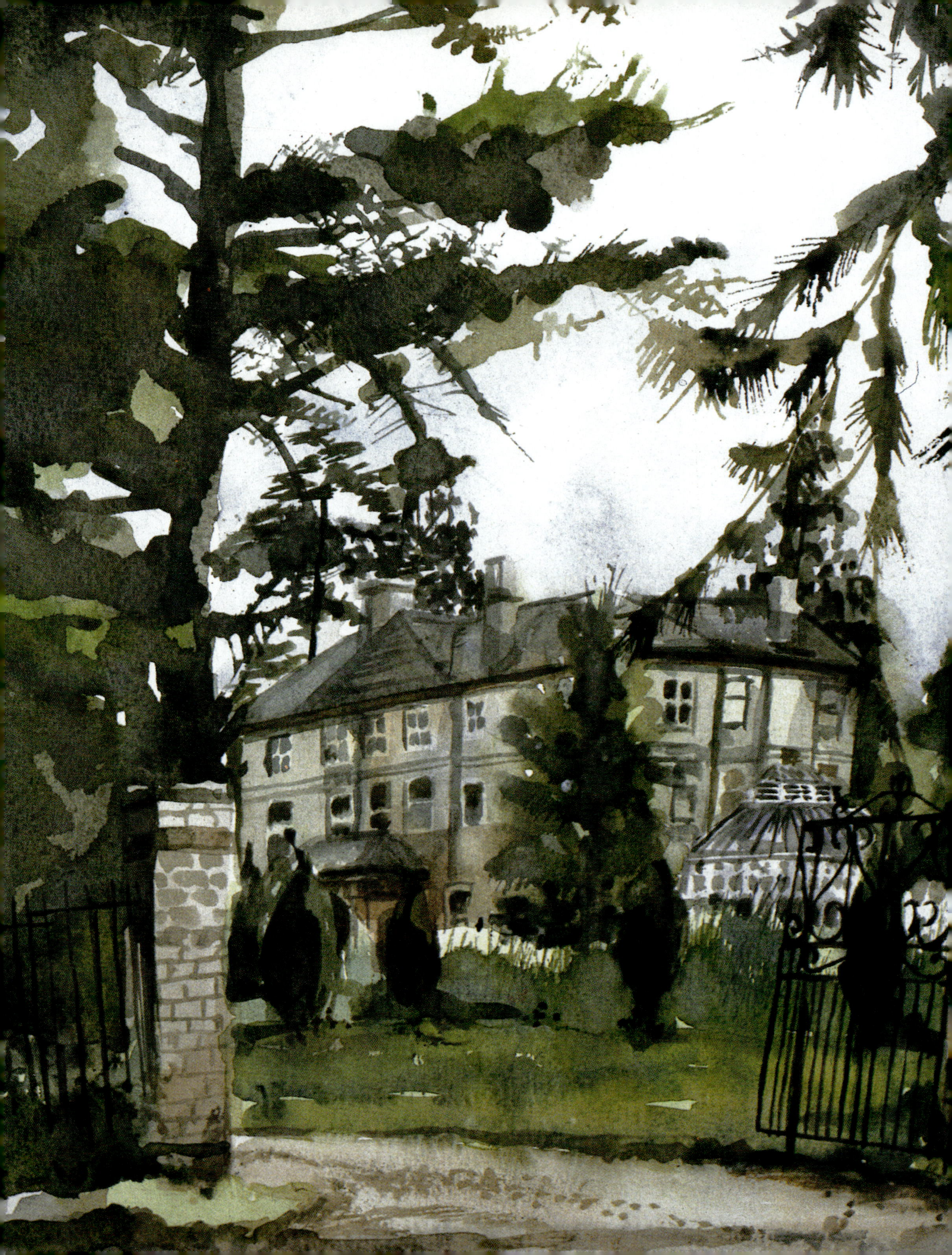

LANDSCAPE

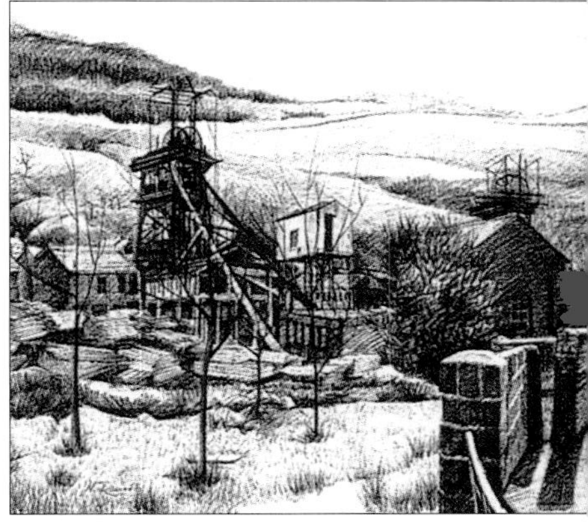

Above A mine in winter: *pencil and conté. The angularity of the machinery is complemented by the clarity and detail of the trees and wall.*

Left *A detailed sketchbook study of a pine tree; the hatching describes the spiny foliage very effectively.*

Far Left *A study in pencil and watercolor wash; here the brush has been used with great skill as a drawing instrument.*

Landscape is the preferred subject matter as a first introduction to painting and drawing. This is very understandable because it combines so many pleasures. There is not only practice in drawing but there is the added delight of being in the countryside "communing with nature." Landscape as subject matter is less exacting for the beginner than say, portraiture, and a pleasing and satisfying result can be achieved quite early on.

In Europe there is a long tradition of landscape painting and drawing, although it became recognized as an independent art form in the 17th century. Before that time most landscapes were backgrounds in compositions where figures or groups of figures played the most important role.

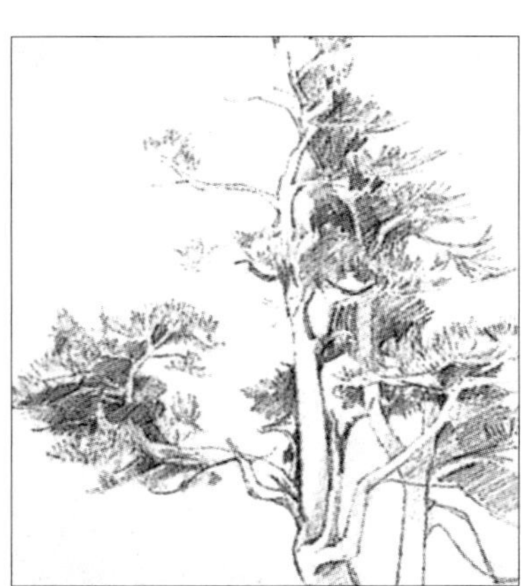

Two of the most revered exponents of landscape painting, John Constable and J.M.W. Turner, are familiar names to many people whether they have any interest in art

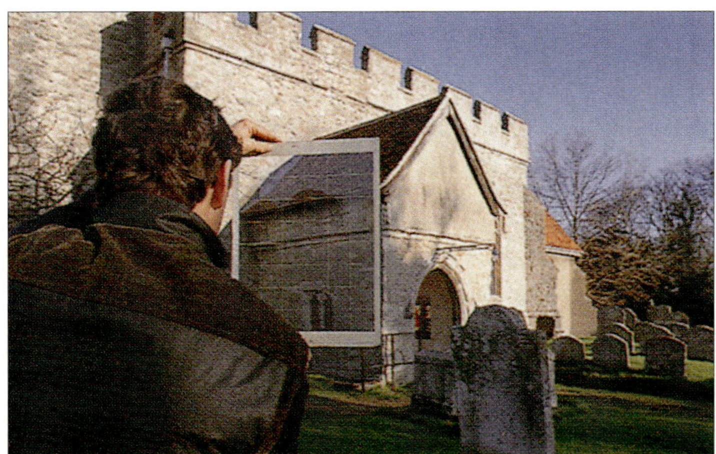

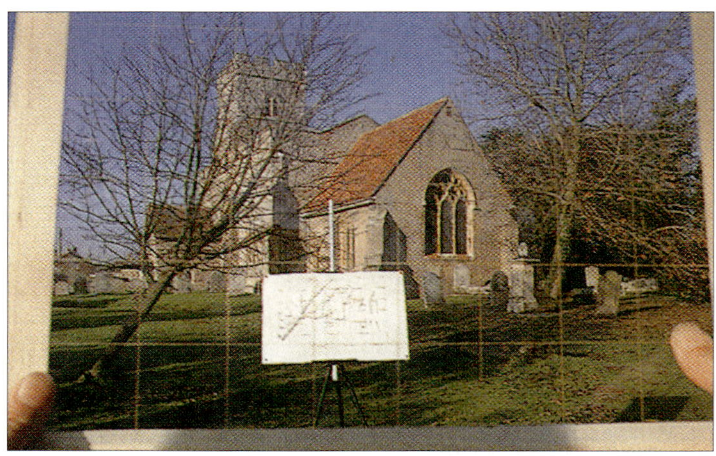

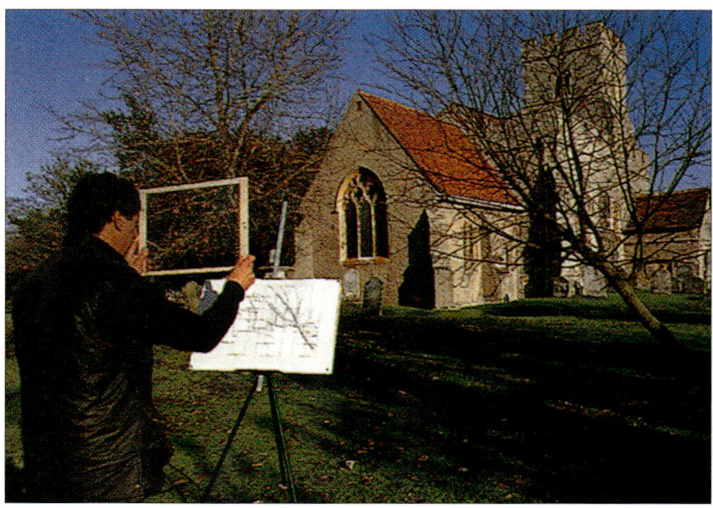

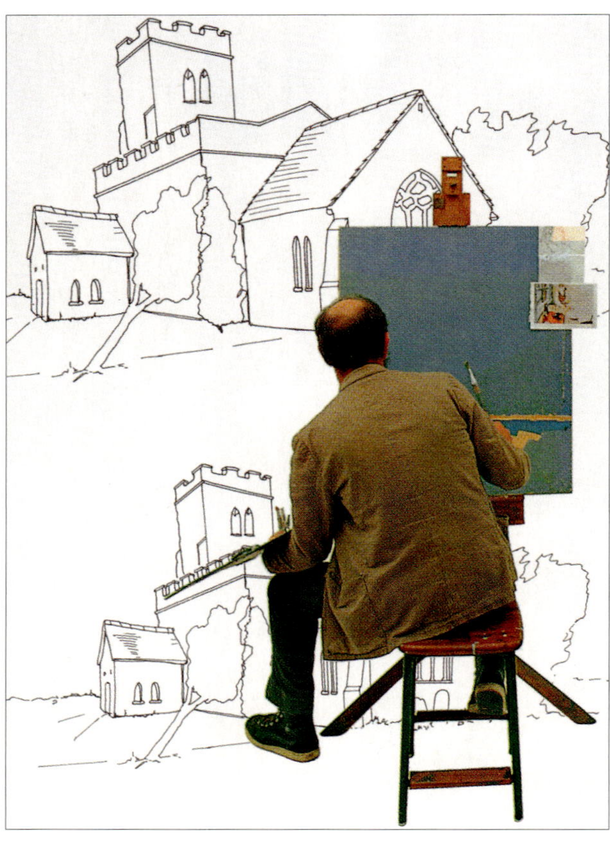

Left & Above *If you intend to take a drawing to a finished state it is most useful to have a sketching stool and easel. Although not essential, it is more comfortable. Position yourself in such a way that you can see that part of the landscape that you wish to draw, also your drawing, without moving your head too much. You are looking at a landscape through an imaginary picture-plane which you are then transposing onto paper. Try to avoid having direct sunlight on your paper, as the glare can be very tiring on the eyes.*

or not. We tend to see these artists' works as representations of a countryside pictured in an idyllic past. To Constable and his contemporaries they were a view of rural life as it actually was in the 18th century and early 19th century. There is a tendency among amateur artists now to look for similar subject matter—for example, thatched cottages and

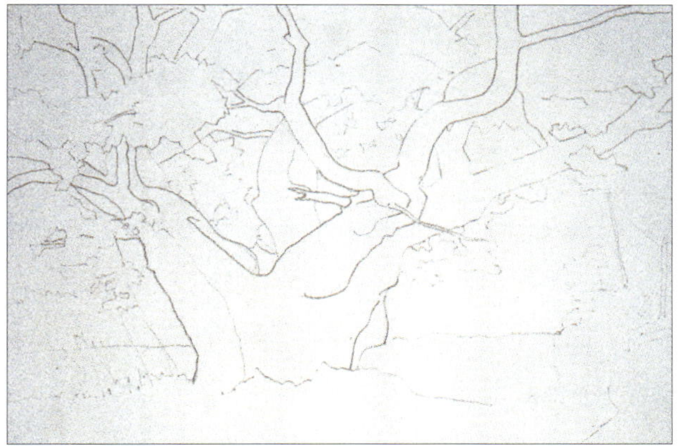

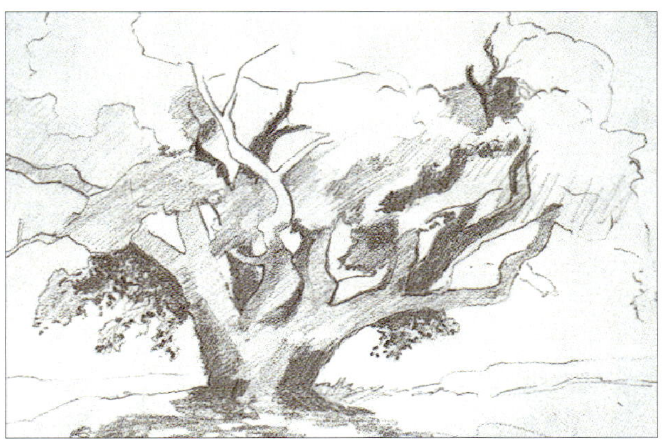

Top *This drawing shows the completed first statement. The major elements of the landscape are entered, and the structure of the composition has been decided within the designated picture plane. Every effort should be made to get to this stage without a break. Do not keep stopping, standing back and considering what you have done. If you do, you will lose the overall feeling of the drawing.*

Above *You can now see large areas that are in shadow in this drawing. They have been altered and very lightly cross-hatched. Again it should be stressed, do try and avoid concentrating too heavily on one particular area. If the drawing is going to be used as the basis for a watercolor painting to be completed when you return home you probably have sufficient information.*

Top Right *A beginner's attempt at watercolor by the direct method. This entails no preparatory drawing and therefore great skill and confidence are required to work directly with the brush. This example has become slightly confused, and under normal circumstances it is recommended that the beginner makes preparatory drawings.*

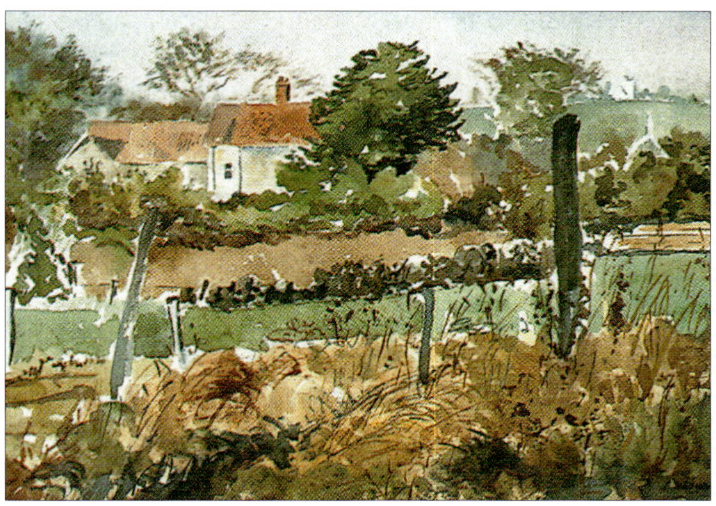

water mills—and to leave out of their paintings modern intrusions, such as power cables, tractors, and vapor trails from jet aircraft.

It is not necessary to live in an area of outstanding natural beauty to successfully produce a landscape drawing. There are numerous examples of interesting paintings and drawings of industrial canals, gas and petroleum plants, major road flyovers, and suburban backyards. Try to draw those things that are familiar to you and are around you. By working in your immediate environment you will make a drawing that in its own way will be as relevant an observation of our world as Constable and Turner made of theirs.

A convenient way to start drawing a landscape is to view the landscape through a viewing frame. This helps to choose the best pictorial composition. Start by drawing a rectangle on your paper. This is to represent the picture-plane as seen through the viewing frame. Do not at this stage get involved in any detail because that could interfere with the overall structure of the drawing. Once all the large features are drawn, add lines designating all the large areas that are in shadow.

Obviously the initial drawing is very flat because all the objects are treated with the same intensity of line—quite light—irrespective of where they are spatially in the drawing. Those things furthest away in the drawing, such as trees or hedges on the horizon, need not be worked any more than they are at this point. In the middle ground, select those details that really are dominant and emphasize them. It is only those parts of the landscape really near to you that should be treated in any great detail.

Now start to outline the areas which are in deeper shadow within the already drawn area of shadow. Shade both these areas again. Now concentrate in greater detail on those areas of the composition that you have decided to make the focal point. If the focal point of your composition is in the middle distance, again, do not over-embellish. Successful drawings may depend far more on what is suggested than what actually is.

Up to now all the exercises have involved the use only of the most basic of drawing instruments, the graphite pencil. To the beginner the pencil is the most obvious and commonly used drawing medium—indeed, the lay person often considers that a drawing can be done only with a pencil. There is nonetheless, of course, a great variety of media, the most commonly used of which are chalk, charcoal, conté crayon, and ink.

Charcoal has many advantages for the beginner. Large areas of tone can be put in very rapidly, and the intensity can be varied by rubbing, blowing or brushing, etc; if you want to alter the form—i.e., shape—it can be easily done with a soft putty eraser. The richness of tone achievable with charcoal is immense, from the palest of grays to the blackest of blacks, and with the addition of white chalk and a putty eraser to bring out highlights, charcoal is a versatile medium.

There are however two distinct disadvantages to charcoal when working out of doors. It is not unknown to have a drawing in an advanced state when a sudden gust of wind removes half your hard-won image before you have had time to apply a fixative. Incidentally, for charcoal-drawing, a paper with a good tooth is necessary and a fixative to secure the charcoal to the paper is also absolutely essential.

Conté crayon and compressed charcoal behave in a not dissimilar manner, and the range of blacks to grays—particularly if used in conjunction with white conté—is equally as encompassing. The facility to be able to spread it with your fingers or rub it out is much

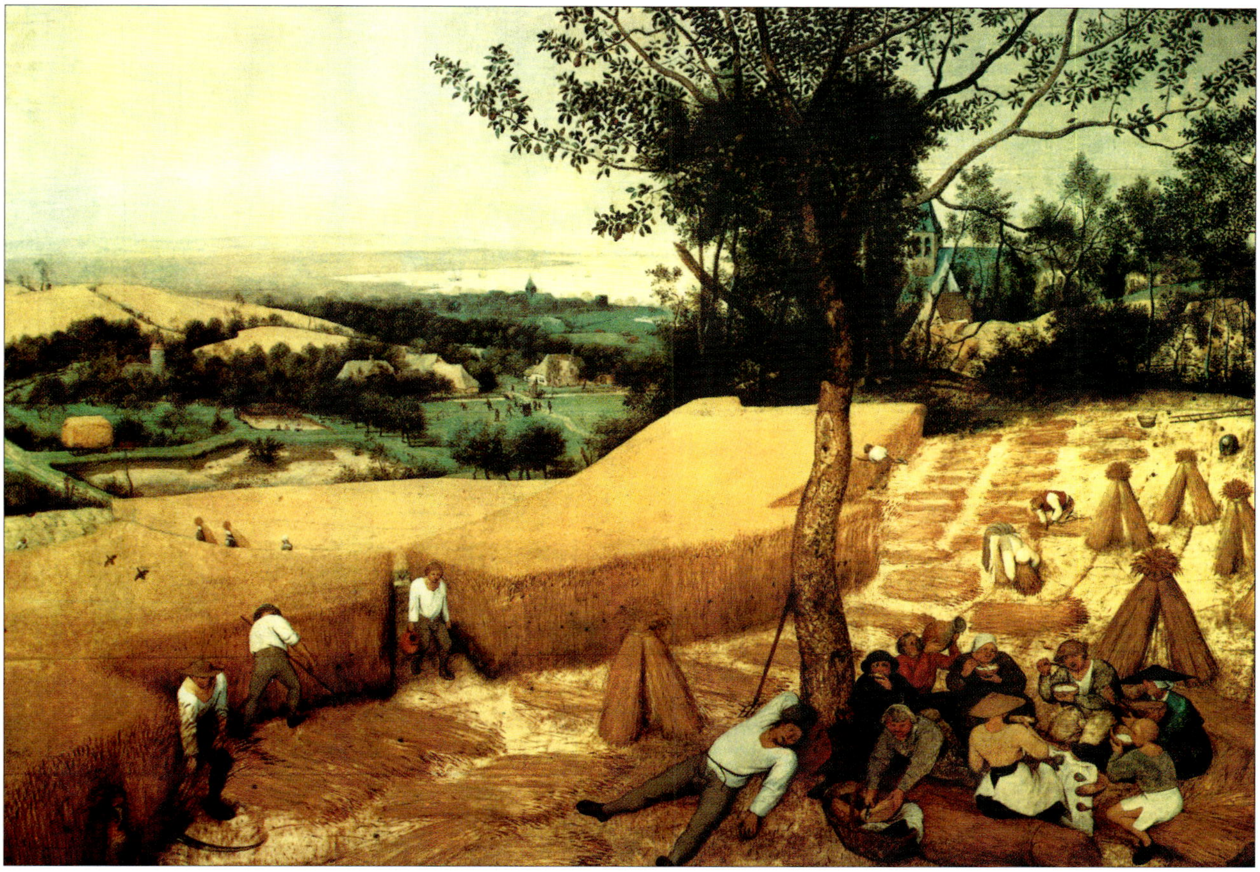

Above & Right *In Bruegel's painting* The Cornharvest *(1568) we have a very fine example of the use of strong geometrical form being used in a landscape painting. It is often thought, incorrectly, that landscape only comprises very soft and rounded shapes. This composition works particularly well as it contrasts the soft, rounded shapes of the trees with the hard edges of the cut cornfield. Such contrasts are even more apparent in modern landscape. It is often a good idea to make tracings from postcards of paintings you have seen to help clarify the compositional devices that might be missed if only a casual observation is carried out. Notice how the sheafs, the path between the corn, the corn laying on the ground, and the curve of the scythe held by the figure on the left, all help to turn the eye toward the main group of figures resting under the tree, which is the central subject matter.*

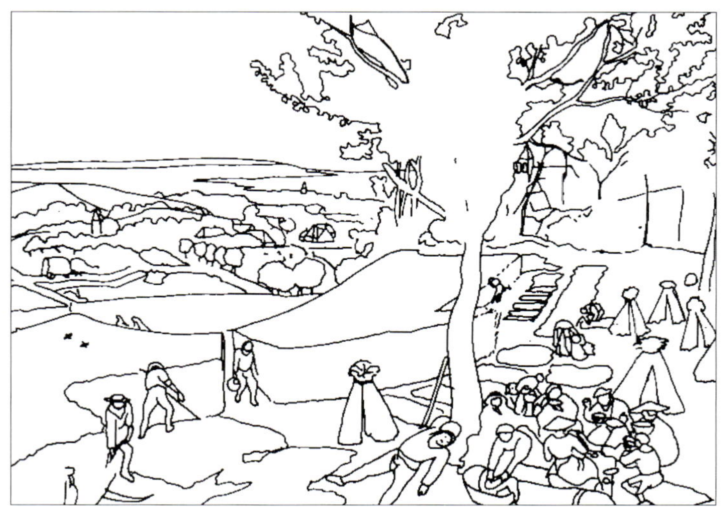

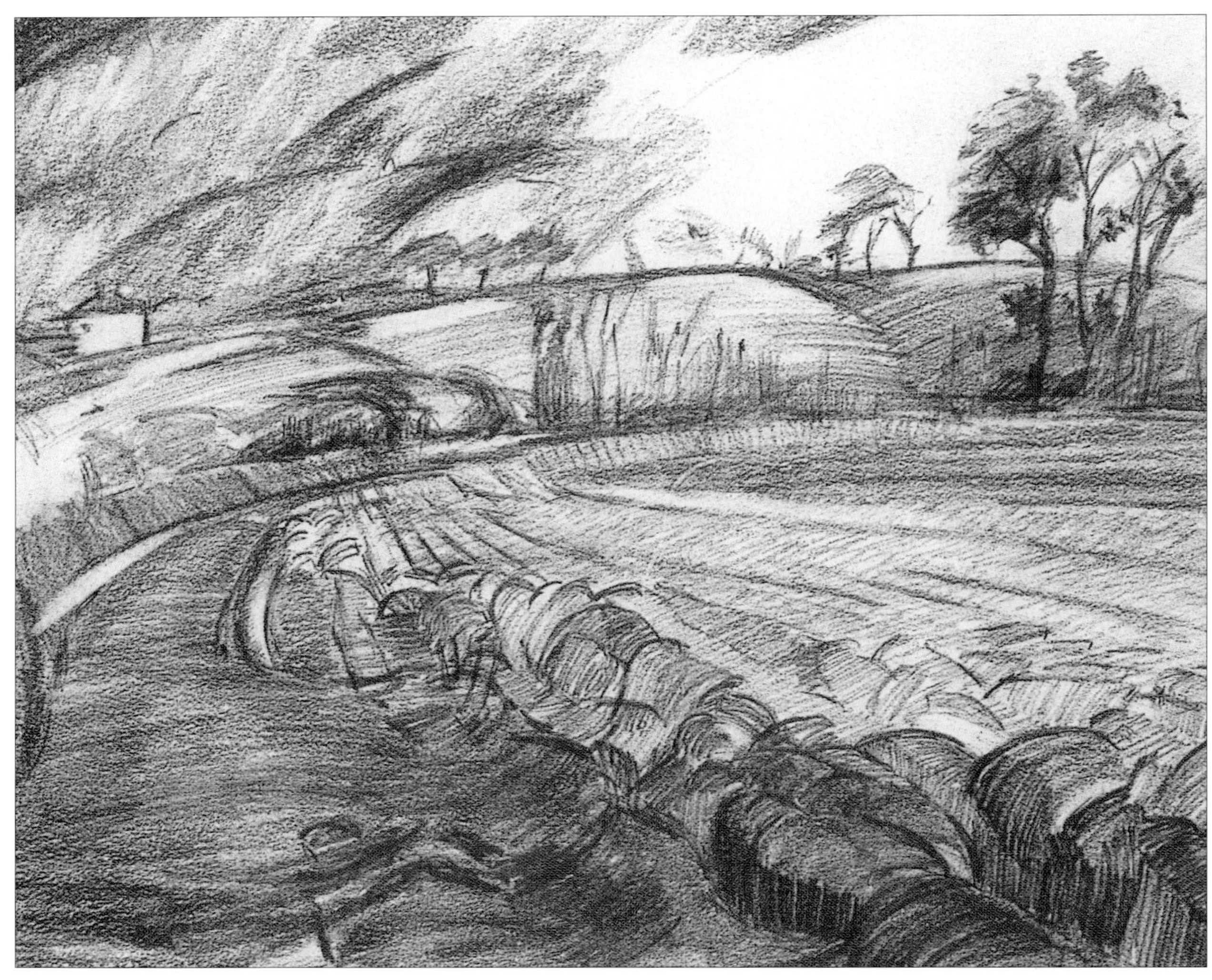

Above *In this pencil drawing made on a late Fall day, the strong lines of perspective of the freshly ploughed field lead the eye into the middle distance. This is an excellent example of the theory of perspective put into practice.*

reduced, so it is necessary to have quite a positive approach to drawing. This is often best achieved by drawing in the large areas first using the conté very lightly to get the palest of grays possible and using this as a base from which to start building the intermediary grays right up to an intense black.

One of the most important elements in landscape is the sky, and cloud formations in particular. Many beginners find it extremely difficult, particularly with a pencil, to make a satisfactory rendering of clouds and sky. Unless you are working in color, the cloudless blue of a Mediterranean sky is almost

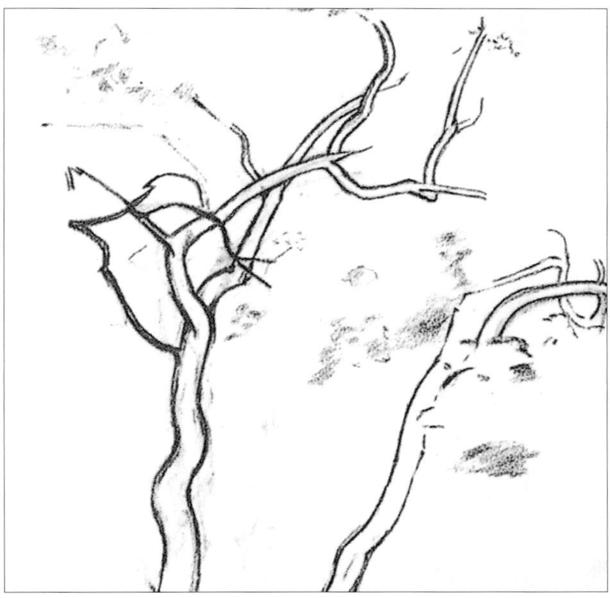

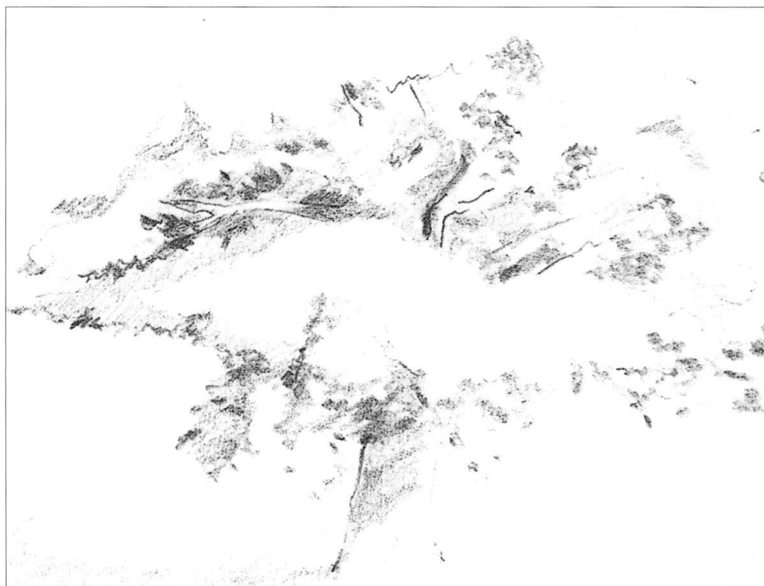

Above Left *This small sketch book study of an oak in full summer leaf rendered in graphite pencil shows the contrast between this medium and charcoal. The main difference is the intensity of the dark shapes. The pencil drawing only measures 8 X 6 in. (20 X 15 cm). Although it would not be impossible, it would be extremely difficult to render a drawing this size in charcoal.*

Above *In this conté drawing emphasis has been placed on the taut, twisting old cherry trees, and the hard, crisp line is an ideal vehicle for expression when using conté, which smudges far less than charcoal. Conté can often be handled with more confidence by the beginner.*

impossible to draw or express. The only solution is to leave that part of your drawing completely untouched; the brightness of the light is then expressed by the vividity of the objects in the landscape and the intensity of the shadows being made by these objects, both of which give a visual clue to the glare of the otherwise blank sky.

Many artists find charcoal and conté a more suitable medium for a composition where the cloud formations play a dominant role.

Ink may be a very satisfactory medium for landscape drawing, particularly when it is diluted with water and used with a brush. This approach allows for detailed tonal information to be recorded out of doors for use in the studio later. The technique of pen-and-wash drawing is very similar in approach to watercolor painting, in which the major part of the image is laid down with a brush, and only parts that must be sharply distinguished are rendered with a pen.

The theory of perspective, which has already been mentioned, is basically a pictorial device to work out the proportions of objects in space which are more or less the same size, but which have to be represented so that those that are nearer to you appear larger

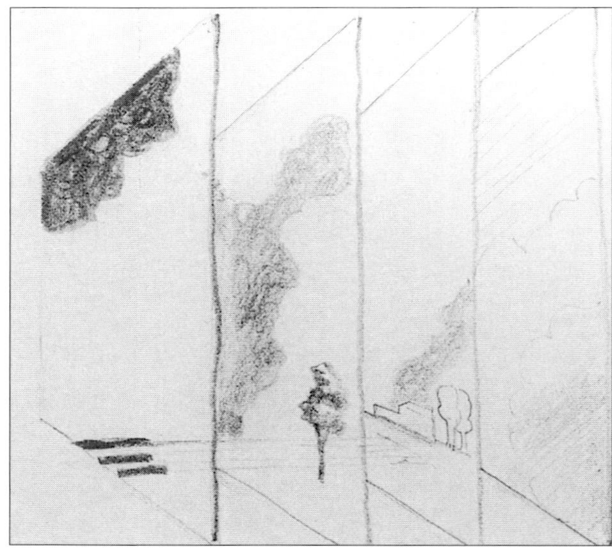

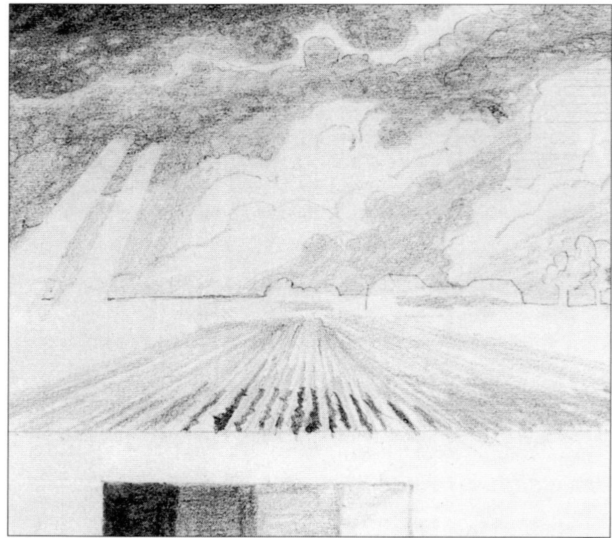

Top & Above *To illustrate the ploughing on the field here, normal linear perspective can be used, but how do you create atmospheric perspective in a monochrome drawing? Imagine that the picture is made up of four sheets, and that which is nearest to you is the darkest and on the first sheet, that which is in the middle distance is on the next sheet, and that in the furthest distance is on the next. The fourth sheet represents the endlessness of the sky. The sky is often represented as a backdrop to the landscape, but this is a mistake. The clouds also are represented on each of the "sheets", the closest ones are darkest, fading toward the horizon. In this way, atmospheric perspective is applied both to the land and the sky.*

than those that are further away. If you are looking out to sea, you could use perspective to determine the relative size of the waves as they recede toward the horizon. When this theory is applied to the sea, a greater sense of space is achieved than merely drawing the waves in an arbitrary manner.

Aerial perspective is a further development of linear perspective. Instead of following a structural framework, it is based on the idea that what is nearest to you can be seen in sharper detail than the same object would be seen in the middle or distant ground. This theory in particular applies to color.

The result of this ratio between intensity and distance is called "value". To translate value where color is not being used, it is necessary to find an equivalent in grays to represent these differences. An exact representation of color is of course impossible.

Another method of applying this theory is to draw an object that is nearer to you in a darker line and with more detail, lightening the intensity of the line and reducing the amount of detail until you arrive at the furthest distance, which is then just lightly outlined. The reverse is true in terms of highlight. The brightest highlight is used only for an object that is near to you, again diminishing, becoming more gray as it moves back in space.

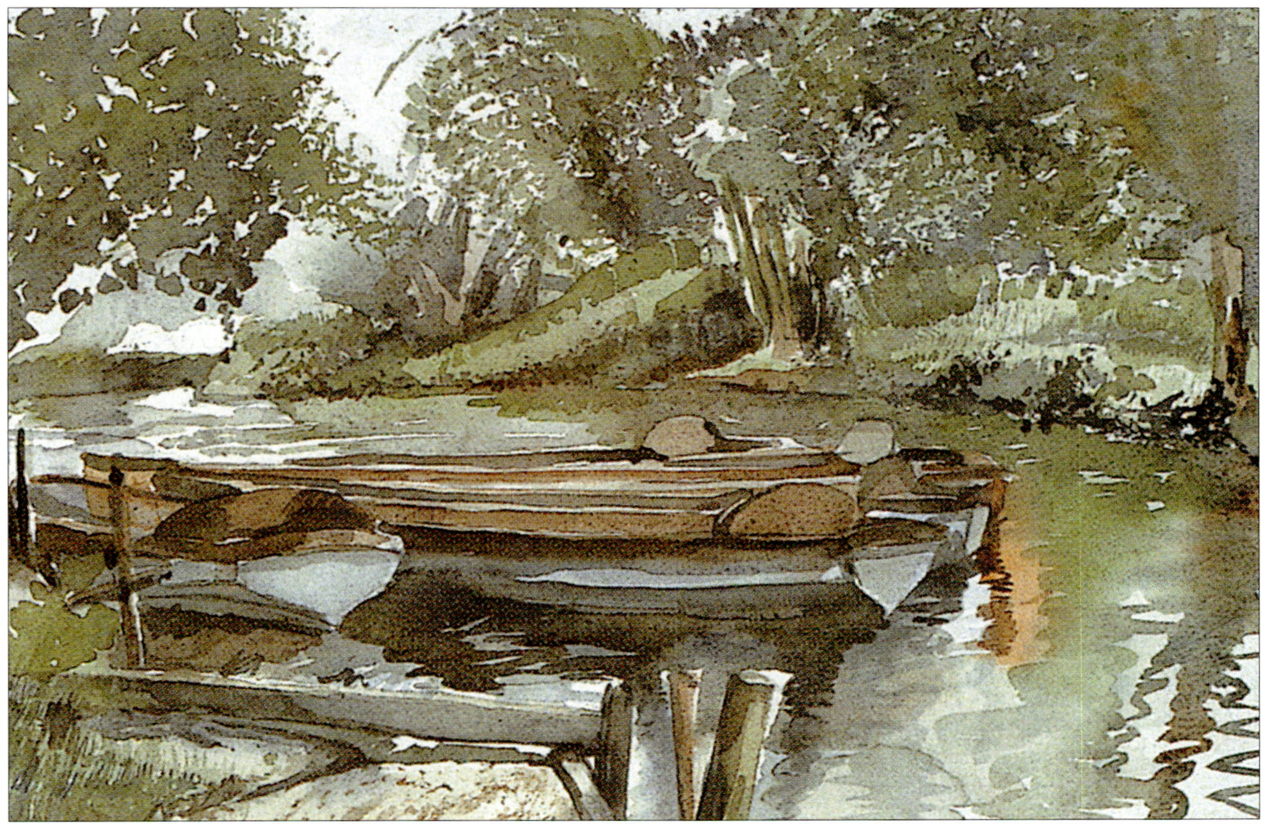

Above *In this watercolor good use has been made of the white paper to emphasize the highlights. The work started as an on-field pencil study and developed in color later in the studio.*

With practice beginners will likewise start to develop their own particular ways of dealing with tone and color. The most commonly used device is to actually write on the drawing a description of the color, time of day, and weather conditions, with cross-hatching to show areas in shadow (cross-hatching closely areas near to you and broadening the hatching out to show distance), and with arrows showing the direction of the light.

Another device is to take for example a point on a hedge, follow down a natural line of perspective, and at intervals develop part of the hedge in more detail. The eye naturally follows down those areas of more visual activity, thereby combining linear perspective and aerial perspective in one statement.

The beginner often finds this theory of aerial perspective the most difficult to comprehend. It is better, therefore, to have some idea of the basic concept at this stage and let it develop with experience; to let the actual experience of drawing teach you by practical application.

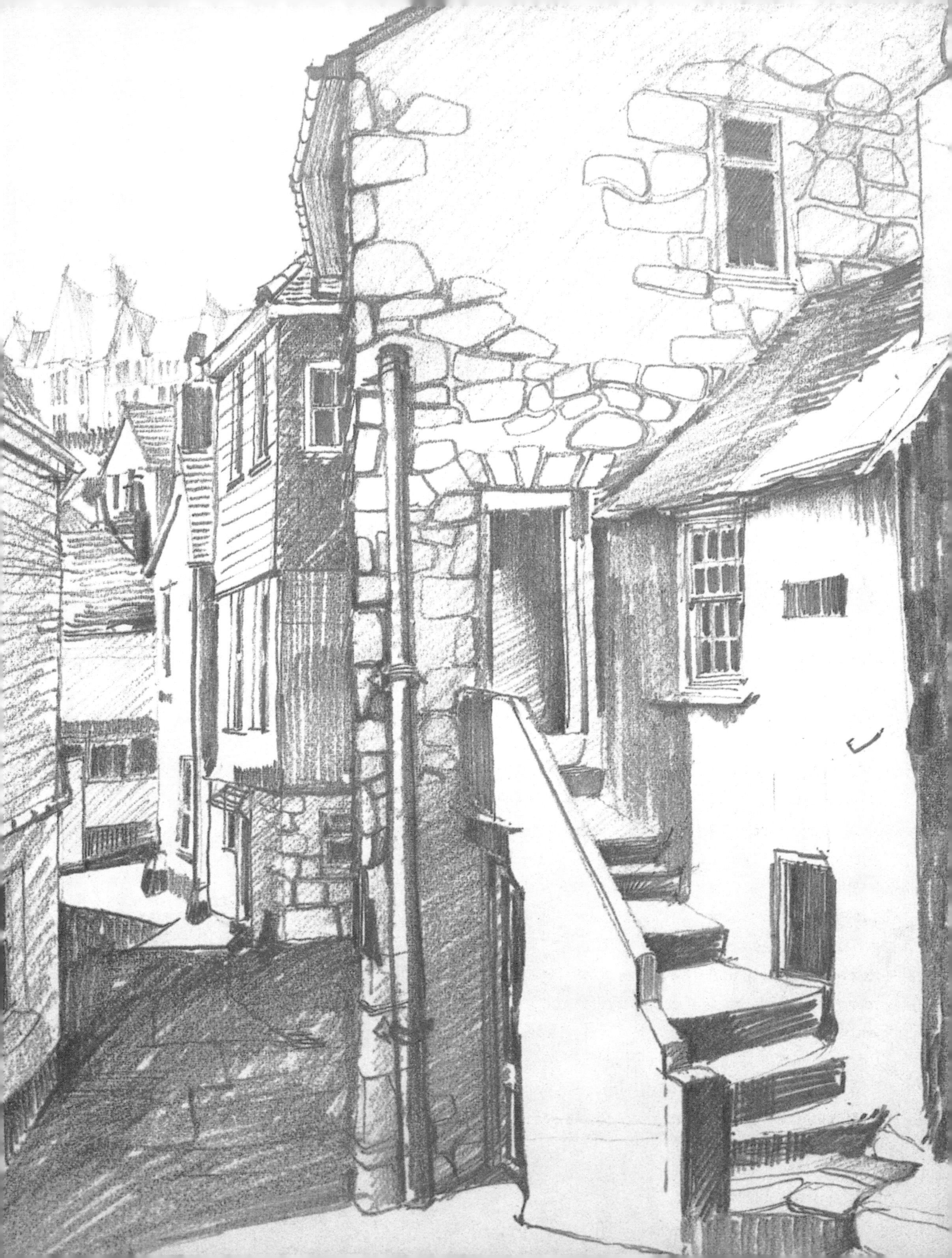

5 BUILDINGS AND TOWNSCAPE

All the theories and pictorial attitudes that have already been discussed in the chapter on Landscape apply equally well to the study of Townscape and Buildings. The geometrical precision of buildings when used in contrast to natural landscape can create a visual tension, and the same is equally true in reverse of a row of trees lining a central city street, which add an organic contrast to the geometrical hardness of the adjacent buildings.

There are many artists who have found a lifetime of subject matter in an urban environment. Several notable artists have painted street scenes completely devoid of any figures. Canaletto's fascination with his native city of Venice, where the effects of the crisp northern Italian light brought a supreme degree of clarity to that architectural subject matter, greatly influenced many artists of succeeding generations. Even today, many photographic souvenir postcards are taken of that city and others in a way that echo his archetypal view. It took succeeding generations of artists to realize and come to terms with the idea that cities cannot always be seen in a clean, clear light that makes every detail of the architecture visible.

Our own contemporary environment presents just as many possibilities. Brightly colored motorcars stacked in rows in a drab

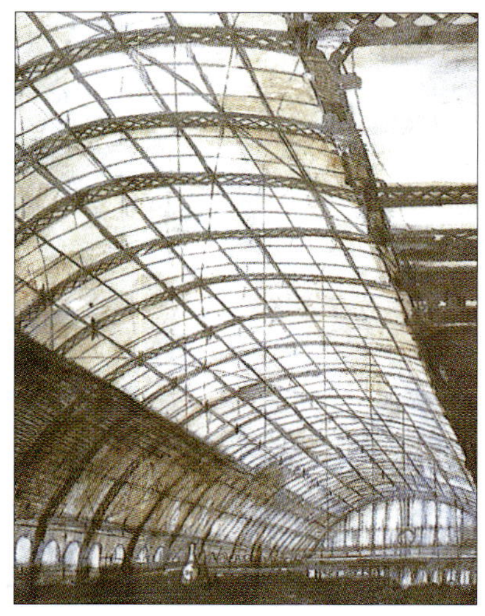

Above *A pencil and wash study of the glass roof of a Victorian railway station, London. This drawing relies upon a painstaking control of perspective as well as silhouette to create a cavernous expanse of glass and steel.*

Left *This pencil study is a good example of multi-point perspective.*

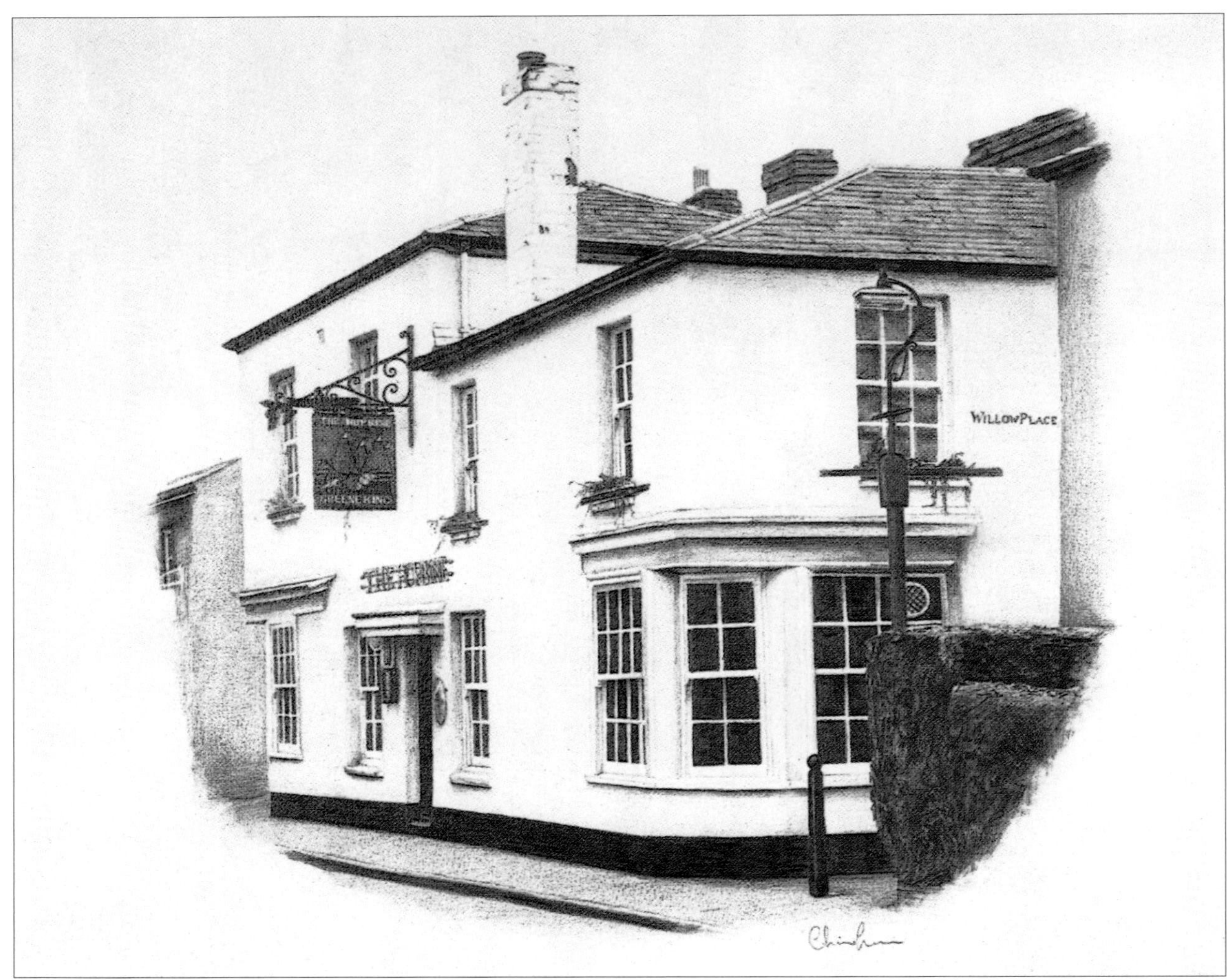

concrete multistorey car park could quite easily be turned into an interesting pictorial study. The grotesque silhouette of an industrial plant, which obeys none of the proportions necessary in an inhabited building, can give the artist a whole range of visual possibilities: such structures obey their own strong logic governed by the industrial processes they are designed to serve. The city at night can be particularly visually exciting, its multitude of light sources casting shadows in all directions.

Above *Pencil study of a public house depicting the building in a clear and concise manner. No attempt has been made to include people on what would normally be a busy thoroughfare. The subject of this drawing is categorically the building*

For those students who wish to represent the townscape in a less impressionistic manner, a working knowledge of perspective is very useful. But because few streets are built dead straight or uniformly, simple, two-point perspective is essentially too limiting and an understanding of the laws of multi-vanishing-point perspective is more useful. However, if the pictorial basics of good observation and the picture-plane are clearly understood, an exciting rendition of a townscape can be successfully completed with the minimum of perspective knowledge.

Take any street scene and view it as you would a landscape, through a viewing-frame.

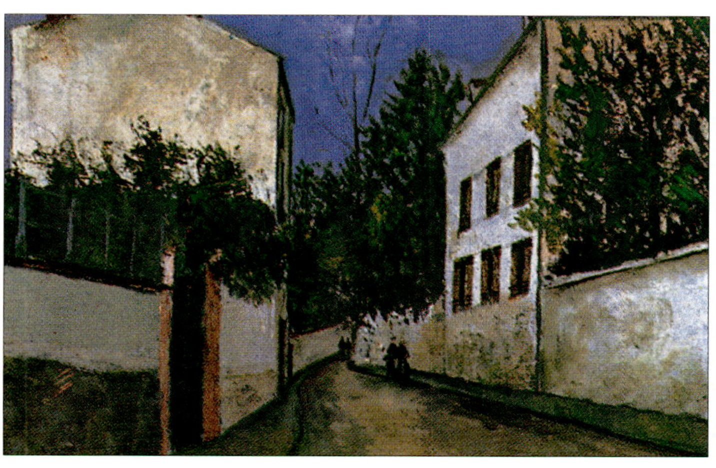

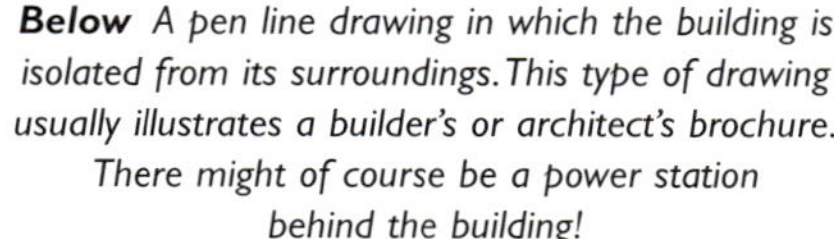

Below *A pen line drawing in which the building is isolated from its surroundings. This type of drawing usually illustrates a builder's or architect's brochure. There might of course be a power station behind the building!*

Above *The French artist Utrillo had a very different approach to the contemporary urban environment. Utrillo's paintings convey an eerie emptiness and sense of isolation. The city is not used as a backdrop for figures but is used to create a melancholy mood.*

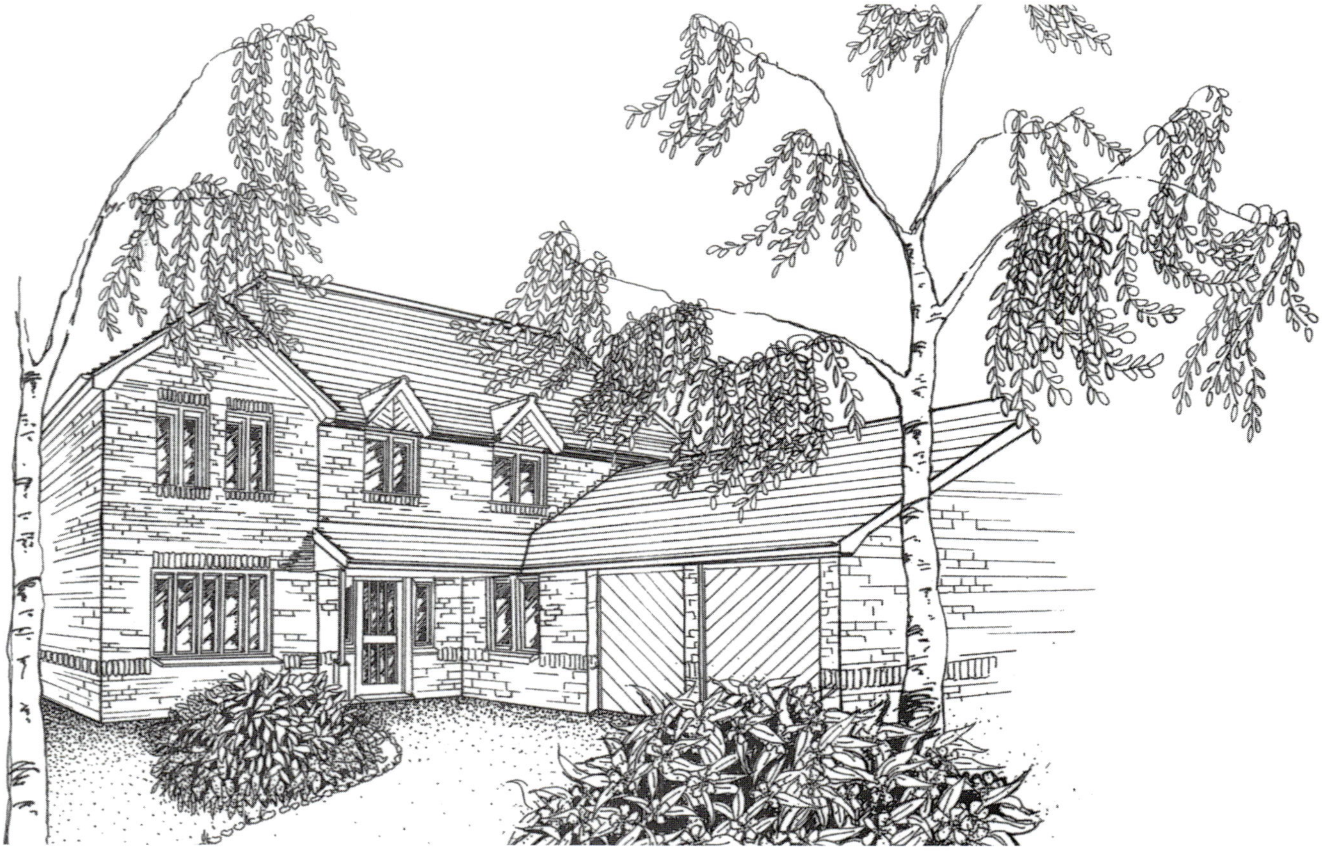

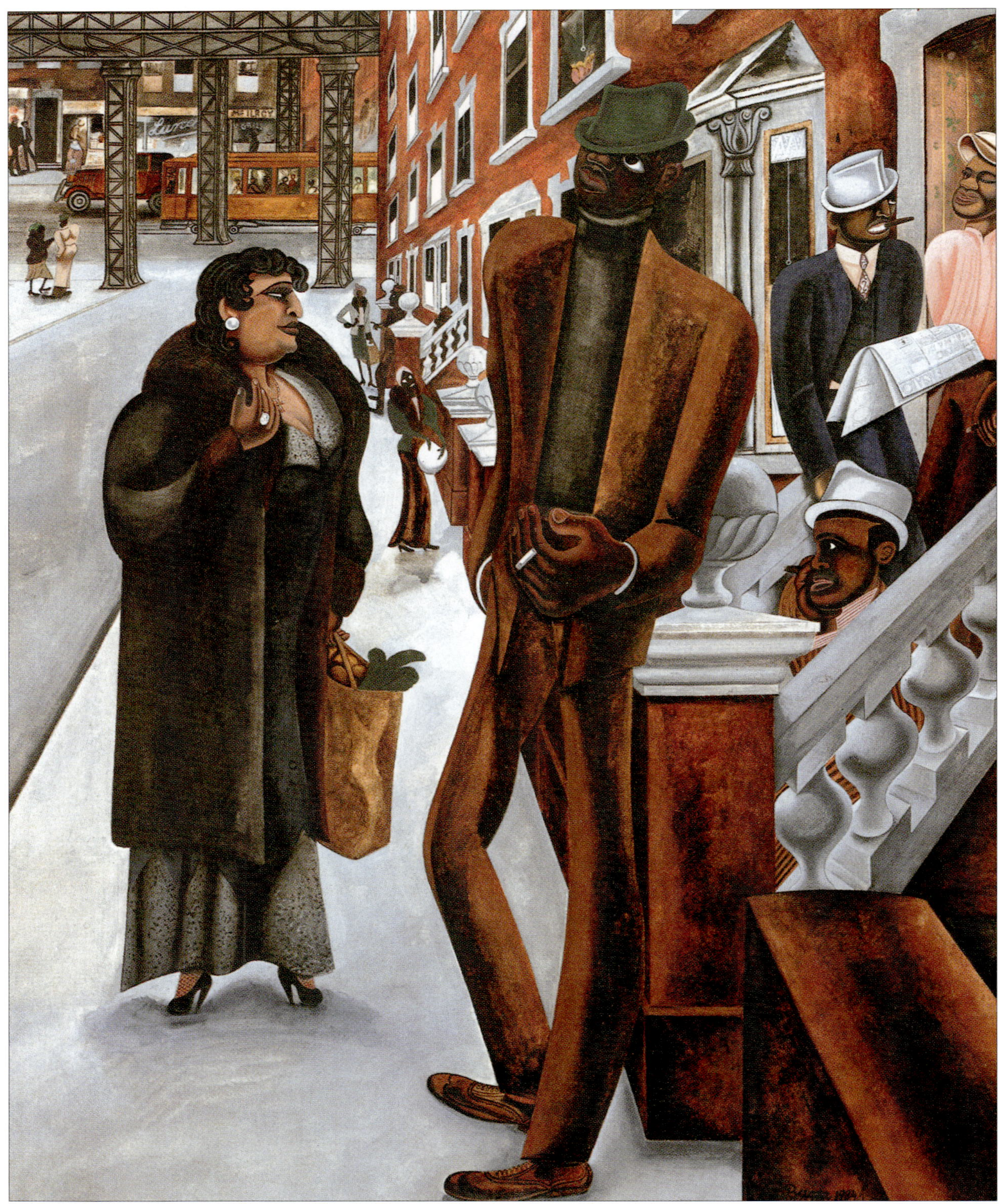

Draw a picture-plane on your paper. Now draw a continuous line corresponding first of all to the overall silhouette of the major buildings nearest to you. Try to avoid seeing each building individually. See the whole street as a continuous shape that is divided into individual buildings by the addition of the features that make each building separate from its neighbor. Observe how a large building at the end of the street appears smaller than a more modest one nearer to you. Again the main problem is in believing what you see and having the confidence to record it.

The first attempt for those who do not have easy access to a town could well be to portray a local church. This is a much-worked subject for beginners, and many of the resultant drawings are quite uninteresting because the drawing is carried out in purely topographical terms. But there are other ways in which to tackle such drawings, and indeed with imagination this type of subject has many possibilities. Street scenes of villages and small towns have considerable visual potential. Corner shops, squares and market places, statues, and war memorials, all hold great

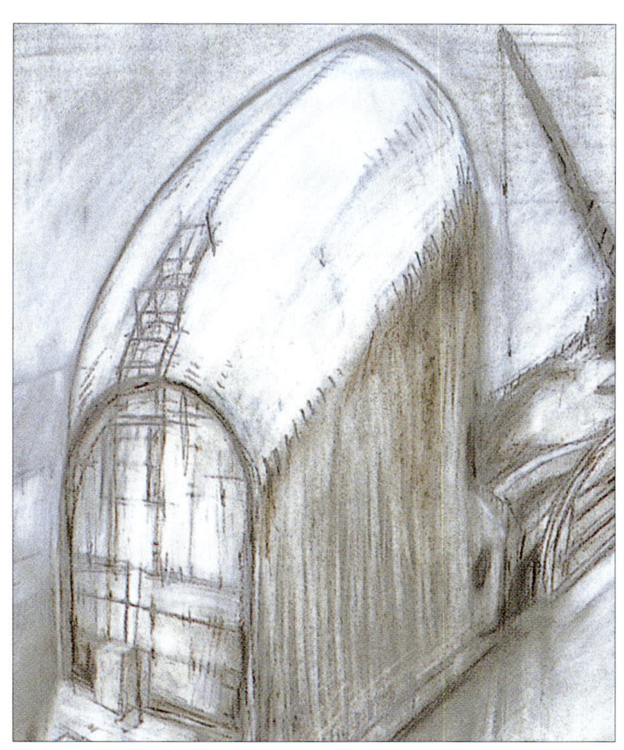

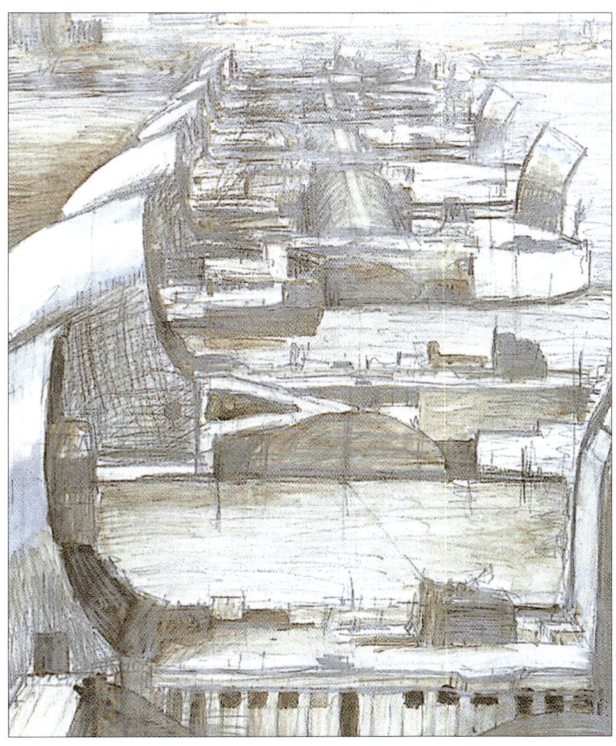

Left Harlem *by Edward Burra; the vibrancy of the city is captured in the juxtaposition of hard and soft textures and the peculiar perspective.*

Top Above and Right *Pen and wash studies of the Thames Barrier, London; in these two drawings, an optimistic view of man's achievement in the urban environment is presented.*

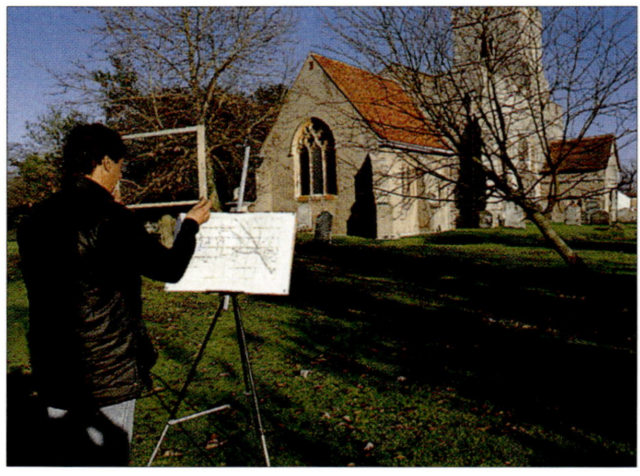

Above *Use of the squared screen can be of great assistance both in landscape and townscape drawing as a device for finding interesting angles of composition. It can also eliminate the complicated use of multi-point perspective. The artist is working from the squared screen onto squared paper.*

Below *Churches can be a good architectural subject for the beginner, because they are sometimes situated where a lengthy study can be undertaken without too much disturbance. The drawing in sepia conté crayon is typical of a beginner's approach. An attempt has been made to depict the building in a clear and concise manner. The result is not outstanding, either in composition or drawing technique, although it is quite competent. It has little interest in itself to anyone who is not familiar with this particular church.*

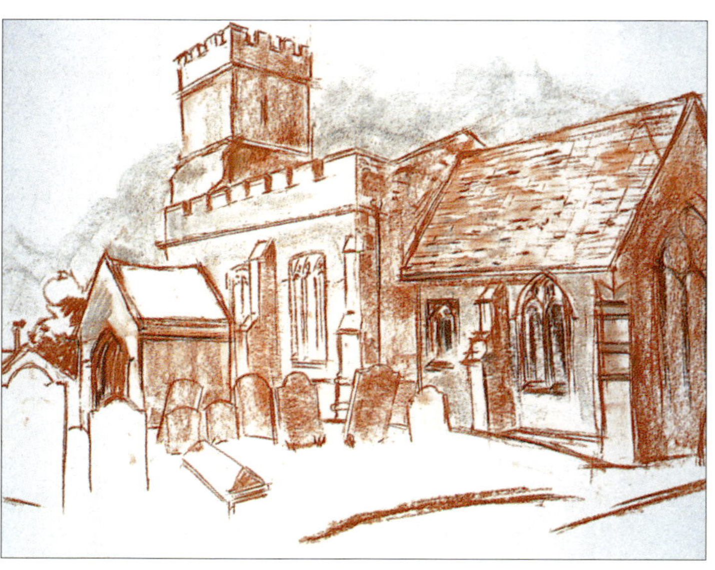

pictorial value. Again it is often the contrasts of architectural periods in buildings and their proximity to contemporary constructions that can give an interesting visual twist to a contemporary scene.

As in drawing a landscape, try not to ignore those things that you might feel to be an intrusion of modern life on the town, such as traffic signals and signs, refuse containers, etc. Many beginners omit these things from their drawings in an attempt to portray a street scene of predominantly older buildings. Works carried out in this frame of mind inevitably look unconvincing because many other pictorial elements that would have been present in the 19th century are not there—say, horses or figures in period costume. Try to see the view in front of you in terms of its pictorial value in a specifically contemporary sense.

Artists in the 20th century tended to look at the city in an expressionist and abstract manner. A cool, analytical, perspective study of a city street can often miss the essential quality of vibrance, noise, and excitement that the city expresses to those who live in it. Expressionist drawings may not be accurate representations of the city, but they may poignantly and emotively convey a sense of urban vibrance. A work like this is conceived pictorially on more than one level. Similarly, Edward Burra's watercolor *Harlem* (1934) displays a peculiar perspective which suggests that the windows are disattached from the buildings (see page 44). It is not too fanciful to say that such a work has the disjointed atmosphere and vibrant harmony of a jazz composition. Compare the work of Canaletto, Lowry, Utrillo, and Burra to discover the four main approaches to townscape. Many of the expressionist works of the 20th century take this multi-point view in one work.

It would often be impractical or very difficult to approach drawing a townscape in the same manner as drawing a landscape; there is not least the difficulty of trying to set up an easel and stool in a busy shopping street, and it is the tackling of such a subject surrounded by physical complications that brings a full realization to the beginner of the usefulness of a sketchbook.

Artists have different ideas about working from sketchbook notes but a useful approach is to think of your sketchbook as a

Below *With the use of a squared screen, the artist found a more interesting and unusual aspect of the same church. The artist exploited the fact that the sun was low on the horizon on the left-hand side. The last of the sun catches the tombstones in the foreground and sets them brilliantly against the dark shadows. With the early moon in the righthand corner, this pastel study has an eerie melancholy; a marked contrast to the pedestrian study of the other side of the church.*

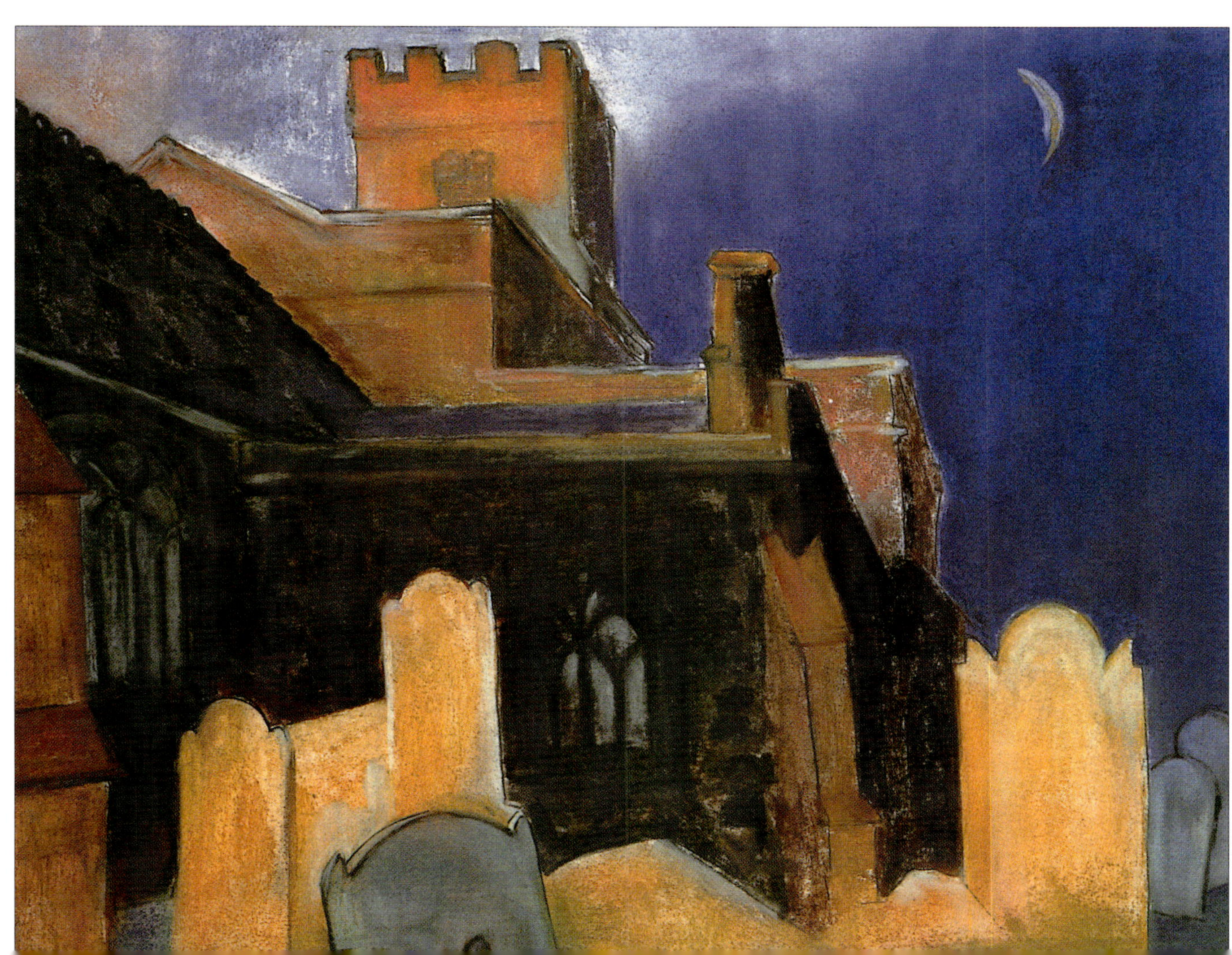

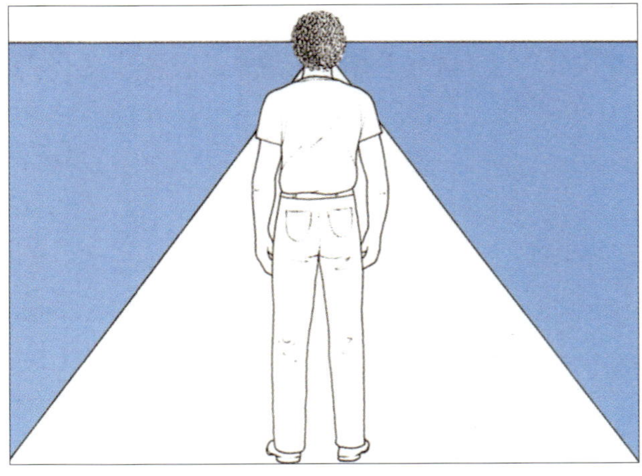

1

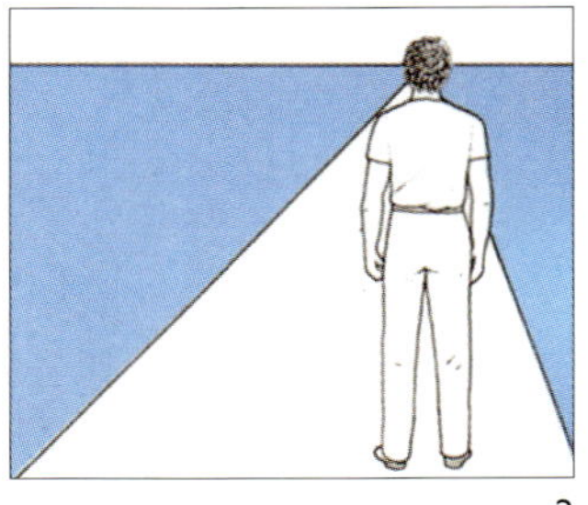

2

Above and Left *All parallel lines which recede into the distance eventually converge at a point, called the vanishing point (above). The angles at which these lines converge depends upon the spectator's position.*

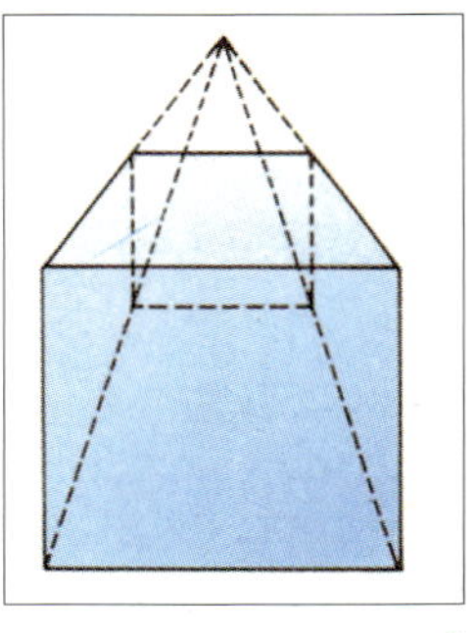

3

Left *In one-point perspective, only two faces of the cube are visible. One side is seen straight on, and there is only one vanishing point.*

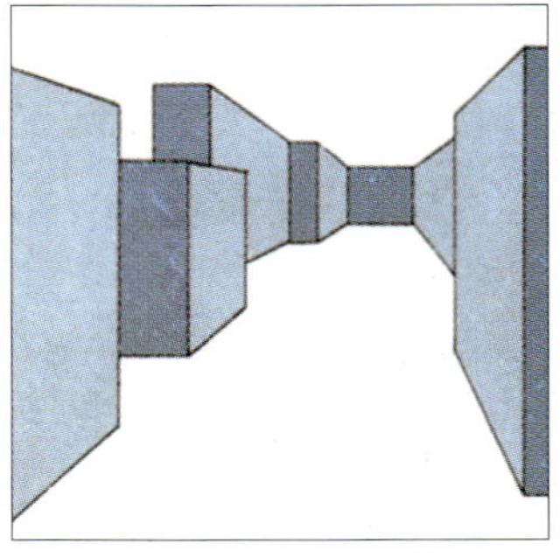

4

Left *Vanishing points are often obscured by buildings or other objects. When this occurs, it is nevertheless crucial to know where the vanishing points would be located, so you are able to judge the correct angles.*

visual diary in which on a day-to-day basis you record those things that are visually stimulating, gathering as much visual information in your quick drawings as possible. Beginners often get the wrong impression about what a sketchbook is for, and fill it with ill-conceived and rather scribbled drawings which two days after they have been done are visually unreadable and carry insufficient information to be of any real value in the studio. The sketchbook should be considered the training ground for quick, accurate drawings in which every line and every mark conveys the maximum of visual information. The real function of a sketchbook is to record accurate visual information that can be useful in the studio, that can be included in a larger composition, and that can impart to the final work authority and meaning.

Most artists dealing with a townscape subject make their finished works in the studio using a whole range of visual notes collected over a period of time. For example, the overall composition may be decided from a quite simple continuous line drawing, but it may then be found to have insufficient information about doors and windows. Drawings of such details should be drawn separately in a sketchbook on a larger scale. Your work might require a group of people on a corner waiting to cross the road. These could well have been drawn on another corner in another town, but if they fit the

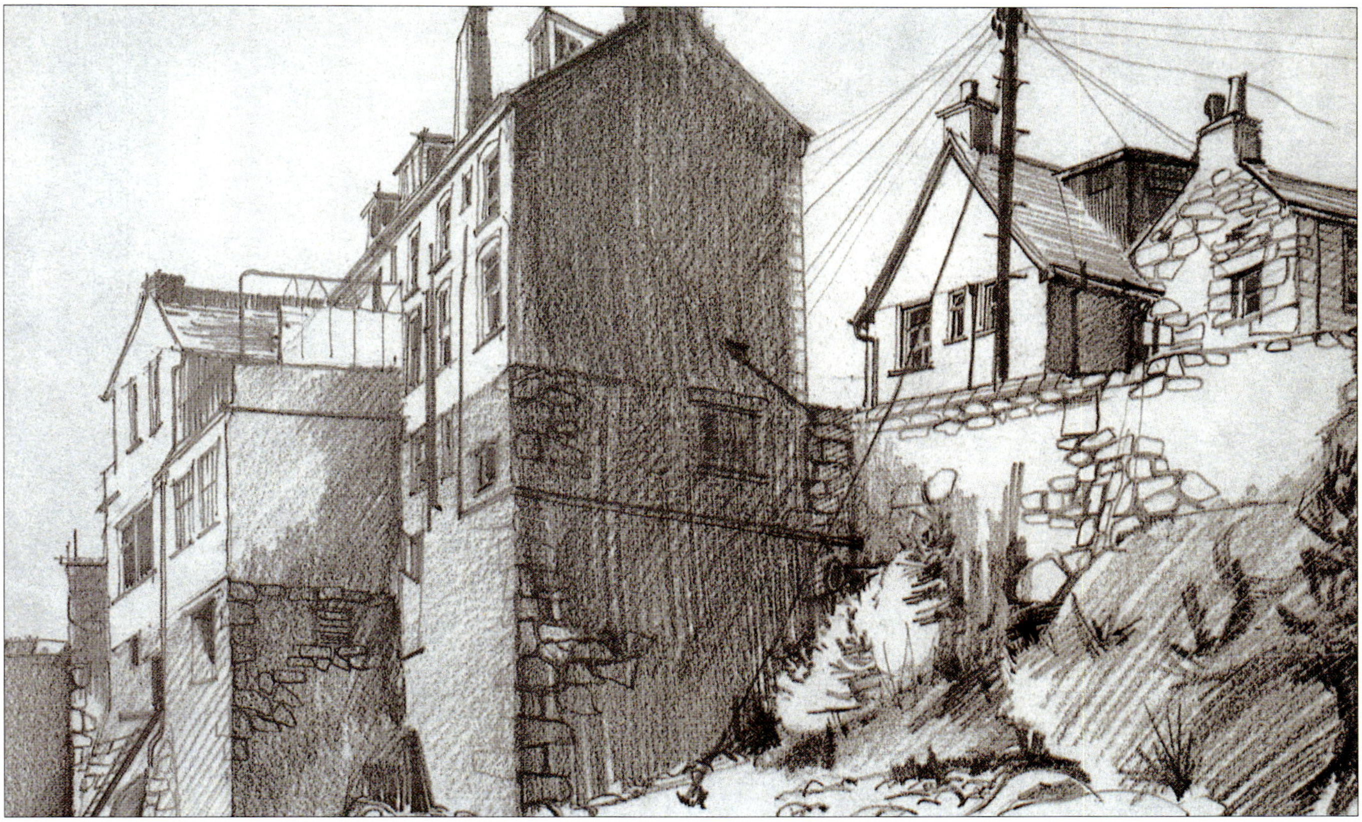

Above *A vacation sketchbook study in pencil; the strong perspective gives a sense of towering scale. Again, a squared viewing frame helps to find and isolate matter that has pictorial value.*

Below *Leonardo da Vinci's pen and ink preparatory study for the background to the* Adoration of the Magi. *The vanishing point is to the right of center.*

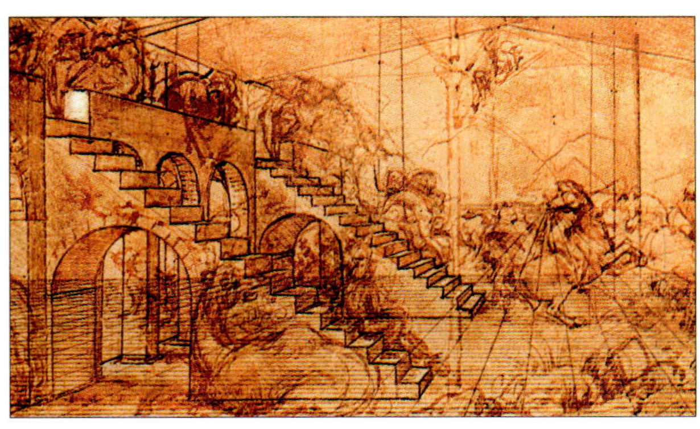

composition they can be used. Your original drawing for the composition would, in any case, be too small in size to carry the amount of detail that you require to complete a finished work.

As an exercise, try making a drawing from a series of sketches and notes done in one location. When you start to draw your townscape in the studio from your sketches, you will soon discover the sort of information that you should have recorded. Go again to the same location and make some more sketches. In this practical way you will soon understand what you need to record for the sketches to be of any real value.

Obviously, not all finished townscape drawings have to be a composite of work from a sketchbook; many works can be finished on location. There will inevitably be interruptions by people looking over your shoulder when you draw in a busy place, and although this can be quite embarrassing, and disturbing, for a beginner you will, after a few attempts, become quite brazen and indifferent to the comments of passers-by. A more positive approach is thus required for townscape drawing than is required for the more lonely activity of drawing in the countryside.

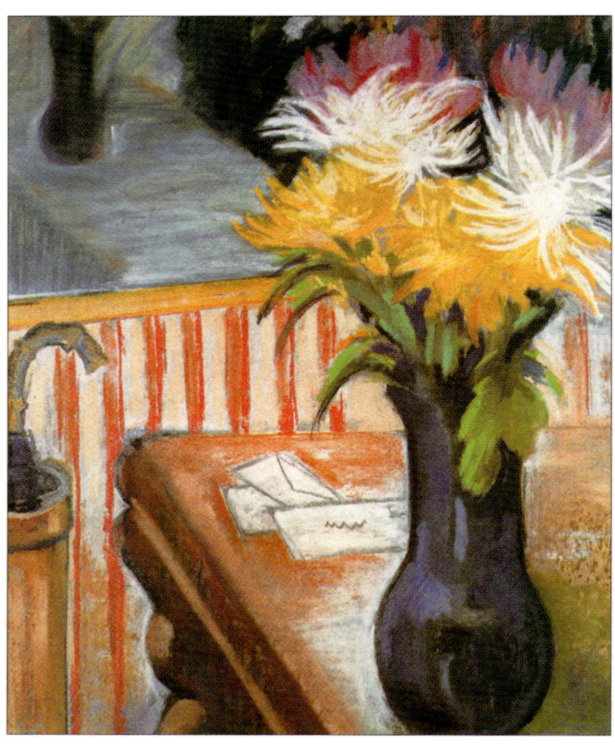

Above *This pastel drawing uses the mirror as a device to thrust the drawing back into the space being occupied by the viewer. A touch of mystery is added by the figure at the door. Are they leaving or entering? This pictorial device was much used by artists in the 17th and 18th centuries.*

Still life as subject matter has a long history. There is literary evidence of wall paintings of fruit and flowers in the ancient Greek period, and although no actual examples survive to this day, there are numerous examples from the Roman period which are probably copies of earlier Greek motifs.

Throughout the Middle Ages there was a strong accent in all the arts toward religious subjects, and it is only in a secondary role that nature and still life were depicted. It was not until the Renaissance that realistic representations of the natural world were again considered acceptable subject matter for the artist, and in northern Europe—where a striving for realistic representation took a stronger hold in the 16th and 17th centuries—still life again came to be treated by the artist as a genuine subject in itself.

The words "still life" come from the Dutch words, *stil leven*, which describe any painting or drawing of inanimate objects.

In the famous painting by Holbein all the objects between the two figures represent by themselves a wonderfully descriptive still life, but they are of secondary importance to the main subject, the two figures. Here the objects of the still life give an indication of the two noblemen's interests in music, astronomy, and navigation. Even as late as 1533, when Holbein painted *The Ambassadors*, the majority of still lifes were incorporated as secondary visual subject matter, often for narrative reasons. A generation or so later, in Caravaggio's *The Supper at Emmaus*, the beautifully rendered still life in the foreground is also used as a narrative visual device. However, a few years previously, Caravaggio had painted an almost identical, independent still life arranged in the same manner. There is, though, no record of Holbein's making an independent painting of the musical instruments as a still life painting.

By the end of the 17th century, Willem Kalf's paintings had many of the commonly recognized features of still life painting as an independent art form. Many of his still lifes were of tables laden with various kinds of food, often with symbolic overtones.

Symbolism of the kind employed by Kalf, in which the object depicted represented the interests of the commissioners of the work, was common throughout the 17th and 18th centuries, particularly in Holland, where the art of still life rose to a fullness of expression and painting skill that remains unsurpassed. This style of still life was used as a model of how the subject matter should be handled into the late 19th and early 20th centuries.

It took such artists as Van Gogh, Braque, and Picasso to breathe new inspiration into and create a contemporary approach to still life. However, Braque's and Picasso's works in still life are of a Cubist and abstract nature; their works are not representational and are therefore outside the remit of this book.

The Chimneypiece by Edouard Vuillard brings still life painting in its representational form into modern times. Vuillard painted many

Below *A pencil and wash study of the glass roof of a Victorian railway station, London. This drawing relies upon a painstaking control of perspective as well as silhouette to create a cavernous expanse of glass and steel.*

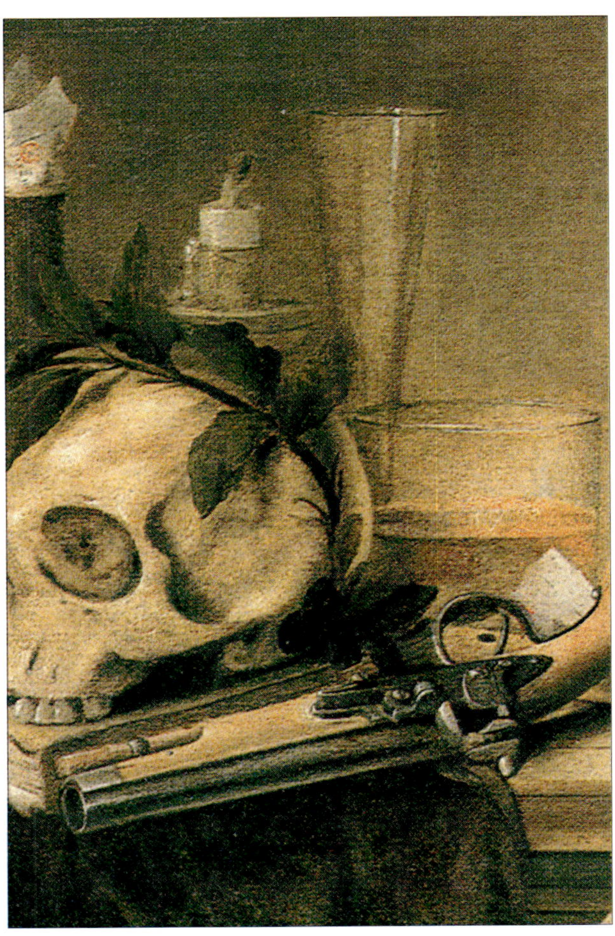

works similar to the one illustrated right up until his death in 1940. In this painting there are no people present, but the haphazard nature of the objects about the room give the viewer an intimate insight into the occupants' lives. The summer flowers set the time of year; the medicines imply either illness or hypochondria. The somber tones of the work and the washing drying by the fire suggest a dull, rainy, rather claustrophobic summer day. The apparently casual placing of all the objects in the painting also suggests an easy intimacy.

It is clear, thus, that the dullness commonly associated with still life is to a large extent due to the objects chosen and the forced and unconvincing way they are arranged as a subject for drawing and painting.

With your drawing board, and without any preconceived ideas as to what would make a good subject, just walk around your

Below The Supper at Emmaus *by Caravaggio; the still life group clearly forms a central part of the composition, an arrangement to be found in many of the artist's works. The fruit is autumnal, (the wrong time of the year from the biblical account) a pointer to the very secular approach to the religious subject. The foliage seen through the window is suggestive of a Japanese print.*

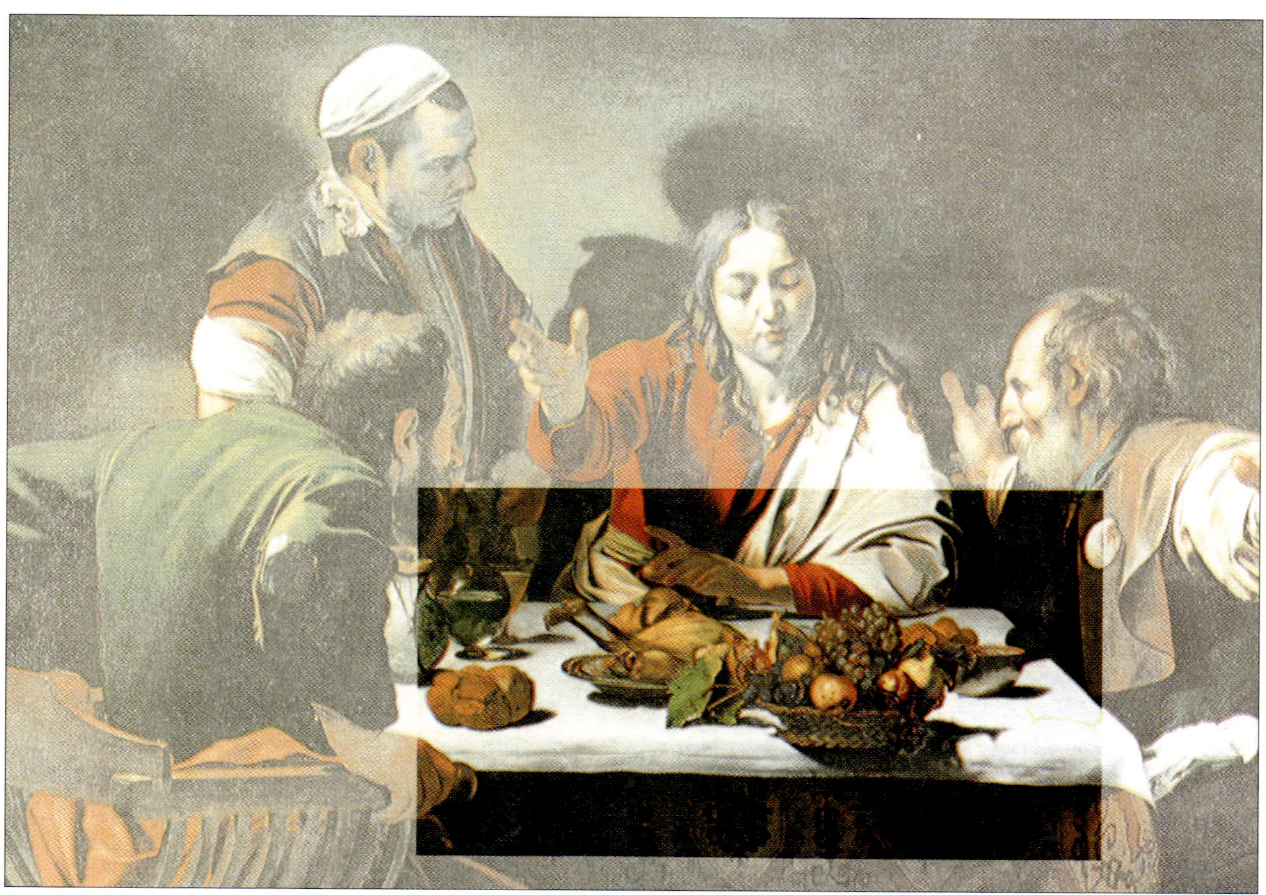

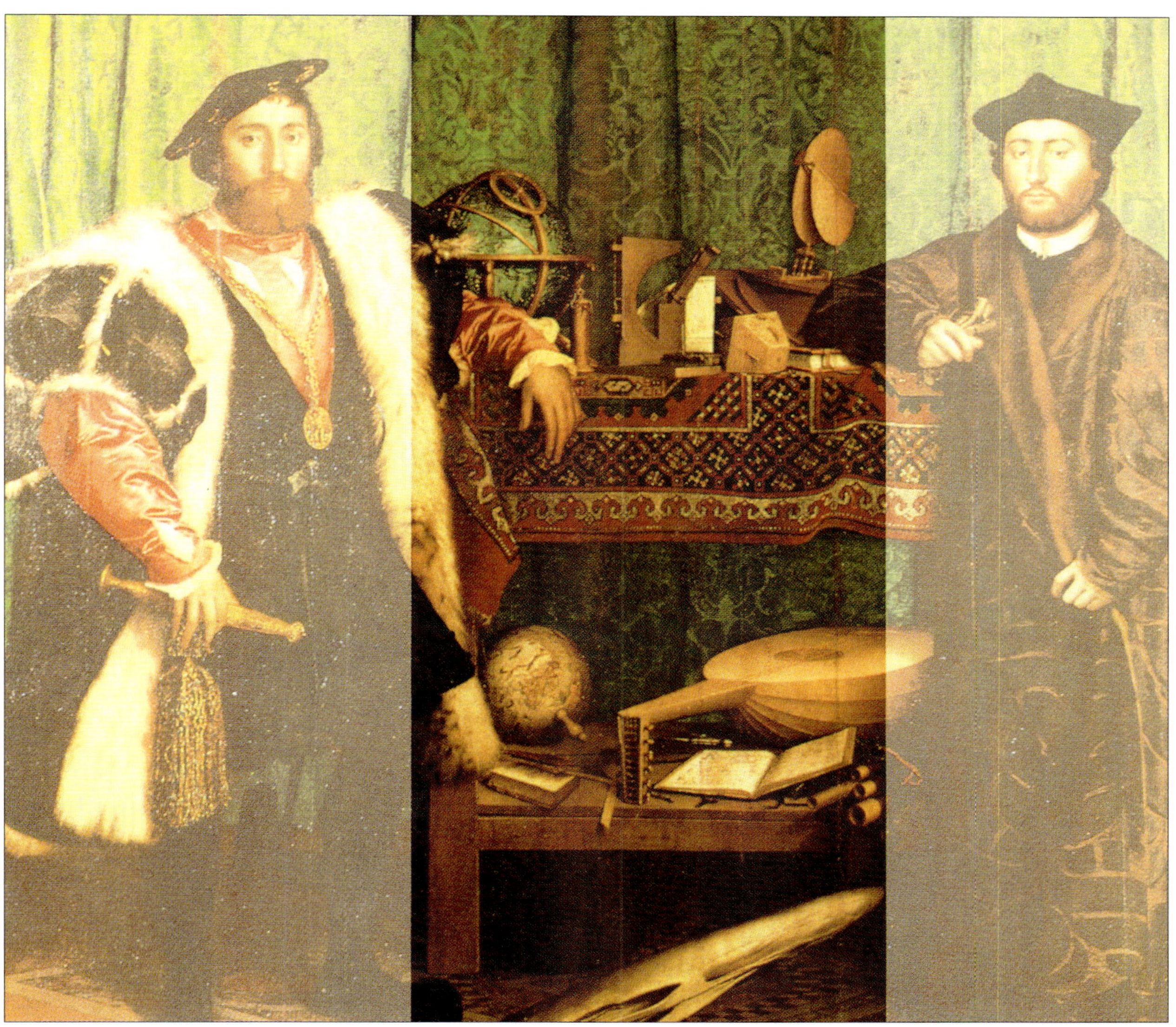

Left The Ambassadors,*Hans Holbein, commissioned in 1533; the still life central section is symbolic of the interests of the two men and emphasizes their Renaissance learning and culture. It also divides the two figures, indicating a formal, rather than an intimate, relationship. Note the distorted skull at their feet, a grim and curious counterpoint to the secular, worldly self-confidence above.*

home and find an interesting corner, bathroom shelf, or bedside table. Do not rearrange anything. The objects' unintentional and natural positioning may well be visually more interesting than any arrangement you could make. Start by making a simple line drawing. Try to resist the temptation to see the objects individually at first. Draw the main shapes and their inter-relationships. Always remember that, when you draw, the shapes being made on the paper are all interdependent on one another. The negative shapes are just as important as the positive shapes.

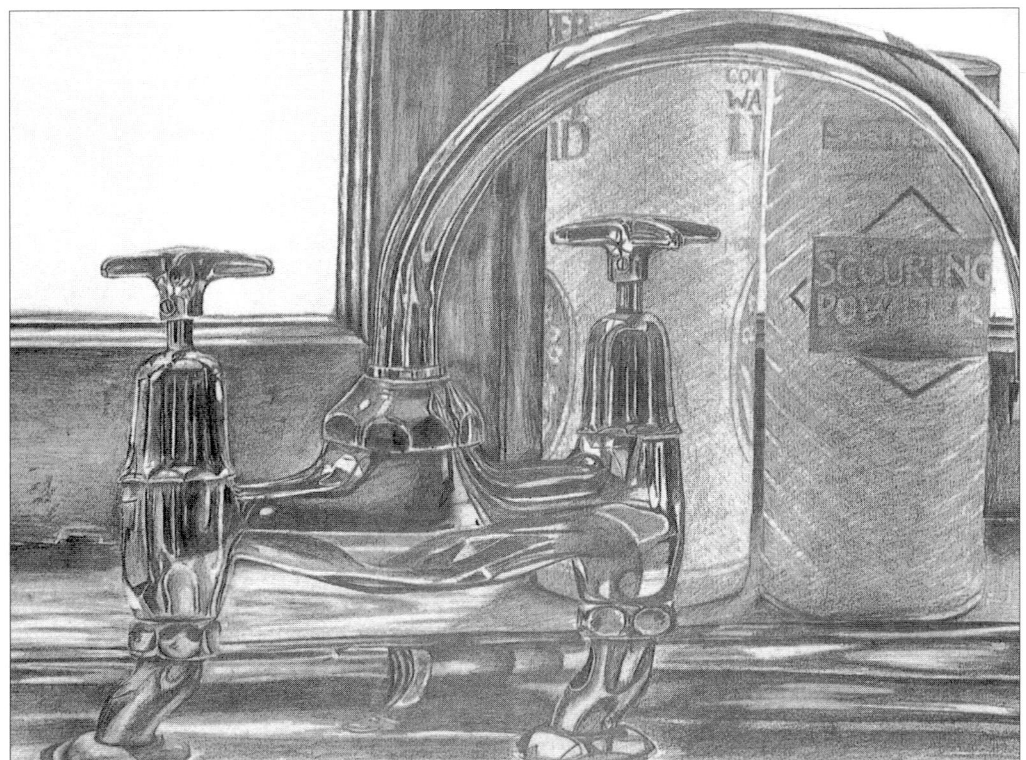

Left *This pencil study shows the influence of Baroque still life painting in a modern study. Note the complexity of the reflections used to depict a highly complex reflected surface.*

In your search for subject matter, a viewing-frame can be very useful. Do as many drawings as you can to practice looking for subject matter. Do not be too selective: do not think that what is familiar to you is not worth the effort to draw. One of the great problems that the beginner has in still life and in landscape is indecision over choosing what to draw, often caused by the fact that to make a drawing demands a considerable effort from beginners and they therefore feel that their view must be directed toward a subject that warrants such effort on their part. This results in their simply dismissing many highly pictorial subjects because the assumed status of the view in front of them does not appear to warrant the effort involved. The commonplace object can nevertheless become a special, highly interesting, and emotively charged object when drawn by an artist.

Things also change by the light in which they are seen. What could be a very uninteresting landscape on a bright, sunlit day might on a cloudy and stormy day be most interesting and exciting. The play of light is one of the most important elements, and the shapes and colors of objects change constantly under the effect of changing light.

As an exercise, collect together four or five household objects that are no longer required for everyday use. Give them a coating of white emulsion paint so that they all appear to be made of plaster. The whiteness of the objects will help you to see the effect light has in causing shadows. Set up your still life in a convenient corner, and with the aid of an adjustable lamp, direct light from one specific direction onto these now white but familiar shapes. Keep your drawing board as upright as conveniently possible and, remembering the picture-plane concept, outline the pattern of the objects in front of you. Then draw around the shadows. Notice that there are two distinct types of shadow. One is the shadow that is present on the side of objects away from the light source. This is called "actual" shadow and is more difficult to see, particularly on a cylindrical or round object, as the dark side gets progressively darker, and the exact line where the grayness begins is sometimes difficult to see. Because the objects are painted white, however, this should be easier to recognize. A

Below *A finely rendered pencil study which captures the delicate textural differences with almost photographic precision; the reflection in the glass has been achieved with the use of an eraser to bring out the highlights.*

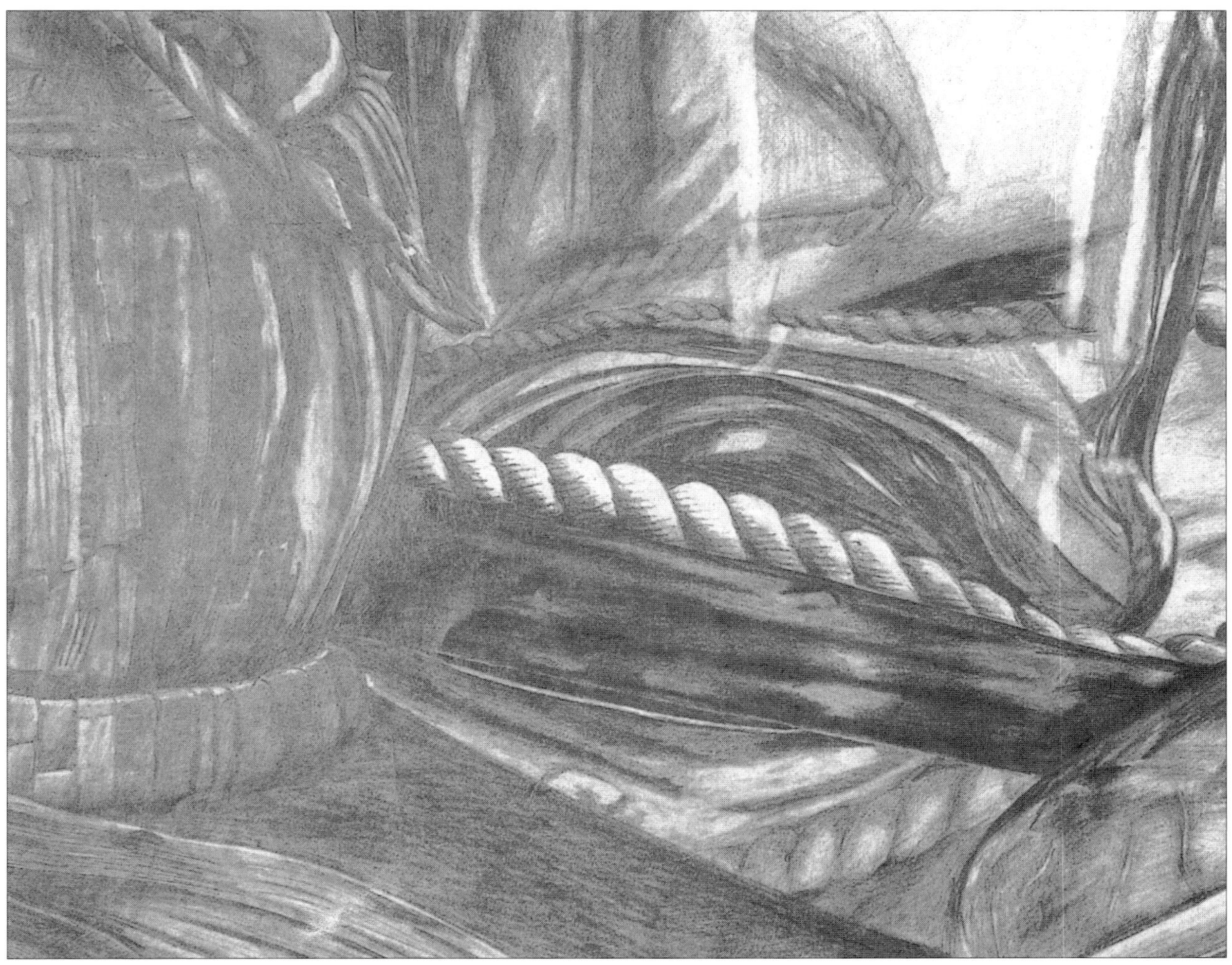

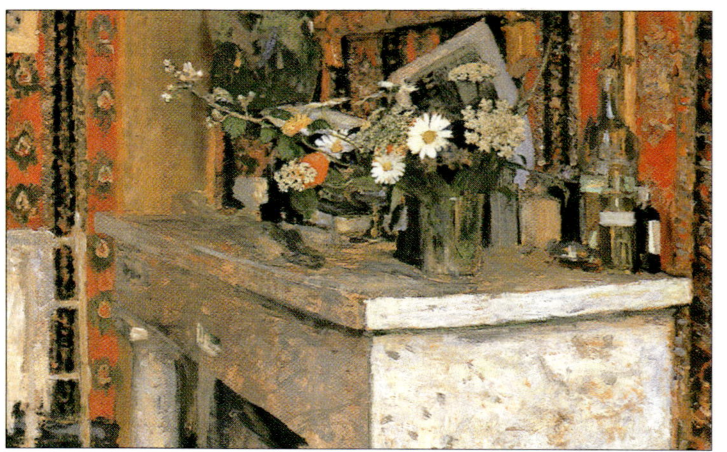

Left *This early 20th century still life painting by Edouard Vuillard,* The Chimneypiece, *painted in 1905, is very different from 17th century Dutch Baroque painting. The very informality of the arrangement of the subject matter makes this painting appear a casual observation of a corner of a well-used room. The meaning of this painting relies almost entirely on the inter-relationship of extremely commonplace objects.*

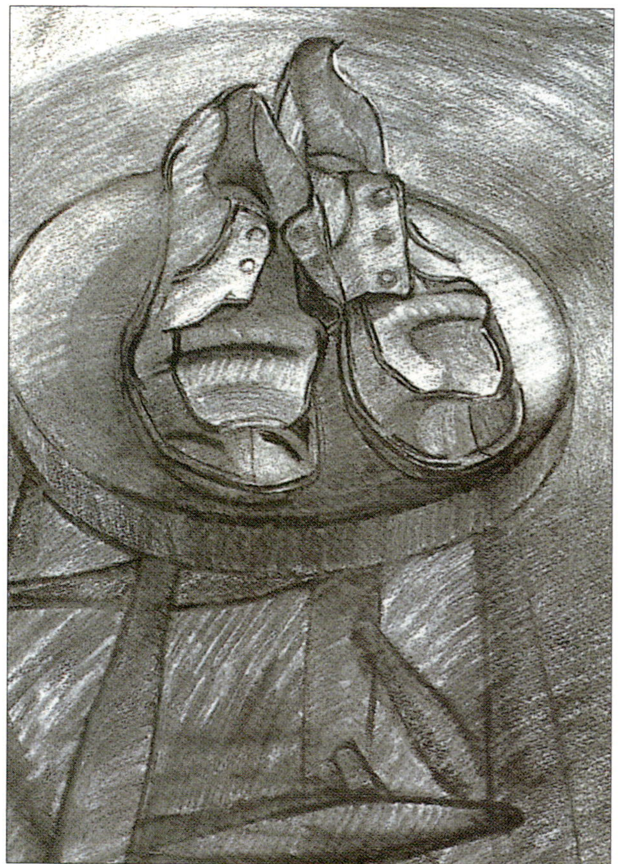

Above *This charcoal drawing of a well-worn pair of shoes on a stool has been rendered in a way to give a sense of the character, not only of the shoes, but also of the wearer.*

simple way for the beginner to draw the actual shadow is to decide where the darkest part is and shade this as dark as possible. Then decide where the lightest gray is. Divide the area between the lightest shade and the darkest shade into four, and graduate the shading accordingly.

The other type of shadows are "cast" or "projected" shadows. A cast shadow is that area that light cannot get to because there is an object in the way. Because light travels in a straight line, a cast shadow's shape is a version—perhaps a distorted version—of the shape of the object that is casting the shadow. Draw around the cast shadows, and you will notice that there is no variation in the darkness of a cast shadow. If there is, this variation is caused by light reflected off an adjacent object and shining into the shadowed area.

Now, change the position of the light (not the arrangement), and draw the same subject matter again. Notice that all the patterns and shapes in your second drawing are very different from those in your first, although you have not moved the objects or altered the position from which you are drawing them.

Now have another look round your home and find a potential subject that is lit by a

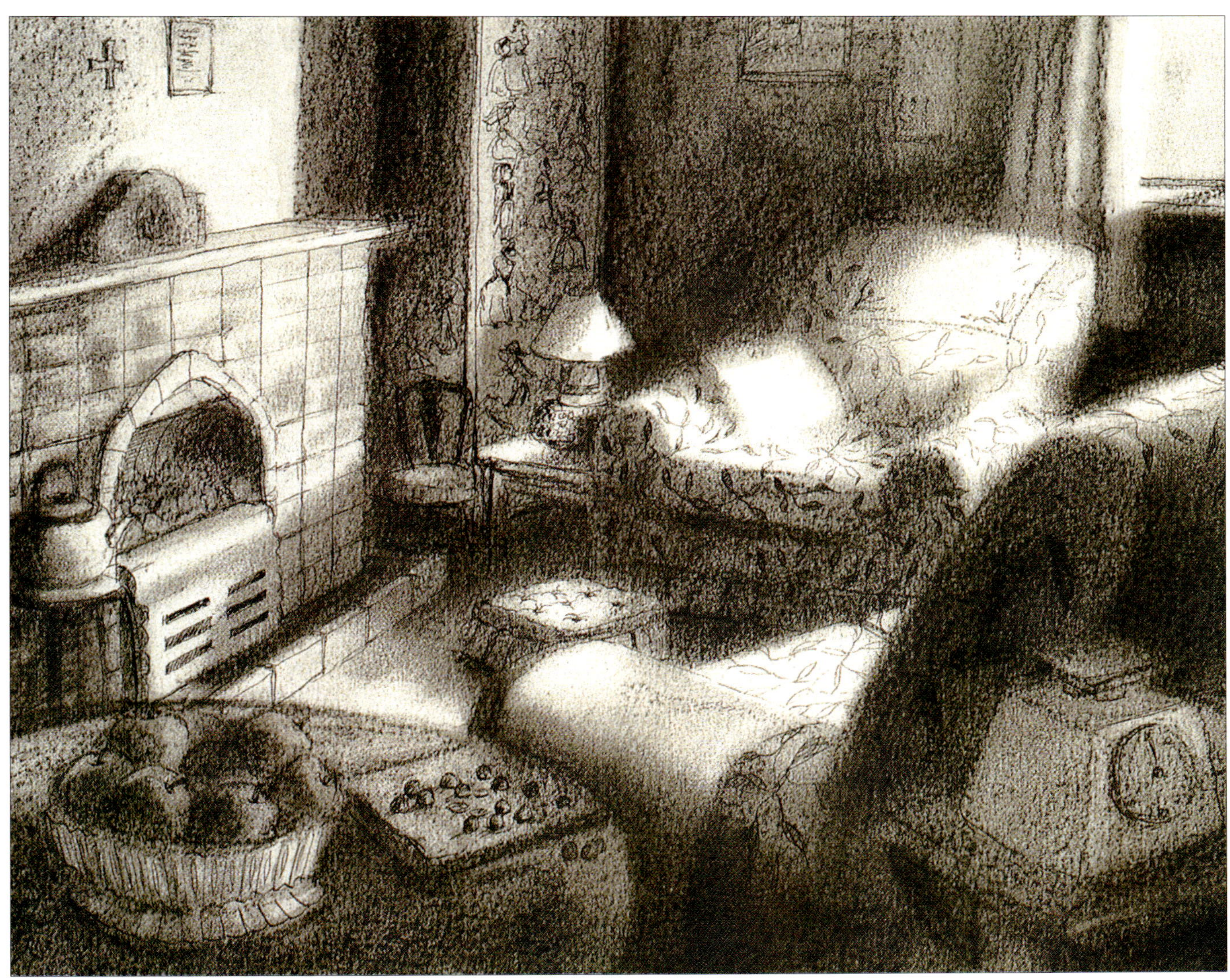

table lamp or a single light source. Set yourself up to make a drawing of it. The first thing to notice is that because all the objects in view are not white but their rightful colors, it is much harder to see the shadows.

So, in drawing as a method of recording, considerable clarity is required. Think of your sketchbook more in terms of a notebook or reference book. For example, if you do a study

Above *What makes this pen and conté drawing particularly interesting is the use of the bright light coming through the window, and it is as much a study of light and dark as it is a study of particular objects. Any alteration in the position of the light would place a different emphasis on the composition.*

of a child's bedroom, and then of a child at a different time and probably in a different situation, the drawings in your sketchbook should be sufficiently clear in the information they hold to enable you to combine the two

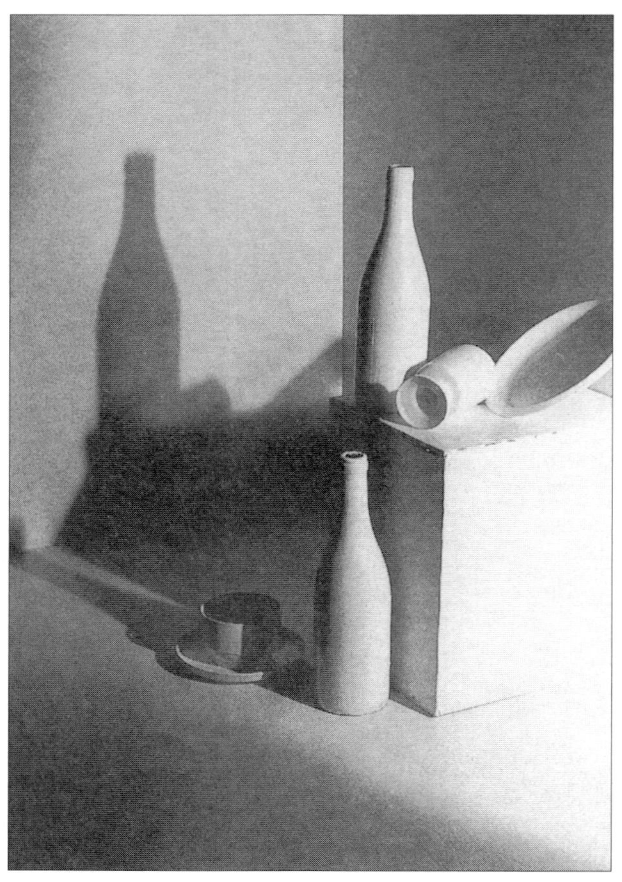

drawings together and make from them an interesting painting or drawing. Professional artists look through their old sketchbooks to find a suitable tree, boat, car, or person, that they need for inclusion in a composition. Unfortunately, the word "sketch" seems to indicate something hurriedly and indecisively drawn.

Try not to restrict your drawings in a sketchbook to scenic compositions. Careful studies of wild flowers, rock formations, and all manner of natural forms may be exceedingly useful to you. Also make studies of cars, bicycles, windows, doors, people, and animals. Many people are restricted in the time of the year at which they can draw and paint, and the visual information on flowers gathered at the height of summer can be crucial to the successful completion of a landscape painted

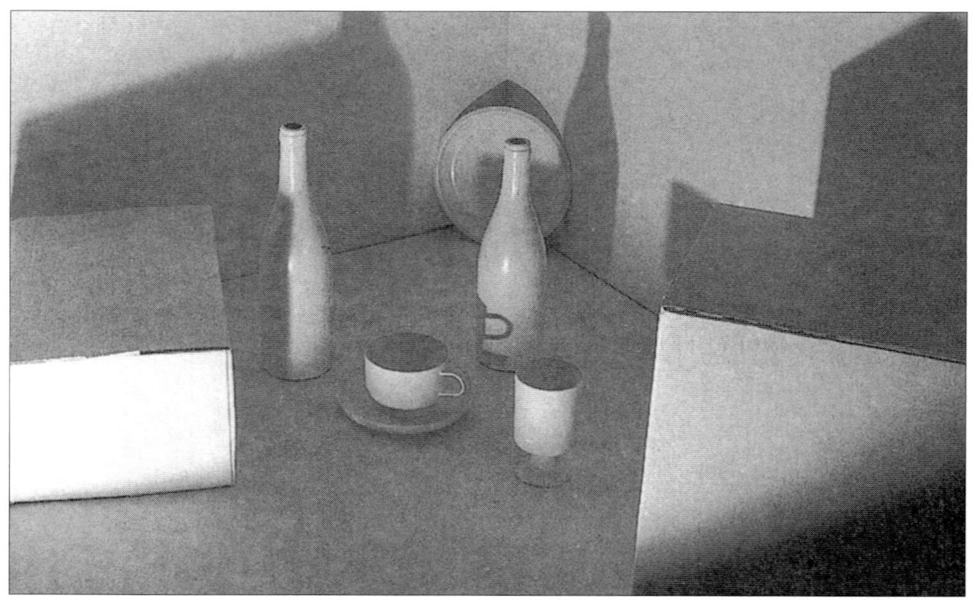

In the four photographs we have objects painted white. In each photograph, the single source of light has been moved, giving them all different two-dimensional patterns of lights and darks.

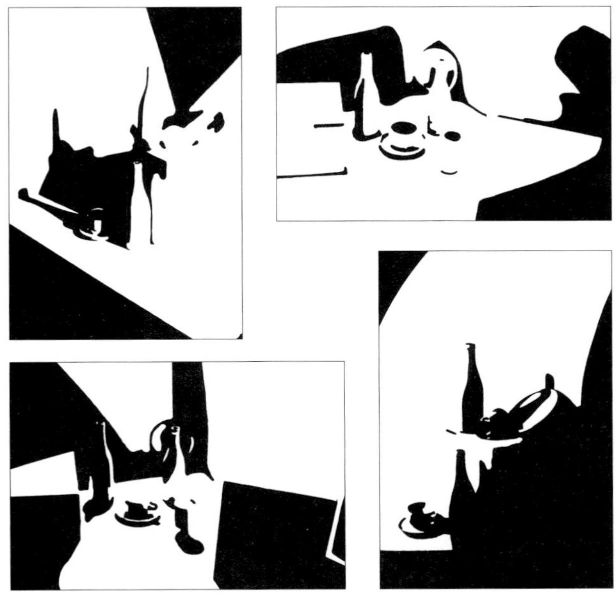

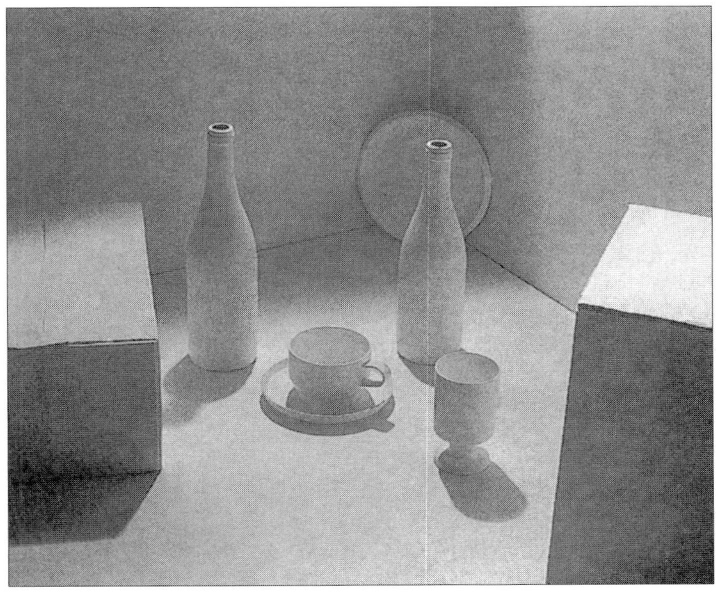

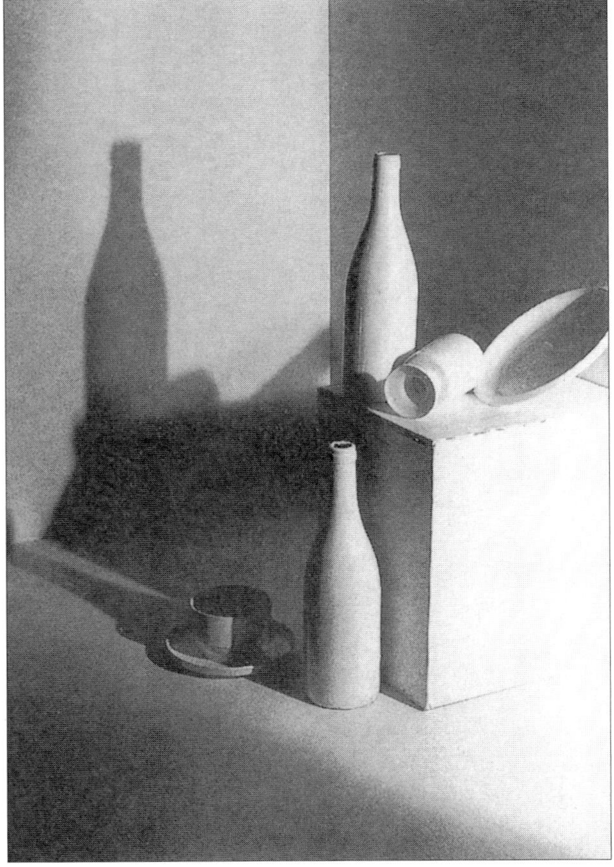

or drawn at home in the depths of winter.

It is often the desire to use color that makes this subject most attractive. However, many beginners' paintings of flowers rely on an exuberant use of color at the expense of form. Drawing flowers without the use of color might, in fact, at first seem not a very rewarding pursuit.

There is, however, a need to concentrate on the form or construction. A flower is not a haphazard splash of color. Some varieties of wild flowers, such as the thistle, have a sculptural and pictorial quality that makes them ideal subjects to be drawn as a separate entity and unrelated to other objects. The drawing of flowers and plants demands great sensitivity and observation; for the student who is particularly attracted to working in a detailed way, the possibilities are extensive.

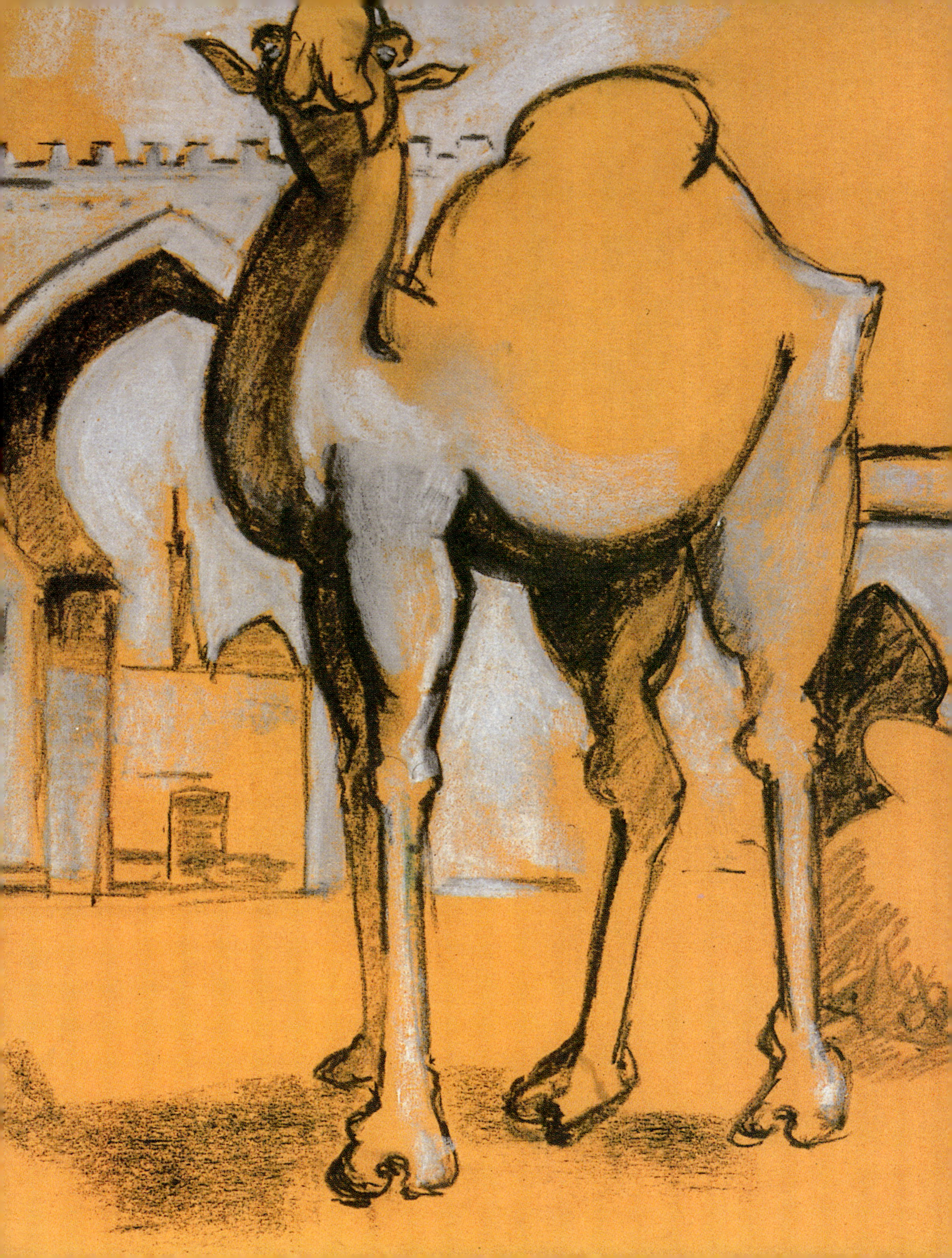

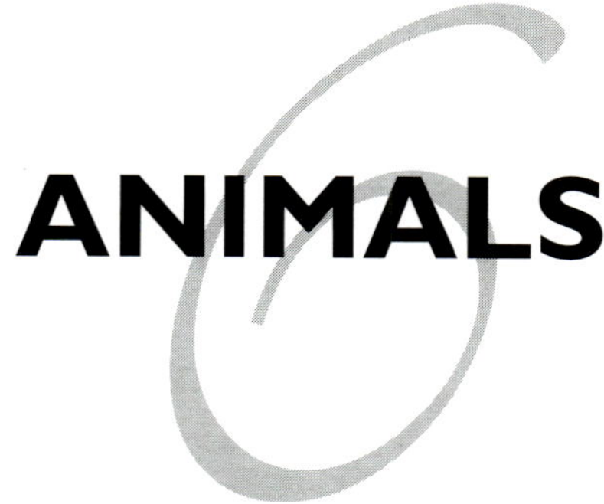

ANIMALS

Animals as subject matter for the visual arts have a longer history than any other subject. The first images drawn by the human race depicted the animals that were hunted for survival: the prehistoric cave drawings at Niaux (Ariege), in France, are some of the best preserved examples. Lions, tigers, and hippopotamus were frequent subjects for wall paintings in ancient Egypt and for relief carvings in ancient Syria. There are numerous Greek and Roman examples of animal images in mosaic, bas-relief, and sculpture. There is no period in art when animals have not played a major role.

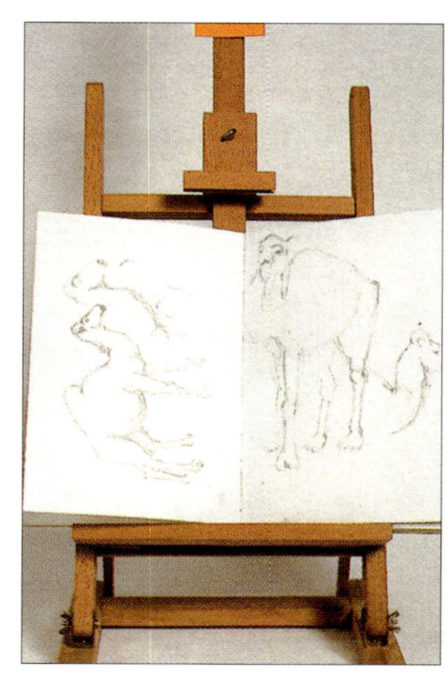

Left *Sketchbook studies of camels were combined with a vacation photograph to create this conté drawing on orange paper. The color of thepaper suggests the heat of the Middle Eastern setting.*

In modern times, everyday contact with animals has become more distant than at any other time in human history, so that first-hand experience of animals for many Western people comprises the particular relationship between man and his domestic pets. Art has tended to reflect this change in social conditions with the result that many animals tend to be represented in art as cuddly and lovable, and the images are full of sentimentality. This has tended to turn animal representation into a secondary art form considered only fit as images for greetings cards. Our contemporary approach to this genre of painting is a far cry from the savagery and excitement depicted with such clarity in such works as the Syrian bas-relief of the lion hunt in the British Museum, London. It is not surprising that we find it difficult to draw animals with the directness with which our forbears saw them, for our sensibilities to, and our relationship with, the animal kingdom has changed so much.

William Blake, the 18th-century poet, engraver, and pamphleteer, might give us an indication of an approach to visual images of the animal kingdom more appropriate to today. His stunning engraving of a tiger with eyes burning bright to illustrate his poem *The Tyger* depicts a primitive savagery—but on reading the poem it is equally possible to come to the conclusion that the content is more about the conscious and unconscious savagery of humankind and that the tiger is used as a metaphor for the human condition. "What immortal hand or eye/Dare frame thy frightful symmetry" is a relevant question for today's artists, so isolated from the animal kingdom. It is perhaps by taking this philosophical attitude to drawing the animal kingdom—portraying animals as a metaphor for the human character and condition—that it might be possible to

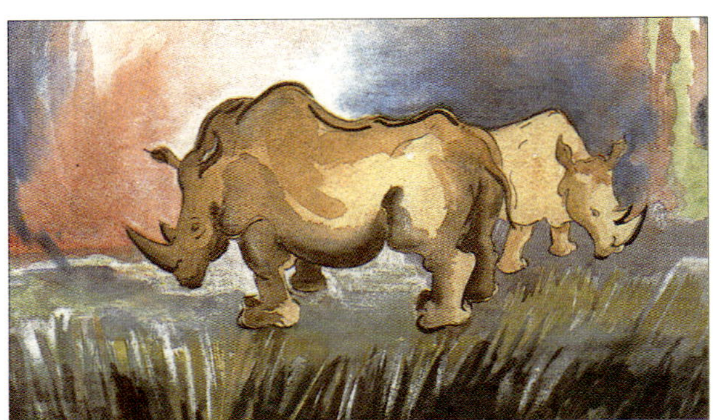

Right *Pen, watercolor, and pastel drawing of two rhinos; this drawing was made from a series of rapid sketchbook studies drawn at the zoo.*

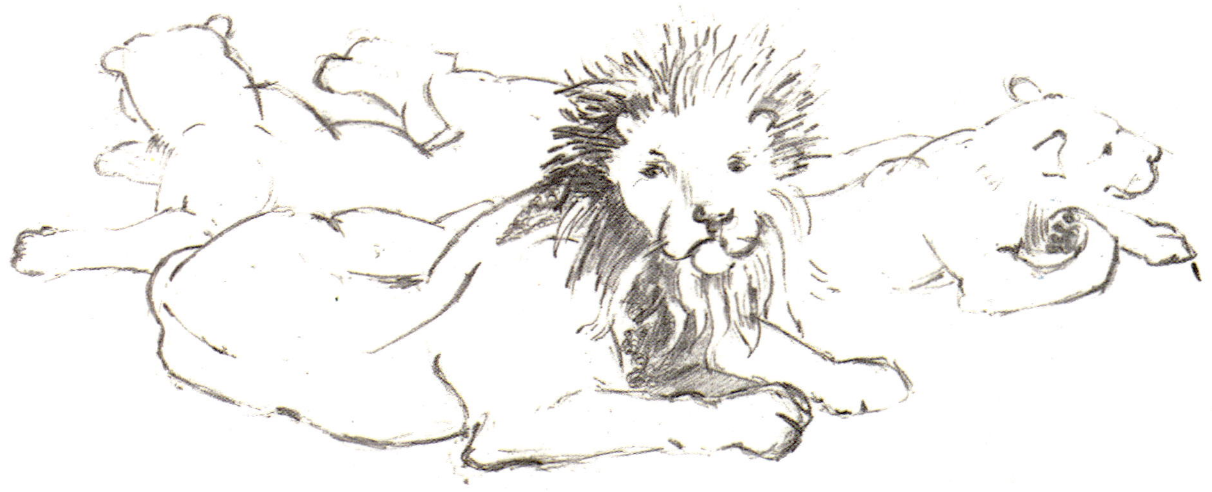

Below *This pencil study of a pride of lions resting in the heat was a composite of several separate sketches; the body of the lioness is actually a reversal of the lion's body, using tracing paper.*

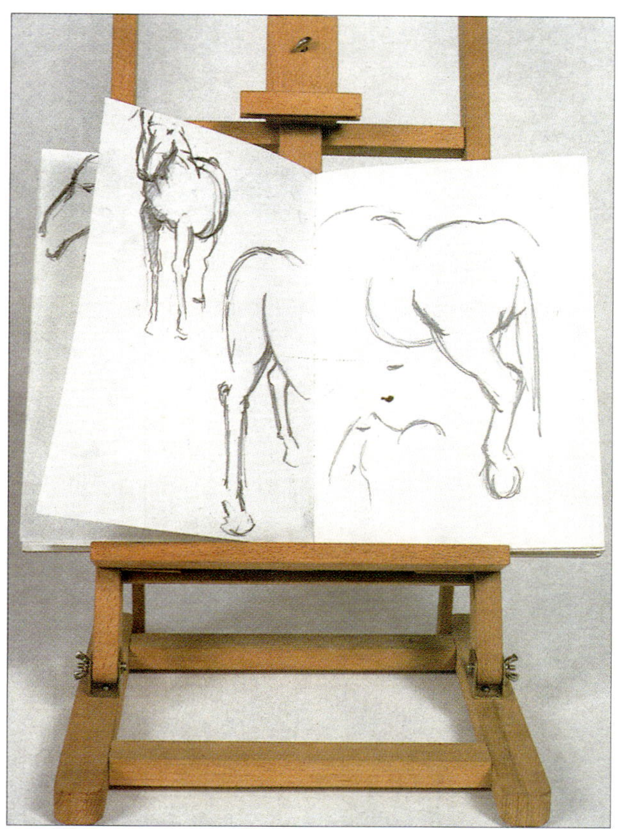

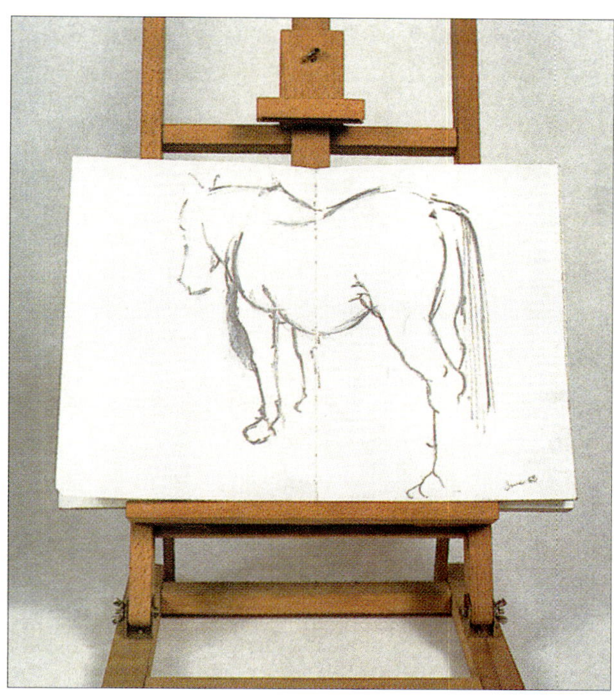

Left & Above *A composite sketch of horses was later made from preliminary sketches of the same horse seen from different angles; the first stage is a simple line drawing copy of the sketchbook notes arranged in an interesting way (as seen on the Left). Notice how the eye level runs through all the horses just below the top of the neck. This ensures that all the horses are represented as being the same size.*

break away from the sentimental imagery so often depicted. We are all familiar with animals being used as metaphor and in caricature by the political cartoonist, where the assumed character of a particular animal takes on the features of a person in the public eye. Many animals are associated with particular human traits—the courage of a lion, the infidelity of a monkey, and a baying pack of jackals are commonly used as metaphorical images.

The drawing of animals presents several pictorial problems unique to the subject matter. Unlike human beings, few animals obey a command to remain still. The use of a viewing-frame or squared-up paper is thus of little assistance. Even for a skilled artist the constant movement of a tiger pacing an enclosure in a zoo can present tremendous difficulties. Speed and subtlety of observation are required to draw animals in this environment. Before any attempt is made to put pencil to paper, therefore, observe the animal for some time—how it moves, the size of its head, the proportion and weight of the limbs—and then with the animal in front of you create a drawing that is made as much from your visual memory and imagination as it is from direct representation. When the beginner first tries to draw animals at the zoo, he or she should try to arrange that the time spent there includes feeding time. This is the one time when, although the animals are no less active, they are more generally in one place. The drawing of birds often presents even more of a problem, although they can be drawn quite easily when they are resting on a perch. When they are in their natural environment, or in flight, however, to represent birds as members of a recognizable species is a skill that only an ornithologist is likely to develop.

For those who wish to become deeply involved in this fascinating subject, some basic understanding of anatomy is a great help. For example, a knowledge of the pelvis and leg bones of a horse enables the beginner to understand the shapes visible on the surface of a horse's flank. As in drawing the figure, the points of articulation are the most important anatomical features to be aware of, and much useful work can be undertaken toward an understanding of animal movement by studying individual species at a local natural history museum. A simple book on animal anatomy would help if there is no easy access to real skeletons in a museum. In general, it is probably

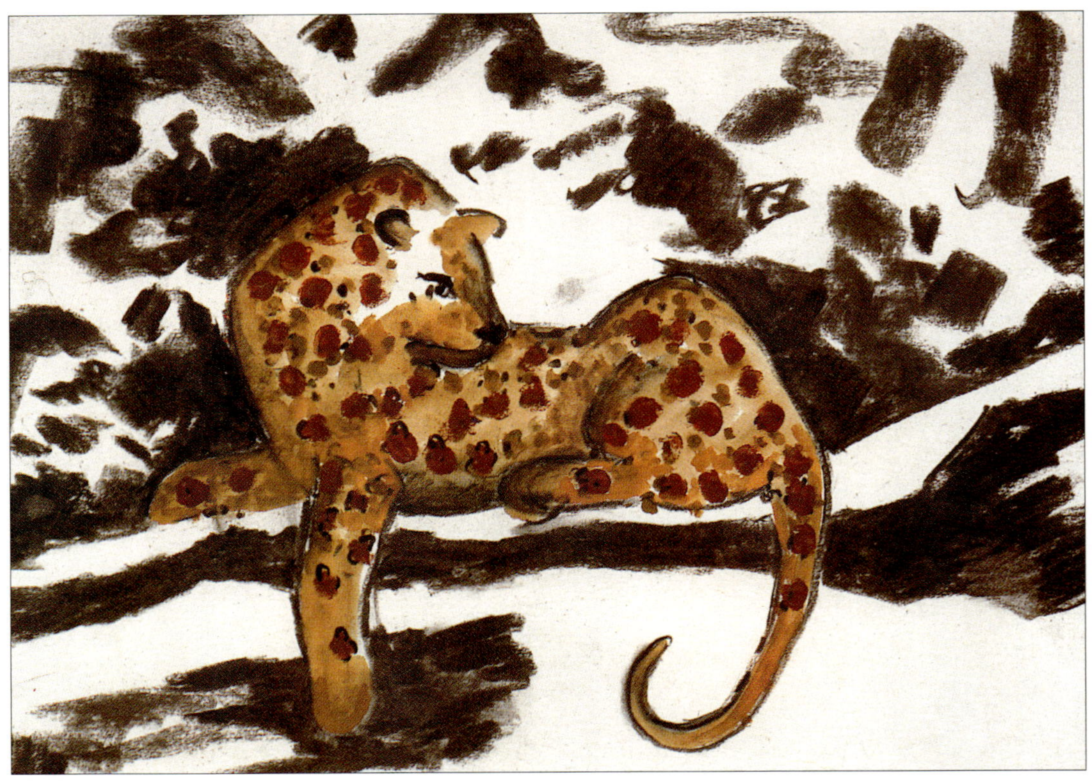

Left *A charcoal and gouache study of a resting leopard; no actual sketch was made of a leopard in this particular pose and it is a composite of snatches of visual information hurriedly drawn. In a zoo, even when animals are reasonably relaxed, some are almost constantly in movement.*

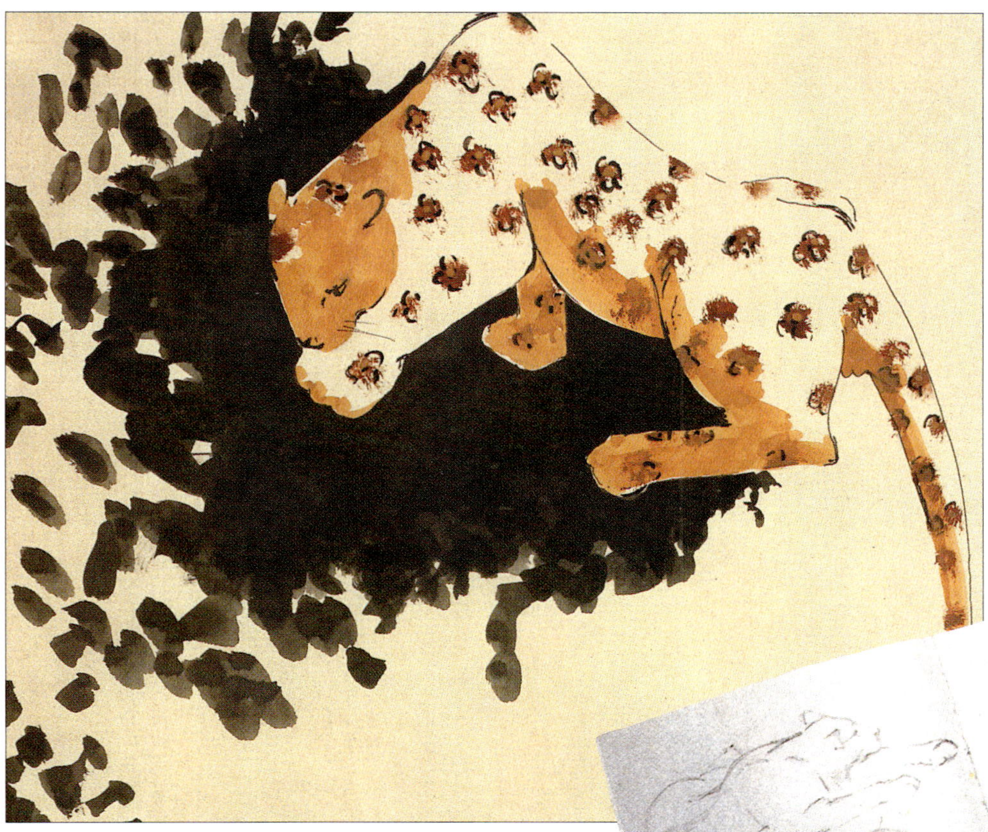

Left *This drawing on pale-yellow cartridge paper in pen and gouache was made from the small sketch in the bottom right-hand page of the sketchbook. The sketch was reversed through the use of a tracing.*

Below *Pencil studies of leopards and lions in various attitudes of rest.*

better if you try not to make drawings that are mere anatomical studies, but concentrate on your own visual responses to the animal.

Most drawing media are suitable: selection really depends on personal choice. The speed at which charcoal can be used with little pressure perhaps has a certain advantage for the beginner.

Photographic reference may also be of some help but should, if possible, be used in conjunction with visual notes made in the presence of the animal that is to be drawn. It does not matter how good or faithful to life the photograph of a tiger might be, there is no substitute for the first-hand experience of seeing the sheer power and size of a fully-grown tiger on the move, even in a zoo enclosure.

If you use photographs, it is far better to use photographs you have taken, for they will act not only as a reminder of the visual appearance of the animal, but they will also remind you of your own feelings toward it.

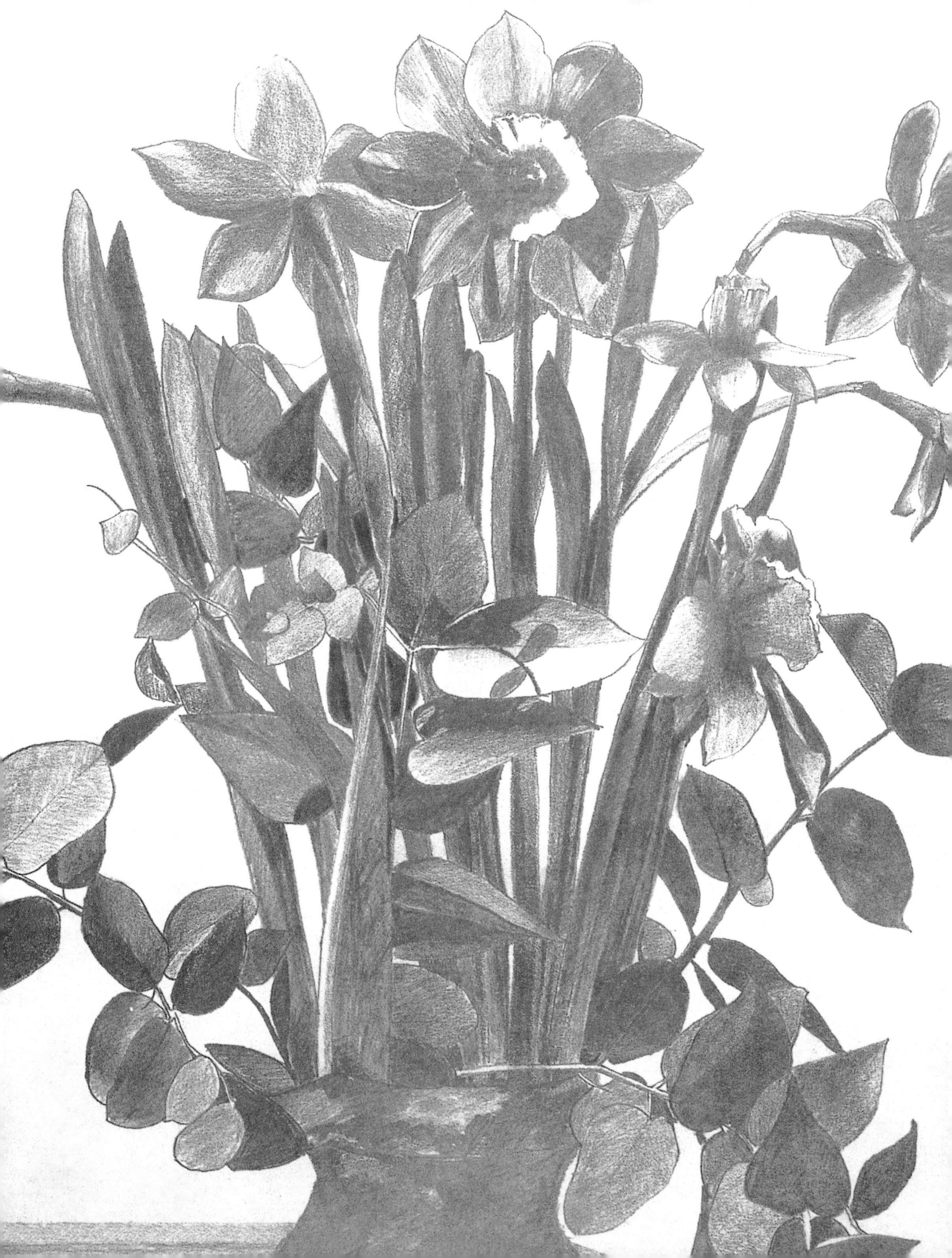

7 NATURAL FORM

During the 18th century the great voyages of discovery in search of new lands were also linked to serious scientific expeditions to record the natural world. This required totally new forms of drawing. The demands for accuracy of representation required by map-makers and others formed a relationship between the mathematician, the natural scientist, and the artist. This new demand for accuracy of observation naturally spread to the recording of plant life, animals, birds, insects, geological formations, and topographical landscapes.

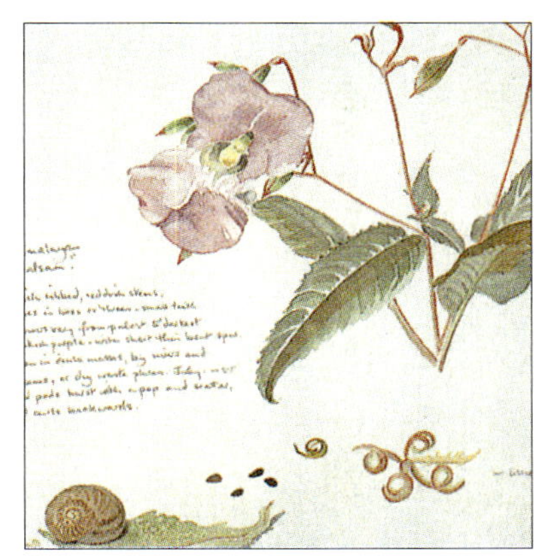

Above *A student drawing in the style of an 18th-century botanical study. The fine watercolor wash and written notes help identify the plant as a particular species. The snail eating a leaf adds a further touch of graphic interest.*

Left *This pencil study shows a very different approach to the one above. It has not been drawn to identify the plant, but is concerned with the vibrance of the lights and darks.*

This type of drawing also demands a clarity that can be easily translated into print, and from early on it was found that pen and ink or hard pencils produce a clear and definable line, the results of which are highly refined and delicate drawings. In studying reproductions of beautiful 18th-century botanical drawings, framed, and gracing the walls of a modern suburban home, it is often not realised that these drawings were carried out for scientific and not for decorative purposes.

Unlike those days, though, the contemporary student has no need to toil over difficult materials. There is now available a whole range of reservoir pens that produce a very fine and even black line.

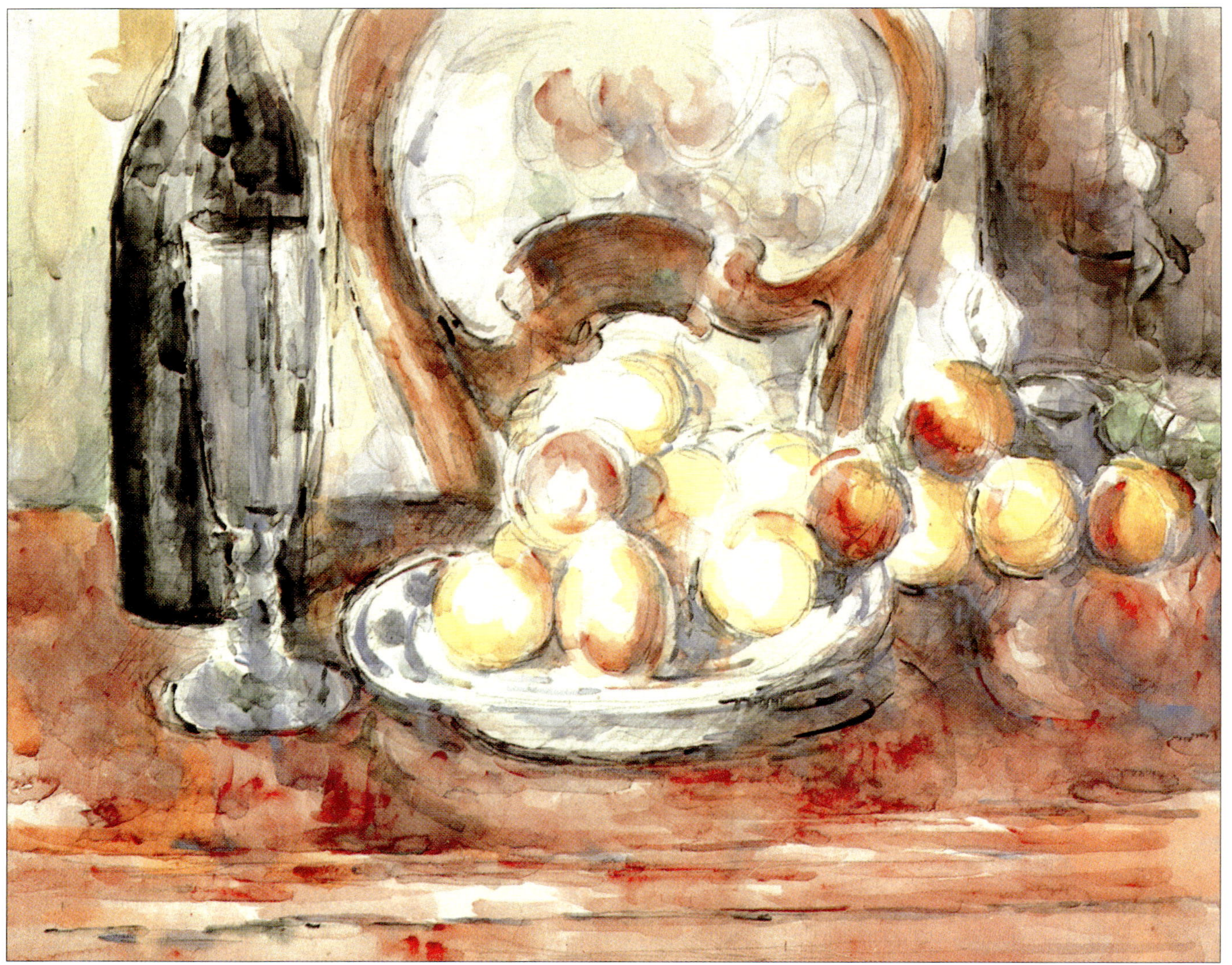

Left Chair, Bottles and Apple; *Cezanne used still life to explore the relationships of forms and their interaction on various spatial planes.*

Right *A study of daffodils in pencil and oil pastel; the diagonal application of color gives the composition visual excitement.*

The fact that ink cannot easily be erased encourages careful consideration before any mark is put to paper.

Many beginners start by making a pencil drawing first and then inking over this primary study. Although the student may feel this is a safer way to proceed, the end result can be disappointing, for the inked line inevitably looks very dead. This is due to the fact that the student is no longer looking at the subject matter when inking over the pencil line with the pen. Really, it is essential that you develop the confidence to use the pen directly—there are no easy shortcuts.

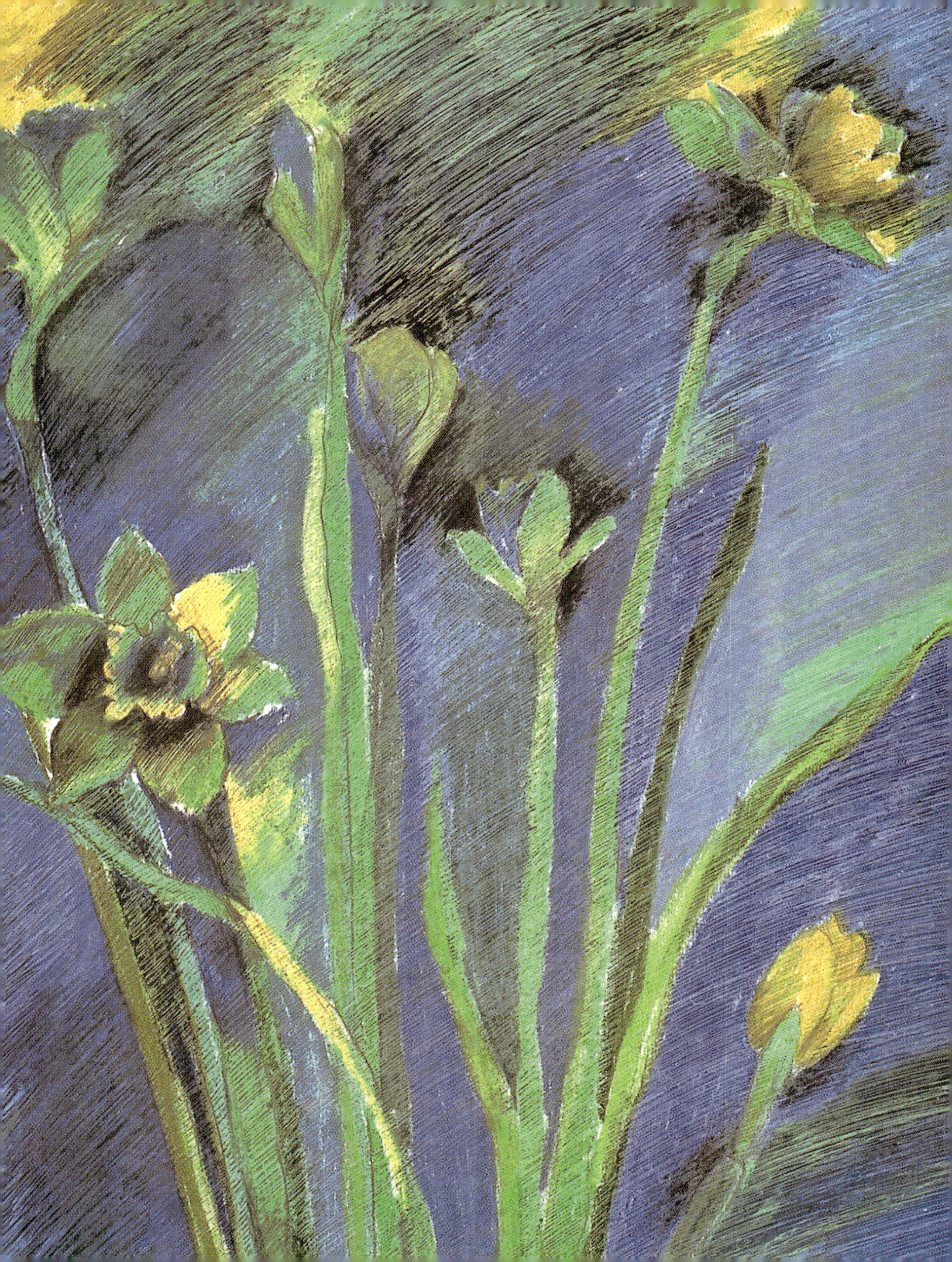

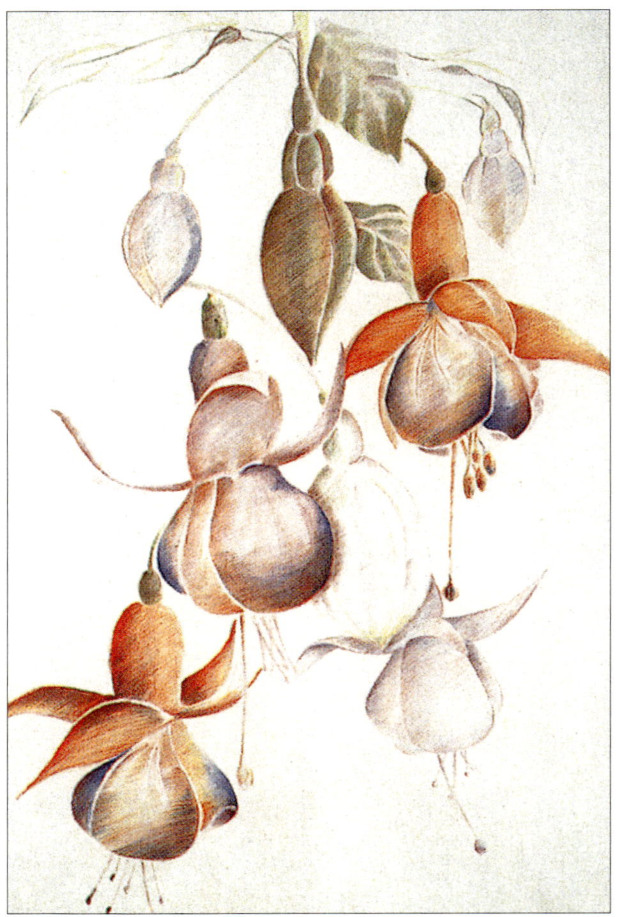

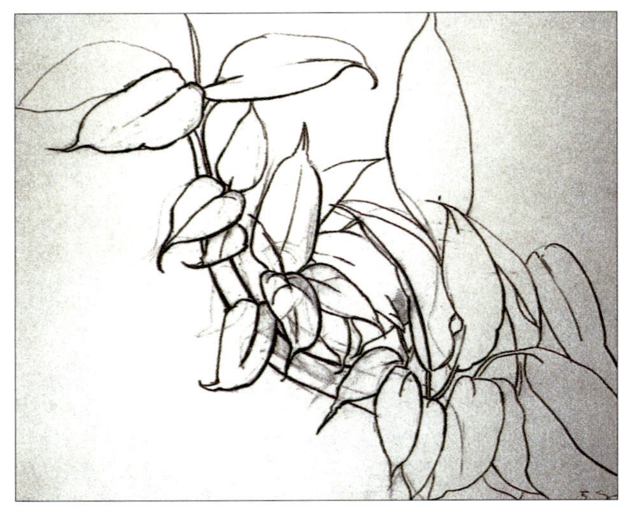

Above *This plant study in charcoal displays a linear approach with no attempt at shading. The fineness of the line has been achieved because the study is larger than would normally be expected of a plant drawing. It measures 38 X 27 in. (95 X 68 cm), which allows sufficient space to use charcoal in a linear manner. Although not an impossible medium for plant drawing, charcoal is not suitable for detailed studies.*

Left *Fuschias drawn in pencil and wash, reminiscent of the elegant style of the botanical draughtsmen of the 18th and 19th centuries. It is evident, though, that this work is far more concerned with the evocation of formal beauty than it is with plant recognition.*

Start by taking a single flower and recording all that you see as accurately as you can. Turn the same flower to another aspect and draw it again. Take the same approach with insects, fruits, vegetables, leaves, or any natural object that catches your eye.

For the student wishing to study natural form beyond a passing interest, a large (naturalist's) magnifying glass and stand is a necessary piece of equipment through which to view the fine structures of the objects being drawn. Some students may find this analytical approach too restrictive, and indeed objects of natural form can be drawn in a more expressive and personal manner. Works that divert from the scientific and analytical approach are nearer in content to still life, which allows the student much greater freedom both of expression and material resources. A painting such as Van Gogh's *Sunflowers* is essentially the same subject matter as an 18th-century botanical drawing, but the purpose behind the Van Gogh painting could not be further removed. Van Gogh's rendition of sunflowers was an expression of his personal feelings and was not intended as an analytical study of the plant species.

A fine pen is used to make fine marks—but now take a flower or other plant form and draw it in charcoal. It is soon evident that a charcoal drawing would be unsuitable for botanical recognition, but that charcoal is ideal for expressing the growth and virility of a plant, or expressing the abstract pattern created by plant form.

Something must be said at this stage about the use of color in representing natural form. Although very interesting drawings can be made in black and white, the importance of color cannot be totally ignored in this particular area of study. Watercolor wash was used in almost every work by 18th-century artists because color is so important in the recognition of species. The student may wish to try laying some simple washes on a pen or pencil drawing.

Other useful media are pastel—both dry and oil pastels—and colored pencils, with which the riot of color in nature can be recorded in a more forceful manner than watercolor wash normally allows. In art schools, the drawing of natural form has long been associated with mixed media, and a combination of pencil and oil pastel can result in some very exciting work. Ink and gouache also work very well together. One of the great advantages of drawing natural form is that it enables the student to experiment more freely and without inhibition with a range of materials that might create difficulties if used in drawing landscape or the figure.

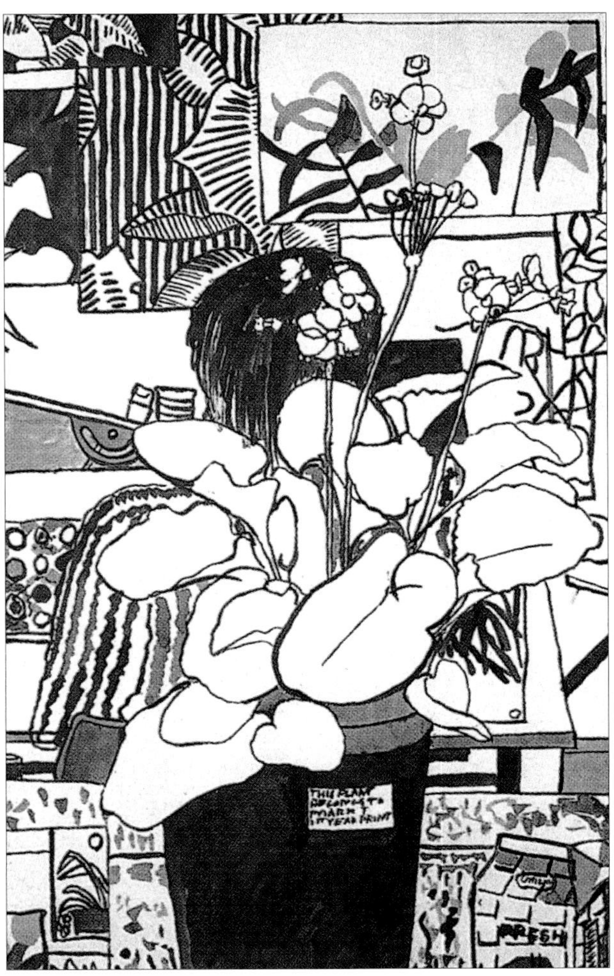

Right *This pen and ink study has been produced as a two-dimensional abstract design, and although it is a drawing of a plant, the manner of its composition makes it much more an exercise in still life than an accurate representation of natural form.*

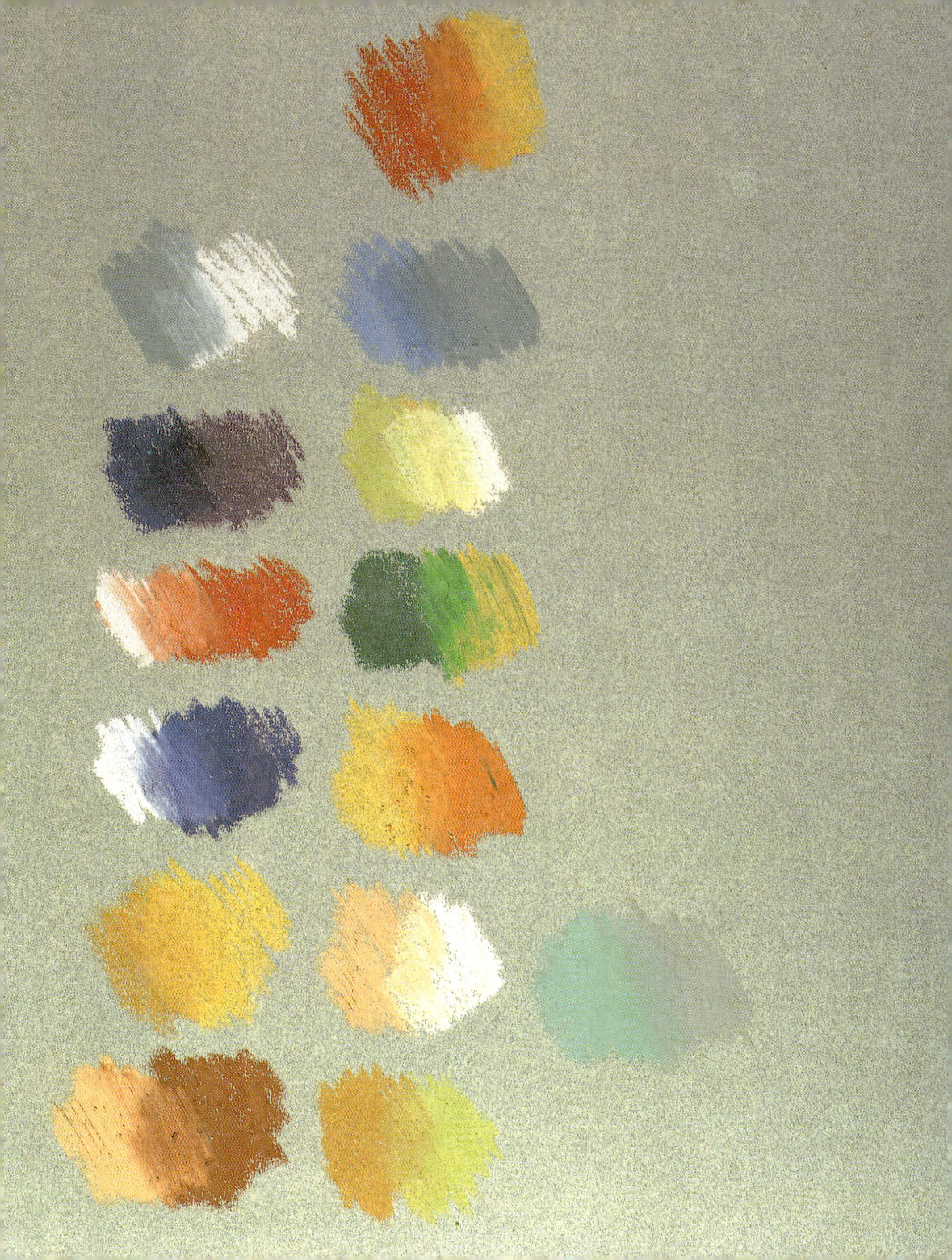

MATERIALS, EQUIPMENT AND PRESENTATION

It is recommended that a beginner keeps the materials and equipment as simple as possible. Modern chemistry and technology have produced an incredibly wide range of new media totally unknown to the Renaissance artist. These appear extremely attractive to the beginner, who feels that wonderful results are bound to spring from these apparently easy-to-use materials. Nevertheless, until you are reasonably confident, it is best to work mainly with the traditional materials that behave in a manner that can be anticipated.

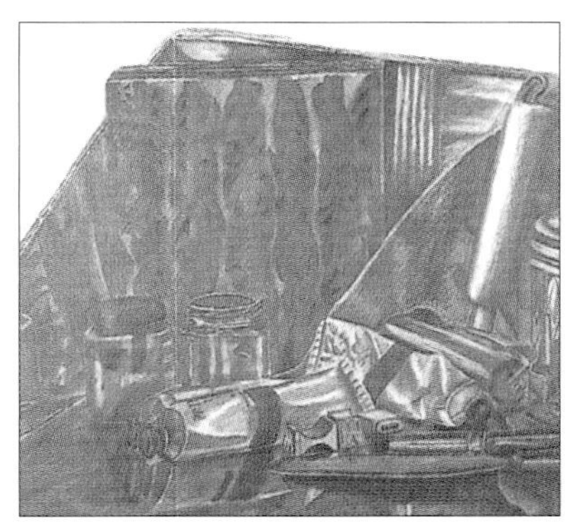

Above *This drawing was done with a single pencil of medium hardness. The reflections and different surfaces are competently rendered, but a greater range of tones would have enlivened the overall gray in this drawing. Using pencils of different hardness would have made this easier.*

Left *Oil pastels are an adaptable medium; the colors can overlay one another or be blended more completely with the fingers.*

With natural charcoal, a variety of papers can be used— but for the beginner a medium-toothed hot-pressed paper will probably secure the best results. The heavier-toothed papers require a little more confidence as the marks are smudged and moved less readily. Compressed charcoal and conté can be used on a grained (toothed) paper, but some of the quality of hard, black line which these media can make is lost. If the drawing is intended to be predominantly linear, a harder-surfaced paper is more suitable.

Pastels behave very similarly to charcoal and conté, and come in a variety of grades from very soft to a hard stick. Many beginners find that their first approach to color is through this medium. When using pastels

Left There are many types of easel on the market, not all of which are suitable for all purposes. If, for example, you intend to work indoors, and particularly if you wish to use watercolor washes, then the radial studio easel (illustrated) is fine, because it allows you to position the paper horizontally. It is, however, too bulky to be carried around for outdoor work.

care should be taken in the selection of the paper. With the harder variety of pastels, which behave more like crayons, a hard, smooth paper can be quite suitable and a very clear and detailed image can be produced. With soft pastels, a paper with a tooth is almost essential for a satisfactory result because the tooth of the paper is necessary to hold the soft pastel marks.

Pencil covers a wider range of medium than is commonly thought. The lead pencil is now quite an uncommon medium, although still available. The lead pencil's light, silvery, gray line can produce an effect not dissimilar to that of silverpoint which, before the innovation of the modern graphite pencil, was the main linear drawing instrument, particularly among Renaissance artists. The graphite pencil is still often incorrectly called a "lead pencil." A relatively new drawing instrument, it has been in common use only for about 200 years.

The solid graphite stick is also very useful for larger, tonal pencil drawings, and is often used in conjunction with a regular pencil. Many artists have been drawing with raw graphite powder, rubbing it into the paper to make large tonal marks, then bringing out highlights with a rubber and more detailed areas with a regular pencil. This method is suitable for very large works.

A pencil can be used in a variety of ways but is most commonly employed in making a line—the result is a crisp, clear drawing. Shadow can be produced by hatching or crosshatching, which is a set of parallel lines or two opposing sets of parallel lines, respectively. Darker tonal areas can also be shown by a series of regularly spaced dots. The softer variety of pencil can produce very soft areas of tone using the finger or torchon, or by spreading with a rubber. Harder, smoother-surfaced papers are generally the most suitable for pencil drawing. A good-quality cartridge paper is most commonly used and is readily available in most areas. Coarser-toothed papers can produce some very interesting results with a softer-grade pencil, but generally the rougher papers are used less commonly with pencil.

A very large selection of colored pencils and crayons is available, most of which are suitable for use in drawing, although some of the wax crayons have a tendency to fade quickly if exposed to strong light. Wax crayons should really be used only for work of a temporary nature, such as for visualizing an idea in terms of its color scheme.

A modern variant of the wax crayon is the oil pastel, which has a much greater pigmentation and therefore does not have a fading problem. The richness of the colors available is similar to that of oil paint. Oil pastels can be mixed on the paper to a limited extent, but they do not blend as readily as regular pastels. Blending is best achieved by overlaying one color on top of another, although some very interesting results are obtained by putting the oil pastels on the paper straight from the stick, and with the aid of a brush and turpentine an effect can be produced not unlike an oil sketch on paper.

Although oil pastels can be used with other media, it must be remembered that they are oil-based and do not readily interact with water-based or chalk-based media. For work out of doors, the oil pastel has many advantages, particularly for the artist whose

Below *Crosshatching does not have to be a grid of parallel lines; curved crosshatching, or crosshatching in multiple directions, are particularly effective.*

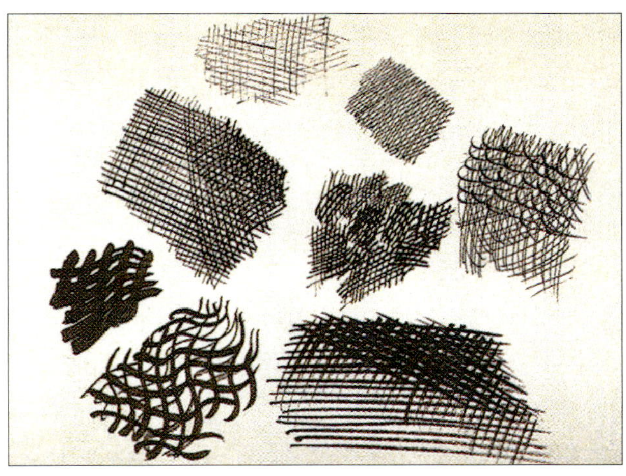

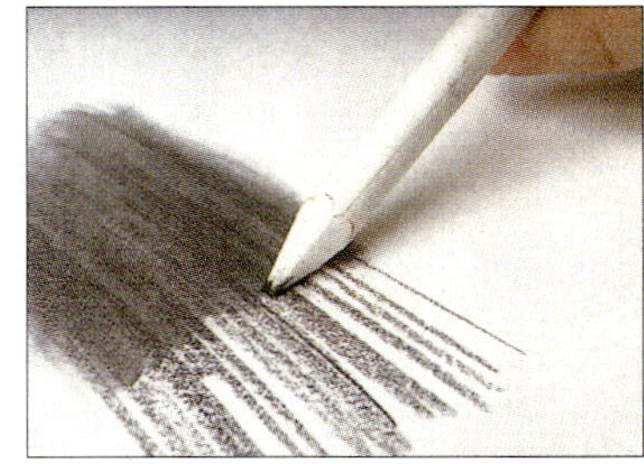

Right *Blending conté crayon with a piece of paper tightly rolled allows more control over small areas than blending with the fingers.*

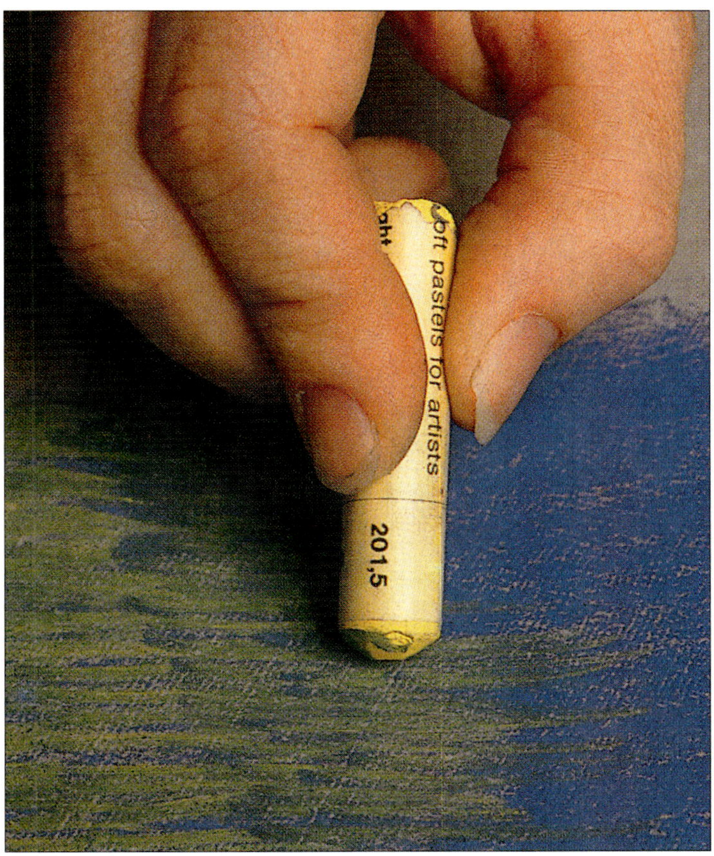

Above *A completely blended effect is not always required when using pastels. In the example illustrated above, the artist has decided not to rub in the colors entirely. Instead, he is blending them roughly with the use of short strokes, thus preserving the contrast.*

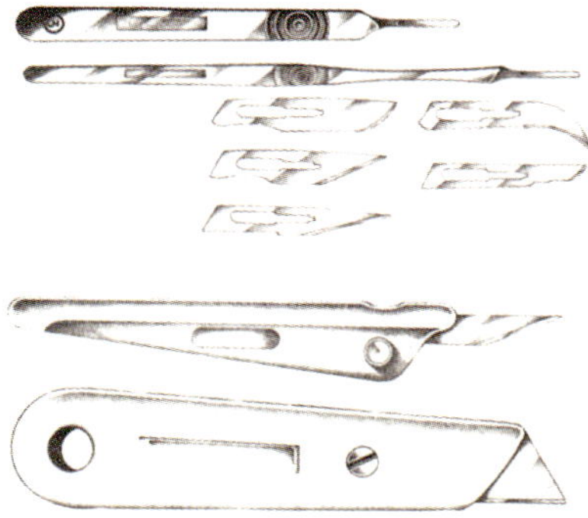

Left *Scalpels, craft knives, and trimming knives are surprisingly useful when drawing, for sharpening pencils and trimming paper, and even working on the drawing itself; for cutting fine lines into crayon, for example, or scraping away small areas of colored pencil. A veritable must for every artist!*

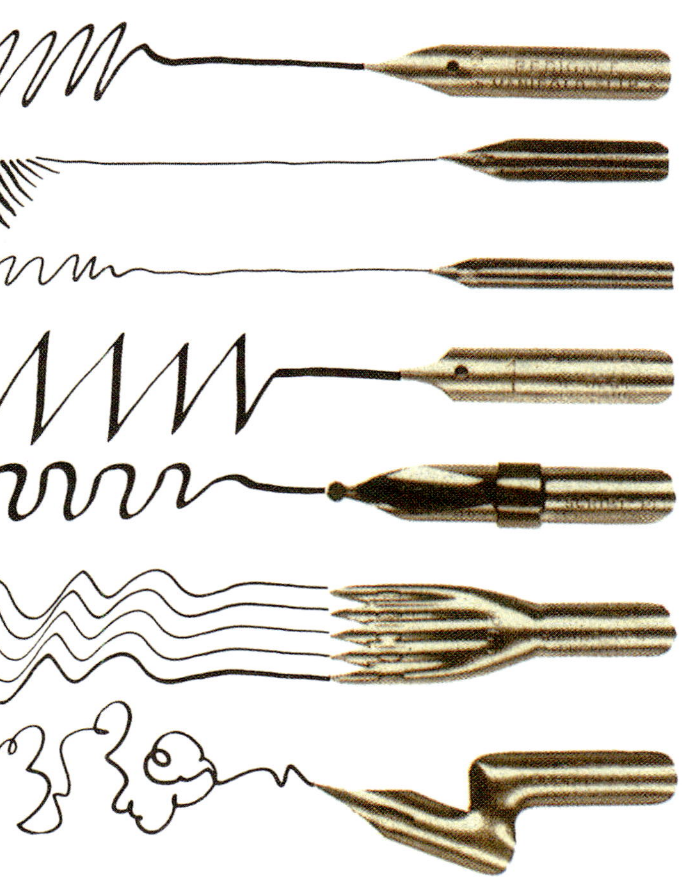

Above *Nibs for dip pens. The slip nib (1) produces a fluid line; the map pen (2) will give a line of varying width depending on the pressure applied. The crow quill (3) gives a consistent line width. The thick and thin strokes of the italic nib HI are more angular than those of the script nib (4). The five-line nib (5) is perfect for regular crosshatching. The copperplate nib (6) is angled to accommodate both vertical and horizontal strokes.*

finished work is predominantly in oils, because the colors are very similar in richness to oil paint.

Designers' colored pencils are more permanent than wax crayons, although again they have a tendency to fade, some colors fading much quicker than others.

The real advantage of using colored pencils out of doors is that you require no extra equipment such as brushes and water, and for creating colored notes from nature in a sketchbook there is no more highly recommended medium. For the beginner a box containing about ten colored pencils should be sufficient.

Most types of paper can be used with colored pencils and crayons. It is advisable to use fixative on most drawing media such as charcoal, conté, soft graphite pencil, and crayon pencil. With wax crayons and colored pencils it is not necessary and could even cause some damage to the work.

Fixative is applied either from an aerosol can or a mouth-activated spray. The aerosol cans are convenient but the ecologically conscious would almost certainly prefer to use a spray. The fixative can be obtained ready-mixed in a bottle. There are in addition a number of old and well tried formulas for mixing fixatives. If the work is in a horizontal position, some care should be taken not to over-apply the fixative because it may cause runs, or to have the spray too close to the work. Beginners are recommended to lay the work horizontally and to spray the fixative evenly across the surface so that it falls gently and evenly onto the work.

Ink, like charcoal, is one of the oldest media used for drawing. In modern times the most common way of using ink is with a steel-ribbed pen. The beginner normally starts with a line drawing and crosshatching, and a great variety of hatching lines can be produced with the pen. Artists such as Rembrandt drew almost exclusively in pen and ink, putting in large areas of tone with a brush and creating dramatic effects of light and dark. It was a common sight to see Rembrandt in the countryside around Amsterdam with an ink bottle tied to his belt, recording the dramatic effects of light in that flat watery landscape.

Ink comes in a variety of forms and a very full range of colors. It is recommended that the beginner use a watersoluble ink, in color either black or sepia. This type of ink allows for a full range of tones when used in conjunction with a little water.

Below *Watercolor brushes for drawing need to be of good quality. Pure sable brushes are the best but the most expensive. There is now a very wide range of student-quality nylon brushes on the market which serve reasonably well.*

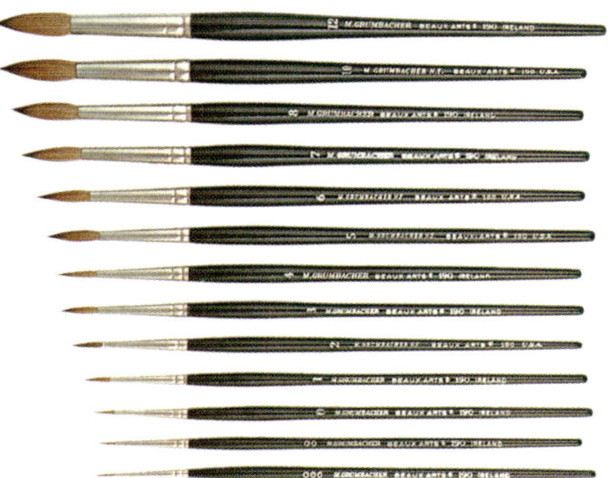

There is also available a full range of water-soluble felt-tip pens. The very finest of these can produce a line as fine as that produced by any mapping pen. It is advisable to check, when purchasing one of these pens in black, that the ink when thinned with water is in fact black and not dark blue.

The harder, smoother-surfaced papers and coated boards are the most suitable for pen and ink drawing. A toothed (grained) paper can be used for colored or tonal wash drawings where the amount of pen work is minimal. It is advisable to shrink the paper before you start. This is particularly true for pen and ink drawings intended to be tinted with watercolor.

It is often a good practice, irrespective of the medium being used, to preshrink the paper. This is done by immersing the paper in water for about five minutes to get it thoroughly soaked, then laying the paper on a drawing board (which should be at least two inches bigger in every dimension than the paper). Sponge off surplus water and attach the paper to the board around all its edges with regular gummed brown paper. Allow the paper to dry naturally in a flat position. Once dried, the paper will not cockle again when washes in inks or watercolors are applied.

There is a great variety of sketching easels available. The traditional folding wooden sketching easel is still widely used, but there is also a good selection of metal easels. For any work that is going to take more than about half an hour to complete, the use of an easel of some type is recommended. The sketching easel also doubles as a studio easel for smaller work.

The regular hard eraser is an essential item of equipment. However, for charcoal and pastel drawing a putty eraser should be used. It is very soft and can be molded in the hand to make a point for lifting charcoal and pastel in areas of great detail.

The most effective method of erasing ink is with a sharp blade, so that the ink is actually scratched off the surface of the paper. Care should be taken, however, because deeply scratched-out alterations can cause ink to run to the fibers of the scratched-out area if that area is redrawn. Ideally, the erasing of ink should be left until the very last stage, when the drawing has virtually been completed.

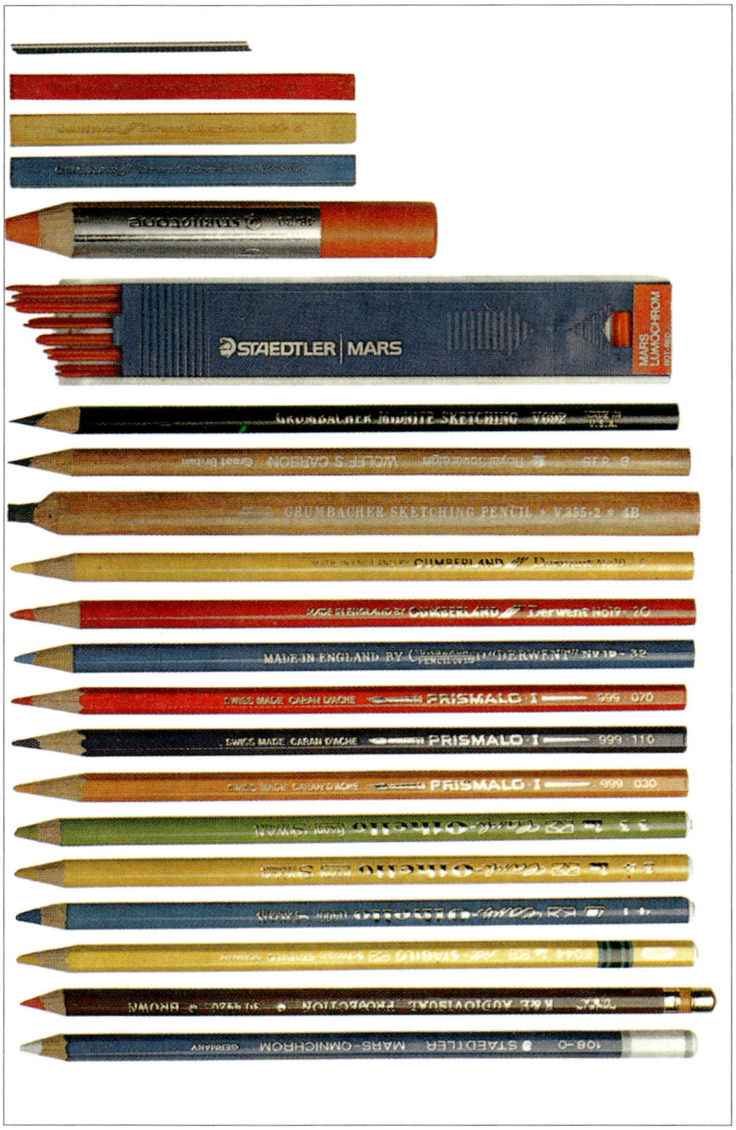

PENCILS AND OTHER DRAWING MEDIA

The word "drawing" suggests to many a work executed in pencil, but a variety of tools has always been available and this selection is increasing so that the draftsmen of today can choose from a very wide range of materials.

Left *The pencil is a wonderful thing; not only is it infinitely various, it's cheap. Charcoal and carbon pencils produce a very black line. The constituents of colored pencils—filler, binder, and lubricant—result in a soft lead which can usually only be removed with a blade.*

ASSEMBLING A FRAME

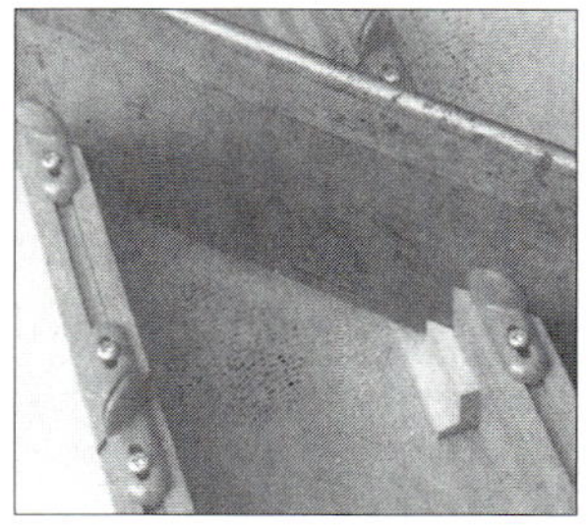

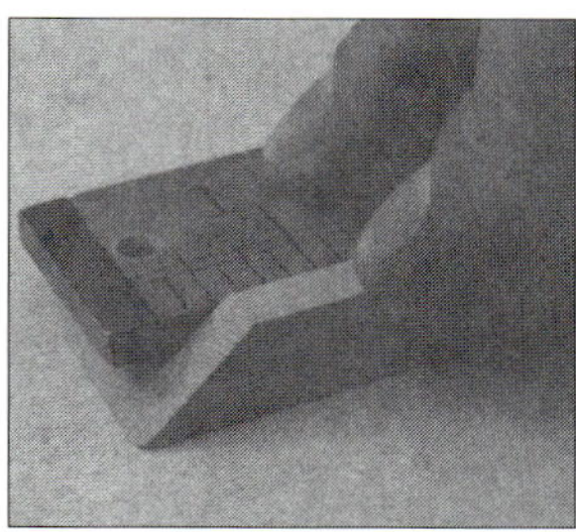

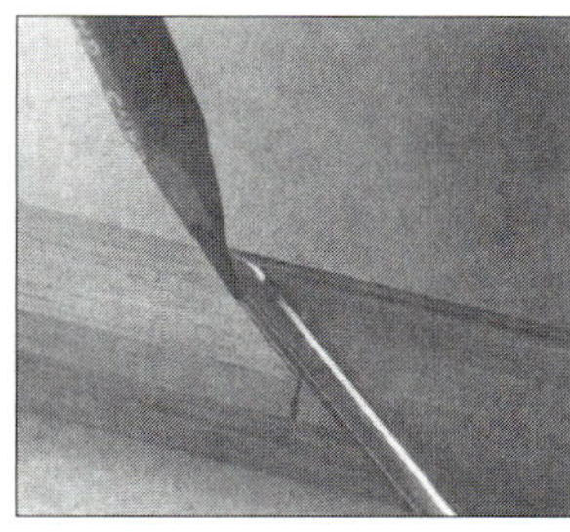

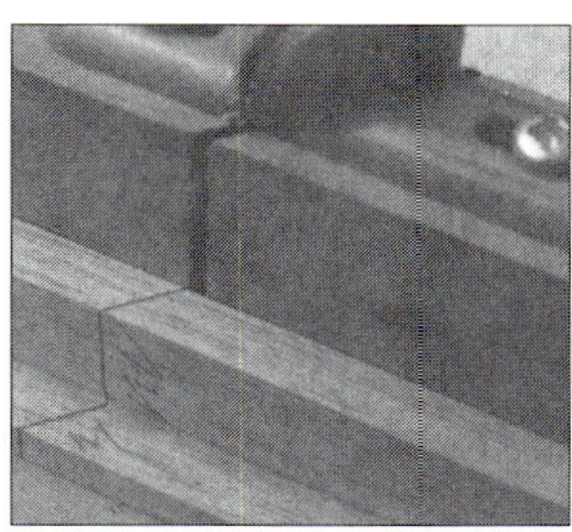

1 *Secure a length of molding, position the saw and make the first cut.*

2 *To measure the molding, align the ruler as shown above.*

3 *Mark the other end using a set square to obtain the 45° angle of the meter.*

4 *Position the molding in the miter board; saw it through.*

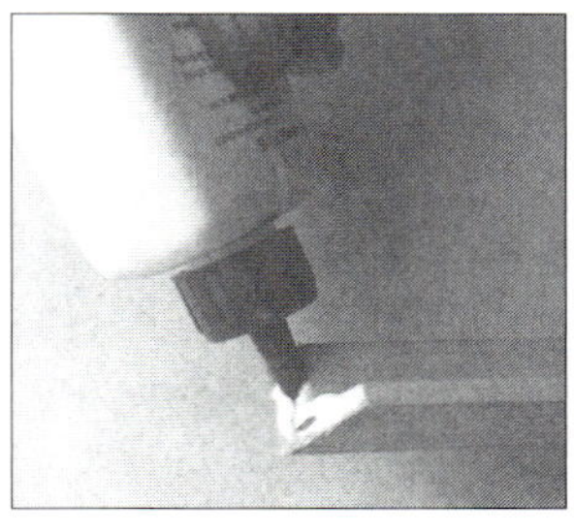

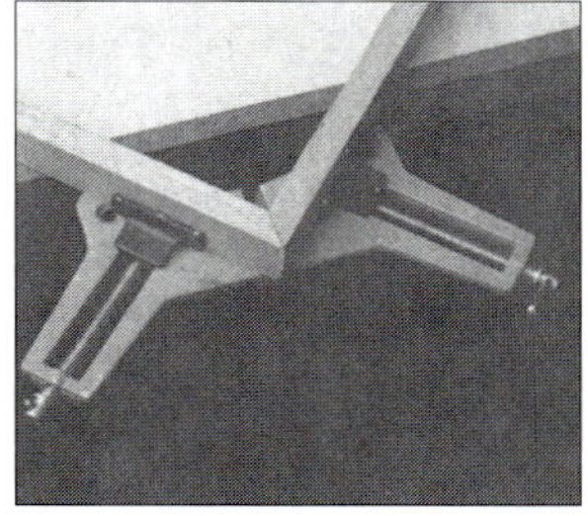

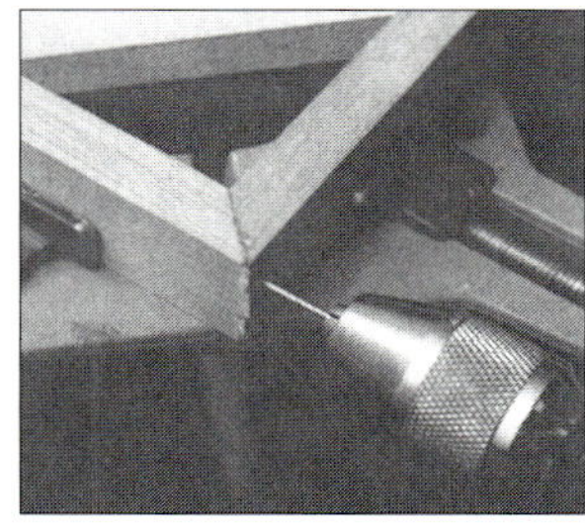

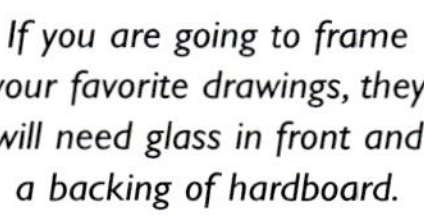

If you are going to frame your favorite drawings, they will need glass in front and a backing of hardboard.

5 *Cut frame; apply adhesive to the mitered ends of the molding.*

6 *Lay molding flat; secure two mitered ends together in a corner clamp.*

7 *Drill small holes into each corner. Secure the pieces with panel pins.*

Pencil

The most common instrument used for drawing is the pencil (from the Latin work *pencillus,* meaning "little tail"). Pencils are graded by the H and B systems. H through to 8H indicate increasing hardness of lead, whereas B through to 8B denote increasingly soft cores. It is important to experiment with a wide range of pencils. Their characteristics may vary

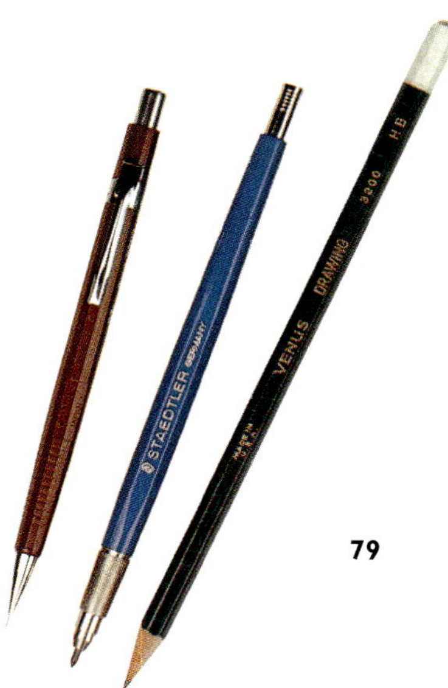

Right *Pentel and Steadtler Mars clutch pencils, and Venus graphite drawing pencil.*

according to the paper used, a hard pencil, for instance, making a fainter mark on a smooth, coated paper than on a coarsely textured one. Similarly, a very soft pencil, say a 5B, will make an intensely dark, coarse, and rich line on textured paper, so much so that marks may prove difficult to control. Often the best way to exploit the pencil fully is to combine several different grades. Paul Hogarth (b. 1917), for instance, is an example of a leading contemporary artist who demonstrates the use of various grades within the same work.

The early forerunner of the pencil was silverpoint, a sharpened stick made from an alloy: lead and tin. The study of a man in a helmet by Leonardo da Vinci shows a refined technique comprising many fine shaded lines, netting across the paper surface to record the image. Various pressures are employed to give due emphasis and stress, seeming almost to caress the paper at times. Contrast this with the vibrant figure studies of the great French sculptor, Rodin (1840-1917). Here the line seems to be a continuous tracing on the paper, full of energy conveying somehow a prediction of the next intended movement.

Charcoal

Charcoal is made of sticks of wood, often willow, burnt to carbon. Various grades are available, ranging from hard to very soft, and the latter particularly need to be fixed to the paper on completion of the drawing.

Charcoal pencils, containing compressed powdered charcoal and a binding agent, offer more control and a cleaner instrument with

Left *Graphite pencils are available in a wide range of degrees of hardness or softness, ranging from 8H, which is very hard, to 8B, the softest lead. In order to illustrate the differing effects, the appropriate pencil has been used to draw each of the selection shown here. The hardest appears fainter than the dark, smudgy effect of the softest.*

PENCIL TECHNIQUES

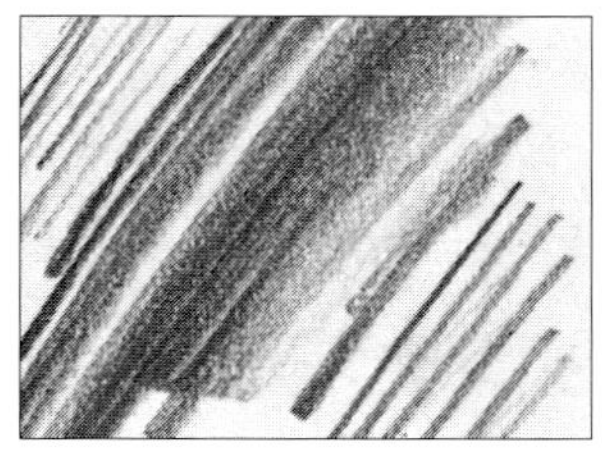

1 *Combinations of pencil and paper produce a wide range of effects. (Used here, 2B)*

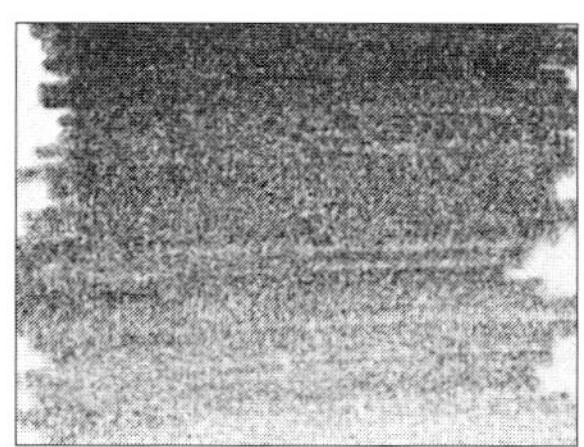

2 *A fairly soft pencil (4B) creates a gradated tone on a moderately smooth paper.*

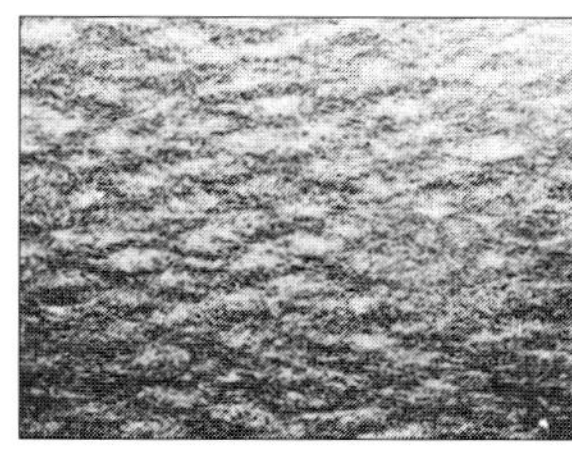

3 *Used on a rough paper, this same 4B pencil gives a much less even result.*

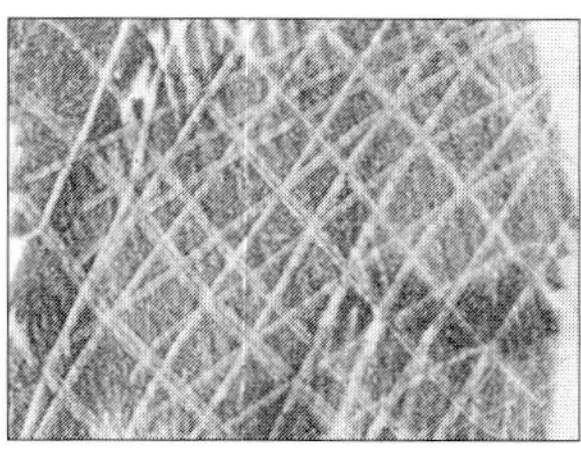

4 *Draw with the reverse end of the pencil to create indentations, then shading.*

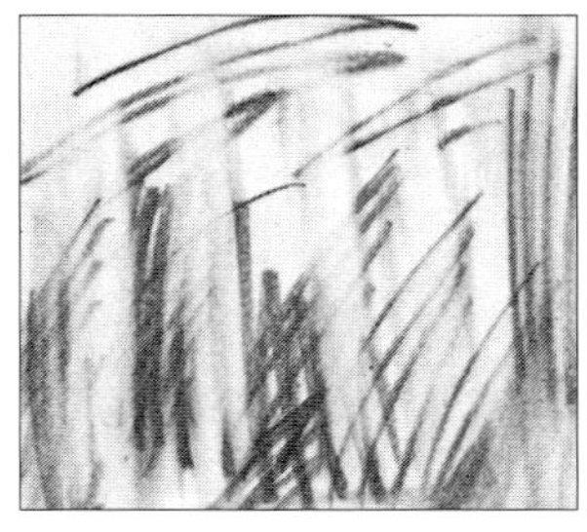

5 *2B lines partially erased to show the effects produced with an eraser.*

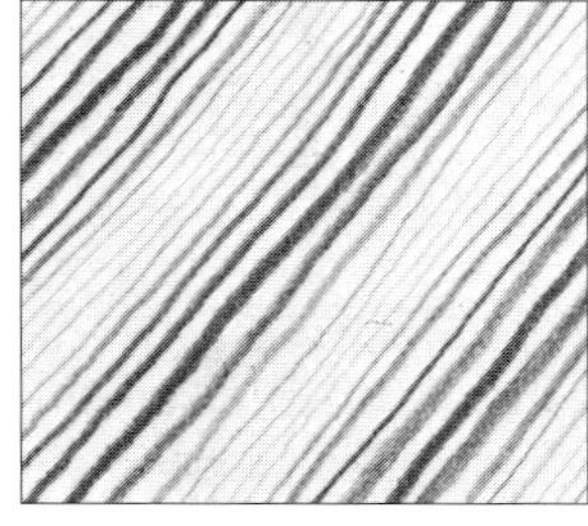

6 *Differences in weight, shown by lines drawn with 6H to 6B pencils.*

7 *For dramatic effect use carbon paper on top of your drawing surface.*

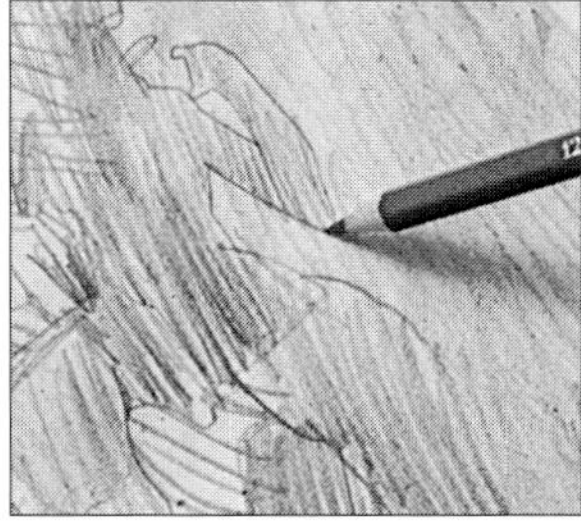

8 *Pencil can be used to produce tone as well as line effects. (Used here, 2B)*

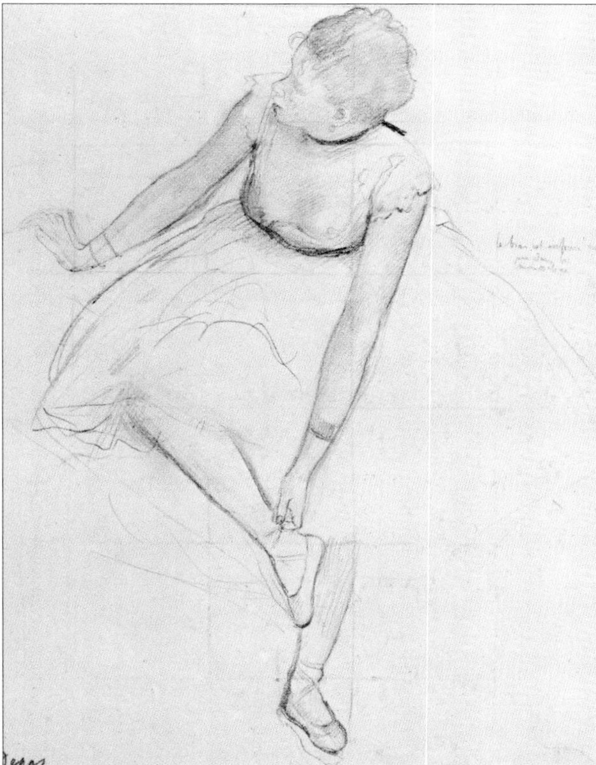

Above: *The studies of ballet dancers by Edgar Degas invariably capture an immediacy which is crucial to the subject. This pencil study,* Dancer Adjusting Her Slipper *vividly recalls his vibrant pastel drawings, but has its own formal qualities which show his understanding of this delicate medium.*

CHARCOAL TECHNIQUES

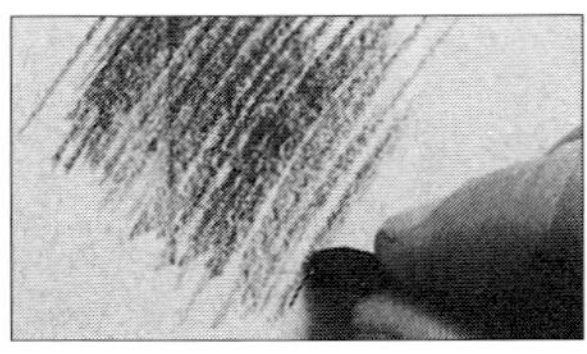

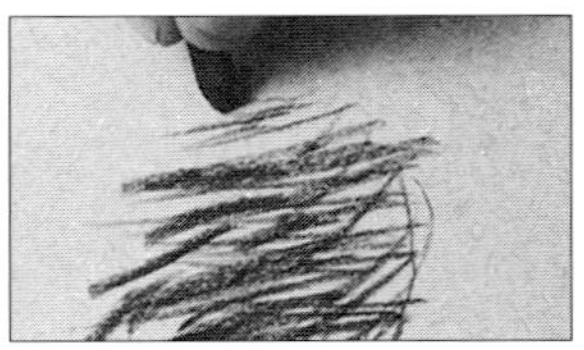

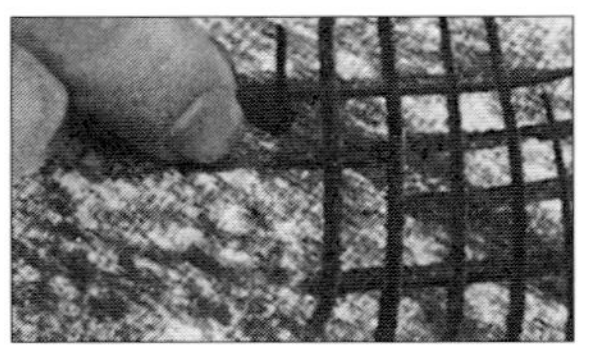

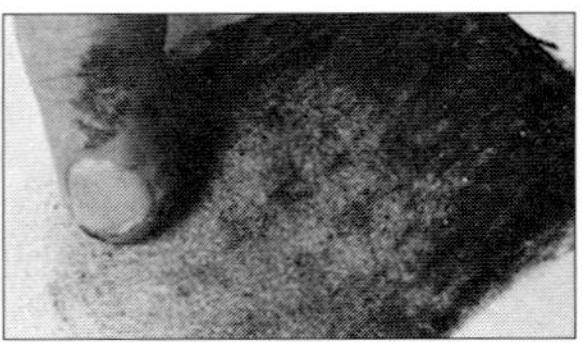

1 *Fine, hatched line builds up graded tone, working in one direction with varying pressure.*

2 *Loose crosshatching is an alternative method of building up tonal areas.*

3 *Lay areas of tone with the side of the charcoal stick; crosshatch over for a richer texture.*

4 *Use finger to spread charcoal dust evenly over the paper or to vary the tone.*

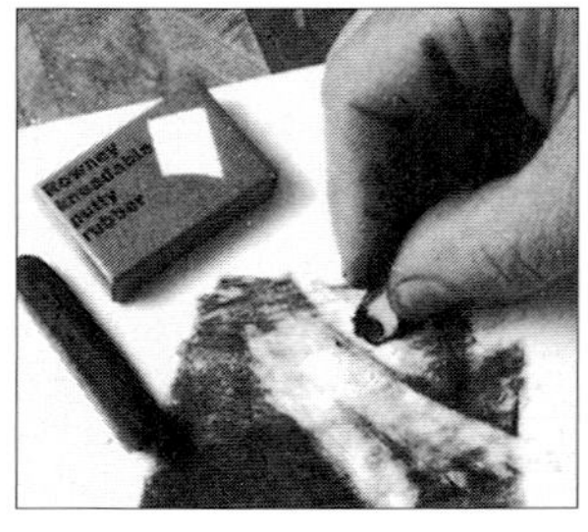

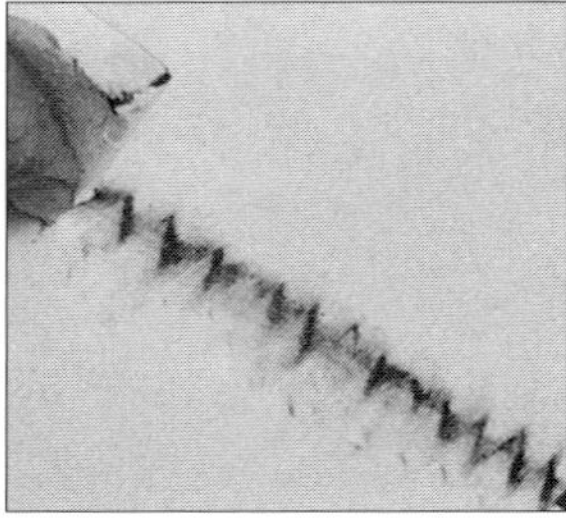

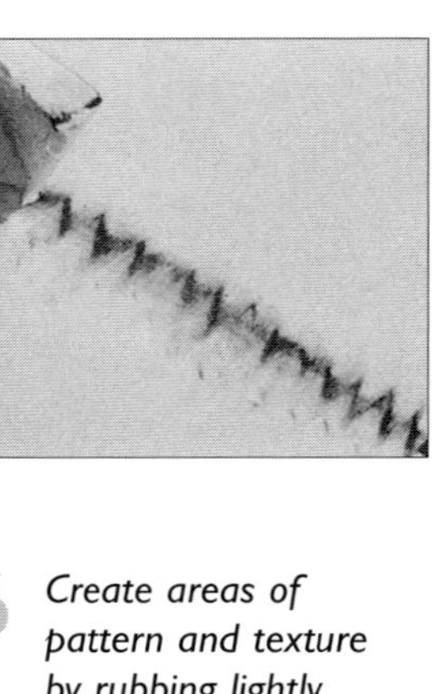

5 *Work lights or erase charcoal by using a clean, soft putty eraser.*

6 *Create areas of pattern and texture by rubbing lightly with a putty eraser.*

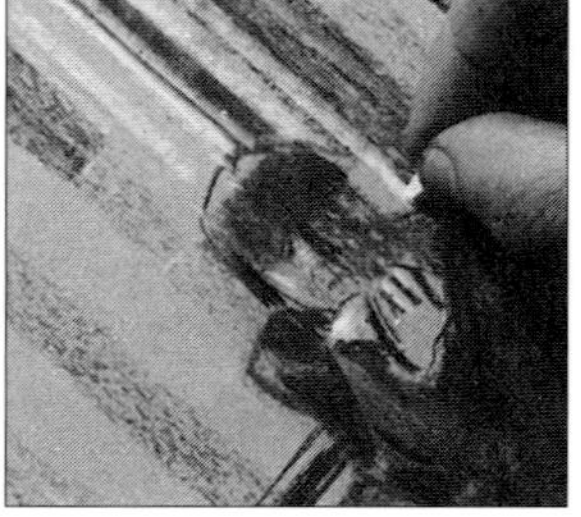

7 *Work gently with a soft brush and clean water to use a charcoal wash.*

8 *Highlights can be added by using a white chalk or pastel.*

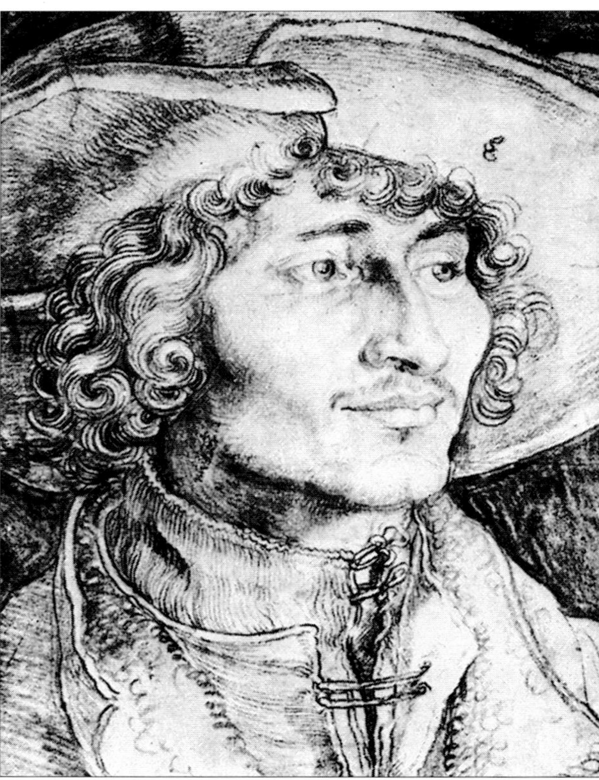

Above Portrait of a Young Man *by Albrecht Durer illustrates the precision that can be achieved if charcoal is handled confidently. It is sometimes regarded as a clumsy medium, but here crisp lines in the hair and subtle modeling of the face are achieved with great skill and delicacy.*

which to work. The density of mark will vary according to the proportions of pulverized charcoal to oil (or wax); a softer pencil contains more binder, a harder one less. In general a toothed paper or board is most suitable for use both with sticks and pencils.

Charcoal techniques

Charcoal can be used to good effect for strong and vigorous linear works and it is especially suitable for making tonal drawings working from the darks, a technique in which the surface of the support is covered with a consistent layer of powdered charcoal forming a flat, mid-gray tone. From this surface, by the use of a kneaded or putty rubber, the lighter parts of the design are provisionally picked out, leaving the gray sheet punctuated with patches of white. Into this beginning can be introduced the positive marks, using lines and smudges of

PASTEL TECHNIQUES

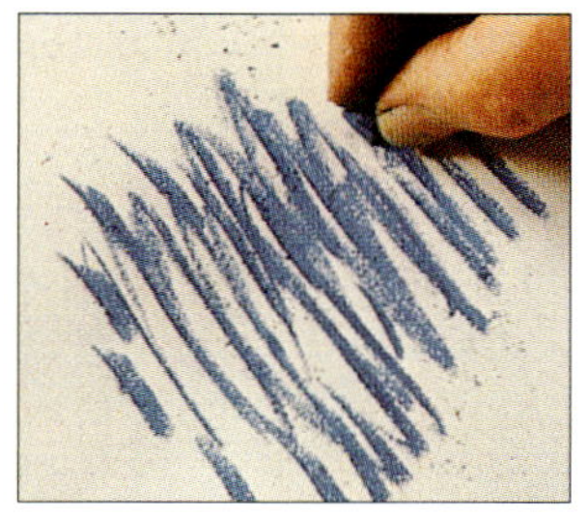

1 *For diagonal hatching, use the side of the stick; more pressure, thicker lines.*

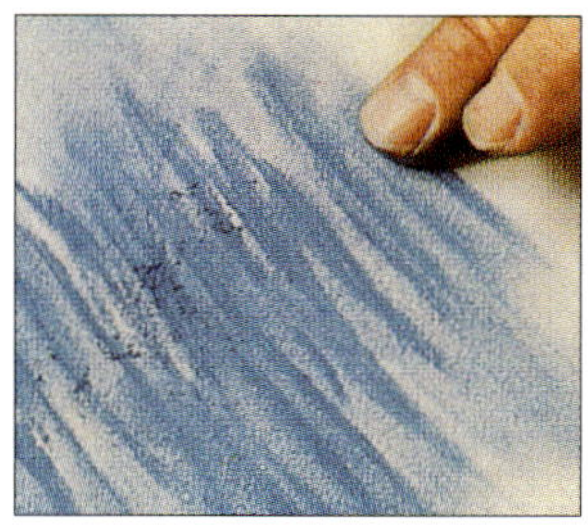

2 *Rubbing the hatched lines spreads the colour to give a hazy effect.*

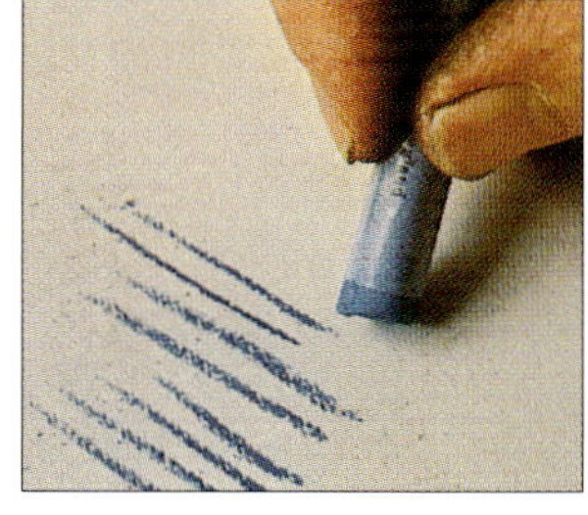

3 *Use the side of the pastel and press lightly in order to obtain crisp, fine lines.*

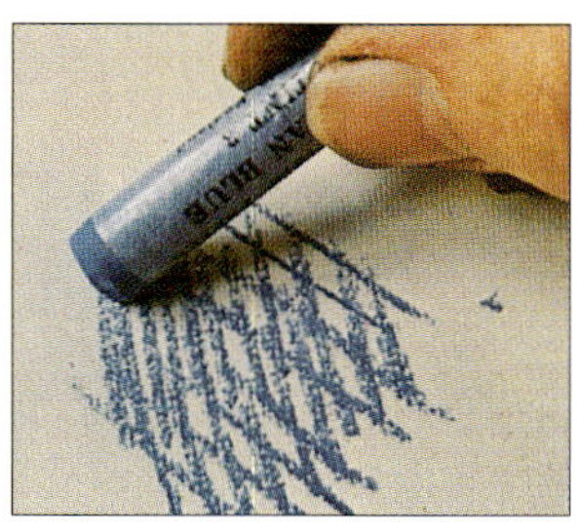

4 *Work across lines in the opposite direction for a crosshatched texture.*

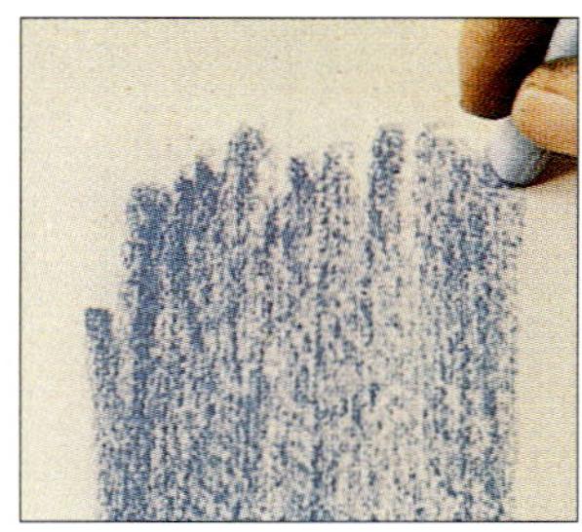

5 *Work with blunt end in one direction to lay an area of colour.*

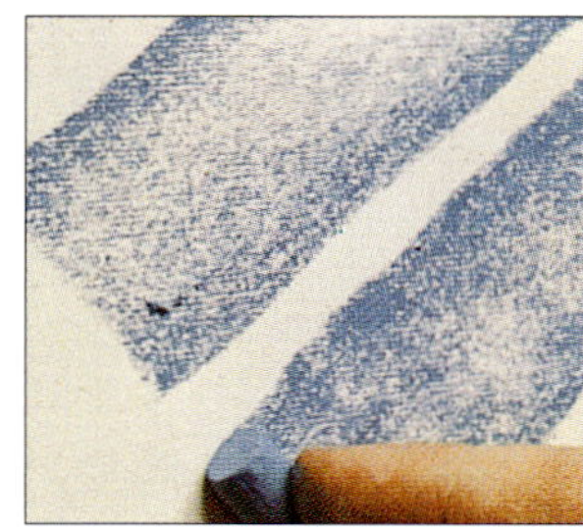

6 *Peel back cover paper and hold the pastel flat for broad strokes.*

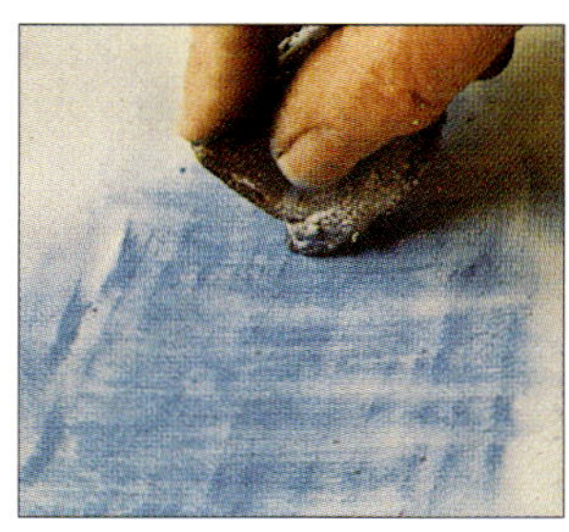

7 *Use a kneaded rubber to lift off color and achieve paler tones.*

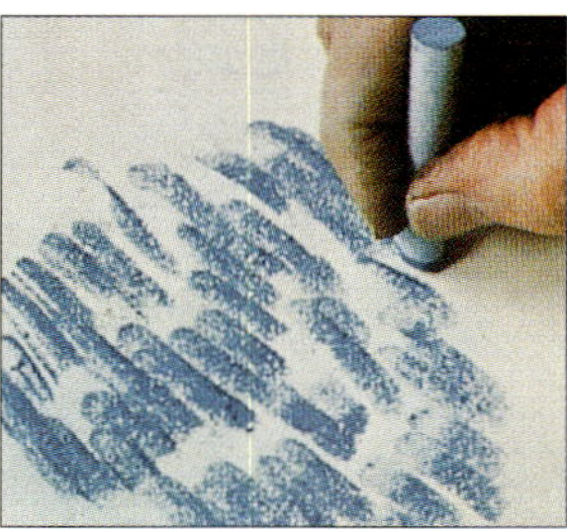

8 *Make brisk strokes across the grain of the paper for stippled effect.*

charcoal. Development through the consolidation both of the negatives (the wiped-off areas) and the positives allows great scope for adjustment and even major correction. One of charcoal's prime advantages over other drawing media is this capability of being changed. Degas tended to use charcoal in a similar way to chalk or pencil, enclosing the figure forms by firm, positive strokes, but exploiting the material's versatility by rapid indication of varying areas of tone. Matisse made figure drawings in charcoal combining line with the soft smudges, left as ghostly traces, of corrections having been made.

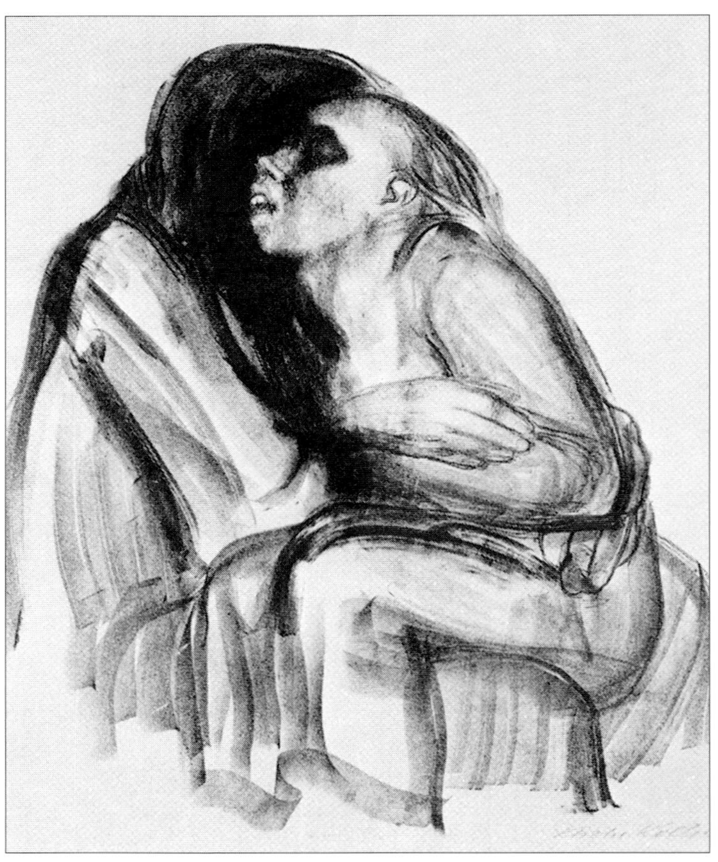

Pastel

Color is used in drawing both to arrest a memory and to enliven the picture surface, but it can also be used to describe the world-as-seen or to propose schemes for works in other media. Pastel drawing was at its height as a popular medium for portraits in the 18th century, but since that time it has been used by a number of artists, either as a unique technique or in conjunction with other materials. Traditionally pastels are made from powdered pigments mixed only with sufficient gum or resin to bind them into stick form. Pastels tend to be softer than pencils or chalks; they are still, however, defined according to grade, depending on the amount of gum used in their manufacture. The primary advantage of the medium is its immediacy of effect, it being necessary only to rub the stick over the surface for it to release the characteristic fresh pure

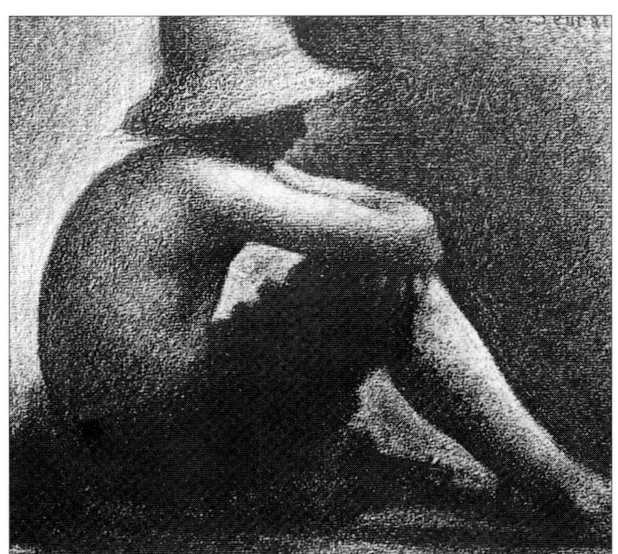

PASTEL EFFECTS

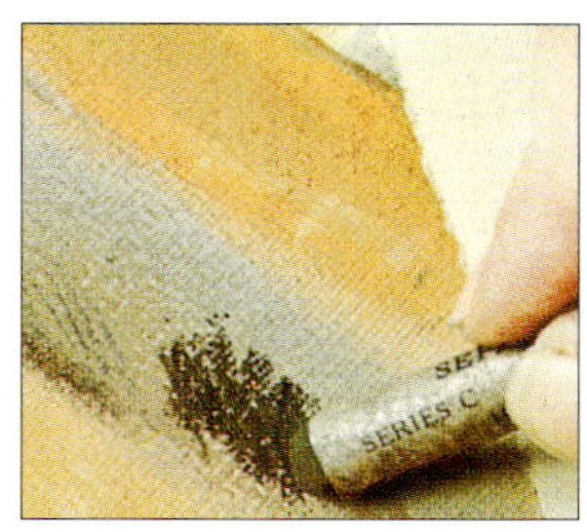

1 Use blunt end of the pastel to draw in a fairly small area of thick color.

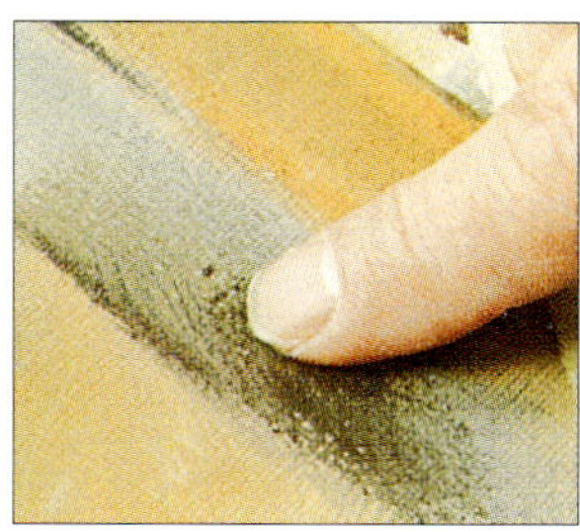

2 Work the color over with fingertip and spread lightly from the center.

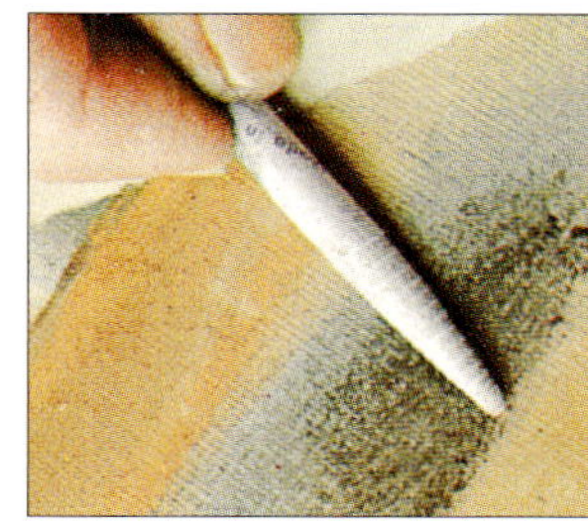

3 Paper folded to make a point is more accurate than the fingers.

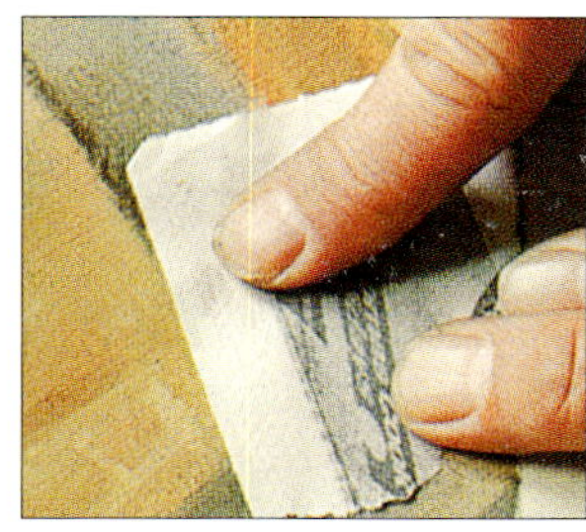

4 Rub with newspaper to push the pastel into the support.

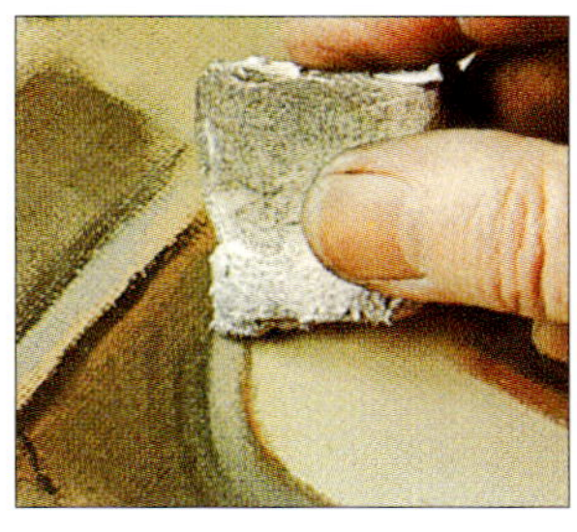

Highlighting with a kneaded rubber by manipulating a rubber to a point.

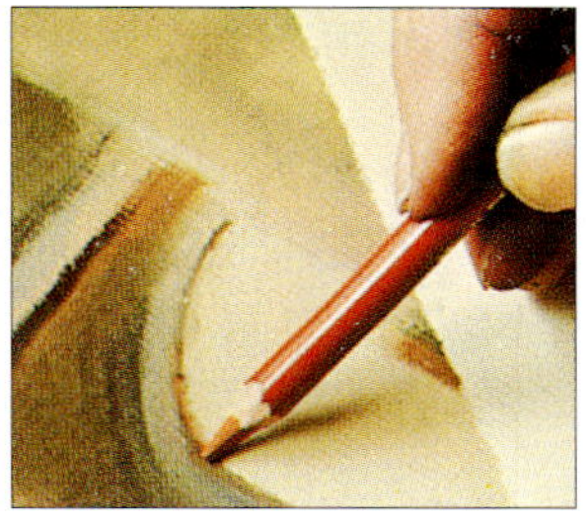

Adding detail with a pastel pencil, an easily sharpened, suitable medium.

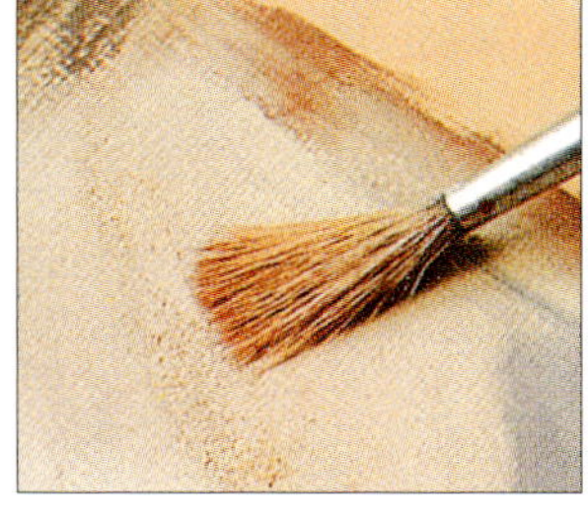

Lifting excess pastel colour gently, and easily, with the use of a soft paintbrush.

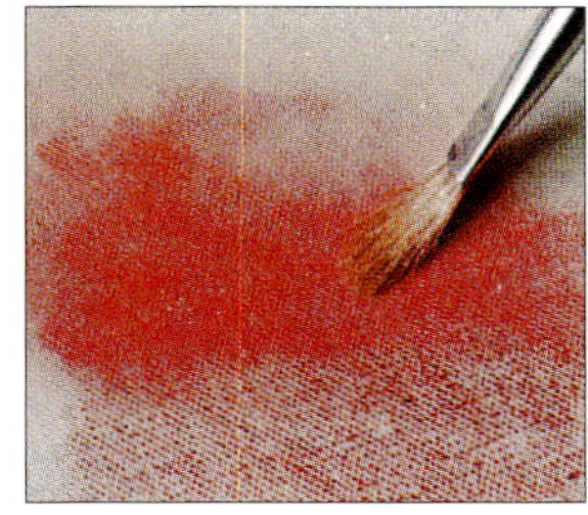

To lay an oil pastel wash, use turpentine not water to spread the colour.

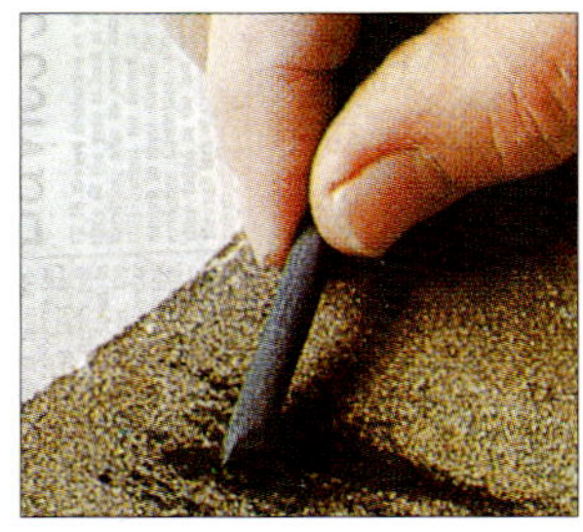

Adding detail with charcoal sharpened by rubbing on sandpaper.

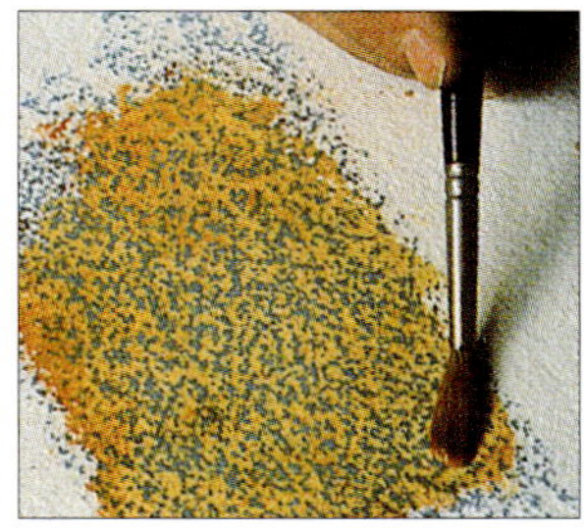

Adding detail with charcoal sharpened by rubbing on sandpaper.

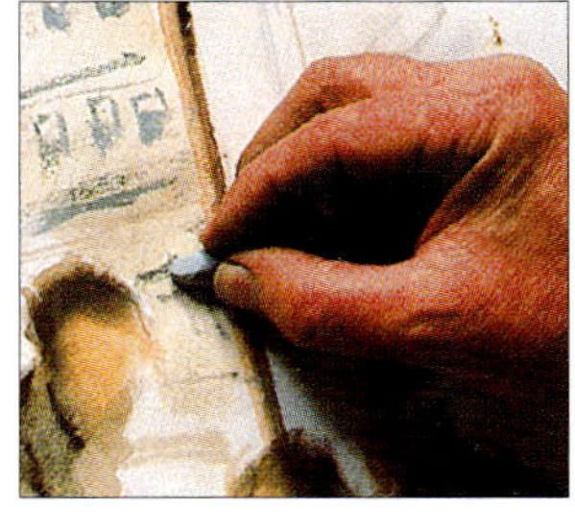

Ordinary pastel will be spread by, and mix with, the watercolor.

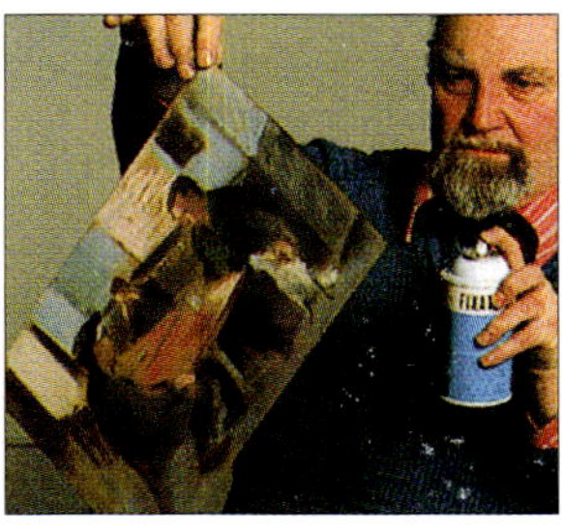

Spraying fixative from behind prevents dulling of the color.

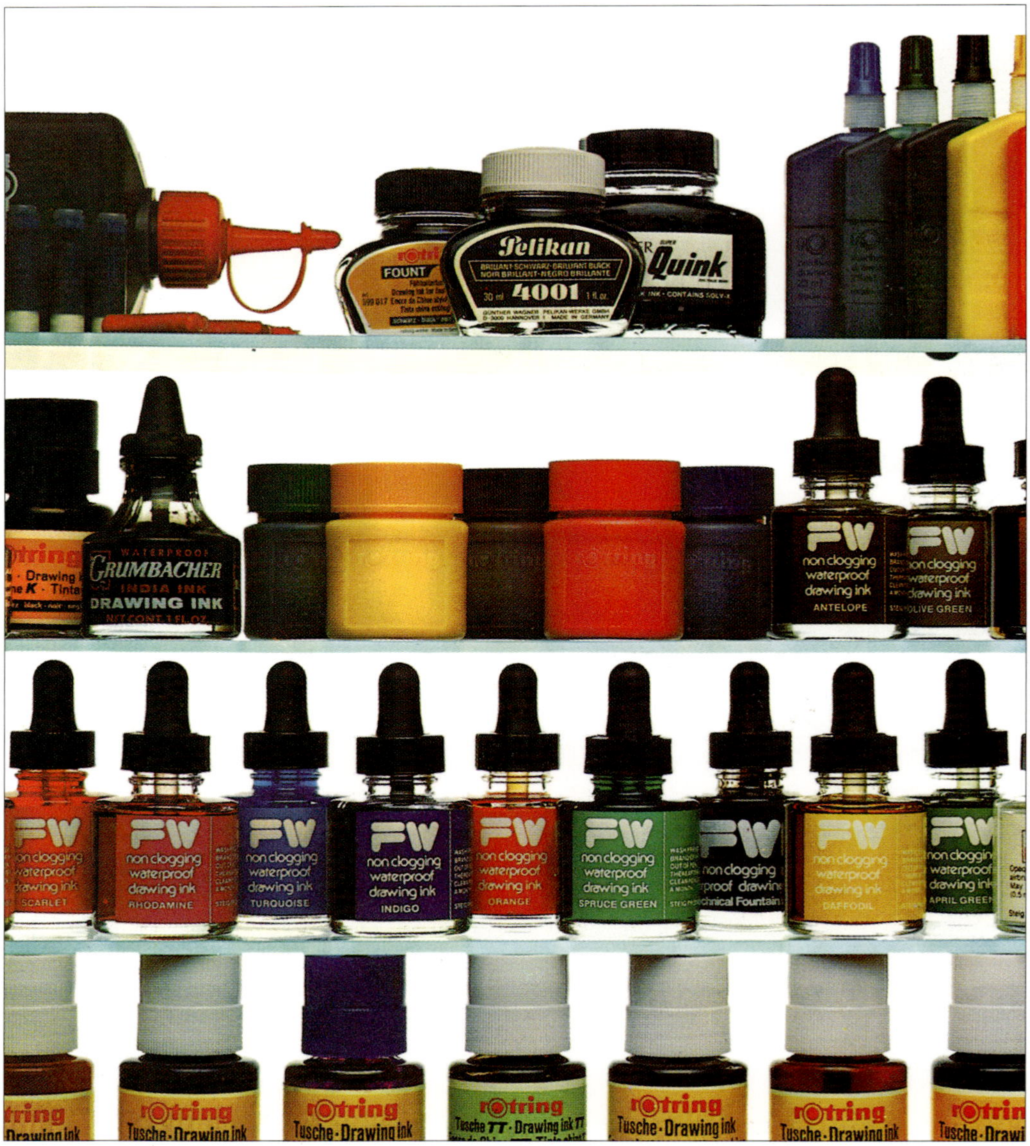

Left *A wide selection of inks is available. Artists' drawing inks are waterproof, drying to a glossy film which can be overlaid. They come in many colors, though black Indian ink is most commonly used for drawing. Non-waterproof inks dry matt and have the effect of diluted watercolors; they can be further blended when water is washed over them with a brush.*

Top Row, Left to Right: *Rotring special drawing ink, ink cartridges, Rotring, Pelikan and Wuink fountain pen ink, smaller bottles of Rotring special drawing ink.*

Second Row *Rotring and Grumbacher Indian ink, jars of Rotring special drawing ink, FW waterproof drawing ink.*

Third Row *FW waterproof drawing ink and Pen-Opake.*

Bottom Row *Rotring drawing inks.*

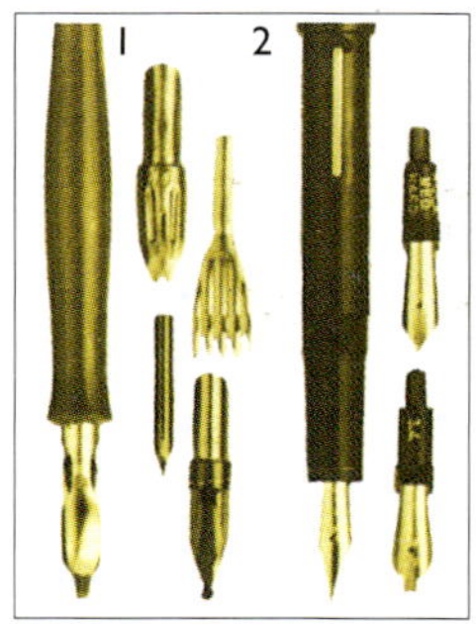

Left *Dip pens (1) have long been the traditional tool of pen and ink illustrators and are still extremely popular. The nib itself is known as the "pen" and the main shaft is the "penholder." Many nibs are produced; they can be used with any type of ink, but should be cleaned regularly under running water to prevent the ink caking. Fountain pens (2) are sometimes more convenient but the range of nibs available is much smaller. They are often filled by suction.*

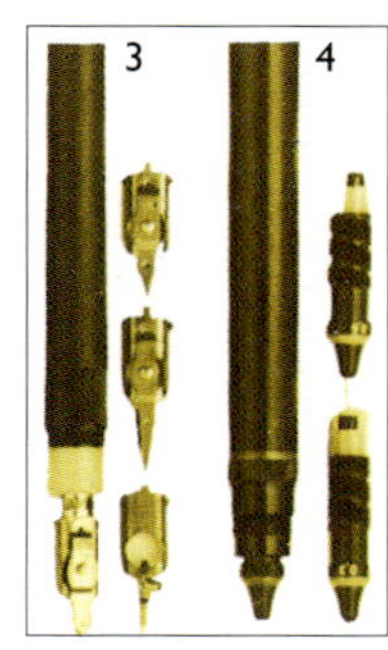

Left *Reservoir pens, as their name suggests, have an ink holder which is filled by pouring in the ink rather than by suction. Suitable inks are waterproof and available in a wide range of colors. The graphos pen (3) can be fitted with nibs in a variety of sizes and styles, while the stylo tip pen (4) has tubular nibs, in varying widths, giving a constant line width.*

color. The support used is often pastel paper—a surface made with pastel drawing specifically in mind and usually colored.

Oil pastel

Oil pastel is a relatively recent development and has an entirely different range of possibilities from traditional pastel. Limited by its relative clumsiness in use, this medium nonetheless contributes its unique qualities to the repertoire of the draftsman. Used in association with, for example, pens or watercolor, it lends the richness of oil-bound pigment, but it is also an important medium in its own right. Although not really suitable for use in the small pocket sketchbook (some

PEN AND INK EFFECTS

Pen and ink is an extremely versatile medium. It is important to try different pens and techniques in order to find those which best suit your style of drawing. Stylo tip pens are particularly useful for drawing straight lines of uniform thickness and for producing a dotted effect (top row). Indian ink, full strength or diluted, and dip pens can be exploited to create a huge range of results (bottom row).

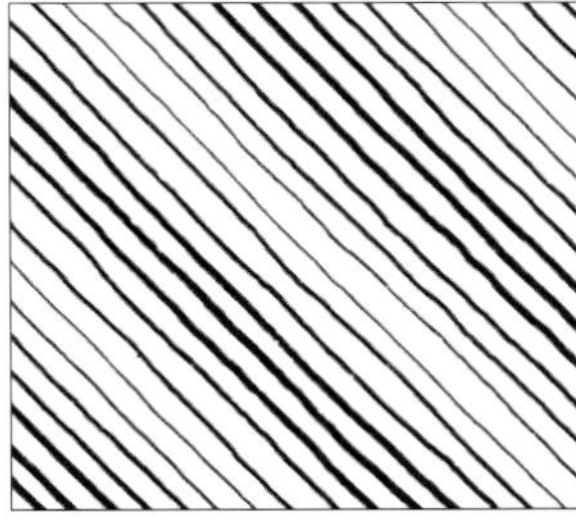

Using a stylo tip, lines of varying widths are drawn freehand with different nibs.

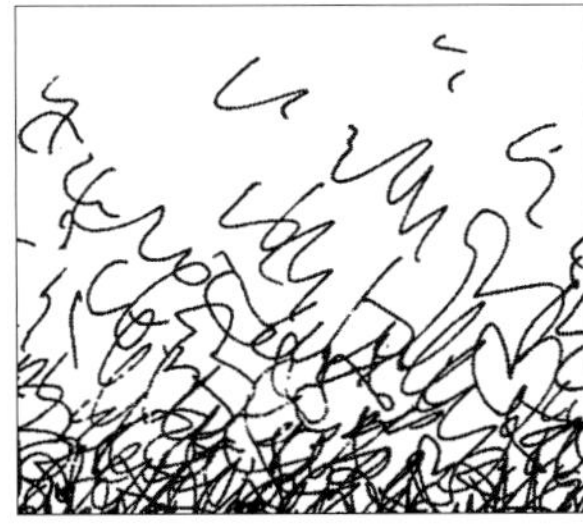

Simple stylo tip scribbles can be profuse and dense, or spare and delicate.

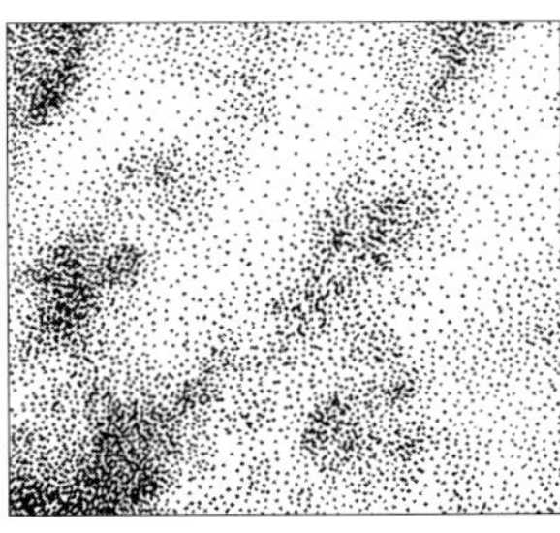

This dotted, or pointillist, pattern has been created by using a fine stylo nib.

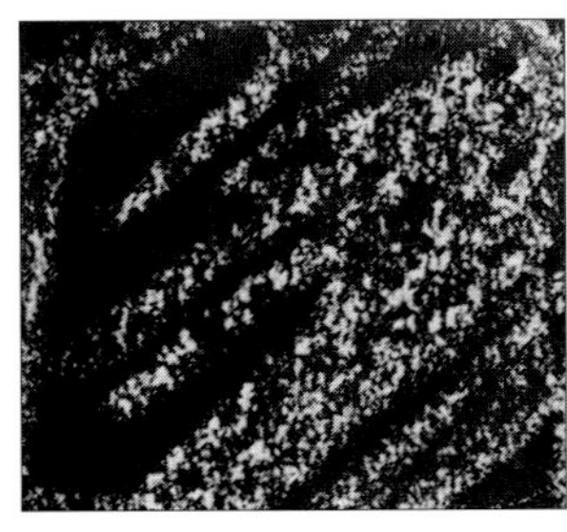

Candle wax repels ink and can be rubbed over the paper to leave highlights.

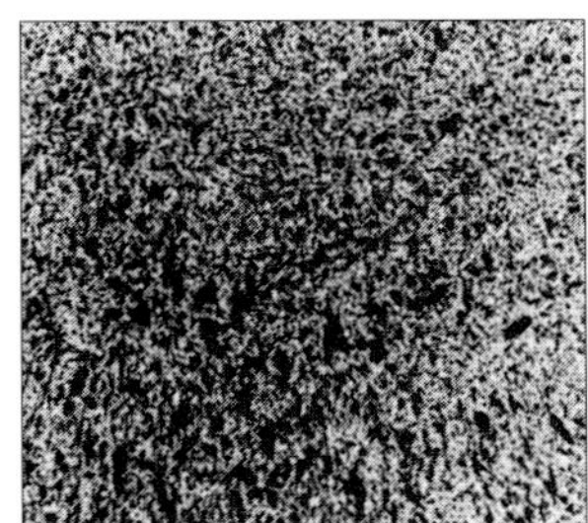

Use an old toothbrush to splatter ink over a surface, blotting it off if a softer effect is required.

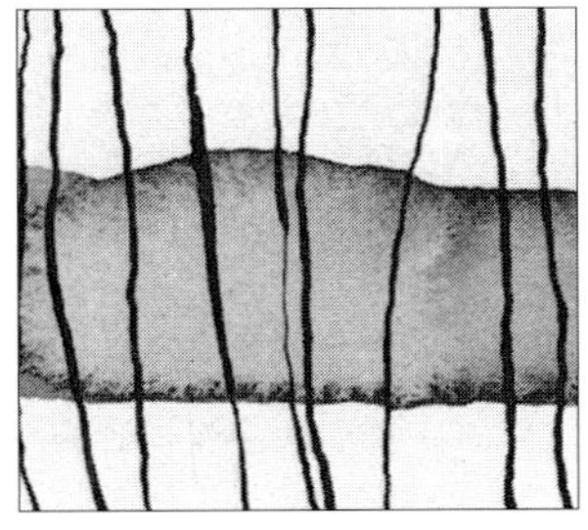

Line and wash requires both brush and pen. Let wash dry before adding pen lines.

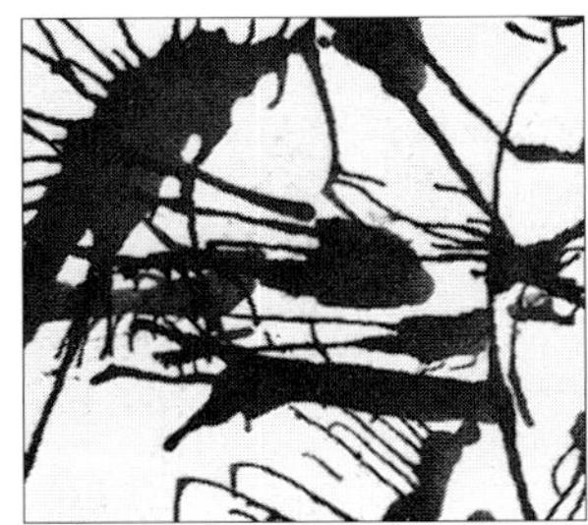

A blob of wet ink blown across the support to create random splodges and streaks.

people achieve even this), it is very suitable for quickly worked interpretations of figure or landscape. Control can be aided by the use of a little masking paper to lay beneath the working hand, thus preventing unwanted smudging and smearing. In common with traditional pastel, this new material shows well on a colored support but is perhaps at its best on white.

It is as part of a mixed media drawings that the oil pastel is unique, not only when overlaid by watercolor, gouache, and inks but in association with pen drawing, traditional pastel, black chalk, and pencil.

Chalk

Chalk is a harder medium than pastel, pigments being mixed with wax or oil to make them usable in stick form. As well as silverpoint and, later, pencils, chalk has long been used for drawing. Many of the drawings best known to us, through reproductions, by Michelangelo, Andrea del Sarto, Toulouse-Lautrec, and Watteau, all made brilliant use of the medium. Some used black chalk, some red, and others mixed the two and even used white to bring out highlights.

Pen and ink

Despite the popularity of newly invented pens intended for use primarily by graphic designers, traditions die hard, and the ink-dipped nib in the traditional penholder remains the most popular instrument among professional artists. This is probably because the range of possible marks is very wide, and such flexibility is highly valued by the artist.

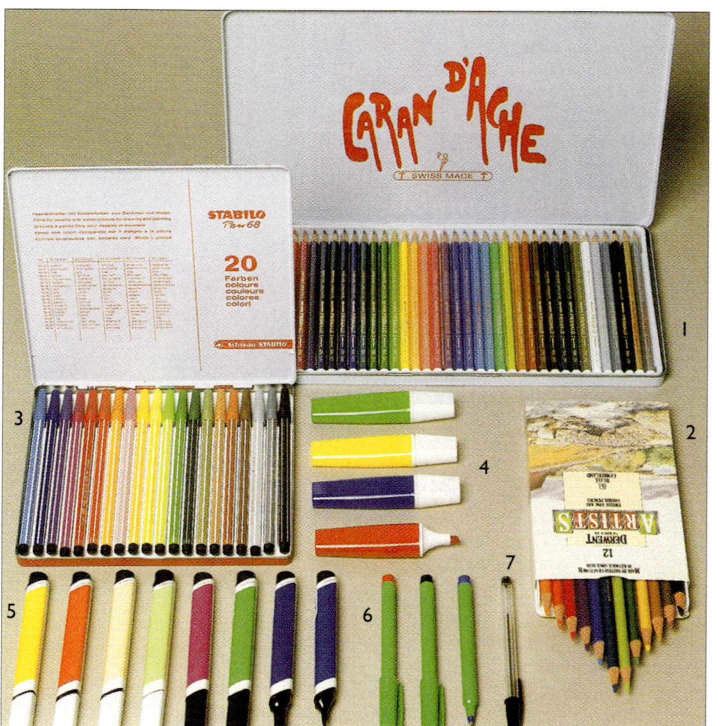

Left *Colored pencils are available in an enormous range of subtly varying hues. Some are soluble in water (1) so that a basically linear style of drawing can be softened by spreading color with a damp brush. The ordinary colored pencils (2) are usually soft enough to allow delicate shading, while sharpening easily to a point. Fiber tip pens (3) have relatively fine points made of tough material. The color is usually water-soluble and can be blended with a brush. Felt tips and markers (4, 5) are often spirit-based as they are used by designers needing stable color overlays. They are available with broad or fine tips and in many beautiful colors. Prices vary and a good set of markers can be quite expensive. For more delicate work. Fine ball tip pens (6) have largely replaced ballpoints and fountain pens as they are convenient and reliable writing implements, and for the same reasons they are useful drawing tools also. The color range is restricted, as is the range in ballpoint pens (7) but this type of pen is more easily carried and used for sketchbook work, for example, than other drawing media.*

MIXED MEDIA

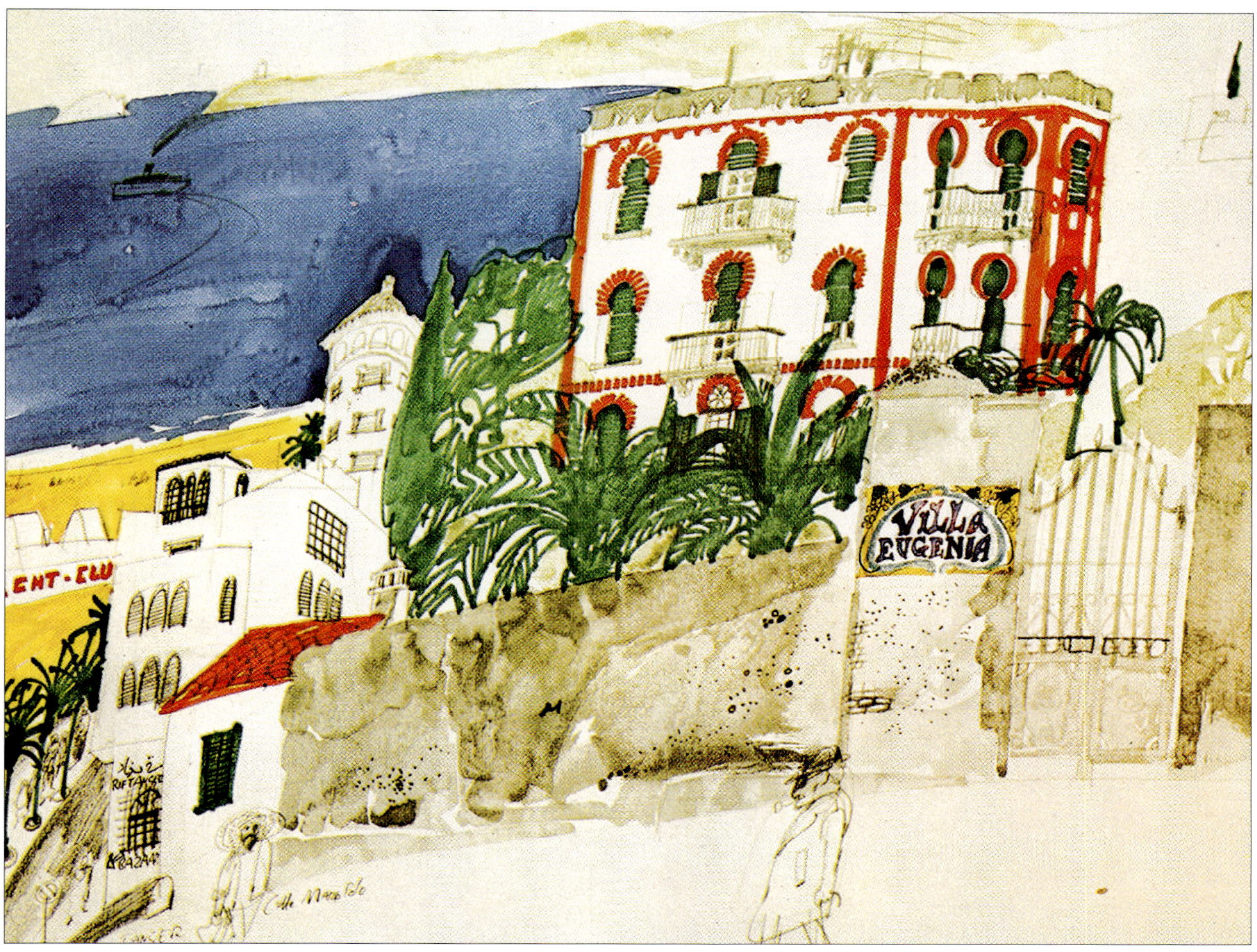

Above *This drawing demonstrates the impact of a controlled use of the bright colors which are characteristic of marker pens. In* Calle Marco Polo, Tangiers, *Paul Hogarth has combined felt tips with pencil, ballpoint, ink wash, watercolor, and an ordinary dip pen to build up the textures, tones, and colors.*

For styles of pen and ink drawing that are better served by a regular flow of ink, cartridge pens come into their own. It is extremely difficult to vary the width of line obtainable, and if care is not taken the resultant drawing can seem wiry and insensitive. With the addition of the brush line, however, this can easily be overcome.

Colored ink

Drawing in colored inks, both with a limited and a comprehensive range of colors, can stretch the possibilities of pen and ink drawing further. These inks add dimension, not only as washes of color but also when used to describe objects in their identifiable local colors. Pens and nibs can be varied and a wide range of colored inks used, perhaps consolidating the tones by the addition of a stronger, neutral ink. Tones can present a problem, it being imperative that all colors conform to an overall tonal scheme within

COLORED PENCILS

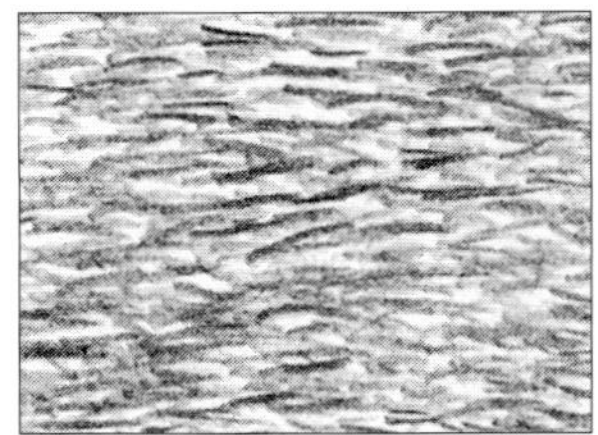

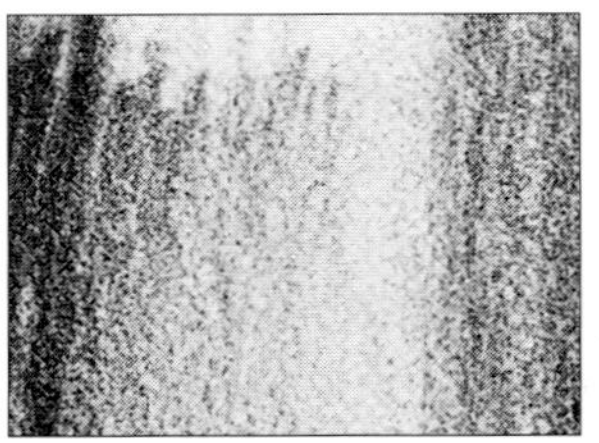

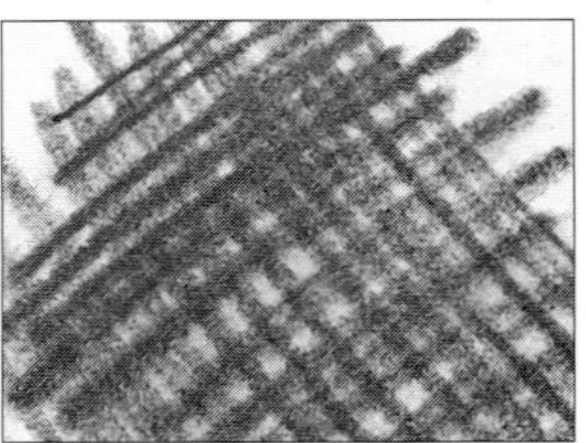

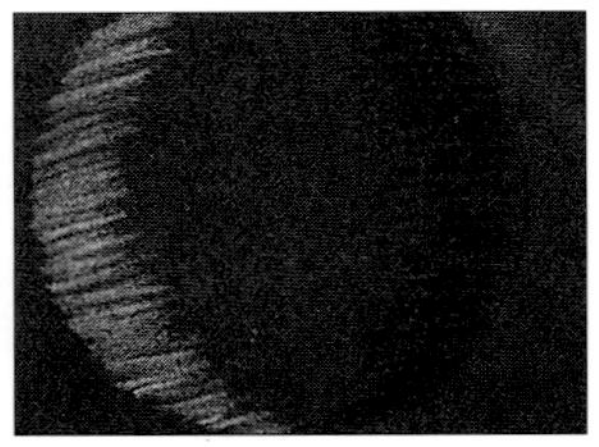

1 *Small dashes are overlaid and blended to make a graded tone.*

2 *Even layer of soft, water-soluble pencil melts into second color.*

3 *Crosshatched lines are softened by washing over with a clean, wet brush.*

4 *For solid effect on toned paper, work in black, highlight with white.*

FELT TIPS

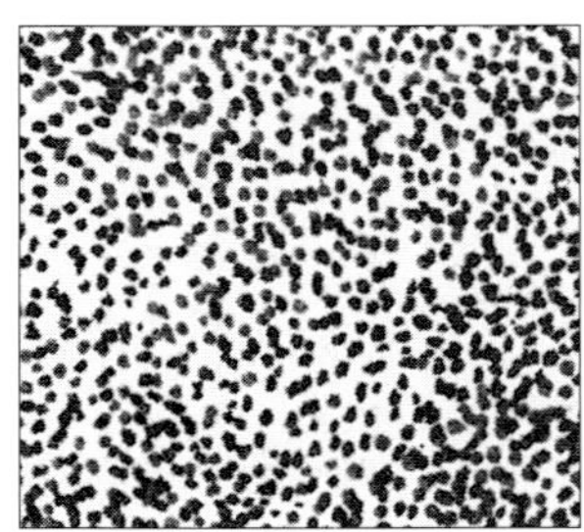

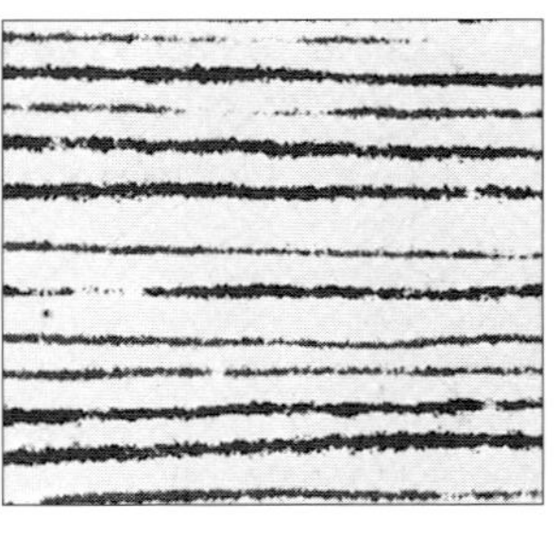

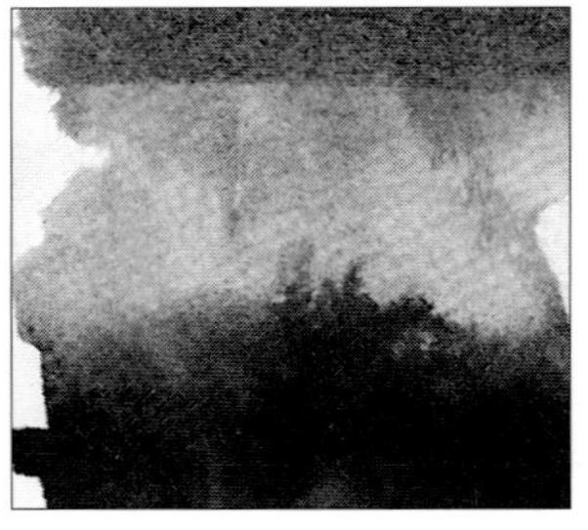

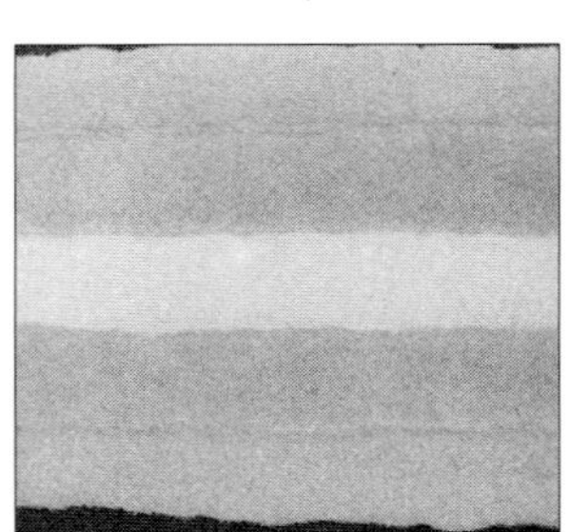

1 *An intriguing pointillist technique is composed simply of random dots of color.*

2 *For blurred effect, draw through a piece of tissue paper onto your chosen support.*

3 *A transparent wash on water-based ink causes color to spread in a cloudy pool.*

4 *On thin paper, spirit-based pens tend to saturate the surface with color.*

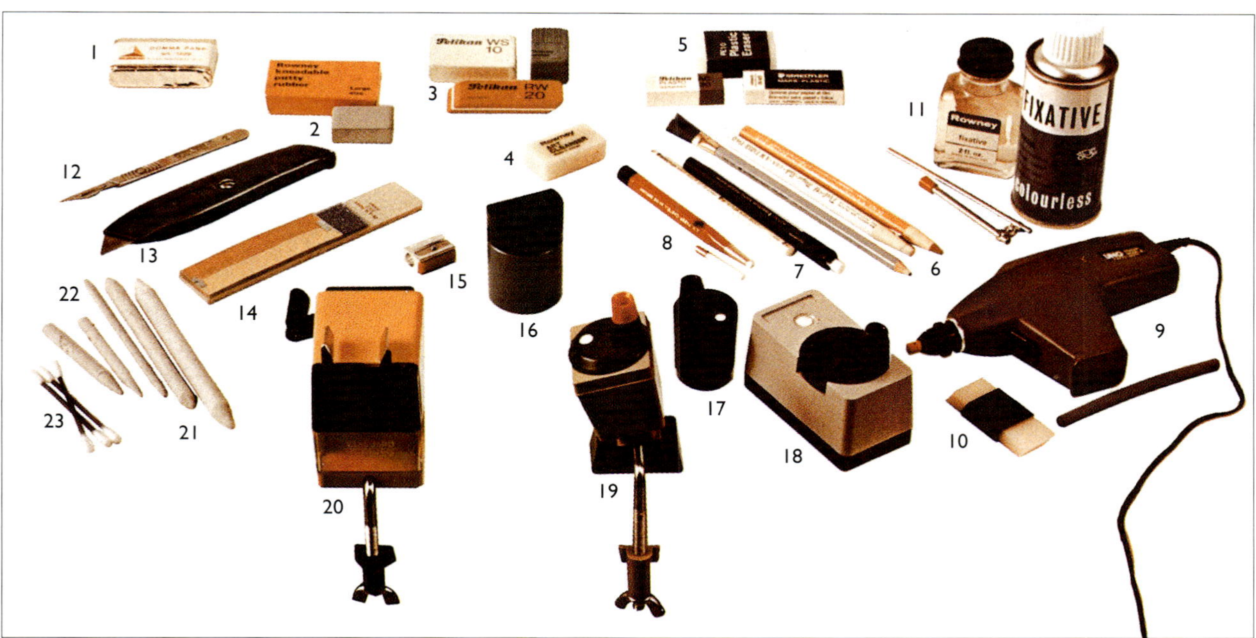

the piece. A well resolved monochromatic drawing might prove the best foundation for color, used either as the juxtaposition of lines in various colors to effect an optical color mix, or as single colors to describe objects.

Choosing a pen

There is a great variety of pens and other instruments suitable for making ink drawings. The reed pen, made by selecting a length of reed, cutting a suitable shape and splitting it carefully to hold drawing ink, was used in earlier times. The character of the line achieved is exemplified by the trailing of the drying nib and the fullness of the main strong lines. Bamboo will produce a similar but less flexible implement, and very good bamboo pens are now made by the manufacturers of

Above Equipment *Erasers are now made in a variety of forms. A bread rubber (1) was the earliest type, largely superceded now by kneadable putty rubbers (2), which can be used in a solid mass or drawn into a pointed shape for greater precision. Soft rubbers (3) come in a number of shapes and sizes and the art eraser (4) is specially composed to have non-smudging properties. Plastic rubbers (5) give a clean, sharp edge and are suitable for erasing pencil, ink, and graphite. Eraser pencils (6) and cores (7) can be used with accuracy and fibrasor (8) will rub out drawing ink, which is often difficult to correct. An electric eraser (9) is also marketed and the core in this can be changed to suit work in ink or pencil. An ink eraser made particularly for designers (10) may be found to have a use in a drawing studio. Fixative (11) is vital for protecting work in pencil, pastel, charcoal, or chalk. A scalpel (12) or general purpose knife (13) may be useful for sharpening pencils and crayons and will also come in handy in work incorporating collage. A glasspaper block (14) refines the point of a pencil and also sharpens charcoal sticks. There are many different types of pencil sharpeners from the most simple (15, 16) to clutch models (17, 18) which hold the pencil steady, and for studio work a table sharpener (19, 20) fixed to the worktop can be a convenient device. Stumps (21) are resistant sticks which are used to spread chalk, charcoal, or pastel when shading a broad area and torchons, or tortillons (22), made of heavy rolled paper, serve the same function. Cotton buds (23) can also be used but are less precise.*

artists' materials. Although these methods of applying ink to the support are associated with the past, they are nonetheless extremely interesting for contemporary use and it is well worth experimenting with them. The most common tool is a steel nib, which until the advent of ballpoint pens was universal not only for drawing but also for writing in ink. These are available in a range of sizes and on a scale of flexibility ranging from stiff to bendy.

Robust supports

A well-sized paper surface is appropriate for use with pen and ink because it holds the mark well and does not bruise or break as is the tendency with softer surfaces. A support prepared with a gesso or acrylic base, say on cardboard or millboard, will make a suitable surface and can be polished to a hard glossy finish to allow richly worked and overworked drawings.

It enables corrections to be undertaken by overpainting errors with fresh acrylic paint and reworking the offending parts. Even on a softer paper such as cartridge, mistakes are often remedied by painting out and overdrawing. Various opaque white correctives are available, quick drying, and very hard, and all are useful to have to hand. If work is being made on a card or illustration board then a common technique employed to

STRETCHING PAPER

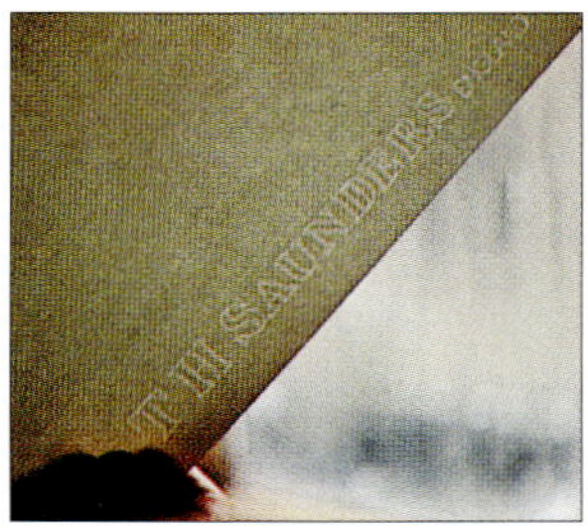

1 *Hold your paper up to the light to read watermark correctly and check right side.*

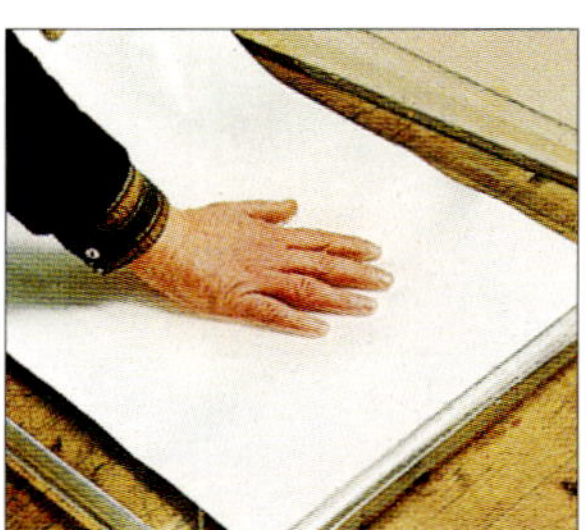

2 *Soak your piece of paper in a photographic developing tray, or a bath of water.*

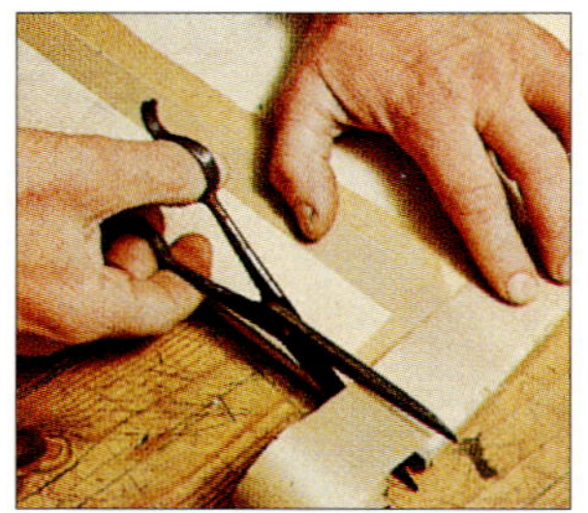

3 *Cut lengths of gummed paper tape to the size of each side of the drawing board.*

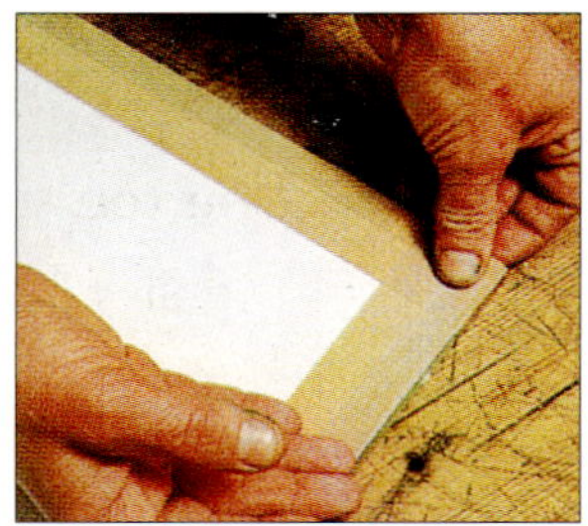

4 *Drain paper, lay on board and stick tape along the sides. Allow to dry naturally.*

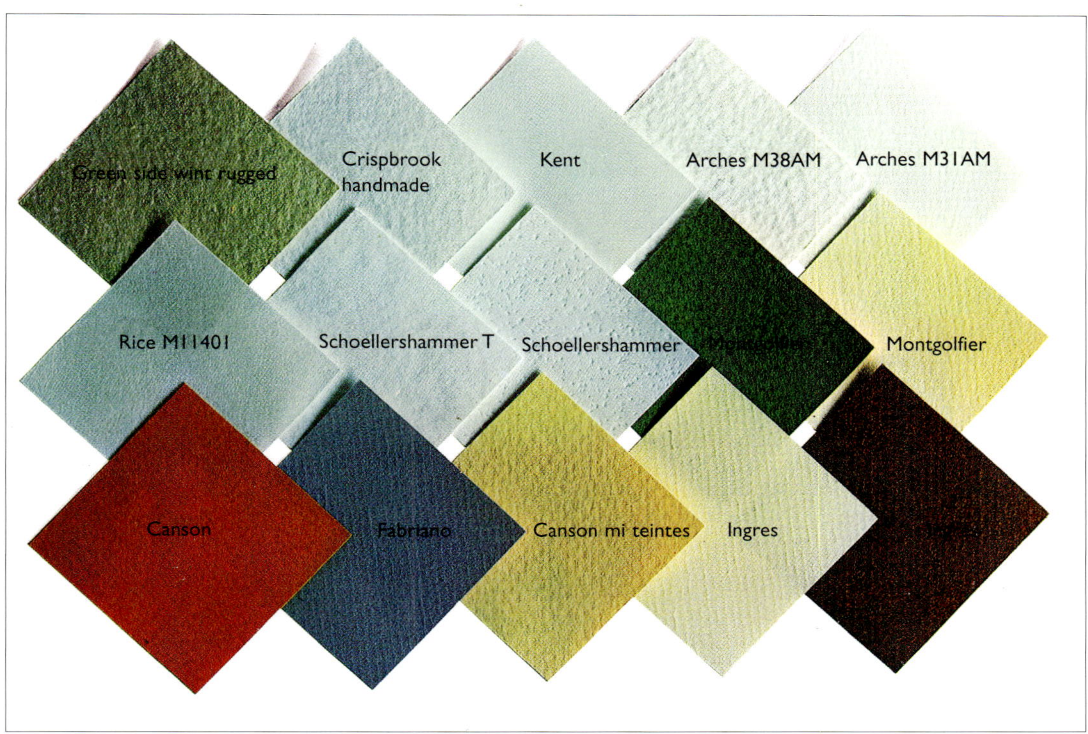

Right *The range of papers can be bewildering. If you are unsure about what best suits your purpose, buy only a few sheets at a time, some specialist shops will provide you with samples. Weight is one factor to be taken into consideration. It is necessary to stretch lighter grades before starting work. Toned papers provide a good middle ground from which to work darks and lights; a good alternative to buying toned paper is to lay a wash over your support. Paper comes in three textures—hot-pressed, the smoothest, cold-pressed, or "not," with a medium texture, and rough.*

make adjustments and even major corrections is to scrape the top surface off, using a sharp craft knife or a single-edged razor blade. It is essential that the cutting edge, in this case the scraping surface, is kept almost flat against the support so that mistakes can be erased without tears or scratches. If they do appear, the area affected should be burnished flat.

Colored pencils and felt tips

The increase in the range of colored pencils available has been a recent exciting development in the repertoire of the serious draftsman. Not only is the variety of colors most impressive, but the differing compounds used to make up the lead filling have many different characteristics.

Colored pencils can be exploited in other ways. Several brands have leads which are soluble in water, allowing an extension of effect within any one drawing. Areas of color applied with a pencil, will contrast well with areas where the color has been "melted" by the simple process of spreading it with clean water.

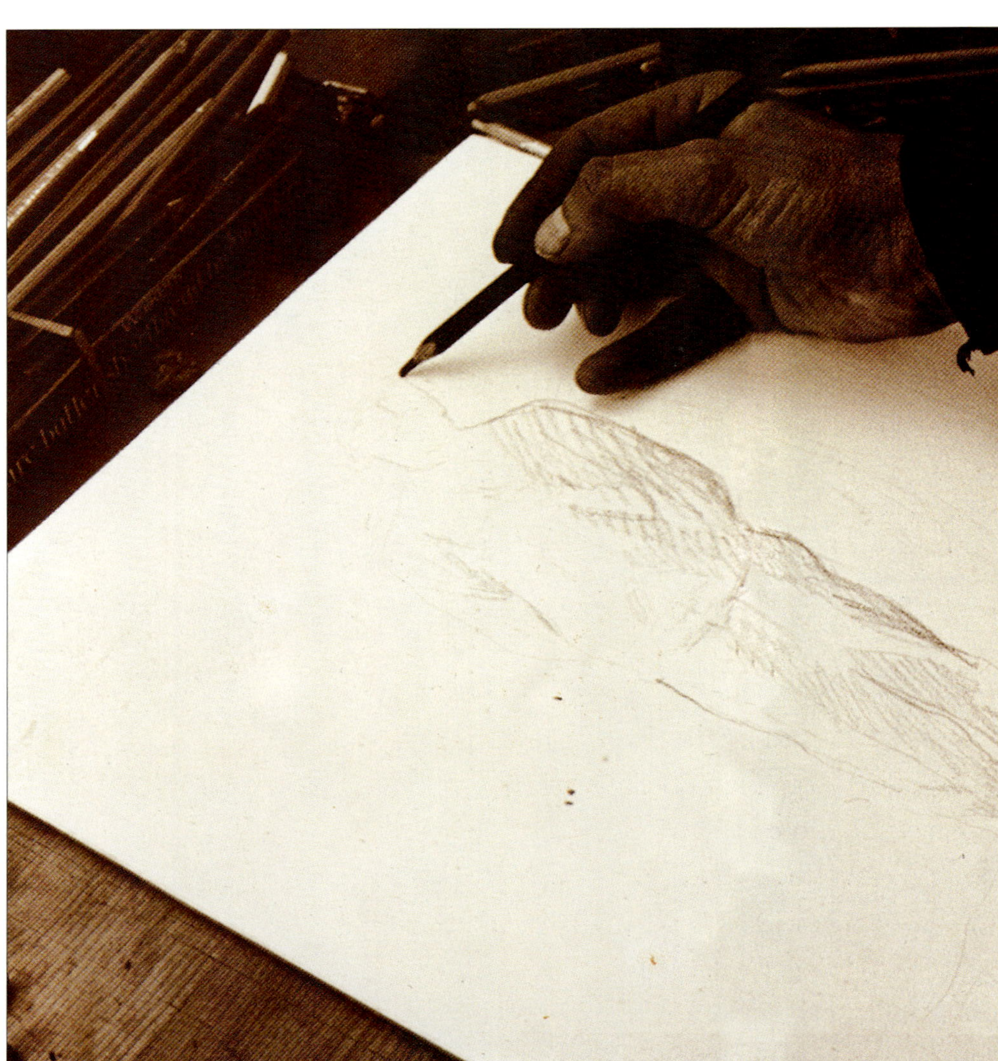

Right *There are no hard-and-fast rules about the way in which you should organize your materials for drawing. It is, however, essential to adopt some sort of sensible system so that you are not held up by being unable to find a particular piece of equipment at a critical moment. Ensure that you position yourself so that your working hand neither smudges completed areas nor blocks the light from your support.*

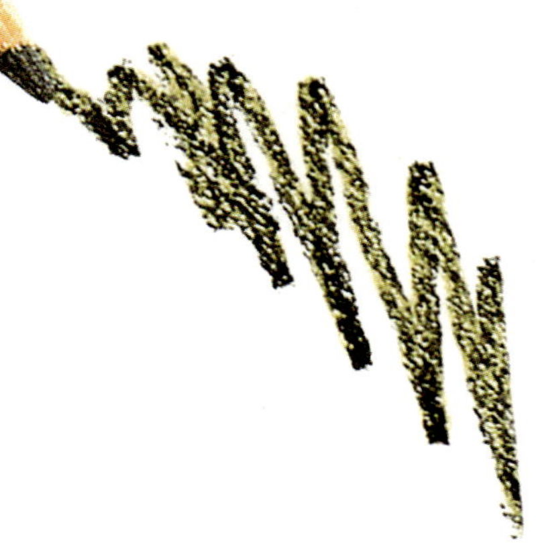

Felt tip pens have water or spirit-based colors saturated into strips of felt. They have become popular in recent times, particularly among graphic designers and illustrators, mainly because they tend to be brash and strong in color and make a highly contrasted tonal result suitable for reproduction in books and magazines.

This very advantage to the commercial artist is the reason for some reticence on the part of painters. However, these characteristics have their own potential—strength, high contrast, and directness are often the ingredients of high drama in a drawing. Some of these characteristics may, indeed, be well worth investigating.

CHECK LIST

INDOOR MATERIALS:

- Easel, desk, or table
- Chosen medium
- Erasers
- Fixative
- Prepared support

OUTDOOR MATERIALS:

- Portable easel (if required)
- Pencils or other drawing implement
- Sketchbook, sketchblock, or paper
- Stretched on drawing board
- Erasers
- Fixative

Erasers

Traditional burnishers comprised a handle, not unlike a brush or pen handle, with a piece of agate or other semi-precious stone attached to one end. This nodule of stone was rounded and smooth and was used across the surface in a caressing, gentle rubbing, followed by firmer, stronger strokes to polish the surface.

Nowadays, by-products of the oilfields are used to make synthetic erasers and they come in a number of sizes and textures.

Hardgum-like sticks can be used to pick out faults among otherwise acceptable work, while softer rubbers can erase a larger area without damaging the paper surface. The putty, or kneaded, rubber is used in the positive/negative technique recommended for charcoal.

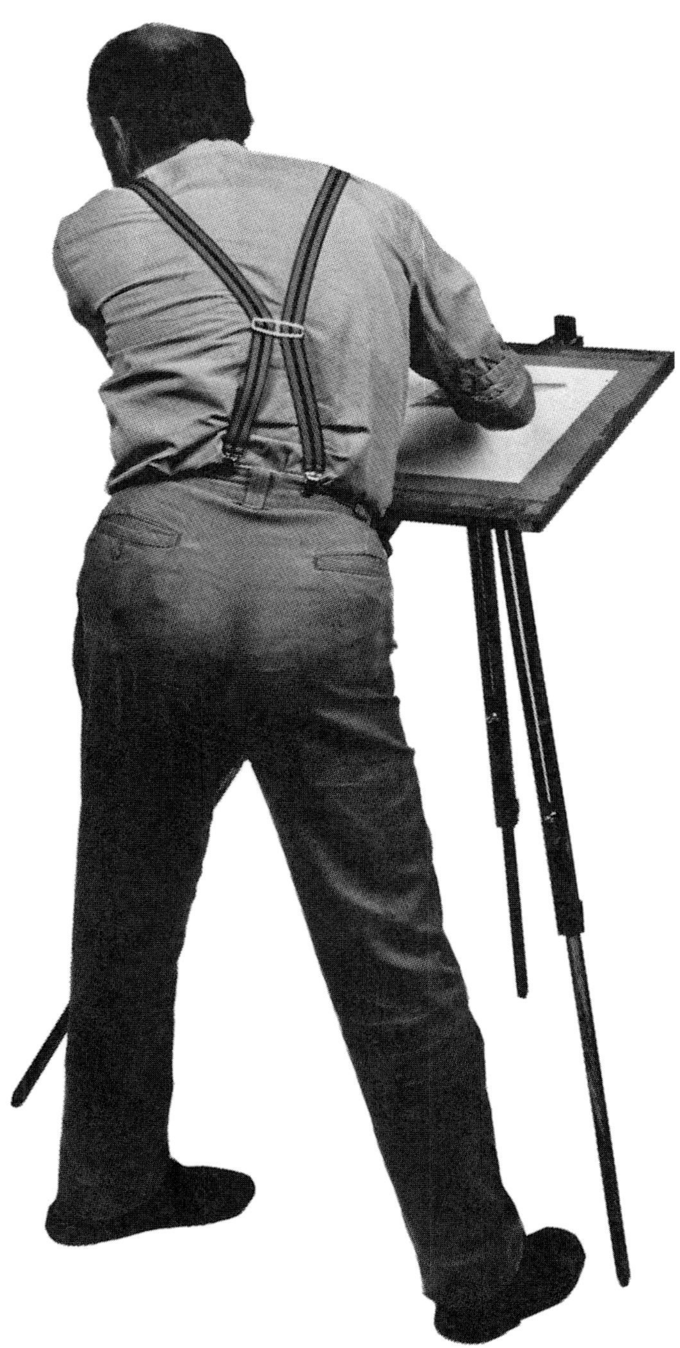

Above *Many draftsmen find that a desk or table is a perfectly adequate surface on which to work. It may, however, be worthwhile investing in the type of easel that can be adjusted to several heights and positions so that you can work either standing or sitting; a portable easel is sometimes useful when working in the field.*

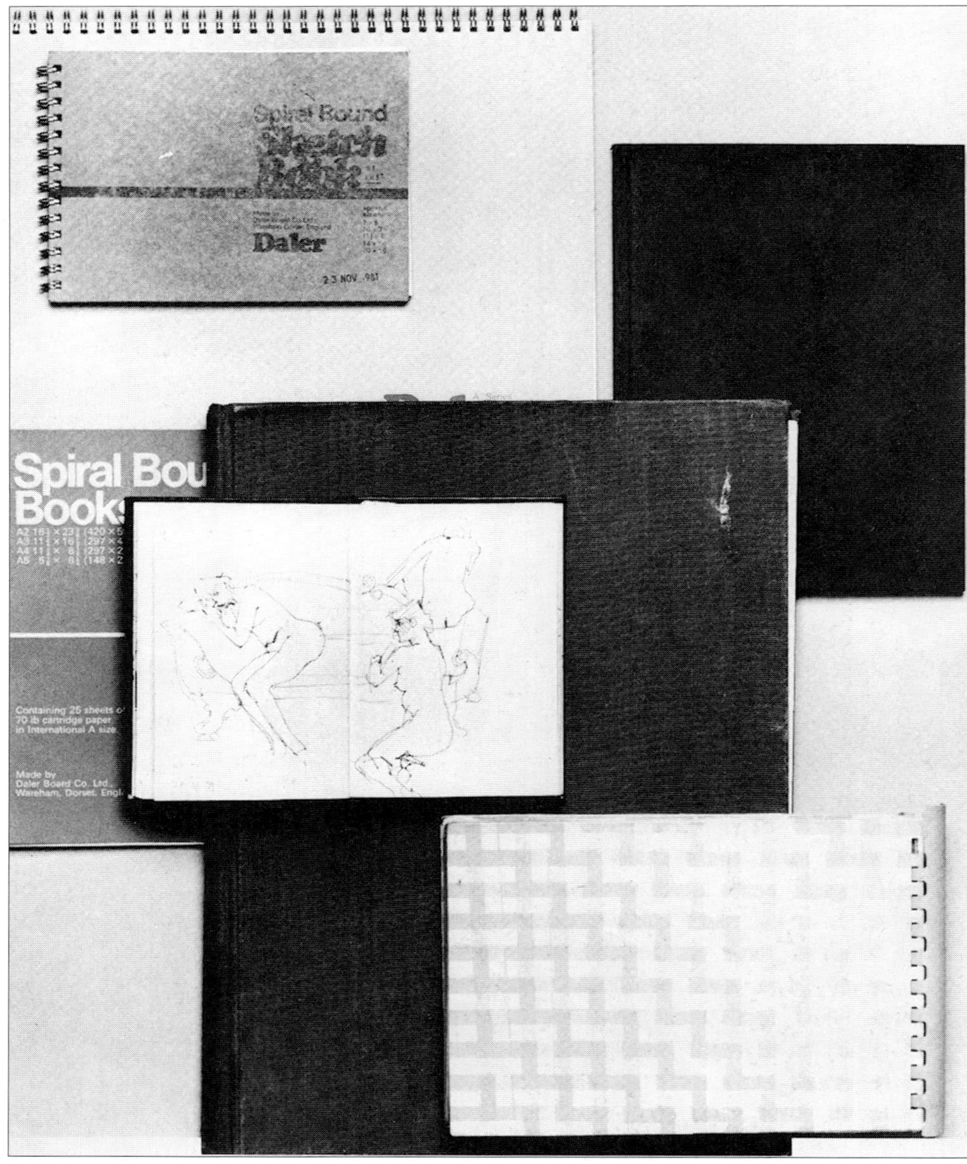

Left *Color notes can be made with words and often an HB pencil and small notebook provide a practical solution. Ballpoint pens and pentels are permanent, requiring nofixing; charcoal smudges easily; oil pastels and watercolor can block in large areas at great speed.*

PAPER

Paper is often the critical factor in a drawing and this is true no matter what the chosen medium. Although not the only support available, paper is by far and away the most common, for the good reasons of cheapness and portability. Variations in color, texture, weight, and surface make for additional appeal. The manufacture of paper has been a highly refined skill for centuries and although most is factory-made today, there remains a core of hand-made papers for the use of artists.

Drawing papers are made by machine in three types, hot-pressed, not, and rough, the texture coarsening in that order. Hot-pressed (or HP) is much used for pencil and for pen, ink, and wash: its surface is relatively smooth but not completely so. Not, really "not hot-pressed," has a more textured surface and a medium tooth very suitable for coarser media such as chalk or soft-leaded pencils. Rough is paper with a positively-textured face, especially favored by watercolorists but also suitable for certain drawing purposes, or for mixed media works.

Charcoal paper is a heavy, rough-textured paper usually with a colored finish. It does not take kindly to the use of a hard eraser, as its surface is very easily damaged; the putty (kneaded) rubber comes into its own here.

Above *This sketchbook drawing contains a lot of information, partly because of its larger size. Pencil is used to make tone as well as line and effect is carefully wrought and assessed. Despite this care, the drawing has been carried out with urgency, to make the most of the fleeting ray of light.*

Pastel papers are available in a wide range of colors, unlike the majority of drawing supports which are usually white, light, or at least neutral. The artist gradually fills in details in the work until evidence of the underlying color of the paper is apparently obliterated. In fact it never is, for the whole work will be influenced in its mood by the color of the support.

Rice papers are very fragile but are sometimes suitable for work in brush or pencil. All varieties are highly absorbent if watercolor or ink washes are used, but as with all "limitations", this can be turned to advantage.

Some recommended papers, suitable for all drawing media, are Kent turkey mill, Ingres papers (in several colors), Saunders, Fabriano, David Cox, and De Wint. Others are available both under manufacturer's names and anonymously made as cartridge papers of various qualities.

Experiment until you discover the best combination of paper, board, or other support and instrument to trace, score, or hatch out the drawing.

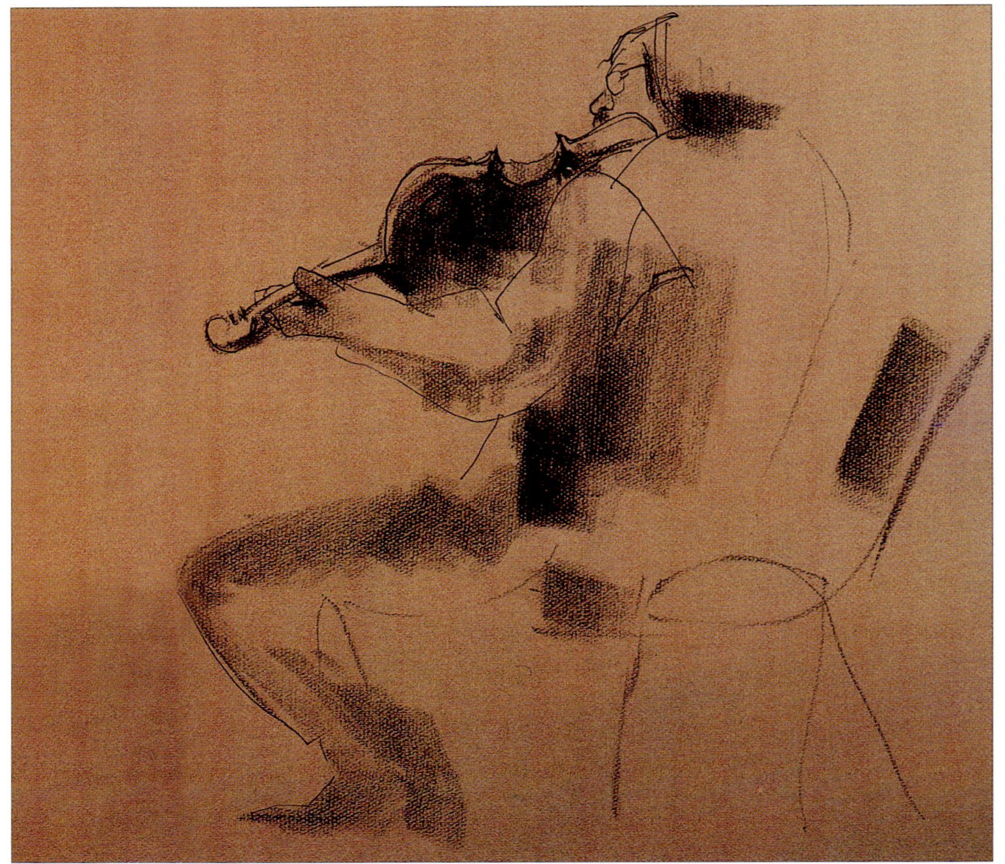

Left: *This drawing,* The Violinist *by Carole Katchen, has been made at great speed, the whole composition being created with just a few "slabs" of shading made with the side of the pastel stick plus some touches of pen line. By seizing on the most significant aspects and avoiding unnecessary detail, the artist has given a powerful suggestion of the musician in performance.*

Right: *In this dramatic and atmospheric drawing of a mining landscape by David Carpanini, there are almost no lines; the charcoal stick has been used on its side to build up dark areas, and smudged in places to create soft effects. The occasional spraying of fixative helps build the charcoal up thickly.*

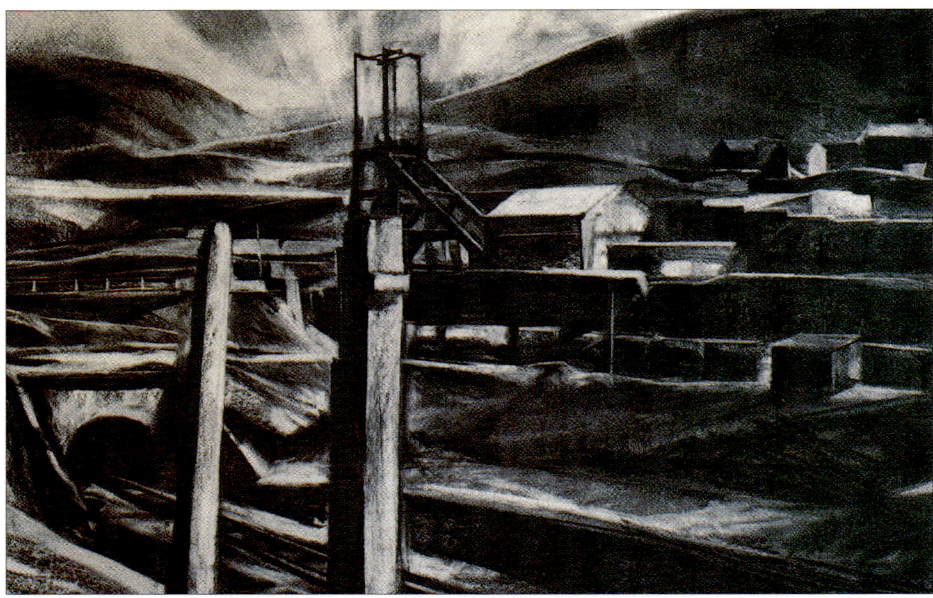

DIFFERENT WAYS OF LOOKING

This drawing course puts the emphasis on seeing, and so it will be no surprise to find as you read on that the projects in the next few pages, which involve drawing objects, are concerned mainly with looking and not with techniques. At first sight, the projects that follow may seem to be only for absolute beginners, but this isn't the case. They could be returned to time and time again by experienced artists, and lead to a widening of their horizons and an escape from seeing in a preconceived way.

THE AIM OF THE PROJECTS

'Looking' in different ways
Identifying character of objects
Developing skill in using line

WHAT YOU WILL NEED

- **Pencils, pens, charcoal, conté crayon**
- **Sheets of A3 size paper**

TIME

You should spend at least 1 hour on projects 1 & 2, and at least 2 hours on project 3.

The way you decide to draw is one of the factors which determines the way you look at an object. For example, if you are making a line drawing, you look at the outline shape of the object. If, however, you decide to make a drawing without any lines then the lightness or darkness of the object will be important.

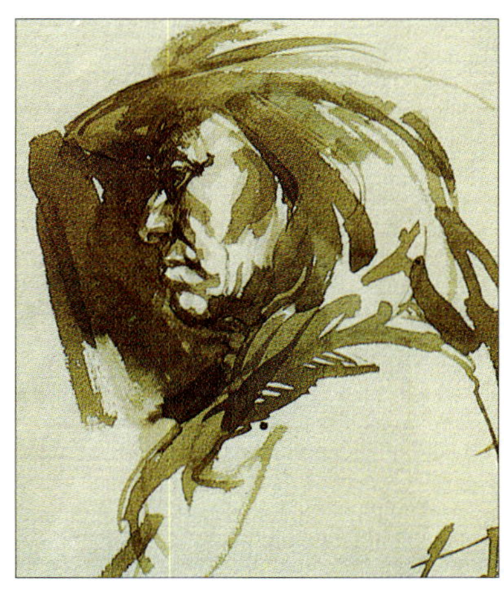

Above *The ink has been used both at full strength and diluted in this portrait drawing by John Houser. A dry brush has been used for the dark background which throws the profile into relief. The brush can be a very sensitive drawing implement, and has been used here with skill and confidence.*

PROJECT ONE

CONTOUR DRAWING

Pick any uncomplicated object—a pair of shoes, gloves, or a cup and saucer and plate. Place them on a table and make certain you and your board are in the right position for drawing.

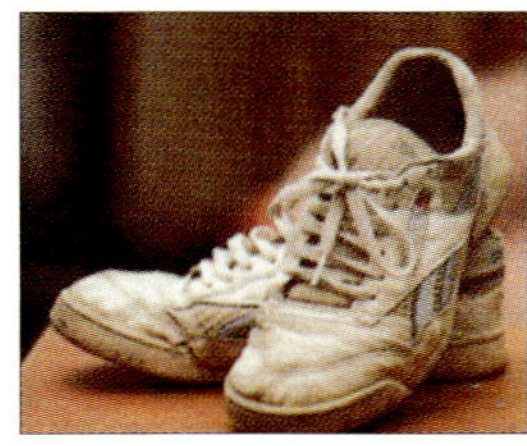

Choose any medium suitable for making a line drawing, then fix your eyes at a particular point on the outline shape of one of the objects and rest the point of your pencil (or other instrument) on your paper. The point on the paper must be the same one that you are looking at in the subject. You are now going to draw without looking at the paper. Very slowly make your eyes feel their way around the contour shapes of the objects—don't look at the paper—and equally slowly and deliberately, in pace with your eyes, make your hand describe what you see.

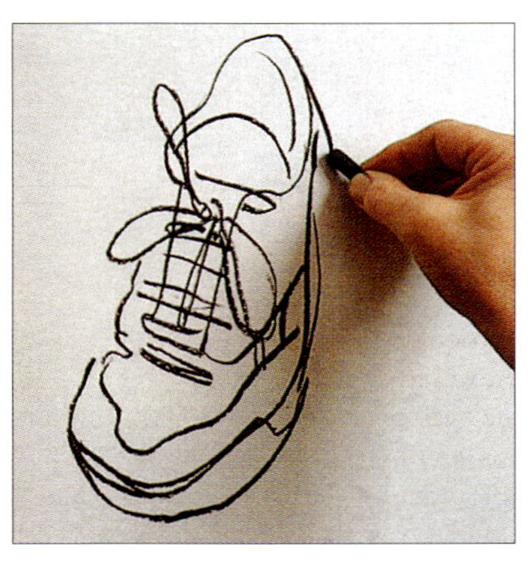

1 *The artist is feeling her way around the contour of one of the shoes with the sharp edge of a conté crayon.*

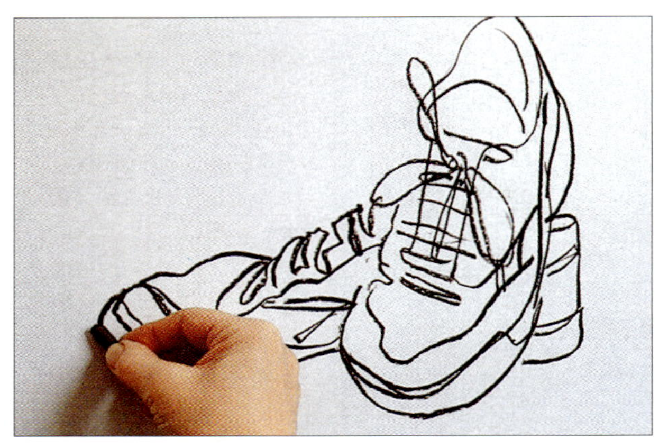

2 *The second shoe is introduced in the same flow, unless there is a change in direction.*

If your hand and eye get out of step, relocate your pencil at a particular point on your drawing, fix your eyes at the same point on the contour of your subject and continue. Don't rub out any lines. Keep on until you have drawn the complete contours of your subject and only then look at your drawing.

If you have really followed the contours, your drawing will not be just a silhouette because in some places your eyes will have been led inside the outline shapes to

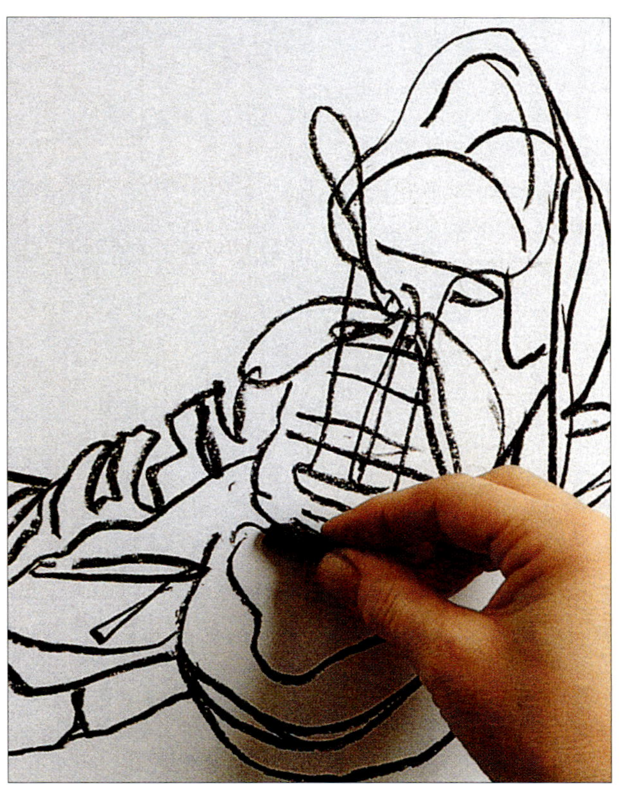

3 *The drawing continues, with the contour of the second shoe leading back to the first one.*

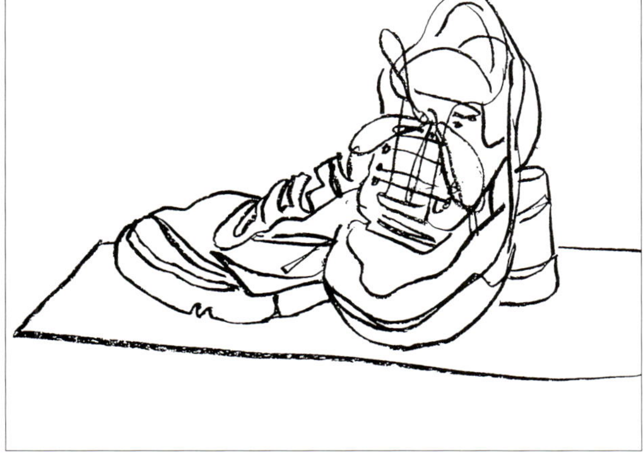

4 *The complete drawing gives a remarkably good idea of the shoes, although it was done quickly and with no hesitation. The artist has also related them to the surface beneath, by drawing an outline of the paper they rest on.*

describe, for example, the rim of a cup. It will probably take some time to produce a drawing which looks right. Your first drawing may not look anything like the subject, but it doesn't matter. Learning to feel with your eyes is what is important.

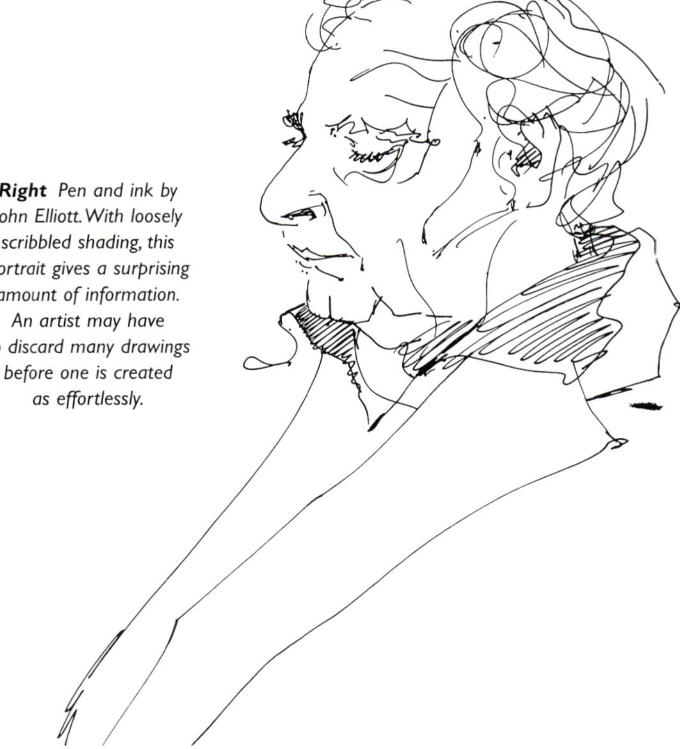

Right *Pen and ink by John Elliott. With loosely scribbled shading, this portrait gives a surprising amount of information. An artist may have to discard many drawings before one is created as effortlessly.*

PROJECT TWO

INNER FORCES

Looking within the contours, to see if you can identify some particular characteristic—like finding 'movement' in static figures—there, is another way of describing an object.

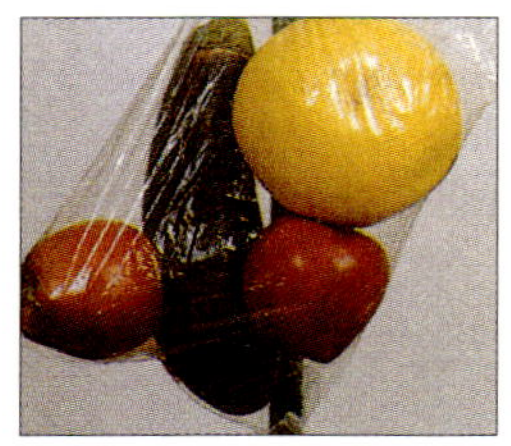

A table or a chair, and in fact, most static objects, has a feeling of its weight pressing it onto the floor, and even a sack dumped in the corner of a barn will bulge to suggest the character of its contents.

Choose an object to draw which looks heavy or has some other kind of internal tension. You might suspend an object from a hook to see how it sags under its weight. I then want you to make drawings which describe these inner forces. They shouldn't be drawings of the external appearance of the objects, but should show the particular internal characteristics of the subject. Draw in line, only using a different medium from the one used in the last project. Draw quickly, using a continuous line without taking your pencil from the paper, though this time you can look at the paper as you draw. Let your drawing instrument dart about describing how the object seems to twist, thrust, or fall. Make the action of your hand describe the movement in the object.

As your line describes its movement you will sometimes be drawing through the center of the object, and sometimes in your efforts to give your drawing its true dynamic you may end up drawing outside the object altogether. Draw with absolute freedom, and above all don't follow the contours of the object, because this won't describe the inner forces.

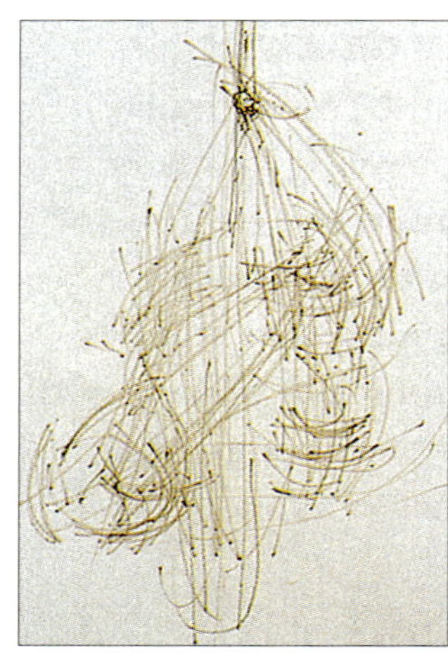

Fruit in a plastic bag provides an excellent subject and, using fine fiber-tipped pens, the artist is starting to draw the way the objects hang their weight and their downward forces.

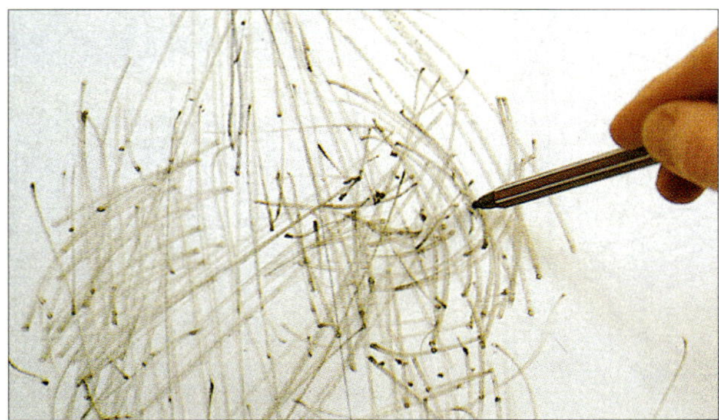

2 *Direction lines, describing the downward thrust of the fruit, are drawn in series of delicate but decisive lines.*

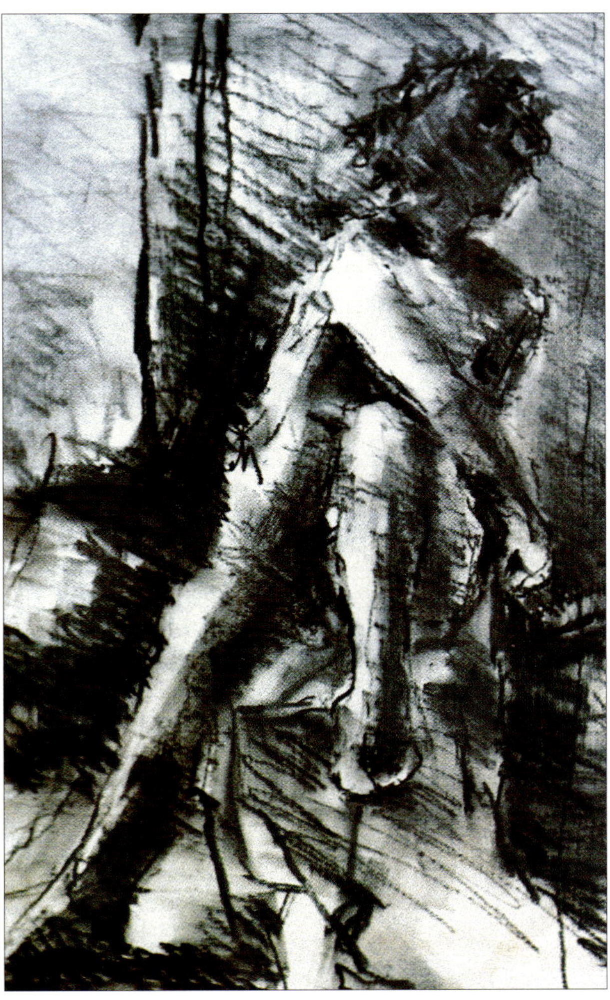

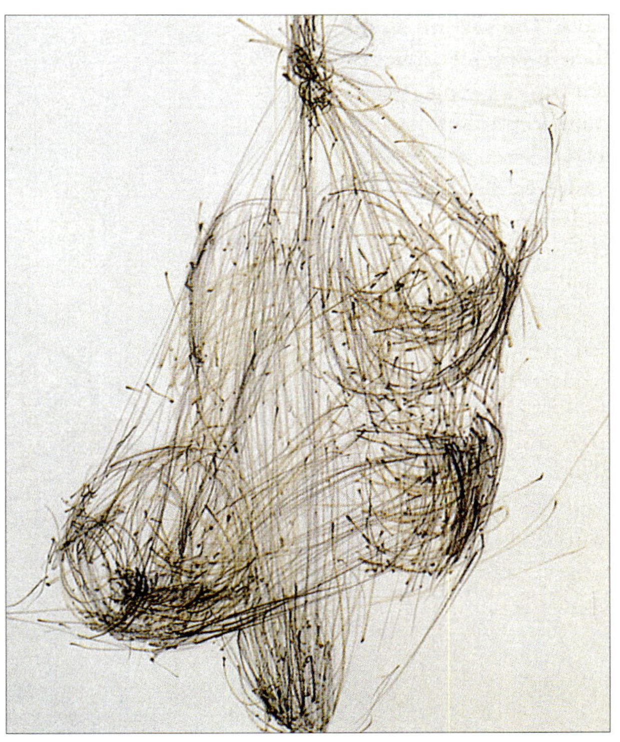

3 *The finished drawing gives a feeling of suspended weight without following the contours of the fruit or bag. The artist has allowed her hand to follow the implied movement of the objects. This has given the drawing a dynamic quality which describes the inner forces of the subject.*

Left *Charcoal is the ideal medium for broad effects, and in* Life Drawing II *by Joan Elliot Bates, it has been used very freely to describe both the play of light on the pose and the dynamic qualities of the pose. Shading has been done by scribbling, hatching, and smudging, and the vigorous use of the medium gives the drawing life and vitality.*

PROJECT THREE

OUTER AND INNER

I want you to now consider what happens in between the "edges" of an object. You will need a basically cylindrical object which can be placed vertically or horizontally.

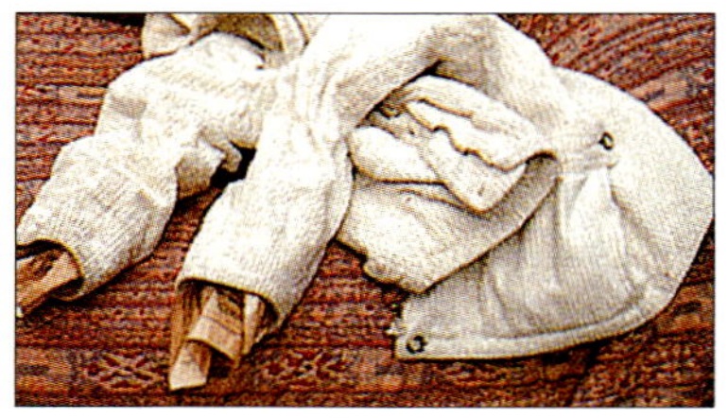

The sleeves have had paper stuffed inside them to make them round so that folds and creases in the fabric run round the arms like irregular corrugations.

A similar subject could be made with a pair of trousers, but the object doesn't have to be a garment. A vase with a striped pattern, a log of wood, or a few cups stacked one inside the other would all be excellent. What is needed is a set of positive lines running in from the edges of a tubular form.

Draw in line, use a medium which you haven't used so far in this lesson. Make your eyes follow the stripes or folds as they run across the form you are drawing and use line to describe what you see.

If you are drawing a garment you will see that there isn't a continuous outline around its edge. The line will frequently turn inward to describe folds, for example, and as it does it may provide an accurate cross-section of the object.

Lines that run around forms are very important in making objects appear to be three-dimensional, and often in drawing classes students are told that they must learn to draw across forms and not merely remain on the edge. The project should compel you to do this.

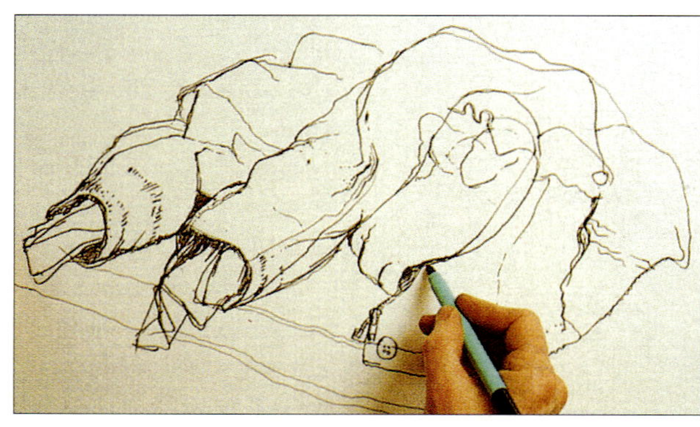

A fine black fiber-tipped pen is being used to follow the folds and creases in this jacket. The lines describe the cross-section of the garment rather than just its outline shape.

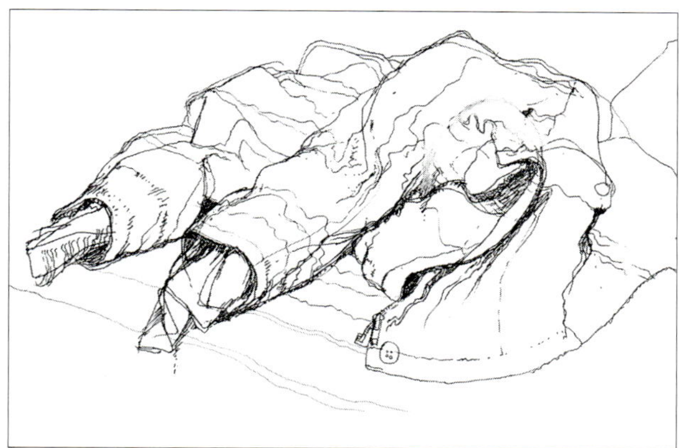

2 *The undulations of the folds of the jacket have been drawn in much the same way as the hills and hollows of a landscape might be described. It is very important that when you are drawing you realize that the "middle" of the object matters as much as its edges.*

Right Chairs *by Paul Bartlett shows how a close-up view of upholstered furniture has been drawn by using the distinctive pattern and texture of the upholstery fabric as a series of contour lines to build up the forms.*

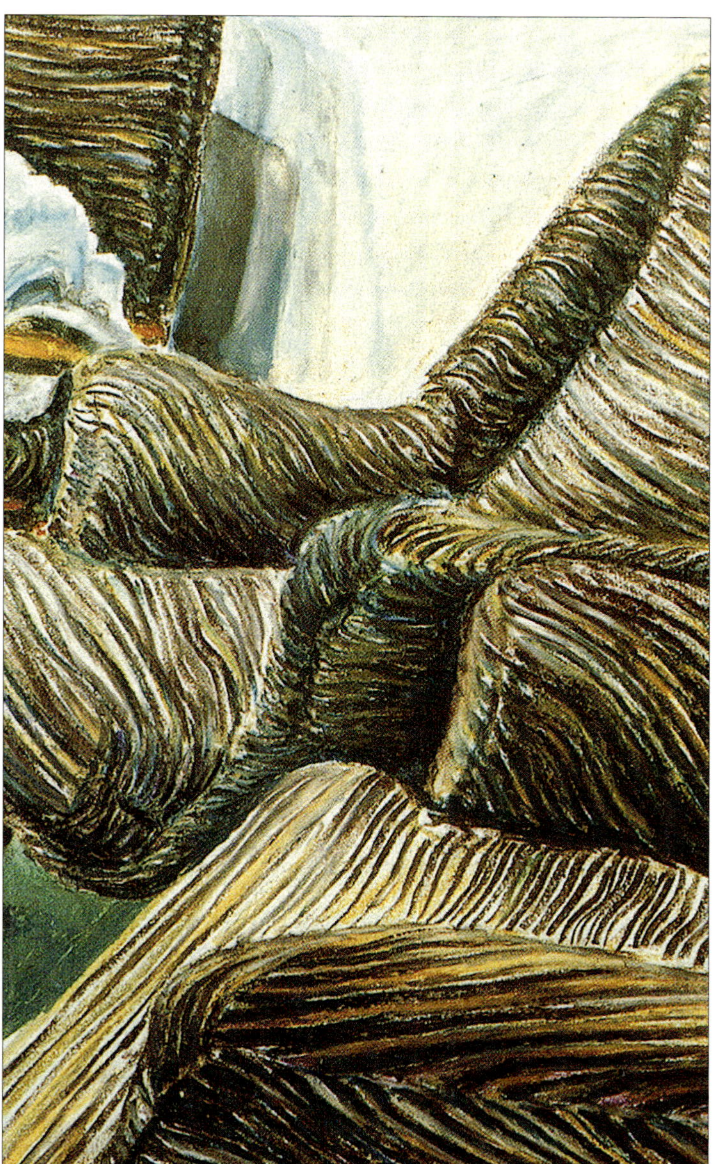

Below Lilies in a Black Vase *by Barbara Walton. You can try using more than one medium in a drawing. Here, the artist has combined charcoal, pastel, and touches of acrylic to produce a well-integrated drawing with a strong feeling of movement.*

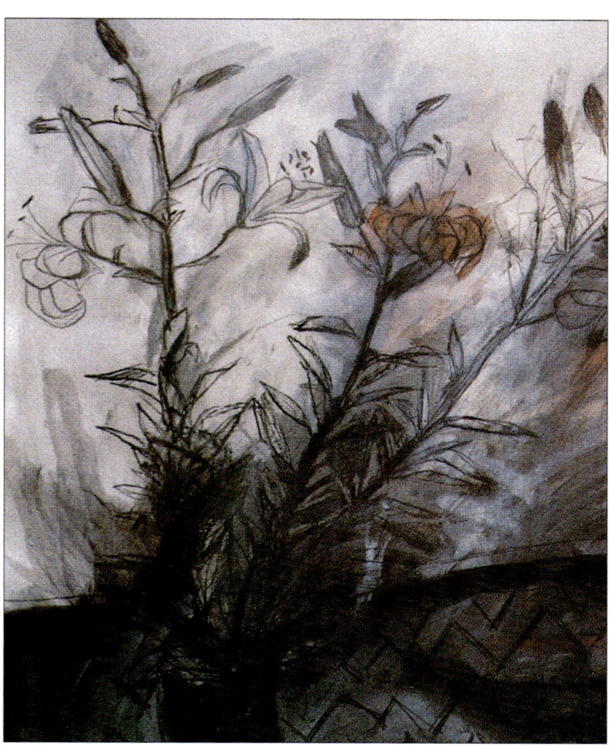

DRAWING TWO DIMENSIONS

When you draw the shape of an object you only have to consider two dimensions, height and width, but it is not always easy to make an accurate outline drawing. In this lesson you will be learning how to relate shapes of an object to a background, first by drawing on a grid of squares, and then by using background features as a cheek for shapes.

If your drawings are not entirely accurate at first, don't be disappointed. To be able to see shapes clearly and draw them well demands concentration and practice. Some people have the idea that they should be able to sit in front of an object with a line pouring

***Below** Four different views of a violin have provided the artist, John Houser, with an exciting relationship of subtle curved shapes. No shading has been attempted.*

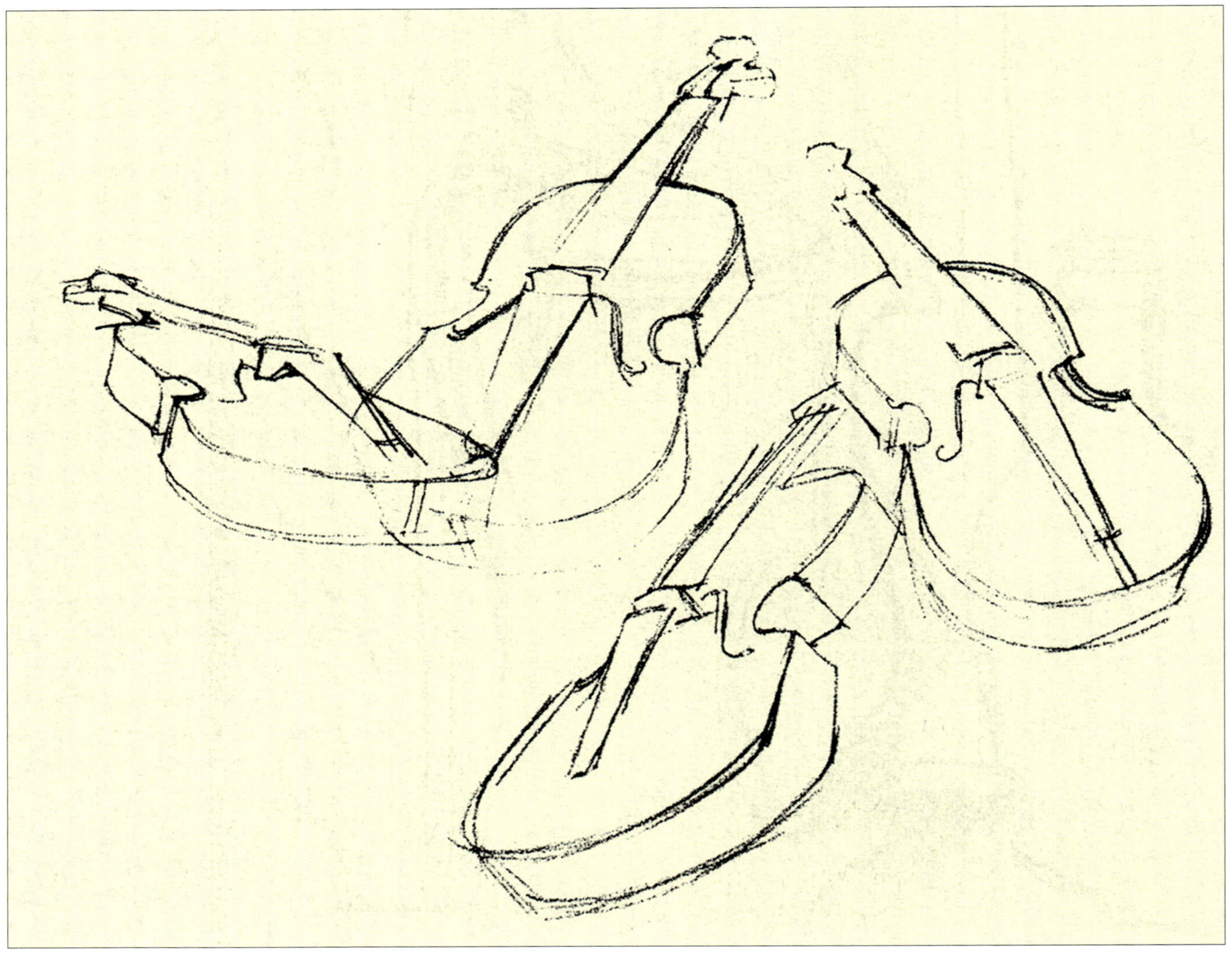

THE AIM OF THE PROJECTS

Relating an object to its background

Learning to see accurately

WHAT YOU WILL NEED

- **Your drawing board, three A2 sheets of cartridge paper (or two and one piece of white card), a ruler, a B or 2B pencil, and a pen.**

TIME

About 1 ½ hours.

out of their pencil and automatically tracing the shape onto their paper, but this is a myth. Some may have greater drawing facility than others, but what counts most is training yourself to see. When you begin to notice discrepancies between the shape of the object and the shape in your drawing, then you are learning to draw.

The projects in this lesson will make you realize how important it is to compare shapes and directions when you draw. Usually people see objects in isolation; for example landscape is seen as first one tree, then another, and then a background. In learning to see and compare all these features simultaneously, you are learning to see in the way that an artist does.

In drawing classes students are often advised to hold a pencil vertically as a drawing aid, or to use a pencil held at arm's length to measure the different sizes of two shapes. In my experience these methods are unreliable, and I recommend that you make comparisons between objects, seeing how they relate to each other and to their background. This drawing habit may take a little time to learn, but once you have acquired it you will be able to draw in this way automatically.

PROJECT FOUR

RELATING AN OBJECT TO A GRID

Choose an object that has a handle, spout, and other projections. Your drawing is to be made on a grid of squares, with another identical grid placed behind the object, so draw the grids first.

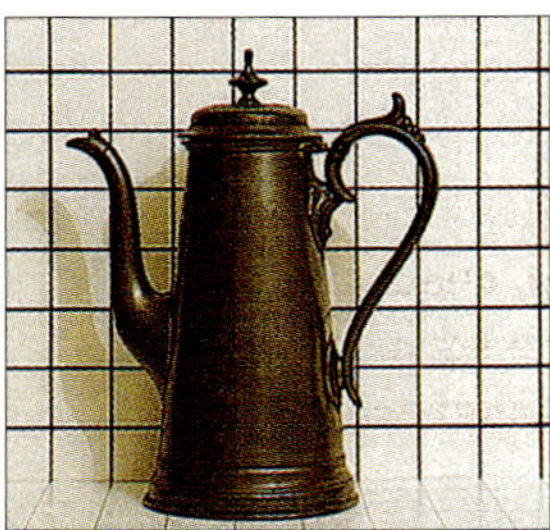

Draw 1.5 in. (4 cm) grids on both papers. Pin one up behind the object. This grid must be propped up absolutely vertical and not turned at an angle.

Place the object on the table not more than 2 in. (5 cm) from the grid. Draw the shape of the object, in line only, checking constantly to make sure that your drawing on your grid relates to the grid placed behind the object.

Check your starting point is in relation to the background square for accuracy. Continue to plot the shape of the jug in relation to the grid. Do not rub out if you get lines in the wrong place; draw and redraw the shape until it is as accurate as possible. Then spend a few minutes comparing your drawing with your view of the actual object.

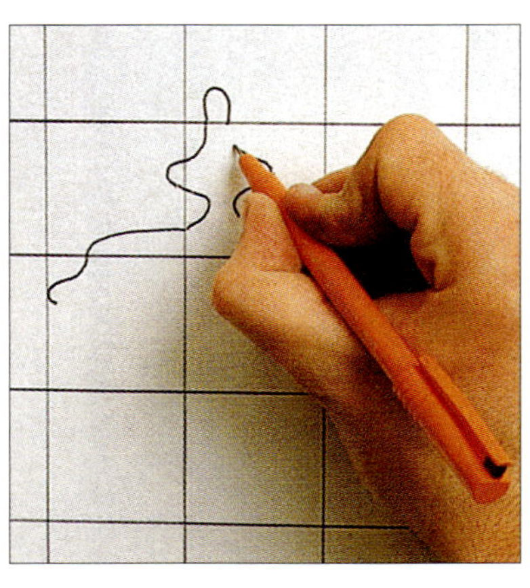

1 *Using a black fiber-tipped pen, the artist carefully draws the shape of the lid, checking that it corresponds correctly against the squares of the background grid.*

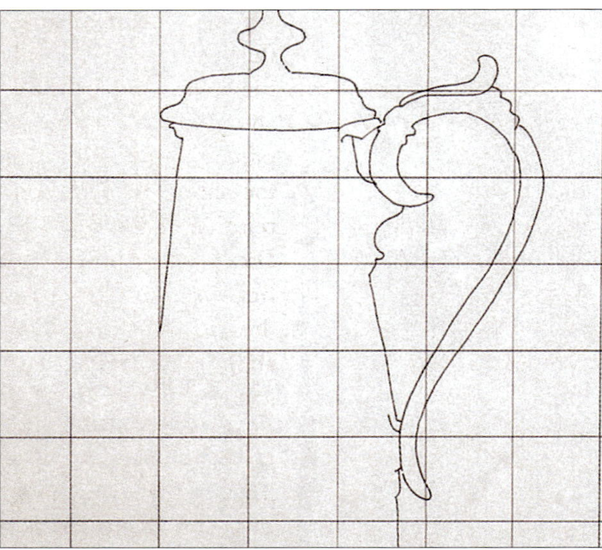

2 *As he develops the drawing, he continues to check the shapes against the background squares. This helps with the relative proportions of different areas of the object.*

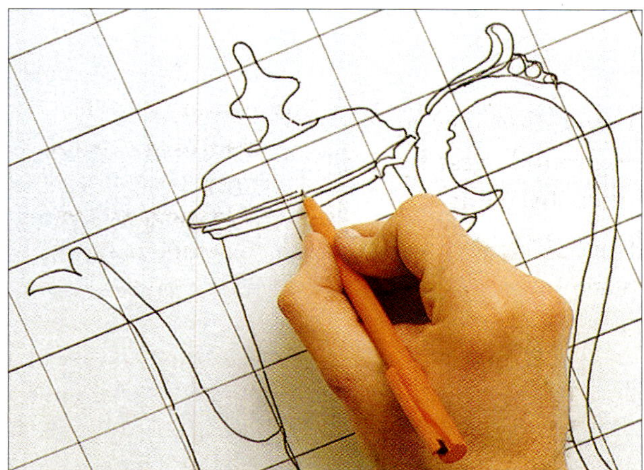

3 *It is important not to change your viewpoint in any way, as this will alter the relationship of the object to the grid.*

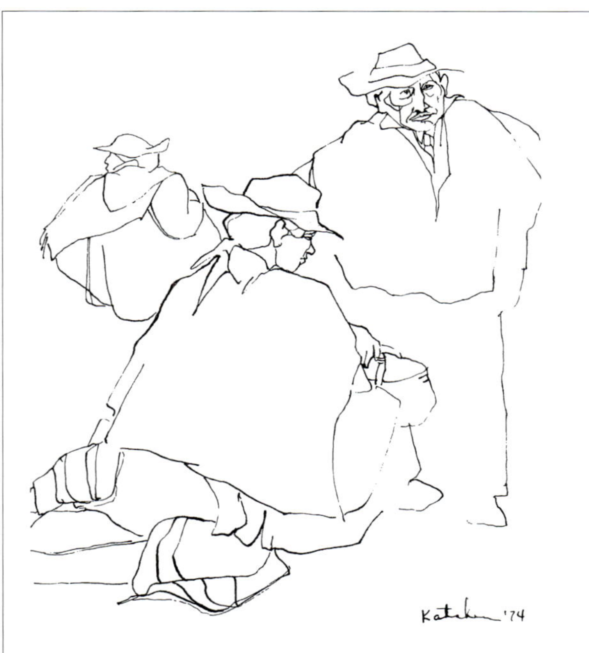

Above *As in the drawing of the violins on page 106, the artist here has been primarily interested in the relationship of the shapes, and has arranged them to create an elegant composition. But even so, she has described form by following contours across the figures, the hats, scarves, and jacket, which provide the visual clues about the three-dimensional forms.*

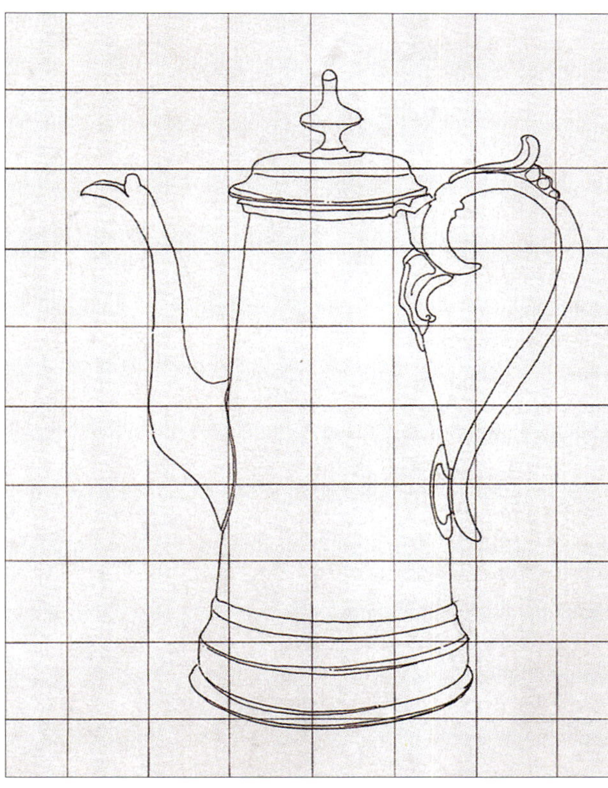

4 *Because the artist is an experienced draughtsman, he completed the drawing with no revisions. A student will almost certainly need several attempts to produce an accurate drawing. If you have to make some corrections, don't erase the earlier lines.*

SELF-CRITIQUE

- **Did you find it difficult to decide on the exact position of the object in relation to the squares on your drawing?**
- **Did you find out anything unexpected about the object? Is its shape precisely symmetrical, for instance?**
- **How would you rate the accuracy of your drawing on a scale of 1-10?**
- **Did you find that you concentrated on drawing one object and lost sight of its relationship to everything else?**

PROJECT FIVE

ROUNDED FORMS

I want you to make a drawing of a group of fruit. Apples and pears would be best because of their smooth surface, so you are not distracted by texture.

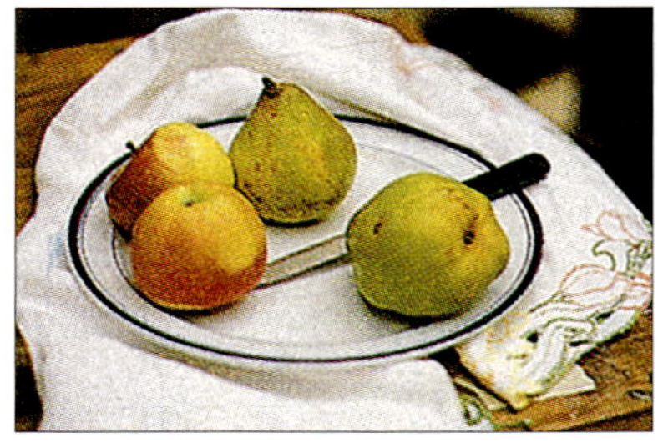

Put the fruit on a table on a plain, light-colored surface. The most important thing is the lighting, as it is this that describes the forms. The group needs to be illuminated from one side only, so if you are drawing by daylight you may have to move your table near a window.

Using soft pencil, charcoal, or conté crayon, draw them as large as possible, paying careful attention to the way the light falls, and trying to identify the darkest and lightest areas of each fruit. Concentrate on drawing only what makes the objects look solid. From time to time look at your drawing critically and see whether the fruit look three-dimensional. A common mistake is to make the outlines too strong, which destroys the effect of the shading, and another is to make the shadows too dark.

You will find it worthwhile to make several drawings of the same objects, changing the direction of the light and experimenting with different media and ways of shading. If you used charcoal in the first drawing, you could try ink wash for another one. Or if you found charcoal too soft, try hatching and crosshatching with a pencil.

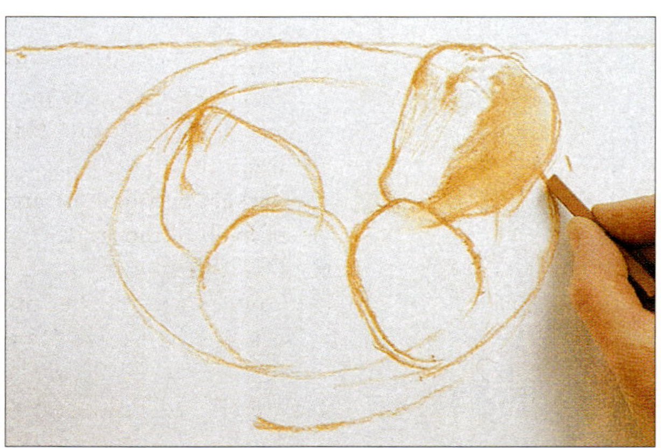

The shapes of the fruit and the plate have first been drawn in lightly in line with conté crayon. The artist now starts to use shading to indicate the direction of the light.

2 *The forms of the fruit are described by identifying the lightest and darkest areas. Note that the artist is developing the whole drawing at the same time, not just concentrating on one object.*

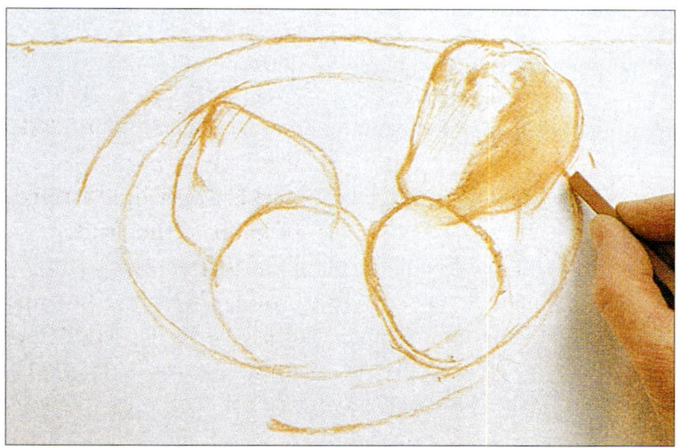

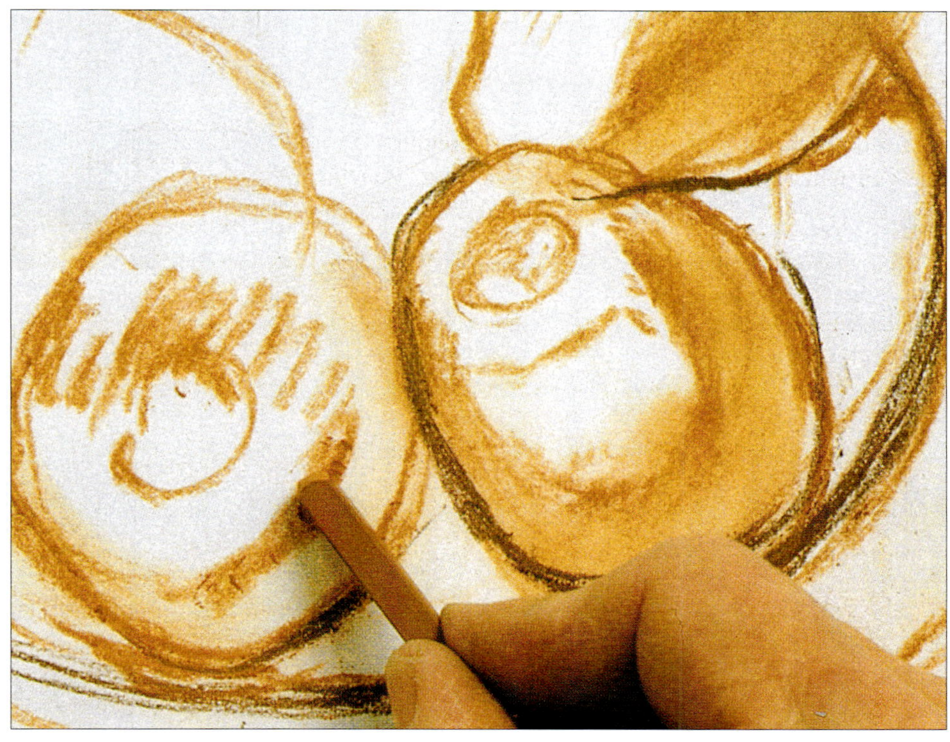

3 *A darker brown conté has now been introduced into the background. Although the outlines on the fruit are quite dark, the shading is sufficiently strong to make the objects appear solid. The artist has ignored some elements. The shadows cast by the objects, for example, have been ignored.*

Right *A certain amount of smudging can be seen in this charcoal drawing, but line predominates, used both as a means of describing the shapes of some of the objects and for hatching and cross-hatching to build up areas of tone. This drawing is much more concerned with the character of the individual objects than with lighting effects.*

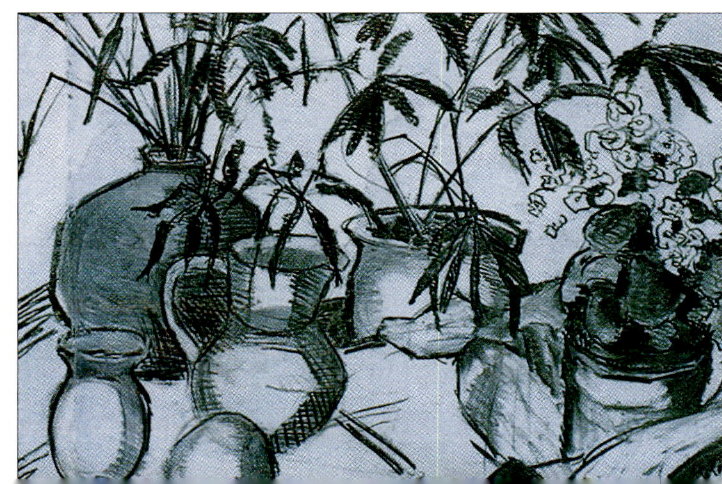

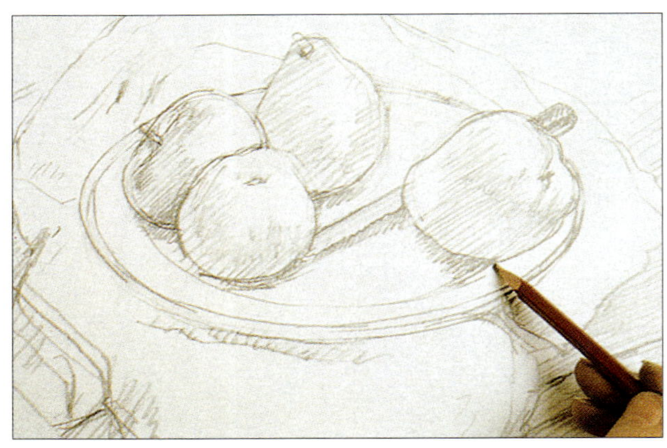

1 *In this pencil drawing, shadows have been seen from the beginning as important. As well as establishing the shapes of the fruit on the plate, the artist has also related these objects to the near edge and corner of the table and to the cloth under the plate of fruit.*

2 *In this drawing the light is coming from the right, and the artist now builds up shading to describe the dark areas of the fruit.*

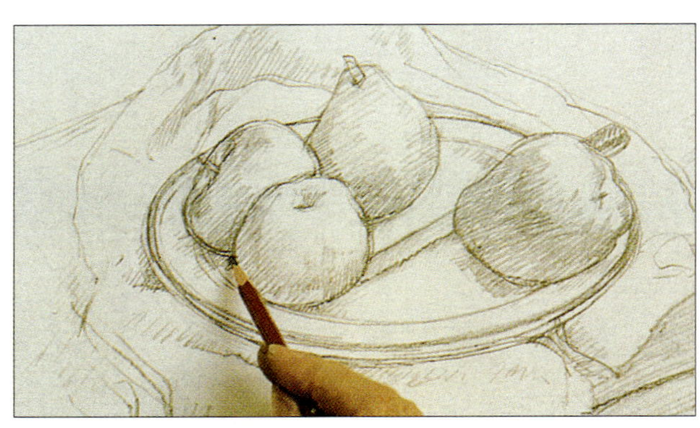

3 *This close-up detail reveals how the artist has carefully described the hollows at the tops of the apples and the subtle undulations on the surface of the pear. The shading is made with freely scribbled lines which give the drawing a certain vitality.*

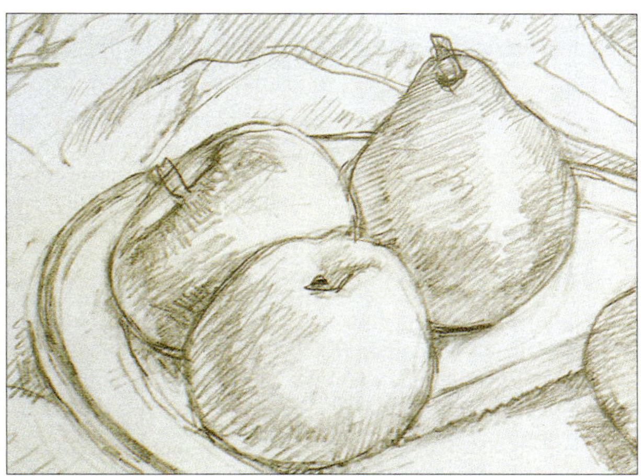

4 *As the artist worked, she became interested in the different three-dimensional forms in the subject. She has used line and shading to describe the hard, sharp corner of the table, the rounded forms of the fruit, and the soft crumpled form of the cloth under the plate.*

SELF-CRITIQUE

- **Could the fruit look more solid and three-dimensional?**
- **Have you concentrated too much on the outline shapes?**
- **Have you confused matters by drawing in the shadows?**
- **Would you have been happier using a different drawing medium?**

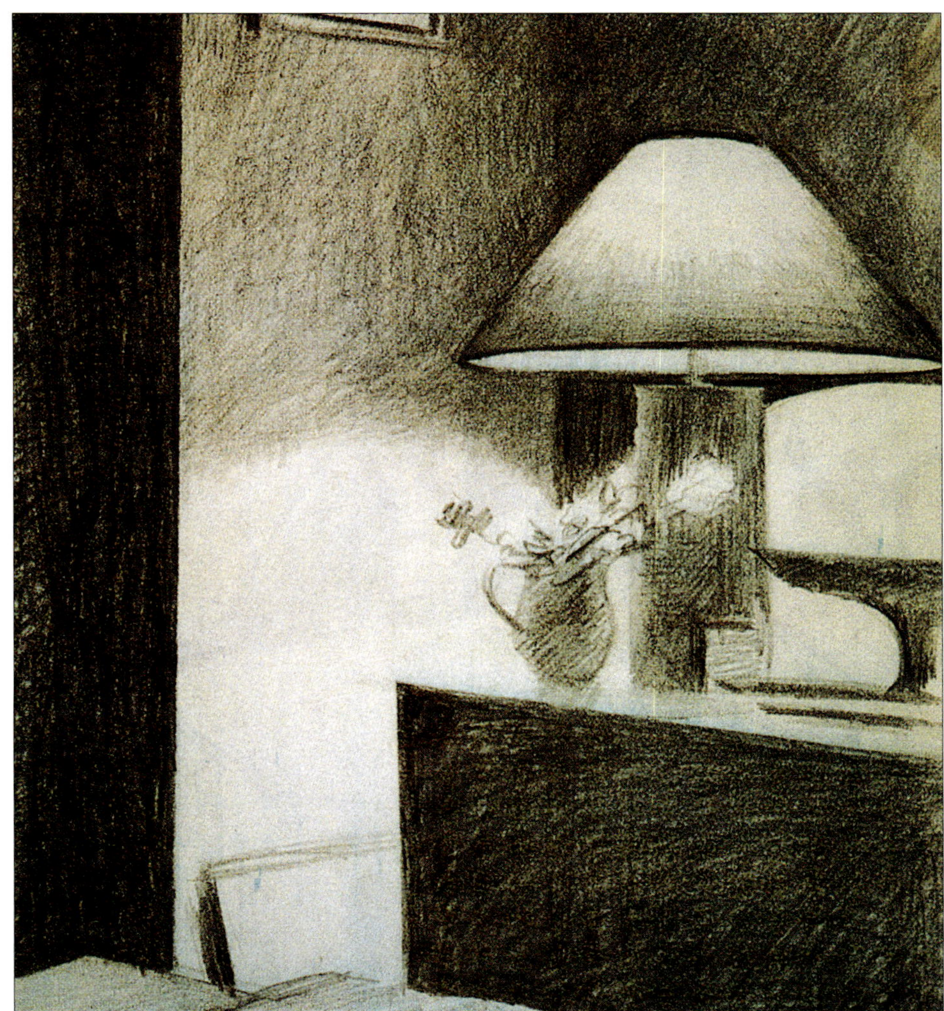

Right *A very soft pencil has been used here, in a carefully controlled technique of hatching, smudging, and blending. The strong pattern of light and dark, and the organization of the subject into simple shapes, makes a powerful drawing, which is deceptively easy. The impact comes from the way the artist has selected only the important features of the subject; the best way of appreciating the skill needed to make a drawing like this is to try to visulize all the things the artist has probably left out.*

PROJECT SIX

DESCRIPTIVE COLOR

You can use any color drawing medium you like for this project, but before you start, experiment with your chosen medium so you know how to mix colors and have an idea of the range of colors.

How you begin depends on the medium you are using. For pastel, you can start by making a drawing of the main shapes in charcoal, or you can use one of the pastel sticks for the drawing. If you are working in colored pencils, use a light neutral color for the drawing. For inks or markers, make a light drawing in pencil first.

Now start to use color to describe the objects, bearing in mind what you discovered about tone in the previous project, but this time considering hue and color intensity as well. Remember everything has a color if you look for it. Shadows, for instance, are not merely gray or black. Keep asking yourself what color it is; how dark it is; how intense it is. Unless there is an area that you want to leave white, cover all the paper with color. If you are using pastels you may need to fix your drawing between stages as well as at the end.

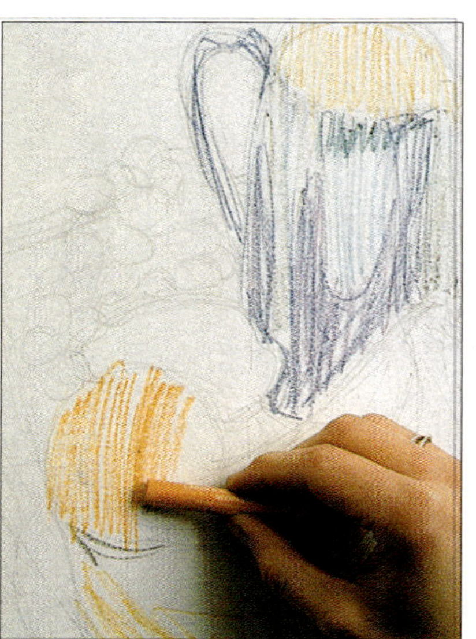

1 *Having worked the main shapes with charcoal, the artist nows draws in color.*

2 *(Right) With this medium the color has to be built up gradually, and as a first step the artist is identifying the main local colors in the subject.*

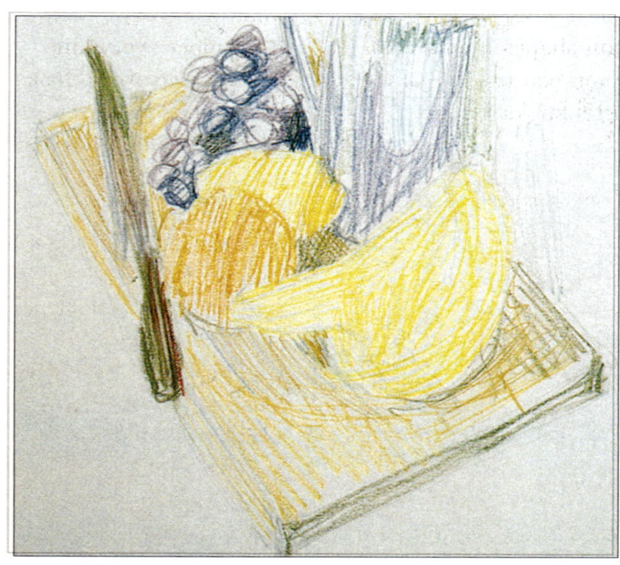

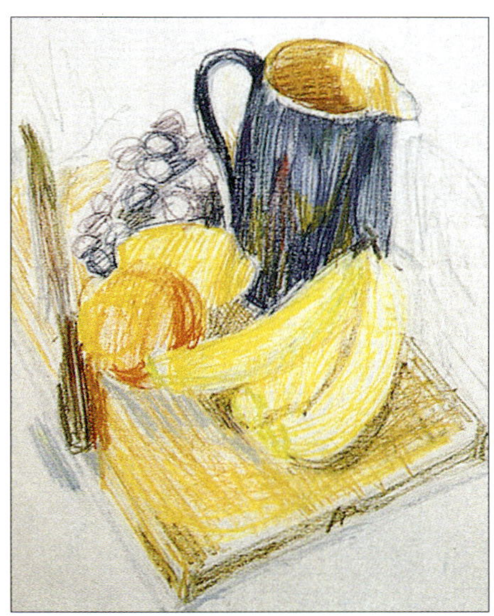

3 *Careful attention must be paid not just to identifying the color of an object but also its tone. The jug is not simply blue, it is also much darker in tone.*

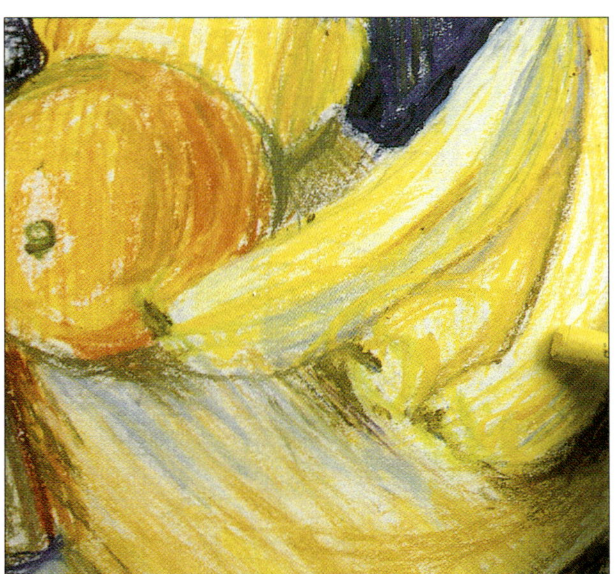

4 *The colors are built up by laying various layers. Notice the cool greens and grays of the bananas, in contrast with the warm, rich colors of the orange.*

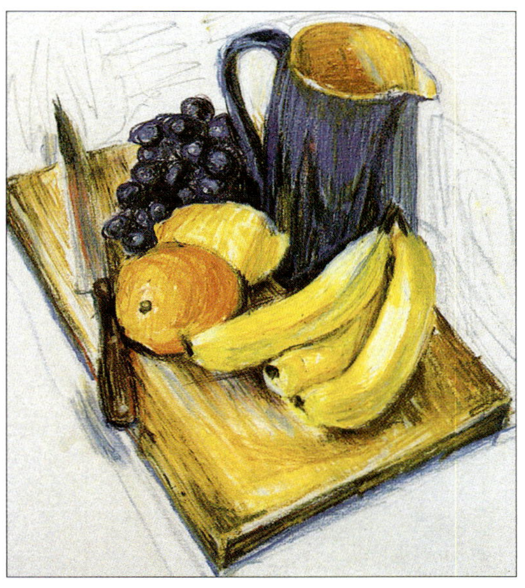

5 *The drawing is now complete, with the colors developed and the tonal contrasts preserved.*

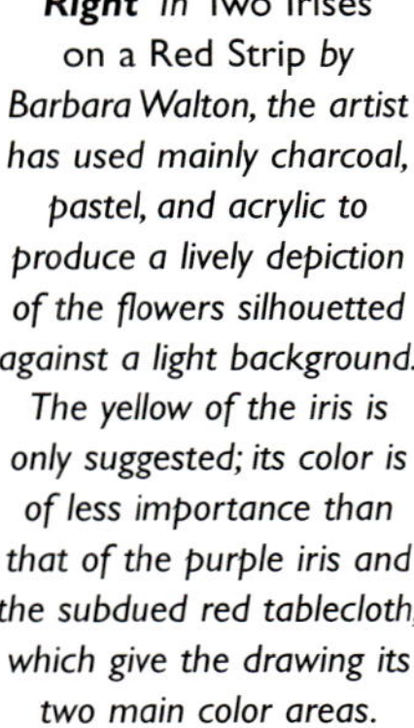

Right *In* Two Irises on a Red Strip *by Barbara Walton, the artist has used mainly charcoal, pastel, and acrylic to produce a lively depiction of the flowers silhouetted against a light background. The yellow of the iris is only suggested; its color is of less importance than that of the purple iris and the subdued red tablecloth, which give the drawing its two main color areas.*

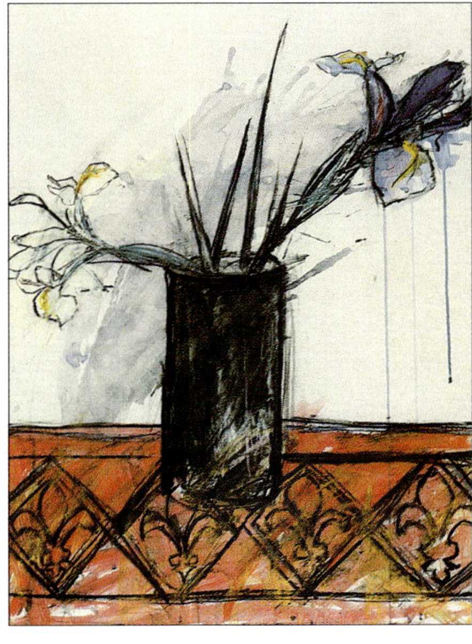

CREATIVE USES OF COLOR

In the last lesson you used color to provide your drawing with an additional descriptive element, but color has other uses; e.g., to enhance the illusion of three-dimensional space or to express emotions.

Colors are often arranged around a circle, called a color wheel, starting with red and proceeding in steps through orange, yellow, green and blue to violet. The greatest contrasts are between complementary colors, those opposite each other on this circle, for example red and green. Harmonious colors are next to each other on the color circle (yellow and orange).

There is also another very important kind of color contrast, which is of the greatest importance in creating an illusion of three-dimensional space—color "temperature." Reddish hues are described as "warm", and bluish hues as "cool." Generally, warm colors appear to advance to the foreground of a drawing and cool colors recede into the background. This can't be taken as a firm rule; if you have an intense blue in the foreground and a muted red in the background, for example, the intensity will compensate for the tendency of blue to recede.

Below *In this pastel drawing, the artist has ignored the actual colors of most of the objects and given the drawing a wistful, slightly melancholy color scheme in keeping with the theme.*

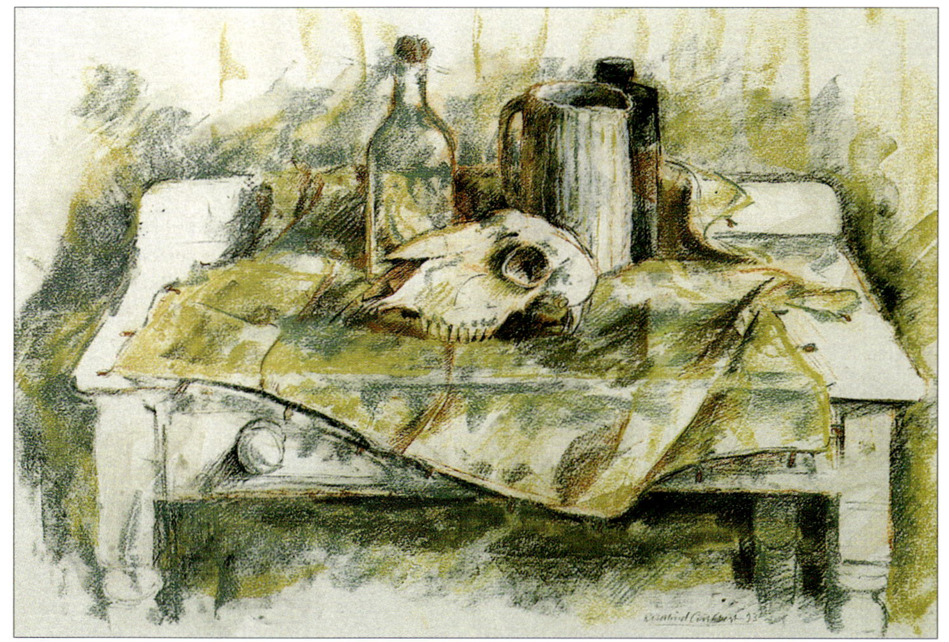

THE AIM OF THE PROJECTS

- **Making color recede**
- **Contrasting colors**
- **Learning to express yourself through color**

WHAT YOU WILL NEED

- **Your chosen color-drawing medium, paper. If you are using pastel, this would be an opportunity to try a colored paper. Choose an unobtrusive mid-tone for your first attempt.**

TIME

Project 1: about 2 hours.

PROJECT SEVEN

CREATING SPACE

The difference between this project and the previous ones is that you need to have more depth in your drawing, so position your objects so that you can see well beyond them across the room.

MAKING YOUR DRAWING

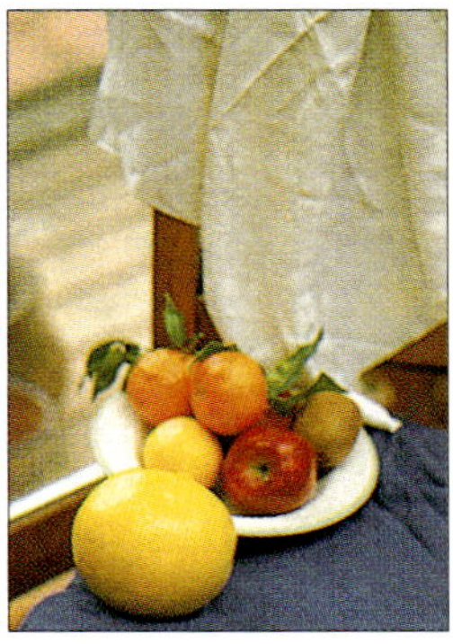

This time, start in color from the very beginning. Use an unobtrusive color (pale blue, for example) to draw the main shapes rapidly, but as soon as possible try to establish the main colors in your drawing. The aim in this drawing is to identify warm and cool colors, and by emphasizing these color qualities create a feeling of depth.

The colors of shadows tend to be cooler than the lightstruck areas, and using blues or greens in the shadows will help you make them look solid. Also, the colors in the background are cooler than the foreground. Experienced artists use warm/cool contrasts automatically; soon, you will also learn to identify the colors.

1 *The main shapes of the group have been drawn in line, using gray pastel reinforced in places with blue, which the artist has already identified as a color which will be important in the drawing.*

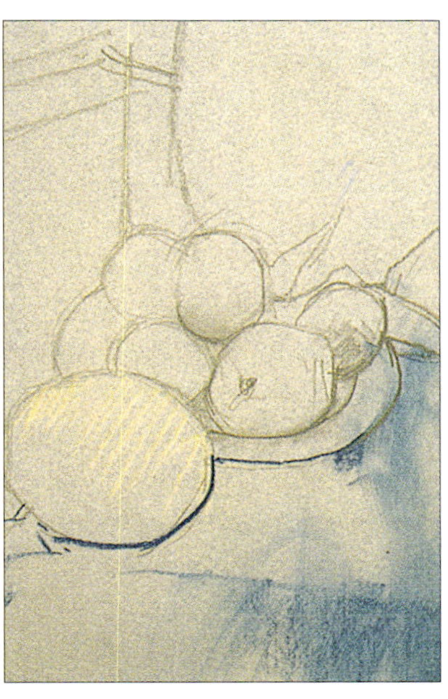

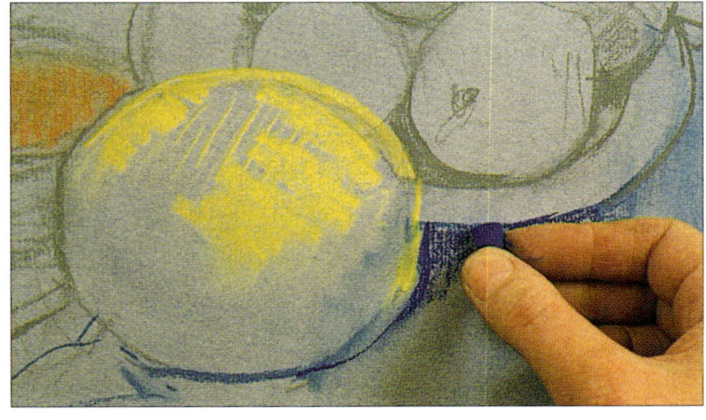

2 *Patches of yellow were introduced to help the artist assess the depth of color needed for the blue cloth. This is now slightly intensified.*

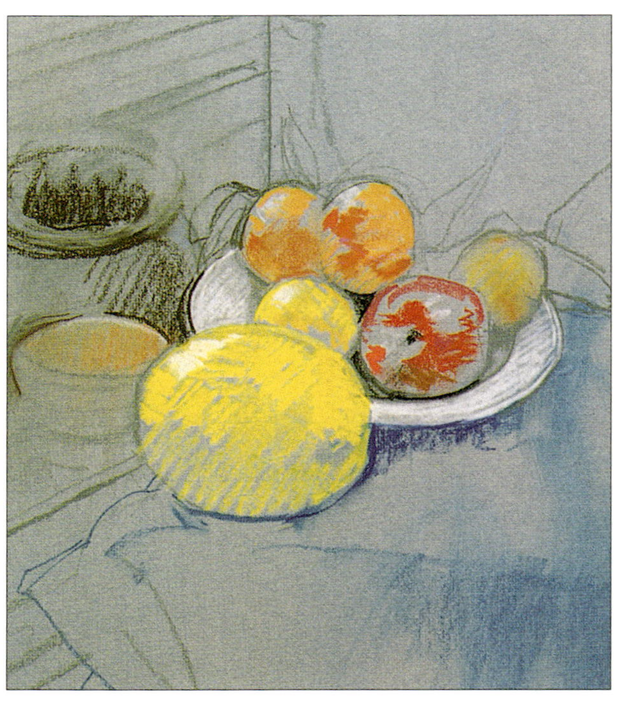

3 *The drawing is now well established and the main colors blocked in. The cool gray of the paper has been left uncovered.*

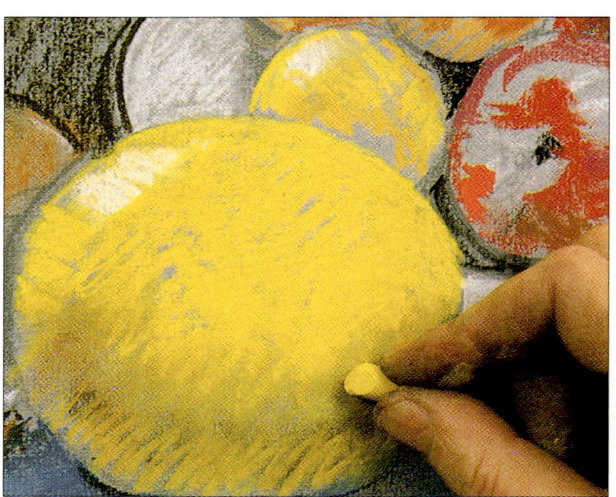

4 *The color of the grapefruit, the largest foreground object, is built up; the other colors are gauged against the immediate foreground.*

5 *The objects are developed into a more complete statement. Here the artist is rubbing pastel with a finger to create an area of soft color.*

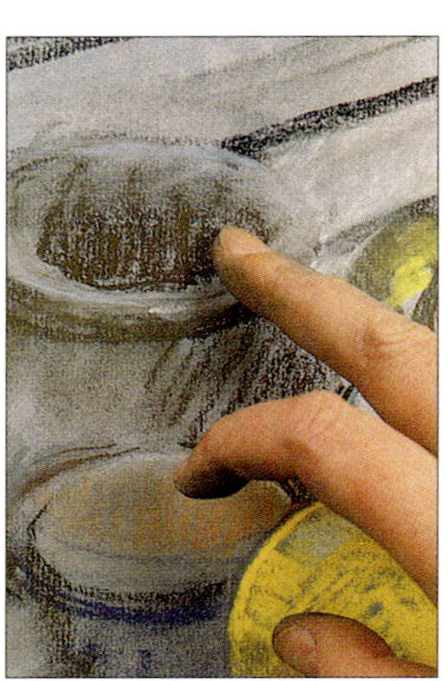

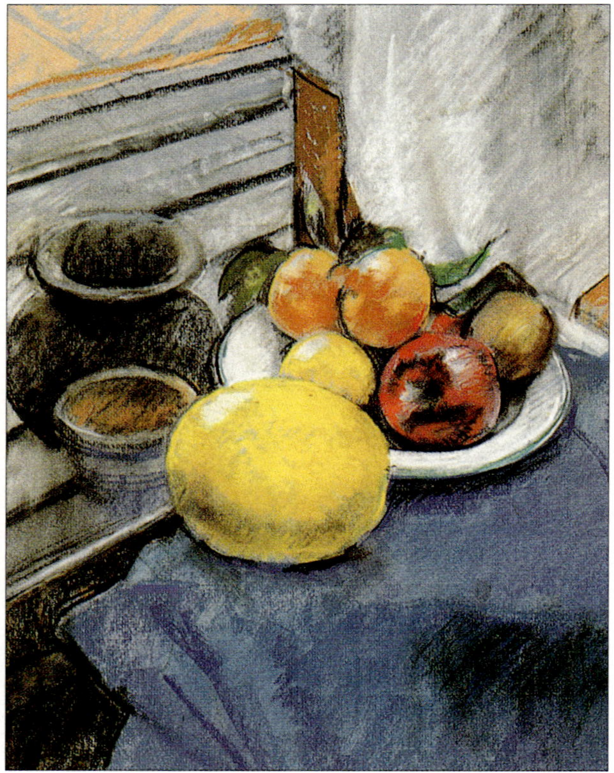

6 *Blue can be a "recessive" color, but in this case its vividness is accentuated by the striking contrast with the yellow.*

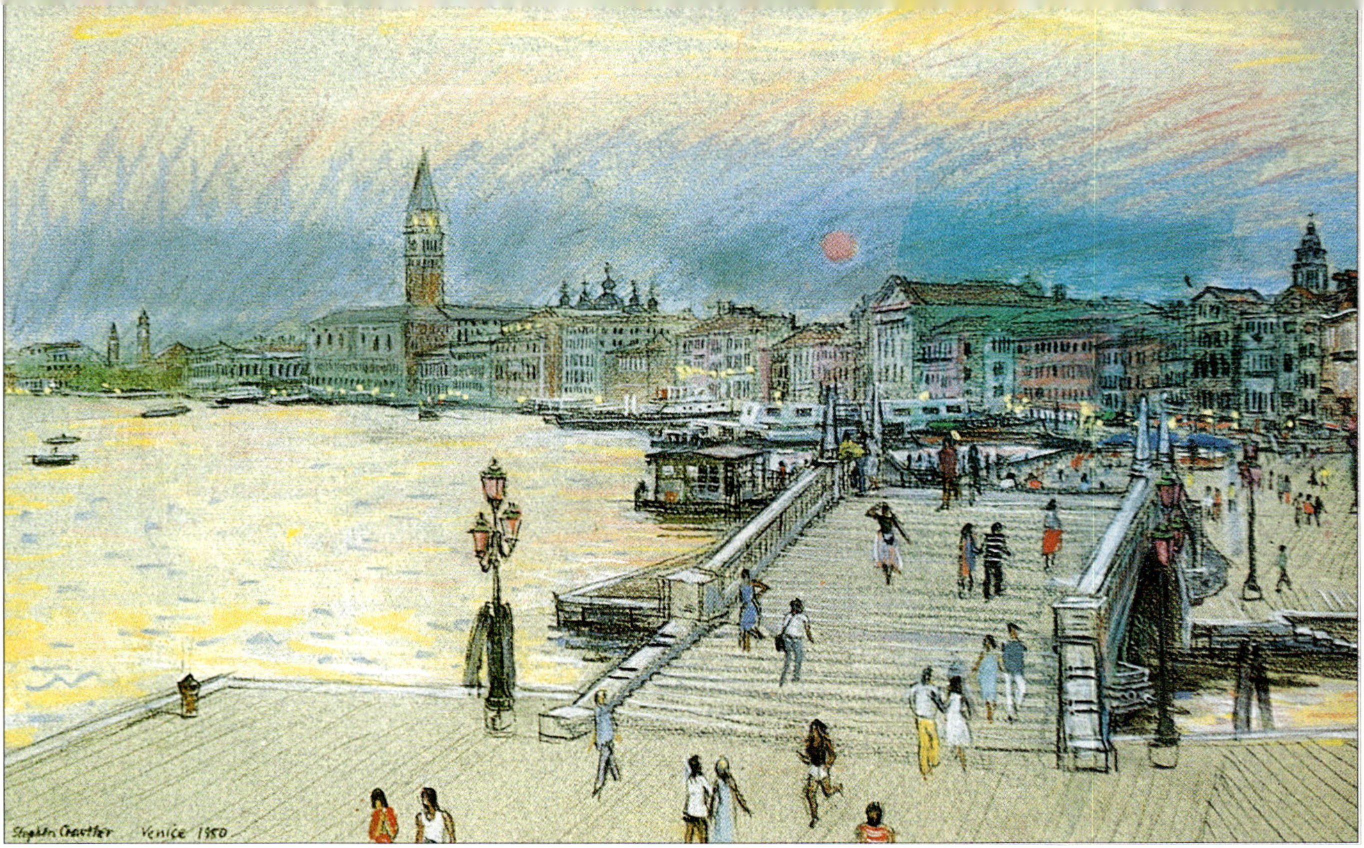

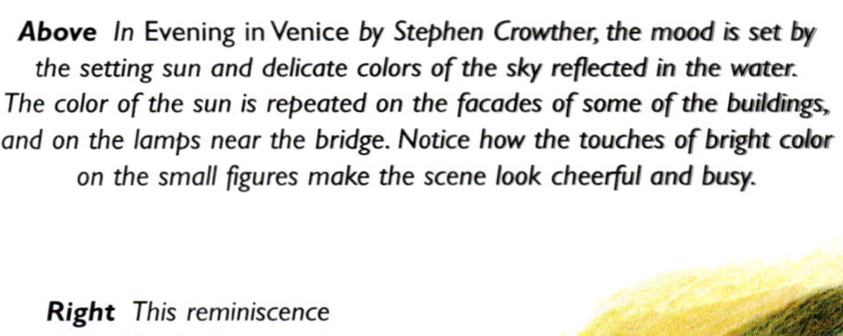

Above *In* Evening in Venice *by Stephen Crowther, the mood is set by the setting sun and delicate colors of the sky reflected in the water. The color of the sun is repeated on the facades of some of the buildings, and on the lamps near the bridge. Notice how the touches of bright color on the small figures make the scene look cheerful and busy.*

Right *This reminiscence of a holiday looks just right due as much to the choice of colors as to the objects.*

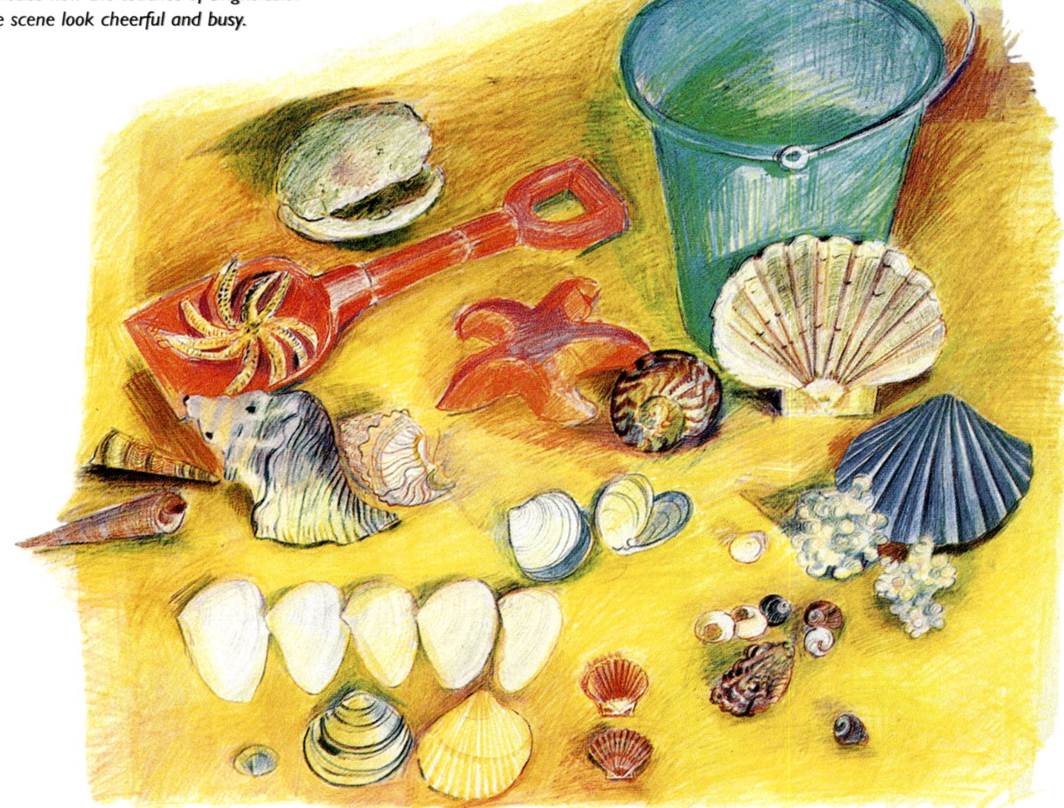

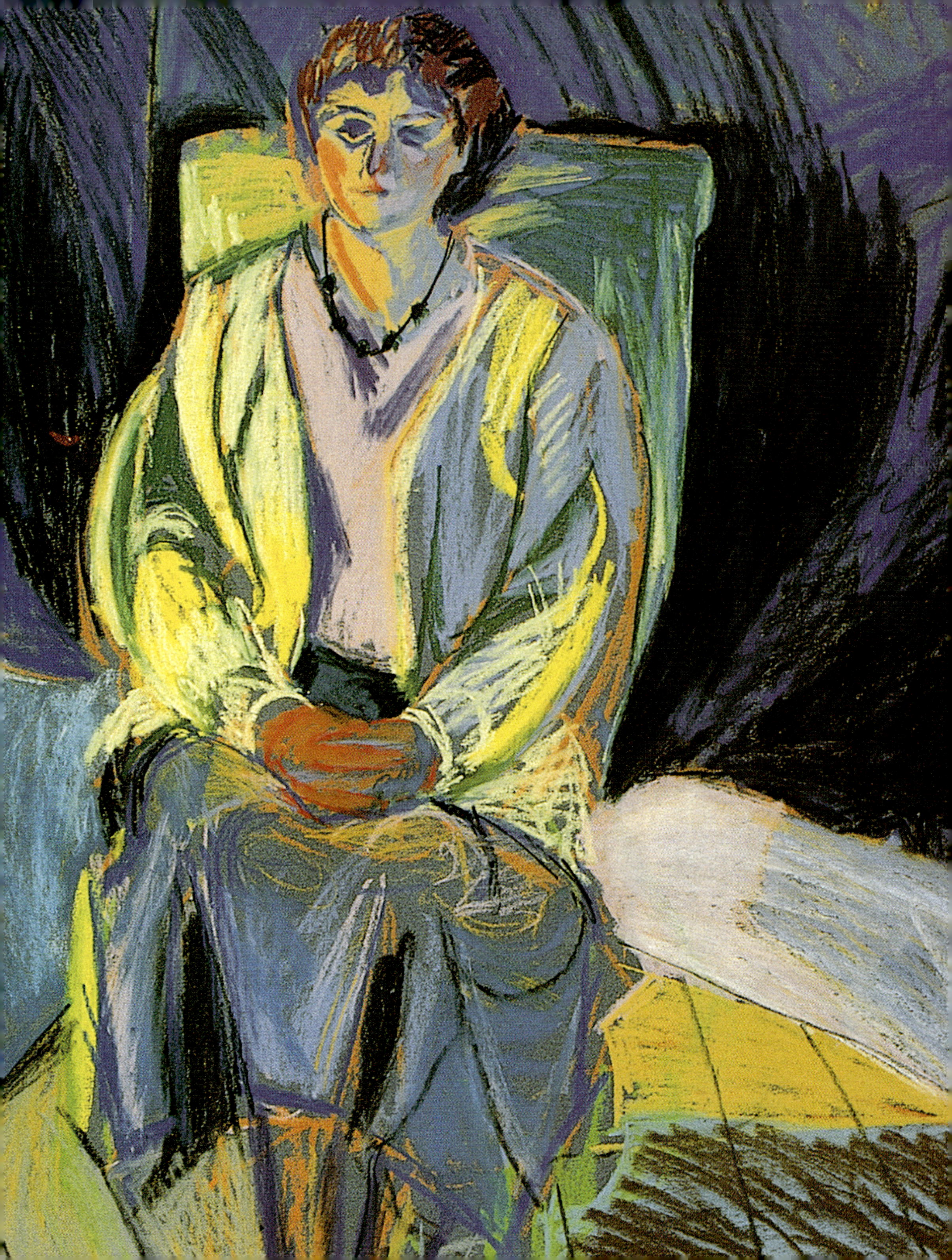

10 DIFFERENT APPROACHES

As was mentioned earlier, drawings can be the first stage in developing a work in another medium, or they can be works of art in their painting. When a drawing is an exploration of a subject, it may be done partly to investigate the compositional potential of the subject.

COMPOSITION

Composition is the art of combining the various elements of a drawing for painting into a satisfactory visual whole. In a good composition the various shapes, forms, and colors (if color is used) are arranged so that the work continues to hold the viewer's interest after it has made its initial impact. When you look at a well-composed drawing you should feel that its composition is not weighted in one direction or the other, but that everything is held in balance.

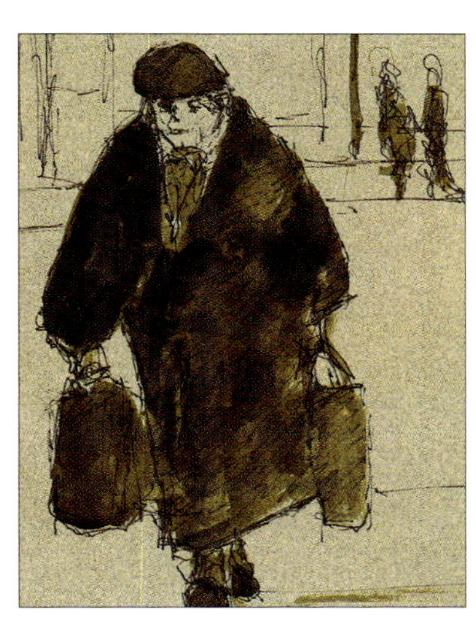

Above *In John Denahy's pen and wash drawing* The Shopper, *the overall shape is a triangle, balanced by the background figures set within an inverted L-shape.*

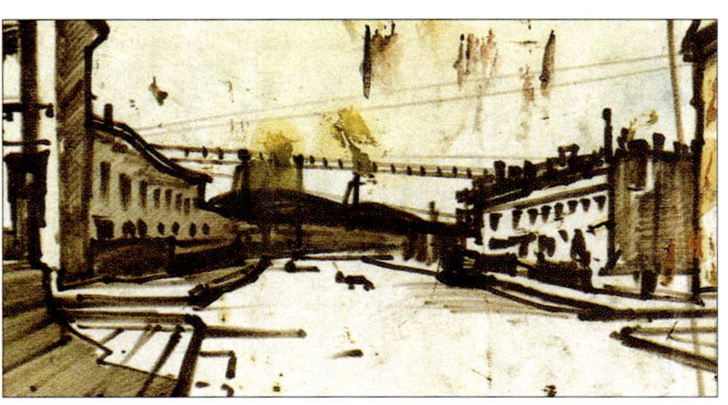

Left *Christopher Chamberlain's pen and wash drawing of a London cityscape has an almost symmetrical balance, but the strong verticals and diagonals have been cleverly used to avert predicability.*

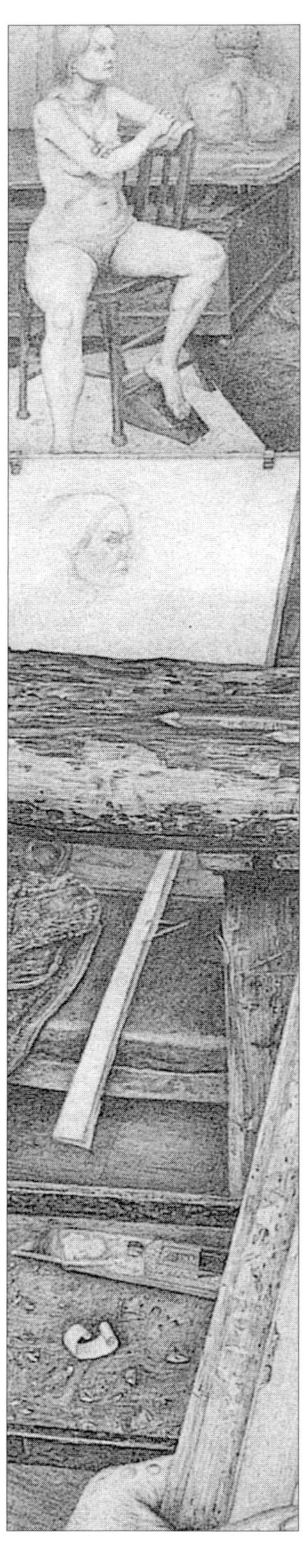

***Left** Paul Bartlett's unusual pencil drawing* First Term in the Life Drawing Room *gives an excellent impression of the narrow view you often have as you look between the other students in a life studio. The foreground hand directs you toward the model, but the directional forces are balanced by the many near horizontal lines.*

THE DYNAMICS OF THE RECTANGLE

You begin to tackle the all-important problem of composition as soon as you put the first mark on a piece of paper. On its own, a rectangle is static, but anything introduced into it, even the merest mark, disturbs its equilibrium and has an effect on how the rectangle is perceived. For example, a mark put in the top right-hand corner will lead your eye immediately to this point. The inclusion of tone will make further changes in the balance of the rectangle, and the introduction of curved shapes will change the balance yet again.

SIZE AND SHAPE

There is no reason why a drawing should not be planned within a circle or oval, but the majority of drawings are rectangular. These shapes, depending on whether they are horizontal or vertical, are usually known as "landscape" or "portrait" format respectively. Traditionally, these subjects have been drawn and painted in these particular shapes, but they do not have to be; an upright landscape can be very effective when you want a composition with a vertical emphasis. What is important is that the shape suits the subject.

DIFFERENT APPROACHES

There are two main ways in which you can approach composition in drawing. The first is to draw without being concerned about the shape the drawing will finally take, and only as it nears completion decide on the best proportioned rectangle to contain it. This can be done by masking off your drawing with strips of paper or two L-shaped corners cut from card or paper until you are satisfied that you have the best shape.

The second approach is to treat the rectangle itself as the starting point and compose your drawing within it. In the history of art many drawings and paintings have been based on simple geometric designs. The drawing rectangle was divided in particular ways, and the main features of the composition made to conform to this predetermined design. Many compositions, for example, are based on a triangle.

THE GOLDEN SECTION

Formal geometric compositions have often been based on a proportion called the golden section, in which a line or rectangle is divided into two parts so that the ratio of the smaller to the larger is equal to the ratio of the larger to the whole line. This ratio (approximately 8:13) has been known since antiquity, and was believed to possess inherent aesthetic virtues, bringing art and nature into harmony. The golden section proportion was used extensively by Renaissance artists. Although it is considered less important today, it is interesting to note that many drawings and paintings, when analysed, reveal the use of this proportion even though the artists concerned did not use it consciously.

BASIC RULES

The fundamental rule of composition is that the picture surface should not be divided symmetrically. Pictures require a form of equilibrium which is much more complex and subtle than this, and the balance must not be too apparent. A well composed drawing is one that remains satisfying after you have looked at it for some time, rather like peeling an onion—each layer reveals something new.

The basic rule of asymmetry in composition can be extended to provide further rules. For example, it is courting disaster to place a standing figure in the center of your paper or position a fence so that it runs horizontally across your drawing, equally dividing the distance from the bottom edge of your drawing to the horizon line. There are, however, no rules that can't be broken. There are times when artists do make symmetrical compositions work well. It is important to remember that composition is something to be aware of and to respect, but just as following a set of rules does not guarantee success, breaking them does not always mean failure.

THREE-DIMENSIONAL COMPOSITION

So far I have put the emphasis on two-dimensionnal design, but it is equally important that a drawing is balanced in depth,

Above *The shape of David Carpanini's pencil drawing* The Brothers *echoes those of the heads of the standing men. The horizontal provided by the terraced houses, together with the lines of the roofs and angular shapes of chimneys, provide a counterpoint to the curves and repeated ovals.*

with the intervals of space between foreground, middle distance, and background as varied as the surface pattern. In creating an illusion of space, the depth of the drawing has to be composed as carefully as the balance of the main shapes and the divisions of the rectangle.

This is easier for some subjects than for others. A typical example of a difficult composition is a close-up view of the facade of a building—a subject which seems to have a fatal attraction for many drawing students. It will be virtually impossible to create an interesting composition in depth, even if a satisfactory arrangement of two-dimensional shapes can be selected. A subject where the main interest is in the middle distance can be equally difficult, as you will have to find means of organizing the foreground so that the eye is led through interesting intervals of space into the picture. Most subjects, however, approached carefully, can be used to provide an interesting composition.

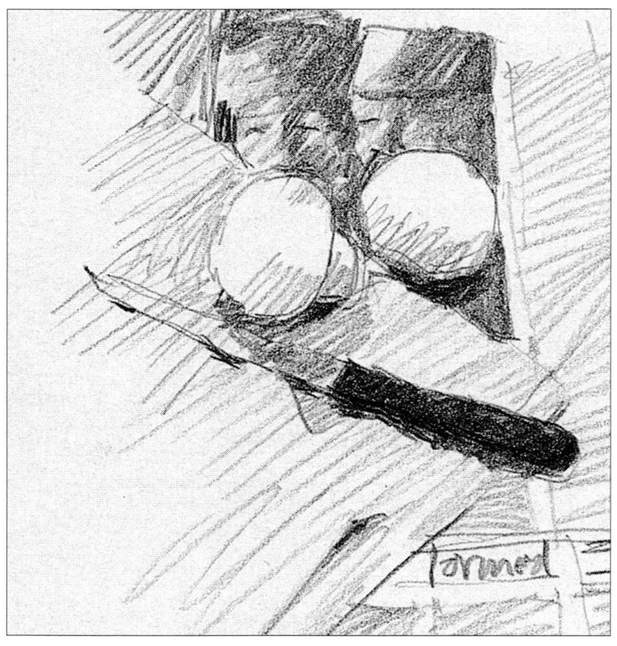

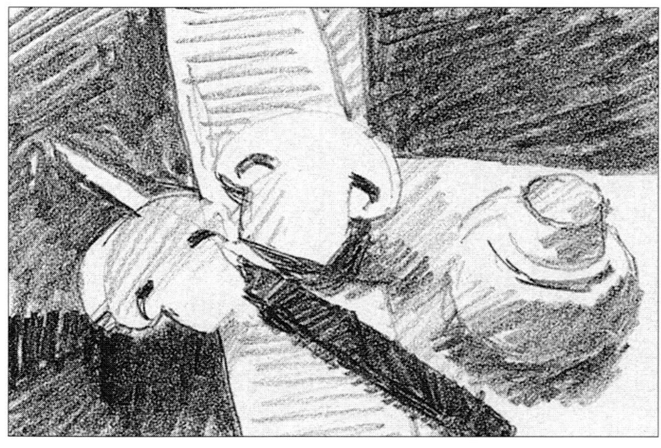

SELECTION

Selecting the key elements and discarding unimportant ones, is an essential part of the process of composing. The kind of composition you decide on can also determine the amount of detail you include. For example, if you have decided that the foreground of your drawing has to be kept simple so that your eye can move through this area into an interesting incident in the middle distance, don't be tempted to add unnecessary details.

As you decide what to include and what

Left Above and Left *In these two pencil sketches, compositional studies for a still life painting, Ronald Jesty has tried out two variations on a theme—the contrast between oval and angular shapes. In the second sketch, the mushrooms have been cut in half, producing two further shapes.*

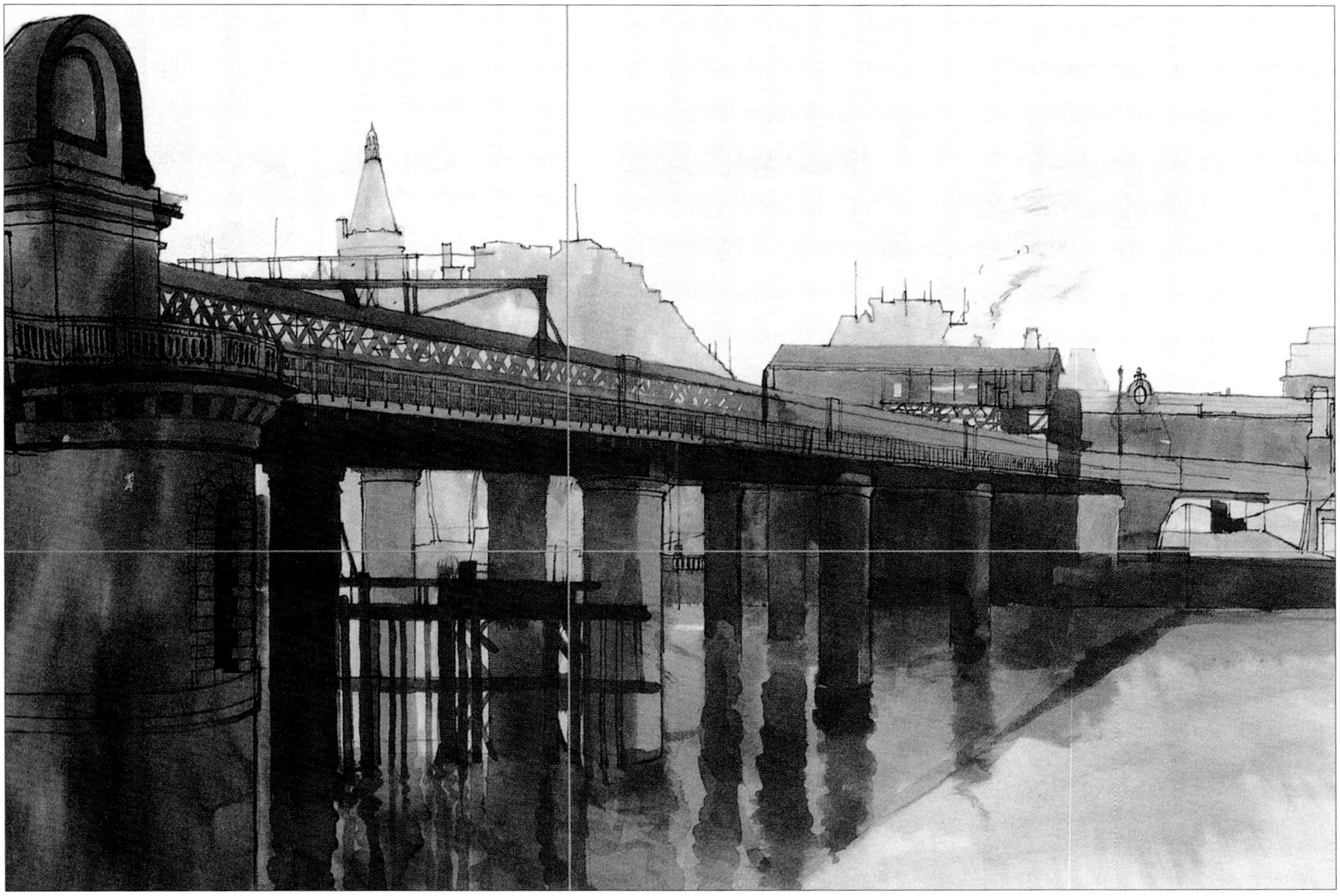

Above *Ian Simpson's pen and wash drawing of Hungerford Bridge was done on the spot. No definite shape was chosen in advance, but the rectangle the artist eventually decided on shows that the far bank of the river and one of the bridge's strong verticals divide the drawing into Golden Section proportions.*

to leave out of your drawing, bear in mind that objects which are incidental to the subject might add something to the composition. A telegraph pole, for example, may look out of context in a view of a village but it may provide a very useful vertical emphasis. Always think about how each element can contribute to the composition.

If you find it difficult to make these

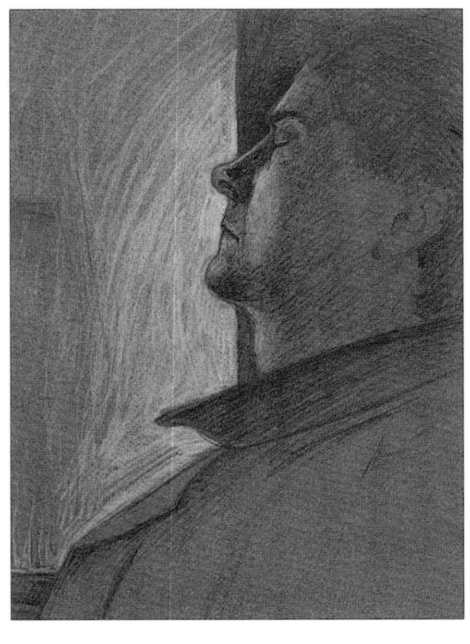

Right *In her pastel drawing* Sleeping Passenger, Morning *Rosalind Cuthbert has achieved a cleverly balanced composition in which the symmetry of the emphatic central vertical is broken by the overlapping profile.*

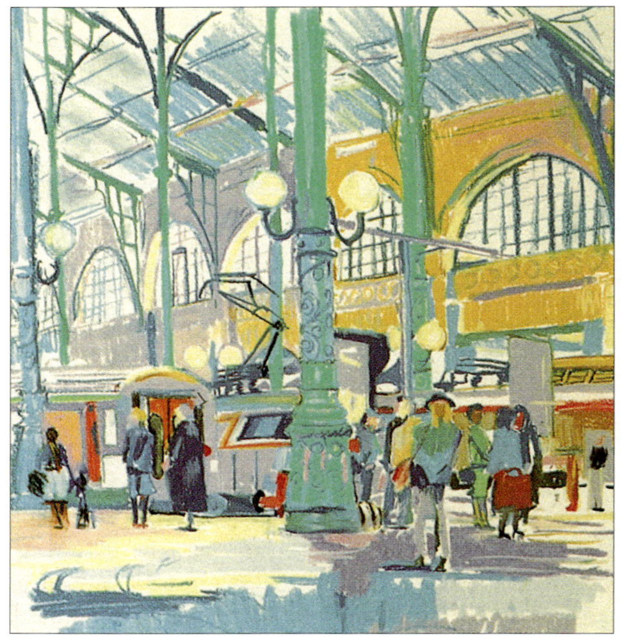

decisions—and it can be—break the subject down into simple shapes. Once you see how these work two-dimensionally, you can progress to selecting more detail and building up the composition gradually.

CROPPING

Until the mid-19th century, the conventions of composition required that the main interest in a picture was entirely contained within the picture rectangle. No vital element was cut off at the edges of a drawing or painting. The advent of photography brought

Above *Peter Graham's pastel drawing* Gard du Nord *has several verticals, giving it an upward direction. This is balanced by the arched windows and the figures on the platform.*

Below *In Pip Carpenter's mixed media drawing, the curving lines of the field take the eye rapidly to the background, but it is then led back by the intervening three-dimensional space.*

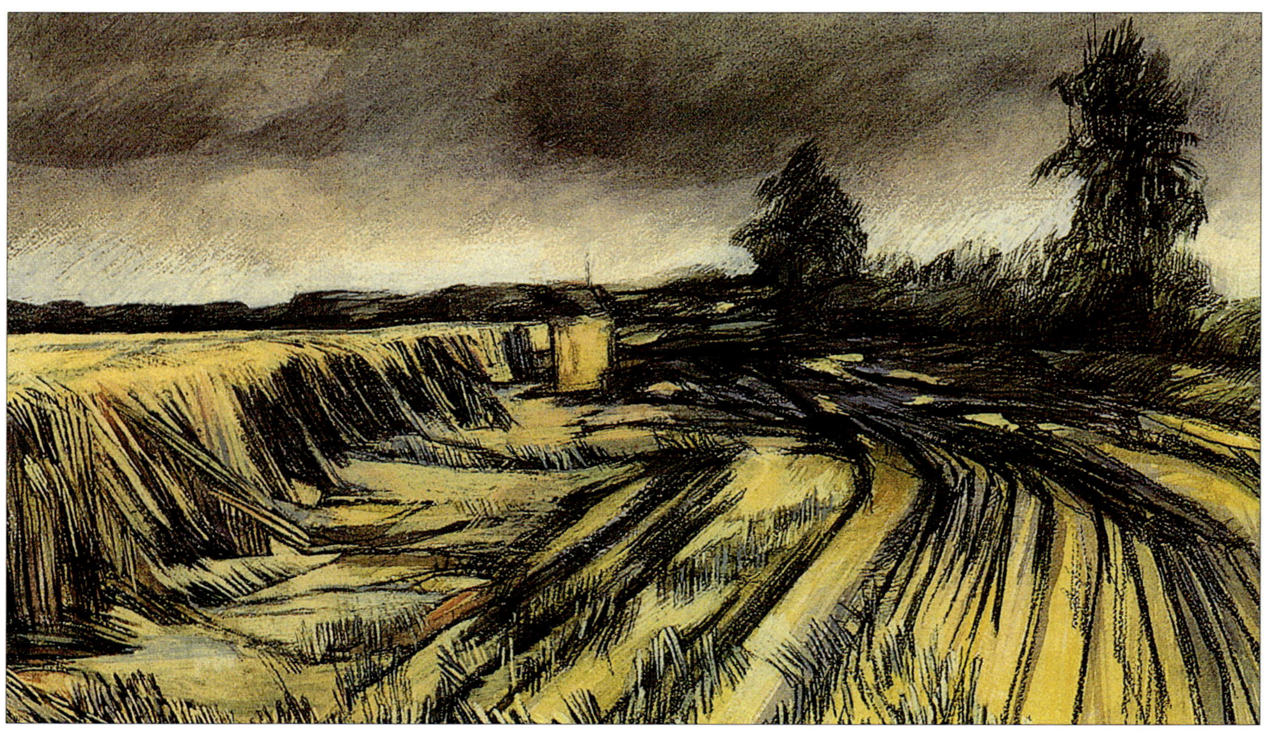

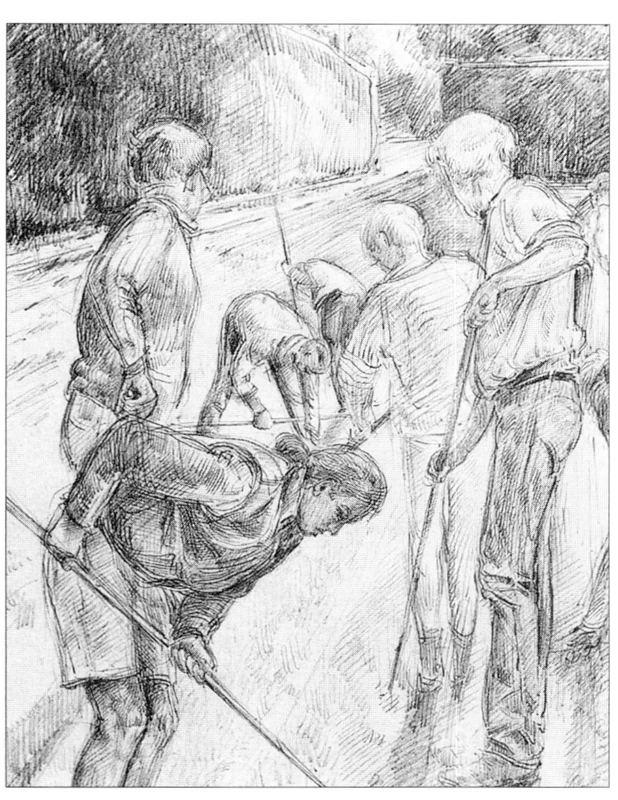

Right *Timothy Easton's pencil drawing* The Hoeing Team *takes the eye through a series of three-dimensional intervals between the working figures to the archway in the middle distance. This route is balanced by the road on the left which passes between verticals to the landscape in the background.*

about important changes in how composition was seen, and artists began to experiment with similar effects. Dramatic effects could be obtained by "cropping" a figure or object. Many artists also found that other photographic effects could be useful, for example, having part of a picture indistinct and out of focus, which could add to its sense of depth and drama.

Part of the process of selection is to decide where the outer edges of your drawing should be and how they should contain the subject. If you are cropping an object or figure, consider the way the edges of the drawing rectangle cuts across them; if the cropping is awkward the composition can look casual and unplanned.

OPEN-ENDED DRAWING

A drawing can be begun with no preconceived notion about either what it is to include or what its ultimate purpose will be. This open-ended approach to drawing is seen in its most obvious form in doodles and similar kinds of spontaneous drawings where the drawing is given a life of its own and allowed to develop as it will. Chance effects created in this kind of drawing may be exploited only to be discarded later if another

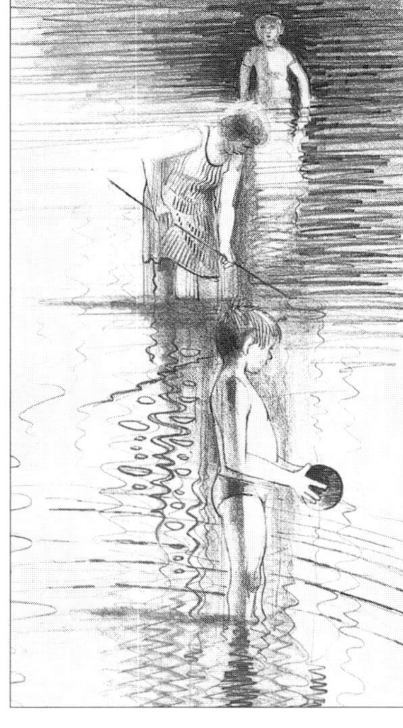

Right *Ray Mutimer has rejected anything that would detract from the composition of his pencil drawing. The figures create an interesting vertically, balanced by the swirling curves and horizontals of the water and the diagonals of the striped pattern on the middle figure's dress.*

accidental effect is preferred.

There are, however, many other open-ended ways in which drawings can be made from the visual world. If a subject excites you, you will be trying to identify the elusive features which create this excitement when you draw it. Or you may start to draw something which doesn't particularly appeal to you, searching for some arrangement of shapes and forms which will suddenly intrigue you.

Even if you haven't started to draw with the idea of enquiry at the forefront of your consciousness, you will often make discoveries when drawing. In trying to decide the best composition, you may discover aspects of the subject which are much more significant than those you had identified at first.

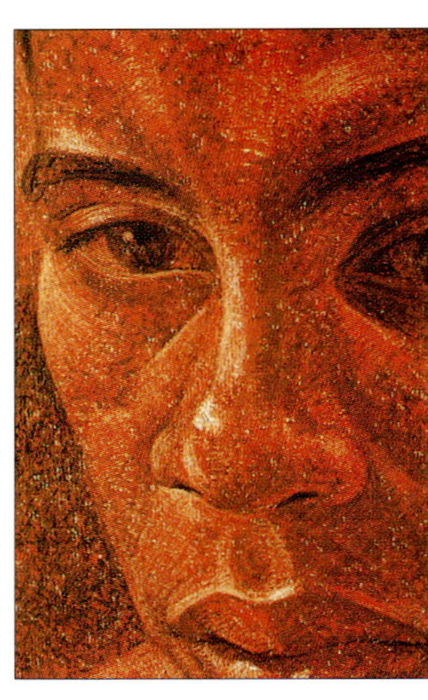

Right *The form of dramatic composition seen in Robert Geoghegan's pastel* Head Study *is more often associated with photography than with drawing.*

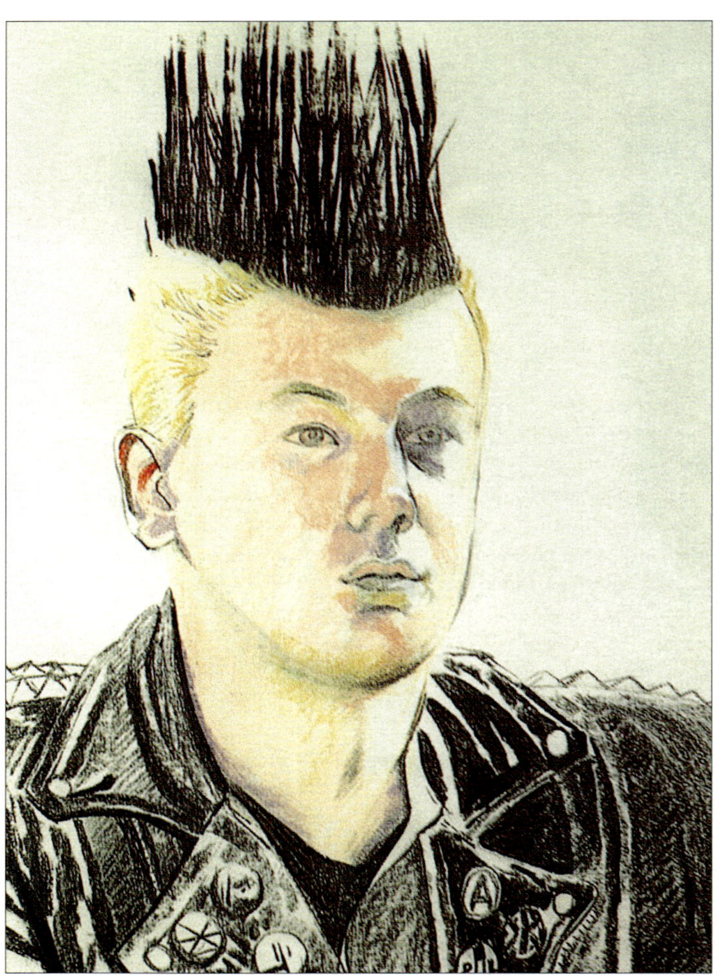

Left *The hairstyle and clothing were obviously the key elements here, so Rosalind Cuthbert has wisely left the background of her pastel drawing plain in order to emphasize both these elements, as also the delicate drawing of the face and features.*

DRAWING THE PARTICULAR

There are many drawings which give perfectly accurate descriptions of a scene or person but which tell you nothing more. A good drawing, however, should provide you with more than information about the subject; you should be able to see what it was that intrigued the artist, and what they felt about it.

When you draw you should avoid merely making a generalized statement and concentrate on the particular aspects of the subject which are important to you. These will often be things that you can't describe in words, and may even be something that you only recognize when you see it in your drawing. This search for the particular rather than the general is what will give your drawings the individuality which will make your work easily recognizable.

DISCOVERING A PERSONAL LANGUAGE

Usually the work of great artists is instantly recognizable. As well as having found important new things to say, they have also found new ways to say them. As you draw more and more, you will find that a particular style of drawing begins to develop. That's not to say that your drawings will become strikingly different, but that your work will acquire a distinctive personality. As the actual "handwriting" of your drawing develops, the way you use things will become more personal. To a large extent, this will come from greater eye, brain, and hand coordination that will come with practice.

As your work becomes more accomplished, however, there are some dangers to look out for. One is that your work becomes mannered, that is, the same shapes, forms, and effects appear frequently in your work without being related to the particular visual experience. Another danger is developing a superficial slickness which produces what at first glance look like reasonable drawings, but where all the shapes and forms look similar and generalized. The way to develop a personal language while guarding against mannerism and

OTHER ARTISTS TO STUDY

PAUL KLEE

(1879–1940) Klee produced some 5,000 drawings, probably the largest graphic output of any 20th-century artist, which he filed away in portfolios. One of the most imaginative and individual artists of the century, he believed that art does not reproduce visible things but that the artist makes things analagous to nature. "Now it is looking at me," he would say of a work in progress, and the titles of many of his drawings have been suggested by the works themselves. "My hand is wholly the instrument of some remote power," he wrote.

PABLO PICASSO

(1881–1973) Picasso is an essential study for anyone interested in drawing. It has been said of him that "No man has changed more radically the nature of art." He was not satisfied with the limited possibilities of the traditional mode of representation. Throughout his long career his drawings constantly searched for new means of expression. There are several series of drawings where a subject such as the bullfight or the artist and model are investigated in many different ways. Even when he was experimenting with extreme forms of non-representational painting, he frequently returned to making realistic drawings.

ARTISTS' SKETCHBOOKS

One of the best places to see drawing as a process of investigation and discovery is in sketchbooks. There have been exhibitions of Picasso's sketchbooks, and many museums have artists' sketchbooks on display. A number of publications have also been devoted to sketchbook drawings because this private and personal work best illustrates the artist's character, working methods, and reactions to the world.

slickness is to search for the elements of the subject which seem to you to make it unique. This could be described as discovering something not seen at a first glance—finding the extraordinary in the ordinary.

Because drawing is the most direct way of recording visual information, artists' drawings are often more revealing than their paintings, giving special insights into their thinking and approaches to the visual world. And the most revealing drawings are frequently those which have been produced quickly and spontaneously. When you draw outdoors, for example, you have to work at speed, and sometimes when you look at the drawings later you see things in them which

Below Landscape near Montmajour *by Vincent Van Gogh. Reed pen and sepia ink, with touches of black chalk. Van Gogh frequently made drawings of the subjects he painted, which—although they are investigations of the possibilities of subjects—appear to have been seen as ends in themselves.*

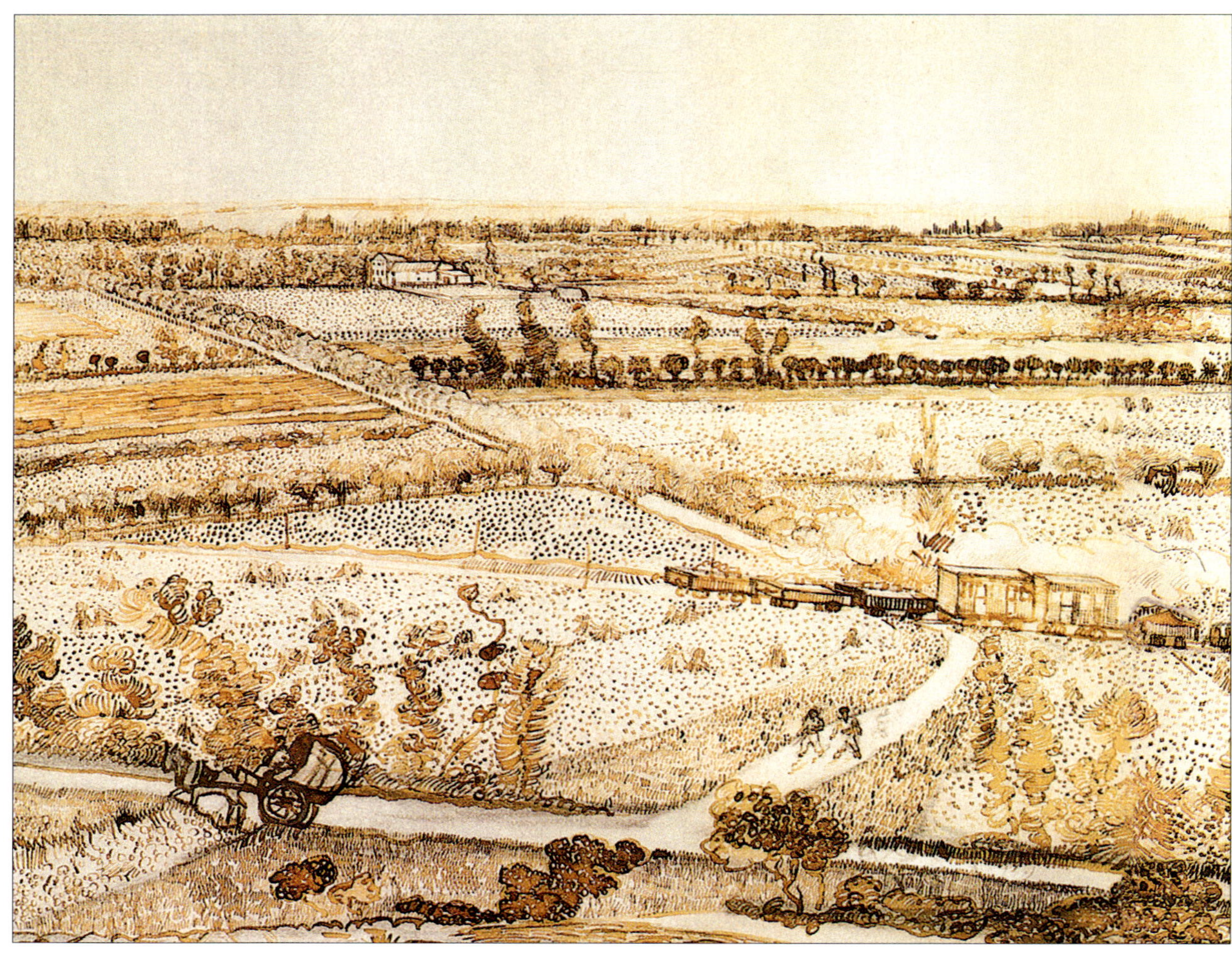

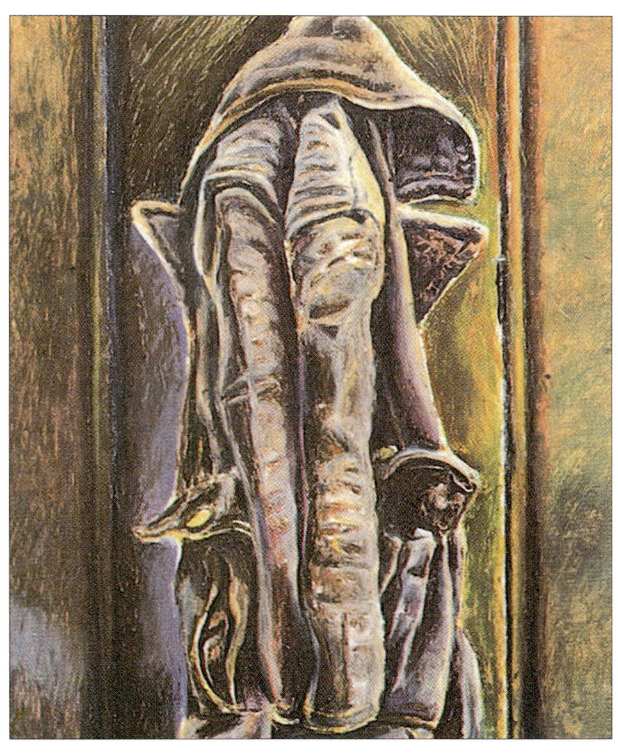

Left *Charcoal drawing by Peter Willock. While the play of light on the figure is an important part of this drawing, the artist's primary concern has been to explore the human figure as a series of planes and semi-geometric shapes linked to the surrounding objects.*

Below *An oil pastel by Paul Bartlett. A very ordinary subject has inspired a most dramatic drawing. The sleeves have been simplified into a contrasting pattern of light and dark to give a feel of the material.*

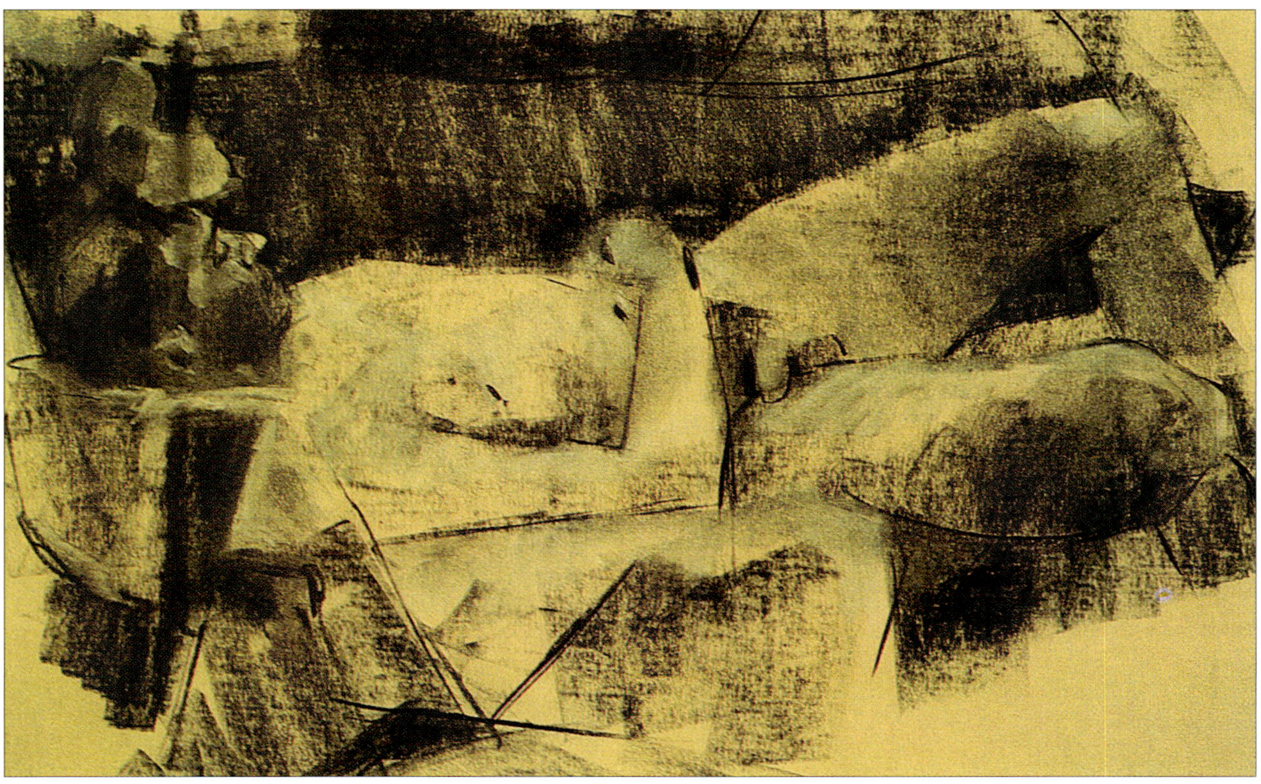

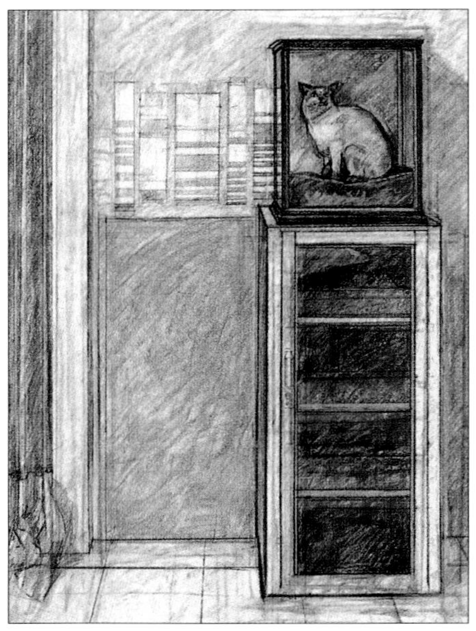

Left *Drawing in pencil, charcoal, and chalk by John Sprakes. The contrast between the areas of freely drawn tone and the precise lines in this drawing gives it an interesting tension. Depth is created by the use of perspective. The darkest lines and tones have been reserved for the cabinet topped by the cat in the glass case, which will be the central feature of Sprakes's painting.*

you don't remember and can't imagine having drawn. Drawing is not only a medium for making discoveries about the external visual world; it is also good at giving us insight into ourselves.

DRAWING AS INSPIRATION

Although it may seem a contradiction, drawing can be a means of discovering things to draw. If you are ever stuck for a drawing subject, the best advice is just to start drawing—anywhere and anything. The French painter Pierre Bonnard was a compulsive draftsman. He took a pencil and a scrap of paper everywhere he went, but he was particularly adept at discovering new subjects (or new things to say about old subjects) in his immediate surroundings. A catalog of the pictures he produced while living at one particular house records that he made seventy-four paintings of the dining room and twenty-one paintings of the bathroom. Many of these were developed from ideas which he had quickly drawn in his diary.

DRAWING DETAIL

There is no rule about how much detail a drawing should contain; it depends on the type of drawing and the artist's interests. Drawings which are not intended to be works in themselves but are done as a means of gathering information may be concerned only with a single aspect of the subject, such as tone or texture. But even when a drawing is the artist's complete statement it may not go into elaborate detail. A drawing of a figure

THE PROJECTS

PROJECT 1

Seeing through the Medium

To some extent the medium determines how you draw the subject; if you only had a fine pen you would be compelled to look for linear features. Choose a detailed subject, such as a bush with small leaves or a similar plant, and make some drawings using only ink and a brush not smaller than a No. 4. The medium will not describe the objects easily, so you will have to find a way of translating what you see to suit its characteristics.

PROJECT 2

An Object Hanging

In earlier lessons you have spent some time making things and figures stand properly in your drawings. Now see if you can discover how you can make objects hang so that they look heavy. The subject can be anything heavy which you can hang up, such as a full shopping bag.

OTHER ARTISTS TO STUDY

WILLIAM HOGARTH (1697–1764)

Hogarth was an excellent painter, particularly of portraits, but his fame, both in his lifetime and now, rests mainly on his masterly satirical engravings. He wrote, "My picture is my stage, and men and women my players, who by means of certain actions and gestures, are to exhibit a dumb show." His subjects—the first three were *Harlot's Progress, Rake'sm Progress,* and *Marriage a la Mode*—are full of information which is superbly organized. Each moral story is told in a series of pictures and as well as appreciating each picture as a whole, it is necessary to read them detail by detail. They contain fascinating and shrewd observations of people, places, and attitudes.

EDGAR DEGAS (1834–1917)

Degas had a traditional training in drawing and was a great admirer of the classical draftsman Ingres (1755–1814). He also embraced the ideas of Impressionism, and by taking the best from both worlds, he produced some of the most original and compelling drawings ever. From around 1873 onward he became interested in drawing and painting women at work, women dressing and bathing, dancers and cabaret artists. There are some monumental drawings, often in charcoal, of figures in repose with simple contours containing beautifully drawn details. The heads, hands, and feet, and the muscle and bone structures in these drawings are keenly observed and very subtly suggested.

seen against the light, for example, may contain little detail of the figure's features because they would detract from the main point of the drawing—a dark shape silhouetted against a light background. Deciding how much detail to include in a drawing is part of the important process of deciding what to include and what to ignore.

Detail isn't something with which to decorate drawings. If your drawing is to be highly detailed, the detail must serve a purpose. Sometimes, particularly in the 17th century, the amount of detail in a drawing or painting was an indication of the artist's virtuosity. Detail in drawings, however, can be used for other purposes. It can bring the attention of the viewer to particular parts of a drawing and provide a contrast with other areas of the drawing which are more simply treated. In a landscape, detail can be used to increase an illusion of space by describing the foreground more minutely than the background.

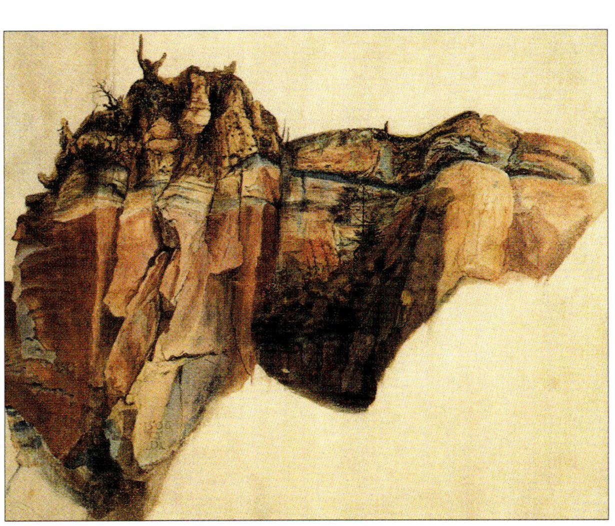

STATED OR IMPLIED DETAIL

But detail does not have to be drawn in this way; many drawings of the highest quality which at first glance look to be broad statements, turn

Left A Study of Rocks by Albrecht Durer *(1471–1528). This is a brush drawing in watercolor. It is difficult to think of anyone in the history of art who was able to cram more information into such a small pictorial area. This not withstanding, the initial impact is made by the dramatic and unusual shape of the rock.*

out on closer examination to be quite detailed. Edgar Degas is an excellent example of an artist who is a master of this kind of understatement. His figure drawings in charcoal and pastel often give an impression of being a brilliant translation of the main features of a particular pose, and it is only when you have looked at them for some time that you realize how detailed they actually are. The bone structure, for example, at the wrists, knees, and ankles—important points of articulation which are often disregarded in drawings—are beautifully suggested, but Degas doesn't allow detail to interfere with what he considers the most important features of the pose.

SCALE AND DETAIL

In drawing detail, one of the things you have to be constantly aware of is that it is easy to get it completely out of scale. This is sometimes due to a common problem which I have already mentioned: when we focus our attention on

Below The Lake of Geneva *by Joseph Mallord William Turner. (1775–1851). Turner's visual memory was exceptional; he claimed to be able to remember the exact look of the sky during a storm in the Alps long after he had seen it. An eye-witness account from a copassenger in England records how Turner thrust his head out of the open window of a stationary train and kept it there for several minutes in a howling gale. This was to fix in his memory a scene which he had later recreated in his famous painting* Rain, Steam and Speed.

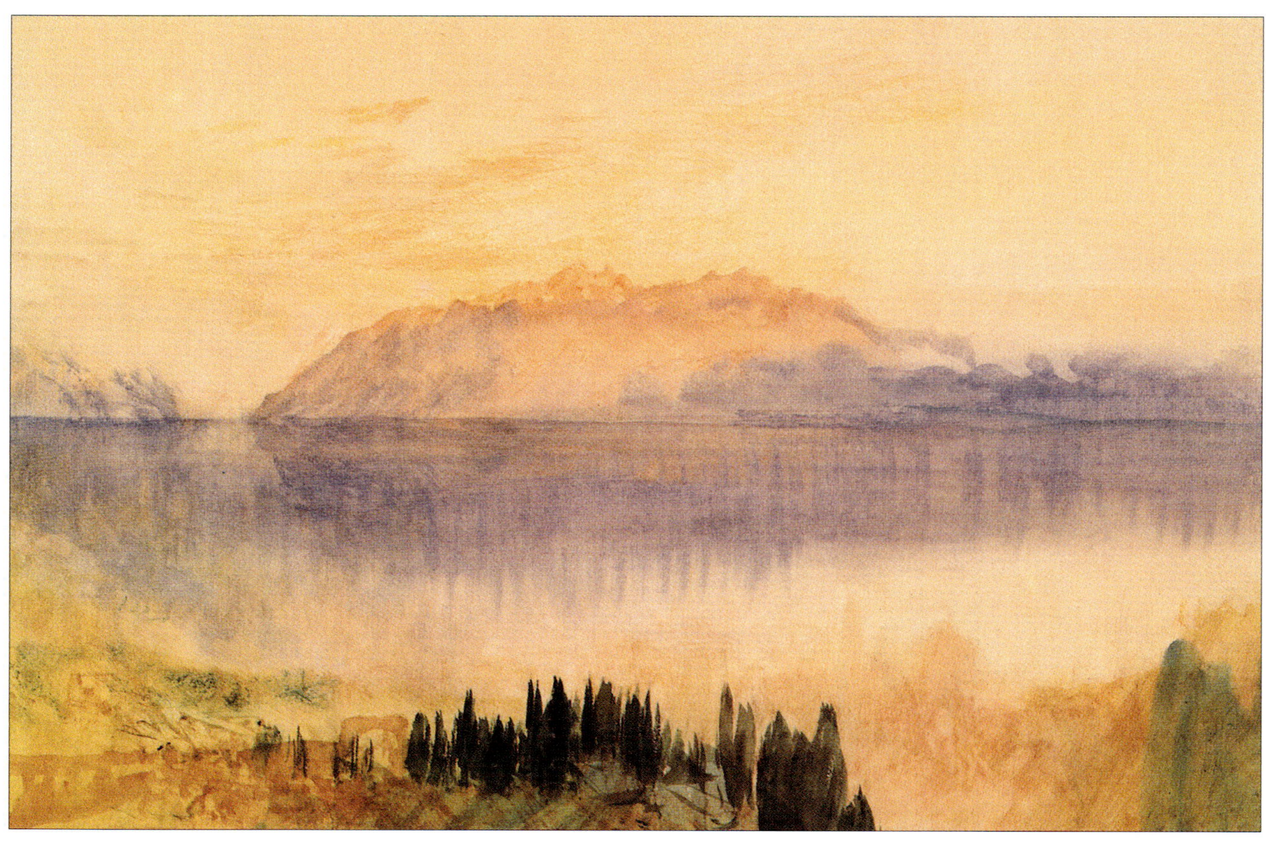

OTHER ARTISTS TO STUDY

PAUL GAUGUIN
(1848–1903) Gauguin was another advocate of working from memory. He wrote, "It's good for young artists to have a model, but they should draw a curtain across it while painting… then the work will be your own." The filtering of the visual world through memory was very important to him, and he advised against copying nature. "Art is an abstraction: draw it out of nature while dreaming before it and think more of the creation."

JAMES ABBOTT McNEILL WHISTLER
(1834–1903) Whistler, an American who studied painting in Paris and lived mainly in England, is renowned for his masterly etchings as well as his paintings. As a friend of Lecoq's student Fantin Latour, he had imbibed the idea of working from memory, and described his famous Nocturne series of paintings as "painted from my mind and thought." He stressed that what mattered was not the subject, but the way in which it was translated. His most famous—and enormously popular—painting is a portrait of his mother entitled *Arrangement in Gray and Black*.

WALTER RICHARD SICKERT (1860–1942)
Sickert was influenced by Whistler and worked in a similar way, omitting unnecessary detail. Many of his subjects were scenes at the theater and incidents in the shabbier parts of town. He never painted on the spot, relying on memory, drawings, and sometimes newspaper photographs and picture postcards. He made many drawings, sometimes several slightly different versions of the same subject.

one aspect of a drawing, we tend to lose sight of the whole. The bricks or stones in a wall or building are often drawn much too large, particularly if they are in the foreground, which immediately destroys the credibility of the structure. And if an object is some distance from you, say a tree in the middle distance, and you draw individual leaves too large, you will also lose the sense of space.

Making a detailed drawing requires, above all, patience. You must be sure that the basic shapes and the main features of your drawing are right before you focus in on details. Generally, this kind of drawing is an additive process, with visual information being added until you know that you have created the statement you require.

DRAWING FROM MEMORY

To some extent, all drawing is memory drawing because it is impossible to look at the subject and the drawing at the same time. When you are drawing from objects, the visual information only has to be carried in your memory for a second or two, but it is surprising what a difference it makes if this time is a fraction of a second longer.

Many people feel they couldn't draw anything without having it in front of them, but visual memory can be improved by training yourself to memorize shapes, tones, and colors. This is useful, as drawing from memory is sometimes the only means by which you can recreate a subject. When you draw a moving figure or animal, you can only do so by remembering them in one particular position. If your memory is good enough, you will also be able to add things to a drawing

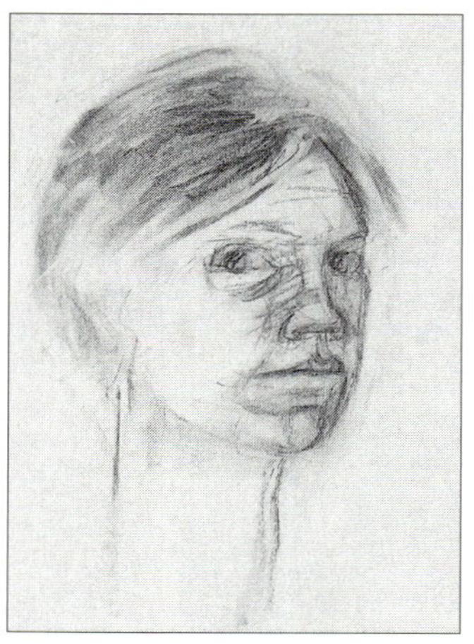

Left *A self-portrait makes a good starting point for an exercise in memory drawing. This drawing is done in charcoal by Karen Raney. Try to work on form rather than concentrating on the features. Here, the artist began by establishing the forms and planes of the face. The drawing works as a three-dimensional structure as well as being a reasonable likeness.*

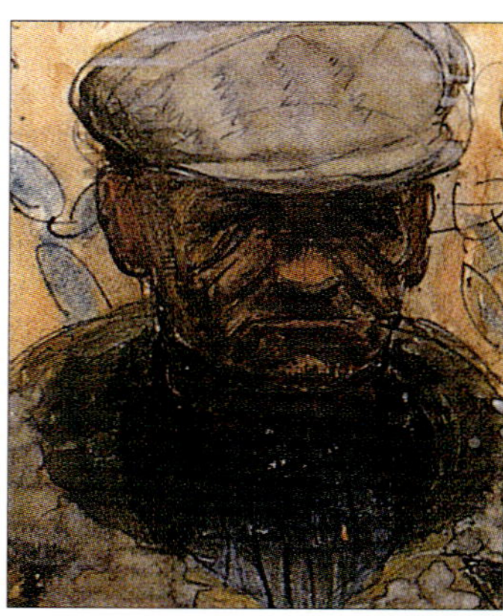

Right *This powerful and expressive drawing,* Durham Miner *executed in pen and gouache by Stephen Crowther, is a detail of a sketchbook study done from memory. The original drawing showed more of the man's body and the surroundings, but the artist later decided to isolate the head only and exhibit the drawing in this form.*

THE PROJECTS

PROJECT 1

Drawing by Touch

This is not strictly memory drawing but it is an interesting variant. Take several objects which are small and hard, perhaps some pebbles, a shoe horn and a pair of scissors, place them on a table and look at them for about three minutes. Try to fix in your mind their positions on the table and their relationship to each other. Then put the objects in a bag made of some kind of thin non-transparent material. Make a drawing of the group of objects as you remember them but feeling them through the bag from time to time, so that you can remind yourself of their appearance without actually looking at them.

PROJECT 2

A Head of Memory

Get someone to pose for you for not more than five minutes, and try to fix their features and characteristics in your mind—the shape of their head, the form of their nose, their particular kind of chin, and lips. Then make the most detailed drawing you can from memory. Try to avoid it looking like a police identikit picture, where each feature looks as if it has been remembered separately. Close your eyes from time to time and see the head you are drawing in your mind's eye.

that are not actually there.

Setting out to memorize something so that you can draw from it demands a degree of conscious analysis. If you spend five minutes looking at an object which you intend to draw later, you will not only have to retain a number of images in your mind but also to organize them into categories of relative importance. When you start to draw, you will find that although the fact that the object is not in front of you has the advantage of curbing your urge to copy irrelevant details, it can also make it very difficult to recapture the precise forms or tonal relationships.

A 19TH-CENTURY DEBATE

The importance of the visual memory to artists was much debated in the middle of the 19th century. In Paris, which was then the center of the art world, a tradition of academic drawing had developed, embodying a system of learning and a conventional visual language. Most drawing was from the figure, but first, students had to learn a technique of finely gradated shading by making drawings of plaster casts of Classical statuary. The Classical proportions and simplifications learned from this process was then in effect superimposed on the living models drawn in the studios.

The rigid conservatism of the bastion of academicism, The Ecole des Beaux-Arts in Paris, was challenged by the appointment of Horace Lecoq de Boisbaudran as Director of the Ecole Royale et Speciale de Dessin. Lecoq described drawing as "looking at the object with eyes, and retaining its image in the memory whilst drawing it with the hand." He set out to train the memory, since he believed that left to itself it was inclined to store irrelevant information. His memory-training exercises progressed from simple objects to moving figures, working outdoors as well as in the studio, and he stressed that the flexibility of his teaching encouraged invention.

Henri Fantin-Latour, best known now for

Below The Deluge, with Neptune and the Gods of the Winds *by Leonardo Da Vinci (1452–1519). The spiral and other techniques used here were later used by many artists. The drawing has almost certainly been made from imagination, but it is no doubt based on Leonardo's personal experience.*

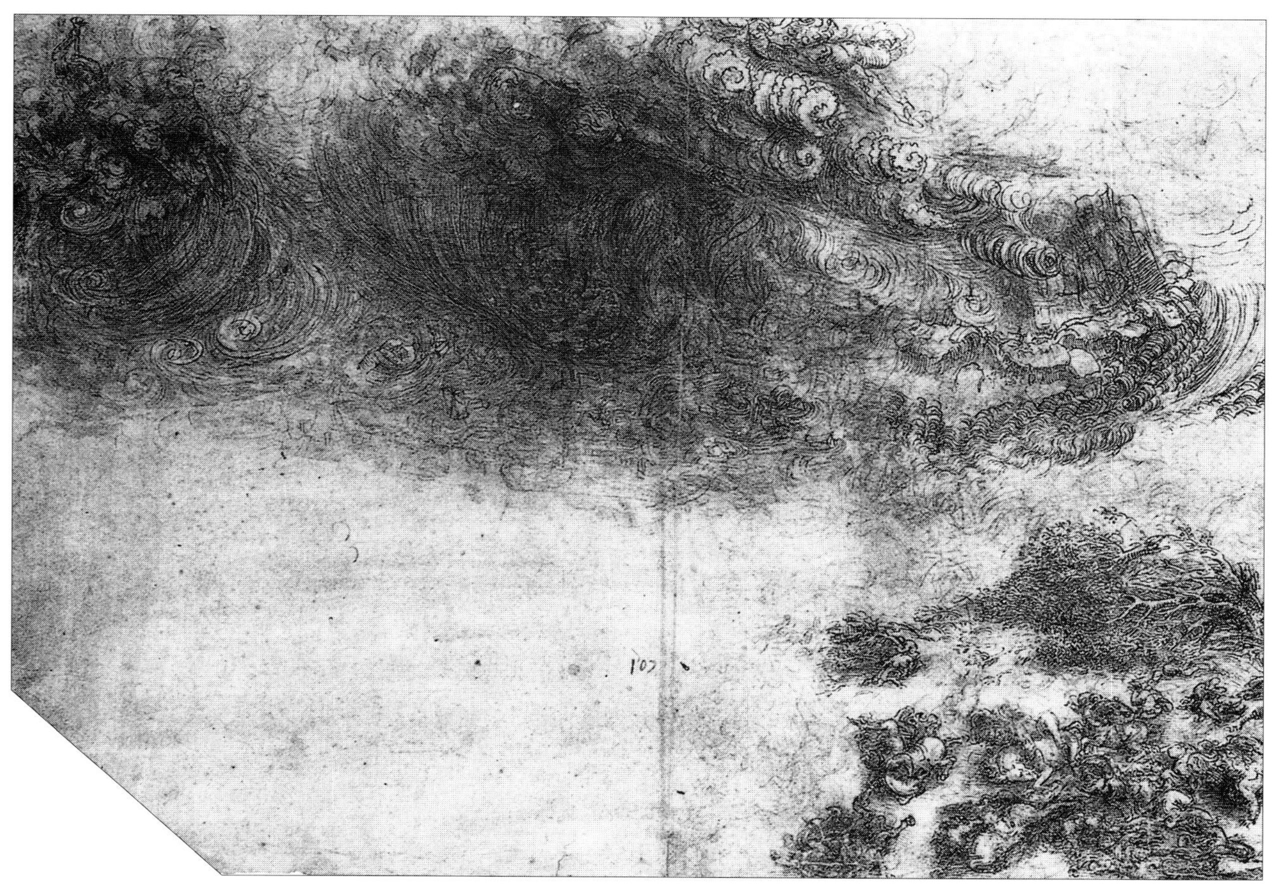

his exquisite still-life paintings, was a student of Lecoq, and because Fantin-Latour was friendly with most of the progressive artists of his day, Lecoq's ideas on the importance of the memory filtered into Impressionist circles. To quote Pissarro, "The observations you make from memory will have far more power and originality than those you owe to direct contact with nature. The drawing will have art—it will be your own."

AIDS TO MEMORY

Theoretically Pissarro's advice may be sound, but it probably needs the thorough training in memory drawing which Lecoq provided to make it bear fruit. In practice, when most people draw from memory the drawings are not so much original as vague and generalized. However, memory will help you if you combine it with rapid note-making. These may be scribbles on the back of an envelope, or the main shapes of the subject quickly drawn in a sketchbook with some accompanying written notes. Many artists develop their own "drawing shorthand"—visual notes which might mean little or nothing to anyone else, but to the originator contain vital information. Also, the simple act of drawing helps to commit a scene to memory in a way that simply looking does not.

DRAWING MOVEMENT

There have always been drawings made from moving objects, in fact the earliest drawings we know, made some 15,000 years ago, are cave drawings of moving animals. The aim in most drawings of moving objects, however, has been to make a static record of them, that is, "freezing" the movement at one moment in time rather than showing them in motion. Often even this has proved extremely difficult as our eyes find it impossible to seize and preserve a single point in a complex movement, particularly if it is a rapid one.

The way the legs of a galloping horse move was not identified until the development of photography; previously

OTHER ARTISTS TO STUDY

AUGUSTE RODIN (1840–1917)

Rodin, the most celebrated sculptor of the 19th century, opposed the academic tradition in sculpture in much the same way as the Impressionists did in painting. Both he and painters like Delacroix and Degas became increasingly interested in drawing a moving figure, and his freely drawn, multiple-contour drawings of nudes, often made in line and wash, give a marvellous sense of movement and energy.

HONORE DAUMIER (1808–1879)

The interest of the Impressionists in drawing moving figures had been prefigured by Daumier, painter and cartoonist, who made over 4,000 drawings for journals, many of them bitter satires. His free handling of line and tone made one critic of his time write that he "transformed muscles into rags hanging from a framework of bones." He was, however, adept at describing movement; his lines coming together to create a vivid impression of motion.

OTHER ARTISTS TO STUDY

MARY CASSATT (1844–1926)
Cassatt, an American who settled in Paris and became a friend of Manet and Degas, exhibited at the Impressionist Exhibitions between 1879 and 1886. She made some beautiful drawings and paintings of domestic scenes which are often informal portraits. Children, like animals, are subjects which often produce very sentimental drawings, but Cassatt's drawings of mothers with babies are tender without ever descending to trite sentimentality.

SIR STANLEY SPENCER (1891–1959)
Many of Spencer's drawings and paintings could be called informal portraits; he incorporated recognizable people into his religious paintings. He also produced formal portraits which are carefully observed and skillfully simplified, and he made many "portraits" of landscapes and houses around Cookham in Berkshire, where he lived for most of his life. His drawings, which combine a strong sense of pattern with a stylized representation of three-dimensional form, show an eye for unusual detail and great technical certainty.

DAVID HOCKNEY (b.1937)
In the 1970s, at a time when abstract painting and conceptual art were regarded by the art establishment as the only forms worth pursuing, Hockney was one of a small number of artists who swam against this powerful current and promoted figurative art. He did try his hand at abstract art, but found it too barren. Hockney is an excellent draughtsman, and many of his most brilliant works are spontaneous informal portraits of his friends. There are also more formal portraits, including drawings of his parents and portraits of people and buildings, which are produced by ingenious use of photography. Although Hockney has always denied being a pop artist, this is how he is perceived by many.

artists had drawn horses in movement with their legs in completely inaccurate positions. Sequences of photographs like those made by Eadweard Muybridge in the 1870s not only showed how a horse's legs moved as it trotted, cantered, or galloped, they also demonstrated how a sequence of pictures showing an object gradually moving from one place to another could give an impression of movement.

LINE AND MOVEMENT

There are a variety of ways in which movement is depicted in drawing. Some of these can be seen most clearly in the graphic conventions used in strip cartoons. A rapidly moving figure is often shown followed by "movement lines." Our eyes readily follow

Below *Note the subtle and delicate modeling around the mouth, nose, and eyes.*

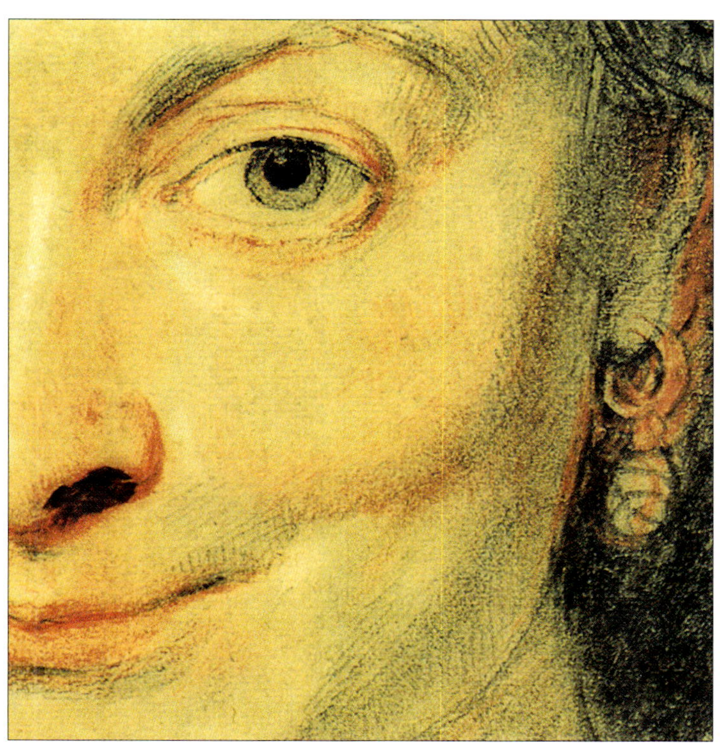

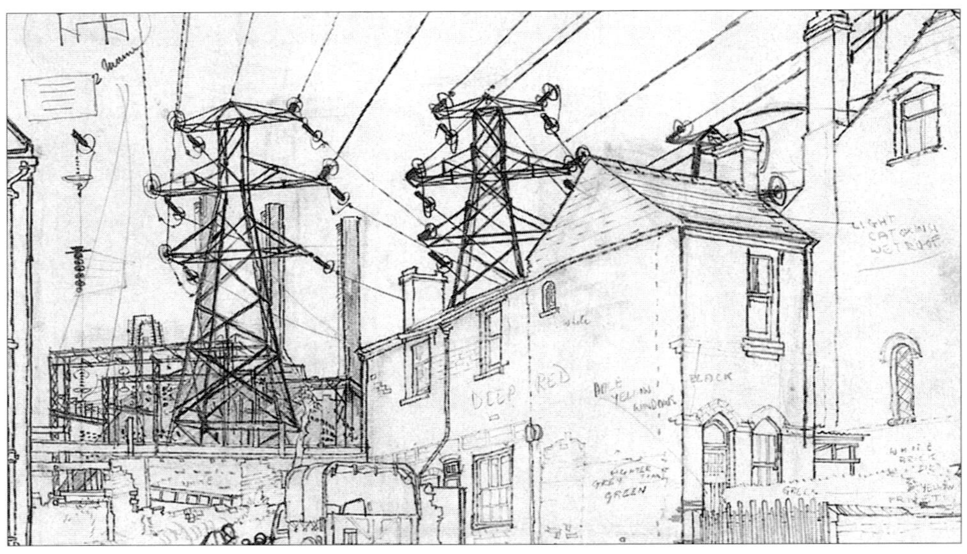

Right *In* Near Stoke on Trent *by Christopher Chamberlain, different qualities of line have been skillfully used to convey the textures of paving stones and the hard, dark structures of the pylons. The artist has seized on the significant features of what to some would seem a mundane subject. This drawing, made as a reference for a painting, incorporates some notes on color.*

strong linear directions, and this can give a line the attribute of movement.

The way the line is used is of the utmost importance. One kind of movement may be best described with bold, vigorous pen strokes, or fluid brush drawing, while another can be most effectively recreated with swirling lines made with a pencil using free sweeps of the hand. Generally some realism has to be sacrificed to create an illusion of movement in drawing. The energy which comes from sweeping strokes of the pen, pencil or other drawing medium is much more important in generating a feeling of movement than the realistic description of detail.

CHANGING THE VIEWPOINT

So far I have assumed the artist would be in a fixed position and the object moving. A sense of movement of a different kind can be created when the artist moves, drawing a sequence of different views of the subject. If these drawings are drawn (or later arranged) side by side they will give a fairly strong sense

Left *In* Frigiliana *by Joan Elliot Bates, the artist has produced a convincing likeness of a small town nestling between hills. Although simplified, all the features of the town and its surroundings are included, and there is a distinct "sense of place."*

of the passage of time and can provide an accumulative experience of an object.

As in some Cubist drawings, drawings from different viewpoints can be superimposed so that you have two or more views in the same drawing.

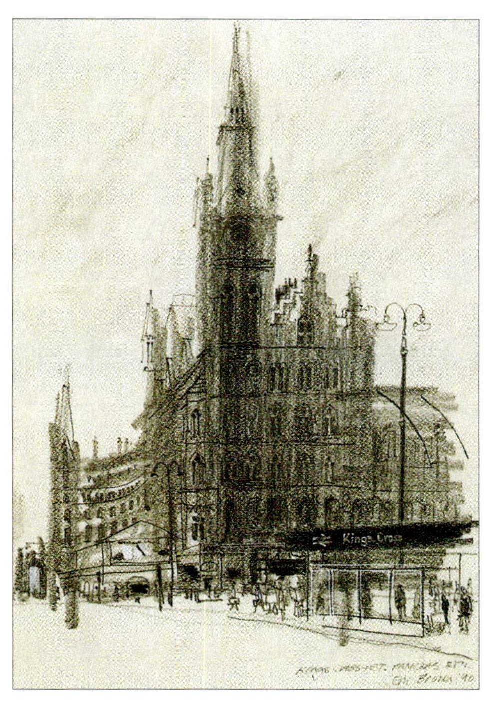

Right *The distinctive, dark silhouette and towering size of this famous London landmark, St Pancras station, make it instantly recognizable. Although not a detailed architectural drawing, it works perfectly as a "portrait" because all the important features are included, and the proportions are accurate.*

ABSTRACTION THROUGH DRAWING

Abstract art is based on the belief that shapes, forms, and colors have intrinsic aesthetic values and thus don't necessarily have to relate to a real subject. Some 20th-century artists have found drawing and painting what they see too restricting. They have looked to music and seen that it can exist as an art form capable of communicating in all kinds of ways without imitating natural sounds. Why then, they have asked, should art not also be able to exist in a similar way?

This idea is not new. As long ago as the 4th century BC the Greek philosopher Plato had seen the artistic potential of

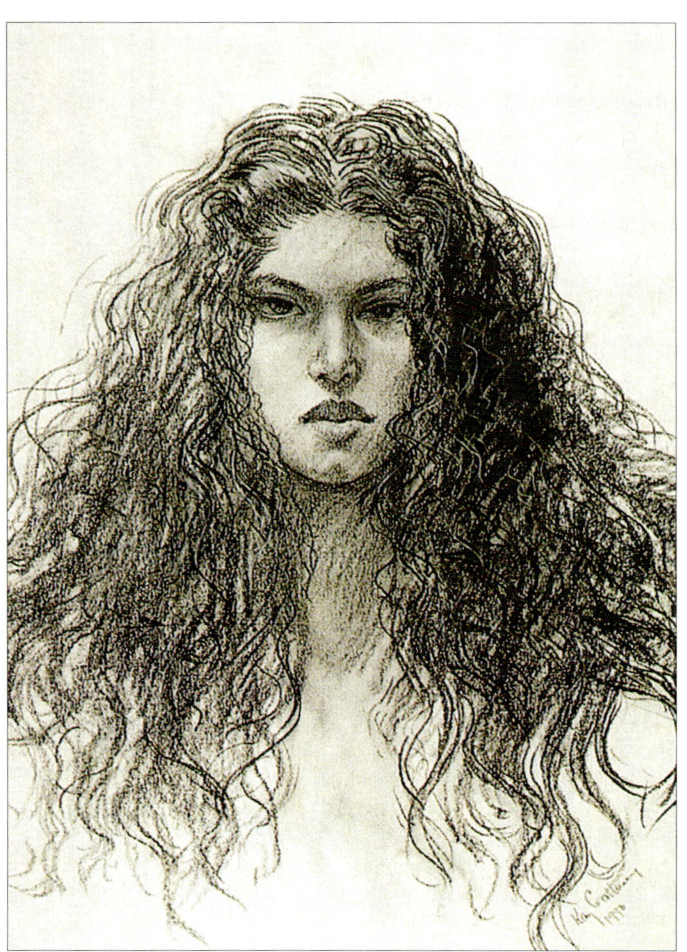

Left *The dominant feature of this drawing is the flowing hair, drawn in long, curling lines, but careful attention has been given to the features also. The eyes and mouth have been drawn in considerable detail, and shadows and reflected light used to model the distinctive forms of nose and chin. This drawing has been executed in black pastel by Kay Gallwey.*

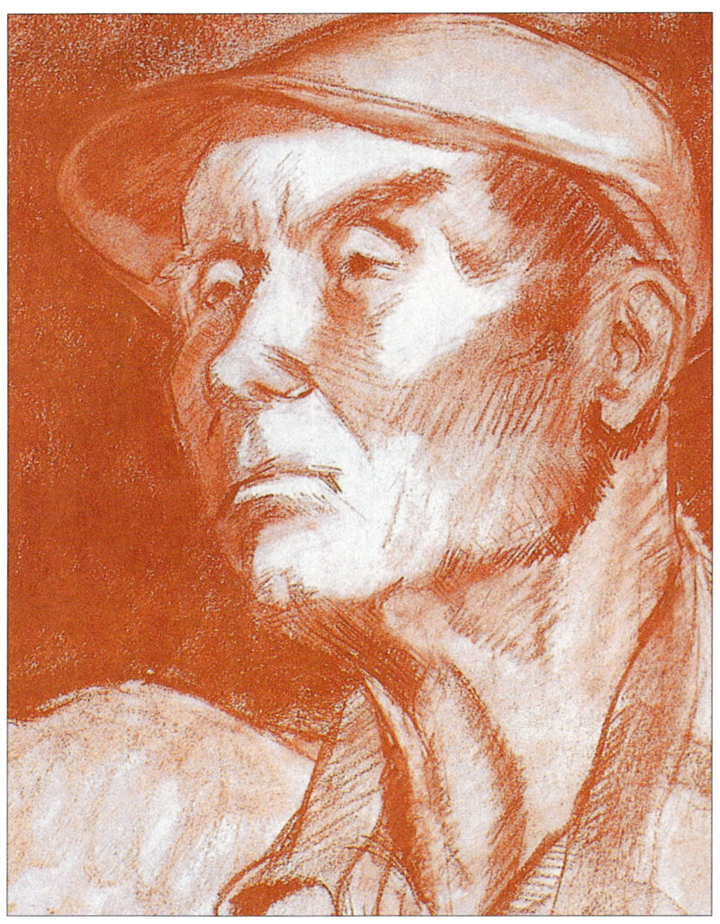

Above *Conté crayon has been used in this lively drawing, which conveys atmosphere as well as describing the features, the head has been simplified into two main tones with a third and darker tone for the background.*

Abstraction takes from a subject those shapes, forms, and colors that have the greatest pictorial significance. When you are abstracting from nature, you don't have to worry about whether your drawing looks realistic; indeed you can select and exaggerate shapes, forms, and colors until the subject is completely unrecognizable. Most people find it difficult to draw anything without it creating an illusion of reality, so you may find it easier to work from a drawing you have made previously. Make another drawing from the first one, extracting the important shapes, abstract shapes and forms. He wrote, "I do not now intend with 'beauty of shapes' what most people would expect, such as that of living creatures… but straight lines and curves and the surfaces of solid forms produced out of these by lathes and rulers and squares… These things are not beautiful relatively like other things, but naturally and absolutely."

THE PROJECTS

PROJECT 1

Portait in a Setting

Although a likeness depends primarily on selecting those particular features which seem to be unique to the sitter, a good portrait should also say something about their character. You can often give an extra dimension to a portrait by hinting at the person's occupation or interests, and placing the sitter in an appropriate setting. A gardener might be drawn with her garden or greenhouse as a background, for instance, or a writer drawn in a booklined study. Make a drawing which is a likeness and describes as much as possible about the sitter's personality.

PROJECT 2

A Particular Place

Choose as your subject a building or some scene which you feel you can draw like a portrait—your own house, or a single tree in a park. Remember that the success of the "portrait" will depend on selection, not on merely trying to draw as much detail as possible. As you draw, try to discover its most telling features and be prepared to emphasize or even exaggerate them so that the subject is recognizable as one particular house or tree.

forms, textures, and tones.

If you work directly from a subject, start by blocking in the main shapes with tone or color and develop your drawing by selecting and exaggerating the shapes, forms, and colors which you see as significant. You may need to turn away from the subject periodically and develop the drawing independently, as otherwise you may find it impossible to prevent yourself from describing it realistically.

A CONCEPTUAL THING

Because line drawing is so familiar to us and using lines seems such a natural way to draw,

Below Beach in Cornwall *by Victor Pasmore (b.1908). Pasmore developed a Basic Design course based on abstract principles of design. In his transitional stage from realism to abstraction, Pasmore made many drawings like the one here, which uses only line; the clouds and rocks are translated into interlocking shapes with the sea wedged between. A spiral motif began to be introduced into his drawings as a translation of movement, and it appears in a rudimentary form in the sea in this drawing. It is interesting to note that Leonardo had used a spiral in his deluge drawings and Turner in his sea pictures.*

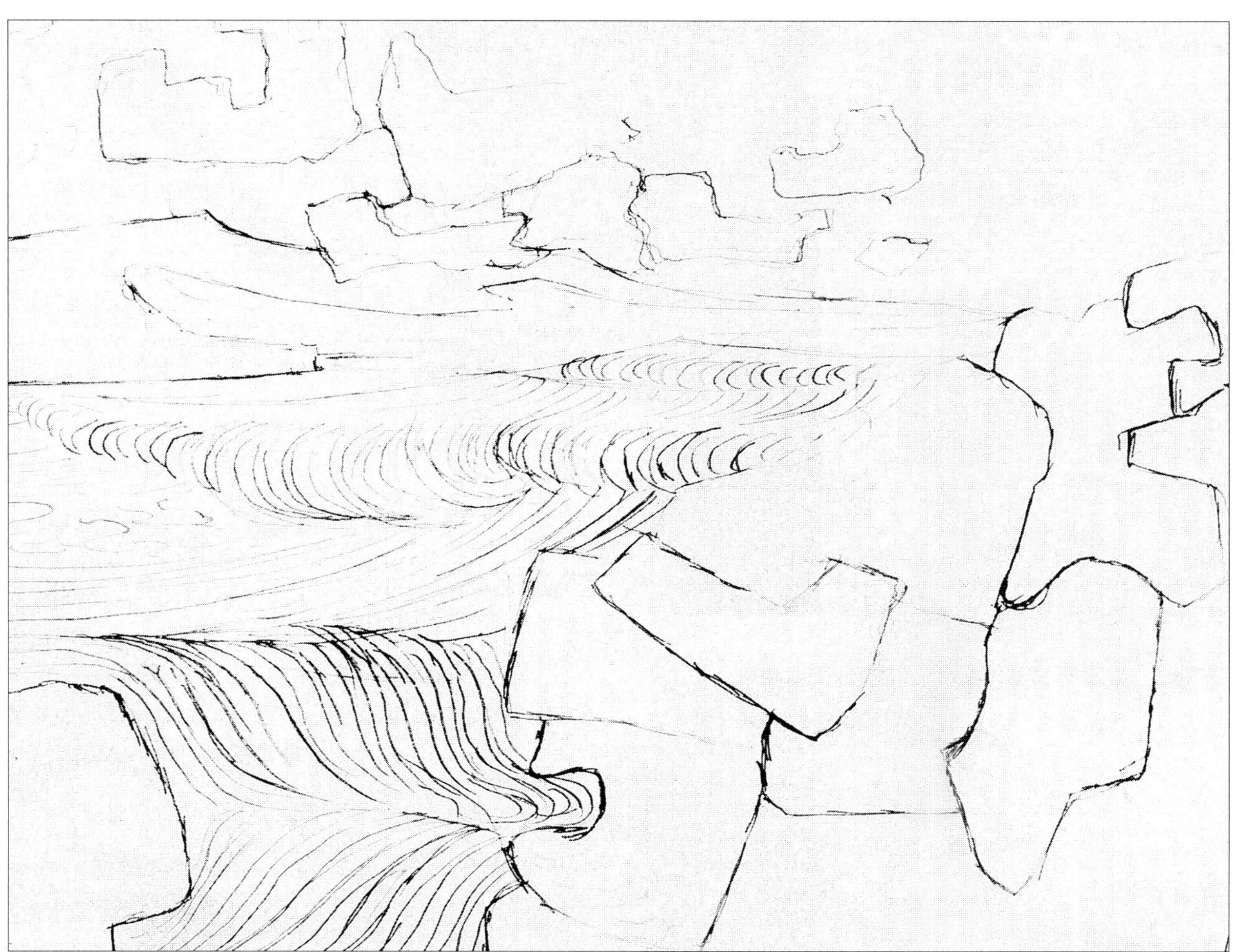

it comes perhaps as a surprise to realize how conceptual line drawing is. There are no lines in nature. The line is used as a means of describing where one object stops and another starts. Blake wrote, "Nature has no outline, but imagination has."

Below Woman Seated in a Garden *by Henri De Toulouse-Lautrec. Lautrec drew and painted scenes from the Paris dance halls, cafes and brothels, the cabarets, and the circus, and many prostitutes, nude or partially dressed. He depicted them while washing or dressing, just as Degas painted them, or waiting for clients. He hated posed models, and prostitutes provided him with the informal poses he needed.*

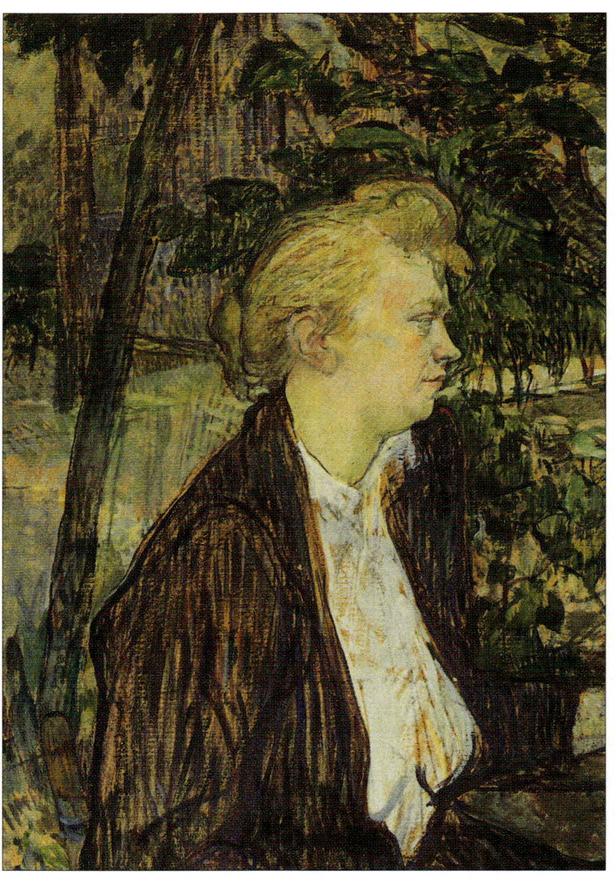

THE PROJECTS

PROJECT 1

Abstraction from Still life

A good place to start making abstract drawings is with still-life subjects, as the Cubists generally did. You may like (as they did) to use bottles, musical instruments, and other objects with clearly defined shapes.

PROJECT 2

A Flat Expanse

The aim in this abstraction is to make a drawing which is concerned with pattern and has very shallow depth. Find a flat vertical area, such as an old wall, with stains, perhaps moss, cracks, and general signs of wear, and make as exciting a drawing as you can, treating it as an intricate abstract design.

PROJECT 3

A Tree or a Hedge

In this project the idea is to make an abstraction from a single natural form. There are some fascinating drawings and paintings of thorn hedges and other natural forms by Graham Sutherland (1903–1980) that you might like to look at before you start. The silhouettes, the textures, the intertwining shapes of branches and leaves are all possibilities for abstraction.

DRAWING THROUGH PAINTING

There is a widely held belief that in order to paint you must first learn to draw. This view has its origins in the academies of the 19th century, where students only graduated to painting after completing a rigorous course in academic drawing. Even at that time, however, there were those who questioned the validity of this approach. Some of the Impressionists rebelled against the academic dogma, and Paul Gauguin, who prided himself on being

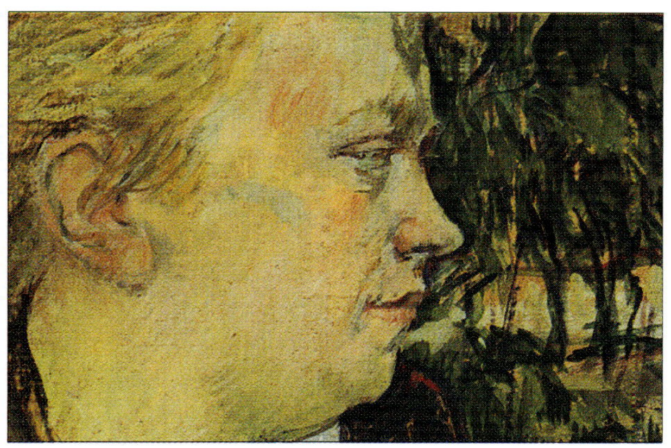

"untouched by the putrid kiss" of academic education, said, "One learns to draw and afterward to paint, which amounts to saying that one begins to paint by coloring in a ready made contour, rather like painting a statue." John Ruskin, the most influential British art critic of the 19th century as well as an artist and meticulous draftsman, pointed out more than a century ago that "while we moderns have always learned, or tried to learn, to paint, the ancients learned to draw by painting." By "ancients" Ruskin meant the artists of the Renaissance. He went on to observe that you never saw a childish or feeble drawing by any of the "ancients" because they had only turned to drawing when they were already accomplished painters.

DRAWING WITH PAINT

We automatically think of drawing as lines and of painting as areas of paint. But

OTHER ARTISTS TO STUDY

ALBERTO GIACOMETTI (1901–1966)

Sculptor, painter, and poet, Giacometti trained in Italy and France and is best known for his sculptures of extremely tall, thin, single standing figures. As a painter, his subjects were usually interiors, sometimes empty and sometimes with a single figure. The color range he used was deliberately limited almost to monochrome and the paintings, carried out in thin lines made with a brush, look very much like drawings, but with a peculiar atmosphere and intensity. Working with great concentration, Giacometti found that the more he stared at his subject the less it seemed to remain static, and it was this that accounted for the almost frenzied attempts to fix the positions of the objects by stating and restating lines. He was often in despair as he found it impossible to record his visual sensations.

CLAUDE MONET (1840–1926)

Monet's early works include some most accomplished drawings and brilliant caricatures—he had a facility for obtaining a likeness. It is interesting that many of his later drawings were made from paintings rather than for them. Most of his paintings were made without elaborate preliminary drawings, and in his mature years his drawings were usually rapid sketchbook studies of possible subjects to paint, where he often tried out different viewpoints. These give an impression of impatience, as if he couldn't wait to start the painting itself. From the 1880s the paintings became the drawings, and there was little, if any, preliminary drawing on the canvas. His paintings, particularly the last large Nympheas (waterlilies) pictures, were really drawings on a grand scale, arrangements of intertwining colored lines drawn with a brush.

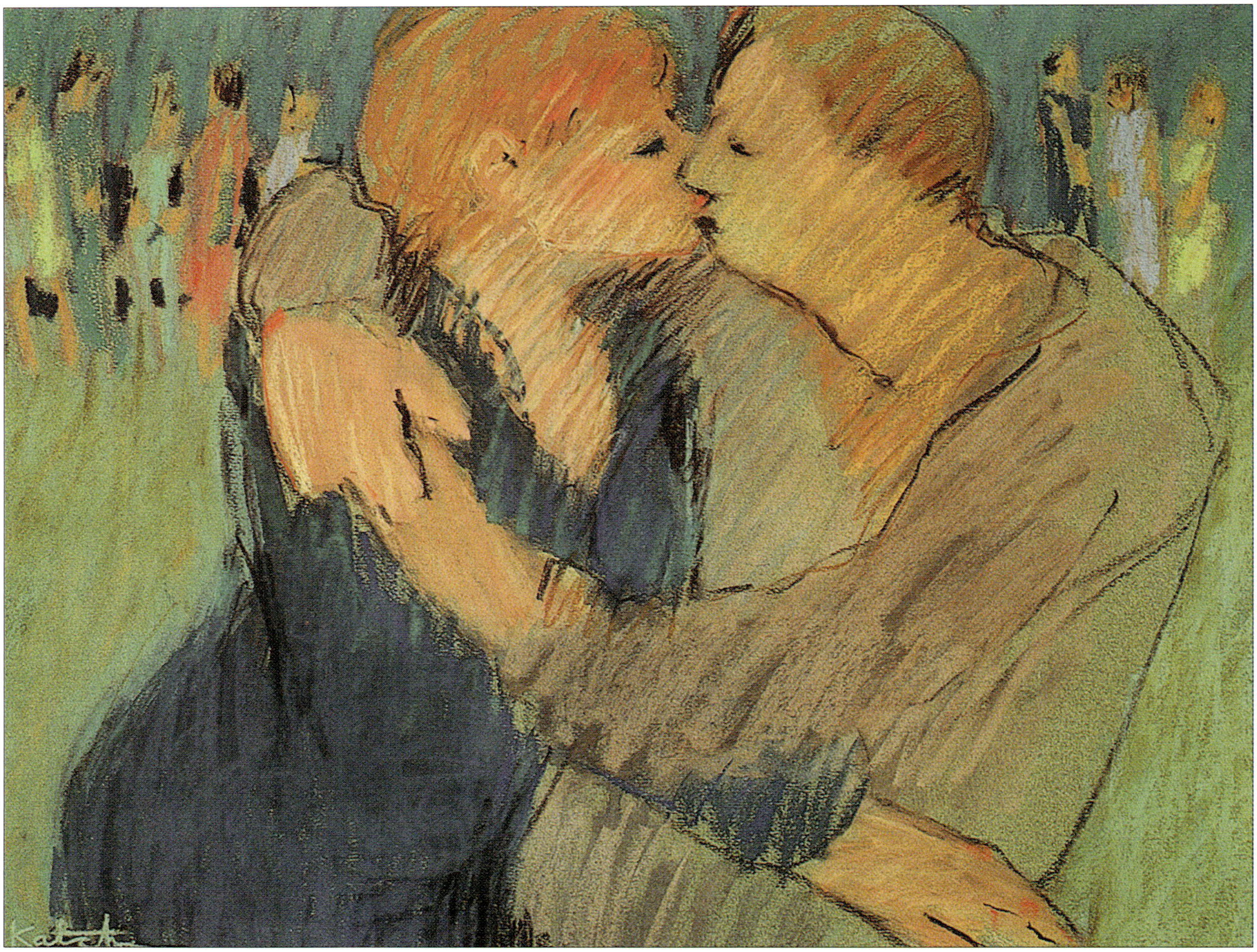

Above Turquoise Kiss *by Carole Katchen. There is some similarity between the way Katchen uses pastel in this drawing and the way Lautrec used oil paint in* Woman Seated in a Garden. *The background figures are blocked in slabs of color, while the foreground has freely applied colored lines.*

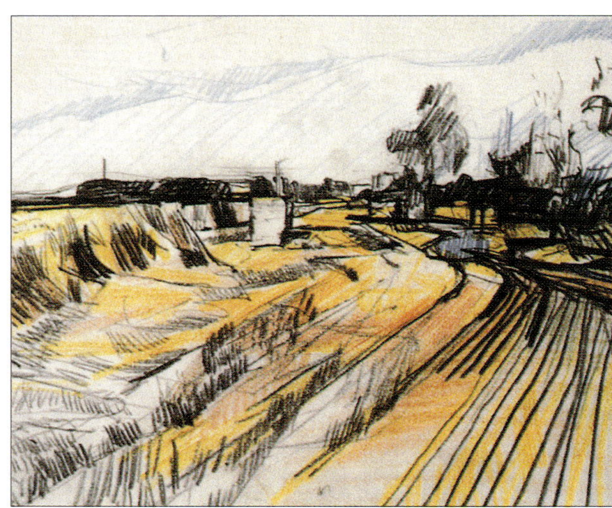

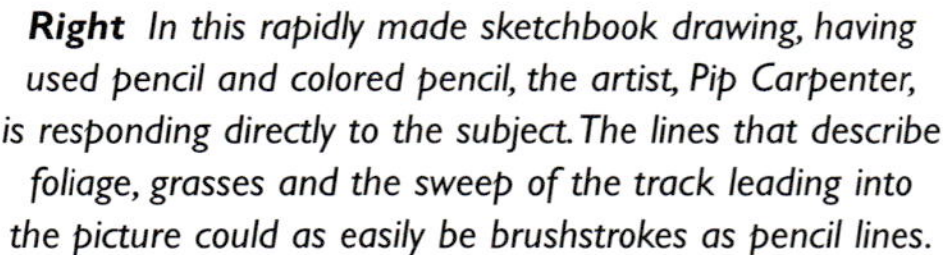

Right *In this rapidly made sketchbook drawing, having used pencil and colored pencil, the artist, Pip Carpenter, is responding directly to the subject. The lines that describe foliage, grasses and the sweep of the track leading into the picture could as easily be brushstrokes as pencil lines.*

THE PROJECTS

PROJECT 1

No Preliminaries

Using all your marker colors (or paints) this time make a drawing directly from either a landscape, a figure, or a still life, with no preparatory drawing and no guidelines drawn on the picture surface before you start to paint. Start describing the subject directly in color and move everything around on the picture surface until you are satisfied that you have a good composition.

PROJECT 2

A Colored Ground

Lautrec used a warm gray-colored board to unify his "drawings in paint." There is less contrast between the paint lines and the painting surface than with a white ground, and the color of the board can become an intrinsic part of the painting. You can use paints if you have them, with thin brushes, or pastels again, but don't blend the colors. Build up with a series of lines in the way that Lautrec did in *Woman Seated in a Garden*. The subject could be a figure outdoors, a landscape, or perhaps a still life with flowers.

although it is generally advisable to keep line to a minimum when you paint, not all artists work in this way. For some, their paintings are drawings, and they use the paint very much as they would a drawing medium. Swiss artist Alberto Giacometti was convinced that everything had to be discovered through drawing, and drawing on a canvas with paint provided him with the most sympathetic surface on which to draw and redraw what he saw.

Many of Toulouse-Lautrec's paintings also have a linear quality. Indeed, the essence of his painting style was his drawing. A superb draftsman who excelled at capturing movement, he could convey a sense of his subject in a few lines or brush strokes.

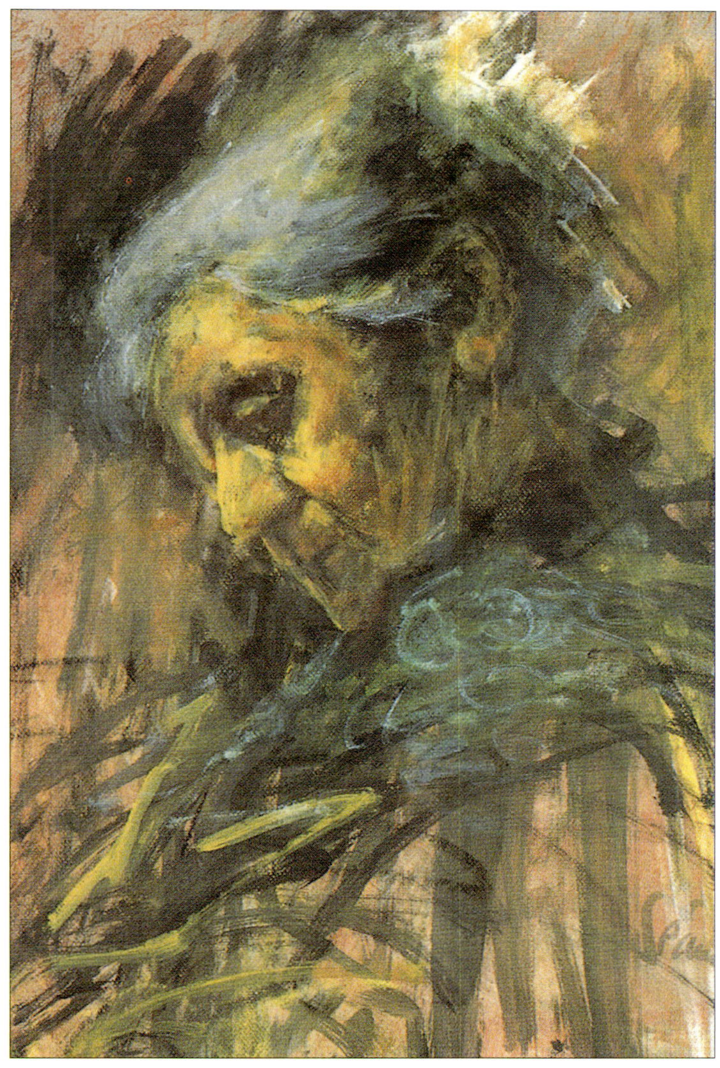

Above Amelia *by Ken Paine. Paine's watercolor technique is unusual, perhaps because he works predominantly in pastel. Amelia has been painted by building up the image with a series of linear brushstrokes, so that the result is more drawing than painting. The color of the paper has been allowed to show in places to become part of the finished picture.*

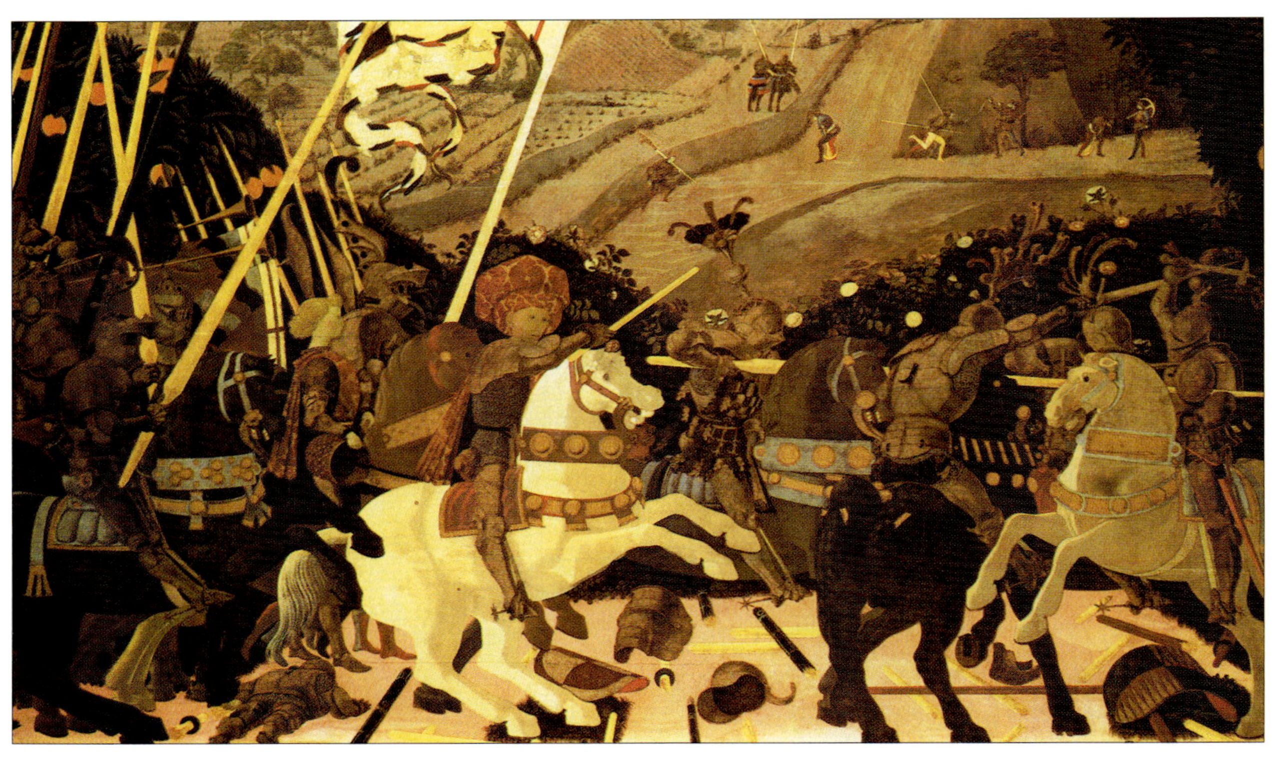

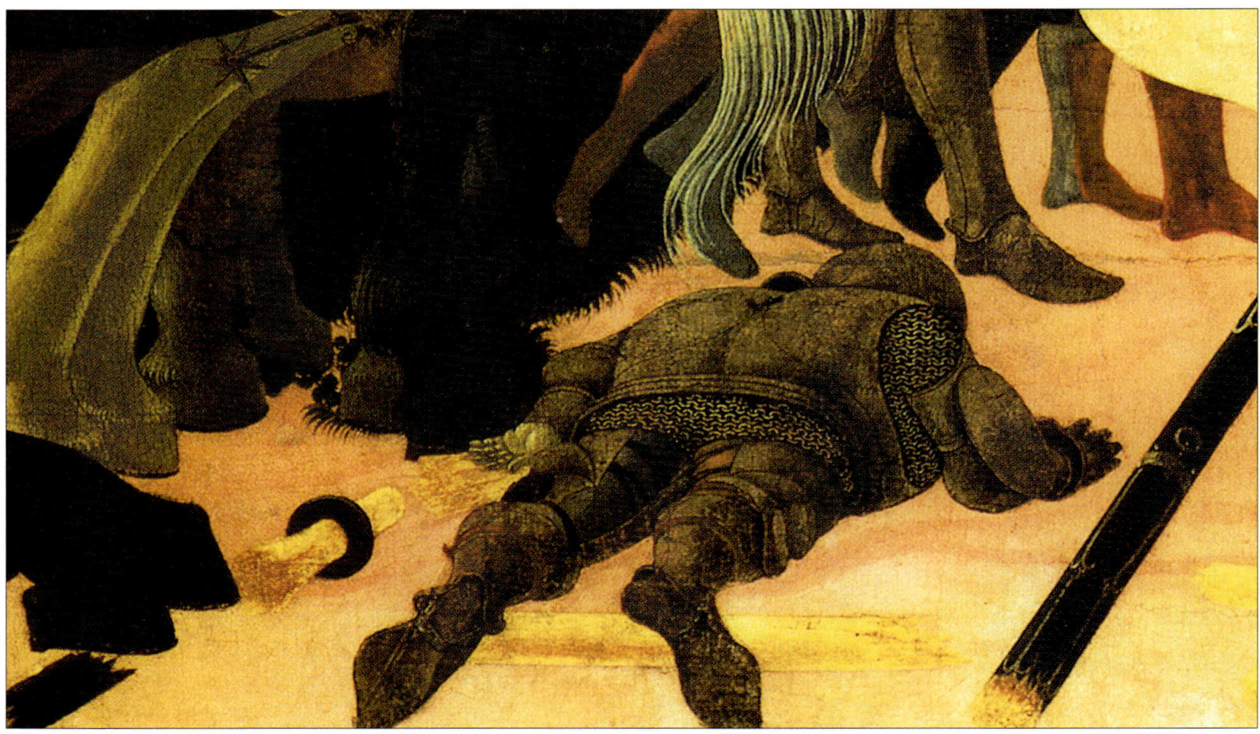

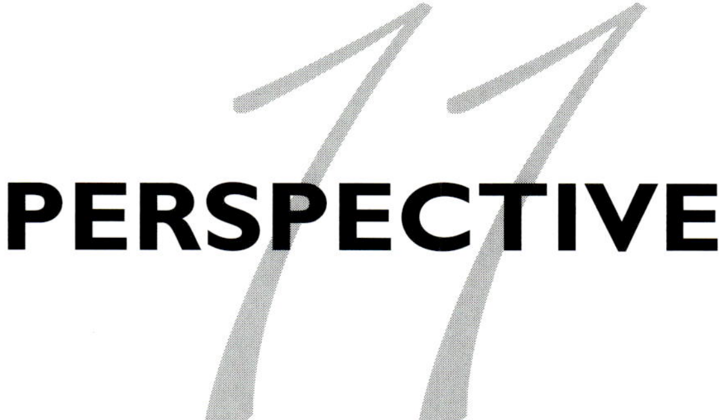

PERSPECTIVE

In a sense perspective has always been there, but it was only when artists became intrigued by the accurate measurement of distance that it could be discovered. The simplest way of illustrating what Brunelleschi interpreted in mathematical terms is to look at an ordinary rectangular doorway, first with the door closed and then with it open, as shown in the photographs.

Far Left *Uccello's painting does not really succeed in describing three-dimensional space. As far as perspective is concerned, the most important part is the foreground. The soldier lying on the ground, although out of scale with the foreground horseman, is a convincing representation of a foreshortened figure.*

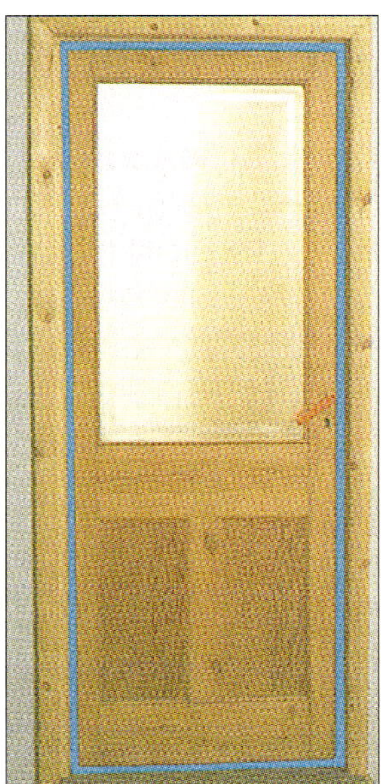

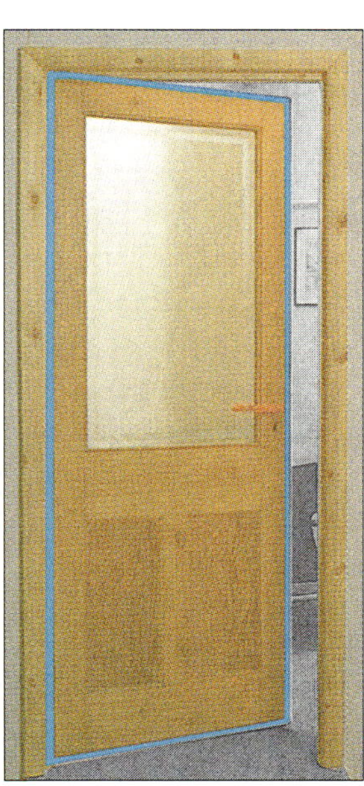

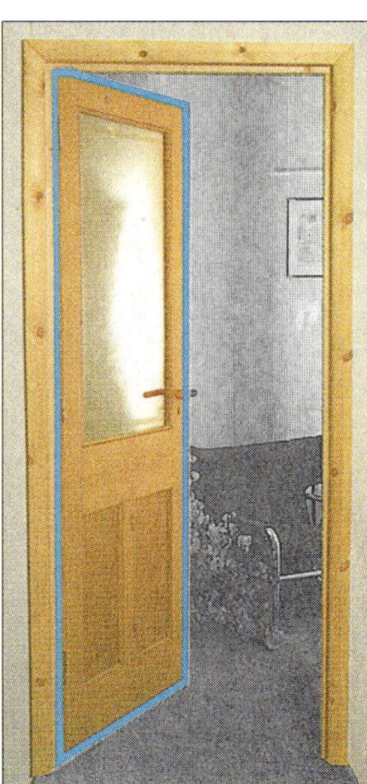

Left *It is easy to underestimate the effect of perspective; it's the old problem of being unable to discard preconceived ideas. We know that a door is rectangular. You may find it helpful initially to hold up your pencil and tilt it to assess the angle. Also check the negative shapes—the space you see at the top, bottom, and side of the door.*

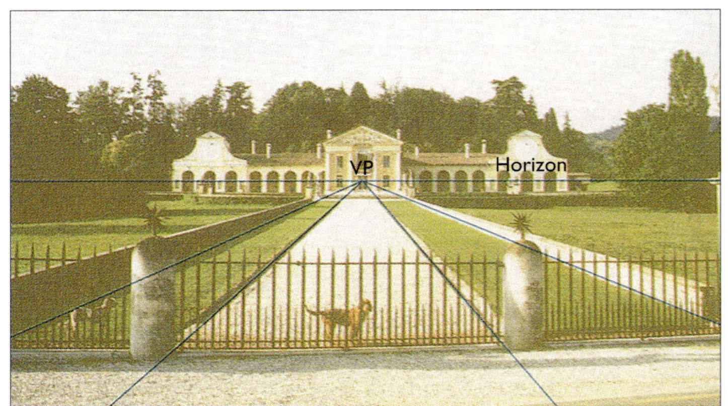

Left *The effect of the parallel lines appearing to meet at a vanishing point is seldom quite as obvious as in this frontal view. Often you will have to cope with bends or irregularities at the edges of a path, or it may be running slightly up or down hill, which affects the level of the vanishing point.*

Now, if you look again at the open door first from a sitting position and then standing, the door will change its shape as you change your position. These simple exercises in observation illustrate the basic principle on which perspective is based. Receding parallel lines (the top and bottom of the open door) would if they were extended meet at a certain point. This point is called the vanishing point (VP), and is always at the level of your own eyes, often referred to in books about perspective as the "horizon line" or simply the "horizon." The reason that the door appeared to change shape when you moved from a seated to a standing position is that your eye level had changed, and with it, the point where the two parallel lines meet.

To put it simply, perspective relies on a consistent viewpoint. Providing you accept this limitation, knowing the rules of perspective will then enable you to draw, for example, the receding walls of houses or relate the height of a person in the foreground to someone in a garden a hundred meters away.

Right *These diagrams show clearly what happens when you move your viewpoint even slightly. Trace shapes on a glass pane, then move away from where you stand. The objects don't fit the lines any longer. If you look at something with one eye closed, then open that eye and close the other, everything appears to shift to the right or left.*

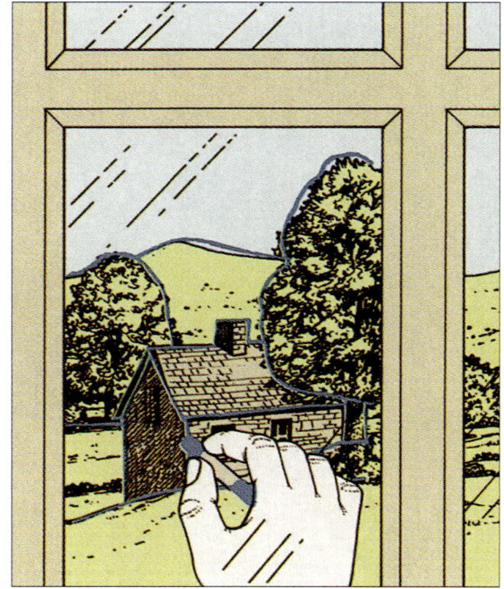

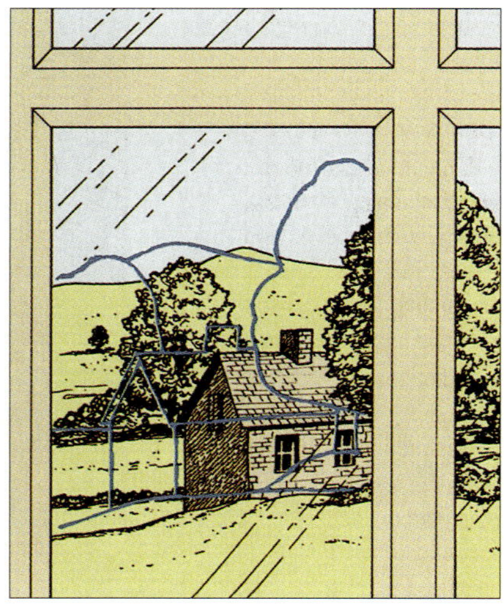

VP Horizon

Below *If you are drawing a simple object, either in parallel perspective (bottom left) or angular perspective (bottom right), you may find it helpful initially to mark in the vanishing points.*

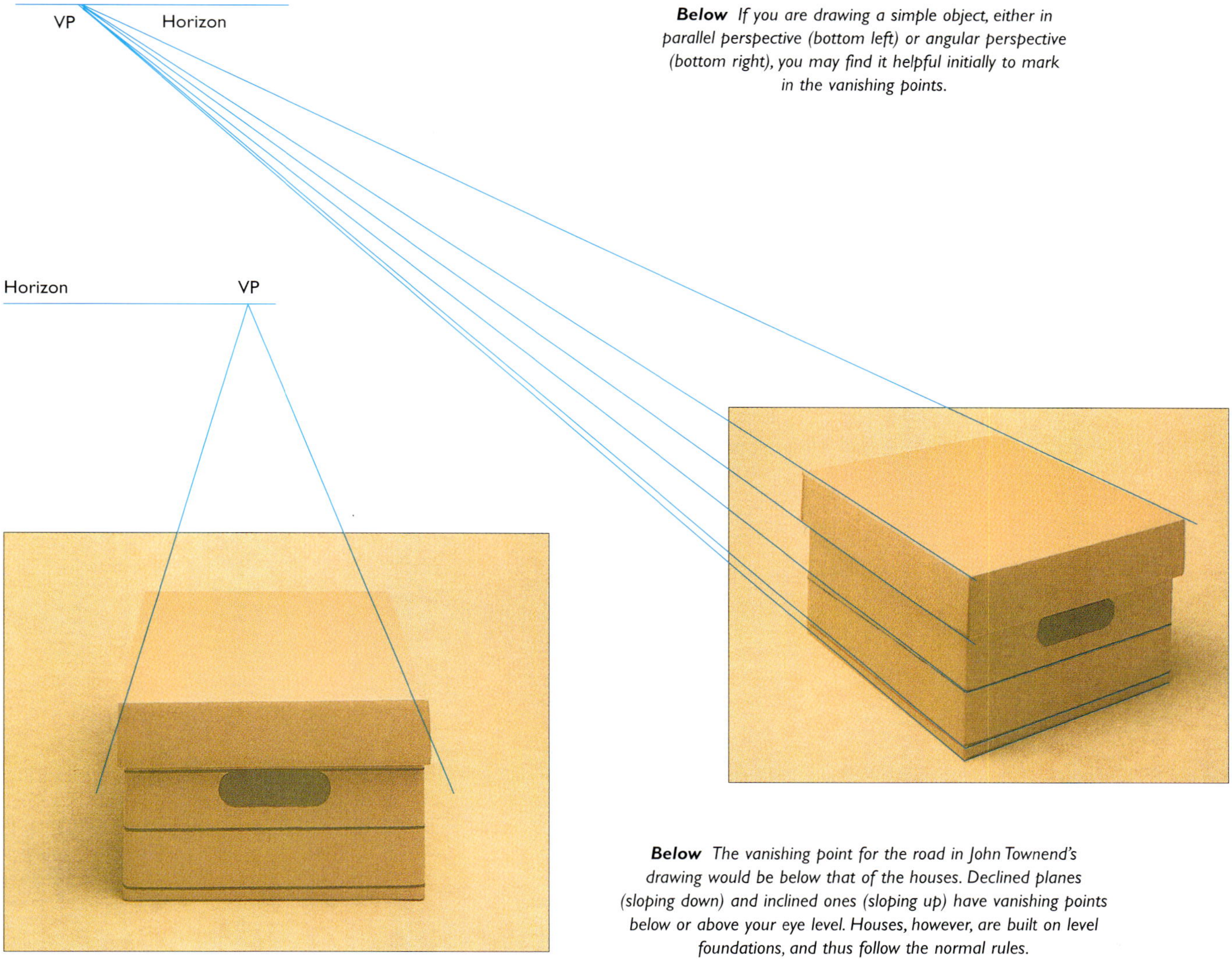

Horizon VP

Below *The vanishing point for the road in John Townend's drawing would be below that of the houses. Declined planes (sloping down) and inclined ones (sloping up) have vanishing points below or above your eye level. Houses, however, are built on level foundations, and thus follow the normal rules.*

DIMINISHING SIZE

As we have seen, when the door was opened, it ceased to be a rectangle and became an irregular straight-sided shape, with the vertical edge at the back shorter than at the front. As objects become further away from you they become smaller and smaller, until they disappear altogether on the horizon. This optical shrinking gives rise to the

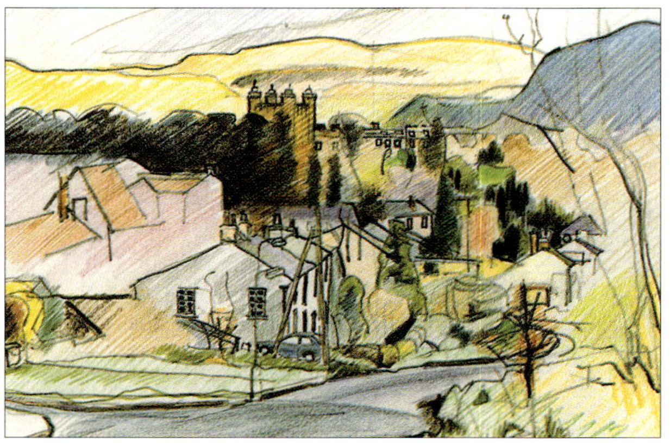

Right *Circles and ellipses are the bugbear of many drawing students, even some professional artists. They change according to your eye level, so keep a consistent viewpoint.*

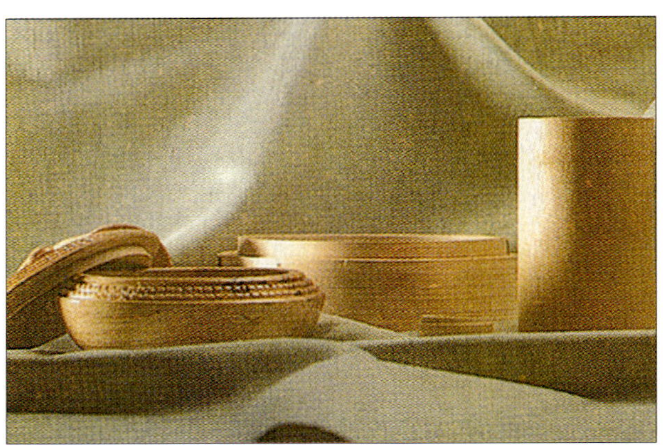

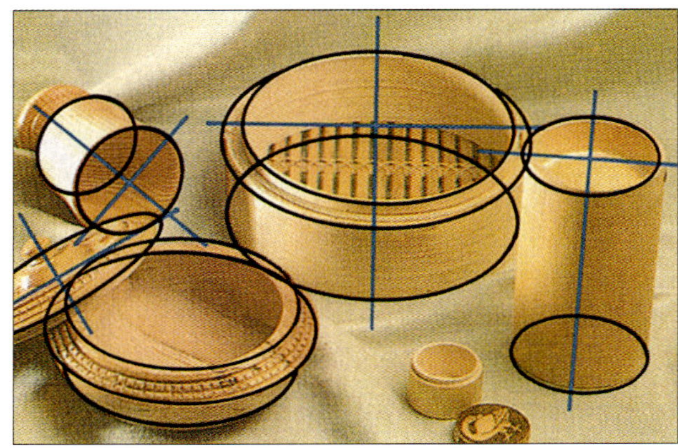

phenomenon of foreshortening, which—after receding lines—is the next consideration in perspective. When Uccello drew his foreshortened soldier he probably worked it out mathematically. Nowadays it is more usual to judge by eye, but foreshortening involves a fundamental problem. Nearly always, when objects are drawn from direct observation the extent to which they are foreshortened is underestimated, because you know their real size and so fail to see how much smaller they become when pushed back in space.

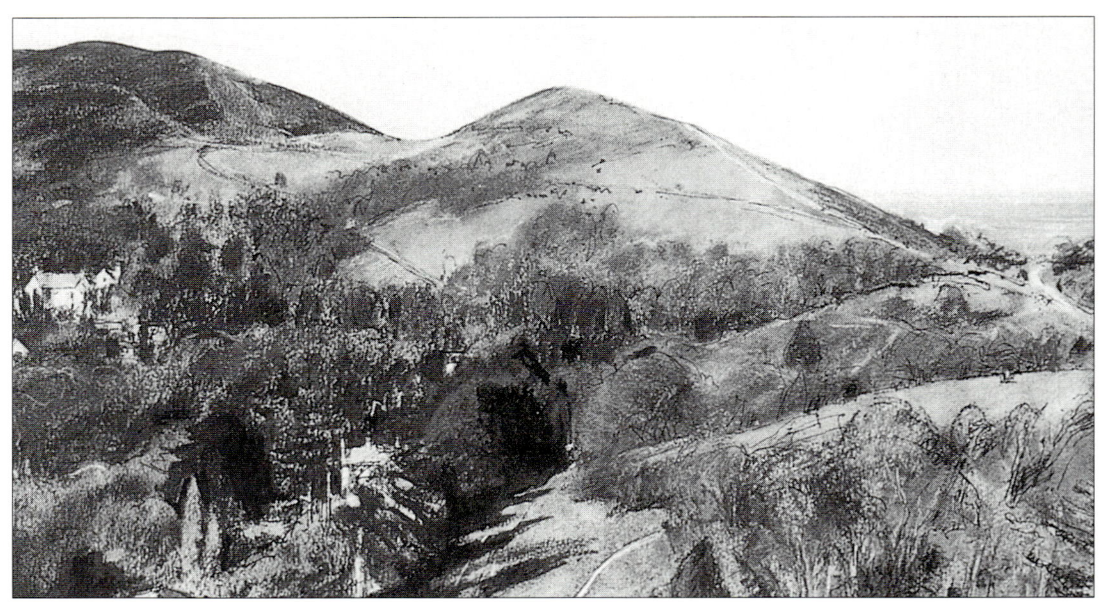

Left *The rules of linear perspective and aerial perspective have been used very skillfully in David Prentice's ink and chalk drawing to convey a marvelous sense of space. Notice also the way he has used the ribbon-like curves of the winding mountain paths to help describe the contours of the hills.*

THE AIM OF THE PROJECTS

- Drawing objects in parallel perspective
- Assessing angles and foreshortening
- Experiencing the relationship between linear perspective and what you actually see

WHAT YOU WILL NEED

All your drawing materials, and at least seven sheets of white cartridge paper. A long ruler or straight edge (a piece of wood about a meter long is ideal). Gumstrip, or something similar for joining pieces of paper in project 2

TIME

Project 1: about 1/2 hour.
Project 2: about 1 hour.
Project 3: about 2 hours.

Above *In this sketchbook drawing, the foreground wall and buildings with the terrace of houses behind have provided the artist with a fascinating angular perspective problem.*

ANGULAR PERSPECTIVE

Initially all pictures in perspective were drawn with one plane of the main object parallel to the picture plane. The limitations of parallel perspective made it impossible to depict corner-on views of objects.

For views of this kind angular perspective was developed where, for example, two sides of a building which are actually at right angles to each other can be drawn receding to separate vanishing points.

CYLINDERS AND ELLIPSES

Students often have difficulty drawing circular and cylindrical objects in perspective. There is a simple rule that can help you here—circles fit into squares, so once you can draw a tabletop or a box, you can draw a circle or cylinder within that shape.

The other important thing to remember is that circles change shape according to your viewpoint. Perspective makes circles appear to be ovals, usually called ellipses. The shape of the ellipse depends on where it is placed in relation to your eye level.

USING PERSPECTIVE

The projects here are concerned with drawing from observation, but making use of perspective systems. You won't have to make elaborate perspective or axonometric drawings; though it would add to your experience if you do practice the various drawing systems.

PROJECT ONE

FORESHORTENING BY EYE

To demonstrate the extent to which receding objects become foreshortened, I want you to first make a drawing of the shapes of two identical-sized postcards.

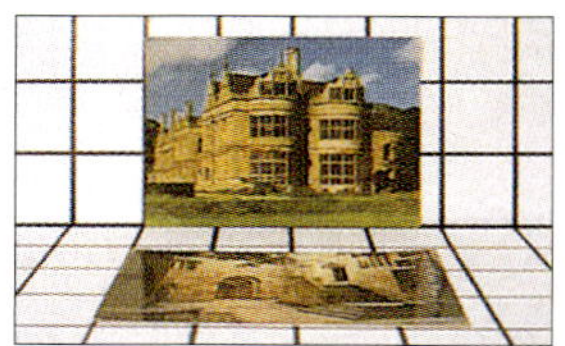

Place them as shown here, and make a line drawing of the shapes of the cards. The vertical card will be a perfect rectangle. The horizontal card will be foreshortened, the effect of which can be compared to the other card.

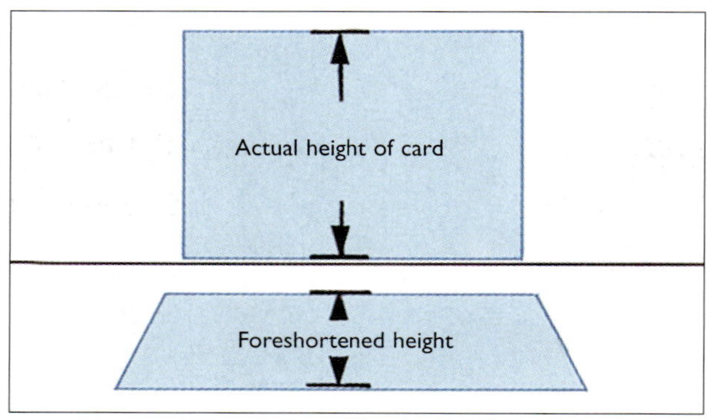

PROJECT TWO

MORE FORESHORTENED RECTANGLES

Place two books of the same size on a table, with one away but directly behind the other. Support another two books on a glass so that they are flat but at different heights above the table.

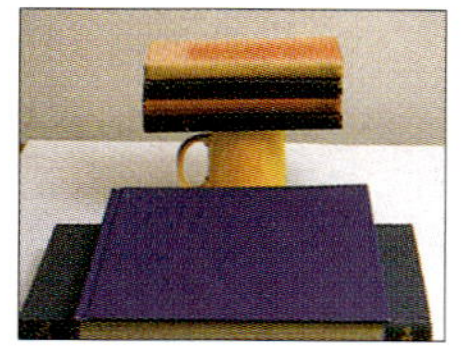

Make a drawing of the four books. When you have drawn the books as accurately as you can, look straight ahead and decide where an imaginary horizontal line projected from your eyes, your eye level, would be in your drawing. Mark this in with a ruler. Each pair of receding sides (of the book) is parallel, and the lines formed by these sides, if extended, will meet on your eye level at the same vanishing point. Extend them in your drawing and see if they do.

1 *Colored pencil has been used to draw the books and the mug on which the top books rest. Although the latter is not part of the exercise, the drawing would have looked odd without it.*

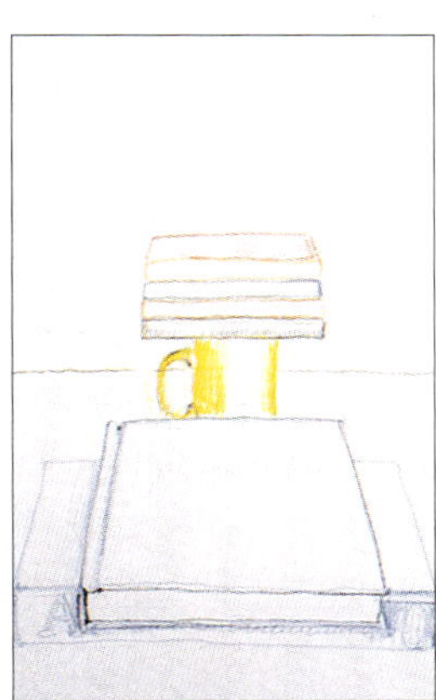

2 *The artist has drawn in his eye level and is using a long ruler to extend the sides of the books to check whether they meet at the same point on the eye level.*

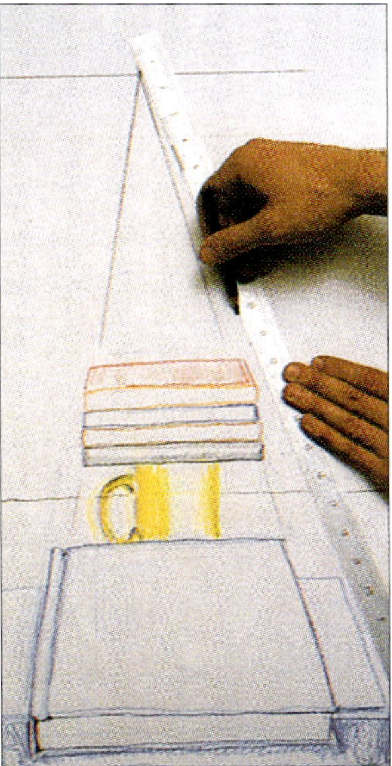

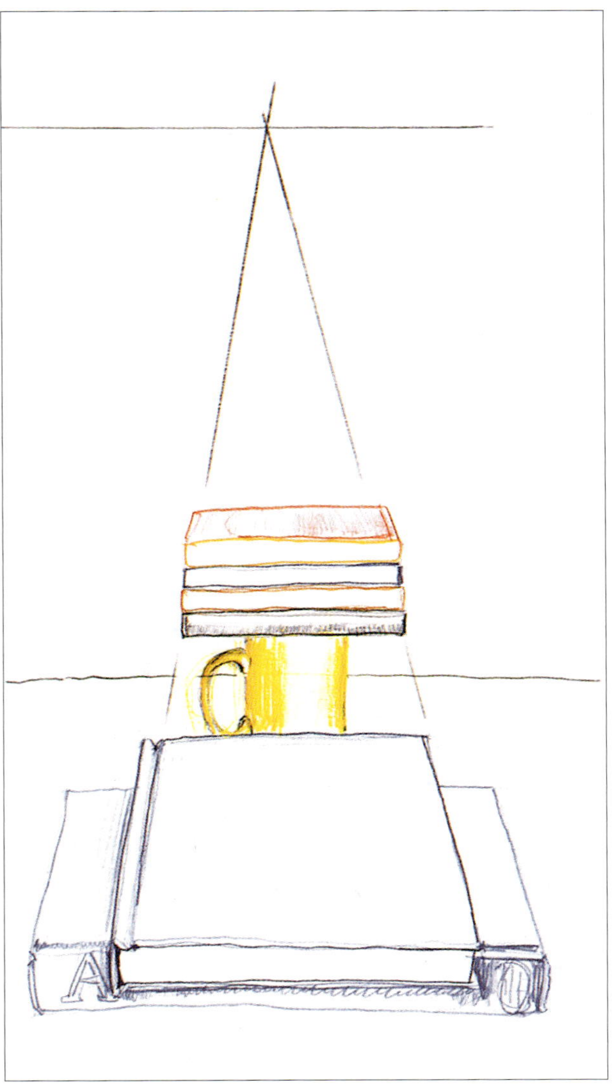

3 *Take care to check the angles of their receding sides against the horizontal sides. You can see in the final drawing that the sides of all the books, if extended, would meet on the eye-level line at the same vanishing point, irrespective of the height they are placed at.*

PROJECT THREE

ANGULAR PERSPECTIVE

Angular perspective helps us draw angled views. To understand this, arrange six or more books of any size so that they are all corner-on to you, with some at an angle on top of others.

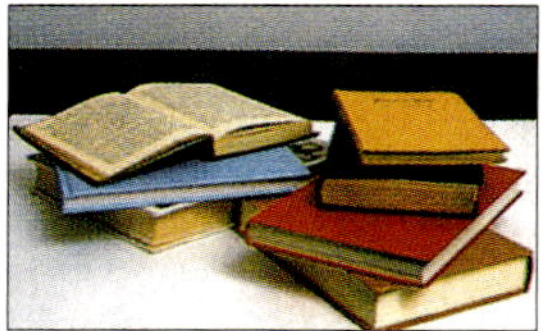

When you have drawn the books as accurately as you can by eye, draw in your eye level as in the previous project and extend the sides of the books until they meet. If any of the books are actually parallel to each other, each pair of parallel sides should meet at the same vanishing point. Otherwise, each book will have two vanishing points, but they will all be on the same eye level.

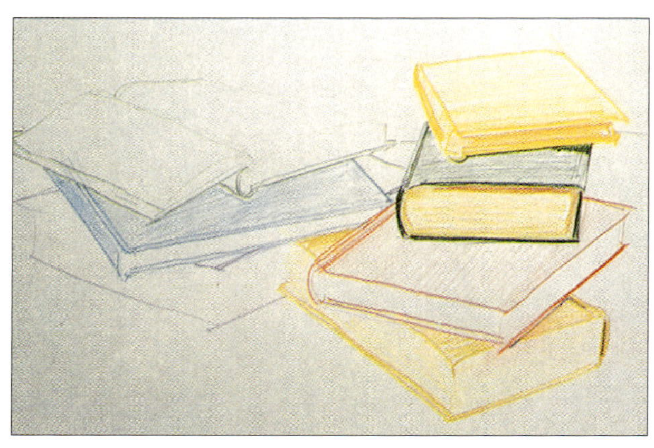

2 *Even when you are drawing what may seem a dull subject, the way you use the medium can make the drawing interesting. Here the artist makes good use of colored pencil.*

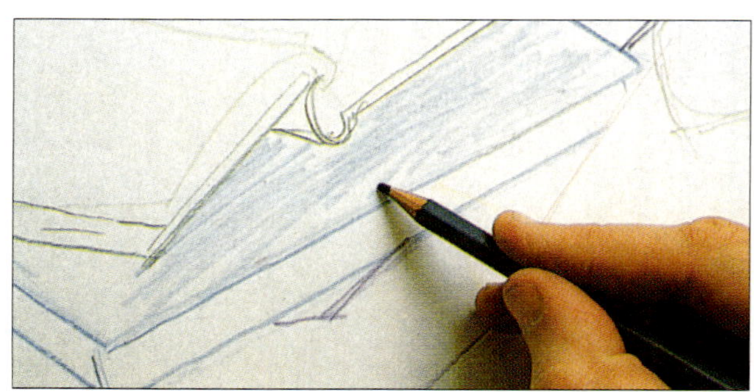

1 *Here, the artist has to assess angles without the help of any horizontals. This is considerably more difficult than drawing objects in parallel perspective.*

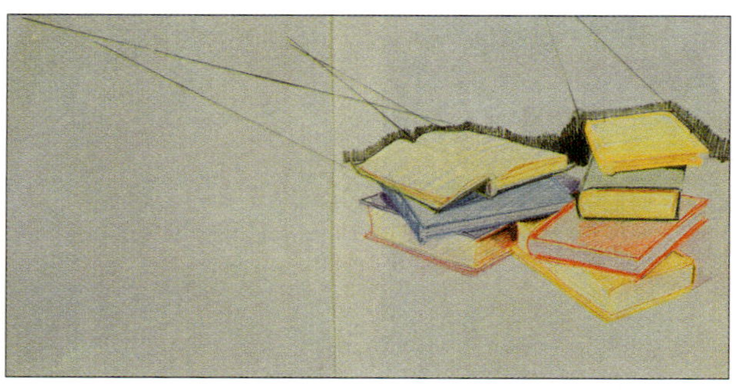

3 *Another sheet of paper has been added to the drawing so that the eye level can be extended and the vanishing points for the receding sides of the books checked.*

PROJECT FOUR

AERIAL PERSPECTIVE

The effect of the atmosphere on tones and colors is best seen toward evenings or on misty days. To understand this, you need a view from where you can relate distant and close-up objects.

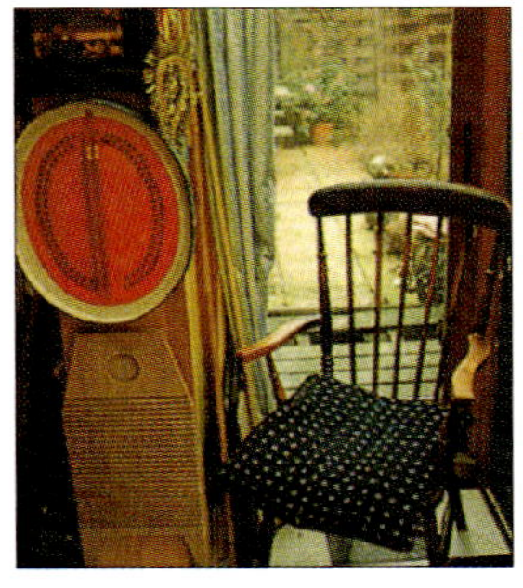

A view from a high window looking down your garden or across rooftops would be great. Look at the way that tone contrasts are less and less distinct the further they are from you. Use line as little as possible and translate what you can see into a tonal drawing using conté, charcoal, or wash. You can include color in your drawing if you wish to create a feeling of depth through the blueness of distant colors.

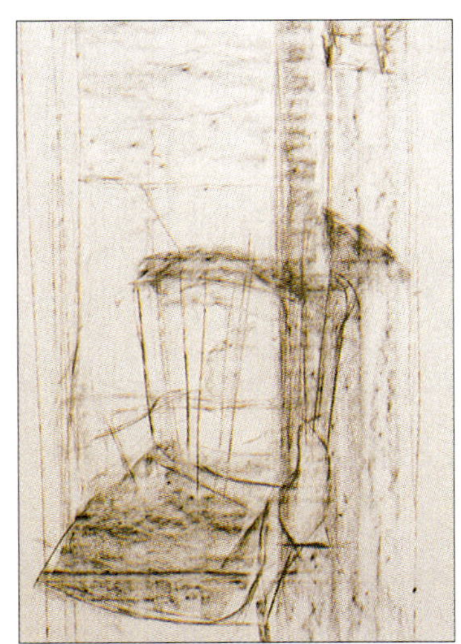

1 *Using charcoal, the artist starts by establishing the positions of the chair and the window behind.*

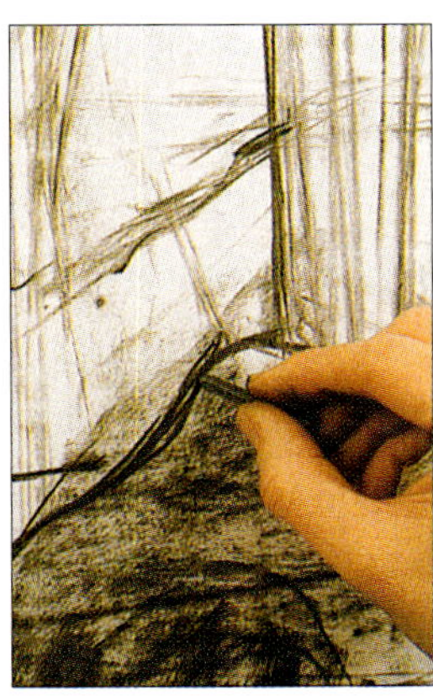

2 *She now strengthens the drawing of the chair, which is the most prominent foreground object. Note how this part of the drawing is done with a certain attention to detail.*

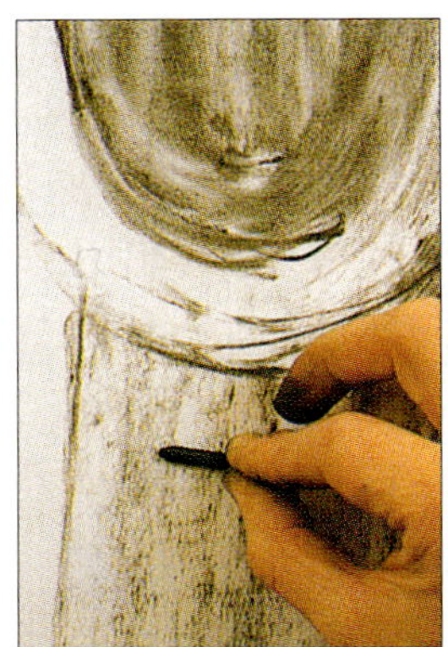

3 *Shading is done by using the charcoal flat on its side. The artist is now beginning to build up the tones and colors in the drawing.*

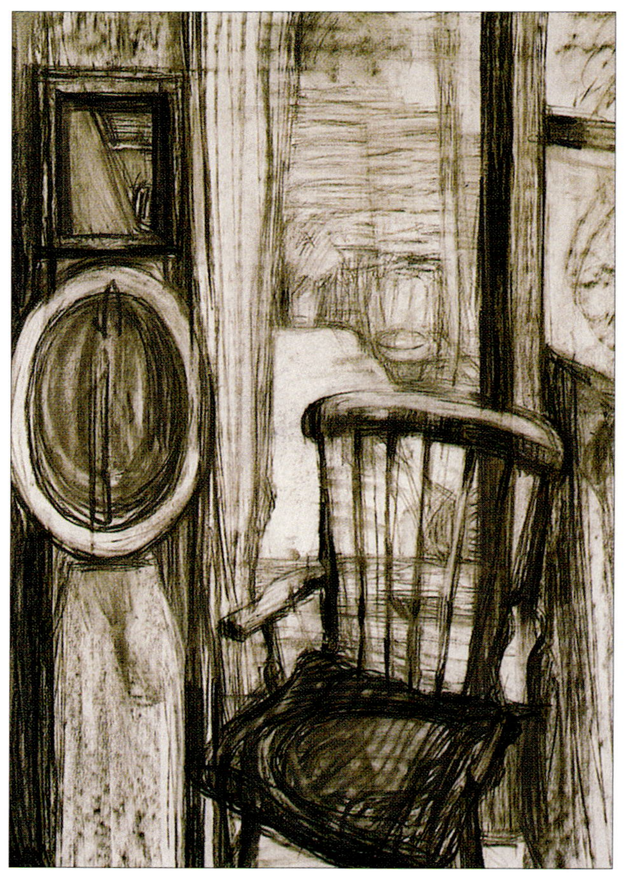

4 *In the final drawing a sense of depth has been created by the strong tone contrasts in the foreground. As you look out through the door and down the garden, the contrasts become less distinct and less clearly defined.*

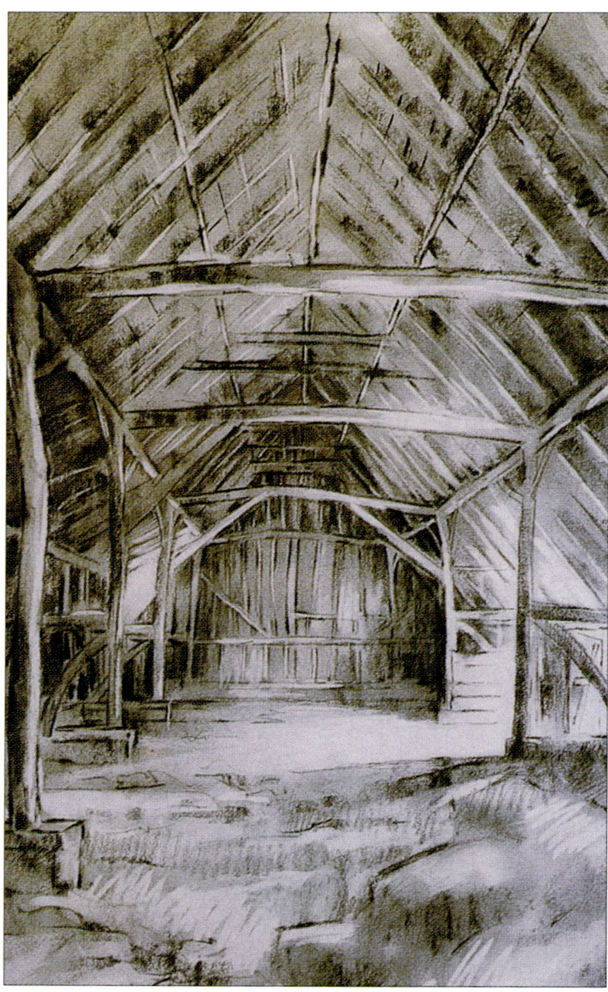

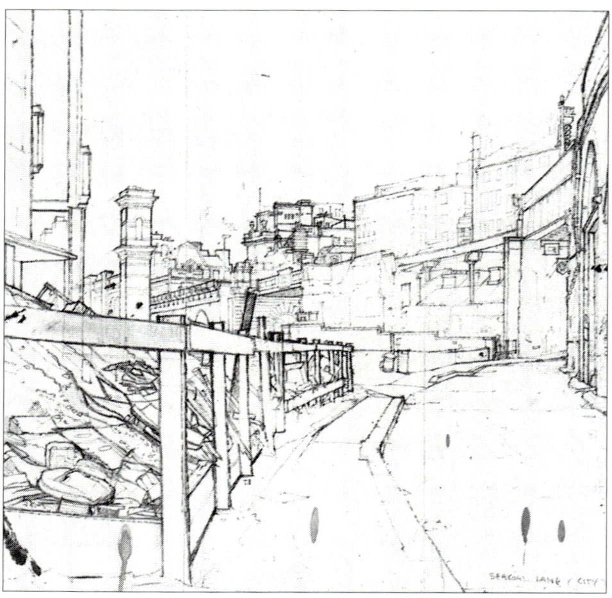

Above *A charcoal and pencil drawing by Geoff Masters. Even though the beams in this old barn are not perfectly straight,* Lower Farm Barn *is a drawing with a single vanishing point. As well as being beautifully observed in terms of perspective, the drawing conveys a strong feeling of atmosphere.*

Left *Pencil drawing by Christopher Chamberlain. The artist chose a view which gave him an extremely complex perspective problem.*

ALTERING THE SCALE

The size you draw objects can be very important. Scaling up or down isn't always easy to do. If you try to enlarge a small object you will probably find that the drawing will get smaller and smaller as you continue. It is equally difficult to scale down a large foreground object; often the subject runs off the page. Also, to keep it within the page, you may distort the scale and proportions.

SIGHT SIZE

Drawing objects the size you see them rather than the size they are is usually described as drawing "sight size." Make a rapid line drawing of the silhouette of any object you can see in the room you are in. Now, close one eye and measure on the pencil the main proportions of the object. Compare these measurements with your drawing. If you do this carefully, the measurements in your drawing will probably be identical.

THE AIM OF THE PROJECTS

- Drawing objects larger than you actually see them
- Drawing objects smaller than you see them

WHAT YOU WILL NEED

You will need A4 size paper for Project 1, and A2 sheets or a sketchbook for Project 2. Color isn't important in this context, so I suggest that you make your drawings in monochrome using line and tone.

TIME

About 3 hours for each project.

PROJECT FIVE

ENLARGING

I want you to make three drawings for this project, spending about an hour on each. To begin with, I want you to make an enlarged drawing of something small, such as a toothbrush.

Your drawing is to fill an A4 sheet of paper, so look at your subject carefully and try to imagine it the size of a building which you can walk around. Quickly draw the silhouette and then proceed to construct a detailed drawing, with attention to the shapes of the different surfaces and the shading. When you have got the idea of drawing larger than you see, choose a screwed-up handkerchief which you can visualize on the scale of a vast landscape.

1 *You will find it easier to enlarge if you use a medium that makes you draw really boldly. Here conté crayon has been chosen.*

2 *Attention has been paid to the ridged pattern on the handle and the shadow beneath, both of which describe the object's shape and give it solidity.*

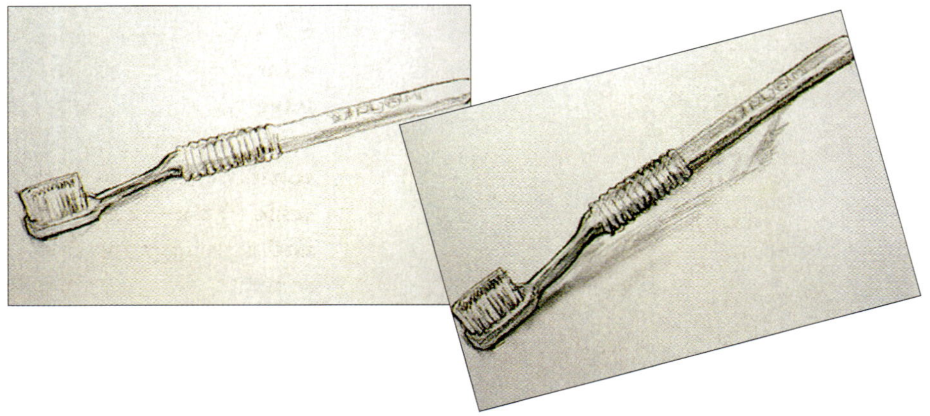

3

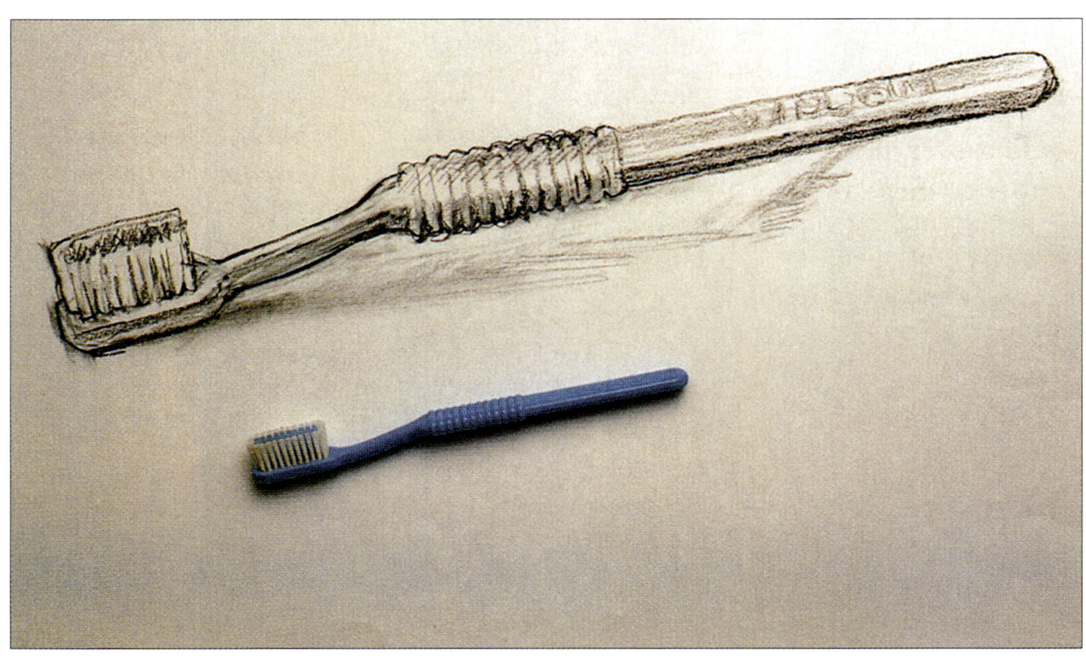

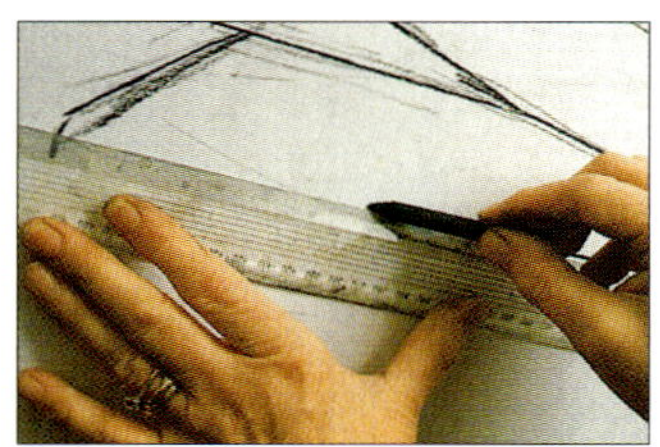

1 *The clean edges of a man-made object are very much part of its character; so the artist uses a ruler to draw.*

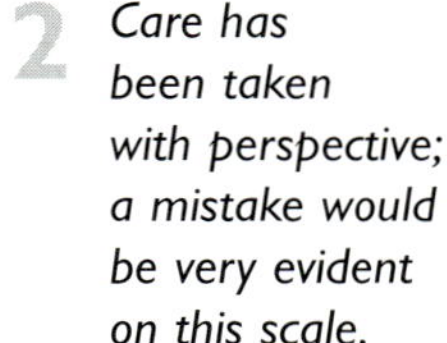

2 *Care has been taken with perspective; a mistake would be very evident on this scale.*

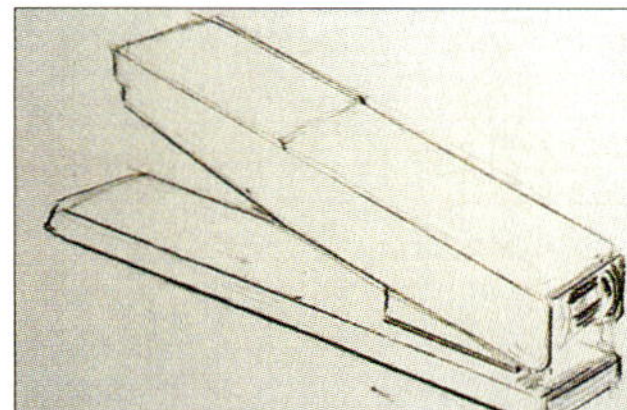

3 *With the shading completed, the giant stapler looks entirely convincing. An object like this is ideal, as its architectural qualities become more apparent in enlargement.*

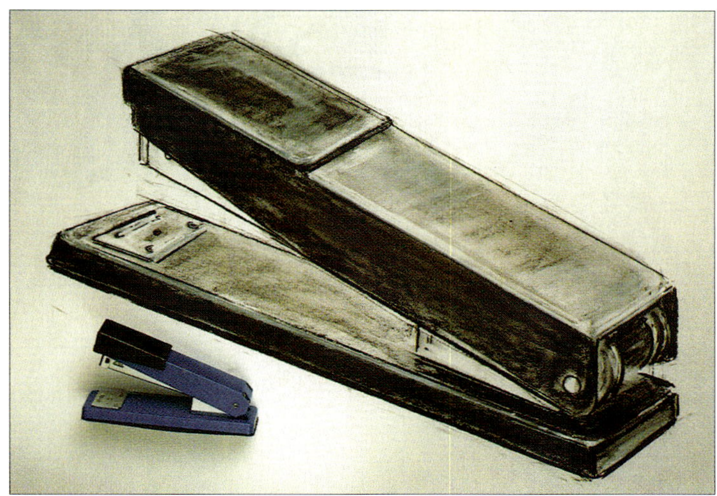

ENLARGING AND REDUCING

There are two semi-mechanical methods of scaling objects up or down—squaring up and pantograph.

For squaring up, a grid of squares is drawn over your sight-size drawing and a similar grid of larger or smaller squares on another sheet of paper. The drawing is then transferred, line by line, to the second grid. A pantograph is a simple adjustable copying instrument. It looks like several rulers joined together at the ends so that they pivot, and it has a point at one extremity and a lead for drawing at the other. By tracing your drawing with the point, the lead will automatically draw an enlarged or reduced version of it. The scale depends on how the "arms" of the pantograph are adjusted.

Squaring-up and the pantograph have their uses, but they are essentially devices for copying or tracing, and they remove any vitality and spontaneity from a drawing. It is essential to be able to reduce and enlarge by eye if many of the qualities which are most important in drawing are to be preserved.

SELF-CRITIQUE

- **Have your enlargements made you get the proportions of the objects wrong?**
- **Did you find any of the objects easier to enlarge than the others?**
- **Were the forms of the soft object, like the crumpled handkerchief, easier to enlarge than the more precise forms?**
- **In making your enlargements, did you try any measuring?**

PROJECT SIX

REDUCING

This project also requires you to make three drawings. To begin with, choose a large piece of furniture such as a kitchen dresser, or a wardrobe with the doors open revealing the contents inside.

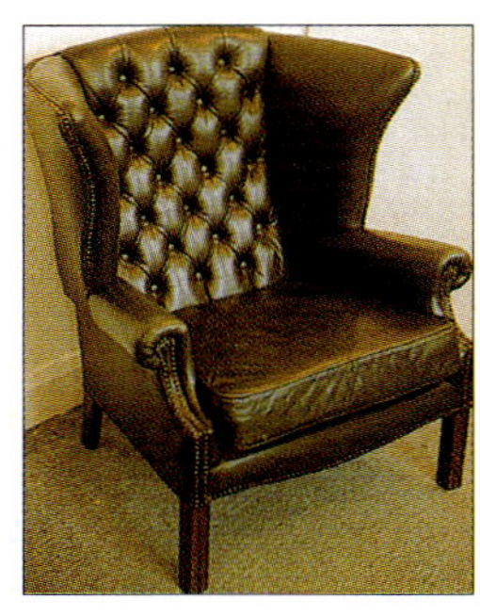

Decide where you are going to position yourself to draw, but before you begin your drawing make a sight-size measurement of the width of the piece. I want you to make your drawing not larger than half this size. Mark on your paper the width you intend the object to be and then draw the overall shape of the furniture within this dimension. Continue your drawing, adding details such as drawers, shelves, and handles. Pay particular attention to the proportions of the furniture and the scale of its details in relation to the whole piece. When you have finished this drawing find two quite different subjects for making drawings which are much less than sight size. You could draw the corner of a room or another building seen through a window. You need subjects which compel you to fit a great deal of detail into large overall shapes. This will enable you to see, once the general size of an object has been decided, whether you can continue to draw to the same scale. Try to see how small you can draw without losing any important detail.

It is surprisingly difficult to draw smaller than you see, particularly on a large sheet of paper. The artist, therefore, began by setting a margin for the drawing. It also helps to use a medium that encourages small, detailed work, such as a fine-tipped pen.

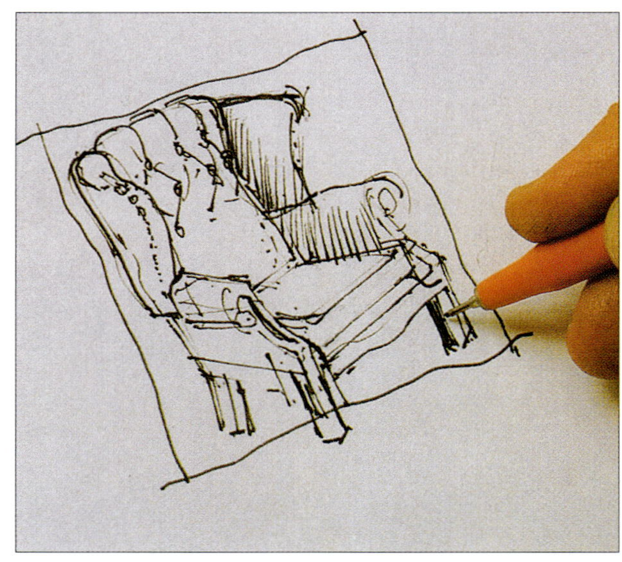

2 *Although both drawings have expanded slightly beyond their boundaries, they are very successful; the proportions of the chairs are correct.*

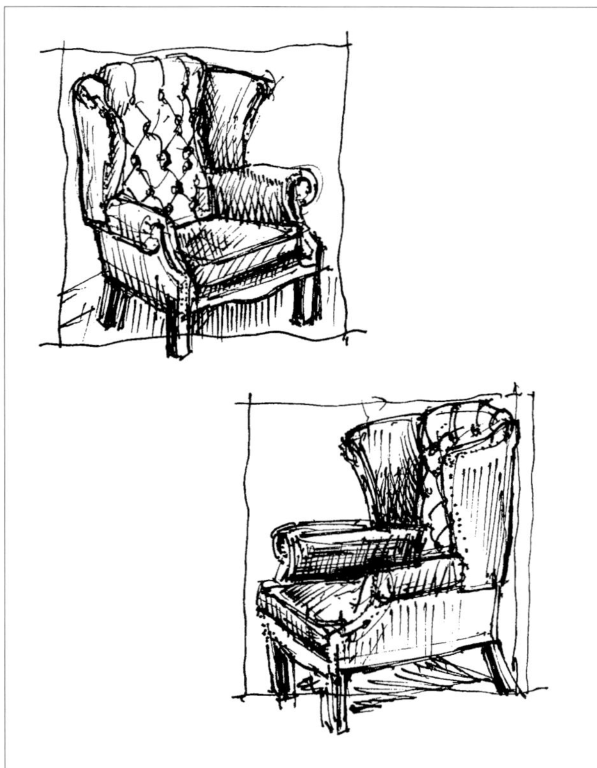

SELF-CRITIQUE

- **Did you manage to get detailed information into your drawings?**
- **Did you find that there didn't seem to be enough space to fit everything in?**
- **Are your small-scale drawings better than the enlargements in the previous project?**

Right and Below *These three drawings in pen and ink are sketchbook studies of the artist's studio, done specifically to practice reducing the scale. You will need to make a good many drawings before you can do this with confidence, but it will become easier in the course of time.*

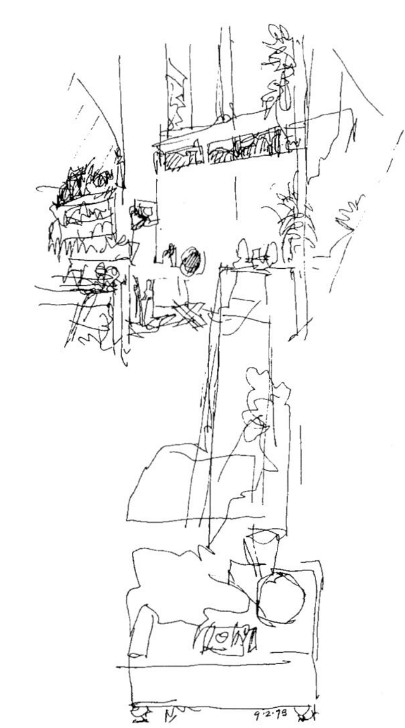

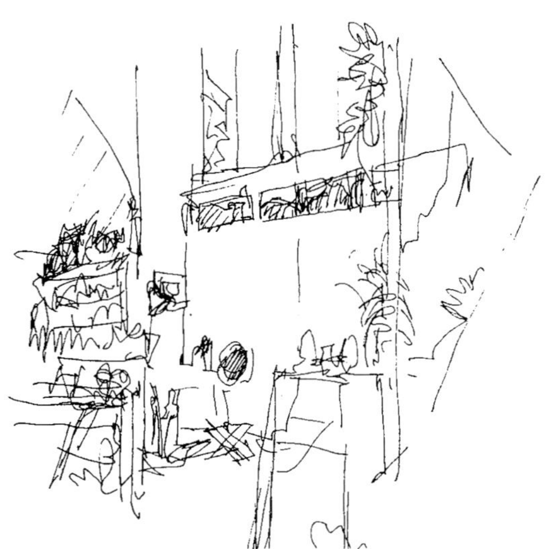

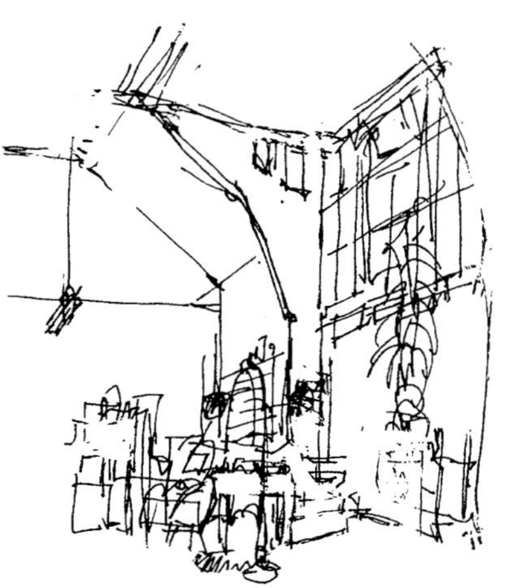

DRAWING ON LOCATION

Drawing on the spot puts pressure on you to work at speed. The light changes constantly, and people move. Besides, all kinds of things can happen in your drawings that you see only when you get home. The subjects in this lesson won't have specially arranged objects, and much more will be left to chance when you draw. But chance happenings often produce better drawings than a highly controlled approach.

THE AIM OF THE PROJECTS

- Producing spontaneous drawings from outdoor subjects
- Working quickly and exploiting chance efforts
- Choosing good subjects and including their most important features
- Making a composition

WHAT YOU WILL NEED

An A2 size sketchbook is needed for the larger drawings but if you have an A3 sketchbook, you can draw across two pages. Alternatively, the larger drawings can be made using your board and A2 paper. You will need all your drawing materials, and you can use color if you wish.

TIME

About 3 hours for each project.

PROJECT SEVEN

TOWNSCAPES

Choose a convenient location and make at least three quick studies (taking about twenty minutes for each) and a larger A2-size drawing on which you should work for at least two hours.

If you can't do all the drawings in one session, make two trips, saving the larger drawing for the second. You will need an unbroken period of at least two hours for this, and if you stop and plan to continue later you will probably discover after the break that things look so different that you won't know where to begin again. It is best, therefore, that you choose a place that is comfortable and convenient.

SELECTING

Once you have decided where to draw, you will find the first problem is what to draw. This is the purpose of the preliminary studies, which will help you to decide what will make the best subject for your larger drawing. All the studies may be variations of the same view, perhaps adding more foreground in one and trying more on the right-hand side in another. Or each could be a different view drawn from the same place. You will find a "viewfinder," a piece of card with a rectangular hole in it, a good aid to get you started.

THE LARGE DRAWING

When you have completed the studies, decide which one will be best to develop as a larger drawing. If possible, make this drawing A2 size, but if not, make it as large as you can. It should be in both line and tone and you may wish to use color. Make as complete a drawing as you can on location. If you put the drawing away for a couple of days and then look at it again, with the studies, you may see some fault that you can put right, such as a feature that needs strengthening. Change as little as possible, though, because altering a drawing once you are away from the subject seldom improves it.

Below, Right and Overleaf *These three rapid pencil sketches have been made from different viewpoints to explore the compositional possibilities of the subject. The one below was finally chosen.*

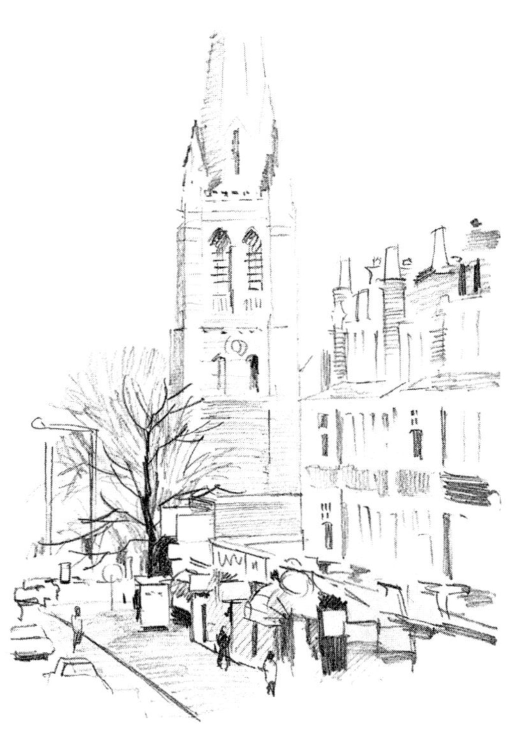

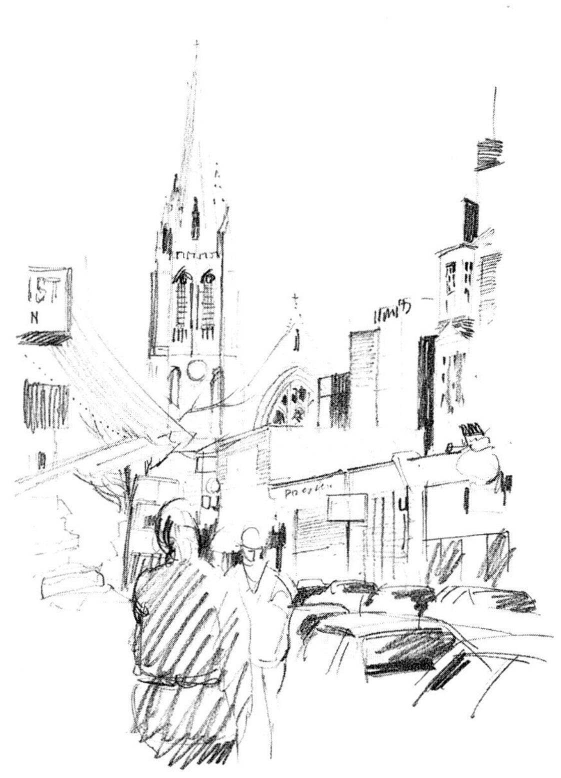

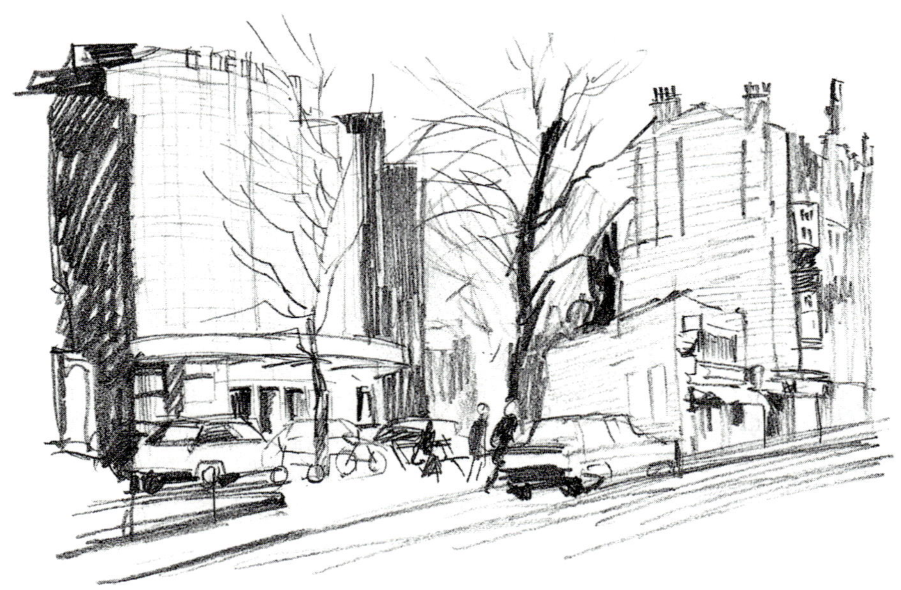

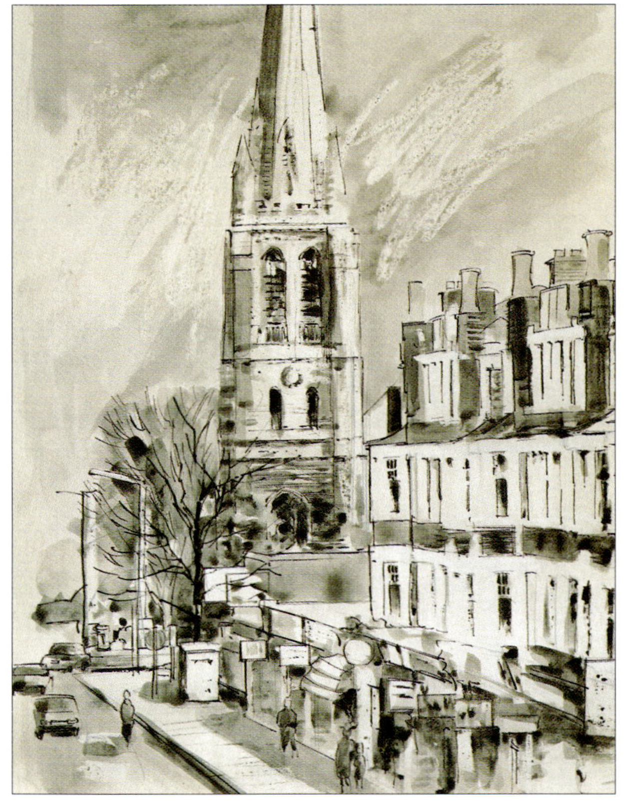

SELF-CRITIQUE

- **What do you feel about your studies and your drawing?**
- **Did you include things which surprise you?**
- **Do you now feel that you chose the most interesting study to develop?**
- **Do you think that the larger drawing does justice to the subject?**
- **Have you learned anything which you know you can put into practice in your next drawing?**

2 *For the finished drawing, the artist has turned to a different medium, pen and wash, which he uses frequently and finds ideal for urban subjects. The suggestion of cloud on either side of the church steeple was made by the wax resist method.*

PROJECT EIGHT

LANDSCAPE

Urban and village scenes offer a wide range of locations and different subjects, but for many it is the desire to make contact with nature that encouraged them to draw in the first place.

Drawing the landscape can be very rewarding. It was what the French painter Eugene Boudin advised the Impressionists to do "study, learn to see and to draw, paint, landscapes. The sea and the sky are so beautiful—animals, people, trees, just as nature has made them with their personalities, their real way of being in the air, in the light just as they are."

The word "landscape" is not intended just as a generic term for hills, mountains, fields, and trees; parks and gardens are also landscapes. A greenhouse or a garden in an urban home can provide a kind of "interior landscape," and even a windowbox can be a landscape in miniature.

You could, of course, make your

Right: *It is hard to believe that a drawing containing so much intricate detail could have been done on the spot, but the artist here, Martin Taylor, always works on location, whether he is painting or drawing, sometimes returning to a subject over a period of days. In poor weather he retreats to his car, which he uses as a mobile studio.*

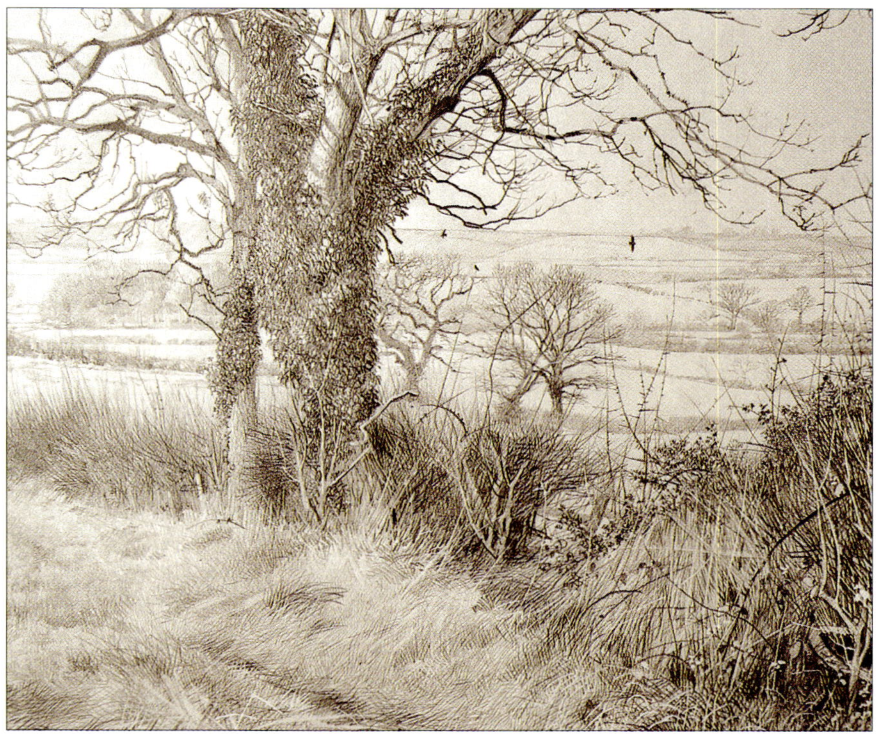

landscape drawing from a window that has a convenient and open view. But it is wisest to take Boudin's advice and draw in the open air. Parks are particularly good places. A number of them even provide seats!

STUDIES AND A DRAWING

Plan your work as you did the last project—three preliminary studies and a large drawing. You should try to finish a single session without a break. Work in line and tone or in color, but consider using a different medium from those you used in the last project. When you have completed this project pin up your work, and also the drawings from the last project, and compare them.

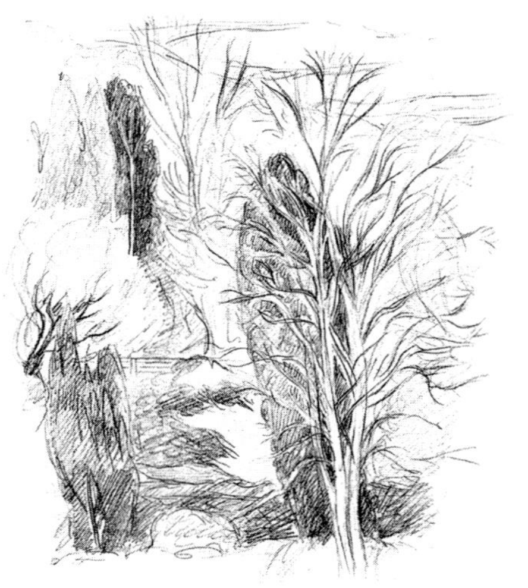

Having worked out the basic composition in the first two sketches (above), the artist made further studies of the shapes of the trees beside the house.

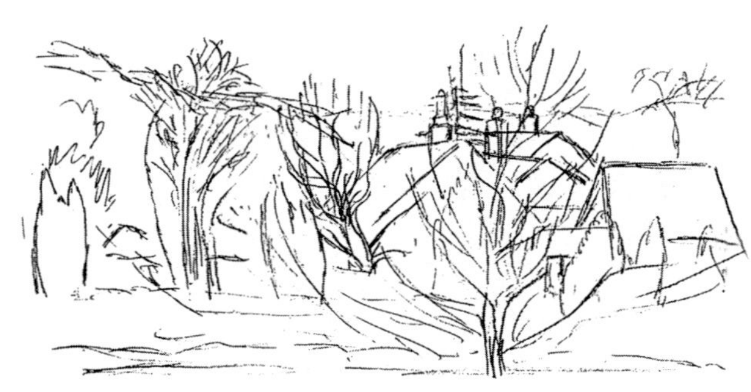

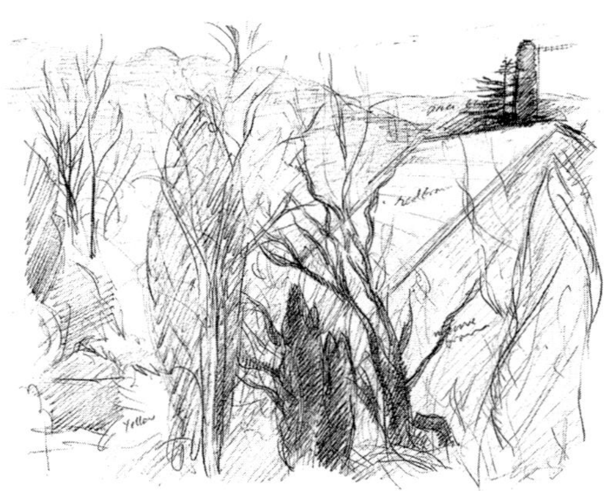

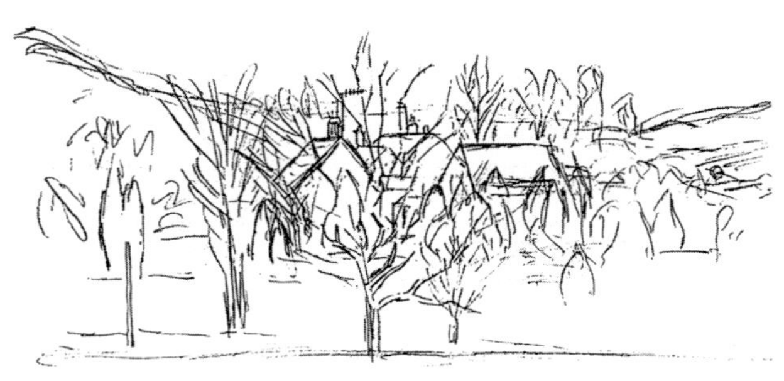

SELF-CRITIQUE

- **Did you find that the experience you gained from the townscape project helped you to draw landscape?**
- **Which of the drawings or studies do you feel best captures the subject?**
- **Have you discovered anything new about the medium you used?**
- **Did you find the trees and plants more difficult to translate than the more clearly defined forms of buildings?**

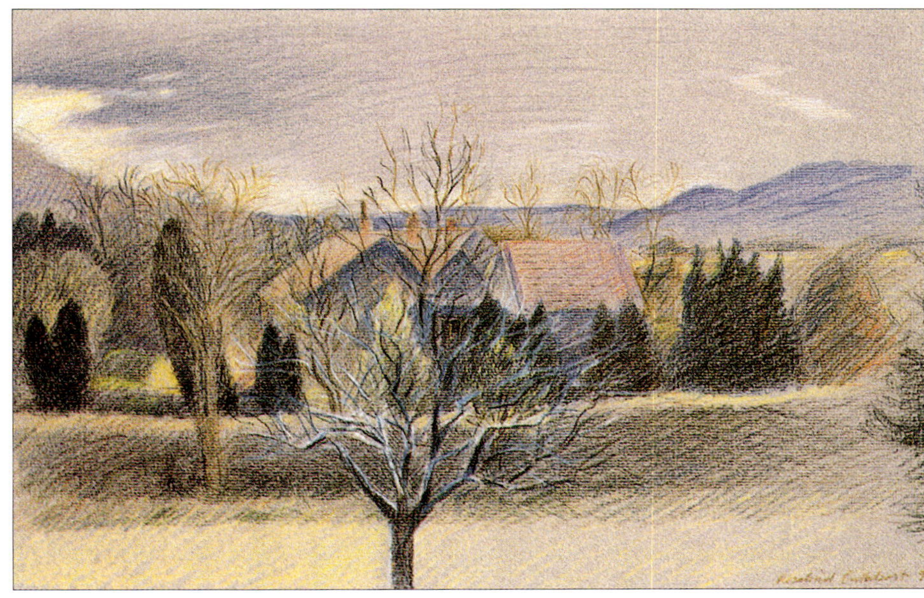

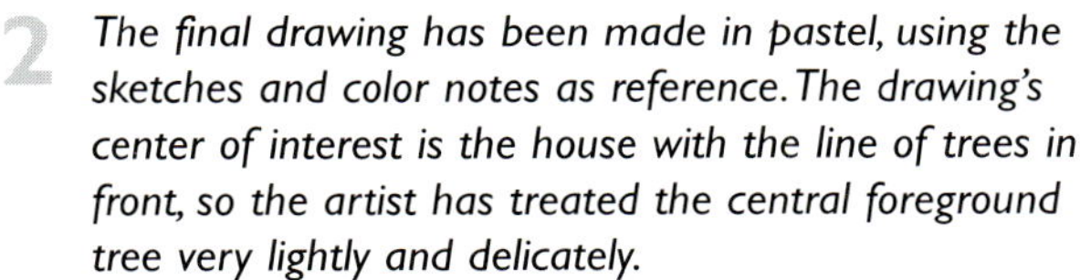

2 *The final drawing has been made in pastel, using the sketches and color notes as reference. The drawing's center of interest is the house with the line of trees in front, so the artist has treated the central foreground tree very lightly and delicately.*

Below *Drawing by Stephen Crowther using charcoal and conté. Although many of his drawings are studies for paintings, this one,* Supreme Endeavor, *was seen as an end in itself. The composition has been planned with care; notice the balance of light and dark tones and the way the triangle made by the quay and pier reinforce the irregular triangle of the boat's bows.*

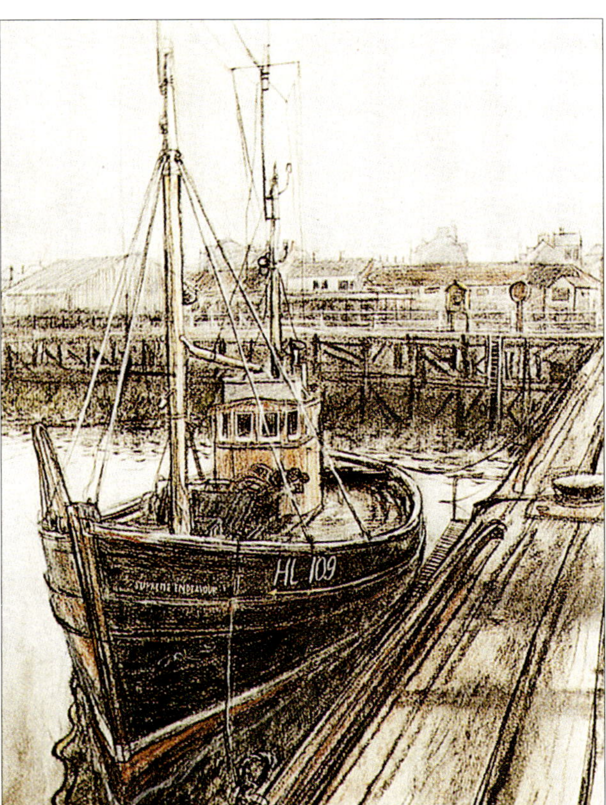

Below *Charcoal and white chalk drawing by Joan Elliot Bates. Time is often limited when you are working out of doors, and decisions have to be made about how much to include. In this simple but beautifully balanced drawing, the artist has limited herself to exploring the balance of shapes and tones.*

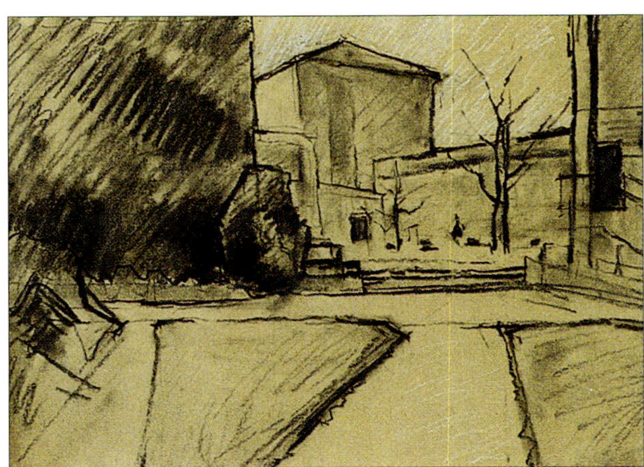

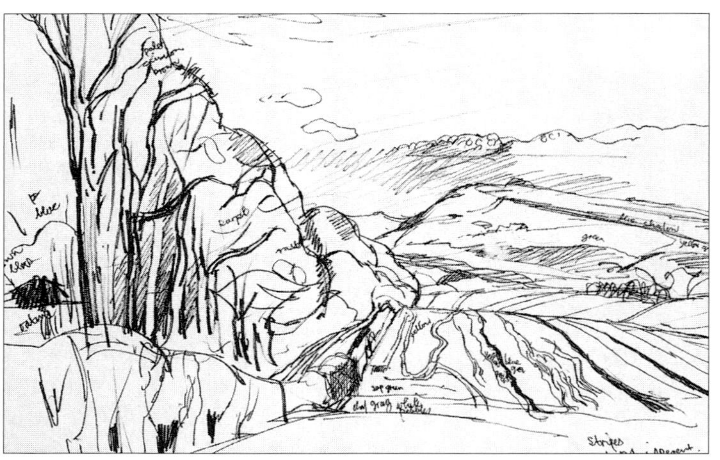

Above *Gordon Bennett is primarily a landscape artist. He draws on location and paints in the studio, constructing his paintings from sketches like this. The drawing, although rapidly executed, includes a series of color notes.*

Below *This working drawing by Bruce Cody has been squared up for transfer. A small grid of squares is made on the drawing and a larger one on the painting surface.*

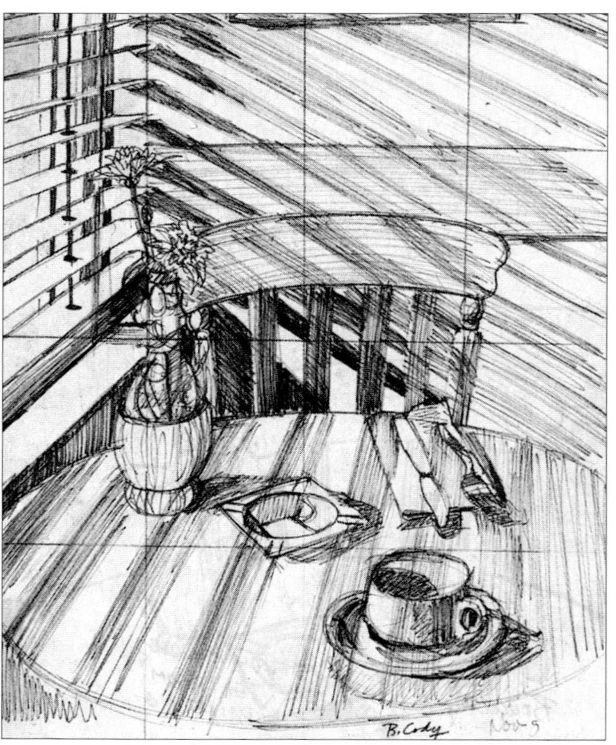

DRAWING FOR PAINTING

A drawing can be an end in itself—a finished work of art—or it can be a means to an end. Drawing is often used by artists in the latter way, as a means of exploration and discovery, and it is widely used by painters for trying out ideas and collecting information.

A drawing from which a painting is to be made is different from one made for its own sake, as it must not only be effective in itself but it must also have all the information you will need when you begin to paint. It must usually be capable of being enlarged, and it must have all the information on shapes, tones, and colors that your painting will require. In order for such drawings to be really useful, it is necessary always to bear in mind the eventual painting. You must concern yourself not with making what you consider to be a beautiful drawing, but with recording the kind of information from which you can later paint.

Drawings which are made as a step toward a work in another medium are often called working drawings. Drawing is very important in relation to painting because it is the quickest way to respond to a visual idea. A few lines, drawn in as many seconds, can effectively conjure up the first idea of a painting. Drawing is quicker even than taking a polaroid photograph and much more use, because in order to make any drawing you have already had to decide which aspects of the subject are significant and commit them to paper.

A drawing from which you intend to develop a painting should first be an investigation of the subject. You must restrict yourself to recording only information from which you can paint. If in the slightest doubt, be prepared to ruin the drawing in order to record sufficient information for the painting.

Sometimes, it is better to make separate studies of shapes, tones, and colors and use all three as references for the painting. This is not absolutely essential, though.

Don't let the dimensions of the original sheet of paper dictate the outcome of the drawing, even if this means that you end up with a drawing larger than your board. You don't need to decide where the edges of your picture will be until you start work on the painting. Pencil, charcoal, or a pen are ideal for this kind of drawing.

TONES AND BRUSH MARKS

Charcoal or conté crayon are both effective for making tonal drawings. You can draw freely and broadly with them to recreate the pattern of tones you can see, and you can use

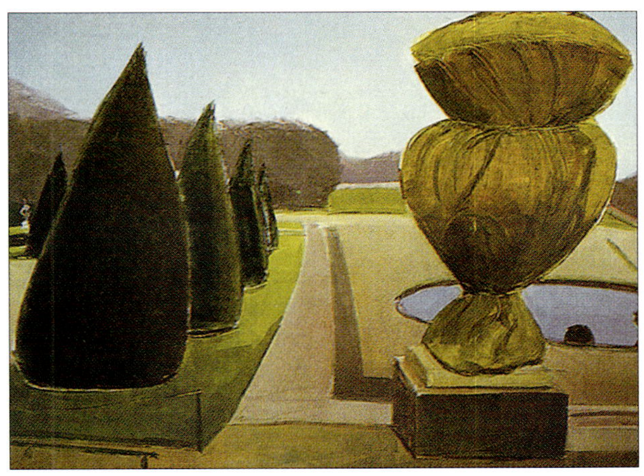

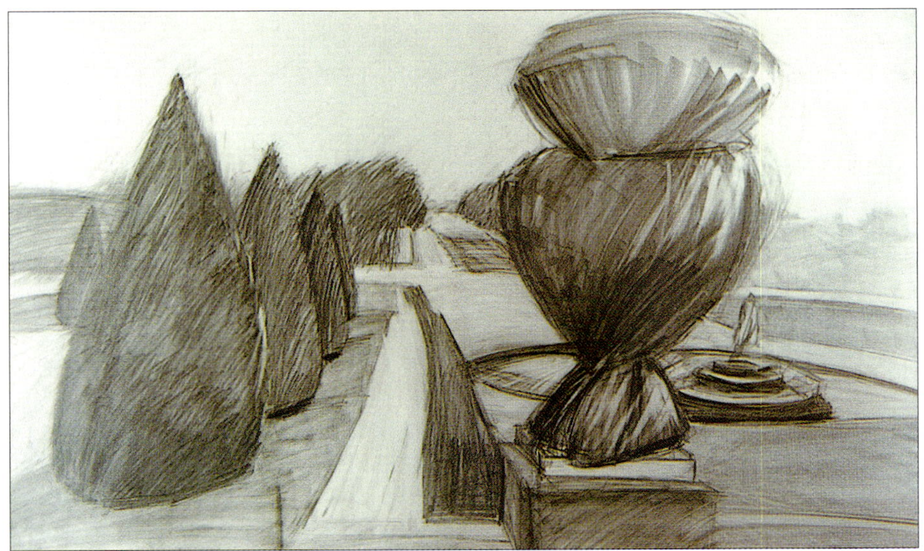

Top and Right *Joyce Zavorskas's graphite drawing,* Wrapped Urn and Trees, *is one of a series of study sketches exploring the possibilities of the subject for the monotype print below. Some artists will make just one drawing, while others will make several preparatory investigations of this kind.*

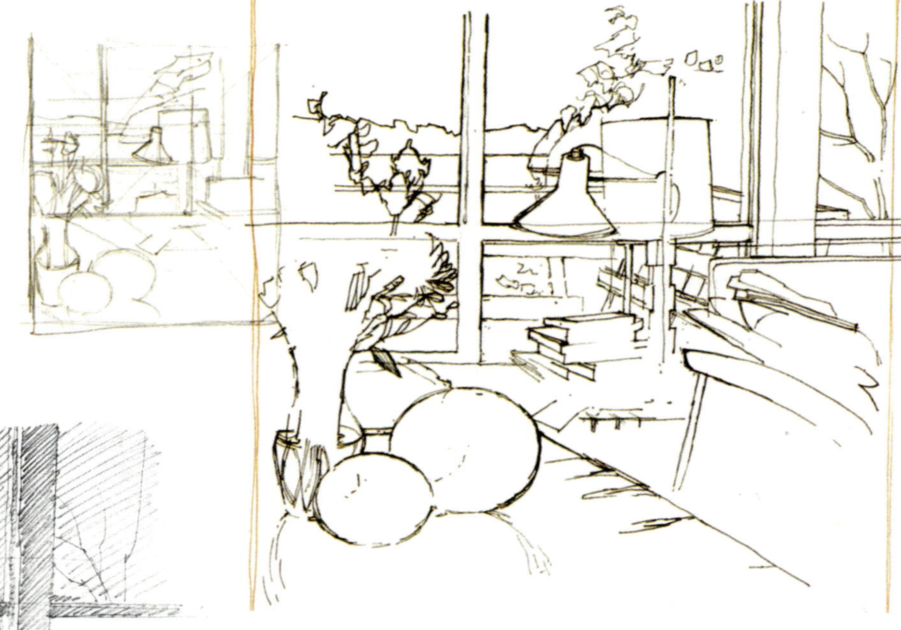

Right and Below *The kind of drawings you make for paintings depends on your personal visual interest. In Ronald Jesty's paintings, both shapes and tones are important, so he has made two separate studies, one in line and the other in tone.*

them in much the same way as you will use your brushes when you paint.

A good way of starting a tonal drawing is to draw the main shapes, then decide the tonal limits of the subject—which are the lightest and which the darkest areas. Decide next how many tones to have between these limits. There may in fact be a great many slightly different tones to be seen in the subject, but usually it is necessary to reduce these to two or three so that there is an adequate balance between contrast and harmony.

COLOR INFORMATION

Some artists write notes about color on their drawings. This is very useful, but only when you have learned how to describe colors. To be effective, a color note has to tell you, perhaps months after making it, what you need to know to recreate the intended color. Merely writing "blue," for example, is not going to be much use when you begin to paint. "Warm blue" or "purple blue" would be better, and "prominent warm blue" or "receding purple blue" even more informative.

DEVELOPING A SHORTHAND

Because working drawings are made only as a step in a process, they need only mean something to the artist concerned. A quick method of making visual notes is extremely valuable: it enables you to record something which might soon change, like a particular atmospheric effect; and also because it enables you to draw in inconvenient places, where speed is of the essence, perhaps on the steep bank of a river or near a busy street.

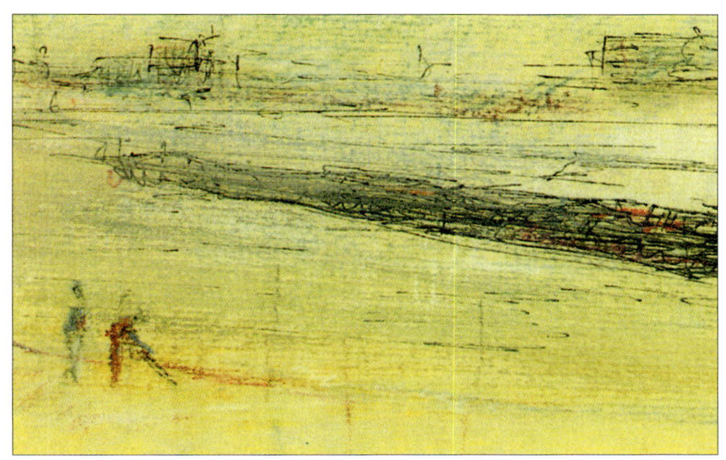

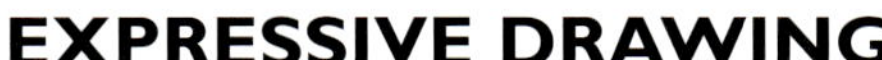

EXPRESSIVE DRAWING

Some artists are less interested in faithfully depicting objects or scenes than in expressing the feelings that these subjects invoke. The Norwegian painter Edvard Munch described the overpowering feeling of a scene. "I was walking along a road one evening—on one side lay the city, and below me was the fjord.

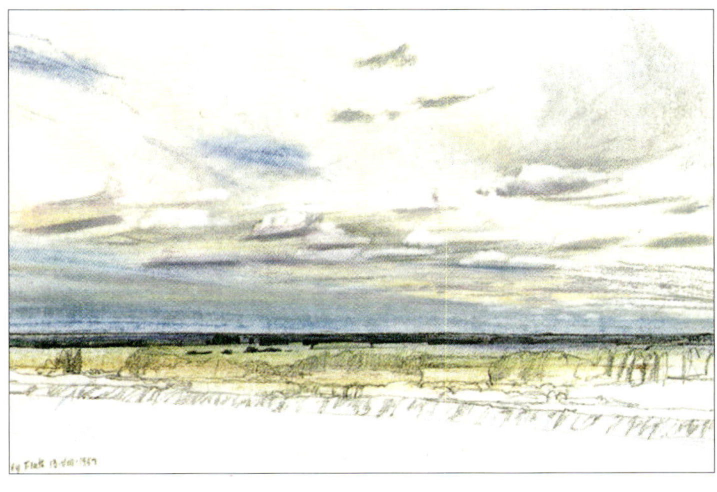

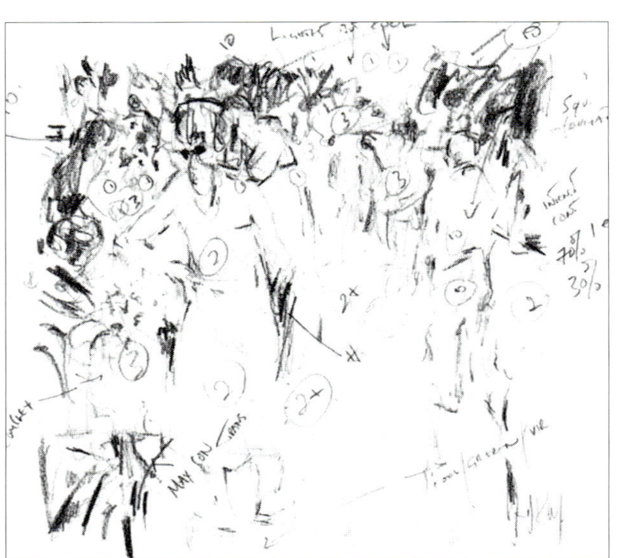

Above *James Morrison's pastel and pencil drawing was done in a large-format sketchbook, of which the artist has several. With a large format sketchbook, you are not caught in a location where you would like to do a study that contains several details and not have enough space to do it in.*

Top Above *In John Denahy's sketch for* Thames Barges*, a combination of pastel and ink has allowed him to record small details as well as color. This information is useful when working in the studio later, for it reminds the artist of his initial response to the subject he was sketching.*

Left *Looking at this drawing it is hard to believe that a painting could be made from it, but Arthur Maderson has developed a highly effective personal "code," numbering the colors and tones and sometimes also writing more elaborate notes on his sketches. The function of a sketchbook is to serve as a reminder of the artist's initial impressions.*

The sun went down—the clouds were stained red, as if with blood. I felt as though the whole of nature was screaming—it seemed as though I could hear a scream." From this emotional experience, Munch produced his famous painting *The Scream*, where the screams of a distorted head are echoed by curving lines.

You will be relieved to hear that you don't have to be in Munch's disturbed emotional state to make expressive drawings, and it is not always necessary to exaggerate shapes and forms to give emotive content to a subject. The French Impressionist painter Alfred Sisley wrote, "Every picture shows a spot with which the artist has fallen in love," and you can express this love for a subject, as Sisley did, without departing significantly from what you actually see.

USING THE MEDIA EXPRESSIVELY

Allowing your hand and eye to respond directly to a subject is one of the main ways in which your drawing will shift from descriptive to expressive. Another way is by the use of tone. Sharp contrasts of black and white will, for example, help to evoke the brilliant sunlight of a summer's day. A drawing which is almost entirely black will have a feeling of doom and despondency.

WIDE-ANGLE VIEWS

It is customary to draw with a narrow angle of vision because otherwise objects at the edges of your drawing tend to become distorted. Widening your angle of vision to include what you see from more than one viewpoint sometimes produces strange drawings. Widening your angle of vision in this way would result in joining together two different views of the figure. With figure drawing this kind of distortion is usually obvious, but in other subjects, such as landscapes or interiors, the distortions are less apparent, indeed you might not notice them unless you were familiar with the subject. And distortion is not necessarily wrong; used intentionally, it can be an important feature in your drawing.

SCANNING

If you draw joining together the viewpoints you get by turning your head around, it will have the effect of stretching and flattening the objects.

Make a very quick drawing from your feet to the ceiling above your head. This might involve four or five movements of your head

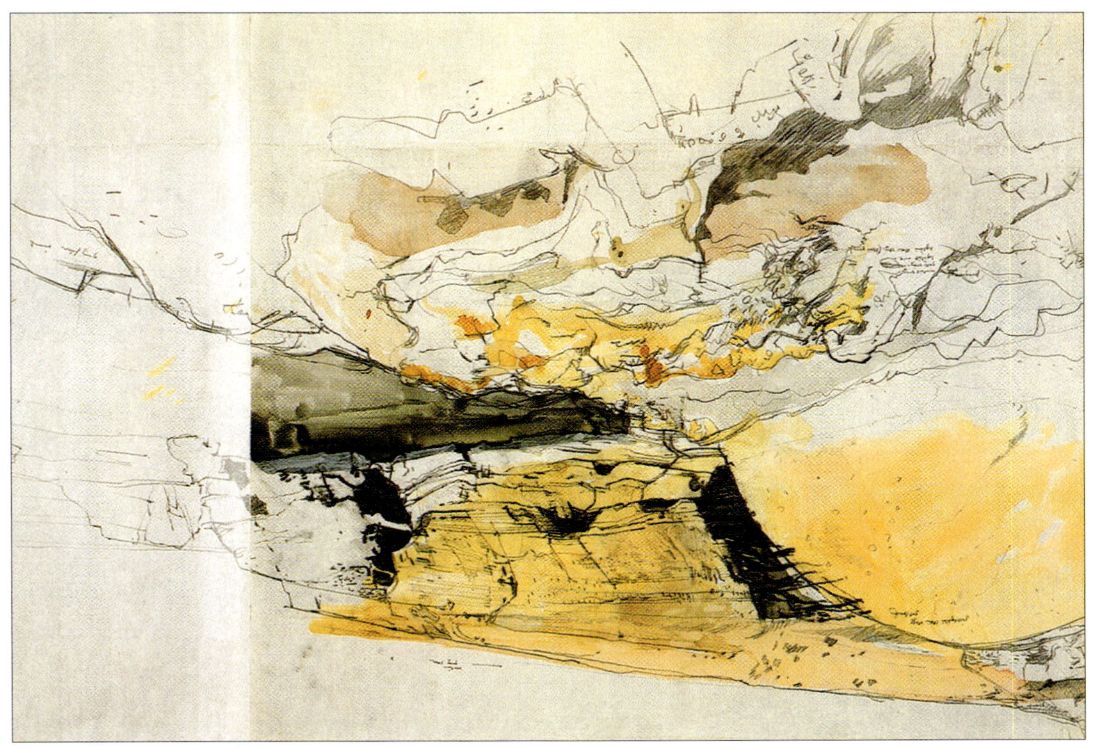

Above *This drawing by Ian Simpson contains many different viewpoints. The artist began by scanning the landscape from the sky down across the rocks. At a later stage he also decided to extend the view to the right, making it necessary to add a sheet of paper to the right side of the drawing. Washes of acrylic color were used to describe the main tones and colors, and there are also some written tone and color.*

and will, in effect, be four or five views joined together. The result might surprise you. Perhaps it will demonstrate that you don't have to restrict your view. You can draw what you see naturally and produce unusual effects and images.

THE AIM OF THE PROJECTS

- Drawing with an emphasis on expression
- Using different media expressively
- Responding to different kinds of mood and atmosphere

WHAT YOU WILL NEED

You will need all your drawing materials, and you should be prepared possibly to work outdoors.

TIME

Each project will take about 3 hours.

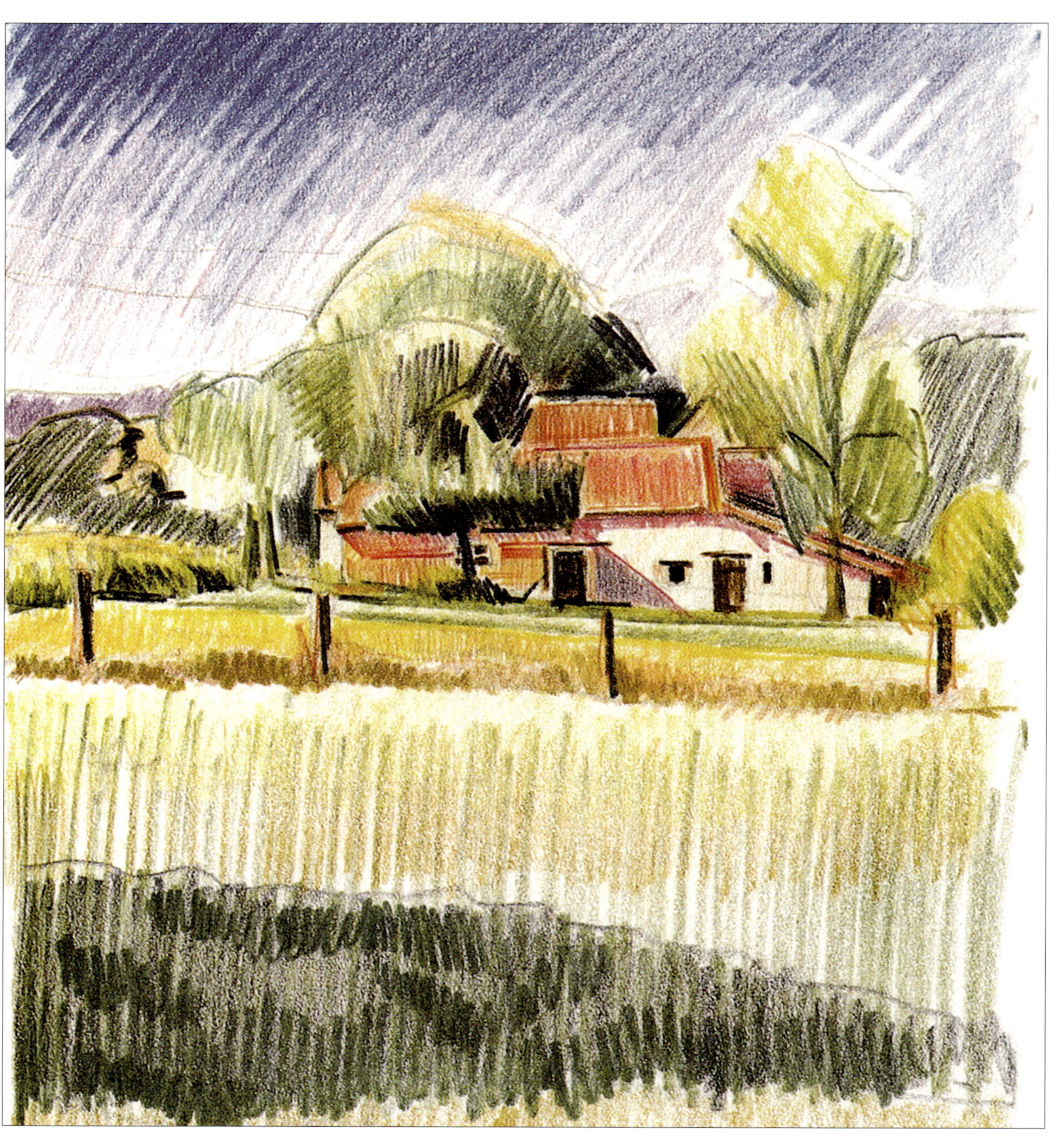

Above *The artist's personal "handwriting" is very apparent in this lively and rapidly made location drawing. Notice the variations in the direction of the lines—diagonal marks for the sky, vertical ones for the foreground field, and multi-directional ones suggesting the different growth patterns of the trees.*

12 DIFFERENT MEDIA AND METHODS

Drawing is about discovery, and you should constantly be finding new subjects or finding new things to say about familiar subjects. Experimenting with media and techniques can help you along on this process of discovery, and this chapter may point you in different directions by offering new insights into how you treat your own visual experiences and artistic expressions.

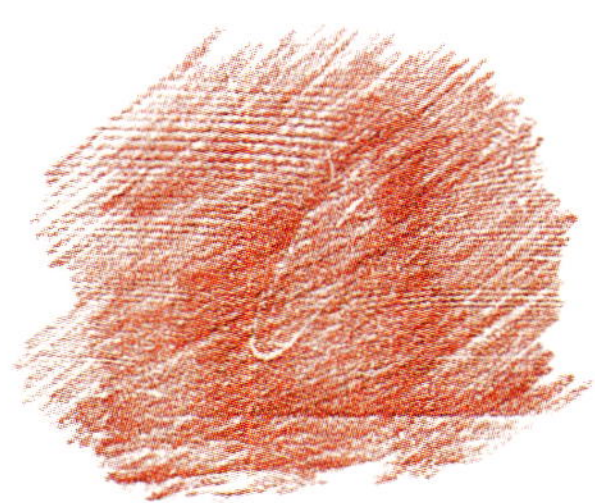

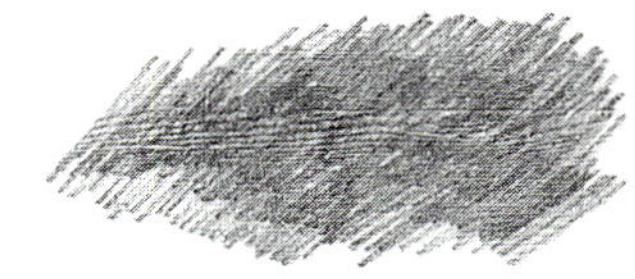

Above *Wood grain is a popular subject for frottage (tracing the patterns or textures of an object by placing a paper on it and rubbing softly with pencil or pastels).*

PENCIL AND COLORED PENCIL

In spite of the ever-increasing range of drawing materials now available, many still prefer pencils to any other medium. It is not hard to see why. The pencil is a convenient and versatile tool, capable of achieving many effects from fine, delicate lines through hatching, crosshatching, and scribbling, to dense areas of shading. The effects you can obtain depend on several factors: the grade of the pencil (its hardness or softness); the pressure you exert; the speed of the line; the surface of the paper; and last but not least, the way the pencil is held.

Because we write with pencils, there is a tendency to hold a pencil for drawing as we do for

Left *Frottage; the effects you achieve with this technique are affected by both the thickness of the paper and the implement used for making the rubbing. Both these examples were made from the same object, a patterned tinfoil ornament.*

HATCHING AND CROSSHATCHING

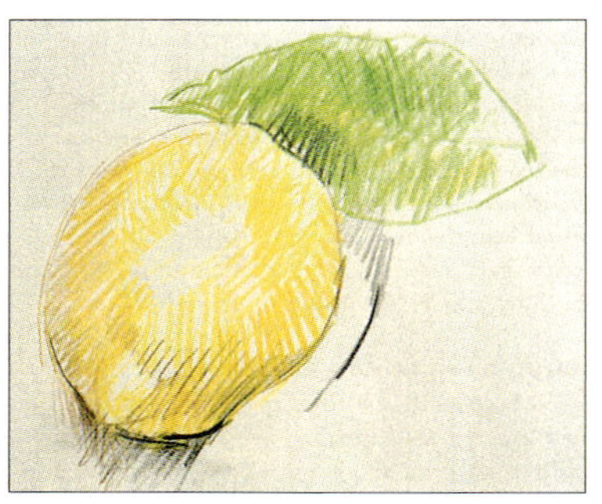

1 *There is no rule about the direction of the criss-crossing lines; here the artist has begun with roughly diagonal hatching lines which she then overlays with crosshatching.*

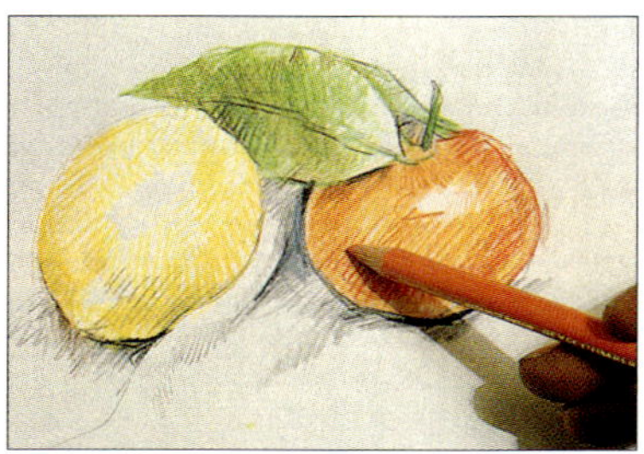

2 *Further crosshatching builds up forms and colors. The artist increases pressure where she wants denser color.*

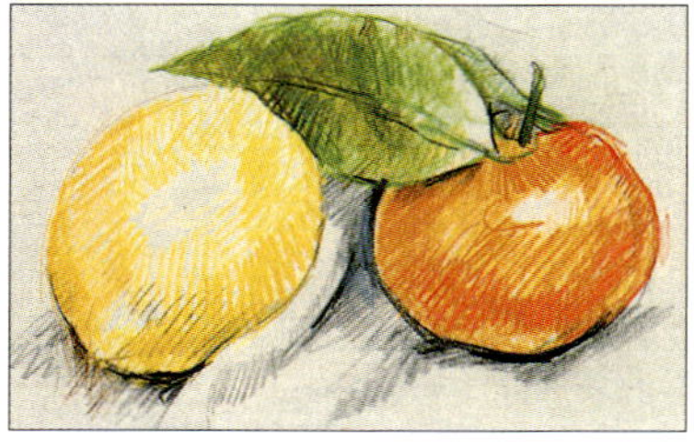

3 *The painter has used rich colors, and the vigorous use of the pencils gives the drawing an attractive feeling of liveliness.*

writing. This gives maximum control and is fine for detailed areas of shading and line, but it can lead to rather stiff, unexpressive drawings. Holding the pencil in different ways, even if they seem unfamiliar at first, can enable you to make freer sweeps of the arm. Try different ways of using pencils, perhaps drawing with a sharp point in one part of a drawing, and a blunt end in others. Don't restrict yourself to one grade of pencil in a drawing, either; you can use two or three different ones, thus extending the possible tonal range.

COLORED PENCIL

Colored pencils are a much newer invention than graphite pencils, and because of their popularity with illustrators, the range is becoming more and more varied. The pencils vary in character—from soft, chalky, and opaque, or soft and waxy, to hard and translucent. These variations are caused by the different proportions of binder used—the substance which holds the colored pigment together.

As with graphite pencils, you can mix different types in the same drawing, and you may need to build up a selection of different brands to provide a comprehensive color range—the pencils are sold singly as well as in sets. You can also mix colored pencils with graphite pencils; the two are natural partners.

BUILDING UP COLORS AND TONES

Colored pencils, being easy to handle as well as light and portable, are an excellent medium for rapid drawings and outdoor sketches. They can also achieve intricate, highly detailed effects and rich blends of color.

Hatching and crosshatching have

traditionally been used to build up areas of tone in monochrome drawings, but they are equally effective with colored pencils. Shading can also be used for mixing and modifying colors, and to achieve a softer effect than is attained by hatching.

BURNISHING

This is a technique sometimes used to increase the brilliance of colors. After the color has been mixed on the paper, the surface is rubbed with a finger or a rag to produce a slight sheen. The rubbing action sometimes smooths the grain of the paper and it grinds down the colors and presses the particles of pigment into the paper, so that they blend together in a way that can't be achieved by any other method of overlaying colors.

You can use a torchon (a rolled-paper stump), a plastic eraser, or one of the pencils themselves for burnishing. Torchons and erasers are most suitable for soft, waxy pencils. Drawings in hard colored pencils are sometimes burnished with a white or pale-gray pencil, using close shading with a firm pressure. This process tends to fuse the colors in the same way as a torchon or eraser. The difference is that the underlying colors will be modified by this form of burnishing.

White-pencil burnishing is a method well-suited to drawing highlights on highly

SHADING

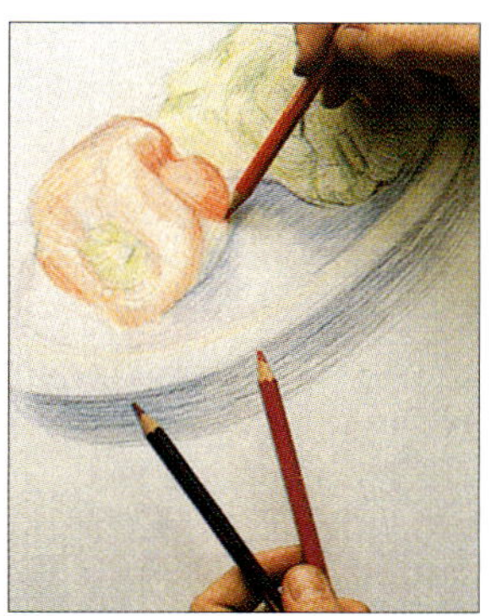

1 *The artist begins by laying in the colors lightly. Note how certain areas of the paper have been left white for the inclusion of highlights at a later stage.*

2 *With the addition of a dark shadow, the artist is better able to judge how much further shading is needed to build up the colors.*

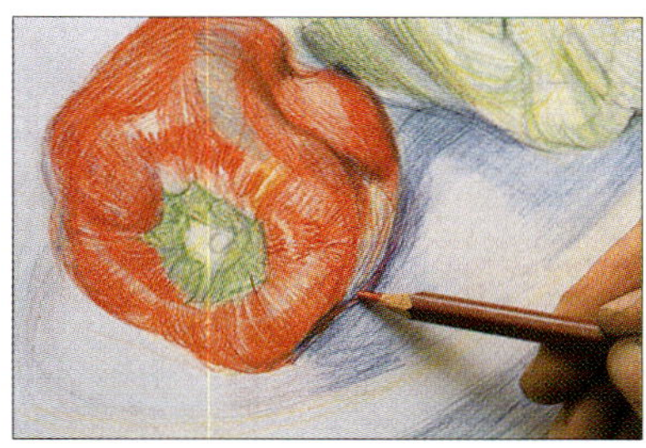

3 *With the addition of a dark shadow, the artist is better able to judge how much further shading is needed to build up the colors.*

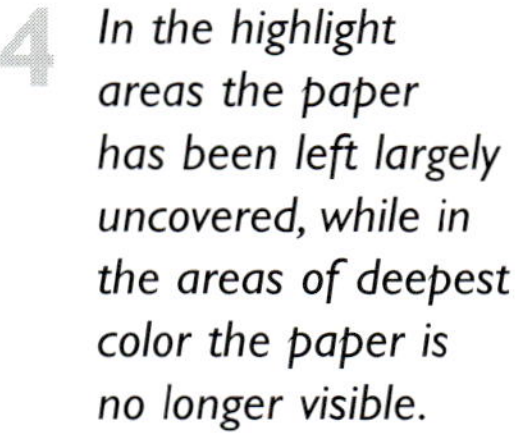

4 *In the highlight areas the paper has been left largely uncovered, while in the areas of deepest color the paper is no longer visible.*

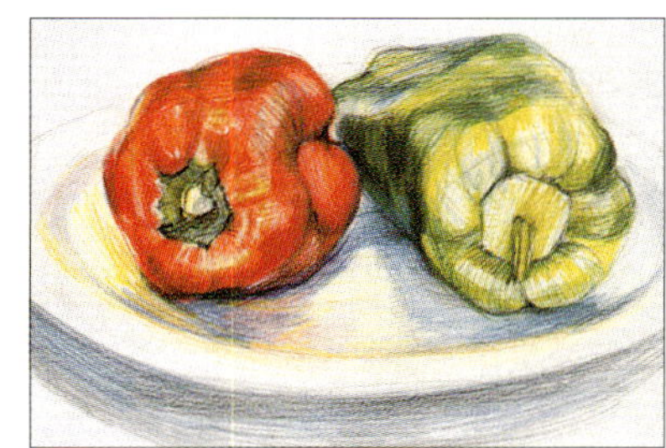

BURNISHING

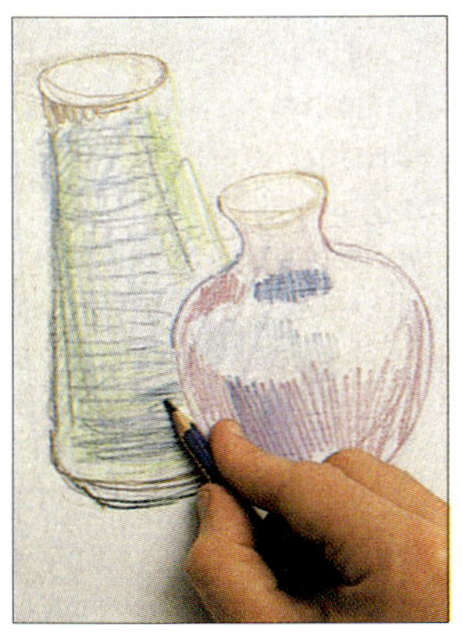

1 *Burnishing—a technique used to increase the brilliance of colors—is always a final stage in a drawing. First, all the colors must be established and built up as thickly as desired.*

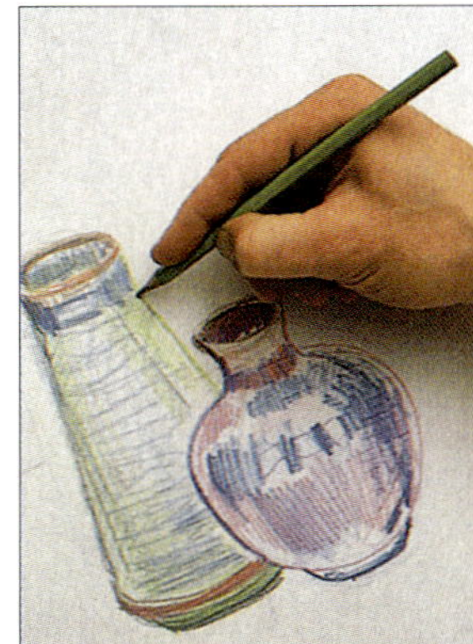

2 *The artist continues to lay colors, using the shading and hatching techniques. Notice that on the body of the green vase he has used curving lines that follow the contours.*

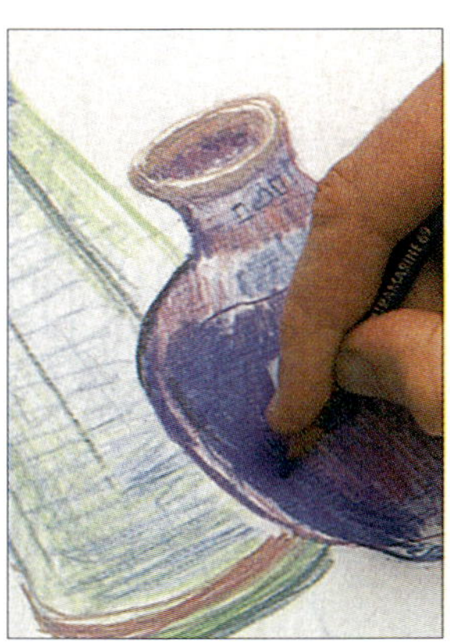

3 *A dark-blue pencil is now used to press the color into the paper, creating a small area of dark reflection, where tonal changes are often very abrupt, with a distinct, hard-edged boundary.*

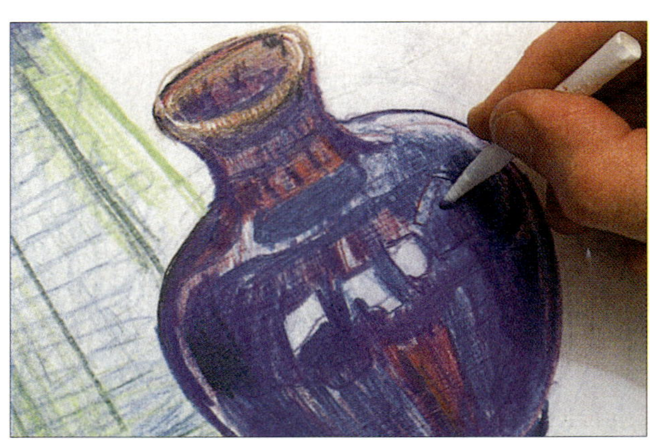

4 *Where the colors merge more gently, the artist "pushes" the colors into one another and into the paper by rubbing with a torchon.*

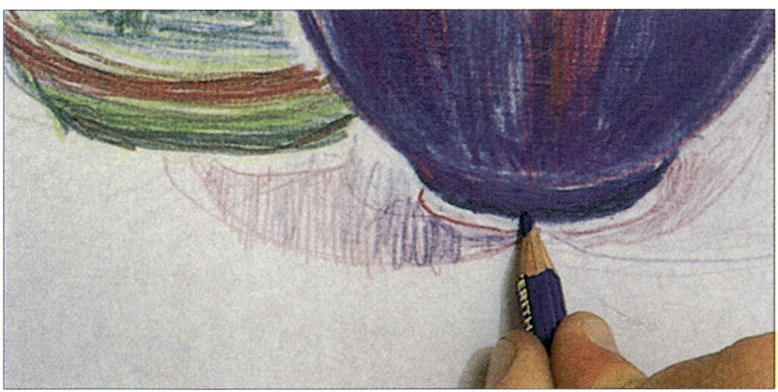

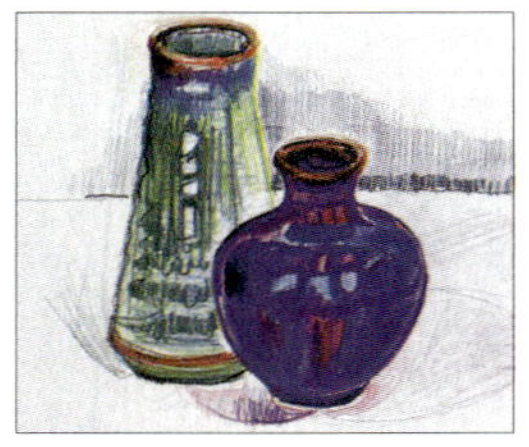

5 *The bottom of the small vase is now darkened. Notice how it remains in shadow because it curves away and under the body of the pot.*

6 *The contrast between the rich burnished colors and the sparkling highlights creates an impression of the pot's shiny surface.*

IMPRESSION

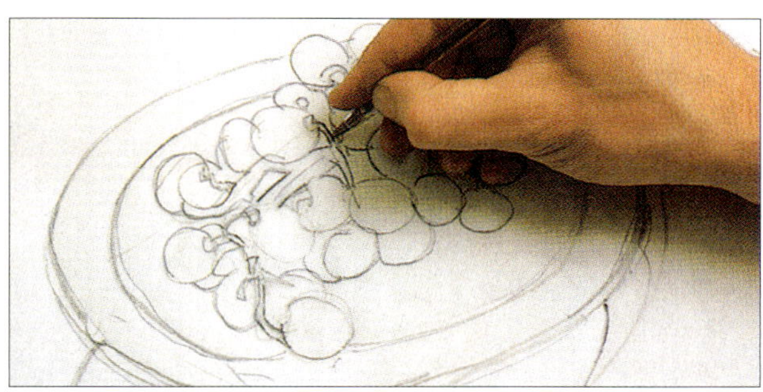

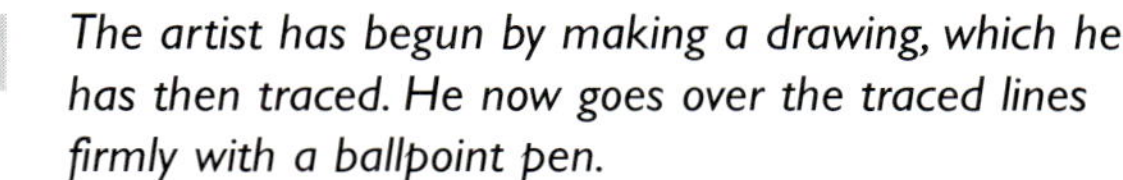

1 *The artist has begun by making a drawing, which he has then traced. He now goes over the traced lines firmly with a ballpoint pen.*

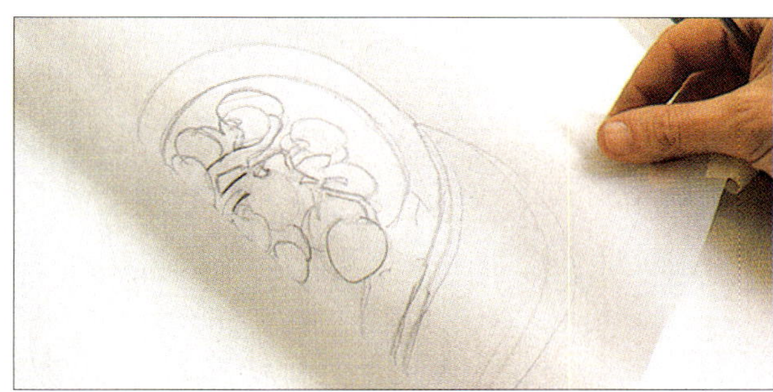

2 *He draws firmly over all the lines, and removes the tracing paper. The impressed lines will appear when pencil is laid on top.*

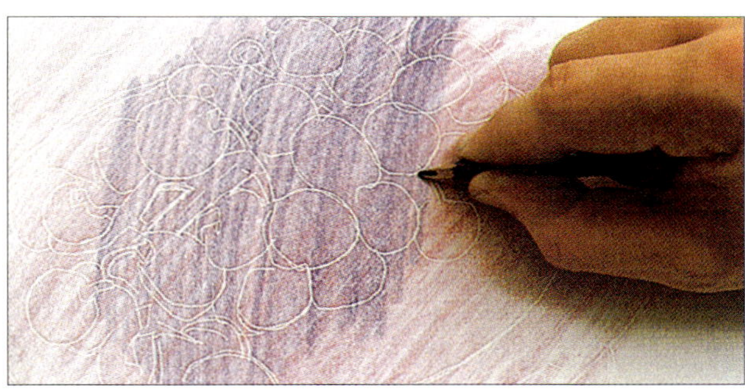

3 *Note how the colored pencil glides over the impressed lines. The more strongly you lay on the color, the more strongly these impressed lines will emerge.*

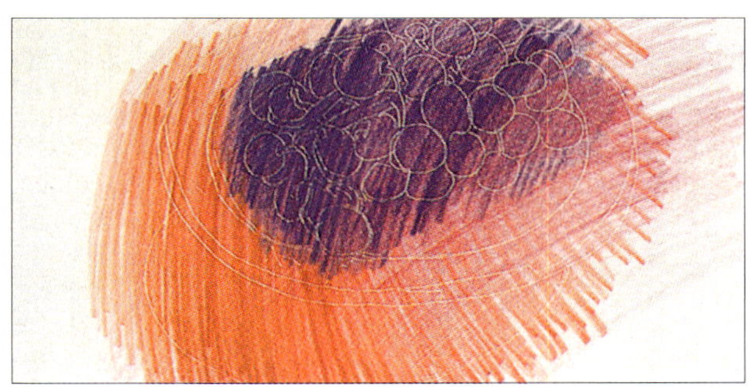

4 *A second color has now been added, and the rim of the plate has become visible. The drawing could be built up further, with subsequent stages of impressing.*

reflective surfaces. Burnishing is a slow process, and is often restricted to one area of a drawing, perhaps to describe a single metal or glass object.

PASTEL AND OIL PASTEL

Pastel can be either a drawing or a painting medium, depending on how it is used, which illustrates that there is no real dividing line between the two activities. With a linear medium such as colored pencil, the variety of different marks you can make is limited. The beauty of pastel sticks, whether you are using the soft (also known as chalk pastels) or the hard variety, is that you can draw with the side of the stick as well as the tip, which

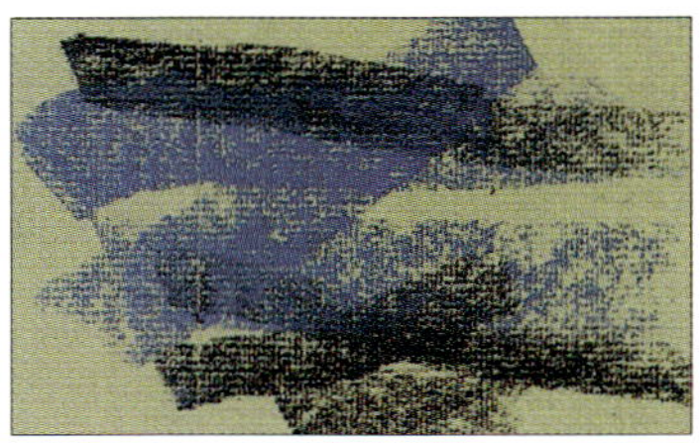

SIDE STROKES

To lay in broad areas of color, the quickest method is to use the side of a short length of pastel. Pressure can be light or heavy, the strokes can follow any direction, and you can mix colors by laying one color over another.

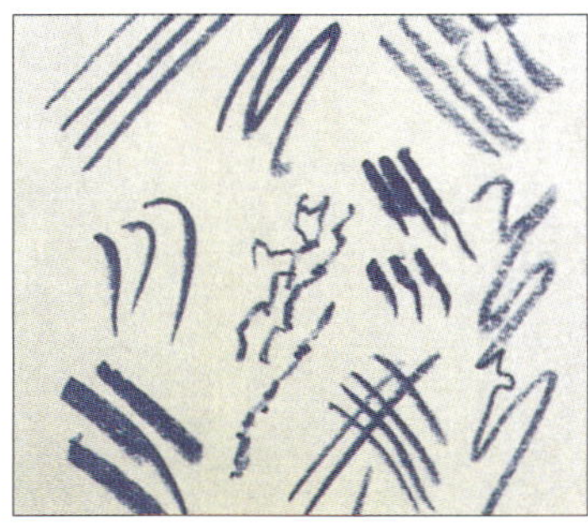

LINEAR STROKES

These can be more or less infinitely varied according to the relative softness of the pastel, the sharpness of the tip or edge, and the way you hold the pastel stick. The more variety of line you can introduce into a drawing, the more expressive it will be.

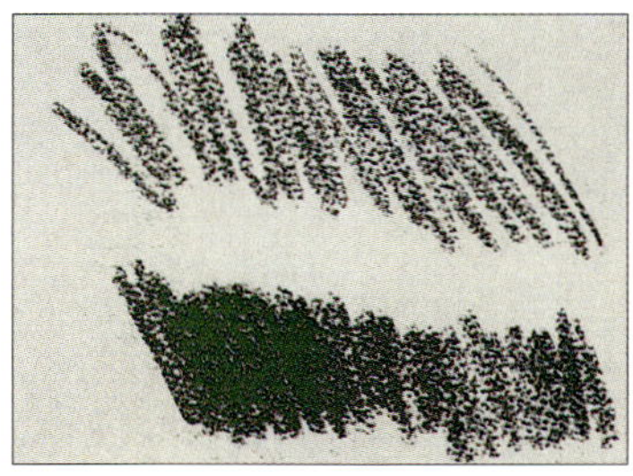

WATERCOLOR PAPER

Some pastellists love this; others hate it. As you can see, it breaks up the pastel colors, giving a speckled effect, and it is virtually impossible to push the color right into the grain.

allows you to range from broad, sweeping lines to fine, precise ones, which can be further varied by increasing or decreasing the pressure.

Side strokes are best done with a fairly short length of pastel, so snap a stick in half. You will be able to draw lines with the resulting sharp edge. You can achieve very fine lines in this way.

SURFACES FOR PASTEL WORK

The texture of the paper will also affect the appearance of your pastel strokes. Pastels are almost pure pigment, with just a little gum tragacanth used to hold the colored powder together (hard pastels have a higher proportion of this binder). If pastels are used on smooth paper, such as cartridge, the pigment will tend to fall off, so the papers made for pastel work have slight "tooth," or texture, which "bites" the particles of pigment and holds them in place. The two best-known papers sold for pastel work are Ingres, which has a laid pattern of small, regular lines, and Mi-Teintes, which has a pattern resembling very fine wire mesh. But there are many other suitable surfaces, including watercolor paper, which breaks up the strokes and gives a slightly speckled look.

Unless very heavily applied, pastel marks don't cover the paper as thoroughly as paints or inks. For this reason pastels are usually done on colored paper, otherwise little flecks of white jump out and spoil the effect of the colors. This is not to say that you can never work on white paper; if your approach is mainly linear you may find it quite satisfactory, but for a more "painterly" drawing you will find colored paper helpful.

BUILDING UP COLORS

If you are using a fairly small range of colors and want to achieve subtle effects or rich, dark hues, you will have to "mix" colors on the paper by overlaying. If you are working on heavily textured paper you can make a good many such overlays, but lighter paper becomes clogged with pigment more quickly, and you may need to spray with fixative between layers.

The color-mixing technique particularly associated with pastel work is blending, in which two or more colors are laid over one another and then rubbed with a cotton ball, your fingers, or a torchon (good for small areas) so that they fuse together. This method allows you to achieve almost any color or tone, but it is not wise to overdo blending, as it can make your drawing look bland.

OIL PASTELS

These come in two different versions, oil pastels and wax oil pastels. Both in fact are bound with a mixture of waxes, but in the wax-oil type the wax content is much more

INGRES PAPER
This paper is made especially for pastel work, and is also popular for charcoal and conté drawing. It is not suitable for a very heavy build-up of overlaid colors.

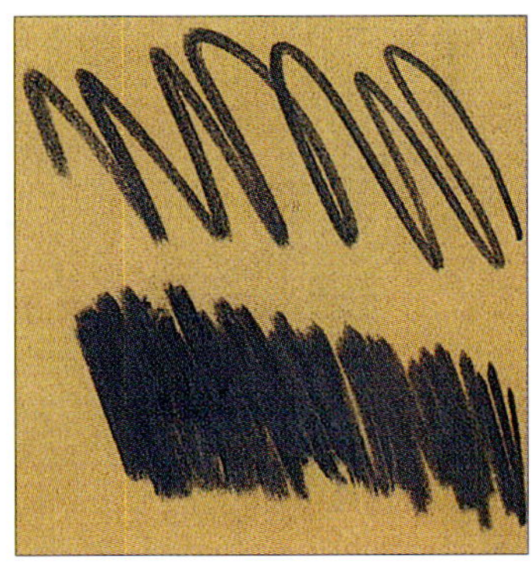

MI-TEINTES PAPER
This is the other "standard" pastel paper. Some find the heavy grain over-obtrusive, and prefer to use the "wrong" side, which is smoother but still has sufficient texture to hold the pigment. Both this and Ingres paper are made in a wide range of colors.

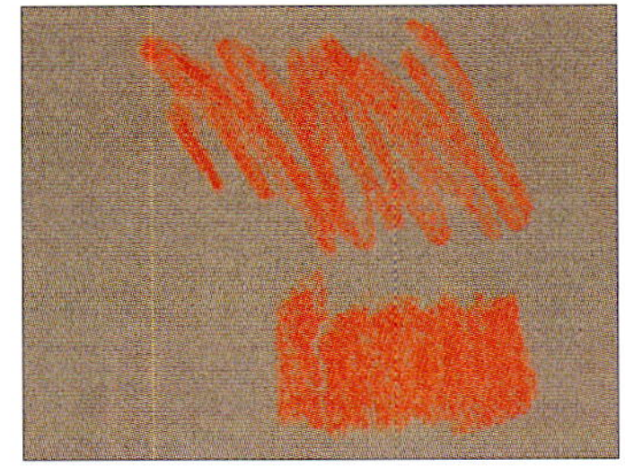

VELOUR PAPER
This is expensive, and only available from specialist suppliers. It gives an attractive soft line, with no paper showing through, and is ideal for those who like to build up thick layers of color.

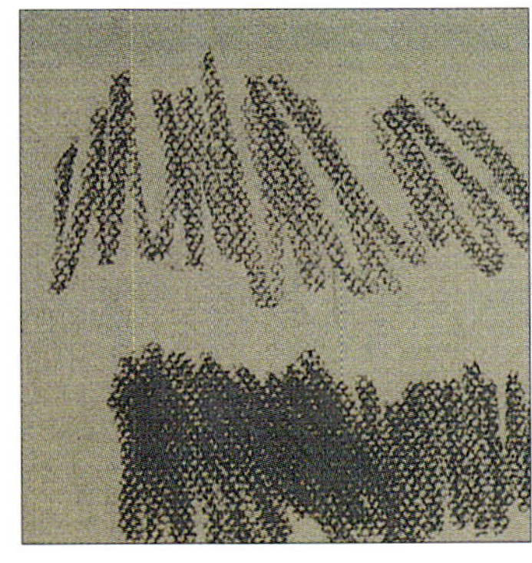

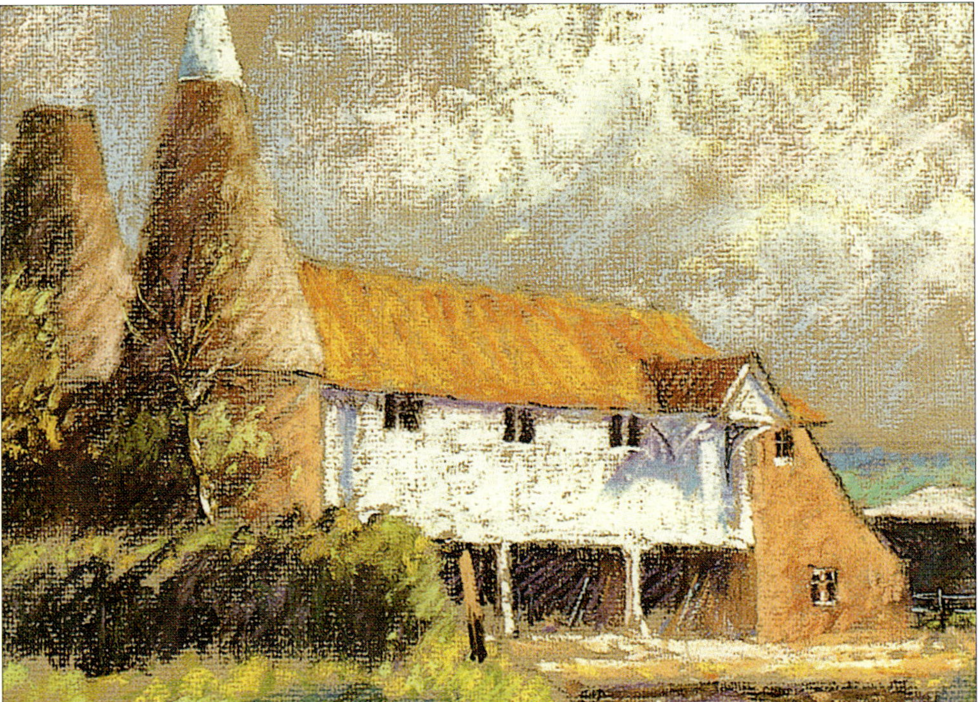

Left *Soft pastel drawing by Alan Oliver. In pastel work, the color of the paper is as important as the texture. Here you can see how well the light brown—clearly visible in the foreground and parts of the sky—blends in with the overall warm color scheme of the picture.*

BUILDING UP WITH LINE

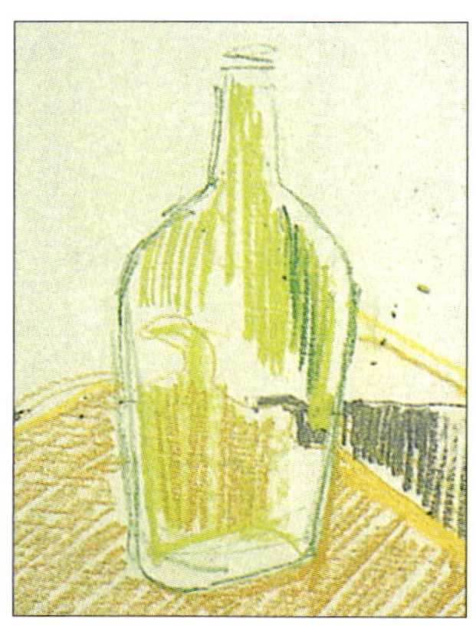

1 *This artist works mainly in colored pencil, and he uses pastel in a similar way, laying a series of firm hatched lines.*

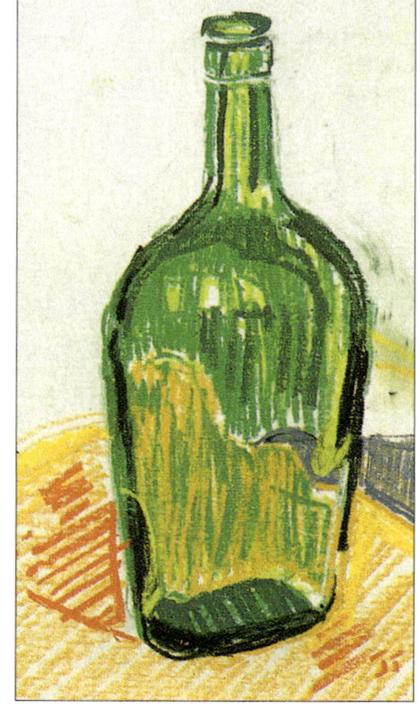

2 *He now introduces darker colors, using the same method.*

3 *Notice how the artist has varied the direction of the lines to express the forms of the bottle and the two separate horizontal planes in this drawing.*

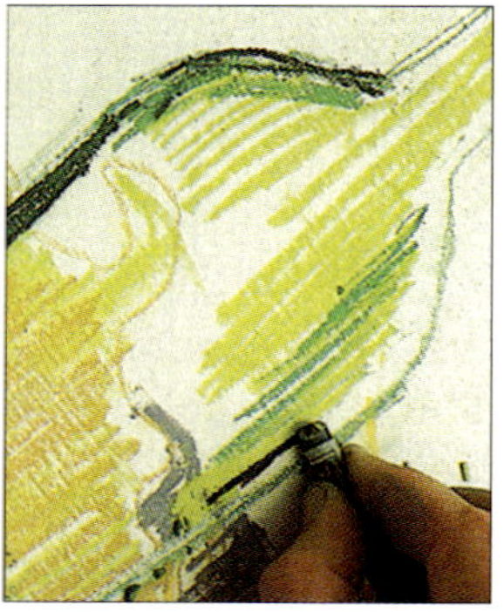

apparent in use. These are extremely useful for the wax resist technique, but some find them less suitable for general drawing than the non-wax type, which is softer and more malleable. Oil pastels can't be blended by rubbing, but the color can be melted with turpentine or denatured alcohol, so that you can mix them on the paper very much as you would mix paints on a palette. The other great virtue of oil pastels is they don't need fixing, and you can build up layers of color without worrying about the top layer falling off. A disadvantage is that in hot weather they tend to melt even without the aid of turpentine, becoming both messy to use and difficult to handle.

SGRAFFITO

Oil pastel is a relatively new medium; artists have, therefore, approached it without preconceptions. One of the techniques becoming increasingly associated with the medium is sgraffito, in which one layer of color is scratched away to reveal another one

BLENDING

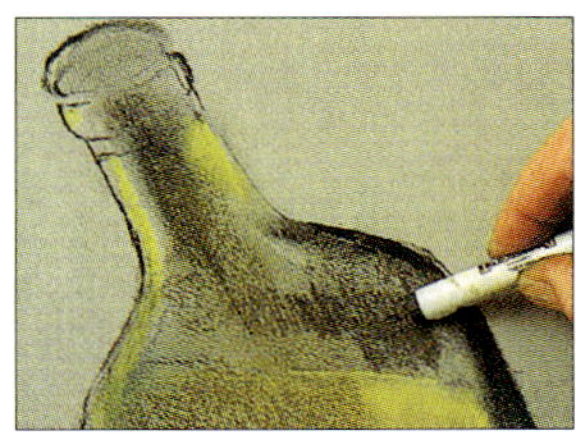

1 *This artist rubs the colors into the paper to create a soft effect. Here she modifies the green with a touch of white.*

2 *Rubbing with a finger blends one color into another. A gray paper has been chosen, as this makes it easier to judge both the darks and lights.*

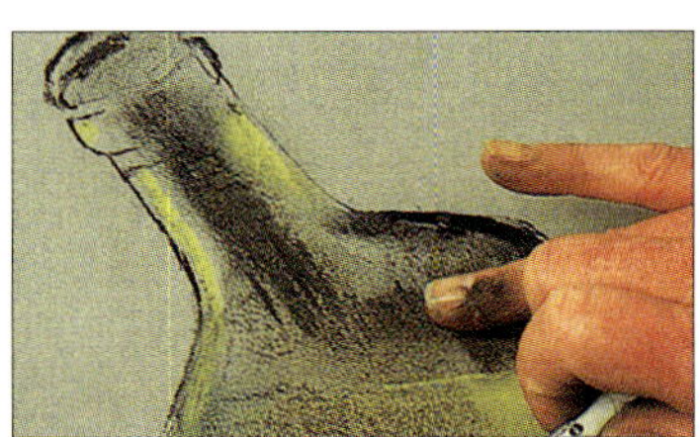

3 *A finger would be too clumsy an implement for the blending on the side of the bottle, so a cotton swab is used. The artist prefers these to torchons, as they are softer and have a gentler action.*

4 *With pastels, light colors can be laid over dark ones, if there isn't too much build-up of color. The highlights are thus left until last.*

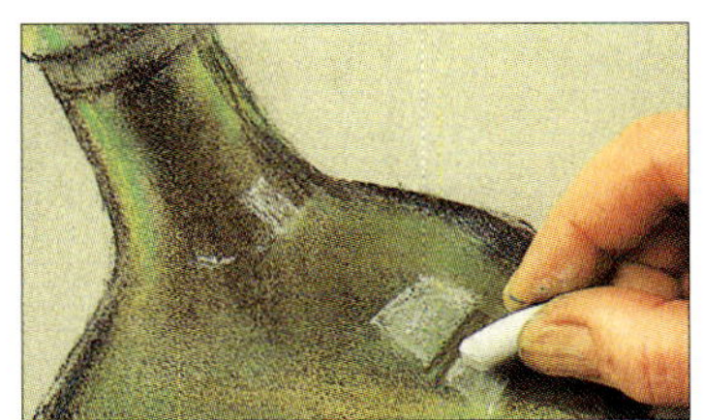

5 *This makes an interesting contrast with the demonstration opposite; here there are no visible lines. The two methods can be combined in one drawing.*

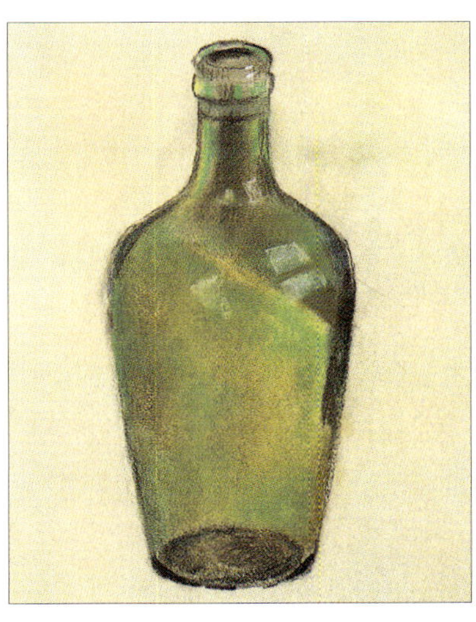

below. You will need to work on a reasonably tough paper for this technique.

Start by laying down a layer of solid color; oil pastel covers the paper thoroughly if heavily applied. Then put another color on top and use a sharp implement such as a craft knife or scalpel to scrape parts of it away. You will find that you can make a variety of different effects: try using the point of the blade for fine lines and scraping lightly with the side of it to create areas of broken color by only partially removing the top color.

CHARCOAL AND CONTÉ CRAYON

Charcoal, one of the oldest of all the drawing media, is made by firing twigs of wood such as willow at high temperatures in airtight containers. It is a wonderfully versatile medium, and is often recommended by art teachers because it is less inhibiting than pencil or pen, encouraging a free approach.

OIL PASTEL AND DENATURED ALCOHOL

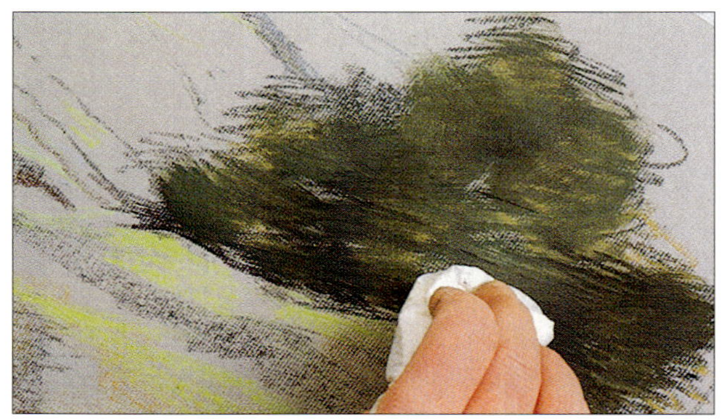

1 *To begin with, the artist spreads the dark color on the paper with a rag dipped in denatured alcohol.*

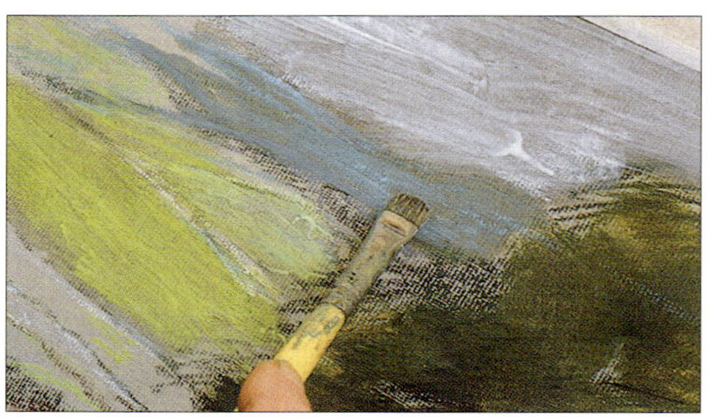

2 *A brush, similarly dipped in denatured alcohol, is now used to spread the color in the sky areas.*

3 *The artist draws over the spread color with a pastel stick tip, introducing a more linear element into the foreground of the landscape.*

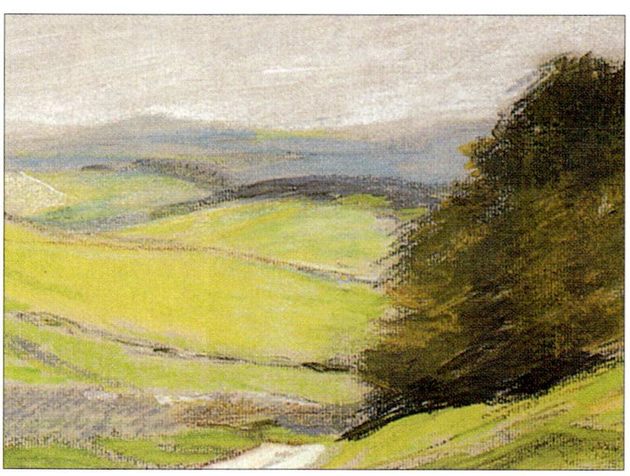

4 *This combination of drawing and painting is a very quick and effective way of building up areas of color, ideal for location work.*

SCRATCHING BACK

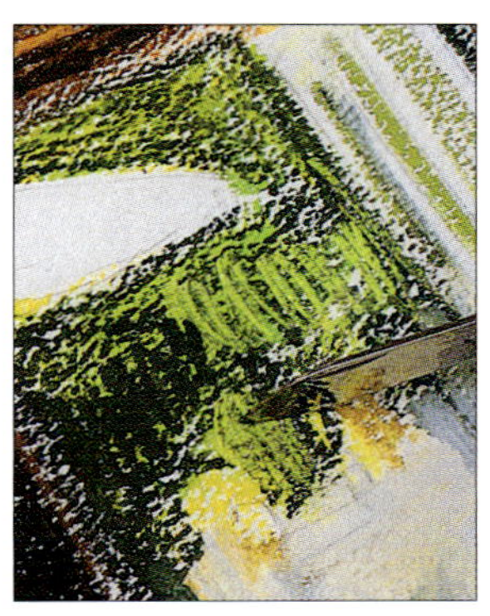

1 *The effect of this technique varies according to the paper you use and the implement used for the scraping. Here the artist is working on watercolor paper, and is using a penknife.*

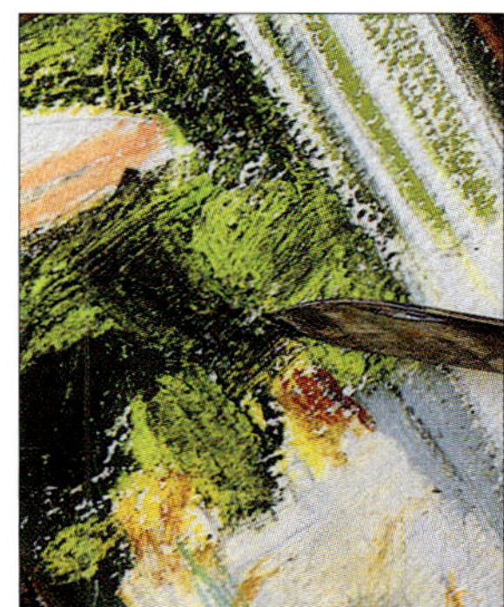

2 *The penknife is used in this case very much as a drawing tool, to manipulate the colors into shapes suggestive of trees.*

3 *The sgraffito effect adds movement to the focal point of the picture—the group of people. Here, the artist has set up echoes by using similar colors in the foreground, applied in diagonal strokes that lead the eye into the drawing.*

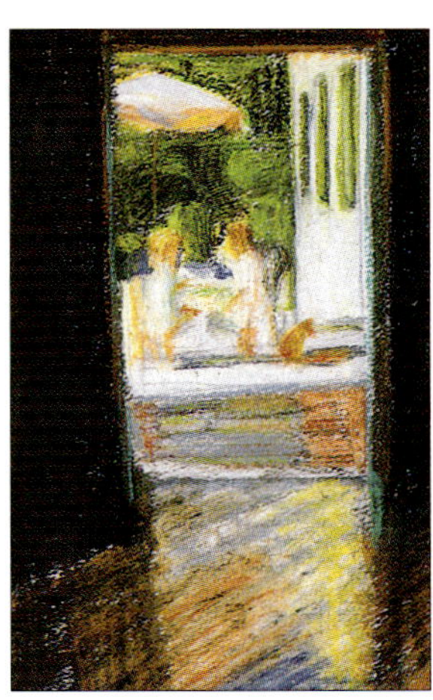

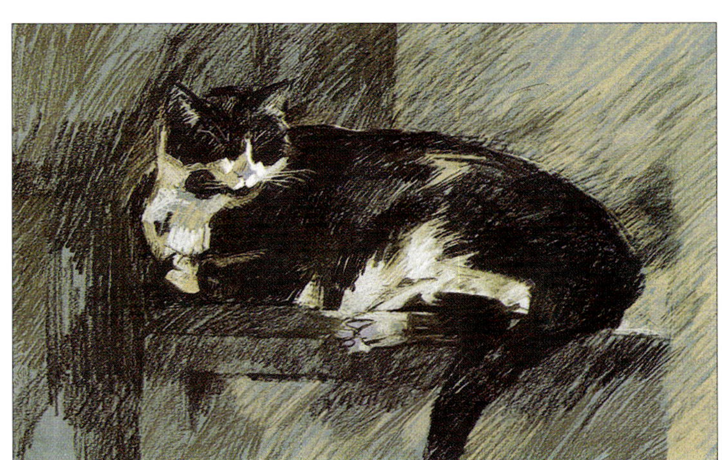

Right and Above Right *Drawings in hard pastel by Pip Carpenter. Pastel, whether hard or soft, is the perfect medium for rapid drawings. The artist has caught the cat's relaxed poses beautifully, and has managed to suggest the texture of the fur simply by varying the direction of the pastel strokes. In both cases, she has worked on a warm, mid-toned paper, which contrasts with the cool grays and blues in the drawings.*

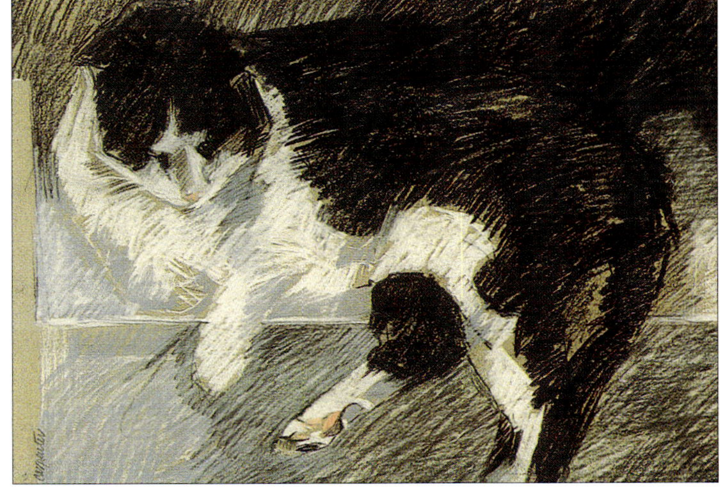

PAPER TEXTURE

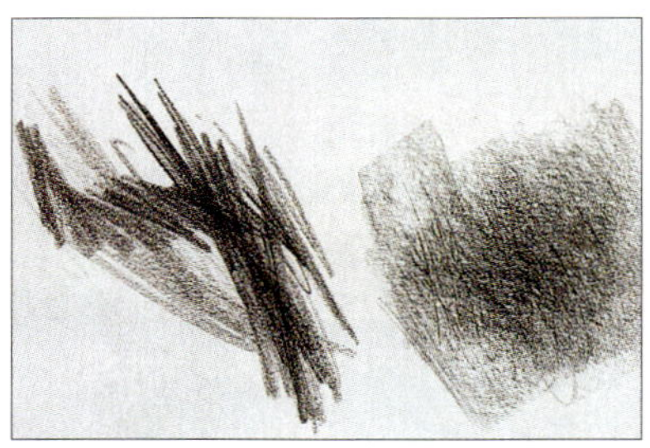

Left *In charcoal, pastel, and conté crayon drawings, the texture of the paper is an important factor. This photograph shows conté crayon on cartridge paper, which is relatively smooth and does not break up the strokes to any great extent.*

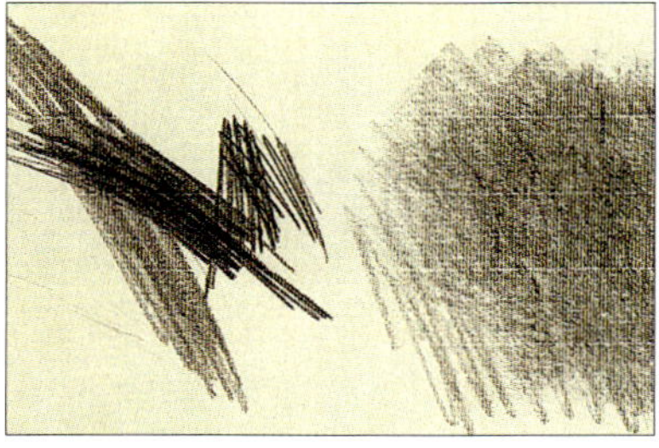

Left *Charcoal paper is made with a laid pattern of even lines which will show through unless the conté is very heavily applied. Sometimes advantageous, this makes it difficult to achieve dense blacks.*

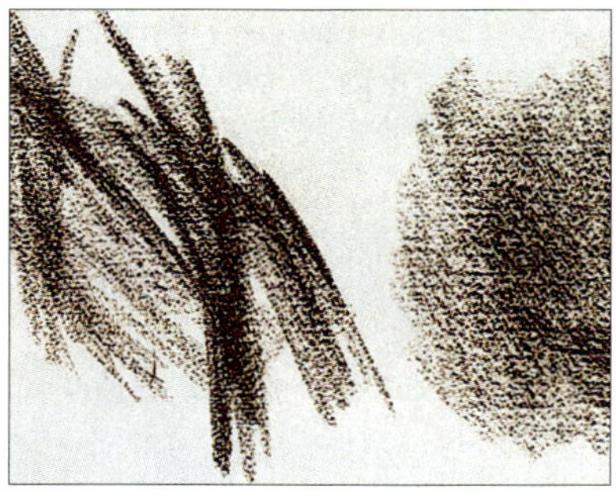

Left *Watercolor paper has a very pronounced texture, and because the conté will adhere only to the raised grain, creates a distinct speckling. This can be effective for a drawing in mainly light and mid-tones, but not for one where you want solid blacks.*

LINES AND TONES

Charcoal is very responsive to the slightest change in pressure, so you can produce a line that varies from the faintest possible tone to a deep, positive black. The marks you make are also affected by the way you apply the charcoal. For instance, pushing it gives a stronger line than pulling.

It is easy—and very quick—to create areas of tone simply by using the side of the stick. If you want a flat, even mid-tone, you can rub the charcoal into the paper with your fingers. This effect can be darkened later with a further application. If you are working with willow charcoal, you may wish to use a fixative on the drawing from time to time, especially if you want areas of very dark tone. It is well worth experimenting with these varied techniques, and developing your own "signature" style with charcoal.

FROM DARK TO LIGHT

Normally, darks are gradually built up in drawings, but with charcoal it is also possible to work the other way round, beginning with the dark tones and "subtracting" the light ones, using a putty eraser. This is an exercise often given to art students, as it has a liberating effect, particularly on those who become over-dependent on using line. You can draw any subject in this way, but it should be something that has strong tonal contrasts.

The method is simple. You begin by covering the whole of the paper with charcoal—compressed or scenepainter's charcoal are best. Rub the charcoal well into the paper so that it becomes dark gray, then draw the subject on this gray ground. Don't put in too much detail, and don't erase if you make a mistake; just rub the lines into the background and redraw them. When you have finished the drawing, lightly rub over the lines so that they are still visible but merge into the background gray. The strongest highlights should be picked out first, so look at the subject carefully and decide where they are, and then use the eraser to "lift" them out. Next, begin to work on the midtones and strengthen the darker areas if necessary.

CONTÉ CRAYON METHODS

Like charcoal and pastels, the tip or edge of a conté crayon can produce a fine line or they can be used on their sides to create broad areas of tone. You can also exploit different textures of paper. Heavy pressure on smooth paper such as cartridge will achieve solid blacks, while a rougher surface such as watercolor or pastel paper will break up the tone to create a lively speckled effect. Their main disadvantage is that they are more or less impossible to erase, but they smudge less easily than charcoal, and don't need to be fixed.

As mentioned earlier, conté crayons are made from natural pigments, and are available in four colors—two browns, black, and white—and in both stick and pencil form. The reddish color, often called red chalk, or sanguine, has a particularly pleasing quality, and has been widely used for figure drawings, portrait, and landscape studies throughout the history of art. A warm cream or buff paper is often chosen to enhance the quality of the red ocher pigment.

CONTÉ IN THREE COLORS

1 *Because the conté colors do not match the still-life group, the artist chooses light brown as a tonal equivalent.*

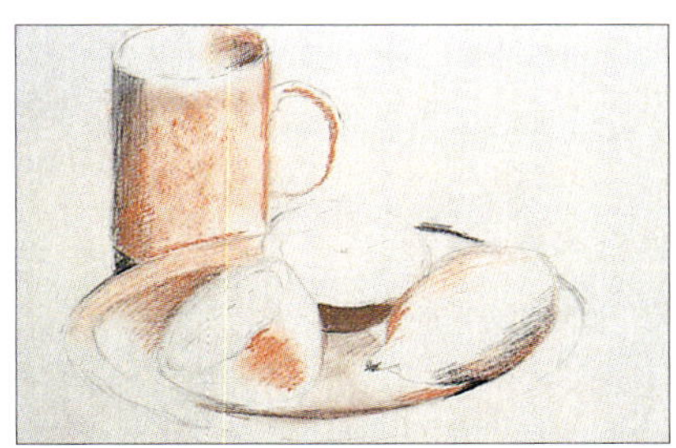

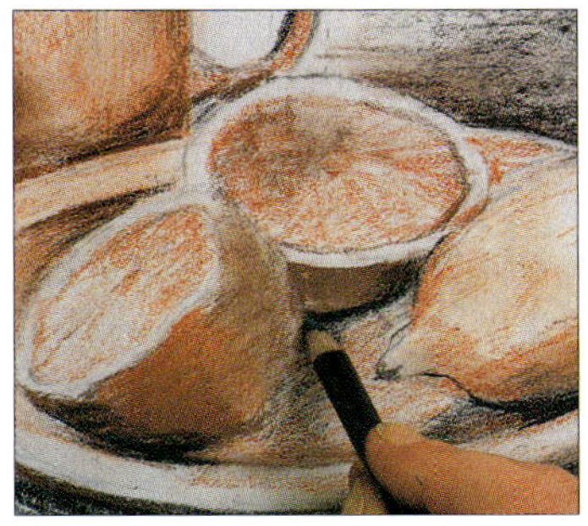

2 *The darker brown and black are brought in for shadow. A conté pencil rather than a crayon is used here for more definition.*

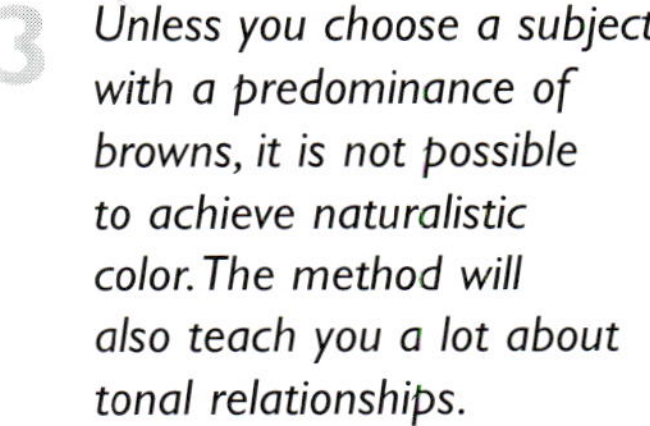

3 *Unless you choose a subject with a predominance of browns, it is not possible to achieve naturalistic color. The method will also teach you a lot about tonal relationships.*

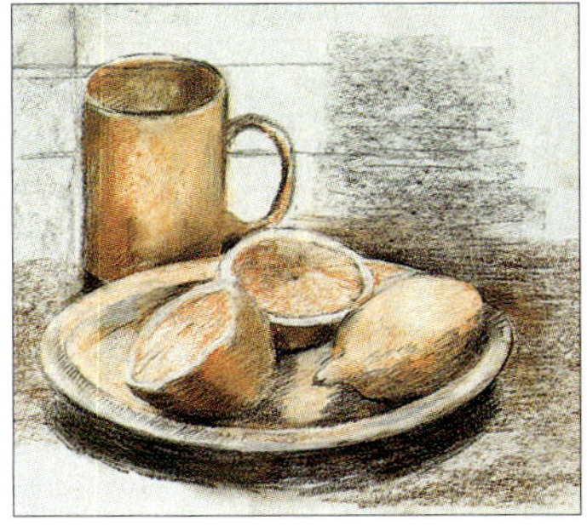

INK DRAWING

Ink is the oldest of all the drawing media. In ancient Egypt, reed pens were used with some form of ink for both writing and drawing, and in China, inks were being made as early as 2,500 BC, usually from black, or red ocher pigment made into solid stick or block form with a solution of glue. They were then mixed with water for use. These inks, later imported into the West in their solid form, became known as Chinese inks or Indian inks.

PEN AND INK

From late Roman times until the 19th century the standard pen was the quill, made from the feathers of a goose, a turkey, or sometimes a crow or gull. The reed pen, however, continued to be used and still is. Both Rembrandt and Van Gogh exploited its sensitive line with consummate skill. A similar

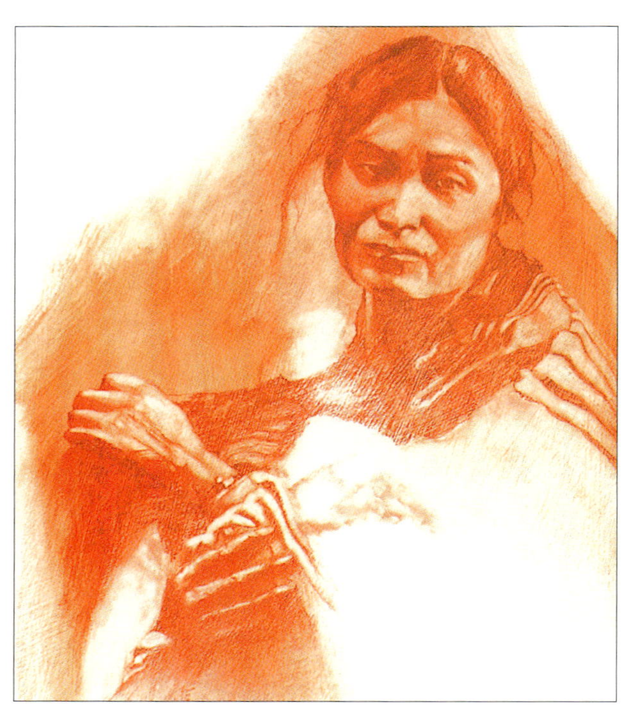

Above *The artist here, Leonard Leone, likes a smooth surface for his conté work, and in this drawing of a Navajo Indian he has used a primed wood panel. This would not be suitable for charcoal because it would not provide enough texture to hold the charcoal, but conté has a higher degree of adherence.*

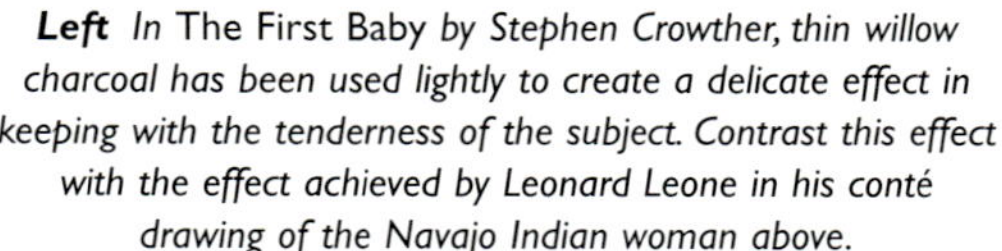

Left *In* The First Baby *by Stephen Crowther, thin willow charcoal has been used lightly to create a delicate effect in keeping with the tenderness of the subject. Contrast this effect with the effect achieved by Leonard Leone in his conté drawing of the Navajo Indian woman above.*

DARK TO LIGHT

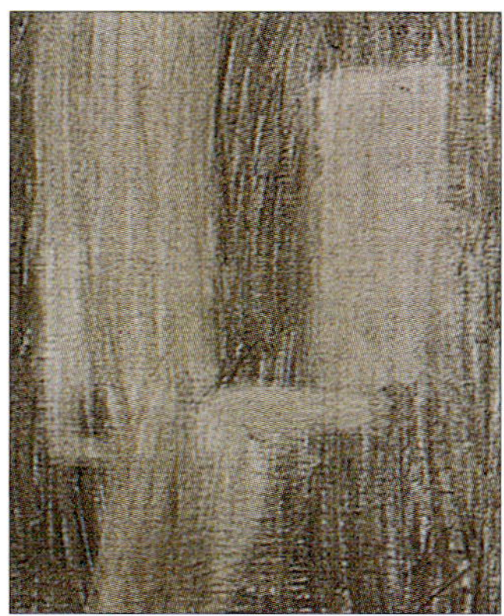

1 *Having spread charcoal evenly on the paper, the artist's next step was to lift out the larger areas of lighter tone with a putty rubber.*

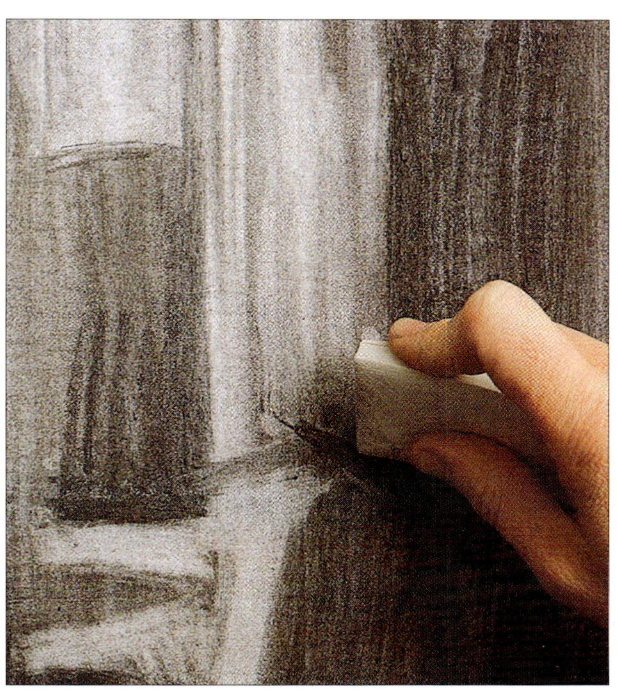

2 *She now uses the corner of the putty rubber to remove more charcoal, thus "drawing" the light front edge of the door. A putty rubber can be used almost as precisely as the charcoal.*

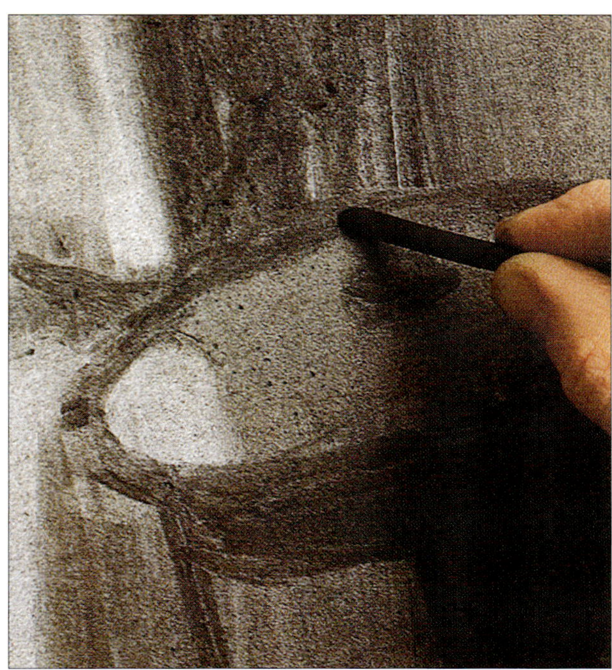

3 *The marble-topped table in the foreground is beginning to take shape, and more charcoal is applied to darken and define the rim.*

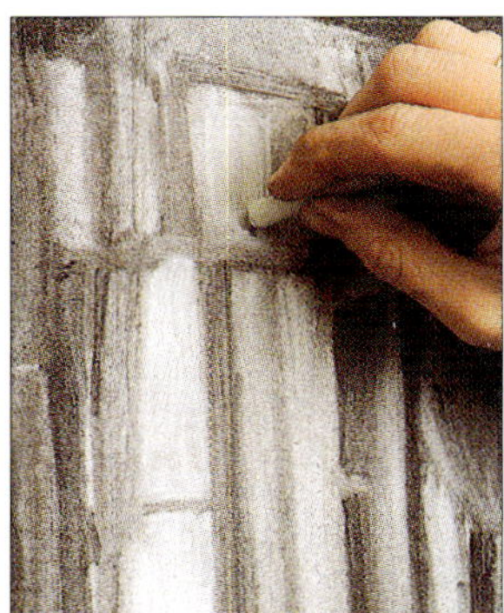

4 *It is not always possible to remove all the charcoal, and this area needs to be pure white, so a little white pastel is used.*

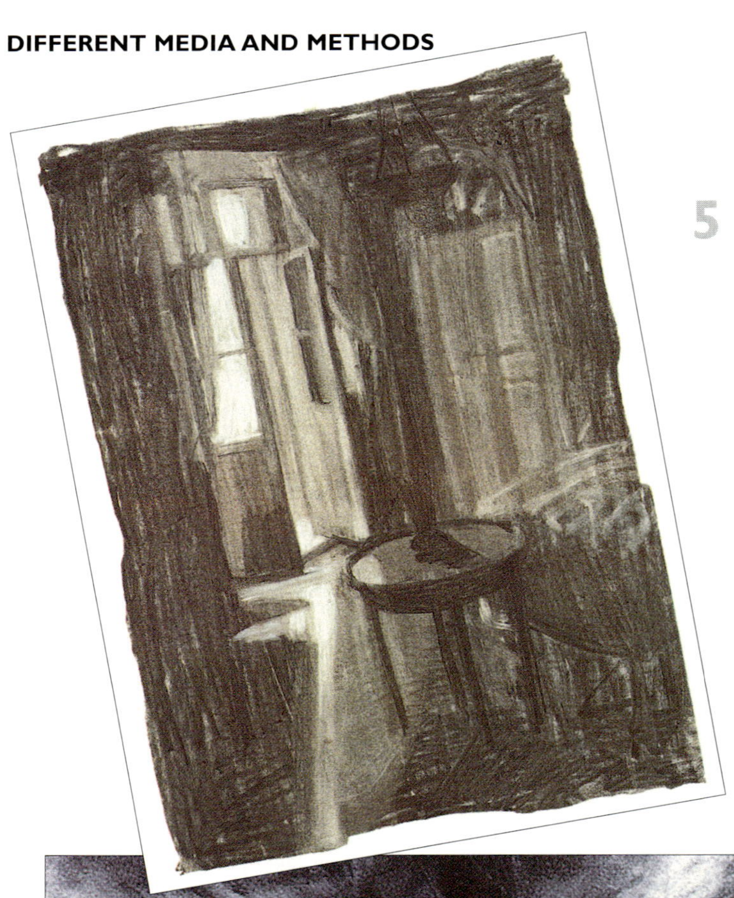

5 *The drawing has a pleasing atmospheric quality. The charcoal can be fixed after all the light areas have been lifted out or darkened with further applications of charcoal.*

Below *Here is a powerful sense of atmosphere, but what is most impressive about* St Gabriels *by David Carpanini is its drama and movement. The swirling clouds in the drawing are echoed by the wave-like shapes of the fields and hills. The small church stands quietly as the stable center of a landscape in flux.*

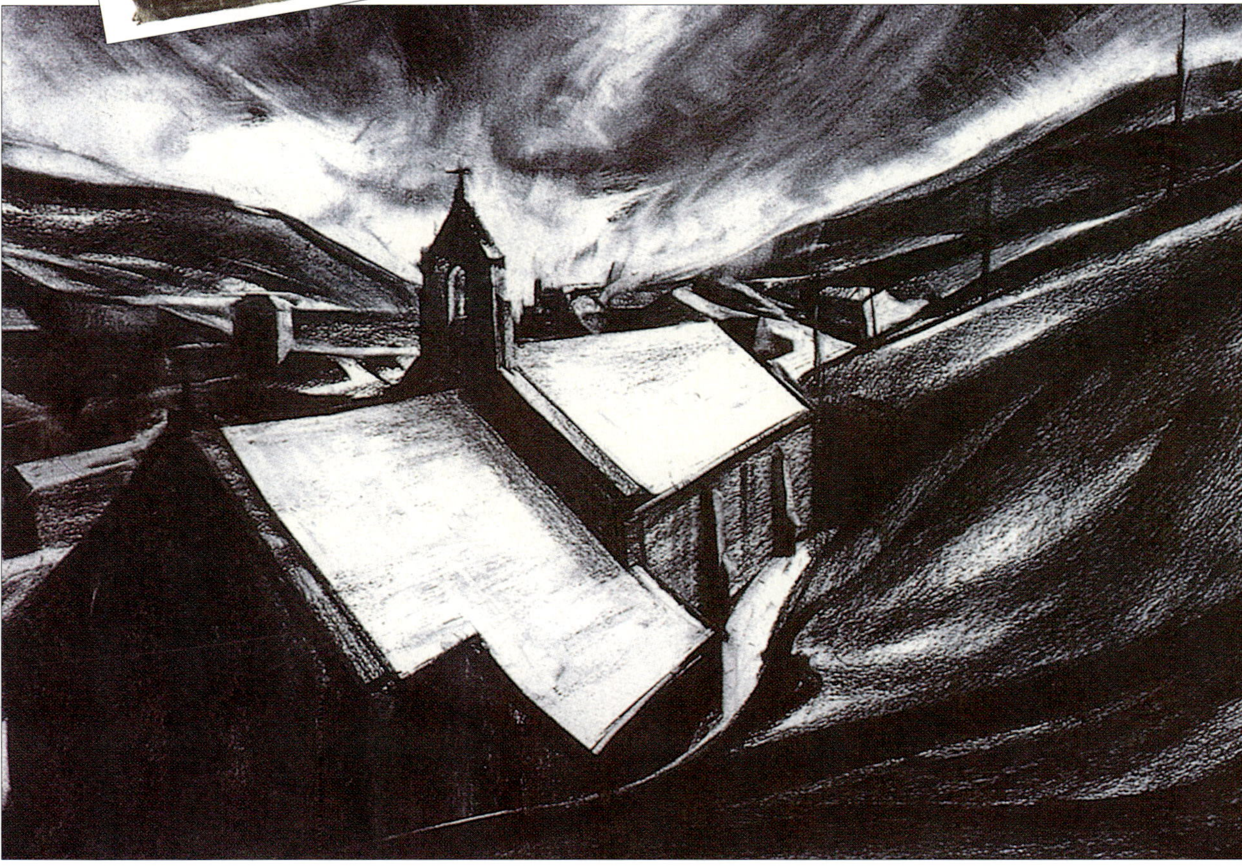

1 Bamboo pen
2 Reed pen
3 Quill pen

Top *Bamboo pen. These are used by both artists and calligraphers, and are available from calligraphic suppliers. They are versatile and exciting to use, but you will need some practice.*

Middle *Quill pen. These were in the past the standard tool for both writing and drawing. They are very sensitive, and provide a range of different kinds of line.*

Right *Reed pen. Similar to the bamboo pen but slightly thinner, reed pens are well worth trying out. David Prentice's drawing opposite was done with a reed pen.*

kind of pen, made from the bamboo, has been used for centuries in the East.

There are a great many different drawing pens on the market today, from the old-fashioned dip pen to reservoir pens and various ballpoints, felt-tips, and fiber tips. Ballpoints and felt-tips don't offer much variety in the kind of lines they make, but they are convenient for outdoor sketching. Dip pens and bamboo pens are more versatile as drawing implements, but less practical for location work, as they require you to carry a bottle of ink.

BUILDING UP TONE

The traditional method of building up a tonal drawing with a pen is by hatching and crosshatching. Remember that although hatching and crosshatching lines should be roughly parallel, they don't have to be straight and completely even. If you are drawing a solid form like the trunk of a tree, or a figure, try letting the hatching lines follow the contours of the form. This is called bracelet shading, and was pioneered by the great German artist

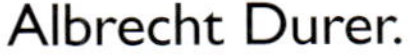

Albrecht Durer.

An equally effective but harder-to-handle method for defining tone is scribble line, which was used by Picasso. The pen is moved freely and randomly backward and forward until the right density of tone is built up. This method creates a wonderfully free and energetic effect. It is difficult, however, to achieve very precise effects with this method.

LINE AND WASH

Another method of achieving depth of tone is to combine ink drawing with a wash, either a monochrome wash of diluted ink, or colored washes of watercolor, or colored ink. Because you do not have to rely on the pen line to provide tone, it can be a freer and more rapid

BUILDING UP TONES

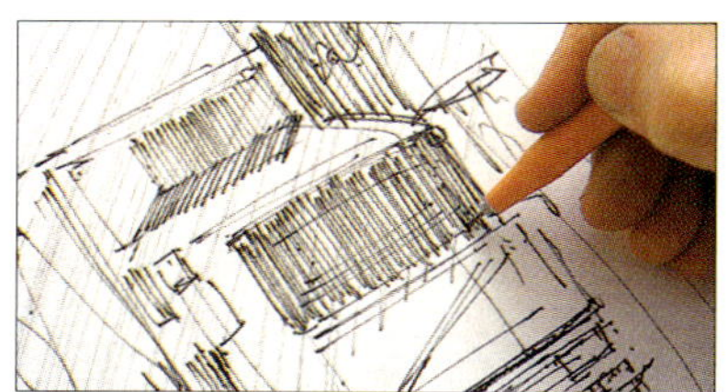

1 *Using a fine fiber-tipped drawing pen, the artist lays in a set of hatching lines.*

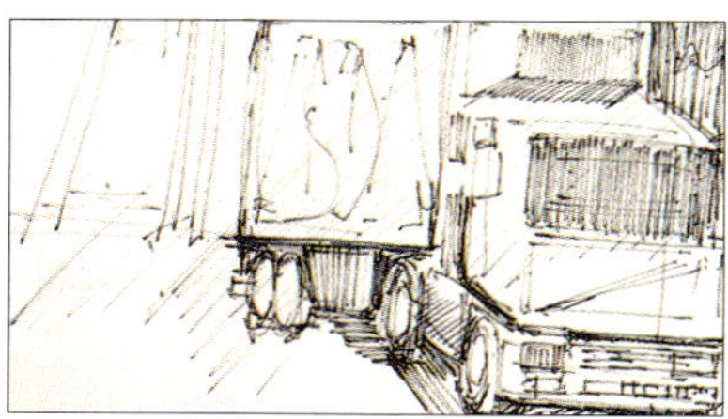

2 *He is now ready to build up the darker tones. Until you are experienced, though, it's wise to work with a light pencil drawing.*

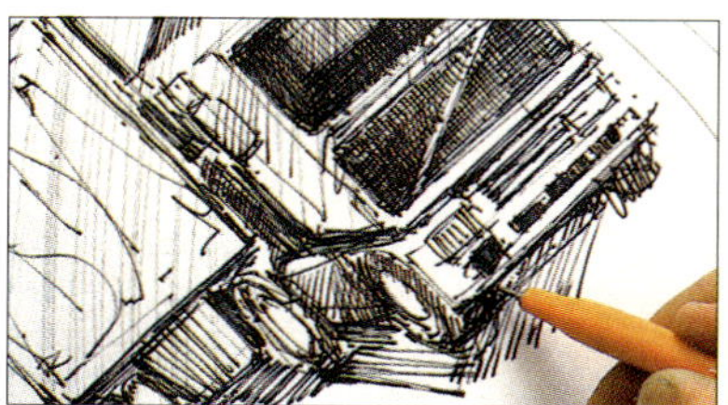

3 *Crosshatching is used to produce areas of dark tone. The diagonal lines here describe the flat plane of the windscreen.*

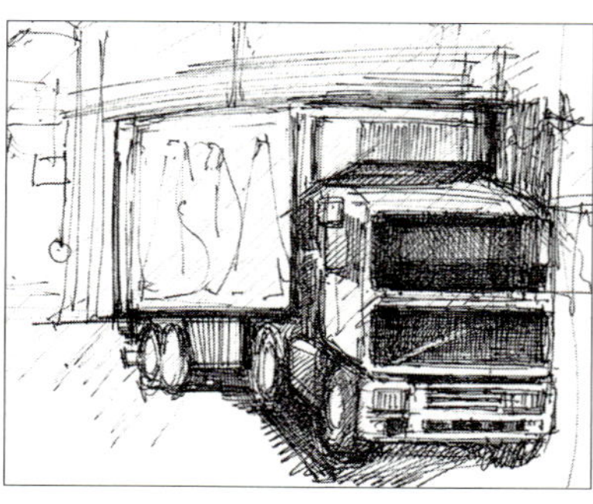

4 *Notice how the artist has varied the hatched and crosshatched lines to suggest the different shapes and planes.*

drawing method than when hatching with pen and ink. Forms and impressions of light and shadow can be suggested with a few brush strokes, strengthened with touches of line where necessary.

It is important to develop both tone and line together, rather than using drawing as an outline. If you are new to this technique, you might begin with a light pencil drawing which will act as a guide for the first areas of tone. You can then add line and further tone as the drawing demands or you work with a pen with water-soluble ink, which you can spread by washing areas of the drawing with clean water.

BRUSH DRAWING

Brush and wash is a similar technique where lines are made with the point of the brush alone. This is an excellent method for making quick tonal landscape studies.

The brush is a very sensitive drawing implement, capable of producing an almost endless variety of different marks. For centuries, Chinese and Japanese artists have produced beautiful brush and ink drawings.

The marks you make are dictated by

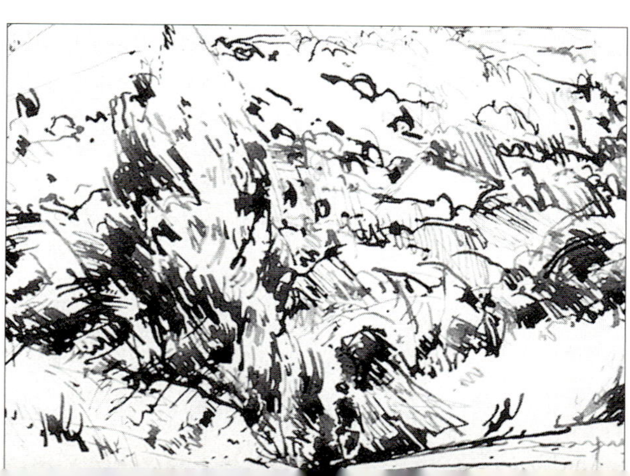

Right Under Black Hill *by David Prentice shows the sensitive and varied line you can achieve with a reed pen.*

SCRIBBLE LINE

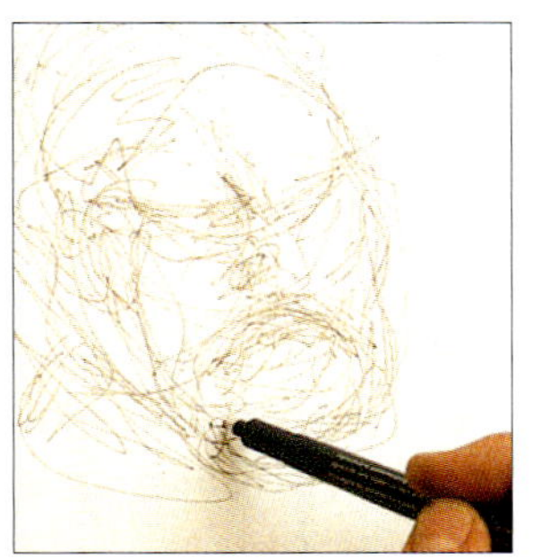

1 The artist begins with a series of loosely drawn lines roughly following the main forms of the head and face.

2 As the network of lines becomes more intricate, a definite impression of the head begins to emerge, though there is as yet no attempt to define the features in detail.

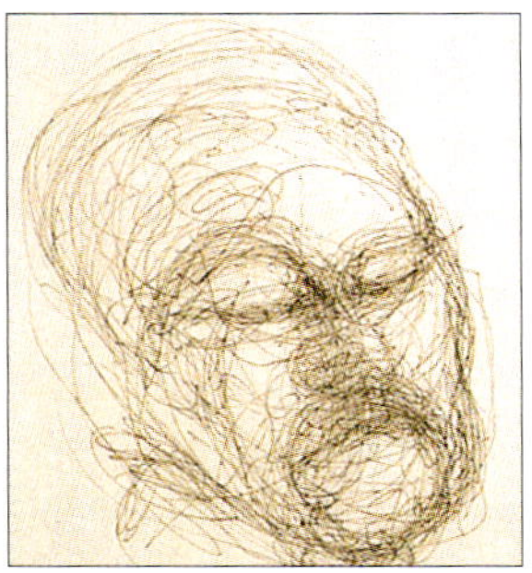

3 In the final stages, further scribbling has built up the forms of the head and body, and the drawing gives an excellent impression of the slumped posture of the sleeping man. The effect is softer than that produced by crosshatching.

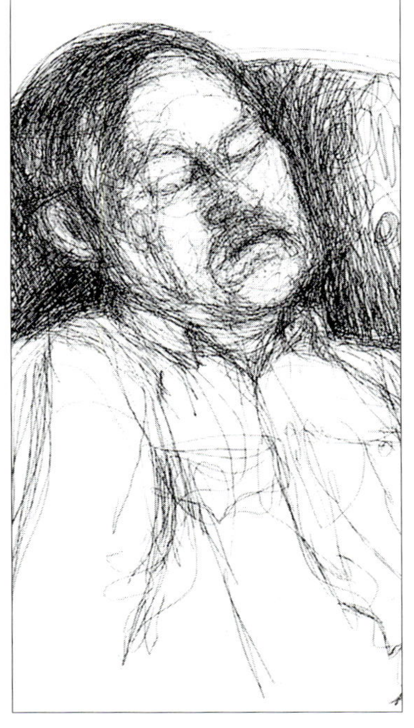

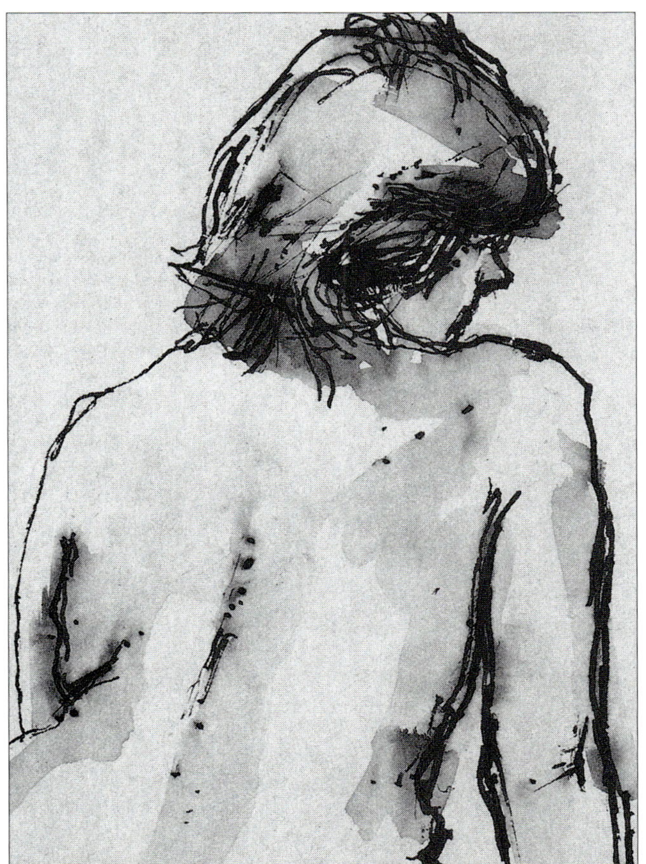

Left Line and wash drawing by Joan Elliott Bates. For this drawing, the artist has used an experimental technique. Instead of the conventional pen, she has drawn with the stopper inside the lid of the ink bottle, which has produced an interesting and varied quality of line. The wash has been kept to a minimum, with just a few deft touches of pale gray suggesting the planes of the body and head.

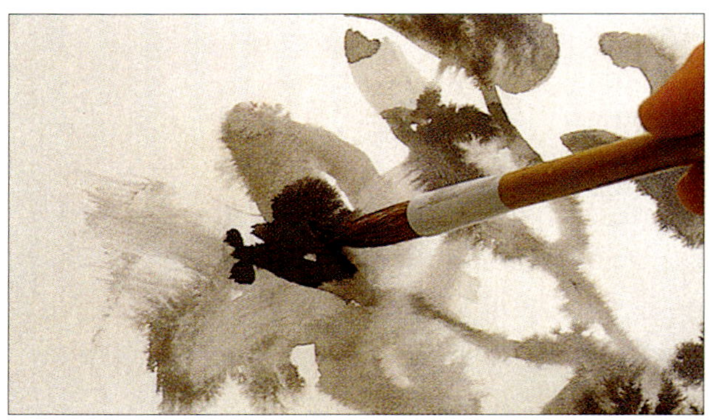

1 *To create the effect of the soft petal, the artist is working on damped paper, which causes the ink to diffuse. She now drops undiluted ink lightly into a paler, dilute wash.*

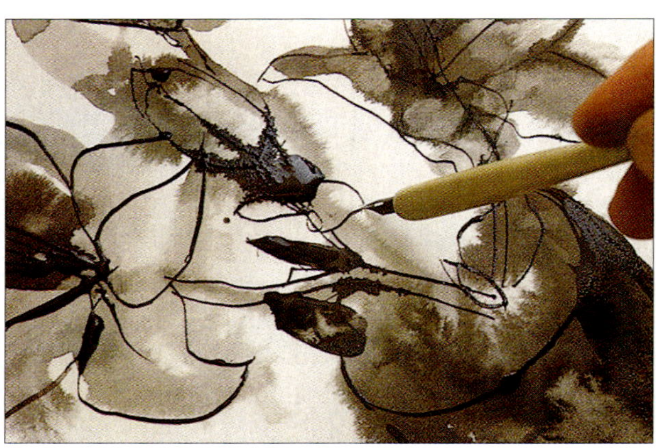

2 *The first washes are allowed to dry before a dip pen is used to add definition to the stems and petals of the flowers.*

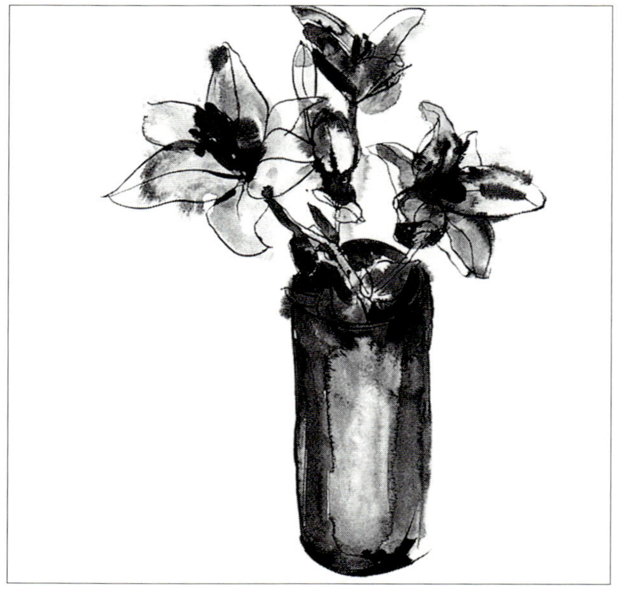

3 *Further areas of wash were added after the pen lines to pull the drawing together. Care must be taken to prevent the lines from dominating the drawing.*

the type and size of brush you use, the direction and pressure of the stroke, and the way the brush is held. You can use any good-quality brushes, preferably sable, as these are firm and springy, and hold the ink well. Or you might like to try Chinese brushes, which are now readily available and relatively inexpensive. Try different ways of holding the brush. Oriental artists and calligraphers have developed a series of different hand positions, and often work with the brush held vertically and the working surface horizontal.

INK AND BRUSH

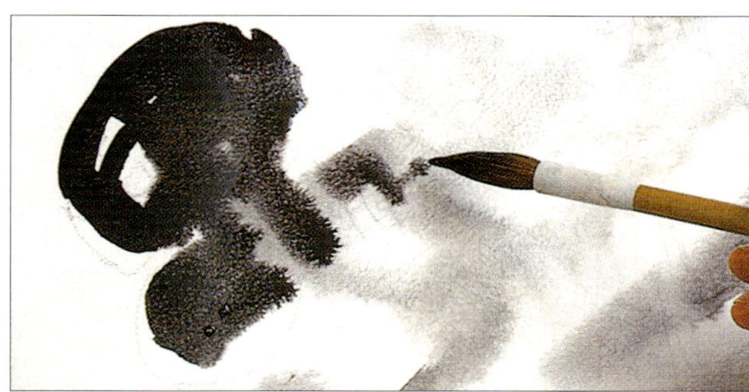

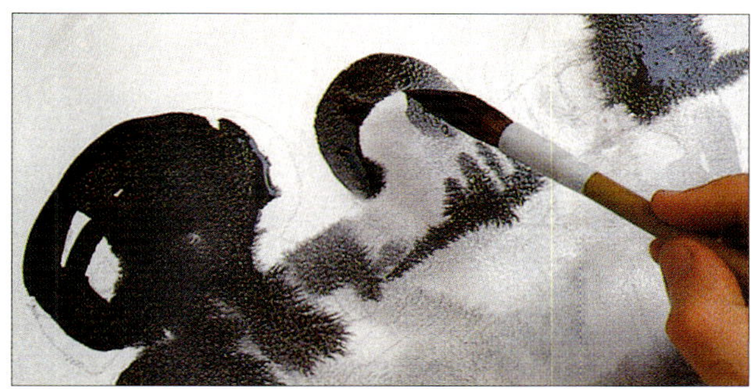

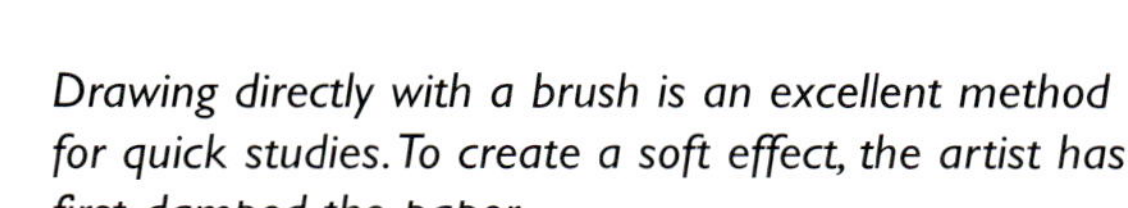

1 *Drawing directly with a brush is an excellent method for quick studies. To create a soft effect, the artist has first damped the paper.*

2 *Undiluted ink is now laid over a still-wet paler wash. This causes the undiluted ink to diffuse somewhat.*

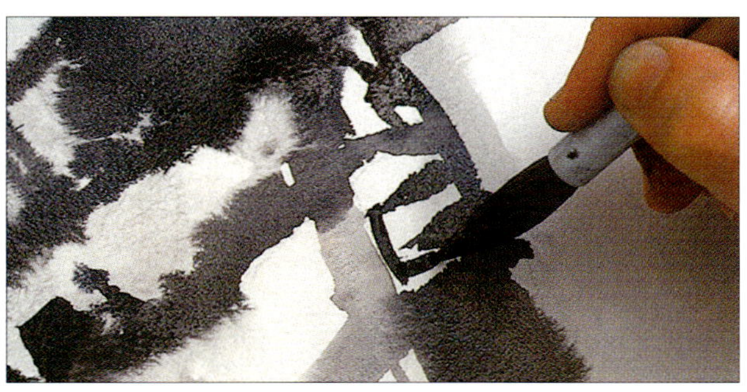

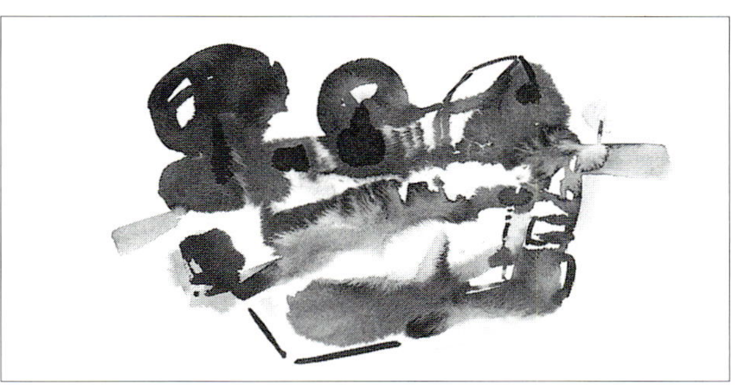

3 *The Chinese brush is a sensitive drawing tool. Here it is used to make both bold lines and small pointed shapes suggestive of trees.*

4 *Although unfinished, the drawing gives a good impression of the fields and trees; the effect of the spreading ink is attractive in itself.*

MIXED MEDIA

In mixed-media work you need to consider the physical characteristics of the media as much as the subject you are drawing, and decide whether the effects they create are compatible.

For example, charcoal and pastel are natural partners, as they both have the same soft, smudgy quality. Similarly, colored pencil and graphite pencil go well together, and the classic example of compatible media—which have been used together for so long that they are hardly now considered as mixed media—is line and wash.

On the other hand, fine pen lines would be unlikely to marry well with black conté crayon, though you might use conté and a broad, black felt-tip, or conté and ink. By experimenting, you will discover which combinations work best for you, and you may find that you can create exciting effects by mixing media that seem quite incompatible.

WAX RESIST

One of the mixtures of incompatible materials that has now become very well

WAX CRAYON AND INK

1 *She has begun by scribbling lightly over the trees with wax crayon. It takes some trial and error to discover how much pressure to apply, but in general, the denser the application the more successful the resist.*

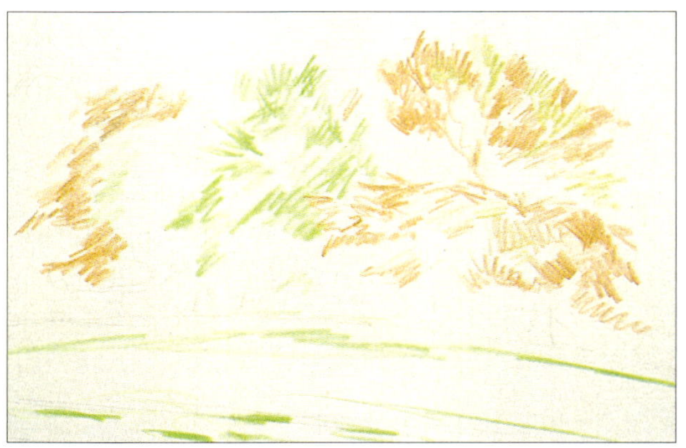

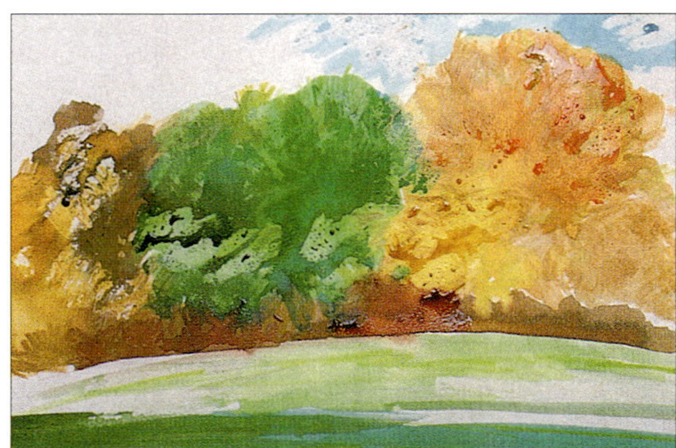

2 *The first application covered the crayon too thoroughly, so the drawing was left to dry before more wax was added, and then more ink. You can see how the color has slid off the waxed areas. This technique is called the "wax resist" method.*

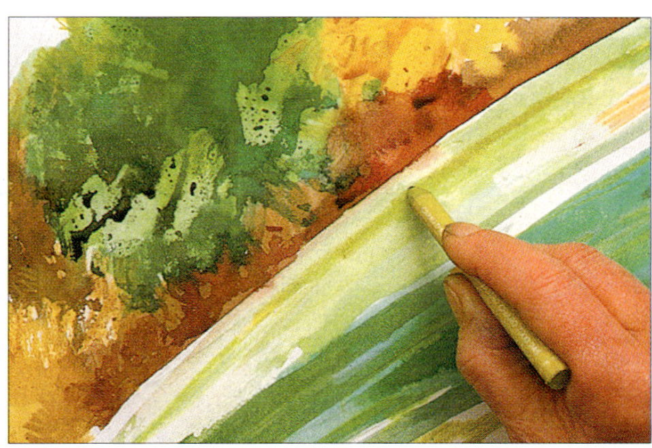

3 *In this area the wax resist is not intended to be very obvious, so she uses a color dose to that of the ink which will be used on top.*

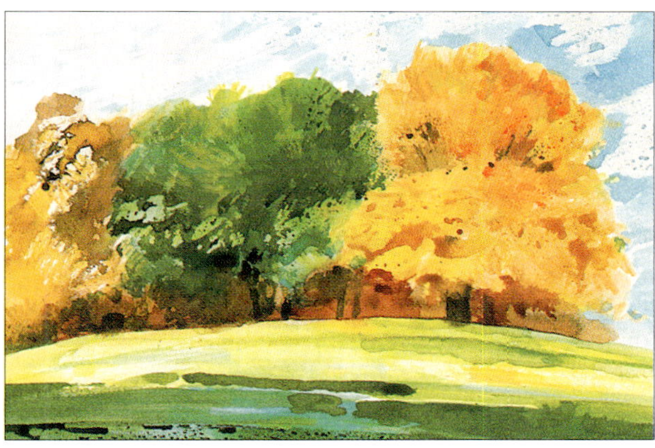

4 *Here, the effect shows very clearly, with the ink forming irregular blobs and pools. The technique has an exciting element of chance.*

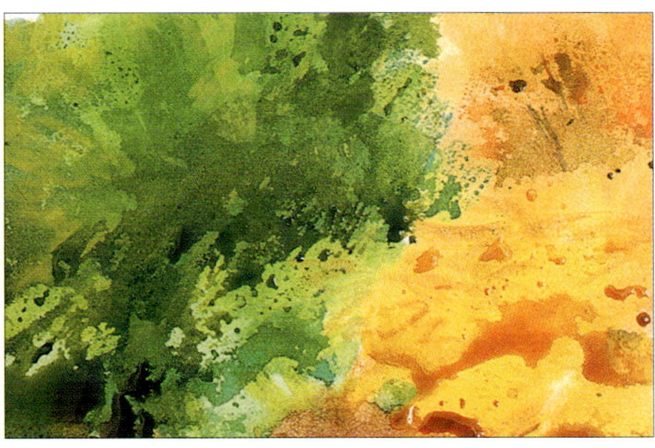

5 *As she worked, the artist discovered that the lighter oil pastel colors resist the ink more effectively than the darker ones. Notice how the white used for the clouds has completely blocked the ink.*

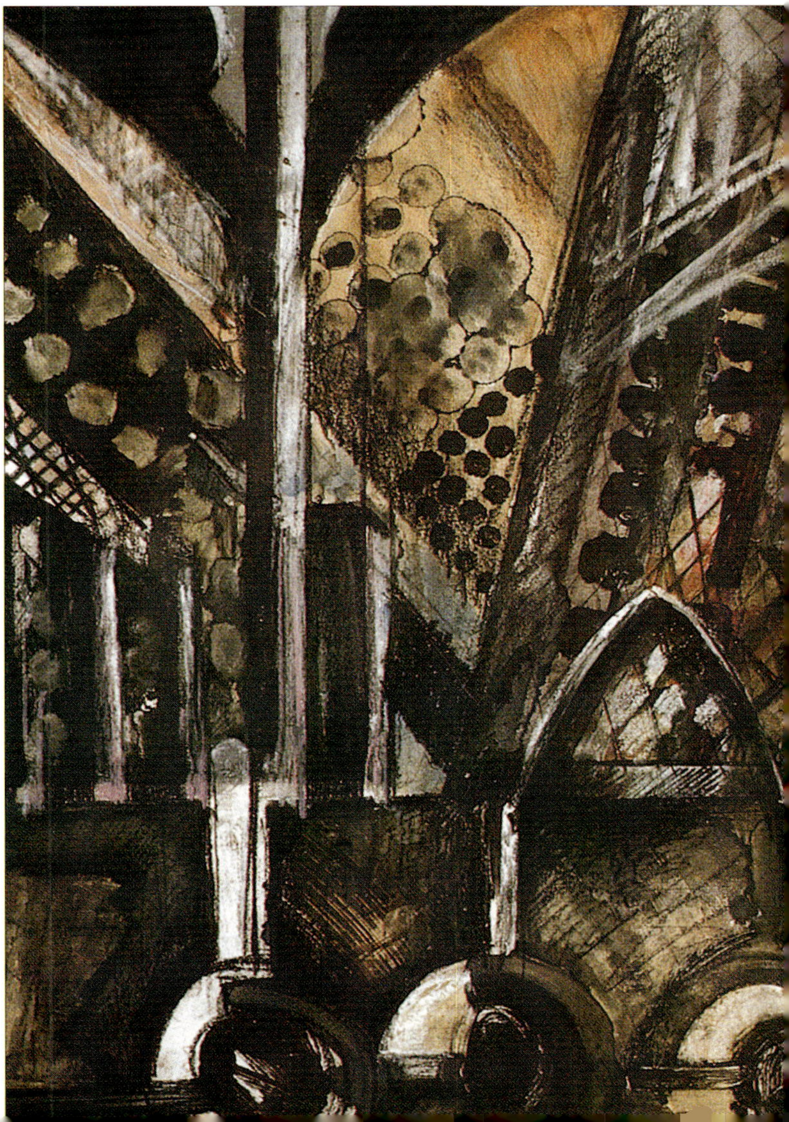

Right *Monoprint and drawing by David Ferry. To achieve the rich effects seen in Cathedral, the artist began with a monoprint—a "one-off" print made by placing the drawing paper on top of an inked-up sheet of metal or piece of glass. He then drew over the print first with colored pencils, then with black oil pastel, and finally with colored drawing inks.*

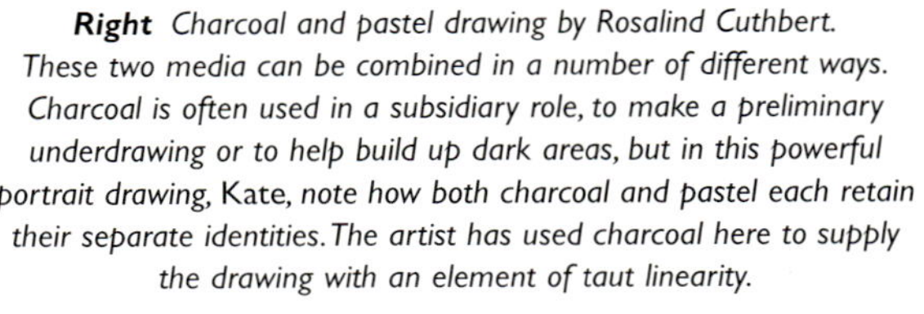

Right *Charcoal and pastel drawing by Rosalind Cuthbert. These two media can be combined in a number of different ways. Charcoal is often used in a subsidiary role, to make a preliminary underdrawing or to help build up dark areas, but in this powerful portrait drawing,* Kate, *note how both charcoal and pastel each retain their separate identities. The artist has used charcoal here to supply the drawing with an element of taut linearity.*

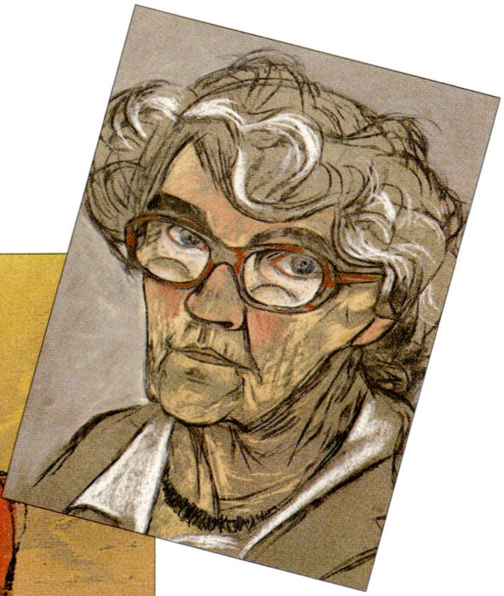

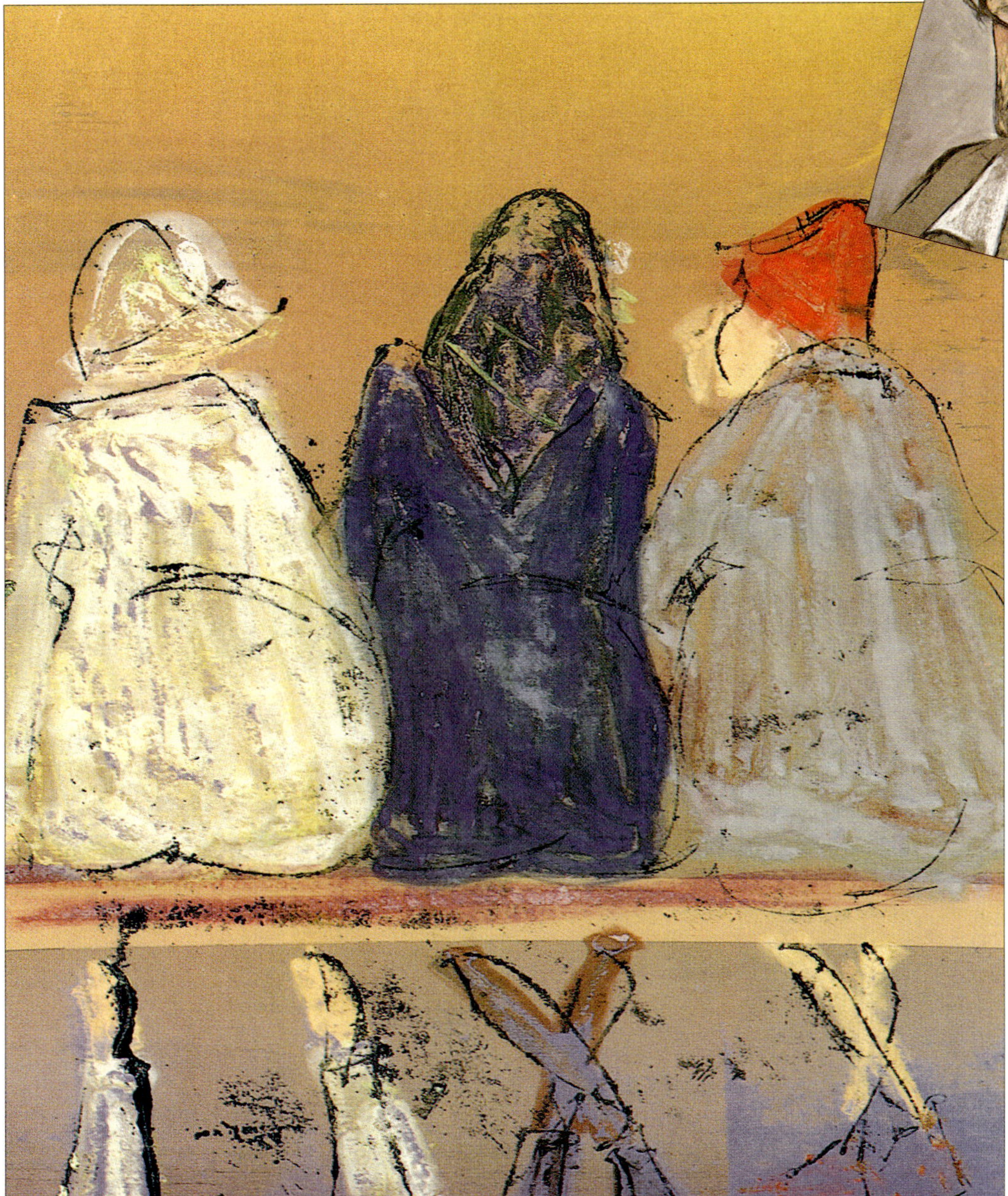

Left *Drawing using mixed printing methods and oil pastel by Samantha Toft. The background of* Three Portly Women *was screenprinted in order to create the soft gradations of tone, and the drawing of the figures is in oil pastel. The fine black pen-like lines were achieved by a monoprint process. The paper was placed face down on a metal plate spread with printing ink and a pencil was used to draw on the back, thus transferring the ink onto the paper selectively.*

PHOTOCOPY DRAWING

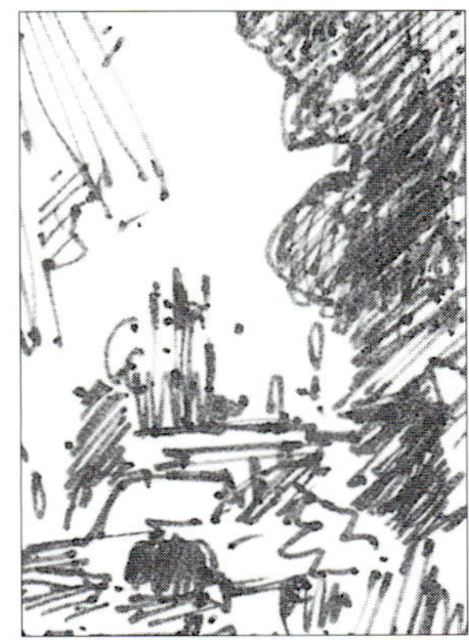

1 *This small sketch in felt-tipped pen was made from a painting by Constable, which the artist particularly admired.*

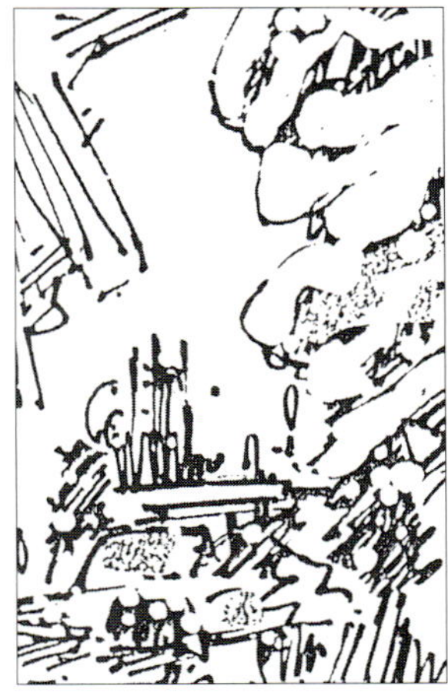

2 *It seemed a suitable subject for a Christmas card, so the artist made a photocopy, on which he used correction fluid to paint the trees white, giving the effect of snow-laden boughs. Further copies were then made, of which this is one.*

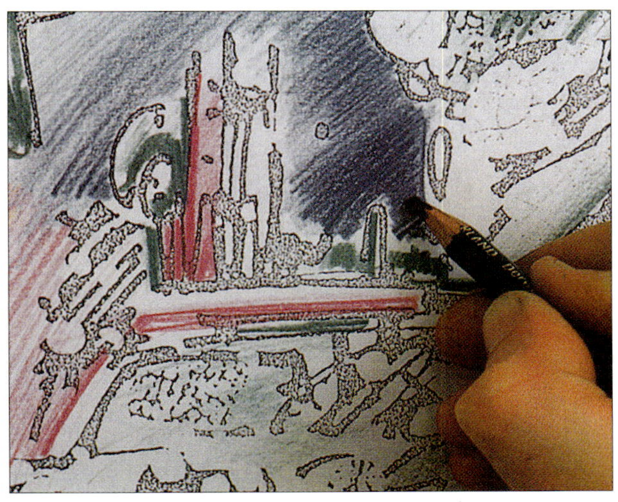

3 *At a later stage, the artist decided to take the photocopy that he had made one stage further and rework it in colored pencil.*

known and is used both in drawing and painting is that of oil and water. If you draw with a wax crayon and then put down a wash of diluted black ink or colored ink, or draw over it with a marker, the wax will repel the color so that the drawing stands out clearly.

Wax resist is an enjoyable and exciting technique because it has an element of unpredictability—you can't be sure of how the drawing will look until you have put on the color. You can simply make some broad splodges with white wax crayon, or a household candle, to create areas of texture or color in a background, but you can also build up a whole drawing by a layering method, applying colored wax crayon, then ink or marker, then more wax crayon, and so on. You can even scratch into the wax in places using the sgraffito technique.

MOUNTING

The procedure for mounting a drawing is

PAPER COLLAGE

1 *Using the photograph as reference, the artist tears pieces of paper.*

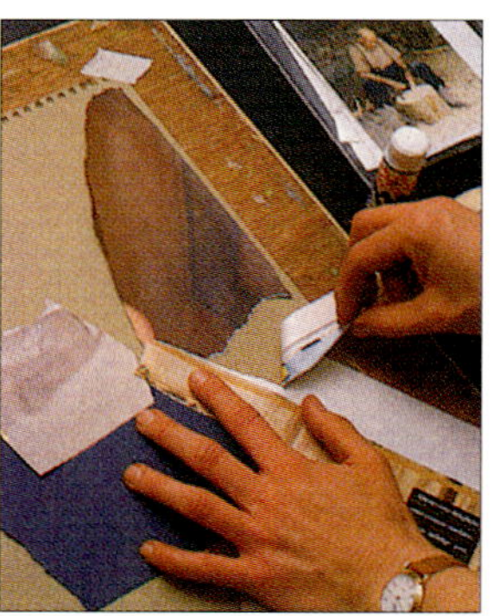

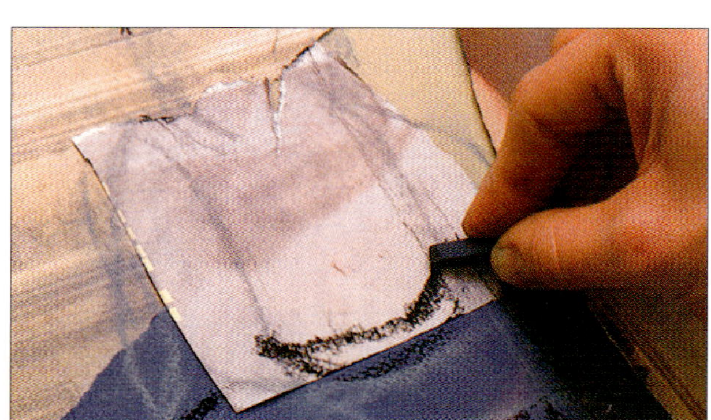

2 *Roughly torn pieces are laid on the area that the artist has determined for the figure, and the main shapes are then defined with conté crayon.*

3 *The color scheme was planned in general terms before work began, and the artist decided on a range of relatively low-key colors with one or two strong darks. She is using a mixture of plain paper and pages from magazines, which provide hints of pattern and texture.*

different from that for a painting. A drawing is usually set within a mount inside a frame; this mount is either of white card or of a restrained, neutral tone that is sympathetic to the work. Once the drawing has been mounted, one or several lines may be drawn round the inner edge of the mount using colors that either reflect or contrast with those used in the mount or the drawing.

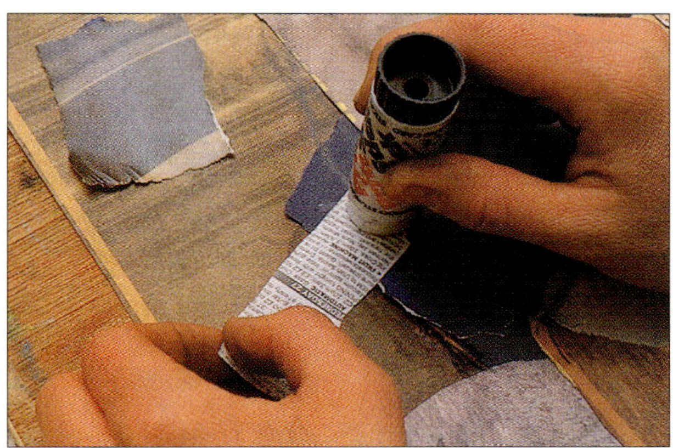

4 *The contrast between cut and torn edges is important in collage. The thick paper has mainly been torn and the thinner magazine paper cut.*

5 *Notice how cleverly the artist has chosen paper to suggest texture. You can see the effect clearly on the foreground objects and the man's arms.*

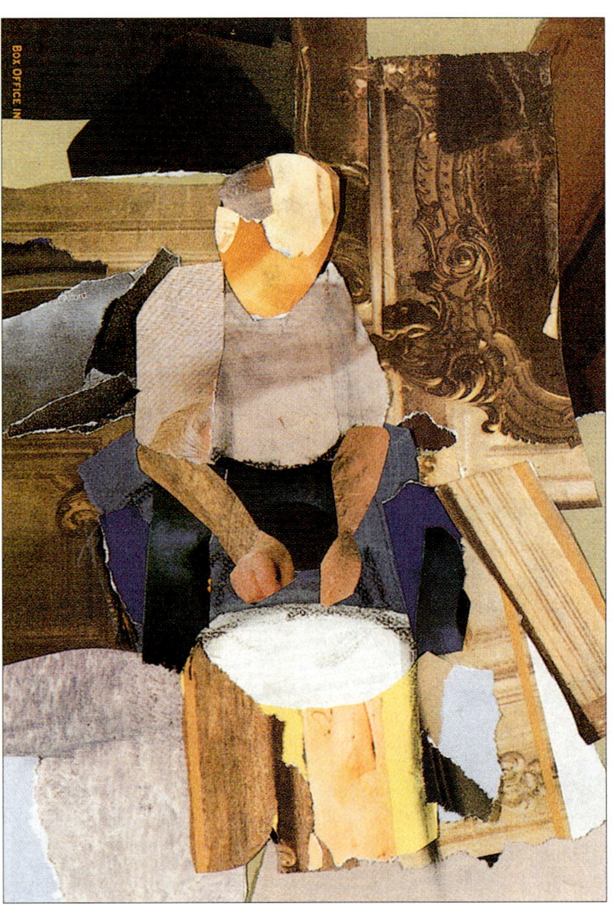

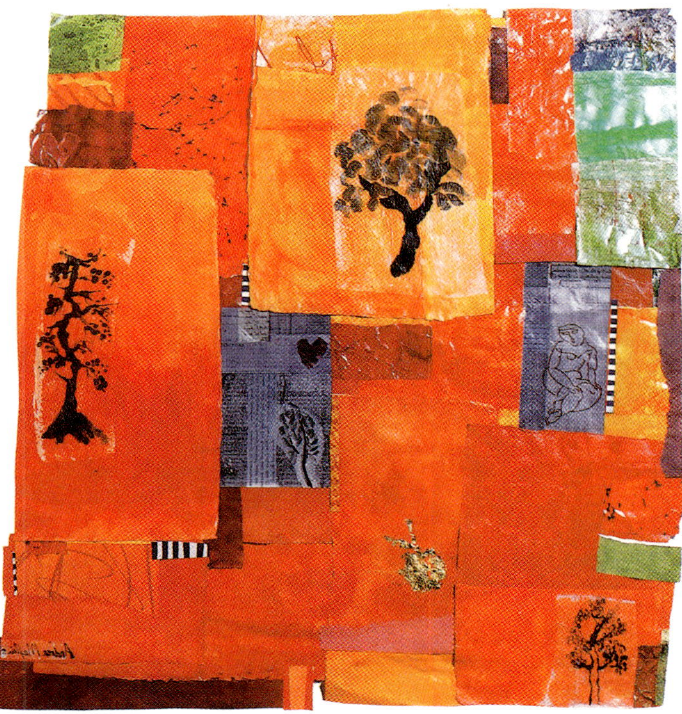

Above *Collage and ink drawing by Andrea Maflin. Here a wonderfully rich effect has been achieved with colored papers and small areas of brush drawing. The artist usually paints the papers before collaging, and uses waterbased glue to prevent discoloration. She has built up a wide collection of papers for her work, and experiments continually with different textures and paint effects.*

By tradition, oil paintings are unglazed—framed without a glass cover—but watercolors and drawings usually are glazed. The reason for this is that whereas oil, acrylic, or other non-water soluble media can be wiped clean of dust, watercolors and drawings cannot and so must be protected.

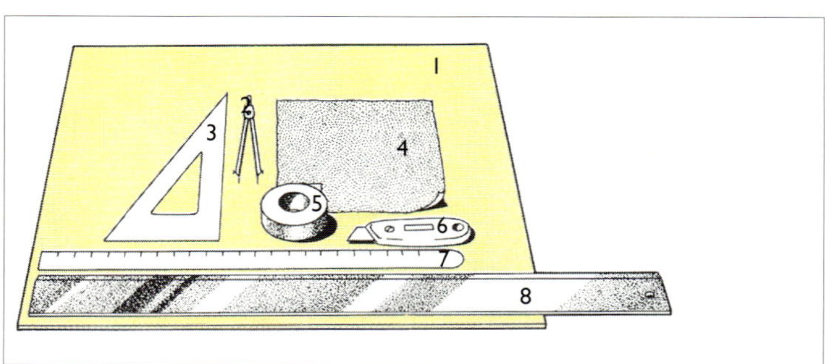

Left *If you plan to mount your drawings yourself it is worth investing in the correct equipment; this will help to ensure that you make a good job of finishing off your work. 1. Cutting board; 2. Dividers; 3. Set square; 4. Fine sandpaper 5. Masking tape; 6. Craft knife; 7. Long steel ruler; 8. Long straight edge*

CUTTING A WINDOW MOUNT

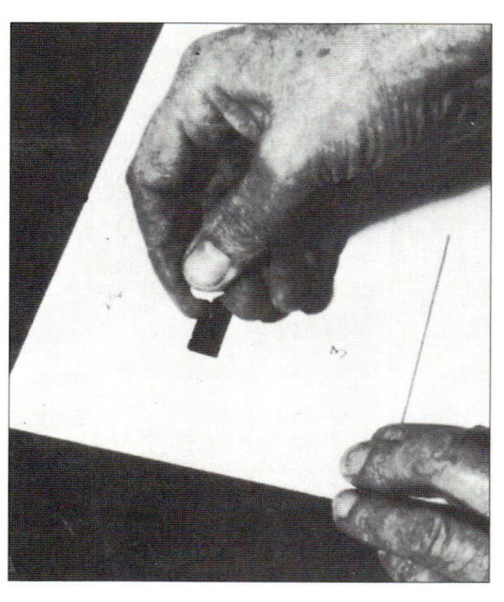

1 *Cut the board to size. To mark the inside edges, cut a template by measuring the width of the borders outward from a hole cut in a card. Place this template with the card and make marks on each corner of the board through the hole.*

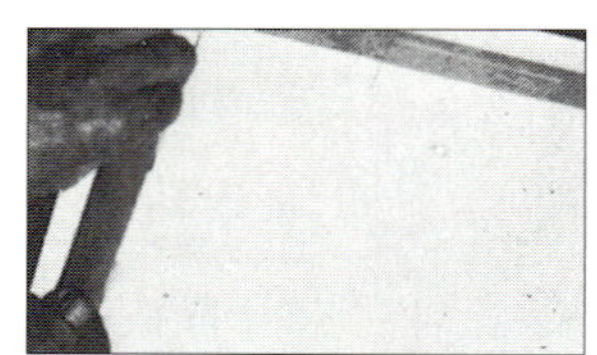

2 *Cut carefully from one mark to another in the corners, using a sharp Stanley knife and a metal ruler.*

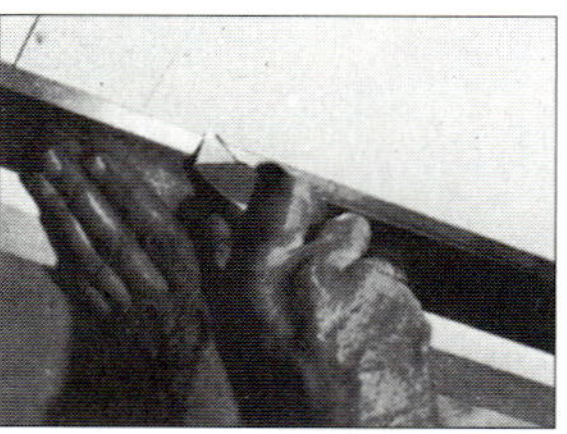

3 *Check the fit of your picture under the window you have cut. Once you are satisfied with the position, tape it securely.*

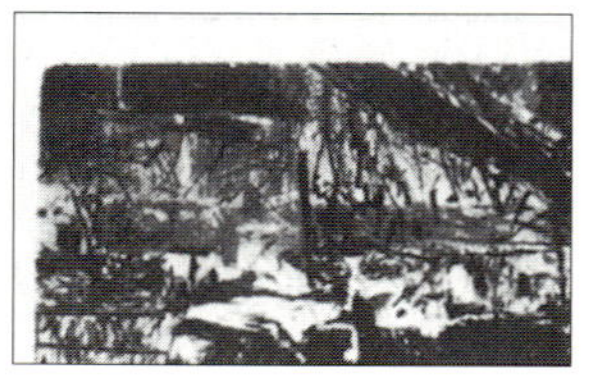

4 *This mount has been cut with a bevel edge, at an angle of about 45°.*

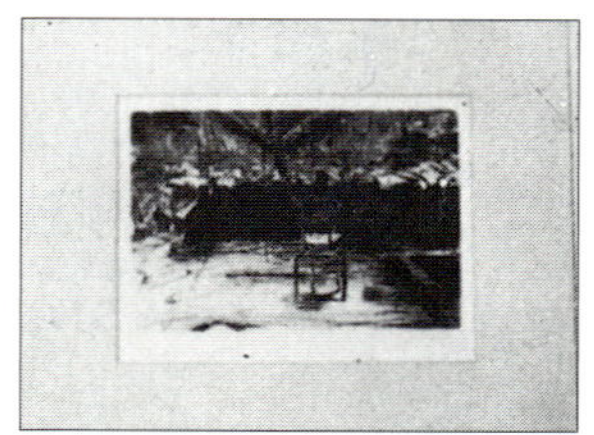

5 *An optical illusion makes it necessary to have the mount slightly deeper at the bottom so it looks centrally placed.*

CUTTING GLASS

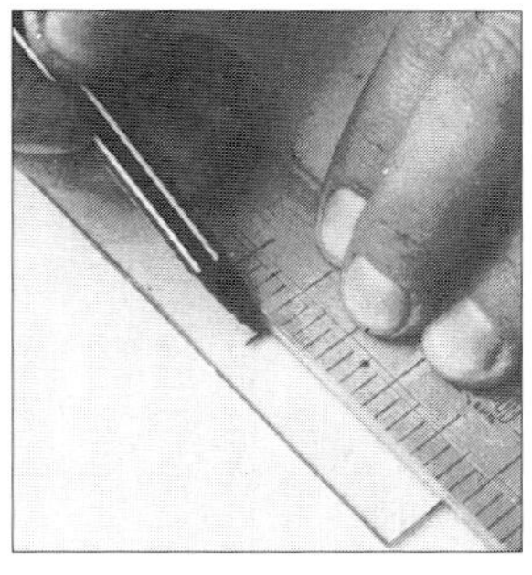

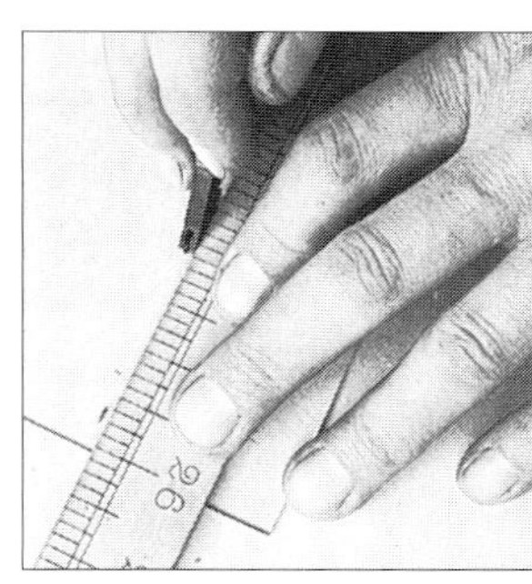

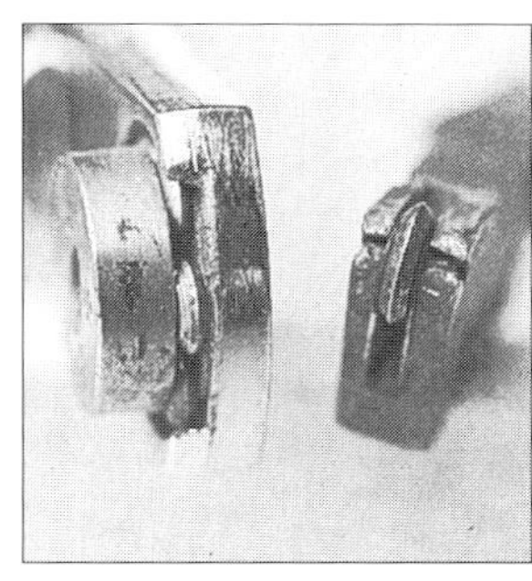

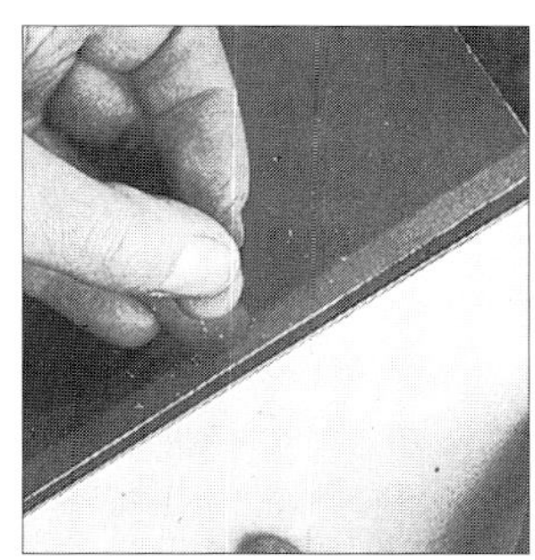

1 *Mark the glass for your frame with the measurements, checking these carefully and using a set square and ruler.*

2 *Rest the glass on a flat supporting surface, place a metal rule between your marks and guide the cutting tool along the ruler.*

3 *Glass-cutting tools are available in different sizes. The head of the tool is set so that the wheel which makes the cut is centered.*

4 *Make a score and place along the edge of a table, letting the excess glass snap. Cut your glass smaller than the frame so it isn't wedged in.*

DRYING MOUNTING WITH AN IRON

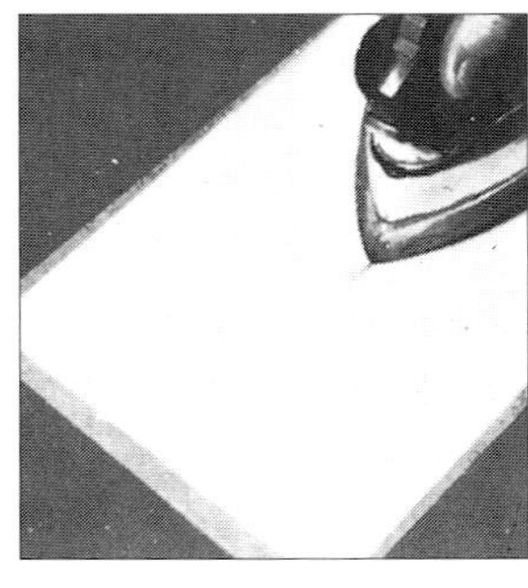

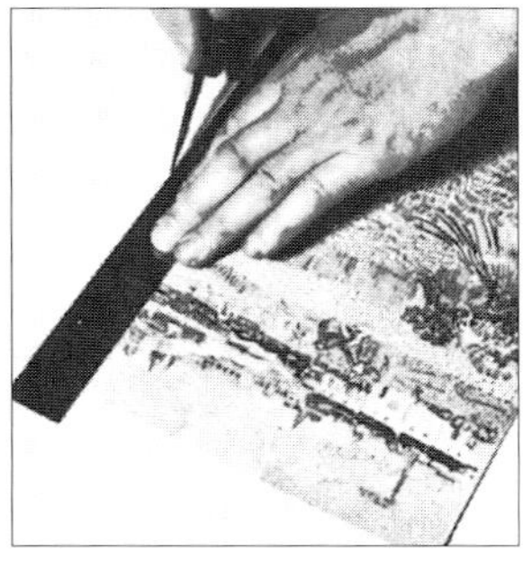

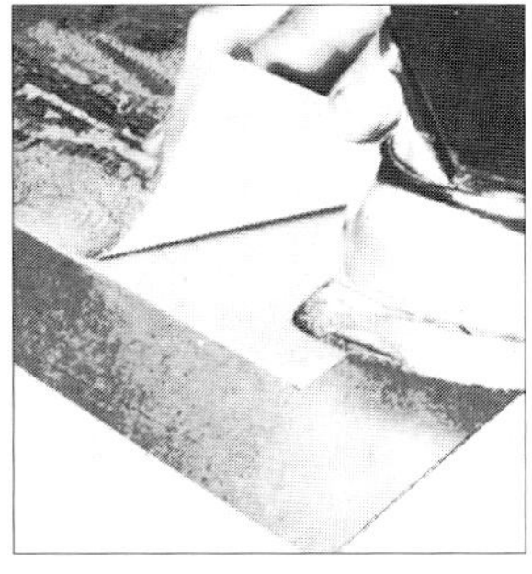

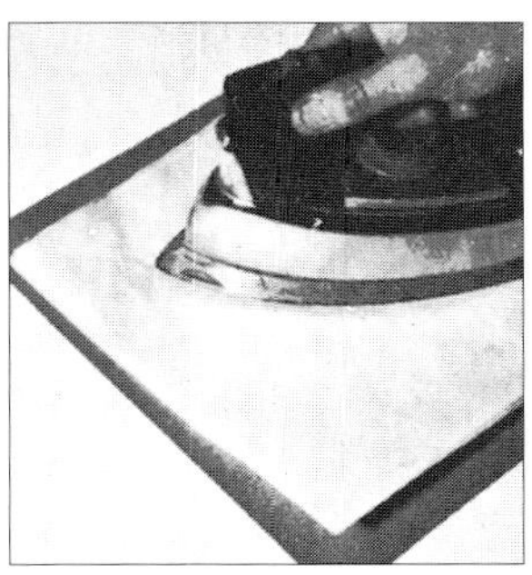

1 *Cut a sheet of shellac tissue slightly larger than the picture you intend to mount and tack it to the center-back of the picture using a cool iron.*

2 *Trim off the edges of the shellac tissue to the exact size of the picture you are planning on mounting, using a steel ruler and scalpel.*

3 *Position picture and tissue on your mounting card, and lift the corner of the picture to enable you to tack each corner of the tissue to the mount.*

4 *Lay a sheet of heat-resistant paper over your picture and iron carefully over this protective layer, working gently from the center outward.*

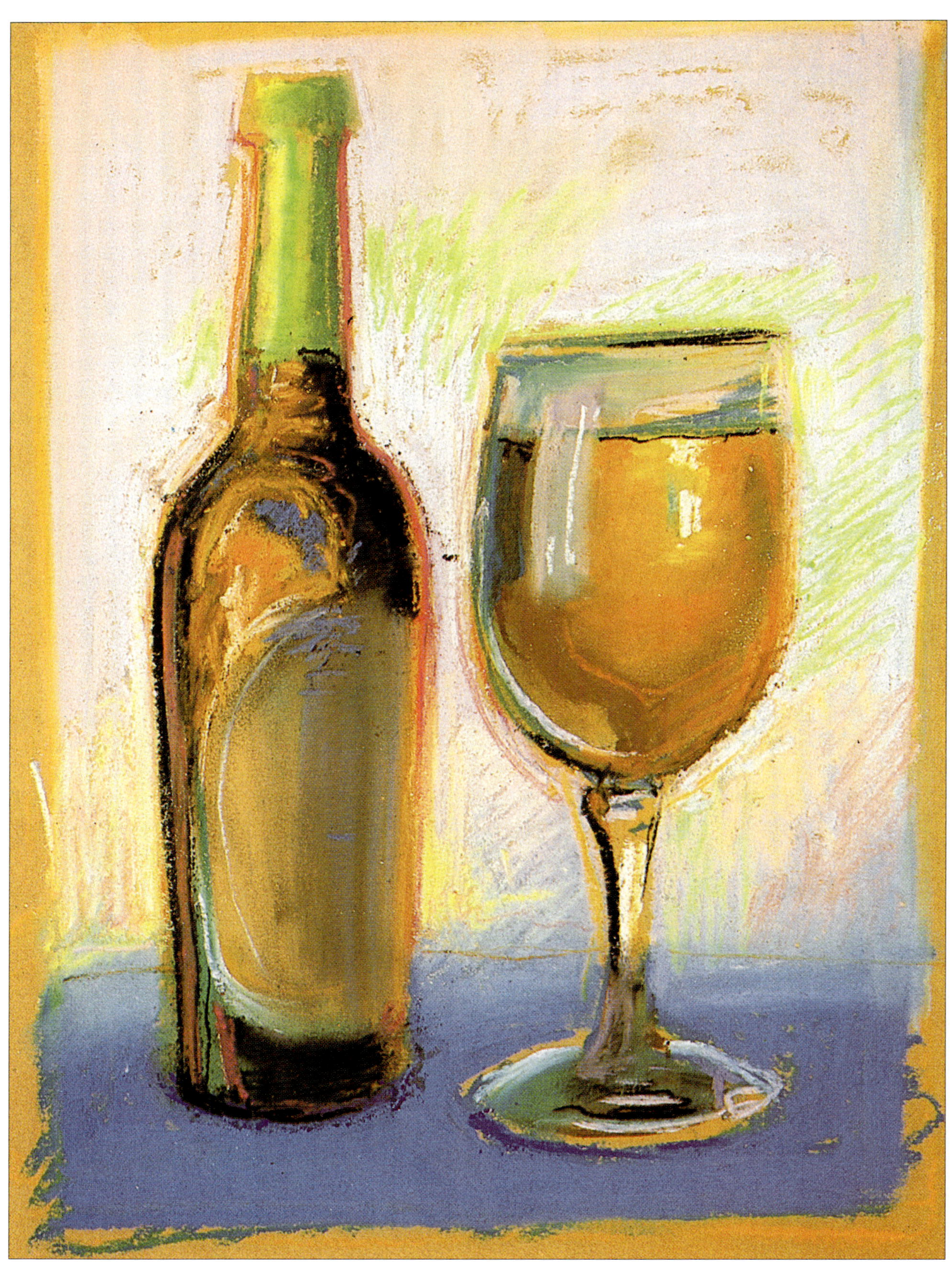

13 LANDSCAPE AND ARCHITECTURE

It should be the aim of the landscape artist to encourage others to view the familiar surroundings amongst which we live as though never seen before. There is a great deal of pleasure to be found in attempting to view things afresh, with a personal vision, and transmitting this unique approach via the final picture; bringing features so little regarded into a tighter focus will encourage the viewer to look again, and more intensely, at the landscape.

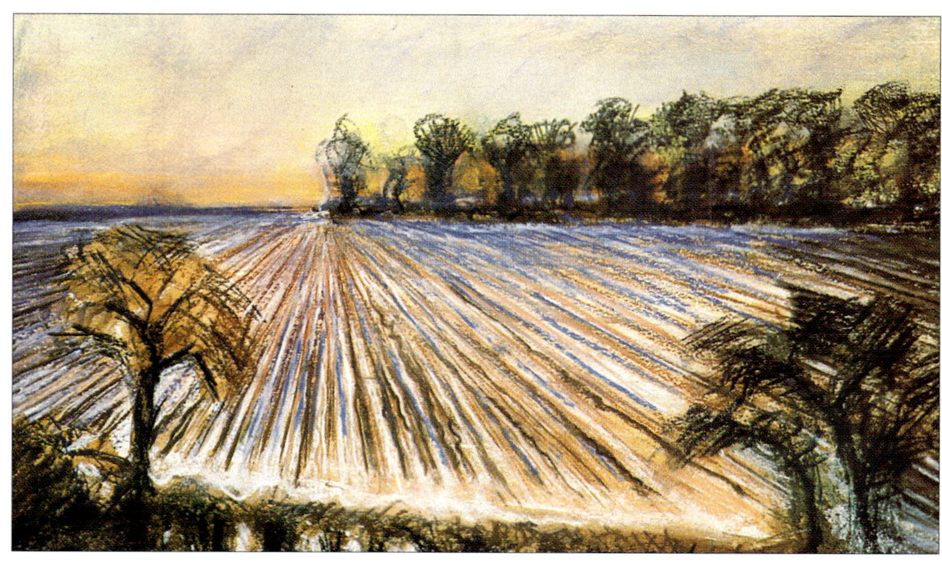

Left *Different media and styles of drawing can help bring a sense of freshness and discovery to familiar views. Tony R. Smith has used pastel and conté crayon over wash to make an effective drawing of an agricultural landscape.*

Far Left Study of Bottle and Glass *drawn in oil pastels. It is not difficult to find suitable subjects for a still life drawing, basic everyday objects that are readily available can make pictures.*

It is not enough simply to copy exactly what you see; adjustments are often necessary, perhaps in the scale of relative parts or in tones. When selecting a point of view, bear in mind the quality that inspired you to choose the scene in the first place, possibly a good skyline or the varied character of some tree. Urban scenes can provide just as much interest as the more obviously beautiful rural views. You may find it necessary to remove a feature altogether if it is spoiling your view; the perfect landscape is very hard to find and the results you achieve will depend on what you can do with the material available.

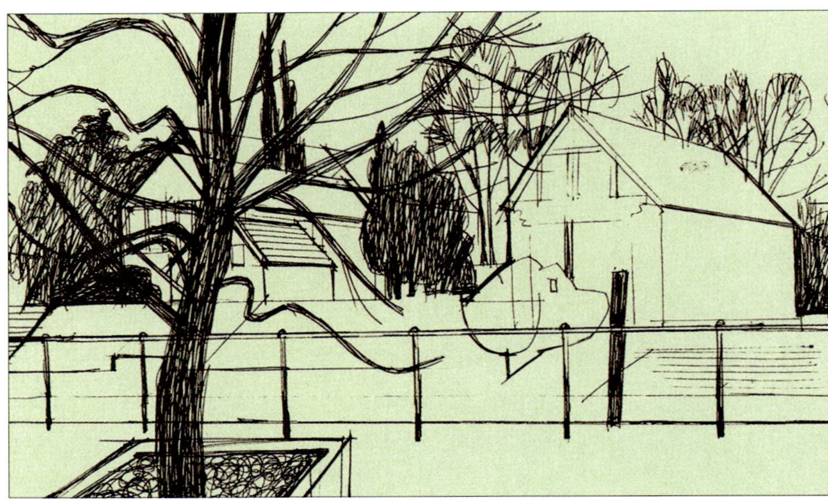

Left *The composition of this drawing of boathouses and trees on the banks of a river was arrived at by means of a series of preliminary sketches (below). It is just one solution to the problems presented by the view chosen by the artist and is a combination of some of the ideas sketched out in an exploratory way.*

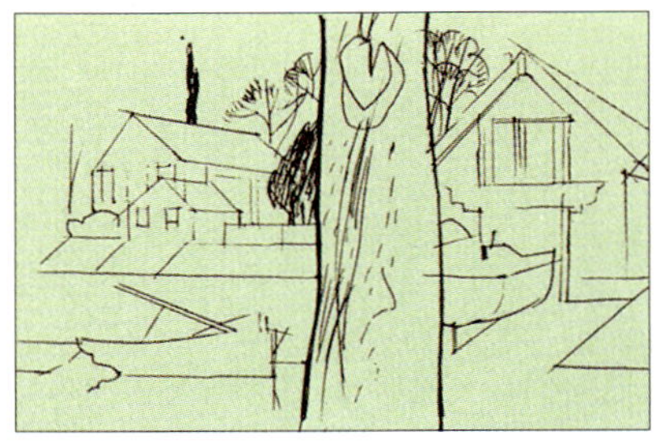

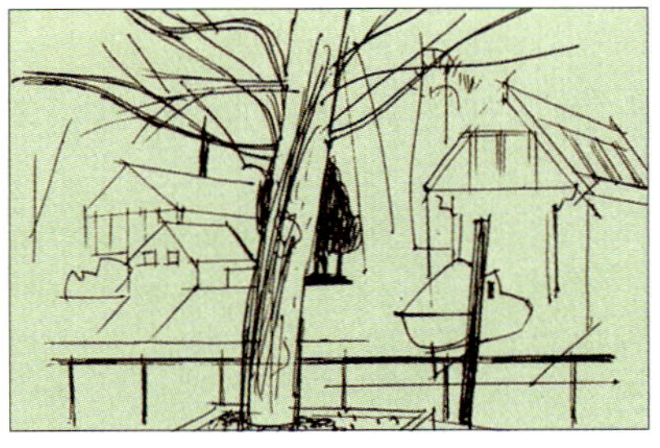

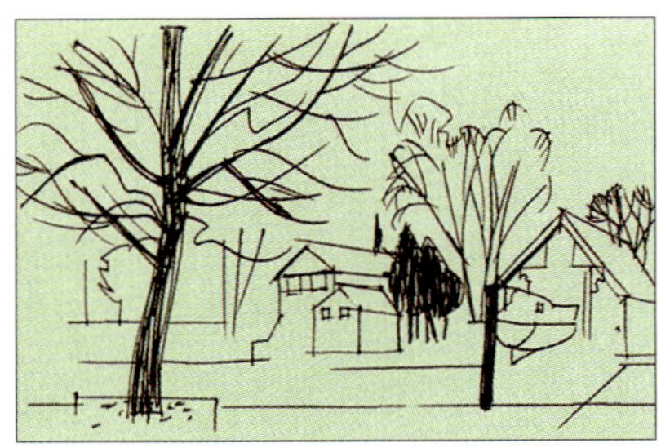

View 1: *It is an unsatisfactory solution; allowing the tree, not a particularly interesting form in itself, to occupy about one fifth of the drawing, the boathouses, occupying most of the rest, are too symmetrically balanced.*

View 2: *The draftsman has moved back to let more of the view enter the frame. Tonal stress is more varied, and a railing gives the foreground a stronger sense of vertical and lateral structure.*

View 3: *With this shift in position, he can see much further. An unfortunate coincidence of verticals divides the picture into three and the mooring post on the right coincides with the edge of the boathouse.*

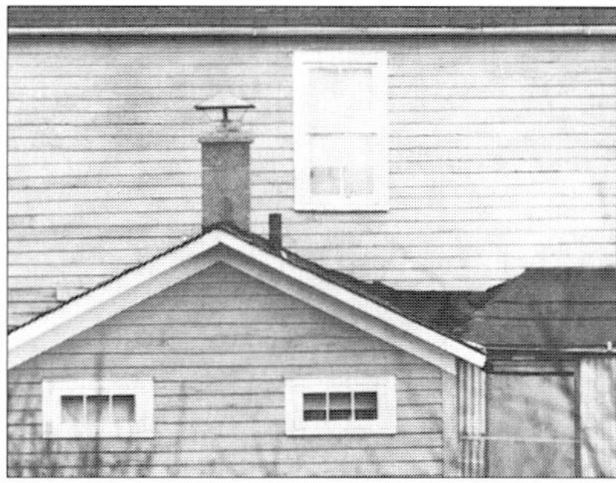

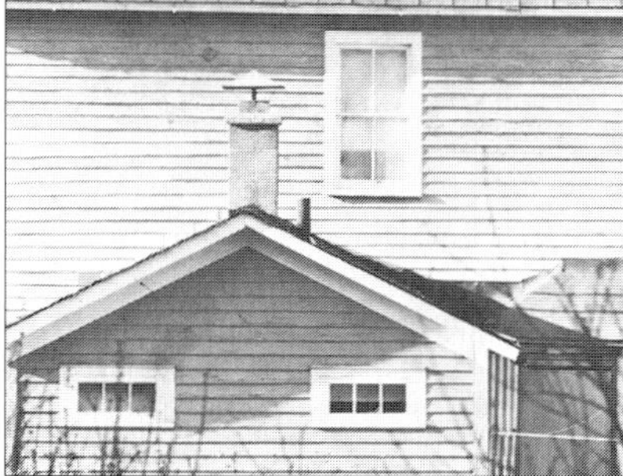

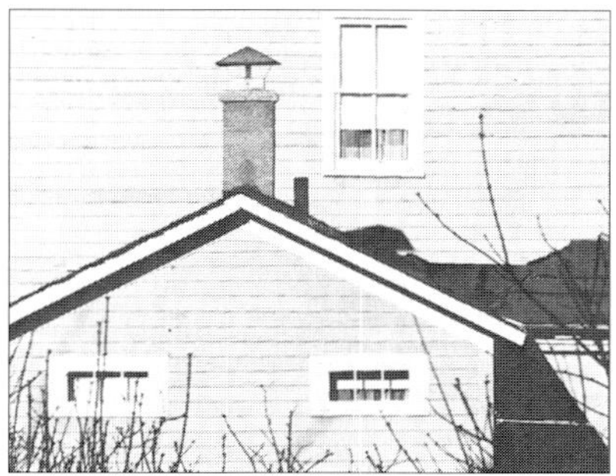

Above *The same view, but completely different effects. Lighting is one of the most important factors to be taken into consideration when planning a landscape drawing; as an exercise, it is well worth taking the trouble to return to the same place at different times of day and make sketches to compare the view under different lighting conditions.*

Below Right *It is its sheer mass and architectural form that make more of an impact, with only the contrasting irregularity of the trees to detract from the strength of the visual image. In contrast with the large masses of complete buildings, you may prefer to concentrate on a detailed drawing of smaller areas. The verandah (below left) is an excellent example of a subject worth a minutely detailed approach.*

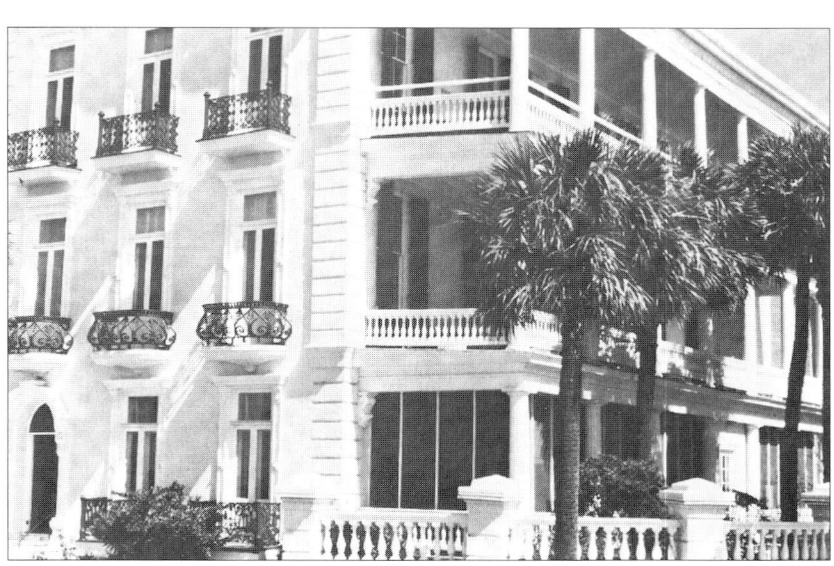

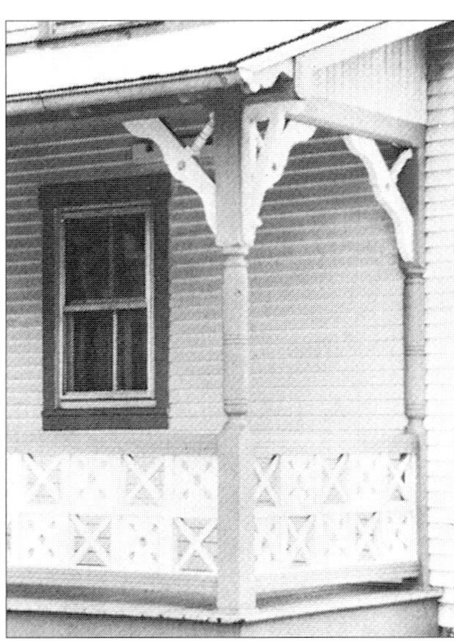

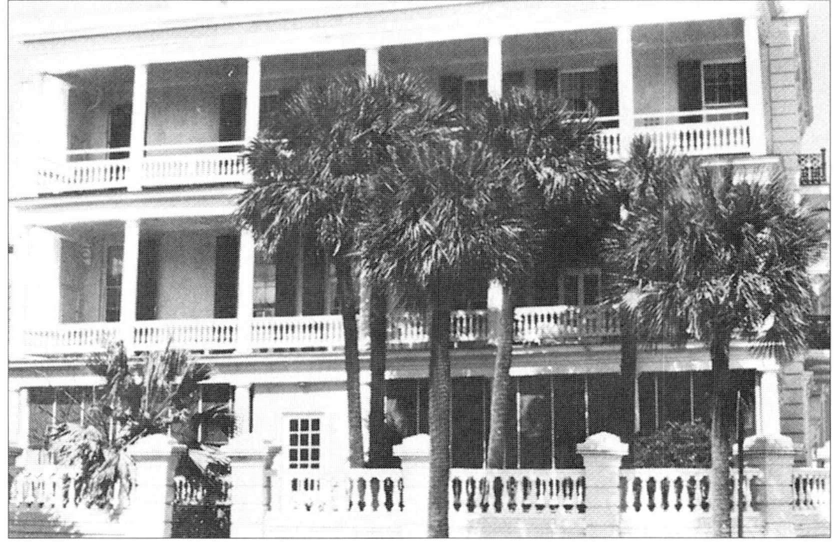

LANDSCAPE ANALYSIS

One of the most important aspects to be taken into consideration by the landscape artist is that of the composition or proportion of his drawing. A well known formula put forward as a guideline is that of the Golden Section; if you were to take a number of landscapes produced entirely instinctively it would be interesting to note how many of them conformed to this ideal, particularly as regards the division between the sky and land masses.

Rules, however, should never be allowed to become a stranglehold on the picture being produced; they should be resorted to as a useful starting point, as for instance when working a large-scale work from a tiny sketch containing information but little else. Thumbnail sketches, scribbled fairly quickly, can be a great help, perhaps covering several variations in location and a different selection of elements.

Light plays an important part in determining the atmosphere of your drawing. As well as creating the general mood, it can also be responsible for dramatic effects, with strong light giving rise to deep, dark shadows or an unusual quality causing a weird unnerving glow. Geographical location will affect the quality, as will the time of day. The qualities of thin, early morning light, of midday sun high in the sky, or of warm evening light can totally alter the scene.

LANDSCAPE

We all are affected by the landscape around us; it has a profound influence upon the way we live and our view of life. We appreciate it not simply through our eyes, but with all our faculties; the changes of weather, wind, sun, the dark, and the dawn all become a part of our experience.

All these factors have combined over the centuries to form an intrinsic part of the artistic tradition, together with the different reactions each individual view produces. This occurs on two levels. The apparently limitless horizons of moor and downland, or the sea, obviously encourage different reactions to those produced by the harsher lines of a dense cluster of buildings. How these reactions are interpreted, however, totally depends on the nature of the artist. He or she can produce a romanticized view of a rural landscape, or a dour and somber one of a townscape; equally, the townscape could be approached romantically and the rural scene more realistically.

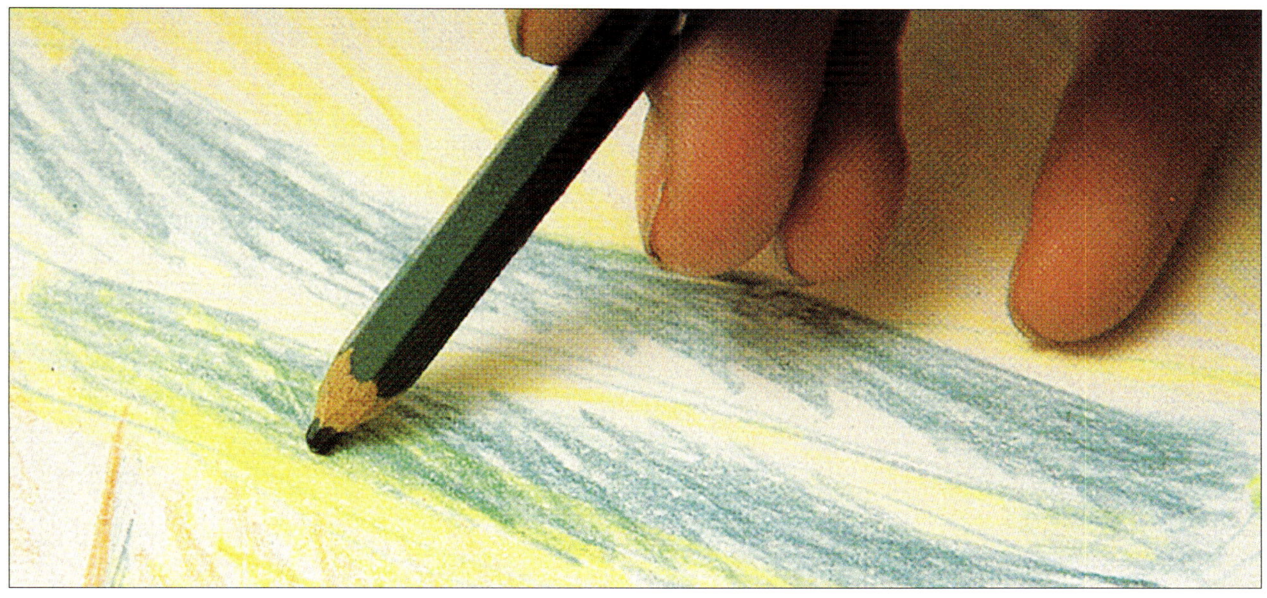

GARDEN SCENE

Above *Use a technique of hatching and crosshatching to build up several layers of color.*

Right *Finished drawing. When practicing landscape drawing it is often unnecessary to travel far to find appropriate subjects. Your local park or, in this case, garden, can provide plenty of interest and variety. The strong, dark shapes of the yew trees contrast with the bright, delicate flowers. above*

Below *Test the effect of a dark background by cutting out a piece of dark paper of an approximately similar shape and holding it in the appropriate area.*

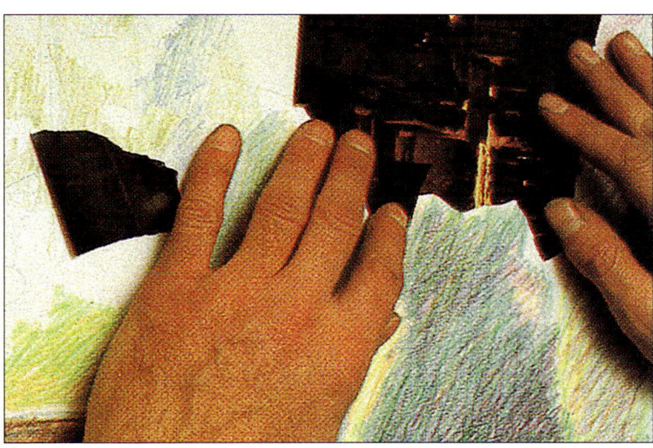

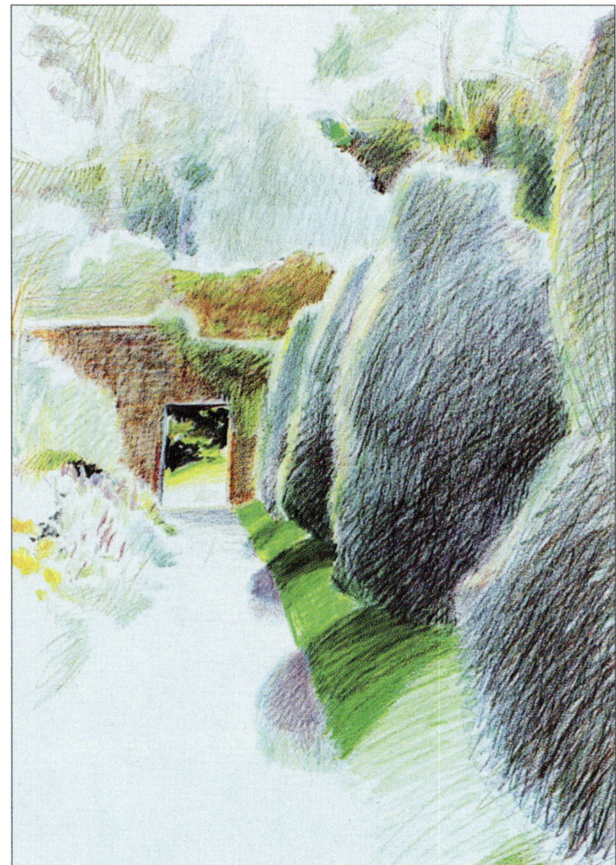

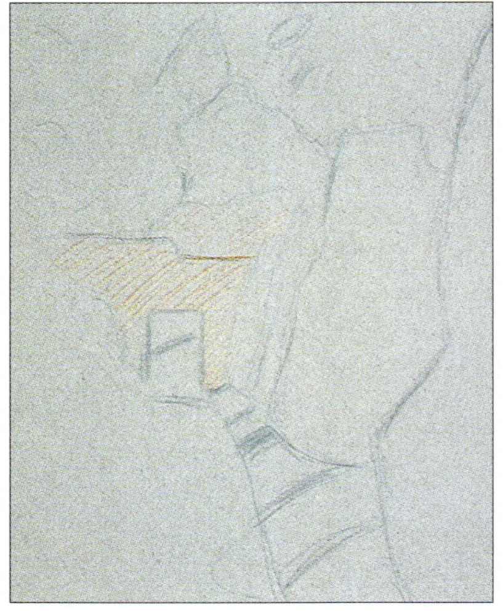

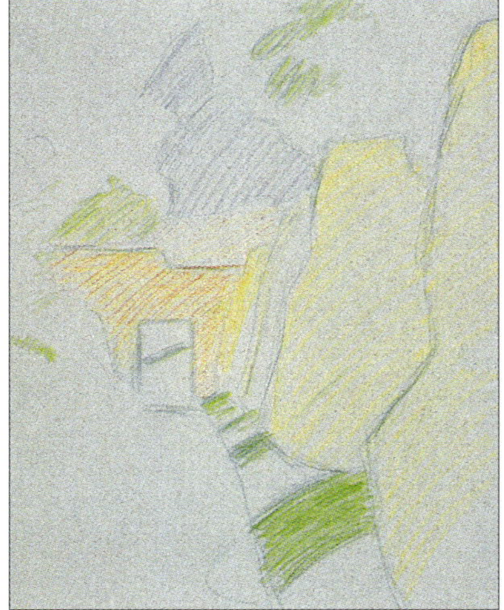

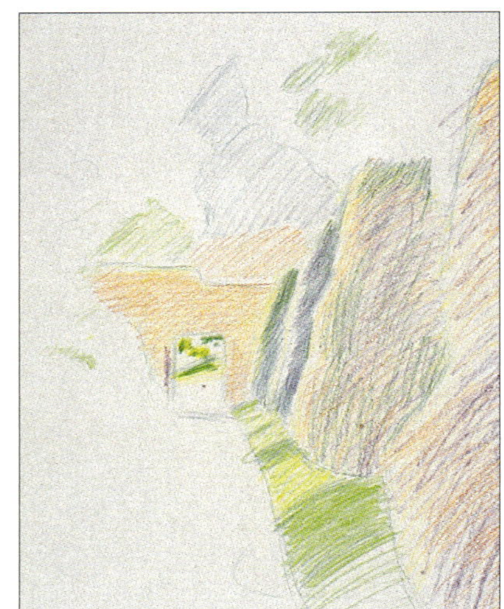

1 *Lightly draw in general composition, paying attention to the yew trees, which are the strongest forms, and their shadows.*

2 *Block in the masses by building up layers of hatching, using an underlying Naples yellow or Cream for the yews.*

3 *Allow the overlapping of various colors—a bluish green, a bright dark-green, purple, burnt sienna, and vermillion red.*

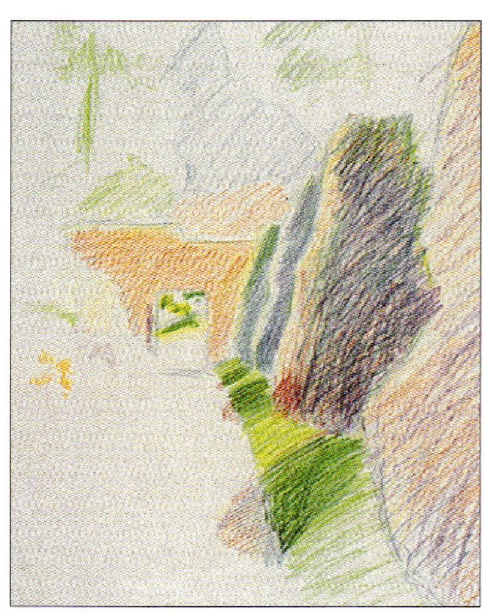

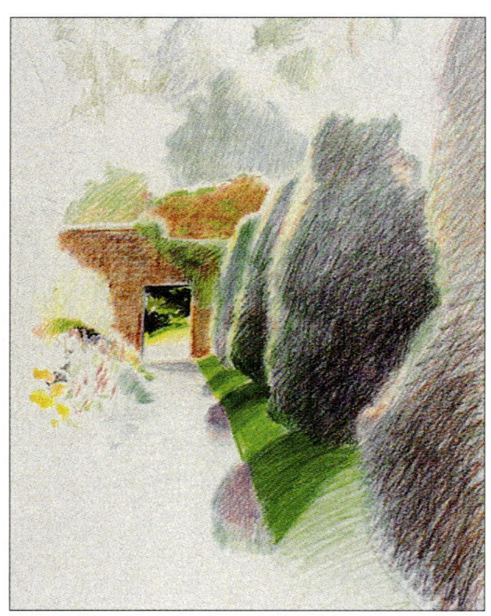

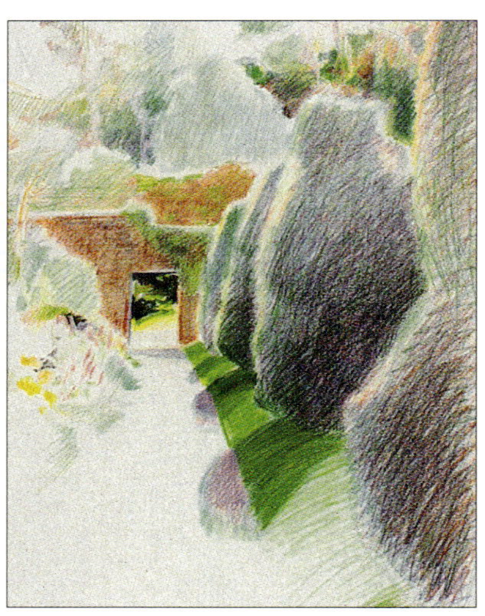

4 *Put in crosshatching to build up color until the final effect is achieved. You can wait until the next stage to work in more details.*

5 *Add definition using orange, crimson lake, and yellow, as you work in details into the background and middle area of the drawing.*

6 *Put in a dark background—tuscan red, black, real green, peacock green, a red; buttermilk to lighten real darks.*

TREES IN PEN AND INK

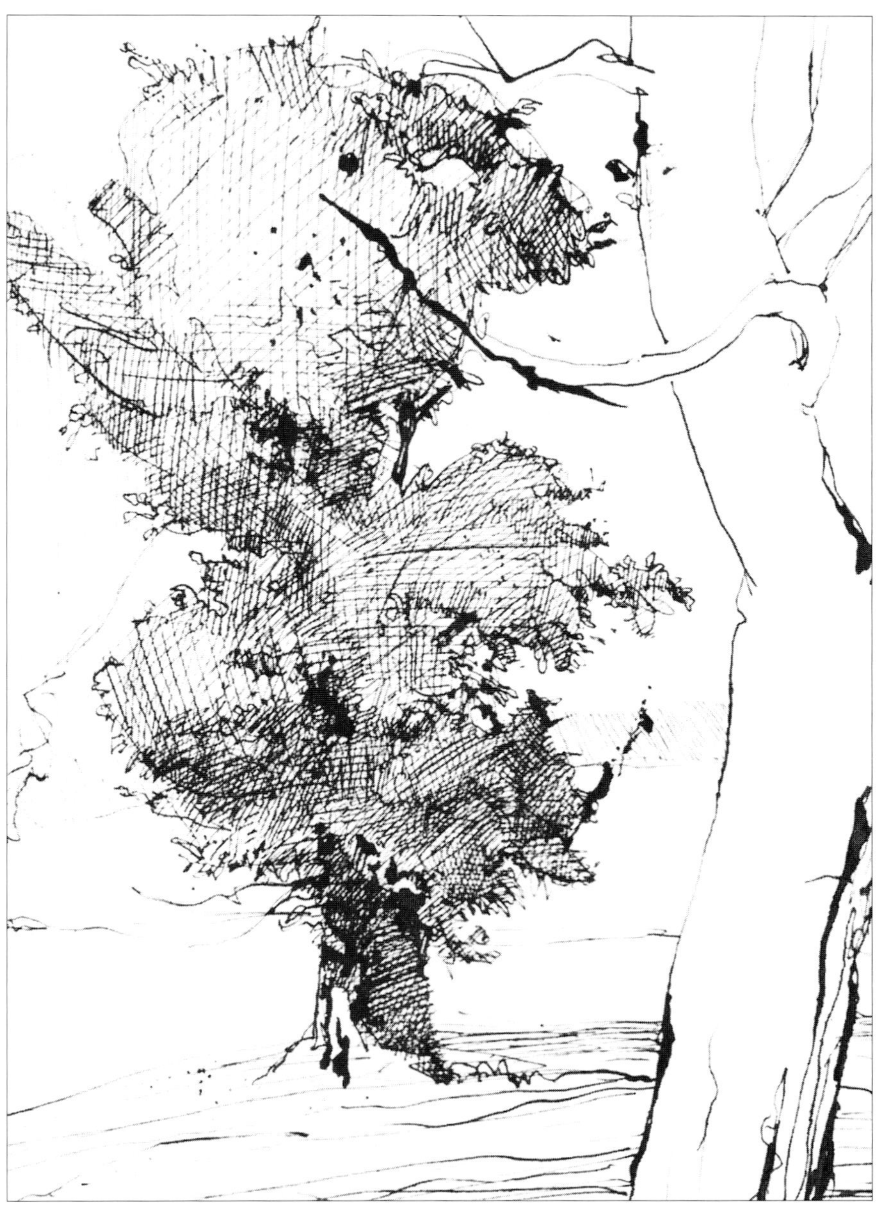

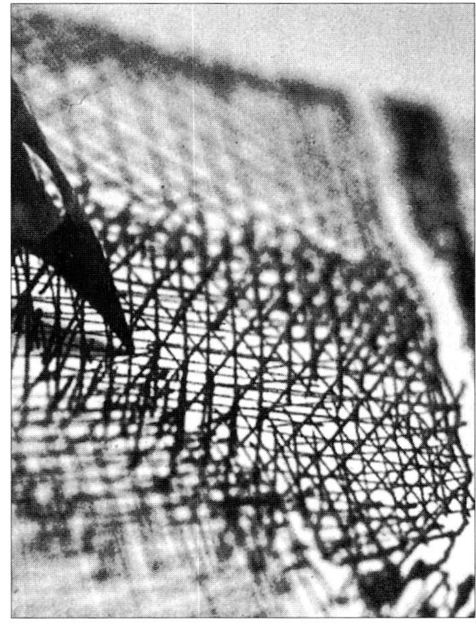

Above & Right *When drawing trees, the most interesting aspect is generally the overall shape, whether concentrating on one tree (above) or placing several in a landscape (next page). With very little pressure, allow the pen nib to move around freely to achieve a very loose effect. Many layers of overlapping are possible; you can cover your tracks as you go. Try to work with a light pressure. If you press heavily you will both wear the nib down making the line less interesting, and pick up too much paper, so that it acts as a blotter. Crosshatching (right) can be used to develop dense and varied tonal areas.*

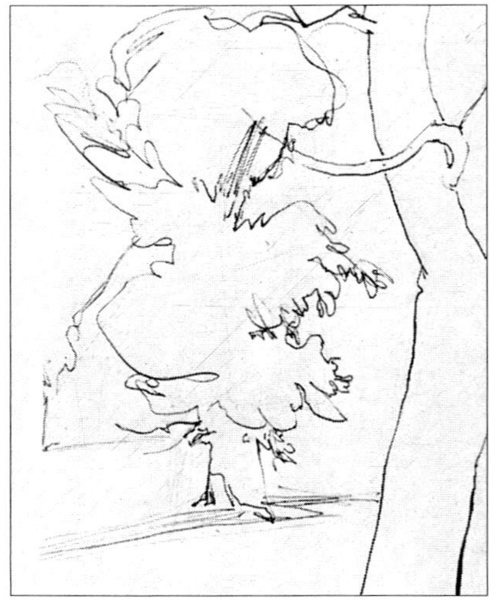

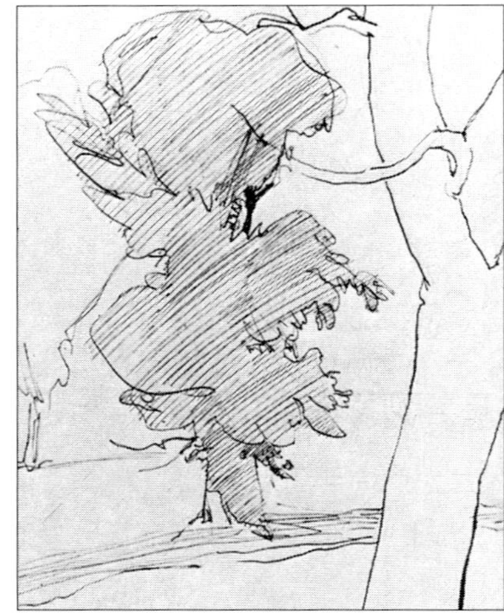

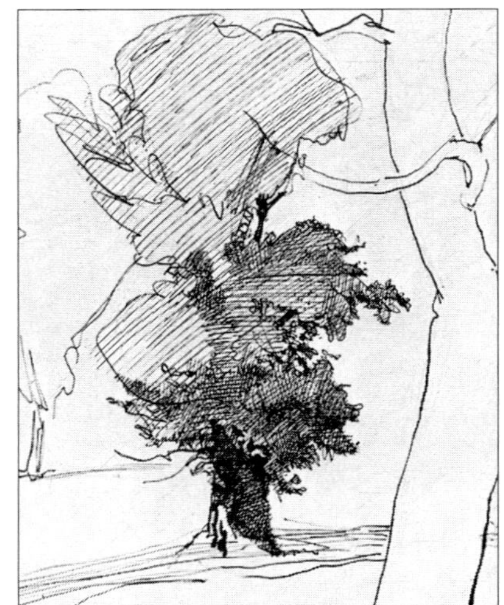

1 *Block out the three planes in the general composition. Put in hatching to develop the middle tree, the most carefully indicated part.*

2 *Use crosshatching to round this tree out into dumps; for leaves, suggest multiplicity by intervals between dots and tiny marks.*

3 *It is easier to put in the back tree by hatching than with a line. Dark lines on the front tree suggest the foreground plane.*

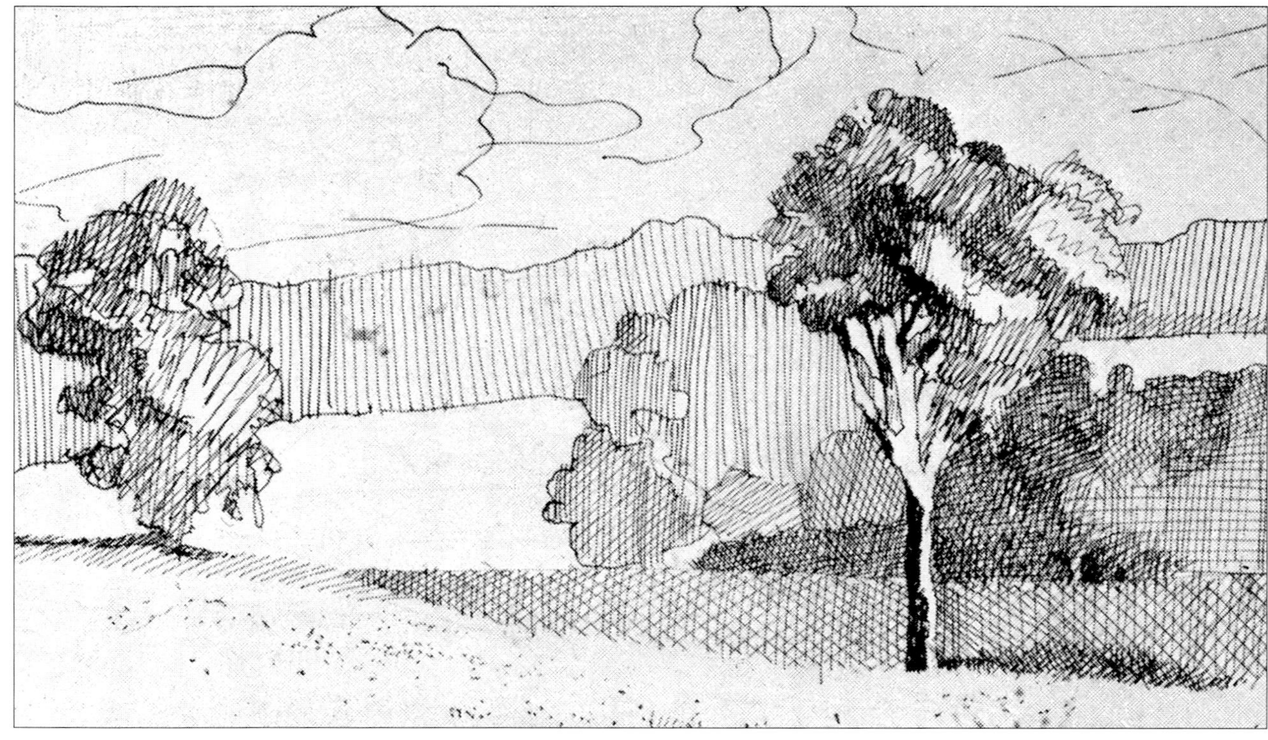

What you should aim for are inventive and surprising angles, views and atmosphere. Edward Hopper's *New York Rooftops*, for instance, differ from the landscape etchings of Rembrandt, just as the places shown vary. Start with a familiar subject and look at it in the most concentrated way possible, even before making a single mark on your support. This kind of concentrated consideration will often surprise you and your eventual drawings can only benefit as a result.

As you explore the possibilities, you will find that landscape is a subject with many advantages. It stays still, except when blown by winds or lashed by storms! It can take on many different and interesting moods. Light moves across fields and trees, for instance, to bring rapidly shifting relationships of tone and color.

Skies, which are sometimes thought to be the single most important feature in a landscape drawing or painting, also vary widely. They can range from leaden gray, dark, and threatening, against which features stand out as bright and highly contrasted, through the huge, cloud-filled variety to a bright, clear backdrop to rich foreground detail. Never fall into the trap of disregarding the sky, or relegating it to the status of insignificance.

Bring this same perception to the

ABSTRACT LANDSCAPE

Right This drawing, done with pen, brush, and waterproof ink, adopts a simple approach to perspective. Although the forms are given impression rather than detail, the carefully noted differences of scale and tone in each area of the image serve to suggest distance and recession. Indentations on the pathway are indicated to lead the eye through the foreground plane and the rolling moor behind, studded with dark patches representing trees and scrub, describes the dip and rise of the skyline.

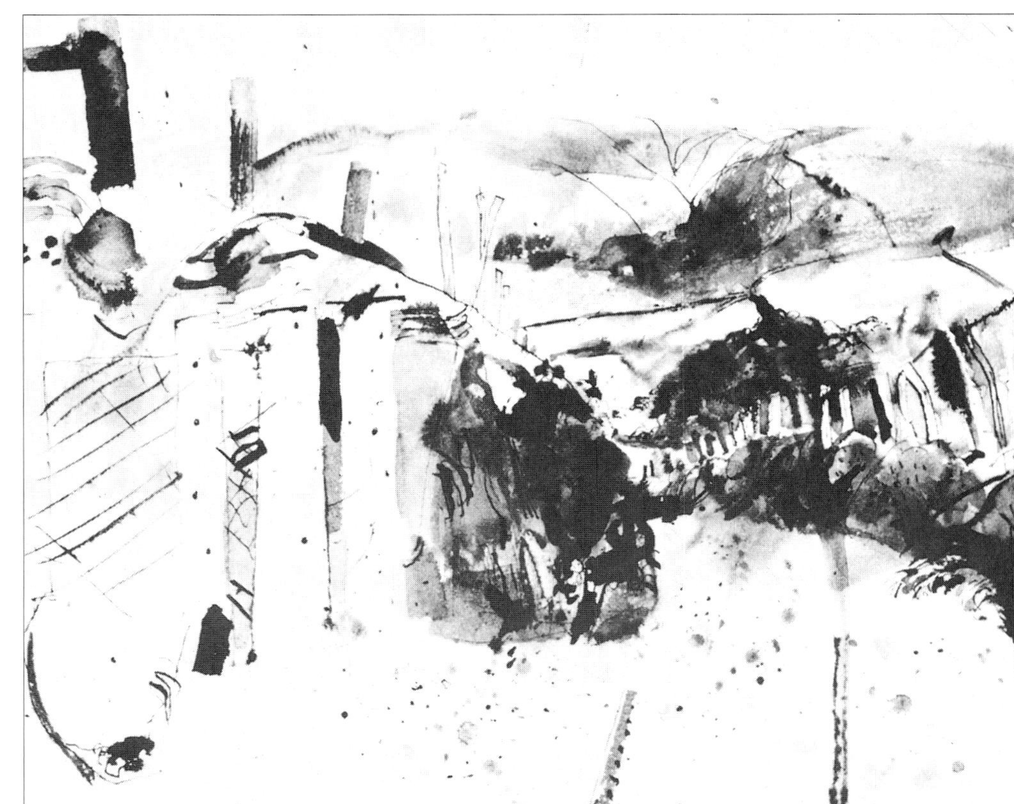

question of color. Green is the dominant color of landscape, but it requires real sensitivity to achieve an effective, living, vibrant foliage. You can only achieve this by constantly varying the range of color with which you are working.

Each element of a successful landscape will have the same degree of careful consideration brought to bear on it. Here, associations and identifications are likely to be involved and decisions made accordingly. Wind, for instance, causes movement. It bends trees in the direction in which it is blowing, while the sky will generally be light in tone. Therefore, all parallel surfaces, such as lakes, fields, and rivers, will tend to be light. Objects standing against the sky—vertical forms such as trees and buildings—tend to be dark. Use such simple, basic guidelines to help you select a viewpoint and a theme, or subject.

URBAN ARCHITECTURE

For many people, an urban environment is the most familiar setting for both work and recreation. This makes it an immediately accessible subject for drawings, and it may renew your interest in your neighborhood to walk through it with an eye to aesthetic features. Complex arrangements of walls and rooftops and the rich colors and textures of buildings invite interpretation in various media

FARM OUTHOUSE

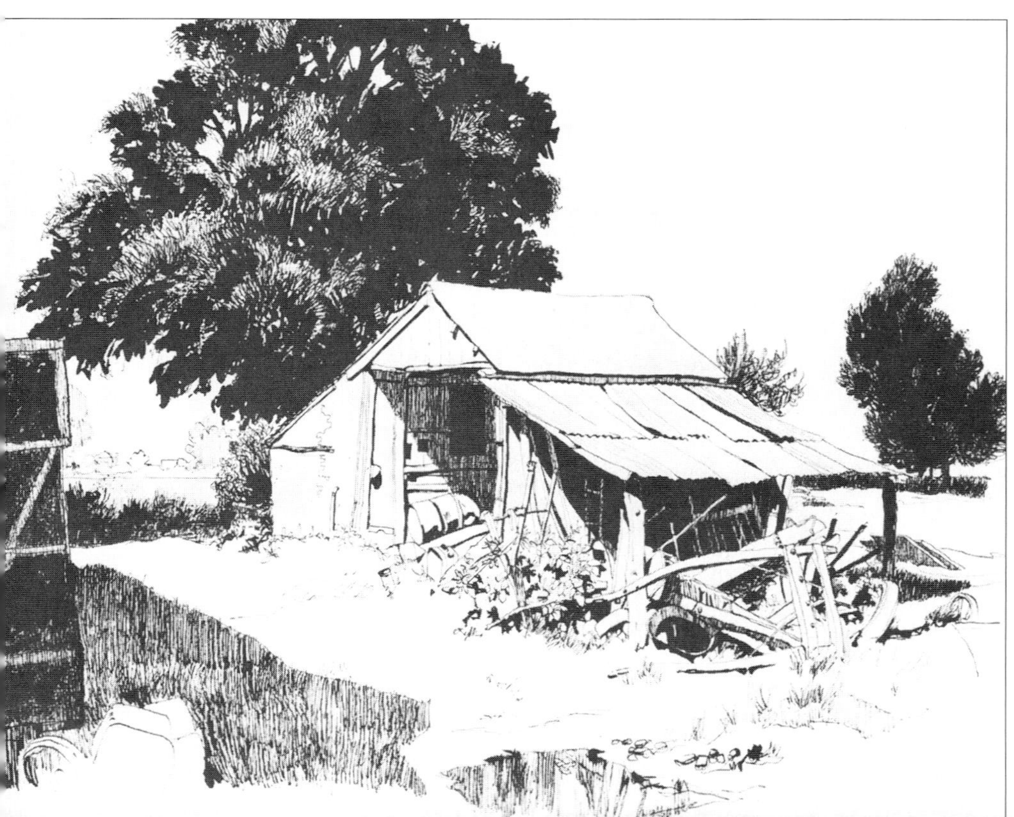

Left *The subject chosen here enables the artist to relate strong areas of dark tone to line drawing of a highly descriptive kind. Heavy cast shadows and the dense foliage of the trees are put down in black, but because of the nature of the pen marks, this is not a flat, lifeless tone, but is enlivened by small areas of white and rough texture. The dark tone is carried right through the space described in the drawing.*

and techniques.

Landscape can be created effectively in monochrome. Here, bulk and the sense of massive distance and weight of the parts involved are the things you should aim to achieve. An archaeological site, for instance, is ideal for such a treatment; large standing stones, or deep ditches, will take dramatic shadows, just as trees do in a different context. Avoid the pitfall of sitting square to lines—whether of stones, trees, or hedgerows. Taking a diagonal view can bring additional visual interest, if properly exploited. The composition, too, should be thought of as endlessly changeable, as is the stuff of nature itself.

Obviously, it is best to work on location, whenever possible, though your sketches can serve as a basis for a reinterpretation of the subject in the studio later, if you so desire. Some artists use photographs as visual reference points and certainly the photographic technique of backlighting—used to sharply delineate the silhouettes of trees, for instance—is a telling effect that can form the basis for an inspiring interpretation.

Do not feel inhibited by the conventional approach to media. Graphite powder, rubbed onto the surface to create textures and lay in general tones, is an

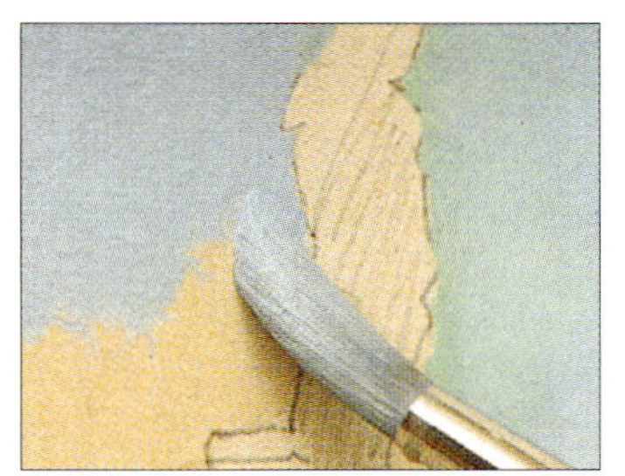

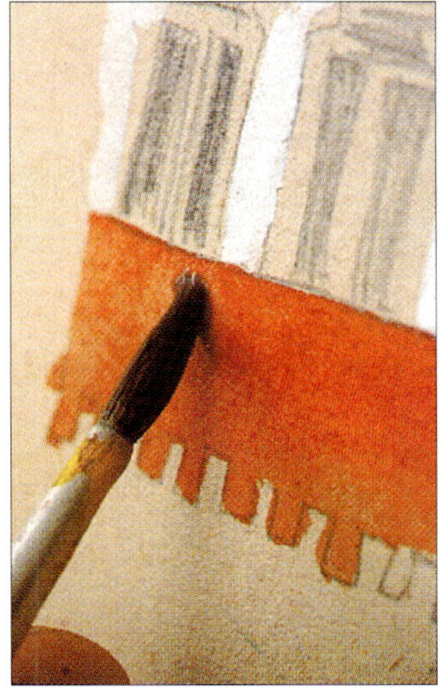

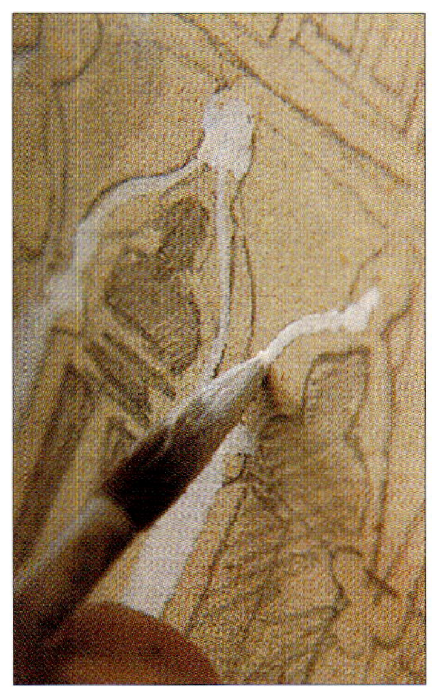

Above & Left *A combination of pencil, gouache, and watercolor on toned paper allows the artist to include many details of line and color in this architectural study, which is not slavishly faithful to the structure.*

excellent way of beginning. Use a torchon with it and elaborate on this basis with pencils, or pen and ink. Remember you will need to fix your work with the appropriate spray if this method is adopted.

You can use colored pencils to build up layer upon layer of subtle color, the end result being almost transparent in texture. Pastel also produces subtle results and can be blended with the fingers to produce areas of solid tone. Crosshatching is a valuable foil when trying to achieve differentiation in tone and emphasis. When using graphite pencils, a putty rubber helps create highlights, while pen and ink lends itself to spattering and other interesting effects.

Never reject a possibility as too difficult to tackle. Rain, for example, brings in its wake fresh visual excitement, while the late evening sun, shining red through low cloud, will create long shadows and warm lights. Snow, or mist, will transform even the most familiar of landscapes into something exciting and

Below *The line drawing is approximate rather than a slavish rendering of rigid structure and this gives the work its original character. In the same way, the color is not strictly accurate, but it establishes an idea of light and shade. A careful look at the watercolor washes shows that the pencil drawing dominates the structure of the composition, color being laid carefully into quite complicated outlines.*

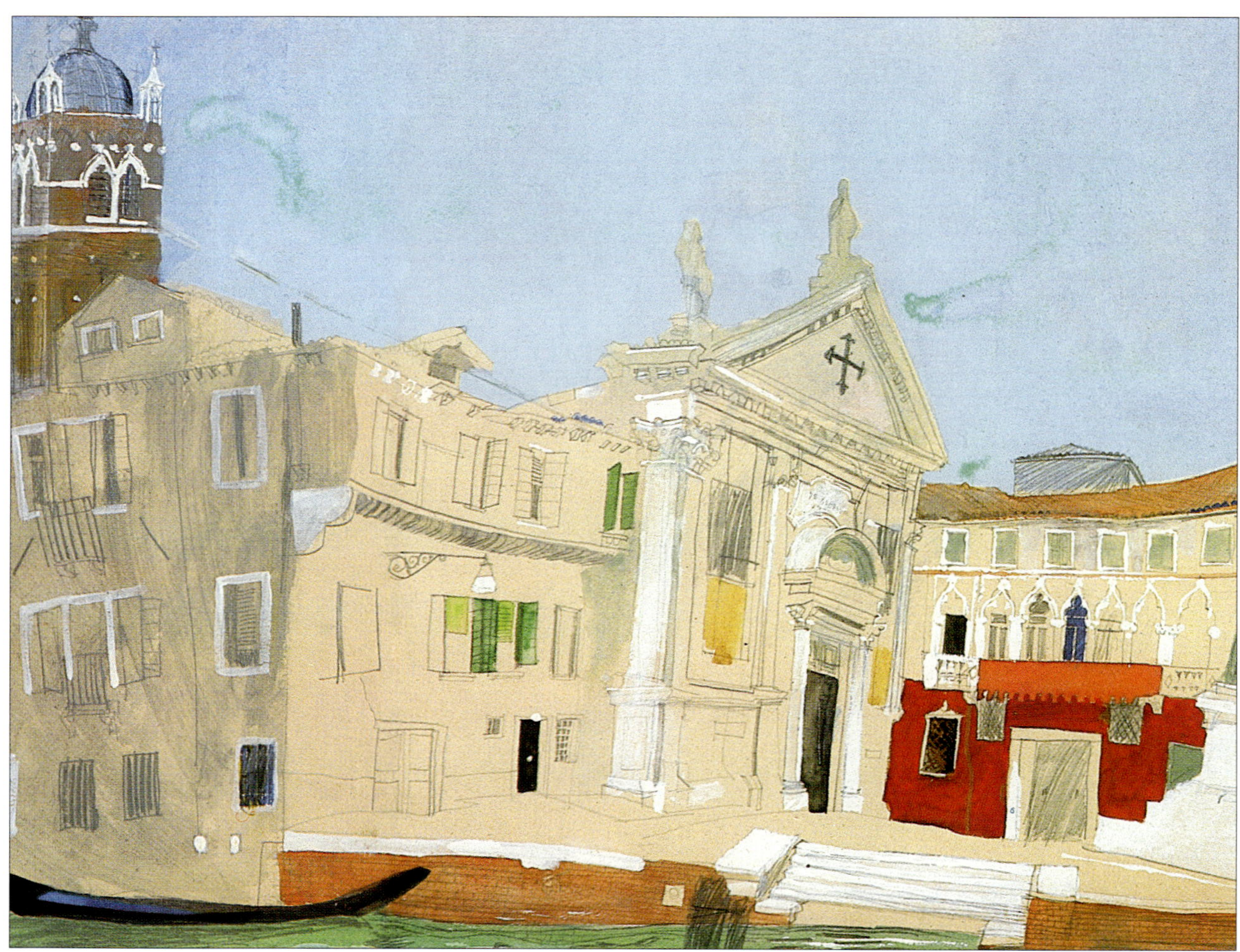

TERRACED HOUSES

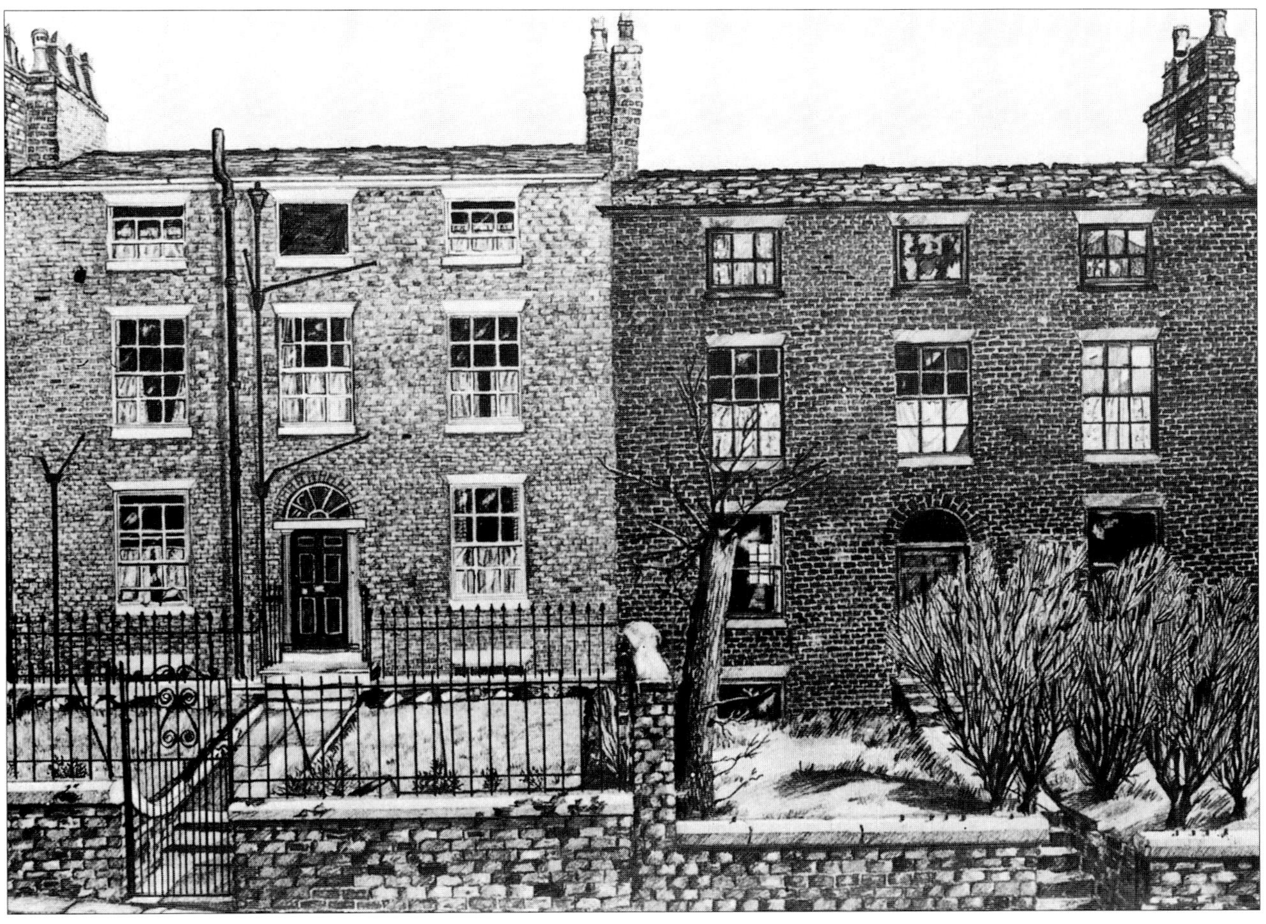

Above *Pencil is an excellent medium for drawings in which the artist wishes to include all the complex details of a densely textured subject. Such a drawing requires patience, skill, and minute observation, and the results can be highly rewarding. A 2B or 3B pencil can be given a fine point for linear detail, but is also soft enough to provide a good range of tones. Heavier pencils may be useful for putting in areas of pure black or grainy gray tones.*

different.

The range of possibilities is almost endless and the suggestions given here are no more than ideas.

You will need some knowledge not only of linear perspective, but also of aerial, or atmospheric, perspective. The latter is the effect of distance on definition, with objects in the foreground being stronger in tone and tonal contrasts within forms than those in the middle distance. These, in turn, are stronger in relation to things in the far distance.

As the tones lessen in strength, they take on an increasing blueness. A range of hills or a building in the far distance, for example, is likely to be almost entirely seen as a limited scale of light blues and blue-grays. Objects in the middle distance will appear to be a

ST PANCRAS STATION, LONDON

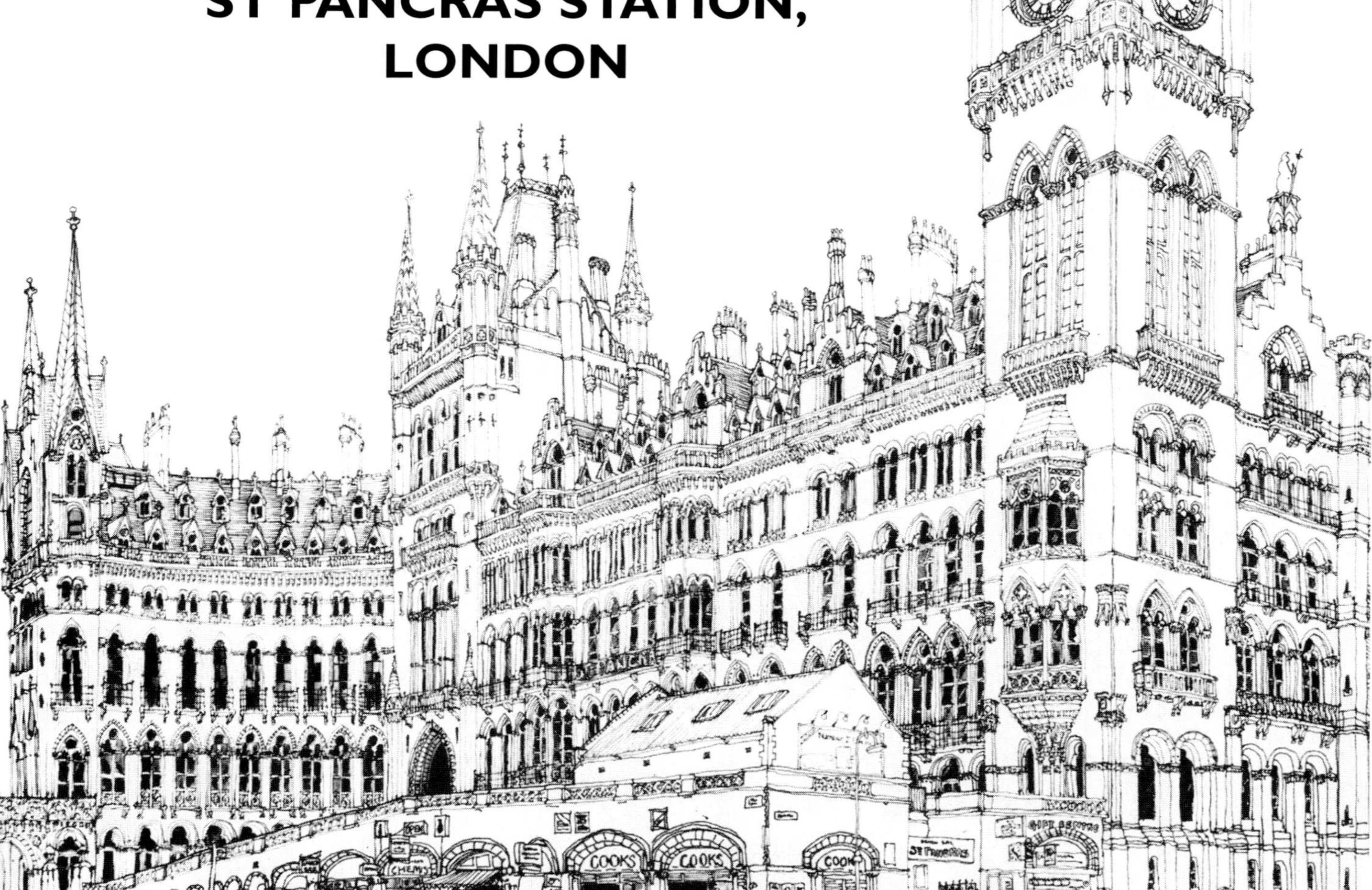

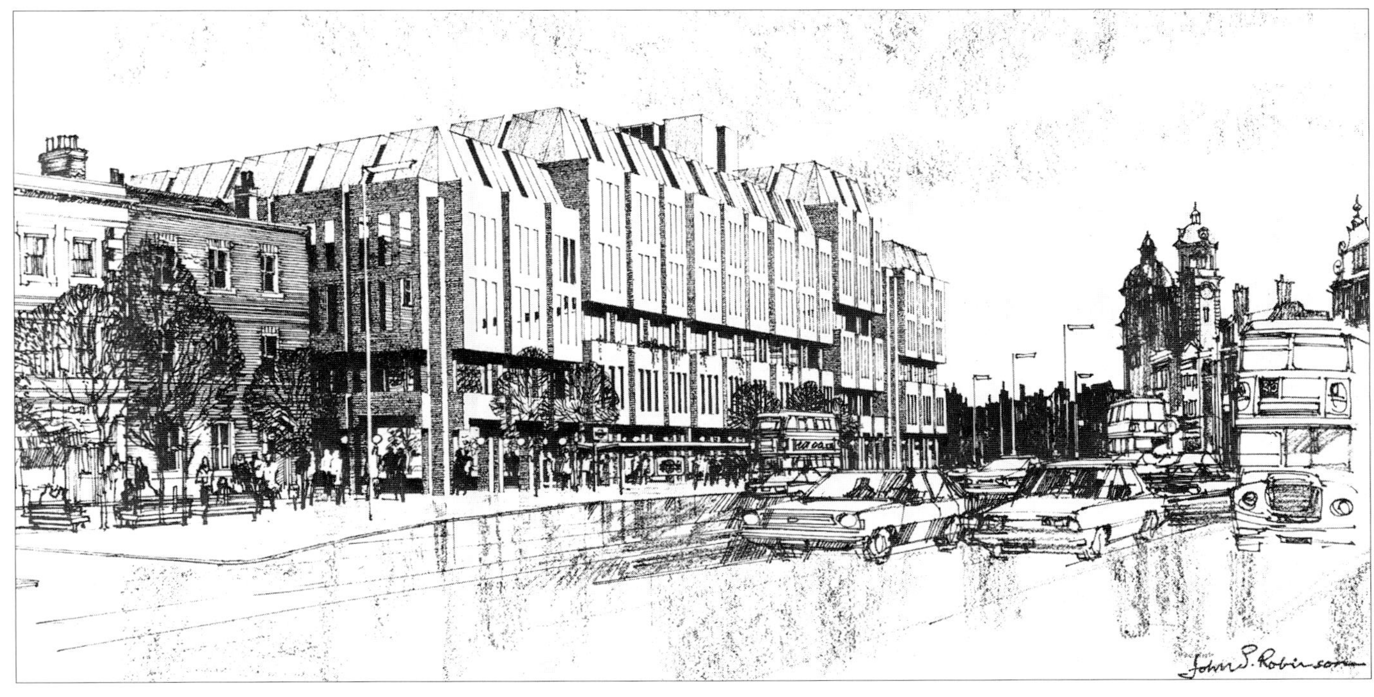

Above *Experiment with different media to find the best way of rendering skies, trees and brickwork; conté crayon and felt tips can create some particularly interesting effects.*

greenish blue, while foreground features will appear in the full range of colors and tones, almost as if existing independently.

You must formalize these visual facts into a reliable system of working. Examples of how this can be accomplished can be seen in the work of Poussin, Turner, and others, while Leonardo da Vinci makes reference to it in his writings on painting.

Remember, too, that although it is important to be true to nature in your choice of colors and so on, it is almost inevitable you will have to make some adjustments in your version of the natural scene. It is a good idea to use a viewfinder at the outset to help you select a suitable composition, while the composition itself can be strengthened on occasion by moving an object within your drawing, or even introducing an element into it! Such creative licence has been used by many of the greatest landscape artists over the centuries.

Above all, be practical, especially when you are working in the field. Always pre-plan your day as far as possible, so that you can limit the amount of equipment you are taking with you to what is really necessary for the drawing in hand.

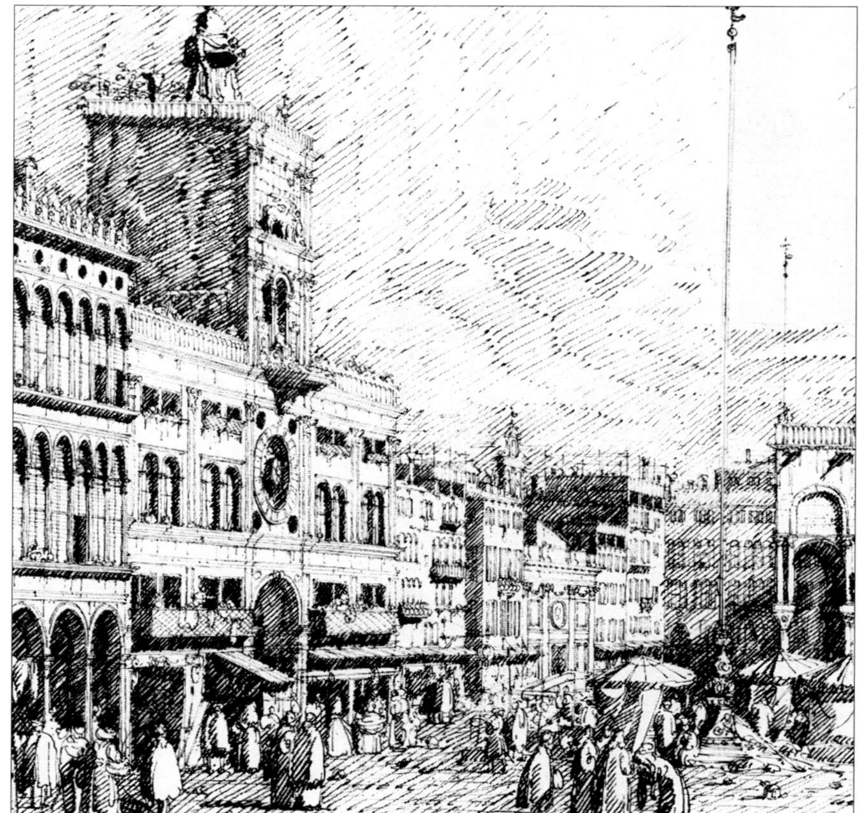

Left *The 18th century Venetian artist Canaletto was an expert in the use of realistic linear perspective, as exemplified in* The North East Corner of Piazza San Marco.

Below *This work provides ample evidence of the fact that atmospheric perspective can be conveyed by methods other than that of varying colors. Without this means at his disposal, Van Gogh has succeeded in creating an impression of depth in his pen and ink drawing,* View of Arles.

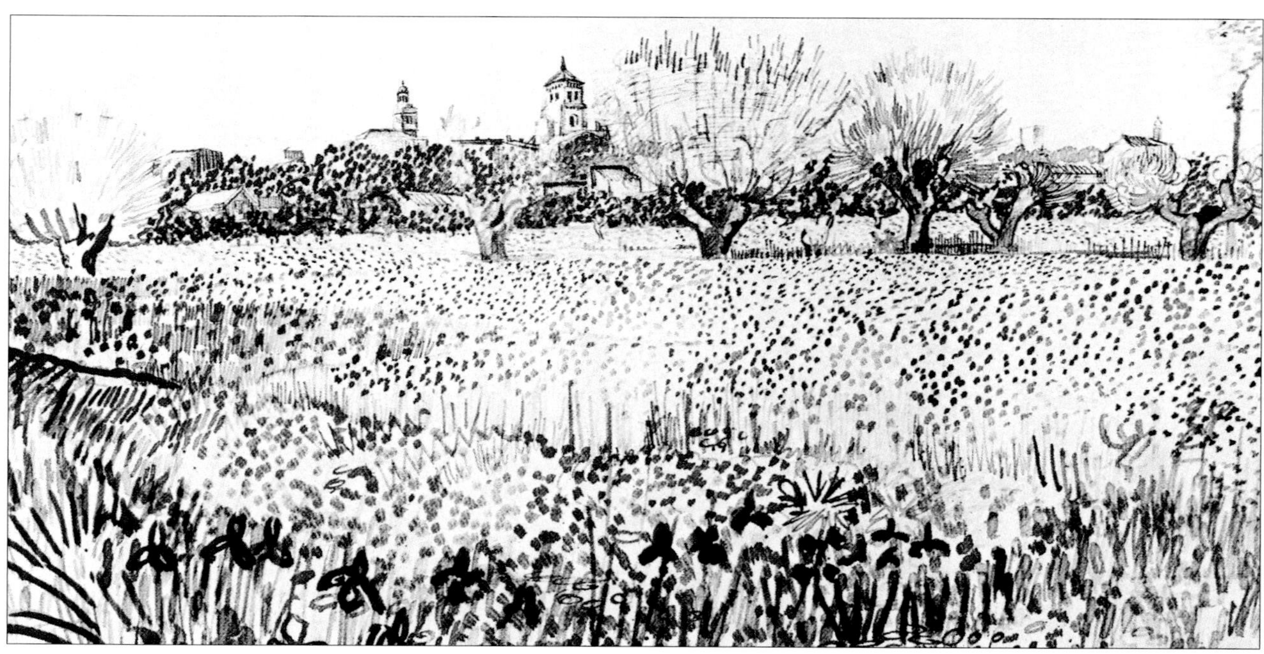

Right *Ruskin's drawing of the* Market Place, Abbeville *employs a combination of the accurate linear perspective to depict the foreground buildings and the blurring of the more distant buildings, which is a device of atmospheric perspective.*

Below *An impression of strong sunlight is quickly achieved in the scene showing figures seated in deckchairs, by the vibrant contrast between heavy-cast shadows and the bright color of the foreground plane. The colors used in this drawing are closely related and each is carefully given a suitable intensity to indicate spatial positions rather than local color.*

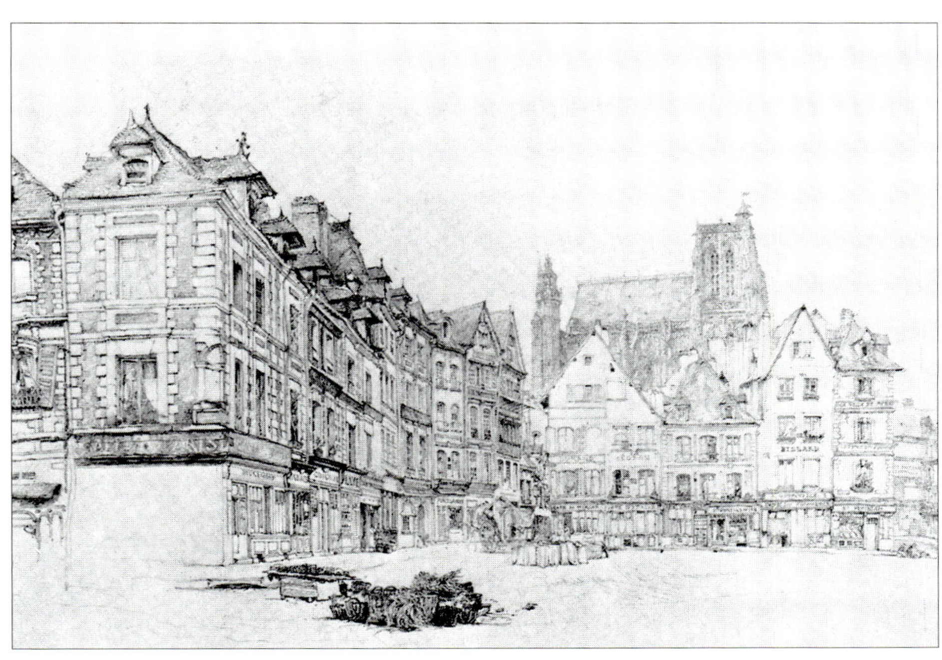

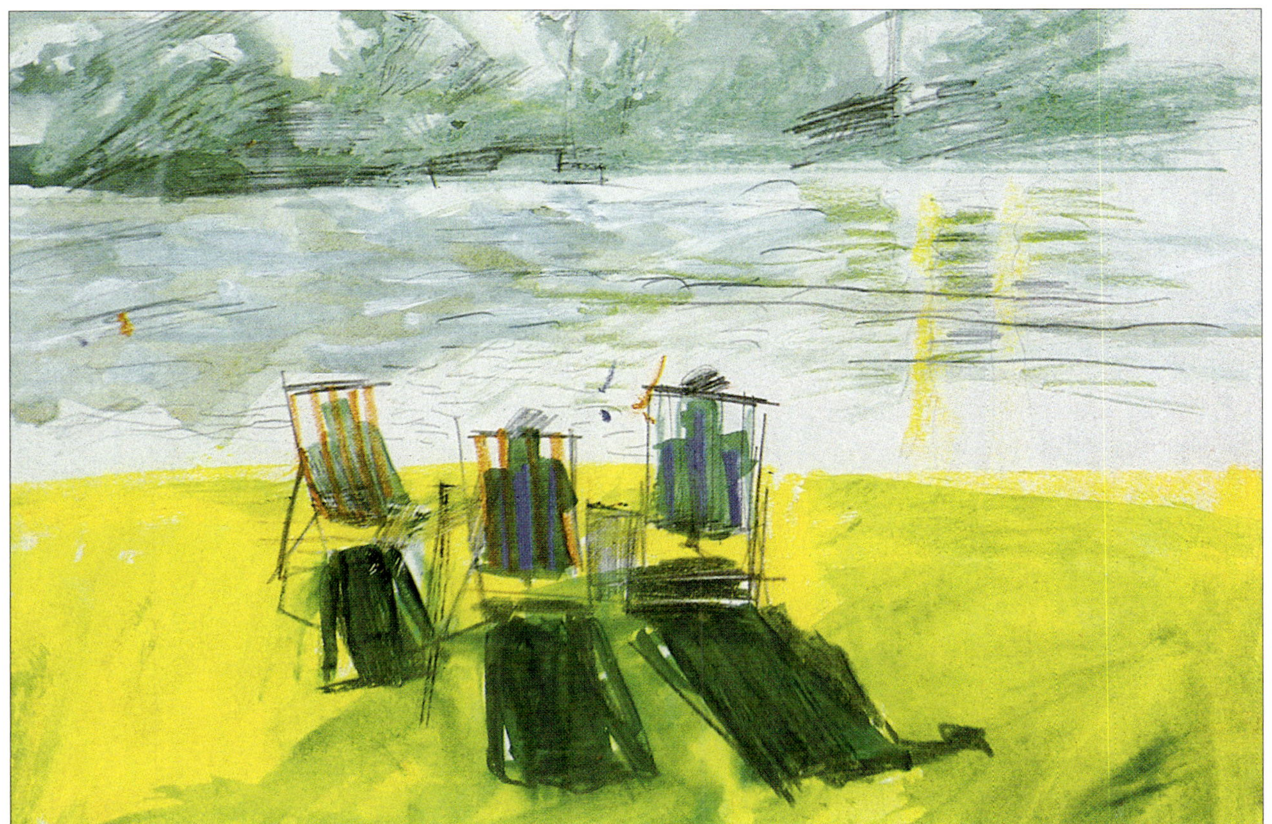

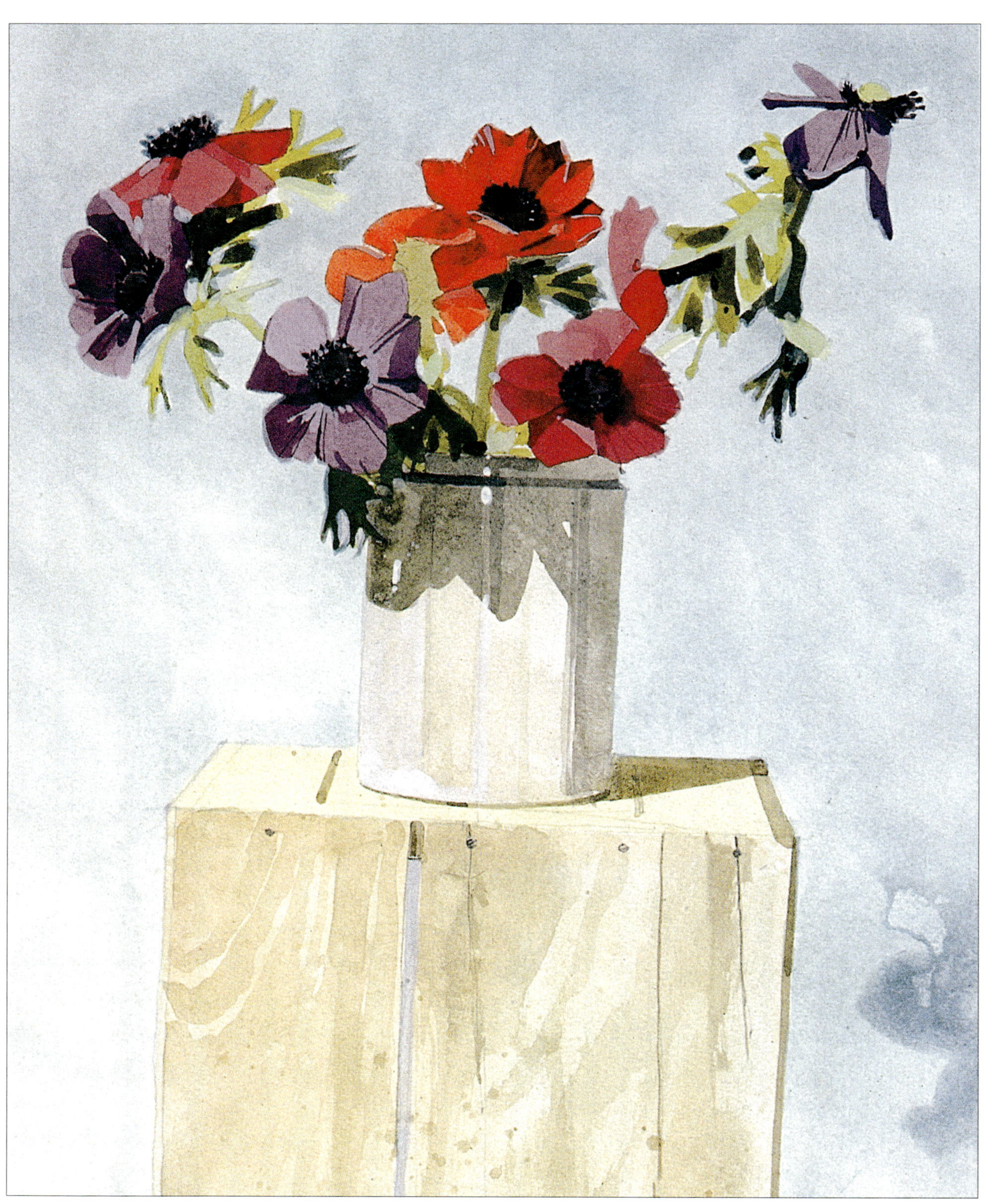

PAINTING

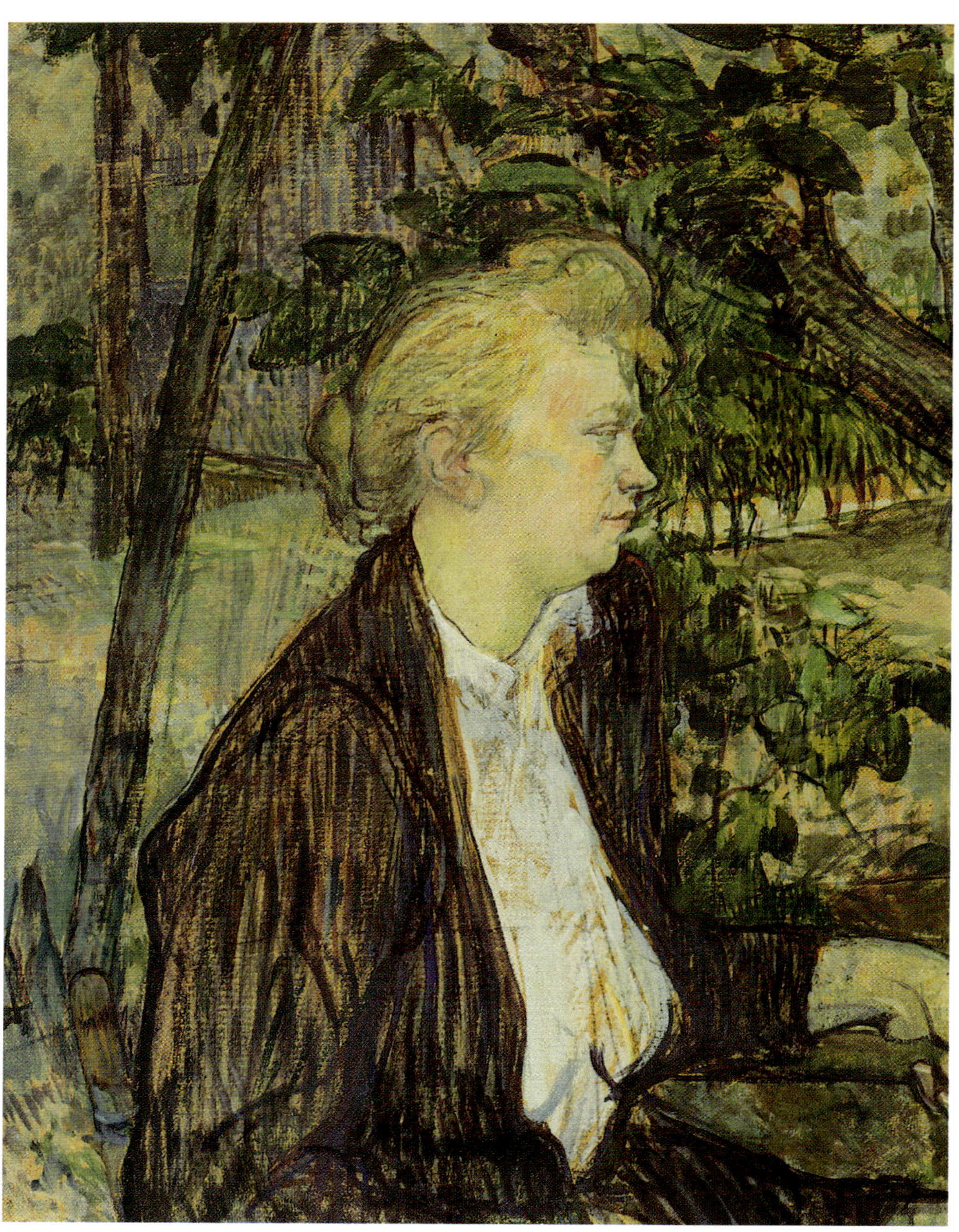

Above Woman Seated in a Garden *by Henri De Toulouse-Lautrec. Lautrec was deeply influenced by both Degas' technique and his choice of subject, and his works, like Degas', are a record of his personal life. He drew and painted scenes from the Paris dance halls, cafes, and brothels, and the circus; actresses, clowns, and many prostitutes. He depicted them while washing or dressing, or waiting for clients. He hated posed models, and prostitutes provided him with the informal poses he needed. He also painted many informal portraits, often in outdoor settings. This one is typical, and it shows his technique of building up forms with a succession of colored lines drawn with a brush. It is done on unprimed board with the oil paint heavily thinned with turpentine, a technique Degas pioneered. The profile of the head and the leaves behind the figure give the painting a sense of pattern, as in the Japanese prints that Lautrec and his peers so admired. The brush lines, with the warm gray color of the board showing through, lend a feeling of vitality.*

INTRODUCTION

There has been, for long, much debate about whether drawing and painting are organically linked. Many 19th century academics believed that until you have mastered the art of drawing, you cannot begin to paint. This was rigorously applied in the academies of the time, with students graduating to painting only after a comprehensive course in academic drawing. The view continues, to this day, to have both supporters and detractors.

The Impressionists were the first to rebel against this approach. Paul Gauguin, one of the few major artists of the period who had no first-hand academic tutoring, derided the academies' "cookery school approach." Similarly, art critic John Ruskin suggested that the artists of the Renaissance had got it right. He said they only turned to drawing when they were already accomplished painters, because of which you never saw a childish or feeble drawing by any of them.

Herbert Read, another distinguished writer and critic, suggested in his book *The Meaning of Art*, published in 1933, that the drawings of the Old Masters "constituted a separate art, distinct from painting, ancillary to it in that they provide a means of rapidly noting moments of vision or of thought which can later be translated into painting, but having no immediate relationship with the paintings."

Some see drawing as an integral part of painting or any other art activity. Every mark made by a painter's brush, for example, can be regarded as a form of drawing with color. In an interview, the contemporary sculptor Michael Kenny said that he thinks the term "drawing" is a misnomer when used to describe work in a particular medium, such as pencil or ink. He regards drawing as a "process of ordering," concerned with selection and deciding what is significant and what can be dispensed with—a process which he feels has been used by all great artists. He believes that every kind of art activity is a form of drawing.

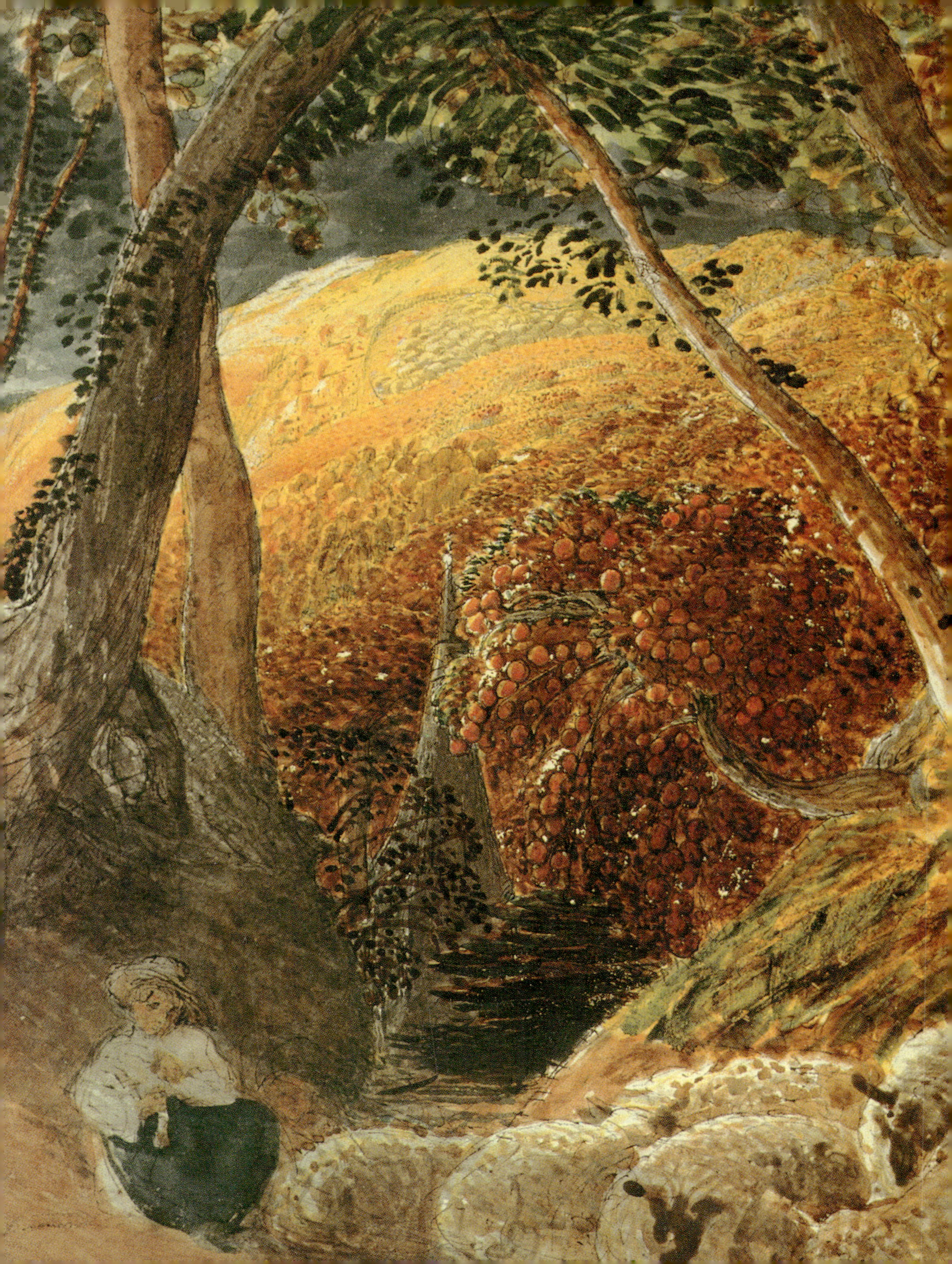

Watercolor

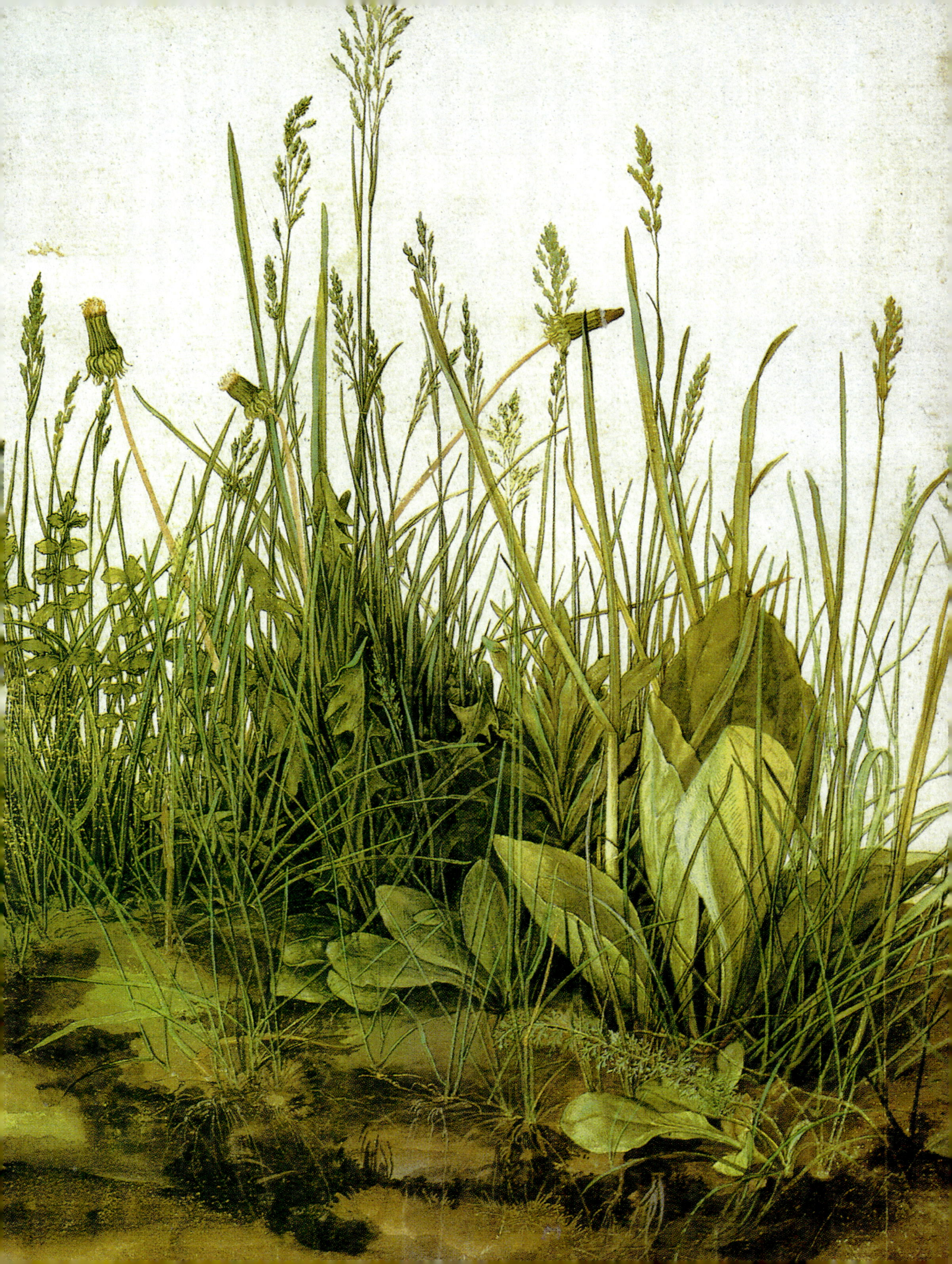

1 INTRODUCTION

Left The Great Piece of Turf *by Albrecht Durer, who found watercolor a particularly sympathetic medium for detailed studies of nature. We cannot be sure of his precise method, but he probably began by using transparent washes to establish broad areas, such as the large leaves, and then built up intricate details with tiny strokes of opaque paint (or body color).*

"I don't do watercolor; it's far too difficult," is a remark often heard from amateur painters, even those who regard themselves as reasonably proficient in other media, such as oils. This very attractive medium is sometimes unpredictable, but this very unpredictability should be regarded as a virtue, not a drawback. What people really mean when they make this kind of remark is that watercolors cannot be altered over and over again as oils can; a color or wash, once laid down on the paper, must stay there. To some extent this is true, and it is understandable that people should feel a certain nervousness when approaching a watercolor. But, in fact, many alterations can be made, and often are, as a painting progresses: a wash in a color that has not come out quite right can be changed dramatically by applying another wash on top of it; areas can be sponged out or worked over; and if the worst comes to the worst, the whole painting can be put under running water and washed away.

Watercolor has many virtues, its main attraction for artists being its freshness and translucence, making it ideal for a variety of subjects, especially landscapes and flower paintings. As its name implies, pure watercolor is mixed with water and is transparent, so that it must be applied from light to dark, unlike oil paint or acrylics which are opaque and can be built up from dark to light. Highlights consist of areas of the paper left white or very pale washes surrounded by darker ones. A certain amount of preplanning is necessary at an early stage to work out where the highlights are to be, but some planning is always needed for any painting or drawing, whatever medium is being used.

No one ever quite knows how watercolor will behave, and the medium itself will often begin to "take over" a painting, suggesting ways of creating interesting effects and lending a sparkle and spontaneity to the work. The purely practical advantages of watercolor painting are that you need little expensive equipment, the painting can be done more or less anywhere provided there is enough light, and paints can be cleared up quickly, leaving no mess. Since the paper is relatively cheap, experiments and mistakes are not very expensive.

THE MEDIUM

Watercolor, like all paint, is made by mixing pigment with a binding agent, in this case gum arabic, which is soluble in water. There are two types of watercolor, "pure" or "classical" watercolor, which is transparent, and gouache, or "body color," which is the same pigment made opaque by adding white pigment to the binder.

THE HISTORY OF WATERCOLOR PAINTING

It is commonly believed that watercolor was invented by the English landscape painters of the 18th century, but this is far from so. Watercolor has been in use in various forms for many centuries. Indeed the ancient Egyptians used a form of it for painting on plaster to decorate their tombs; the great frescoes of Renaissance Italy were painted in a kind of watercolor; it was used by medieval manuscript illuminators, both in its "pure" form and mixed with body color; the great German artist Albrecht Durer made use of it extensively, and so did many botanical illustrators of the 16th century and the Dutch flower painters of the 17th century.

It was, even so, in 18th-century England that watercolor painting was elevated to the status of a national art. A new interest in landscape painting for its own sake culminated in the work of John Constable the forerunner of the Impressionists. Watercolor was at last fully exploited and given its due recognition.

The greatest watercolorist of all, J.M.W. Turner achieved his fame as an oil painter, but he produced watercolors of an

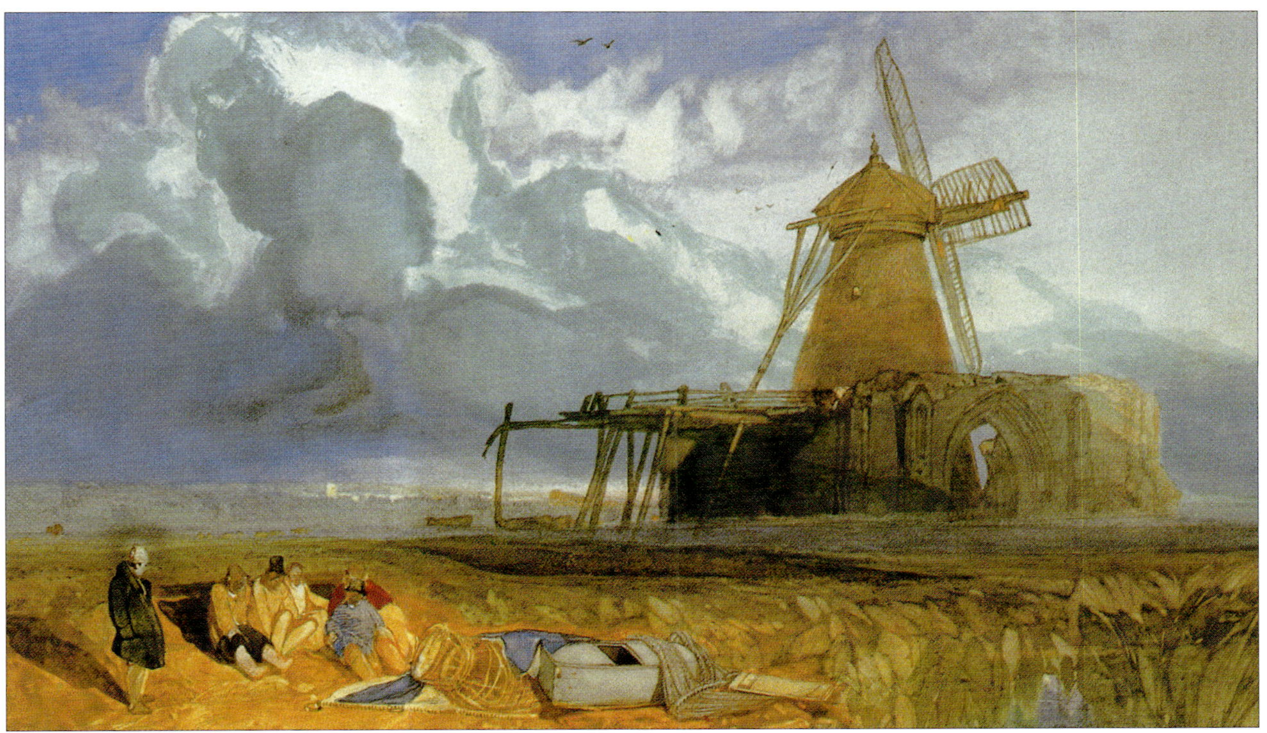

Above *John Sell Cotman was the leading watercolorist of the 18th century British School. In paintings like this one,* St Senet's Abbey, Norfolk, *he used paint in a bold, free, and imaginative way to create marvelous effects of space, light, and texture. Notice particularly the broad, overlapping brush strokes in the foreground and the swirling, directional ones in the sky.*

amazing depth and richness. He exploited accidental effects like thumbprints and haphazard blobs of paint, turning them into the most magical depictions of light and color that have ever been seen in paint. Throughout the 19th century the techniques of watercolor continued to be developed. The poet and artist William Blake evolved his own method of conveying his poetic vision in watercolor, as did his follower, Samuel Palmer, who used swirls and blocks of opaque color in his visionary and symbolic landscapes. With the end of the Napoleonic Wars in 1815, travel became easier, and the topographical tradition reached new heights in the work of artists like Samuel Prout, a very good draftsman who painted buildings and scenery in faithful detail.

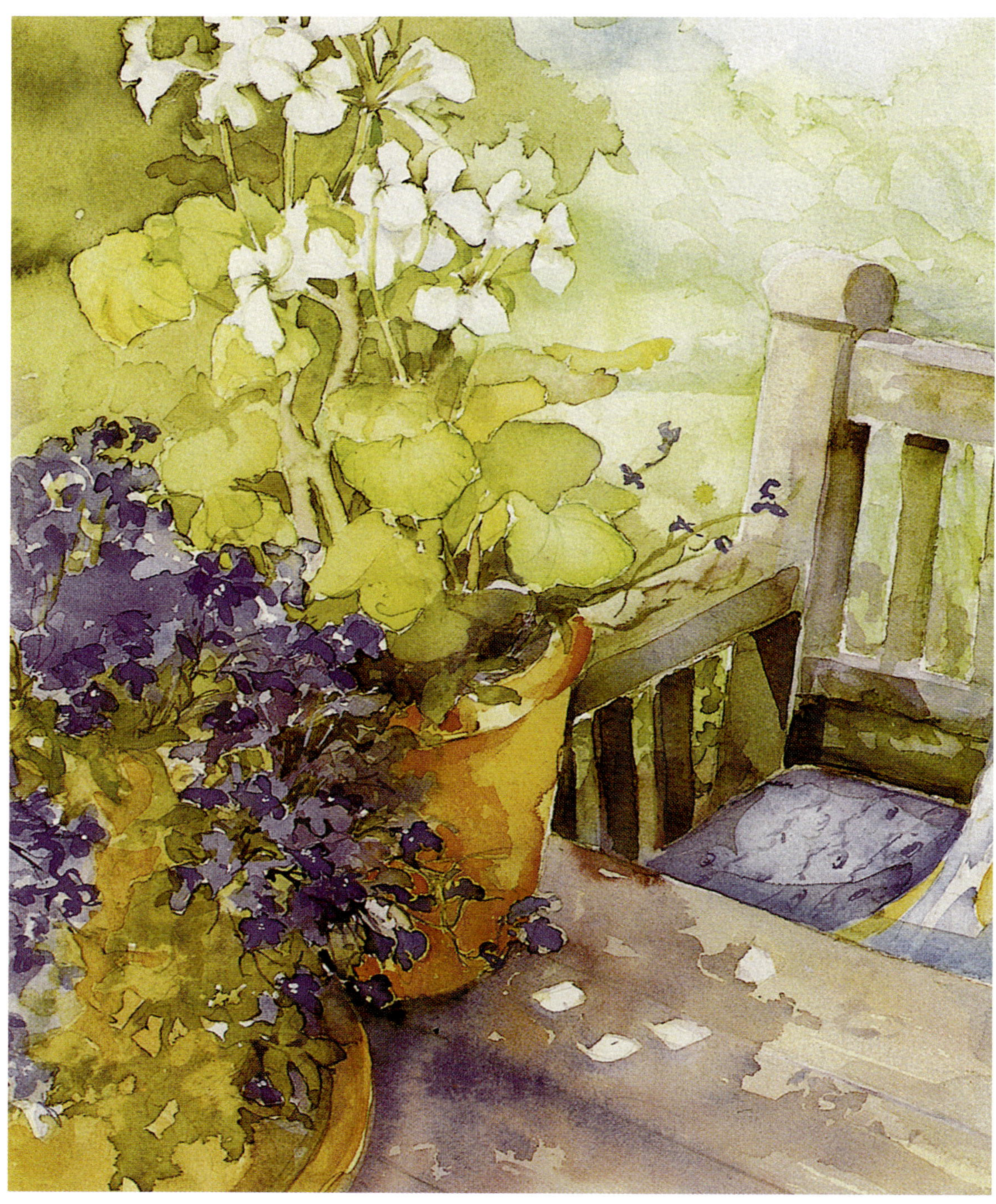

Above *Elisabeth Harden started to paint this composition,* Lobelia and Geranum, *as a view down a garden, but became increasingly attracted by the patterns and colors created by the brilliant overhead sunlight. It became necessary to paint the lobelia as an overall mass and then to pick out details, otherwise the paint would have become bitty and fussy. The areas of pattern on the pot are echoed in the patches of shadow and light on the table and the patterning on the fabric. Subtle reflections of color are echoed round the composition.*

2 MATERIALS AND EQUIPMENT

Perhaps the greatest single adventure of watercolor painting is that only a small amount of equipment is needed, equipment that is easy to store. Paints and brushes, although not cheap, last for a long time; indeed, brushes should last virtually for ever if looked after properly. Hand made paper is, of course, expensive, but beginners will find that many perfectly satisfactory machine-made papers are available from artist's suppliers.

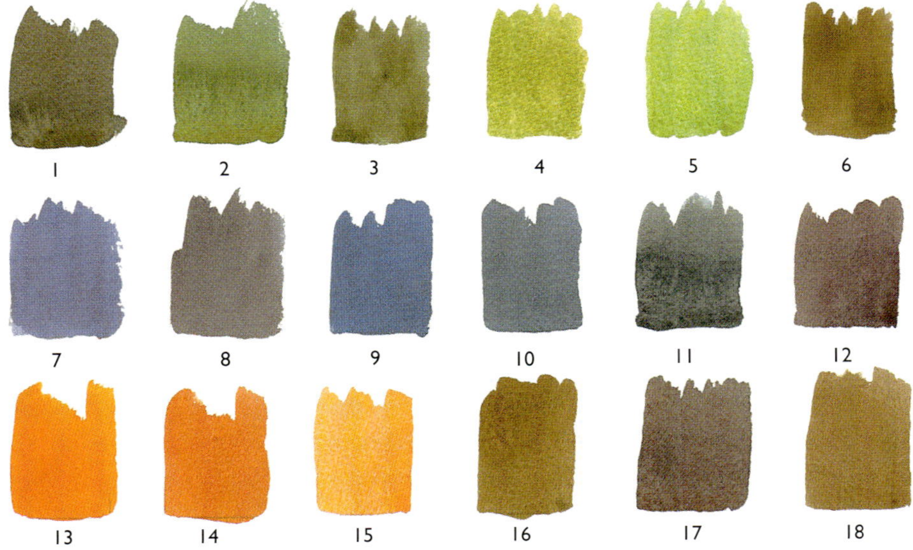

Left *1. Payne's gray + cadmium yellow. 2. Prussian blue + cadmium yellow. 3. Cobalt + cadmium yellow. 4. Prussian blue + lemon yellow. 5. Viridian + lemon. 6. Black + cadmium yellow. 7. Cobalt blue + alizarin crimson. 8. Payne's gray + alizarin crimson. 9. Prussian blue + alizarin crimson. 10. Cobalt blue + Payne's gray. 11. Black + Prussian blue. 12. Black + alizarin crimson. 13. Cadmium yellow + cadmium red. 14. Alizarin crimson + cadmium yellow. 15. Lemon yellow + cadmium red. 16. Burnt umber + black. 17. Payne's gray + cadmium red. 18. Burnt umber + cobalt blue.*

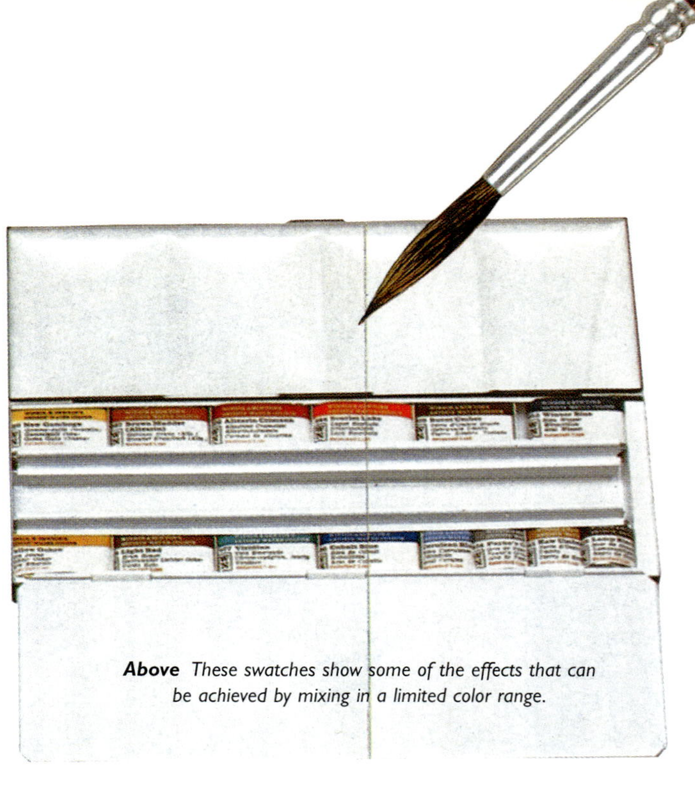

Above *These swatches show some of the effects that can be achieved by mixing in a limited color range.*

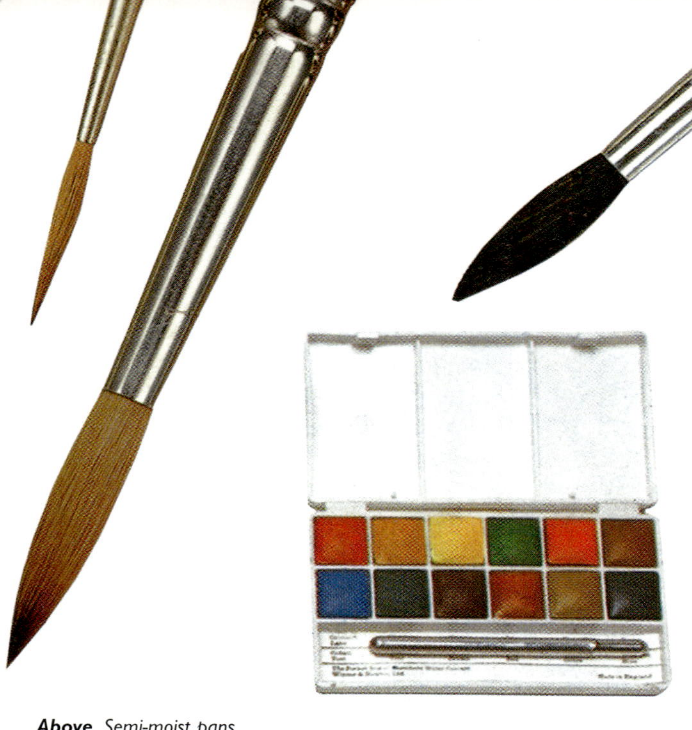

Above *Semi-moist pans must be carried in tins and boxes, which can then be used as palettes.*

Above *A pocket set of watercolors is particularly useful when painting out of doors, or when traveling.*

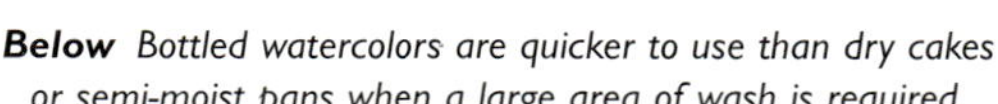

Below *Bottled watercolors are quicker to use than dry cakes or semi-moist pans when a large area of wash is required.*

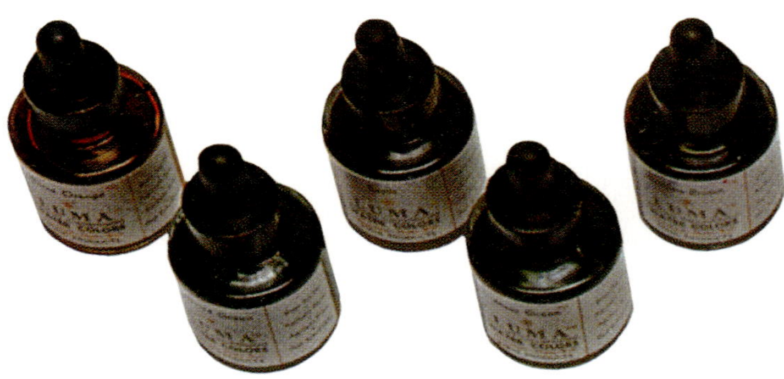

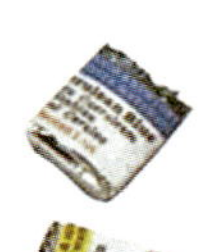

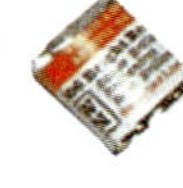

Above *Half-pans are available individually as well as in sets. The artist can replace the most frequently used colors as and when required.*

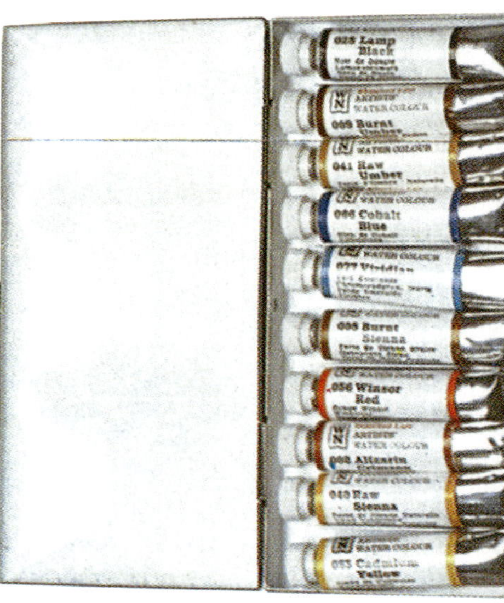

Below *Gouache is available in tube or pot form in an enormous range of colours. From left to right: lamp black, zinc white, burnt sienna, raw umber, yellow ocher, cadmium red (pale), Winsor emerald, cobalt blue.*

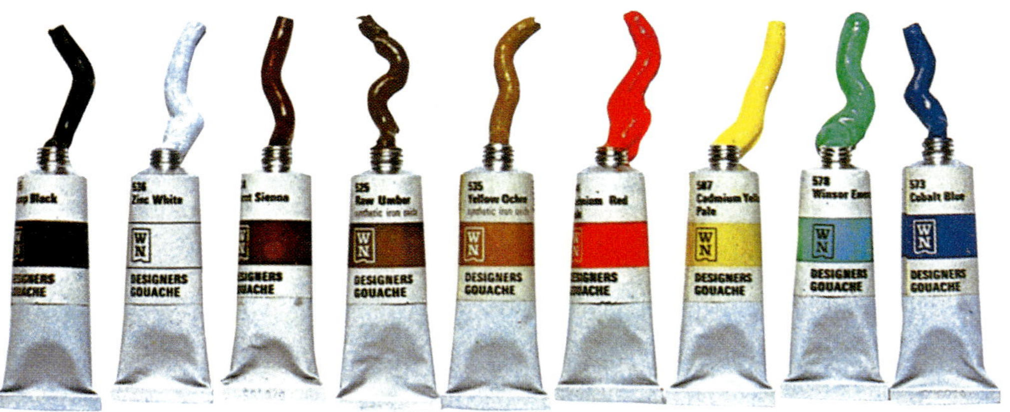

Above *Watercolor in tube form is popular and convenient. Do not squeeze too many colors onto your palette at a time, or they will run together.*

PAINTS AND COLORS

Readymade watercolor paint is sold in various forms, the commonest being tubes, pans, and half-pans. These all contain glycerine and are known as semi-moist colors, unlike the traditional dry cakes, which are still available in some artist's suppliers, but are not much used today. Dry cakes require considerable rubbing with water before the color is released. Gouache paints, or designer's colors as they are sometimes called, are normally sold in tubes. These paints have chalk added to the pigment to thicken it, and are thus opaque, unlike true watercolor. Watercolors themselves can be mixed with Chinese white to make them opaque or semi-opaque, so that they become a softer and

Below *The heavier papers are more expensive but can absorb large amounts of water; they do not, therefore, need stretching, which makes them useful for outdoor work. Toned papers provide a convenient middle ground for some subjects, from which to work darks and lights.*

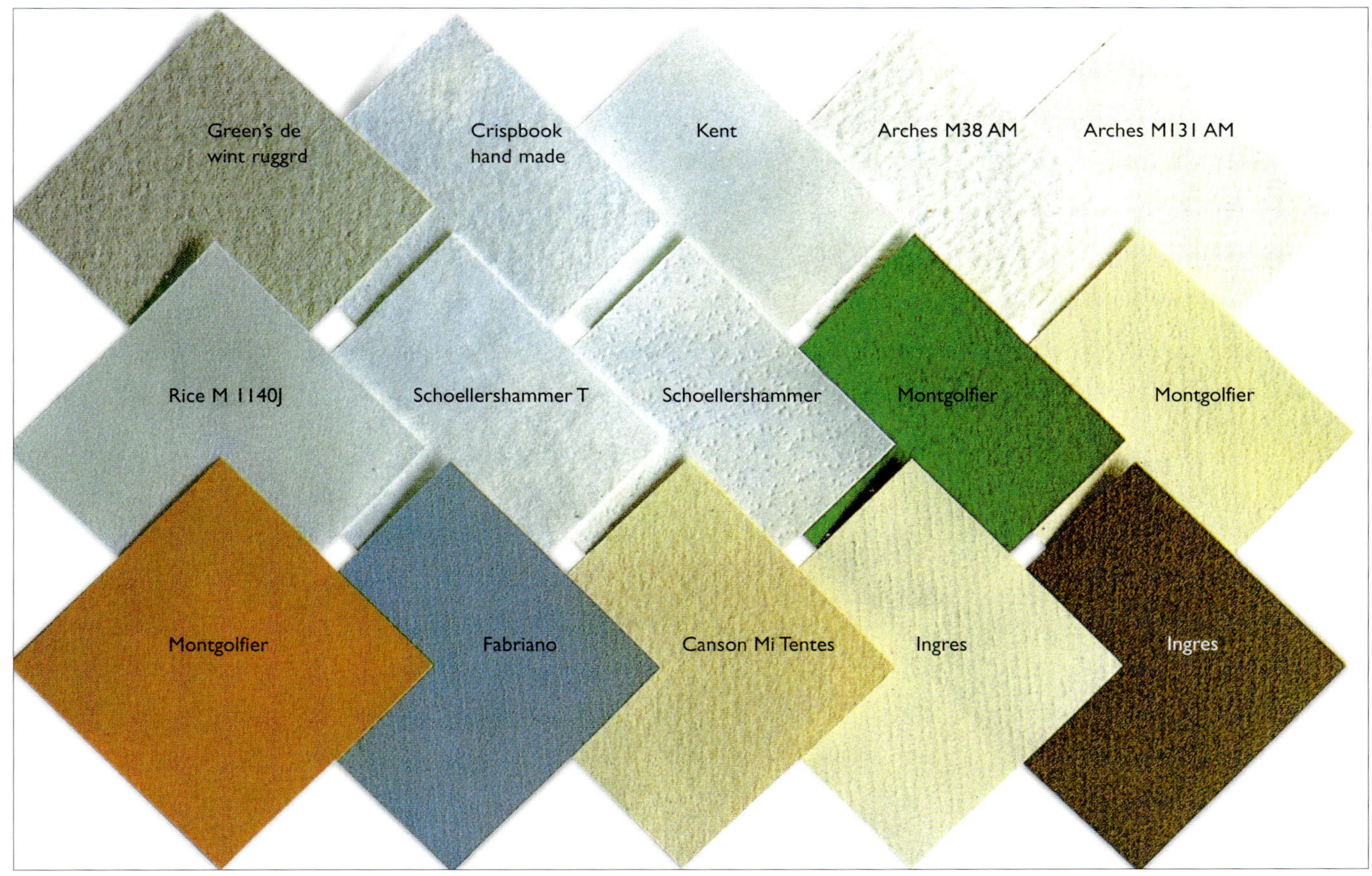

STRETCHING PAPER

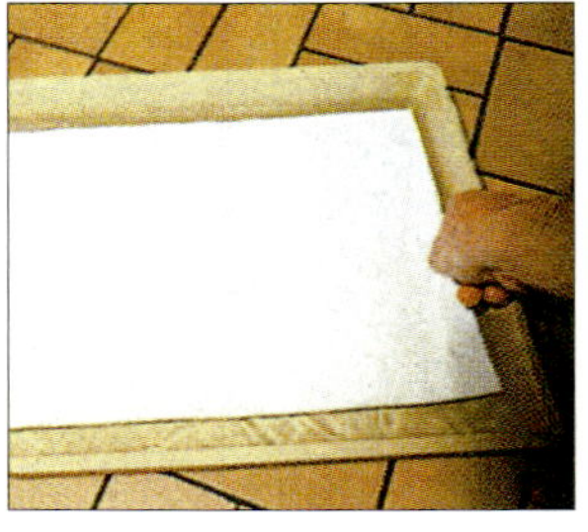

1 *Place paper right-side-up in a tray of water. Soak for a few minutes.*

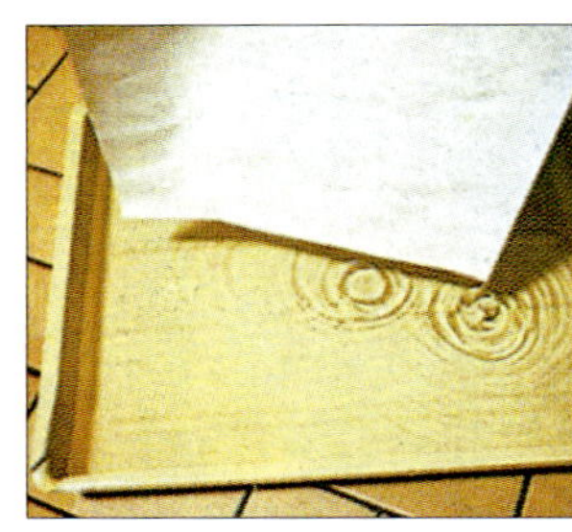

2 *Lift out the paper and carefully drain off the excess water from it.*

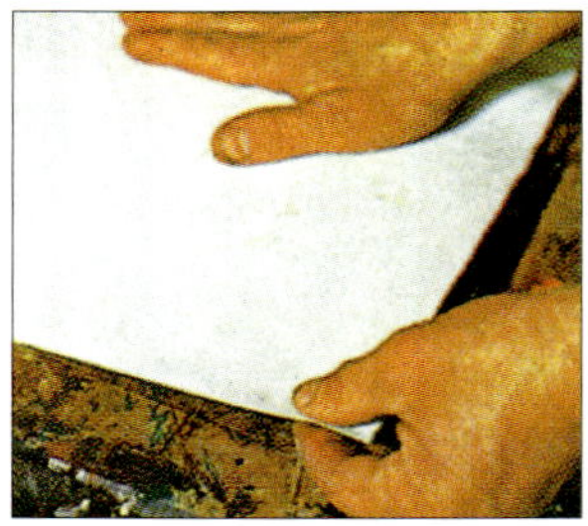

3 *Lay on a board at least 1 in. (2.5 cm) larger than the paper itself.*

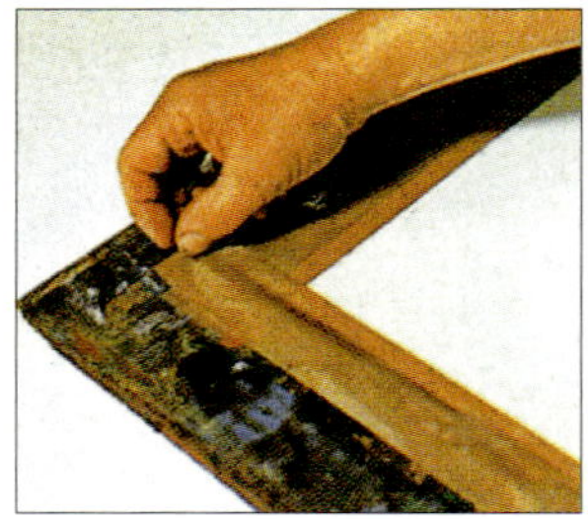

4 *Smooth the paper quite flat and stick gumstrip around the edges.*

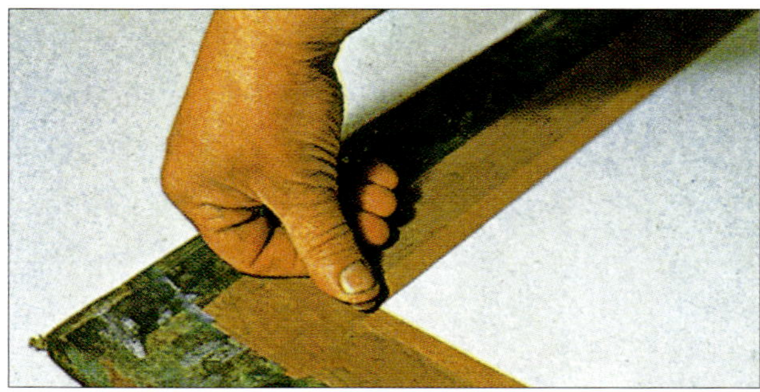

5 *Put a drawing pin in each corner. Do not dry the paper in front of a fire, which will buckle it.*

more subtle form of gouache.

Whether to use pans, half-pans,, or tubes is a personal choice. Tubes are excellent for those who work mainly indoors on a fairly large scale, as any quantity of paint can be squeezed out of them on to the palette. Any paint left on the palette after a painting is completed can be used again later, simply by moistening it with a wet brush. Pans and half-pans, which can be bought in sets in their own palette and are easy to carry, are the most popular choice for working out of doors on a small scale. Watercolors can also be bought in concentrated form in bottles, with droppers to transfer the paint to the palette. These are eminently suitable for broad washes which require a large quantity of paint, but they are less easy to mix than the other types.

Nowadays there is such a vast range of colors to choose from that a beginner is justified in feeling somewhat bewildered, but, in fact, only a few are really necessary. One point to bear in mind is that some colors are considerably less permanent than others, which may not be an important consideration for quick sketches and "note-taking," but clearly is for any painting that is intended to be hung or exhibited. A wise course, therefore, is to rule out any colors classified as "fugitive." These are not always marked on the tubes or pans, but they appear on the manufacturers' color charts.

Few watercolorists use more than a dozen colors. For landscape painting, for example, useful additions to the basic palette are sap green, Hooker's green, raw umber, and cerulean blue, while monastral blue (called Winsor blue in the Winsor and Newton range) is sometimes recommended instead of Prussian blue.

PAPER

The traditional support—the term used for the surface on which any painting is done—is white or pale-colored paper, which reflects back through the transparent paint to give the translucent quality so characteristic of watercolors.

The three main types of machine-made paper are hot-pressed (HP), cold-pressed (CP), which is also rather quaintly known as "not" for "not hot-pressed" and rough. Hot-pressed paper is very smooth and, although suitable for drawing or pen-and-wash, is not a good choice for building up layers of washes in the standard watercolor technique as it becomes clogged very quickly. Coldpressed paper, which is slightly textured, is the most popular and is suitable for both broad washes and fine detail. Rough paper, as its name implies, is much more heavily textured, and the paint will settle in the "troughs" while sliding off the "peaks," giving a speckled effect which can be

Right *The difference between a quality sable brush (bottom), or synthetic sable (middle), and the kind of cheap brush sometimes provided in watercolor boxes (above), are self-evident here.*

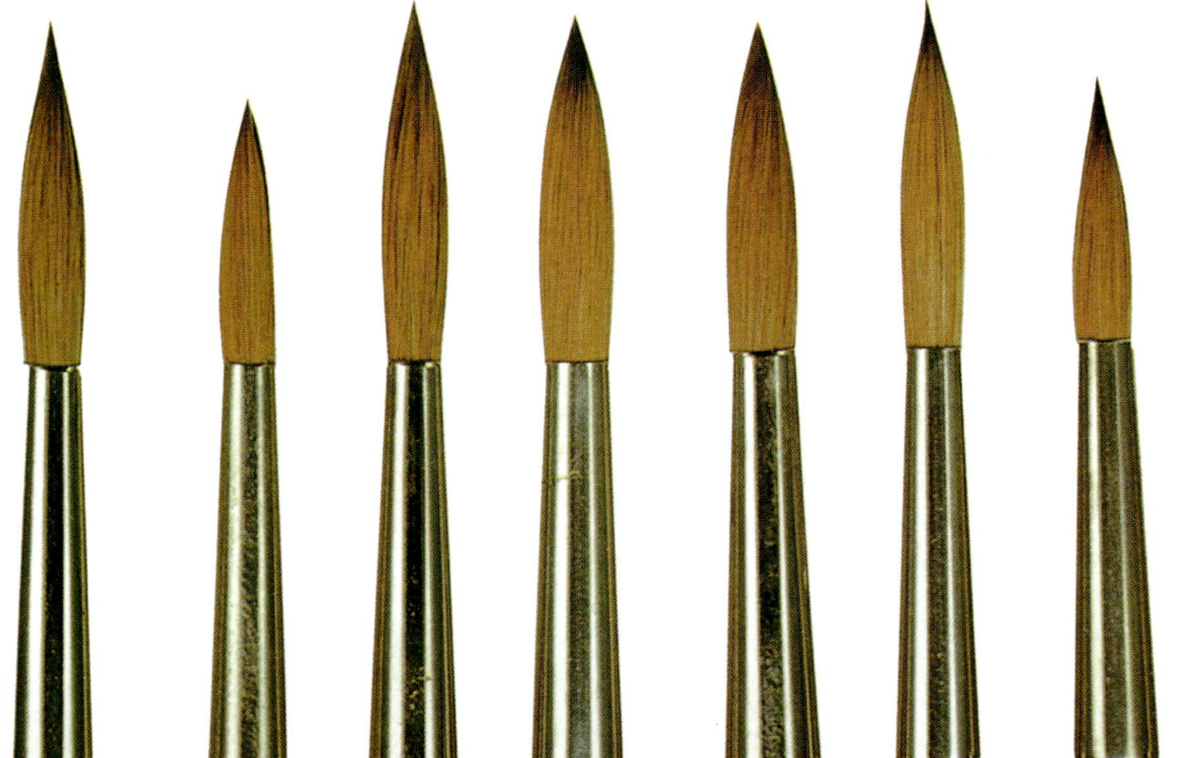

Below *Japanese and Chinese brushes are versatile, and are very well suited to fine calligraphic work, but they require some practice and are not recommended for beginners.*

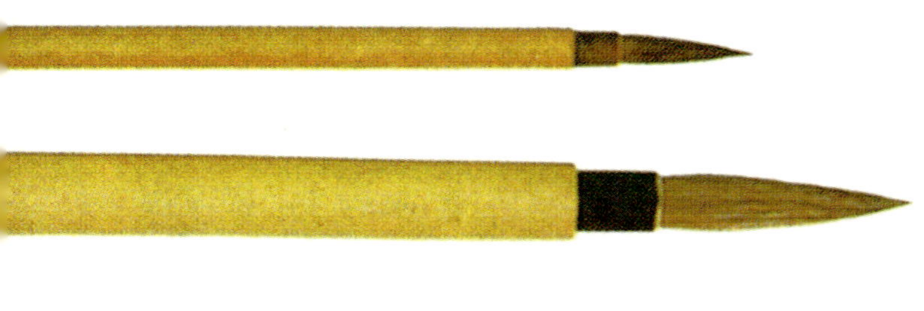

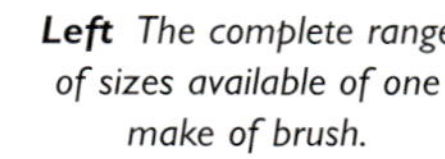

Left *The complete range of sizes available of one make of brush.*

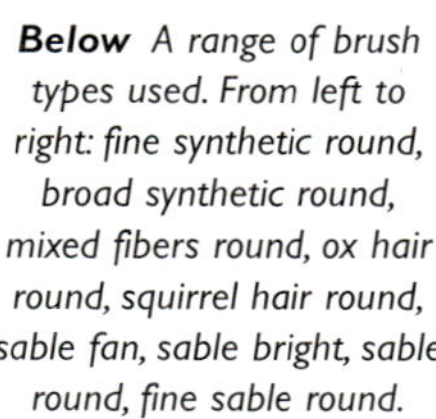

Below *A range of brush types used. From left to right: fine synthetic round, broad synthetic round, mixed fibers round, ox hair round, squirrel hair round, sable fan, sable bright, sable round, fine sable round.*

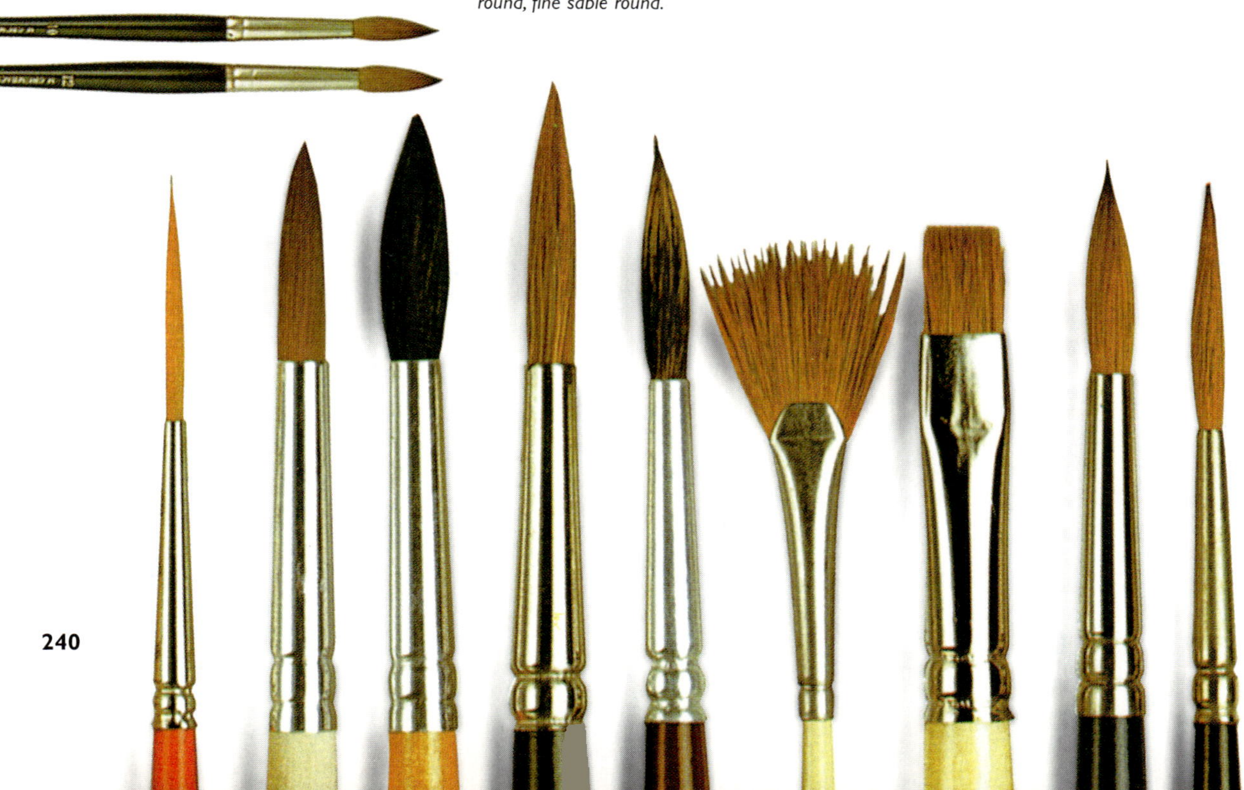

effective for some subjects but is difficult to exploit successfully.

STRETCHING THE PAPER

Watercolor papers vary widely in weight, or thickness, and the lighter ones (less than 200 pounds) need to be stretched or they will buckle as soon as wet paint is applied to them.

Stretching paper is not difficult, but it takes some time to dry thoroughly and needs to be done at least two hours before you intend to start work. Cut the paper to size and wet it well on both sides by laying it in a bath or tray of water. When it is well soaked, hold it up by the corners to drain off the excess water, then lay it right-side-up on a drawing board and stick down each edge with the gummed brown paper known as "gumstrip." Finally, place a drawing pin in each corner. The paper will dry taut and flat and should not buckle when paint is applied. Occasionally, however, stretching does go wrong and the paper buckles at one corner or tears away from the gumstrip; if that happens there is no other course but to repeat the process.

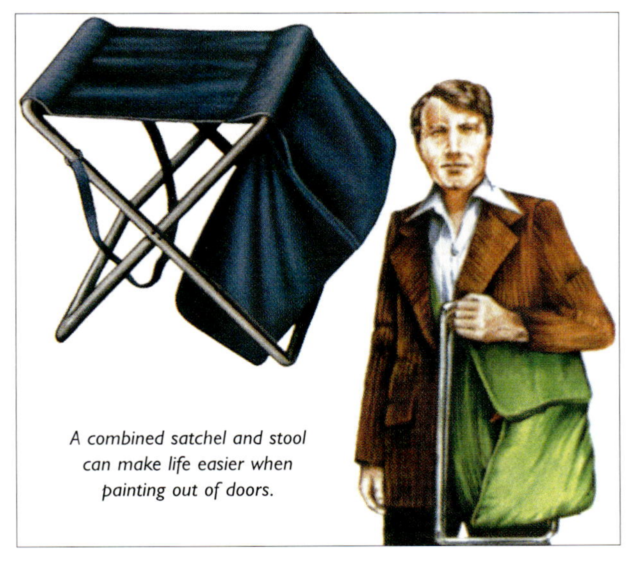

A combined satchel and stool can make life easier when painting out of doors.

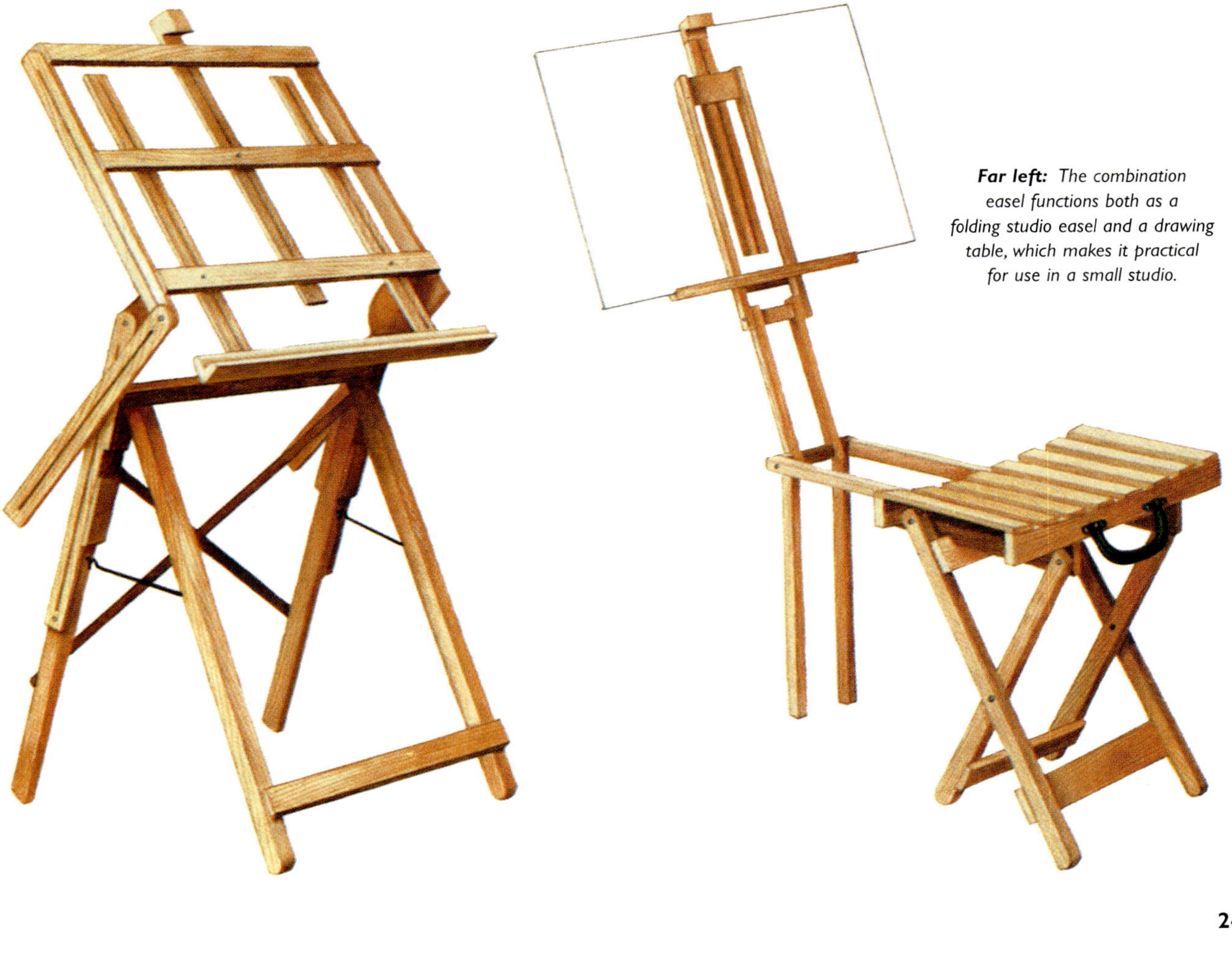

BRUSHES

Soft brushes are normally used for watercolor. The best ones are sable, made

Far left: *The combination easel functions both as a folding studio easel and a drawing table, which makes it practical for use in a small studio.*

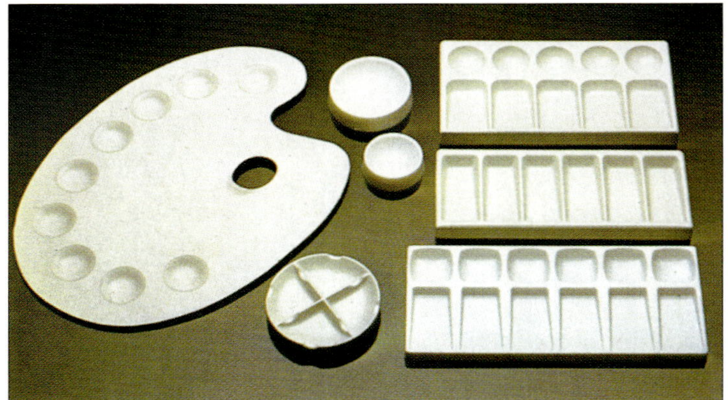

Left *Any plate or dish can be used for mixing watercolor, but there are several specially made palettes on the market. The thumbhole variety is especially useful for outdoor work.*

Below *These colors, and a combination of these, will provide watercolor artists a perfectly adequate range for most needs. Some artists work with even fewer colors. From top to bottom: cobalt blue, Prussian blue, viridian, yellow ocher, cadmium yellow, lemon yellow, cadmium red, alizarin crimson, burnt umber, Payne's gray, and ivory black.*

STARTER PALETTE

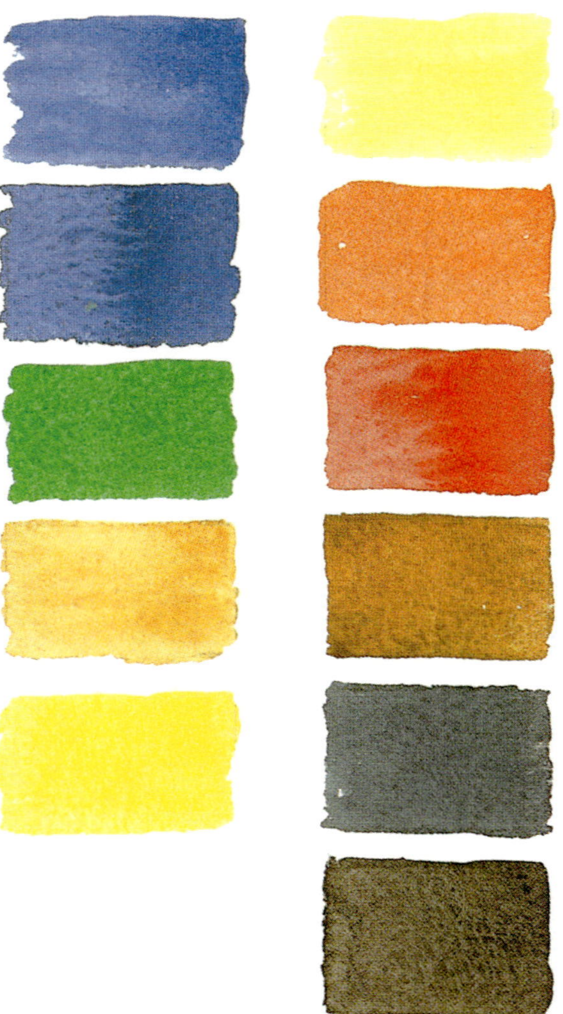

from the tips of the tail hairs of the small rodent found chiefly in Siberia. Sable brushes are extremely expensive, but if looked after properly they should last a lifetime. Watercolor brushes are also made from squirrel-hair (known as "camel hair" for some reason) and ox-hair. These are good substitutes for sable, but have less spring. There is now a wide range of synthetic brushes, usually made of nylon or a mixture of nylon and sable, and although they do not hold the paint as well as sable and are thus less suitable for broad washes, they are excellent for finer details and are very much cheaper. It is not necessary to have a great many brushes for watercolor work; a practical range would be one large chisel-end for laying washes and two or three rounds in different sizes.

EASELS

Watercolors, unlike oils, are best done at close quarters, with the support held nearly horizontal, so that an easel is not really necessary for indoor work. However, an easel can be helpful. It allows you to tilt the work at different angles and move it to the best light, which is more difficult with a table.

OTHER EQUIPMENT

Various other items can be useful and inexpensive aids for watercolor work. Small sponges can be used instead of brushes to apply washes, to sponge out areas, and to create soft, smudgy cloud effects; kitchen roll, blotting paper and cotton wool can be used in much the same way. Toothbrushes are useful for spattering paint to create textured effects, to suggest sand or pebbles on a beach, for example.

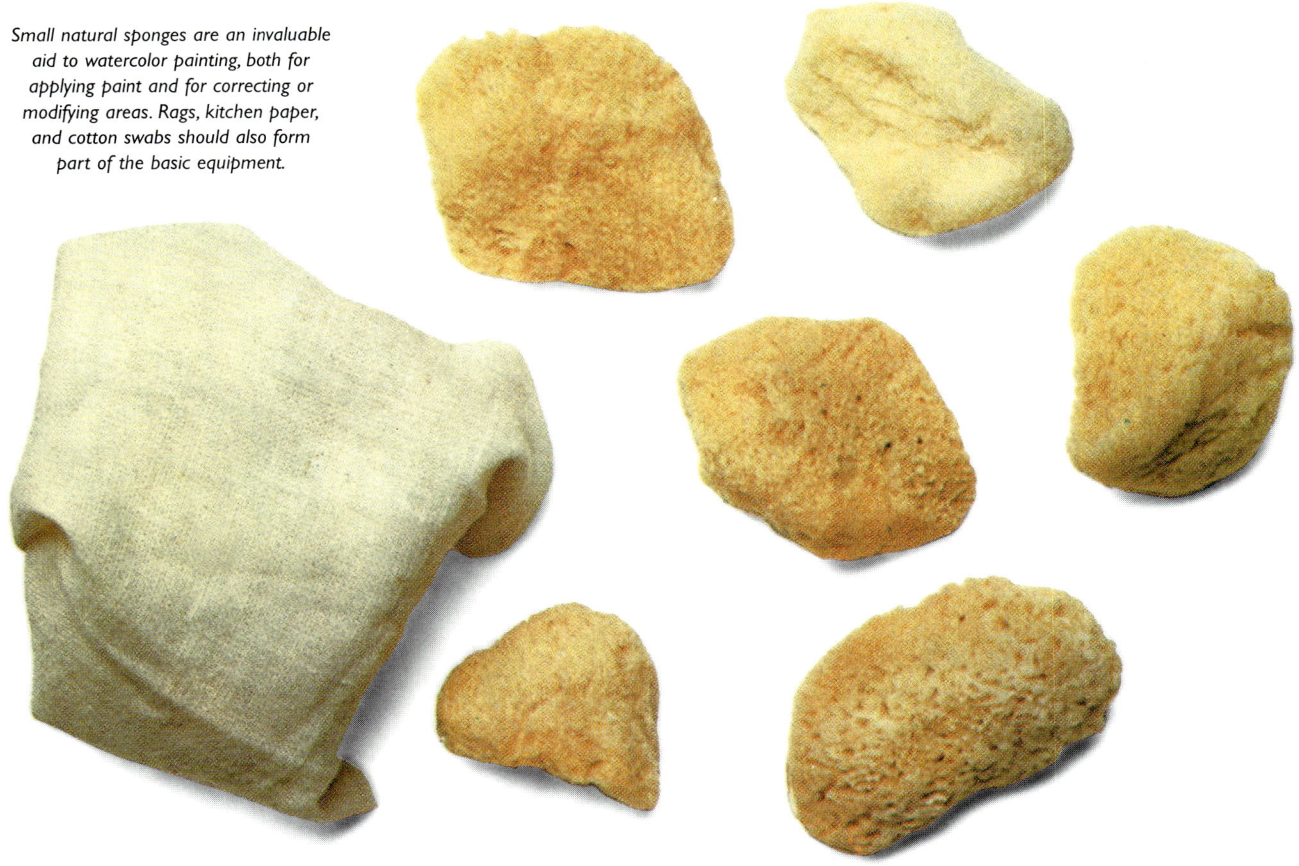

Small natural sponges are an invaluable aid to watercolor painting, both for applying paint and for correcting or modifying areas. Rags, kitchen paper, and cotton swabs should also form part of the basic equipment.

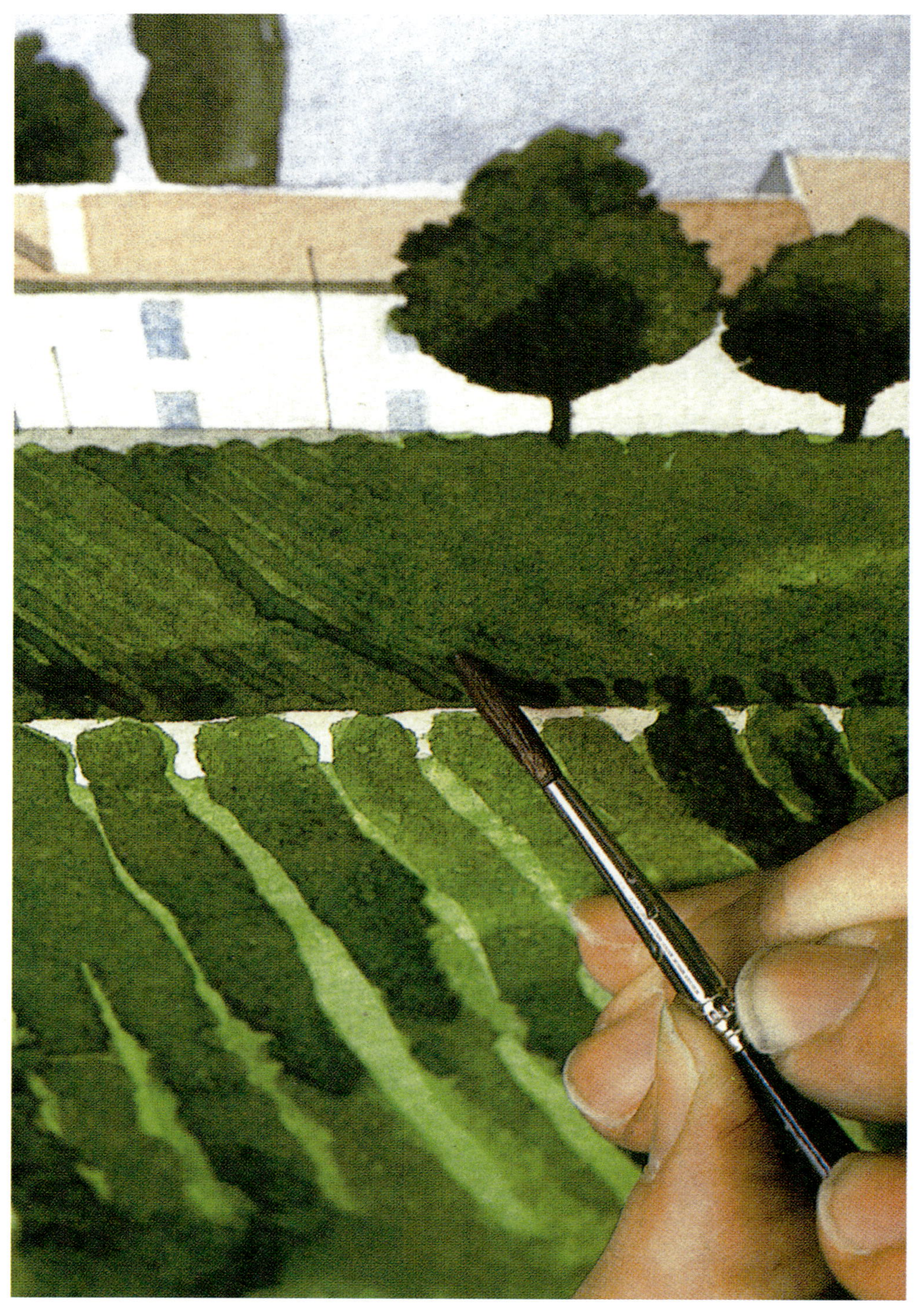

Above *A detail of a French vineyard: the artist decided that the converging lines were too heavily colored. He loosens the color with a soft brush and water, and lifts it off with tissue.*

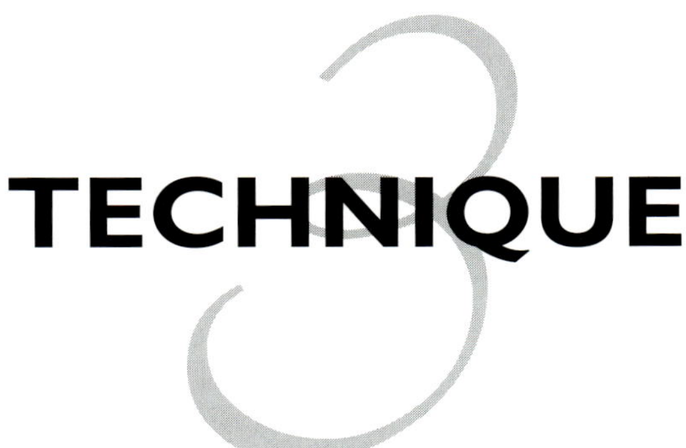

TECHNIQUE

Pure watercolor, being transparent, must be applied from light to dark. The paper itself is used to create the pure white or light tones which, with opaque paints, would be made by using white alone or mixed with colored pigment.

Any area required to be white is simply "reserved," or left unpainted, so that when it is surrounded with darker washes it will shine out with great brilliance. Pale tones are created in the same way, with a light-colored wash put on first and then surrounded with darker tones. Light reflected off the paper, back through these thin skins

of paint known as washes, gives a watercolor painting a spontaneity and sparkle which cannot be achieved with any other medium.

FLAT WASH

A flat wash in a vivid color is being laid on dampened paper with a broad, flat-ended brush. It is not strictly necessary to dampen the paper (many artists prefer the slightly "dragged" look given by working on dry paper) but dampening facilitates an even covering. Tilt the board slightly so that the brush strokes flow into one another, and work backward and forward down the paper until the whole area is covered.

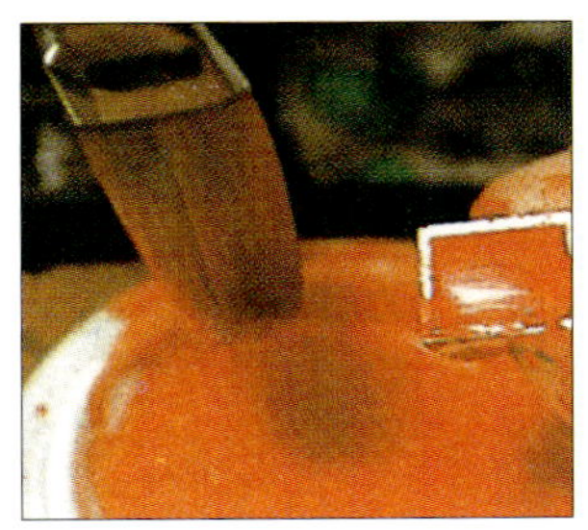

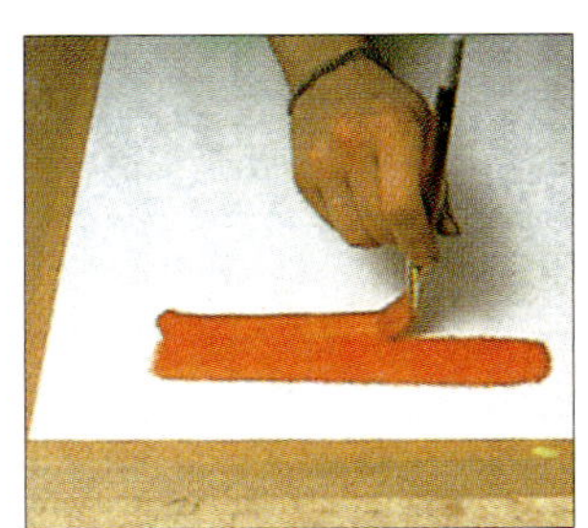

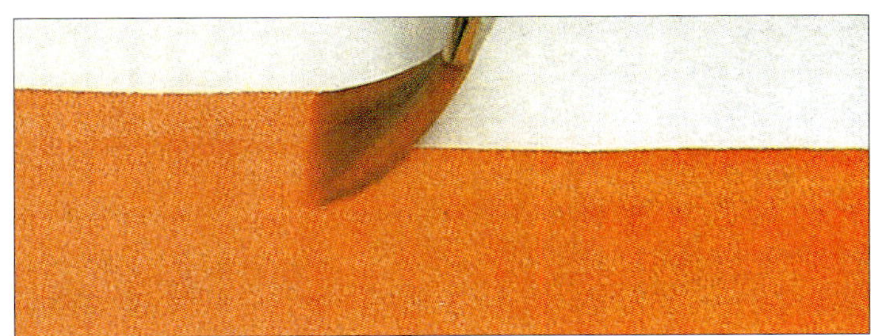

SPONGE WASH

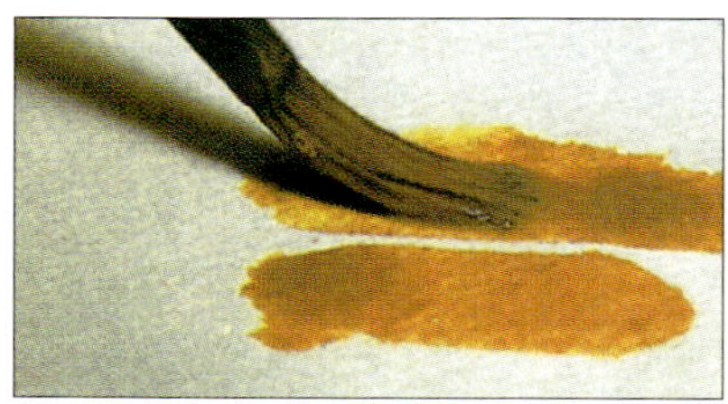

A wash needs to be slightly textured; for this use a sponge.

1 *The wash is mixed with a brush and tested on paper.*

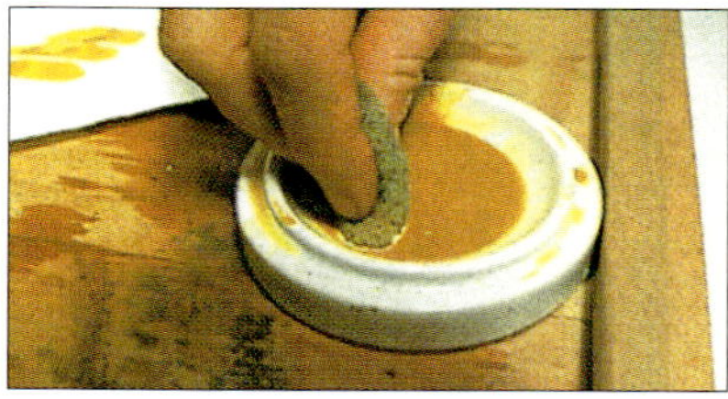

2 *Paint is mixed as needed. For a lighter covering, some paint can be squeezed out of the sponge.*

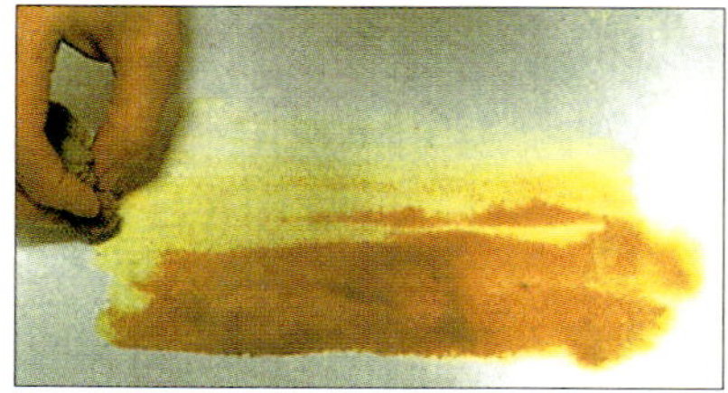

3 *A variegated effect is achieved by applying the paint thickly with the first stroke, thinly with second.*

4 *The final wash can be worked into with wet sponge in order to lighten some areas, for a soft effect.*

VARIEGATED WASH

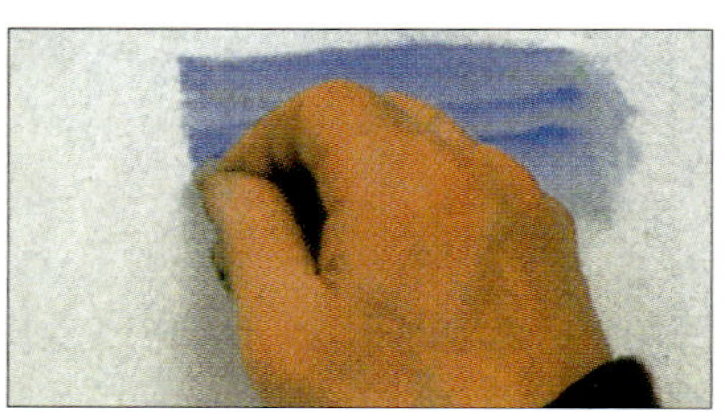

1 *The paper is dampened with a sponge and a thin wash of color is applied.*

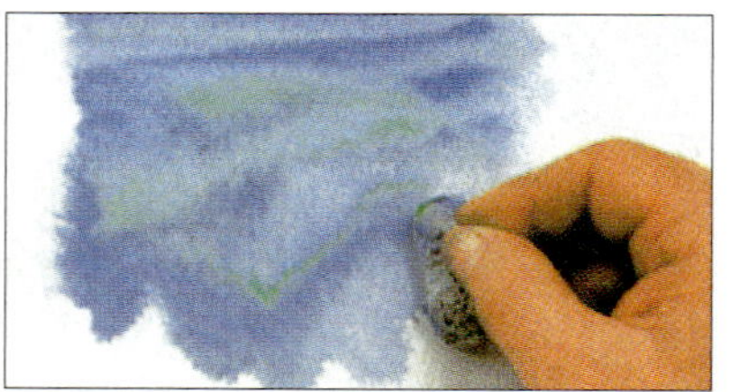

2 *A second color is flooded on, using the sponge tip, so the two run together.*

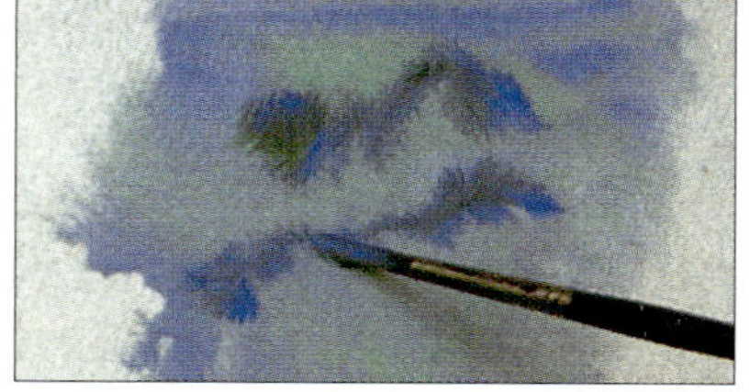

3 *A brush is used to touch in darker areas in the still wet paint. Very subtle effects can be created this way.*

Left *Prussian blue and alizarin crimson have been allowed to run into one another, as with a wash of one color.*

Middle *Laying one wash on top of another often gives textural variety as well as intensifying the color. Notice that the bottom band, a pale wash of Payne's gray, is quite even, while the one at the top, a third application of the same wash, shows distinct brush marks.*

Right *The possibilities of working wet-into-wet may be explored by producing this kind of doodle in a matter of minutes. The wet-into-wet technique is often used in the early stages of a painting, or for the background, more precise work being done at a later stage or in another area of the painting.*

The two most important facts about watercolor are, first, that it is always to some extent unpredictable, even in the hands of experts, and, second, that because dark is always worked over light, some planning is needed before beginning the painting. It is not always necessary to do a detailed and complicated drawing on the

DRY BRUSH

Dry brush work is an excellent method of suggesting texture, such as that of grass or a cornfield. Here a number of similar colors have been used over a pale underlying wash to give tonal variation.

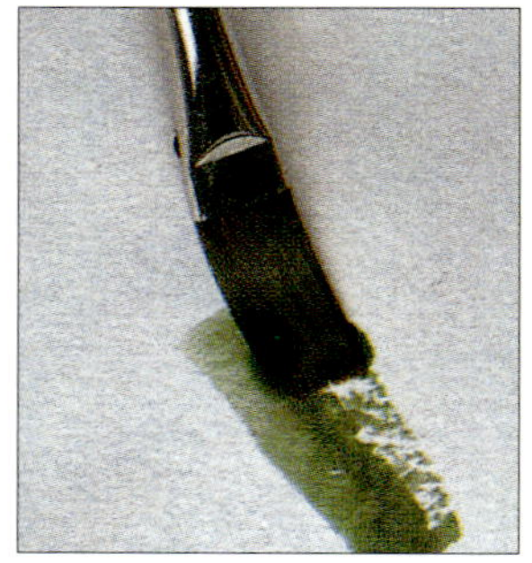

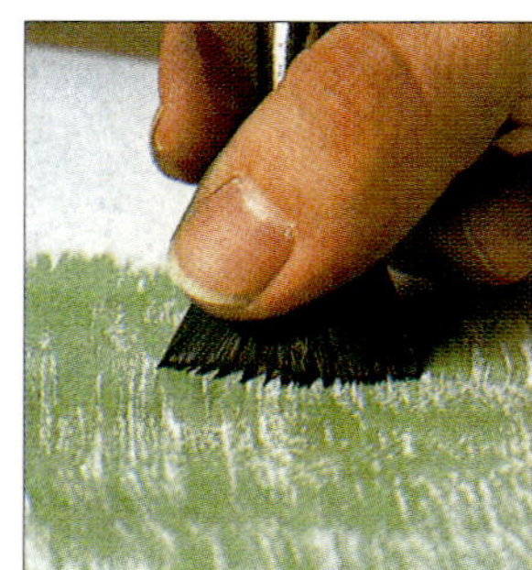

paper, only enough to work out the basic shapes and design; this really should be done however, or you will begin without really knowing which areas are to be left white or pale and how they will fit into the painting as a whole.

LAYING A FLAT WASH

The wash is the basis of all watercolor painting, whether it is a broad, sweeping one, covering a large expanse, such as a sky or the background to a portrait, or a much smaller one laid on a particular area. The support should be tilted at a slight angle so that the brush strokes flow into one another, but do not run down the paper. For a broad wash a large chisel-end brush is normally used; for a smaller one, or a wash which is to be laid against a complicated edge, a smaller round brush may be more manageable. Laying a wash must be done quickly or hard edges will form between brush strokes.

Therefore mix up more paint than you think you will need. Start by damping the paper with clear water (this is not actually essential, but helps the paint to go on evenly). Working in one direction, lay a horizontal line of color at the top of the area, then another below it, working in the opposite direction, and continue working in alternate directions until the area is covered. Never go back over the wet paint because you feel it is uneven or not dark enough, as this will result in the paint's "flooding" and leave blobs and patches.

Leave the wash to dry before working on adjacent areas of the painting. Watercolor dries much paler than it appears when wet, and washes can be laid on top of the first one to strengthen the color or darken the tone, though too many will turn the painting muddy.

COMPLEX EDGES

Sometimes a wash must be laid against a complicated edge, for example, a group of roofs and chimneys with an intricate outline. The wash must then start from the edge rather than end at it. You may have to turn the board sideways or upside down to achieve this. When dampening the paper before putting on the wash, take care to dampen only up to this edge; otherwise the wash will flow into the areas you intend to reserve.

SPATTERING WITH A MASK

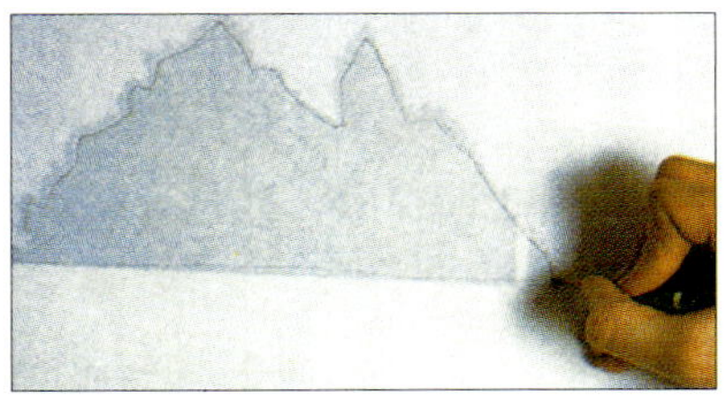

1 *The artist uses detail paper to trace the area he wants to mask.*

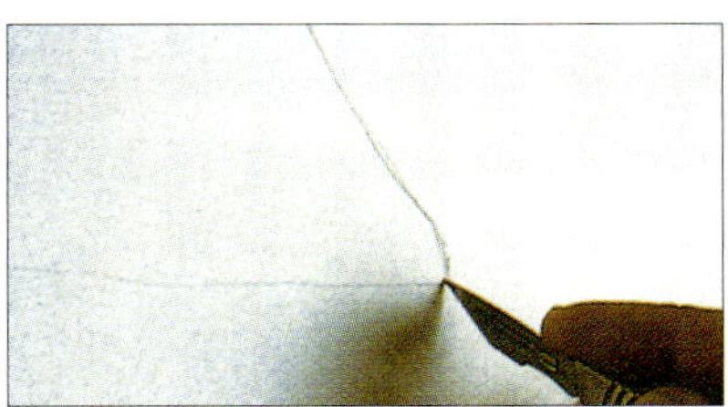

2 *He then carefully cuts the mask with a scalpel.*

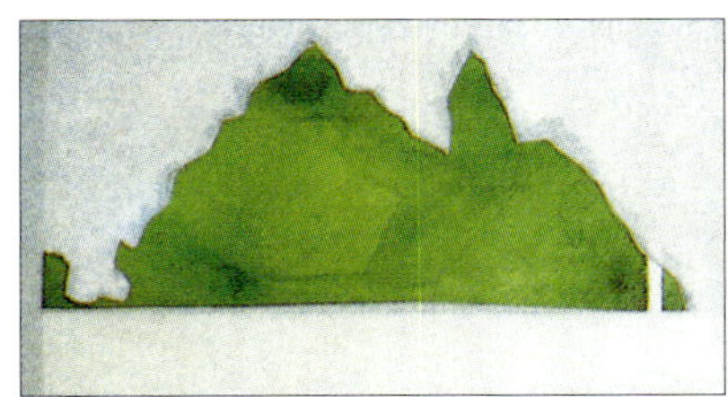

3 *The mask is applied and the tree is painted in sap green.*

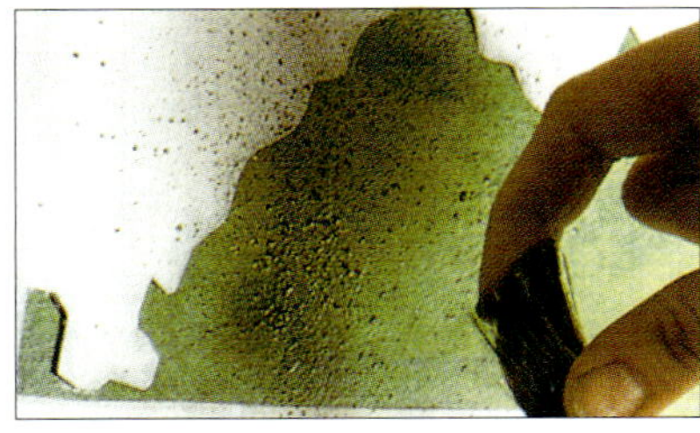

4 *Sap green is spattered on the area with a brush.*

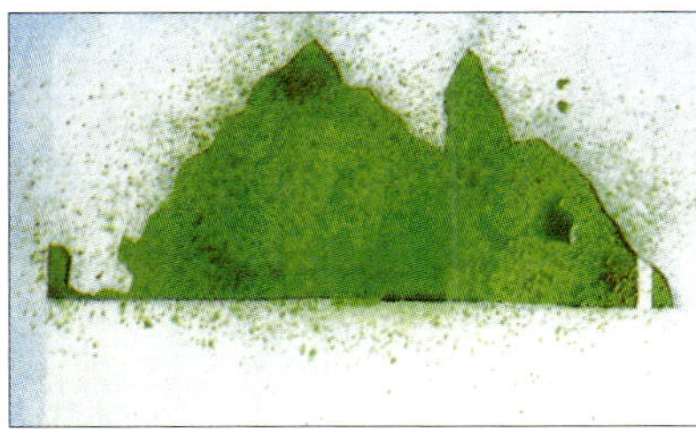

5 *The slightly irregular stippled effect is clear.*

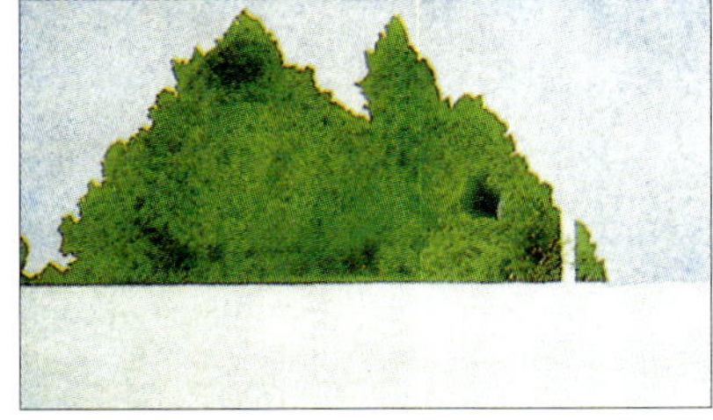

6 *The mask is removed, leaving a clean outline.*

USING A MASKING FLUID

Masking fluid provides a way of painting in "negative," which can give very subtle and exciting effects.

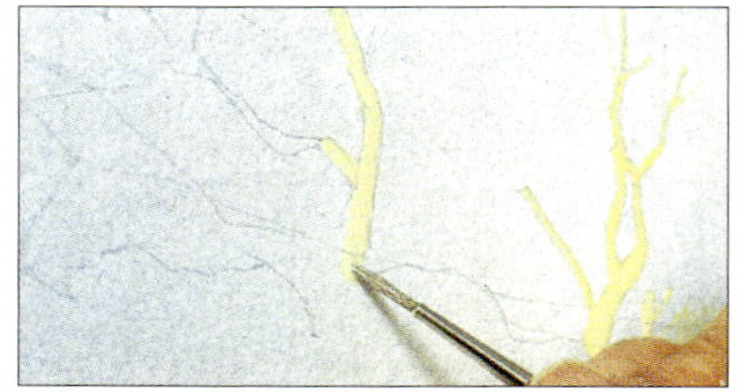

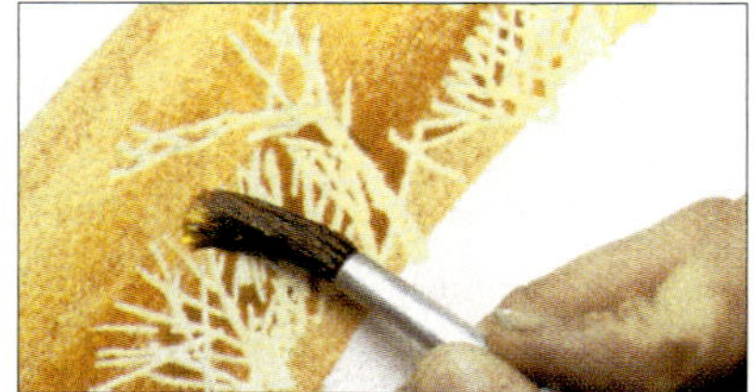

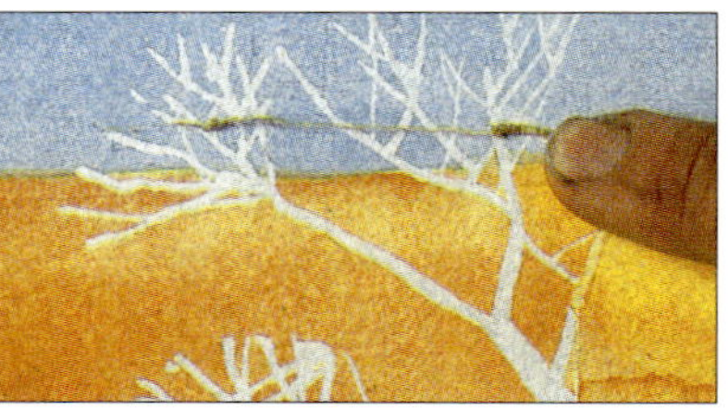

1 *The fluid is applied with a brush to the marked areas.*

2 *The fluid is allowed to dry and a wash is laid on top.*

3 *The fluid is peeled off by gentle rubbing with a finger.*

GRADATED AND VARIEGATED WASHES

Colors in nature are seldom totally flat or one solid hue. It is often desirable, therefore, to lay a gradated wash, which becomes darker or lighter at the top or bottom, or changes from one color to another. For a gradated wash, simply mix more water with the paint to make each successive strip lighter or more pigment to darken them.

For a variegated wash, mix up the two or more colors to be used, dampen the paper as usual, and then lay on the colors so that they blend into one another. The effect of such a wash cannot be worked out precisely in advance, even with practice—you should be prepared for a happy (or unhappy) accident.

DRY-BRUSH AND TEXTURAL METHODS

Painting with a small amount of paint on a fine brush which is almost dry is a method most frequently used for the fine details of a painting, but dry brush is also a technique in its own right and can be used very effectively for large areas. For landscape work it can be used to suggest the texture of grass, trees, rocks, stone walls, and the like. For portraits and still lifes it can model forms more easily than washes of wet paint can.

Like all watercolor techniques dry-brush requires practice. If the paint is too wet it will go on as a solid wash; if too dry it will not go on at all. The brush normally used for large areas of dry-brush work is a large chisel-end, with the bristles slightly splayed to produce a series of fine lines, rather like hatching and cross-hatching in drawing. One color and tone can be laid over another, and the brush strokes can be put on in different directions as the shape suggests.

MASKING OUT AND CREATING HIGHLIGHTS

Many watercolorists use masking fluid and masking tape for reserving areas of white paper. Masking fluid, which is specially made for the purpose, is a kind of liquid rubber sold in small bottles and applied with a brush. Stopping out with masking fluid is a method of painting in "negative," the precise and subtle shades made by the brush remain when the liquid is removed.

The paper must be quite dry before the fluid is applied, and the fluid itself must be allowed to dry before a wash is laid on top. Once the wash has dried, the fluid can be rubbed off with a finger or a soft eraser, leaving the white area, which can be modified and worked into if required. Masking fluid should never be left on the paper for longer than necessary, and care must be taken to wash the brushes immediately; otherwise fluid will harden in the hairs and ruin them.

MIXING MEDIA

Many other media can be used in combination with watercolor; indeed, the mixing of media is now commonplace, whereas in the past it was regarded as breaking the rules. Watercolor used with pen and ink has a long history; in the days before watercolor became recognized as a medium in its own right, it was used mainly to give touches of color to drawings or to tint black and white engravings. Nowadays there are many other media—some old and some new—that can be used with watercolor to good effect.

One traditional way to change the nature of paint by thickening it is to mix it with a little gum arabic, which gives it both texture and lasting luster. Soap can be used in much the same way, and it makes the paint easier to scrape back. Soap can also be used to make imprints of objects such as leaves or flowers. Coat the object with soap, apply paint to it, and then press it on to the paper.

Watercolors can be drawn into with pens, pencils, crayons, or pastels, and areas can be stressed or lightened with gouache or Chinese white. Watercolor pencils and crayons, a relatively new invention, are particularly suitable for this purpose. When dry they behave like crayons or hard pastels,

Gum water, which is gum arabic diluted in water, adds richness to watercolors and keeps the colors bright. It can also be used, as here, as a sort of resist method to create highlights.

1 *The tree and hedge are painted in with pure watercolor.*
2 *A further wash of green is applied, this time mixed with gum water.*
3 *The area of the central tree is spattered with water, flicked on with a household brush.*
4 *The central tree is blotted with a rag, so that small areas of paint are lifted off, the gum being soluble in water.*
5 *The lighter patches of color give an extra sparkle to the tree, while the addition of the gum water imparts richness to the dark green on either side.*

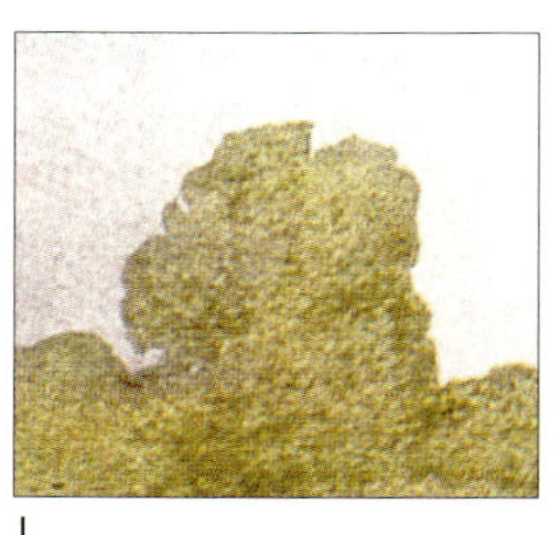

1

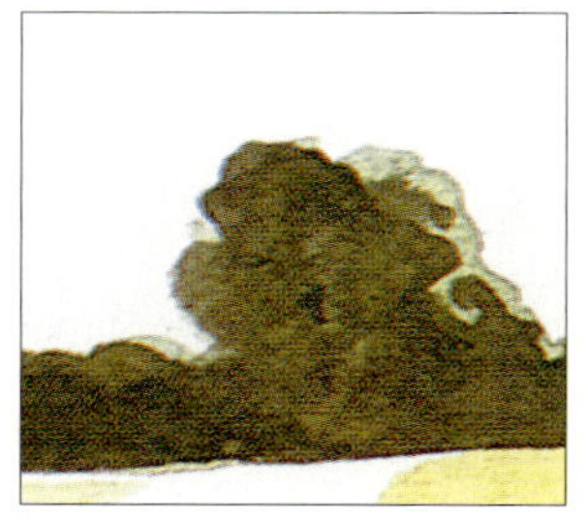

2

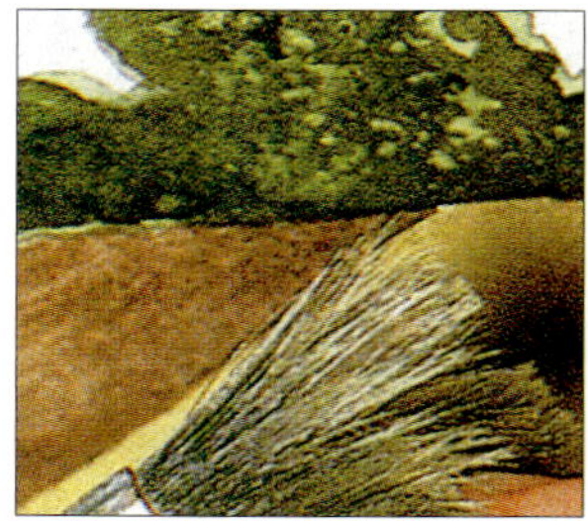

3

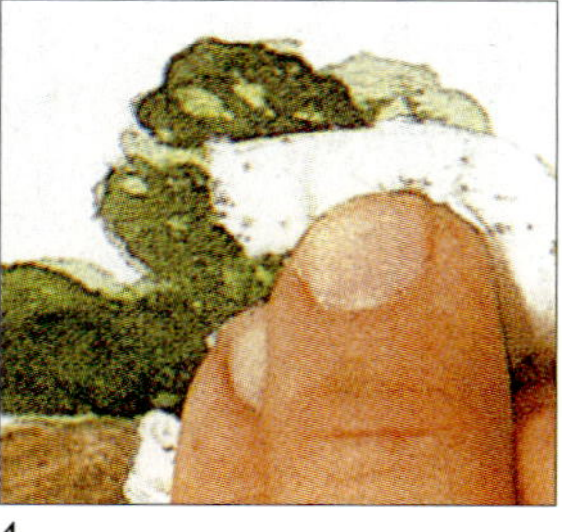

4

5

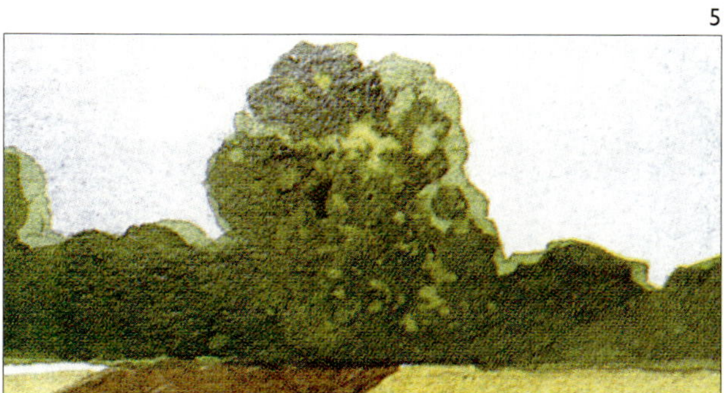

but if dipped in water or used on wet paper they will dissolve, forming a wash. Using these, or ordinary pastels, on top of watercolor can turn a painting which has "gone wrong" and become dull and lifeless, into something quite new and different. It is always worth experimenting with such media on a painting that you are less than happy with; you may evolve a personal technique that you can use again. Wax oil pastels can create interesting textured areas when laid underneath a wash, as can treating the paper, or parts of it, with white spirit before painting, which has a similar effect. The possibilities are almost endless, and experimentation is sure to reward you with interesting discoveries.

PROBLEM-SOLVING

Although watercolors cannot be altered so drastically or so often as paintings in any of the opaque media, changes are possible. It is a mistake to abandon a picture because a first wash has not gone on quite right.

The first thing to remember is that a wash which looks too dark or too vivid on a sheet of otherwise white paper will dry much lighter and may look quite pale when surrounded by other colors. If the first wash looks wrong, let it dry. If you are still quite sure it is not what you intended, sponge it

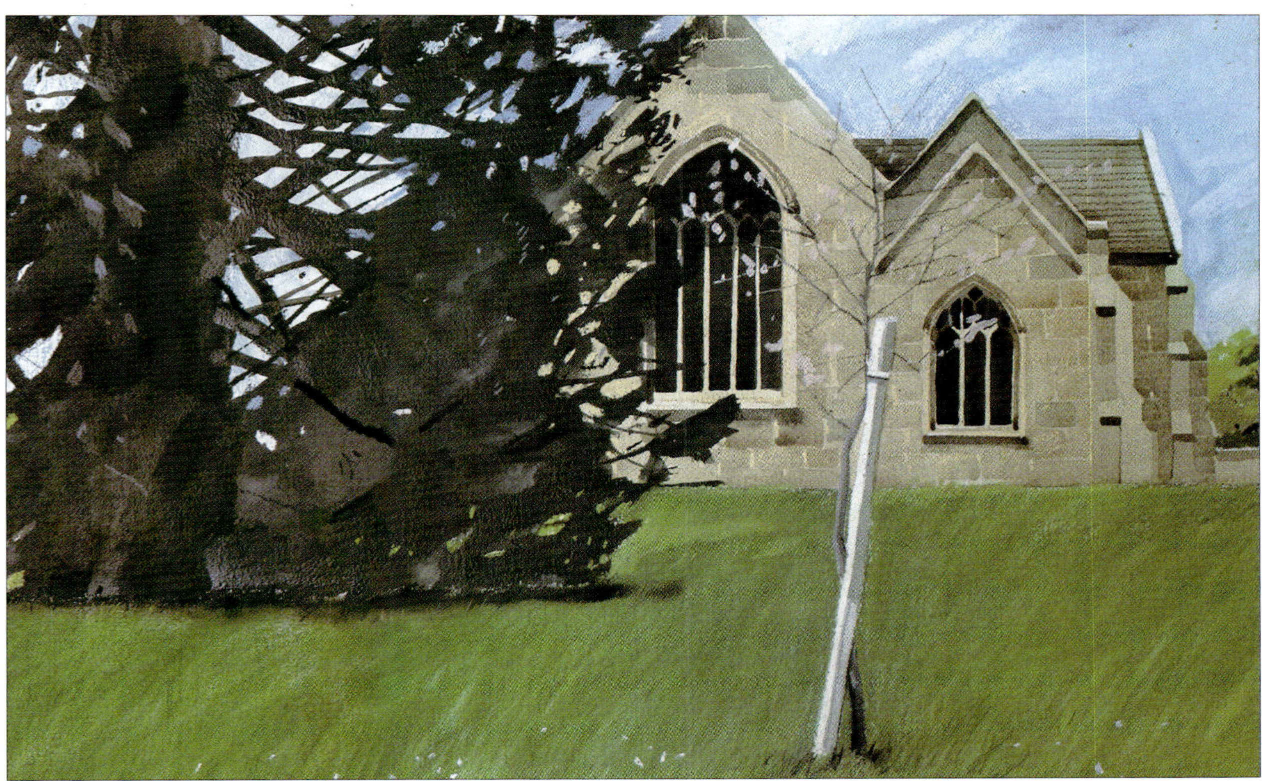

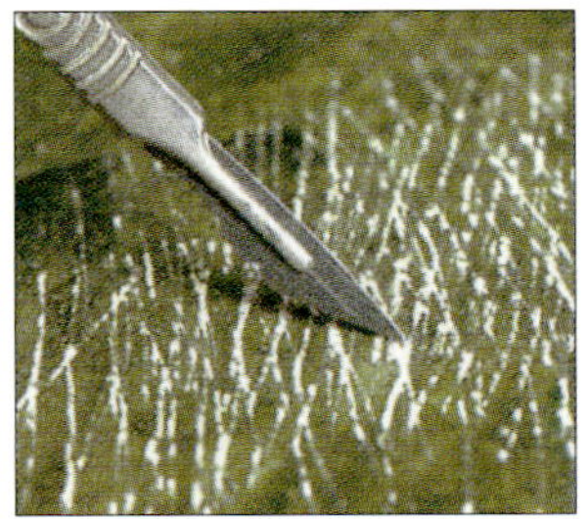

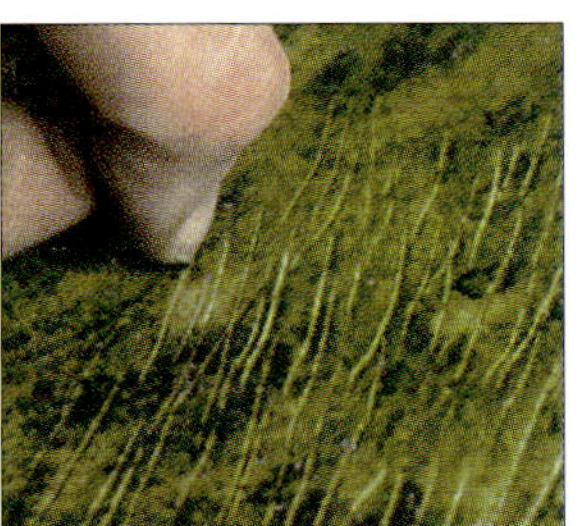

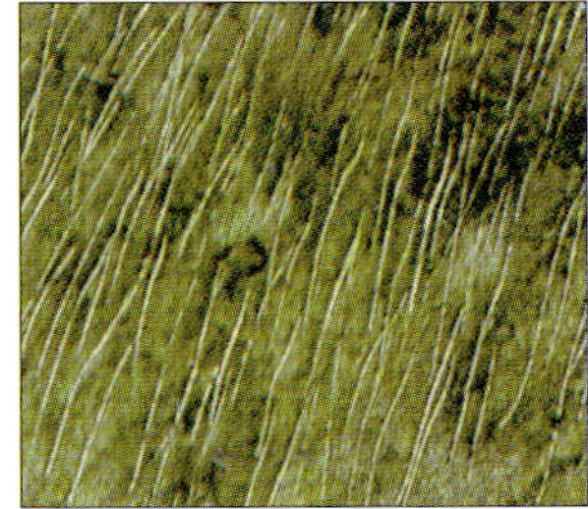

Above *Watercolor has been used in conjunction with pastel to give liveliness and textural contrast to this painting. Both the building itself and the dark tree on the left are in pure watercolor, while the foreground grass is pure pastel. The sky is a combination of the two.*

Left, Middle and Right *Sharp, clean lines and highlights can be made by scraping into dry paint with a scalpel or other sharp knife. Take care not to damage the paper by pressing too hard.*

out with a clean sponge and clear water. This may leave a slight stain on the paper, depending on the paper used and the color itself (some colors stain the paper, like a dye, while others do not), but when dry it will be too faint to spoil the new wash.

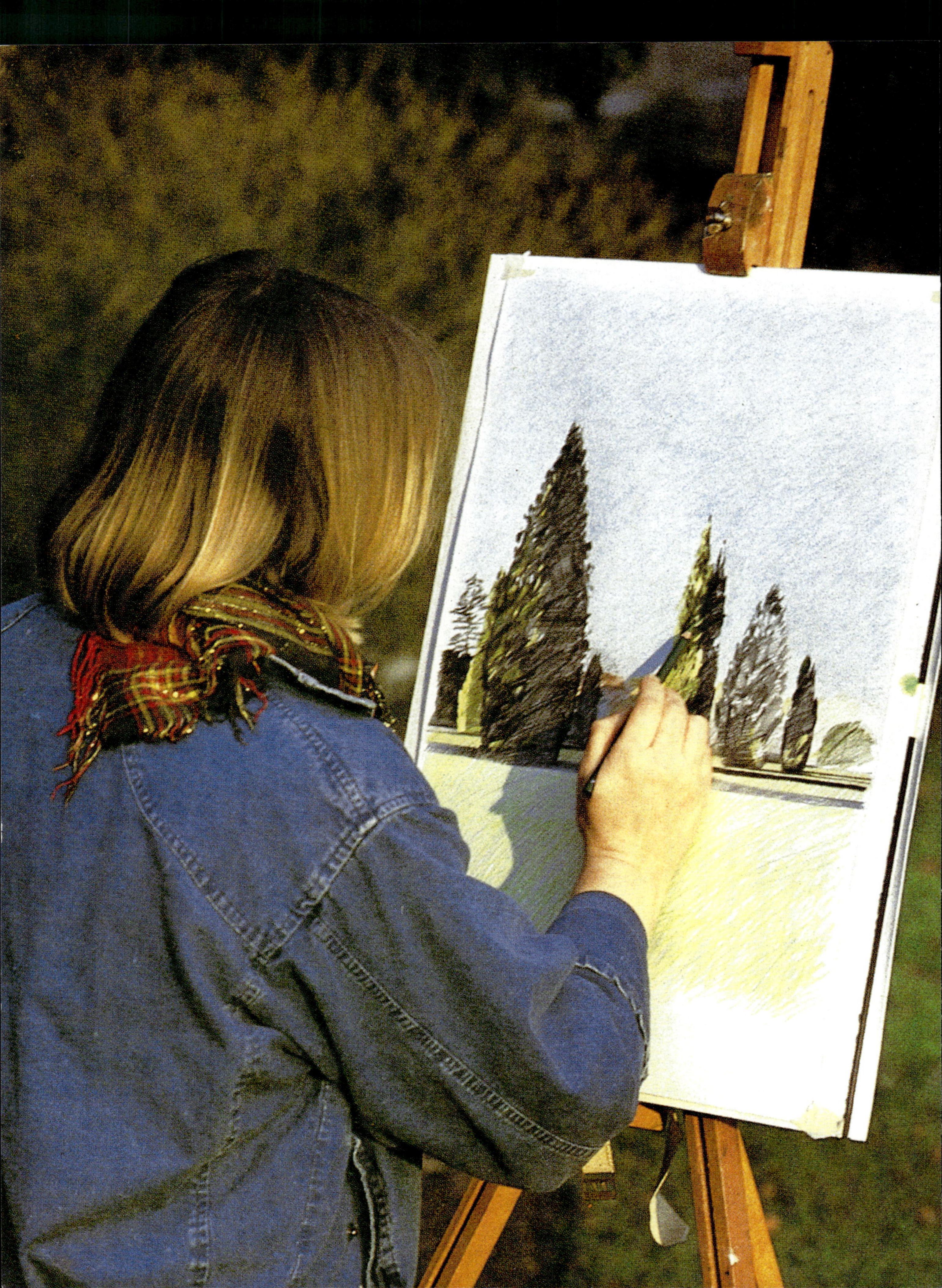

4

BASIC RULES FOR ARTISTS

Every painter, working in whatever medium, needs to understand the basic rules of his craft, even if sometimes only to break them. The underlying principles of such things as composition, perspective, drawing itself, apply to all kinds of painting. The novice watercolorist, who needs to plan his paintings especially carefully, should have a firm grasp of them from the beginning.

COMPOSING AND SELECTING

Whether your chosen subject is a landscape or a single flower in a vase, you need to have a clear idea of what the main elements are and of how you will place them on the paper before you begin to paint. Painting a landscape requires you to decide where the view is to begin and end, whether to emphasize or alter features in the foreground, and so on. For a portrait or still life, you must decide how much to show, the proportion of the figure in relation to the background, the general color scheme and the balance of lights and darks. Composition and selection thus go hand in hand: an artist first selects which aspects of the subject are important and then composes the picture by placing them in a certain way.

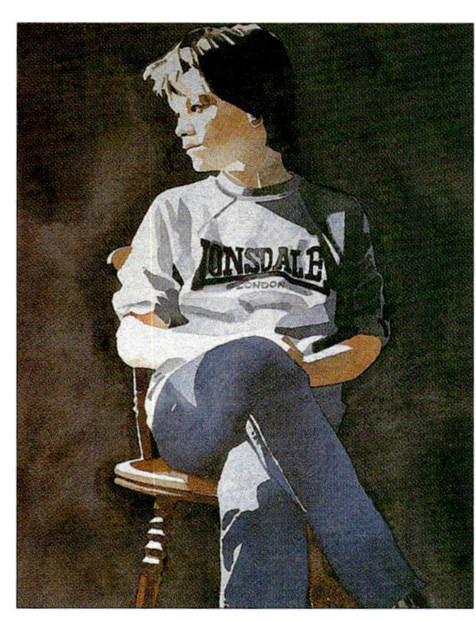

Above *Here the artist has placed his subject in the center of the picture, with the diagonal of the leg balancing the angle of the head. He has allowed one leg and the legs of the chair to "bust" the frame at the bottom, thus bringing the figure forward.*

Left *Working out of doors. Some artists find that they work best with the subject in front of them. Others will only work from reference material.*

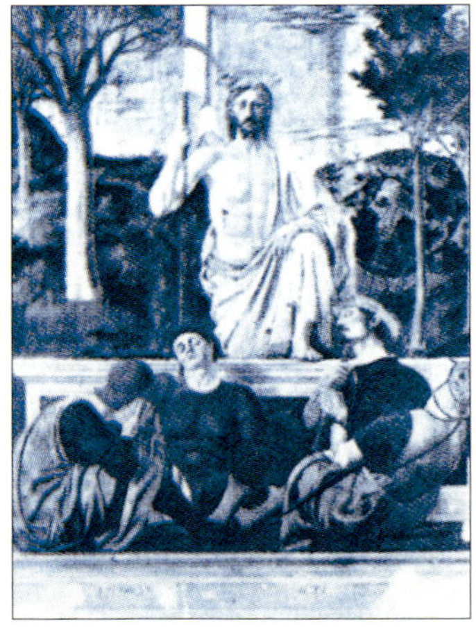

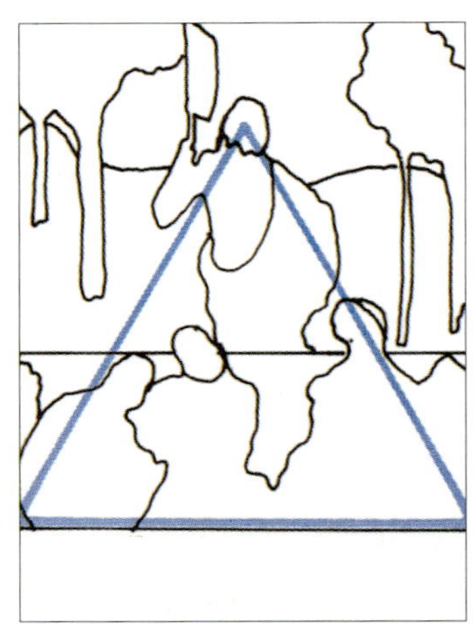

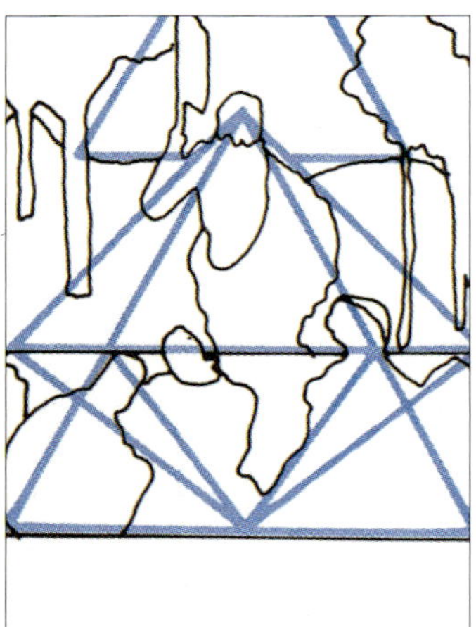

Painters of the Renaissance usually planned the composition of a painting on a geometric grid structure. This example, by Piero della Francesca, is based on a triangle, a common compositional device which is still much used, as are circles and rectangles. The drawing here the right shows how other triangles can be discerned within the main one formed by the figures.

There are well-tested mathematical rules for "good composition". The ancient Greeks, for instance, devised the system known as the Golden Section (or Golden Mean), in which the area of the painting is divided by a line in such a way that the smaller part is to the larger what the larger is to the whole. This ensures that the picture plane is divided in a balanced and symmetrical way, and countless artists have made use of the principle. The triangle is another basis for composition (many paintings are based on the framework of a single triangle), as is a series of intersecting geometric shapes such as squares, rectangles, and circles. It is unlikely that someone sitting down to an outdoor watercolor sketch will need a full knowledge of such principles, but there are some simple and practical ones that should be

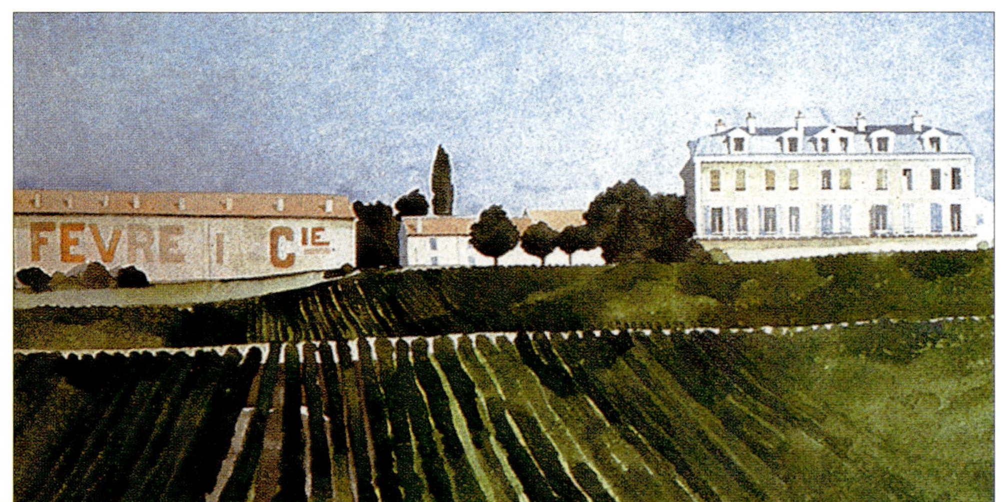

Left *Converging lines in landscapes are often used to lead the viewer's eye to the focal point, in this case the buildings. Unusually, the artist had divided the picture into two nearly equal parts, the land and the sky. It is believed that the viewer's eye should not be led to one part of the painting to the exclusion of others, but there should usually be a "focal point." But monotony has been avoided by allowing the buildings and the trees to break into the skyline and by dividing the foreground by the broken line of the white road in the middle distance. Compositional devices like a road or path, stream, plowed field, or fence, used in this way could help break the painting thus.*

borne in mind. Basically, a good composition is one in which there are no jarring elements—all the parts of the picture balance one another in a pleasing way, and the viewer's eye is led into the picture rather than out of it. Whatever the subject, it is almost never advisable to divide the painting into two equal halves, such as sea and land, or table-top and background in a still life. The result is at once monotonous and disjointed. The viewer's eye should not be led to one part of the painting to the exclusion of others, but there should usually be a "focal point." For example, a group of buildings in a landscape can be used simply as a counterpoint to other elements, such as trees and hills, or they may be what interests you most about the scene, with the trees, hills, and foreground used as a "backdrop." The buildings need not be large, nor placed directly in the center of the picture (this is not normally advisable); what matters is that the eye should be consistently led to them as the focal point. Compositional devices often used to lead the eye in this way are the curving lines of a path, stream, plowed field, or fence, along which the viewer's eye must travel. Such lines should never lead out of the picture unless for a deliberately sought effect.

The focal point of a portrait is almost always the face, the eyes in particular for a front or three-quarter view, and care must be taken not to detract from it by placing too much emphasis on other elements, such as the background, or the hands. Hands and clothing are often treated in a sketchy way so that they do not assume too much

TRANSFERRING THE IMAGE

Below *In portraiture precise drawing is very important. It is often wise to make preliminary drawing and then transfer it to the painting surface, thus avoiding too much erasing on the surface itself. Too much erasing might spoil the surface. Here the artist has worked from a photograph, enlarged to the required size by means of a grid. The drawing line transferred to the support by using a form of carbon paper called iron-oxide paper, which provides a clear outline.*

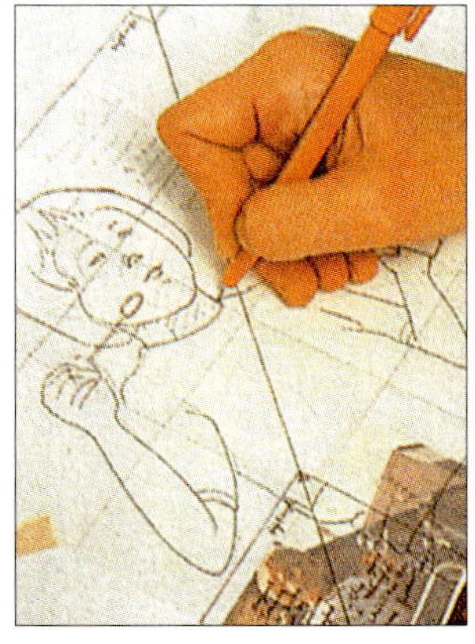

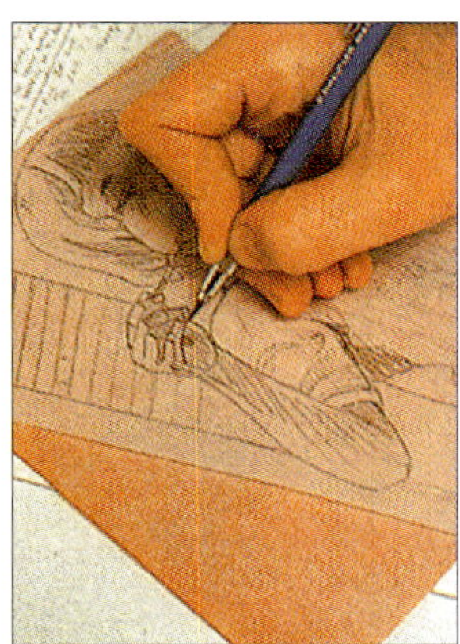

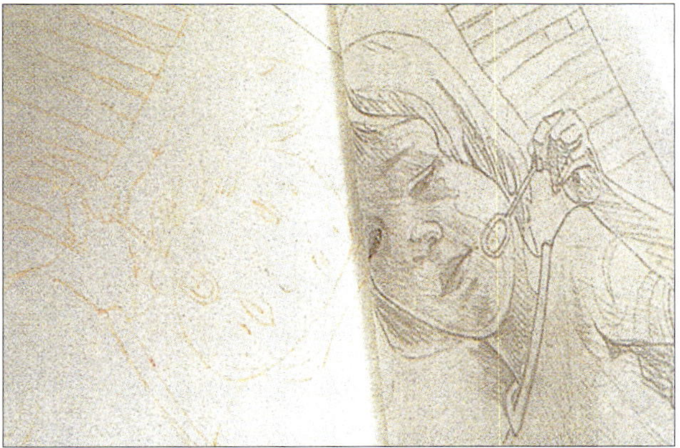

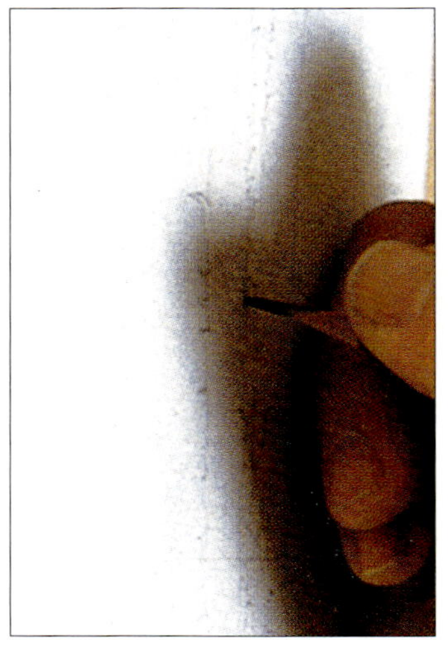

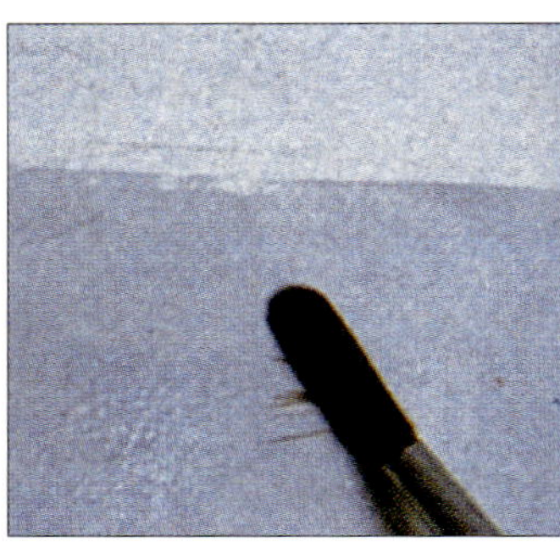

Left *This study of a motel required a careful outline drawing to enable the artist to place his first wash accurately.*

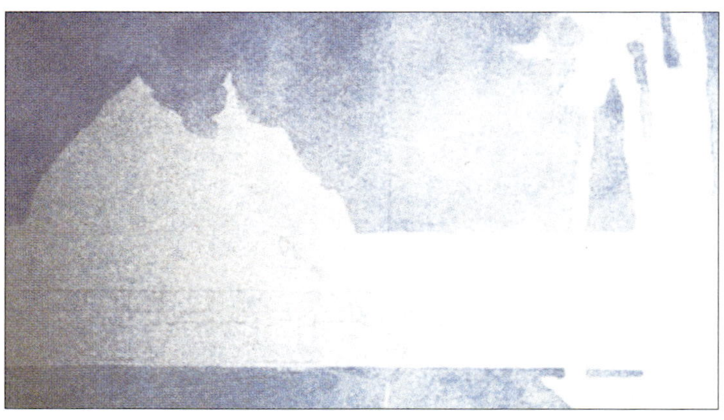

Top Right and Above *Since only an outline was needed, the drawing was done directly on the support. The first wash was then laid around the shapes of the building and trees.*

importance. A figure or face should be placed in a well-considered and deliberate way against the background to create a feeling of harmony and balance. There should not be too much space at the top. Nor, usually, should the subject be placed squarely in the middle of the picture, though a central position can sometimes be effective. Backgrounds are part of a portrait painting, as are skies in landscapes, even when they are quite plain and muted in color. If a picture is placed against a stark white background, the white areas will have their own shapes and thus make their contribution to the balance of the painting. Such flat areas are known as "negative space."

Viewing frames for outdoor work or polaroid cameras for indoor work might help an artist work out a satisfactory composition. Making small, quick sketches, often referred to as thumbnail sketches, is another good way to work out a composition.

DRAWING

Drawing is the basis of all painting. Indeed, painting is simply drawing with a brush and color. Although much of the more detailed drawing in a watercolor is done at the final stages with a fine brush, it is nearly always necessary to make some form of pencil drawing on the paper before beginning to paint. Without this, you will have no idea where to place the first wash or which areas to reserve as paler ones.

Few people draw with the ease and assurance that produce the confident and flowing lines of really fine drawings. However, a drawing which is to be used only as the guideline for a painting need not be

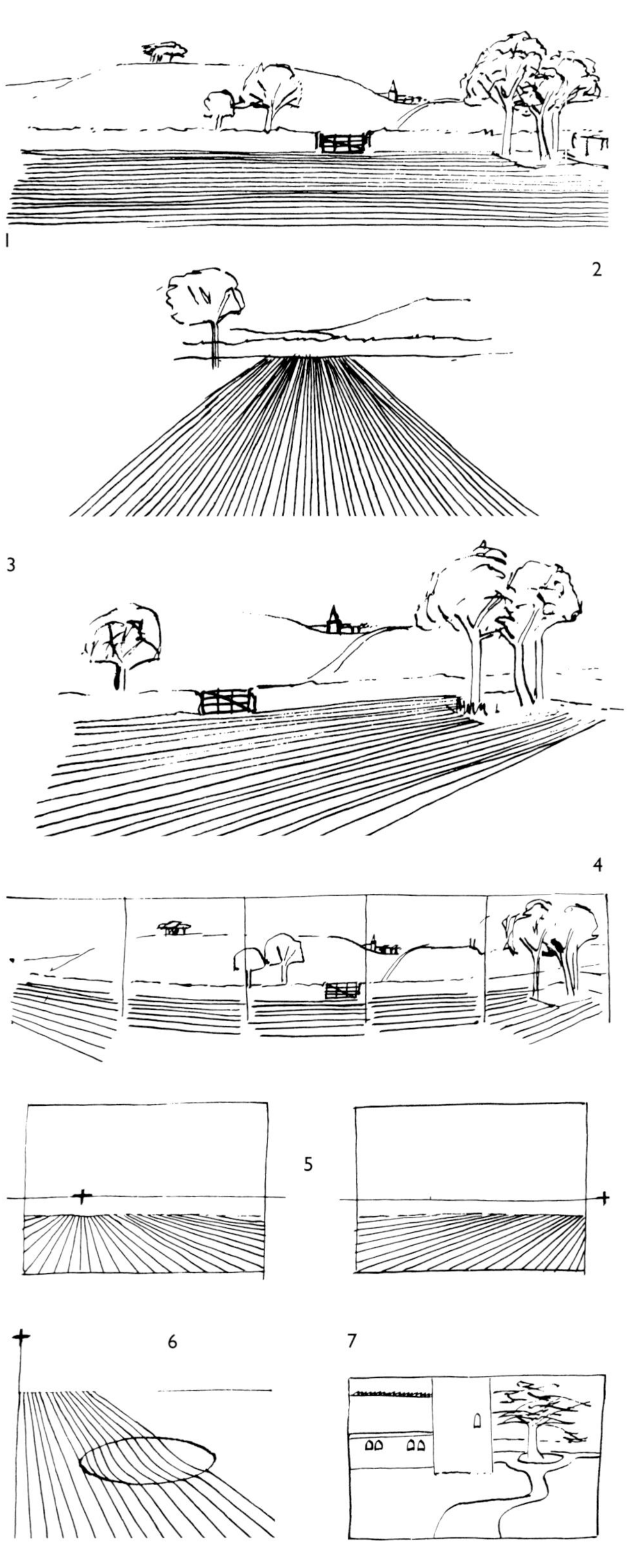

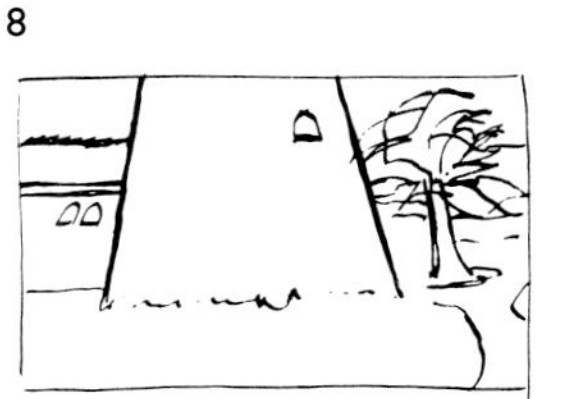

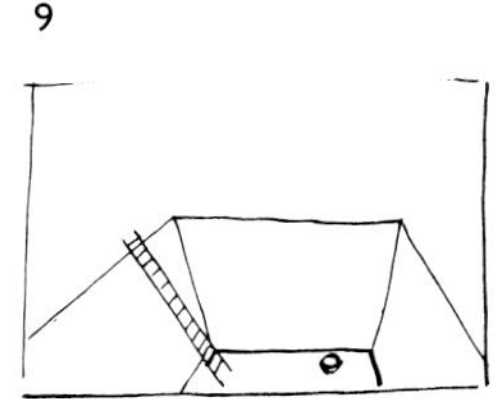

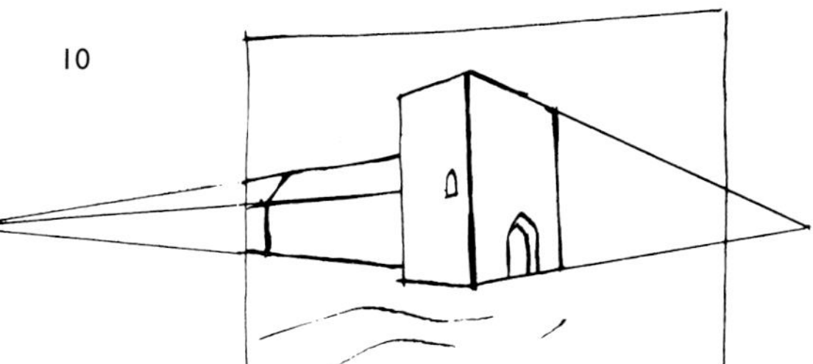

PERSPECTIVE

Perspective governs everything we see; even in a simple landscape of fields and hills, the way, in which the furrows of a plowed field change direction explain the lie of the land and help to create a feeling of form and recession.

1 The spaces between furrows in a plowed field becoming progressively smaller as the field recedes.
2 Now our viewpoint is altered, so that the furrows run away, converging at a vanishing point on the horizon.
3 In this mid-view, the lines still converge on the horizon, but the vanishing point is some way outside the picture.
4 This wide-angle view shows that we do not really perceive the lines of the furrows as straight.
5 The vanishing point must always be on the horizon, but it will be within the picture area only if viewed square-on.
6 If there is a dip in the ground the furrows will follow it, thus taking their vanishing points from the angle of the indentation.
7 When viewed from a distance, the two sides of a church tower appear to be vertical.
8 However, when seen more closely, the side walls seem to converge. The lower the viewpoint, the sharper the effect.
9 When seen from above—thus, a higher viewpoint—the sides appear to converge at the bottom.
10 When the tower is seen from an angle, each side will have its own vanishing point.

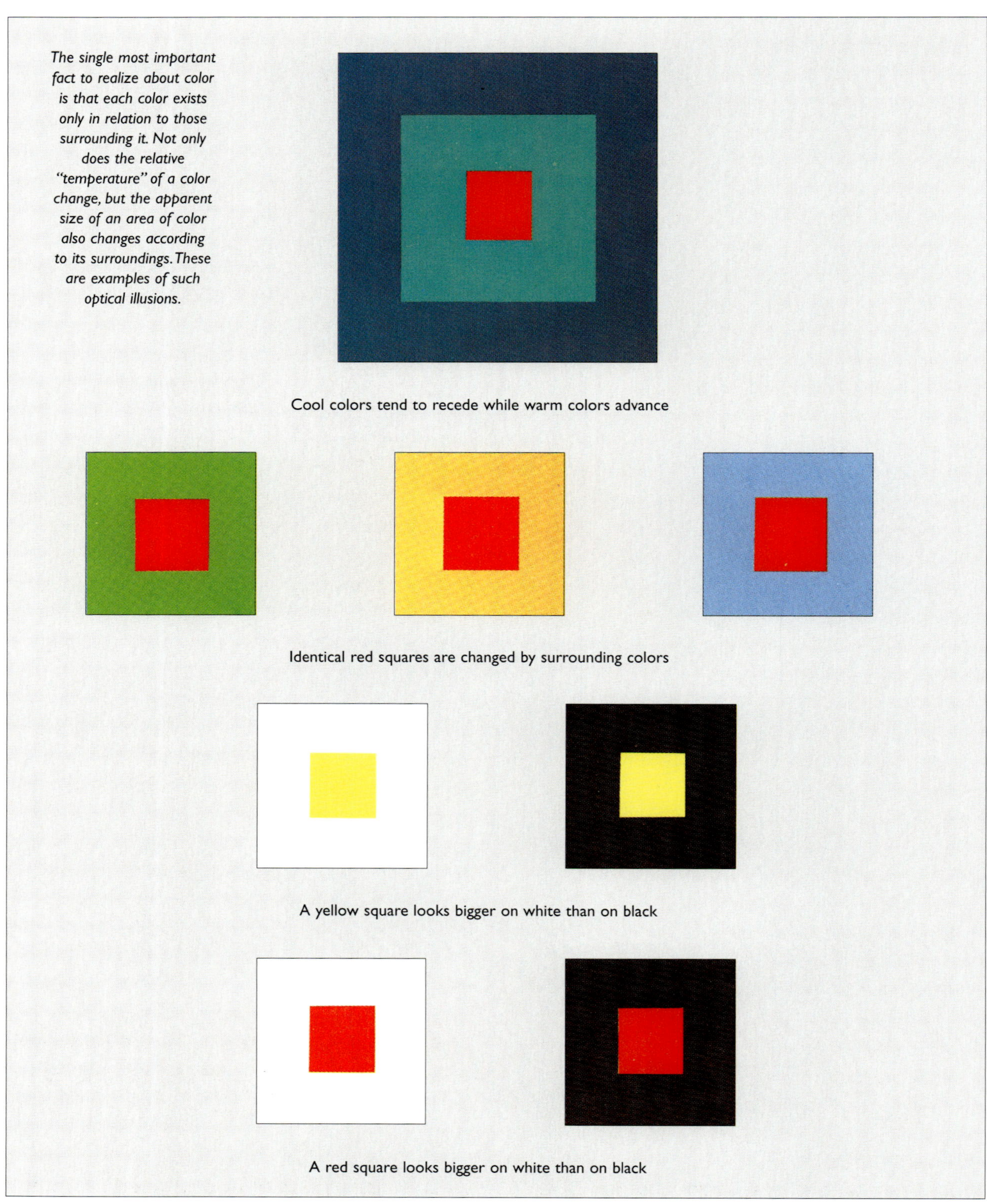

Cool colors tend to recede while warm colors advance

Identical red squares are changed by surrounding colors

A yellow square looks bigger on white than on black

A red square looks bigger on white than on black

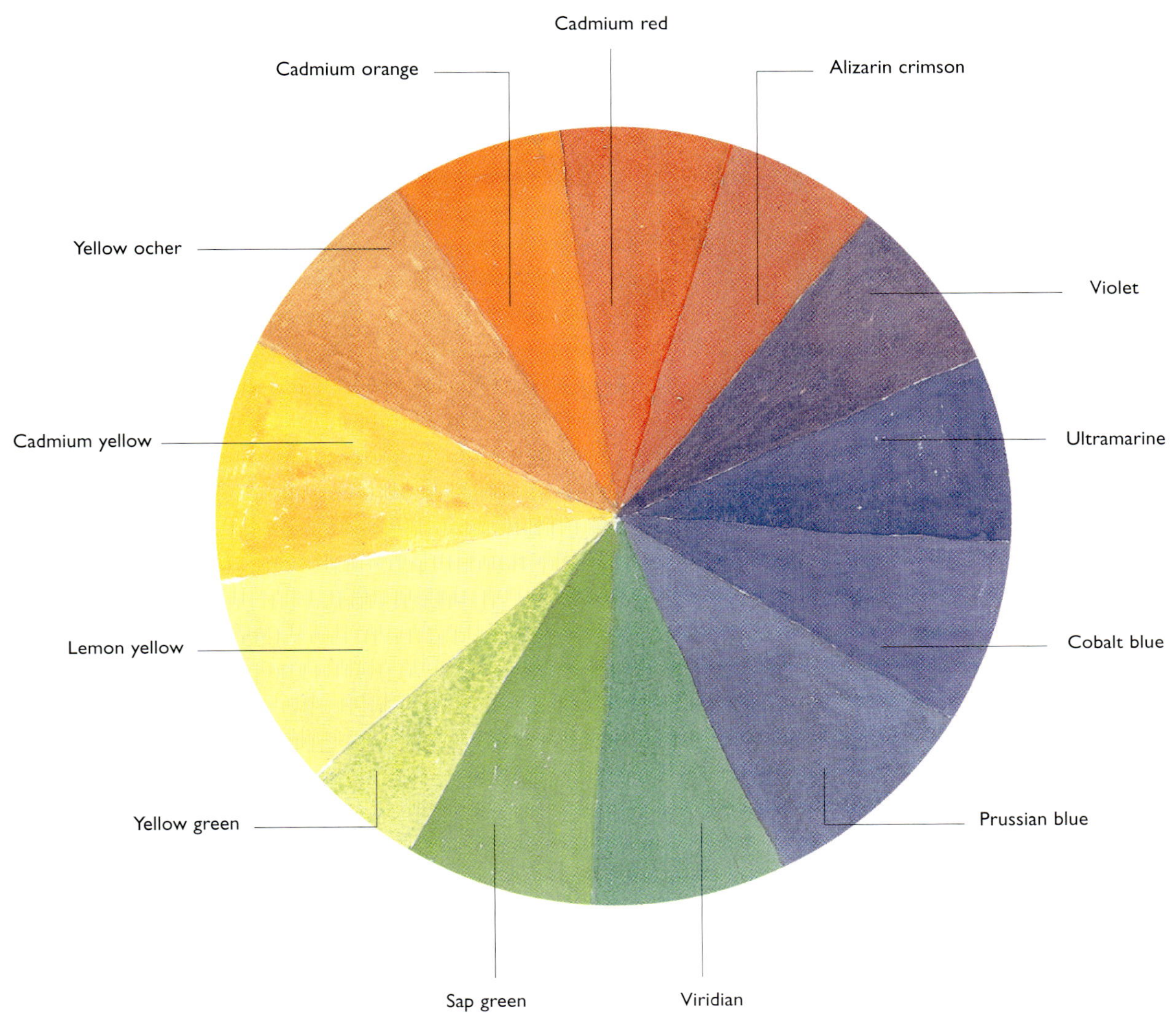

Above *The color wheel, which is really just a spectrum bent into a circle, is a useful device for working out combinations of complementary colors. Notice how the colors on the red and yellow side appear warm, while those on the green and blue side are much cooler.*

of high quality. What matters is getting the proportions and shapes right.

Never try to draw any subject from too close a viewpoint, which distorts the view. And make sure that you do not have to move your head to see different parts of the subject. Your line of vision should be central. Try to make sure that you are reasonably comfortable (not always possible when working out of doors) and hold the

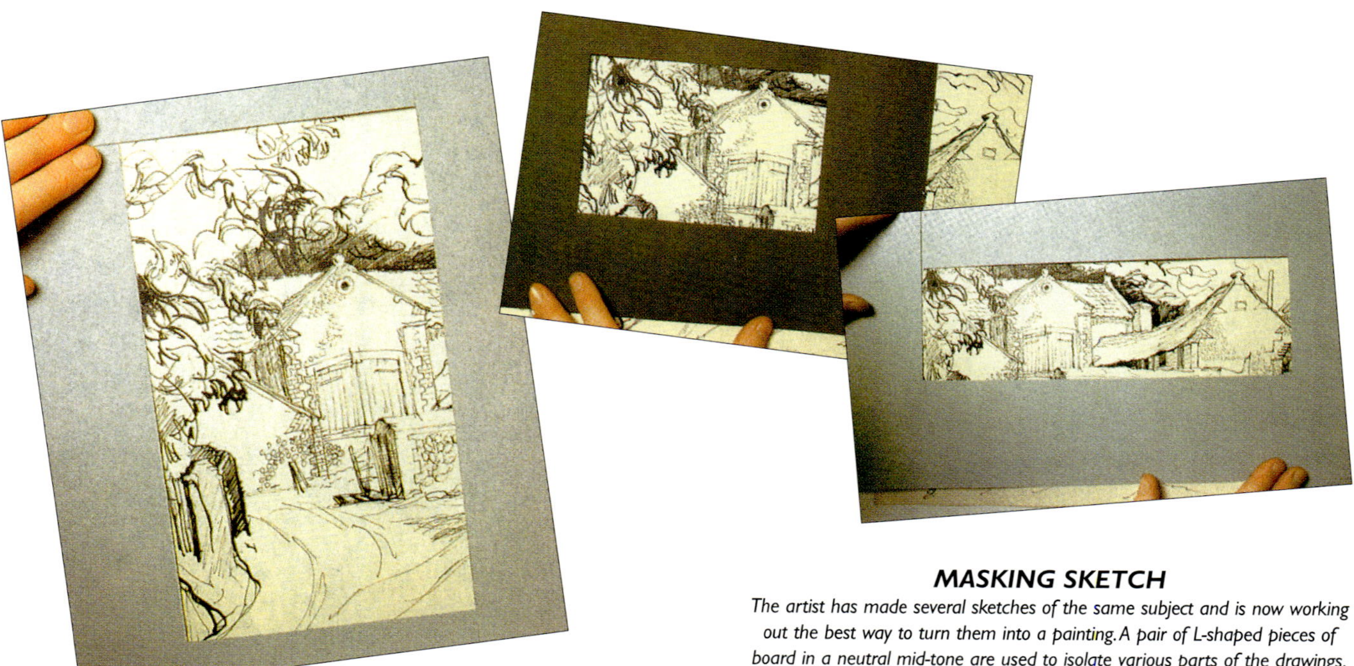

MASKING SKETCH
The artist has made several sketches of the same subject and is now working out the best way to turn them into a painting. A pair of L-shaped pieces of board in a neutral mid-tone are used to isolate various parts of the drawings.

drawing board in such a way that it does not obscure any part of the subject. Check sizes and measurements continually by holding up your pencil and moving your thumb up and down on it, closing one eye to measure distances. Avoid making the drawing too fussy. Too many pencil marks may muddy the paint. An HB or B pencil is the best to use, as softer ones may smudge the paper. The drawing can be erased at any stage during the painting as long as the paper is quite dry.

PERSPECTIVE

Perspective is sometimes believed to be the concern only of those who paint buildings. In fact, the laws of perspective govern everything, simply because drawing and painting transfer three-dimensional shapes on to a two-dimensional surface.

The "golden rule," which most people learn at school, is that receding parallel lines meet at a vanishing point. The real difficulty in drawing complex perspective subjects, such as urban scenes, is that buildings have several different planes, each with its own vanishing point, and sometimes one building or group of buildings is set at angles to another, giving yet another set of points, many of which will be outside the picture plane. These must be guessed at to some extent, but the pencil-and-thumb measuring system described earlier is helpful, or a small plastic ruler can be held up to assess the angles of parallel lines.

TONE AND COLOR

Color theory can be enormously complicated. But there are really only a few facts about color which the average painter needs to know. Color has two main components, tone and hue, the former being its lightness or darkness and the latter its intensity, or vividness. If you were to take both a black-and-white photograph and a color one of a landscape composed almost entirely of greens, the black-and-white one would show the tones quite clearly as a series of dark grays and light grays shading to white and black. It is important to balance tones, or lights and darks, in a painting, but they can be rather hard to assess, particularly outdoors in a changing light. You may wonder whether the sky is lighter or darker than the sea or land, or whether the leaves of a tree are lighter or darker than the hills behind. Tones are much easier to judge if you half-close your eyes, thus eliminating distracting details.

In the landscape photograph, you may notice that the brightest colors are in the foreground, where the contrasts in tone are also the strongest, those in the background tending to merge into one another and become barely distinguishable in places. An understanding of this phenomenon, called aerial perspective, is crucial. As a landscape recedes into the middle and then the far distance, objects appear much less distinct and become paler and bluer because the light is filtered through dust and moisture in

Below *Peter de Wint, an English painter of Dutch extraction, was drawn to flat, panoramic landscapes. His great sweeping views seem to extend beyond the confines of the paintings themselves. Observe the sure and confident handling of the trees and water in* Walton-on-Thames, *and the tiny area of unpainted paper which give extra sparkle to the picture.*

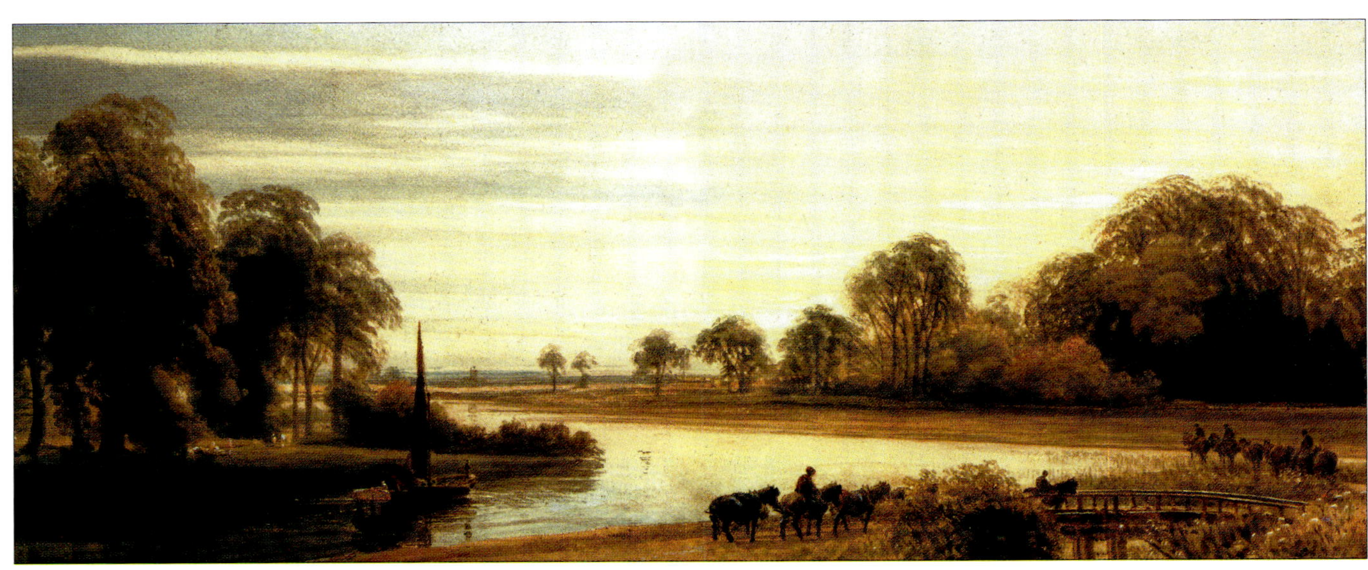

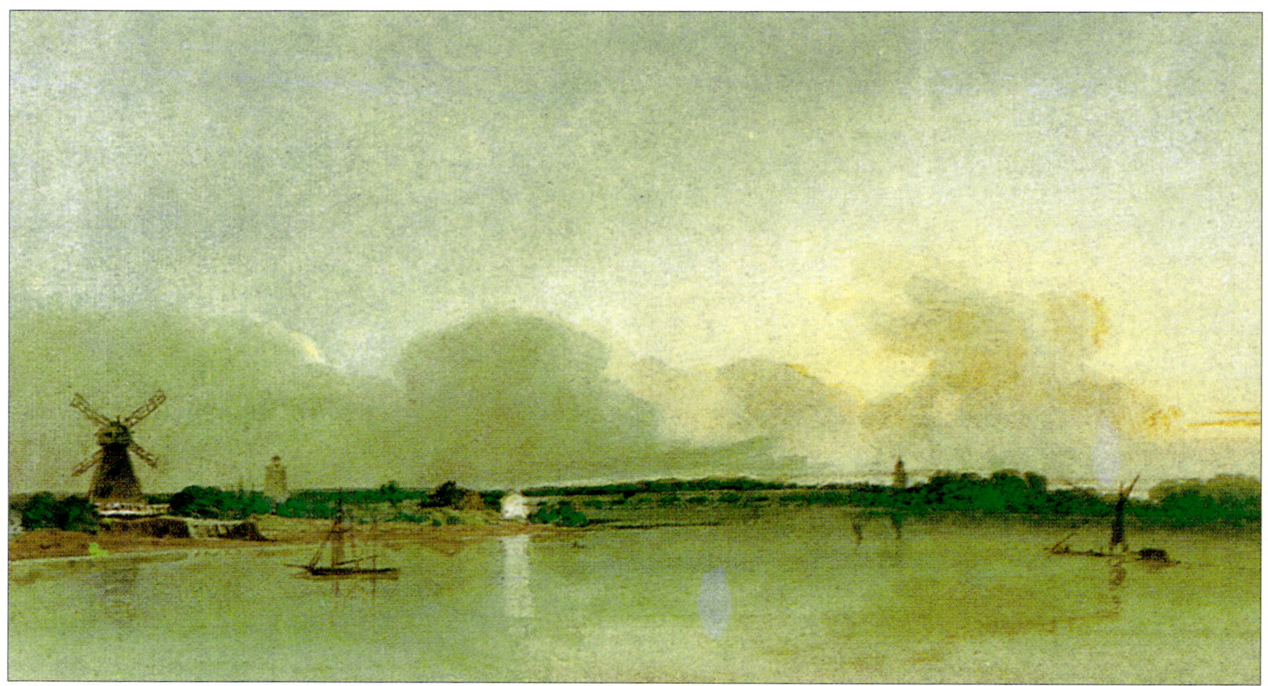

***Above** Thomas Girtin was a pioneer of watercolor painting. He worked with only five colors – black, monastral blue, yellow ocher, burnt sienna, and light red – to create subtle evocations of atmosphere.* The White House, Chelsea *shows both this fine sense of composition and his mastery of tone and color.*

the atmosphere. It is possible to suggest distance and recession in a painting by using this kind of perspective alone.

Colors in the foreground tend to be "warmer" than those in the background as well as brighter in hue. All colors can be broadly classified as either "warm" or "cool." Reds, yellows, and oranges, for instance, are warm, and tend to push themselves forward, or "advance;" blues, and colors with blue in them, such as blue-gray and blue-green, will recede. However, colors can be perceived as colors only in relation to one another, and some blues are warmer than others while some reds are cooler. You can see this by placing ultramarine blue, which is relatively warm, next to the cold Prussian blue, or alizarin crimson, which is quite cool, next to cadmium red, which is warm.

USING REFERENCE MATERIAL

Paintings do not, of course, have to be done from life: many fine landscapes are painted in the studio, and excellent portraits are done from photographs or drawings or a combination of both. You may think that you remember a scene very well, but you will be surprised how the details escape you as soon as you sit down to paint it. It is, therefore, wise to amass as much reference material for visual stimulus as possible, even if it seems to be much more than you need.

Right *A watercolor of stones at Avebury. The cool tones express the calm grandeur of this ancient monument.*

Below *Francis Towne's work was not appreciated in the 19th century, but has since been widely recognised. He was fascinated with grand mountain views, finding much of his inspiration in the wild scenery of the Alps, North Wales, and England's Lake District. This painting,* Grasmere by the Road, *is typical of his technique, in which pen outline is used to isolate areas of contrasting color.*

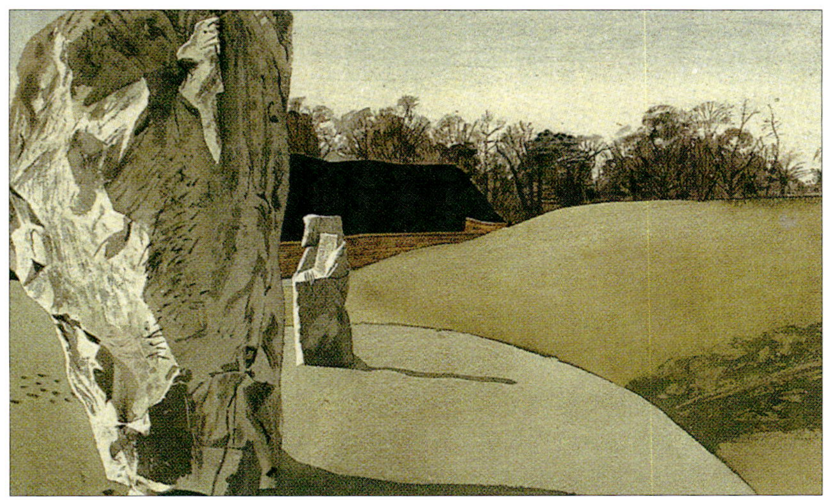

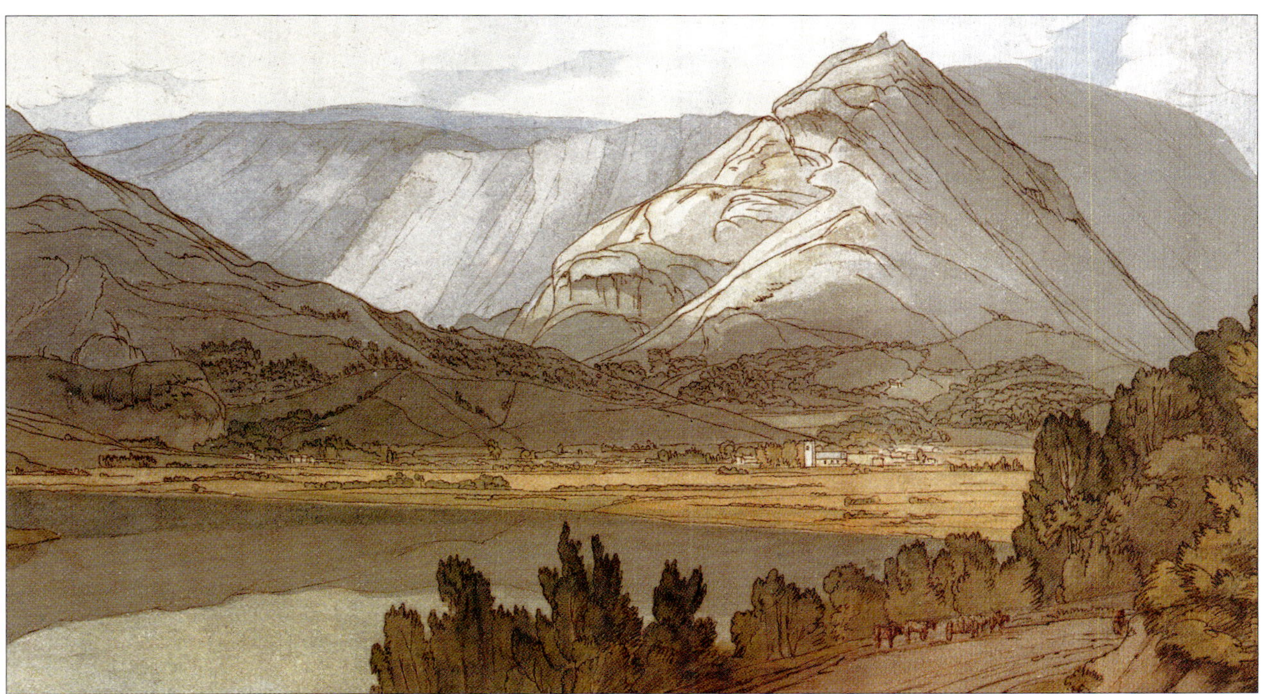

PRACTICAL HINTS FOR OUTDOOR PAINTING

Once landscape had become an "official" subject for painters, working out of doors directly from nature became increasingly common, the more so after the French Impressionists set the example. It is now not so popular.

Photographers queueing up to record a beauty spot are a more usual sight than artists doing so. It is, however, an excellent discipline, which forces you to look hard at

Below *Although Turner's watercolors are less well known than his oils, they rank among his finest works. He was clearly extremely taken with watercolor and used it brilliantly and experimentally to express his preoccupation with light and atmosphere, often making use of the semi-accidental effects that occur in watercolor painting. In* Venice from the Giudecca *he has created a feeling of hazy, shimmering light.*

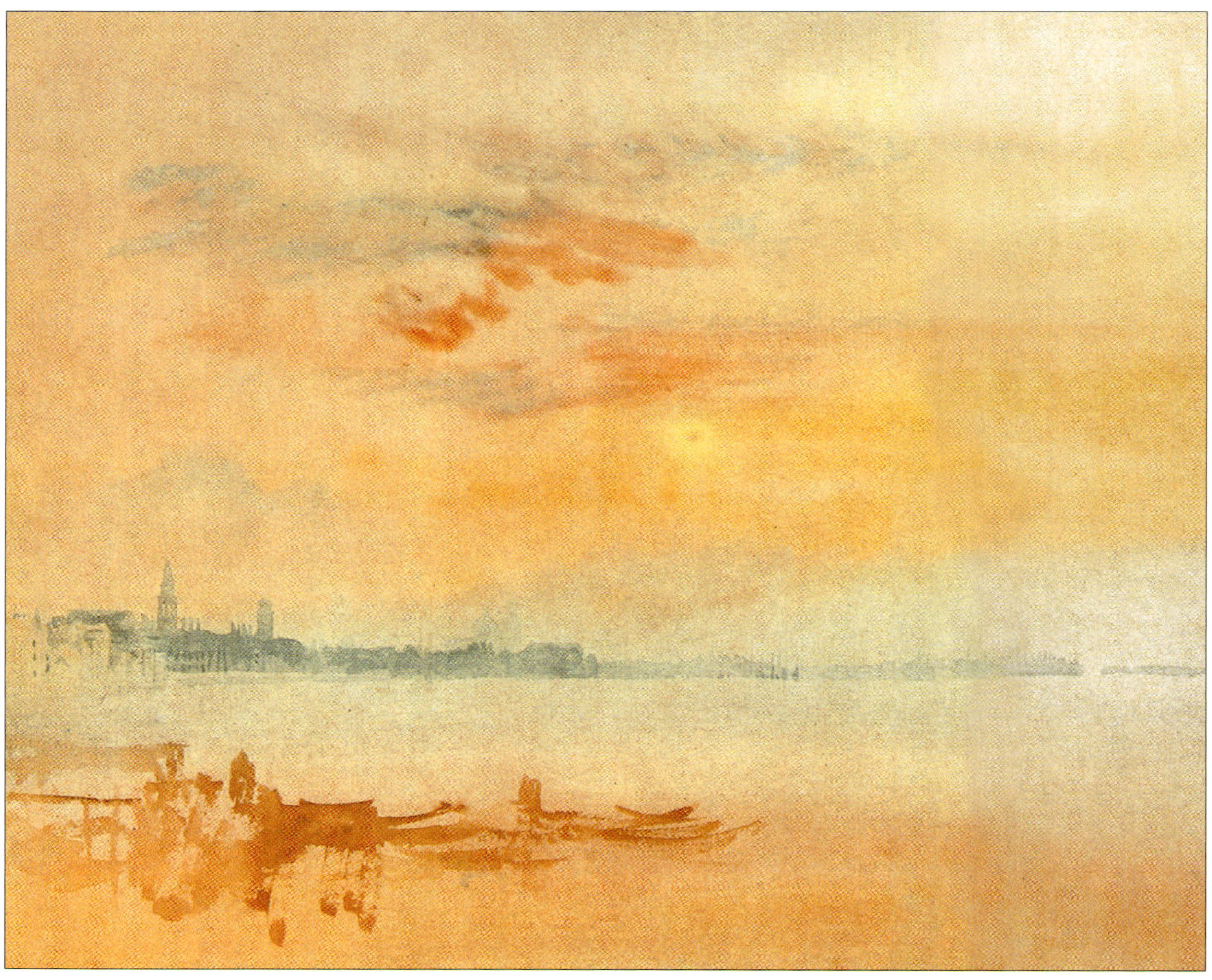

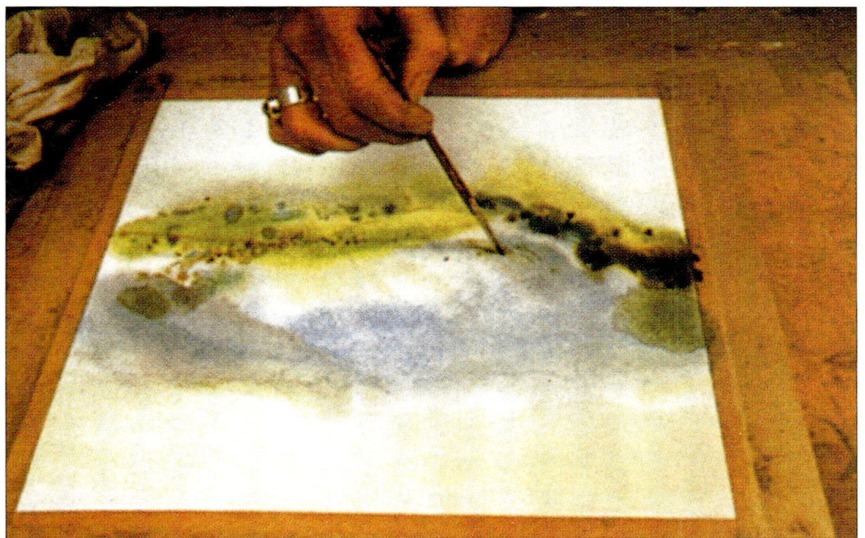

The paper was stretched before use and the board was laid flat, not propped at a slight angle as it would be for laying flat washes. In this way the paint was allowed to mix on the paper without running down it uncontrollably.

a subject and make rapid decisions about how to treat it and lends immediacy and spontaneity to the work itself.

Watercolor is a light and portable medium, ideally suited to outdoor work, but on-the-spot painting, whatever the medium, always presents a different set of problems.

Chief among them is the weather. You may have to contend with blazing heat which dries the paint as soon as it is laid down, freezing winds which numb your hands, sudden showers which blotch your best efforts, or wash them away altogether, and changing light which confuses you and makes you doubt your initial drawing and composition. If the weather looks unpredictable, take extra clothes and anything else you can think of for your comfort, such as tea or a radio.

MATERIALS USED

SUPPORT:
Pre-stretched watercolor paper with a Not surface, measuring 9½ x 13 in. (24 x 33 cm).

COLORS:
Hookers green, oxide of chromium, Indian yellow, Naples yellow, raw sienna, raw umber, cobalt blue, ultramarine, and permanent rose, plus a little Chinese white.

BRUSHES:
A selection of soft brushes and a small household brush.

SUMMER PAINTING

This landscape is a fine evocation of the drama of the everchanging countryside, here

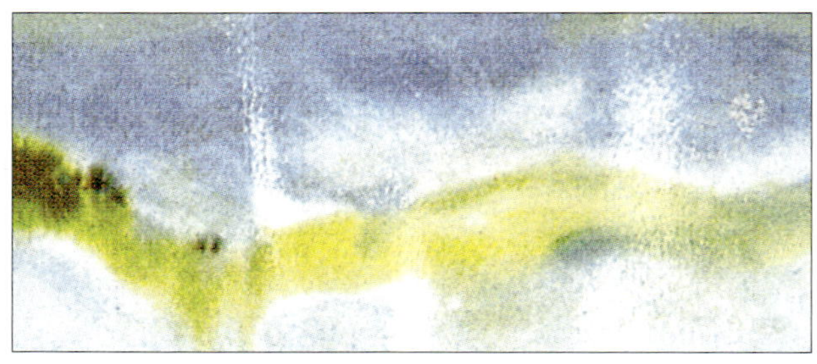

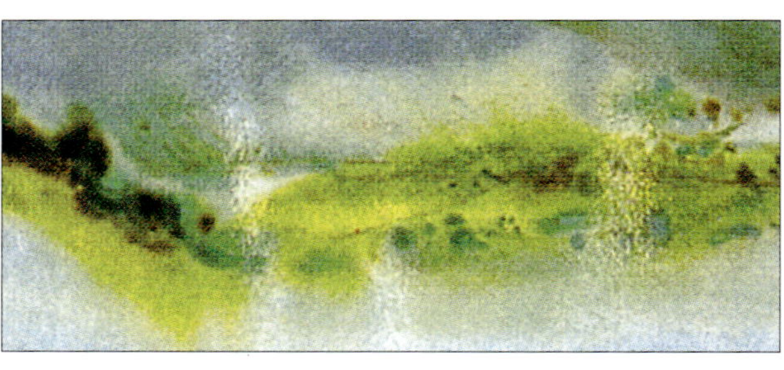

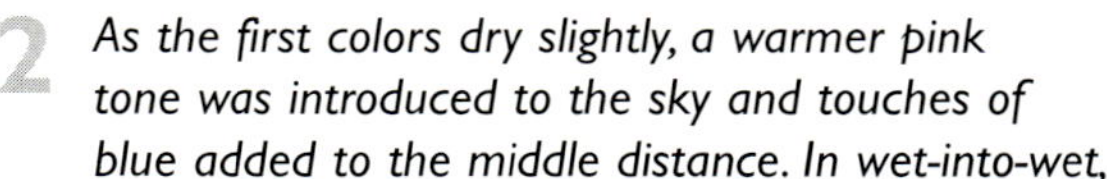

2 *As the first colors dry slightly, a warmer pink tone was introduced to the sky and touches of blue added to the middle distance. In wet-into-wet, the paint is never allowed to dry entirely. But if new paint is added when the first layer is too wet, it will flood, not merge softly.*

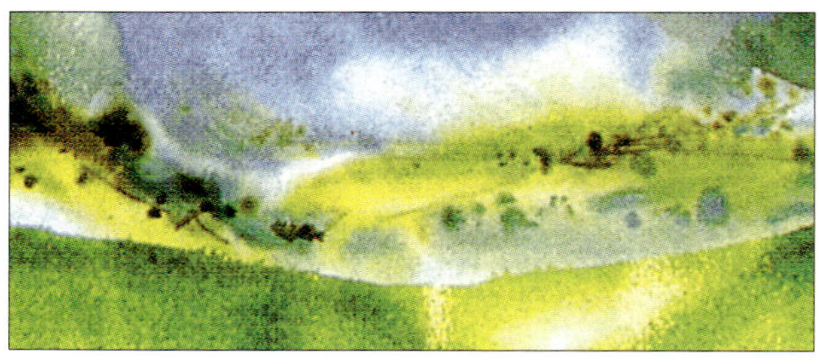

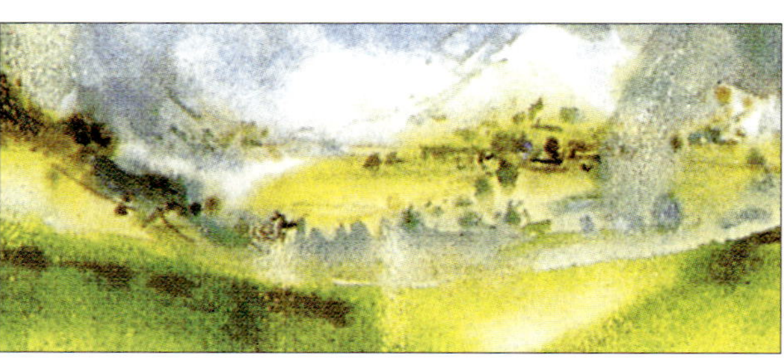

3 *A broad bristle-brush was used to block the foreground; the greens being chosen to balance the yellow-green sunlit hills. Oil painting brushes and household brushes can often be used in watercoior painting to create particular effects.*

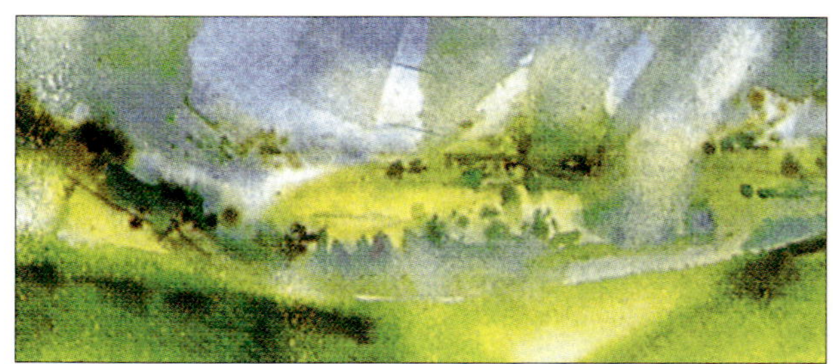

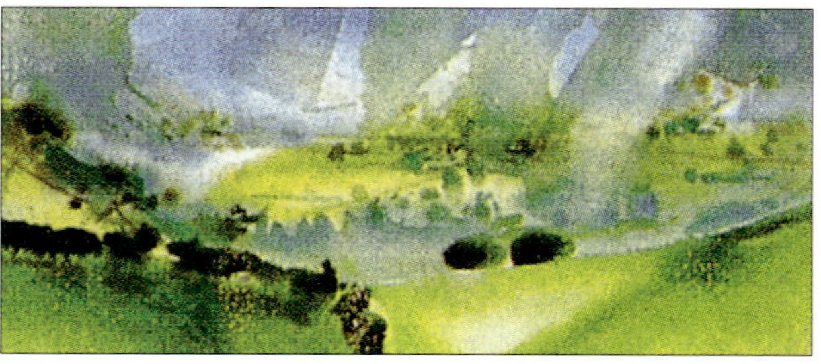

4 *Next, bold brush strokes were introduced into the sky to indicate the rain clouds, and the sky was given a yellow hue. This was then overlaid with gray-blue. At the same time the foreground colors were strengthened and further definition was added.*

SUMMER PAINTING

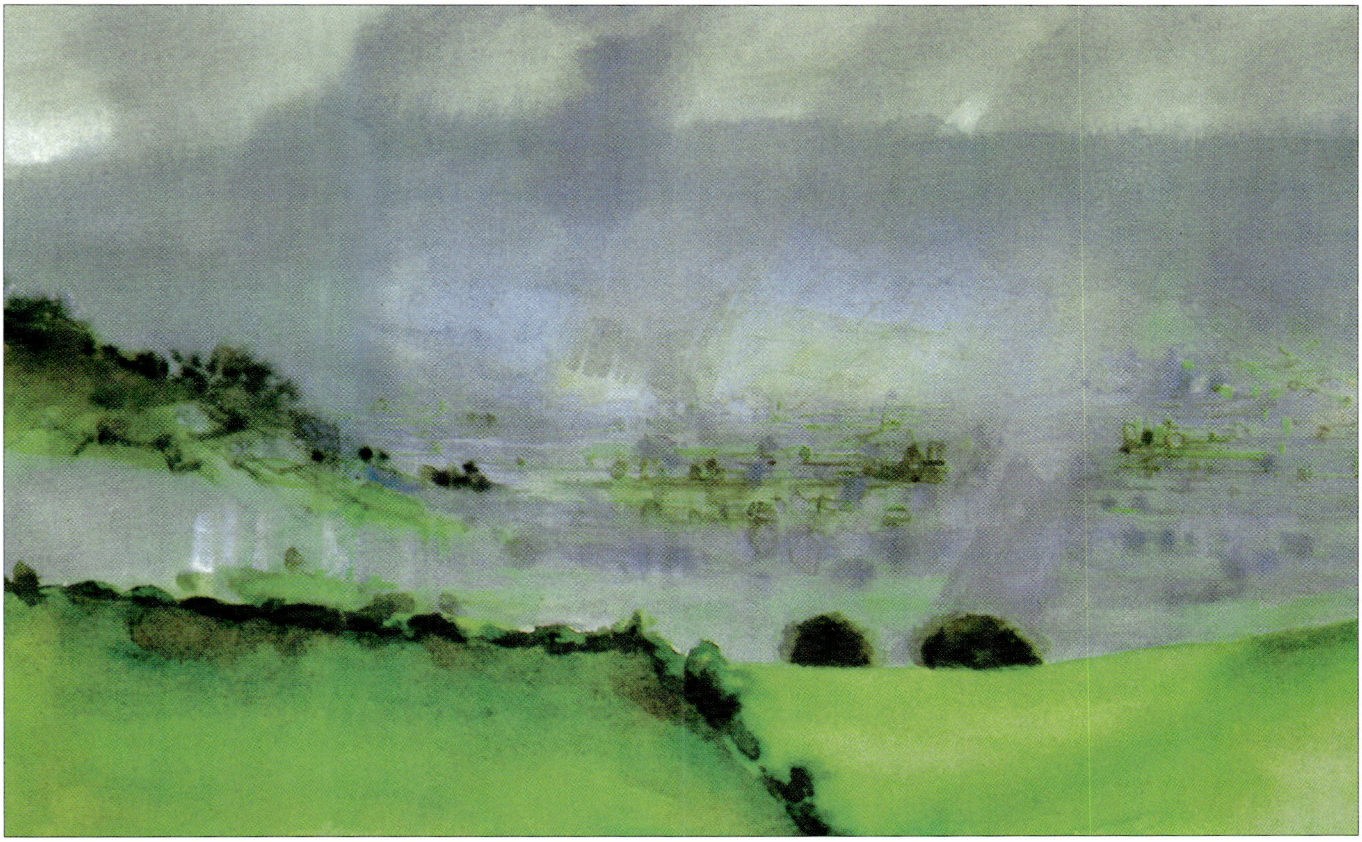

5 *Finished painting: to give a softer, more blurred effect to the rain, a little white has been added to the paint in the final stages. Adding white to watercolor gives an effect quite unlike the harsher one provided by gouache paints, but if used well ahead of completion, it might muddy the other colors.*

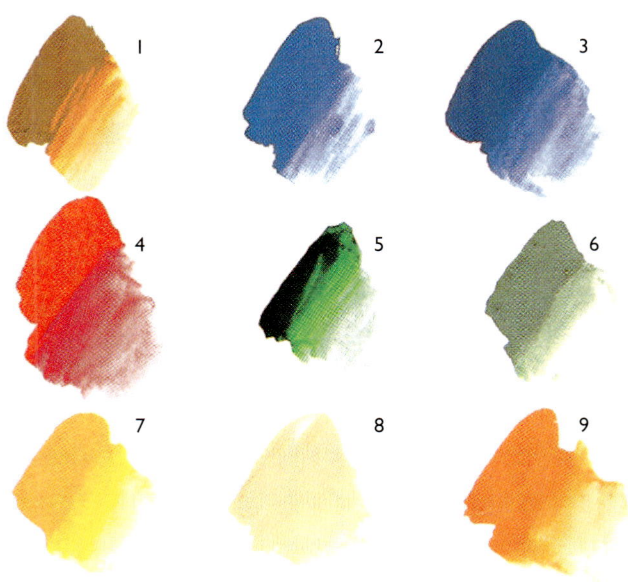

Right *1. Raw umber; 2. Cobalt blue; 3. Ultramarine; 4. Permanent rose ; 5. Hooker's green; 6. Oxide of chromium; 7. Indian yellow; 8. Naples yellow; 9. Raw sienna*

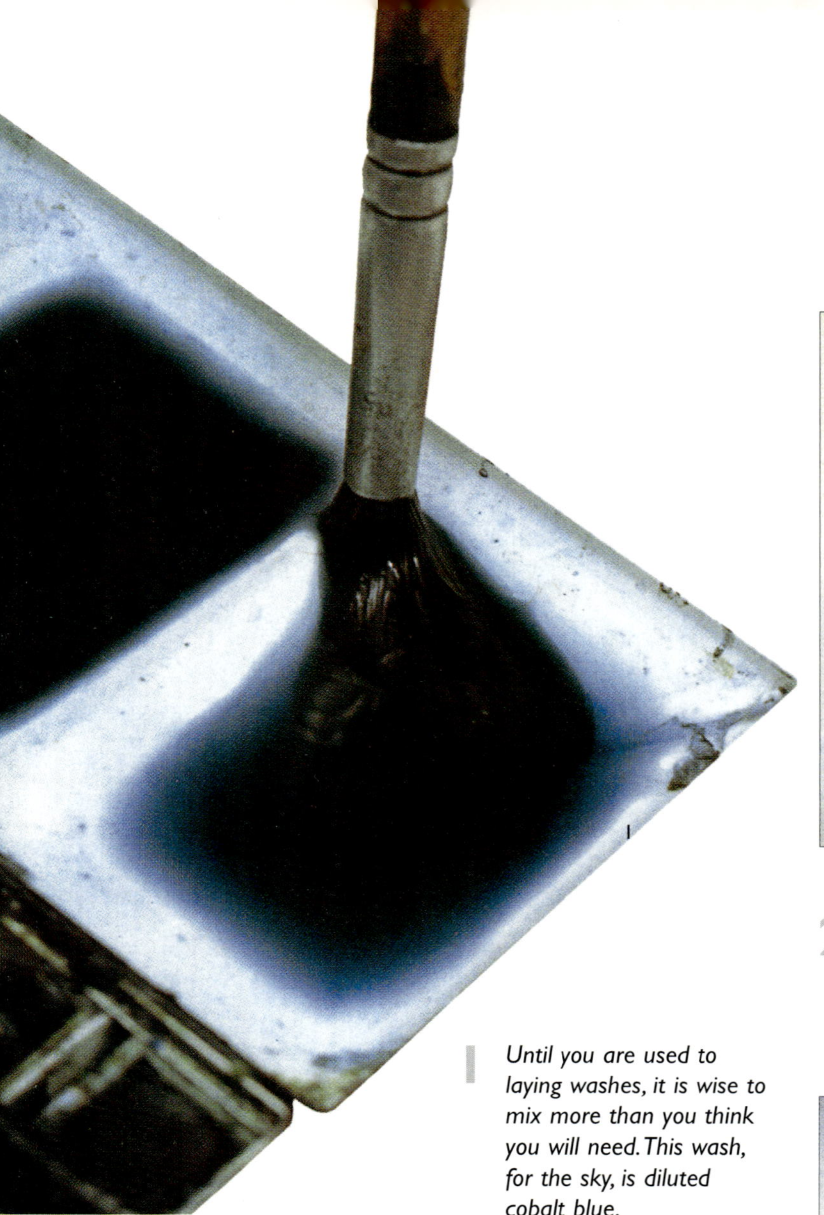

1 Until you are used to laying washes, it is wise to mix more than you think you will need. This wash, for the sky, is diluted cobalt blue.

2 Put on with a No. 10 squirrel brush, the sky was deliberately laid slightly unevenly to suggest a pale blue sky with a light cloud cover. In a landscape painting, clouds are a very important compositional device.

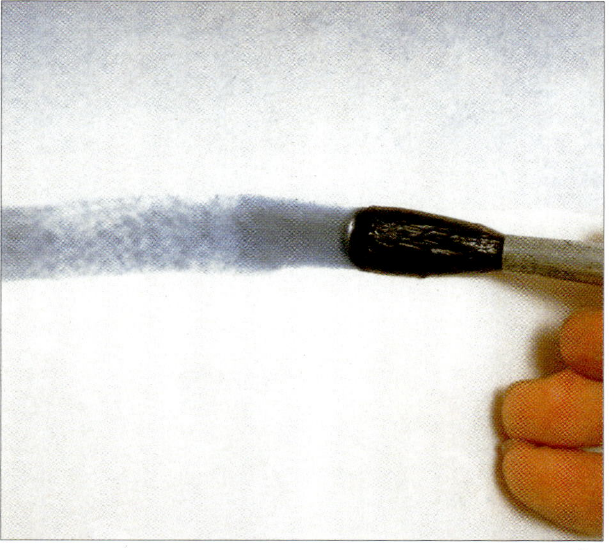

3 When dry, the same squirrel brush was used to put on a darker shade for the sky portion of the painting, with Payne's gray added to the cobalt blue, to the far hills.

seen under the kind of summer squall of rain which causes the sky and hills to merge into one another. Watercolor is an ideal medium for capturing such atmospheric effects, but although the painting looks spontaneous (as the artist intended) it is actually very carefully planned.

The technique could not be more dissimilar to that used in the following example. Here an unusually large selection

4 *The second wash had to be darker than that for the sky but not too dark, as the artist knew that he would have to increase the tonal contrasts in the middle distance to suggest its relative nearness to the picture plane.*

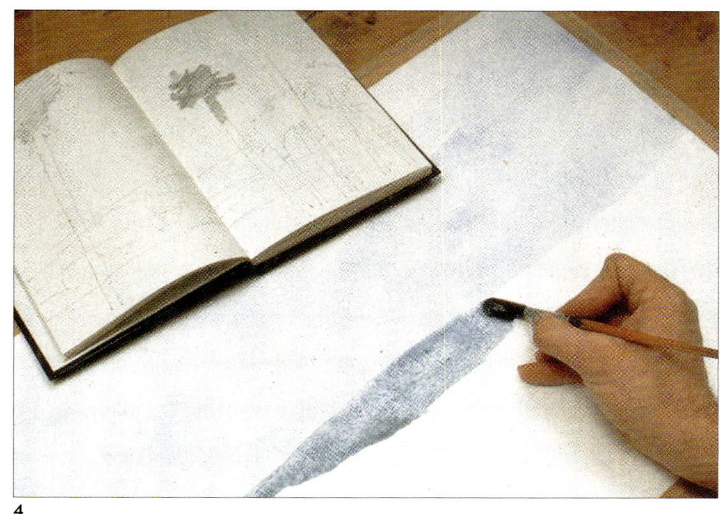

4

5 & 6 *As each wash has to be allowed to dry before putting on the next, in this particular technique, a hairdrier is sometimes used to hasten the process. The third and fourth washes were laid on next, leaving the whole of the foreground and middle distance still untouched.*

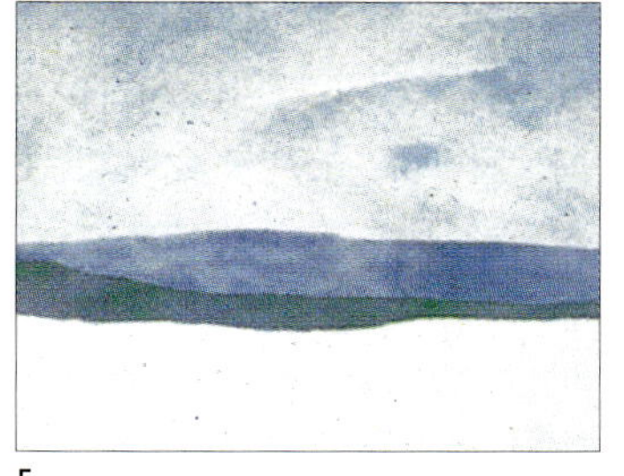

5

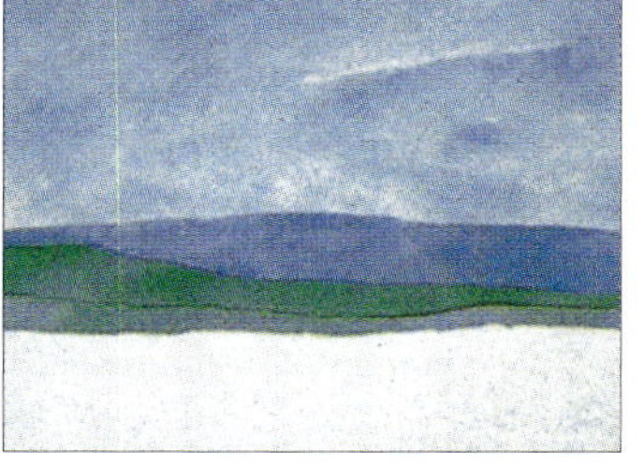

6

7 *The tone of the darker area of the middle distance had to be very carefully calculated to make it appear to be in front of the far hills. This wash has been put on slightly thicker in places to suggest the shapes of the trees.*

7

of colors has been used, and they have been deliberately allowed to mix on the paper to create soft, blurring effects. The natural translucence of watercolor has been exploited to the full to allow the bright colors, such as the greens of the foreground and the patch of sunlight on the hills, to shine out with brilliance and clarity.

Since the time of Turner the effects of light have been among the prime concerns of landscape painters, where the landscape is subject to sudden changes. It is not easy, however, to capture light and atmosphere with brushes and paints, and a painting like this one relies for its success on a deliberate use of certain techniques as well as on fast working—freshness and spontaneity is quickly destroyed if the brush work becomes too labored. Here the brush strokes themselves form an integral part of the painting. There are no totally flat washes anywhere in the painting. Even in the distant hills different tones and colors are visible, but a feeling of space has been rendered by the use of very bright colors and greater tonal contrasts in the foreground.

MATERIALS USED

SUPPORT:
Pre-stretched watercolor paper with an HP surface, measuring 14 x 2l in. (35 x 53 cm).

COLORS:
Cobalt blue, Payne's gray, raw umber, and sap green.

BRUSHES:
A No. 10 squirrel and a No. 4 sable.

ADDITIONAL EQUIPMENT:
A selection of ceramic palettes for mixing the paint; a little gum arabic for mixing with the water.

8

8 *The trees in the foreground were worked on next, the darker paint being taken over the background and sky washes. This device is most successful when the colors are similar; for instance, red-brown tree trunks over bright green middle distance would give a third color, which could provide a jarring element.*

9 & 10 *Both background and foreground were complete, but the area between them was unpainted. Because warm colors tend to advance and cool ones recede, the artist laid a warm greenish wash there to make it come forward toward the picture plane.*

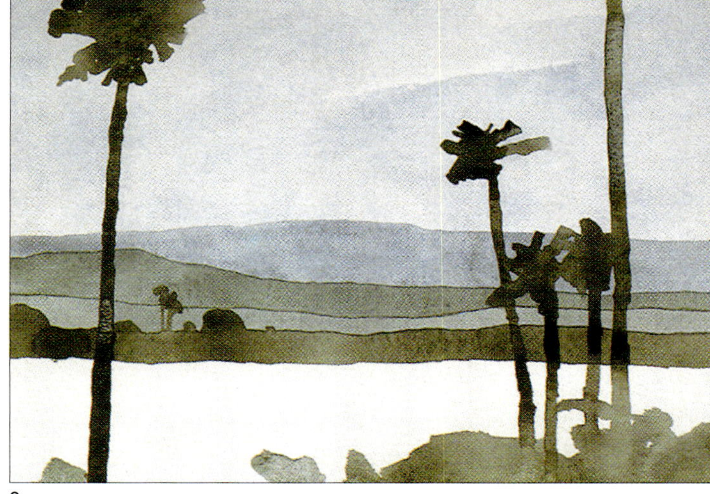

9

10

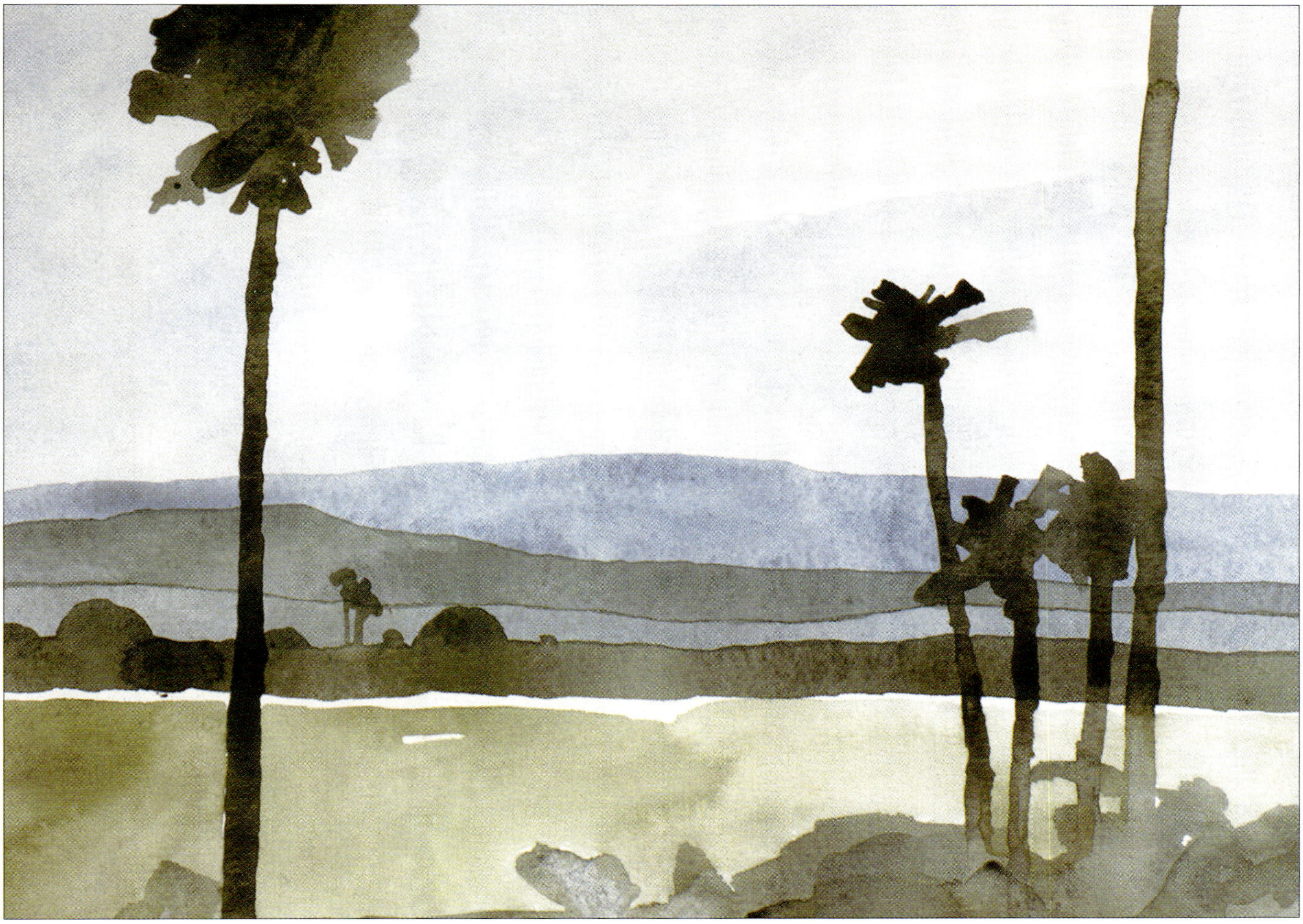

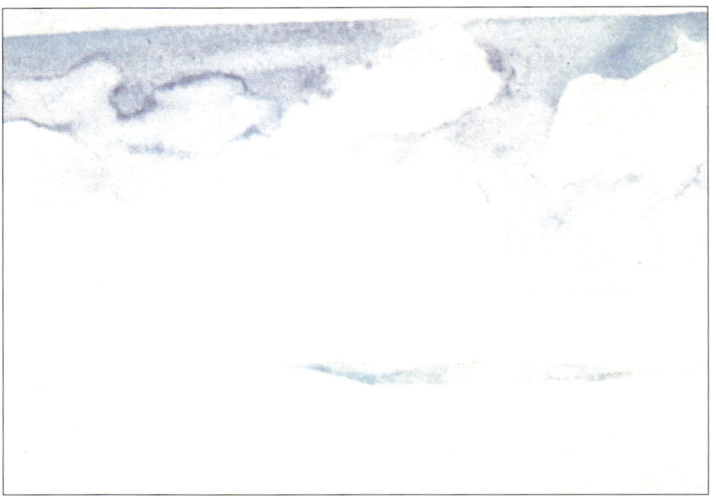

1 *The artist started with some pencil lines to indicate the position of the horizon and the river. He then began to lay wet washes on the sky and distant hills, using the brush to draw the shapes of the clouds.*

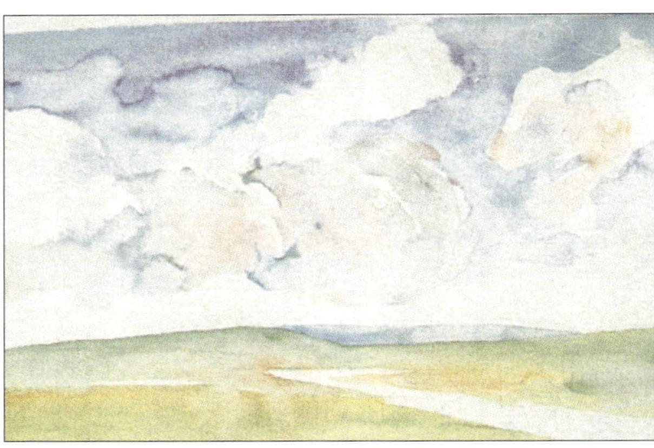

2 *The artist continued to carefully build up wet washes. At this stage, he is taking care to keep the middle ground fairly light, and repeating the warm pink tones on the undersides of the clouds.*

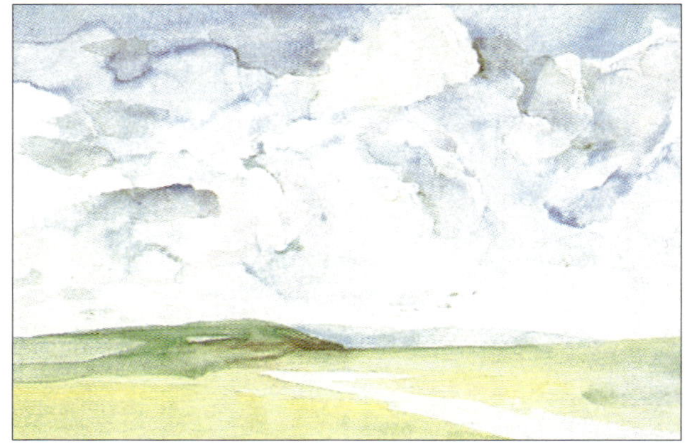

3 *The hills on the left have now been deepened in tone, so that they separate themselves from the more distant hills behind. At the same time, further modeling has been added to the clouds by building up the mid-tones.*

DISTANT HILLS

One of the artist's main concerns was to indicate the spaciousness and recession of the landscape. He used two methods to do this. The first was aerial perspective and the second was to allow the tree on the right to go out of the frame at the top, thus clearly indicating that the group of trees is on the front of the painting.

The painting provides an excellent example of the "classical" approach to watercolor, in which the paint is laid on in a series of thin washes. Each wash, once laid down, has been left without any further paint being laid on top, and the painting was worked from the top downward, with the foreground trees painted over the washes for the sky and hills.

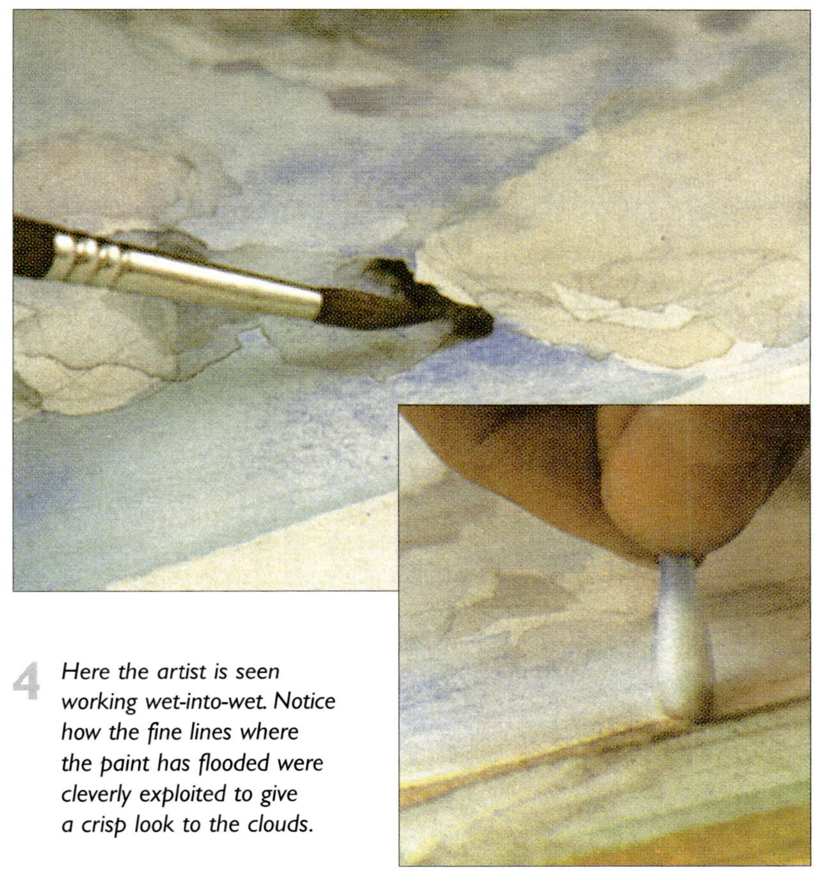

4 *Here the artist is seen working wet-into-wet. Notice how the fine lines where the paint has flooded were cleverly exploited to give a crisp look to the clouds.*

MATERIALS USED

SUPPORT:
Pre-stretched watercolor paper, measuring 10 x 14 in. (25 x 35 cm).

COLORS:
Ultramarine, cobalt blue, olive green, burnt sienna, cadmium yellow, alizarin crimson, and Payne's gray.

BRUSHES & OTHER EQUIPMENT:
Nos. 12, 8, and 4 soft brushes, cotton swabs.

5 *Sponges and cotton swabs can be used to soften edges, as here, or to draw paler shapes into an existing wash.*

6 *Lastly, some definition was added to the foreground and the intensity of the blue above the clouds was darkened.*

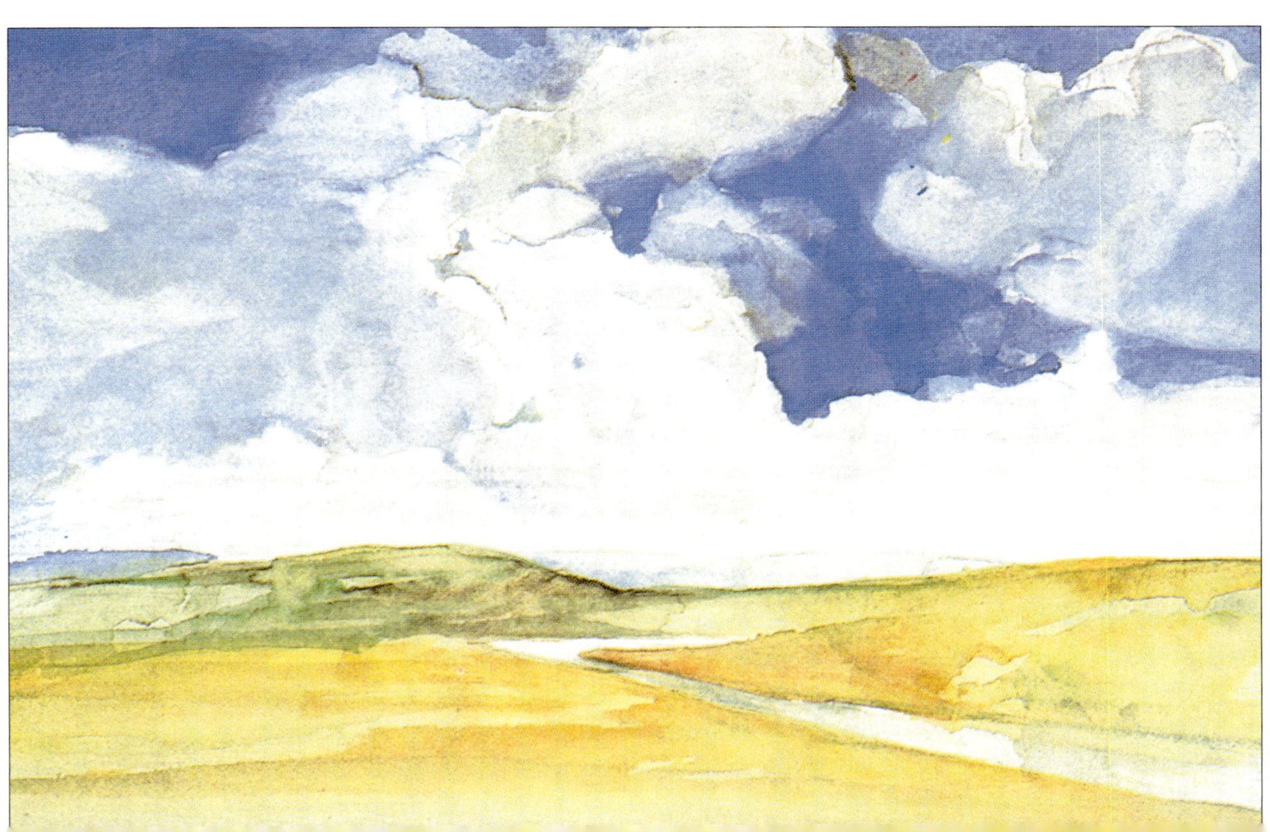

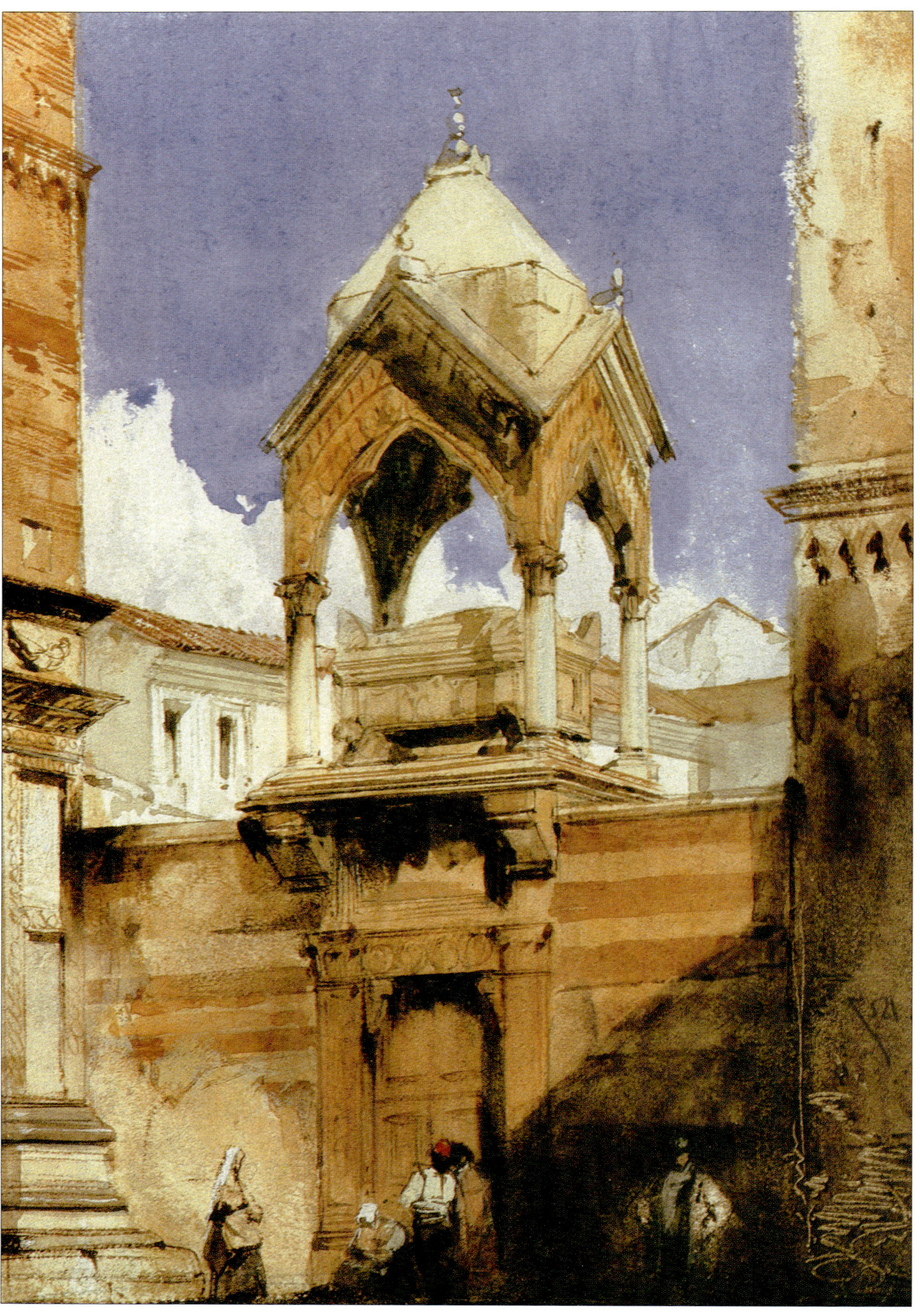

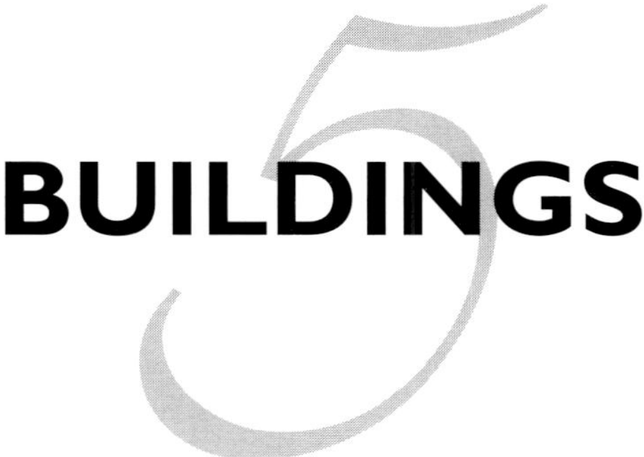

BUILDINGS

Left Bonington's paintings, in both oil and watercolor, were much admired in his lifetime. He died of consumption at the age of 26 without having fully exploited his gift. As a colorist he was superb, and he was a pioneer in the use of watercolor, but it is said of him that he never fully understood perspective. In this painting, Castelbarco Tomb, *the subject is sufficiently simple to disguise any possible weakness.*

Although paintings which take a building or a group of buildings as their subject are usually regarded as a branch of landscape painting, it is more practical to regard architectural painting and drawing as a separate subject. It presents its own problems, not the least of them being the intricacies of perspective. Obviously not all paintings of buildings need to be as accurate and precise as an architect's drawings—this is seldom desirable—but a painting of a house, church, or ruin is similar to a portrait. It is that particular building you want to paint, because you are attracted to its shape, color, or general atmosphere. It is therefore important to get the proportions and perspective right, just as you would the features of a face.

PRACTICAL HINTS

The most important factor is close and careful observation, which leads to a good foundation drawing. Try to work directly from the subject itself wherever possible: photographs, which distort the perspective, are not the ideal source of reference for architectural subjects. The drawing can be done on one day and the actual painting later. A photograph might then be used as a reference for the color only.

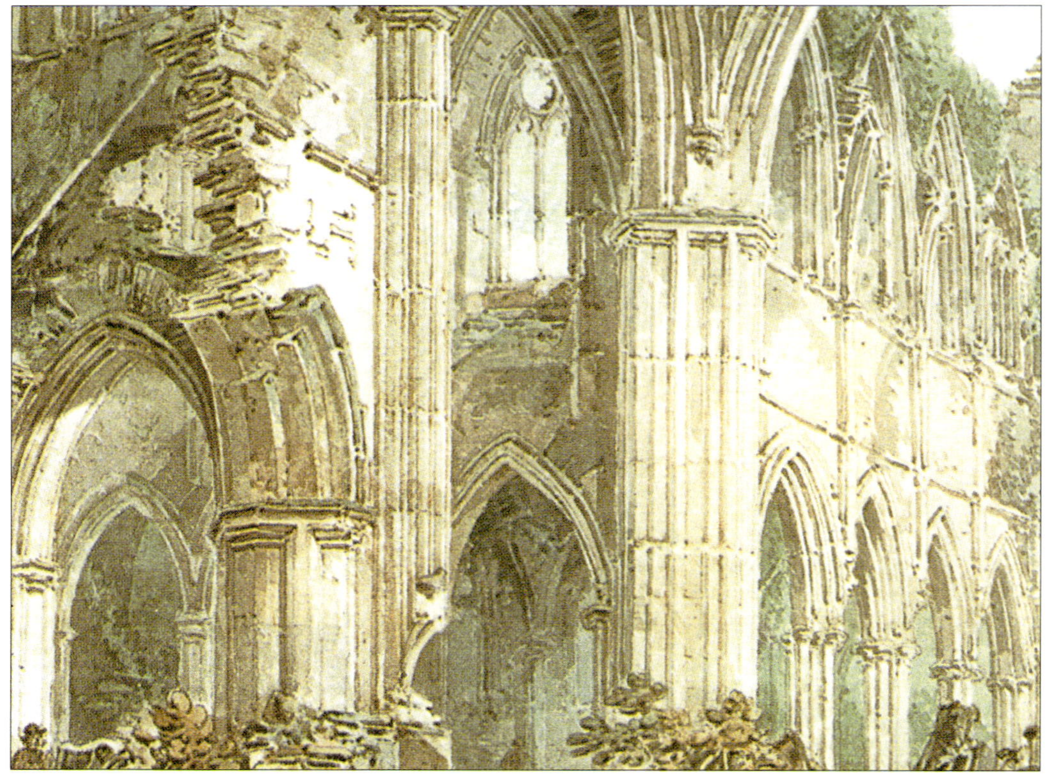

Left *Turner was a master of every kind of painting he turned his hand to, and he could portray the intricate details of a building with the same skill and sensitivity that he brought to atmospheric landscapes. This detail from his* Study of Tintern Abbey *shows a combination of the draftman's precision and the painter's eye for mood, tone, and color.*

Below Seaside Pavillion, *by Moira Clinch, is a good example of an intricately detailed architectural study which retains the freshness of more spontaneous sketches. Light and shade are cleverly handled, the clear, fresh, pale colors of the regular squares of paving stones providing a pleasing contrast to the deeper blues of the sky. On the pavillion itself every minute detail of the position itself has been recorded with faithful accuracy.*

A small ruler is a useful addition to your drawing kit as it can be used to check angles, verticals, and horizontals by holding it up at arm's length and to draw guidelines on the paper.

When the first washes have been laid on, texture can be suggested carefully with a fine brush. The final touches are often added with a pencil or pen and ink to give a more crisp definition, but they must be handled carefully. A heavy, black line can destroy the delicacy of a painting.

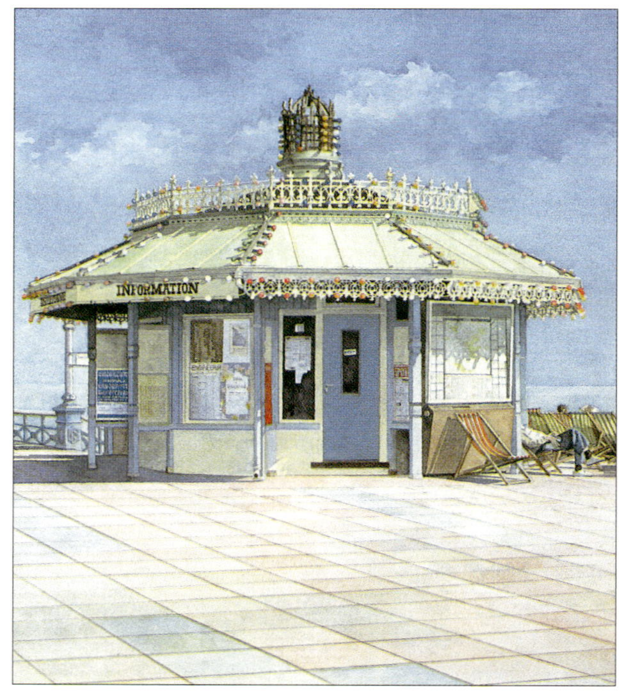

1 *When painting on the spot, making a preliminary sketch is a good way to sort out your ideas before committing yourself to paint. It is absolutely essential to be sure of the most important elements of a landscape. Resist the temptation to put everything in just because it is there.*

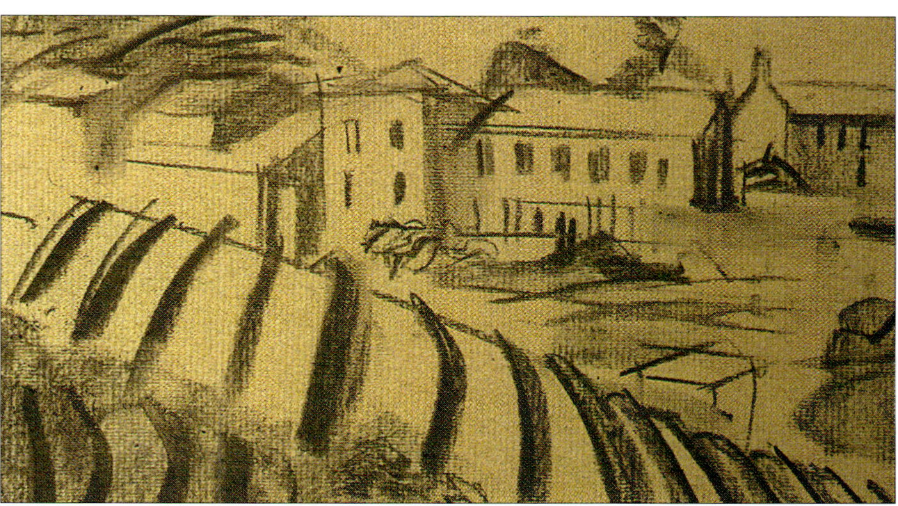

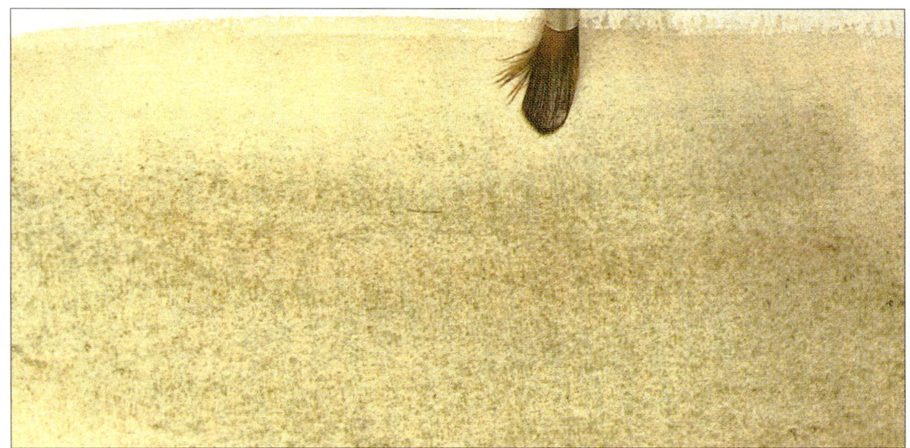

2 *The artist's first step was to lay a neutral wash on the foreground. This was a mixture of raw umber, Prussian blue, and permanent yellow. He then laid a second wash over it, using the same mixture, to create slight tonal differences and texture.*

3 *Having laid broad washes on the rooftops and shadowed sides of the buildings, the artist puts on an area of loosely applied bright green, thus juxtaposing complementary colors and establishing a key for the rest of the painting.*

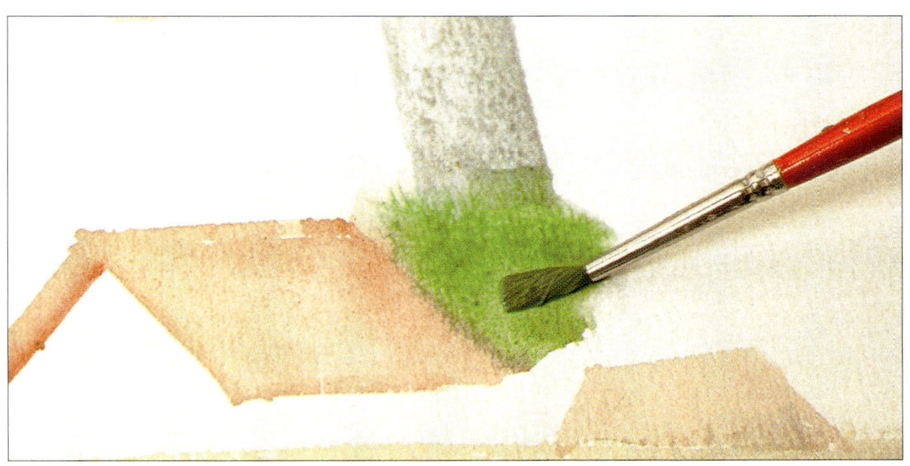

4 & 5 *Here the artist had to lay a wash against a complicated edge, the rooftops. He first wet the paper only in the area to be covered, then worked paint into it, and finally dabbed it with blotting paper to absorb some of the excess paint, lighten the tone, and provide an even texture to the area.*

MATERIALS USED

SUPPORT:
Pre-stretched watercolor paper, with a Not surface measuring 12 x 16 in. (30 x 40 cm).

COLORS:
Raw umber, burnt umber, Payne's gray, terre verte, Hookers green, yellow ocher, permanent yellow, Prussian blue, and cadmium red.

BRUSHES:
Nos. 4 and 11 sable.

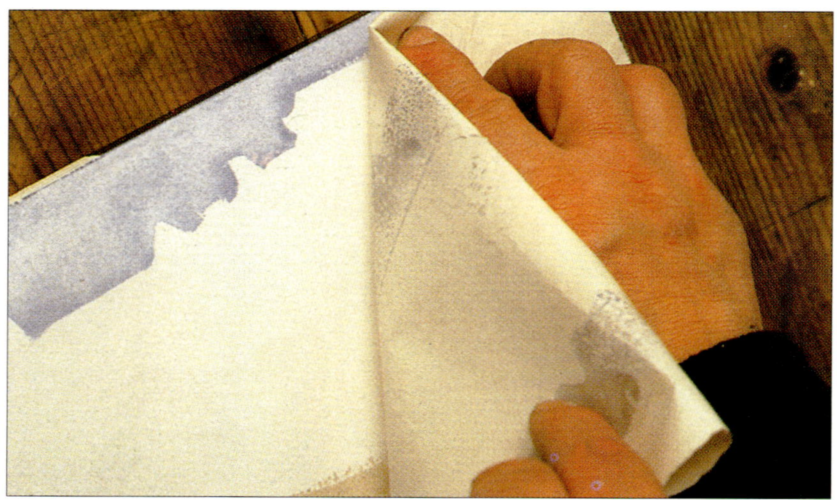

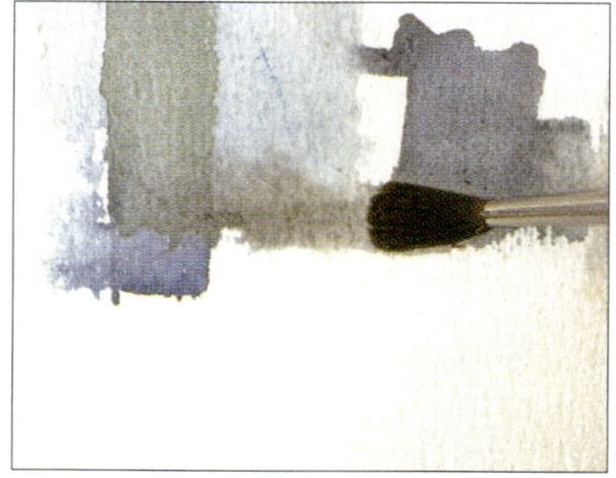

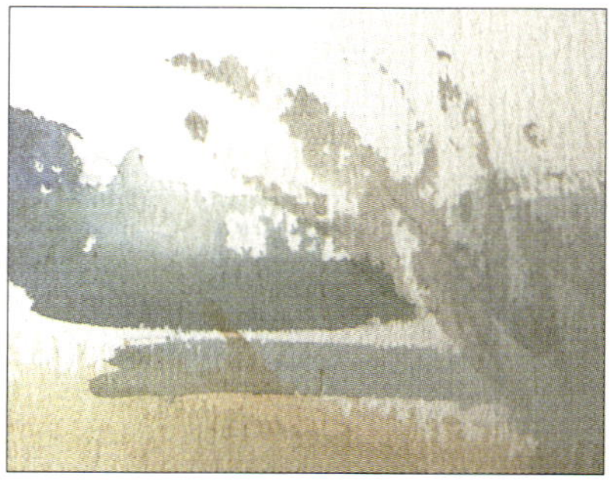

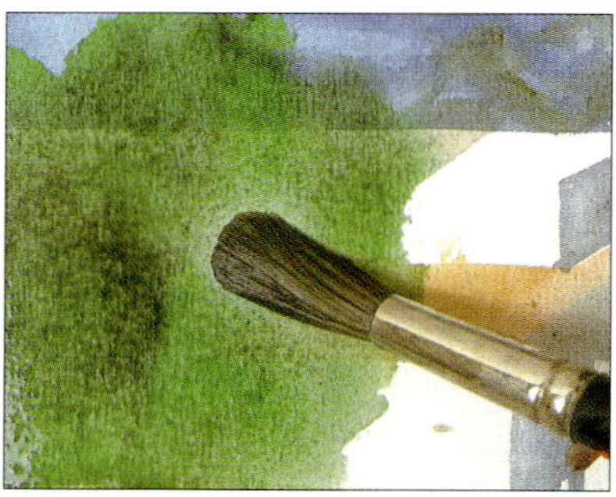

6 *The artist is defining the shadows on the unlit sides of the buildings, allowing the paint to mix in order to produce a soft effect.*

7 *He uses a combination of Prussian blue and Payne's gray to achieve relatively strong tonal contrasts.*

8 *A large soft brush is used to apply dark green over the light red of the roofs and the blue of the sky, so that the colors blend.*

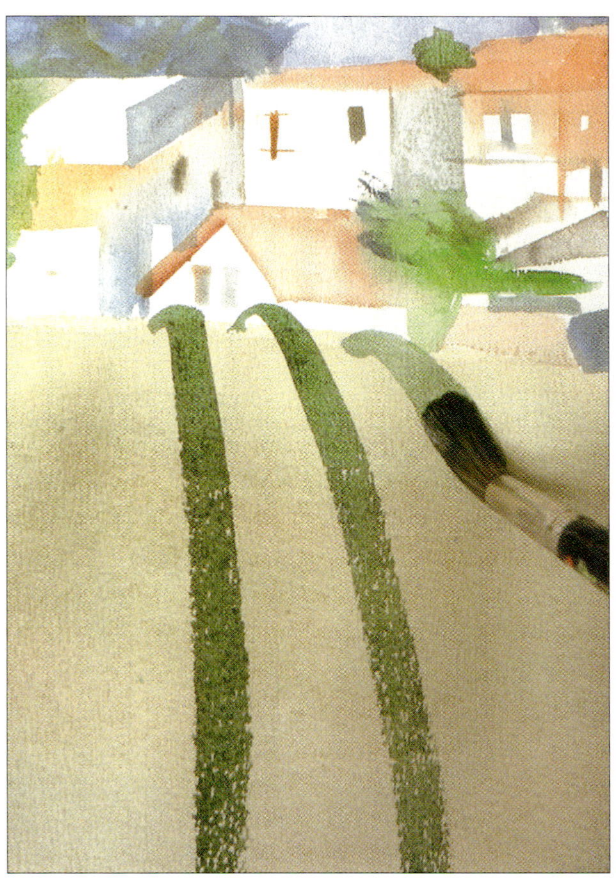

9 *The lines of the veins are laid on with bold brush strokes and darkened in places to hint at shadow, without describing it in detail. Strong tonal contrasts help to bring the foreground forward toward the picture plane.*

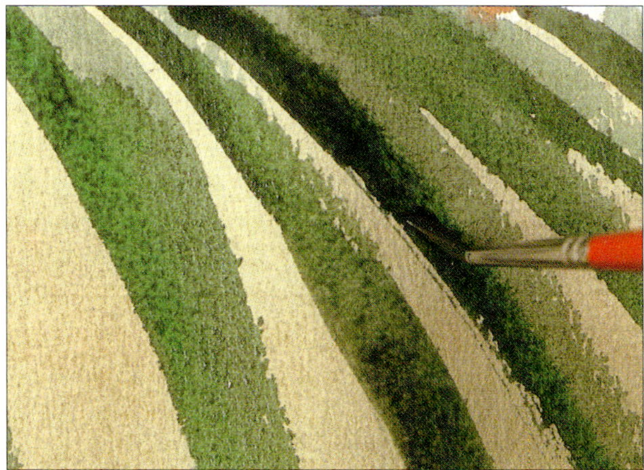

10 *The rows of vines are reinforced with terre verte and Payne's gray. Shadows are not merely darker shades of the same color, but have their own colors.*

VINEYARD IN ITALY

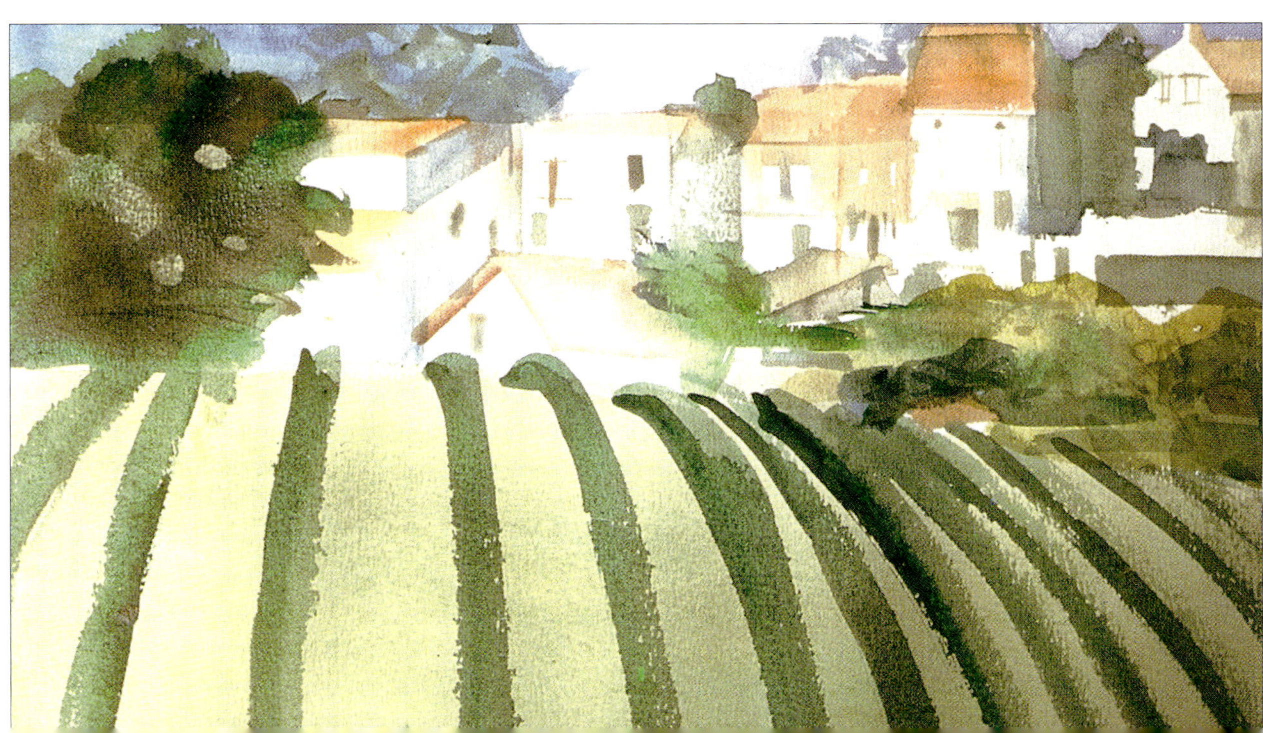

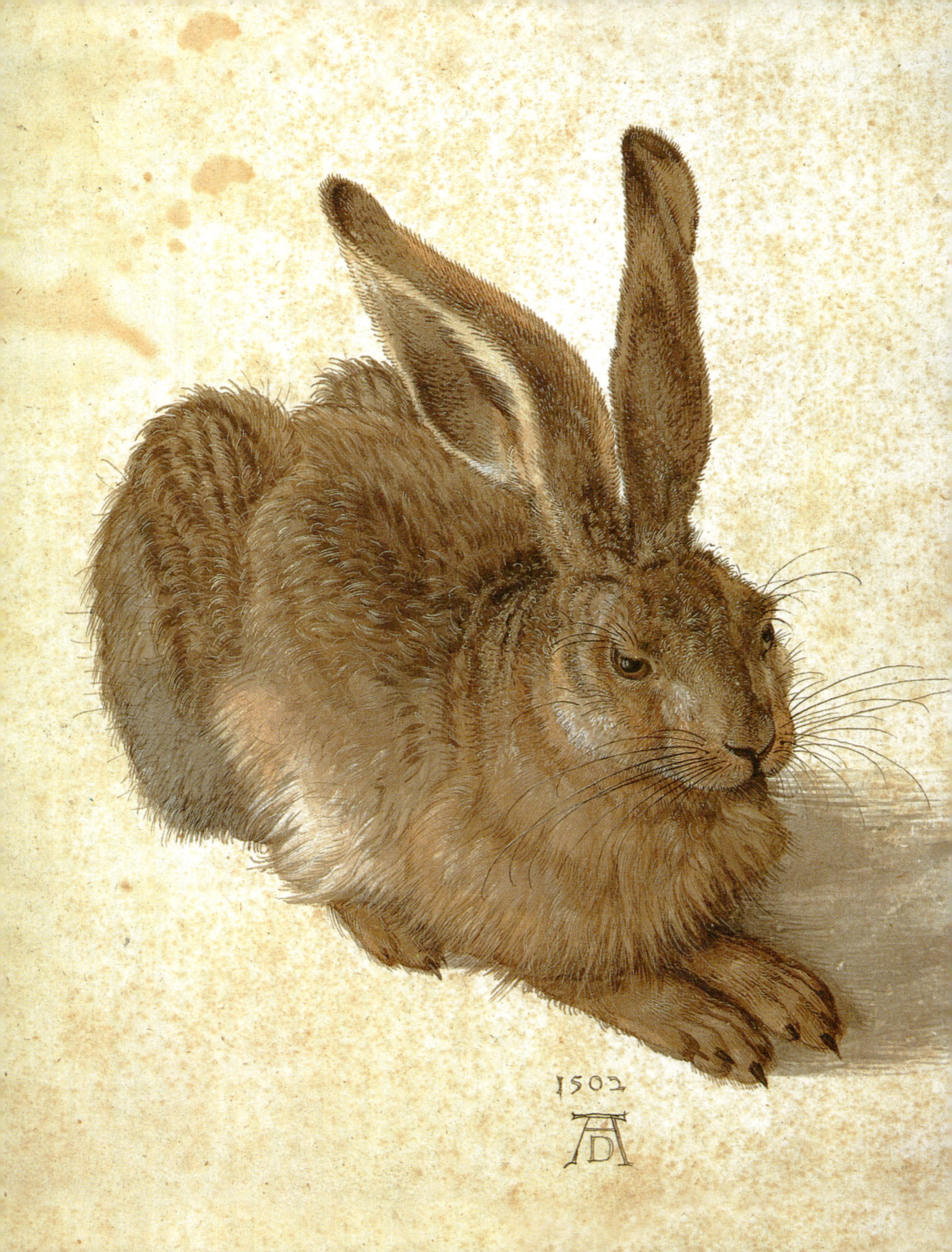
1502

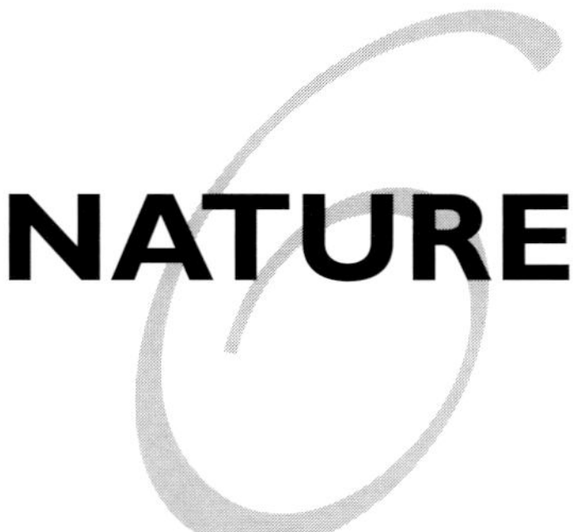

NATURE

Left Durer's accurate and precise drawings and watercolors of plants and animals are possibly the best examples of natural-history painting. The Young Hare was probably begun with broad washes of transparent paint to establish the main form. The fine details were then built up with tiny brush strokes of opaque paint; every hair and whisker has been precisely described, but the hare is still quite evidently a living, breathing creature.

From the 16th century onward watercolor became a favored medium for botanical illustration, which, with the great upsurge of interest in describing and cataloguing plants and flowers, was very much in demand. Just as it did for architecture, the medium proved ideal for the detailed and delicate work demanded by such subjects.

NATURAL HISTORY PAINTING

In the early years of the 16th century Durer pioneered the use of watercolor with body color for botanical subjects, and such works as *The Great Piece of Turf* and *Young Hare*, faithful renderings of nature, laid the basis for a tradition of botanical and natural history painting which has continued down to the present day.

In the 18th and 19th centuries the majority of natural-history painters and illustrators made their initial watercolors as bases for engravings. Some, notably the famous French flower painter Pierre-Joseph Redoute mastered the art of engraving themselves, the techniques of which in turn influenced styles of painting. In America natural-history painting in watercolor reached new heights with the marvelous bird paintings of John lames Audubon, paintings which became familiar to a wide public through the hand-colored

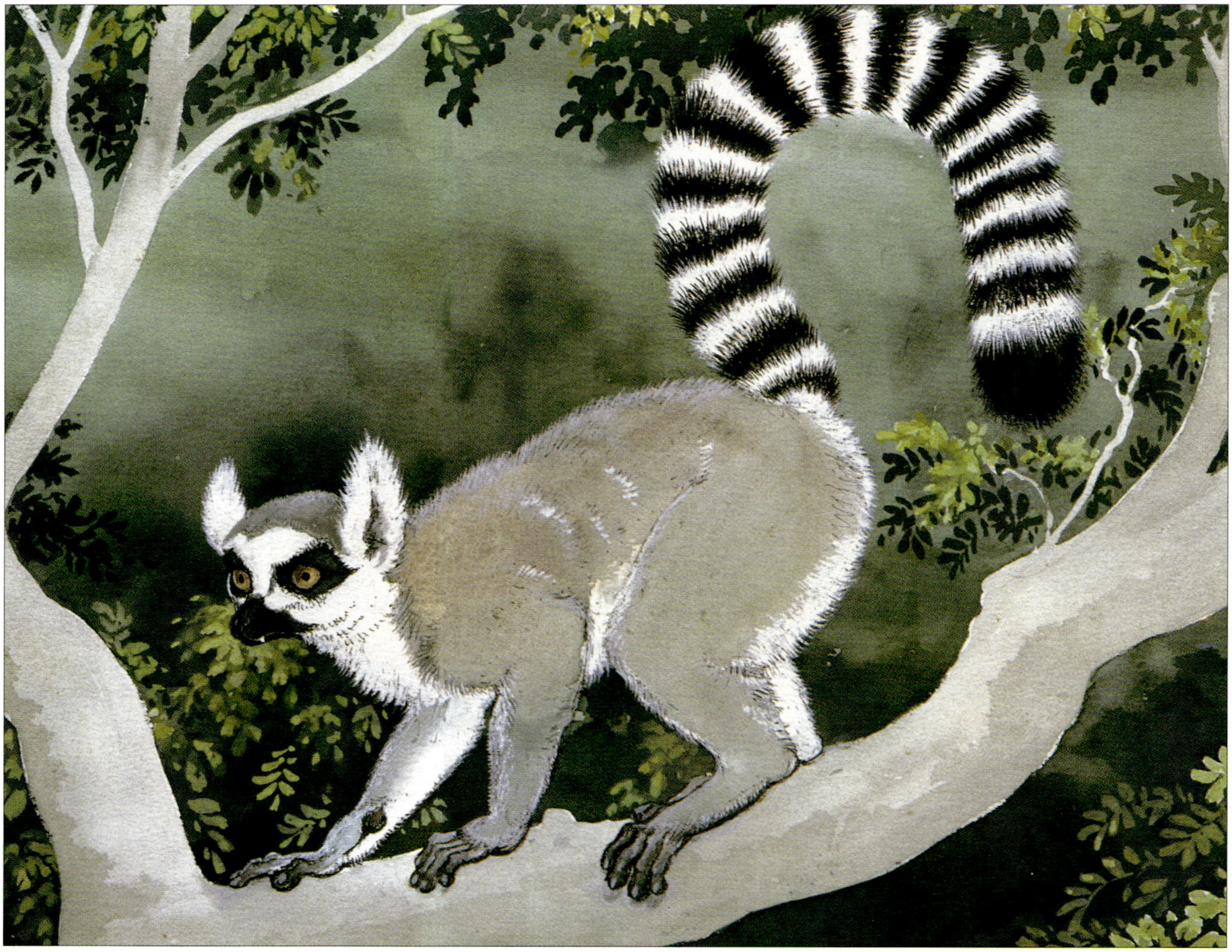

Above Ring-Tailed Lemur, *by Sally Michel, has something of the quality of Durer's work. She works in watercolor and pastel, and always from life, though she takes the occasional polaroid for reference.*

Right *This study of waterlillies, by Marc Winer, was painted on the spot, with much use of the wet-into-wet technique. The artist allowed some colors to run into one another in a semi-random way, sometimes creating more gentle transitions, an effective way to suggest the soft wetness of the leaves and flowers floating in water.*

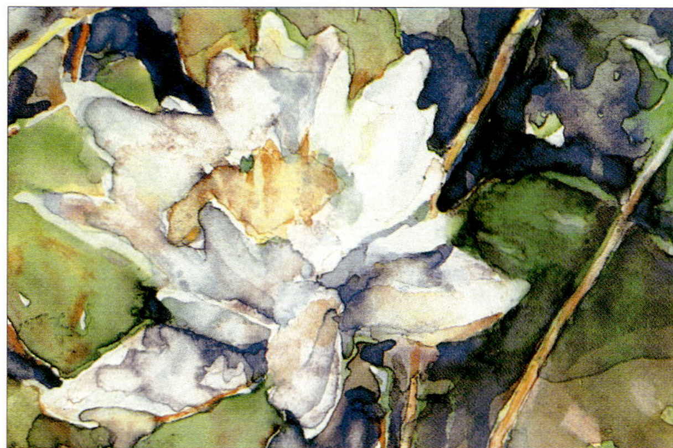

engravings done from them. These works, although they are in the illustrative tradition of accurate observation, are now regarded as art rather than illustration and change hands at staggering prices.

Watercolor is still much used for precise botanical and natural-history illustration, but it has also come into its own as a medium for depicting nature in a more painterly way, either in its natural environment or as still life.

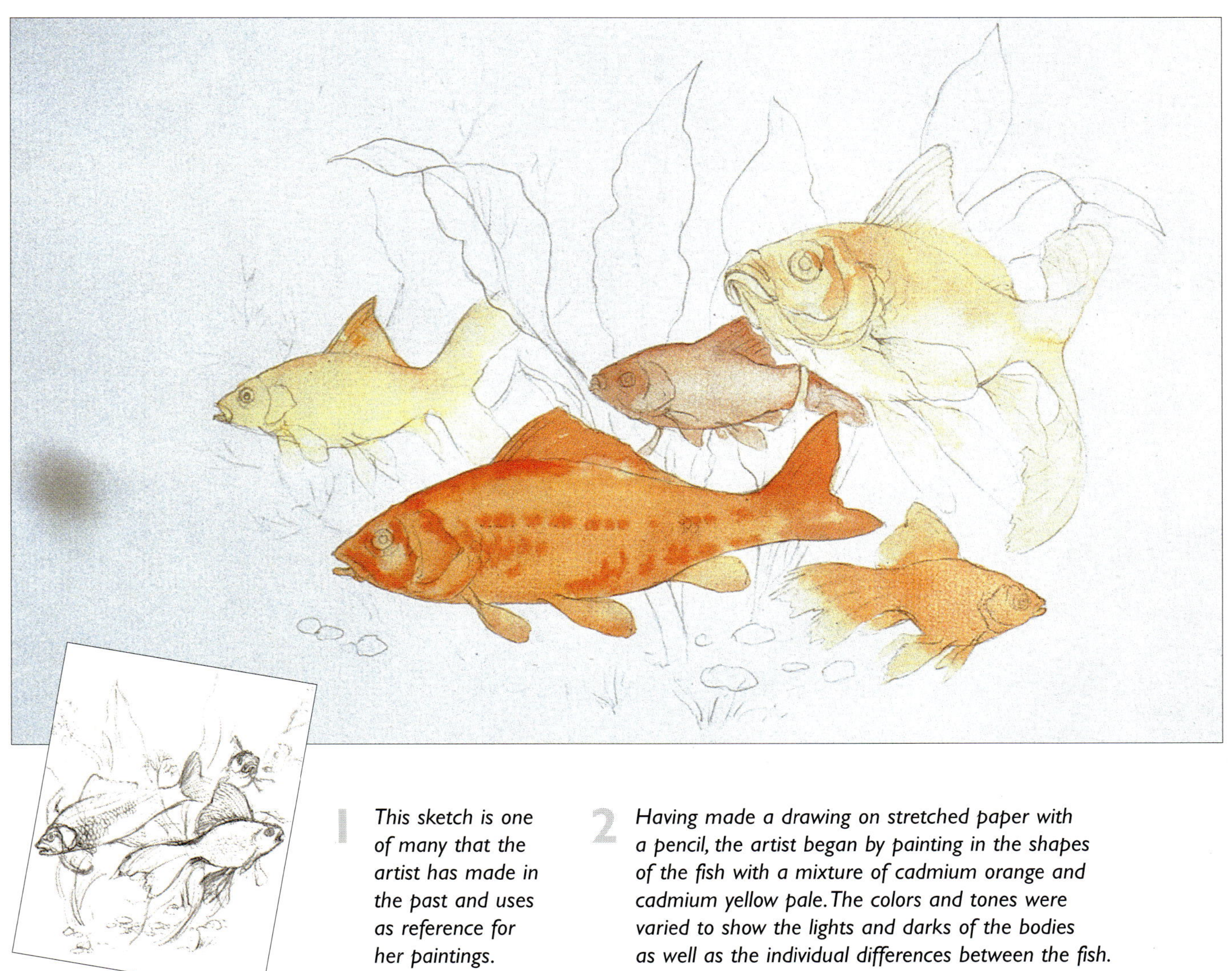

1 *This sketch is one of many that the artist has made in the past and uses as reference for her paintings.*

2 *Having made a drawing on stretched paper with a pencil, the artist began by painting in the shapes of the fish with a mixture of cadmium orange and cadmium yellow pale. The colors and tones were varied to show the lights and darks of the bodies as well as the individual differences between the fish.*

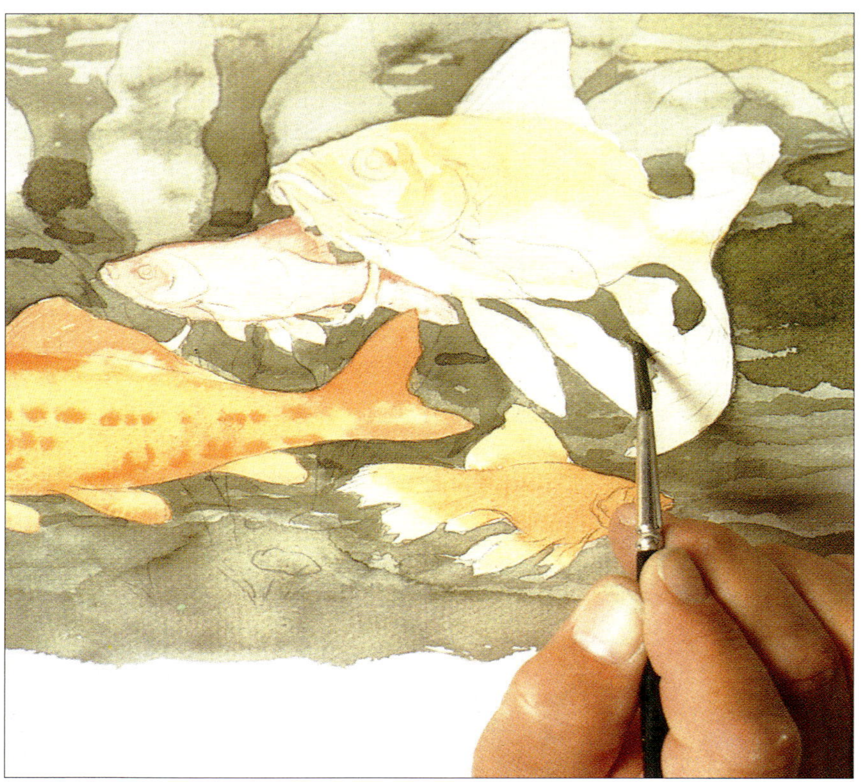

3 *The background color was a mixture of black and lemon yellow, which gives a warmer color than blue and yellow. When laying the wash the artist took special care to work precisely and accurately between and around the fins and bodies in order to preserve the clean, crisp lines that are such a vital feature of the painting.*

4 *When the background has been laid in with deliberately uneven washes to suggest ripples, the painting was allowed to dry. Further layers of color were then added, so that the water became darker around the fish and lighter at the top, where the proportion of yellow to black was increased.*

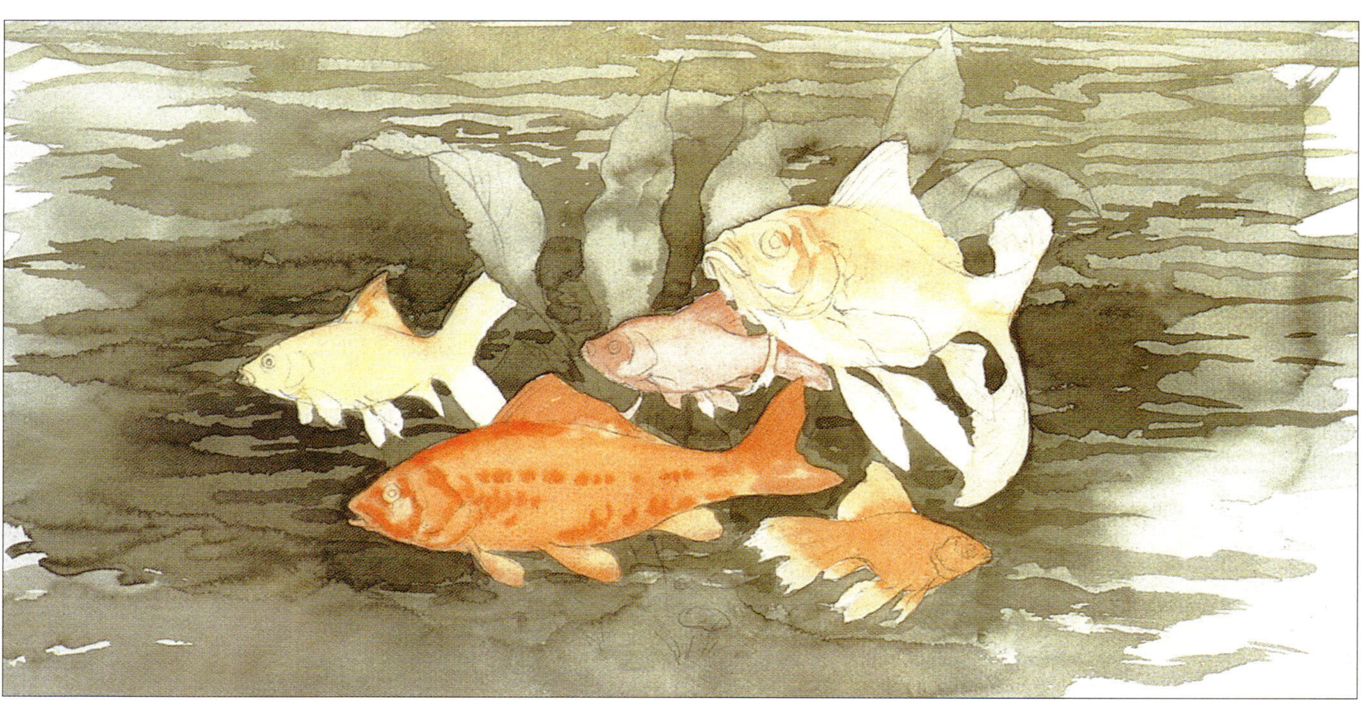

5 *The artist paints the leaves with a fine brush in a very strong lemon yellow, barely diluted. This covers the original pale wash and is slightly modified by it.*

6 *A very fine sable brush is used to paint the delicate details of the scales, and touches of white were added. When doing detailed work, make sure the area below is quite dry or you may smudge the painting.*

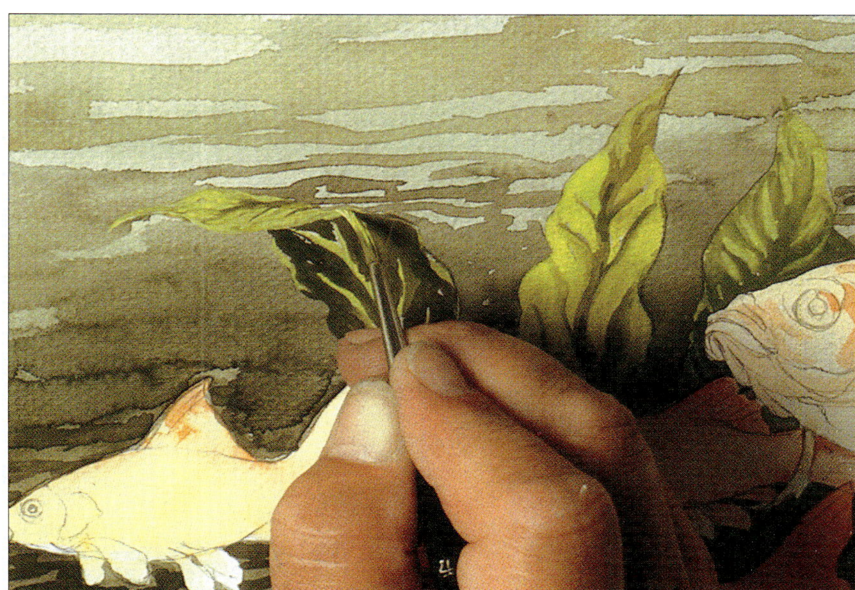

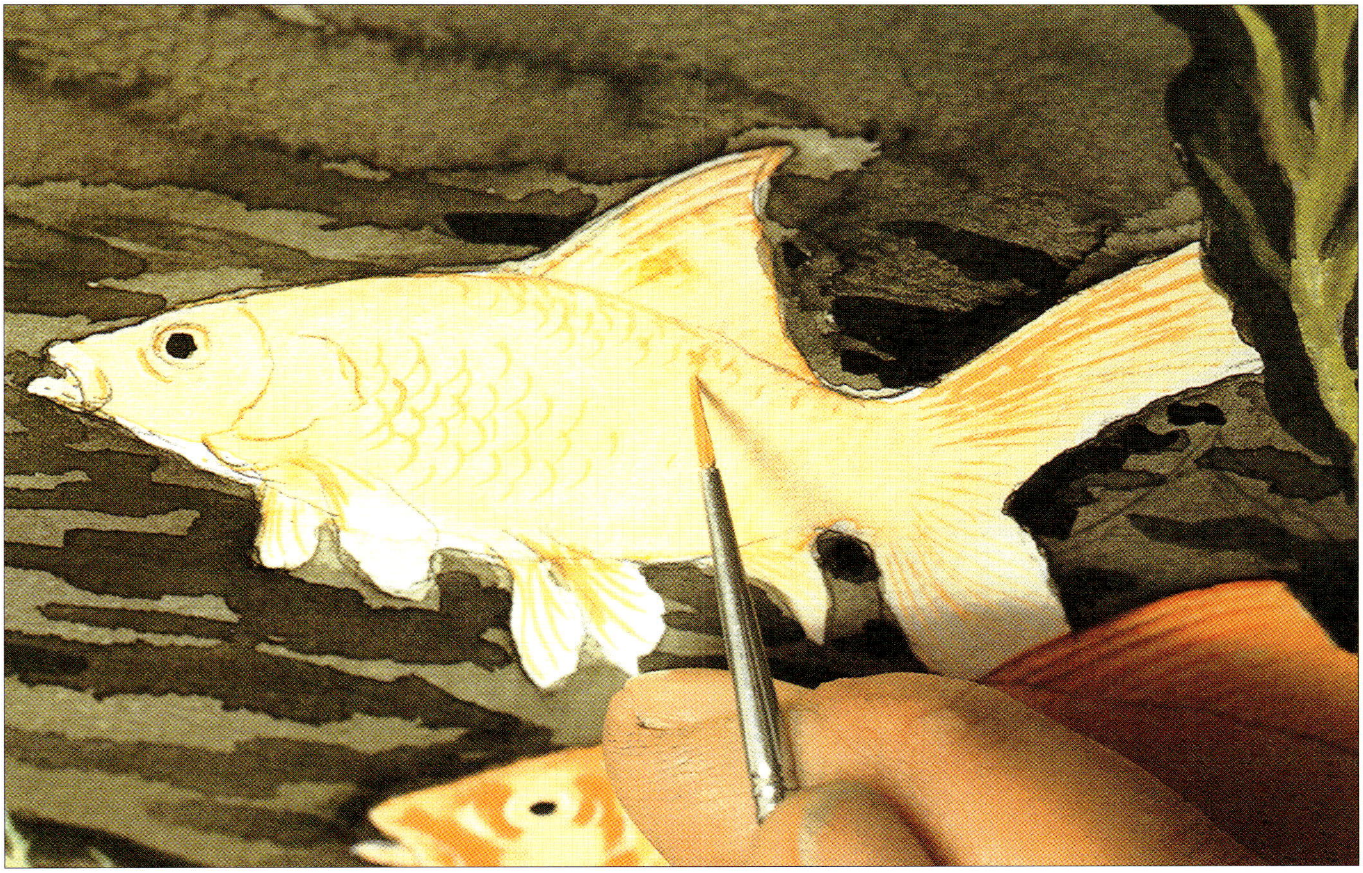

TROPICAL FISH

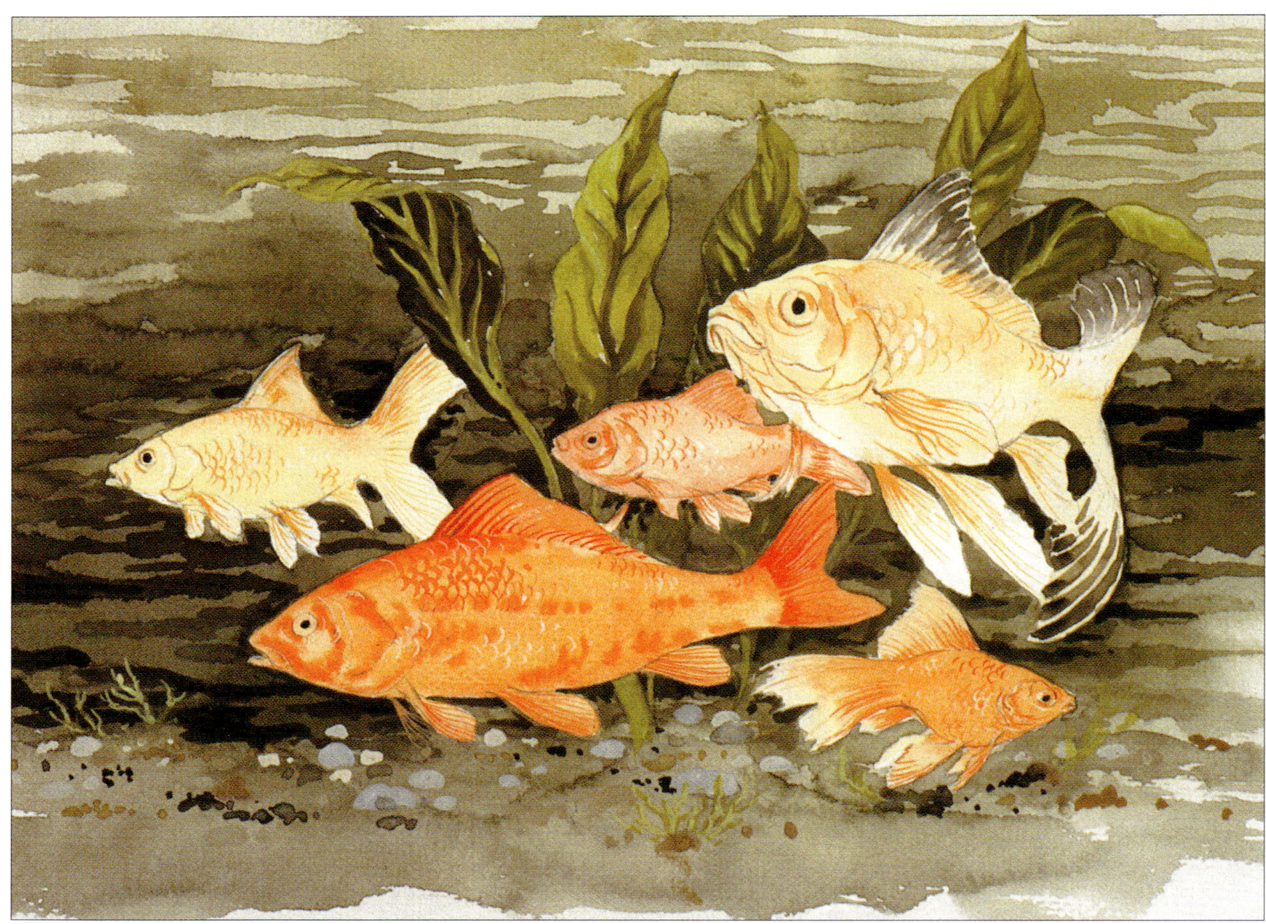

7 *Final touches deepen and enrich the colors of the fins and tails and give definition to the foreground, hitherto left as an area of water. Opaque Chinese white is mixed with the watercolor to produce grays and ochers, which are then used to pick out the pebbles. Opaque paint should be used sparingly and only in the final stages.*

MATERIALS USED

SUPPORT:
Pre-stretched watercolor paper with a Not surface, measuring 14 x 20 in. (35 x 50 cm).

COLORS:
Cadmium red, cadmium orange, cadmium yellow pale, lemon yellow, yellow ocher, sap green, Payne's gray, and black, plus a little Chinese white.

BRUSHES:
Nos. 7, 5, 3, and 00 sable.

PRACTICAL HINTS

Flowers and plants always make attractive subjects and present no particular problems other than the usual one of getting the drawing right. However, many people frequently buy a bunch of flowers and paint them at home. There is nothing at all wrong with the still-life approach, but plants or flowers do tend to look more at home in their natural setting.

Animals and birds present much graver problems; they simply will not sit still. For most professional wild-life artists, birds or animals are a life-long passion, and they have often made a long study of their chosen subject from books and museums before beginning to sketch and observe from nature.

A family pet, however, can often be prevailed upon to stay in one place for long enough to be sketched—especially if it has just had a good meal—and photographs can sometimes be used in combination with sketches as the basis for a painting. Animals and birds must be observed both in movement and in repose. You may think you know exactly what your dog or cat looks like, but if you try to draw it from memory you will soon realize the limits of your knowledge.

TROPICAL FISH

It can be difficult to find natural-history subjects that remain still for long enough to be observed and studied by the artist, but fish in a tank almost beg to be looked at and admired, and although they are always on the move, at least they do not move very far. This painting was done from a series of drawings and from past observations of the structure and colors of the fish. It makes use of both the wet-into-wet technique, in which new color is applied to a wash before it is dry, and the wet-into-dry technique, in which wet washes are laid over dry ones so that they overlap in places. The hard and soft edges formed in this way create the illusion of rippling water, a very important element in the painting. The background washes had to be applied extremely carefully so that they did not spoil the crisp edges of the fishes' bodies and fins. A careful drawing was made before any paint was put on.

Although people often think of watercolors as pale and delicate, the colors can be made as vivid as you like, simply by being less diluted.

FIELD OF DAISIES

A painting like this one presents a technical problem that is not easy to overcome by traditional methods. Since watercolor must

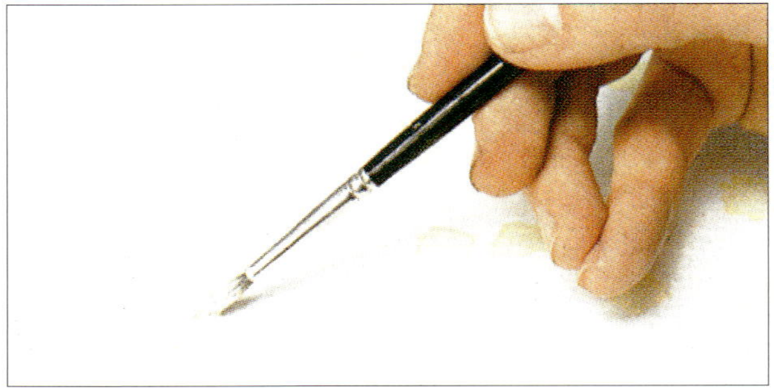

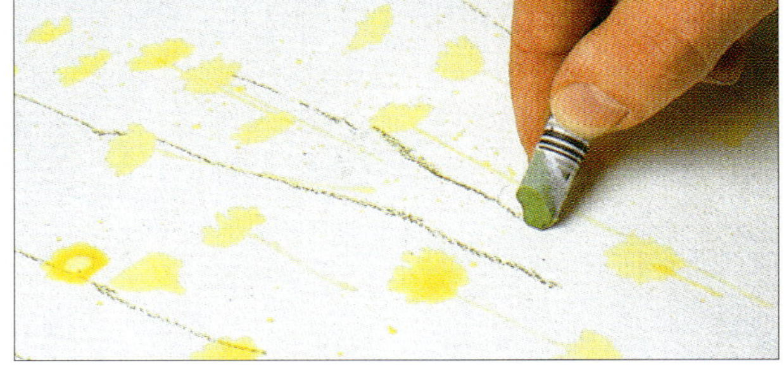

1 *Without making a drawing on support, the artist began by picking out the flower heads with masking fluid. Since this takes some time to dry, it is best if you do this in the very early stages.*

2 *Here the artist is using oil pastel to draw the stems, keeping the strokes as free as possible. When the washes are applied, the paint will slide off the pastel, leaving the stems as clear lines.*

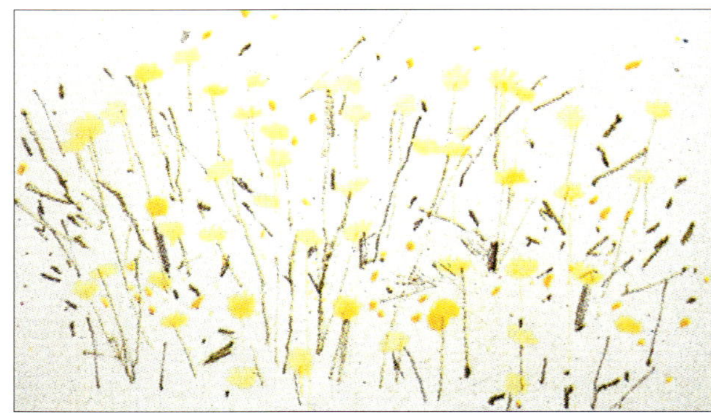

3 *Before any paint was put on, the artist had already established the overall pattern of the painting with masking fluid and with lines and dots of oil pastel.*

4 *Next, the whole picture area was covered with a wash of sap green and yellow, deliberately applied loosely. The brush strokes were used to suggest a windy day.*

always be worked dark over light, white or pale shades are created by painting around them. Here the white shapes are intricate, and if the artist had attempted to lay washes around them, the painting would have been tired-looking. He has solved this problem by using masking fluid for the heads of the flowers, laying washes of varying intensities on top and then removing the fluid to reveal the white paper.

It is difficult to draw really fine lines with it, however, as it is viscous. The artist has, therefore, used oil pastel to draw the stems. This works as a resist medium in the same way as masking fluid; the oil repels the water, creating clear lines and interesting

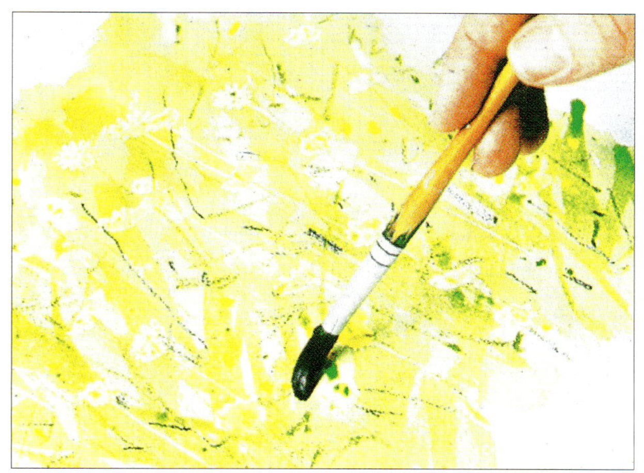

textures. Although some artists believe it is a medium only for graphic artists, masking fluid is a useful device.

TEXTURING

The green wash is enlivened by the strong brush strokes. This is purely a textural effect. The color, therefore, is exactly same as the first. It is applied to give the painting a certain fineness of look by suggesting the texture of the subject.

5 *Once the first wash was laid, the artist began to strengthen the color in places with a dark mixture of chrome green and black. A slight sheen was given to the paint by mixing it with gum water.*

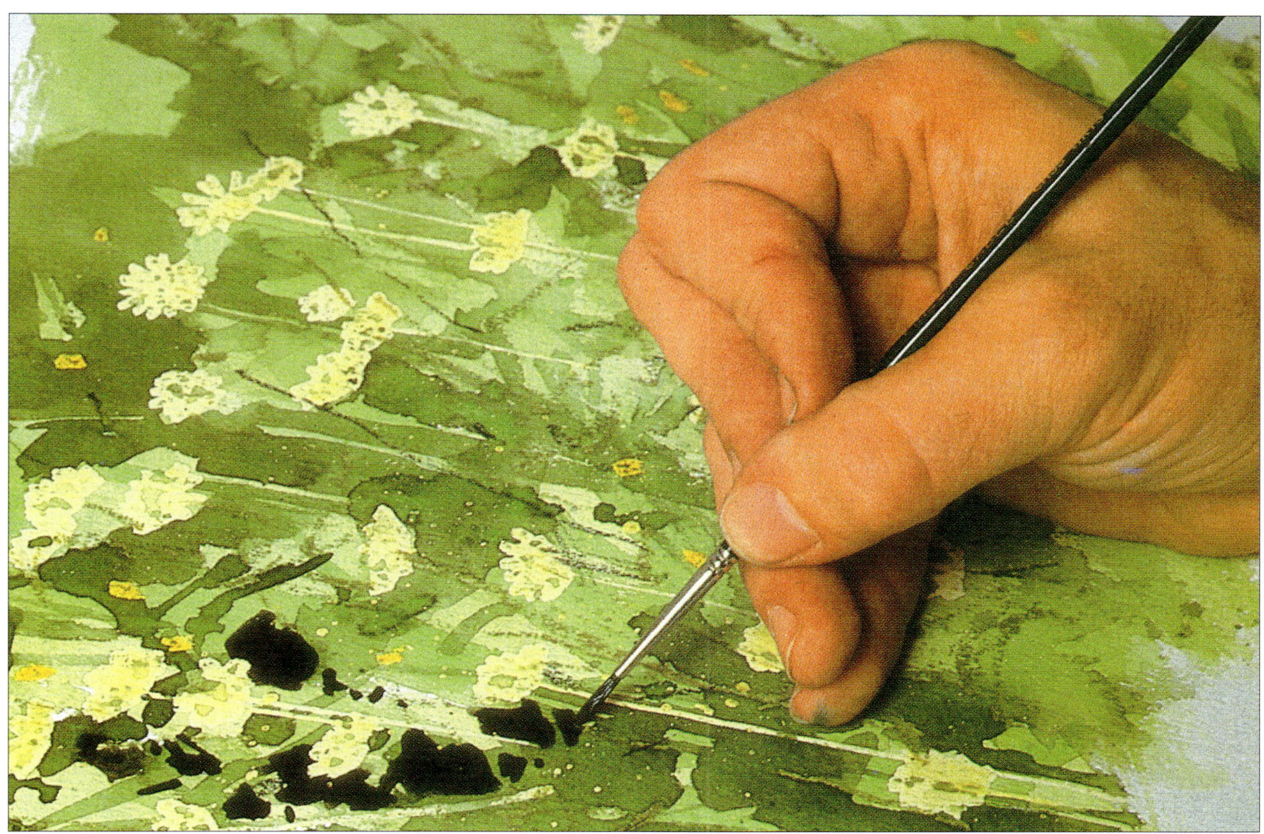

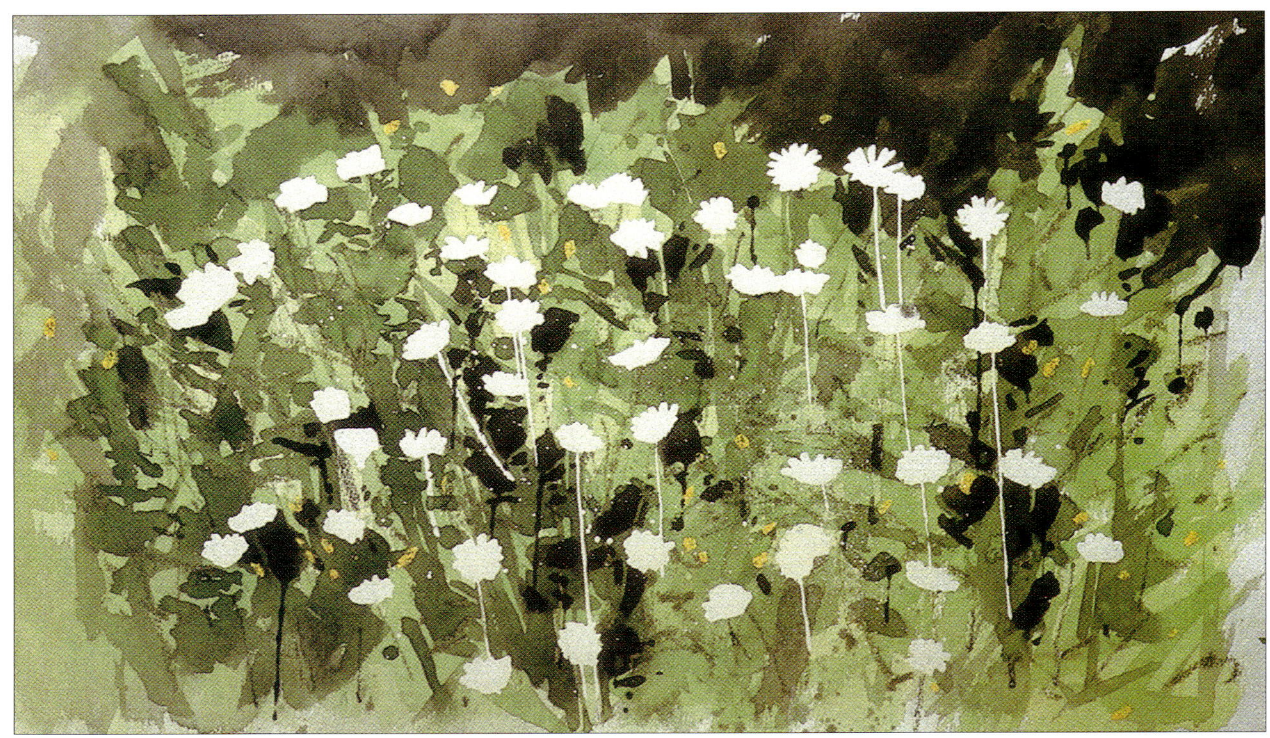

REMOVING MASKING FLUID

6 *The deepest shadows in the foreground have now been painted and the background has been darkened. The darker green areas were carefully drawn with a fine brush. This is the stage when more accurate definition can be put into the painting.*

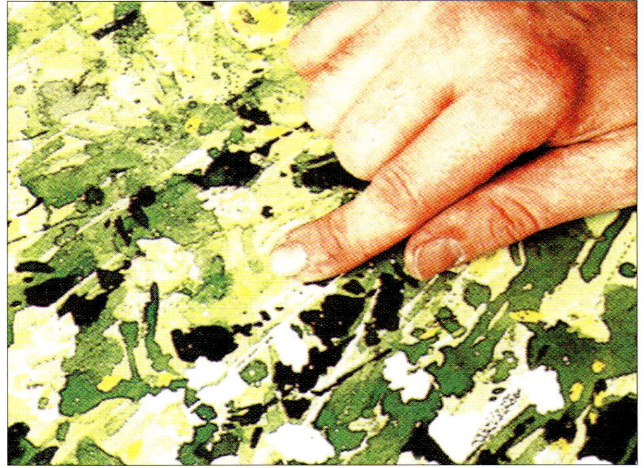

Above: *Before removing masking fluid by gently rubbing with the finger, make sure that the paint is quite dry and that no further alterations or additions are needed.*

MATERIALS USED

SUPPORT:
Arches watercolor paper with a Not surface, measuring 12 x 18 in. (30 x 45 cm).

COLORS:
Watercolors in sap green, chrome green, cadmium yellow, and black; oil pastels in olive green and yellow.

BRUSHES & OTHER EQUIPMENT:
Nos. 6 and 4 sable brushes, a small household brush for spattering, gum water, and masking fluid.

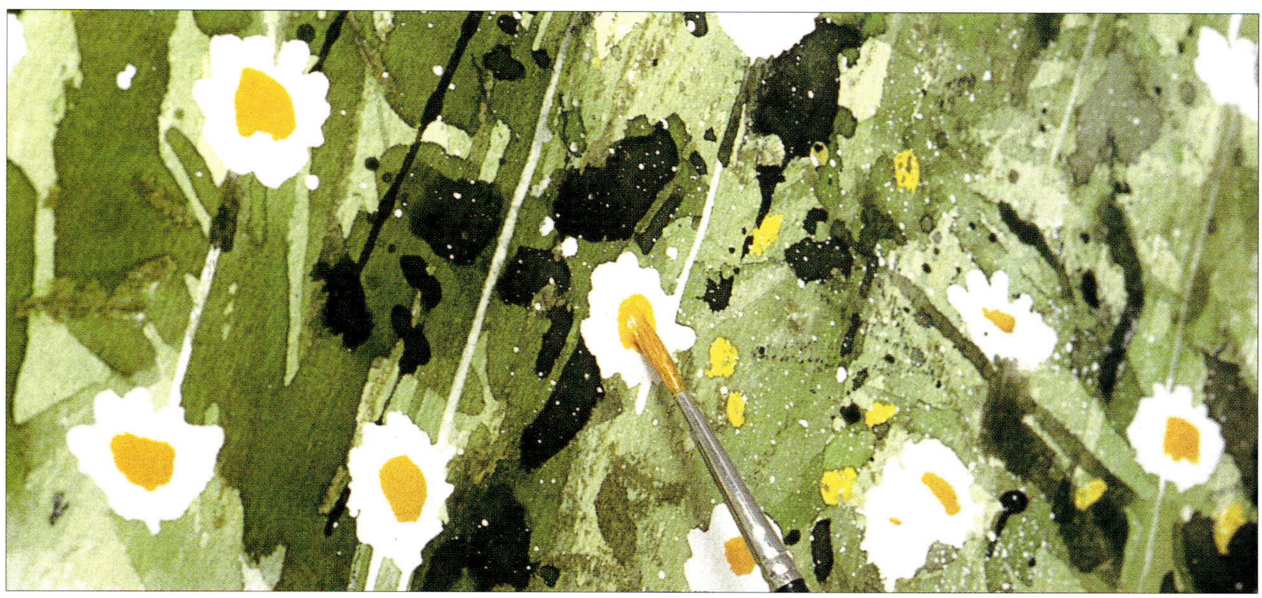

7 *The final touch was to paint in the flower centers with cadmium yellow.*

FIELD OF DAISIES

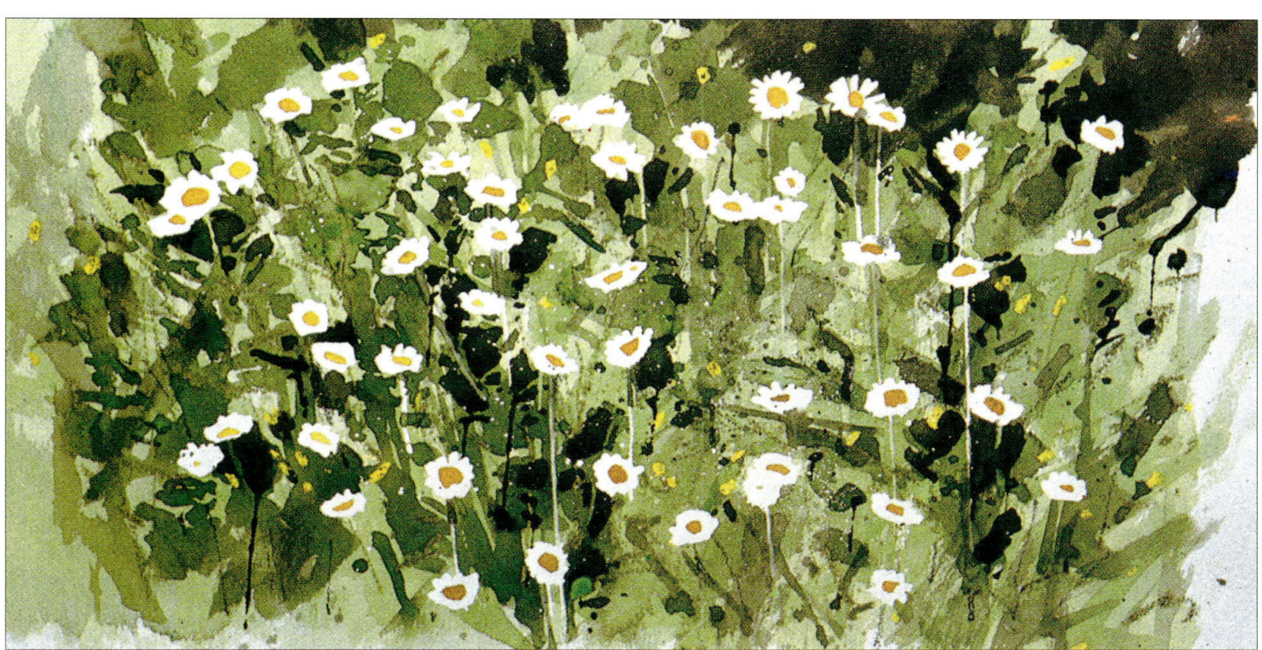

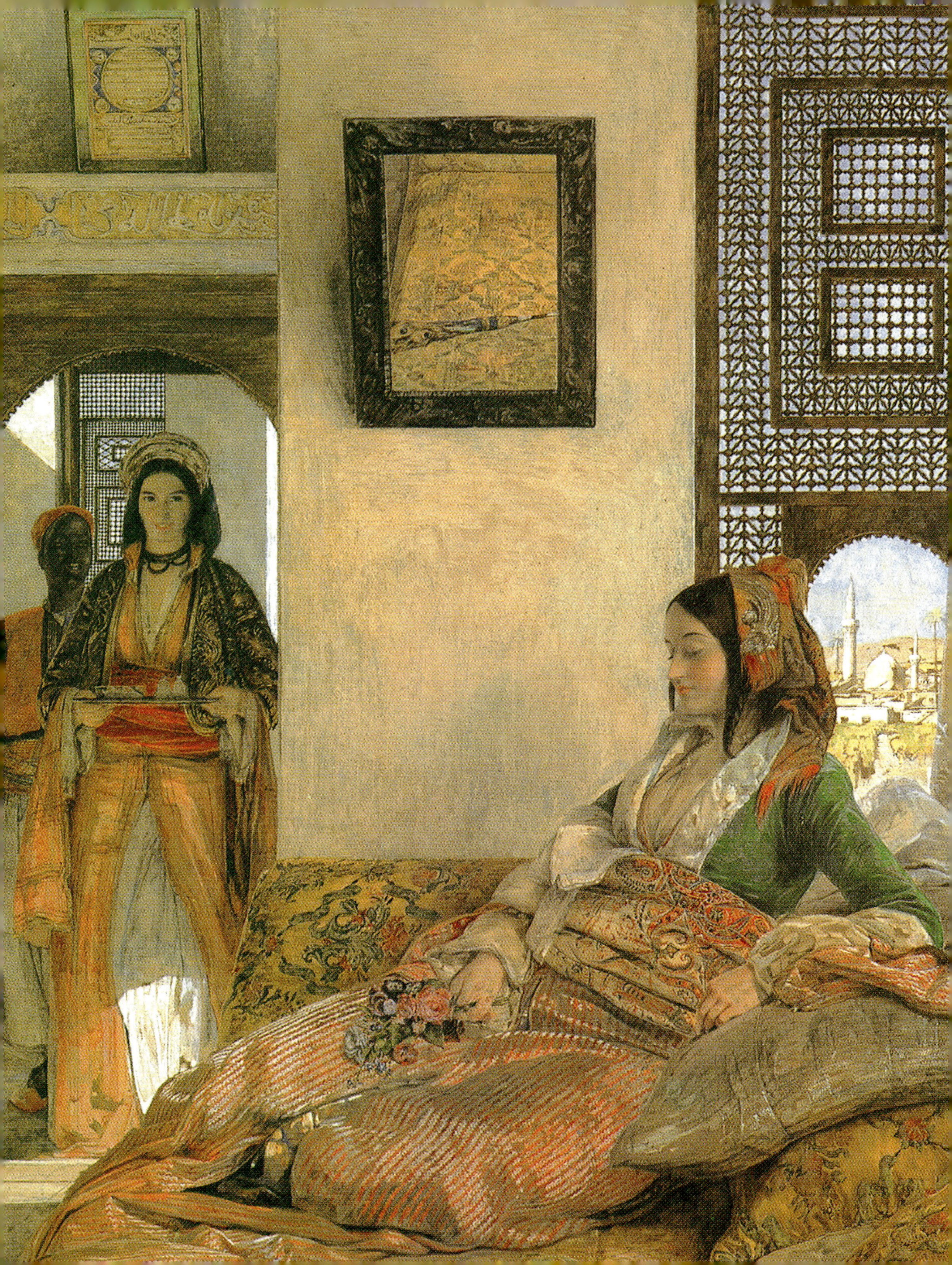

7

PORTRAIT AND FIGURE

As more and more artists succumb to the charms of watercolor, it is becoming an accepted medium for portraits and figure paintings, hitherto regarded as the province of oils. Its softness and translucence make it ideal for capturing the living qualities of skin and hair, but it needs particularly careful handling in this branch of painting if the surface is not to become muddy and dull. Accurate drawing is also vital, especially for portrait work. Try to draw from life wherever possible and avoid the temptation to put the paint on before the drawing is right.

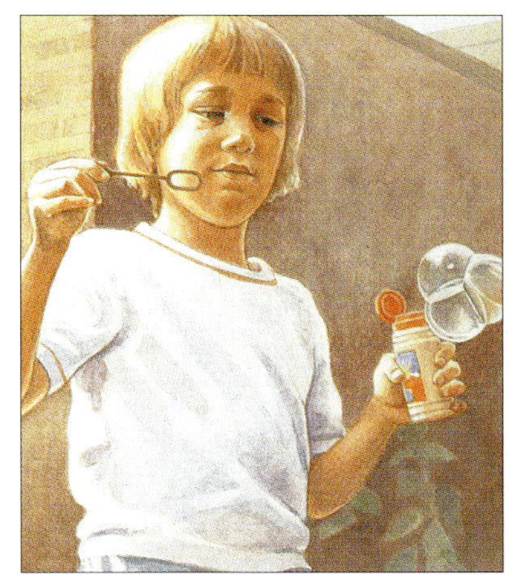

Above Blowing Bubbles *by Elaine Mills was built up in a series of thin washes, the colors kept light and clean. The artist has tried to capture the child in motion, not as a stiff figure.*

Left *John Frederick Lewis was attracted by the rich colors and textures of the East and in* The Harem *he rendered their bright, jewel-like quality in a painstaking technique typical of the watercolors of the period.*

PAST AND PRESENT APPROACHES

Although artists have always used watercolor or pen-and-wash to make quick studies of faces and figures, there is really no tradition of portraiture in watercolor, and until this century paintings of the figure have also usually been in oil. The reasons for this have nothing to do with any inherent unsuitability of the medium itself. In the past portraits were the artist's bread and butter—they were seldom done for pure pleasure as they are today—and the sitter who paid to have his image or that of his family hung on his wall wanted a large and imposing painting as well as one that would stand up to the ravages of time. Watercolors, although we have better ways of preserving them now, as well as more permanent pigments, are prone to fade, and the paper can become mildewed and blotched. Figure paintings were also traditionally fairly large, and most artists found that they called for a slower and more deliberate approach than that normally used for watercolors. Nowadays we have a different attitude to such subjects. A rather sketchy and impressionistic treatment of a figure, either clothed or unclothed, is not only acceptable but often desirable, and can suggest light and movement more easily than a more heavily worked painting.

Figure paintings in watercolor became more usual during the 19th century, partly as a result of the far-reaching influence of William Blake's symbolic and allegorical paintings. The Pre-Raphaelites and Edward Burne-Jones pioneered new techniques, such as rubbing in dry color and scratching out. Another 19th-century artist, influenced by the Pre-Raphaelites was John Frederick Lewis, whose paintings of Middle Eastern scenes such as *The Harem* (see page 294) glow with a jewel-like brilliance. A comparison of *The Harem* with *Girl in Armchair* reveals startling differences in technique. It is difficult to believe that the same medium has been used. Painters such as Lewis used watercolor almost like oil, with the minimum use of washes and much fine-brush work, but his paintings never look tired, as an over-worked watercolor easily can.

Below *In this painting, the artist was interested in light and color rather than in achieving a likeness, and the paint was kept fluid and free, with the minimum of detail, thus enhancing the relaxed mood of the light-flooded figure in the armchair. Note the lack of detailing.*

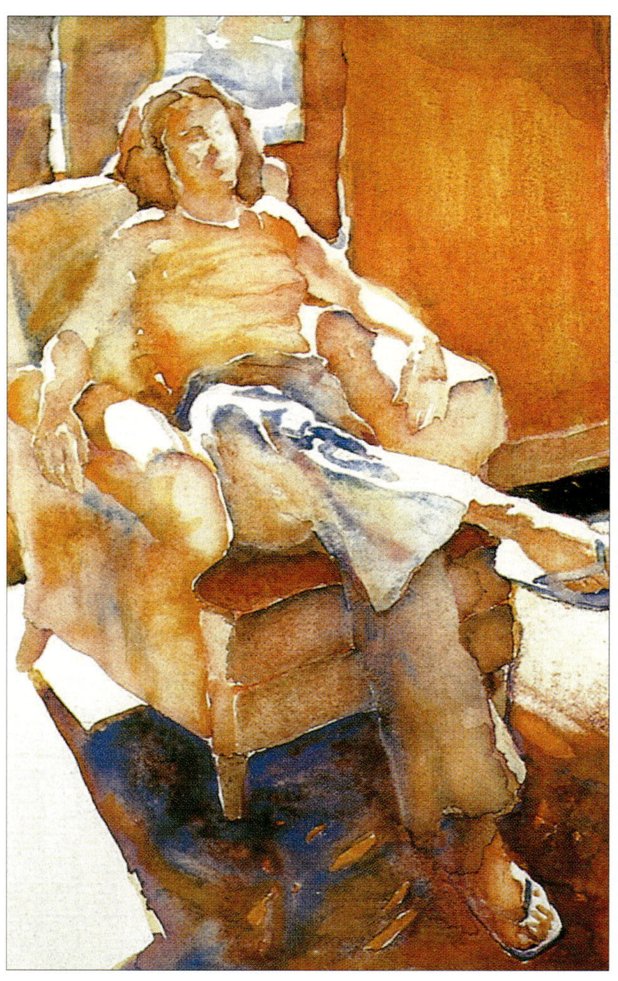

PRACTICAL HINTS

Photographs provide a very useful source of reference for portraiture and figure work, particularly if the subject is a figure in motion. *Blowing Bubbles* is an example of a painting done almost entirely from a photograph. It is advisable, even so, to work from life wherever possible, and since a watercolor study is not likely to take as long as an oil, it should not be difficult to persuade people to sit.

Good drawing is essential for human subjects, since a misplaced eye or an ill-drawn hand or foot can completely destroy the harmony of a painting. Never start painting until you are sure that the drawing is correct; and as you draw, check proportions and measurements constantly. When you are drawing a figure, it often helps to look at the space behind the head or between limbs. Foreshortened limbs, an arm resting on a chair for example, are difficult to get right, but they can usually be checked by using some part of the background as a reference point. You can see at which

1 *(Inset) The photograph shows how different the actual colors were from those the artist has chosen. Even the strongly patterned blanket, which is prominent in the painting, is much paler and more muted.*

2 *(Right) The drawing was made with a mechanical lead-holder into which different leads can be inserted for different purposes. Any unnecessary lines were carefully removed with a soft putty eraser.*

3 *(Bottom) The area around the eyes and brows is one of the most difficult to draw accurately, and the artist pays special attention to the structure and the way the eyes fit into the sockets.*

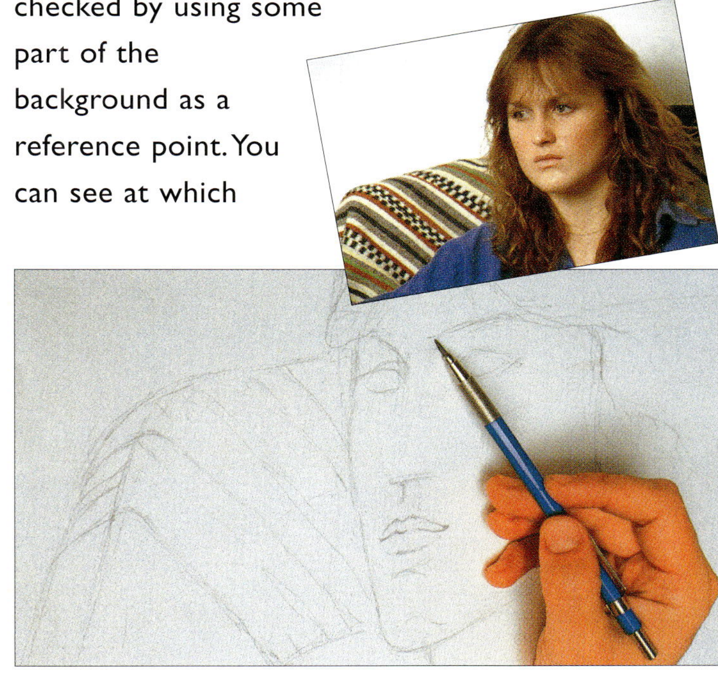

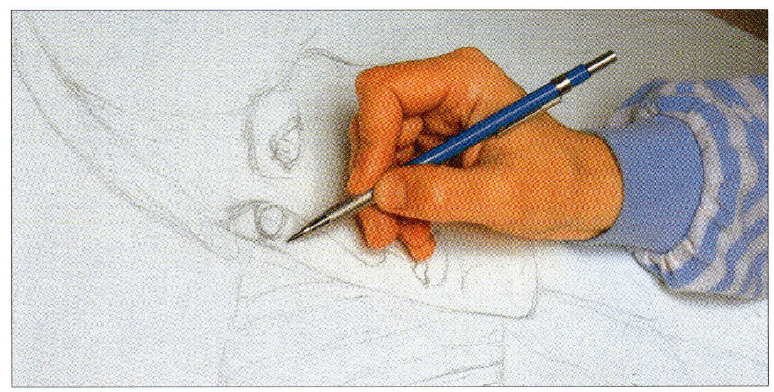

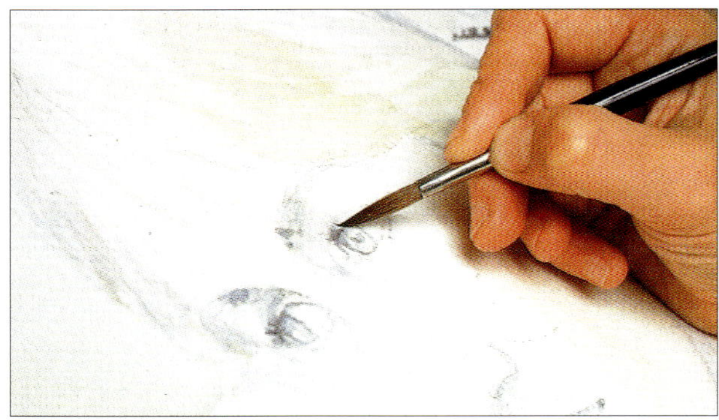

4 *When the pencil drawing was complete the artist began to draw with the brush.*

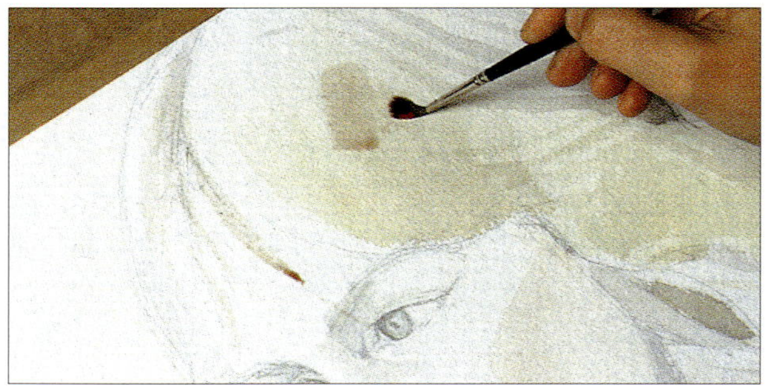

5 *The next step was to get rid of some of the white paper by applying a pale wash.*

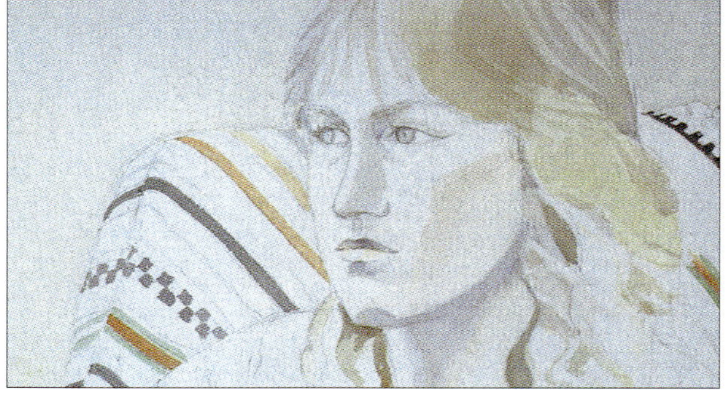

6 *The stripes of the blanket were intensified before further work was done on the face.*

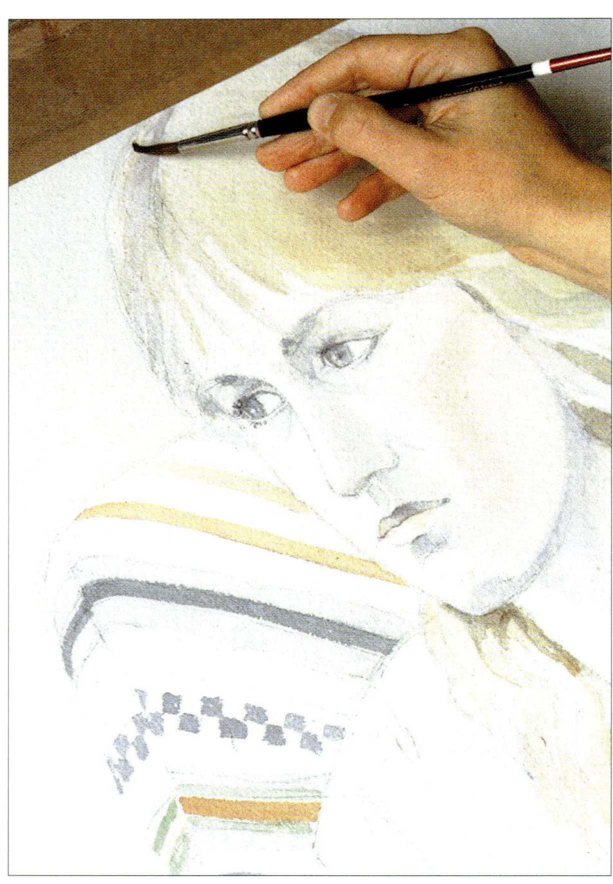

7 *Here the artist paints the darkest part of the hair, using a mixture of violet, Payne's gray, and Indian red. The hair had been mainly yellow ocher with touches of Indian red.*

MATERIALS USED

SUPPORT:
Pre-stretched Bockingford paper, 18 x 16 in. (45 x 40 cm).

COLORS:
Indian red, yellow ocher, violet, Payne's gray, cobalt blue, ultramarine, alizarin crimson, cadmium red, and sap green.

BRUSHES & OTHER EQUIPMENT:
Nos. 6 and 4 sable brushes, a mechanical lead-holder, and a putty rubber.

AGAINST A STRIPED BLANKET

8 *The painting was still weak, the flesh tones too pale and cool. The artist therefore intensified all the tones, adding warmth to the flesh and giving a more solid feel to the face. The final touches were to paint in the pattern of the blanket and add definition to the hair, forming a pleasing pattern.*

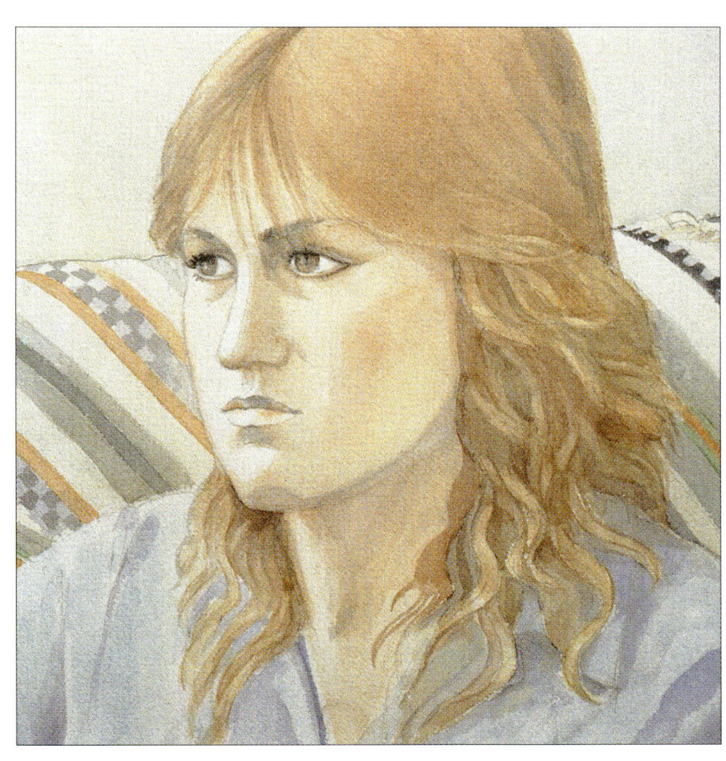

particular point the arm would be intersected by a vertical line formed by the wall behind, or how the hand lines up with the lees of the chair.

AGAINST A STRIPED BLANKET

This is an unusually large painting for a watercolor. The head is almost life-size. The colors are gentle and muted with the minimum of tonal contrast. This type of color scheme, in which there are no dark tones or colors, is known as "high-key." Some artists always work in a high key, others always in a low one (using dark or vivid colors with strong contrasts); yet others are happy to work in both, the choice depending on their approach to the subject.

This portrait was done from life. The artist makes the positions of her hands and feet so that she could resume exactly the same position after breaks. In a painting as subtle as this, the drawing had to be very accurate and the tonal contrasts and variations extremely tightly controlled. The first stage was to draw a very careful outline, establishing the composition so that each wash could be placed quickly and accurately. The pale colors, as well as the sheer size of the painting, ruled out the possibility of major alterations once the painting had begun. Drawing is particularly important in a portrait, since if the proportions of the features are wrong, the painting will not only fail as a likeness, but will also lose structural credibility. The drawing need not be elaborate, but it must be clear and accurate enough to provide a guide for the painting.

PORTRAIT OF PAUL

This sensitive study is much more graphic in approach than the previous portrait. The artist has used a combination of drawing and painting, enabling her to express the character of the sitter in a way she found suited his thin, somewhat aquiline, features.

She used a quill pen made from a goose feather, a drawing tool much favored by such artists as Rembrandt, but the medium was dilute watercolor instead of the more traditional ink. A quill pen produces a less mechanical line than a metal nib, because strokes of different thicknesses can be made by turning the quill. By this means, and by varying the strength and colors of the paint itself, the artist has produced a series of contrasting lines—thick and soft, short and stabbing, fine and taut. She used a Chinese brush and a quill, both to lay washes across the whole image and to soften the line in places by dipping it in a little clean water. Using watercolor gives an artist more freedom to modify or alter lines.

A simple pose, seen directly from the front, was chosen for the painting, because it gave the artist the opportunity to explore fully the lines and contours of the features. No preliminary pencil drawing was made, since the painting was in itself a drawing, which could be corrected as the work progressed.

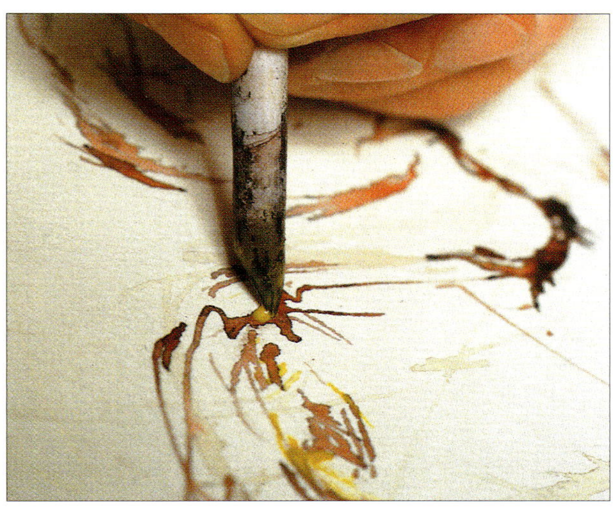

2 *(Left) The artist used three different mixtures: raw sienna and cobalt blue; Prussian blue and cadmium red; and yellow ocher and cadmium yellow.*

3 *(Left Bottom) Here the artist has found that she is not satisfied with the line of the cheekbone; so she lightens it with a brush dipped in water before redrawing it.*

4 *(Below) A Chinese brush was used to apply small areas of color all over. No attempt was made to render the colors precisely. The idea is to create an overall effect.*

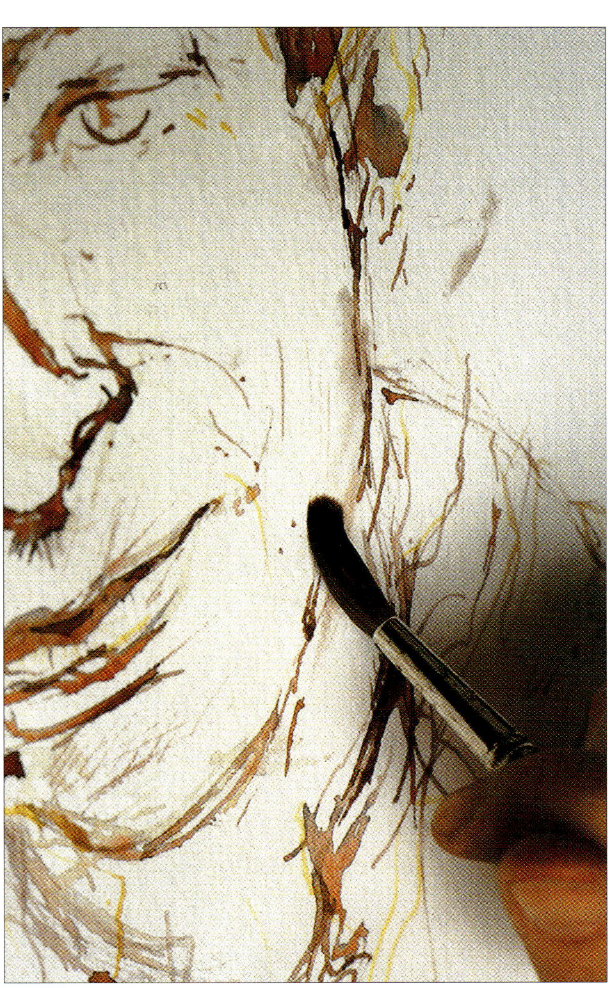

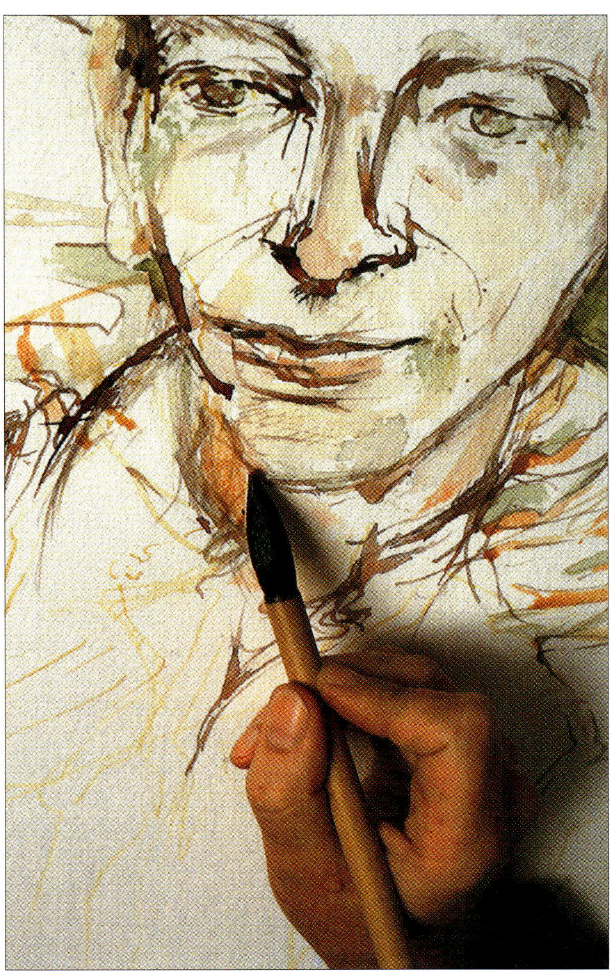

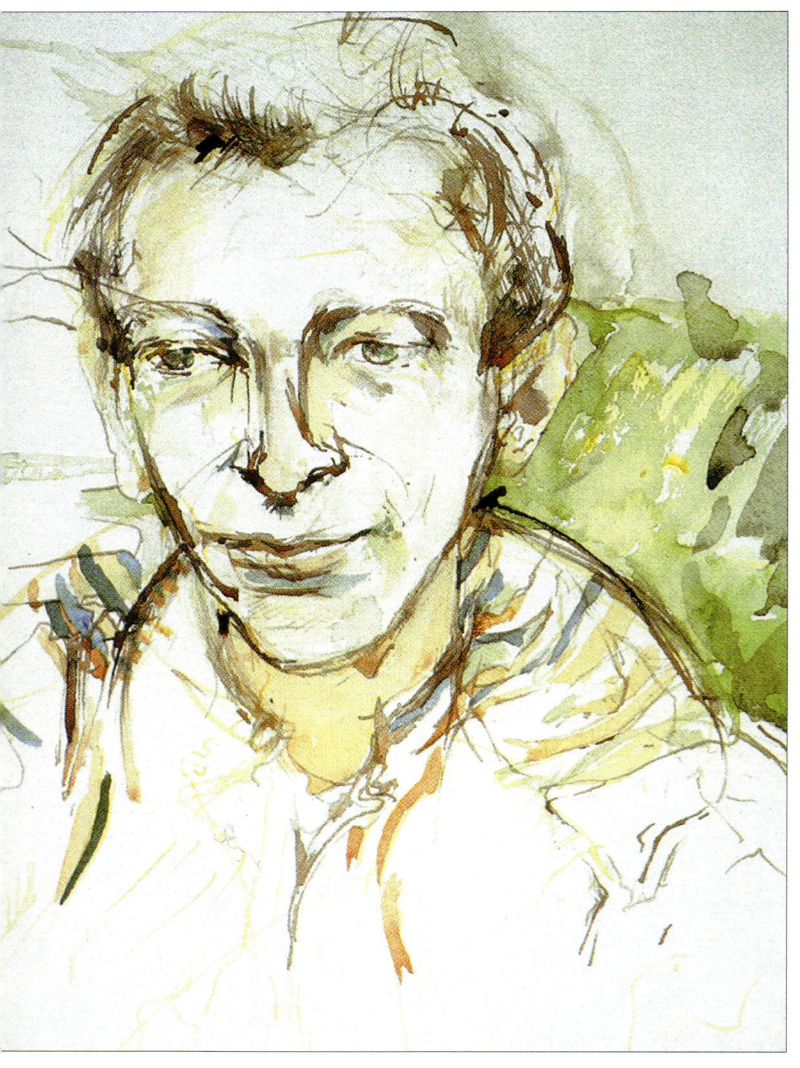

5 *The artist has made little use of the traditional watercolor technique of flat washes. Instead, she has allowed the brush marks to become part of the painting—a sort of combination of drawing and painting. The background was applied with two different brushes, a No. 9 sable round and a Chinese brush.*

PORTRAIT OF PAUL

6 *Once the lines had been firmly established and the artist was satisfied with the drawing, she laid a loose wash over the face and neck to build up the form and add warmth to the flesh. She finds that using watercolor gives her the freedom to modify and alter lines to create the effect she wants of this portrait.*

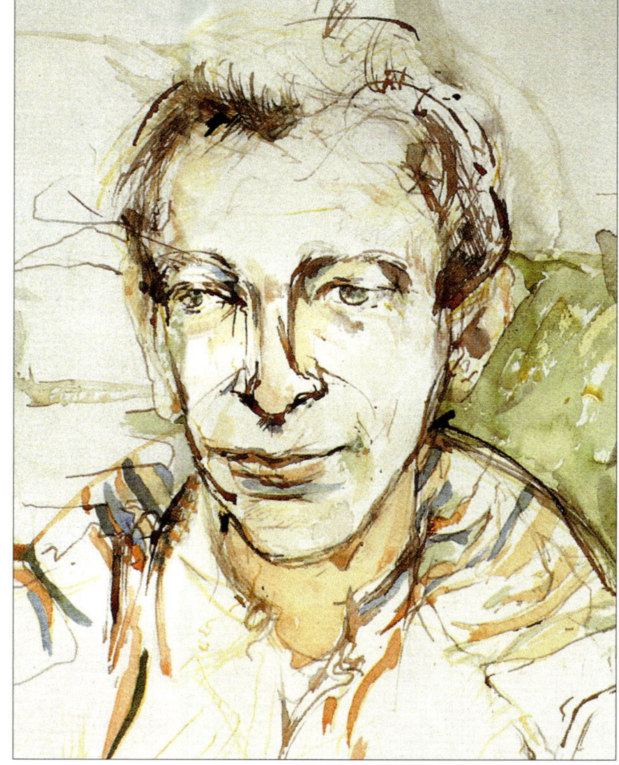

CHINESE BRUSHES

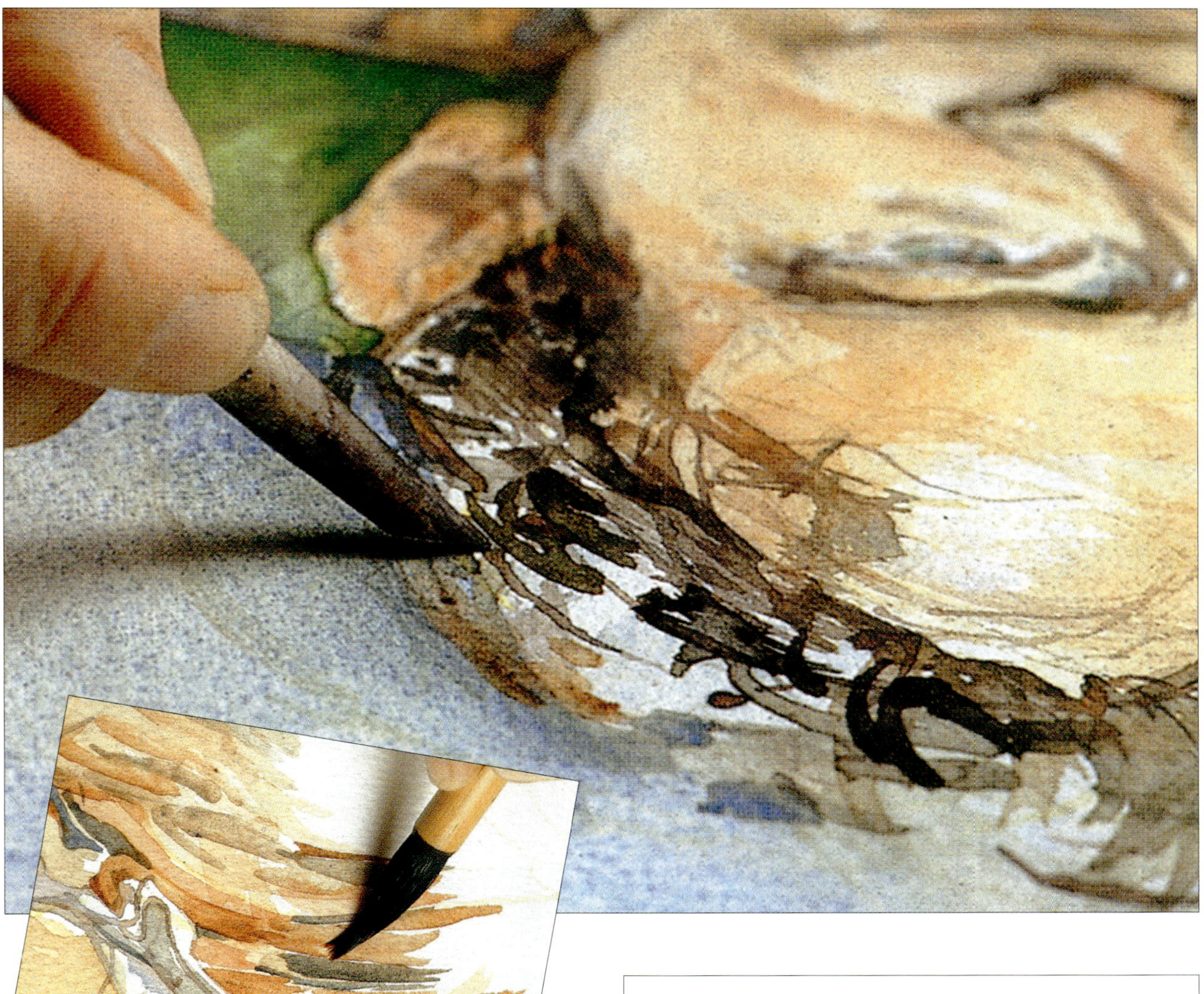

Although color is not the most important aspect of the painting, it has been used boldly and sensitively. Here the artist is using a Chinese brush to apply small patches of bright color to the clothing and darker tones to the hair. She used a Chinese brush and a quill, both to lay washes across the whole image and to soften the line in places by dipping it in a little clean water. She has also used a quill pen to produce a series of contrasting lines—thick and soft, short and stabbing, fine and taut.

MATERIALS USED

SUPPORT:
Watercolor paper, Not surface, 12 x 10 in. (30 x 25 cm).

COLORS:
Raw sienna, cobalt blue, Prussian blue, cadmium red, cadmium yellow, and yellow ocher.

BRUSHES & OTHER EQUIPMENT:
A No. 9 sable round, a Chinese brush, and a goose-feather quill pen.

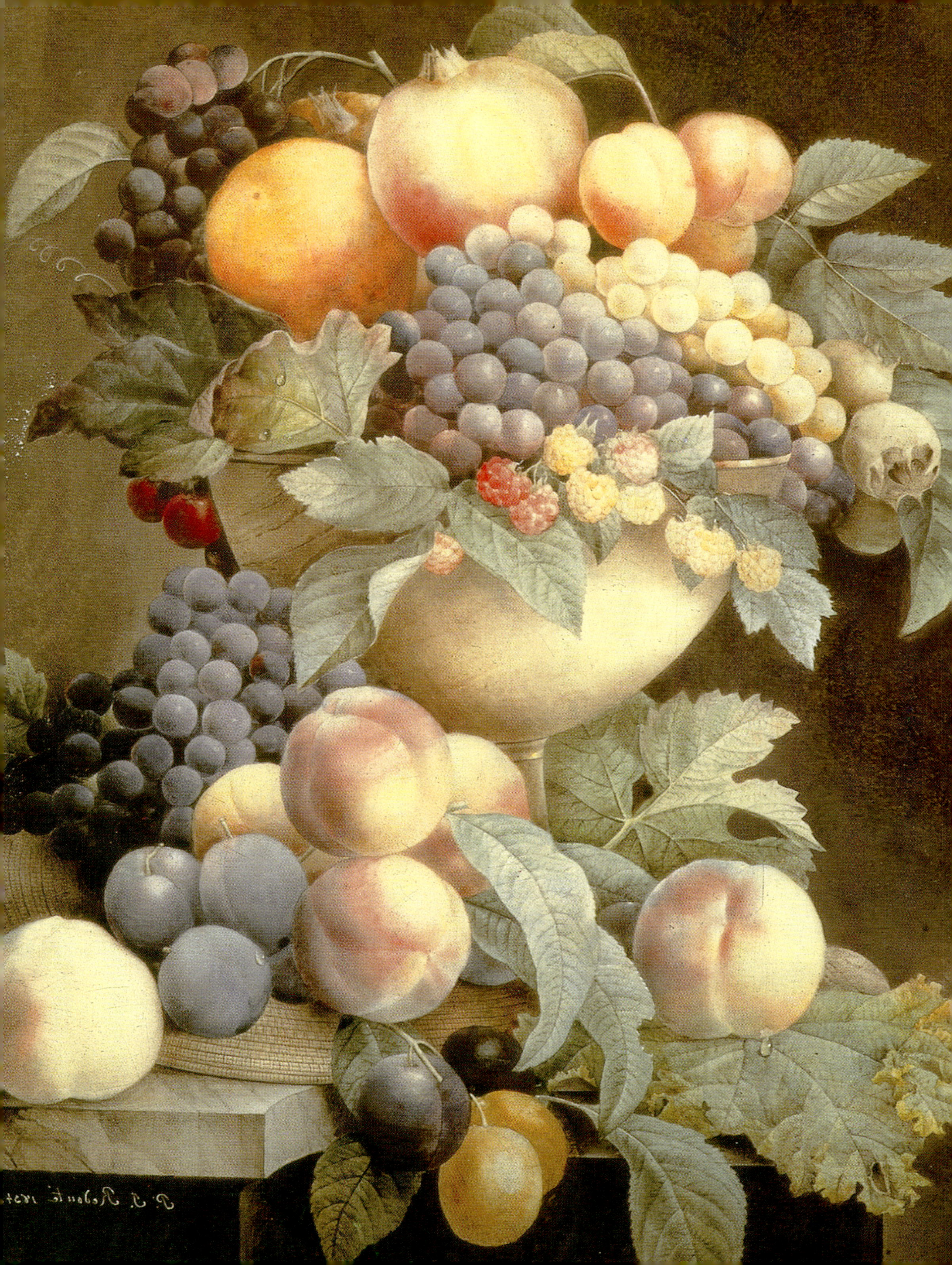

8

STILL LIFE

Still life, as its name implies, simply means a composition of objects that are not moving and that are incapable of doing so, usually arranged on a table; the French rather depressingly call it "dead life" (*nature morte*).

The subjects can be whatever you like, but traditionally the objects in a still-life group are in some way associated with each other—a vase of flowers with fruit; a selection of vegetables with cooking vessels; and sometimes dead fish or game with a goblet of wine, or with a bunch of parsley.

Good paintings can be made from homely subjects. Vincent Van Gogh made a moving still life from just a pile of books on a table.

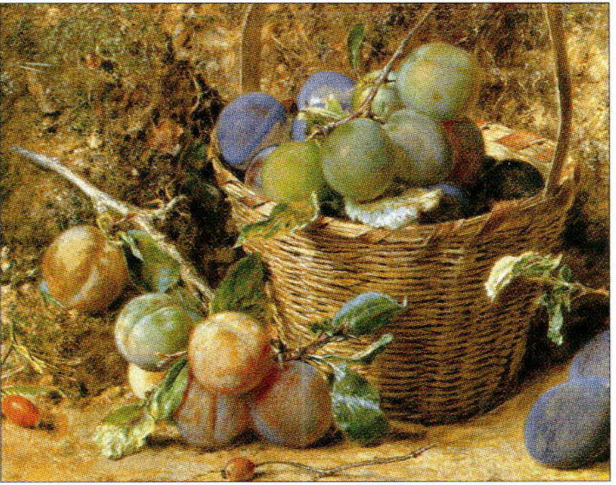

Far Left *Pierre-Joseph Redoute was primarily a flower painter, official artist to Marie Antoinette and later to the Empress Josephine. His detailed flower studies are well known to us through prints; his watercolors and drawings of other subjects are much rarer. This still life, done in 1834, towards the end of his life, shows a wonderfully fresh and skillful handling of watercolor.*

Bottom Left *Cezanne used still life to explore the relationships of forms and their interaction on various spatial planes. He usually worked in oils, but* Still Life with Chair, Bottle and Apple *shows his understanding of watercolor.*

Bottom Right *William Henry Hunt produced charming portraits as well as genre subjects, using his paint rather dry to depict colors and textures with great accuracy.* Plums *is an unusual approach to still life, as it has an outdoor setting but it was almost certainly done in the studio from preliminary sketches.*

Because the subject of a still-life painting can be controlled, as can its arrangement and lighting, still lifes present an unusual opportunity for experimenting with color and composition. The greatest master of the still life, Paul Cezanne, found that the form allowed him to concentrate on such fundamental problems as form and space.

SETTING UP A STILL LIFE

There are no specific problems in painting a still life once it has been set up. The wisest rule to follow is to keep the composition simple. It is also best to have a theme, so the objects do not look uneasy together.

Keep arranging and rearranging until you have achieved a good balance of shapes and colors. Drapery is often used to balance and complement the main subject, and it is useful to have a selection of fabrics on hand. Many artists make small sketches to work out whether a vertical or diagonal line is needed to balance the painting. Finally, look at the arrangement through a viewing frame to assess how well it will fill the space.

Lighting is very important. It defines forms, heightens colors, and casts shadows—all vital components.

CYCLAMEN

Flower arrangements are among the most popular of still-life subjects. Nevertheless, these come with the same problems and the major advantages of being a captive subject.

Here, the composition is simple but very effective: the table-top, with its checked cloth, provides foreground interest to balance the pattern formed by the flowers against the background. It also adds to the impression of solidity and its intersecting diagonal lines provide a pleasing contrast with the curved shapes.

1 *A drawing was made, then painted in with a mixture of cadmium red and purple lake. The spaces created by the flowers against the background are important.*

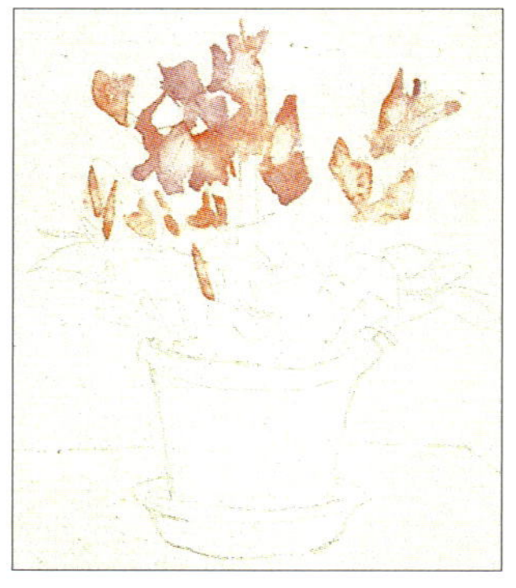

2 *Emerald green, sap green, Payne's gray, and a touch of raw sienna were allowed to mix on the paper. Free brushwork inside & sharper on the edges of the leaves.*

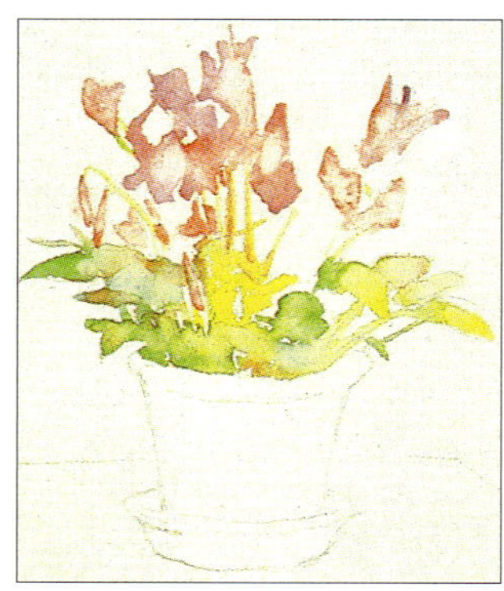

CYCLAMEN

3 *The leaves and flowers were darkened in places and a first wash was then laid on the pot. Here, too, colors put on wet, and then allowed to blend on the paper.*

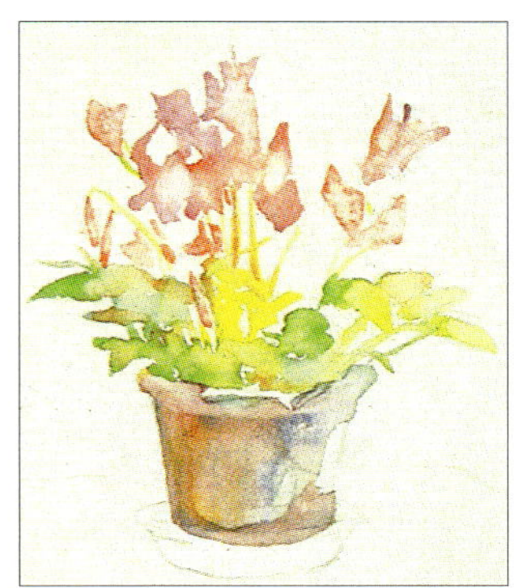

4 *A very pale wash was put on the underside of the dish, leaving the rim white to stand out against the checks. The blue used echoes the blue on the pot.*

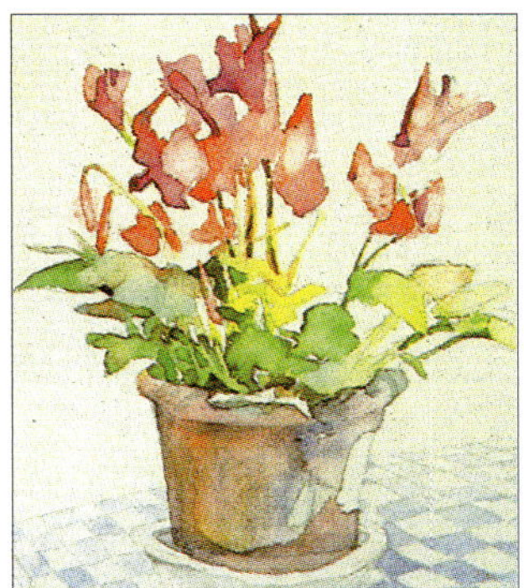

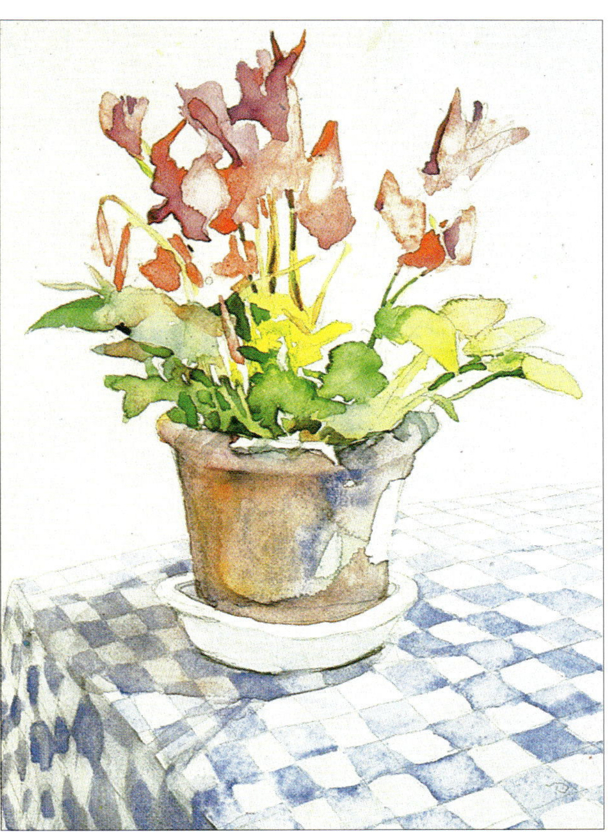

FREEDOM AND LIGHT

5 *The blue checks are varied in size and color to suggest recession, but they are not perfectly straight or regular lines, to avoid a mechanical and monotonous look.*

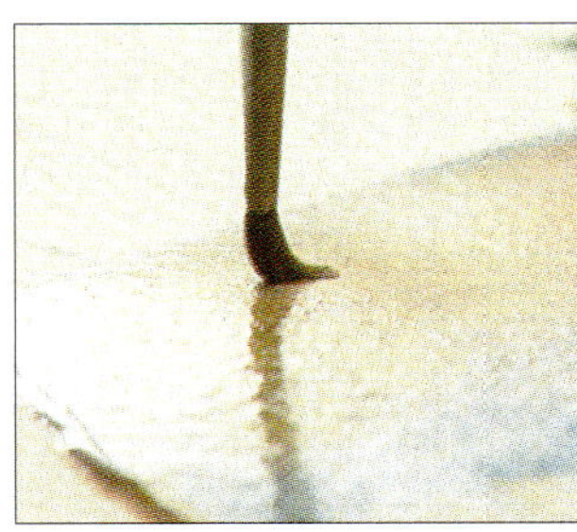

6 *Widely varying colors were applied with plenty of water and blended into one another. If the paint is too wet, or blends in the wrong way, it can be dabbed off.*

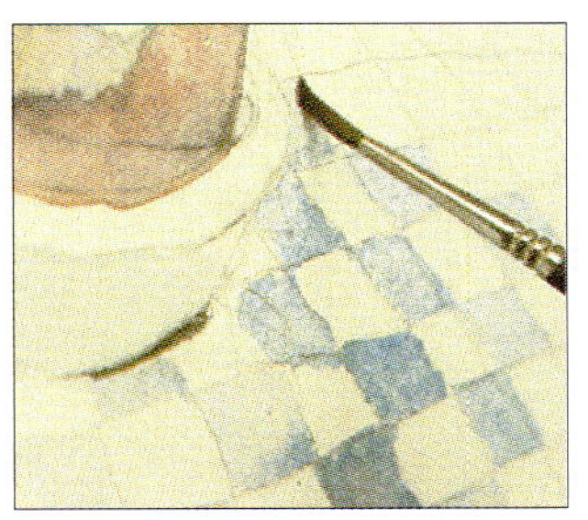

MATERIALS USED

SUPPORT:
Pre-stretched watercolor paper with a Not surface, measuring 12 X 16 in. (30 X 40 cm).

COLORS:
Cadmium red, alizarin crimson, raw sienna, purple lake, emerald green, sap green, lemon yellow, ultramarine, cobalt blue, and Payne's gray.

BRUSHES:
Nos. 7 and 3 sable.

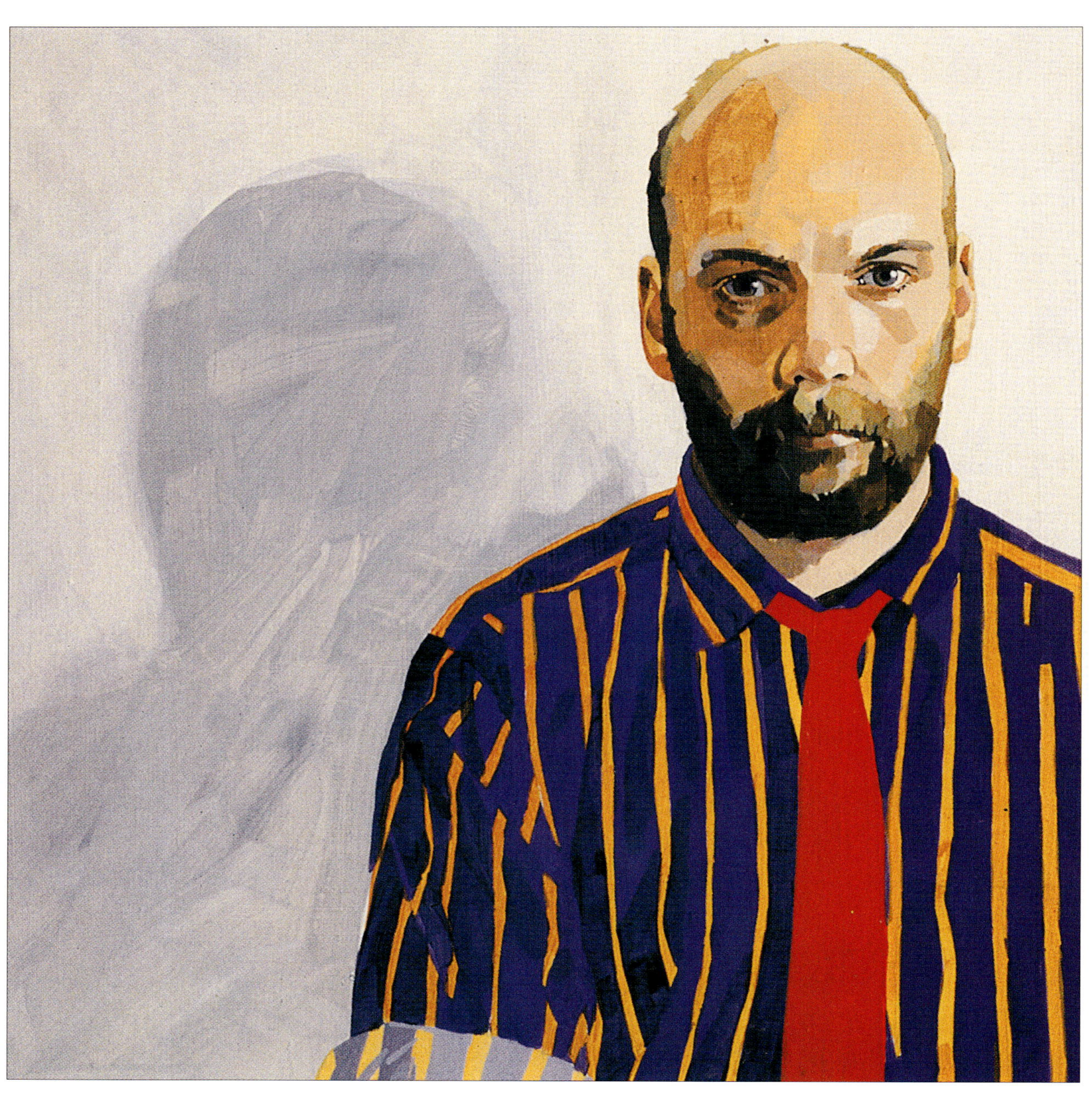

Acrylics

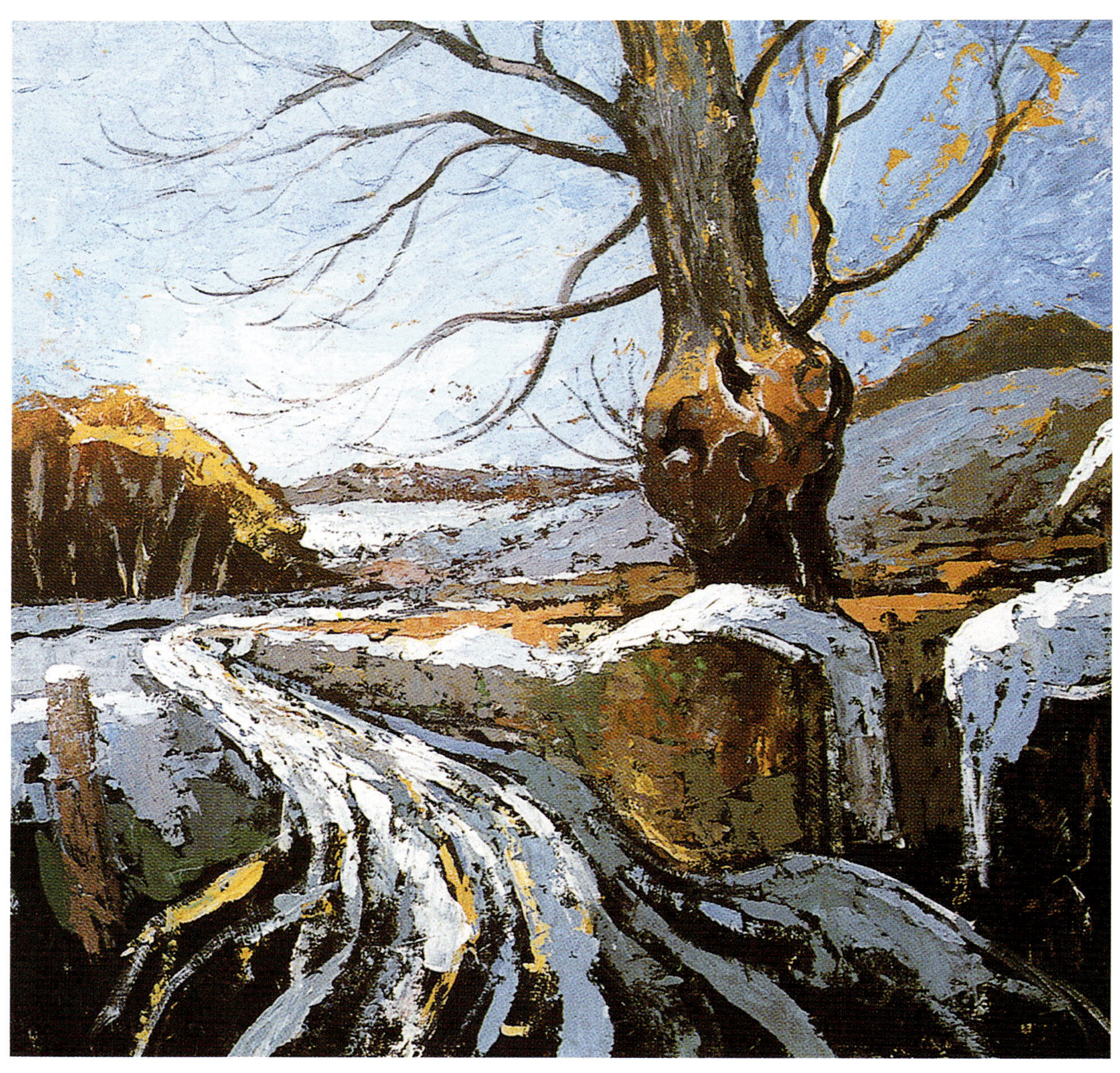

Above *An advantage with acrylic is that light colors can be laid on top of dark. Here, the warm, dark undertones provide a contrasting base to the cold, light tones of the snow and sky.*

Why Acrylics?

Acrylic is a relatively new paint for artists, the first for nearly 300 years. During that time, painters and designers have used mainly oil, watercolor, and tempera. In acrylic, we have a modern paint of enormous value to both artists and designers, whatever fields they are in—painting, illustration, graphic design, textiles, jewelry, mural, and interior design, even sculpture.

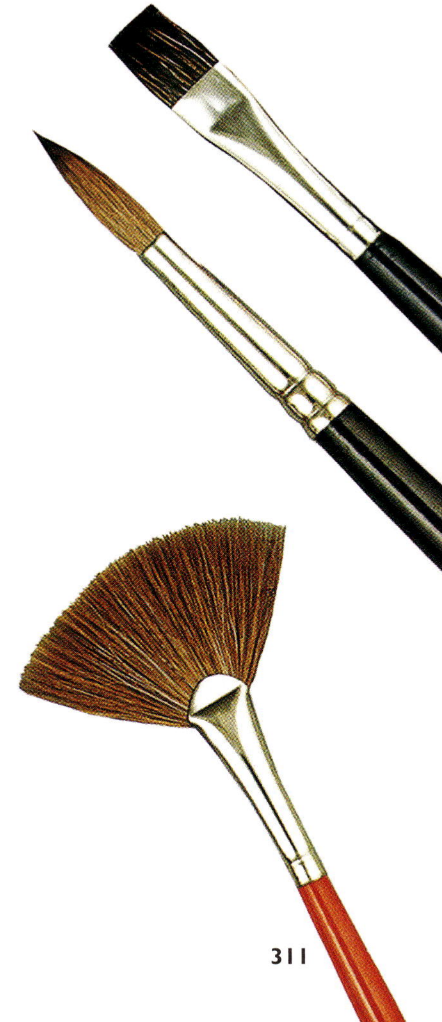

ADVANTAGES OF ACRYLIC

The qualities of acrylic are exceptional. It is certainly more versatile than most other paint. For one thing, it can simulate almost exactly what they can do, in many instances better. It is clean to handle and has only a slight, pleasant aroma. No cumbersome equipment is needed, no special chemical knowledge to make it function satisfactorily. This alone makes it ideal for those who find oil paint somewhat messy, its smell unpleasant, and its use arduous.

One of the advantages of acrylic is its speed of working. It dries rapidly, in minutes if need be, and permanently. Alternatively, drying can be prolonged to suit individual working requirements.

Acrylic dries throughout so thorougly, it can be varnished immediately with either a matt (eggshell) or glossy finish. Another advantage is that acrylic is both tough and flexible.

WHY ACRYLICS?

They are made simple and clean to handle; flexible; water resistant; tough. Acrylics can simulate other paints; smell good; need little special equipment; dry fast; can be cleaned; can be repaired; adhere permanently. It does not peel, crack, or split, and it is water-resistant. The surface of dried acrylic can be gently cleaned should the need arise, and can be repaired easily.

Perhaps the most advantageous characteristics of acrylic are its adhesive qualities. It can be applied, without difficulty, to almost anything, and remain, permanently, without flaking or rubbing off. Unlike oil paint, which can damage the surface of certain materials if applied without the appropriate priming, acrylic can be used without any special preparation if the situation demands.

Among other things, it will adhere satisfactorily to all kinds of wall surfaces, cloth, paper, card (cardboard), hardboard, wood, plastic—almost any object or surface suitable for painting or decoration.

Acrylic is a multipurpose paint; it can be used as a paste as well as a liquid, enabling a variety of surface changes to be carried out and explored. From the perfectly flat, or evenly gradated kind, to the highly modeled, textured surface that has sand, glass, wool fiber, and tissue paper added to it. For among its many accomplishments, the acrylic medium is also a powerful glue.

It will especially suit those who delight in bold, bright, clear colors. Conversely, it can be reduced to subtle tones and carefully gradated tints by the usual methods of mixing.

Acrylic's simplicity of handling is a major advantage, especially for beginners. The simple equipment needed means less initial expense,
a further encouragement to those who have never painted before.

Acrylic is uncomplicated to use, but it is important to learn how it behaves. Practice and experiment will teach you how to exploit the qualities of the paint. Experience with other mediums is not necessary; beginners are at no disadvantage to the more experienced painter in understanding acrylics, and the beginner may be less prejudiced and more adventurous than the painter skilled in other mediums. If you begin with a spirit of inquiry, you will soon grasp the potential of this exciting medium.

THE NATURE OF PAINT

Acrylic is unlike any other paint, but it has affinities with all of them, since all paints contain the same ingredient: pigment. A pigment used in watercolor is identical to that

used in oil and acrylic. The quality is equally high, its brightness and durability the same.

The major difference between one paint and another is not the color but the "binder". The binder largely decides the character and behavior of paints. Binders also play a large part in permanence and drying qualities, and speed of working. They also determine what kinds of diluents (also known as solvents) and varnishes may be used in conjunction with them. For instance, water is the diluent for watercolors and gouache, and turpentine for oil, because of the liquid binders used.

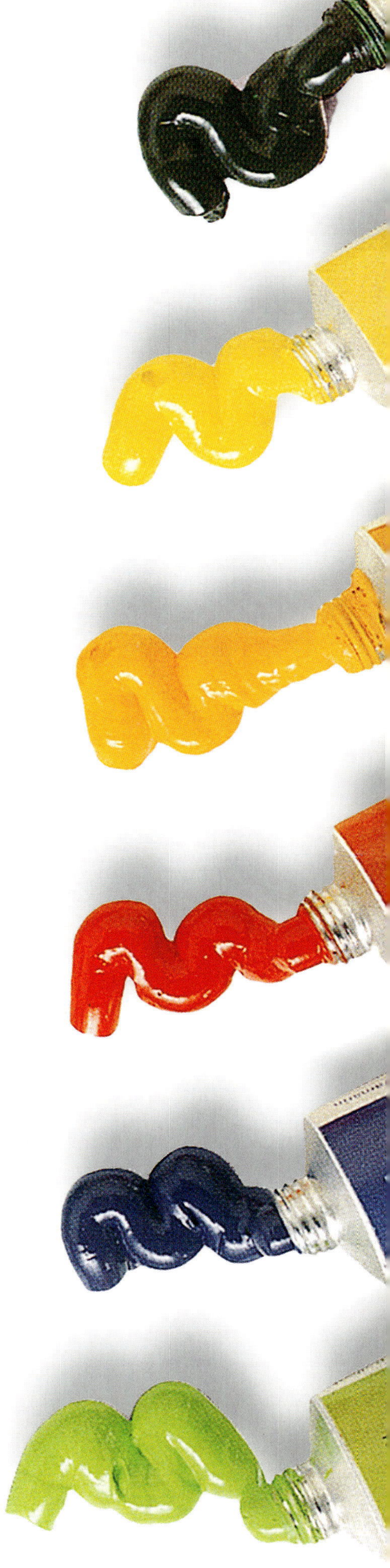

Right *The most convenient way to buy acrylics is in tubes. Acrylic paints are convenient and easy to use, not messy, and do not have an unpleasant smell.*

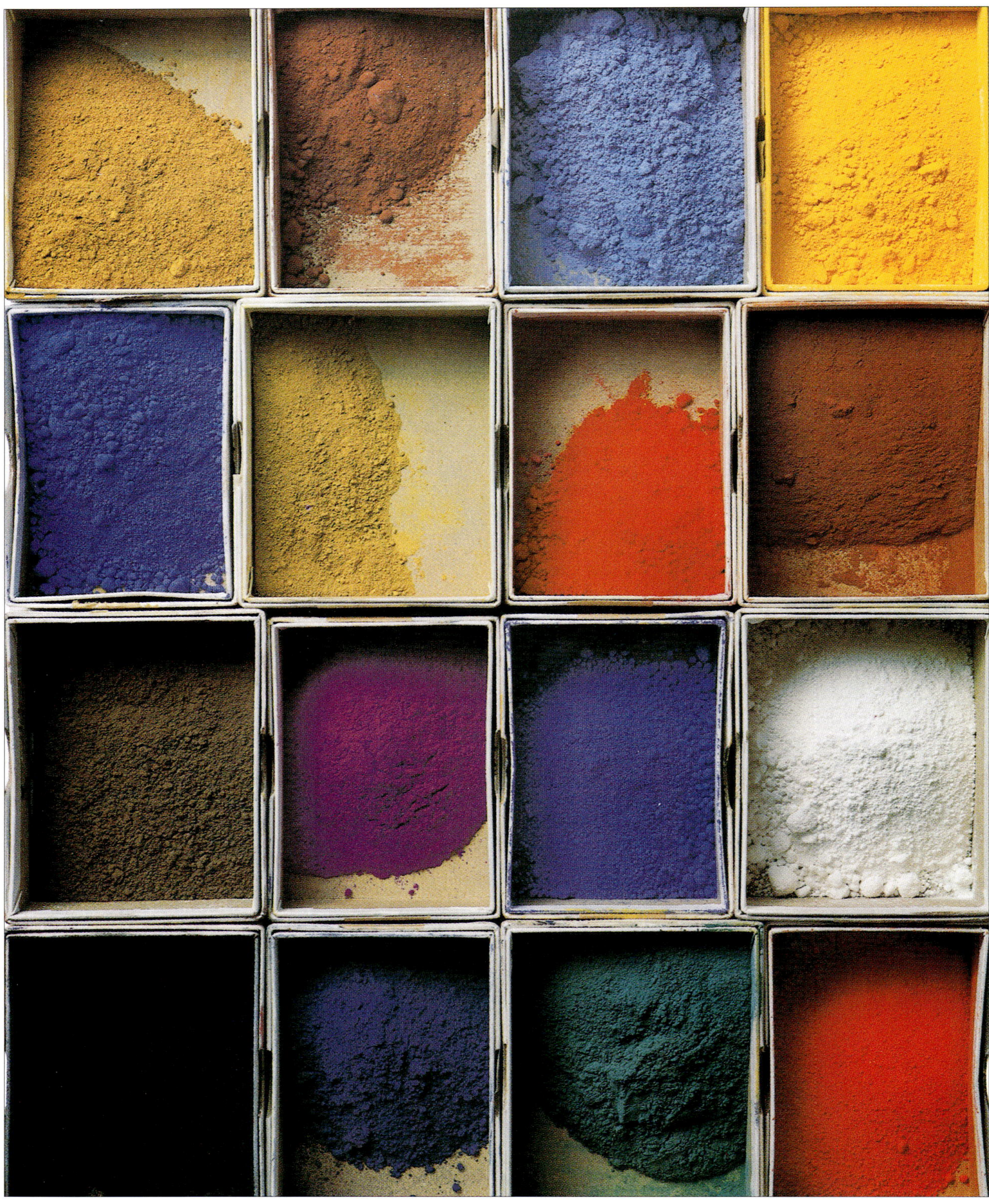

9 Acrylic Paint

Acrylic paint is made by mixing powdered pigment with acrylic adhesive. The adhesive looks milky when wet but becomes transparent when dry, revealing the true color of the pigment. All the ingredients are carefully weighed and tested before use. It is this painstaking precision and control during the manufacture which enables thousands of tubes of paint of almost identical color, consistency, and quality to be turned out at any time.

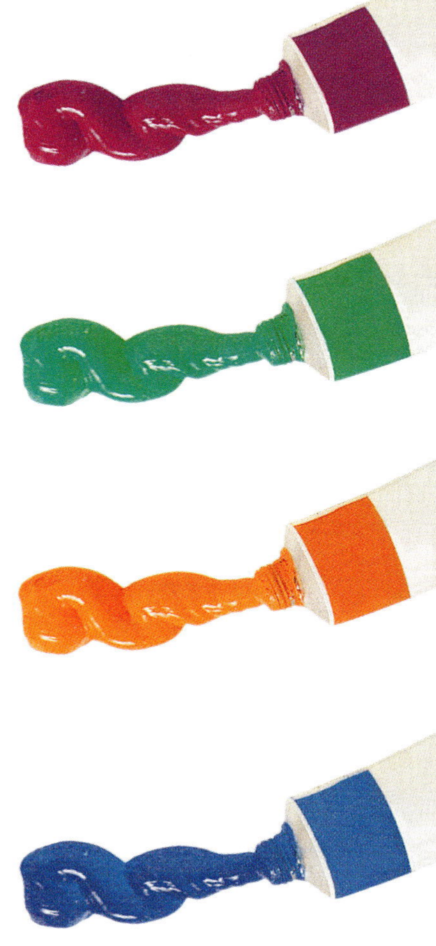

PIGMENTS

Pigments are the coloring materials of paint, and are usually made in the form of powders. Throughout history, bright color was preferred for both practical and aesthetic reasons, having close associations with joy, celebration, pleasure, and delight. Delight in bright color today means a wide range of pigments, and the list of those available is long.

The names of pigments often echo places: burnt Sienna, Venetian red, Naples yellow, Prussian blue, Chinese vermilion; or recall the materials they are derived from: cobalt blue, rose madder, emerald green, ivory black, sap green, geranium lake. Though interesting sounding, the names give little indication of the quality or

HOW ACRYLIC PAINT IS MADE

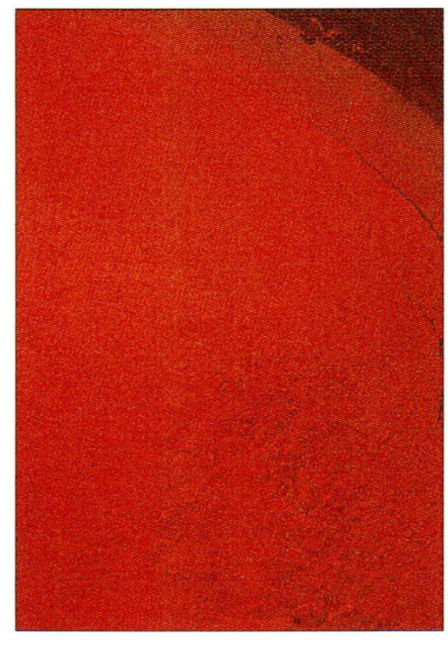

1 *The first constituent is powdered pigment.*

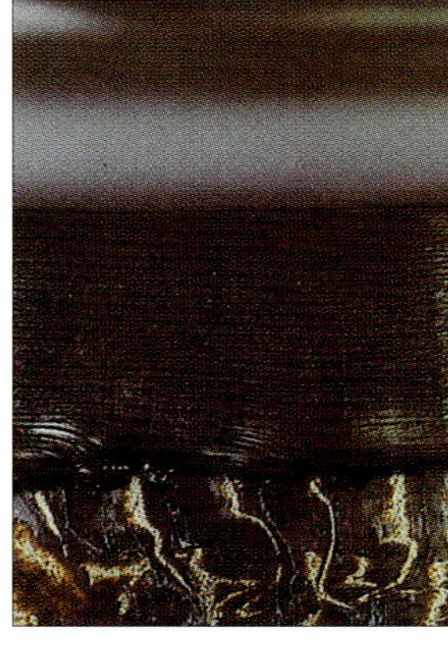

3 *It is then milled between steel rollers.*

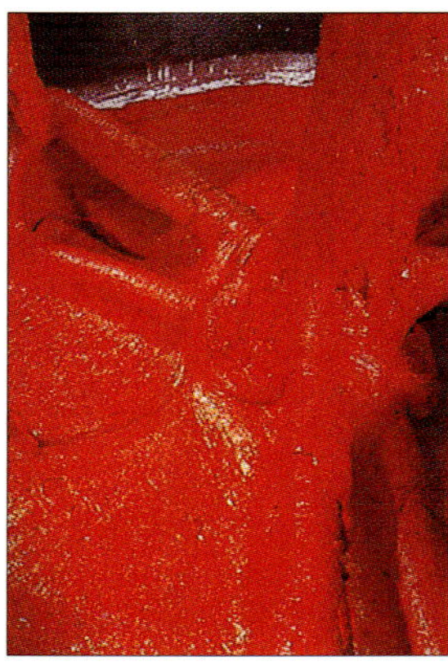

2 *The pigment is mixed with acrylic adhesive.*

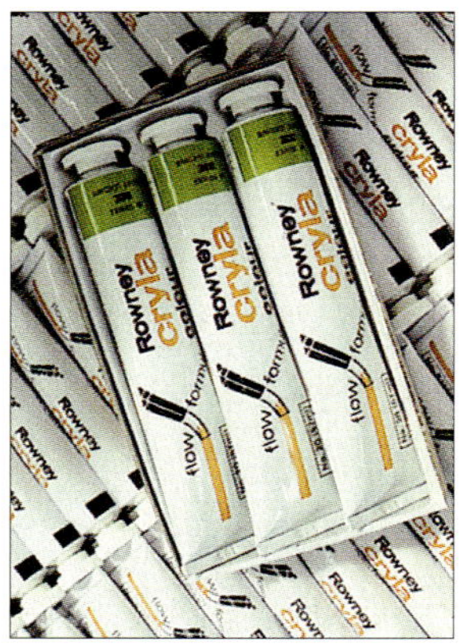

4 *It is inspected, then put into tubes.*

behavior of colors, and some are sold under two or three different names.

Briefly, the requirements for a reliable pigment are that: it should be a smooth, finely divided powder; insoluble in the medium in which it is used; able to withstand the action of light without changing color under normal exposure; and it should be chemically inert. Moreover, it should possess the proper degree of opacity or transparency to suit the purpose for which it is intended, and should conform to accepted standards of color quality.

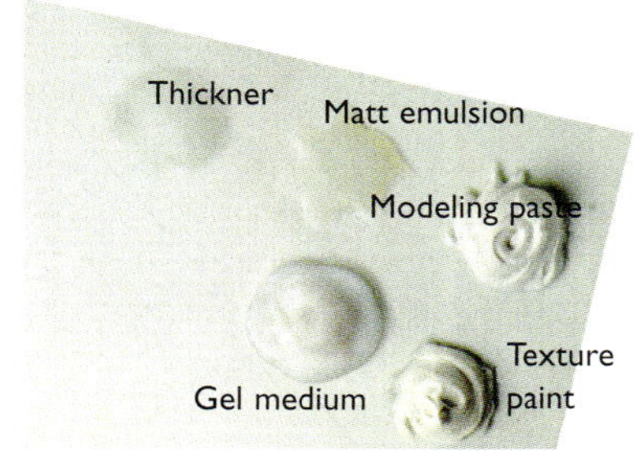

The raw materials used to provide the pigments are customarily classified as inorganic or organic. Inorganic materials are those of purely mineral origin and organic pigments include animal and vegetable substances, as well as complex synthetic substances that have been derived by a chemical process from an organic dyestuff.

PAINTING WITH PIGMENTS

When pigments are seen as powders, they are fresh and bright with a beauty all their own. When mixed with a small quantity of water, a paste is formed that can be painted with. When the water dries the bloom returns, but it also reverts to its former state. What is needed is something to bind the colored grains together to make them adhere. For this purpose some kind of glue or binder must be added to the powder before it becomes paint.

BINDERS

Gum

The earliest form of binder was a gum, probably gum arabic. The popularity of gum arabic as a binder is probably because it dilutes well with water and does not impair the brightness of the pigments. It can also be made into small cakes of paint that are easily stored, and dissolve easily when needed. The only limitation is that watercolor has little body, and is best used transparently, in washes and glazes.

Emulsions

Any sort of paint that is bound with an emulsion that contains oil, but is mixable with water, is called tempera. The tempera most frequently used throughout the Renaissance contained the yolk of an egg. Egg tempera dries quickly, hardly changes color, and is fairly waterproof—sufficiently so not to pick up when over-painted. It has a good surface that wears well, provided it is treated with care. It is by far the best of the mediums, but requires technical knowledge and expertise to handle it well.

There are other drawbacks: speed of working is slow, and it does not cover large areas well. There is always the difficulty of making flat, even coats of color on a large scale because the emulsion binder cannot accommodate huge amounts of pigment—something acrylic can do with ease.

Tempera lends itself to simple images. For more realistic forms of expression, oil paint is more suitable.

Oil

The most common oil used to bind pigment is linseed, and gave the freest possible manner of working for over 300 years. Pigment ground with oil is slow to dry and therefore slow to use, but it brought a softer, more delicate tonality to painting, and did justice to the visual delights of light and shade. Moreover, because of its consistency, it could exploit more surface textures than tempera.

The practical application of oil paint outweighed its disadvantages: that it darkens over a period of time, attracts dirt, is difficult to clean, cracks and peels, and is messy and smelly. Oil paint has to be diluted with turpentine, and brushes and palettes cleaned with white spirit. It can be applied only to primed surfaces. It requires technical expertise and virtuosity and is not an easy medium to master.

ACRYLIC BINDERS, MEDIUMS, VARNISHES, RETARDERS, AND SOLVENTS

Unlike linseed oil, egg, gum, wax, and lime, acrylic binders are made specifically to act as, well, binders. Chemically, they are based on polymer resin, and classed as an emulsion into which pigments are mixed. It is, in short, a clear plastic, with great adhesive properties, and water-resistant. Even though the diluent is water, once the binder is dry, it becomes completely insoluble in water.

Acrylic binders (or more specifically, mediums) can be obtained in three consistencies. With them, not only are we able to achieve what other paints can, but a great deal more besides. These mediums, or binders, come as: liquid, gel, and paste.

When these binders are used to exploit the possibilities of acrylic paint they become in effect mediums: liquid constituents of paint, in which the pigment

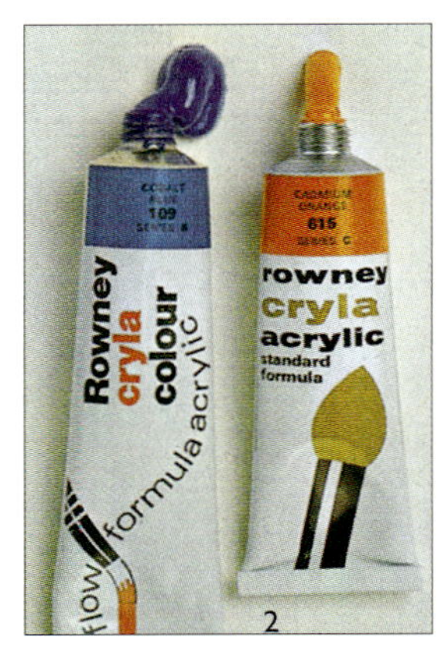

Grumbacher, Winsor and Newton, and Rowney Cryla (2) are some acrylic paints on sale today. Rowney Flow Formula (1) is used for laying large flat color. Prime canvas with an acrylic primer (3) or gesso (4). Mediums are available in gloss (5, 7, 11, 13) or matt (6, 10). Retarding medium (16) slows the drying time. Varnishes can be matt (8, 9) or gloss. Rowney makes a soluble gloss varnish (12). Also useful are gel medium (15) and water tension breaker (14).

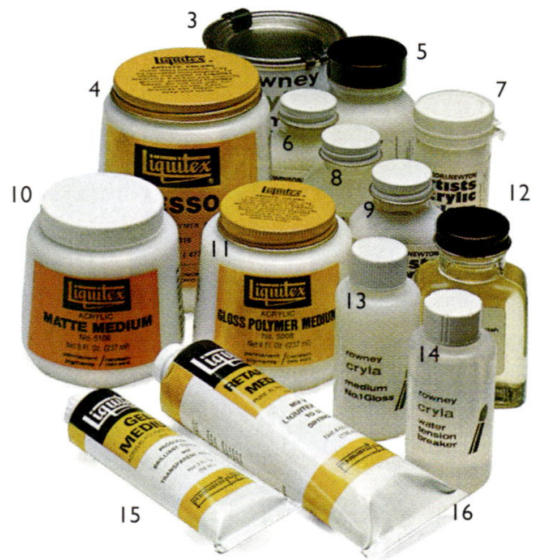

is suspended, or liquids with which the paint may be diluted, without decreasing its adhesive, binding, or film-forming properties.

Mediums can loosely be described as paint additions to make the paint flow or dry more variously, or to produce different results for special kinds of work (impastos, for example, where the addition of a medium will give more bulk to the paint), or, as in the case of acrylic, to transform it into a modeling material. These additions can also thin or thicken to produce a variety of visual effects such as glazes, scumbles, impastos, etc.

Acrylic gloss medium

Acrylic gloss medium increases the translucency and gloss of acrylic colors while reducing consistency to produce thin, smooth paint layers which dry rapidly. A few drops of the medium mixed with ordinary watercolor or gouache immediately transforms them into an acrylic paint, that is, they take on many of the characteristics of acrylic paint: quick-drying, water resistant, capable of overpainting without picking up, and a gloss finish.

Acrylic matt medium

The matt medium behaves in a similar way to the gloss. It is a useful medium to have if you intend to paint matt, so that the tones

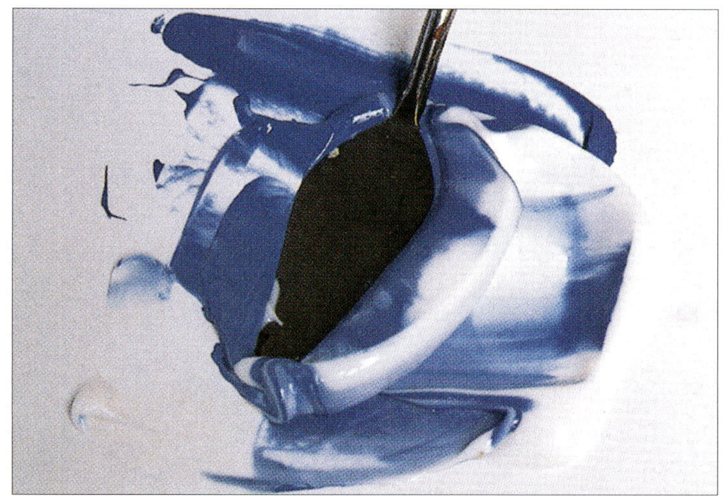

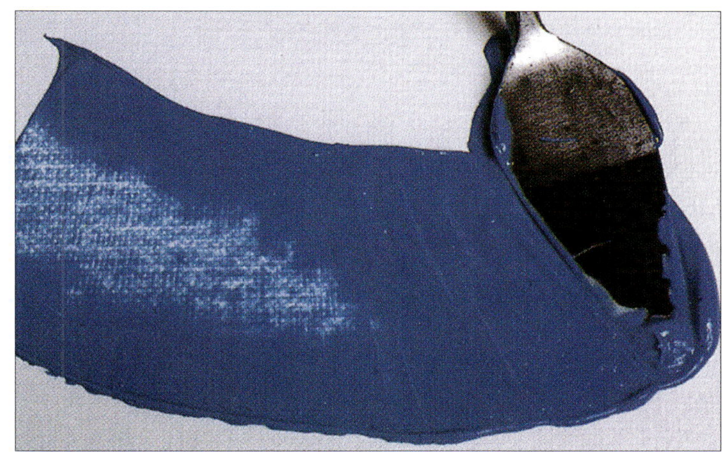

Top *A painting knife is used to mix paint and gel in equal proportions. This is useful for impastos.*

Above *The consistency of the gel is thick, and so it retains the shape of the knife marks.*

of the colors can be properly mixed before painting. There is an appreciable difference in tonality between matt and glossy finishes. The pigment dispersed in either medium may be the same for both matt or gloss, but

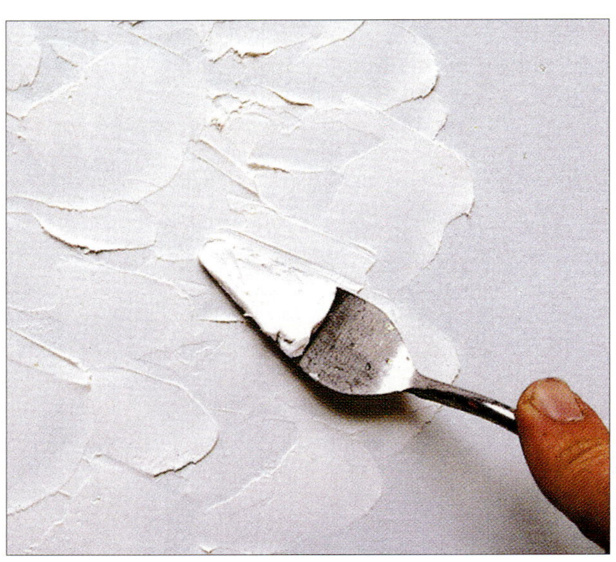

Right *Texture paste is the thickest acrylic medium. Here, it is applied directly to the support.*

the light affects them differently. To allow for this during painting, the addition of a few drops of matt (or gloss) medium in the paint mixtures will ensure that you get exactly the tone or tint you want.

Acrylic gel medium

Gel medium is thicker than the gloss or matt mediums. As its name implies, it is jelly-like in consistency, and like the gloss medium has two distinct functions. First, it enables thick, highly textured impastos to be produced easily while maintaining consistency of color, and second, the colors increase in translucency the greater the proportion of gel medium used. At the same time, the drying rate is retarded to some degree.

Glazes and impastos are an integral feature of acrylic painting. Glazes are made by laying a transparent film of color over another that has already dried. Impasto is thick paint that can be textured by the movement of the brush or by the edge of the palette or painting knife. A particular characteristic of oil paint, gel medium can achieve this effect in exactly the same way as oil paint, with just as much vitality, and is less liable to crack. It dries much quicker than oil, so is less easily spoiled or damaged during painting and, once dried, it becomes very hard to dislodge.

Acrylic texture paste

The thickest, and the most powerful acrylic binder, comes in a carton. Though more dense than the other two binders, it can be watered down without any loss to its adhesive powers. It can be used to make those very heavy impastos that Vincent Van Gogh was so fond of, for this kind of vigorous brush stroke, large brushes will be needed, or a palette or painting knife will serve just as well.

Acrylic water tension breaker

The water tension breaker is a concentrated solution of a wetting agent, which is diluted with water before use. Use of this additive allows easier, more rapid thinning of colors with minimum loss of color strength.

Acrylic gloss varnish

This gloss varnish is water-based and dries to a flexible, transparent, extremely light-fast, glossy film that is water-resistant and scuff-resistant and brings out the brilliance of the colors wonderfully. It both protects and enhances at the same time, which is the major reason for varnishing finished work. Varnishing consequently becomes the normal extension to painting, and should offer few problems if all these points are observed.

Acrylic matt varnish

For very large works, irregular shine will distort the image, or impair the visual effect. The only answer to this is a completely matt surface. Similarly, for those who prefer blonde or high-key colors, a matt finish will be more suitable than a rich glossy one.

__Right__ Acrylic paints can be used very effectively in combination with oil crayons. The properties of the two complement each other nicely, producing an interesting mixed media effect.

Satin on eggshell finish

If you find that a glossy finish is too shiny, or a matt one too bland, there is a way of making an intermediate finish. Simply blend the gloss varnish with the matt in a saucer, and brush on. The resultant midway finish can be adjusted by adding either more gloss or more matt. A prepared satin finish is also available in art supply shops.

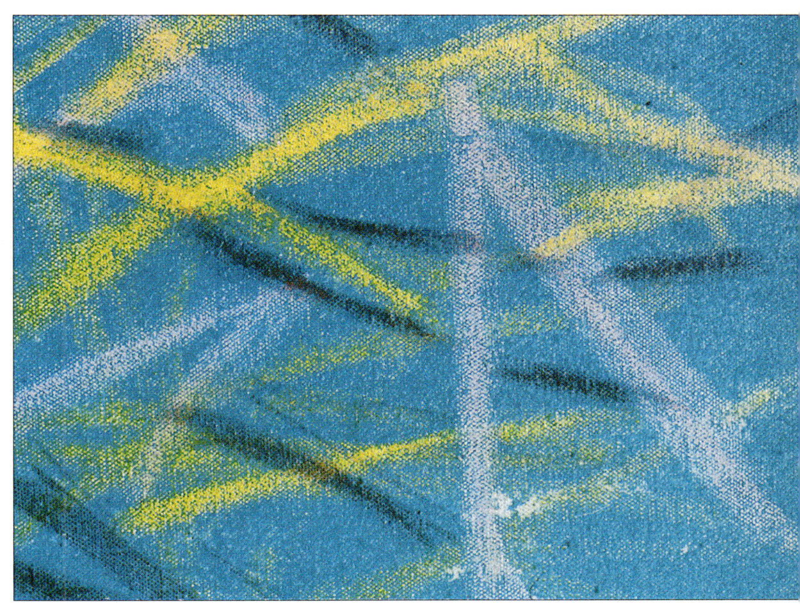

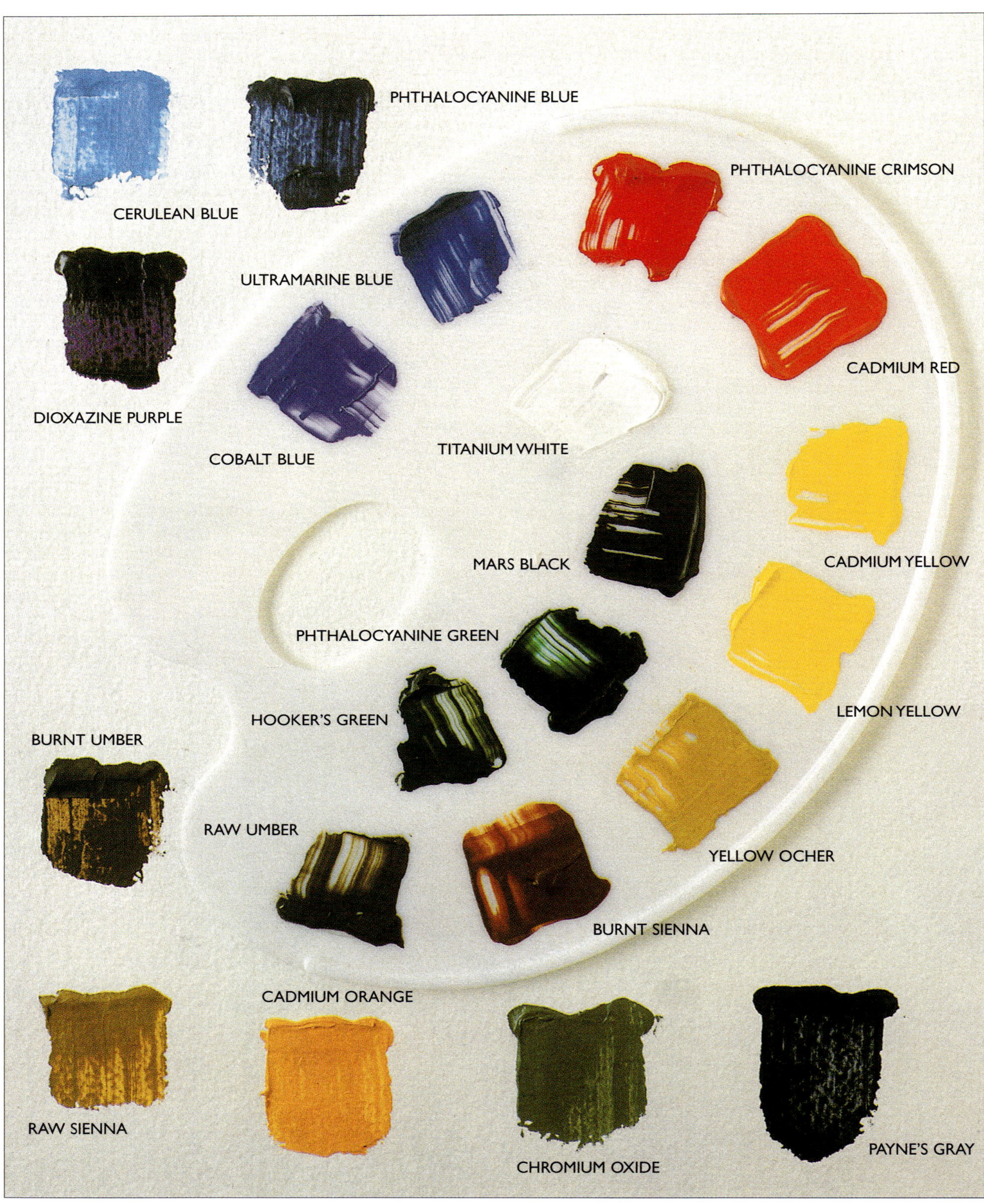
PHTHALOCYANINE BLUE
CERULEAN BLUE
PHTHALOCYANINE CRIMSON
ULTRAMARINE BLUE
CADMIUM RED
DIOXAZINE PURPLE
COBALT BLUE
TITANIUM WHITE
MARS BLACK
CADMIUM YELLOW
PHTHALOCYANINE GREEN
HOOKER'S GREEN
LEMON YELLOW
BURNT UMBER
RAW UMBER
YELLOW OCHER
BURNT SIENNA
CADMIUM ORANGE
RAW SIENNA
CHROMIUM OXIDE
PAYNE'S GRAY

10 MATERIALS AND EQUIPMENT

Painting consists of a number of specific actions, for example smearing, brushing, dabbing, swirling, tinting, staining, spraying, sponging, spattering, and spreading.

The tools needed for this job are usually brushes of varying types and sizes, knives known as painting or palette knives, sponges, airbrushes, and rollers.

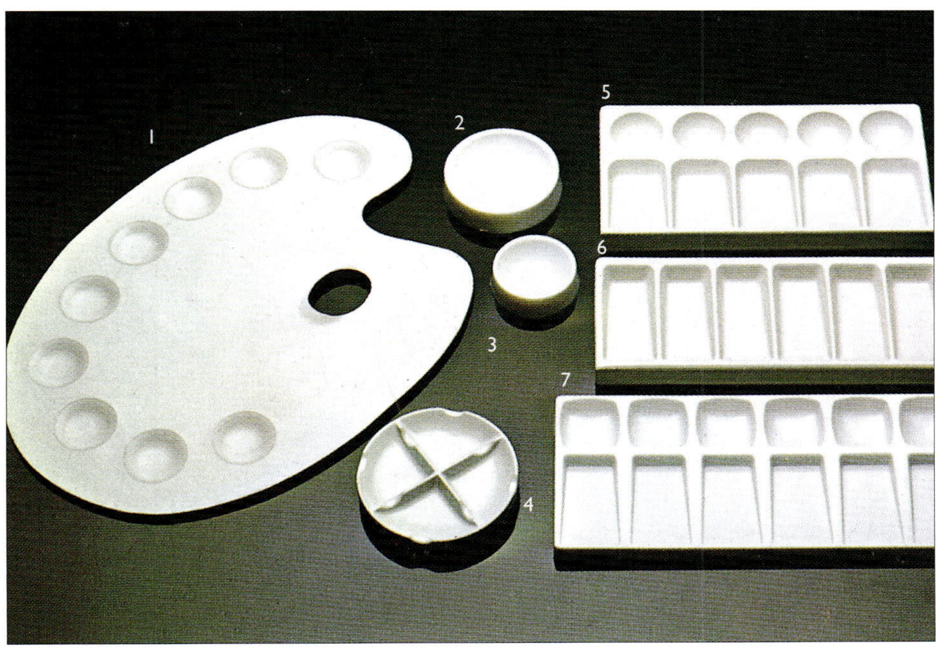

Left *There are many forms of palette. (1) The traditional palette with thumb hole may be held in one hand while painting. (2, 3) Small pots may be used to mix colors separately. (4, 5, 6, and 7) Alternatively, you may wish to keep the colors together in a larger palette with several wells. The palette used is a matter for the artist's personal choice.*

BEST USE OF MATERIALS

- **Mix paint well.**
- **Mix sufficient quantities.**
- **Apply generously.**
- **Keep equipment and tools clean.**
- **Don't hurry the process.**
- **Be gentle, let the tools do their work.**

WATER CONTAINERS

Water is the only solvent, or diluent, needed for acrylic painting, because acrylic paints are water-based. But whether the paint is to be diluted or not, plenty of clean water is essential for keeping brushes clean, and to prevent paint drying on them.

Two containers are not recommended: narrow-necked bottles which restrict movement, and any kind of tin can or container as they are liable to rust and will ruin paint and brushes if they do. Have at least two large containers available, filled with clean water: one for diluting paint and the other for cleaning brushes. Acrylic paint dries when the water in it evaporates, and is then difficult to dislodge. To prevent this, splash a few drops of water on the paint with a brush from time to time, or use a small hand spray.

PALETTES

The next important piece of equipment is a palette. A porcelain or glazed pottery surface is easy to keep clean. If paint dries on it, it can be soaked in hot water for a few minutes and cleaned. A white plate is an advantage. White allows mixtures to be accurately gauged; a colored surface plays optical tricks and is best avoided.

The lip or edge on a plate is only important if the mixtures are rather liquid. For stiffer mixtures, using thicker paints, a pad of paper palettes has advantages. Mix on the top layer, which can be torn off and discarded.

Another possible palette is a sheet of plain white plastic. The advantage here is that it can be bought in any size. Most palettes tend to be small, useful for taking outdoors for sketching trips, but not nearly large enough for working in the studio.

If there is any disadvantage in a plastic palette it might be in the way acrylic paint

IDEAL PALETTE

- **Holds paint well on surface.**
- **Is easy to keep clean.**
- **Has a smooth non-porous surface.**
- **Is white in color.**
- **Has a lip or edge.**

CHOOSING THE PALETTE

- **Large enough?**
- **Practical for your purposes?**
- **Suits your style of working?**

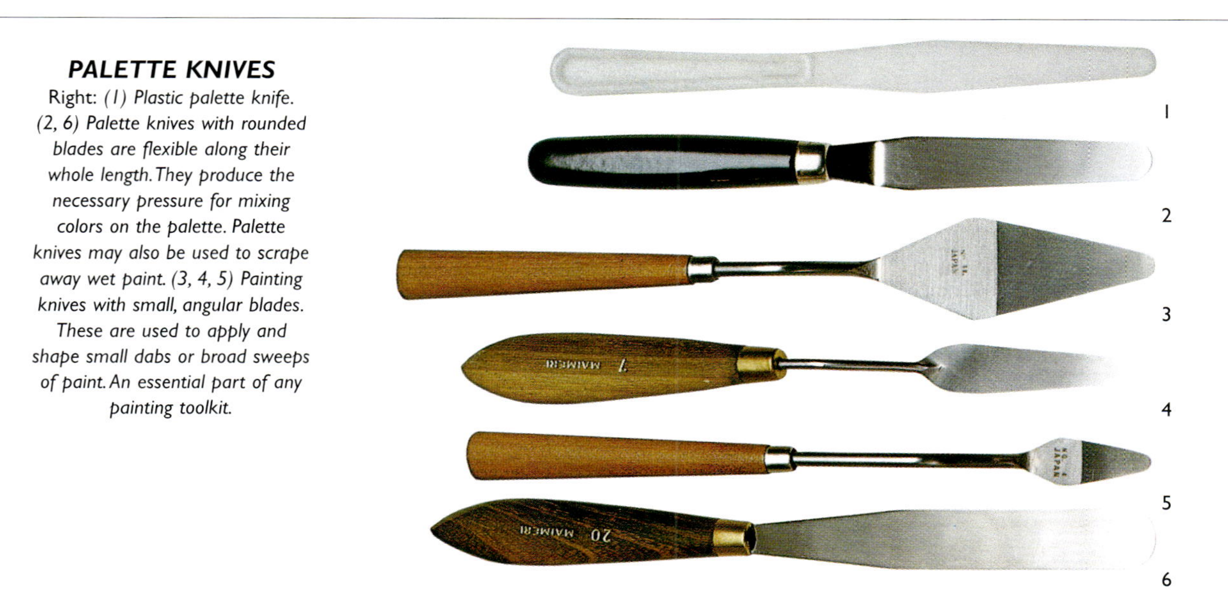

PALETTE KNIVES
Right: *(1) Plastic palette knife. (2, 6) Palette knives with rounded blades are flexible along their whole length. They produce the necessary pressure for mixing colors on the palette. Palette knives may also be used to scrape away wet paint. (3, 4, 5) Painting knives with small, angular blades. These are used to apply and shape small dabs or broad sweeps of paint. An essential part of any painting toolkit.*

clings to it. Some kinds of plastic also have a tendency to stain, unless kept scrupulously dean.

Palette surfaces

Many surfaces will do as palettes, but the palette to avoid is the traditional wooden kind used for oil painting. It has nearly everything wrong with it, from its color to its absorbency. It is difficult to keep clean and is generally impractical for acrylic.

Another surface to avoid is any kind of metal that is uncoated or untreated—with enamel or plastic, etc. Metal has a tendency to corrode, when used with acrylic paint, and if it does, will contaminate the paint. Also avoid old or dirty surfaces, or spongy surfaces like leather or rubber.

MIXING

After palettes come the mixing implements, which can be either brushes—the most common—or palette knives—the most

Below from Left to Right *Red sable round, Russian sable bright, red sable bright, red sable fan blender.*

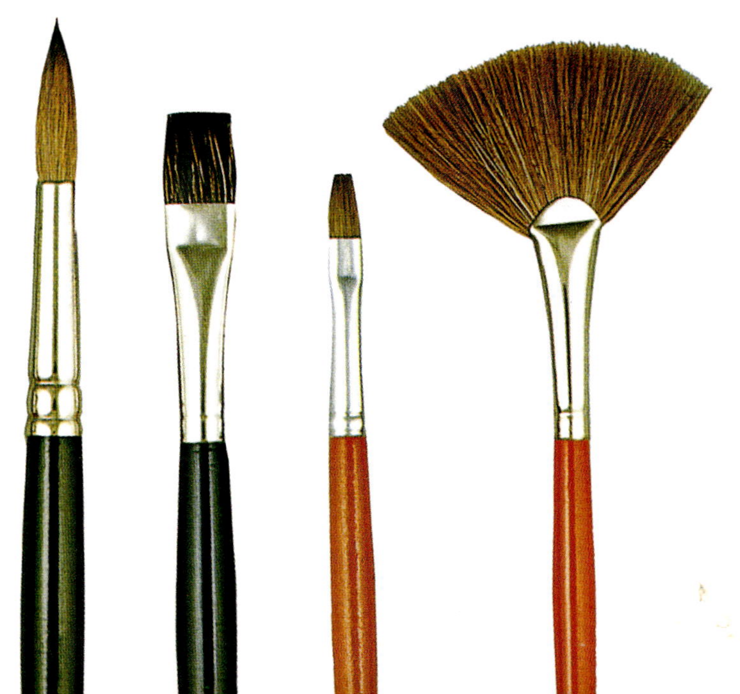

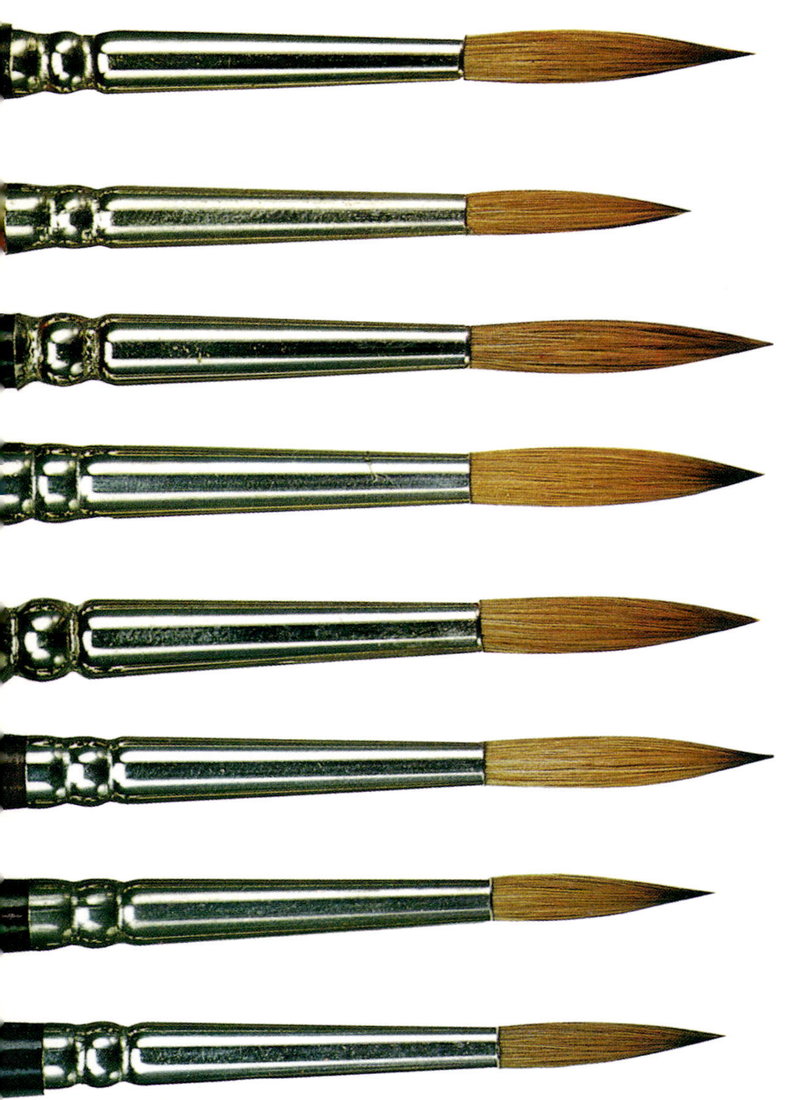

Left *Choice of brushes, as with most other equipment, is a completely personal matter. An artist may wish to use only one type of brush. In this case, he or she will need several different sizes. If the artist wishes to use all types of brushes, three sizes of each may be necessary: small, medium, and large.*

practical. Like brushes, palette knives have more than one function. Both are used to mix and apply paint; the palette knife is also used to clean palettes, which makes it, on balance, a necessary piece of equipment. But this is not all.

A brush wears badly if used for all kinds of mixing—other than small amounts on the palette—and should be regarded primarily as a painting tool, used minimally for mixing.

For mixing (and cleaning) paint, the palette knife is a vital and necessary part of any paintbox, and you can also paint with it. For those who find brushes awkward or difficult to manage, the palette knife will provide the answer. Clean, well-mixed paint can be applied to the support with broad, vigorous strokes. For finer work, specially fashioned knives (known as painting knives) make a variety of delicate marks that are very effective.

BRUSHES

Brushes for acrylic painting can also be used for oil painting.

Sable brushes

Sable brushes are delightful to work with in all mediums. Having specially fashioned points, they can make the most delicate lines and strokes. In addition, they are constructed to hold the paint well, and so spread it with ease and fluency.

They are also expensive, and so must be carefully treated on all counts. If sables are used with acrylic paint, they must be scrupulously washed of all color after use. Acrylic dries hard very quickly, so always keep water handy, to make sure that there is little chance of that happening. Dip your brush in water when not in use.

The range and the variety of sable brushes may appear bewildering initially, but a good start can be made by narrowing the choice down to two: a No. 3 for fine work, and a No. 7 for broad, both round in shape. Other sizes can be added later.

To these can be added ox-hair or squirrel brushes, which are a great deal less expensive than the sable brushes are. Large areas, which would need a very expensive sable to do the job, could be done just as satisfactorily with an ox-hair or squirrel brush.

A good all-round selection of brushes must contain a few soft and hard brushes to meet all possible contingencies. The best hard brushes are hog's-hair.

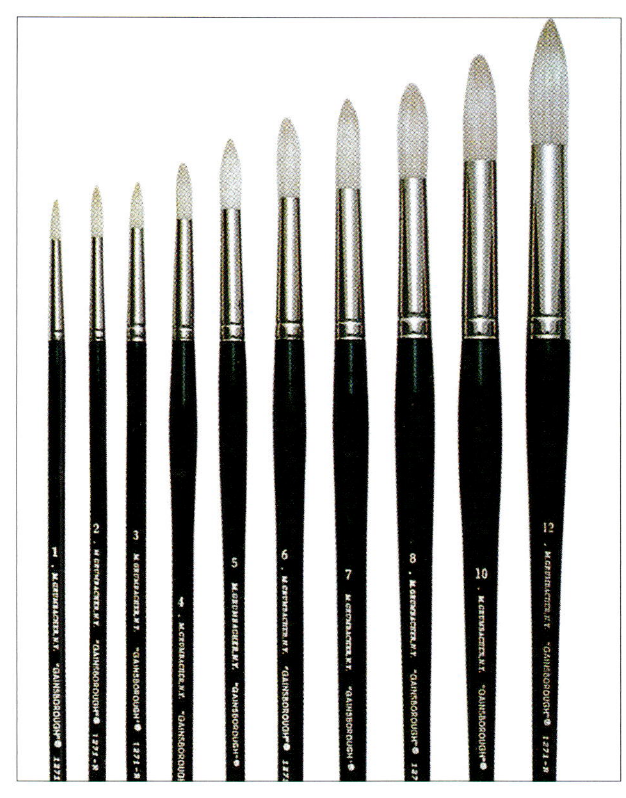

Above *Brushes come in many sizes. Most ranges are numbered from 1 (the smallest) to 12. Extra large brushes (numbered up to 36) are also available.*

Hog's-hair brushes

Hog's-hair brushes were mainly used for oil paint, until the introduction of acrylic, for which, painters have since discovered, they are admirably suited.

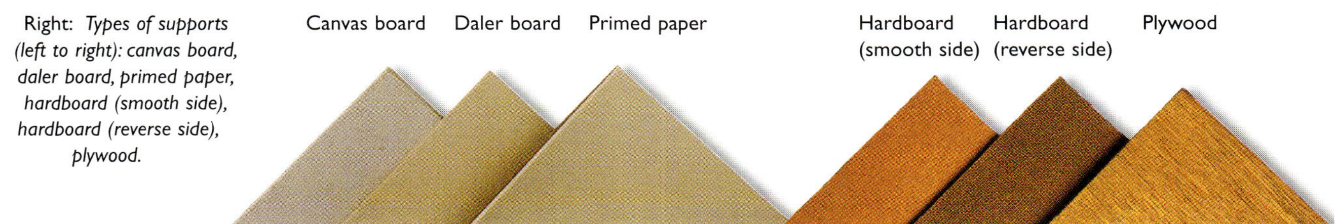

Right: *Types of supports (left to right): canvas board, daler board, primed paper, hardboard (smooth side), hardboard (reverse side), plywood.*

CARE OF BRUSHES

- **Keep them clean.**
- **Store them when not in use—any box will do.**
- **Add a moth repellent.**
- **When in use, arrange in a jar, or bottle, heads up splayed out, to avoid damage.**
- **Don't use the same brush too often; give it a rest occasionally.**

They differ from sables in a number of ways: whereas the majority of sables are round in shape, hog's hairs come in four quite distinct shapes: round, bright (or square), flat, and filbert, which are capable of a great variety of marks.

Hog's-hair brushes are made from real bristle, and are dressed and shaped according to the natural curve of the hair. They are so skilfully put together that they always retain their shape no matter how much paint is on them and how vigorously they are used. They still require careful attention, though.

Choosing a selection of these brushes may be done in the same way as with sables: a small and a large from each type—say a 3 or 4 small, and a 7 or 8 large, depending on individual preferences and cost.

Synthetic brushes

Nylon brushes have improved a great deal since they were first introduced. They perform well, clean easily and, as sable brushes have become very expensive, are good alternatives to sable and the finer hog's-hair. Synthetic fibersare robust and wear well under vigorous use. They are cheaper than other brushes and well worth trying.

CLEANING A BRUSH

1 *Rinse the brush in a wide-necked jar of clean water.*

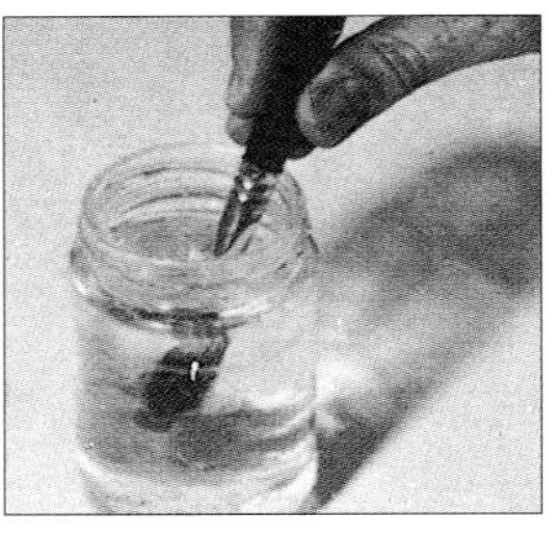

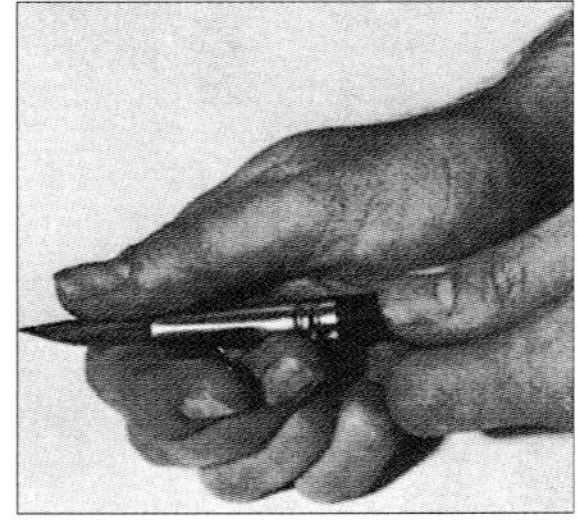

2 *Reshape the brush by drawing it backward through the palm.*

3 *Allow the brush to dry by storing it up-ended in a jar.*

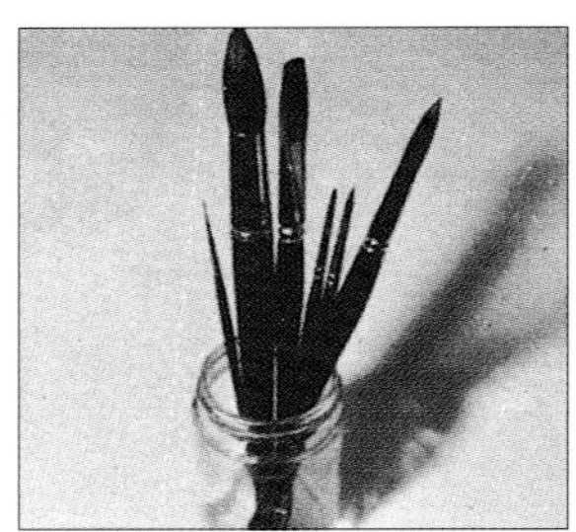

SUPPORTS FOR ACRYLIC PAINTING

Anything upon which a painting is executed is called a support. Traditionally they were wood panels, walls, and canvases; today we also use paper, card (cardboard), and hardboard.

Every painting or painted surface consists of three elements: a support—the material upon which one paints; the ground—which covers the support (also referred to as priming); the paint itself, usually put on in layers.

In theory, you can use almost anything as a support for acrylic painting. There should be no problem if you bear in mind these six points:

- All surfaces must be absolutely clean to ensure adherance.
- Make sure it has not oil or wax in manufacture.
- Do not use oil-primed wood, canvas, or board.
- Very smooth surfaces require tooth before use.
- Avoid silk, unseasoned wood and large sheets of hardboard.
- Avoid very rough surfaces.

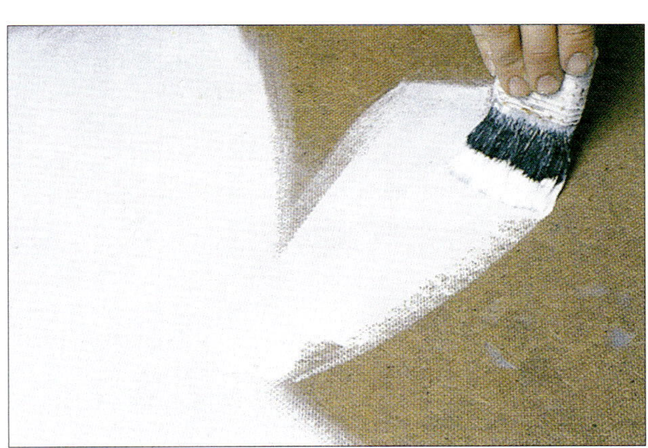

Above: *White arylic primer is applied to hardboard with a household brush.*

HOW TO STRETCH A CANVAS

1 *Wood for stretchers are available in many lengths.*

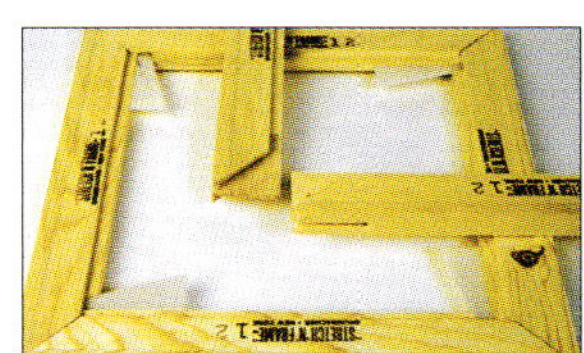

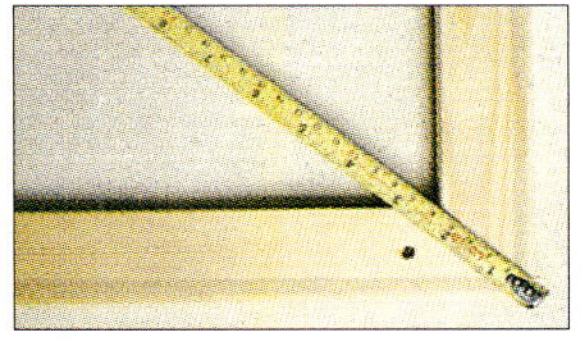

2 *Slot the stretchers together so that the corners are at right angles.*

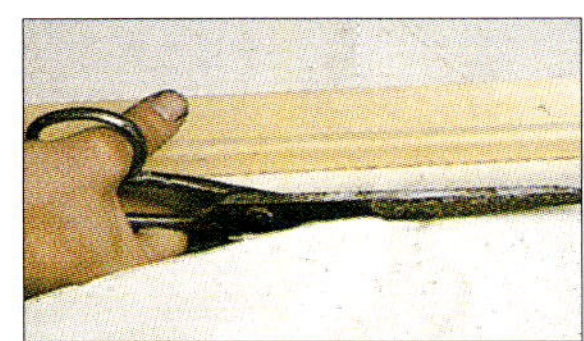

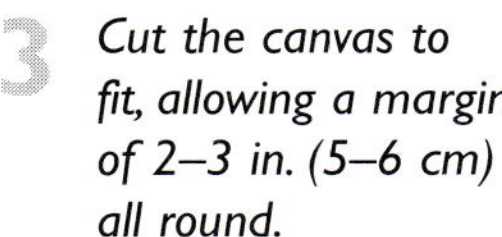

3 *Cut the canvas to fit, allowing a margin of 2–3 in. (5–6 cm) all round.*

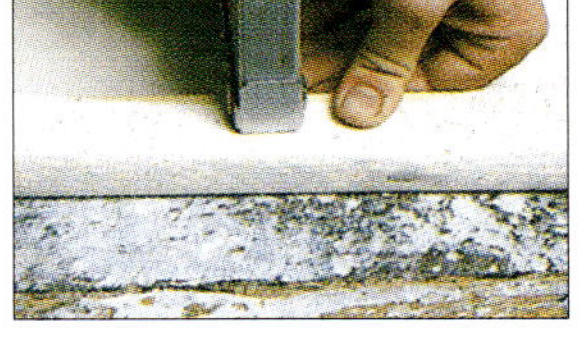

4 *Fold the canvas over and staple it to the middle of the longest side.*

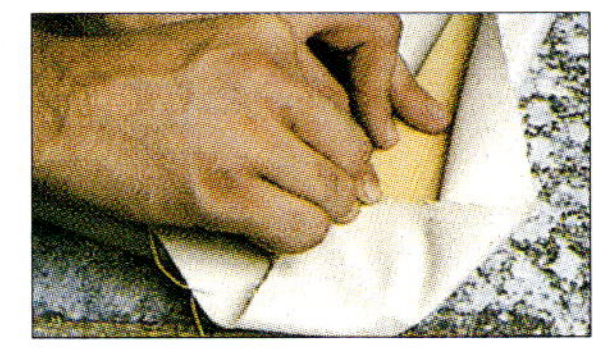

5 *Staple at 3 in. (8 cm) intervals. Repeat on opposite side.*

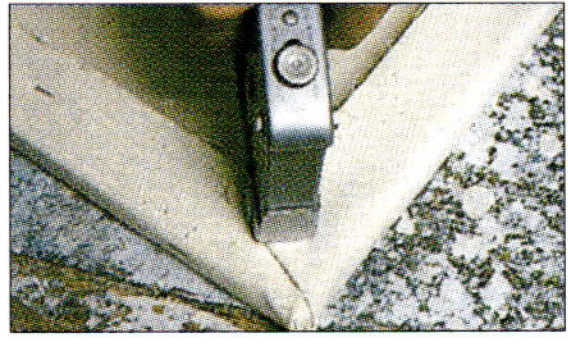

6 *Turn the corners diagonally. Staple both edges firmly.*

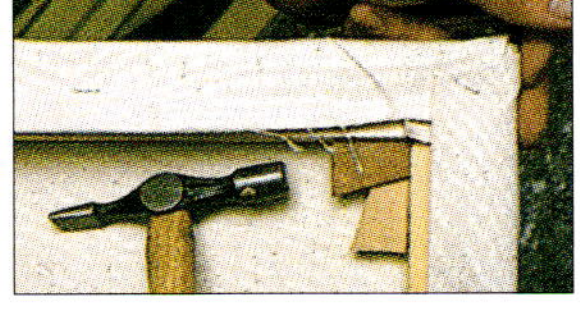

7 *Tap wedges into place. Fabric should be tight.*

1 *Unbleached calico, a cheap cotton weave.*

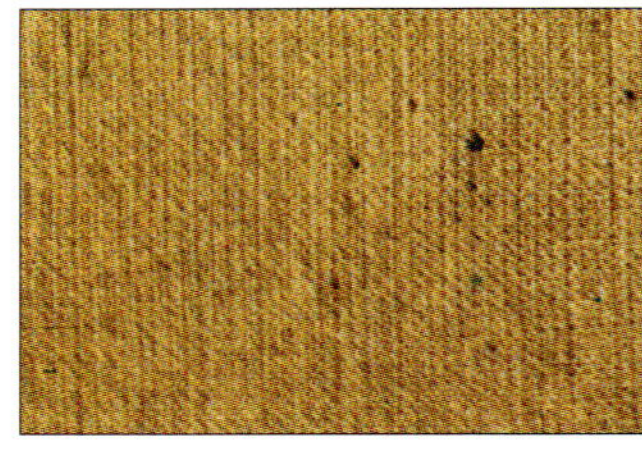

2 *Good canvas; next best thing to linen.*

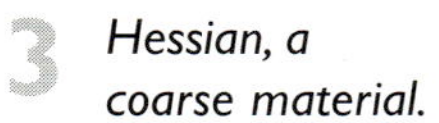

3 *Hessian, a coarse material.*

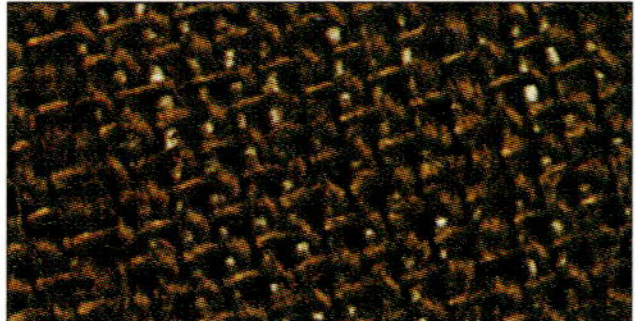

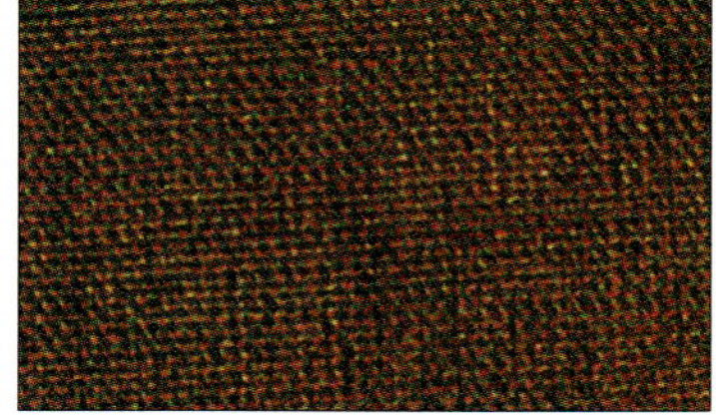

4 *Linen, in a close weave.*

5 *Linen, in a coarse weave.*

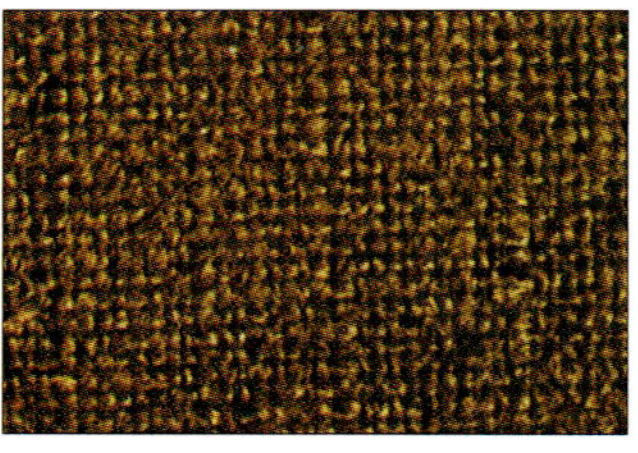

6 *Linen, ready-primed with acrylic.*

Priming

Priming surfaces for acrylic painting requires only white acrylic primer, which is easily and quickly applied with a household brush, roller, or palette knife to wood, canvas, card (cardboard), paper, or hardboard.

Two thin coats should be sufficient to cover a piece of hardboard and one coat might be sufficient for a piece of white cardboard. If you prefer the natural color of the support, you can brush on a thin coat of acrylic medium, matt or glossy, to prime the surface.

Canvases

Ready-made canvases, primed for acrylic painting, can be obtained at most art supply shops. Though light and pleasant to use, it has many disadvantages. Canvas is prone to damage, the expansion and contraction of the cloth in varying temperatures will place a great strain on the priming, and cause cracking and flaking.

Thin coats of acrylic medium might help to stiffen the canvas a little and make it a little less fragile, as would keeping the canvas taut by knocking up the corners with the appropriate wedges whenever possible.

Making your own canvas is not only cheaper, but is also more satisfying if you have the time. A good wide table or the floor will do, provided the canvas can lie perfectly flat. The canvas is made up of two distinct materials, before priming: wood for the stretchers and keys (wedges), and the canvas itself, which might be made from cotton or flax and be woven coarse, medium, or fine.

There are two kinds of stretchers: wedged or fixed. The wedged have a specially cut end that will firmly wedge together. When made up with canvas, they can be stretched tightly by the insertion of small triangular shaped pieces of wood into the specially cut slots. Gently tapping them in with a hammer will pull the canvas tight.

Good art supply shops stock all sizes of wedged stretchers. If for some reason the right size cannot be obtained, making them yourself can be a problem.

As a substitute for a wedged stretcher you can construct a fixed frame, made from bought, 2 by 1 strips of wood. These can be cut to size and properly mitered and glued to ensure that it will take the strain of the taut canvas.

As these frames are rigid, they cannot be tightened at the corners with keys or wedges should the canvas become slack. This means that the only way to keep the canvas tight is to restretch it.

Stretching the canvas

To stretch either raw or primed canvas: cut the canvas 4 in. (8 cm) longer and wider than the stretcher, to allow for overlap. Place on a flat surface and place the stretcher on top of the canvas. Fold one edge of the canvas over the frame and tack or staple it in the center of the side. Then do the same to the opposite side, then to the two remaining sides.

When tacking is completed, make certain that there are no creases at the corners before priming. It is unnecessary to wedge the corners at this stage. When the priming dries out the canvas will tighten automatically, provided the priming is thinly applied.

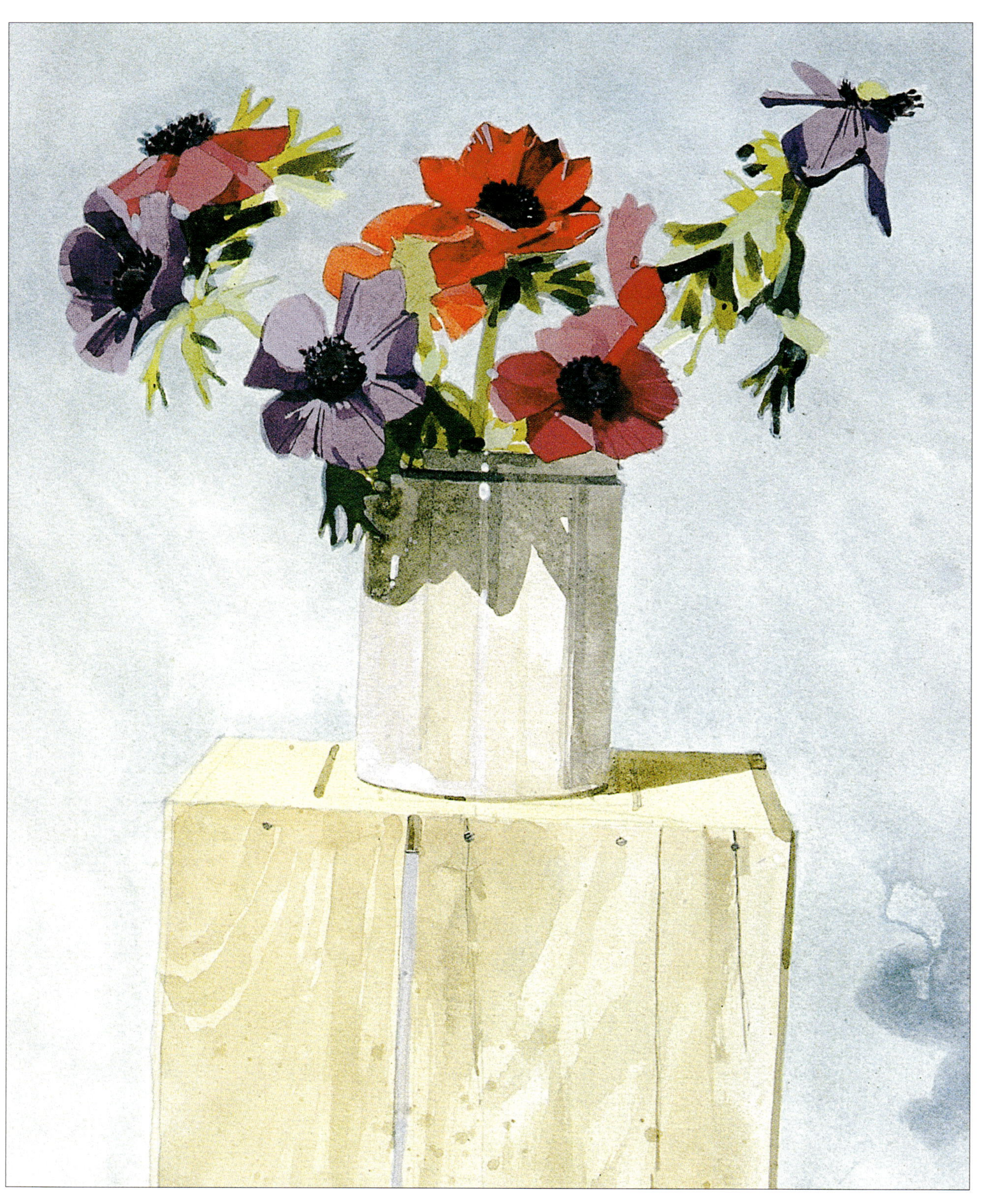

11 PAINTING WITH ACRYLICS

Next to watercolor, acrylics are the simplest of paints to use. The minimum amount needed is a few tubes of paint, some brushes, a palette, and water; because of its basic simplicity, acrylic can give enjoyment from the very start. Many painters and designers make a practice of combining acrylic with other media like colored inks, drawing, and gouache. Acrylic seems to work well with almost any conventional medium, provided it doesn't contain oil.

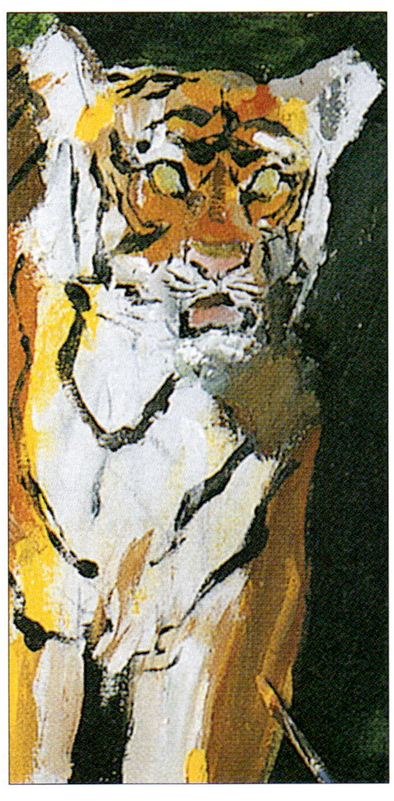

THE INFRASTRUCTURE OF PAINTING

Looking at a painting or design is rather like looking at an iceberg. We only see the tip. We know, however, that a great deal of the iceberg is beneath the water—hence its strength. The strength of a painting, too, lies beneath the surface—and has dangers for the unwary as well as delights. If this fact isn't understood, painting will forever be a mystery.

Actually the principle is very simple and quite easy to understand. It is this: paintings are built up in layers. Even watercolors are built up with layers of washes.

This layering of one coat of paint over another varies with the function of that layer. For example, the function of the primer differs from the function of a glaze: the primer, because it is a sealer and a reflector of light, is thick and opaque; the glaze is thin and transparent because its job is to let the light, or another color, come through.

For painting in oil or acrylic the number of coats or layers could be as many as ten.

LAYERS OF A PAINTING

- Support: paper, card, canvas, hardboard, etc.
- Sealer: glue size or acrylic medium (optional for acrylic, necessary for oil)
- Primer: gesso, acrylic white, lead white, etc.
- Wash or toned drawing
- Blocking in the main areas of color
- Middle layer
- Scumble
- Impasto
- Glaze
- Varnish

The success of any painting depends on how they are amalgamated. The study of paint layers goes hand in hand with a study of colors and the way they interact with each other. Before that, we have to consider another important factor—water.

WATER

The most important of medium used with acrylics is the diluent itself, water.

Water plays a dominant part in painting with acrylics, not only for the vital process of thinning the paint to the required consistency, but also for cleaning brushes and palette.

Literally one must study the behavior of water, for it must play its part throughout the whole of the work. Water is the life blood of acrylics, and though the other mediums extend the range of achievement, one can, at a pinch, do without them—as many of us did when acrylic paint was new and largely unknown. Consequently we were forced to examine just how much we could do with water alone.

It is essential to remember that once the water evaporates the paint hardens and cannot be redissolved with any more water

COLOR TEMPERATURE

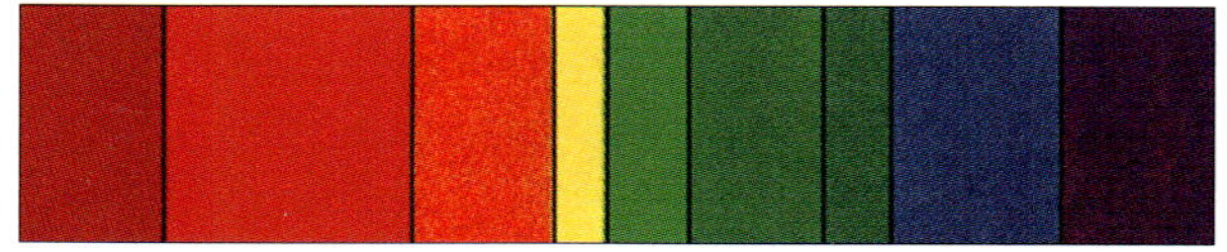

Above *Warm colors are those closer to the red end of the spectrum. Cold colors are those closer to the blue end of the spectrum.*

(as it can with watercolor and gouache). With experience you learn to add just the right amount of water to produce the right consistency and the appropriate drying time to allow for working. This produces the simple rule: the more water used, the thinner the paint and the longer the drying time.

The four main forms of consistency are: thin, thick, transparent, opaque. Some of them can be amalgamated by the use of water alone: thin/transparent; thin/opaque. However, the only way to admix thick and transparent is by the use of a gel. Similarly the only way to get a really thick paint is by the addition of acrylic texture paste. For the rest, water is sufficient.

Because acrylic is a water-based paint, it is always the practice to wet the brush before use, especially for mixing paint. As a general rule, never use a dry brush for anything pertaining to acrylic. You can do the same with a palette knife—moistening it before use—though of course, the knife won't retain as much water.

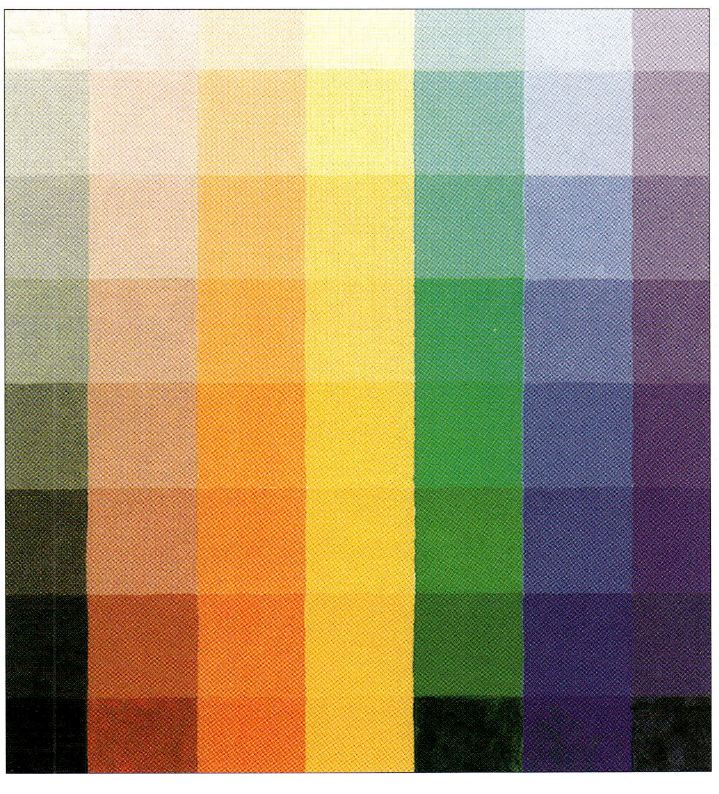

Above *The horizontal and vertical grid. This grid gives us a fair idea about the tones and tints—obtained by mixing white or black to various colors—in various colors.*

CHOOSING COLORS

The next, and most important, stage, is choosing colors, then mixing and applying them. The following color exercises are very basic and, to get the maximum benefit from them, thin opaque paint is recommended.

Choose a palette that will hold the paint well. Thin paint does have a tendency

Left *The grid with separate tones. If you perform the mixing exercises in this chapter, you will soon recognize the different tints and tones in various colors, including black and white.*

to slop about. Another point to note is that once acrylic paint is mixed, it will last indefinitely so long as the water in it doesn't evaporate. Therefore any color that has been mixed, and for any reason isn't needed right away, can be kept in a small jar or container so long as it is properly stoppered.

Choice of colors is the very heart of painting and designing. The question is how to go about it?

The overwhelming compunction on seeing a color chart for the first time, is to want them all—and then give up because the choice is so wide, so it is refreshing to be told that the maximum number of colors needed to make up a palette is five.

FIVE ESSENTIAL COLORS

- White is absolutely mandatory in any palette, for mixing tones and tints, for repainting and as a color.
- Black is essential for tones, and as a color.
- Yellow—primary.
- Red—primary.
- Blue—primary.

The three primaries, yellow, red, and blue can be mixed to make three further colors, or secondaries:

Yellow and red make orange.
Yellow and blue make green.
Blue and red make violet.

MIXING ACRYLIC

To get used to the way acrylic behaves, and to get the feel, as well as the visual impact of a mixture, a sound practice is to begin mixing each color—both primaries and secondaries—with white first, and then with black. Then add black to white mixes, and white to the black.

Mixing white with a color is referred to as a tint.

Mixing black with a color is referred to as a tone.

The point of this is that once the visual experience of mixing colors has taken place it will remain as a guide for future reference. The more mixing that is done now, the more confident will be the results later. The results of these experiments should be kept, at least for a time, as a reminder.

COLOR MIXING

Exercise 1—light to dark

The very first experience with mixing can be with just white and black, before trying out the other colors.

Use six squares, about 0.4 in. (1 cm) in size, which can be conveniently filled with

Left *The tonal scale runs from white to black. Every color—and not just black or white—has a tonal equivalent on that scale between light and dark.*

variegated tones of paint from light to dark, and from dark to light.

Method 1. Add black to white, to make a series of grays, from the palest to the darkest tints, in six steps.

Method 2. Reverse the process by adding white to black.

This exercise can now be repeated with all the colors, one by one, included in the palette, utilising Method 1 to make tones, and Method 2 to make tints. Points to remember, observe and develop:

1. Care should be taken in the mixing, so that each change of tone is clear.
2. When trying any new color, do it this way before using it.
3. The exercise helps sensitize you to what the color looks like when mixed.
4. For best results, white paper or cardboard is recommended.
5. As a variation, colours may be mixed horizontally as well as vertically.
6. Also try mixing without using white; lighten colors with addition of water.
7. Painting can be done with knife or brush; experiment with them all.
8. Try out other acrylic colors—the umbers, siennas, ochers, etc.

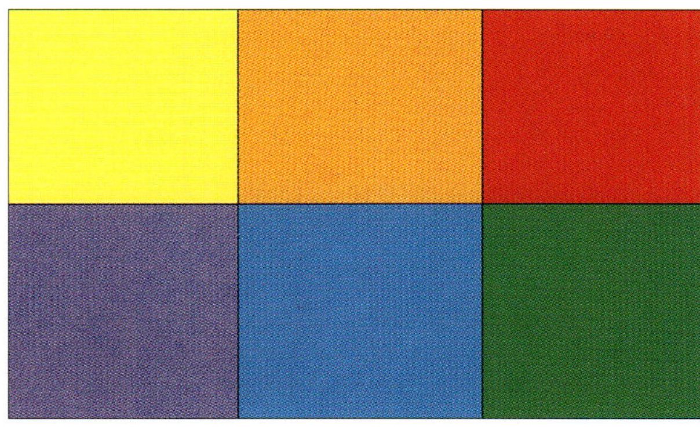

Above *A similar complementary chart to the one below, incorporating intermediate tones and tints. Three of these are primaries (yellow, red and blue) and other three secondaries.*

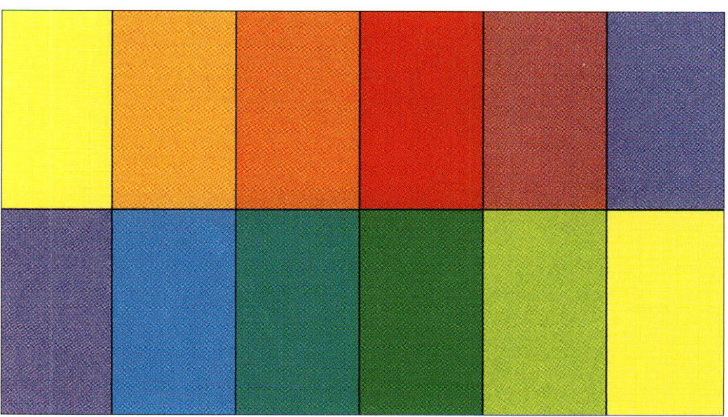

Above *This chart shows the primary colors, yellow, blue, and red with their contrasting complementaries, violet, orange, and green, respectively.*

WHITE PAINT

White plays a most important role in painting and you will need more of it than any of the other colors. If possible buy the larger quantities.

Titanium white is the only white pigment used, at the moment, for acrylic white paint, and is very powerful. A little goes a long way. So one has to be careful when mixing to add the white sparingly, or strong colors will be reduced to tints surprisingly quickly.

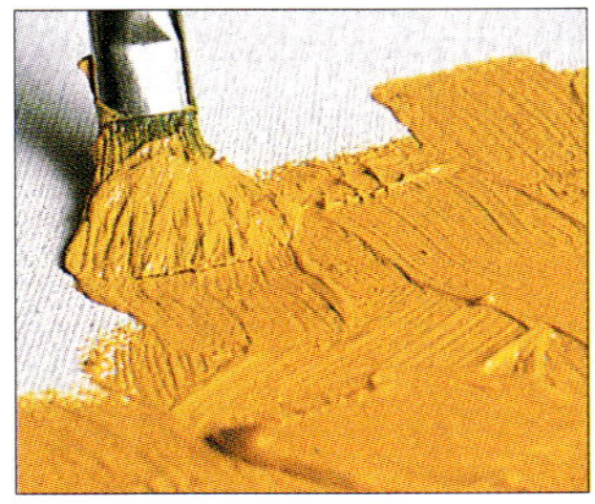

1 *Use knife to mix the paint on the palette, then spread it thickly in broad, textured ridges.*

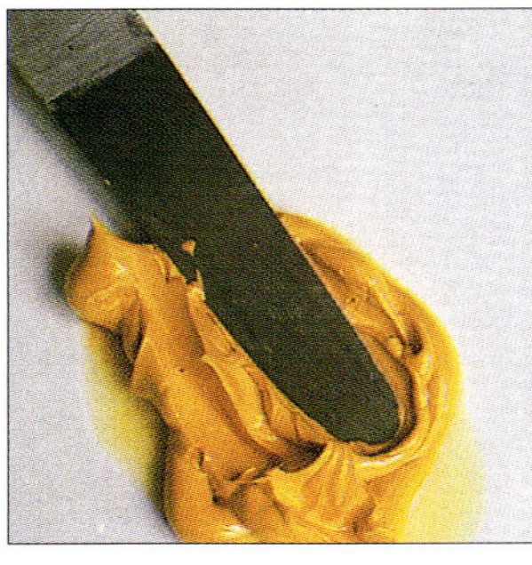

2 *A heavy impasto may be sculpted to produce interesting swirls and ridges.*

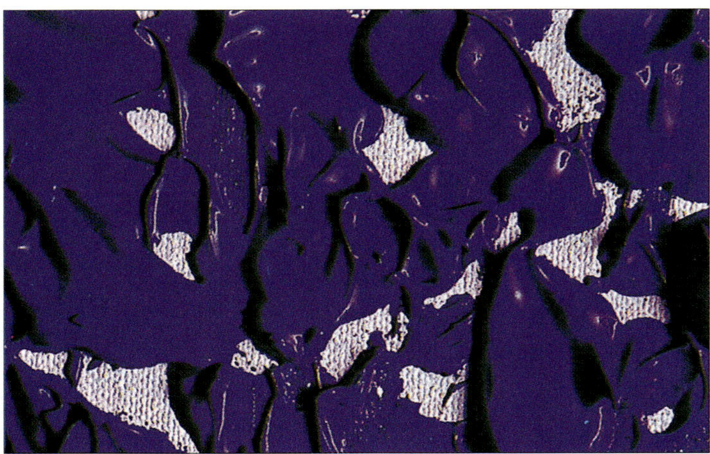

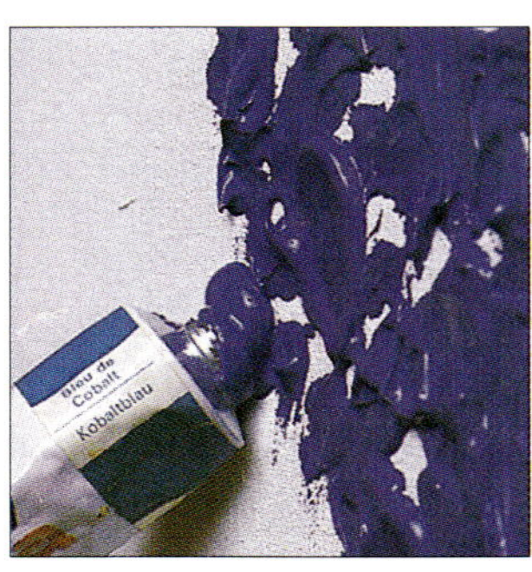

1 *Use undiluted acrylic paint from the tube, or mix with an equal proportion of gel medium.*

2 *Use a knife or a stiff bristle brush to spread the paint on the canvas.*

BLACK PAINT

Mars black, which is absolutely permanent, is manufactured from artificial oxides of iron and is rather powerful so that, like white, it should be mixed sparingly with other colors. Although its use is suggested in the exercises, tones can be produced with many other combinations of color—red and green, for example, make very good gray-blacks, as do blue and umber.

Exercise 2—direct vision

As a bridge from mixing colors on a systematic chart basis as in Exercise 1 to the full examination of color in nature which will lead to the painting of pictures, the following method is a simple and easy step in that direction.

1. Thin, opaque paint.
2. Primed or unprimed paper or card (cardboard), not too big.
3. The choice of the various brushes is again optional.
4. Black and white paint are mandatory.
5. Three primaries only to begin with.

To carry out this exercise, select a number of objects of the same color: red, yellow, or blue.

If a particular color is chosen, say red, to begin the experiment with, it will be immediately noticed that reds vary enormously. Some are warmer, others colder. Shiny reds will appear quite different

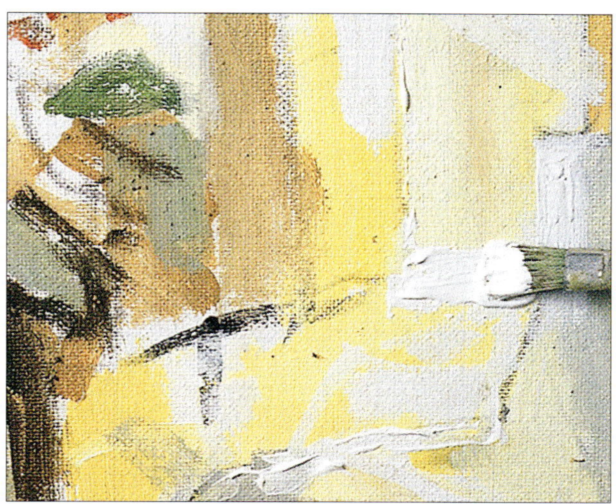

Above *When applying impasto, mix the paint to a fairly stiff consistency and dab onto the support. Spread and shape it as required. The brushmarks will form part of the composition.*

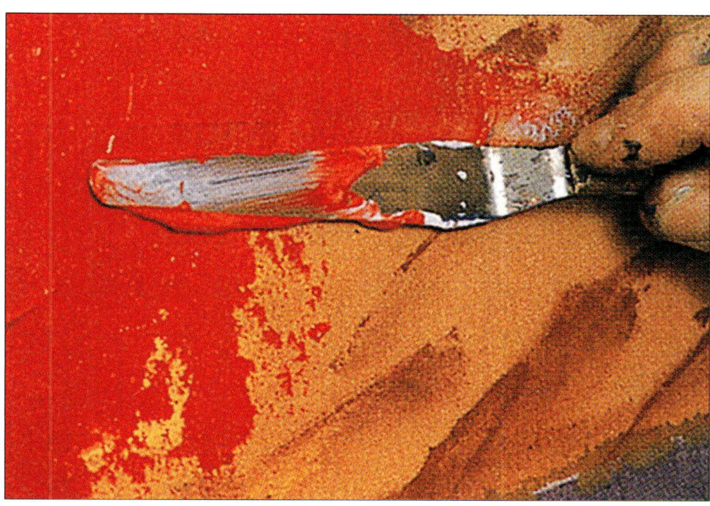

Above *An alternative method of applying impasto is to use a small palette knife. Scoop up some paint and lay it on the support. Spread and shape the impasto.*

from matt, some will be darker than the others, and so on.

Three objects on a similar color background are sufficient to begin with, arranged so as to make the maximum effect of the color obvious.

The object of this exercise, whichever way it is painted, is to mix different tones and tints of the same color. This particular way of observing color will enable you to grasp the essentials of manipulating color.

The suggested method of painting to adopt is as follows:

1. Establish the large areas of color.
2. Build up the shapes of tone with crisp dabs of paint.
3. Make no effort to make the painting look "real"; let the paint and the color dominate instead.

This exercise should be repeated using all the primaries. It can then be followed by exploring the secondaries, green, orange, and violet.

IMPASTOS

Impastos are thick, heavy strokes of paint made with brush or painting knife, and commonly associated with oil paint. With acrylic they can be achieved straight from the tube, like oil paint, and by the addition of either of two acrylic mediums—gel and texture or modeling paste—can be made as thickly as desired. Oil paint, on the other hand, dries slowly and cannot be thickened beyond a certain point without damage to

TEXTURAL IDEAS

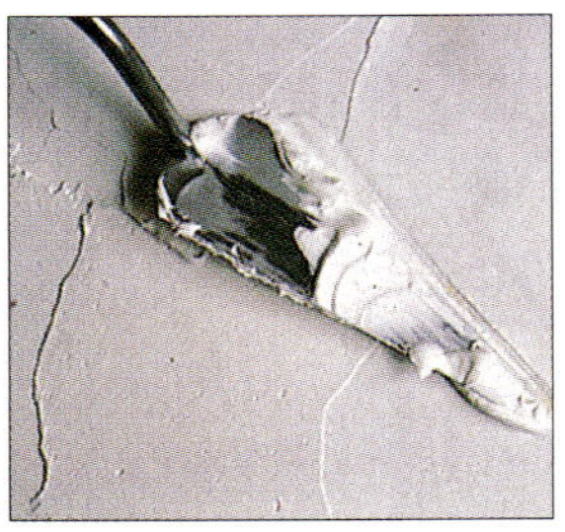

Left: *A thick layer of acrylic mixed with modeling paste is applied with a painting knife and smoothed out.*

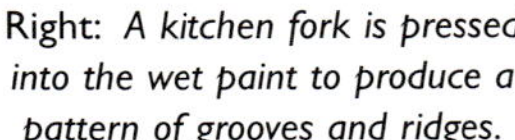

Right: *A kitchen fork is pressed into the wet paint to produce a pattern of grooves and ridges.*

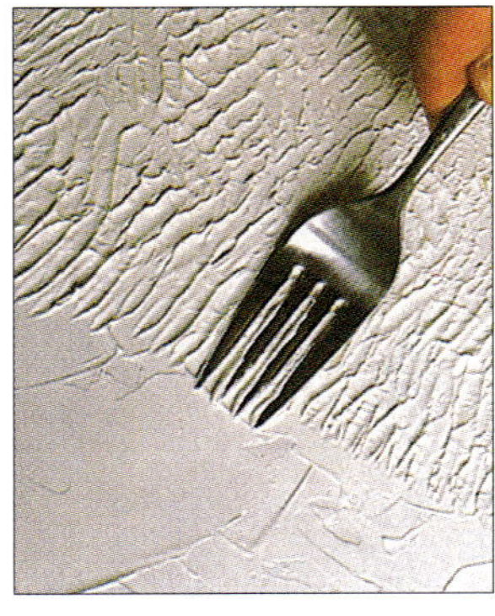

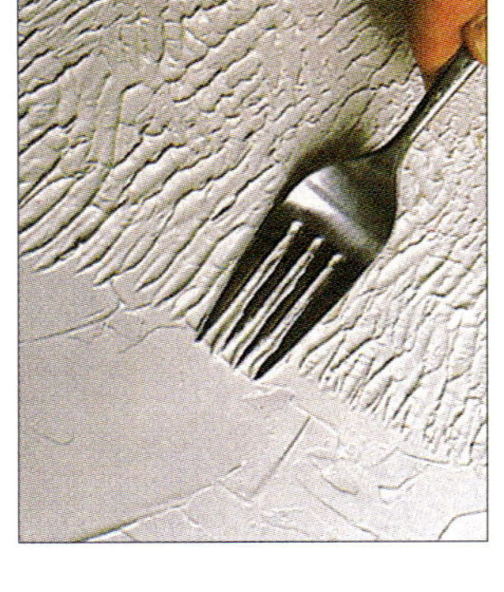

Left: *An adhesive tool is used here. By twisting and turning it, many different patterns may be made.*

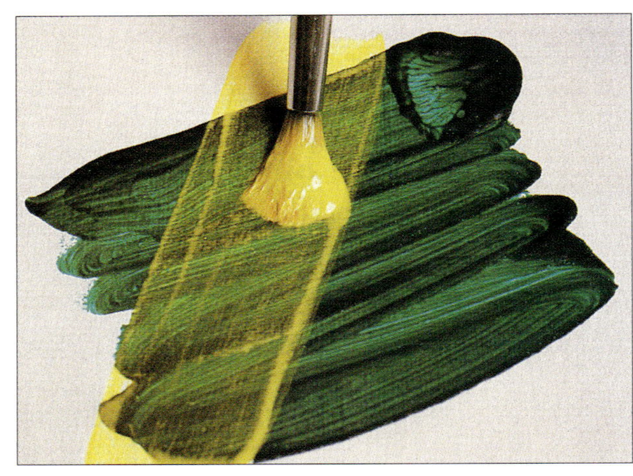

its inherent and visual appeal.

What gives impastos their value is the directness with which they are done. Mess them about by too much overpainting and the vitality is severely reduced: you end with tinted mud. The knife is probably less liable to mess, in spite of being clumsier than a brush. The flat blade of the knife, which is constructed for mixing to begin with, merely remixes the paint when applied to painting. The brush, on the other hand, being less able to mix, will only stir the paint up.

Right: *To make this glaze, mix a small amount of color with a lot of medium. Apply with a soft brush and allow to dry.*

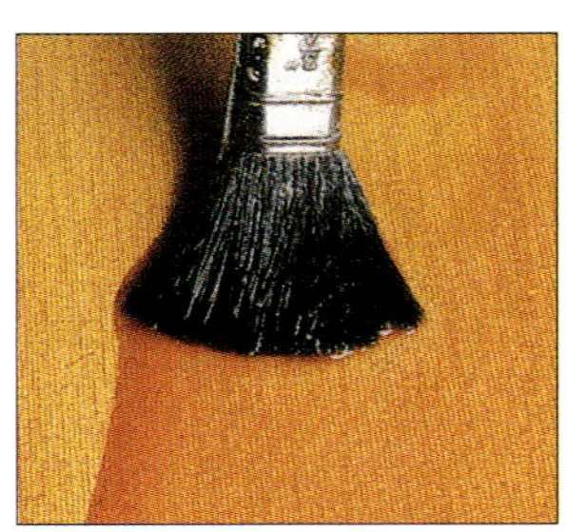

Right: *A more transparent glaze can be made by adding extra matt medium to the pigment.*

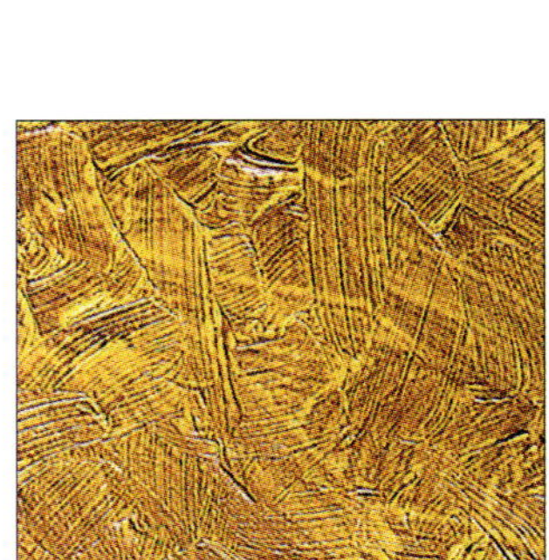

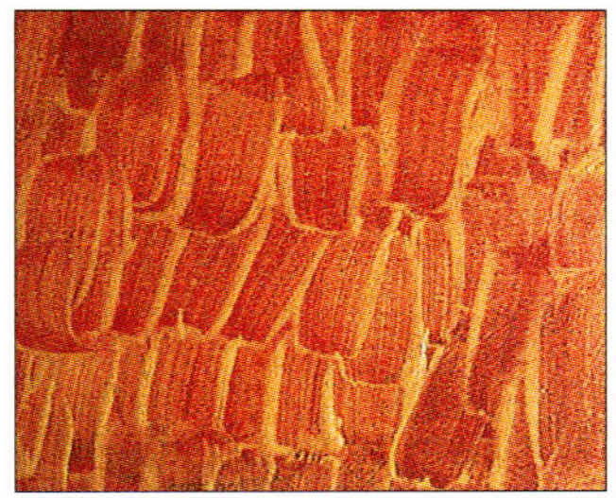

Left *A transparent scumble is made by mixing a lot of matt medium and water with the color to produce delicate scumbles.*

SCUMBLING

1 *Yellow and green are scumbled together but not blended.*

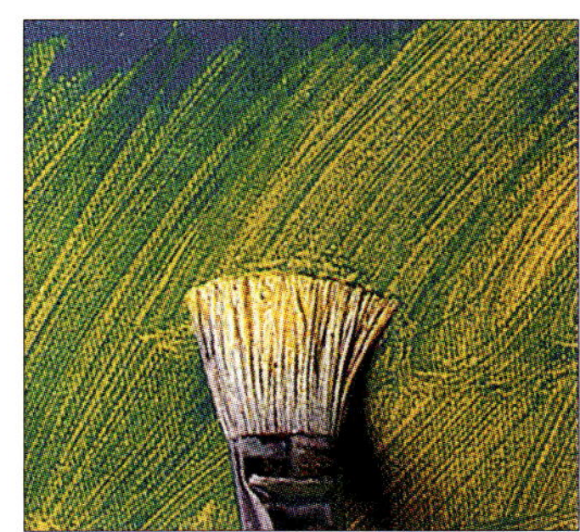

2 *Apply scumbles thinly so that previous applied layers show through.*

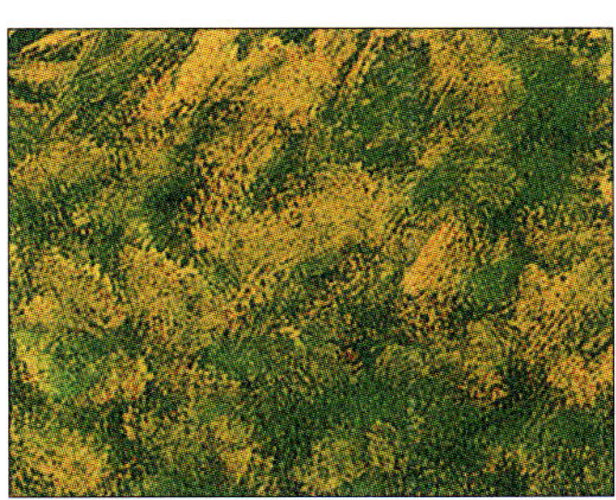

GLAZES

If impastos are the thickest paint used with acrylic, then glazes are the thinnest—thinner even than the washes. Briefly, glazes are a mixture of medium and transparent pigment which is applied over dried underpaintings. Glazes are, in effect, transparent colored windows, and behave not unlike sunglasses—reducing the amount of light, and slightly changing the color.

EXERCISE IN GLAZING

For the exercise only, a small piece of card (cardboard) or paper is necessary. But to get the most out of it, both plain and primed supports should be tried. Glazes should be as thin as possible, which makes them fragile, because the binders are weakened. Therefore the addition of a medium is absolutely vital.

The permutations of this principle are numerous. A few examples:

1. Thin glazes over thin opaque paint
2. Thin glazes over thin transparent paint
3. Thin glazes over thick paint
4. Thick glazes over thin paint
5. Light glazes over light glazes.

SCUMBLING

The brush mark that combines some of the transparent qualities of a glaze with the

Below *Use short, irregular strokes to produce an area of broken, scumbled color.*

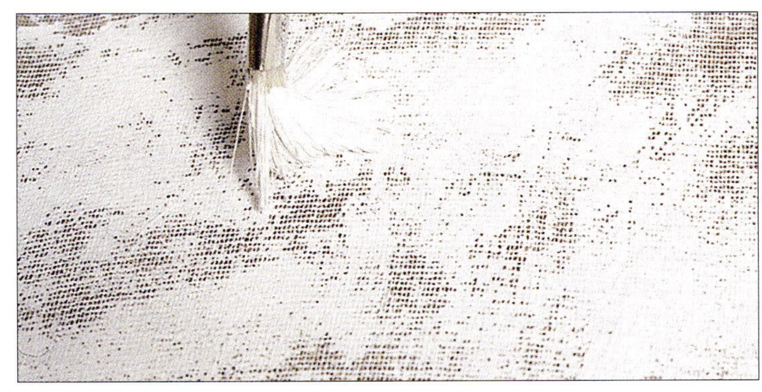

exuberant spontaneity of impasto is a scumble. Scumbling is a somewhat vague term for applying a thin coating of color vigorously brushed over the entire work or parts of it to soften the effect, but the real point of a scumble is to create a free or broken brush mark which will allow the under-painting to show through to animate the color and the surface at the same time.

Scumbling, as its name seems to imply, breaks all the accepted rules for the methodical application of paint. Dry paint, hitherto discouraged as being bad for brushes and palette, is looked upon with favor. "Dry paint" is a stiff rather than thick paint, so that when it is dragged across a surface it will leave a pleasant broken effect. Old brushes or wad of tissue paper are ideal tools.

Scumbling is particularly effective for dragging light paint over a dark ground and vice versa, or dragging one complementary color over another. It is the perfect foil to flat, carefully done painting. Try scumbling over any discarded paintings, and observe how a once-rejected work takes on a new life when scumbled over.

SOME OTHER TECHNIQUES

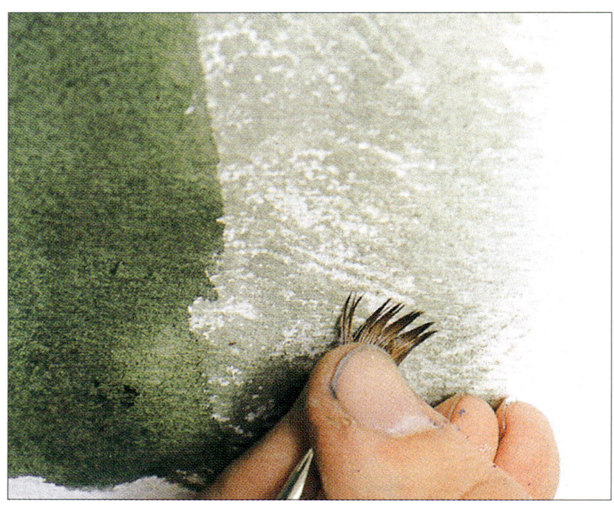

Above *Using a dry brush, pick up color on the brush and move it lightly across the support. The dry brush technique is used to blend or paint areas of finely broken color.*

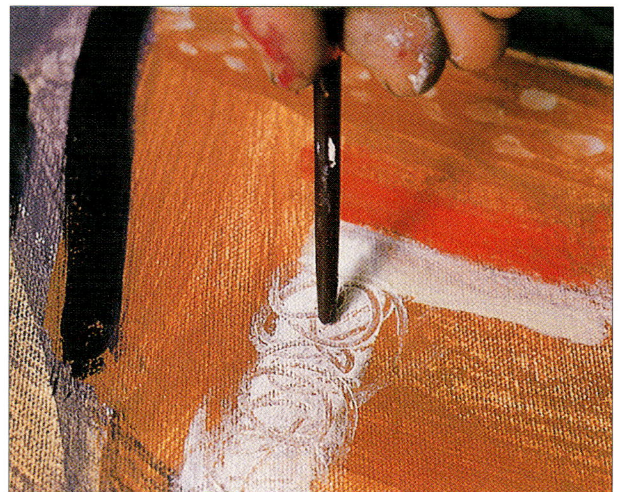

Above *Scratching. Any sharp tool can be used to etch lines and texture into acrylic paint while it is still wet. Here a paint brush handle is being used. A palette knife would have performed adequately as well. The implement would depend on the kind of lines you wish to make.*

WHITING OUT

"Whiting out," or more accurately repriming, enables a painting to be continued indefinitely, or at least until you are satisfied with the result, without the repainted surface showing that it has been reworked in any way whatsoever. Repriming can be done without any difficulty with acrylic because of the quick drying and versatile textural qualities.

Only two conditions need be observed for this to work properly:

1. The surface of the paint must have no impastos or texturing.
2. The white paint (or tinted paint) must be semitransparent.

Dilute some white priming or tube white with water to make a thin semitransparent wash, and white-out the part or parts to be repainted. The density of the paint must be gauged by eye, just so long as the underpainting isn't completely blotted out. Repainting on still-discernible shapes can begin and whiting out can be done as often as necessary. With this method, the whiting-out is done with a painting knife, so that the white paint is spread really thin and the old work shows through better.

Another way of using this method is to use it as an actual technique of building up a work from the start. The design or drawing is painted on unprimed white card (cardboard), or paper, with monochrome washes, and then whited-out over the entire work, letting the drawing or design show through. As a variation, the paint can be tinted with a color. Umbers and ochers are good colors to begin with.

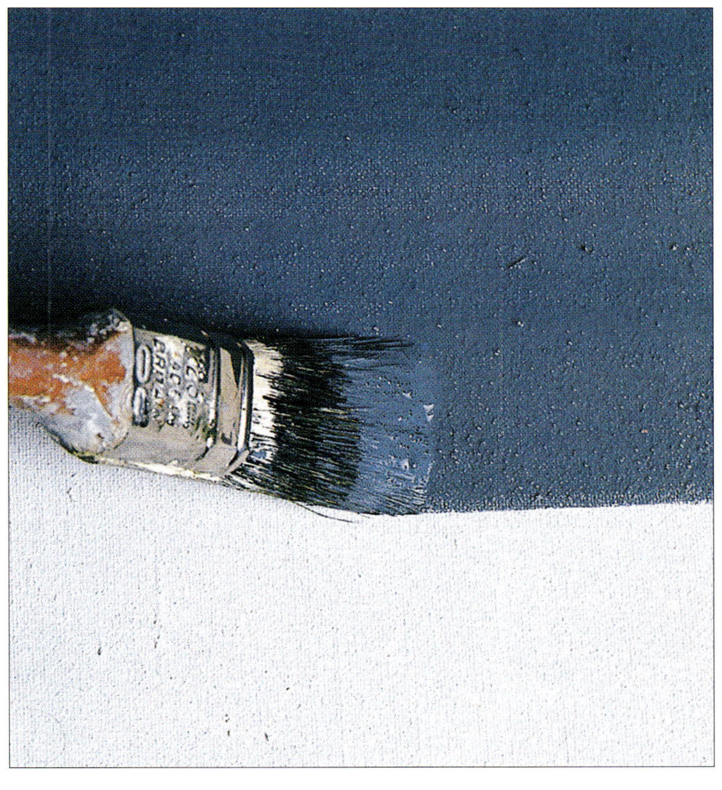

Above *To lay a flat wash, prepare plenty of paint. Use a wide, flat brush and run the strokes in one direction only. Each stroke should slightly overlap the one before.*

WASHES

Although acrylic can be used like watercolor, it must be clearly understood that acrylic washes function differently from watercolor washes. The main difference is the paint composition itself, for though the pigments may be identical, the binders are not. Watercolors can be diluted so thinly that they have hardly any body at all; acrylic, on the other hand, has a binder that imparts weight and substance to the paint.

A useful measure to adopt is always to add a good few drops of the acrylic medium when diluting acrylic paint for washes, as a precaution. It will keep the wash from looking thin and lifeless, and will add a sparkle.

Acrylic, by the very nature of its medium, is less temperamental than watercolor. There is only one rule to observe, that like pure watercolor, once a wash is applied, leave it alone.

Acrylic washes can be formed by:

1. Flooding one wash into another
2. Adding fresh color to a wash
3. Adding color to moistened paper
4. Gradated tones from dark to light
5. Flat
6. Animated by brush strokes
7. Overlay
8. Allowing the surface to play its part
9. Allowing the wash to run freely.

The following experiments should give a great deal of experience. They should be tried on paper, card (cardboard), and even canvas, with and without priming. Vary them by using both smooth and textured surfaces.

Above Left *Experiment 2. To achieve a gradated effect, work quickly, adding water to the paint in increasing quantities with each successive band of color.*

Above Right *Experiment 4. Wet-in-wet: the artist began with a graded wash of cobalt blue and added a wash of lemon yellow.*

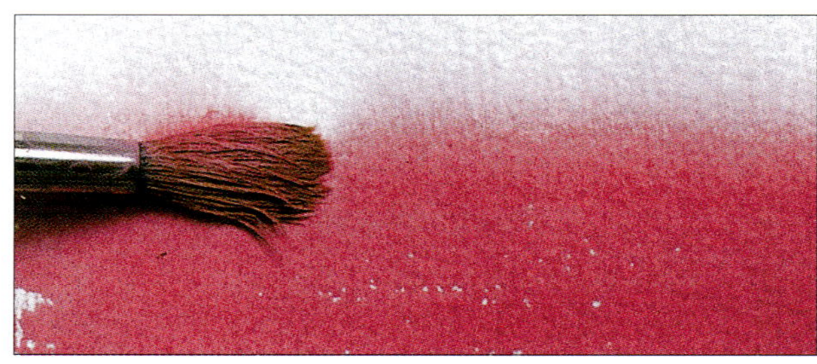

Above *Experiment 3. Single color wet-in-wet wash, made by covering the support with a layer of water.*

Experiment 1—laying a flat wash

- Squeeze out 1/2 in. (1 cm) of paint into a clean container.
- Add water to dilute, mix well to make sure that there are no lumps.
- Add a teaspoon of acrylic medium.
- Spread with a large brush, working from the top, to make a flat wash.
- The application can be carried out upright or on the flat. If upright the wash will run down rather quickly.

OVERLAY

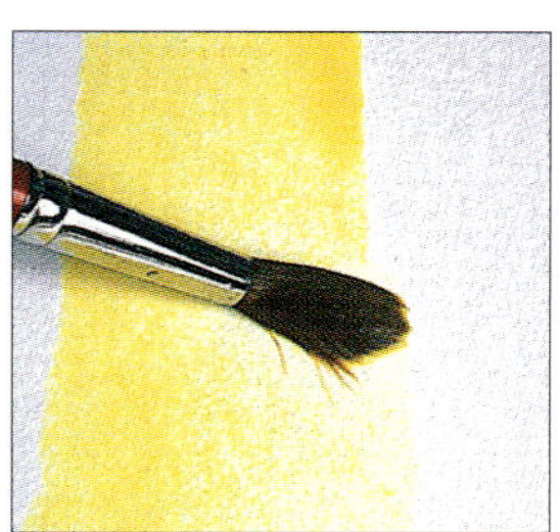

Left *Lay the palest colors first, so that the light reflects off the white paper.*

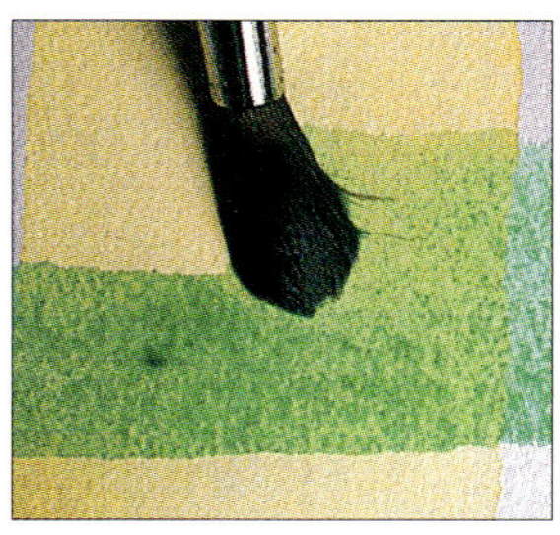

Left *It is vital to allow one color to dry completely before applying the next one.*

Left *The artist applies a thin wash of Hooker's green over the first color. Where the two washes cross, a third hue is produced.*

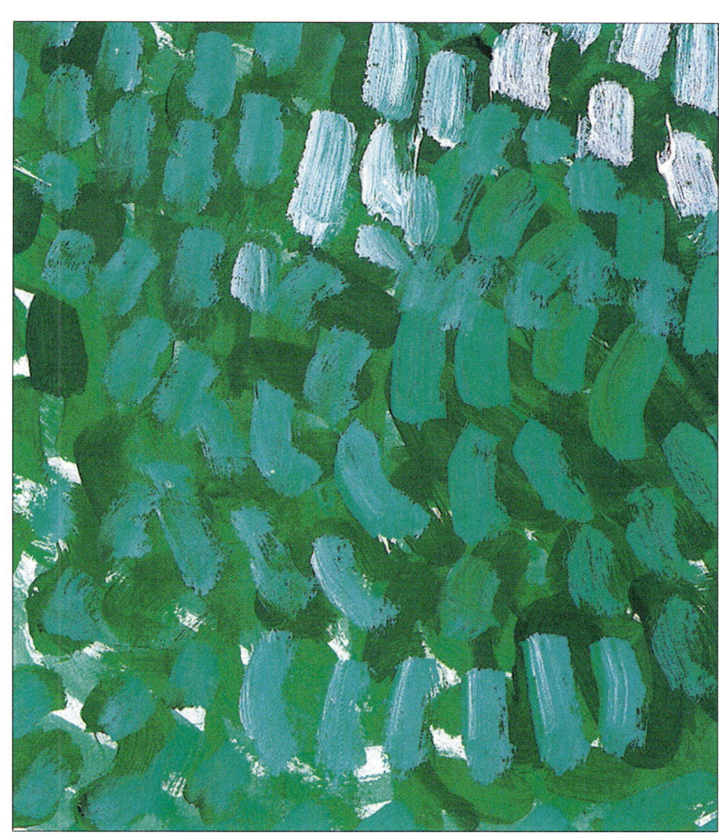

Above *The use of animated strokes with a hog's-hair brush produces a very active texture. These vigorous strokes are better made with hog's hair than expensive sable brushes.*

Experiment 2—gradated tones

Halfway through, continue with clean water and let the color blend into it.

Experiment 3—moistened paper

First cover the paper with water. Then, before it has properly dried, flood a wash into it as above.

Experiment 4—adding color

Proceed as above, and before the color dries flood another color into it.

Experiment 5—overlay

After color dries, apply further washes over the dried paint.

HATCHING

Hatching consists of the criss-crossing of hundreds of small lines over each other to produce a rich variegated tone. The more these fine lines are hatched the more dense

Above *An old, splayed brush was used to create this slightly rough, hatched texture in acrylic. The underlying color glows through overpainting to great effect.*

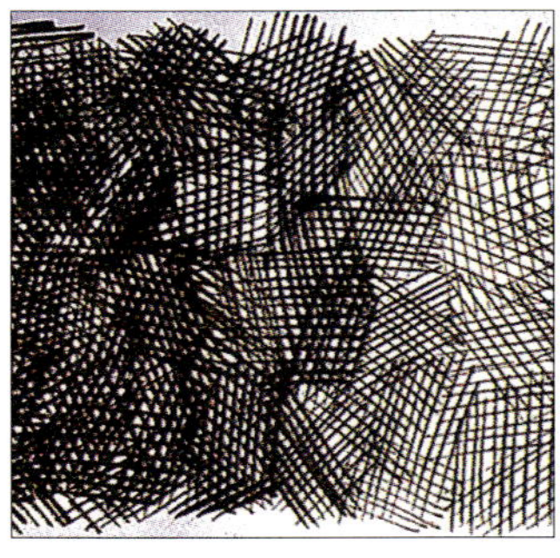

Left *Hatching using ink. By varying the density of the lines, a wide variety of tones is achieved. Freely drawn lines look more lively than perfectly straight, mechanical lines.*

the tone becomes. In painting with a hatching technique, the open network of lines means that not only are the tones gradated, but the underpainting can filter through as well, thus enhancing both tone and color.

Hatching with acrylic will involve small sable brushes (0, 00, or 1) as well as thin paint, which can be either transparent or opaque.

Experiment in hatching

Draw a small grid of 1 in. (2.5 cm) squares. Four squares will suffice. Try filling them with a variety of hatching as follows:

1. Crosshatching with one color
2. Crosshatching from dark to light
3. Crosshatching out from the center
4. Crosshatching in from the outside.

STIPPLING

Stippling is somewhat like hatching in that it is the building up of tone with hundreds of tiny marks. But with stippling, dabs are made with the point or end of the brush.

Stippling can be very hard on brushes unless used with a very gentle kind of stipple, which is not easy to do as the dabbing action is a forceful one. As with hatching, the process is a painstaking one. The overpainting of hundreds of tiny dots one on the other gives a pleasing effect, and the tonal gradations are even more delicate than with hatching. However, it is unnecessary to cover the work completely with stippling. You can confine it to the parts with a more telling effect.

Experiment with stippling in the same way as hatching. The paint can be thicker than with hatching, if desired, and stippling can also be carried out with materials other than brushes: sponges, wads of paper, toothbrushes, even fingertips will do very well as interesting alternatives.

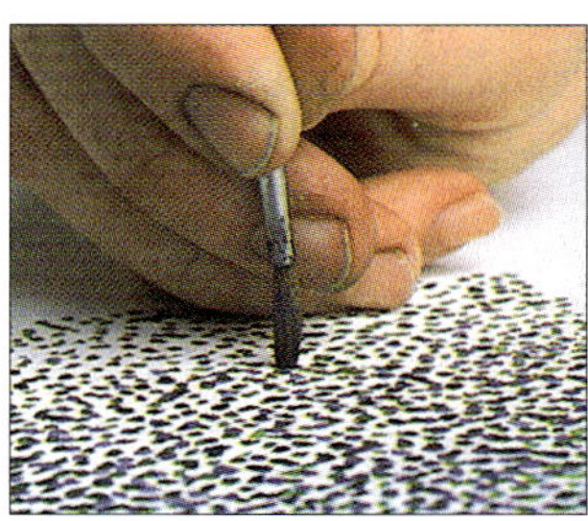

Right *Stippling is carried out by holding the brush at right angles to the painting surface, and repeatedly touching the tip to the surface.*

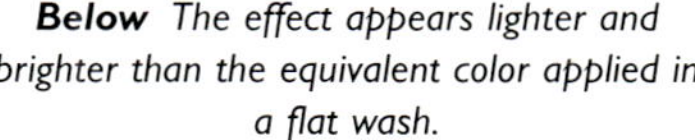

Below *The effect appears lighter and brighter than the equivalent color applied in a flat wash.*

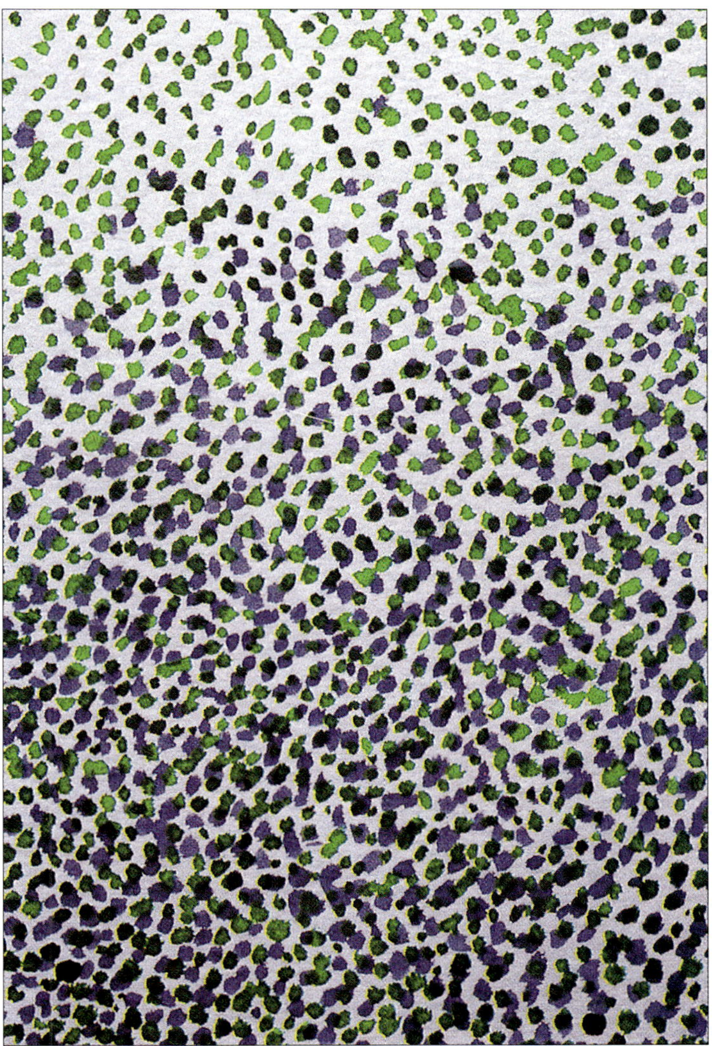

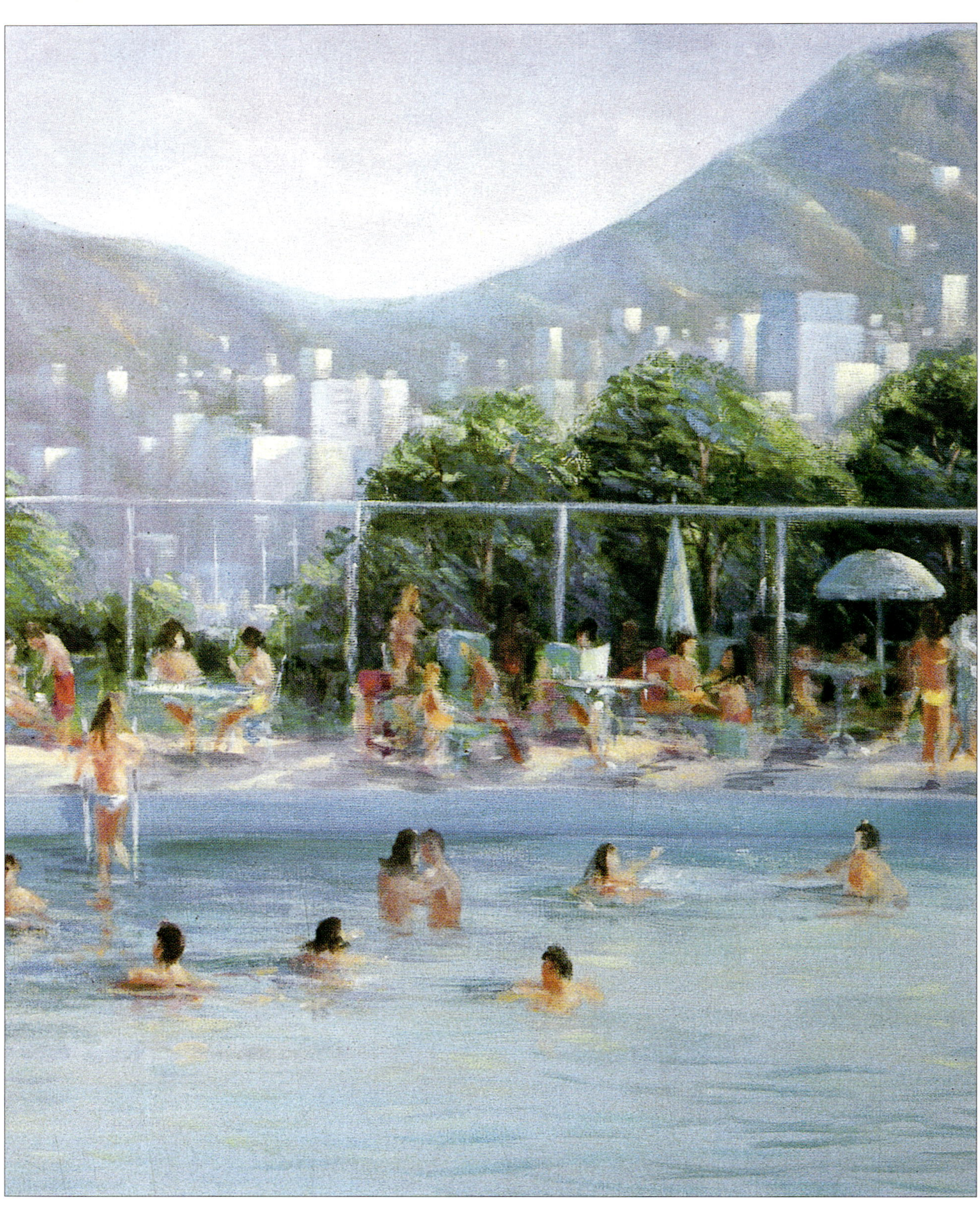

12 THE PROJECTS

Painting is about looking and seeing and translating what you see in the three-dimensional world around you, through selective and imaginative processes, into pictures. Visual source material for your paintings is everywhere around you, on the table in your room, a room in your house, through a window, or even in your mirror. Look at your everyday surroundings with new eyes for a subject and you will find plenty of inspiration.

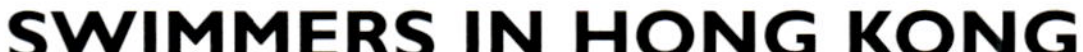

SWIMMERS IN HONG KONG

Waterside pictures are popular subjects for artists, not only because they conjure up holidays, but also because they offer at least three

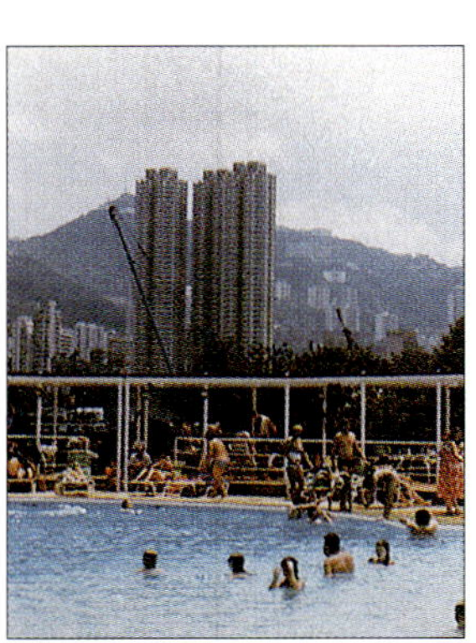

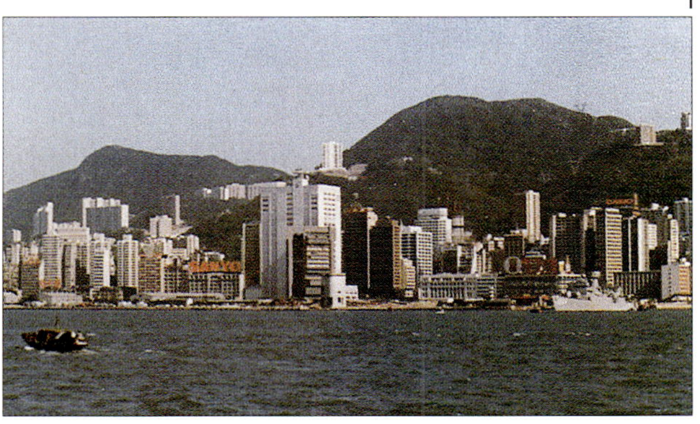

1

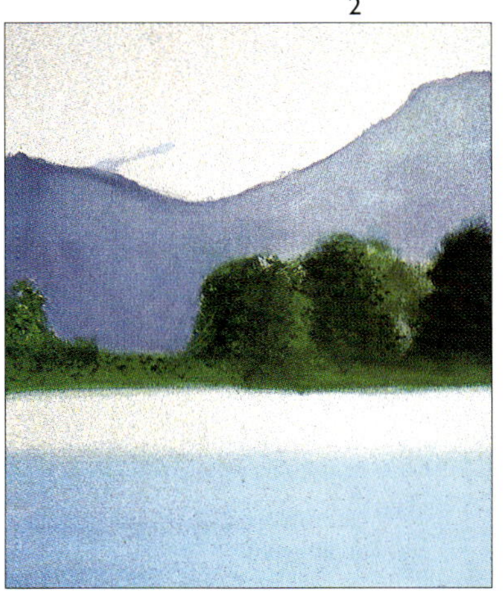

2

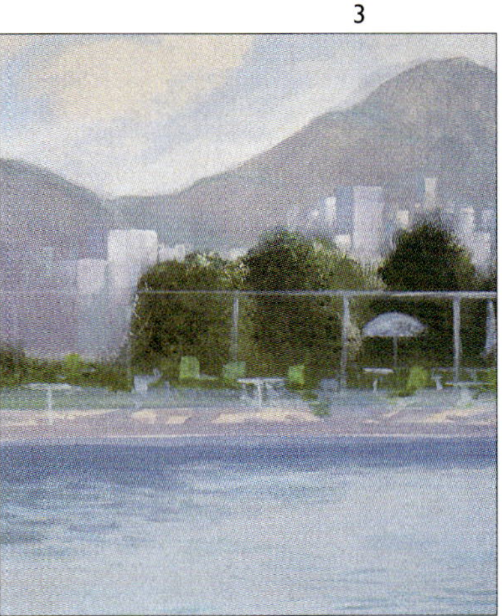

3

1 *Two photographs of the city provide the artist with basic ideas. He will "sandwich" these with other images in his own mind to compose the scene he wishes to paint.*

4

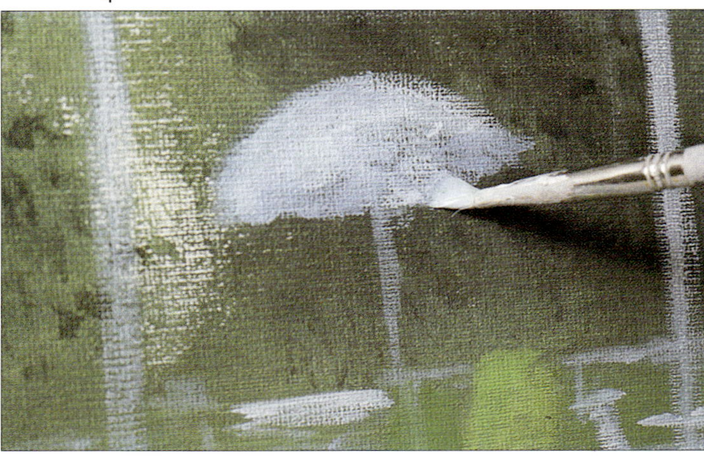

5

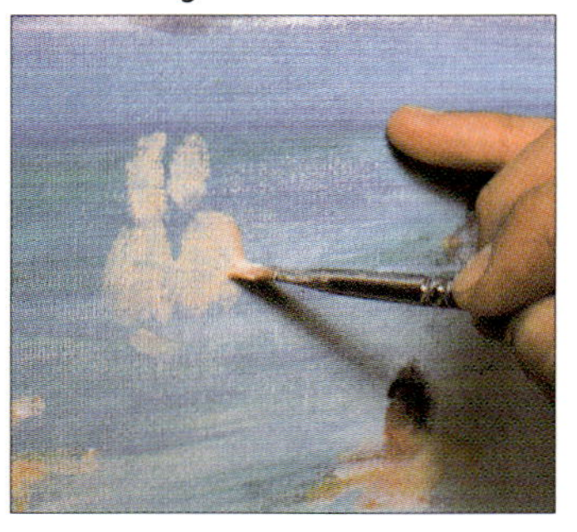

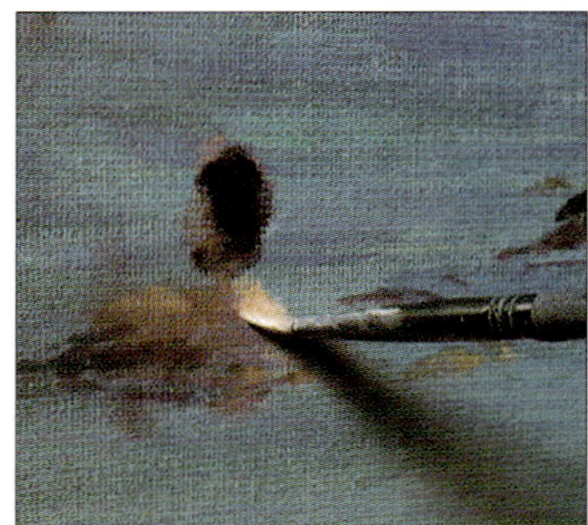

6

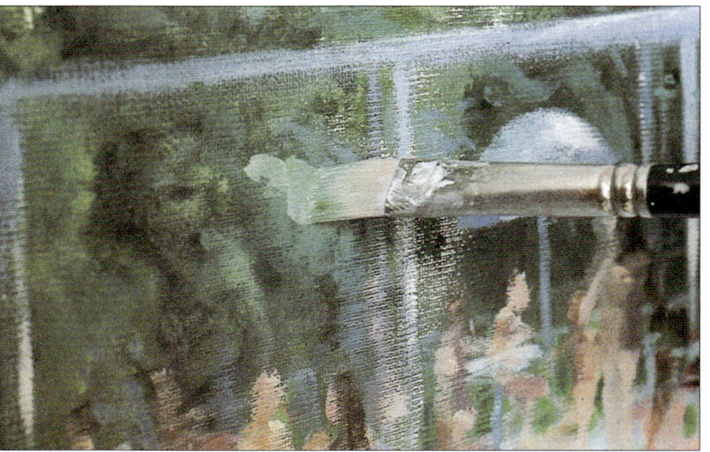

2 *The artist fills the water in primarily with phthalocyanine blue with titanium white which effectively reflect the colors of the sky and the background landscape. The trees in the picture are strengthened with Hooker's green and the hills given more weight and bulk with medium magenta.*

3 *The sky is brought on further with cobalt blue which is also added to the water to deepen and brighten its color. Note how the artist has used different blues for the sky and water.*

4 *Detail in the foreground is now developed, with the correct emphasis on form retained, in keeping with the overall picture. The artist is now building up his painting further.*

5 *Although the figures are very much in the foreground detail would have been impossible here, as the perspective of the composition, with mountains and tall skyscrapers in the background, requires that they be fairly small—maintaining a certain distance.*

6 *The trees are darkened with Hooker's green and highlighted with phthalocyanine green, again in broad brush strokes. Again, the trees are treated with some detail but not intricately.*

MATERIALS USED

SUPPORT:
Prepared, acrylic-primed canvas board, measuring 36 X 25 in. (92 X 64 cm).

COLORS:
Hooker's green, ivory black, phthalocyanine green, medium magenta, titanium white, cobalt blue, phthalocyanine blue, and raw sienna

BRUSHES:
Nos. 2 and 5 round bristle and synthetic, Nos. 2, 4, 6, and 11 flat bristle and synthetic.

7 *The skyscrapers are blocked in with strong, simple strokes; set off against each other with varying mixtures of blues and white.*

8 *The figures have plenty of movement and definition as a result of the careful combination of different colors and tones.*

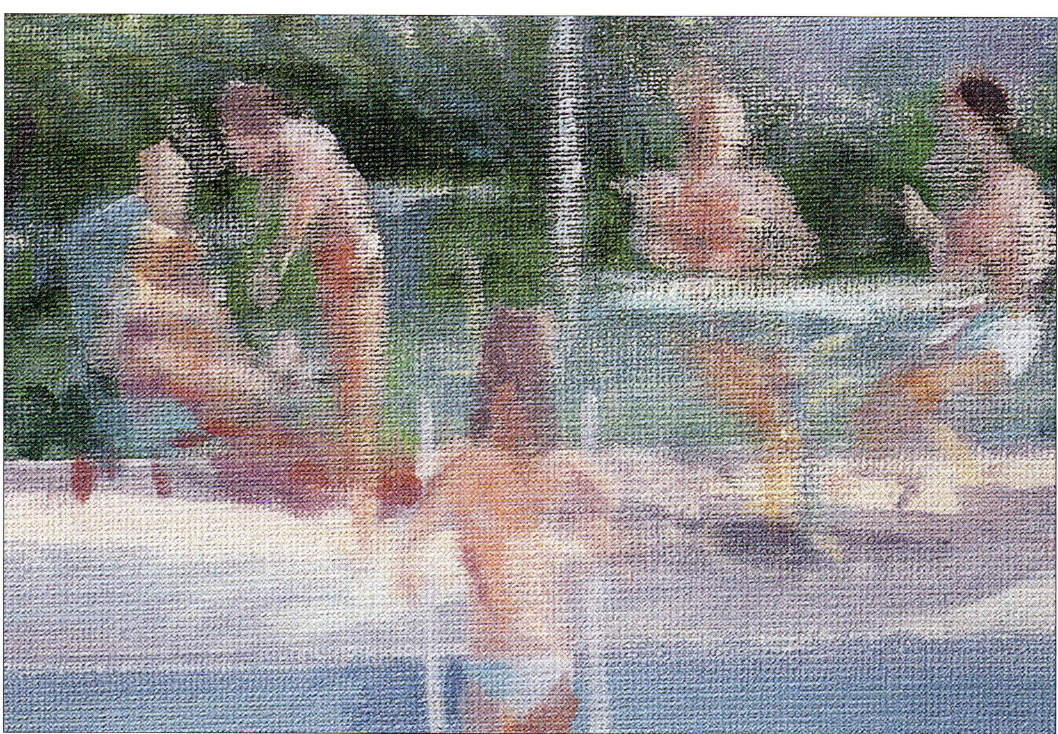

7

8

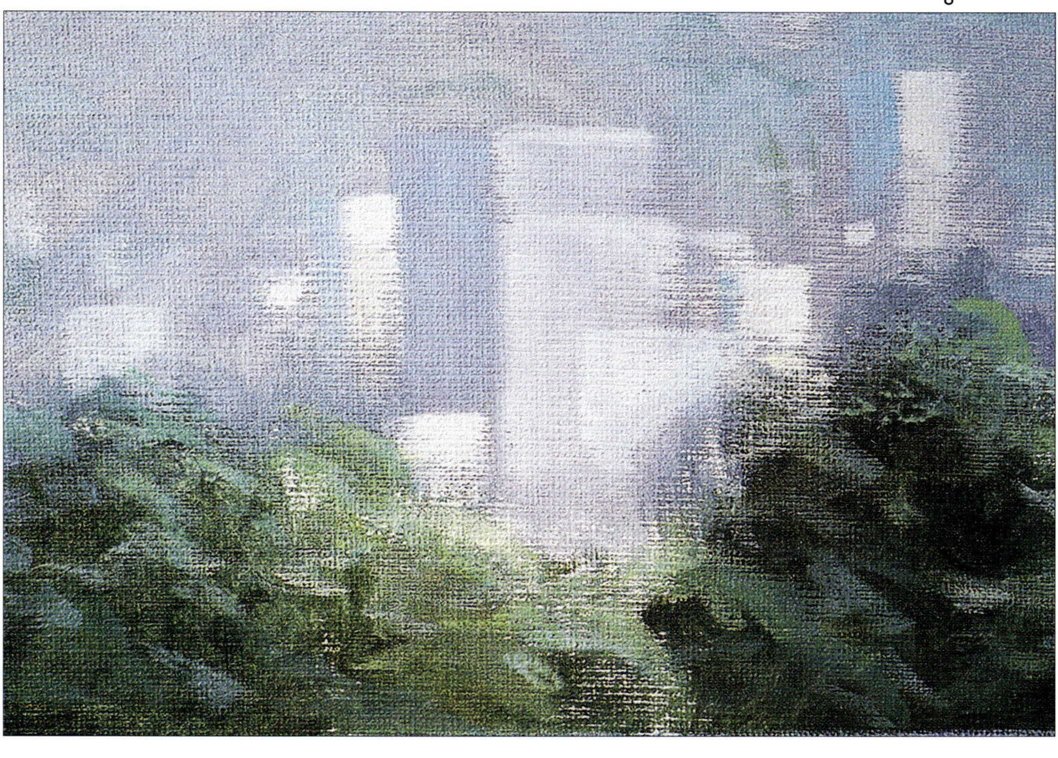

SWIMMERS IN HONG KONG

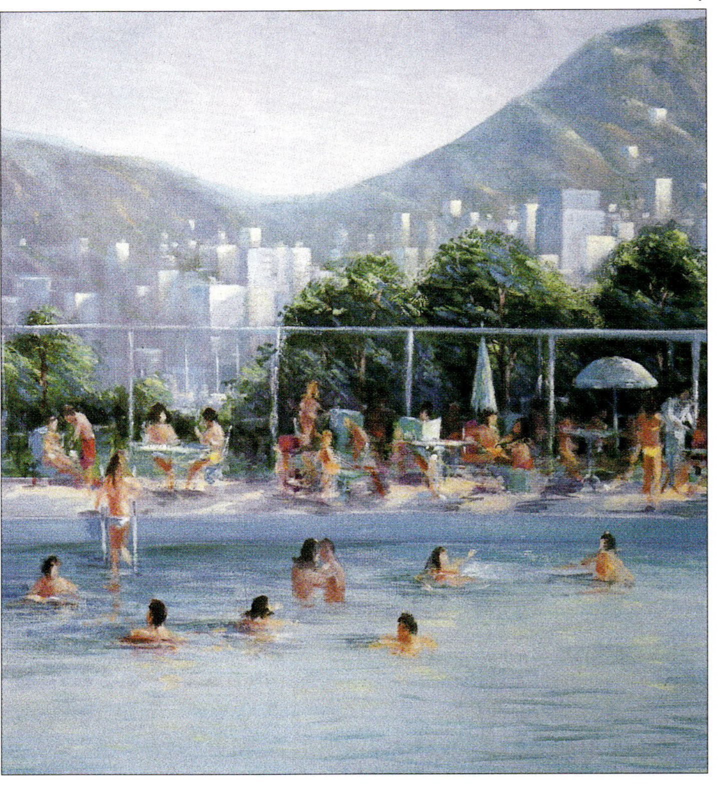

9 *The finished painting owes much of its success to the way in which the brush strokes were applied to the canvas. The texture of the canvas itself has also been used to give depth to the picture and to convey the steamy atmosphere characteristic of Hong Kong.*

quite separate elements to work on, the water, the landscape, and the sky. This picture was painted essentially as a landscape and then brought alive by the addition of figures and buildings.

The artist used the photographs as starting points only, identifying major features in them, particularly the vegetation, the mountains, and the water, before creating his own imaginary landscape. The form of the trees will be treated with adjacent areas of light and shadow while the hazy distant mountains will be emphasized by the use of colors, mainly white and blue.

The almost impressionistic finish was achieved by the use of soft, carefully directed brush strokes and reinforces the relaxed holiday atmosphere which is the central theme of the painting.

INTERIOR

You don't need to travel far and wide in order to find a suitable subject to paint; often the most interesting pictures are those which feature familiar objects and ordinary places. An interior scene, for example—perhaps the very room you are sitting in now—can provide an endless source of inspiration for the creative artist.

As with still lifes, you can arrange the objects in an interior, and also control the lighting, to express a particular mood or to make a personal statement. In this painting, for example, the artist has created a spare, almost abstract composition which captures the melancholy mood of a large, bare room on a cold winter's day. Through the window we catch a glimpse of the gray, wintry landscape beyond. The shadow of the window slants across the cold, empty wall. And in the corner stands a grand piano, half-

INTERIOR

7

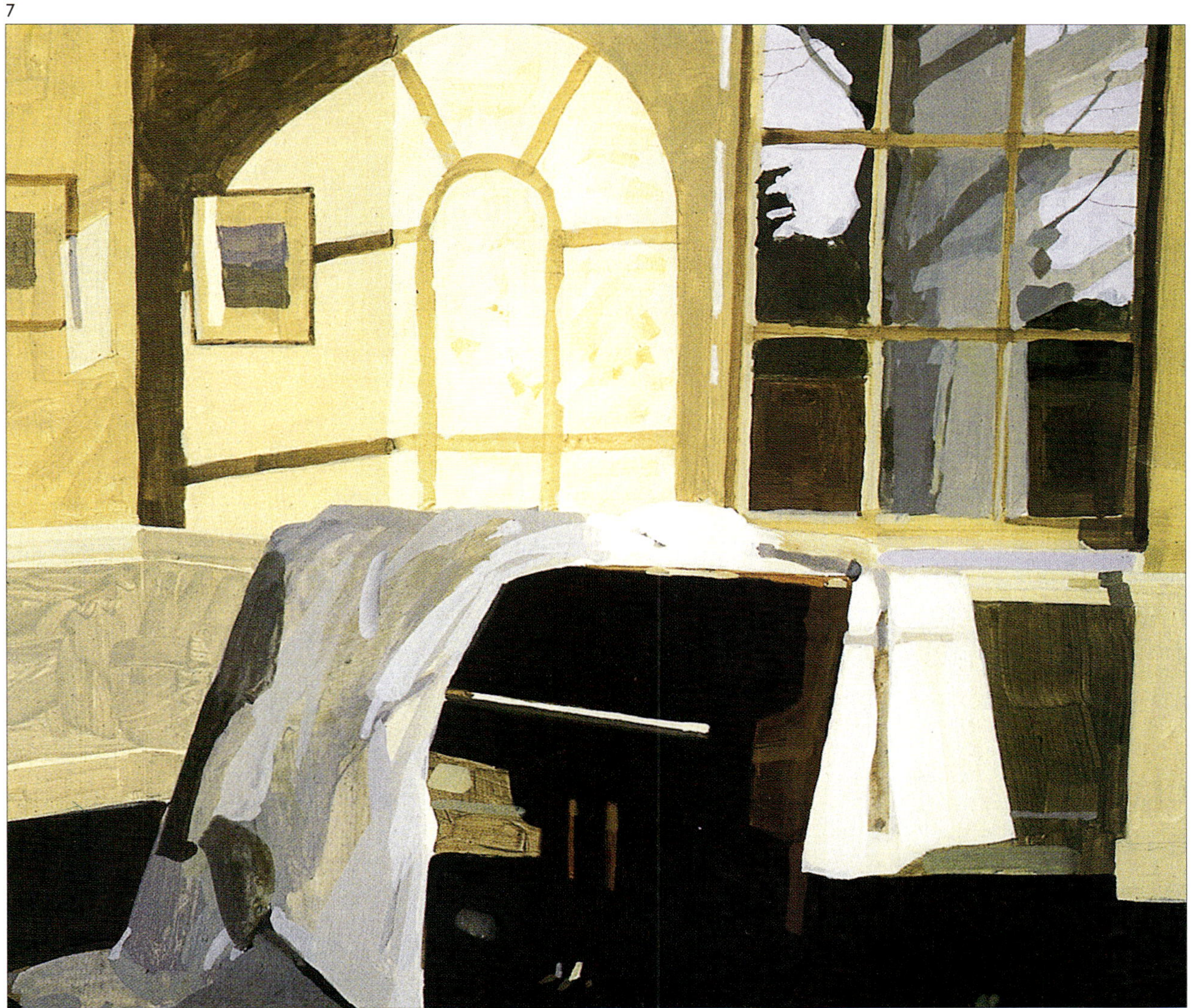

hidden by a shroud-like dust sheet. Altogether, an atmospheric composition.

To capture the mood of the scene, it was essential to work quickly before the light changed—not difficult with quick-drying acrylics. The artist worked with a limited palette of neutral colors, and applied paint onto the canvas with broad, flat washes.

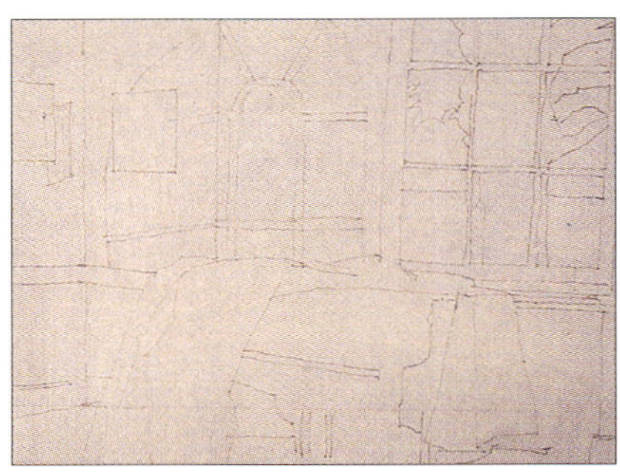
1

1 *The artist begins by making an outline drawing on the support, using a B pencil.*

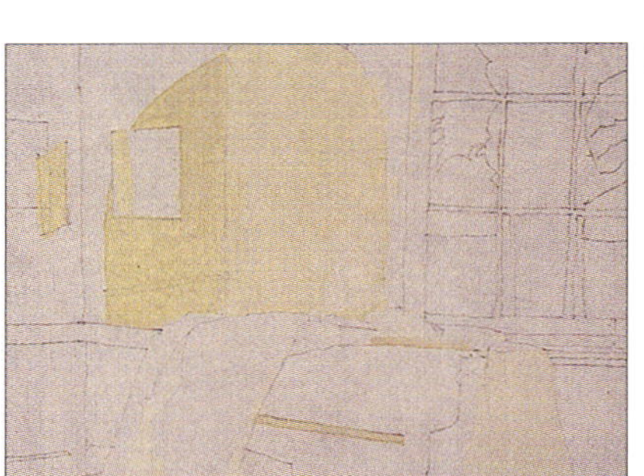
2

2 *The pale tones of the wall are established first using yellow ocher mixed with white, and lemon yellow in the lightest parts.*

3 *Using a No. 4 flat brush, the artist paints in the lines of the window frame, and its shadow, with raw sienna.*

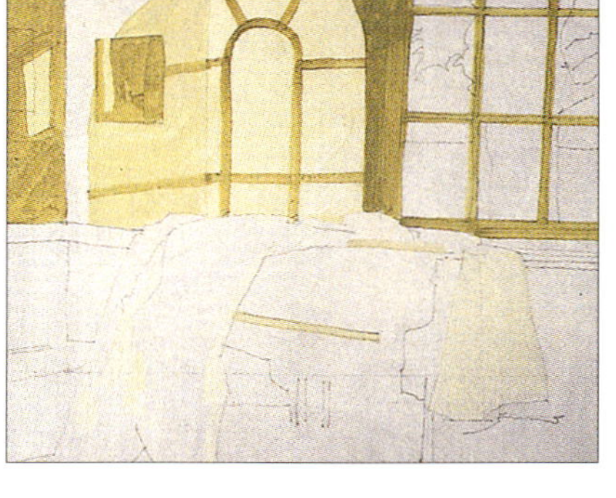
3

4 *The dark tones are blocked in with burnt umber darkened with black color.*

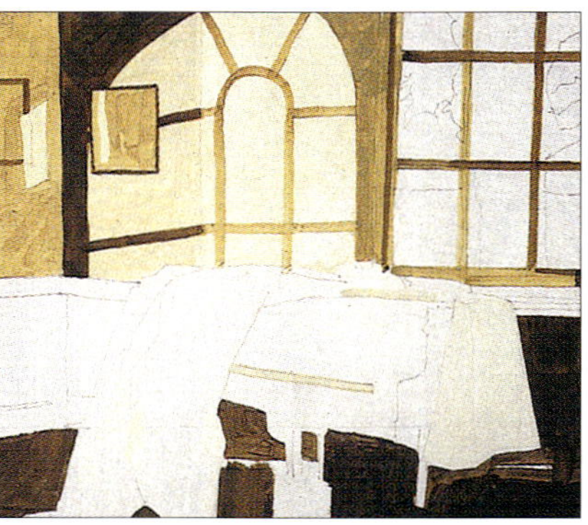
4

5 *The artist paints "negatively," working the dark tones around the white shape of the dust sheet.*

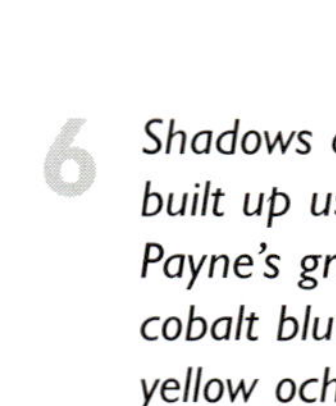

6 *Shadows are built up using Payne's gray, cobalt blue, yellow ocher, and white.*

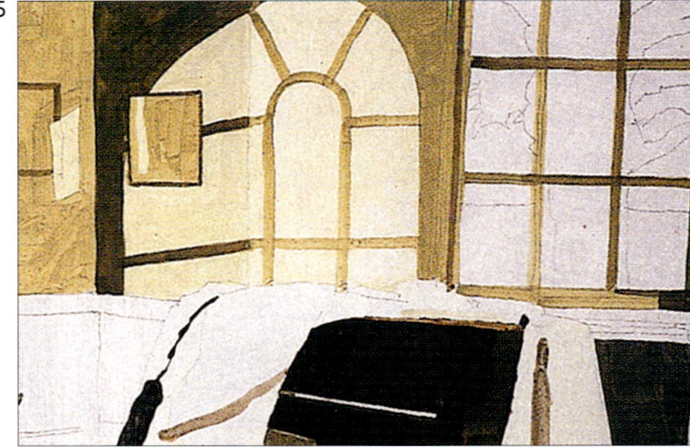
5

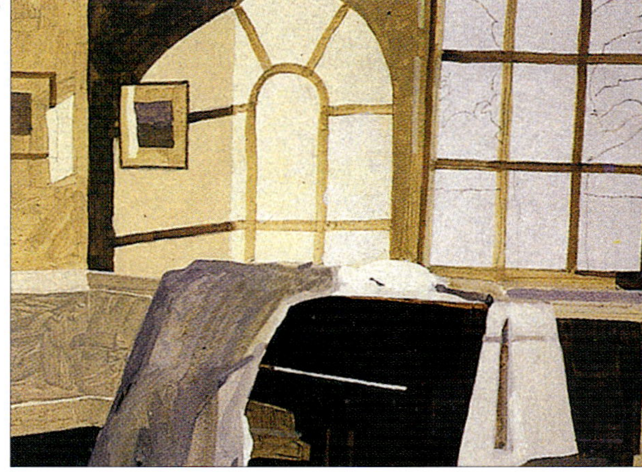
6

7 *Subtle, neutral colors contribute to the quiet, introspective mood of the painting.*

MATERIALS USED

SUPPORT:
Gesso primed hardboard, measuring 10 X 12 in. (25 X 30 cm).

COLORS:
Raw sienna, yellow ocher, Payne's gray, Mars black, titanium white, burnt umber, and cobalt blue.

BRUSHES:
Nos. 4 and 7 flat synthetic hair.

LANDSCAPE WITH SHED

Acrylic is without doubt one of the most versatile painting mediums to date. This landscape demonstrates how techniques and methods borrowed from other mediums can be effectively and harmoniously combined in one picture. For example, the artist has used a sheet of stretched heavy white paper, as one would with watercolor, but has begun the painting using the traditional oil technique of underpainting.

The artist continued to develop the picture using both watercolor and oil techniques. For example, thick paint has been scumbled and dragged in places as in oil paint. In other areas, the wash, a watercolor technique, is used to exploit the underpainting and create a light, subtle tone which complements the heavier, opaque passages. All of which goes to show that there are few rules in acrylic painting, and that a wide range of expressive techniques can be effectively used to get the most out of your subject.

MATERIALS USED

SUPPORT:
Stretched heavy white drawing paper, measuring 20 X 23 in. (50 X 58 cm).

COLORS:
Alizarin crimson, ivory black, burnt sienna, cadmium red medium, cerulean, chrome green, yellow ocher, and titanium white.

BRUSHES:
Nos. 4 and 6 synthetic fiber.

1 *Working on stretched damp paper, the artist begins by lightly sketching in the subject with a pencil. Then he starts to block in the shed wih colored washes.*

1

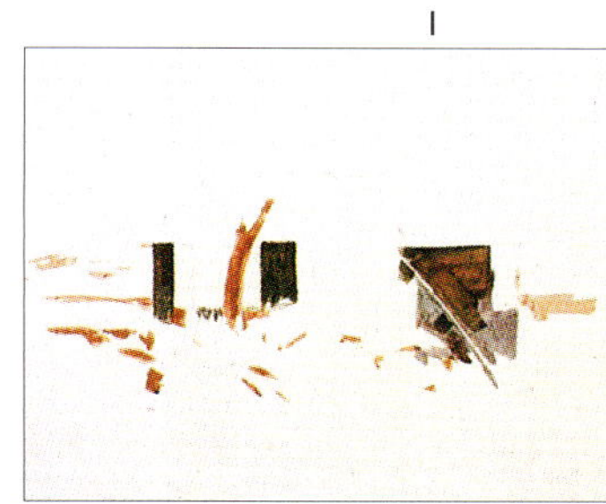

2 *The main shapes and outlines are further developed with very wet washes of burnt sienna. In places the tip of the brush is used to "draw" the outlines.*

2

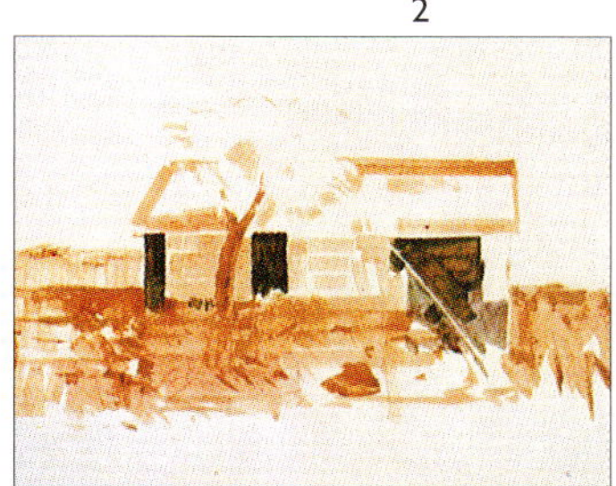

3 *The roof color is put in next, using a mixture of burnt sienna and cadmium red. The darker grass and shrub colors are flicked in with pure chrome green.*

3

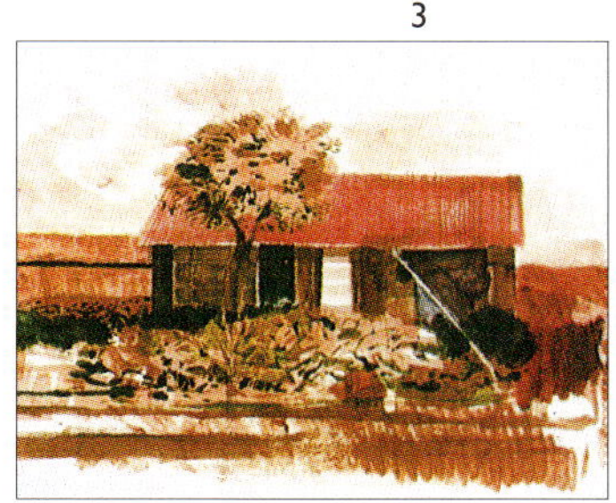

4

5

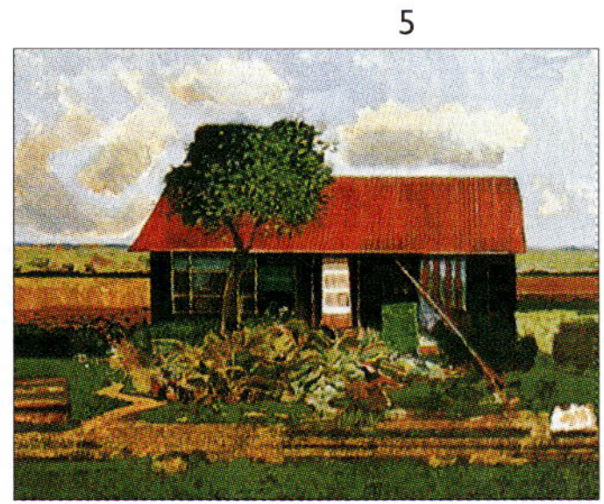

LANDSCAPE WITH SHED

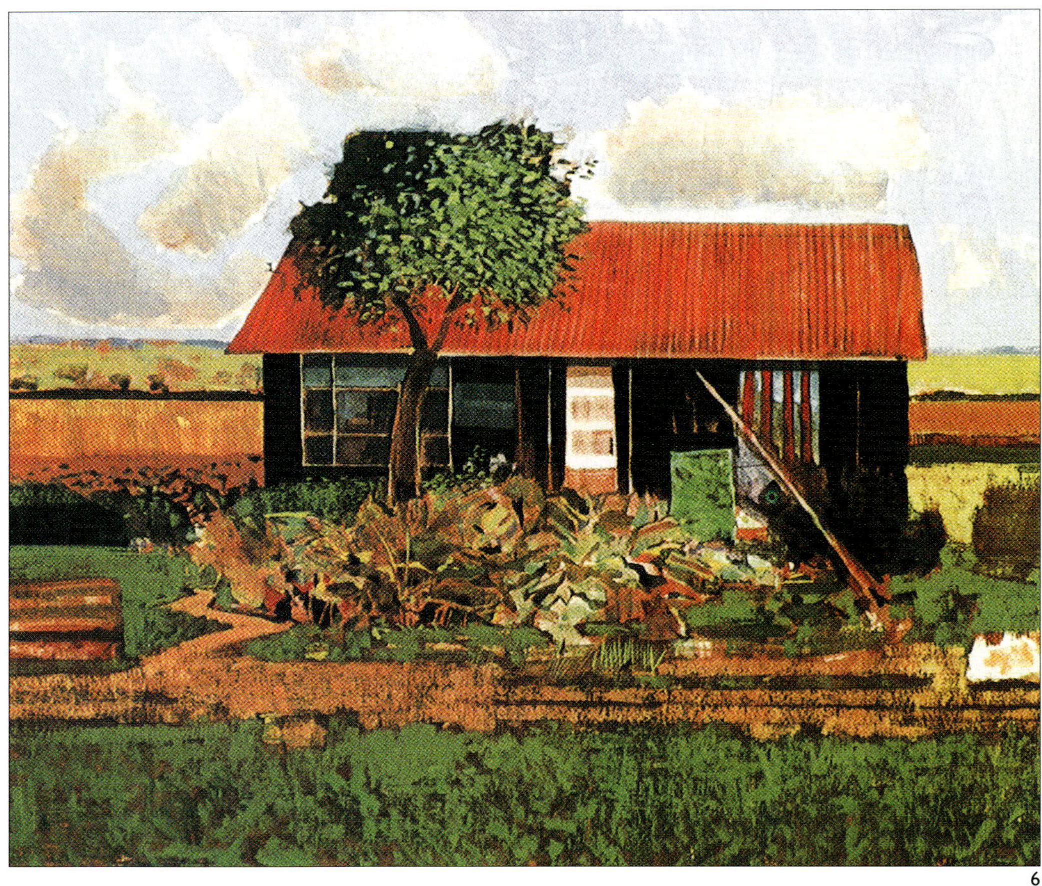

6

4 *A thin wash of cerulean blue for the sky, with pale scumbles of alizarin crimson for the clouds. The tones of the foliage are mixtures of chrome green and white.*

5 *A light green tone is used for the highlights in the foliage, and a burnt sienna wash in the foreground.*

6 *The artist now covers the foreground with a light green tone of dryish consistency, allowing the brown underpainting to show through. Next, he works over the painting putting in the final details. Notice how the artist weaves warm reds and cool greens to create a vibrant color harmony.*

SELF-PORTRAIT

If you are looking for a convenient model for a portrait painting— someone who is inexpensive, reliable, and available at times that suit you—who better than yourself? Painting a self-portrait also has the added advantage that you don't have to worry about flattering your sitter!

Acrylic paints are an especially suitable medium for self-portraits. Their consistency can be varied to suit a whole range of styles, from loose and impressionistic to tight and realistic, depending on the mood you wish to convey.

Strangely, it is usually difficult to "see" ourselves properly. You may think you know

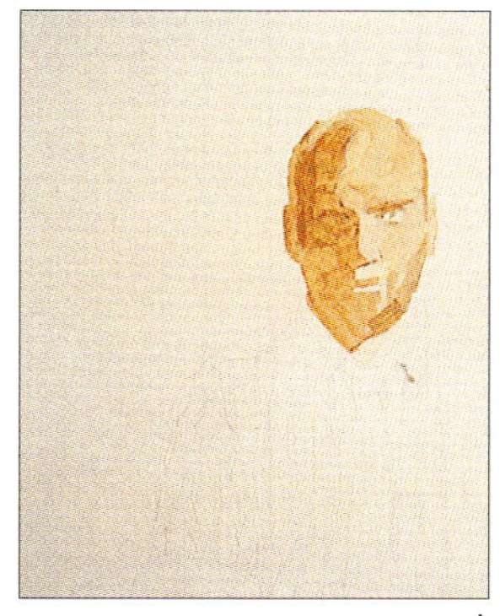
1

1 *The artist begins by making an outline drawing of himself on the canvas. He then blocks in the main light and shadow areas on the face with broad strokes of burnt sienna, diluted with water.*

your own face extremely well, but when it comes to painting a portrait it is essential to study your features as if for the very first time. If necessary, make a series of sketches before you begin the actual painting.

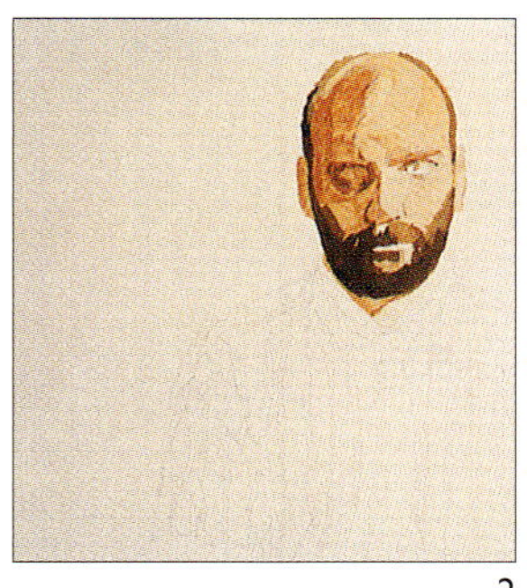
2

2 *Now the dark tones of the hair are put in with burnt sienna darkened with cobalt blue.*

3 *This close-up reveals how the artist is building up the broad masses and planes of the face with washes of color which indicate the light, medium, and dark tones.*

4 *The artist continues to model the face using various tones of earth colors; the eyes are painted with Payne's gray and black, and the mouth with red ocher.*

3

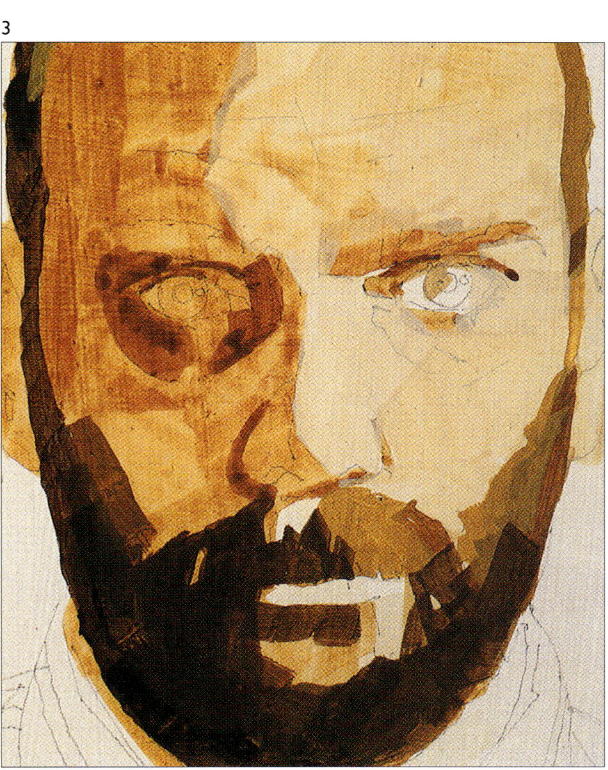

4

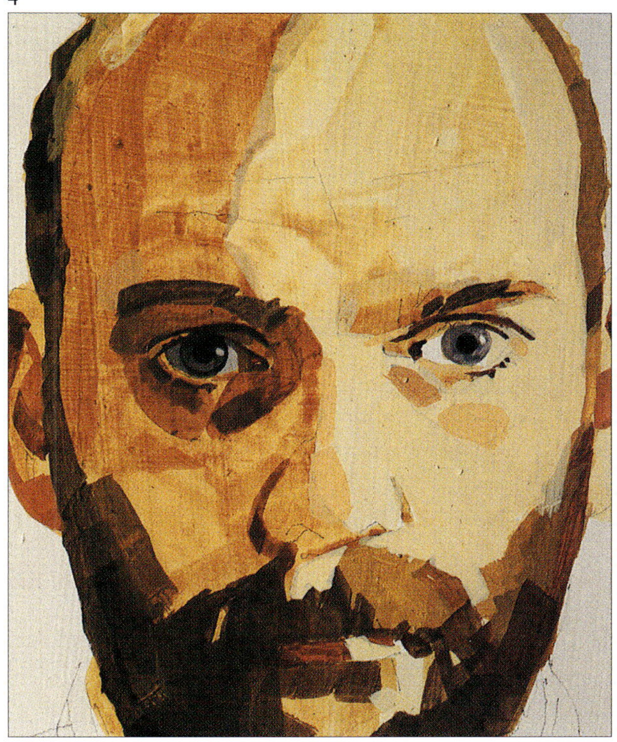

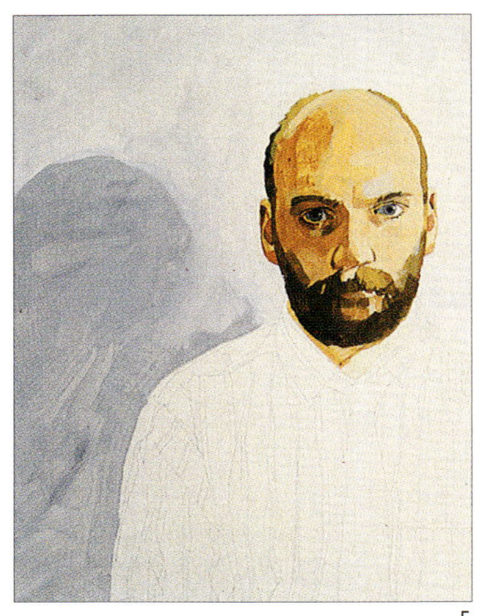

5

5 *Now the cast shadow on the wall is brushed in and a weak solution of Payne's gray, white, and yellow ocher.*

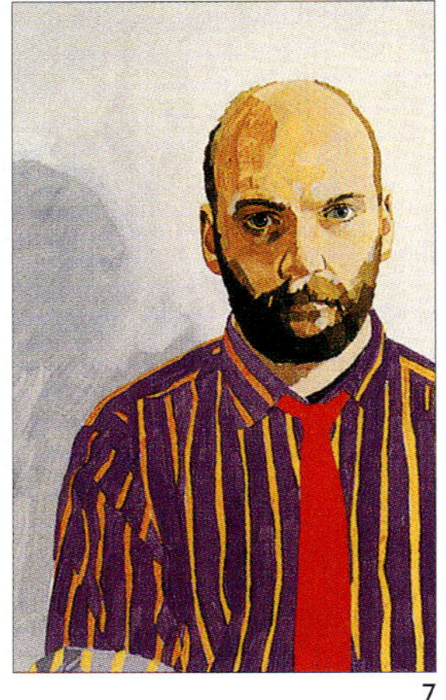

7

7 *Washes of ultramarine blue complete the coloring of the shirt. These bright, vibrant colors are deliberately chosen to bring a touch of vitality to the otherwise somber composition.*

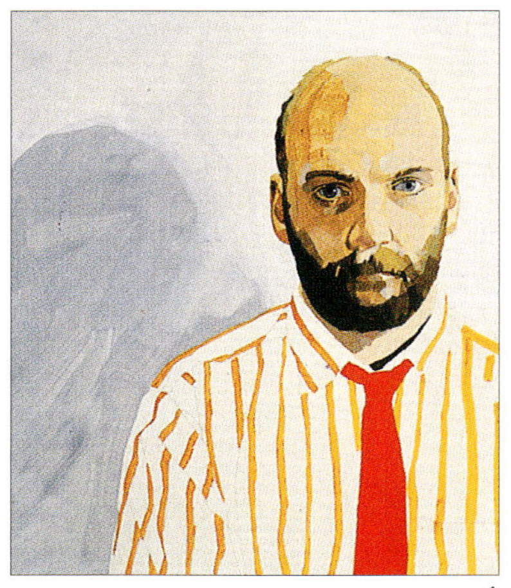

6

6 *The details of the shirt and tie are painted with cadmium red medium and brilliant orange.*

8 *The artist now completes the modeling of the head and the facial features. The highlights in the skin tones are added with thin washes of Turner's yellow and white.*

8

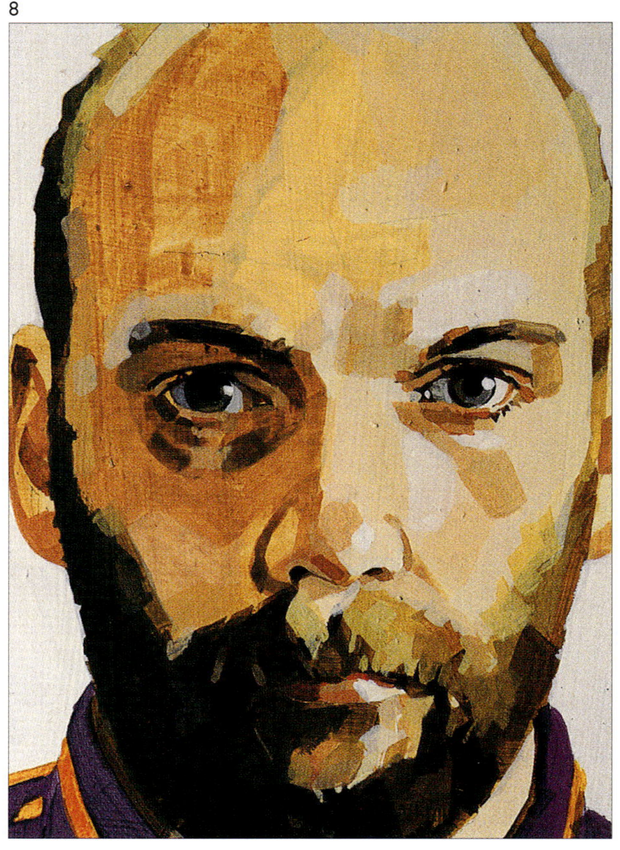

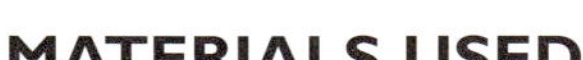

MATERIALS USED

SUPPORT:
Gesso-primed hardboard, measuring 20 X 16 in. (50 X 40 cm).

COLORS:
Burnt sienna, cobalt blue, Turner's yellow, yellow ocher, brilliant orange, cadmium red medium, ultramarine, Payne's gray, and titanium white

BRUSHES:
Nos. 4 and 7 synthetic brush and a 1 in. (2.5 cm) bristle brush

SELF-PORTRAIT

9

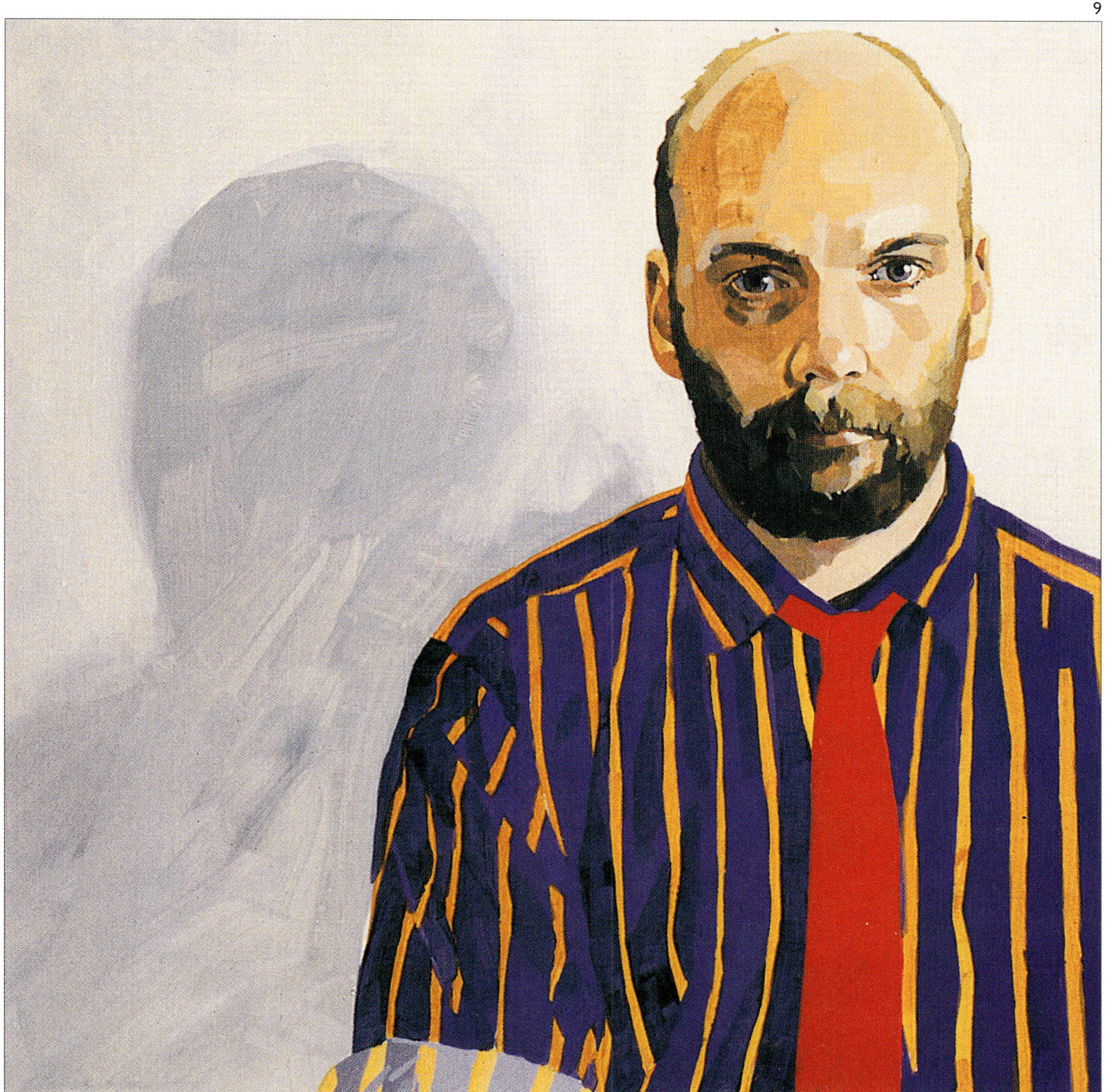

9 *The finished portrait. Notice how the unique placement of the figure and the use of clean, white space around it force the viewer's eye into the face of the subject. Also interesting to observe are the strong colors of the shirt and tie contrast boldly with the white of the paper and create a dynamic visual tension.*

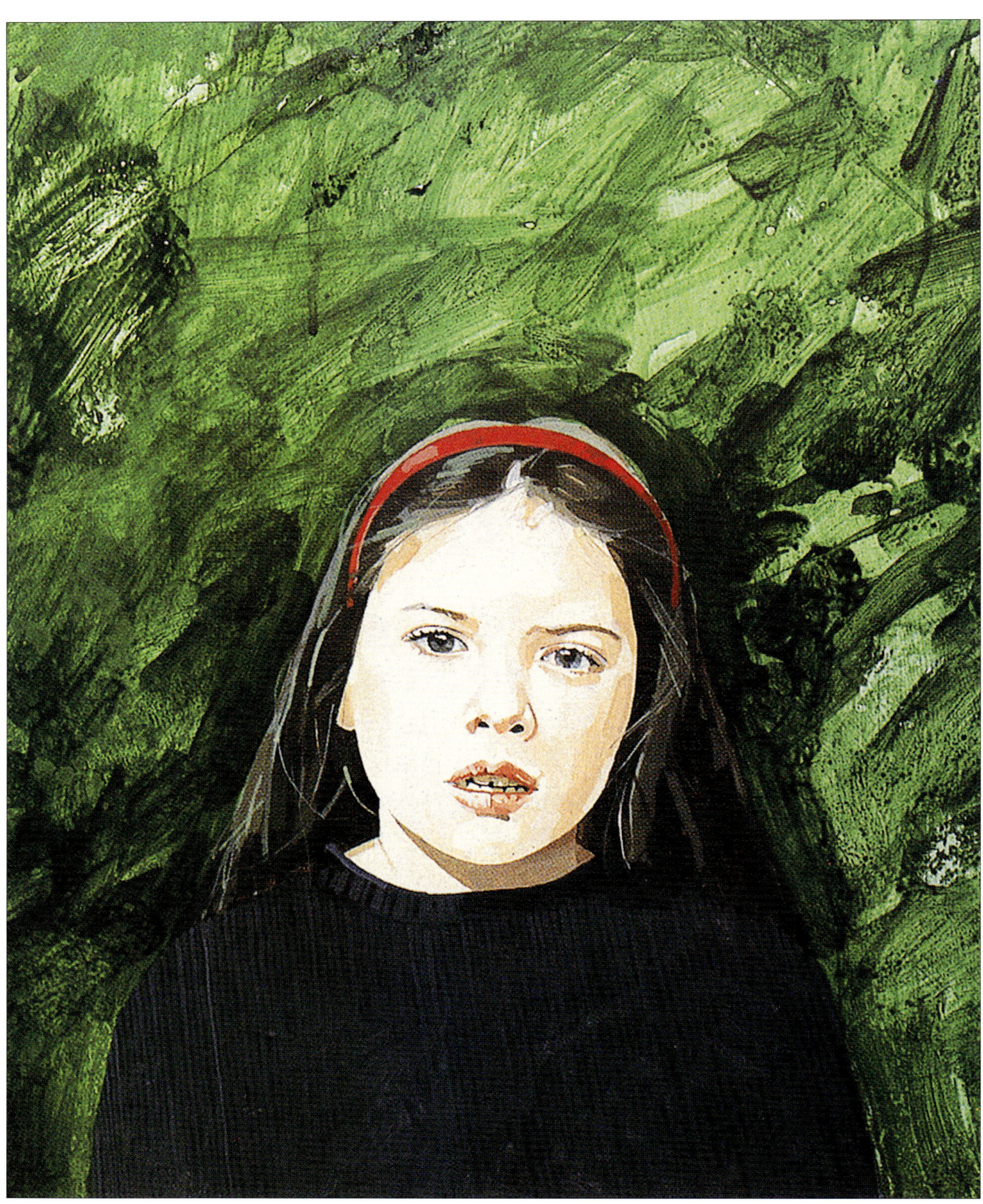

EPILOGUE

Acrylic is a wonderful paint. In fact, a magic paint that can do everything other paints can, and in many instances far better—more transparent than watercolor, more opaque than gouache, and thicker than oil paint. It dries quicker, is more resilient to damage, and more versatile than any known paint today.

Left *This portrait of a young girl was painted on primed hardboard using as reference a color photograph blown up to life size.*

To make acrylic produce wonders is not the province of the manufacturers, but of the user. The magic, alas, won't happen by itself.

Technique will enable acrylic to go some of the way to fulfil its potential, but the magic needs imagination. Whereas oil paint demands years of discipline to allow any magic to come through, acrylic can accommodate lots of imagination to let it happen sooner. You can experiment with acrylic in a way that would seem presumptuous with other mediums. There are no rules you break at your peril, only a few simple conditions that should be observed, to get the magic working. They can be summarized thus: Use plenty of clean water. Keep brushes clean by washing immediately after use. Mix the paint well. Don't be cautious about adding extra acrylic medium to mixtures; additional medium always makes paint flow better. To produce the maximum visual qualities of acrylic in a subtle and arresting way, let the painting show on its surface the effect of the layers beneath. Vary the layers and allow each one to show through. Starting with lean paint, and finishing with thick is better than starting with thick paint, because once acrylic is dry it is almost impossible to remove. Allow washes to show the white surface through the transparent layers. Unlike glazes which can cover any surface or underpainting, both thick and thin, washes depend on the white surface to give the sparkle needed. When in doubt white it out—an easy process with acrylic. Enjoy the process.

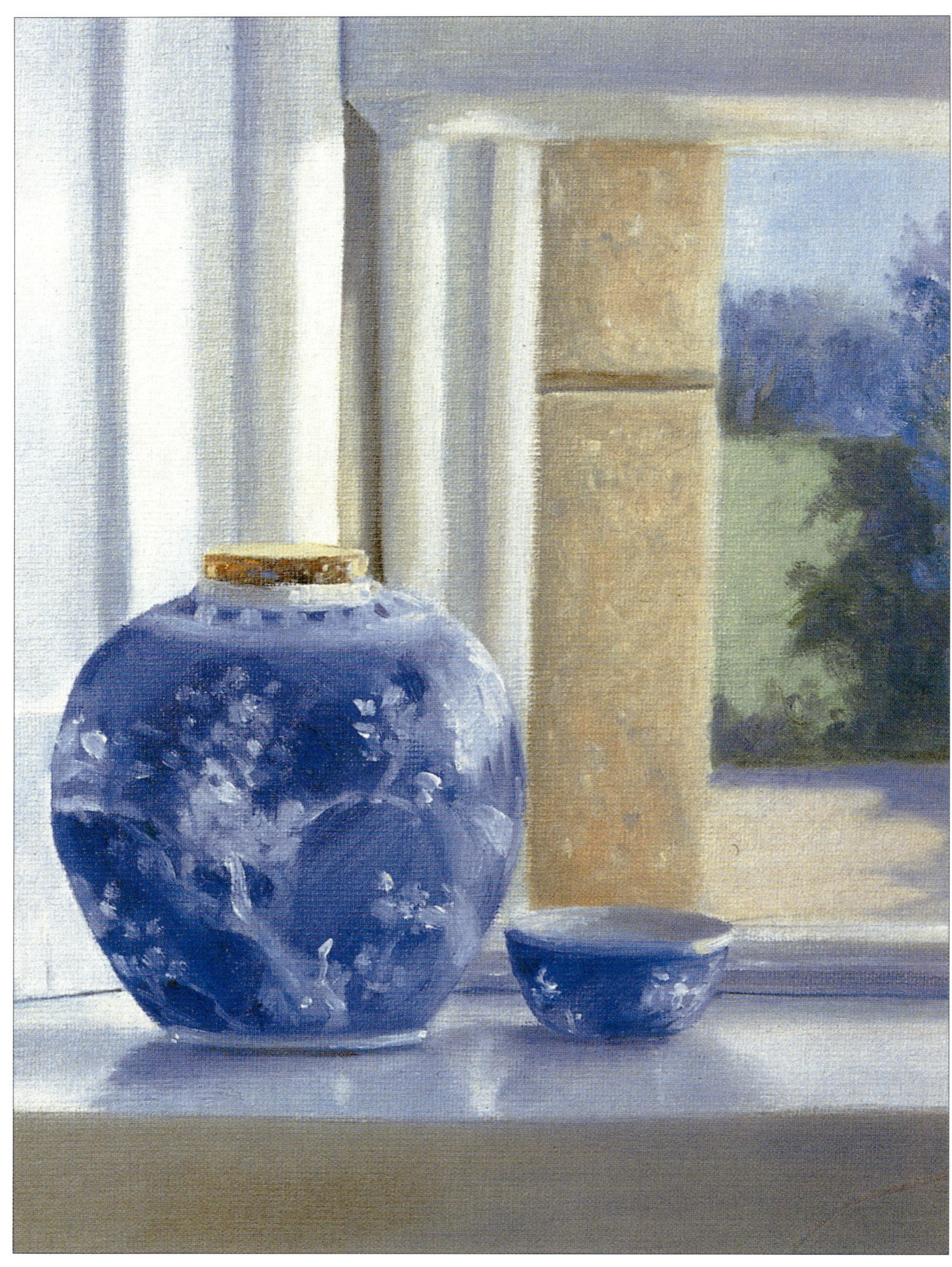

Oils

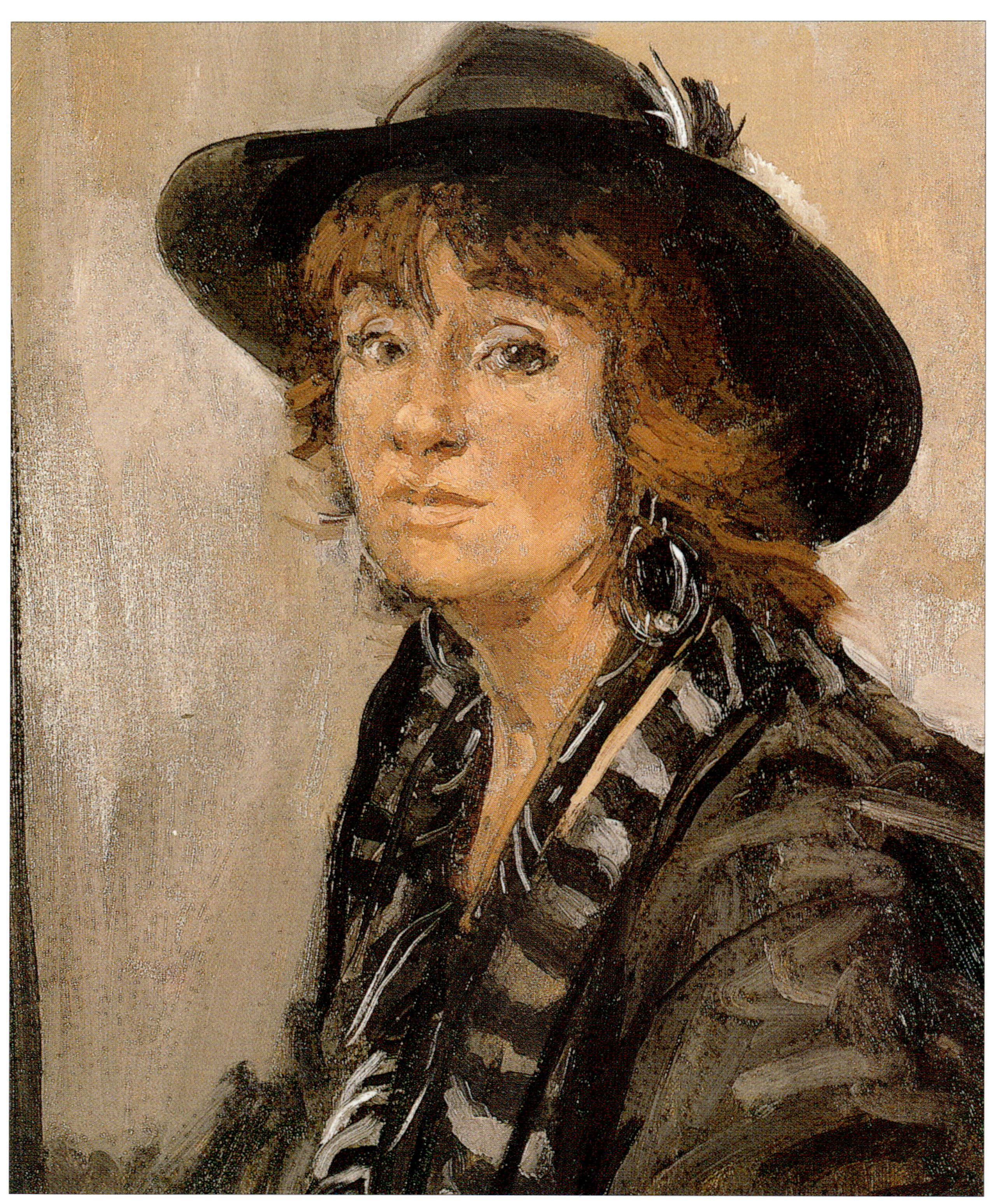

13 WHY OILS?

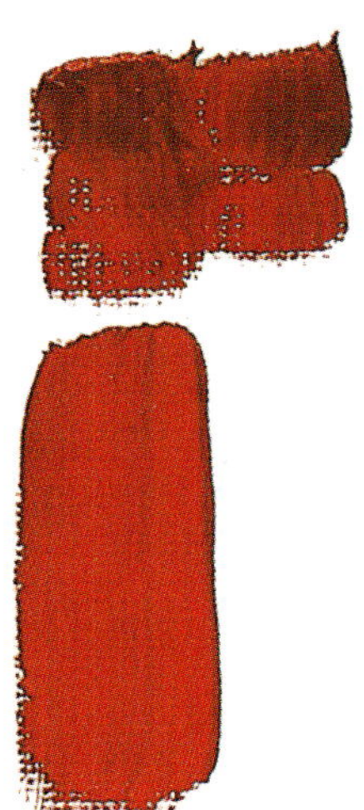

In recent decades there has been an amazing proliferation of new materials for the artists and designers. Why, then, are oil paints still so popular with professional artists and "Sunday painters" alike? There are two main reasons for this, the first being that oil paint is the most versatile of all the painting media, and can be used in any number of ways to suit all styles, subjects and sizes of work. The second is that it is the easiest medium for a beginner to use. Which is not to say, of course, that a novice will automatically be able to create a masterpiece at first try—that is most unlikely. But because oil paint can be manipulated, scraped off, and overpainted, built up and then scraped down once again, it enables you to learn by trial and error, uninhibited by the thought of having "to start all over again," or waste expensive materials. This is not true of any other medium: acrylic, for example, cannot be moved at all once it has been laid down, and watercolor quickly loses its freshness and translucence if overworked. Of course, an overworked oil painting will not be perfect, but it may be a creditable one, if only because of the knowledge gained in painting it.

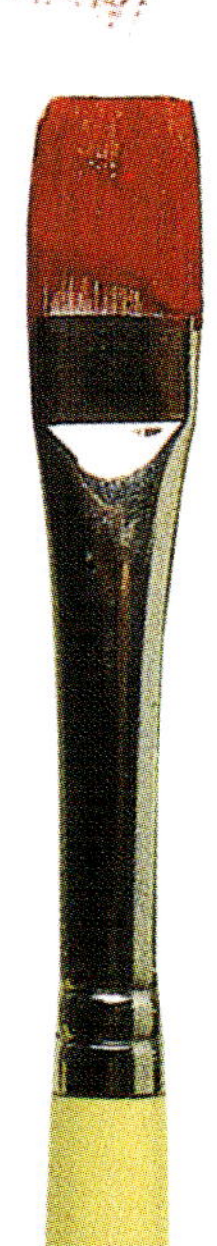

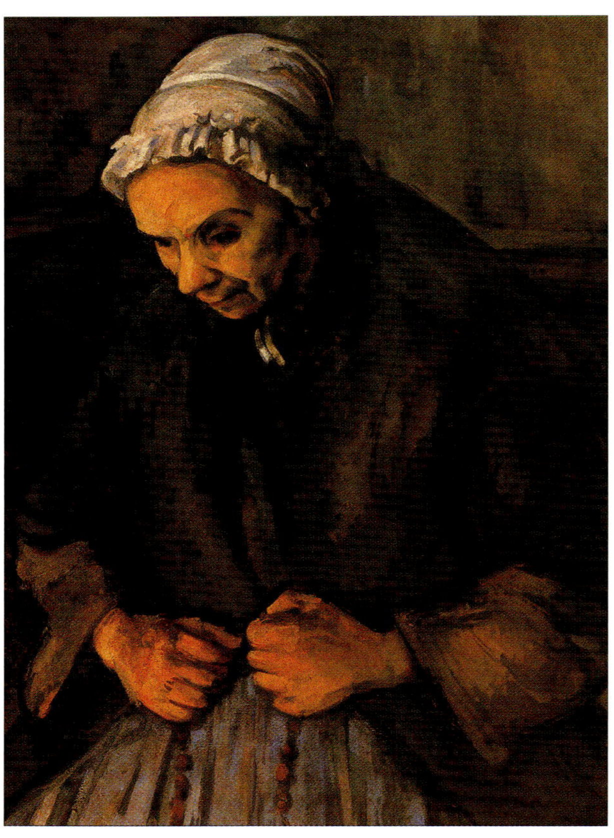

Above Old Woman with a Rosary *by Paul Cezanne (1839–1906). By Cezanne's time, the techniques of oil painting had been largely freed from the earlier restrictions and prejudices. The brushstrokes are an integral part of this dramatic composition, as are the areas of broken color, while the face itself has been treated in a bold manner as a series of planes.*

OIL PAINT IN THE PAST

Oil paint, though regarded as a "traditional" painting medium, is actually quite young in terms of art history. The Flemish painter Jan van Eyck was the first to experiment with raw pigments bound with an oil mixture, when he found that one of his tempera paintings had split while drying in the sun.

The early painters in oil, like van Eyck, used the paint thinly, with delicate brushstrokes that are almost invisible to the eye. In Titian's hands, and later in those of the great Dutch painter Rembrandt, oil paint was at last used with a feeling for its own inherent qualities. Both artists combined delicately painted areas of glazing (thin paint applied in layers over one another) with thick brushstrokes in which the actual marks of the brush became a feature rather than something to be disguised.

The English landscape painter John Constable, and the French Impressionists later in the 19th century, took the freedom of painting to even greater lengths by using oil as a quick sketching medium, often working out of doors. Vincent van Gogh, who was not an Impressionist but is sometimes grouped with them because he was working at much the same time, used great, thick, swirling brushstrokes. (He sold only one painting during his entire lifetime!)

The very diversity of painting techniques in the past has had the effect of freeing us from any preconceptions about the medium. Today's painters use oil paint in so many different ways that it is often hard to believe that the same medium has been used. Interestingly, tempera painting is now undergoing a revival, and some artists working in oil use a similar technique. Other artists apply paint thickly with a knife, so that it resembles a relief sculpture.

New painting media are constantly

being developed in recognition of these different needs; for example, you can choose one type of medium if you want to build up glazes, another if you want to achieve a thick, textured surface using the impasto technique.

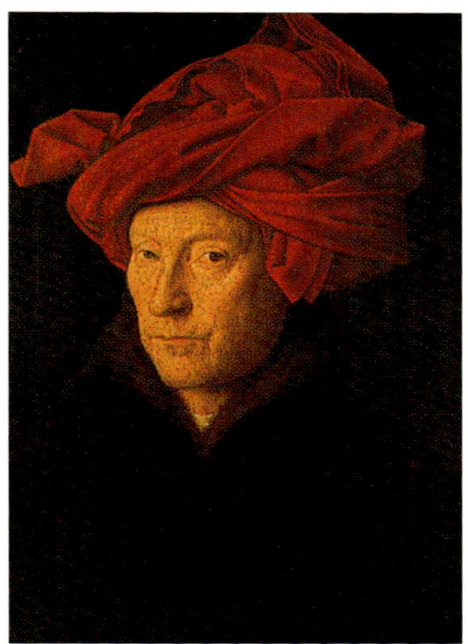

Above Man in a Turban *by Jan van Eyck (active 1422–41). In his oil paintings, van Eyck used much the same methods as previously used for tempera, building up thin layers of paint with glazing. However, oil paint used in this way gives a depth and luminosity, which cannot be achieved with tempera.*

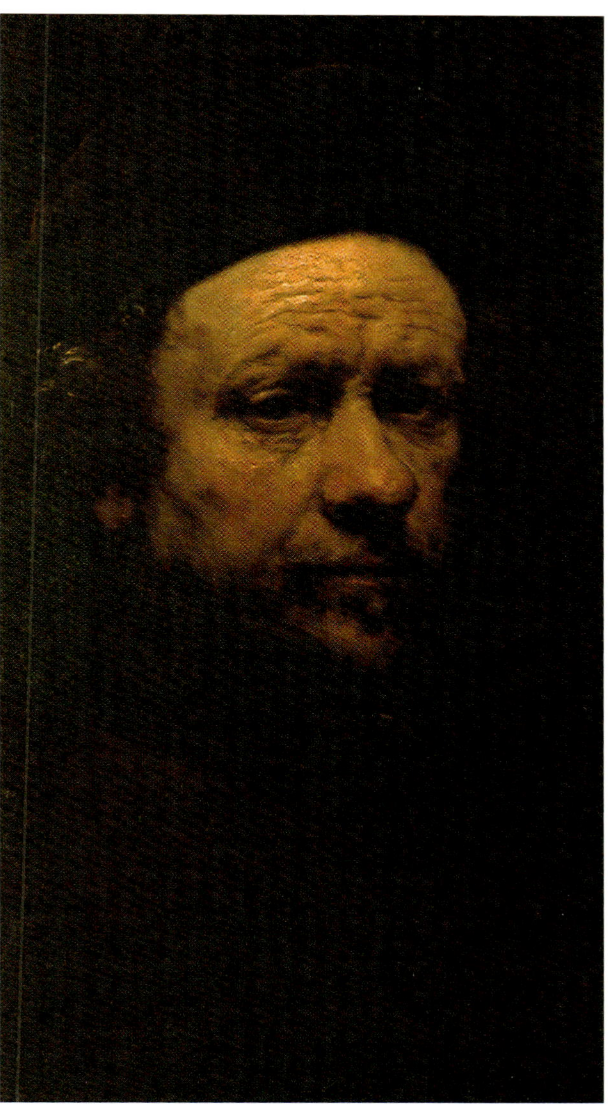

Above Self Portrait *by Rembrandt van Rijn (1606–69). Rembrandt shocked many of his contemporaries by his bold use of paint, which produced thick, textured surfaces. The popular Dutch paintings of the time were characterized by a very smooth finish, with no visible brushstrokes, while in Rembrandt's later work brushstrokes and the paint itself are used to suggest texture, the paint being used almost as a modeling medium in places.*

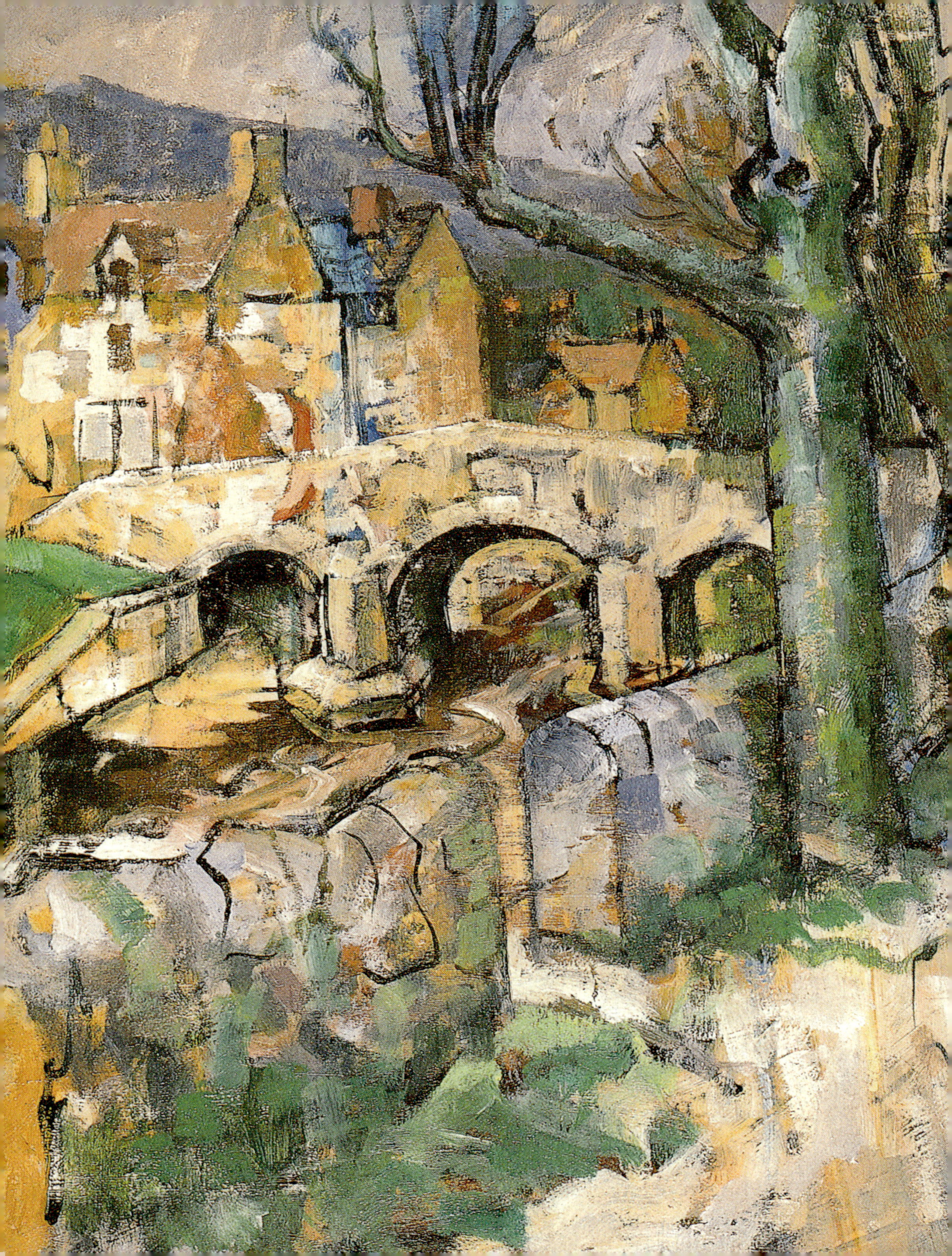

14 MATERIALS AND EQUIPMENT

Materials for oil painting can be costly; so it is advisable to work out your "starter kit" carefully. Begin by buying the minimum and adding extra colors, brushes, and so on when you have progressed to the stage of understanding your particular requirements. For example, someone who intends to specialize in flower painting will need a different range of colors from someone whose chosen theme is seascapes, while a person working on a miniature scale will use brushes quite unlike those needed for large-scale paintings. The photograph shows the colors mixed with varying amounts of white.

Below *A suggested "starter palette." From right to left: white (above), yellow ocher, cadmium yellow, cadmium red, alizarin crimson, cobalt violet, ultramarine, Prussian blue, and viridian. The palette depends very much on the subject to be painted: for instance, violet might not be needed at all, cobalt blue might be used instead of the other two blues, or an additional green added.*

CHOOSING PAINTS

Oil paints are divided into two main categories: artists' and students' colors. The latter are cheaper because they contain less pure pigment and more fillers and extenders, but they cannot provide the same intensity of color as the more expensive range. However, it is possible to combine the two types using the students' colors for browns and other colors where intensity is not a prime requirement and artists' for the pure colors such as red, yellow, and blue. A large-size tube of white works out most economical, since white is used

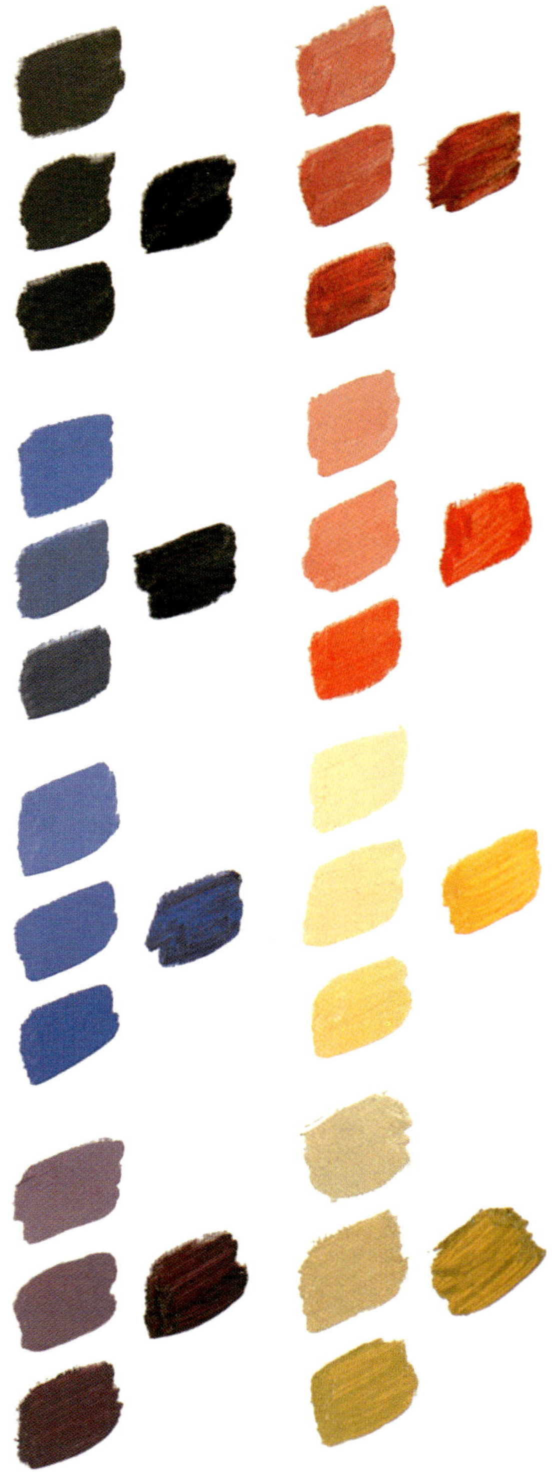

more than most other colors.

It is often said that all colors can be mixed from the three primaries, red, yellow, and blue. To some extent this is true, but they will certainly not provide a subtle or exciting range. In general you will need, as well as white, a warm and a cool version of each of the primaries, plus a brown and a green and perhaps a violet or purple. Good browns and grays are burnt sienna, burnt umber, and Payne's gray. Flake white dries quickly and is resistant to cracking, but it contains poisonous lead; for this reason some artists prefer to use the non-toxic titanium white. The use of black is often frowned upon, and many artists never use it as it can have a deadening effect, but it can be mixed with yellow to produce a rich olive green, and many landscape artists use it for this purpose.

PAINTING MEDIUMS

Oil paint can be used just as it comes from the tube, or it can be a combination of oil and a thinner (what artists call a medium). If you try to apply undiluted paint accurately in a small area, you will see why such mediums are necessary; without them the paint is not easily malleable.

The most popular medium is the traditional blend of linseed oil and turpentine or white spirit, usually in a ratio of 60% oil and 40% thinner. Linseed oil dries to a glossy finish which is resistant to cracking.

There are several faster-drying mediums available, such as drying linseed oil, drying poppy oil, stand oil (which also makes the paint flow well and disguises brushstrokes), and the alkyd-based Liquin.

Turpentine is the most commonly used artist's thinner, though in fact white spirit is just as good and is less likely to cause headaches and allergic reactions. White spirit also has less odor, and stores without deteriorating.

BRUSHES AND KNIVES

For oils, unlike for watercolors, you need more than just one or two brushes, otherwise you will be forever cleaning them between applying one color and the next. The ideal is to have one brush for each color, but a selection of six should be enough to start off with.

The main types of brushes:

Flats have long bristles with square ends and hold a lot of paint.

Brights have shorter bristles than flats and produce strongly textured strokes.

Rounds have long tapered bristles, and produce a wide variety of soft effects.

Filberts are fuller, with slightly rounded ends that make soft, tapered strokes.

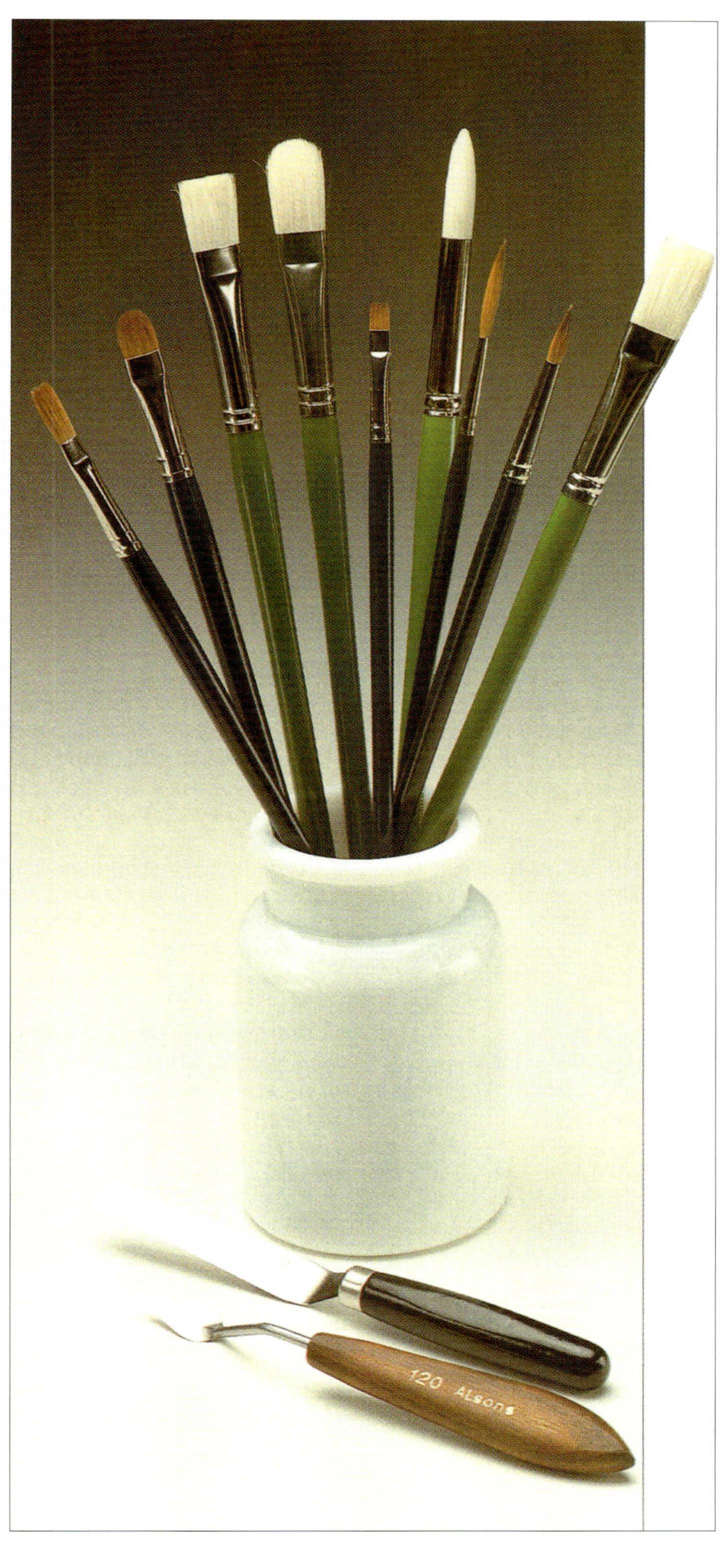

Right *A selection of oil-painting brushes in both hog's hair and synthetic fiber. The four white (hog's-hair) brushes are the basic shapes: from left to right, flat, filbert, round, and bright.*

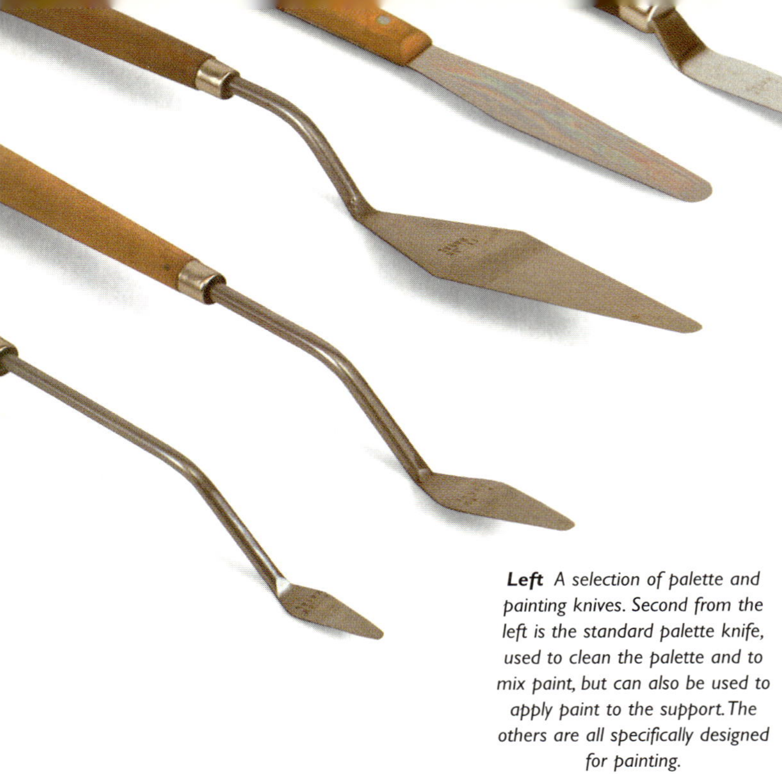

Left *A selection of palette and painting knives. Second from the left is the standard palette knife, used to clean the palette and to mix paint, but can also be used to apply paint to the support. The others are all specifically designed for painting.*

Of the four types of brush, rounds and flats are the most useful to begin with. Brights and filberts can be added later, should you require them.

Each type of brush comes in a range of up to 12 sizes; so choose the size that best suits the style and scale of your paintings.

Hog's-hair bristles and sable hair are the traditional materials for oil-painting brushes; hog's hair is fairly stiff and holds the paint well, while sable gives a much smoother and less obvious brushstroke.

Palette knives, made of flexible steel, are used for cleaning the palette and mixing paint, while painting knives are designed specifically for painting. An ordinary straight-bladed palette knife should form part of your "starter kit."

PALETTES

Palettes come in a variety of shapes, sizes, and materials, designed to suit your individual requirements. Before buying a palette, try out different sizes and shapes to see which feels the most comfortable.

New wooden palettes should be treated by rubbing with linseed oil to prevent them absorbing the oil in the paint. You can even improvize your own palette, from any non-absorbent surface, making it any size and color you like. An old white dinner plate might do, or a sheet of glass with white or neutral-colored paper underneath it. Disposable palettes made of oilproof paper are a boon for outdoor work, and remove the necessity for cleaning.

OIL PAINTING ACCESSORIES

Other essential items include dippers for your painting medium, which can be attached to the palette; jam jars or tin cans to hold white spirit for cleaning brushes; and of course a large supply of rags or kitchen paper (oil paint is very messy). Another useful painting aid is a mahl stick, which steadies your hand when you are painting small details or fine lines. For anyone who intends to do a lot of outdoor work, a pair of canvas separators is very useful.

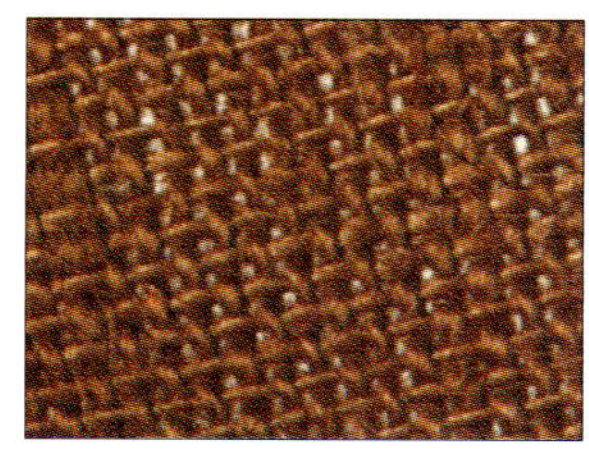

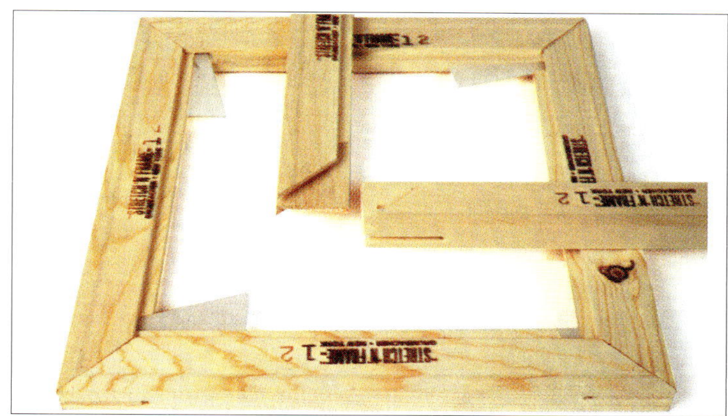

Above *Stretchers can be bought in a range of sizes. They are sold in pairs, which are then fitted together to form rectangles.*

SUPPORTS

The most commonly used support for oil painting is canvas, which provides a sympathetic surface and holds the paint well, while primed hardboard, favored by some artists, is unyielding and holds the paint much less well, so that it tends to slip about. This can be an advantage for someone who paints with thinned, and thus quicker-drying, paint, and makes use of finely drawn detail, but is less suitable for thickly applied paint, as each successive layer will disturb the one below.

Canvas

Canvases can be bought stretched and ready for use, but they are very expensive. Unprimed canvas and stretchers are easily bought. Generally, a coarse weave canvas is suitable for broad, heavy brushwork, while a finely woven texture is best for finely detailed work. Linen canvas, which is undoubtedly the nicest surface to work on, is expensive and could be an unwise choice for a first attempt. Cotton canvas is much cheaper, and perfectly adequate.

Boards and paper

Hardboard is an inexpensive, strong, yet lightweight support which you can buy from any timber yard or builders' suppliers. Either the smooth or the rough side can be used,

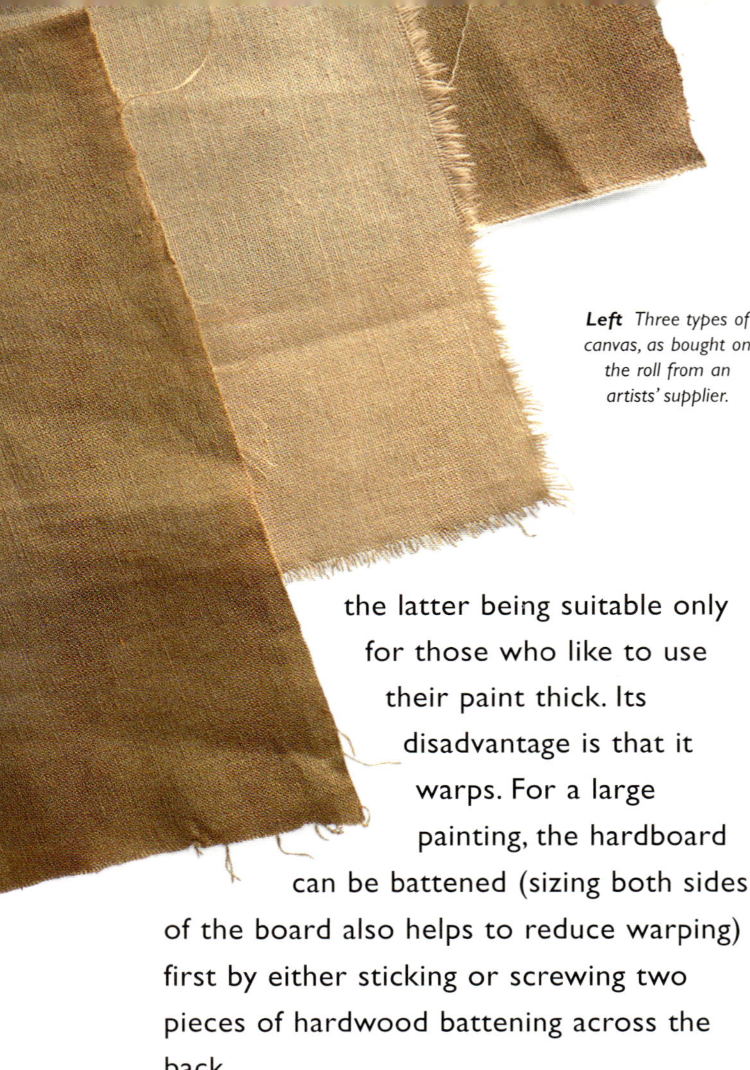

Left *Three types of canvas, as bought on the roll from an artists' supplier.*

the latter being suitable only for those who like to use their paint thick. Its disadvantage is that it warps. For a large painting, the hardboard can be battened (sizing both sides of the board also helps to reduce warping) first by either sticking or screwing two pieces of hardwood battening across the back.

Paper and cardboard make perfectly satisfactory supports for oil painting as long as they are primed (see: Sizing and priming). They are excellent for small, quick sketches, as the paper, being slightly absorbent, allows the paint to dry quite quickly. If using paper, buy a good-quality, heavy watercolor paper, as a thin paper will buckle when primed. Specially prepared paper, called oil sketching paper, can be bought, usually in pads. Some people get on well with this, but others find its surface greasy and unpleasant to work on, like that of the cheaper painting boards.

Sizing and priming

The conventional method of priming all supports is first to apply a coat of the animal-skin size described above, and when dry to apply a coat (or sometimes two) of oil-based primer. However, oil primers do take a fairly long time to dry. An alternative is to use emulsion paint, which dries quickly, or the acrylic primer sold under the (incorrect) name of gesso, which is compatible with oil paint.

The purpose of sizing and priming is to provide a protective layer between the canvas and the oil paint. Some contemporary artists, among them the English artist Francis Bacon (b. 1910), do paint on unprimed canvas in order to achieve special effects, but this should never be a general practice. The oil paint will eventually rot the canvas or other support.

Easels

An easel is a necessity. You may manage to produce one small painting by propping up your canvas on a table or shelf, but you will very soon find out how unsatisfactory this is. Without an easel you cannot adjust the height of your work—essential if you are doing a painting of a reasonable size, as you must be able to reach different areas of it easily and comfortably—and you cannot tilt the work.

There are several different types of easel on the market, from huge, sturdy studio easels to small sketching easels. If you intend to work out of doors frequently you will need a sketching easel. If, on the other hand, you know you are unlikely to paint anywhere but indoors, the heavier radial easel could be a good choice, but this cannot easily be dismantled and put away, so you might choose a portable easel for space reasons.

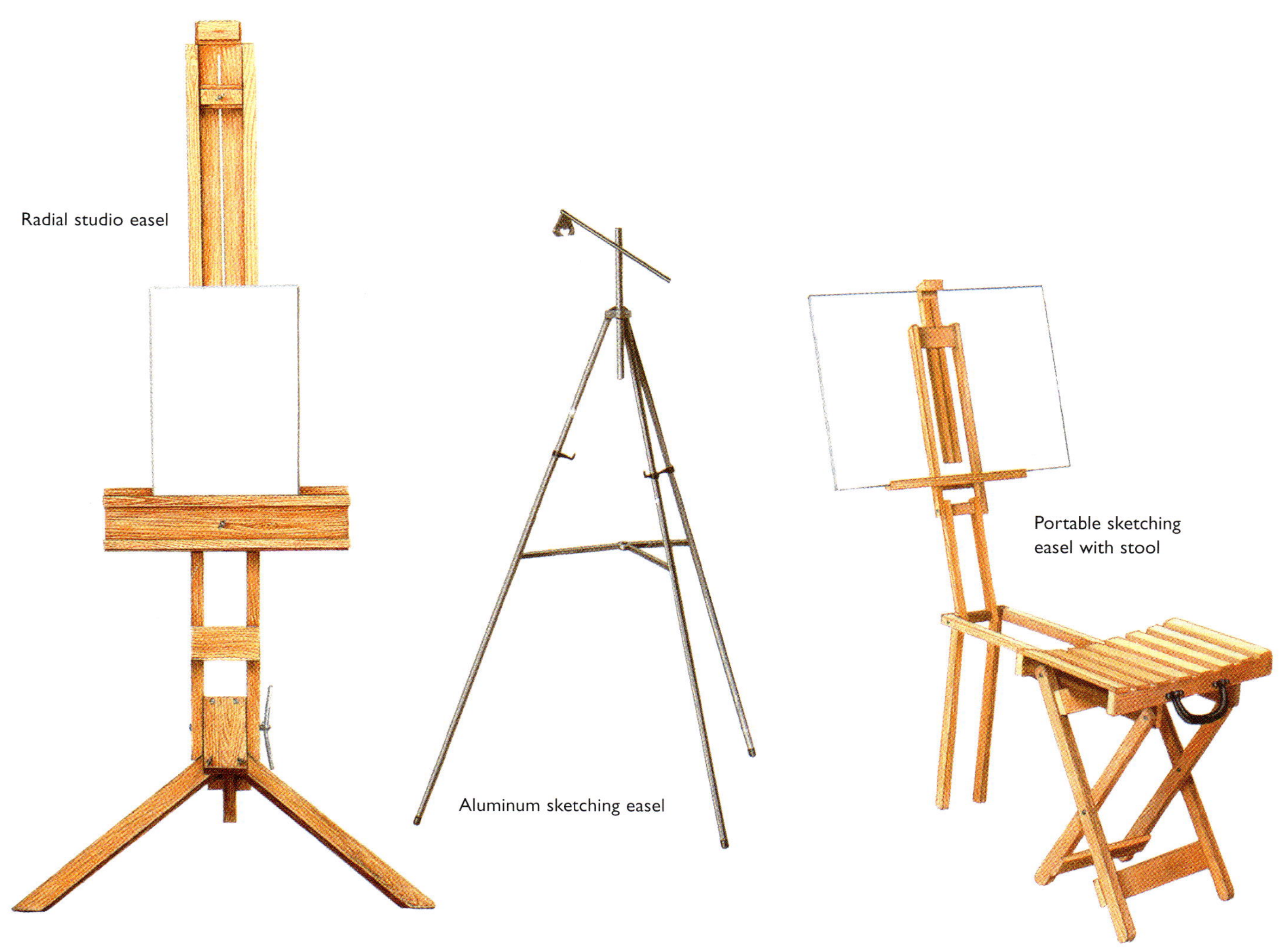

Radial studio easel

Aluminum sketching easel

Portable sketching easel with stool

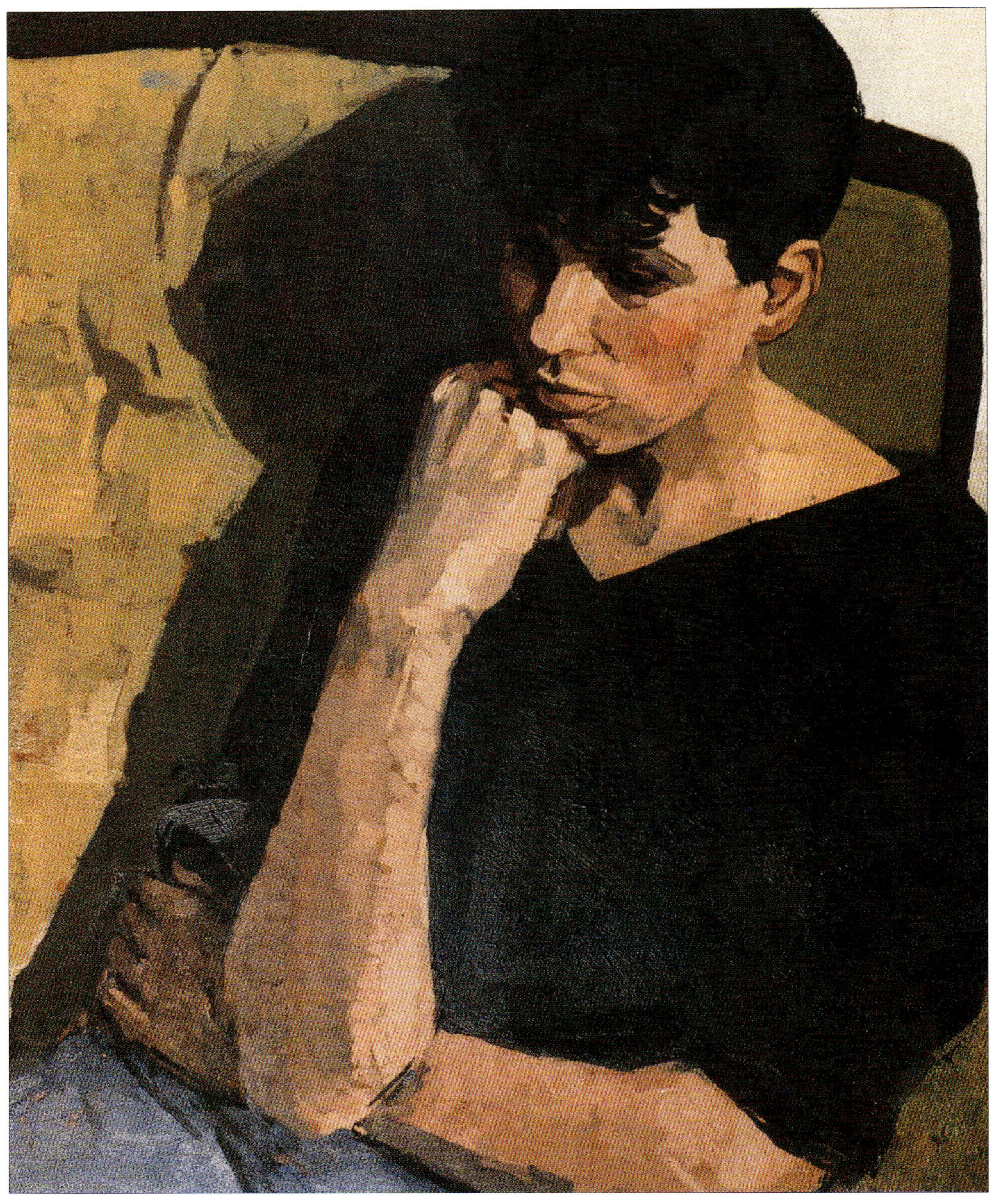

15

THE MECHANICS OF PAINTING

Although there are really no hard-and-fast rules in oil painting, it is helpful to have an idea of the various ways in which artists go about things so that you can experiment with different techniques, color schemes, and compositions. Rules are often useful in a negative way: once you know a rule you can break it for reasons of your own, or "bend" it, as many artists have done with the rules of perspective. This, indeed, is what some of the best-known painters have done down the ages.

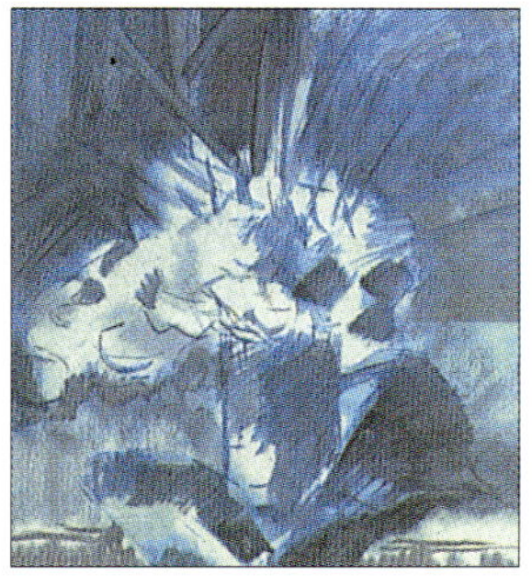

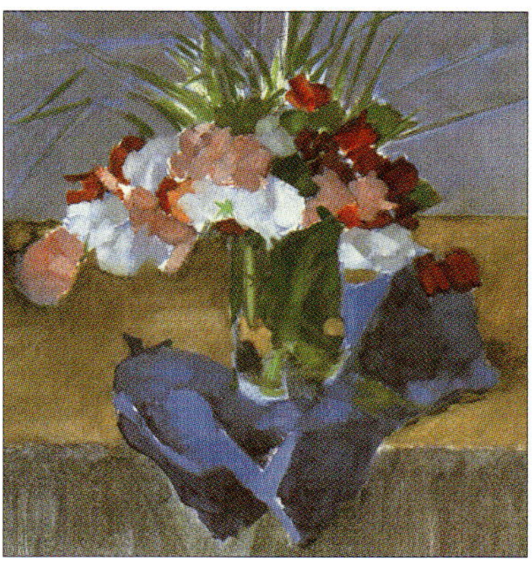

Above, Above Left and Below Left *This painting was begun with a monochrome underpainting in dilute cobalt blue, an unusual but deliberate choice of color, as the blue is repeated throughout the picture. The flowers and drapery were then built up in thicker paint—"fat over lean"—the background and foliage being left quite thin.*

GENERAL PAINTING TECHNIQUES

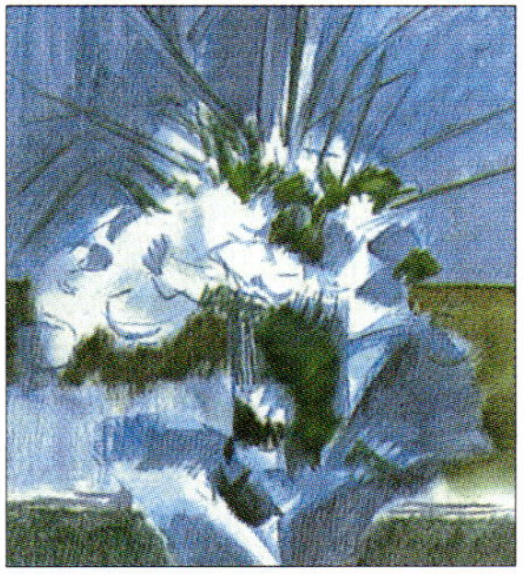

For a complex subject, such as a figure study, or perhaps a landscape including people or buildings, a preliminary drawing on the canvas is usually advisable. This enables you to work out the composition and the position of the main elements within it, and to plan the balance of dark colors and light ones. Careful planning enables you to be more spontaneous later.

Underdrawings can be done either in pencil or charcoal, the latter being preferable, as it is a broad medium, easier to use freely. To avoid loose charcoal mixing with the paint and muddying it, brush it down lightly with a rag before starting to paint. Underpainting—another form of drawing but done with a brush—can be either in monochrome or an understated version of the finished color scheme, in both cases using paint well thinned with turpentine.

A good general rule for oil painting—and a very old one—is to work "fat over lean." This simply means that in the initial stages the paint should be used fairly thin, becoming thicker and oilier as the painting progresses.

Not all paintings, however, are done in stages in this way; many are completed at one sitting, with a minimum of drawing or underpainting. This is known as alia prima painting, and is much used for landscape or quick portrait studies where the painter wants to record his impressions rapidly in a free and spontaneous manner. The paint is used thickly, with each color laid down more or less as it will finally appear. In this method, the colors blend into each other, particularly when one is laid on top of another. This is known as working "wet into wet," and was much exploited by the Impressionists, particularly Claude Monet in his outdoor paintings.

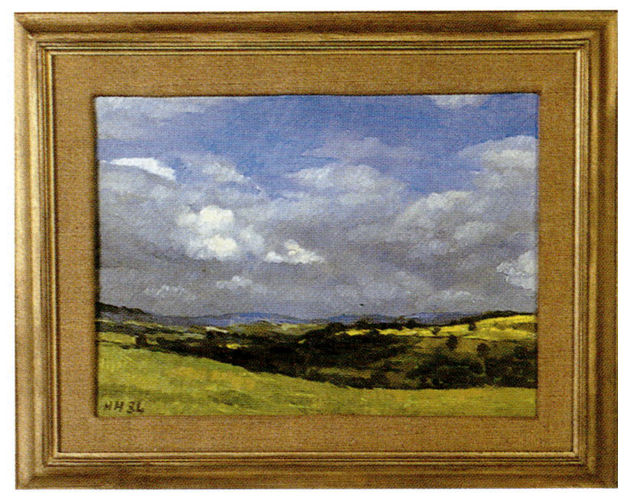

Above *This small painting was done by the alia prima method, with the paint used quite thickly and put down rapidly with little subsequent alteration.*

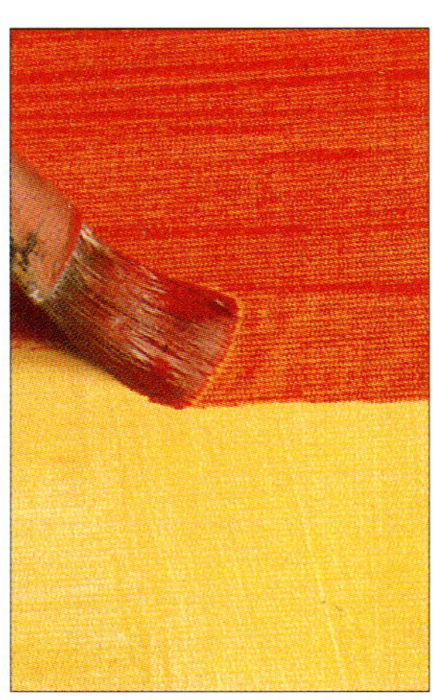

The photograph (Left) shows colors being blended by working wet into wet. A thin layer of transparent red paint (Right) is being laid over a dry layer of yellow. This is the technique called glazing, which gives an effect quite unlike that of one layer of thicker paint, as the color below reflects back.

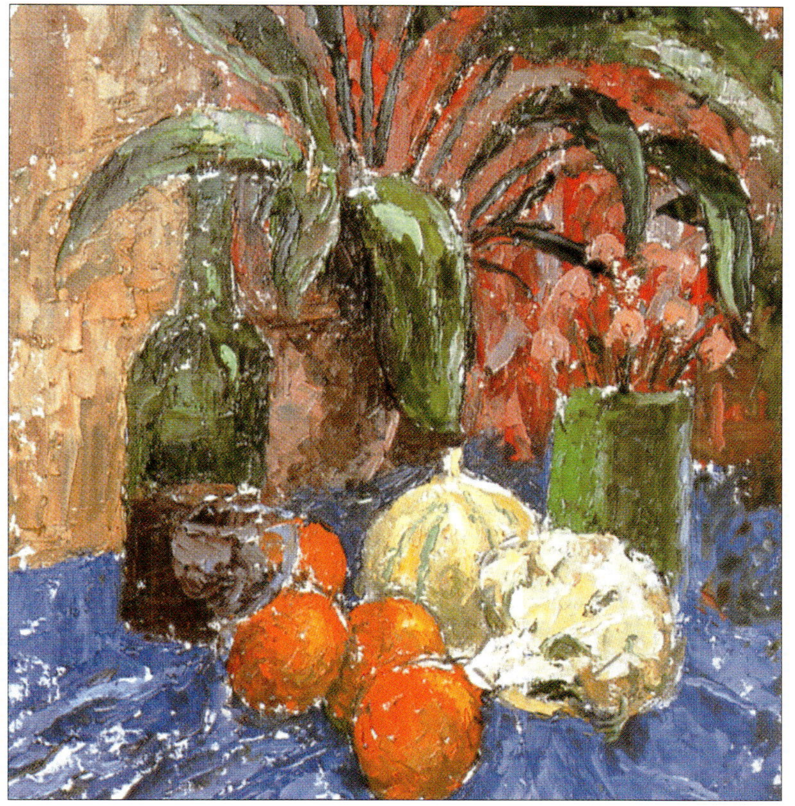

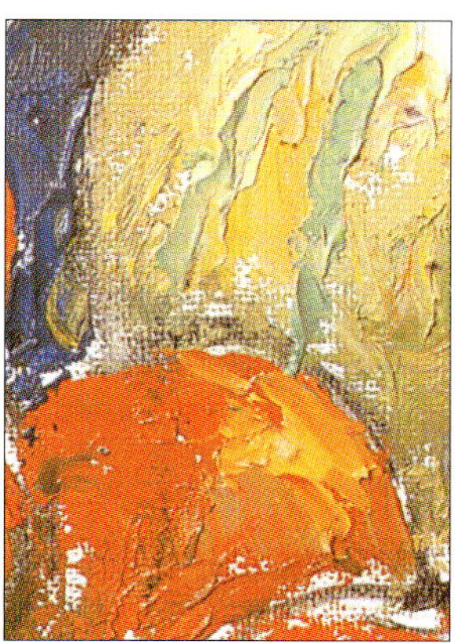

Below *Here scumbling was used to suggest the texture of the chalk cliffs. The paint was scrubbed on with a brush over dry paint below, and in places was worked in with the fingers.*

Above *The paint surface here is an important part of the painting, the broken patches and restless texture of the thickly applied color enhancing the vividness of the subject. The paint was applied with a knife alone, and the detail, (abover right), clearly shows how different is the effect from that of traditional brush painting.*

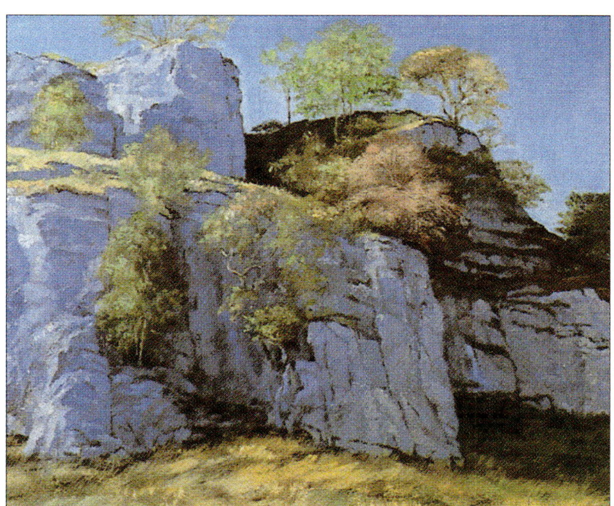

SPECIAL PAINTING TECHNIQUES

There are many ways of applying oil paint, some used almost unconsciously, while others are the result of careful planning. The method called scumbling comes into the first category.

Areas of irregular texture can be made by laying a flat area of color in opaque paint and then "blotting" it, when semi-dry, with non-absorbent paper. As you peel back the paper, it drags at the surface layer of paint and creates a stippled texture. This technique is called frottage.

Another way of creating texture is impasto, in which the paint is laid on thickly, often with a palette knife. In the past, artists such as Rembrandt combined impasto with areas of delicate brushwork, pointing up the differences in texture between, for example, flesh and clothing.

Interesting effects can be achieved by drawing or scratching into a layer of wet oil paint to reveal another color beneath or sometimes the white ground of the canvas. The implement used can be anything pointed, such as a brush handle or a knitting needle. This method is called sgraffito.

A technique that comes into the deliberate planning category is glazing, in which thin, transparent paint is laid over an area of already dry paint. This creates effects akin to the deep glow of wood that has been lovingly polished.

COMPOSING A PICTURE

Composing a painting is mainly a question of selecting, arranging and rearranging. The thumbnail sketches (see: opposite page) illustrate how some artists try out possible compositions for paintings. A "good composition" is one in which there is no jarring note, the colors and shapes are well-balanced, and the picture sits easily within its frame.

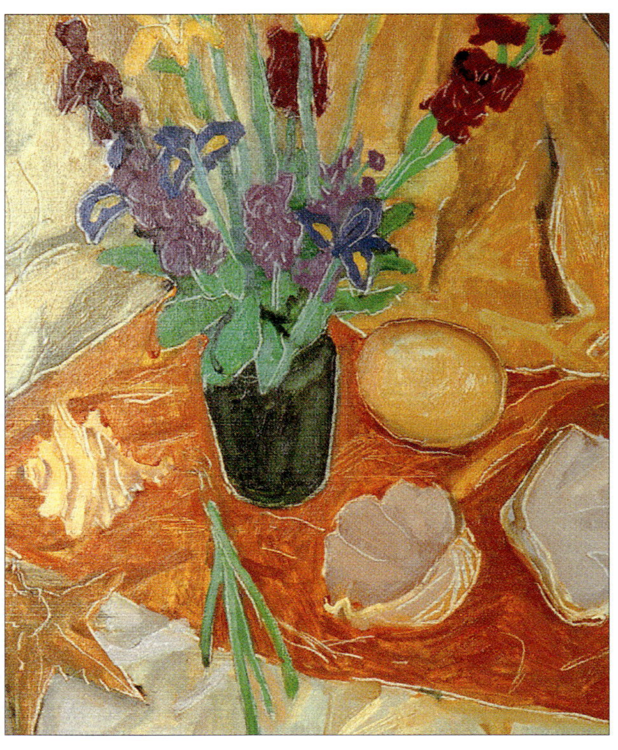

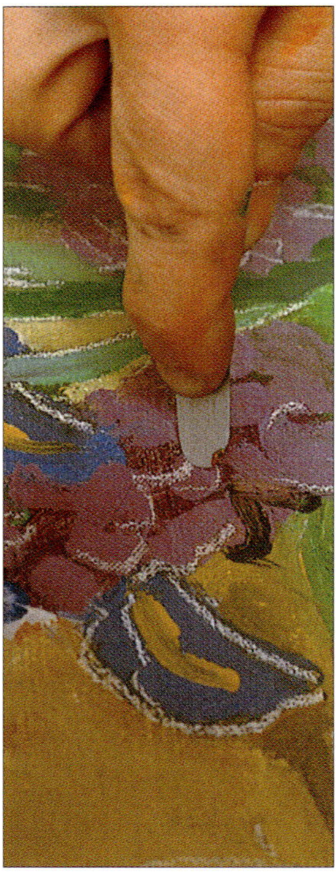

Left *The artist scratches through the paint to reveal the white surface of the canvas. Where there are several layers in a painting, the technique can also be used to reveal one or more of the colors below.*

Far Left *The still life was given sparkle as well as additional definition by the use of sgraffito.*

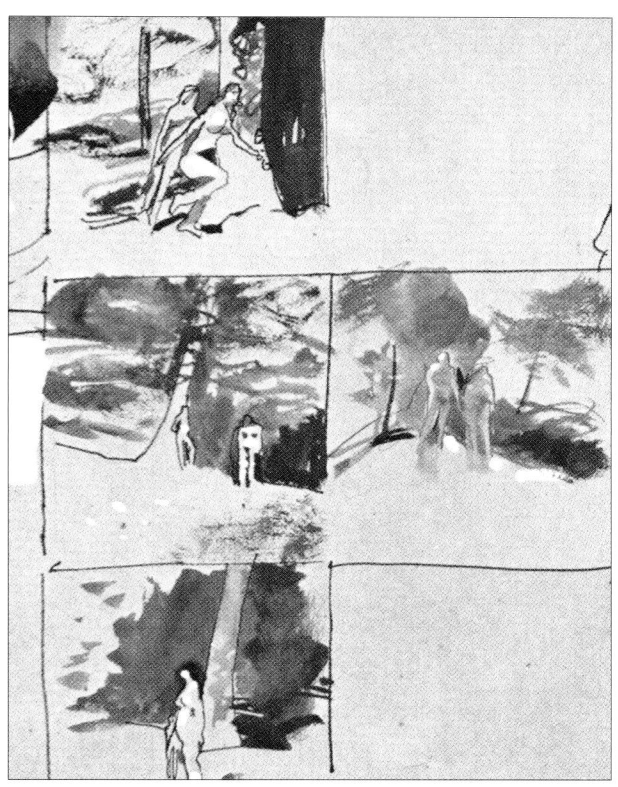

***Above** These thumbnail sketches, of female figures in various poses against different backgrounds, illustrate the way in which some artists try out possible compositions for paintings. Such drawings, which can be done quite quickly and need be little more than scribbles, are an excellent means of working out the arrangement of the mai shapes and the balance of lights and darks.*

There are some basic errors which should be avoided if possible. In general it is not a good idea to divide a landscape horizontally into two equal halves—the land and the sky—as the result will usually be monotonous. A line, such as a path or fence, should not lead directly out of the picture unless balanced by another line which leads the eye back into it.

A still-life or portrait should not be divided in half vertically, while a flower painting is unlikely to be pleasing to the eye if the flower arrangement is placed too far down, too far to one side, or very small in the middle of the picture frame.

In the case of interiors, portraits, still-lifes, and flowers, backgrounds can be used as a device to balance the main elements of the composition. Use part of a piece of furniture behind a seated figure, for example, or a subtly patterned wallpaper which echoes or contrasts with the main shapes and colors in the figure. In landscape painting the sky is a vital part of the composition, and should always be given as much care and thought as the rest of the painting.

COLOR AND LIGHT

Color has two main qualities, tone and intensity, the first being the darkness or lightness of a particular color and the second being its brightness. Colors which are opposite one another on the color wheel, such as red and green, yellow, and violet, are called complementary colors. These can be used in a deliberate way to balance and "spark off" one another.

Colors are basically either "warm" or "cool," and the warm ones will tend to "advance," or push themselves to the front of a painting, while the cool ones will recede. You can make use of the "advancing"

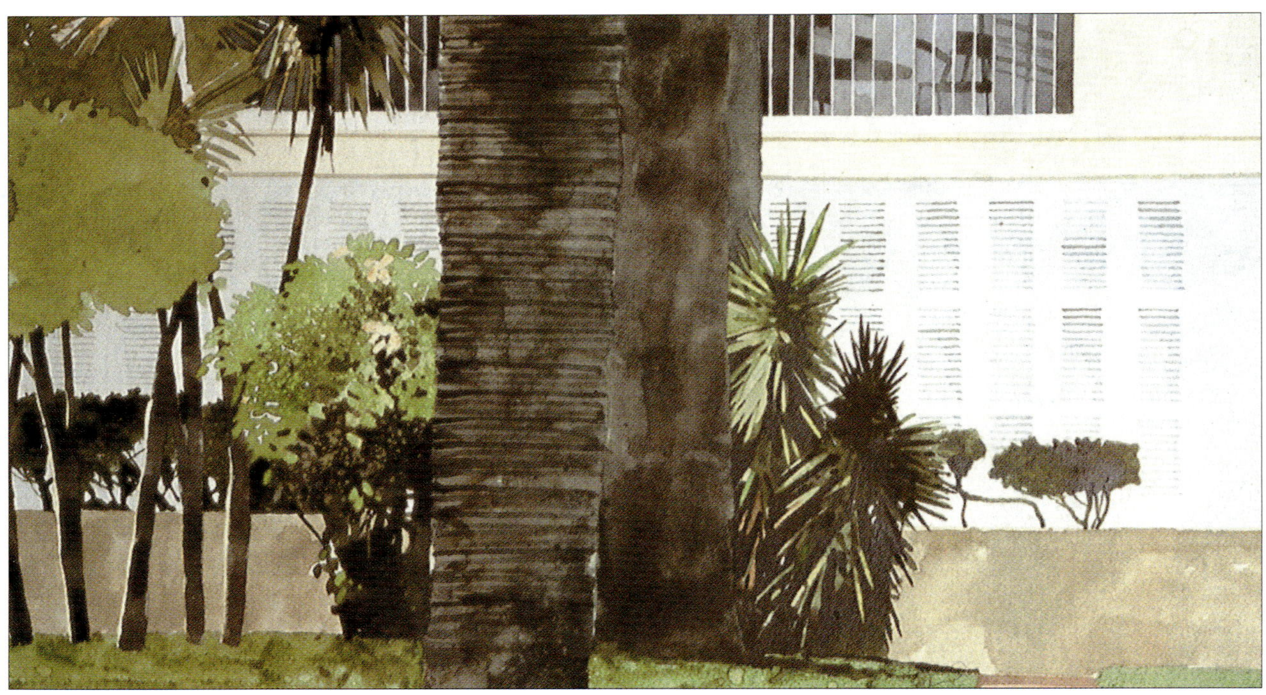

Above *The natural inclination when painting subjects like trees is to try and get everything in, but in this painting the artist has allowed the foreground trees to "bust" out of the frame, giving a stronger and more exciting effect.*

and "retreating" qualities of warm and cool colors in creating a sense of space and depth.

There is no color without light, and the direction, quality, and intensity of light constantly changes and modifies colors. This fact became almost an obsession with the Impressionist painter Claude Monet; he painted many studies of the same subject—a group of haystacks—at different times of the day in order to understand and analyze these changes. You can see the effects very easily for yourself if you look at any scene—the view from a window or a corner of the garden—first on a cloudy morning and then in low evening sunlight.

Light is vital to a painting whether a landscape or a still-life or portrait study. Both photographers and painters of landscape know that the high midday sun is their enemy, as it creates dense patches of shadow and drains the landscape of color and definition. A portrait or still-life can also look flat, if lit directly from above, while a side light can suddenly bring it to life, creating exciting shadows of purple or green and vivid, sparkling highlights.

AERIAL PERSPECTIVE

This is a way of using color and tone to give a sense of space in a painting, and to indicate recession. It is particularly important in landscape painting. If you look at an expanse of landscape, such as one with fields and trees in the foreground and distant hills or mountains beyond, you will see that the colors become paler and cooler in the distance, with details barely visible. The objects in the foreground will be brighter and have much clearer areas of contrast, or tonal differences, which will become smaller in the middle distance and may disappear altogether in the far distance, so that the hills or mountains appear as pure areas of pale blue. It takes some experience to use aerial perspective successfully; if you accidentally mix a rather warm blue on your palette and try to use it for the distant hills you will find that they seem almost to jump forward to the front of the picture. The same applies if you combine a pale color with a much darker one; there will then be a greater tonal difference than is actually present and the

Below *In this painting, the contrast between the dark and light tree trunks has been emphasized by the use of very thin paint. The solid foliage of the evergreens draws attention to the slenderness of the foreground trunks and provides a counterpoint within the picture.*

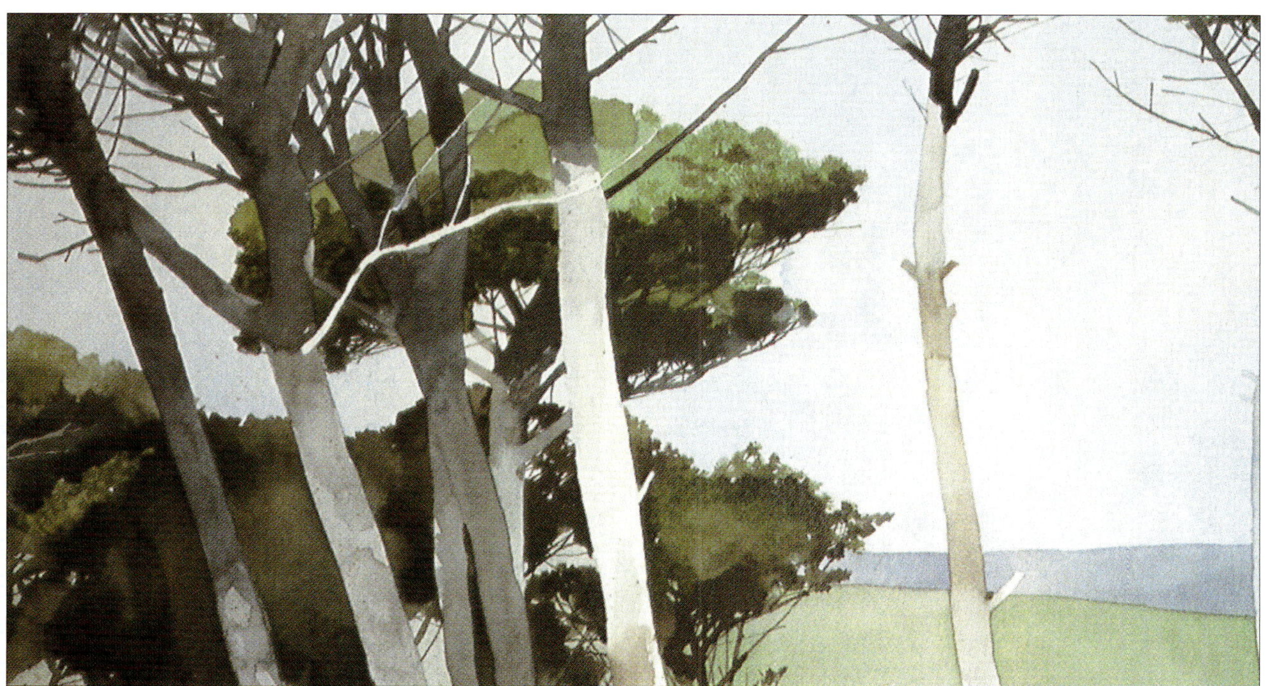

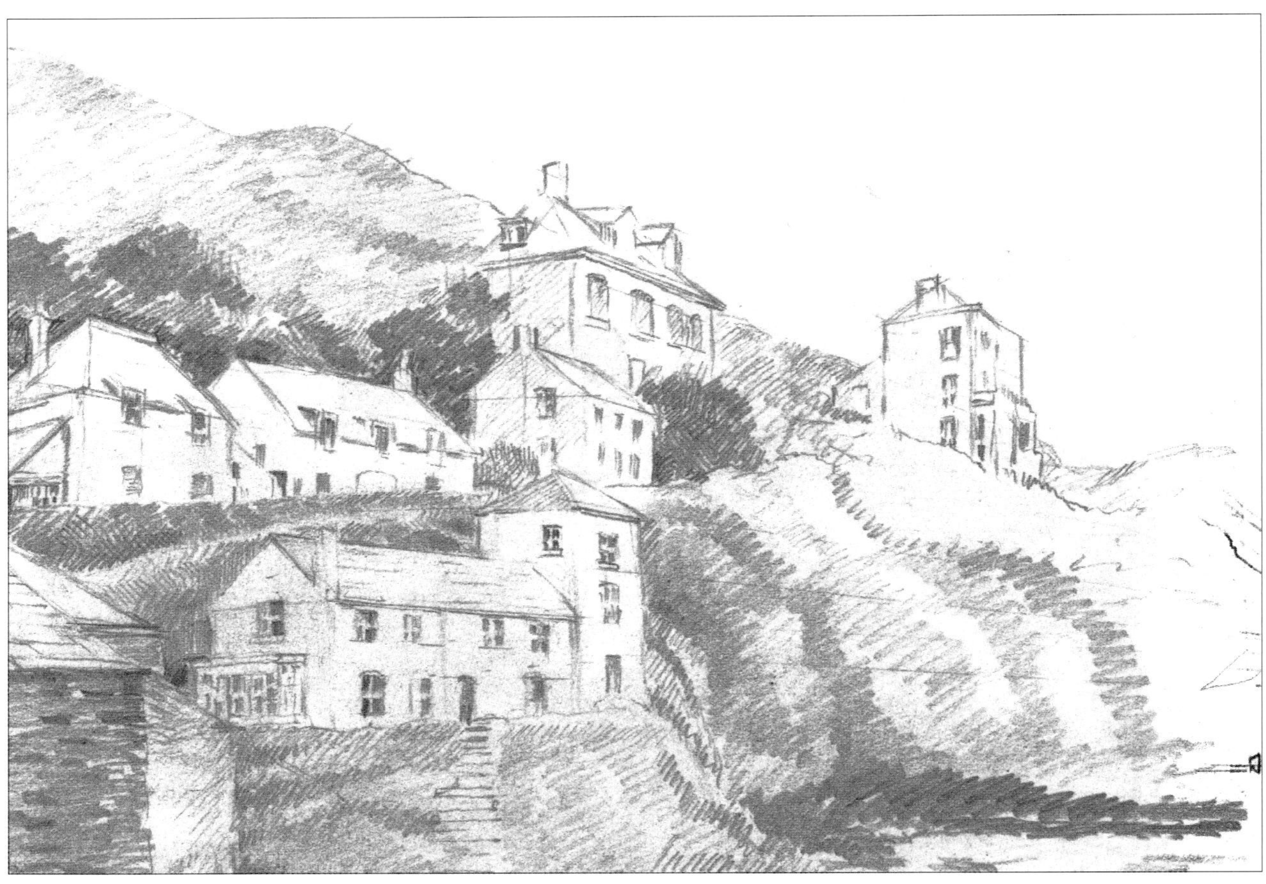

background will begin to vie with the foreground.

Aerial perspective can, of course, be either exploited or ignored. Sometimes, for instance, you might be more interested in creating a flat pattern or you might want simply to use areas of vivid color.

LINEAR PERSPECTIVE

This, like color theory, can be a very complex subject, almost a science. During the Renaissance, when the laws of perspective were first being formulated in a systematic way, artists vied with one another to produce more and more elaborate perspective drawings; for example Paolo Uccello made a study of a chalice broken down into a series of separate receding surfaces which is quite breathtaking in its intricacy. However, unless your particular interest is architecture, you might perhaps want to make a series of detailed studies of the interiors of churches—for instance, it is most unlikely that you will need to understand more than the most

Left *A scene such as this relies on an understanding of the laws of perspective or the effect of the high-perched buildings would be lost. When sketching out of doors, it is often helpful to mark in a horizon line so that the angles can be related to it; the eye alone cannot always judge such angles truthfully.*

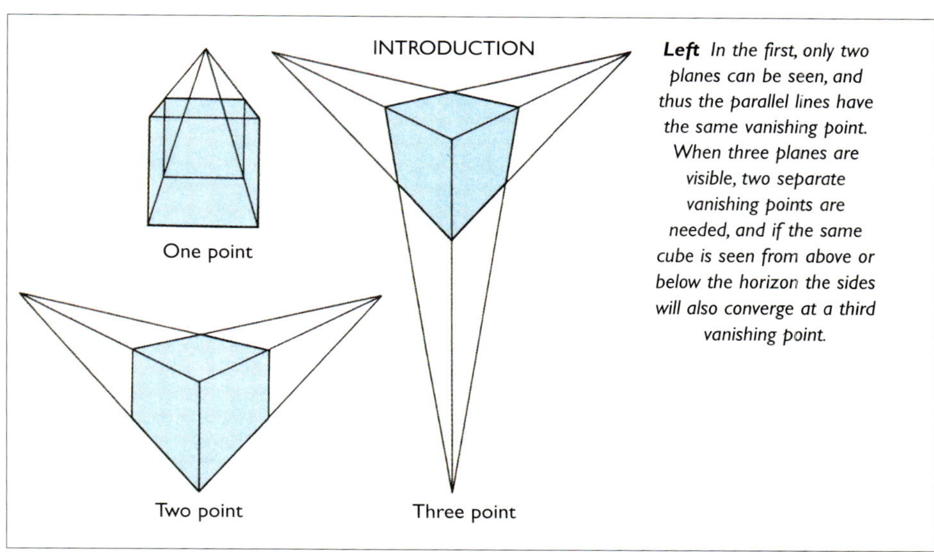

Left *In the first, only two planes can be seen, and thus the parallel lines have the same vanishing point. When three planes are visible, two separate vanishing points are needed, and if the same cube is seen from above or below the horizon the sides will also converge at a third vanishing point.*

basic rules, which are helpful when faced with the problem of how to make buildings look solid or how to indicate that they are being viewed from above.

The primary rule, which many people learn at school, is that all receding parallel lines meet at a vanishing point, which is on the horizon. It is easy enough to learn such rules, but far less easy to apply them. A single building has several different planes, or sets of parallel lines, and a group of buildings, such as a farmhouse with barns and outhouses, has even more, as the buildings are often set at random angles to one another. Where, you may ask yourself, is this horizon at which they will all meet, and how is it determined? This is dependent on your chosen viewpoint. If you are high up, on a cliff or hilltop, the horizon will be level with you, so that you have very little sky and a large expanse of land or sea. You will be looking down at the group of buildings, and the parallel lines receding from you will slope up to the horizon. If you are at a low angle, perhaps sitting on the ground, the horizon, still at eye-level, will also be low, giving a large expanse of sky. The buildings will be above the horizon and the receding parallels will slope down to it.

In the case of parallels running directly away from you, the vanishing point would be within the picture area, but for different planes at angles to them it will be a hypothetical one which can be some way outside the picture area to the right or left.

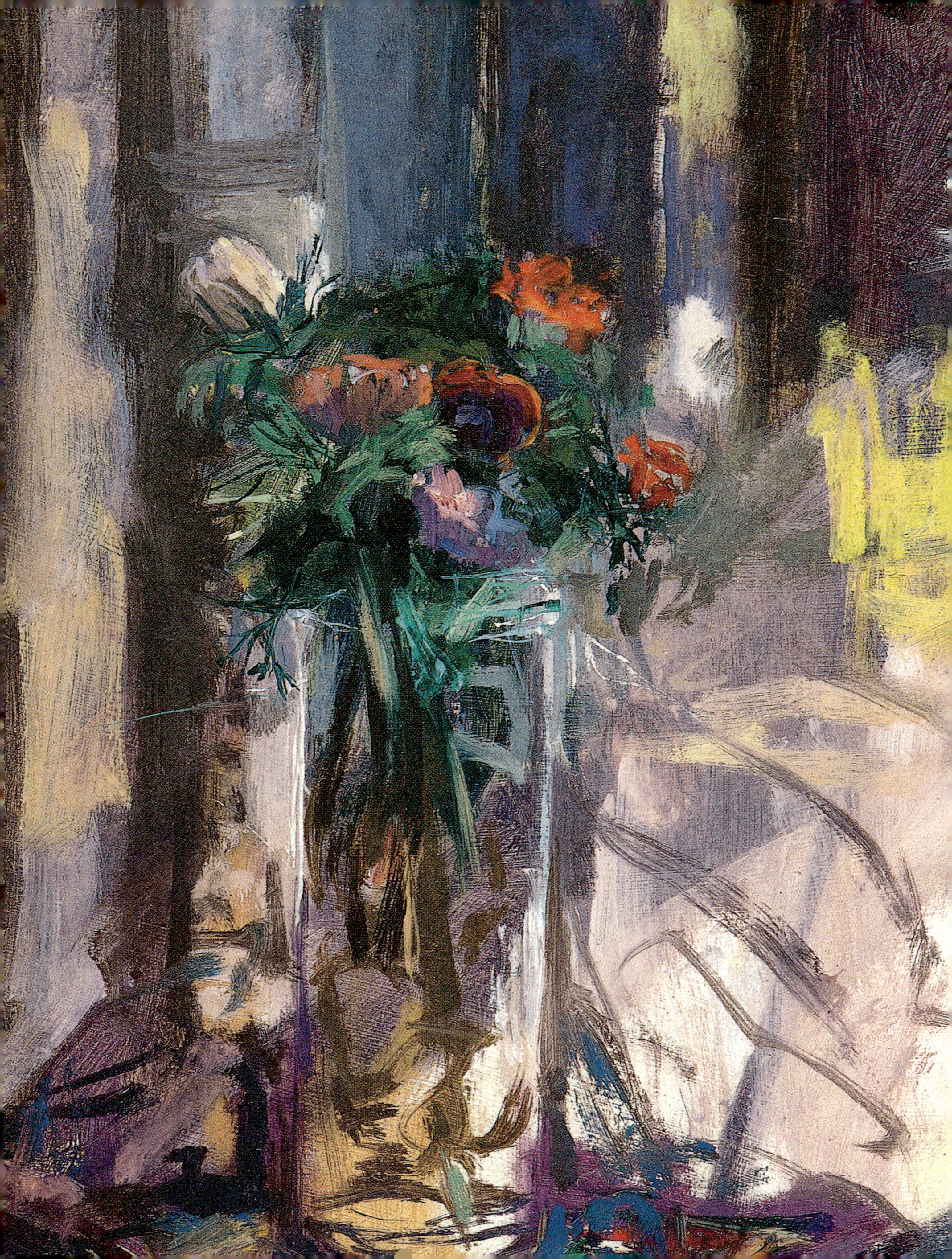

16 STARTING TO PAINT

Many people seem to feel that just as there are "proper" ways of going about a painting, there are also "proper" subjects. This is quite untrue; as we have seen, there is no way of applying oil paint that is more correct than another, nor is there any one subject that makes a better painting than another. Still lifes, flowers, and landscapes are all types of painting hallowed by long tradition, but many artists have made fine paintings of just the corner of a room or a wall with a few flowers against it. Vincent van Gogh made deeply moving and expressive still lifes from such subjects as a pair of peasant's boots or a pile of books on a table.

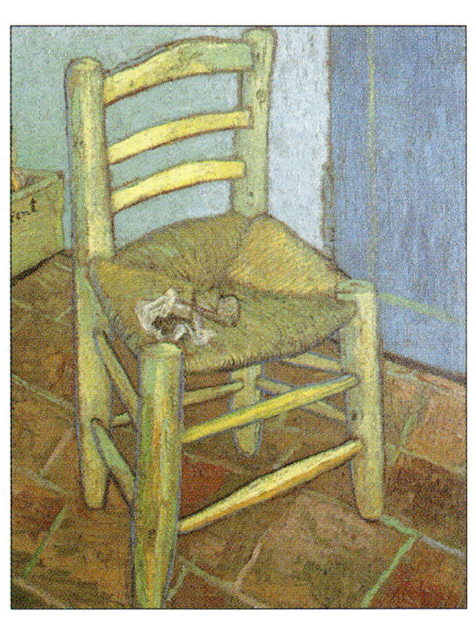

Above *Domestic interiors have been a favorite subject with artists since the Dutch 17th-century masters. These two paintings, Van Gogh's* Yellow Chair *and Gwen John's* A Comer of the Artist's Room in Paris, *although very different, give a strong feeling of serenity.*

It should be said, however, that some subjects are more difficult than others, and it can be discouraging to find you have set yourself a task which your experience is not equal to. Still lifes, flowers, and landscapes all provide good starting points, depending on your particular interests. Subjects for still lifes can be found in most people's homes or the nearest vegetable or flower shop, and you can choose your own arrangement, light it in any way you want and take your time over it. In the case of landscape, if the weather is not suitable for outdoor painting, or if you feel shy about it, you

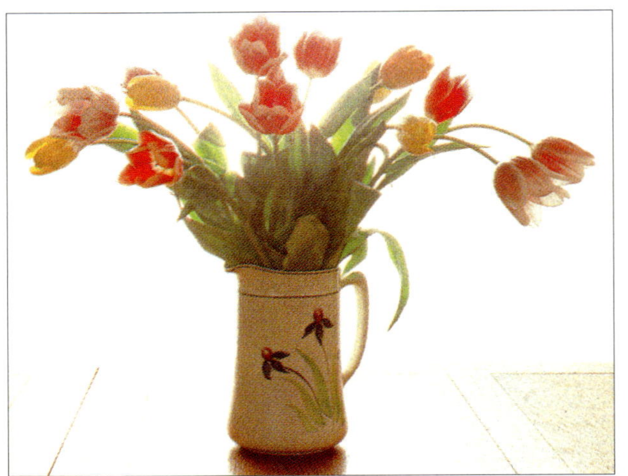

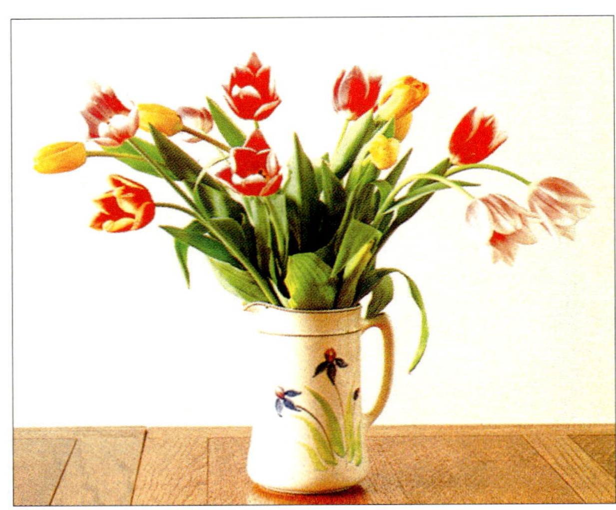

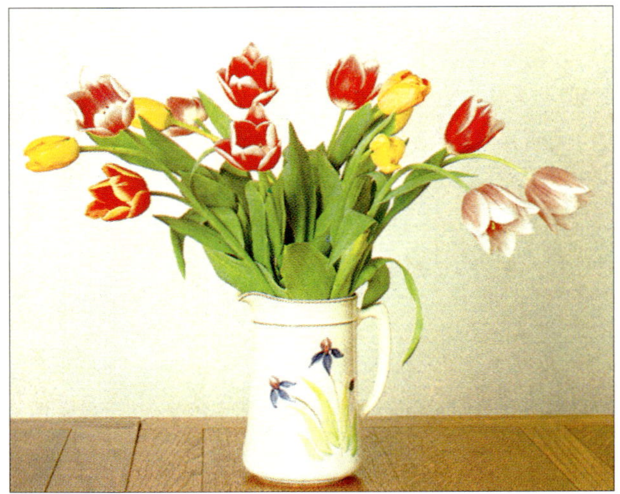

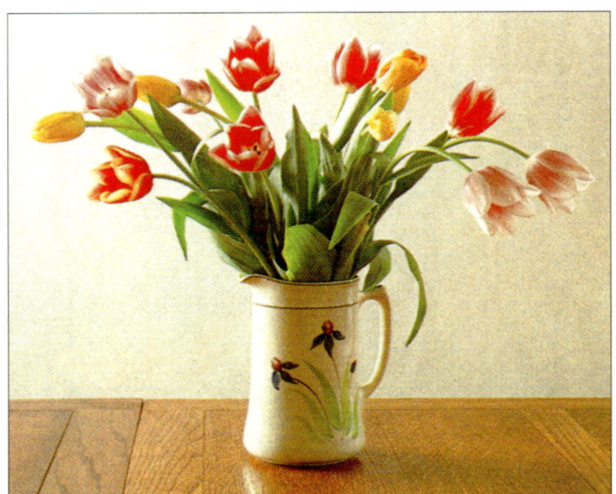

Lighting plays a vital part in the arrangement of a still life or portrait, and a subject can change quite dramatically according to the way it is lit. Back lighting (top left) can be very effective for flowers, as the light will shine through the petals in places, giving a brilliant sparkle, with the front foliage and vase appearing dark. Front lighting (above left) tends to make any subject seem dull, while side or diagonal lighting (top and above right) will define the forms more clearly. Start very small. A good starting size is about 20 X 16 in. (50 X 40 cm), a standard one in which you can buy both boards and canvases.

could start by working from a photograph or you could paint the view from a window.

CHOOSING A SHAPE AND SIZE

This may seem trivial, but in fact both shape and size have an important part to play in the composition and treatment of a painting. A single tree might call for a narrow vertical painting, while a still life with a lot of objects in it could suggest a rather square one.

Size is a very personal matter: some artists work on vast canvases too big to fit in most living-rooms, while others produce tiny, detailed work on supports no larger than a photograph. Until you have established a size which suits you, it is wise to use an inexpensive support, such as a piece of primed paper or cardboard, oil sketching paper or "canvas board."

AVOIDING DISCOURAGEMENT

If your painting goes wrong at an early stage you may feel discouraged. Various suggestions are given here which will help you to avoid or overcome the more common problems.

Tinting the ground

A white surface is "dishonest," as it prevents you from judging the tones and colors correctly. No color exists in a particular way except in relation to the colors surrounding it. A method often used by artists is to tint the canvas in a neutral color, usually a warm brown or gray, before starting the painting. This can be done either by mixing pigment in with the primer or by putting a wash of oil paint, such as raw umber, heavily diluted with turpentine, over the white ground. Acrylic paint can also be used for this since it dries much faster than oil paint.

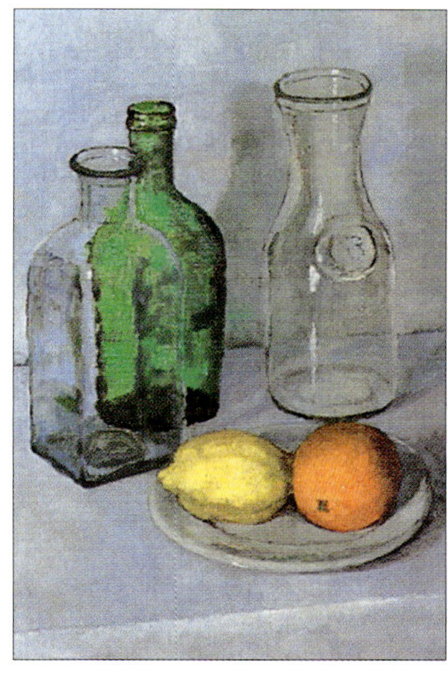

Right *Although still life and flower arrangements need not be elaborate, some thought is needed in the initial setting up if the foreground and background are not to become dull and featureless. Thumbnail sketches and photographs are useful aids in setting up an arrangement.*

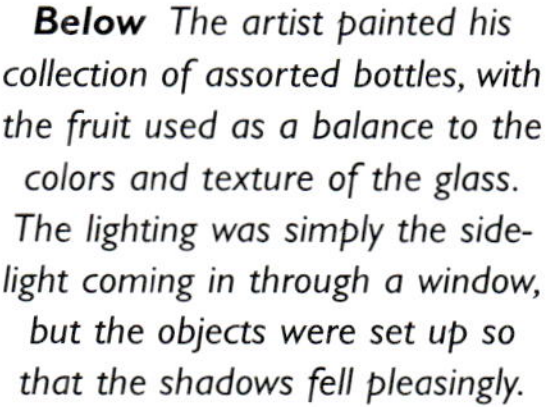

Below *The artist painted his collection of assorted bottles, with the fruit used as a balance to the colors and texture of the glass. The lighting was simply the side-light coming in through a window, but the objects were set up so that the shadows fell pleasingly.*

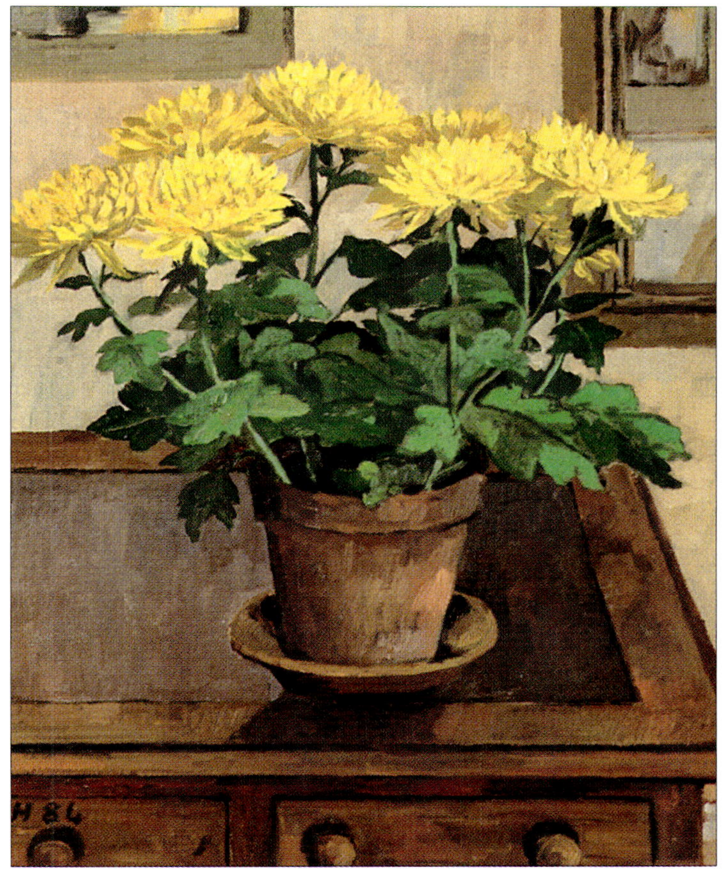

Remember: oil can be used over acrylic, but not vice versa.

Preparation

Always start with an adequate drawing or under-painting. You may be impatient to start on the real business—the laying on of paint—but it does pay to take your time at this stage, for it will avoid a lot of frustration later.

Keeping the picture moving

Try to avoid working in detail on one part of the painting at the expense of others. This approach can lead to a disjointed-looking painting, since you are more likely to tire of it half-way through. Generally, it is better to work on all parts of the canvas at once, so that you have a better idea of how one part relates to another in color, tone and texture.

Avoid getting bogged down in detail too early; fine lines, such as the stems of flowers, small facial details in a portrait, or foreground details in a landscape, are best left until last.

In general, it is easiest to build up oil paint light over dark, as white is the most opaque color; so keep to dark and middle tones in the early stages, working up gradually to the light and bright tones and colors.

Below *These drawings show the different elements of a still life arranged in a variety of ways. A symmetrical arrangement (left) tends to be monotonous, but the arrangement, with the flat plane of the table angled away from the eye and a more varied grouping of the fruit (center), has considerably more visual interest. The drawing of the flower and fruit with draperies (right) provides more linear contrast and a busier background.*

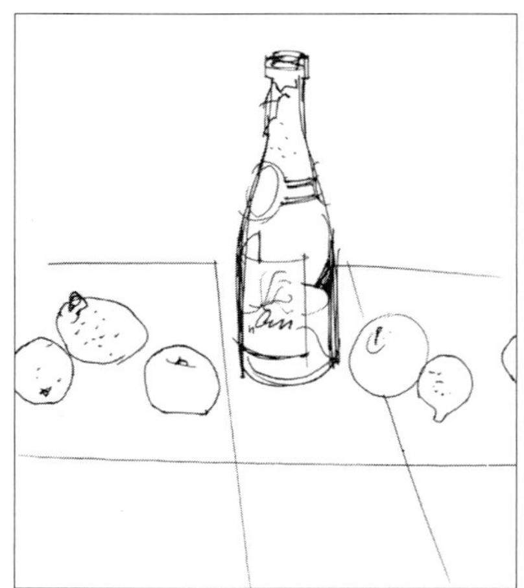

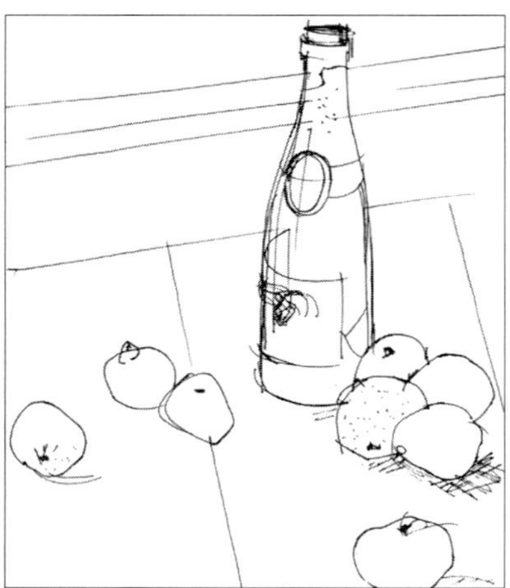

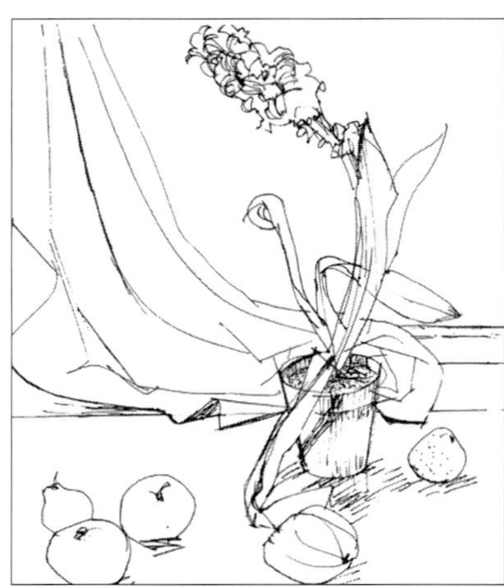

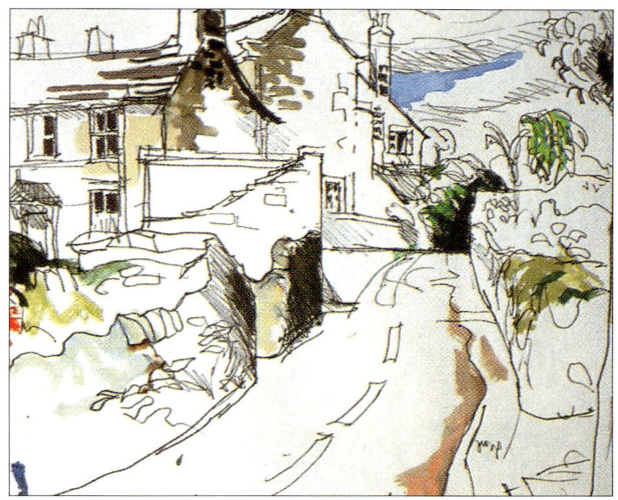

Different artists have different methods of making sketches, according to their individual style and what particular aspect of a scene they want to note and remember. Some do detailed drawings in pen and ink or pen and wash, some make rough pencil sketches with color notes, while others use oil paint, which is an excellent sketching medium because it can be applied so quickly. At any rate, sketching or underpainting helps artists decide upon a composition.

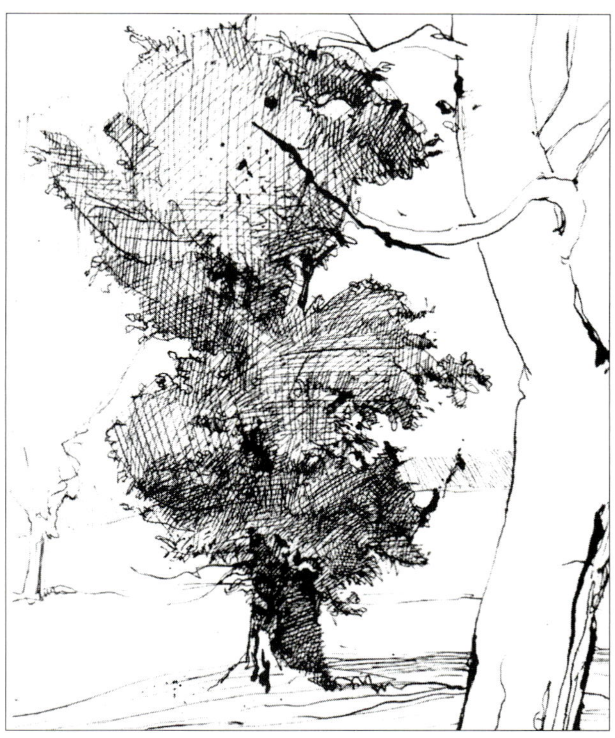

PROBLEM-SOLVING

Even paintings by professionals go wrong, but the beauty of oil paint is that they can easily be altered. If you suddenly notice that your drawing is incorrect and that you have quite misunderstood a shape or color, the best course is to scrape off the area with a palette knife and then repaint it. You may even decide to scrape down the whole painting and start more or less from scratch—this is often more satisfactory than drawing over and becoming so overloaded with paint that you are just churning it up by adding layers.

USING REFERENCE MATERIAL

Painting is about looking at things—a good painter is constantly assessing objects and scenes with a view to translating them into paintings. This kind of analytical vision is largely a matter of habit and training, but few people have perfect visual memories, and for this reason artists often make visual references to use later on. Normally these take the form of sketches, and art students are always urged to carry sketchbooks at all times. Artists also use additional materials, like photographs or texts, to refresh their memories.

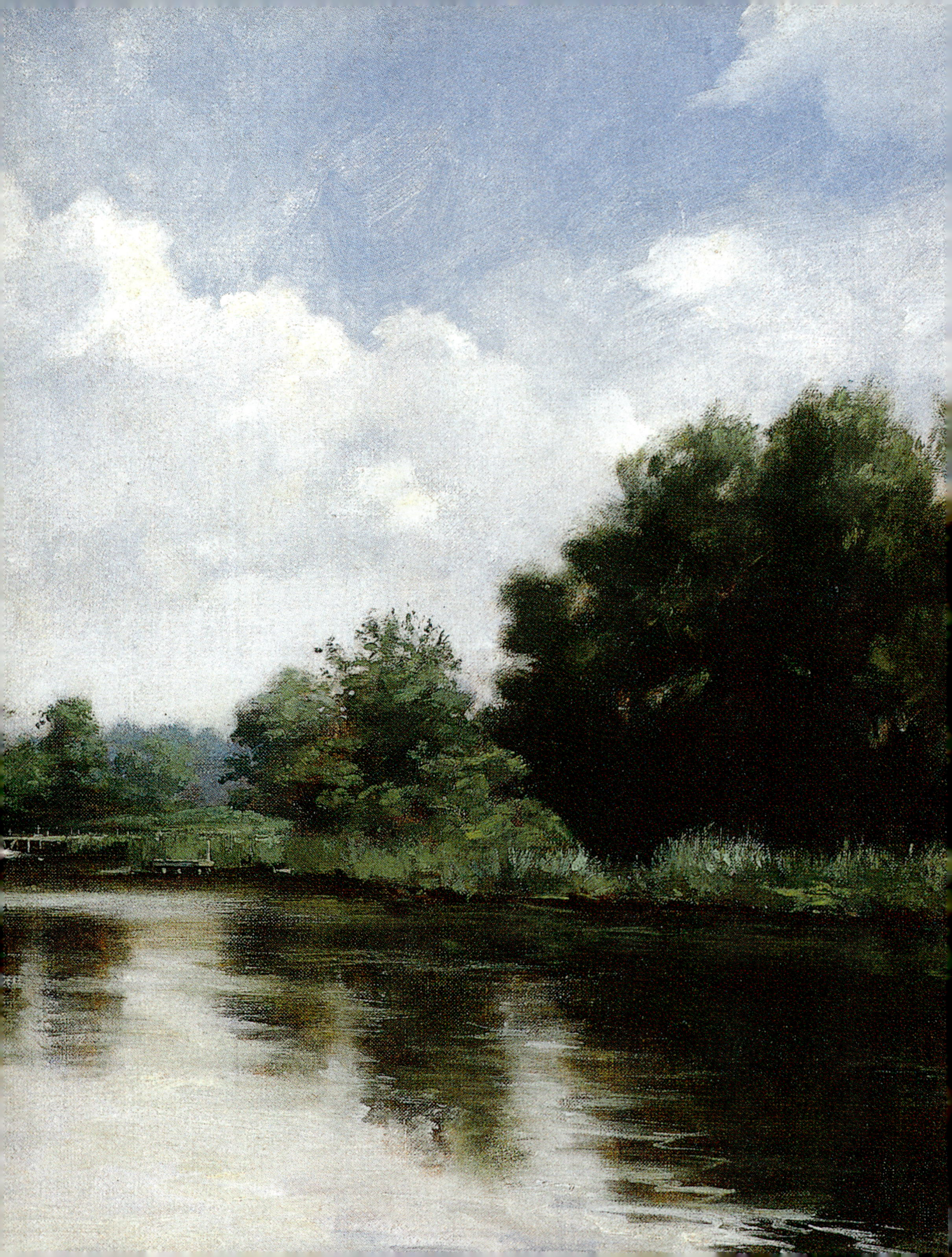

17 OUTDOOR SUBJECTS

All the paintings on the following pages, although very different from one another, fall into the broad category of landscape, a term that can really be used to describe practically any subject that is located outside the walls of the studio or home, even if it is a painting of a building or a single tree. Outdoor subjects such as these need not actually be painted out of doors—indeed many fine landscapes are painted in a studio—but at some stage in the inspiration and evolution of a good landscape, close observation of the outdoor world is vital.

Outdoor subjects thus present challenges and problems very different from those of still lifes or portraits: the painter of landscapes cannot arrange the subject and lighting as he chooses; he can only decide on a scene and then select what he wants to show and what he will leave out. One painter, for instance, may be particularly interested in the way the light falls on a particular scene, or in the ever-changing shapes and colors of the clouds, while another will ignore these aspects in favor of shapes or flat patterns. There is also the aspect of facing the outdoors and painting in an area where you are vulnerable to people's gaze.

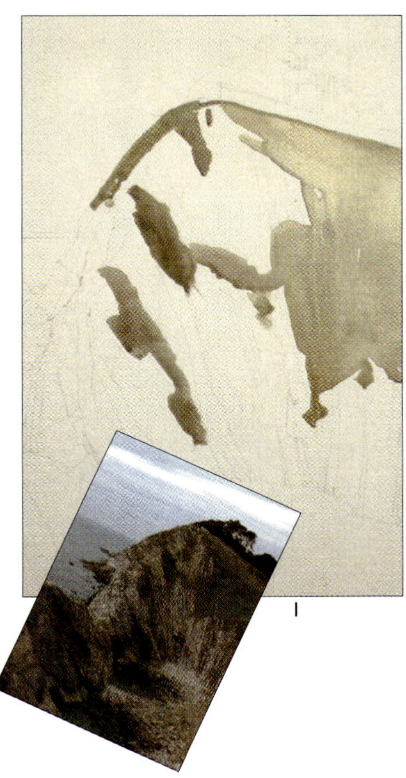

Above *A detailed and precise underdrawing was made with a sharp 3B pencil, after which the first diluted wash of olive green paint was laid down on the area at the top of the cliff.*

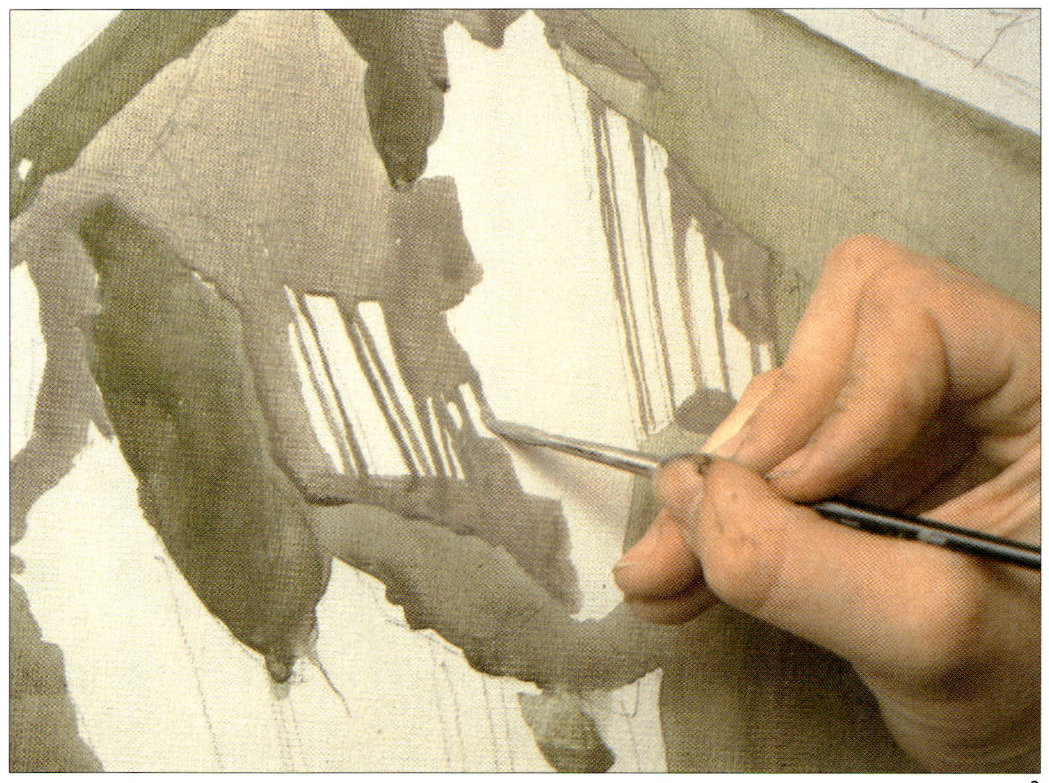

2

Left *More thinned paint was applied with a fine, soft brush, with areas of white being left uncovered. The lines were painted very carefully as this technique does not allow changes to be made. The pencil lines of the original drawing show through the thin paint, but this is not a disadvantage as in this case it adds to the effect.*

3

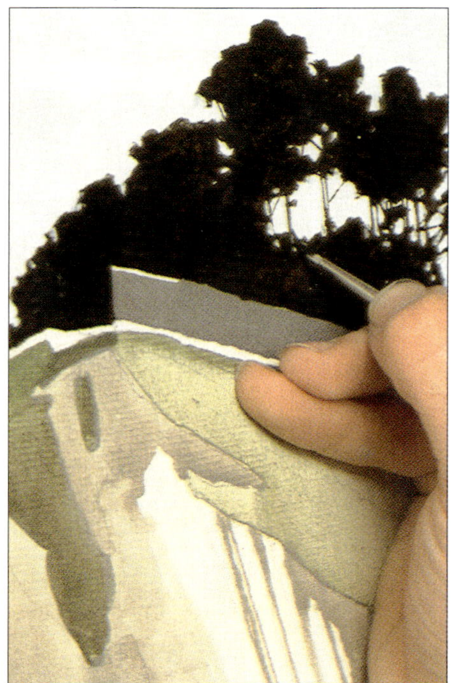

Left *The trees and the wall below them were painted almost as flat areas with a fine sable brush. The painter could safely rest his hand on the painting while doing this detailed work as the paint in that area was already dry.*

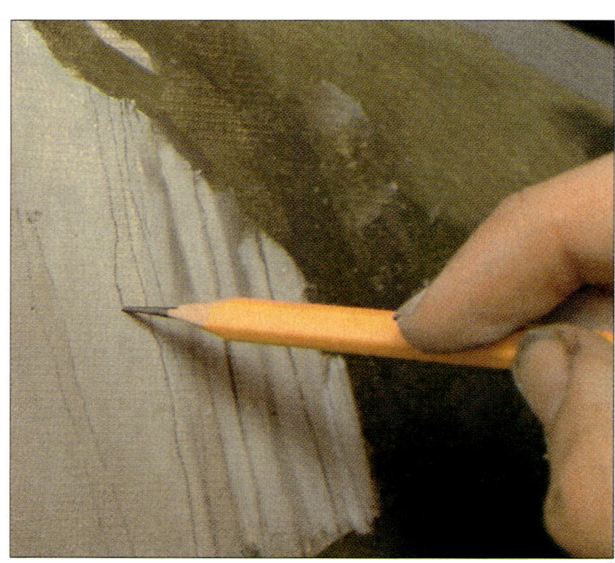

4

Above *A pencil is used to draw into the paint to create the effect of the rocky fissures in the cliff face. The pencil marks would create indentations like those made with a knife.*

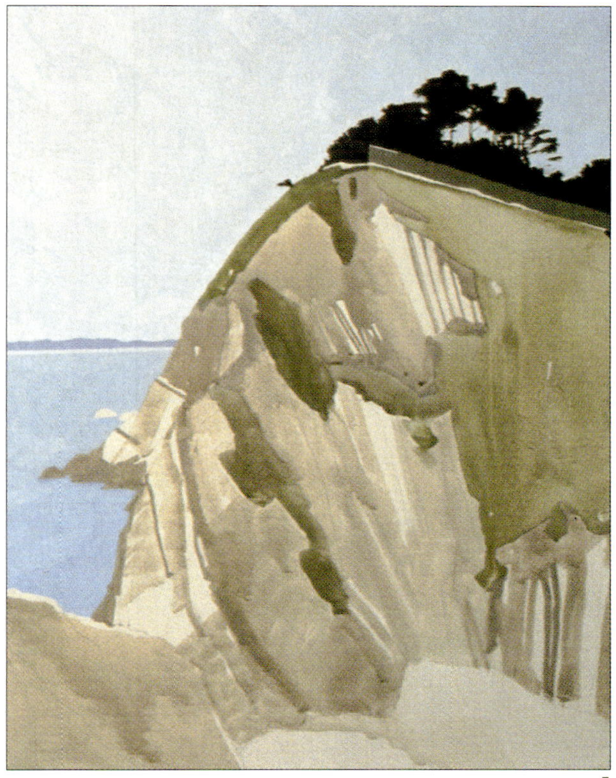

5

Above *Areas of white have been left unpainted, to be treated in a different way. The edges which separate each area of color from the next are sharp and clearly defined at this stage.*

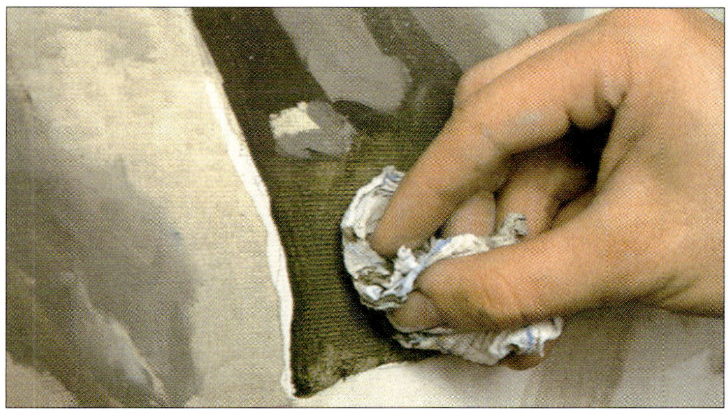

6

Above *The detail shows wet paint being applied to the dark area below the cliff. As illustrated above, a crumpled tissue was used to create texture.*

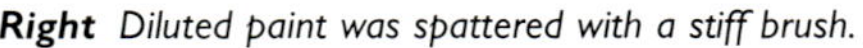

Right *Diluted paint was spattered with a stiff brush.*

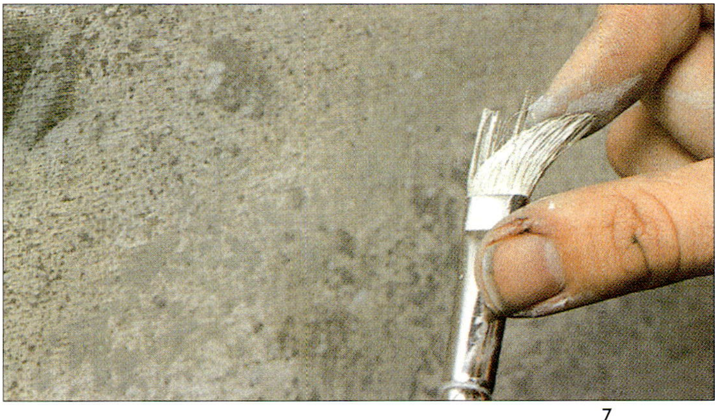

7

8

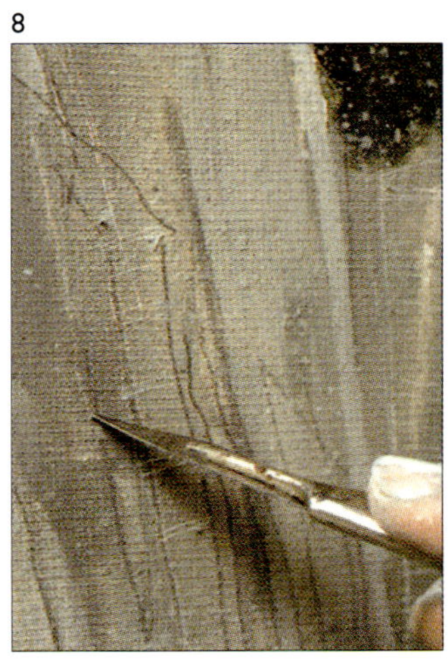

Left *A scalpel was used to scratch into the paint, allowing fine lines of white to show through: the sgraffito technique.*

Right *This detail shows thicker paint in a mixture of white and Payne's gray being used for highlights. The paint was then blended with the finger.*

9

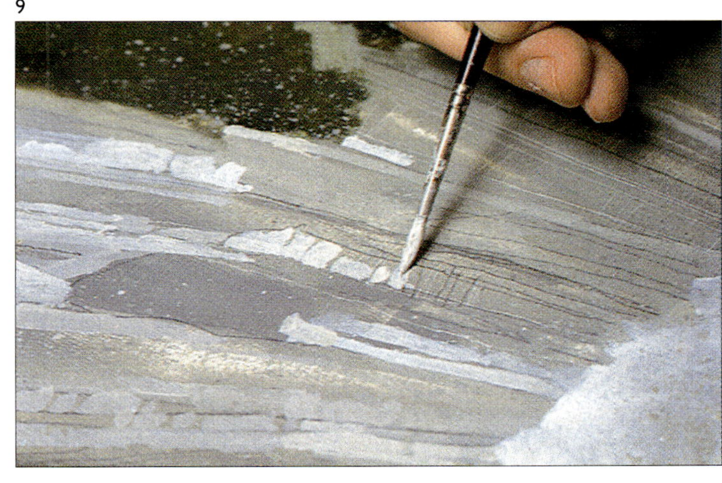

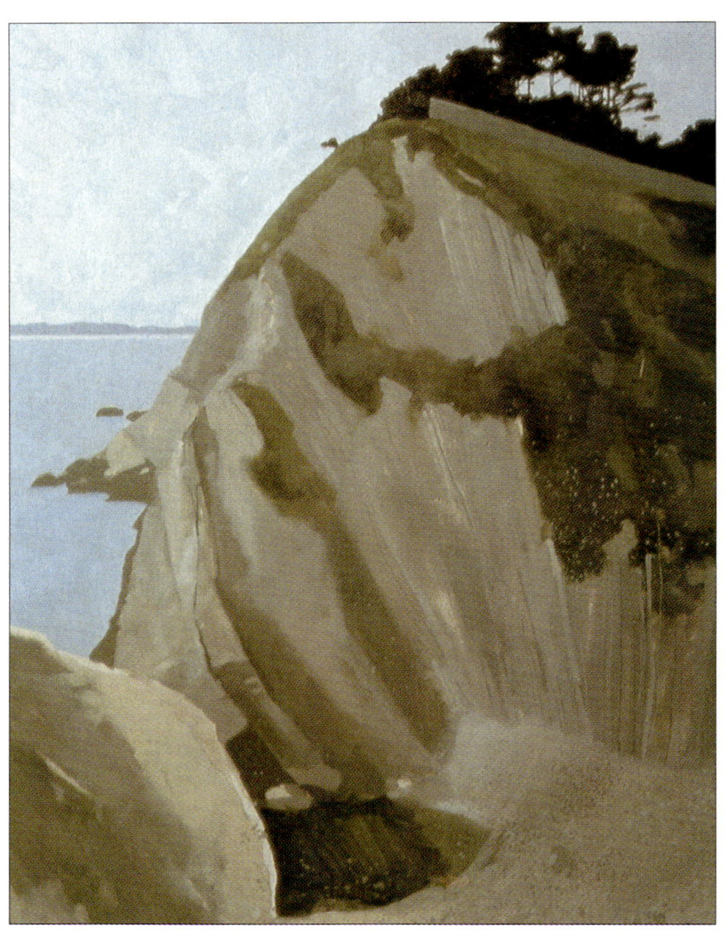

THE HEADLAND

This painting shows oil paint being used in a way more often associated with watercolor—in very thin washes. The paint was diluted so much that it was virtually transparent, and each wash was allowed to dry before the next was applied. Since oil paint mixed with a medium such as linseed oil can take a very long time to dry, turpentine was used in combination with the fast-drying alkyd medium, Liquin, which binds the pigment as well as thinning it; if

MATERIALS USED

SUPPORT:
Finegrained, readyprimed canvas board 30 X 20 in. (76.2 X 50.8 cm)

BRUSHES:
Number 6 sable and a number 6 soft synthetic as well as two flat bristle brushes, numbers 4 and 7

COLORS:
Titanium white, ivory black, cobalt blue, Payne's gray and yellow ocher, thinned with turpentine and Liquin

turpentine had been used alone the paint would simply have dribbled down the surface.

If you look at the photograph of the scene you may see why the painter has chosen to work in this way; it is an extremely linear and angular subject, with the group of trees starkly defined against the sky and the very distinct lines of the cliffs converging at the bottom. Using paint thickly, in a more conventional manner, would have given an effect much softer than the one created in this picture.

Using oil paint in this way requires a rather deliberate approach—again much more like a watercolor technique—and the painting was begun with a very careful drawing in pencil. The color scheme is deliberately somber, with only six colors being used in all, but although the palette is so limited the colors are neither dull nor muddy, with the blue of the sea appearing quite bright in the context of the surrounding grays and greens. The sky, which the photograph shows as containing two distinct areas of tone, has been painted almost, but not quite, as a flat area, thus allowing the eye to concentrate on what is really important—the cliff itself. Painting the clouds as they actually appeared would have detracted from the effect rather than enhancing it. This kind of selection and rejection of elements is an important part of landscape painting. The support chosen for the painting was a tall, narrow one, which suits the vertical emphasis of the subject. The surface of the canvas board shows through in places, and additional texture has been introduced by drawing with a pencil on top of the paint to define the lines of the cliffs, by scratching into the paint with a scalpel and by spattering thinned paint on to the board to suggest the appearance of the shingle beach.

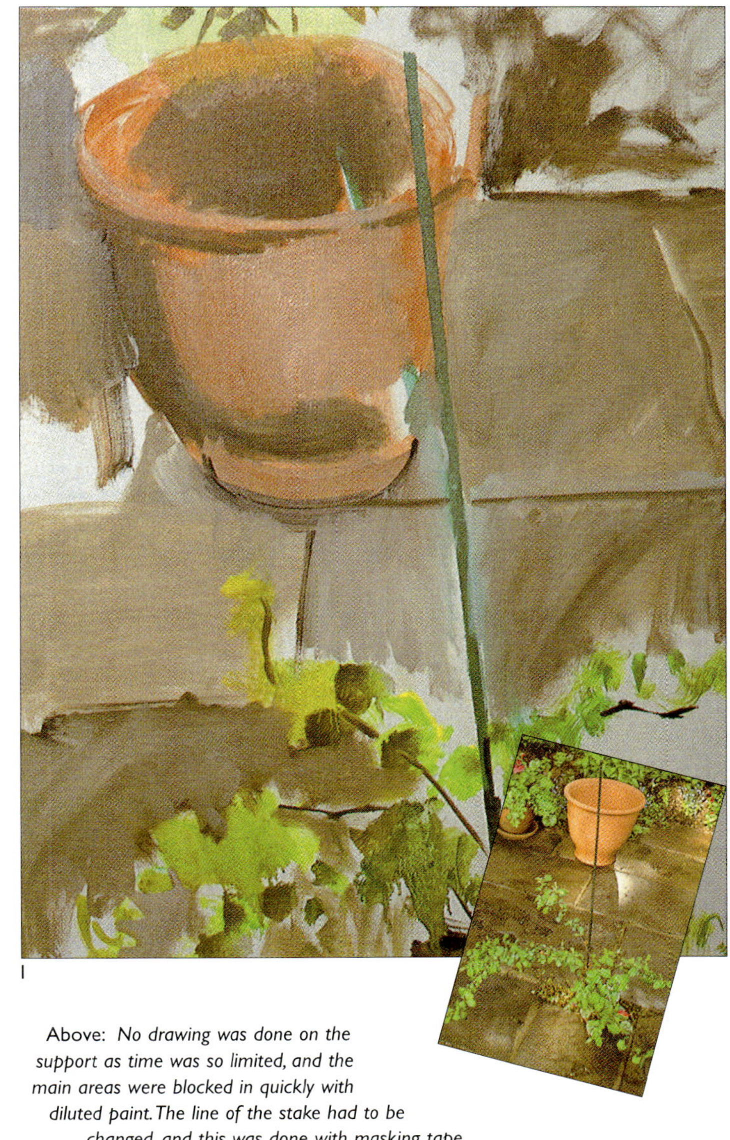

1

Above: *No drawing was done on the support as time was so limited, and the main areas were blocked in quickly with diluted paint. The line of the stake had to be changed, and this was done with masking tape. Two parallel lines of tape were laid down to define the new line, and color was applied rapidly right over it. The tape was then removed, leaving a clear, well-defined line.*

IN THE GARDEN

This painting of a corner of a town garden, while falling within the general category of landscape, is actually more of an "outdoor still life," and it illustrates very well the statement made earlier that subjects for paintings can be found virtually anywhere. If you put two or three people into the same garden and told them to do a painting of some aspect of it, they would probably all

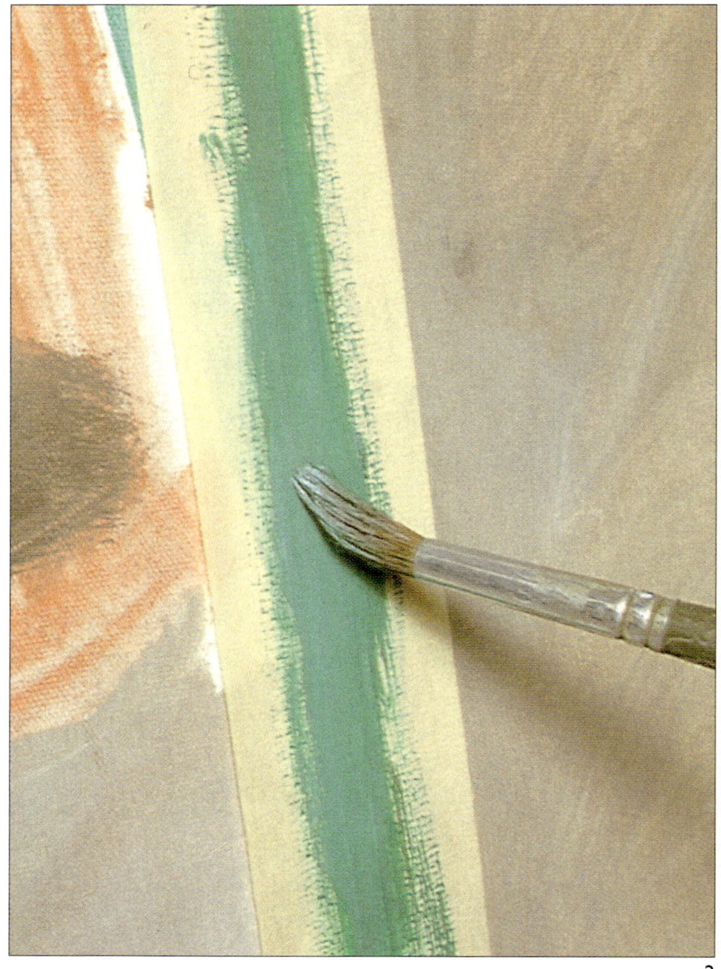
2

choose quite different ones, depending on their particular interest and way of looking at things. This particular artist chose a subject which was literally under his feet, because he was attracted to the colors and patterns of the flagstones, the lines of the pot and stakes, and the texture of the foliage.

The painting was done out of doors in circumstances of some difficulty—the weather, and therefore the light, was changeable—and the painting had to be completed under an umbrella. A comparison of the finished painting with the photograph shows two things: firstly how the camera flattens out both color and perspective, and secondly how various selections, rejections, and adjustments have been made by the artist in order to make a satisfying composition. The foliage in the background, for instance, has been reduced to a few

3
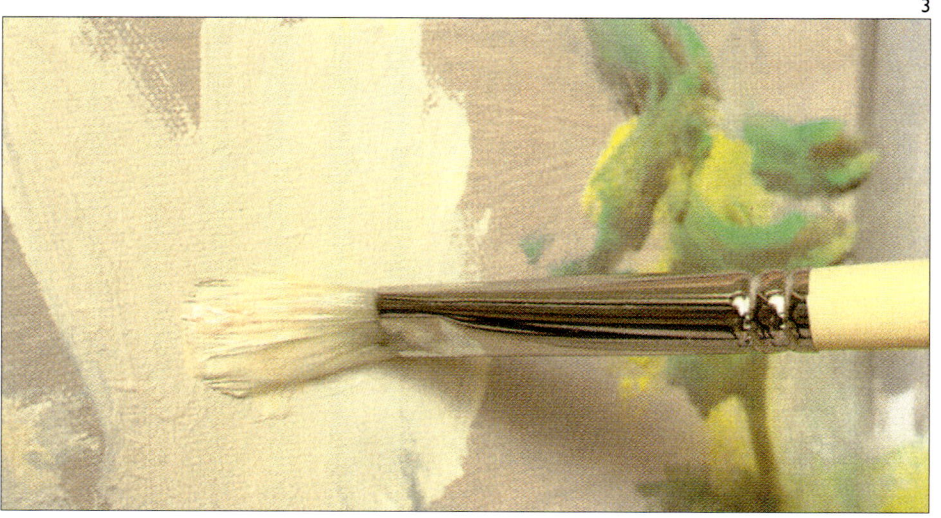

Above *After underpainting, the picture was built up with thicker paint, and more colors were introduced.*

Right *The photograph shows a thick mixture of yellow and white being used for one of the flagstones over an underlayer of pinkish-brown. Other flagstones were painted in shades of blue and muted gray.*

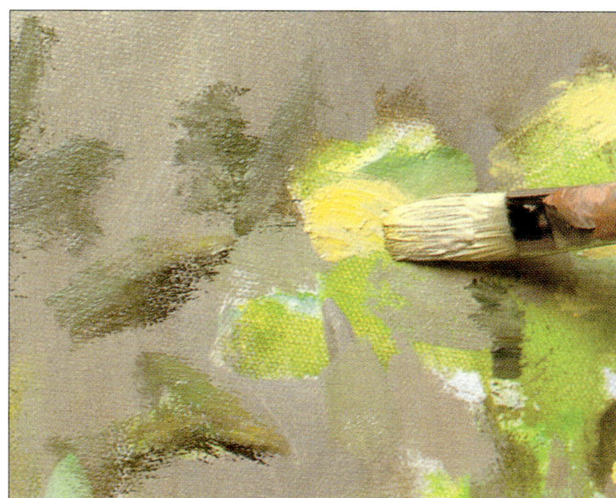

4

Left Thick paint is being applied to define the rim of the pot, and the foliage is being built up (Below) with areas of scumbled paint and thick brushstrokes of yellow-green.

telling brushstrokes (if treated in more detail they could have detracted from the foreground); the colors of the flagstones have been altered and lightened to allow the foreground foliage to stand out, and the line of the stake has been somewhat altered so that it neither cuts the pot in half nor conflicts with the lines of the flagstones.

The painting had to be done quickly as the weather was so unpredictable, and the composition was established rapidly by blocking in the main areas in thinned paint. This degree of certainty about the way a finished painting should look is largely the result of years of observation and practice, but even professional artists sometimes change their minds, and as the painting progressed it became necessary to make some alterations. In the first detail you can see that the line of the stake ran exactly parallel to the line of the flagstone on the

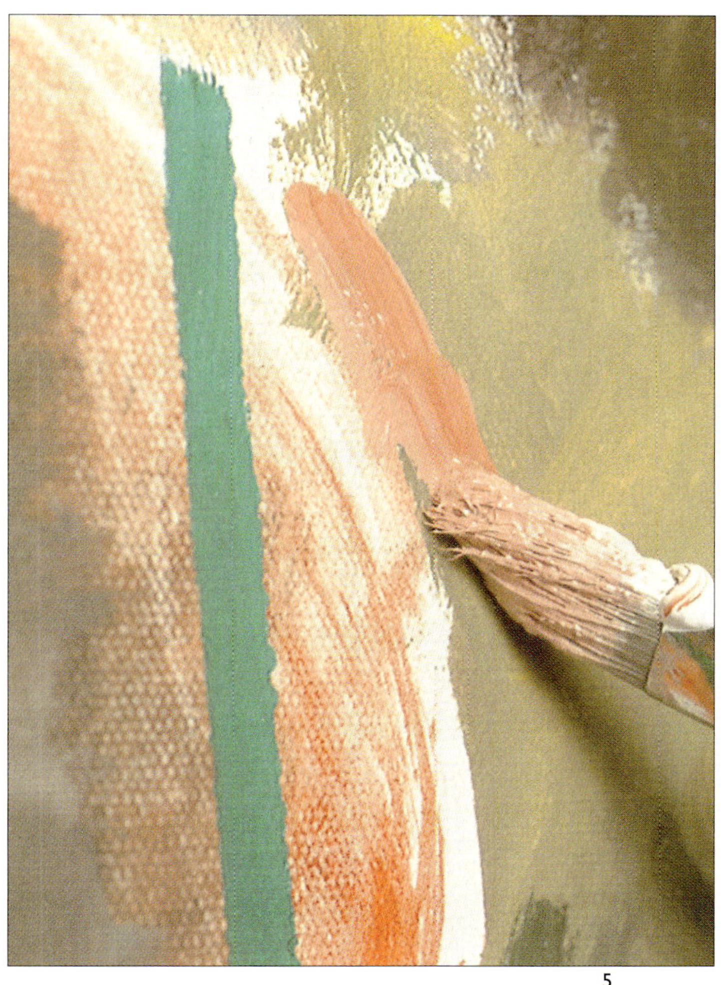

5

right, and led the eye of the viewer out of the picture, which should always be avoided. Thus the artist decided to change it, bringing the stake further over. Once this alteration was done, the paint was built up more thickly over the original thinned color—in one place it was even smudged on with the fingers—and the paint surface in the finished

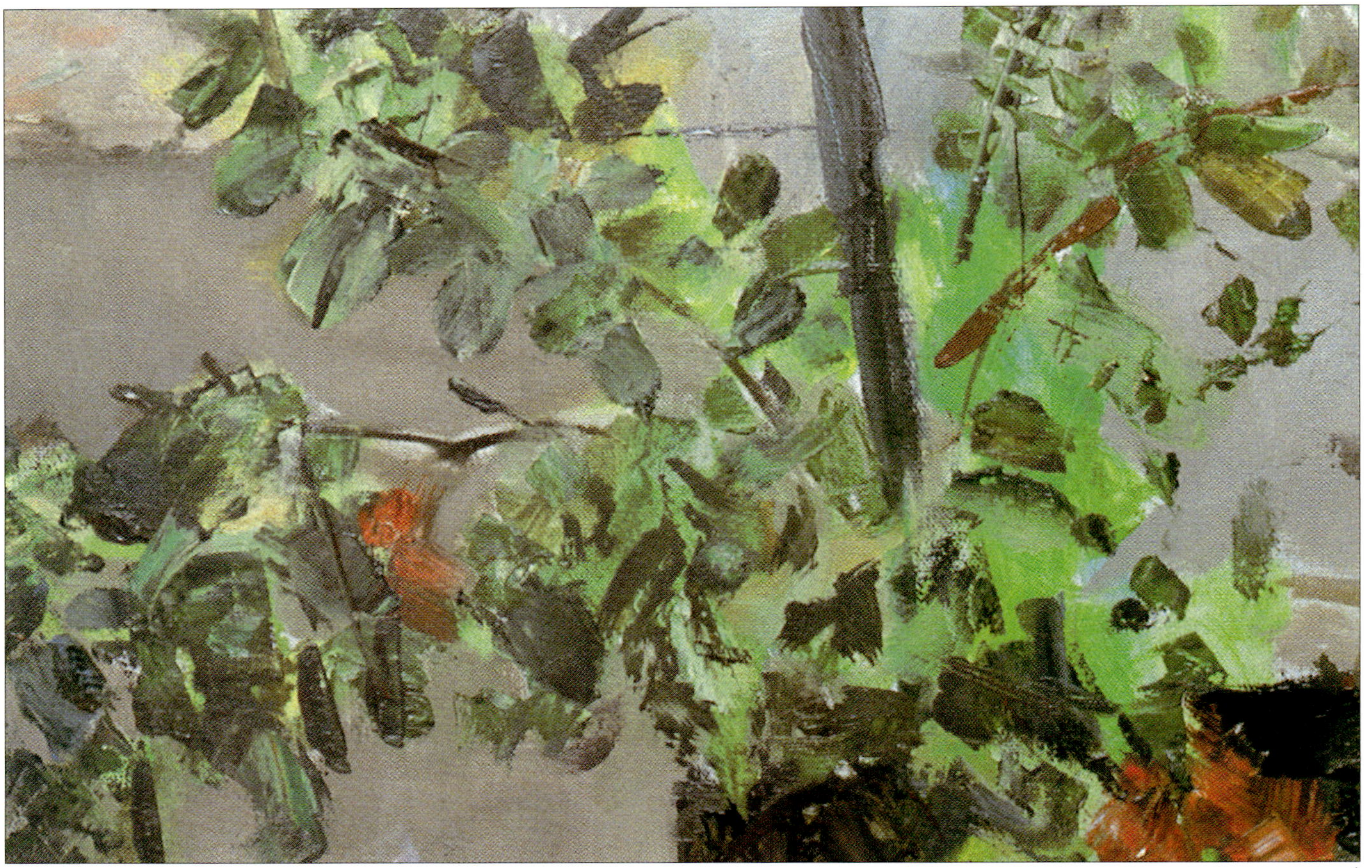

6

Below *The artist uses his fingers to smudge in highlights.*

7

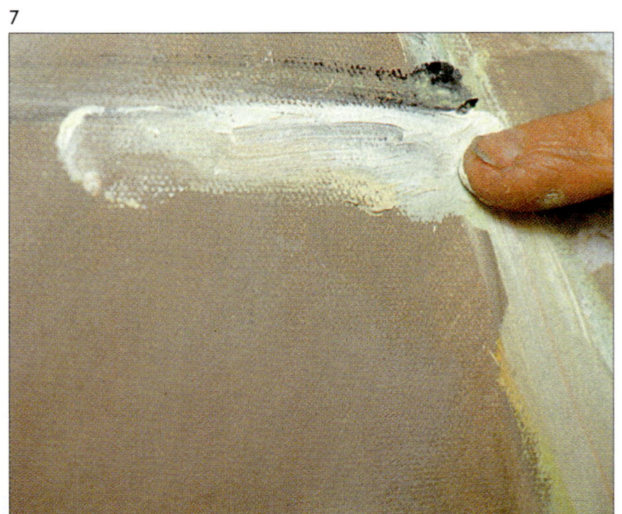

Above *The leaves here are suggested by short, curving brushstrokes, using thick paint over a still-wet layer beneath it so that the color is modified by the one beneath. No attempt has been made to define all the leaves, and some areas have been painted loosely, adding to the spontaneous effect.*

MATERIALS USED

SUPPORT:
Bought, ready-primed canvas 30 X 20 in. (76.2 X 50.8 cm)

BRUSHES:
Two flat hog's-hair, Nos 5 and 12; No. 12 soft synthetic

COLORS:
Titanium white, Payne's gray, burnt umber, raw umber, cobalt blue, cadmium red, Naples yellow, sap green, chrome green, viridian, and chrome oxide

picture is richly textured, particularly in the foreground area, where the brushstrokes have been used in a directional way to suggest individual leaves.

Paint surface is extremely important and plays a more vital part than many people realize in the finished effect of a painting; however well-chosen the colors and however good the drawing and composition may be, an unpleasant, slimy or churned-up paint surface will detract from the picture and may even make it impossible to see its virtues.

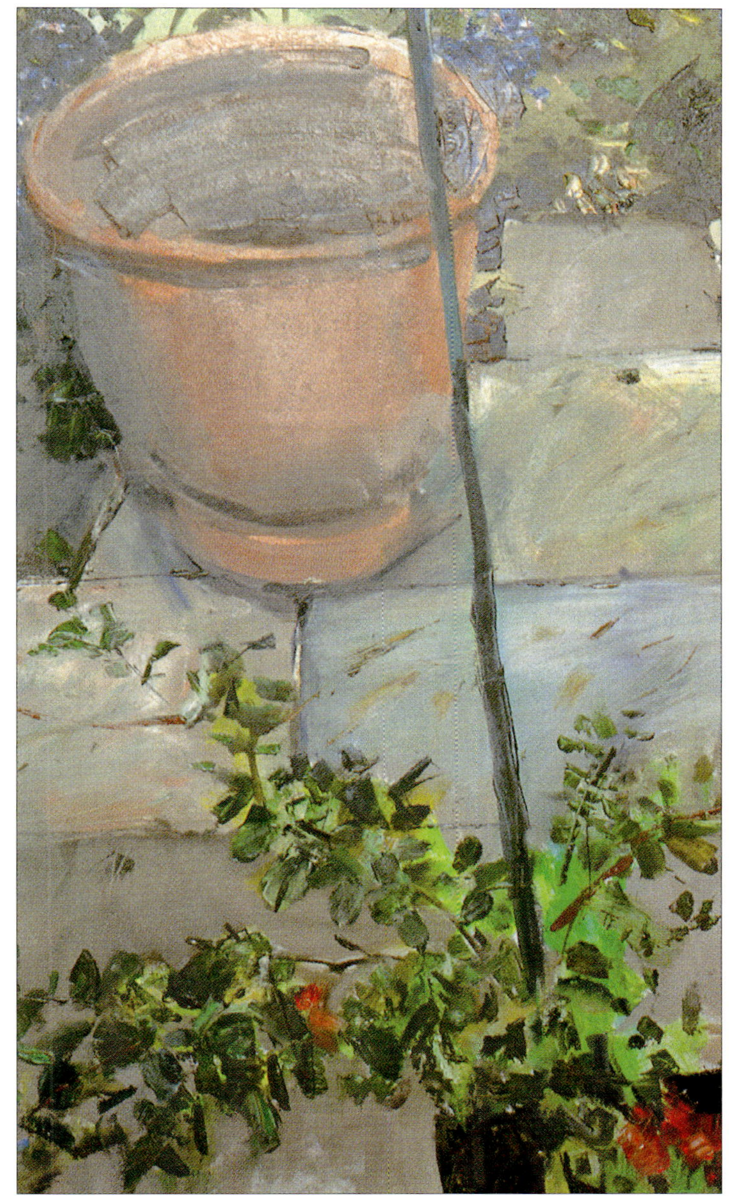

GREEK VILLAGE

This painting was not done on the spot, but it is the result of much sketching and observation of a particular part of Greece, where the painter frequently spends holidays, and it captures the sun-soaked Mediterranean atmosphere very successfully. A series of drawings was made for the painting, together with color notes and photographs, so that the composition and color scheme could be planned and worked out from a wide range of reference material.

The painting shows a view from a window, a subject which often makes an interesting composition as the viewpoint is higher than the usual street-level one and tends to include more varied elements. In this case, the bird's-eye view of the rooftops provides an attractive contrast to the smaller rectangles of window frames and doors, and the straight lines of the buildings are balanced and enhanced by the curves of the trees, foliage-covered walls, and the vegetable patch in the foreground, which lead the eye into the picture. The taut diagonals of the two rows of steps give an effect of movement and rhythm to the whole composition, which is full of interest and detail without being in any way fussy—even the small figures and the chairs and tubs on the balcony play a part in the scene, but are never allowed to dominate it. The balance of lights and darks is particularly important in this painting, as the artist wanted to capture the effect of the bright Mediterranean light, which creates strong tonal contrasts.

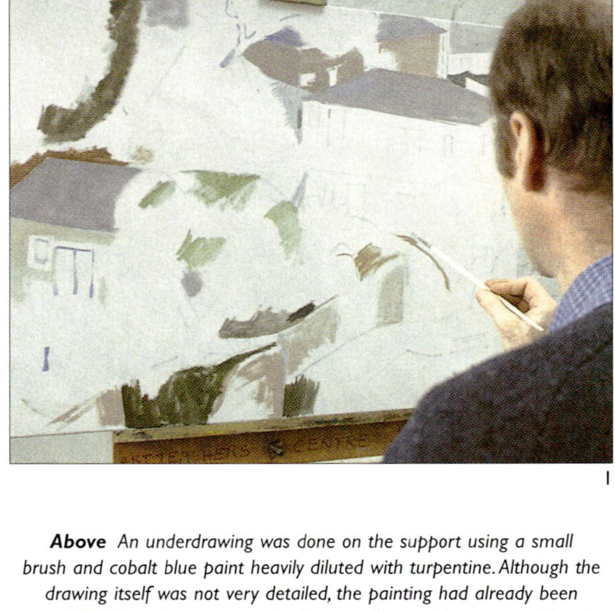

1

Above *An underdrawing was done on the support using a small brush and cobalt blue paint heavily diluted with turpentine. Although the drawing itself was not very detailed, the painting had already been carefully planned, a necessary preliminary for a subject as complex as this one with its many contrasting shapes and tones. The artist then proceeded to block in the mid-tones, using thinned paint. These provided a key for the tones. Another artist might have worked in a quite different way, doing a monochrome underpainting or charcoal drawing to establish the lights and darks first.*

2

Left: *With the mid-tones established, together with the main lines of the drawing, the architectural details of the buildings in the painting could be drawn in with dark paint.*

After all the main tones and colors were established, the painting emerged as a complete entity, whereas previously it had been a series of disparate elements. The feeling of warmth in the grays and shadow areas was achieved by mixing alizarin crimson into the cooler colors, while mixtures of white, yellow ocher, Naples yellow, and burnt sienna were used for the warm browns and yellows. The colors were then modified and some areas developed and clarified, with the paint applied more thickly, and the final details such as the chairs on the balcony were added.

The painting you see here was completed in just one day. The paint was used quite thinly to begin with and then

Right *The artist rests his hand on a mahl stick to steady it while he draws a precise curve. The mahl stick is held in the non-painting hand with the cushioned end resting on a dry part of the canvas, or on the edge of it if the paint is wet. In a painting like this, careful drawing is essential—an inaccurately placed window frame or a crooked roofline would have a jarring effect, and spoil the overall harmony of the picture.*

Far Right *A small round bristle brush was used to paint in the figures, giving detail without being over-meticulous. The artist just hints at the figures, but we get a clear idea of them.*

Below *The areas of foliage were then developed using viridian and raw umber for the dark tones and lemon yellow and cobalt blue for the lighter ones.*

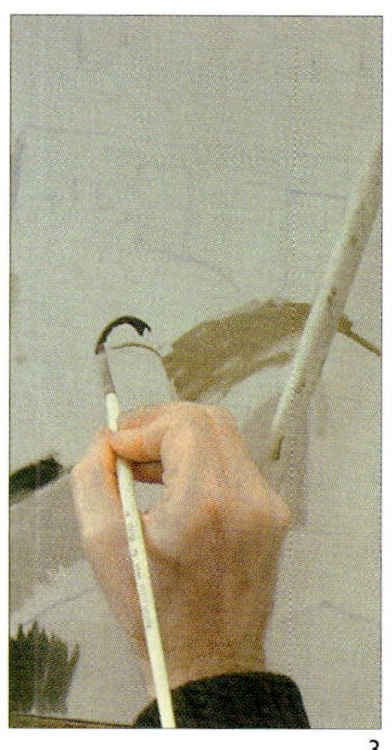

3

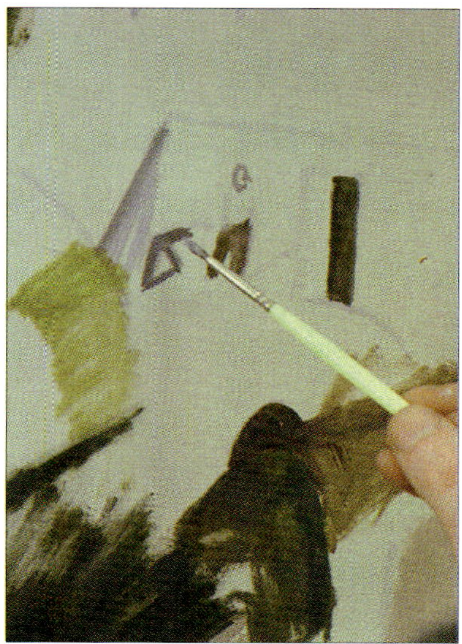

4

5

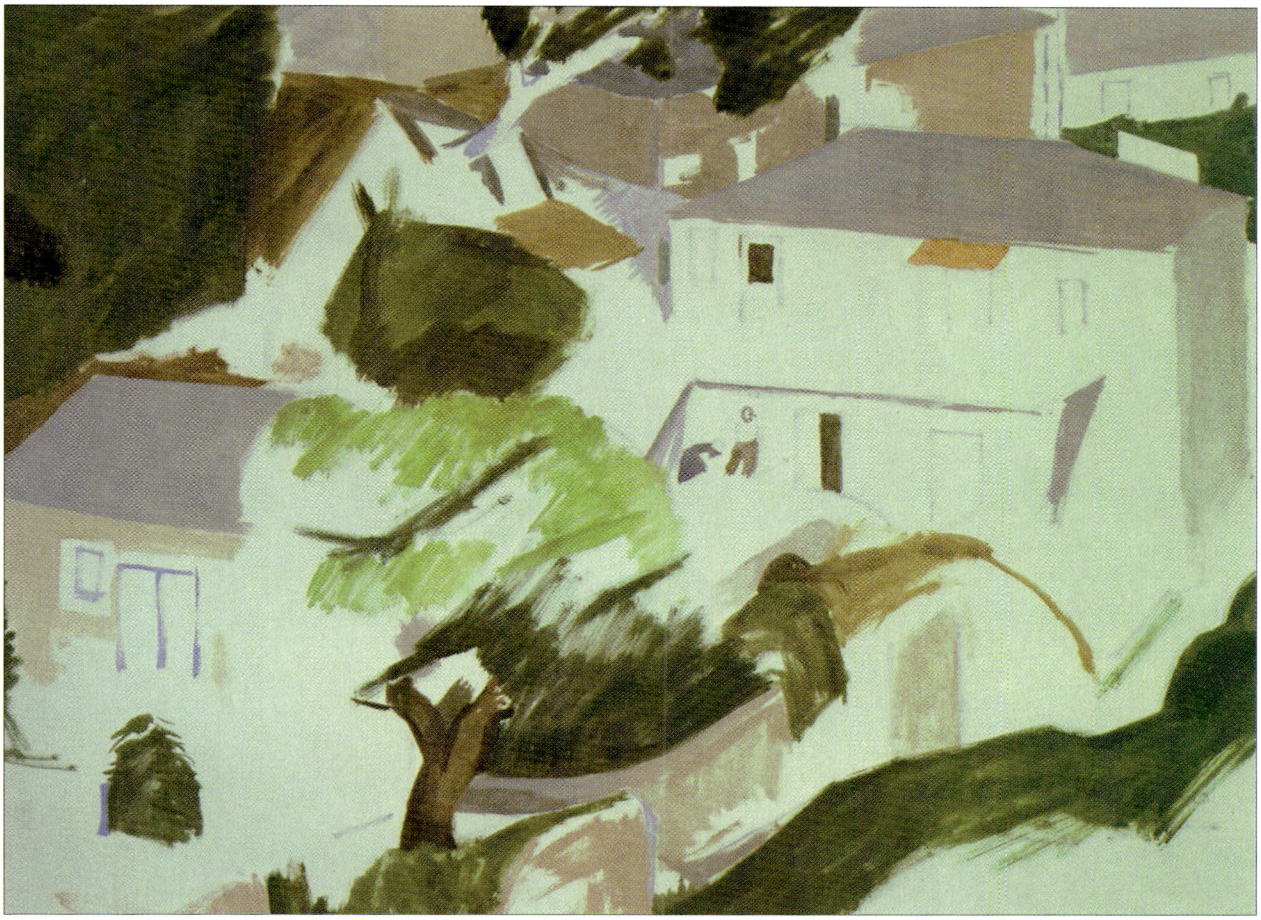

gradually built up to a thicker and richer surface as the work progressed (this is the classic oil painting technique known as working "fat over lean"). Note how the quality of the brushstrokes is in itself an integral part of the painting, and has been

Below and Right *The feeling of warmth in the grays and shadow areas was achieved by mixing alizarin crimson into the cooler colors, while mixtures of white, yellow ocher, Naples yellow, and burnt sienna were used for the warm browns and yellows. The colors were then modified and some areas developed and clarified, with the paint applied more thickly, and the final details such as the chairs on the balcony were added.*

MATERIALS USED

SUPPORT:
Finely woven, readyprimed canvas 36 X 48 in. (91 X 122 cm)

BRUSHES:
A selection of hog's-hair rounds ranging from numbers 6 to 10, with a number 4 sable used for the underdrawing

COLORS:
Titanium white, lemon yellow, Naples yellow, yellow ocher, burnt sienna, raw umber, cadmium red, alizarin crimson, cobalt blue, ultramarine, viridian, and sap green. The painting mediums were linseed oil and turpentine

6

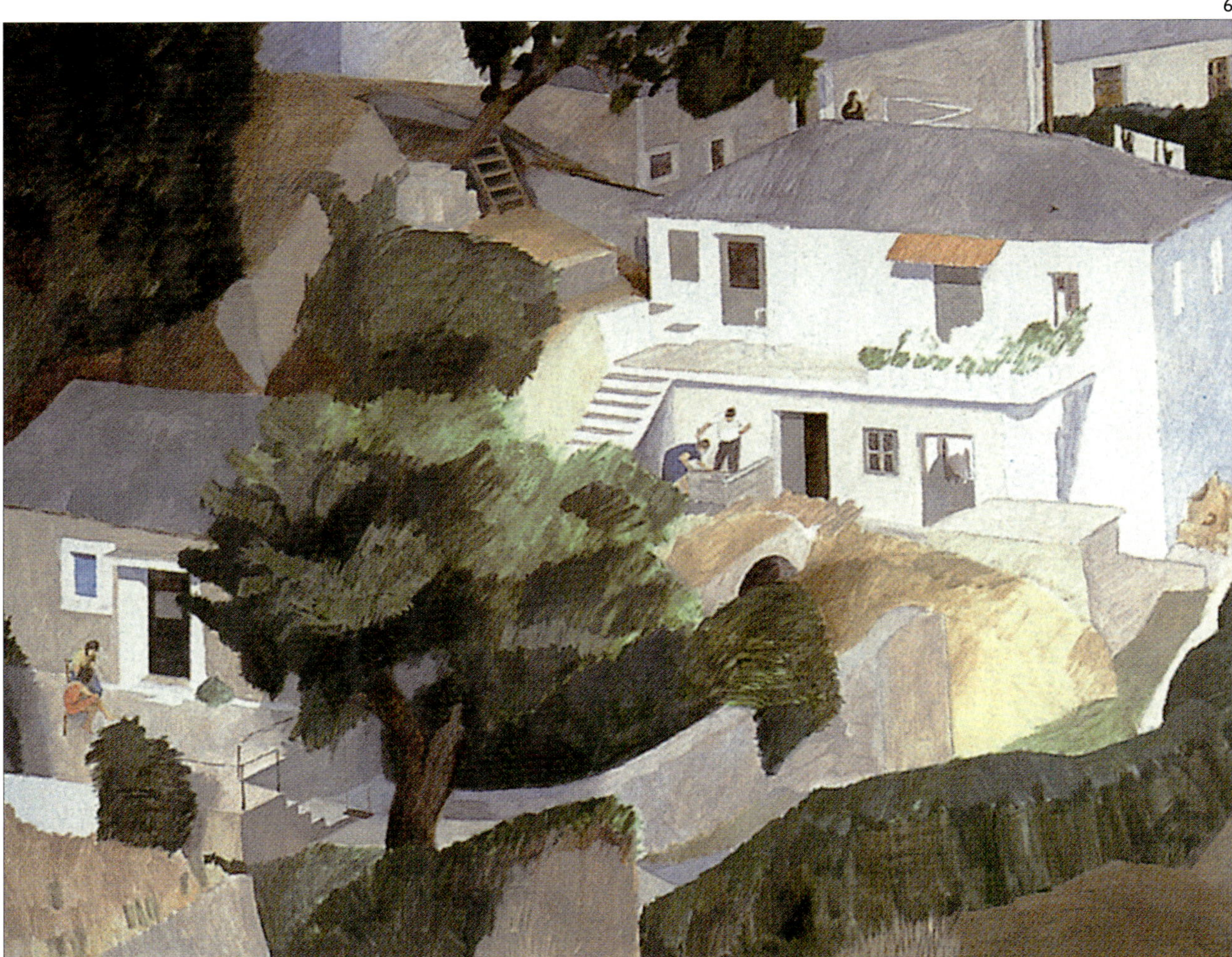

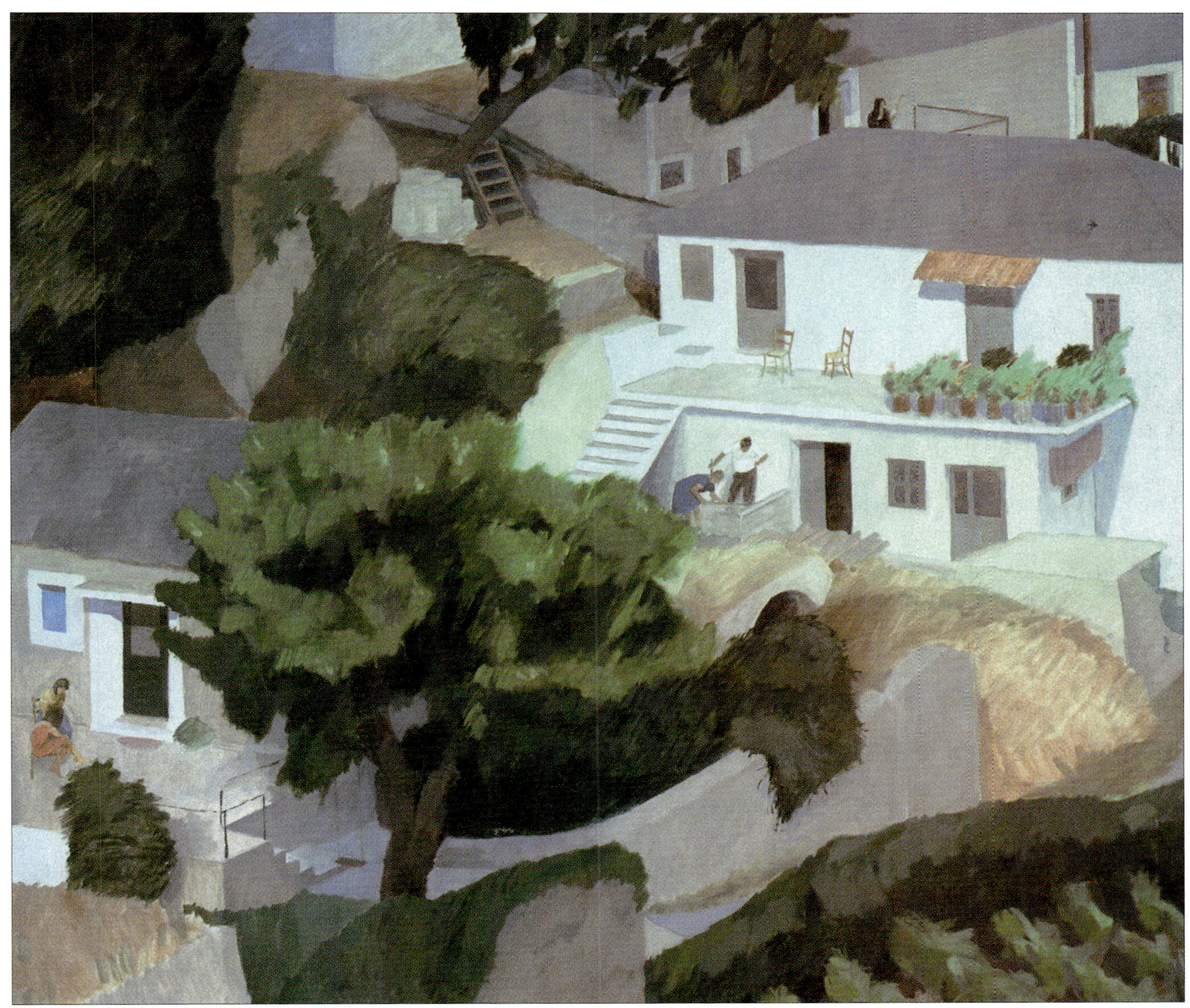

used in places to create textures and suggest forms, such as in the tree and the vegetable patch in the foreground of the painting.

The support was a fine-grained canvas, particularly suitable for a painting with areas of small detail and sharp straight lines, which would be more difficult to achieve on a very coarse canvas.

DERELICT PIER

This subject is an ambitious one in which accuracy of drawing is particularly important; so several careful pen-and-ink

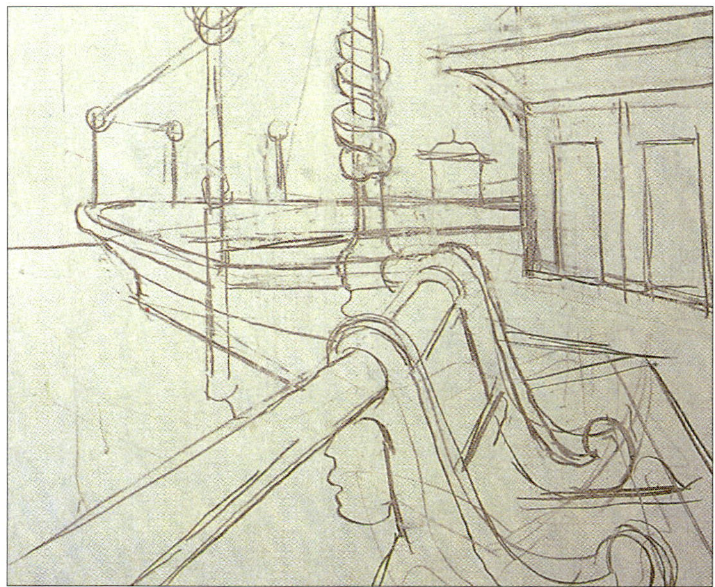

Left The main lines were drawn with willow charcoal. This was then dusted off and the lines were strengthened with thinned black paint applied with a fine synthetic brush.

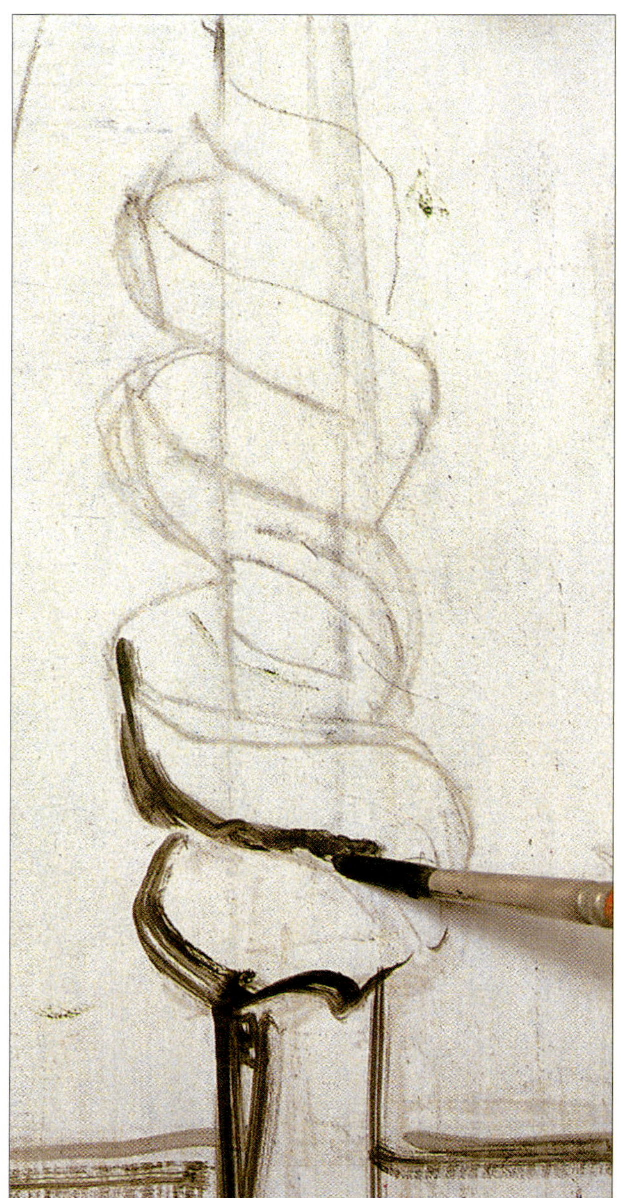

Right The lines of black have been overpainted very little, so that they are still visible as an integral part of the finished work. The artist worked from several sketches, but developed the painting further, so that it is not identical to any of them.

studies were made before the painting was begun. (Rain came before the one illustrated was completed—hence the splashes.) The main lines of the pier, with its railings, seats, lamp-posts, and buildings, were then drawn on to the support with charcoal. Note the diagonal line running through the tops of the lampposts, enabling the perspective to be plotted correctly. The drawing was tightened up and emphasized in places with thinned black paint and a small brush, after which the main color areas were blocked in with gray, green, and yellow ocher. The paint was initially used quite thinly, and applied with flat bristle brushes. Patches of the white support were allowed to show through, but the paint became thicker as the painting progressed; finally built up into a rich scumbled surface which is extremely satisfying to the eye.

The composition is based on the relationship of the diagonal and vertical lines, with those of the railings leading in to the strong vertical formed by the outer edge of the building and then up to the opposing diagonal of the eave of the roof, which takes the eye back to the center. The curves—of the arches, lampposts and seat arms—act as a counterpoint to the angular shapes.

The brushstrokes on the building are straight, following the vertical plane, and they have not been blended or worked together, so as to leave the paint surface clean and fresh. Although bright colors are introduced, they have been very carefully related to each other so that no one color jumps forward or assumes undue importance.

Below and Right *The sea was laid in first as a flat area of green, which was then given warmth and a feeling of light and movement by cross-hatching with brushstrokes of burnt sienna, white and red. There is a strong element of perspective in this painting, and the artist has used the railings against the large blocks of color as a visual device to lead the eye of the viewer straight into the picture. The brushstrokes have been used in a directional way to strengthen the effect; those on the seat follow and accentuate the form* (Bottom right) *and those on the railings are worked round rather than along the forms. This has also helped to suggest the texture of the old metal.*

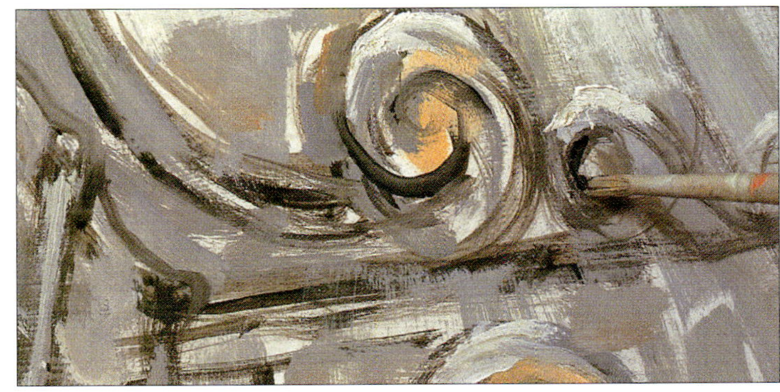

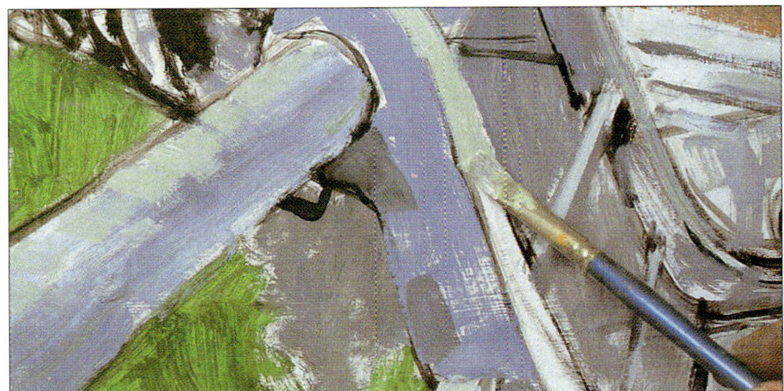

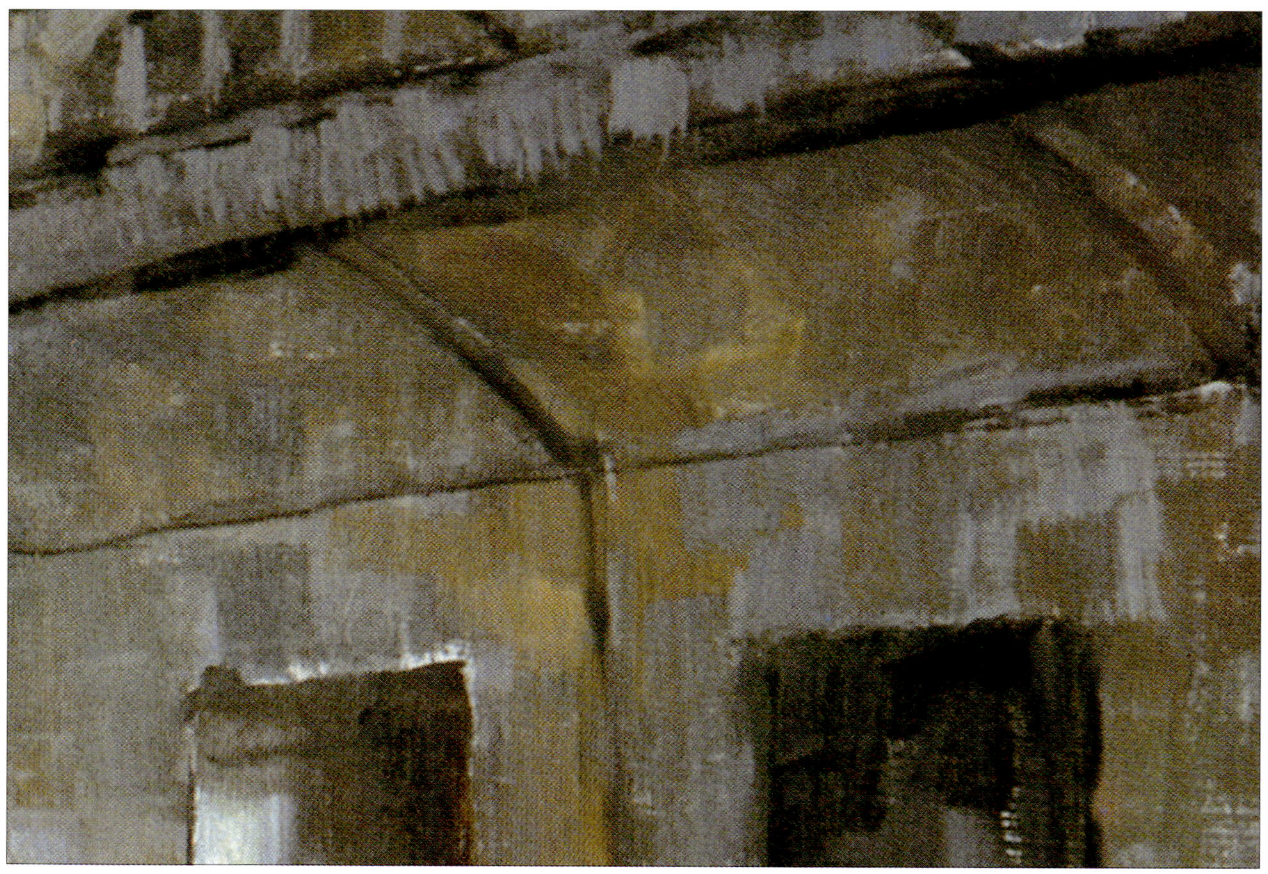

Above *The brushstrokes on the building are straight, following the vertical plane, and they have not been blended or worked together, so as to leave the paint surface clean and fresh. Although quite bright colors have been introduced here, they have been very carefully related to each other so that no one color jumps forward or assumes undue importance. This is much more difficult than it looks.*

The color range is quite limited, but the colors nevertheless glow and shimmer with life, partly because of the way the paint has been physically applied and partly because of the way the colors themselves are juxtaposed. The building on the right, for example, could have been treated simply as an area of flat gray, but here rich color has

MATERIALS USED

SUPPORT:
Smooth side of a piece of hardboard 24 X 30 in. (60 X 75 cm), which had been sanded down before priming to remove the shine. Some of the sanding dust was left on the board to provide texture, and it was then primed with white gesso primer

BRUSHES:
Dalon synthetics Nos. 4 to 11, which are less soft than nylon and give a good, fine point for detailed work

COLORS:
Titanium white, yellow ocher, light red, burnt sienna, ultramarine, sap green, cadmium green, and lamp black, which is warmer than ivory black and gives deep, rich tones when mixed with ultramarine

been introduced, with relatively bright patches of blue and yellow inside the arch, while blues and yellows recur on the front of the building, echoing the greens of the sea and the rich ochers of the pier top. Even the lampposts and seat arms have been warmed and enlivened by touches of muted yellow, which occur again in a stronger form in the area at the bottom of the railings, representing the reflected light from the sea.

Below *The final touches involved more work on the building and the addition of a scumbled texture over the whole painting, heightening the impression of old, crumbling metal.*

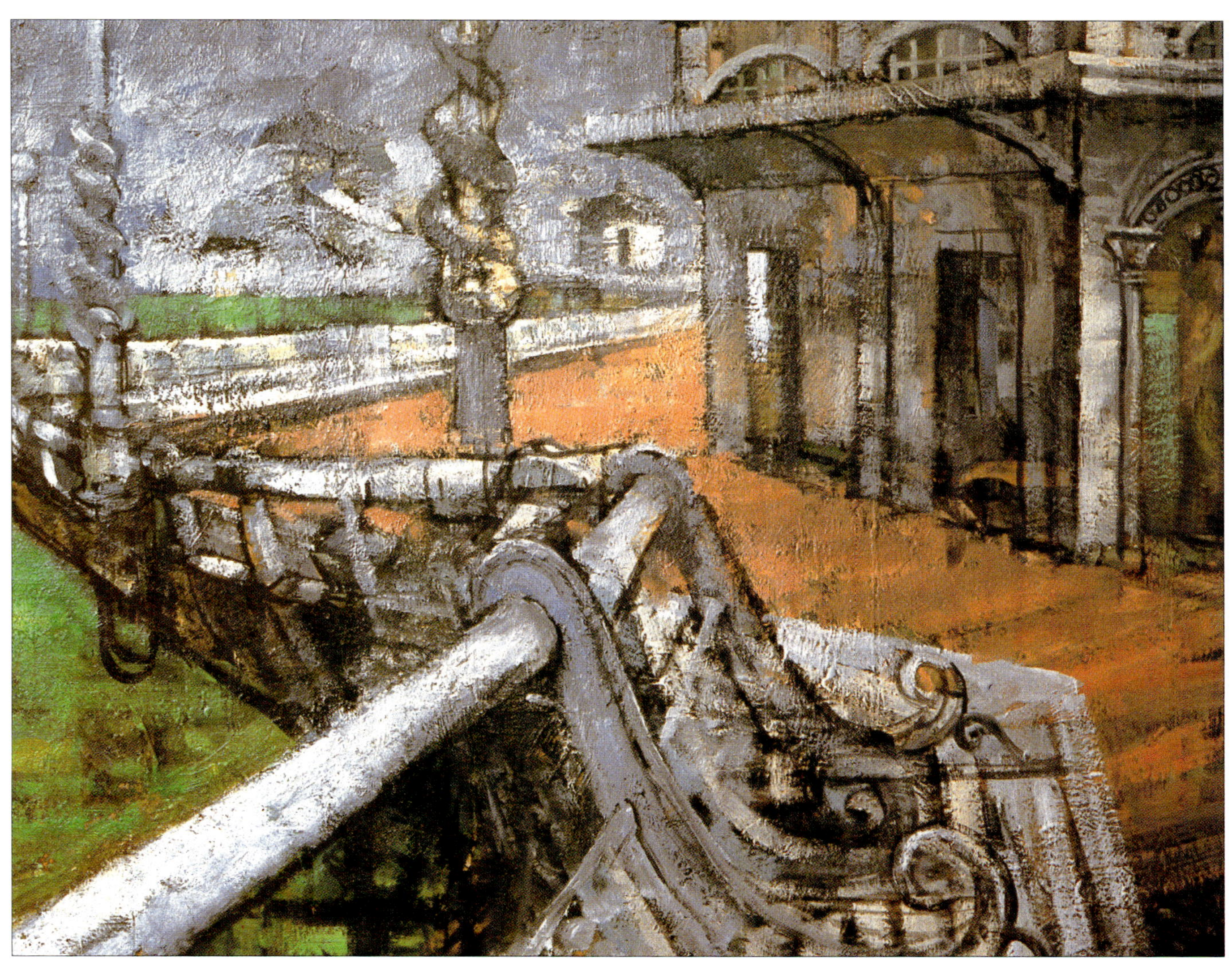

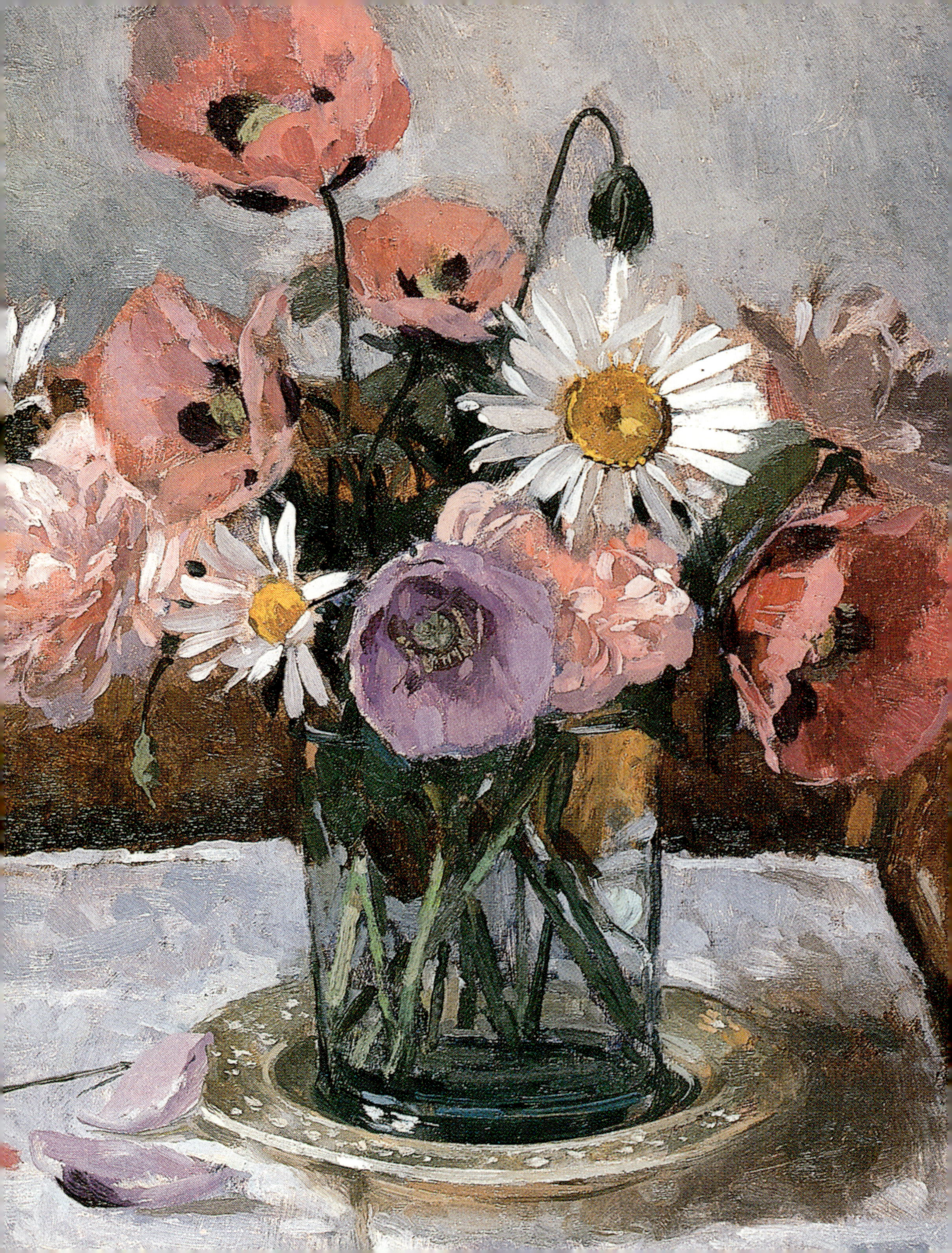

18 INDOOR SUBJECTS

All the paintings that you will examine on the following pages, whether portraits, figure studies, still-lifes or flower paintings, have one thing in common—they have all been done under conditions which are in the control of the artists themselves. A portrait or still-life can be set up in whatever way you want—you can usually dictate what your model should wear and what the background will consist of, and you can decide what objects you want in your still-life or flower painting.

All this can be an enormous advantage, because it means you need not feel rushed; it can, at the same time, also be a disadvantage, because that very sense of urgency you feel when confronted with a subject that must be captured quickly can often produce a more interesting painting. One way of artificially creating this sense of urgency, and thus not allowing yourself to fall prey to the temptation of niggling away at a picture, is to set yourself a time limit. Take as long as you like over arranging and lighting a still-life or doing preliminary drawings for a portrait, but when you start the painting, decide that you will complete it in one or two sessions.

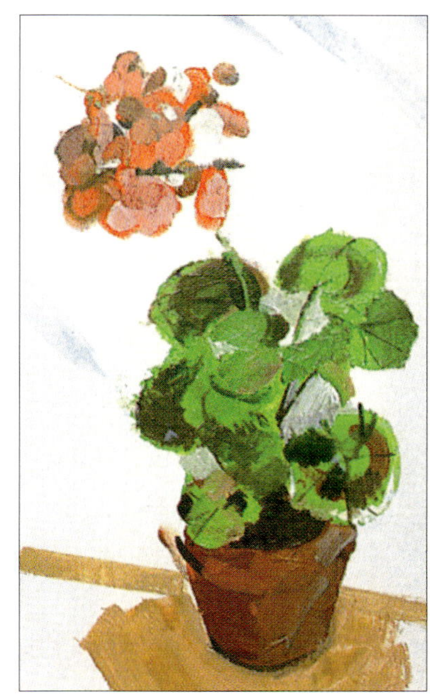

Below *The only drawing for the portrait consisted of a few lines and outlines (1) made with a number 3 bristle brush and thinned paint, after which yellows, blues, and warm red-browns were laid on, to be modified and defined later. (2) A rag was used to wipe off some paint from the forehead, cheeks and chin, (3) thus lightening the highlight areas. It was also used to smooth the previously roughly-applied paint in the background. (4 & 5) Shadows and highlights were built up in the face and hair. Because the painting was done on hardboard, which is not very absorbent, only turpentine was used as the medium. (6) Even so, by the sixth stage the paint had now become too thick and wet to work on satisfactorily, so the whole surface was blotted with newspaper, which removed the excess layer while still leaving a quite distinct image.*

PORTRAIT OF A MAN WITH A BEARD

This portrait was done quite quickly, in only two sessions, and has a fresh and spontaneous quality. Portraits often have to be completed in less time than the painter would perhaps consider ideal, since few sitters have either the time or the

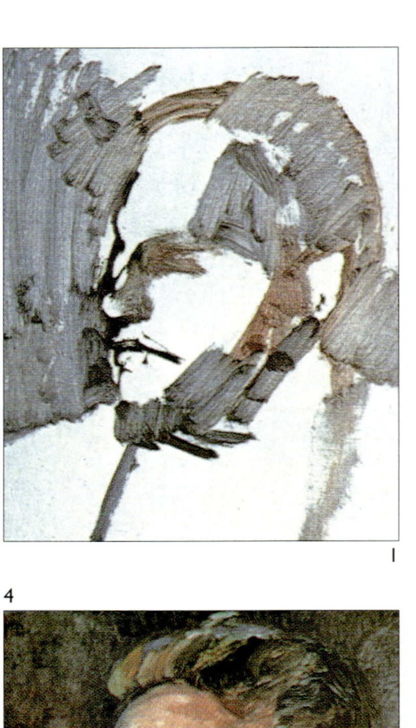

1

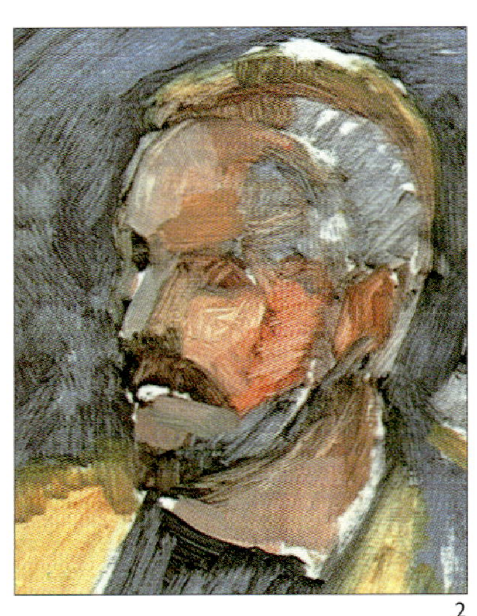

2

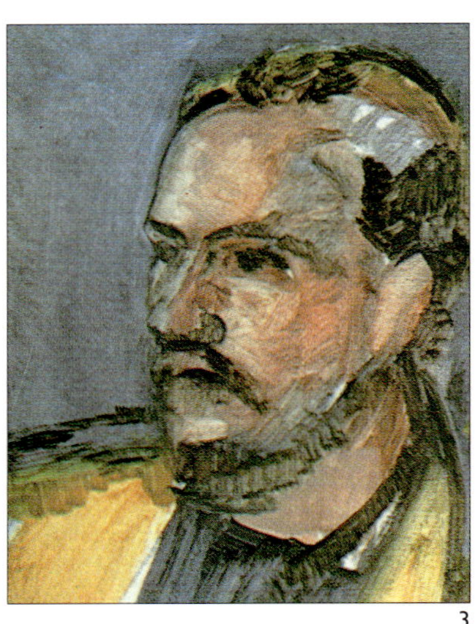

3

4

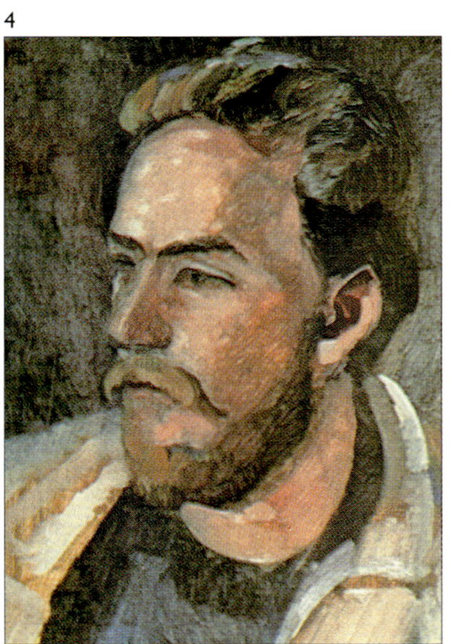

5

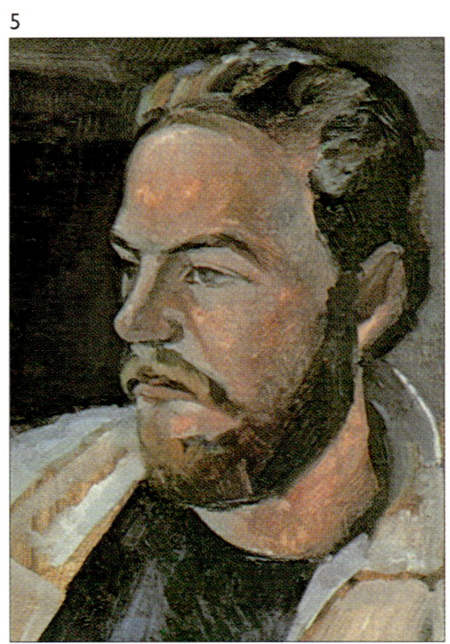

6

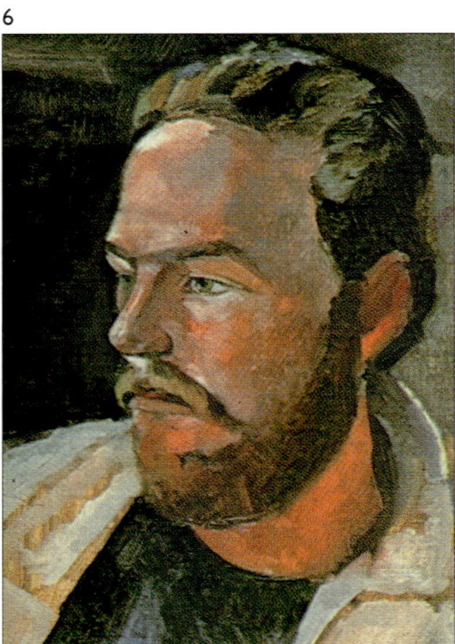

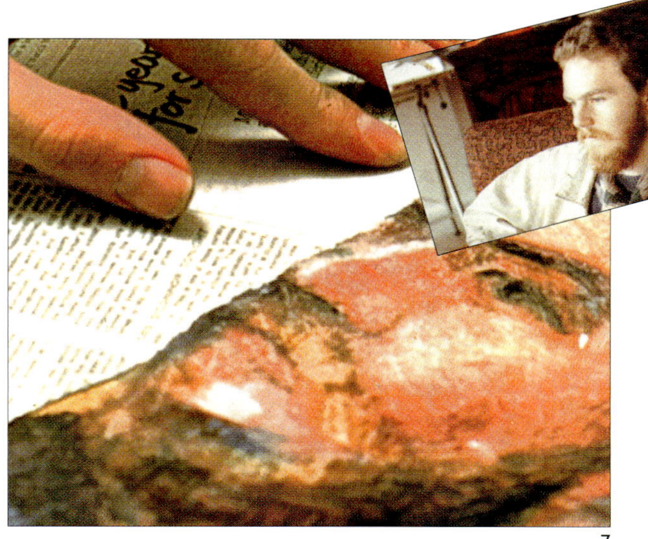

7

Left *A piece of newspaper was pressed lightly and lifted off to remove surplus paint. Blotting paper can also be used for this purpose.*

Right *A rag was used to clean up places where the paint had become too thick.*

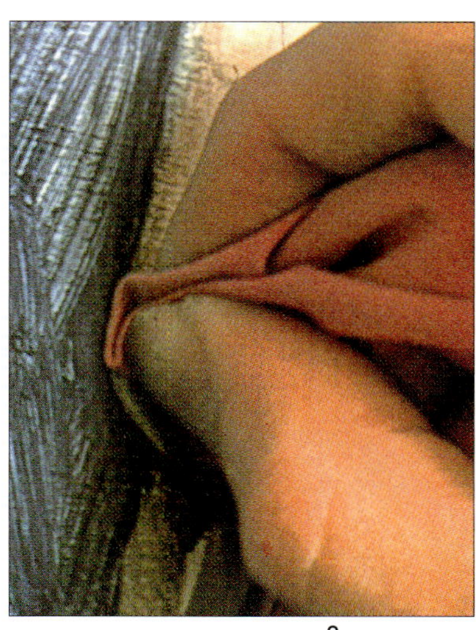

8

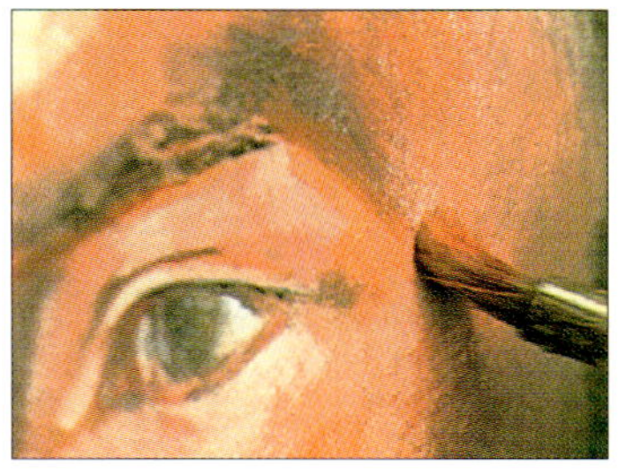

9

Right and Left *Using a small brush, the artist begins to work on the more detailed areas of the painting to define the hitherto vague facial features.*

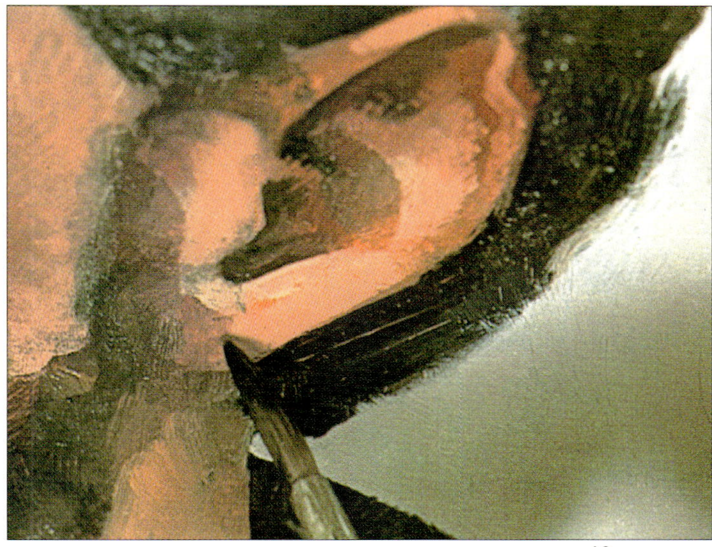

10

Bottom Left and Bottom Right *When the painting was almost finished it became clear that the tone needed to be lightened; so he overpainted the background, also correcting the outline of the face, and then adjusted the colors and tones of the flesh, blending the paint with light brushstrokes. He then altered the right side of the background, so that from being the darker side it became the lighter one. The scarf, seen in the finished painting, was not originally planned as part of the composition, but the heightened tones and colors seemed to need a balance, and it was added as a final touch. This portrait provides an excellent example of the way in which oil paintings can be altered again and again without loss of quality.*

11

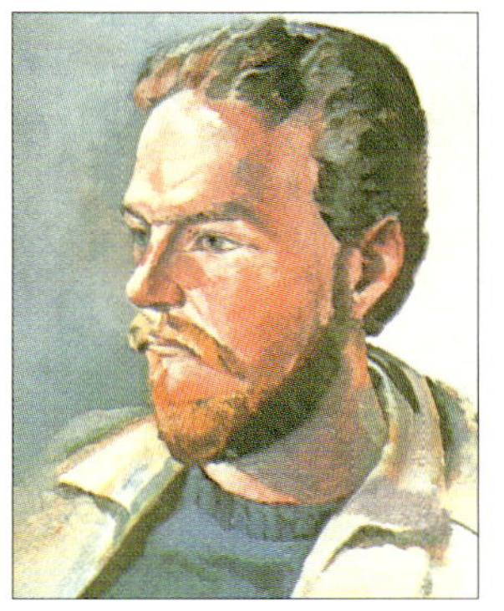

12

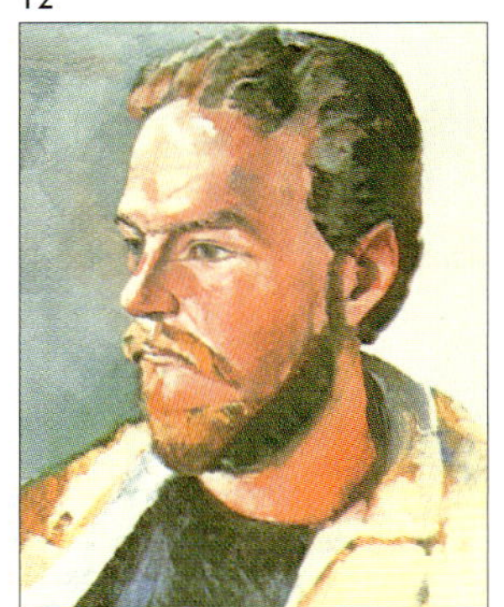

inclination to sit in one position for long periods of time. This particular portrait was actually done mainly from the photograph, which was freely adapted to convey the artist's own impression of the subject's coloring and character. He tried to simulate

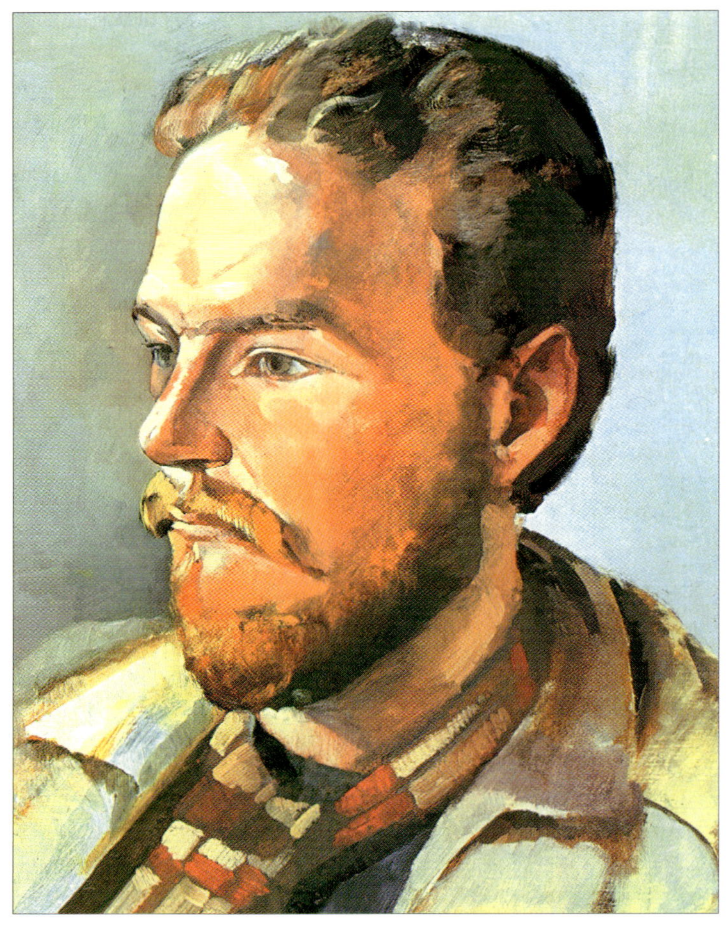

Left *The covering of the face with a reddish glaze, giving a warmth and glow to the flesh, is clearly reflected in both the detail of the brow area and in the finished painting.*

MATERIALS USED

SUPPORT:
Primed hardboard 18 X 12 in. (45 X 30 cm)

BRUSHES:
Number 3 flat bristle and a number 5 round sable for the fine details

COLORS:
Titanium white, ivory black, cadmium yellow, yellow ocher, vandyke brown, cobalt blue, ultramarine, chrome oxide, and vermilion, and the painting mediums were turpentine and linseed oil

the conditions of working from life in order to avoid an overworked, tired painting. It is often a good idea to set yourself a time limit in this way, both with portraits and landscapes, and to try to rely on your original impressions of a face or scene rather than peering at with a photograph.

The painting was begun with an underdrawing in neutral browns and blues, using thinned paint, after which layers of thicker paint were built up. The facial features were left quite undefined in the early stages, emerging only gradually from the broadly treated planes of the face, and the scarf was added later almost as an afterthought. All areas of the painting were worked on at the same time, the whole canvas being covered almost immediately, so that the relationship of the tones and colors could be assessed, balanced and altered where necessary. When the head was reasonably complete the artist decided to lighten the colors of the background, which also gave him an opportunity to correct and redefine the outline of the face. The tones and colors of the flesh were then adjusted in relation to the new background, and the relatively bright colors of the scarf blocked in to balance them.

Because the painting was done quickly, there was no time to allow the paint to dry between stages, so a rag was used to lightly blot the surface, removing the excess paint. A rag was also used to spread the paint in the background areas and to lighten the highlights in the early stages. Such techniques are particularly useful when working on a non-absorbent surface such as hardboard, which can easily become overloaded with paint.

ANITA IN MINIATURE

This is a particularly interesting portrait because, although the treatment is bold and free, the painting is very small, almost as big as the reproduction here. As this artist usually works on quite a large scale, producing a portrait as small as this presented something of a challenge. However, the artist has managed to reduce the scale without detriment to her normal colorful and bold style.

As the portrait had to be completed quickly, a piece of cardboard was used for mixing the colors instead of the

Below *A careful pencil drawing was done first, and was particularly necessary in this case, since for such a small painting inaccurate drawing or a clumsy placing of the head in relation to the background could be disastrous. As you can see by comparing the finished painting with the photograph, the area of the pink blouse has been reduced to just two small triangles; these balance the bright colors of the flesh and lips. The area of background is greater on the left side of the face than the right, thus avoiding monotony. Even in a head-only portrait compositon this is important and should be planned at the outset.*

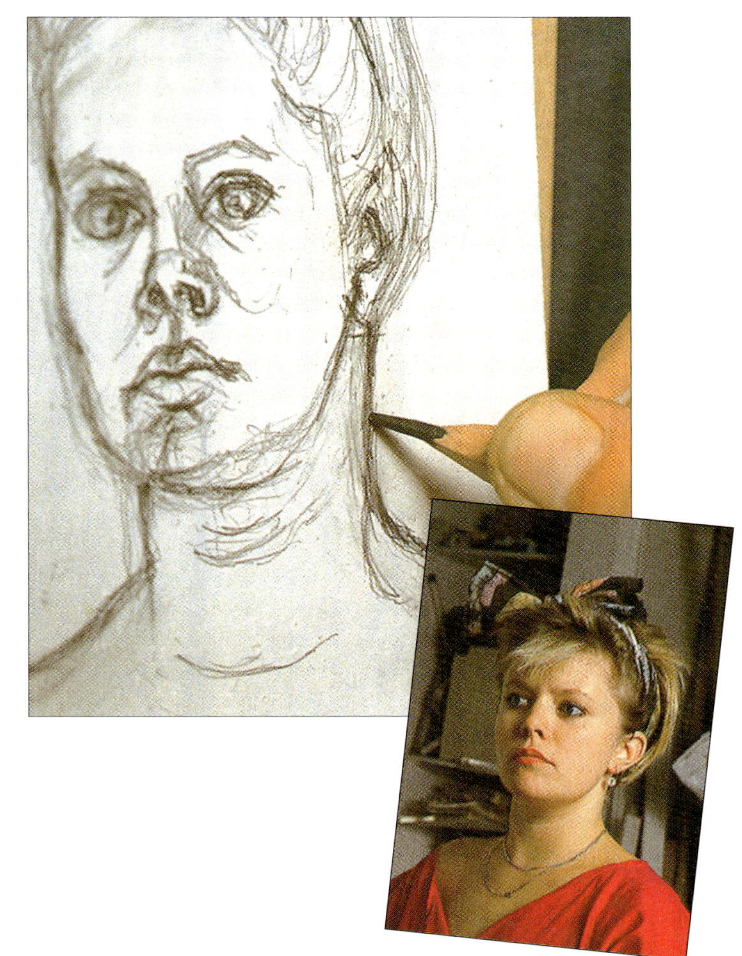

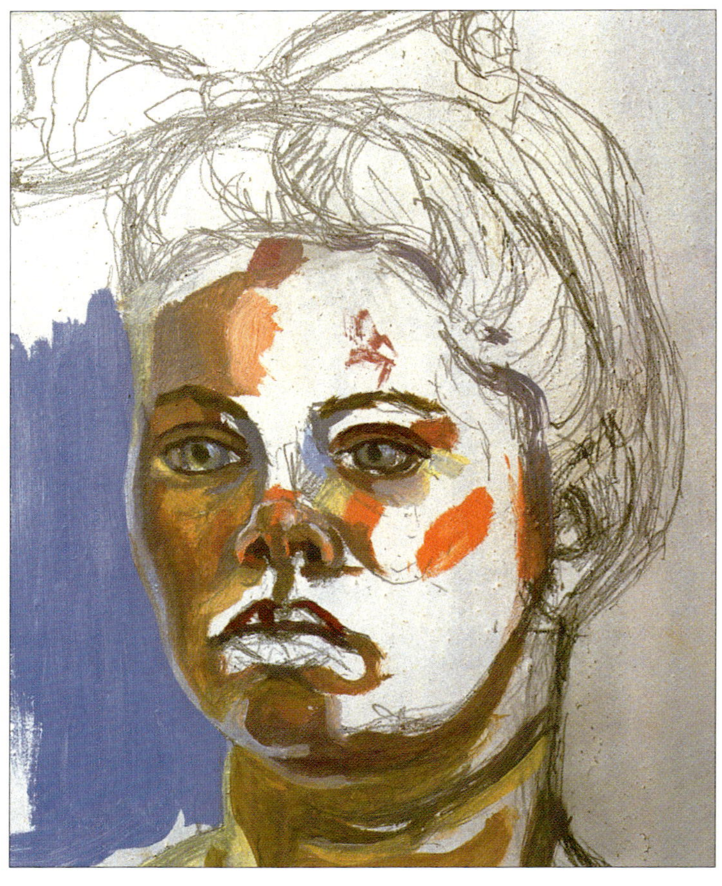

Above *The dense pencil lines were rubbed down lightly before the paint was applied, to prevent the graphite dust muddying the colors. The first flesh tints, mixed from a wide variety of pure colors, were then applied, and the planes of light and shade began to emerge. Note how the strip of cool, pale color down the side of the face—the reflected light visible in the photograph—prevents the similar tones of the background and the shadow area of the face from merging together. The area of blue was blocked in at an early stage so that the flesh tones could be related to the color of the background, and the artist put dabs of color and tone on to the unpainted side of the face to help offset the effect of the glaring white canvas.*

conventional palette, which had the effect of absorbing some of the oil and letting the paint dry more rapidly. Turpentine, used as the medium, also speeded the drying and provided a matt surface, which this artist prefers. Sable brushes were used in place of the more usual bristle ones in order to apply the paint carefully in small blocks, which were then blended lightly into one another. The colors have been considerably heightened and exaggerated, with the background appearing as an area of clear, bright blue and the face itself composed of separate, though related, patches of pure color. This type of color is known as high key, as opposed to low key. The brightness of this painting was deliberate, and is enhanced by the use of a pure white support, with no underpainting; the white is reflected back through the paint, giving the colors extra sparkle and translucency.

GIRL IN PROFILE

This painting was done in a quite different technique from that used in the other two portraits; the paint here is used very thinly, so that the early stages resemble a watercolor. The colors are also much less vivid, the emphasis being on the contrasts of lights and darks.

A profile is a difficult subject, and profile portraits are not often done, the three-quarter view being the preferred one.

This is partly because a profile can look rather boring and unsubtle, and partly because, of course, it does not allow the eyes, the usual focal point of a portrait, to show. Here, an interesting composition has been made by placing the head to one side so that the back and top are cut off, with the line of the hair creating a bold curve to break up what would otherwise have been a stark vertical at the edge of the canvas. The artist has given the space around the head an importance of its own by painting it flat and allowing it to occupy almost as much of

__Right and Below__ The areas of pale flesh tones, mainly mixed from red, yellow ocher, and white are being applied to the neck and taken right up to the background. The paint was used fairly thickly so that it was opaque enough to cover the blue and give a clearly defined line. The bright pink area around the eye, applied with a small brush, reflects the bright rose of the blouse, as does the shadow under the chin.

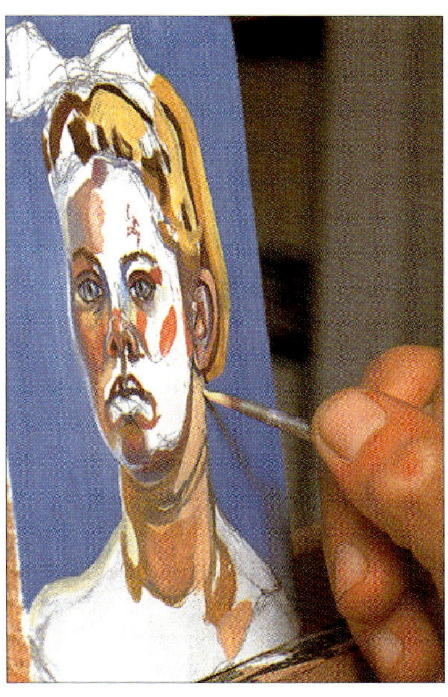

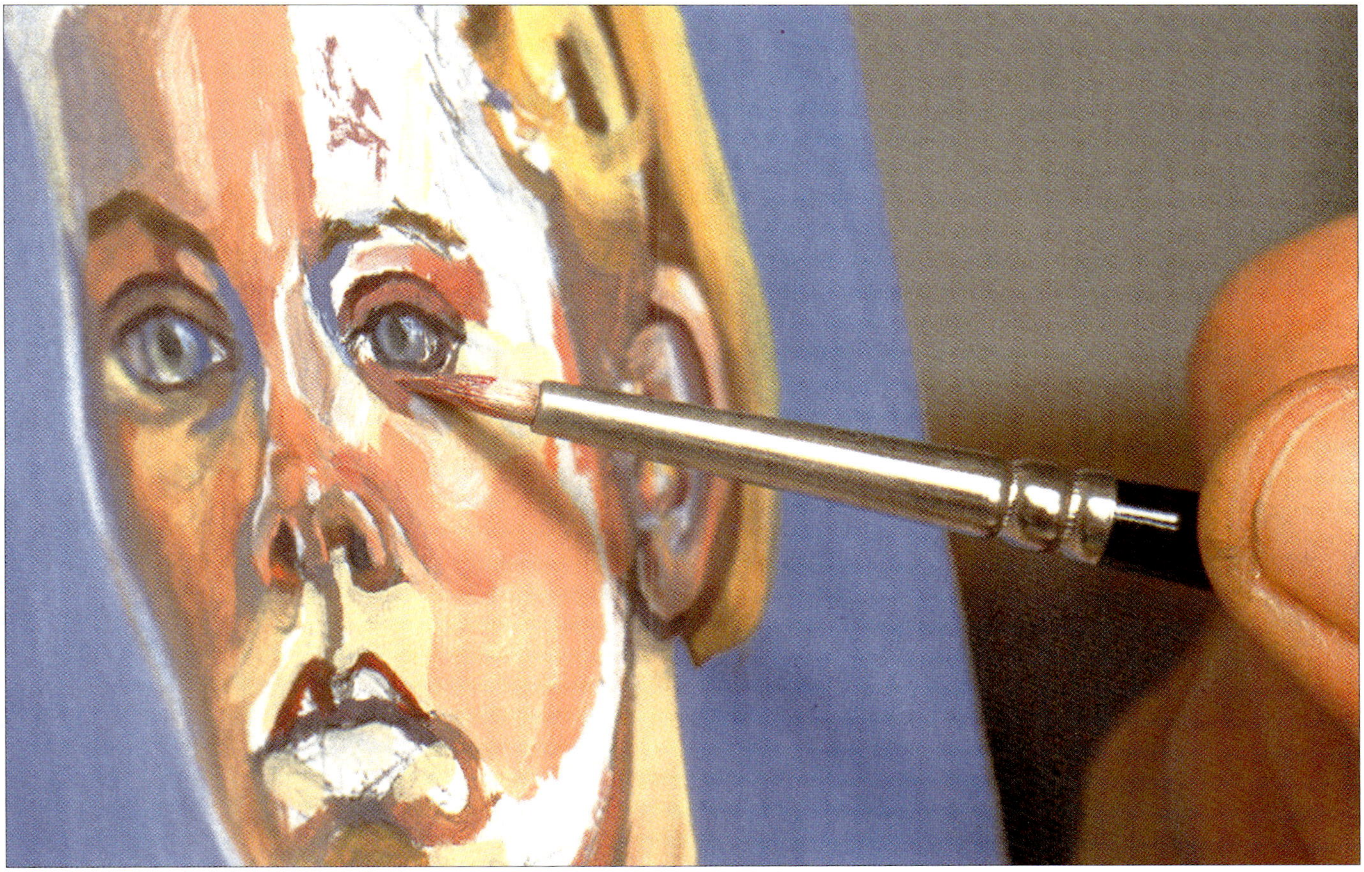

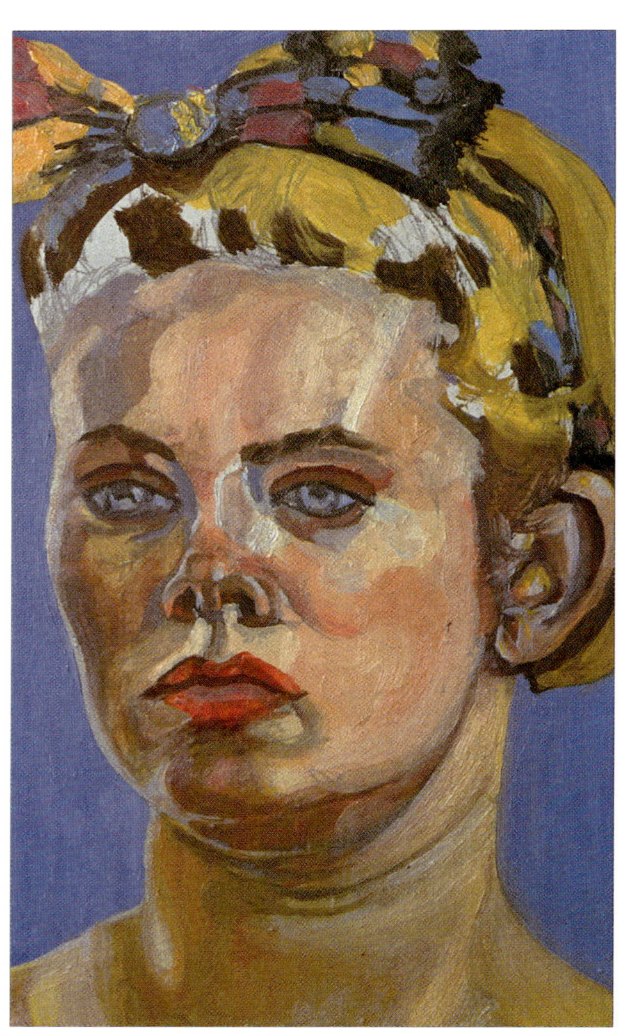

Right *The lips were painted next, and then the patterned scarf, in which each color was carefully related to those in the face itself. When painting in such a high color key, much care and thought is needed to relate the colors to each other, otherwise there will be unpleasant discords. The hair was then modified in color so as to emphasize the bright colors of the scarf, and the fringe was defined with free, bold brushstrokes.*

the total picture area as the profile itself. The picture can thus be seen as two interlocking areas (this is particularly noticeable if you look at it upside down). This concept is sometimes called "negative space," and can form a very important part in a composition, the "negative" space being used to balance the "positive" image.

The luminous quality of the shadow area of the face has been achieved by glazing. It is a particularly suitable technique for painting flesh, and was much used by the early painters in oil, such as Jan van Eyck. In this case, linseed oil with a very little turpentine was used to thin the paint for the glazes, but linseed oil is not actually the best medium for this technique. A special alkyd medium called Liquin is now manufactured and sold specifically for the purpose.

DIANA

This full-length portrait, or "clothed figure study," was done partly from life and partly from the photograph. A comparison of the finished painting with the photograph is particularly interesting in this case as it

MATERIALS USED

SUPPORT:
Primed hardboard about 6 X 5 in. (15.5 X 12.5 cm)

BRUSHES:
Round sable numbers 2, 3, 5, and 8, and the paint was thinned with turpentine alone

COLORS:
Titanium white, yellow ocher, Naples yellow, cadmium yellow, cadmium red, alizarin crimson, Rowney rose, violet, cobalt blue, ultramarine, cerulean blue, and terre verte

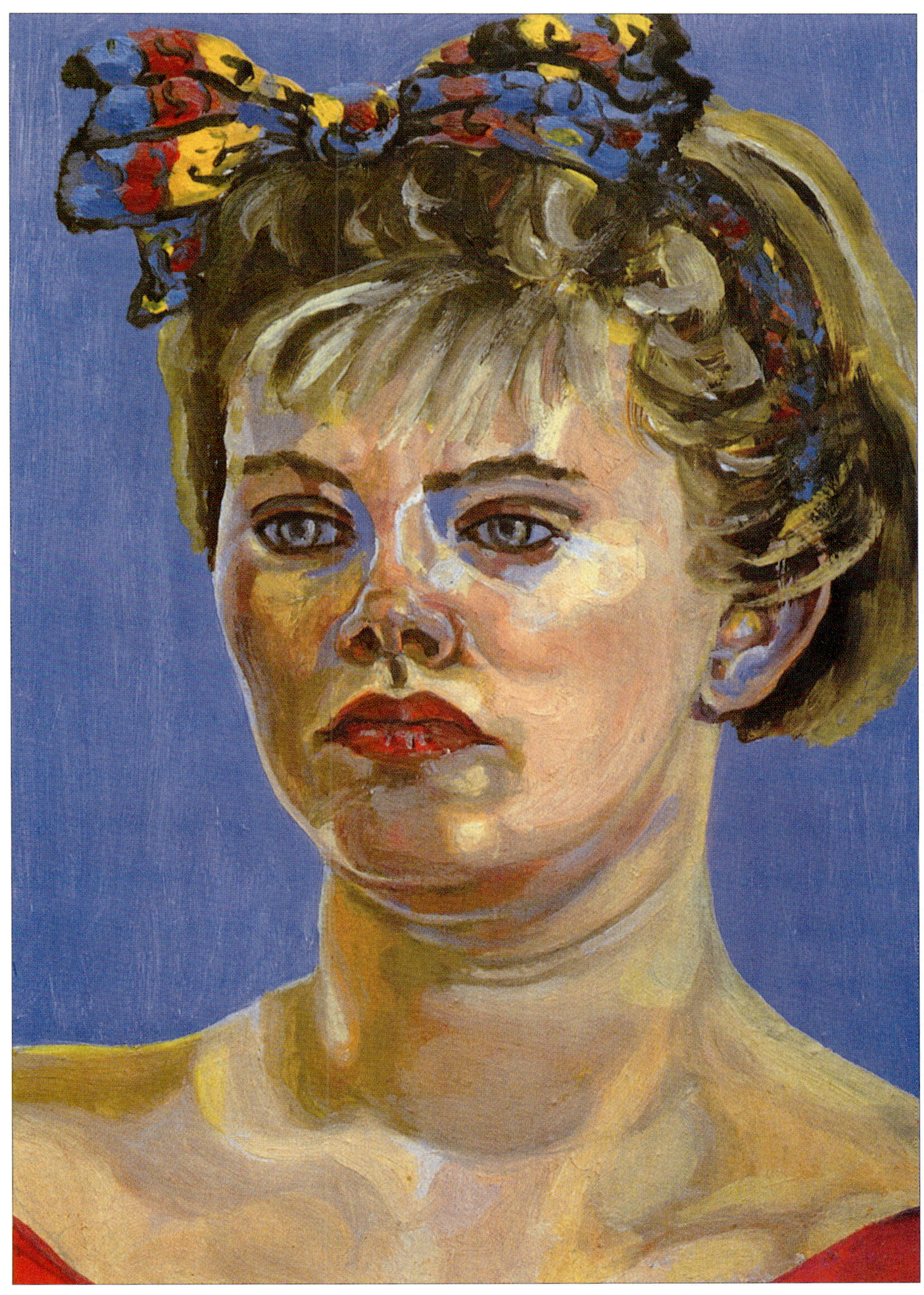

Left *Note how the whole portrait is "lifted" by the patterned scarf and red lips—all the colors suddenly appear brighter and the entire image is crisper.*

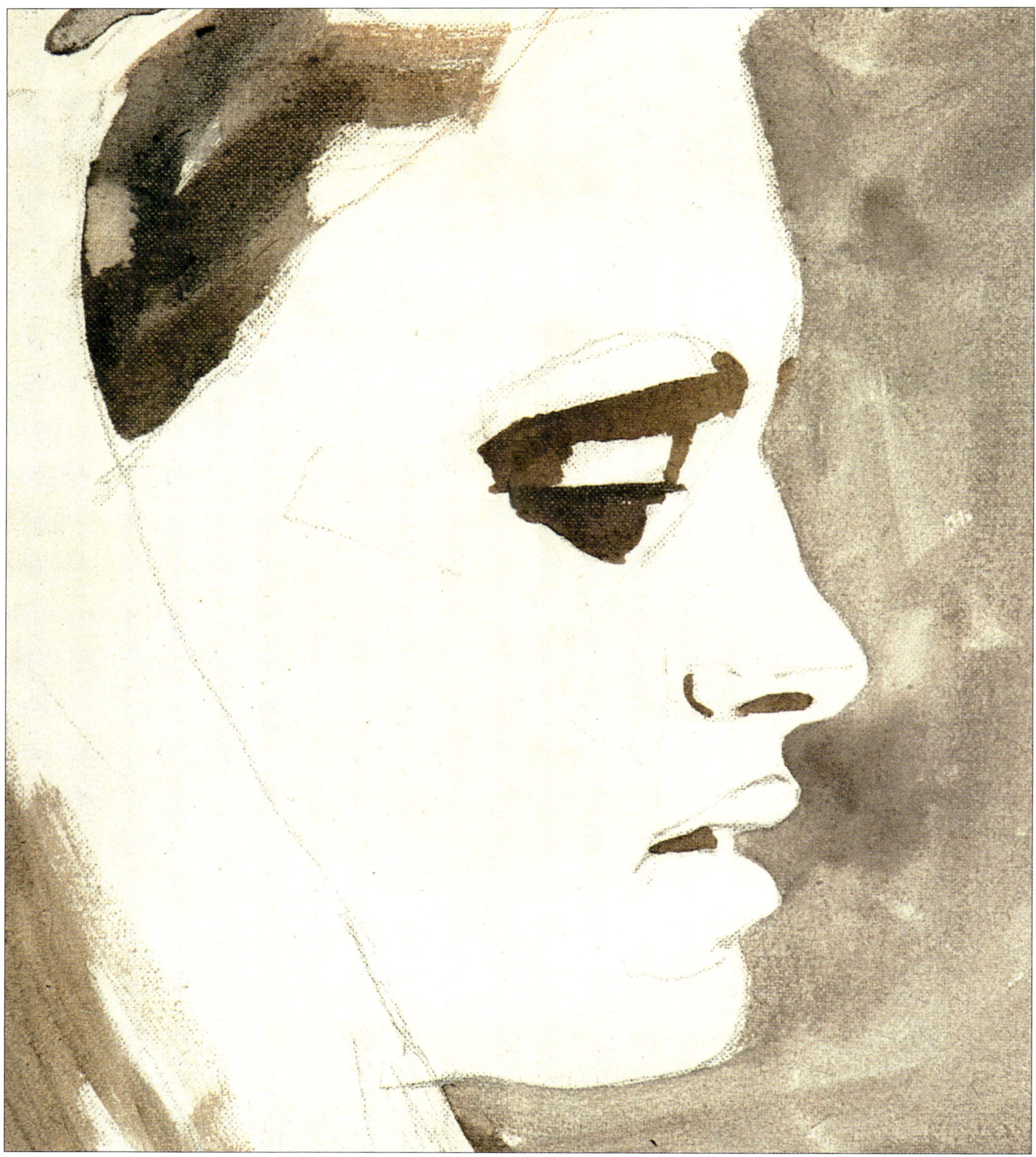

Left *A simple but accurate line drawing was done of the profile, including indications of the shapes of the highlights on the cheekbone, nose, and chin. The background area was then blocked in with a thin wash of gray paint applied with a number 4 flat bristle brush, and a wash of burnt umber was used for the shadow under the brow.*

Right *The warm tones were established next, using a mixture of yellow ocher and white for the hair, and burnt umber, cadmium red, and titanium white for the face.*

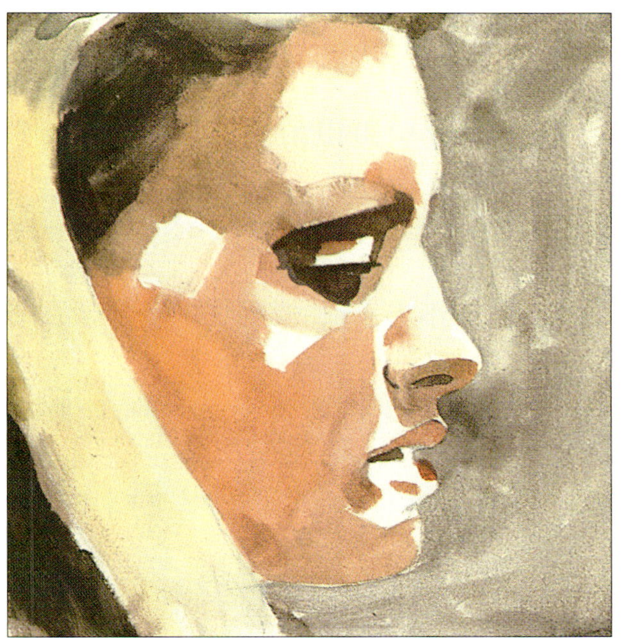

shows how much the artist has simplified the subject in order to deal with what he personally found interesting—the figure itself and the richly glowing blues, violets, and orangey-browns. Another artist painting the same subject might have treated it in a quite different way, perhaps including the view through the window, the pattern on the sitter's blouse, and the details on the cupboard, thus making a much busier composition, but here all the emphasis is on the figure itself, with the background areas treated very sketchily so that they do not compete with the main image.

Color is the dominant aspect of this painting, and the artist has started to place the colors immediately, with only the minimum of underdrawing, using thinned paint in shades of violet and cobalt blue. With the vivid violet of the blouse established, the canvas was then completely covered with thin paint, the color of the background being more or less that which appears in the finished painting.

The background paint was left thin, but the figure itself was built up in thicker paint,

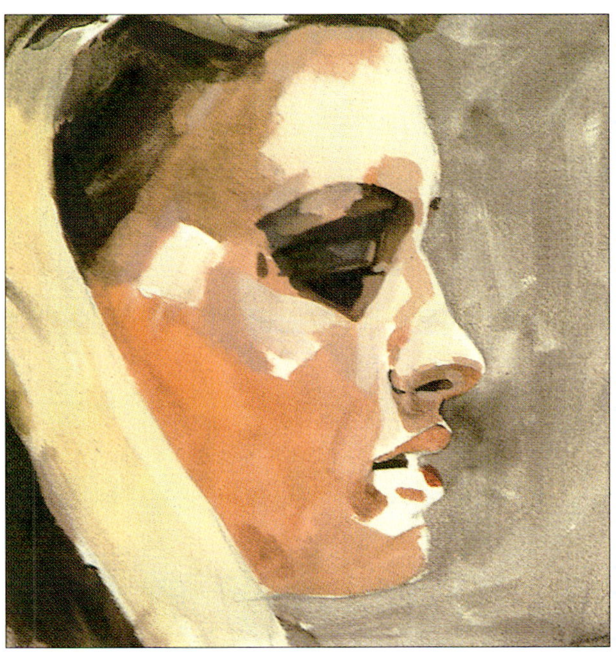

Above *The shadows around the eyes were painted with a smaller bristle brush, a number 2, each separate block of color and tone being carefully delineated.*

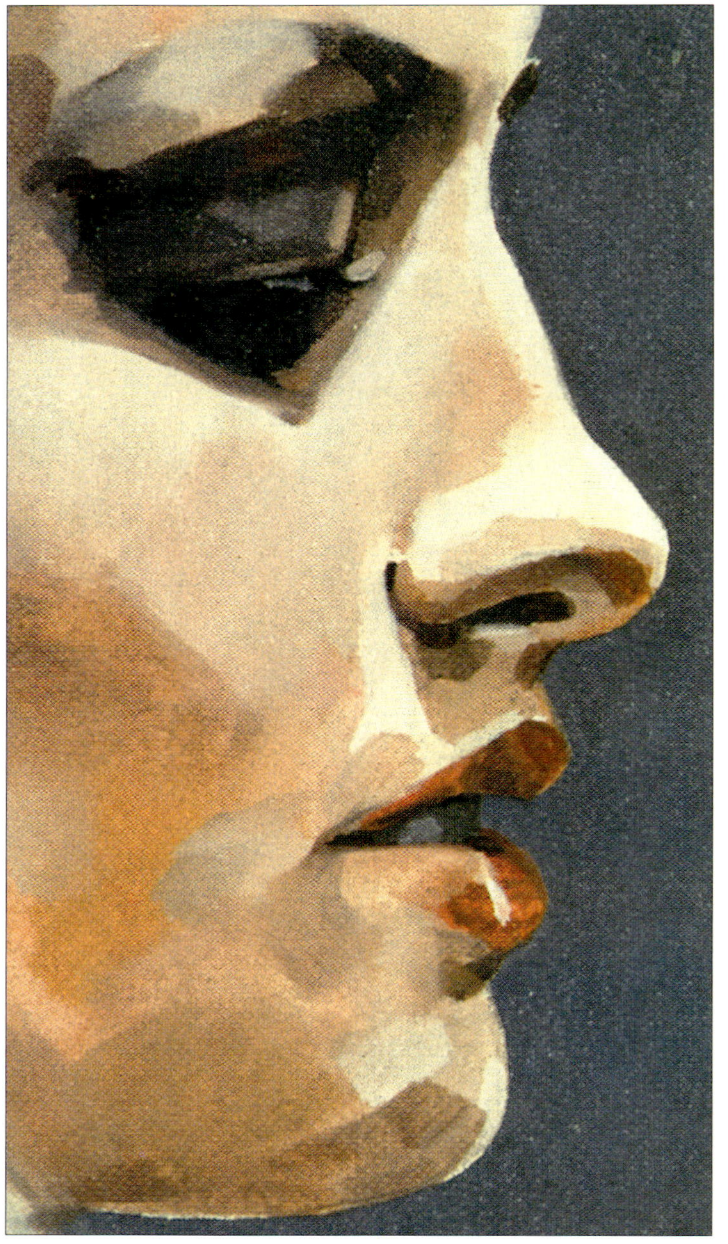

Left The skin tones were developed more fully by applying diluted paint in thin glazes which allow light to bounce off the canvas and back through the colors. This produces a luminous glow which cannot be achieved with opaque paint. Glazes can also be laid over a layer of thick, impasted paint to modify the underlying color, as was done by Rembrandt and Turner. Here, however, all the layers are thin; in the detail the texture of the canvas is quite clearly visible through the paint.

Right As a final touch, fine strands of hair were added above the forehead and beside the cheek and chin, using a very fine brush and a mixture of titanium white and yellow ocher. Note how these few lines "lift" the whole portrait, hinting at the quality of the fine hair and breaking up the large area of background while allowing it still to exist as a definite shape.

MATERIALS USED

SUPPORT:

Small, fine-grained canvas board bought ready-primed, 15 X 12 in. (37.5 X 30 cm)

BRUSHES:

Flat bristle, with a small sable for the fine lines

COLORS:

Titanium white, ivory black, burnt sienna, burnt umber, yellow ocher, cadmium red medium, scarlet lake, and ultramarine. The mediums were linseed oil and turpentine, with a much higher proportion of linseed oil used for the glazing

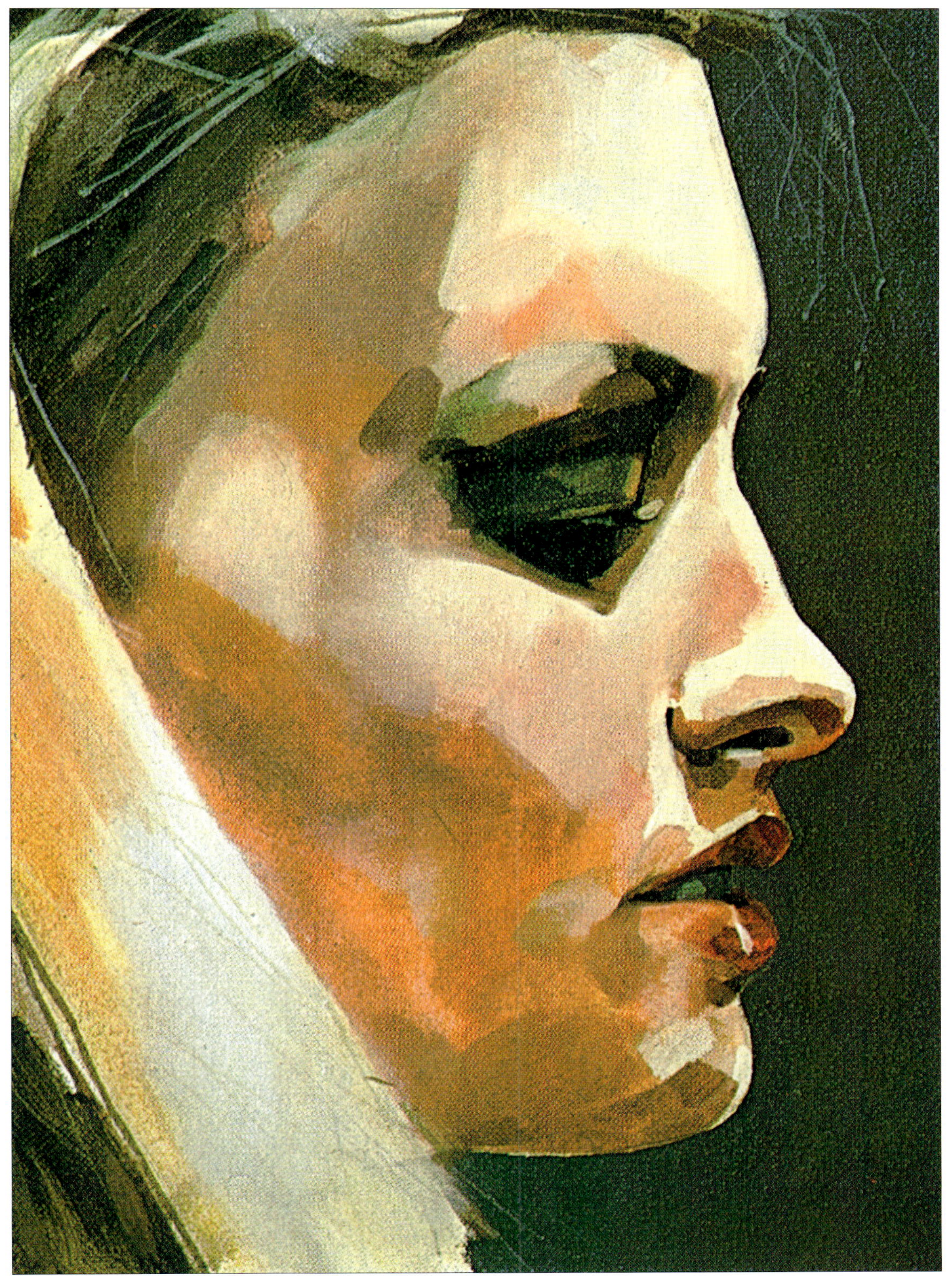

and in places the sgraffito technique—drawing or scratching into the paint with a knife or brush handle—was used to remove paint from the highlight areas, allowing the white ground to show through.

The composition is a simple one, as befits the subject, with the figure itself placed centrally but made to appear less symmetrical by the placing of the unequal shapes on left and right—the window and cupboard. The image has been given movement and interest by the diagonals formed by the bottom of the window frame, the skirting board, and the top and bottom of the cupboard, the latter two leading the eye into the figure. The angles literally point to the figure so that its central position, which might have resulted in an unfocused or flat painting, is quite acceptable. The bottom corner of the window and the top corner of the cupboard form a triangle with the light reflected from the top of the jeans, providing depth. If the background had been on a flat plane with the skirting board as a horizontal, the effect might have been monotonous.

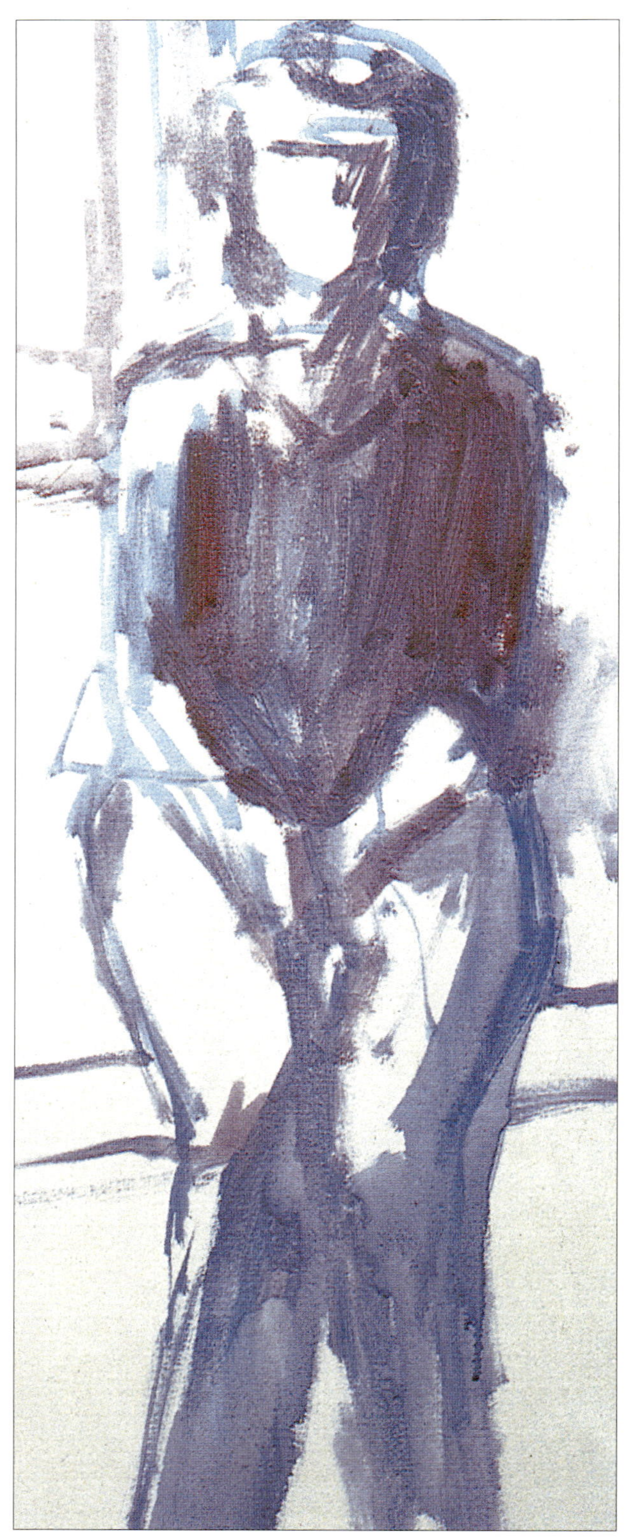

TEA-CADDY ON A WINDOW SILL

This small, quietly harmonious painting, has a limited range of colors and the artist has chosen a simple subject. It illustrates the way in which color and composition can be

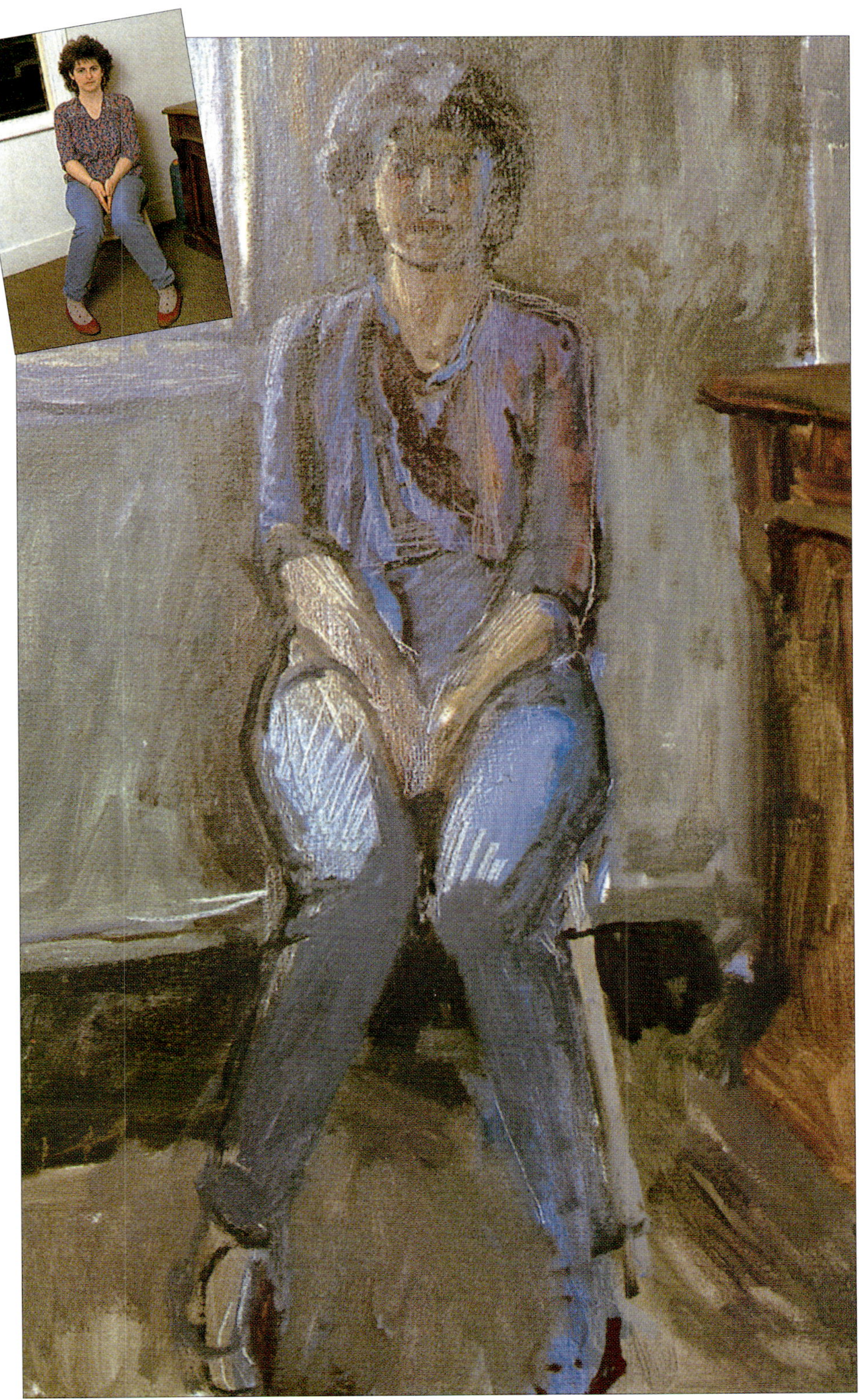

Left *As soon as the whole canvas was covered with paint the artist began to work on the highlights to define and sharpen the forms.*

Far Left *The artist began to lay the color on immediately, using diluted paint so that it would dry quickly. Marking in the vertical and horizontal lines for the cupboard and background helped him to position the figure correctly.*

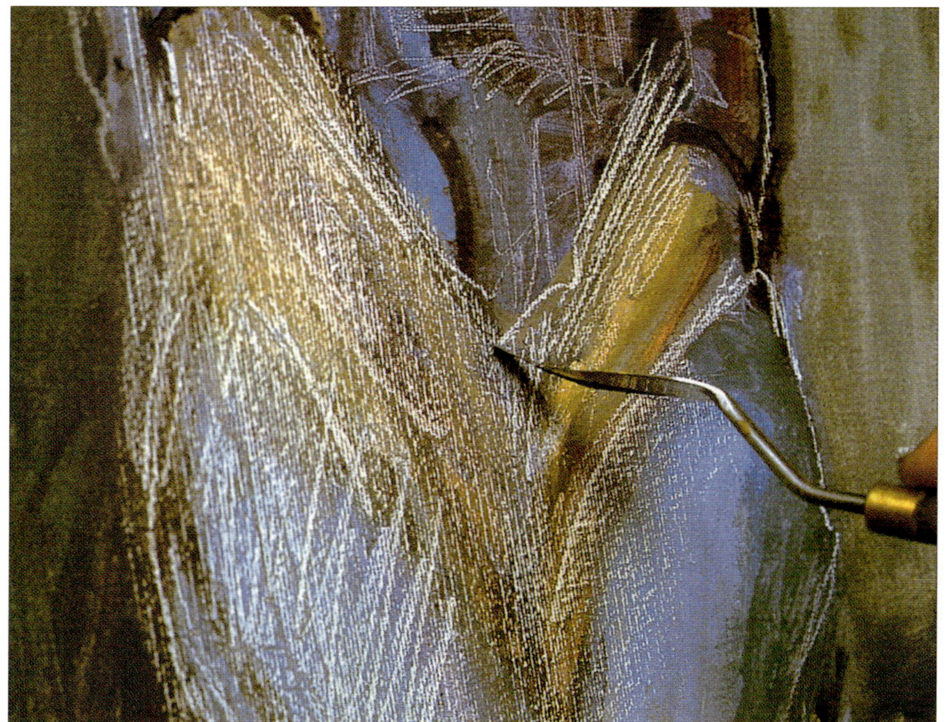

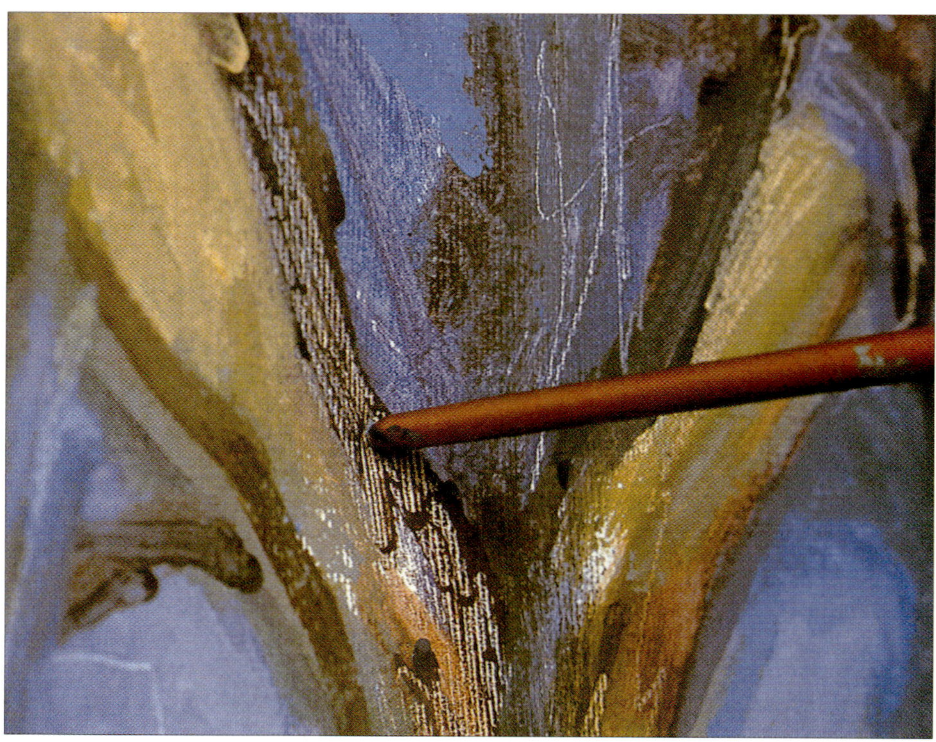

Left *Here a painting knife is being used to scrape back to the white surface of the canvas.*

Bottom *The arm has now been more fully modeled, with a dark line of shadow, and a brush handle is being used to draw into it. Some of the purple color of the blouse has been repeated on the inside of the arm and then scraped away, leaving just enough to suggest the reflected color in the shadow.*

Right *The color of the blouse and jeans is vitally important to this painting, and the artist has chosen to simplify the visual impact by ignoring the pattern on the blouse (visible in the photograph) so that it stands as an area of vibrant blue. However, it was not applied as just one color; mid and dark purple were used for the shadow areas and bright blue for the highlights.*

Bottom *Shadows have a color of their own rather than being simply a darker shade of the highlight color.*

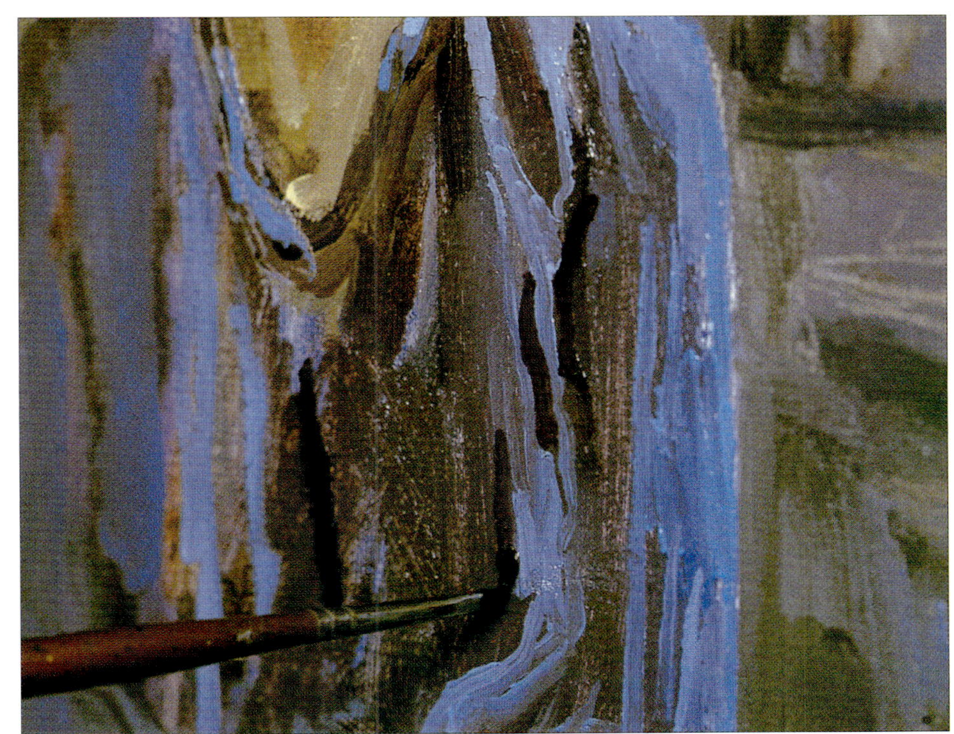

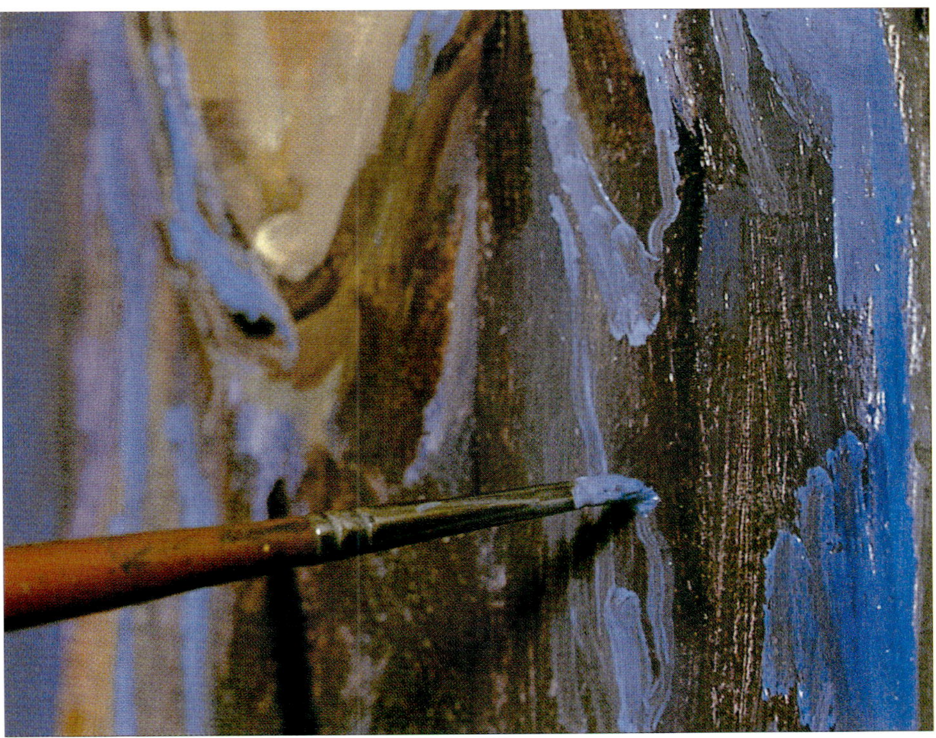

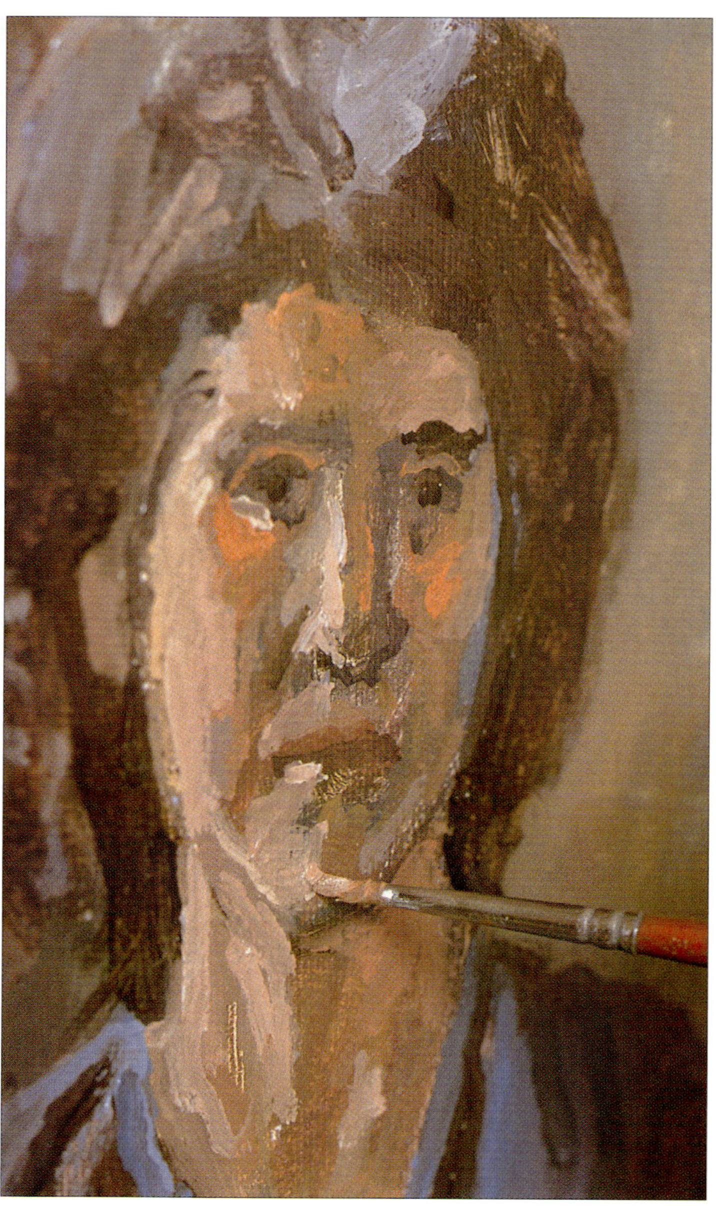

Above *The face has been built up in thick paint, freely but carefully applied so that the features are distinct but not over-meticulous. Little blending has been done, but because the artist is working wet into wet, the colors are modified by the process of laying one on top of another. The line of blue on the right, the reflection from the blouse, has been left quite distinct.*

MATERIALS USED

SUPPORT:
Bought, ready-primed canvas 24 X 18 in. (61 X 46 cm)

BRUSHES:
A selection of bristle and synthetic, a flat bristle being used for the background and small, round synthetics for the face and details of the clothing

COLORS:
Titanium white, cobalt blue, cerulean blue, cobalt violet, light red, alizarin crimson, yellow ocher, burnt sienna and raw umber. No medium was used except in the early stages, where the paint was thinned with turpentine

used quite deliberately to create mood: here there are no jarring compositional elements and no bright or discordant colors, but the effect is far from dull—just pleasantly peaceful.

Most people have one or two items about their homes that seem to suggest an idea for a painting, and in this case the artist was attracted to the swelling curves of the pot and its decorative motif. In order to highlight these qualities, he chose to make the composition a geometric one, in which the horizontals and verticals of the window frame and shutter act as a foil for the curved and rounded shapes. The composition is very carefully balanced, with the strip of blue-gray in the foreground just slightly narrower than the window sill above, and the rectangle on the right large enough to be "read" as the view through the window but not so large as to dominate the

Right *The finished painting shows how the figure has been given solidity by the use of thick paint and strong tonal contrasts, while the background has been left as areas of quite thin and transparent paint. Although there is little detail in the background, it is not flat and uninteresting; different colors have been used to echo and harmonize with those of the figure itself.*

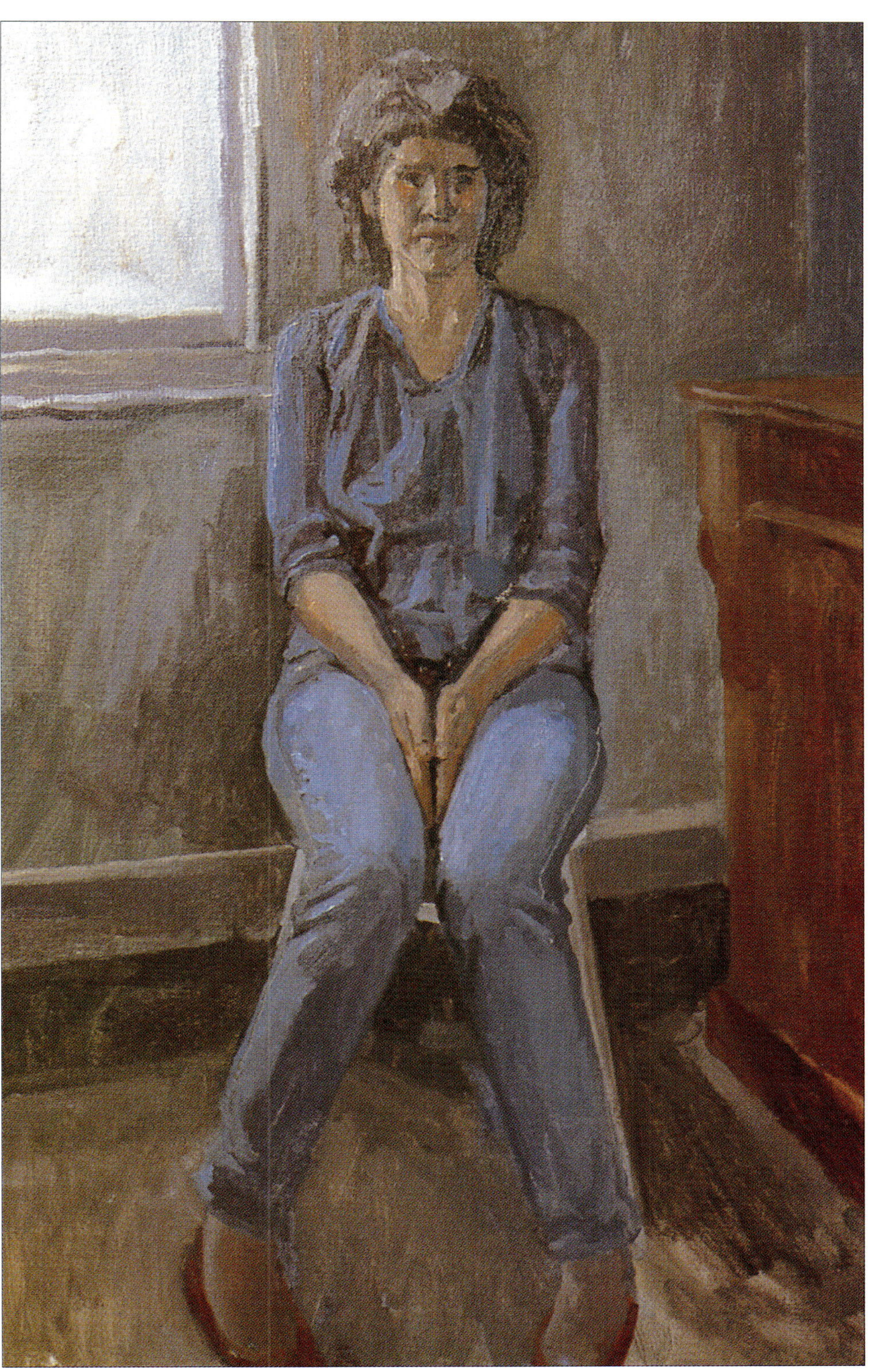

painting. The verticals of the window frame have been carefully planned so that they do not interfere with the dominant shapes of the pot and bowl, and the slanting shadows on the left, which appear in the photograph as very distinct areas of tone, are merely hinted at by a very slightly darker color at the top left.

The paint has been applied very carefully and meticulously, with sable brushes used to build up thin layers, and the support, a fine-grained canvas, was chosen as particularly suitable for this kind of painting. For a picture like this, it is very important that the straight lines should be really quite straight—an accidentally slanting vertical line, for example, would provide just the jarring element the artist has been at pains to avoid—so masking tape was used to aid the process.

At one time such techniques were considered rather "mechanical," and frowned upon. But even experienced artists will agree that it is extremely difficult to draw a straight line freehand, and there is no reason why masking tape or rulers should not be used.

The range of colors used was deliberately very small—just two blues, a green, gray, black, and yellow. It can be a useful discipline

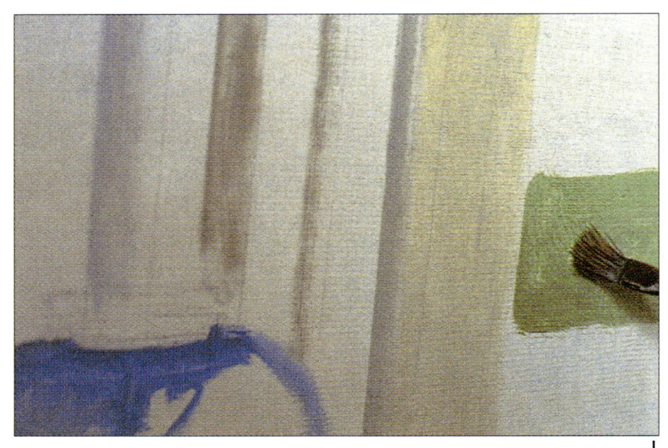

1

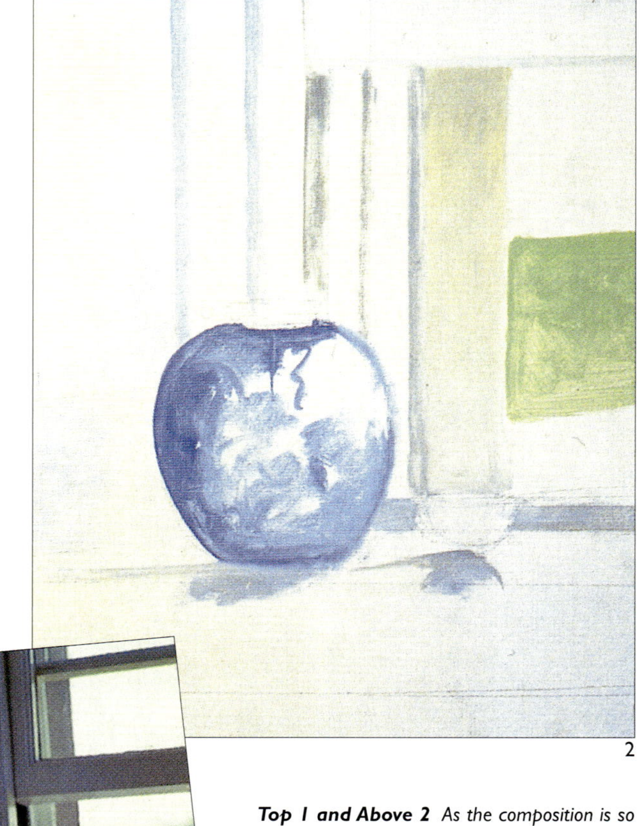

2

Top 1 and Above 2 *As the composition is so simple, no underdrawing was necessary. Instead, the main elements were quickly blocked in, using thin paint and a sable brush, in more or less the colors that appear in the finished painting.*

Right *At this stage a bristle brush was used, as the paint was rather thicker (though still relatively thin). The blue of the pot was built up using a mixture of ultramarine and white, with white and Payne's gray used for the window sill. Payne's gray is a useful and versatile color, with a slight mauvish tinge. Here it appears quite warm in relation to the deep blue. A mixture of black and white would have given a much less "alive" quality.*

Below Right *Masking tape had been applied to the line that separates the edge of the window frame from the little rectangle of landscape that is visible just beyond. This also allowed the artist to apply the paint quite freely on the window-frame area.*

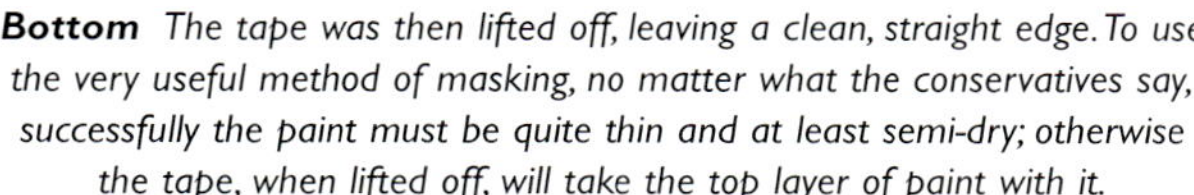

Bottom *The tape was then lifted off, leaving a clean, straight edge. To use the very useful method of masking, no matter what the conservatives say, successfully the paint must be quite thin and at least semi-dry; otherwise the tape, when lifted off, will take the top layer of paint with it.*

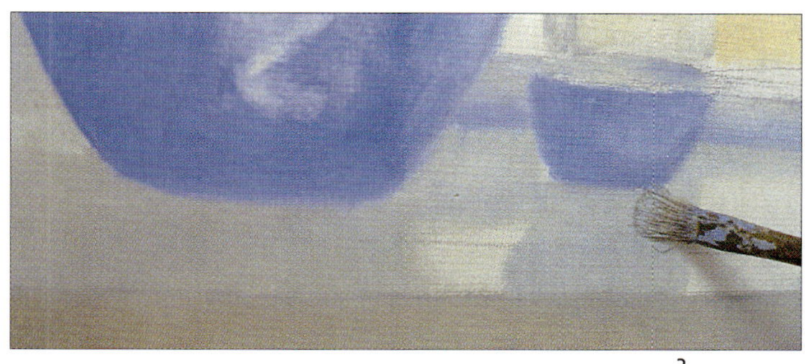

3

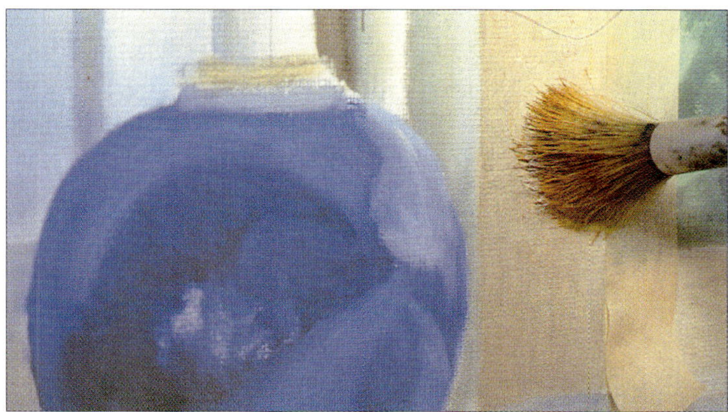

4

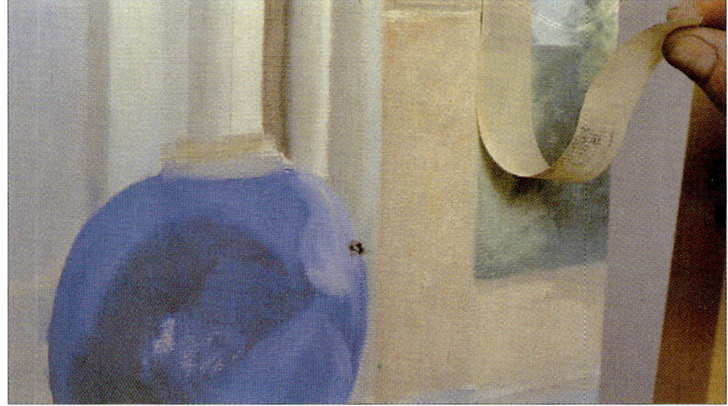

5

to limit your colors in this way, choosing just one or two colors and their complementaries (blue and yellow, as here, or red and green) plus grays and browns. It may cut down your choices, but this can also be an advantage as you will have fewer to make, and you may find that your painting achieves a harmony and unity that it might not have had with a whole range of colors at your disposal. It will also teach you far more about mixing colors than reading a whole book on the subject.

STILL LIFE WITH WATERMELON

This still life, while very different from the one preceding it, has a rather similar atmosphere of simple, quiet harmony. One of the most difficult aspects of still-life painting is deciding on the initial arrangement.

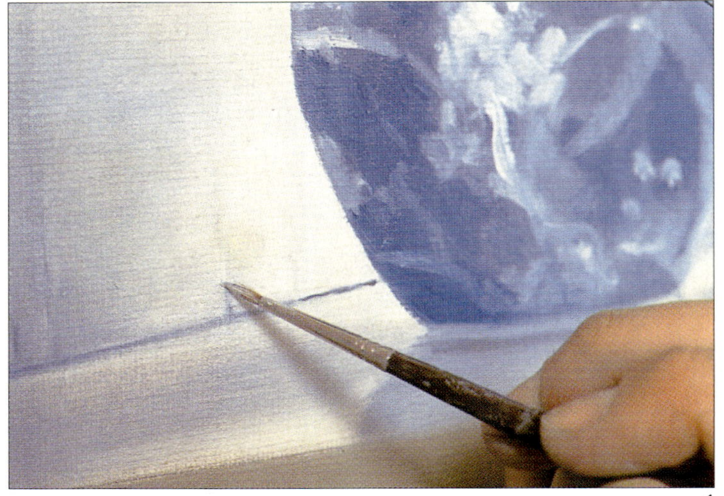

6

Left and Below *Several thin layers of paint had been built up, but the details, which give a crisp definition to the finished painting, had not been added. In the detail (left) a small sable brush is being used to paint the fine lines at the bottom of the shutter. If you look at the finished painting you will see that this delicate diagonal line is actually vital to the composition, leading the eye to the pot and bowl, which are the focal points.*

Right *The brickwork was painted in a mixture of Payne's gray, yellow ocher, and white, with viridian and white used for the mini-landscape through the window. It is important that the artist does this part of the painting with great care. There is always the danger that if the tonal contrast were too great or the colors were too bright, the landscape would "jump" forward, assuming too much visual importance and conflicting with the foreground. Viridian, being a cool, rather blue green, is useful for receding backgrounds.*

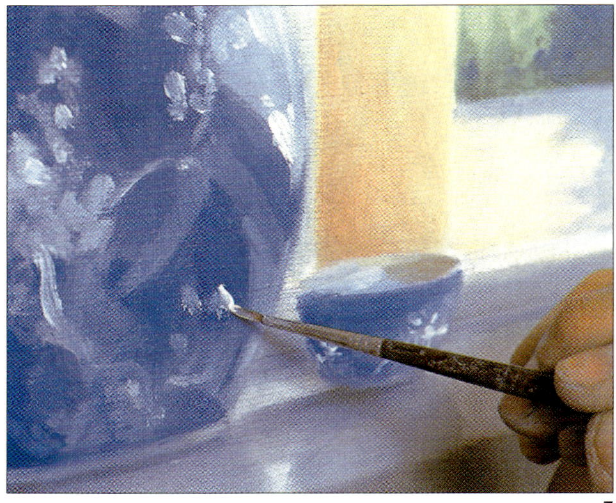

7

MATERIALS USED

SUPPORT:
Primed, fine-grained canvas 12 X 10 in. (30.5 X 25.4 cm)

BRUSHES:
Small sable and a number 8 round bristle

COLORS:
Titanium white, ivory black, Payne's gray, yellow ocher, cadmium yellow pale, viridian, ultramarine, and Prussian blue

It is only too easy to buy up a greengrocer's entire stock and then find yourself unable to arrive at a satisfactory way of arranging the different elements you have set before you, or to rush around the house collecting bowls, plates, and vases which, when placed together, don't seem to add up to anything you want to paint. Here, as can be seen in the photograph, the artist has chosen a simple arrangement, one that could then be arranged in such a way that the shapes are balanced very carefully.

The composition of the painting is based on a triangle with the point at the top left, and the circular shapes of the plate and half melon intersecting at different angles. The smaller piece of melon echoes the triangle, while the strawberries in the foreground both break up the area of white space and give a feeling of solidity by establishing the plane on which they rest. If

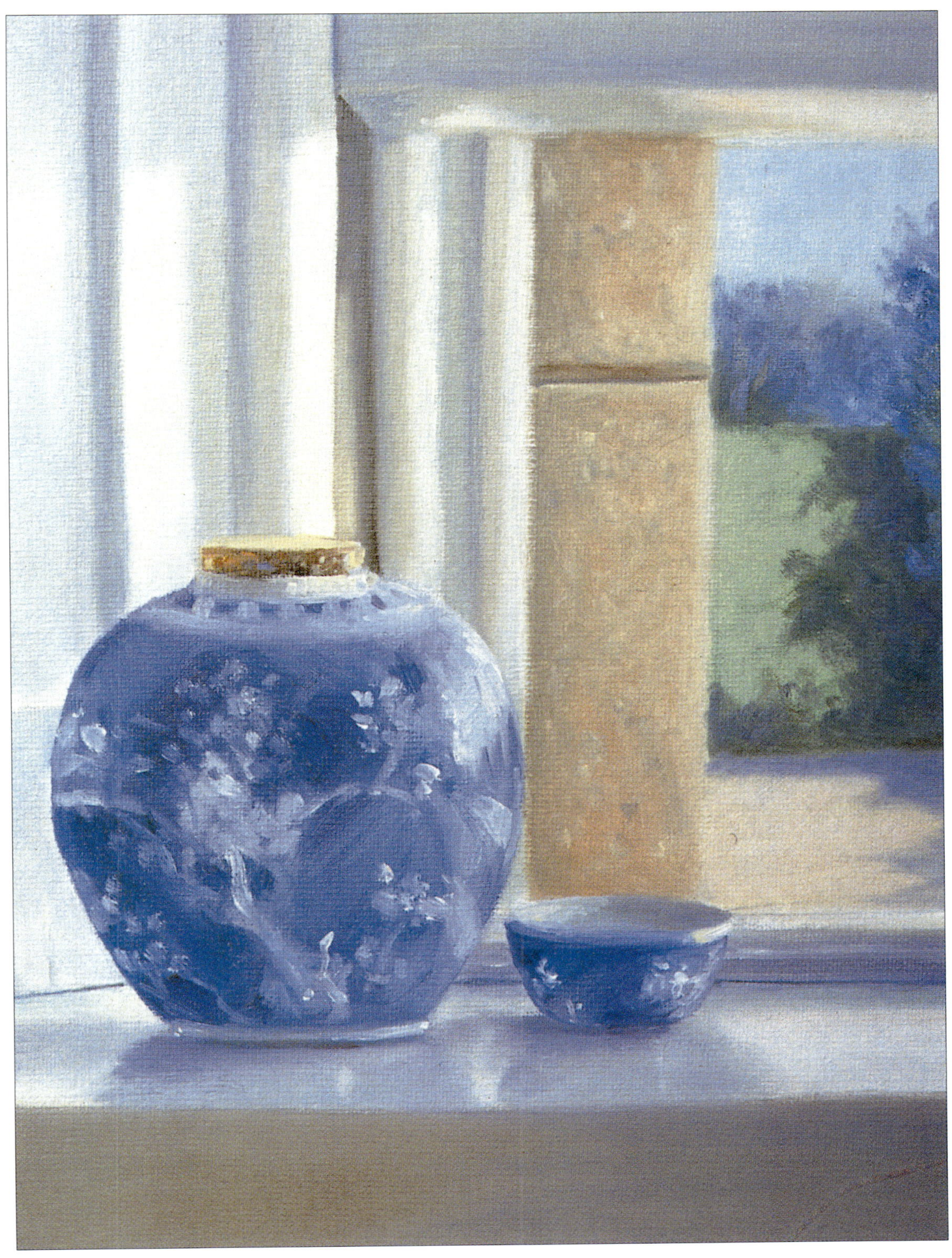

you mask them out with your finger you can see how drastically the composition would be weakened and how the main elements would then appear to float in space. The artist has chosen to ignore the line created by the back edge of the table, treating the table top and background as a flat area of "negative space;" treating the table and wall as separate planes would have detracted from the composition and reduced the importance of the main shapes, which appear almost as though "carved out" of the space.

Below *A faint underdrawing was done with pencil to position the main elements of the composition, which were then blocked in with heavily-diluted paint.*

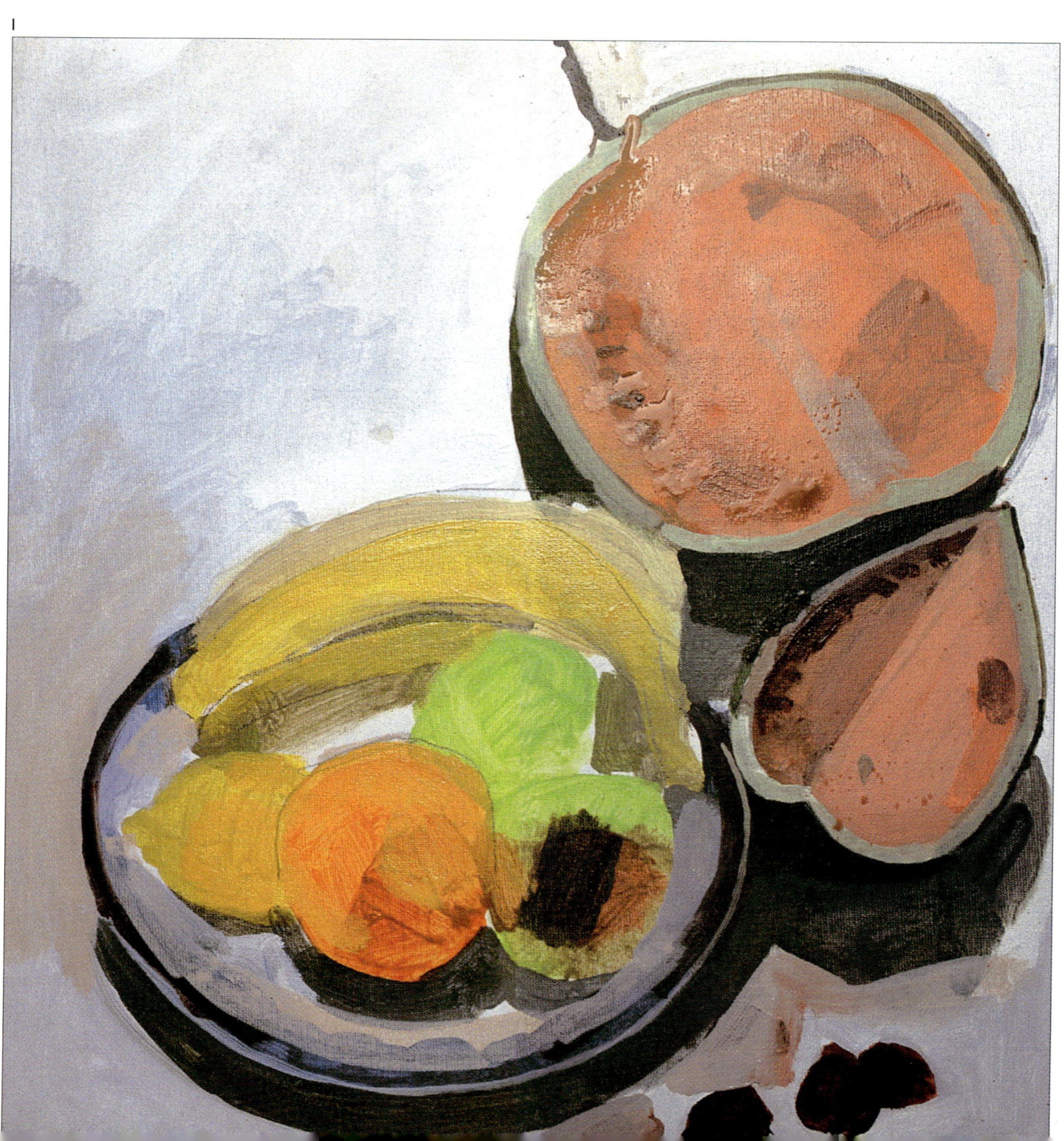

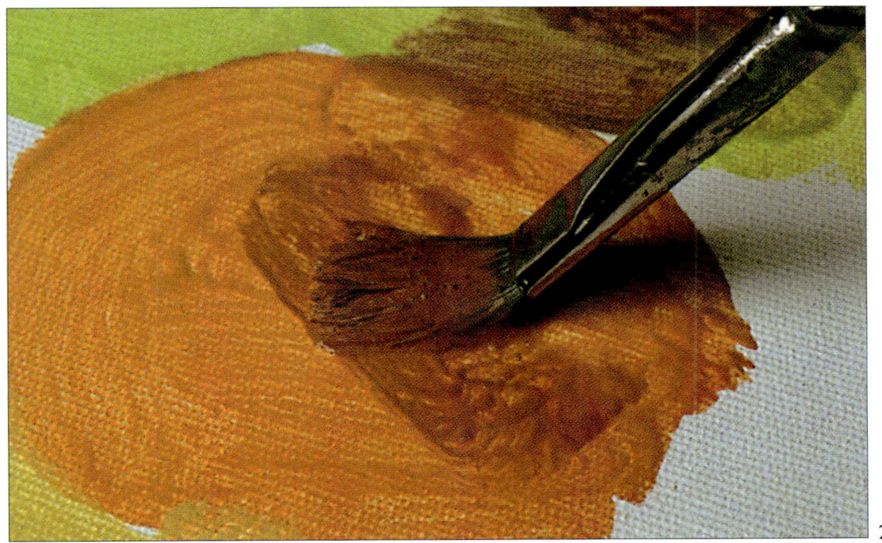
2

Left and Bottom *As soon as the colored underpainting (in very washy colors) was dry, the artist set about defining the separate pieces of fruit, building up the highlights in thick, juicy paint.*

3
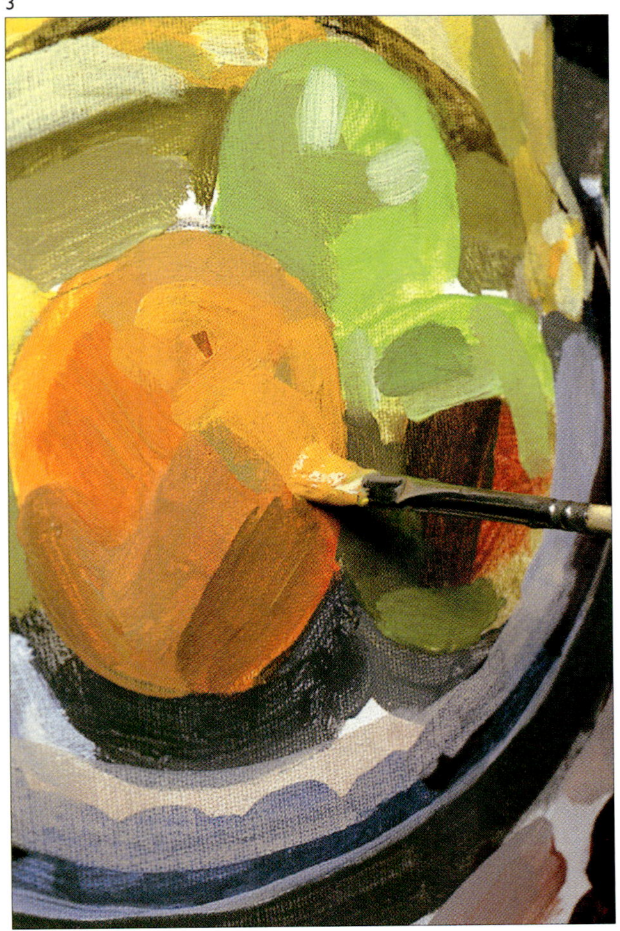

A variety of painting techniques has been used to create an interesting paint surface here; the first step being a colored underpainting in very washy paint, after which areas were built up and defined in much thicker paint. The watermelon was given texture by spattering paint on to the surface from a stiff-haired brush; and a pencil was used to draw through the paint into the fruit. Note how the white background is very slightly textured with just-visible brushstrokes.

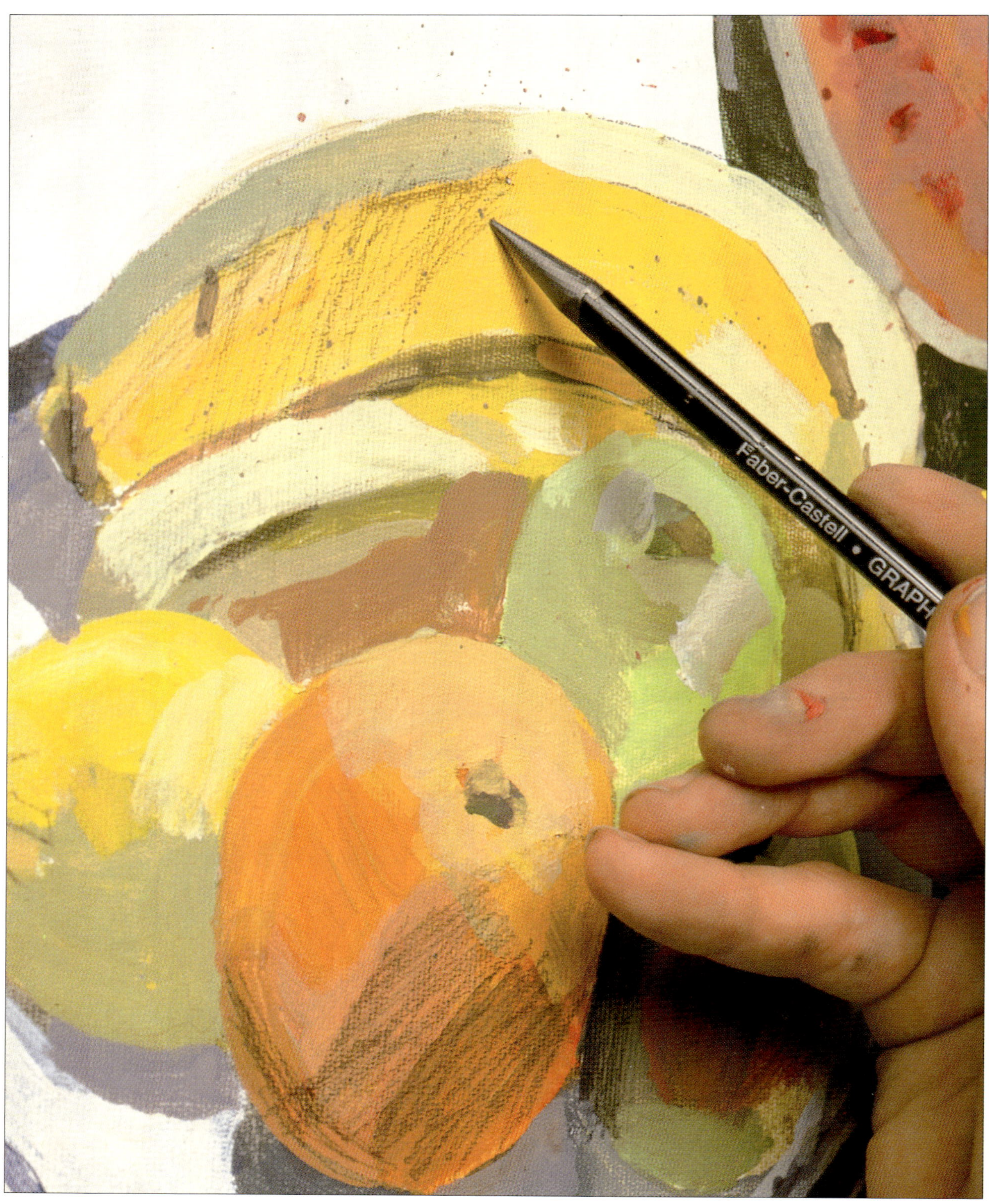

4

***Left** The artist then drew into the dry paint with a pencil—a technique that has a dual function. In this case, it gives a certain kind of texture and visual interest to the fruit. It also has the effect of somewhat muting the tones in the painting without the necessity for overpainting.*

***Right** The strawberries are no longer just brushstrokes. The artist has given them shape and form, painting the highlights in a light pink and the leaves and stems in bright green.*

***Bottom** The artist's final touch was to modify the shapes by working back into them with white paint. Also note how the shadows have been painted in a blue-gray, and clearly outlined on the white background. The plane of the table top has also now been clearly established.*

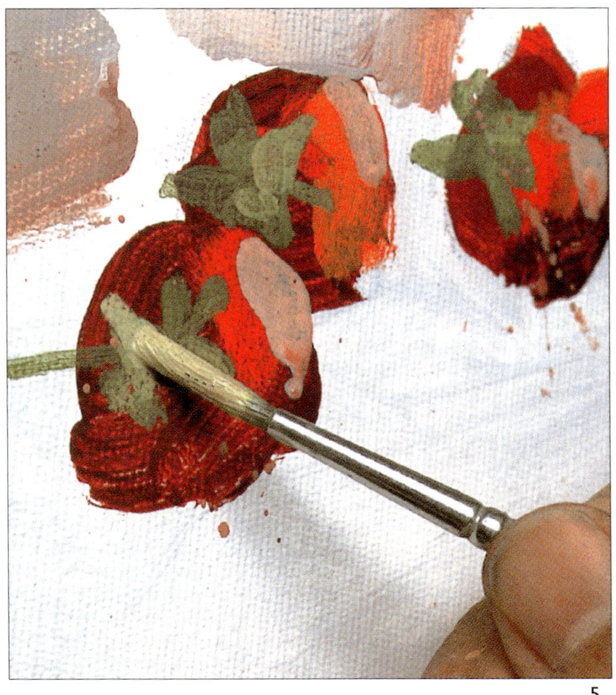

5

6

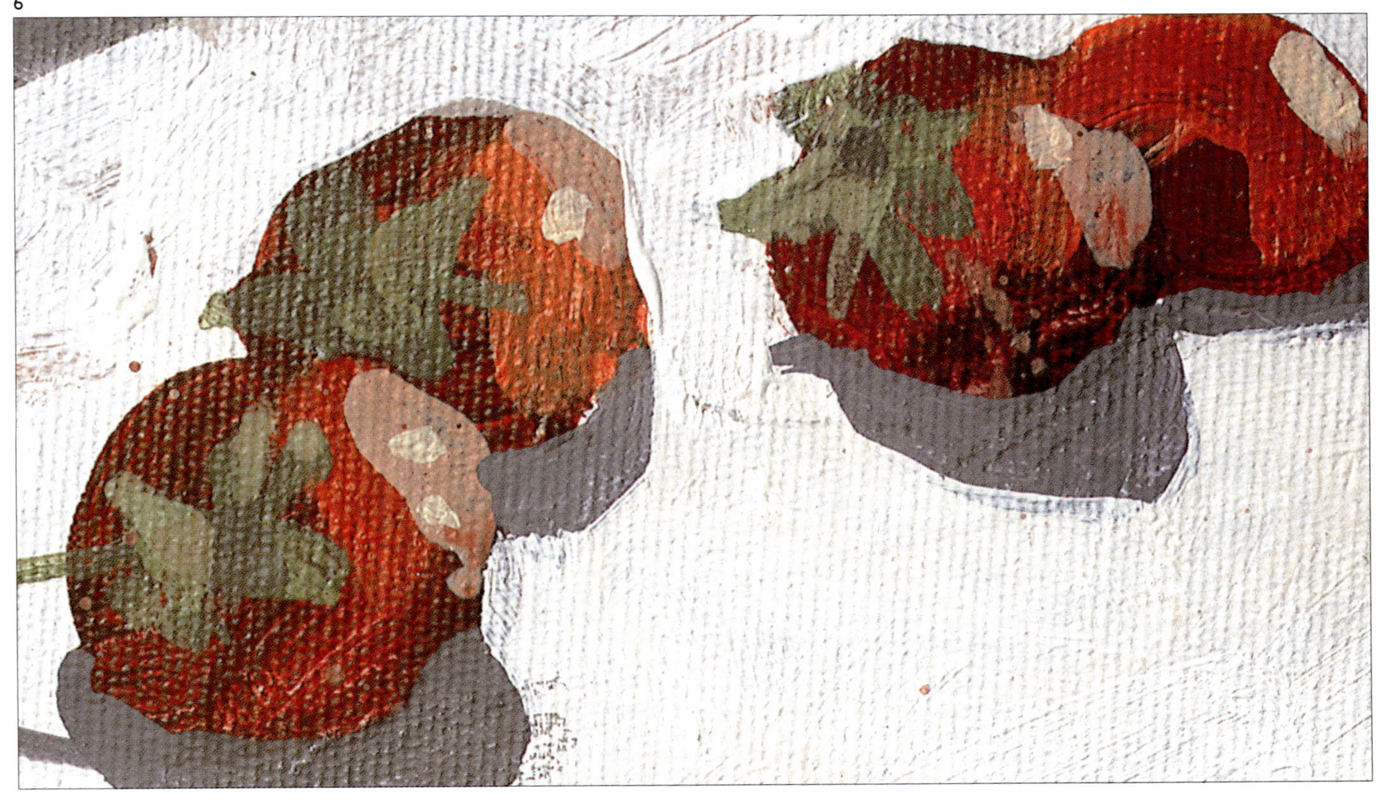

MATERIALS USED

SUPPORT:
Bought, ready-primed canvas board 20 x 16 in. (51 x 40 cm)

BRUSHES:
Number 12 white bristle and a number 4 hog's hair, with a 1-in. (2.5-cm) housepainting brush used for the spattering

COLORS:
Titanium white, yellow ocher, vermilion, cadmium red, cadmium yellow, sap green, cobalt blue and Payne's gray, a range consisting almost entirely of good, strong primaries

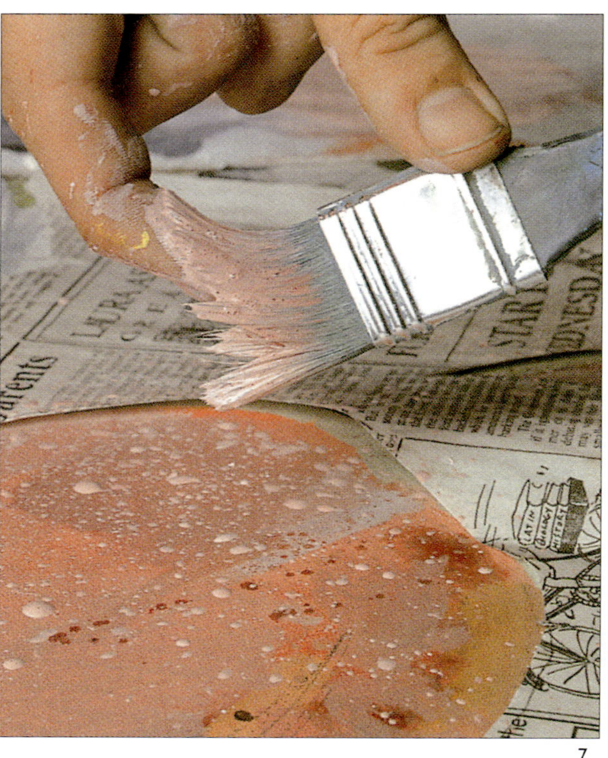

__Right__ The texture of the watermelon is an important element of the painting. The artist has chosen a technique he frequently uses—spattering paint from a stiff-haired brush. In order not to splash paint on the rest of the painting he has cut a mask from newspaper, leaving exposed only those areas that are to be textured. Two tones were used for the spattering, one lighter and one darker than the mid-tone of the underpainting.

7

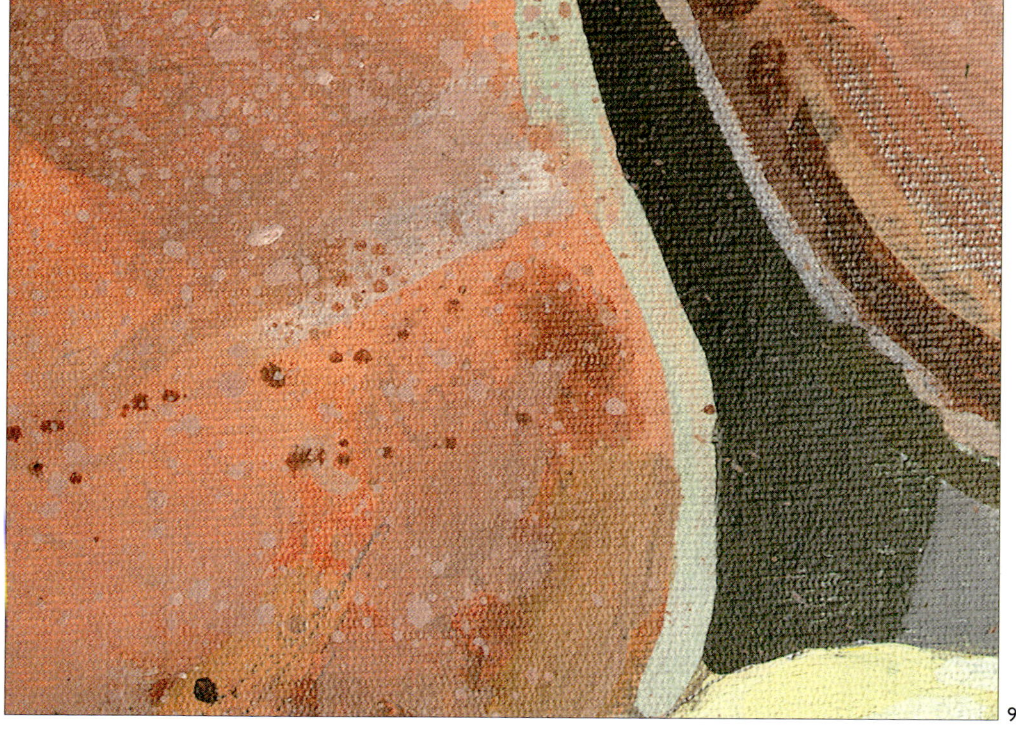

9

__Left__ The tones and colors were chosen with great care as they had to be light or dark enough to show up, but not so sharply contrasting as to "jump" off the surface.

Right *In the finished painting the pencil drawing is still just visible on the banana and the apple, and the same technique has been used on the smaller piece of watermelon and on small areas of the shadow under it and the plate. It is touches such as these that give a painting that special "something," creating extra interest and liveliness; but they should never be allowed to become too important.*

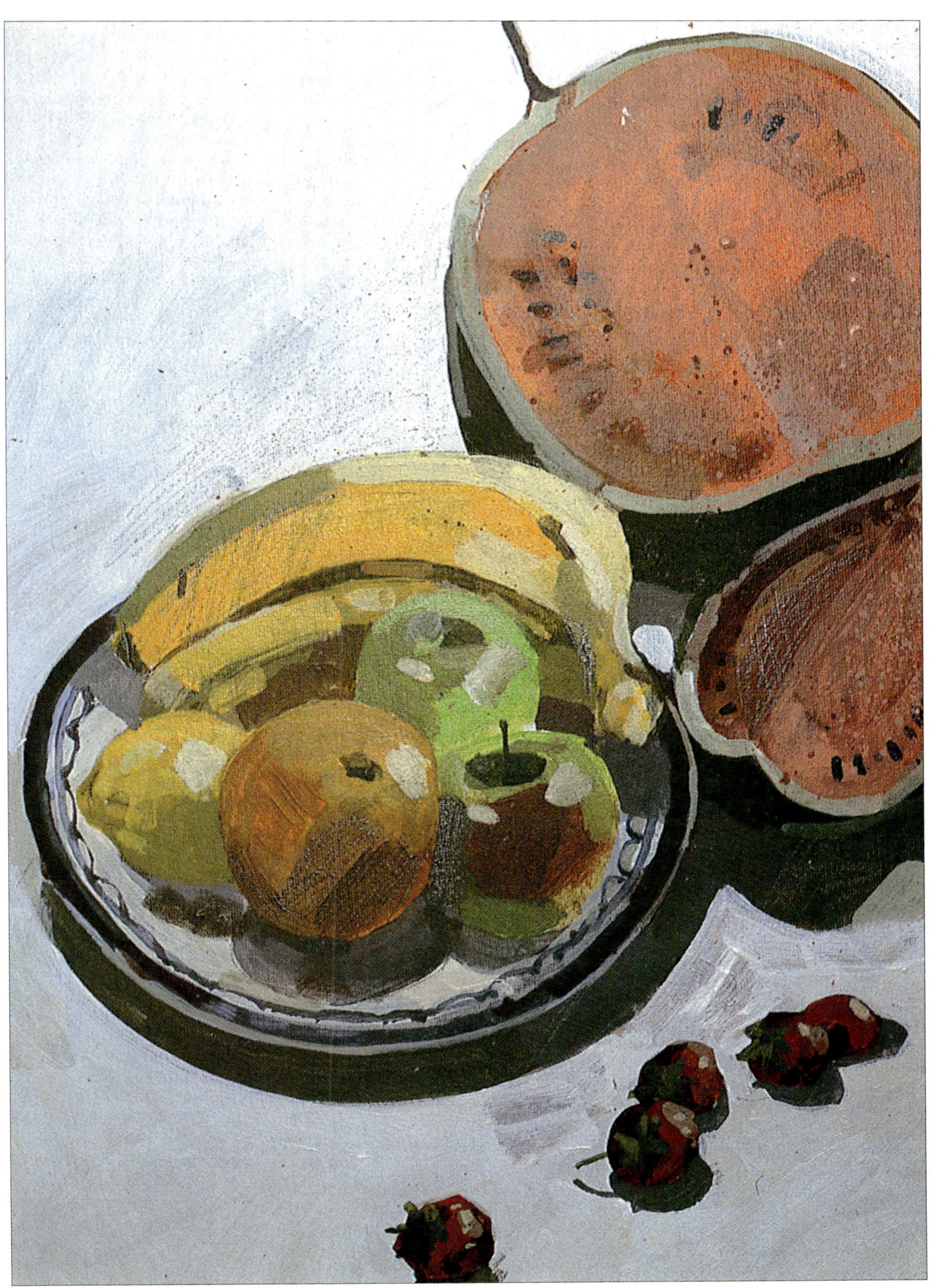

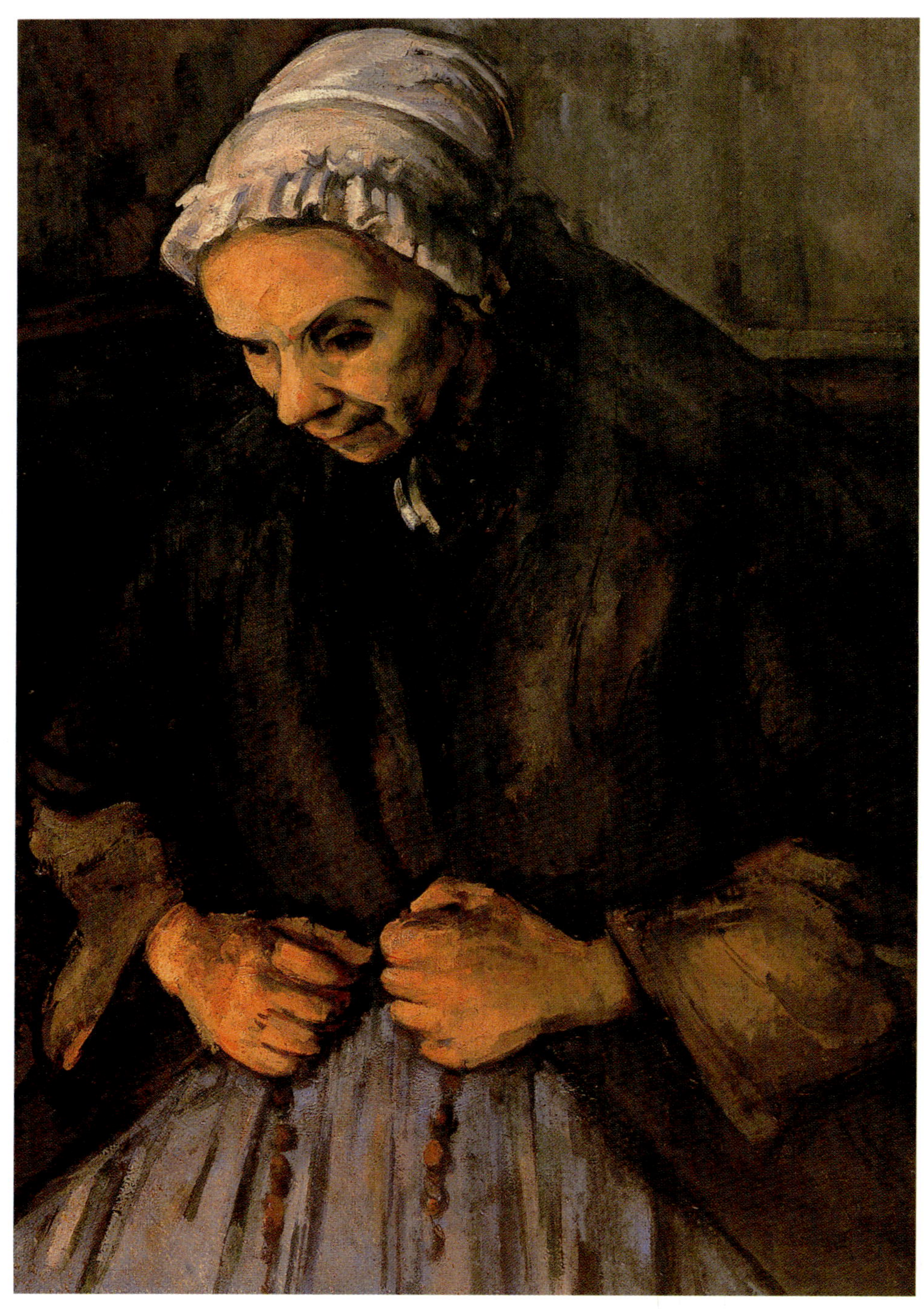

Above: Old Woman with a Rosary *by Paul Cézanne (1839–1906). By Cézanne's time, the techniques of oil painting had been largely freed from the earlier restrictions and prejudices. The brushstrokes are an integral part of this dramatic composition, as are the areas of broken colour, while the face itself has been treated in a bold, broad manner as a series of planes.*

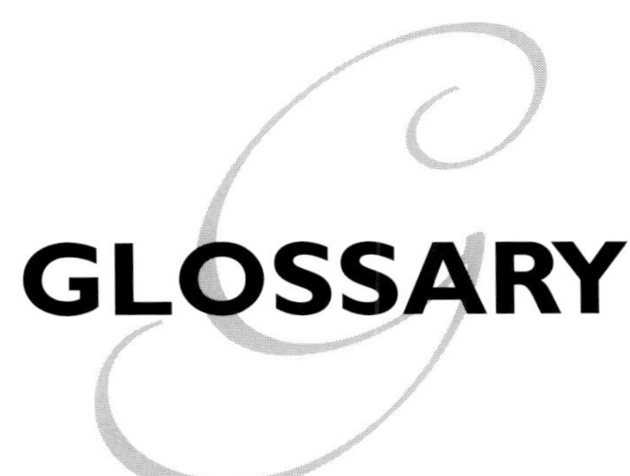

GLOSSARY

Airbrush: Tool by means of which paint is sprayed on to a surface using compressed air
Audubon, John James: 1785–1851; French painter, naturalist and ornithologist, known especially for his depictions of the birds of North America

Blake, William: 1757–1827; English poet, painter and printmaker, well regarded for his hand-illustrated series of poems including *Songs of Innocence* and *Songs of Experience*
Bonington, Richard Parkes: 1802–1828; English landscape painter
Bonnard, Pierre: 1867–1947; French painter and printmaker
Boudin, Eugene: 1824–1898; one of the first French painters to paint outdoors
Braque, Georges: 1882–1963; French painter, one of the inventors of Cubism, which primarily consists of fragmenting objects and forms into abstract shapes
Burne-Jones, Edward: 1833–1898; British painter
Burra, Edward: 1905–1976; English watercolourist

Canaletto: 1697–1768; Italian landscape artist
Caravaggio: 1571–1610; Italian painter
Cezanne, Paul: 1839–1906; French painter, acknowledged as one of the greatest in the Post-Impressionist era
Composition: The plan or arrangement underlying the various elements in a work of art; elements may refer to the degree of lightness or darkness, the perspective, and so on
Constable, John: 1776–1837; renowned British landscape artist
Conté crayon: Drawing pencil, so called after its inventor Nicolas-Jacques Conté
Cotman, John Sell: 1782–1842; English landscape painter who worked chiefly in watercolour

Degas, Edgar: 1834–1917; French painter and sculptor
Dürer, Albrecht: 1471–1528; renowned German painter and printmaker from the Renaissance era

Eyck, Jan van: 1395–1441; Flemish painter known chiefly for his role in establishing the technique of oil painting

Francesca, Piero della: 1420–1492; Italian painter known for his innovations with the use of perspective

Gauguin, Paul: Leading French painter, printmaker and sculptor of the Post-Impressionist era
Girtin, Thomas: 1775–1802; English painter and etcher, helped to establish watercolour as an art form
Gogh, Vincent van: 1853–1890; Dutch painter, generally regarded as one of the greatest in European art history
Gouache: A painting technique wherein watercolours are mixed with a gum to produce an opaque effect

Hatch: Technique for creating effects like shading and modelling, by filling in areas with parallel lines. Crosshatching comprises lines etched at an angle to one another
Hockney, David: 1937; English painter and photographer
Holbein: 1497–1543; Hans Holbein, the Younger, was a German painter well known for his portraits

Hopper, Edward: 1882–1967; American painter, known particularly for his realistic depictions of urban life
Hunt, William Henry: 1790–1864; English painter of watercolours
Impressionism: Movement in painting that developed chiefly in France in the latter half of the 19th century; stressed on recording scenes in terms of their natural light and colour at any given point of time

John, Gwen: 1876–1939; Welsh painter

Kalf, Willem: 1619–1693; Dutch painter of still life

Lewis, John Frederick: 1805–1876; British painter

Matisse, Henri: 1869–1954; influential French painter of the 20th century
Michelangelo: 1475–1564; Italian Renaissance painter, sculptor, architect and poet
Monet, Claude: 1840–1926; French painter, one of the chief developers of the Impressionist style
Monochrome: Painting done in different shades of a colour
Munch, Edvard: 1863–1944; Norwegian painter and printmaker
Muybridge, Eadweard: 1830–1904; English photographer

Palmer, Samuel: 1805–1881; English landscape painter and etcher
Perspective: Technique of graphically representing three-dimensional objects on a two-dimensional plane, while keeping the illusion of the three-dimension space
Picasso, Pablo: 1881–1973; Spanish painter, one of the pioneers of Cubism
Poussin, Nicolas: 1594–1665; French painter
Pre-Raphaelite Brotherhood: Group of English painters who came together in 1848 with the intention of discarding what they thought to be an artificial approach to art
Prout, Samuel: 1783–1852; English watercolour painter

Redouté, Pierre-Joseph: 1759–1840; French painter, official artist at the court of Queen Marie Antoinette of France
Rembrandt: 1606–1669; Dutch painter and etcher, renowned for his numerous self-portraits
Renaissance: Cultural movement marked by renewed surge of interest in classical learning as well as scientific breakthroughs; generally considered to have begun around the 14th century
Rodin, Auguste: 1840–1917; famous French sculptor of bronze and marble figures
Ruskin, John: 1819–1900; English painter who was also esteemed as an art critic

Sarto, Andrea del: 1486–1530; Italian painter
Sisley, Alfred: 1839–1899; French Impressionist painter of landscapes
Still life: Painting that depicts inanimate objects like flowers and fruits
Titian: 1488/90–1576; Italian Renaissance painter, widely regarded as one of the greatest of the time
Toulouse-Lautrec, Henri de: 1864–1901; French painter
Turner, Joseph Mallord William: 1775–1851; English landscape painter

Uccello, Paolo: 1397–1475; Italian painter, recognised for his role in developing the art of the perspective in painting
Utrillo: 1883–1955; French painter

Vanishing point: Point in a drawing at which parallel lines receding from the viewer appear to converge
Vinci, Leonardo da: 1452–1519; Italian painter, sculptor, architect and engineer; among his most well-known paintings are *The Last Supper* and *Mona Lisa*
Vuillard, Edouard: 1868–1940; French painter, printmaker and decorator

Watteau, Jean-Antoine: 1684–1721; French painter
Wint, Peter de: 1784–1849; English landscape painter

INDEX